Baltimore County
Marriage Evidences
and
Family Relationships,
1659 - 1800

Baltimore County
Marriage Evidences
and
Family Relationships,
1659 - 1800

Robert W. Barnes

CLEARFIELD

Published for Clearfield Company by
Genealogical Publishing Company
Baltimore, Maryland
2014

ISBN 978-0-8063-5685-3

Made in the United States of America

To

Allender

Baltimore County Marriage Evidences and
Family Relationships 1659-1800

Table of Contents

Introduction

Dedication

Allender Sybert had been a friend, mentor, adviser and patient listener to my talking about the problems and progress I have made in compiling this book. It is with great pleasure that I dedicate this book to him.

Organization of Sources

After I published *Maryland Marriage Evidences, 1634-1718,*[1] I planned to continue the series, but then other authors brought out their own compilations of Marriage evidences for specific counties. I decided to specialize in Baltimore County, and so this book came into being. Early in my researching I discovered that marriages could not always be found in the church record, even though I knew where the couple lived, and I knew what church they attended. Obviously, one reason was that the records had been destroyed or lost. St. Paul's Parish in Prince George's County, and Sater's Baptist Church and Mt. Zion Presbyterian Church, both in Baltimore County, are examples of this.

Many German Churches contain registers of baptisms, list of communicants, and data on funerals but no marriages. The missing marriage records turn out to have been kept in separate books by the pastors, who took these 'Pastoral Registers' with them when they moved to another church.

Sometimes, however, the records are extant, but individual items are not found. The original records of St. Paul's Parish contain a list of marriages performed by Reverend Thomas Chase, and listed by him on some loose papers, but not entered into the official register. Reverence Chase must have been forgetful towards the end of his life. Six couples were married but the good Reverend, for whatever reason, did not have them recorded by the parish registrar. The witnesses to the wedding came before the parish registrar and testified that they were at the wedding when it had occurred, and the couple had lived together as man and wife ever since then.

Reverend David Love, an Episcopal Priest at All Hallow's Parish in Anne Arundel County returned to England at the outset of the American Revolution because he was a Loyalist. He took with him his marriage register which he was used to document his claim that he had lost income as a clergyman because of his loyalty to the crown. This register was discovered by Peter Wilson Coldham when he was researching his book *American Migrations.*[2]

---

[1] Baltimore: Genealogical Publishing Co., 1995.
[2] Baltimore: Genealogical Publishing Co., 2000.

After seeing the excellent work by Shirley Middleton Moller, *Prince George's County Marriage References and Family Relationships,*[3] I decided to expand the scope of my book to include relationships, such as unhappy marriages, children placed with a guardian, children bound out as apprentices, and children born to single parents. I included names of in-laws found in wills, administration accounts, and land records.

On occasion, people were not always careful to record the births of their children. They may have neglected to do this because they had to pay a fee to register the births, and deaths of their children and slaves. In Maryland a 'lease for three lifetimes' stipulated that the land would be held for the lifetimes of the original tenant and two other people. If the last one named was a child, and hat child died, the tenant may have decided to name the next child born after the deceased infant, thus ensuring the land would stay in the family.

What was the frustrated researcher to do?

This volume contains clues to Baltimore County marriages found in land, court, and probate records, as well as private records such as church vestry proceedings, Bible records, and newspaper records for the years 1719 through 1800. In addition there are clues to marriages and other, 'irregular,' relationships found in administrative records of religious denominations, and in newspapers. Court minutes and other sources gave clues to family relationships other than marriage.

Acknowledgements

Many thanks are due to Henry C. Peden, Jr., and V. L. Skinner, Jr., for their excellent abstracts of records which pointed me to the original sources. The abstracts of Prerogative Court Wills by the late Carson Gibb were also extremely helpful.

To my wife, Cathy, and my friends Robert, Martin, Dolly, and Isaac who listened (Patiently, oh, so patiently!), and offered encouragement and advice, I am deeply grateful.

Thanks also go to Dr. Edward C. Papenfuse, State Archivist at the Maryland State Archives, for creating an environment where research can be conducted and also to Michael McCormick and the Reference Department Staff for their help. I also appreciate the help given by Dr Patricia Anderson and the Library Staff at the Maryland Historical Society, especially Francis O'Neill and Damon Talbot for valuable editorial assistance..

I would thank Dr. Michael Tepper and the entire staff of the Genealogical Publishing Company for publishing this work.

Last, but certainly far from least, I thank my good friend Allender who has acted as confidant, critic and my sounding board as I worked on this project.

---

[3] Lewes [DE]: Colonial Roots, © 2010 by Colonial Roots.

A word of caution about the Index!

As with most indices a name may appear more than once on a page.

Through a mistake on the part of the author, a portion of the Index, covering the names Hatten through part of Hayes was incorrectly paged, and this was not discovered until the Index was being printed. That missing part of the Index will be found on page 557.The author regrets the error.

Bibliography

2BAVP - St. John's and St. George's Parish Vestry Proceedings, trans. by Lucy H. Harrison, at MdHS:

AAAD: ANNE ARUNDEL COUNTY REGISTER OF WILLS. Administration Accounts. MSA C29, CM 85. See Carol G. Mitchell, "Anne Arundel County, MD, Administration Accounts, Liber ED, 1777-1779," *MGSB* 26:293-ff.

AAAL: All Hallow's Parish, Anne Arundel Co. MSA SC 2458; AAAL 1: Register, 1669-1721; AALH 2: Register 1700-1724. (See MSA Card Index 27, *AACR* below.)

AAAN: St. Anne's Parish, Anne Arundel Co. MSA SC 15; MSA M 143; 175. (See MSA Card Index 27, *AACR* below.)

AACR: F. Edward Wright. *Anne Arundel Co. Church Records of the 17th and 18th Centuries.* Westminster, MD: Family Line Publications, no date.

AAJA: St. James Parish, Anne Arundel Co. MSA SC 2497. (See MSA Card Index 27, *AACR* below.).

AAJU: ANNE ARUNDEL CO. COURT (Judgment Record), MSA C 91. See Douglas Hayman, "Orphans Cases in Anne Arundel County Court, Maryland, Judgment Record TB#1, March 1705-September 1709," *Readings* 7 (1) (Jan 2004) 3-8.

AALR: ANNE ARUNDEL COUNTY COURT Land Records. MSA C 97, CM 91. See Rosemary B. Dodd, *et al. Abstracts of Land Records of Anne Arundel County, Maryland.* Pasadena, MD: The Anne Arundel Genealogical Society, n.d. Anne Arundel County Land Records. Volumes I-VIII.

AAMA: St. Margaret's Parish, Anne Arundel Co. MSA SC 2915. (See MSA Card Index 27, *AACR* above).

Adams, Edward BR, pub. in *MHGB* 7 (1) 1.

Allen's Marr. Register: Marr. Reg. of Rev. John Allen for St. George's Parish, 1795-1816 at MSA.

AMG: Annapolis *Maryland Gazette.*

ARMD: *Archives of Maryland.* Volumes 1-70 exist in hard copy. Vols. 71- are located at the Maryland State Archives web site (www.mdsa.net) as *Archives of Maryland on-line.*

AWAP: Peter Wilson Coldham. *American Wills and Administrations in the Prerogative Court of Canterbury, 1610-1857.* Baltimore: Genealogical Publishing Co., 1989.

BAAB: BALTIMORE CO. REGISTER OF WILLS (Administration Bonds) MSA C264.

BAAD: BALTIMORE CO. REGISTER OF WILLS (Administration Accounts) MSA C 261, CM 127.

BACH or BACT: BALTIMORE COUNTY COURT (Chattel Records) MSA C298, CM 133: BACT TR#E is at MSA, as MSA No. C298-1, Location 2/14/11/41; BACT

B#G is at MSA, as MSA No. C298-2, Location 2/14/11/42; BACT Liber 1773-1784, MS 2865 at MdHS; BACT Liber 1785-1788, MS 2865 at MdHS; BACT Liber 1791-1794, MS 2865.1 at MdHS; BACT WG#7, 1800-1801, as MSA No. C298-3, Location 2/14/12/46; BACT Liber 1811-1812, is at the Maryland Historical Society; BACT WG#18, 1813-1814; as MSA No.: C 298-3, Location 2/14/11/43.

BACM: BALTIMORE COUNTY COURT (Minutes) MSA C386: BACM 1: 1755-1763; BACM 2: 1765; BACM 3:1768-1769; BACM 4: 1772, 1775-1781; BACM 5:1782-1786.

BACP: BALTIMORE CO. COURT (Proceedings) 1682-1756, MSA C 400, hereafter cited as BACP.

BACT: See BACH above.

BAGA: BALTIMORE CO. REGISTER OF WILLS (Guardian Accounts) MSA C333.

Baggs BR 1:Printed by M. L. and W. A. Davis, 1801, in MGR 35:89

BAJO: St. John's Parish, Baltimore Co. See; see also SJSG and Peden, *A Closer Look*, below.

BALC: BALTIMORE COUNTY COURT (Land Commissions) MSA C350.

BALR: BALTIMORE CO. COURT (Land Records) MSA C 352, CM 135. See Robert W. Barnes. *Baltimore County Deed Abstracts, 1659-1750*. Westminster: Family Line Publications; see also Louis Dow Scisco. *Baltimore County Land Records, 1665-1687*. Baltimore: Genealogical Publishing Co.

Baltimore Co. Rent Roll # 2, 1658-1771; LAND OFFICE (Rent Rolls) MSA S 18.

Baltimore County Genealogical Society. *The Notebook* of the Baltimore County Genealogical Society: checked vols. 1-25.

BAMI: BALTIMORE CO. COURT (Minutes), 1755-1851 MSA C386; hereafter cited as BAMI

BAML: BALTIMORE COUNTY COURT (Marriage Licenses), C376. See Dawn Beitzler Smith, *Baltimore County Marriage Licenses. 1777-1799*. Westminster: Family Line Publications, 1989.

BAOC: Baltimore Co. Orphans Court Proceedings, MSA C399.

BAOC: BALTIMORE CO. REGISTER OF WILLS (Orphans Court Proceedings) MSA C396.

BAPA: St. Paul's Parish, Baltimore Co. MSA SC 2652. See Bill Reamy and Martha Reamy. *Records of St Paul's Parish*. 2 vols. Westminster, Md.: Family Line Publications. © by Martha Reamy.

Barnes, Robert W. *Maryland Marriages, 1634-1777*. Baltimore: Genealogical Publishing Co., 1975.

Barnes, Robert. "Baltimore County Marriages, 1634-1820, Found in Bibles." *The Notebook*, 7 (3) (Sep 1991), 32-34.

BAWB: BALTIMORE CO. REGISTER OF WILLS (Wills) MSA C 435, CM 188; Selected Wills from Libers 1-6.

BCCP: See BACP above.

BCF: Robert W. Barnes. *Baltimore County Families, 1659-1759*. Baltimore: Genealogical Publishing Co., 1989.

BFD: PREROGATIVE COURT (Balance Books, 1751-1776) MSA S 533, SM 9.

Bible and Family Records of Harford County, Maryland. Compiled by Shirley L. Reightler. 3 vols. Special Publications of the Harford County Genealogical Society, nos. 3, 4, 15.

Biggs BR 1; pub. in *NGSQ* 10:118

BINV: BALTIMORE CO. REGISTER OF WILLS (Inventories), MSA C 340, CM 155.

Black Books. See CMSP.

BOCP or BPET: BALTIMORE CITY REGISTER OF WILLS (Petitions), 1791-1950,
T621.

BR: Bible Record.

BRHA: Governor William Paca Chapter, Daughters of the American Revolution. "Bible
Records of Harford County, Maryland, Families." ms. at MdSA.

Buck BR 3. See Robert Barnes. "Buck Bibles." *The Notebook* 11 (2) (June 1995), 21-24.

Burnham BR, in *The Notebook,* (Baltimore Co. Gen. Soc.010 (1) (March 1994) 7-8.

Burns, Annie Walker, Maryland Marriage References, typescript, Maryland Historical
Society.

Carroll: Kenneth Carroll. *Quakerism on the Eastern Shore of Maryland.* Baltimore:
Maryland Historical Society.

CECH: Henry C. Peden, Jr. *Early Anglican Church Records of Cecil County.* Westminster, Md.: Family Line Publications, 1990.

CELR: CECIL CO. COURT (Land Records), MSA C626, CM 343. See June D. Brown.
Abstracts of Cecil County, Maryland, Land Records. 2 vols. Westminster, Md.:
Family Line Publications, 1998. Checked CELR: 1*, 2*, 3*, 4*, 5 to folio 493

CHAD: CHARLES COUNTY REGISTER OF WILLS (Administration Accounts). MSA C
650, CM 366. See also Carol G. Mitchell, "Charles County Administration Accounts,
1708-1738," *MGSB* 26 (4) 340-ff.

Chaires BR: Chaires Bible Record in FCA, MHS; pub. in *MGSB* 45 (2) 401-404.

CHLR: CHARLES COUNTY COURT (Land Records), MSA C670, CM 394. See Elise
Greenup Jourdan. *Abstracts of Charles County, Maryland, Land and Court
Records, 1658-1722.* 3 vols. Westminster, Md.: Family Line Publications, 1993-
1994.

CHPR: REGISTER OF WILLS (Inventories), MSA C 665, CM 386. See Ruth King and
Carol Mitchell, "Charles County, Maryland, Probate Records, Inventories, 1673-1753,
1753-1779, 1791-1808" *MGSB* 25 (1) 52-91, (2) 136-172, (3) 214-253.

CMSP: *Calendar of Maryland State Papers: The Black Books.* Publications of the Hall of
Records Commission No. 1. 1942. Reprint, Baltimore: Genealogical Publishing
Co., 1967.

CMSP: *Calendar of Maryland State Papers: The Red Books,* Publications of the Hall of
Records Commission No.4, Part 3. Annapolis, 1955.

Coldham, Peter Wilson. *Settlers of Maryland, 1679-1783. Consolidated Edition.*
Baltimore: Genealogical Publishing Co., 2002. Coldham, Peter Wilson. *Settlers of
Maryland, 1701-1730:* checked through p. 57

Collins BR 1 "Collins, Laws, and Polk Bible Records," *HMGB* 6 (3) 25.

Cottman BR: Cottman Bible in FCA, MHS; pub. in *MGSB* 45 (2) 333-335

Cotton, Jane Baldwin. "Extracts from the Early Records of Maryland." *MHM* 16:279-
298, 369-385, 17:60-74, 292-308.

CRSM: See Jourdan below.

CSM: *Chronicles of St. Mary's.*

Culver, Francis B. "Some Old Bible Records of the Emory Family of Maryland." *MG*
1:430-431

DOJU: DORCHESTER CO, COURT (Judgment Records), MSA C704, CM 844. See F.
Edward Wright. *Judgment Records of Dorchester, Queen Anne's & Talbot*

Counties. Lewes, Del.: Delmarva Roots, 2001.

DOLR: DORCHESTER CO. COURT (Land Records), MSA C 710, CM 440. See James A. McAllister, Jr. *Dorchester Co. Land Records,* Repr. Westminster: Family Line Publications.

Emanuel, or Baust's Church, Carroll County, 1792-1800, Records of, in *MGSB* 35:261-ff.

Evans FR: Book started by John Evans of John; transcription at the Methodist Historical Society, #1675.

FCA: Filing Case A, Maryland Historical Society.

First German Reformed Church, Register, Baltimore, at MdHS.

First Presbyterian Church Register, Baltimore, at MdHS.

First Record Book for the Reformed and Lutheran and Congregations at Manchester, Baltimore Co. Maryland (Now Carroll County), in *MGSB* 35.

FR: Family Record.

FRAA: FREDERICK CO. REGISTER OF WILLS (Administration Accounts). MSA C 747, CM 463.

Francis Holland BR, in *MBR* 5:89-90.

FRLR: FREDERICK CO. COURT (Land Records), MSA C 814, CM 485. See Patricia A. Andersen. *Frederick County Land Records, 1748-.* Pub. by the Author.

FRML: FREDERICK COUNTY COURT (Marriage Licenses) MSA C 825.

FRWB: FREDERICK CO. REGISTER OF WILLS (Wills), MSA C898, CM 512. See Donna Valley Russell. *Frederick County, Maryland, Wills, 1744-1794.* New Market: Catoctin Press, 2002.

Garrettson BR (1845), MGRC 1979: 1.

Gillespie BR 1: "Gillespie-Brittain-Brattan Record," *Gen. of PA Fam. from the PA Gen. Mag.* GPC, 3:777-779.

Goslin FR 1: Goslin Family Records (provenance unknown); FCA: MHS.

Gough-Carroll Bible Records. *MG* 2:23-25

Gould BR 1: Robert Gould's Bible (1754); John Baker Brimmer's Bible (1777), FCA: MHS.

Gracey BR 1: Gracey Bible. Philadelphia, 1830; typed copy, DAR, in FCA:MHS

Graflin BR 1: Graflin Bible: 1680; FCA: MHS.

Griffith BR 1: "Griffith Bible Record," *NGSQ* 17:51-ff.

Griffith BR 2: "Griffith Family Register," *MGSB* 18:170-ff.

Guyton BR, in Rev. War Pension Appl. W21237, in *NGSQ* 21:48.

HABFR: *Bible and Family Records of Harford County, Maryland.* Compiled by Shirley L. Reightler. 3 vols. Special Publications of the Harford County Genealogical Society, nos. 3, 4, 15.

Hall, Robert W. *Early Landowners of Maryland: Volume 7: Baltimore County, 1658-1710.* Lewes: Colonial Roots, 2010.

HAML: HARFORD CO. COURT (Marriage Licenses) MSA MSA CM 586. See also Jon Harlan Livezey and Helene Maynard Davis. *Harford County, Maryland Marriage Licenses, 1777-1865.* Westminster: Family Line Publications, 1993.

Hance Nelson BR, in *MBR* 5:128-129.

Hanson BR: *MGSB* 3 (3) 26-29.

Harper, Irma S. *First Kent, Second Kent, Third Kent.* 3 vols. Privately printed. [Abstracts of Kent Co. Land Records for the years 1648-1726.]

Harris and McHenry [Court Reports]. 4 vols., 1700-1779. See also *NGSQ* 53 (below).

Harrison: Lucy H. Harrison: official copyist of the Maryland Historical Society whose transcriptions of early parish registers were the basis of this author's *Maryland Marriages, 1634-1777.*

Harrison: Anne Arundel County Church Registers

Harrison, "All Hallow's Parish Register," Anne Arundel Co., at MdHS.

Harrison, "St. Ann's Parish Register," Anne Arundel Co., at MdHS.

Harrison, "St. James Parish Register," Anne Arundel Co., at the MdHS.

Harrison, "St. Margaret's Parish," Anne Arundel Co., at MdHS.

Harrison: Baltimore County and Harford County Church Registers.

Harrison, "St. George's:" Lucy H. Harrison, "St. George's Parish Register," Baltimore and Harford Counties. at MdHS.

Harrison, "St. James:" Lucy H. Harrison, "St. James Parish Register." Baltimore Co, at MdHS.

Harrison, "St. John's:" Lucy H. Harrison, "St. John's and St, John's Parish Register," Baltimore and Harford Counties, at MdHS.

Harrison, "St. Paul's:" Lucy H. Harrison, "St. Paul's Parish Register," Baltimore Co., at MdHS.

Harrison, "St. Thomas:'" Lucy H. Harrison, "St. Thomas' Parish Register," Baltimore Co. at MdHS.

Harrison, Lucy H. "All Saints Parish Register," Frederick Co., at MdHS

Harrison, Lucy H. "Coventry Parish Register," Somerset Co., at MdHS.

HCBR: See *HABFR.*

Headley, Robert Kirk, Jr. *Married Well and Often: Marriages of the Northern Neck of Virginia, 1649-1800.* Baltimore: Genealogical Publishing Co., 2003.

Heinegg, Paul. *Free African Americans of Maryland and Delaware from the Colonial Period to 1810.* Baltimore: Genealogical Publishing Co., 2000.

Hinchcliff, Helen. "Job Davidson, Cooper in Baltimore, Maryland, and His Long Lost Descendants..." *NGSQ* 94 (2) (June 2006) 85-100.

HMGB: Hayes' Maryland Genealogical Bulletin. Periodical.

Hodges' Marriage References: Maryland State Archives Card Index 5. [It should be noted that some of her citations are obscure. "Liber 1" could refer to MWB 1 or MDTP 1.]

Hood BR in Rev, War Pension Appl. W-3816, in *NGSQ* 20:120-121,

Hook BR, *MGSB* 20 (4) 344.

Hooper, Debbie. *Abstracts of Chancery Court Records of Maryland, 1669-1782.* West-minster, Md.: Family Line Publications.

INAC: PREROGATVE COURT (Inventories and Accounts), MSA S 536, SM 13. See V. L. Skinner. *Abstracts of the Inventories and Accounts of the Prerogative Court of Maryland, 1674-1718.* Westminster, Md.: Family Line Publications.

James Bond BR, *in Gen. of Penna. Families from the Pennsylvania Genealogical Magazine,* Baltimore: Genealogical Publishing Co., 3:581-582.

James McCormick BR, in *MBR* 5:114-115.

Jennings BR, in *HMGB* 2 (2) 9-10.

Jeremiah and Thomas Johnson BR, in *MGSB* 47 (1) (Winter 2006) 6-12.

John Buck of B. BR, in MGRC 31:178.

John Henry Hoppe BR, in *MBR* 3:122-124.

John Trimble, BR, in *MBR* 2:160-161.

Jones Bible Records. *MG* 2:106-109.

Judgments: probably Provincial Court Judgment Records (used by Hodges and Fresco).

Kelley BR, from Rev. War Pension Appl. R5831, in *NGSQ* 20:95.

KELR: KENT CO. COURT (Land Records), MSA C 1068, CM 662. See also Irma S. Harper.

Kemp BR 1: Kemp bible, Printed Philadelphia: Cowperthwait, Desiver and Butler, 1856, in MGR 35: 21-23.

Kent BR 1: Kent Bible, pub. London: 1783. FCA:MHS.

Leisenring, "Maryland Marriages, 1777-1804." MdHS.

Maryland Rent Rolls; Baltimore and Anne Arundel Counties, 1700-1707, 1705-1724: A Consolidation of Articles from the Maryland Historical Magazine. Baltimore: Genealogical Publishing Co., 1976.

MBR: Henry C. Peden, Jr. *Maryland Bible Records.* Lewes [DE}: Colonial Roots, 2003, vols 1-7. It should be noted that while many of these marriages have been found elsewhere, the Bible records and family records often give additional data.

MCHP: CHANCERY COURT (Chancery Papers), MSA S 512.

MCHR: CHANCERY COURT (Chancery Records) MSA S517.

MCW: Md. Cal. of Wills; Maryland Calendar of Wills, vols.1-16. Westminster: Family Line Publications,

MDAD: PREROGATIVE COURT (Accounts) MSA S 531, SM 7. See V. L. Skinner, *Abstracts of Administration Accounts of the Prerogative Court of Maryland. Libers 1-74, 1718-1777.* 11 vols. Westminster, Md.: Family Line Publications.

MDTP: PREROGATIVE COURT (Testamentary Proceedings), MSA S 529, SM 15. See V. V. L. Skinner. *Abstracts of the Testamentary Proceedings of the Prerogative Court of Maryland. Volume I: 1658-1674.* Baltimore: Clearfield Publishing Co., 2004.

*MG: Maryland Genealogies.*2 vols. Baltimore: Genealogical Publishing Co.,

MGR: Maryland Genealogical Committee Reports (located at the DA Library, Washington, D.C.).

MGRC: Maryland Genealogical Records Committee. N.S.D.A.R.

MGSB: Maryland Genealogical Society Bulletin.

MGSJ: Maryland Genealogical Society Journal.

MHGB: Maryland Historical and Genealogical Bulletin.

MHM: Maryland Historical Magazine

Micajah Greenfield BR, in *MBR* 1:97-98.

MINV: PREROGATIVE COURT (Inventories) MSA S534, SM 11. See V. L. Skinner. *Abstracts of the Inventories of the Prerogative Court of Maryland, 1718-1777.* Westminster, Md.: Family Line Publications.

MM: Monthly Meeting of the Society of Friends..

MRR: Maryland Rent Rolls: Baltimore and Anne Arundel Counties. Baltimore: Genealogical Publishing Co., 1976.

MSA Card Index 27: An index of marriages recorded primarily in Protestant Episcopal Churches.

MSA: Maryland State Archives, Annapolis, MD.

MWAR: MARYLAND LAND OFFICE (Warrant Record) MSA S 23.

MWB: PREROGATIVE COURT (Wills) MSA S 538.

→MWB abst. by Carson Abst. by Gibb), accessed at

MWB abst. in Md. Cal. of Wills: see above

NGSQ 53:199-204. Jean Stephenson, "Extracts from Maryland Court Records," *National Genealogical Society Quarterly* 53:199-204.

NGSQ: National Genealogical Society Quarterly. Checked vols. 1-31.

Nicholas Dorsey BR, in *MBR* 3:67-69.

Nicholas Dorsey BR, in *The Notebook*, 10 (3) (Sep 1994), 29-31.

Nicodemus BR, in *MGSB* 39 (1) 73

The Notebook, pub. quarterly by the Baltimore County Genealogical Society.

"Old Maryland Bibles." *MG* 2:270-278.

OSBR: Memory Aldridge Lester. *Old Southern Bible Records*. Baltimore: Clearfield Co., 2007.

Oursler BR, in *NGSQ* 6:32.

Owings BR (1767), in *NGSQ* 5:63.

Owings BR, *in NGSQ* 5:53-64

Owings Family BR, in *HMGB* 3 (3)18-20.

Patterson BR (1) in HCBR 1:10-11.

PCJU: PROVINCIAL COURT (Judgment Record) MSA S 551.

PCLR; PROVINCIAL COURT (Land Records) MSA S552.

Peden, Henry C., Jr. *Bastardy Cases in Baltimore County, Maryland, 1673-1783.* Westminster: Willow Bend Books, 2001.

Peden, Henry C., Jr. *A Closer Look at St. John's Parish* [entered first two sections]

Peden, Henry C., Jr. *Colonial Tavern Keepers of Maryland and Delaware, 1634-1776.* Bel Air, Md. © 2010 by Henry C. Peden.

Peden, Henry C. *Orphans and Indentured Children of Baltimore County, Maryland, 1777-1797.* Lewes: Colonial Roots, 2005.

PGLR: PRINCE GEORGE'S CO. COURT (Land Records), MSA C 1237, CM 782.

Piet: Mary A. and Stanley G. Piet, *Early Catholic Church records in Baltimore, Maryland, 1782 through 1800.* Westminster: Family Line Publications, 1989.

Polk, John, Electronic transcriptions of SOJU 1692-1693, 1693-1694, and 1695-1695, graciously made available to the author.

Provincial Court: term used by Fresco and Hodges; probably to refer to either Provincial Court Judgments or Provincial Court Land Records.

QAJU: QUEEN ANNE'S CO. COURT (Judgment Records) MSA C 1416, CM 844. See Irma S. Harper. "Queen Anne's County Judgments Records." *Chesapeake Cousins* 24 (1) 22-25 (1710-1730), 24 (2) 26-29 (1730-1737), 25 (1) 22-24 (1737-1740).See also F. Edward Wright. *Judgment Records of Dorchester, Queen Anne's & Talbot Counties.* Lewes, Del.: Delmarva Roots, 2001.

QALR: QUEEN ANNE'S CO. COURT (Land Records), MSA C1426, CM 1163. See Bernice Leonard. *Queen Anne's Co. Land Records.* St. Michael's, Md.: Pub. by the Author).

QMES: F. Edward Wright. *Quaker Minutes of the Eastern Shore of Maryland, 1676-1779.* Dover, Del.: Delmarva Roots, 2003.

QRNM: Henry C. Peden, Jr. *Quaker Records of Northern Maryland.* Westminster, Md.: Family Line Publications.

QRSM: Henry C. Peden, Jr., *Quaker Records of Southern Maryland.* Westminster, Md.: Family Line Publications, 1992.

Reamy. *St. George's:* Bill and Martha Reamy. *St. George's Parish Register, 1689-1793.* Westminster: Family Line Publications, 1988.

Reamy. St. Thomas': Bill and Martha Reamy. *St. Thomas' Parish Registers, 1732-1850.* Silver Spring: Family Line Publications, 1987.

"Records from an Old [Owings] Bible." *MG* 2:272-274.

Red Books. See CMSP.

Reformed Congregation of Saint Benjamin's Known as Kreider's Church at Pipe Creek, Maryland [Westminster], in *MGSB* 35:437-ff.

Reverend William West BR, in *MBR* 5:207-209.

Revolutionary War Pension Applications; accessed at Heritage Quest.

Richards Marr. Register: Marriage Register of Rev. Lewis Richards, Pastor of First Baptist Church, Baltimore, 1784-1818. MS 690 at MdHS

Rouse Family BR, in *MGSB* 48 (1) (Winter 2007) 67-72

Russell, Donna Valley, "The Putative Daughters of John Larkin," *MGSB* 45 (1) (Winter 2004) 35-62.

Russell, George Ely, "Portuguese and Spanish Colonists in 17th Century Maryland." *TAG* 76 (April 2001).

Scharf Papers, MS.1999 at MdHS. It should be noted that the Scharf Papers are now at the Maryland State Archives, but the marriages noted here are from photocopies deposited at the Maryland Historical Society.

Sherwood, George [F. T.]. *American Colonists in English Records*. 1921, 1933. Reprint, Baltimore: Genealogical Publishing Co., 1969.

Skinner, Vernon L., Jr. *Abstracts of the Proprietary Records of the Provincial Court of Maryland, 1637-1658*. Westminster, Md.: Willow Bend Books, 2002.

Skordas, Gust.: *Early Settlers of Maryland, 1633-1680*. Baltimore: Genealogical Publishing Co., 1979.

Slemaker FR, *MGSB* 19 (3) 145-146.

SM: St. Mary's Co.

SMRR: MARYLAND LAND OFFICE (Rent Rolls) MSA S 18, SM 130: St. Mary's Co. Rent Roll, 1707; transcribed by Christopher Johnston; microfilm of original is at MHS. Pages given are to the Johnston transcription.

SO: Somerset Co.

SOLR:IKL: SOMERSET CO. COURT (Register of Births, Marriages and Deaths, 1649-1720), MSA C 1739, CM 956. It is interspersed with deeds in a volume of land records. See Clayton Torrence, *Old Somerset on the Eastern Shore of Maryland*. 1935. Reprint, Westminster, Md.: Family Line Publications, 1992, pp. 396-400.

"Some of Bible Records of the Ridgely Family of Maryland." *MG* 2:300-ff.

SORR: MARYLAND LAND OFFICE (Rent Rolls) MSA S 18, SM 130: Somerset County Rent Rolls, 1663-1723, abst. and pub. by Ruth Dryden. Repr.: Westminster: Family Line Publications, n.d.

TA: Talbot Co.

TAG: The American Genealogist.

TAJU: TALBOT CO. COURT (Judgment Records) MSA C 1875, CM 1810. See F. Edward Wright. *Judgment Records of Dorchester, Queen Anne's & Talbot Counties*. Lewes, Del.: Delmarva Roots, 2001.

TALR: TALBOT COUNTY COURT (Land Records) MSA C 1880, CM 1011. See Bernice Leonard. *Talbot County Land Records*. Privately Printed.

Thompson BR 1: "Thompson Bible Record (Eastern Shore of Maryland)." FCA: MHS.

Thompson BR 2: "Thompson Bible:" Baltimore: Fielding Lucas, n.d.; FCA:MHS

Thompson BR 3: Middleton Thompson Bible; FCA: MHS.

Torrence, Clayton. *Old Somerset on the Eastern Shore of Maryland*. 1935. Reprint, Westminster, Md.: Family Line Publications, 1992.

///

Tschudy FR: Family Records copied from Book of Edward Hiner; in FCA, MHS; pub. in

MGSB 45 (2) 412-414; also in *MGSB* 16 (2) (May 1975), 64-ff.

Urath Randall Owings Bible. *MG* 2:270-271.

VMHB: Virginia Magazine of History and Biography.

Walker BR: Walker-Cradock Bible Records, in MdHS, in *MGSB* 39 (4) 530-534).

Welch BR 1: Printed Cambridge: John Archdeacon, 1769; in MGR 35:-96-98.

Wesley Stevenson BR, in *The Notebook* (Baltimore Co. Gen. Soc.) 21 (3) (Fall 2005) 12-15.

Westmoreland Co., VA, Will Book. (See Fothergill above.)

Wiatt BR 1: Bible Records of Solomon Wiatt, in *HMGB* 13:23.

William Ady BR, in *MBR* 5:2-3.

William Patterson BR, in *MBR* 5:143-144.

William Thomas Watson BR, in *MBR* 2:169-171.

Wilson Diary 1: Hezekiah Wilson's Diary, Montgomery County, MD," *NGSQ* 6:27-ff

WWBR: Mrs. Wilbur F. Yingling. "Bible Records Presented Through William Winchester Chapter." MGRC. 1981. typescript, MdHS.

YOLR: York Co., PA Land Records. See Mary Marshall. Brewer. *Land Records of York County, Pennsylvania, 1746-1764.* Lewes; Colonial Roots, 2004.

"Single Names"

[-?-]. Caleb, m. 1 June 1788, Rose [-?-] at St. Peter's Catholic Church, Baltimore (*Piet*: 126).

[-?-], Elinor, servant of John Morgan, was charged with bastardy at the March 1746/7 Court, but her master paid the fine (BACP TB&TR#1:397).

[-?-] Ned, m. 22 April 1792, Sarah [-?-] at St. Peter's Catholic Church, Baltimore (*Piet*: 126).

[-?-], Leonard, m. by license on 28 Dec 1786, Bett [-?-] at St. Peter's Catholic Church, Baltimore (*Piet*: 126).

[-?-], Patience, servant of Walter Falls, was charged with bastardy on 7 Aug 1744; on 6 Nov 1744 she was ordered to serve the county for seven years after her present servitude; her ten month old child Assex was sold to Walter Dallas and ordered to serve him to the age of 31 (BACP 1743-1745:293, 300).

[-?-], Phil, m. 10 June 1792, Clare [-?-] at St. Peter's Catholic Church, Baltimore (*Piet*: 126).

[-?-], Sarah, servant of John Brown, was charged with bastardy at the Nov 1772 Court and fined (BAMI 1772-1781: 84).

"A"

Abbitt, John, and Miss Nancy Little, both of Baltimore, were m. last Thurs. eve. by Rev. Mr. Bend (*Baltimore Telegraphe* 16 July 1798).

Abbott, [-?-], m. by 13 Nov 1800, Ann, daughter of John Buckingham (BAWB 6:327).

Abercrombie, Robert, and Ann Hatton were m. on 6 Aug 1756 (Harrison, "St. John's:" 213). On 29 July 1771 she was named as a daughter of John Hatton (MDAD 66:15).

Abercrombie (Cromby), Robert, m. by 4 Dec 1772, Salathiel, poss. widow of [Henry?] Eaglestone (*q.v.*), she was a daughter of Jarvis and Mary Biddison, and heir of Daniel Biddison (BAWB 3:272; BAAD 8:308, 11:4, 13).

Abrahams, Jacob, of Baltimore, stated he would not pay the debts of his wife (*Maryland Journal and Baltimore Advertiser* 20 Sep 1784).

Achchief?, Isaac, m. by 21 Dec 1799, Elizabeth, legatee and granddaughter of Elizabeth Barrow (BAWB 5:98; BAAD 13: 168).

Ackerman, George, son of George and Christiana, was under age when his father died. On 31 Aug 1790 George Ackerman married M. Bose (Marriage Lic. Returns of Rev. Daniel Kurtz, 1786-1790, Scharf Papers, MS. 1999, MdHS).

Acorns, John, in Nov 1757 was fined for begetting a bastard on the body of Sarah Butram (BAMI 1757-1759:74).

Acton, Richard, in his will dated 8 Oct 1740 named his grandsons Richard and Henry Young (MWB 22:319 abst. in *Md. Cal. of Wills* 8:123). Margaret Acton had m. Suel (Sewell) Young (*q.v.*).

1

Adair, Dr. Alexander, of Kent Co., d. by 11 Oct 1749 having m. Christian, only heir of Thomas Sterling of Kent Co.; Robert Adair was a son of Alexander and Christian (BALR TR#C:297).

Adair, Elizabeth, formerly Wilson, on 6 d. 4 m. 1775, was charged with marrying contrary to the good order ("Minutes of Gunpowder Monthly Meeting," *QRNM:* 65). [No other marriage reference found].

Adams, [-?-], d. by 27 March 1754, at which time Bothia Adams, admx. of James Barnes (*q.v.*) was m. to [-?-] Scarlett (*q.v.*) (MDTP 36:28).

Adams, Henry, on 27 July 1784 was named as a grandson of Rowland Smith, stone mason (BAWB 4:7).

Adams, James, native of Ireland, m. by lic. on 28 May 1800, Margaret Sheney (Chaney), widow of Peter Shirk (*q.v.*) at St. Peter's Catholic Church, Baltimore (*Piet:* 126).

Adams, James, Negro, m. by banns on 21 Dec 1800, Agnes Butler, Negro, at St. Peter's Catholic Church, Baltimore (*Piet:* 126).

Adams, John, printer of Baltimore, and Mrs. Eleanor Reed of Philadelphia were married last Thurs. eve. (*Baltimore Daily Repository* 10 July 1793).

Adams, Richard, m. by Dec 1691, Mary, admx. of John Stansby (*q.v.*) (BACP F#1:136).

Adams, Samuel, teacher of languages, married Mrs. Agnes Thomson, widow and admx. of the late Andrew Thomson (*Maryland Journal and Baltimore Advertiser* 29 May 1789; BAAD 10:109)

Addison, John, and Miss Sarah Leitch were married at Epping, Baltimore Co., by Rev. Coleman (*Maryland Journal and Baltimore Advertiser* 16 Oct 1792).

Addison, Col. Thomas, of Prince George's Co., and Elinor Smith, aged 19 years, daughter of Col. Walter Smith were m. 17 June 1709 (Harrison, "St. John's, Piscataway Parish," Prince George's Co., at MdHS, p. 264; BALR IS#J: 6).

Adieu, Peter, of Baltimore, and Miss Kitty Estafy of Alexandria, were m. at the latter place last Sat. (*Baltimore Telegraphe* 11 Aug 1797).

Adelsberger, George, m. by 11 Oct 1796, Susan, heir of Nicholas Frankforter (BAAD 12:198).

Adkinson, John, and Ann Shepard were m. on 11 Feb 1734 (Harrison, "St. George's:" 281). On 24 July 1738 Ann was named as a daughter of Rowland Shepherd of Baltimore Co. (MDAD 16:247). Adkinson's widow Ann m. 2nd, by 30 Jan 1755 Major David Bisset (*q.v.*).

Adonis, Charles, m by lic. on 6 July 1799, Elizabeth Lachenal, both free Mulattoes of St. Domingo, at St. Peter's Catholic Church, Baltimore (*Piet:* 126).

Adrean, Christian, in his will made 28 Dec 1799 named his daughters Barbara Parsonham *alias* Adrean, Mery Edgen, Elizabeth Morrison, and Hannah Cross or Gross *alias* Sedgwick, and her son Christian Cross (Gross) (BAWB 6:316).

Ady, Jonathan, d. 21 June 1801, and Rebecca York, d. 24 Sep 1800, were m. on 27 March 1743 (Harrison, "St. John's:" 238; "Ady Bibles," *MGSB* 20 (3) (Summer 1979) 237).

Ady, William, b. 8 Aug 1745, son of Jonathan and Rebecca Ady, m. 1770 Chloe Standiford ("Ady Bibles." *MGSB* 20 (3) (Summer 1979) 237, 239; *MBR* 5:2).

Aiken, Archibald, m. by 11 March 1768, Margaret [-?-]; he named a step-daughter Margaret Kelley (BAWB 3:95).

Aikenhead. See Aitkenhead.

Aisquith, [-?-], m. by 7 Dec 1772 [-?-], sister of Mary Hall, widow of Elisha Hall; Mary Hall named her nephew John Aisquith, who was not yet 21 BAWB 3:291).

Aisquith (Asquith), William, and Elizabeth Connell were m. on 2 May 1762 (Harrison, "St. Paul's:" 192). On 15 May 1762 Elizabeth was named as a daughter of John and Mary Connell (BALR B#K: 185).

Aitkenhead, George (Aikenhead), d. by Feb 1781; m. by 11 Dec 1778 Catherine, widow and admx. of Nicholas Hasslebach (BAAD 6:337; BALR WG#C: 210, BALR WG#HH: 296, 301).

Akers, Edmond Francis, m. by 13 Sep 1793 Frances, daughter of Joseph Rawlins (BAWB 5:151).

Albers, Lueber, merchant was m. last eve. by Rev. Mr. Altenar, to Eve Diffenderfer, daughter of Michael Diffenderfer, all of this city (*Federal Gazette and Baltimore Daily Advertiser* 5 Jan 1798).

Albright, John, m. by 11 Oct 1796, Catherine, widow of William Clour (BAAD 12: 195).

Alcock, William, of Baltimore, stated he would not pay the debts of his wife Bridget, who has eloped (*Baltimore Daily Repository* 24 Nov 1792).

Alder, [-?-], m. by 15 Nov 1790 Mary, sister of Catherine Barbara Brown, wife of Jacob Frederick Brown (BAWB 5:35).

Alexander, Dr. Ashton, of this city, and Miss Catherine Thomas of Frederick Town, were m. 26th Dec. by Rev. Bowers (*Federal Gazette and Baltimore Daily Advertiser* 2 Jan 1800).

Alexander, Joshua, of Baltimore Co., m. by 25 March 1749, Mary [-?-] (MDAD 26:33).

Alexander, Robert, son of Robert and Araminta, m. 1764, Isabella Lawson ("Alexander-Lawson Bible Record," FCA at MdHS).

Alkin, [-?-], d. by 13 July 1798, having m. Mary Ashberry, only daughter of Ellen Burneston; Mary Ashberry Alkin m. 2nd, Reuben Gilder by license dated 5 Oct 1790 (BAML). Alkin's widow married [3rd] by the above date John Chalmers the Younger (*q.v.*) (BALR WG#55:430).

Allaert, James, m. by lic. on 28 Oct 1798, Ann Quedan at St. Peter's Catholic Church, Baltimore (*Piet*: 126). James Ellirt [*sic*] and Nancy Quidane were married by license dated 27 Oct 1798 (BAML).

Allain, Lewis, son of Thomas and Jane (Rouboutet) of St. Domingo, m. by lic. on 29 Oct 1799, Ann Boisson, daughter, of Thomas and Adelaide (Cornu), native of Cap Francois at St. Peter's Catholic Church, Baltimore (*Piet*: 126).

Allbright, John Ernest, m. by 3 Nov 1787, [-?-], sister of Elizabeth, the first wife of Frederick Meyers (BAAD 9:116).

Allen, Adam, m. by 15 Sep 1798, Elizabeth, daughter of Michael Earnest (BAAD 12:524).

Allen, James, of Deer Creek, in Nov 1756 was charged with begetting a bastard on the body of Rebecca Gladding (BAMI 1755-1763; BACP BB#C: 311).

Allen, John, d. 2 March 1792, was m. to Mary [Grover?] on 12 Oct 1791 by Rev. John Davis in Baltimore Co. (Rev. War Pension Application of Mary Allen: W-4114).

Allen, Joseph, of Baltimore Co., stated he would not pay the debts of his wife Anne, who had eloped from him, and gone off with a Recruiting Officer and stood a summer's campaign with Col. Brodhead's Battalion (*Maryland Journal and Baltimore Advertiser* 7 Dec 1778)

Allen, Michael, stated he would not pay the debts of his wife Mary (*Maryland Gazette or Baltimore General Advertiser* 31 Oct 1775).

Allen, Nathaniel, d. by 29 Feb 1725 on which date his admx. Frances m. John Mason (*q.v.*) (BAAD 3:178).

3

Allen, Sarah, (later Underwood), on 24 d. 10 m. 1799 was found guilty of having gone out in marriage by the assistance of a hireling minister (("Minutes of Deer Creek Meeting," *QRNM:* 161). [No other marriage reference found].

Allen, Solomon, m. by 31 Oct 1791, [-?-], daughter of John Schleich whose will of that date named his grandson John Allen (BAWB 7:118).

Allen, William, and Elizabeth Wright were m. on 5 Oct 1756 (Harrison, "St. John's," p. 214). On 11 July 1763 Eliz. was named as a daughter of Jacob Wright (BAWB 3:170).

Allen, William, b. 3 Nov 1769, son of Robert and Hannah Allen of Wexford, Ireland, and Hannah Bond, b. 6 July 1779, daughter of Thomas and Catherine Bond, were m. on 12 April 1798 ("Allen-Raymond Family Bible," *HABFR* 2:3). They were m. by the Rev. Mr. Allen (*Federal Gazette and Baltimore Daily Advertiser* 17 April 1798).

Allender, [-?-], m. by 29 Nov 1766 Jane, daughter of Avarilla Lynch who named her daughter Jane Allender (BAWB 3:72).

Allender, [-?-], m. by 4 Dec 1770, Keziah, daughter of Samuel Wheeler (BAWB 3:179).

Allender, John, and Lucina Roberts were m. on 27 March 1749 (Harrison, "St. John's Parish Register:" 157). On 20 June 1756 Lucy was named as a daughter of John Roberts, lawyer of Baltimore Co. (BALR TR#D: 459).

Allender, John, and Hannah Jervice were m. by 25 Nov 1789 in Baltimore ("Marr. Returns of Ezekiel Cooper, Scharf Papers, MdSA S1005," *MGSB* 32 (1) (Winter 1991) 6).

Allender, Dr. Joseph, and Mary Biays, daughter of Major Joseph Biays, all of this city were m. last Thurs. eve. by Rev. Dr. Allison (*Federal Gazette and Baltimore Daily Advertiser* 3 Feb 1800).

Allender, Joshua, m. by 6 Aug 1755, Avarilla, daughter of Edward Day and Avarilla his wife, who later m. Patrick Lynch (*q.v.*) (BACH TB#E: 185; BAWB 3:72; BACT TR#E: 166).

Allender, Nicholas, m. by 16 April 1755, Jane, daughter of Edward Day and his wife Avarilla who later m. Patrick Lynch (BACT TR#E: 166; BAWB 3:72).

Allender, William, m. by 18 June 1766, Anna, daughter of Edward Day and his wife Avarilla who later m. Patrick Lynch (BACT B#G: 93; BAWB 3:72).

Allender, William, m. by 26 July 1781 Sophia, daughter of Walter Tolley who also named his grandson Joseph, Thomas Tolley, Walter, Mary, and Elizabeth Allender (BAWB 3:507; BALR WG#FF: 257).

Allison, Elisha, of Montgomery Co., was m. last Sun. eve. by Rev. Mr. Bend to Miss Ann Sheppard of this town (*Federal Gazette and Baltimore Daily Advertiser* 21 June 1796).

Allison, Rev. Dr. Patrick, b. 1740 in Lancaster Co., Pa., and Polly, daughter of William Buchanan of Baltimore, were married Thursday evening last [13 March 1787] (*Maryland Journal and Baltimore Advertiser* 20 March 1787; *Maryland Gazette or Baltimore General Advertiser* 20 March 1787; "Patrick Allison Bible Record," in MGRC 33:24).).

Almeny. See Almony.

Almony (Almeny), John, married Elizabeth Waddam [not Warhorn] on 6 Feb 1753 (Peden. *A Closer Look:* 1 corrects entry in Harrison's "St. John's"). Their son John was b. on 26 March 1764 ("Benjamin Almony Bible," *MBR* 7:3).

Almony, John, and Mary Watson were m. on 6 Feb 1770 (Harrison, "St. John's:" 260). On 24 Dec 1789 Mary was named as an heir of William Watson (BAAD 10:94).

Almony, John, son of John and Elizabeth, was b. 20 March 1764, m. by 1 Jan 1798, Ann [-?-], when their son Benjamin was b. ("Benjamin Almony Bible," *MBR* 7:3). [No other marriage reference found].

Alricks, [-?-]. m. by 8 Nov 1791, Jane, admx. of Samuel Leggit (BAAD 10:471).

Alter, John, and Susannah Giles, both of this town were married last evening by Rev. Kurtz (*Federal Intelligencer and Baltimore Daily Gazette* 21 Dec 1795; *Federal Intelligencer and Baltimore Daily Gazette* 21 Dec 1795). Their daughter Margaret was b. on 15 Sep 1796 ("John Alter Bible," *MBR* 3:3).

Alter, John, in his will made 23 Nov 1800 named his bro. Christopher Alter, his uncle Jacob Brown and his sisters Susanna Mackenheimer and Mary Tibbles (BAWB 6:373).

Ambrose, Ann, servant of John Parrish, was charged with bastardy at March Court 1730/1, presented at June Court, 1731, and charged again at Nov Court 1737 and presented at March Court 1737/8 (BACP HWS#7:156, 166, HWS#1A: 129, 160).

Ambrose, James, of The Garrison Forest close by Susannah Buchanan's, on 24 Nov 1785 posted bond to administer the estate of Charles Motherby (BAAB 6:338).

Ambrose, William, administrator, on 1 Sep 1796 posted bond to administer the estate of James McKeele (BAAB 8:916).

Ambrose, William, m. by 19 June 1798, Mary, daughter of Mary Parrish (BALR WG#55: 188). Mary Ambrose, formerly Parrish, on 27 d. 9 m. 1775, was charged with having been m. by a priest ("Minutes of Gunpowder Monthly Meeting," *QRNM:* 66). [No other marriage reference found].

Amelin, Mathe..., m. by 3 May 1798, Therese Emille Constance Estienne, legatee of Frederick Estienne (BAAD 12:428).

Amelung, Frederick, was m. at New Bremen on Thurs., 4th inst., to Miss Sophia Furnival, eldest daughter of Alexander Furnival of this city (*Federal Gazette and Baltimore Daily Advertiser* 8 May 1797).

Ami, Francis, native of Lyons, France, m. by lic. on 16 Aug 1795, Ann Tillard, b. in Acadia, at St. Peter's Catholic Church, Baltimore (*Piet:* 126).

Amie, John Baptist Joseph Amable, physician, native of Brignoles, son of John Baptist Joseph and Margaret Louise Julie (Chambeiron), m. by lic. on 27 June 1797, Helen Frances Toullain Dupuy, daughter of Peter Francis Toullain and Margaret Susanna (Monchet). Native of Plaisance, St. Domingo, at St. Peter's Catholic Church, Baltimore (*Piet:* 126).

Amos, [-?-], m. by 22 June 1787, Elizabeth, extx. of William Standiford (BAAD 9:68, 11:348).

Amos, [-?-], m, by 25 Nov 1794, Ann, daughter of Nicholas Hutchings (BAWB 5:210).

Amos (Amoss), [-?-], m. by 29 Aug 1800 Elizabeth, daughter of Robert Cornthwait (BAWB 6:322).

Amos, Ann. See Thomas Sheppard.

Amos, Eleanor, See Eleanor Bull.

Amos (Amoss), James, and Hannah Clark were m. on 29 Jan 1739 (Harrison, "St. George's Parish Register:" 275). On 22 Dec 1755 Hannah was named as a daughter of Robert Clark of Baltimore Co. (MWB 30:221 abst. by Gibb).

Amos, James, son of William, and Hannah Lee on 25 d. 8 m. 1790 declared their intention to marry ("Minutes of Gunpowder Meeting," *QRNM:* 89).

Amos, Joshua, m. by 1756 Mary, daughter of Richard and Mary ([-?-]) Marshall (*ARMD* 31:174-179).

Amos, Joshua, m. by 22 June 1788, Sarah, daughter of Edward Bussey (BAWB 3:245; BAAD 9:217).

Amos, Luke, on 27 d. 12 m. 1794, hath gone out in marriage to a woman not of our society ("Minutes of Gunpowder Meeting," *QRNM:* 95). Luke Amos and Sarah Gallion were m. on 26 Nov 1794 (New Jerusalem Swedenborgian Church Register at MdHS).

Amos, Maulden, son of William, on 27 d, 6 m., 1770, was charged with outgoing in marriage by a priest ("Minutes of Gunpowder Monthly Meeting," *QRNM:*60). "Louldin" Amos [*sic:* prob. Maulden] m. Rachel Bull on 3 June 1770 (Harrison, "St John's Parish Register:" 260).

Amos, Mordecai, and Mary Scott were m. on 16 Feb 1748 (Harrison, "St. John's Parish Register:" 198). On 2 May 1758 Mary was named as a daughter of Elizabeth Scott (MWB 30:493 abst. by Gibb).

Amos, Robert, and Martha McComas were m. on 22 Dec 1765 (Harrison, "St. John's Parish Register:" 228). On 31 Oct 1766 Robert's wife was named as a daughter of Daniel McComas (BAAD 7:192).

Amos, William, m. by 21 Sep 1747 Hannah, dau. of William McComas (MWB 25:488 abst. by Gibb; BAAD 5:75, 135).

Amos, William, Jr., and Susannah Howard, on 26 d. 5 m. 1773, declared their intention to marry ("Minutes of Gunpowder Monthly Meeting," *QRNM:* 64).

Amos, William, Jr., and Elizabeth Hugo on 12 d. 9 m. 1799 declared their intention to marry ("Minutes of Baltimore Meeting," *QRNM:* 234).

Anderson, Andrew, m. 1778, Ann Bealmear ("Watts Bible Record," MGRC 3:64).

Anderson, Charles, and Grace Preston were m. on 2 Nov 1762 (Harrison, "St. George's Parish Register:" 248). On 5 Nov 1728 Grace was named as a daughter of James Preston (MWB 19:778).

Anderson, Charles, m. by 17 Feb 1759, Mary, daughter of Richard Deaver (BALR B#H: 115).

Anderson, Edward E., m. 12 Dec 1797, Susan Chaney ("Watts Bible Record," MGRC 3:64).

Anderson, Henry, merchant of Baltimore, and Miss Crawford, daughter of Dr. Crawford of Hanover St., were m. yesterday by Dr. Allison (*Baltimore Telegraphe* 24 Oct 1799).

Anderson, John, m. by May 1765, Catherine, daughter of Edward Flanagan; John is not named as Catherine's husband but he filed an admin. bond as exec. (BAWB 3:28); on 31 Aug 1772 she posted bond to administer the estate of Edward Flanagan (BAAB 3:97; MDAD 69:392; MDTP 46:127-128).

Anderson, William, and Mary 'Harrard' were m. on 21 Aug 1755 (Harrison, "St. John's Parish Register:" 212). On 2 Nov 1764 Mary was named as a daughter of Susannah Herod or Harrod (BAWB 3:13).

Anderson, William, m. 28 May 1778, Sarah Wayman ("Watts Bible Record," MGRC 3:64).

Anderson, William, m. 1 Jan 1785, Elizabeth Willett ("Watts Bible Record," MGRC 3:64).

Anderson, William, m. by lic. on 25 June 1790, Kitty Anderson at St. Peter's Catholic Church, Baltimore (*Piet:* 126).

Anderson, Capt. William, was m. last eve. at Canton, the seat of Col. O'Donnell, to Mrs. Mary Roe (*Federal Gazette and Baltimore Daily Advertiser* 12 April 1799).

Andrew, Maddox, merchant, and Pamela Kell, both of Baltimore Town, were m. last evening (*Maryland Journal and Baltimore Advertiser* 2 March 1792).

Andrew, William, d. by Feb 1791; his extx. Mary had m. by 17 Aug 1789 Abraham George Hammond (*q.v.*) (*Maryland Journal and Baltimore Advertiser* 22 Feb 1791).

Andrew. See also Andrews.

Andrews, [-?-], m. by 2 March 1747, [-?-], daughter of William Denton, who also named a grandson Abraham Andrews (MWB 25:206 abst. by Gibb).

Andrews, Joseph, d. by Nov 1711, having m. Sarah [-?-], whose sister m. William Holland (MWB 10:243 abst. in *Md. Cal. of Wills* 6:39).

Andrews, Nathaniel, m. by 1800, [-?-], heir of John Buckler (*q.v.*) (BPET: Nathaniel Andrews 1800).

Andrews, Thomas, d. leaving a will dated 24 Dec 1783, proved 3 Jan 1784, naming friend Mrs. Thomasin White and natural daughter Charlotte Andrews, b. 13 Sep 1783, as heirs of entire estate (BAWB 3:572). Thomasin White m. William Gordon (*q.v.*).

Andrews, William, on 16 June 1721 was named in the will of William Holland as the son of the sister of Holland's wife (MWB 10:243 abst. in *Md. Cal. of Wills* 6:39).

Andrews, William, and Mary Bond were m. on 14 Feb 1732 (Harrison, "St. John's Parish Register:" 74). On 4 Oct 1743 Mary was named as a sister of Anne Bond who named her nephews William Andrews and Billy Drew Andrews (MWB 28:564 abst. in *Md. Cal. of Wills* 8:276; see also BAAD 3:271; MDAD 19:266). On 10 Sep 1746 Mary was named as a daughter of William Bond (MDTP 32:14). On 19 Nov 1748 William was named as a nephew and exec. in the will of Elizabeth Lloyd who also named Mary, wife of William Andrew, and Betty Drew Andrew, who was not yet 16 (MWB 25:475 abst. by Gibb). On 18 Dec 1748 he was named as a bro.-in-law in the will of Peter Bond (MWB 25:552 abst. by Gibb). Andrews d. by April 1784, having m. Mary Lynchfield (BAOC 1:112).

Andrews. See also Andrew.

Angler, Mary, was charged with bastardy at June Court, 1756 (BACP TB&TR#1:2).

Anglin, William, and Elizabeth Taylor, widow, were m. on 22 July 1725 (Harrison, "All Hallow's Parish Register," Anne Arundel Co., at MdHS: 425. In 1726 Elizabeth was named as the admx. of Thomas Taylor (MDTP 27:311).

Anlis, Margaret, on 2 April 1731 was named by Simon Pearson as his mother-in-law (BALC HWS#3 #29).

Annadown, Thomas, and Miss Susan Thompson were m. in Philadelphia (*Baltimore Telegraphe* 17 May 1799).

Annis, James, shipbuilder, and Mrs. Rachel Hamilton, both of Baltimore, were m. last Sun. by Rev. Backsler (*Baltimore American* 17 Dec 1799).

Annis (Annisee), Sarah, was charged with bastardy and confessed at Nov 1756 Court; she was fined 30 shillings on 3 March 1746/7; she paid the fine and the charges were dismissed (BACP TB&TR#1:2, 220, 378, 394, 399-400).

Annis (Ennis), Susanna, was charged with bastardy at Nov Court 1750 (BACP TR#6:1).

Ansbach, Frederick, on 29 Dec 1800 was named as a brother-in-law of Henry Zorn (BAWB 6:351).

Ansbach, Henry N. and Miss Eliza Furnival, second dau of Alexander Furnival, Esq., both of this city, were m. last eve. by Rev. Mr. Bend (*Federal Gazette and Baltimore Daily Advertiser* 20 Feb 1799).

Anthony, James, and Magdalen Pindare, French free Negroes from St Domingo, were m. on 8 Feb 1796 at St. Peter's Catholic Church, Baltimore (*Piet*: 126).

Antill, John, in Nov 1760, admitted paternity of Richard Deaver, the illegitimate child of Mary Deaver (BAMI 1755-1763:30).

Aphold, George Nicholas, native of Germany, m. by banns on 13 Feb 1796, Mary Martin, native of Penna., at St. Peter's Catholic Church, Baltimore (*Piet*: 126).

Araughty, Laurence, native of Ireland, m. by license on 8 July 1800, Mary Lewis of Baltimore Co., native of Penna., at St. Peter's Catholic Church, Baltimore (*Piet*: 126).

Arbegast, Peter Christophel, m. by 24 Dec 1769, Margeth Bornin ("First Record Book for the Reformed and Lutheran Congregations at Manchester, Baltimore (now Carroll) County," *MGSB* 35:273).

Arden, John, d. by April 1694 (MWB 7: 23). His widow Sarah m. 2nd, Joseph Strawbridge (*q.v.*). In her will made 30 March 1699, Sarah, widow of Joseph Strawbridge named her daughter Mary 'Harding,' son Samuel 'Harding,' and the latter's father John 'Harding' (MWB 6:260 abst. in *Md. Cal. of Wills* 2:178).

Arding (Harding), [-?-], m. by 1741, Mary, heir of Joseph Strawbridge (BAAD 1:7).

Arieu[?], John Francois, free Negro from St. Domingo, formerly a slave of Mr. Gabriel Arieu, planter of St. Domingo, m. on 24 July 1796, Mary Magdalen [-?-], free Negro, formerly belonging to said John Francis, her actual husband, at St. Peter's Catholic Church, Baltimore (*Piet*: 126).

Armacost, Christopher, b. 24 Dec 1769, d. 1834, and Belinda Murray, daughter of John and Diana, b. 1 Feb 1776, were m. by 1796 when their daughter Diana was b. ("Murray Bible,"*The Notebook* 9 (4) (Dec 1993) 40)

Armacost (Armagost), Christ'r, m. by 8 Dec 1787, [-?-], daughter of Michael Burns (BAAD 9:127).

Armacost (Armagost), John, m. by 15 April 1795, Mary Gittinger, a representative of John Gittinger (BAAD 12:4).

Armacost, Michael, and Ruth Osborn were married by license dated 23 Jan 1793 (BAML). On 10 April 1793 his wife was named as being entitled to £23.5.9 of the estate of Daniel Osborn (BAAD 11:233).

Armacost (Armigost), Stophel, m. by 13 April 1791, [-?-], daughter of Christ'r Armigost (BAAD 10:355).

Armacost (Armagost, Armegist), Peter, and Elizabeth Doyle were married by license dated 5 Sep 1792 (BAML); on 4 March 1796 Sarah Doyle named her daughter Elizabeth wife of Peter Armegost (BAWB 5:369).

Armand, Francis, native of LaRochelle, France, m. by lic. on 3 July 1794, Margaret Lebat, widow, at St. Peter's Catholic Church, Baltimore (*Piet*: 126).

Armagost. See Armacost.

Armiger, Thomas, m, by 11 Dec 1672, Anne, widow of Francis Trippas (*q.v.*) of Baltimore Co. (MDTP 5:377).

Armigost. See Armacost.

Armitage, James, stated he would not pay the debts of his wife Sarah (*Federal Intelligencer and Baltimore Daily Gazette* 9 April 1795).

Armour, David, a non-Catholic, m. by lic. on 14 May 1793, Mary Hillen, at St. Peter's Catholic Church, Baltimore (*Piet*: 126).

Armstrong, [-?-], m. by 13 Jan 1797 Eliza, mother of John Malone, who on that date was bound to Henry Clarke to learn the trade of nailor (BIND 1:162).

Armstrong, James, d. by Nov 1694 by which time his widow had m. 2nd, John Bird (*q.v.*) (BACP D:212).

Armstrong, James, m. by 1 June 1769 Martha, daughter of Elizabeth Chapman (MWB 37:123, abst. in *Md. Cal. of Wills* 14:81; BAWB 3:131).

Armstrong, Sarah, was charged with bastardy at the March 1768 Court (BACP BB: 2).

Armstrong, Solomon, and Sarah Standiford were m. on 2 Aug 1744 (Harrison, "St. John's Parish Register:" 191). On 15 Dec 1744 Sarah was named as the admx. of Ephraim Standiford (*q.v.*) (MINV 30:415).

Armstrong, Solomon, in Aug 1746 was charged with begetting a bastard on the body of Sarah Deason (BACP TB&TR#1:132-133).

Armstrong, William, and Elizabeth Shepherd were m. in March 1735 (Harrison, "St. John's Parish Register:" 77). On 7 Nov 1750 Elizabeth was named as a daughter of Elisabeth Shepard (BACT TR#E:20). He d. by 27 Feb 1754 by which time his admx. Elizabeth had m. 2nd, Archibald Standiford (*q.v.*) MDTP 36:120).

Arnall. See Arnold.

Arnold, [-?-], m. by 24 March 1783, Rebecca, daughter of Jacob Retecer (BAWB 3:570).

Arnold, Anthony, m. Sarah, admx. of John Wright (*q.v.*), and d. by 3 June 1726 when his estate was administered by Charles Wells (*q.v.*) and his wife Sarah (BAAD 3:62).

Arnold, Dr. Benjamin, m. after 27 March 1689 and by 1696, Susanna, widow of James Phillips (*q.v.*), and mother of Anthony (for whom she was extx.), and of James Phillips and Mary Carville (INAC 15:25; BAAD 2:63; MWB 6:81 abst. in *Md. Cal. of Wills* 2:157; MDTP 17:215, 28:215). In his will dated 6 June 1698, Anthony Phillips, son of James and Susanna, named his mother Susanna Arnold, as extx. Susanna Arnold, extx., on 23 May 1699 posted bond to administer the estate of Anthony Phillips (BAAB 2:427).

Arnold, Ellender, Mary Arnold, William Arnold, and **Jacob Arnold,** in Feb 1797 chose Joshua Arnold as their guardian (BAOC 3:208).

Arnold, John, in Nov 1733 was charged with begetting a bastard on the body of Elizabeth Chapman (BACP HWS#9:142).

Arnold, Mary, was charged with bastardy at the March 1728 Court (BACP HWS#6:95). She m. John Cannaday on 2 Dec 1729; their daughter Rachel was b. 7 March 1727 (Harrison, "St. George's Parish Register:" 35).

Arnold, Mary, was charged with bastardy at the March 1746/7 Court (BACP TB&TR#1:378).

Arnold, Richard, and Mary White were married by license dated 9 March 1784 (BAML). Luke White, in his will made 12 Aug 1793, named his daughter Mary Arnold (BAWB 5:493).

Arnold, William, on 16 Dec 1738 was named as a bro.-in-law in the will of Charles Wells (MWB 22:408 abst. in *Md. Cal. of Wills* 8:152).

Arnold, William, in March 1745/6 confessed to begetting a bastard on the body of Mary Trego (BACP TB&TR#1:5-6).

Arrow, Francis, in June 1721 was charged with begetting a bastard on the body of Sarah Perdue (BACP IS#C:15).

Ary, Joseph, m. by 3 Nov 1726, Ruth, extx. of George Yates (*q.v.*) (MDTP 27:353).

Ashby (Ashley), Mary, servant of John Smith, was charged with bastardy at the Nov 1741 Court (BACP TB&TR:178).

Ashcombe. See Askew.

Ascue. See Askew.

Asher, [-?-], m. by 10 May 1775, Keziah, sister of Luke Raven (BAAD 6:325, 7:228).

Asher, [-?-], m. by 10 May 1775, Avarilla, sister of Luke Raven (BAAD 6:325).

Asher, Barnett, m. by 9 June 1795, Sarah Forrest, admx. of John Forrest (BAAD 11:298 12:17).

Ashley, Sarah, was charged with bastardy at the March 1746/7 curt, and again at the June 1750 Court; she was fined and her master paid her fees, but she was ordered to serve him an extra year (BACP TB&TR#1:378, TR#5: 11-12).

Ashman, George, m. by Feb 1685/6 Elizabeth Trehearne, widow of William Cromwell and of William Ball, and mother of Thomas Cromwell (BAAD 1:349, 2:244; MDTP 13:294, 382).

Ashman, George, m. by 28 Oct 1743, Jemima, daughter of Josephus Murray (BALR TR#C:340, 376). They were m. on 9 Dec 1746 (Harrison, "St. Paul's," p. 156).

Ashman, John, was named as a son-in-law in the will made 15 Sep 1719 in the will of John Wilmot, Sr., of Baltimore Co. (MWB 15:226 abst. in *Md. Cal. of Wills* 4:216; BAAD 1:253; MDAD 4:138).

Ashman, William, m. by 10 Nov 1760, [-?-], daughter of William Cromwell (BAAD 4:298). Elizabeth Cromwell, in her will, made 15 Dec 1792, named her daughter Eleanor Ashman (BAWB 6:244).

Ashman, William, merchant, and Miss Rebecca Boyce, both of Baltimore, were m. last eve. by the Rev Dr. Watcoat [*sic*] (*Baltimore Daily Repository* 28 Dec 1792).

Ashmore, [-?-], m. by 29 July 1757, Susannah, youngest daughter of Margaret Leasie (MWB 30:401 abst. by Gibb).

Ashmore, Frederick, in Nov 1756 was charged with begetting a bastard on the body of Ann McLachlan (BAMI 1755-1763; BACP BB#C:312).

Ashton, [-?-], m. by 1 Oct 1781, Hannah, daughter of Richard Chenoweth, blacksmith (BAWB 3:434).

Askew, [-?-], m. by 27 Aug 1777, Keziah, sister of Edward Hanson (BAWB 4:107).

Askew, [-?-], m. by 26 Dec 1785 [-?-], daughter of Jonathan Hanson, who named his grand-children, William Hanson, Elizabeth Hanson, Joshua and Jonathan Askew (BAWB 4:115).

Askew, Joshua, and Elizabeth Williamson were m. on 23 Sep 1784 (Marr. Returns of Rev. William West, Scharf Papers, MS.1999 at MdHS). On 12 Feb 1788 Askew was named as a son-in-law in the will of Thomas Williamson (BAWB 4:379; see also BALR WG#HH:540).

Askew (Ascue, Ashcombe), Richard, m. by 19 Dec 1688, Mary, relict of John Hamond (*q.v.*) and Samuel Brand (*q.v.*), and extx. of Edward Reeves (*q.v.*) (MDTP 14:124, 15A:8, 27; BALR IR#AM:68; BACP F#1:128, G#1:84).

Askew, William, merchant, and Miss Ann Shepherd, both of Baltimore, were m. last Wed. eve. by Rev. Caskery (*Maryland Journal and Baltimore Advertiser* 17 April 1795).

Aspray, John, of Suffolk Co., Va., m. by 9 July 1777, Beersheba, granddau. of Moses Rawlings, dec. (BALR WG#A:204).

Atherton, Ebenezer, d. by 28 July 1781, having m. Hannah, daughter of Nicholas Riffett, of Middle River Upper Hundred, yeoman (BAWB 3:440).

Atherton, Richard, married on 1 Nov 1721, Susannah Norris (Peden. *A Closer Look:* 3 corrects mistake in *Maryland Marriages, 1634-1777*). On 5 June 1723 Atherton gave public notice that his wife Susannah had absented herself from his person (BALR IS#G:143).

Atkinson, Bartholomew, of Baltimore Co. , m. by 29 Nov 1721, Sebra, sister and heir at law of John Alien (Allen) (AALR SY#1:379).

Atkinson. See also Adkinson.

Atticks, Mary, was charged with bastardy at the Nov 1758 Court; her child was named William Atticks (BAMI 1757-1758: 163).

Auger (not Anger), James, married on 1 Jan 1756, Mary James (Peden. *A Closer Look:* 3).

Aughard, John, in his will, made 27 Nov 1746 named his bro. William Hodsworth and his sisters Elizabeth and Sarah Hodsworth (MWB 25:332 abst. by Gibb).

Auld, Capt. Hugh, b. 20 July 1767, son of Edward and Sarah, m. Zipporah Willson, b. 26 Aug 1775, on 26 July 1792 in Baltimore ("Thomas Auld Bible Record," *MBR* 1:15-16; Marr. Returns of Rev. Thomas Hagerty, Scharf Papers, MS.1999 at MdHS).

Austin, Mary, was charged with bastardy, convicted, and fined at the March 1754 Court; Edward Bowen was named as the father of the child (BACP BB#A:35-36).

Avery, John, m. by 8 April 1772, Catherine, daughter of William Towson (BAWB 3:222).

Ayers, [-?-], m. by 6 March 1784 Drue, daughter of Abraham Andrews (BAWB 4:11).

Ayres, [-?-], m by 21 Aug 1797, Elizabeth, daughter of John Almony (BAWB 6:19).

Ayres, [-?-], m by 21 Aug 1797, Rachel (Racher?), daughter of John Almony (BAWB 6:19).

Ayres, Edward, m. Isabel, relict of Abraham Houldman [Holman] of Baltimore Co. (MDTP 2:61). On 20 Nov 1666 he posted bond to administer the estate of Abraham Holdman, in trust for Abraham Holdman, orphan of the said Abraham (BAAB 3:216). Edward Ayers d. by 19 March 1674, leaving a widow who m. 2nd. James Collier (*q.v.*) and a daughter Elizabeth Ayres (MDTP 6:178).

Ayres, Nathaniel, in Nov 1724 was charged with begetting a bastard on the body of Lydia Compton (BACP IS&TW#4:32, 41).

Ayres, Nathaniel, on 11 Dec 1733, warned all persons that his wife Rhodea has left him and he stated he would not pay her debts; however, she joined him in a deed dated 29 March 1735 (BALR HWS#M:15, 271). In Nov 1739, Rhodea was given £100 by Hannah Tench who had it from her aunt Mary Bosreys of Amsterdam, Holland (BALR HWS#IA:365).

Ayres, Thomas, was b. in Baltimore Co. and d. 30 March 1836 in Harford Co., was a Private in the 5th Maryland Line, m. Elizabeth [-?-] on 1 Jan 1784 (Rev. War Pension Application of Elizabeth Ayres: W-8346).

"B"

Bache, Sarah, on 5 June 1795 was named as a daughter in the will of John Tracy (BAWB 5:289).

Backer. See Baker.

Backoven (Bakcoven?), Samuel, stated he would not pay the debts of his wife Kitty (*Federal Gazette and Baltimore Daily Advertiser* 26 April 1799).

Bacon, Martin, m. by 15 Oct 1742, Mary, mother of William Watson who was then aged about 5 (BALR TB#C: 55).

Baconais, Lewis Francis Mary, m. by lic. on 26 June 1798, Constance Agatha Assailly, at St. Peter's Catholic Church, Baltimore (*Piet*: 126).

Badet, John Baptist, native of l'Artibonite Isl., St. Domingo, m. by lic. on 21 May 1794, Jane Frances Carrere, native of Bordeaux, widow of M. Copela, at St. Peter's Catholic Church, Baltimore (*Piet:* 126). (Bride's name is given as Capela in BAML).

Bagby, John, of Calvert Co., m. by 30 Aug 1719 Mary, daughter of John Ford who was a brother of James Ford (BALR TR#DS: 147).

Bagford, James, m. by 1720 Elizabeth [-?-], widow of Richard Sampson (q.v.); she m. 3rd, Samuel Hinton (*q.v.*), and 4th Thomas Stone (q.v.) (MWB 14:43, abst. in *Md. Cal. of Wills* 4:29; BACP IS#C:4; BALR IS#H:328, 385; HWS#M:163; MWB 21:768, abst. in *Md. Cal. of Wills* 7:212). On 4 April 1720 he was named as a son-in-law of Samuel Hinton (MWB 16:255 abst. in *Md. Cal. of Wills* 5:33). Sarah James, aged about 64 years, deposed on 26 May 1735 that 18 or 19 years earlier...James Bagford had m Elizabeth (now the widow of Thomas Stone, dec.), and that she (Sarah James) had been sent for as a midwife to Elizabeth Bagford, and had delivered her of a son, James Bagford, now living with his mother, and that James Bagford, Sr., was present at the birth (BALR HWS#M: 237).

Bahn (Bahon), Stephen, m. by 27 Dec 1787, Barbara Weaver, devisee and extx. of Adam Brandt (BALR WG#BB: 97; BAAD 11:68).

Bahon. See Bahn.

Bailey, [-?-], m. by 21 April 1752 Bridget Ann, daughter of John Legatt, Sr. (MWB 30:81 abst. by Gibb).

Bailey, [-?-], m. by 25 March 1791, Mary, daughter of John Penn (BAWB 4:530).

Bailey Charles, m. by 23 March 1765, Sarah, daughter of John Cotterall (BALR B#O).

Bailey, Enoch, m. by 12 June 1767, Kerrenhappuck, daughter of Joseph Murray (BACT B#G: 230; BAWB 3:216).

Bailey, George, m. by 2 July 1722, Sarah, daughter of Hector Maclane (MWB 18:37 abst. in *Md. Cal. of Wills* 5:126). Bailey d. by 27 Aug 1763 and his widow Sarah, daughter of Hector McClain, conv. property to Elijah and Samuel Bailey (BALR B#L: 468).

Bailey, George, m. by 26 Oct 1741 Rachel, extx. of John Moale; she d. by 14 June 1750 and Thomas John Hammond, her eldest bro., signed her inventory (BALR TB#A: 30; MINV 42:236; MWB 22:249; MDAD 20:85).

Bailey, Groombright, m. Mary Moore on 5 Oct 1757 (Peden, *A Closer Look at St. John's Parish Registers;* the groom's name was incorrectly given as Groom Bright Bayley in Harrison, "St. John's Parish Register:" 216).

Bailey, Hellen, in her will made 11 April 1795 named her daughter Elizabeth Parker and her granddaus. Sarah Calvert and Helen Buck (BAWB 6:405).

Bailey, James, m. Christiana Waideman on 3 Jan 1791 by J. Daniel Kurtz, Pastor of the Lutheran Church of Baltimore (Rev. War Pension Application of Christiana Bailey: W-9342).

Bailey, John, of Baltimore Co., m. by 1 Sep 1739, Hellen Newsam (BALR HWS#1A: 271).

Bailey, John, m. by 1 Aug 1732 Lucy, aunt of John Ryley whose mother Elizabeth had m. 2nd, Francis Russell (BALR IS#L: 267).

Bailey, Josiah, and Avarilla Barnes were m. on 25 June 1776 ("Josiah Bailey Family Record," in *MBR* 7:8).

Bailey, Thomas, on 6 Oct 1725, warned all persons that this wife Katherine "had been very profuse in her illegal ways of living," and he would not pay her debts (BALR IS#H: 191).

Bailey (Bayley), Thomas, and Rachel Towson were m. on 26 Dec 1758 (Harrison, "St. John's Parish Register:" 49). On 8 April 1772 Rachel was named as a daughter of William Towson, who also named a granddaughter Rachel Bailey (BAWB 3:222).

Bailey, Thomas, merchant of Baltimore, and Sally N. Muir, were m. Tues., 17th ult,, by Rev. Mr. Kemp, at Windsor, the seat of John Muir, Esq., in Dorchester Co. (*Maryland Journal and Baltimore Advertiser* 13 April 1792). **N.B.:** The *Baltimore Daily Repository* of 12 April 1792 says the groom was of Wilmington.

Baily, |-?-|, m. by 27 March 1792, Mary, heir and rep. of John Penn of Baltimore Co. (BACT 1791-1794, MS 2865.1 at MdHS: 46).

Bain (Bane), William, and Lydia Johnson were m. on 14 Oct 1761 (Harrison, "St. John's Parish Register:" 222). Lydia was the admx. of Amos Johnson (*q.v.*) (MDTP 38:288; BAAD 6:139; MDAD 47:367, 48:264). She was also admx. of Peter Miles) (BFD 3:154).

Bainer, William, m. by lic. on 25 April 1793, Elizabeth Steiger, at St. Peter's Catholic Church, Baltimore (*Piet:* 126).

Bakcoven. See Backoven.

Baker, |-?-|, m. by 3 Feb 1759, Rachel, daughter of William Gosnell (BAWB 2:143).

Baker, |-?-|, m. by 26 Sep 1787, Elizabeth, who on that date was living in Hopewell Twp., Washington Co., Pa., daughter of John Lane, and sister of John Boring Lane (BALR WG#AA:549). On 10 Nov 1794 William Lane named his sister's son John Baker (BAWB 5:208).

Baker, Alexander, m. by 1750 Zipporah Hilyard, widow of Thomas Floyd (*q.v.*); she m. 3rd, by 11 June 1756, Henry Maynard (*q.v.*) (BALR HWS#1-A:137, BB#1:570; John F. Dorman, "The Maynard Family of Frederick County, Maryland, *NGSQ* 48:177-ff.).

Baker, Catherine, and Benjamin Mead, in Nov 1736, were cited for unlawful cohabitation, they having lived together unlawfully for seven years; they were admonished by the vestry in Nov 1736 (Harrison, "St. John's and St, George's Vestry Proceedings," pp. 14-15). Catherine Baker was imprisoned for debt ion June 1734; Benjamin Mead was ordered by the court to maintain and keep her two children (BACP HWS#9:255).

Baker, Charles, m. by 25 June 1711, [-?-], daughter of William Hawkins, Sr., who called Baker his son-in-law in his will of that date (MWB 13:213; abst. in *Md. Cal. of Wills* 3:195).

Baker, Charles, and Elizabeth Cockey were m. on 9 Jan 1749 (Harrison, "St. John's Parish Register:" 200). On 26 Sep 1753 Elizabeth was named as the mother of John, Edward, William, and Peter Cockey (MDAD 35:165; MWB 30:112, 151; BAAD 6:4). **See Charles Butler, below.**

Baker, Charles, Jr., and Elizabeth Wheeler were m. on 16 Dec 1762 (Harrison, "St. John's Parish Register:" 224). On 19 Jan 1770 Elizabeth was named as a daughter of Leonard Wheeler (BALR AL#A:669).

Baker, Elizabeth, was charged with bastardy in March 1745/6 (BACP 1743-1745:800).

Baker, Elizabeth, with John Roberts on 1 May 1750 was charged by the vestry of St. Thomas' Parish with unlawful cohabitation (Reamy, *St. Thomas' Parish Register:* 54).

Baker (Backer), Jennis Helming, and Susanna Johanna Gerardine Van Noemus were m. on 29 May 1797 by Rev. Dr. Allison (Register of First Presbyterian Church, Baltimore, MS. At MdHS: 3; *Federal Gazette and Baltimore Daily Advertiser* 30 May 1797).

Baker, Joseph, widower, m. by lic. on 23 Jan 1800, Magdalen Fulweiler, widow, at St. Peter's Catholic Church, Baltimore (*Piet:* 126). She was Magdalen Wintzeiler, widow of Francis Foldweider (*q.v.*).

Baker, Kery, was charged with bastardy at June 1765 Court; John Brunts was summoned to appear (BAMI 1765:16).

Baker, Lemuel, and Sophia Meads were m. on 5 March 1739 (Harrison, "St. John's Parish Register:" 137). She was a daughter of Edward Meads (BAWB 2:264).

Baker, Mathias, of Newington, innkeeper, in his will made 21 Sep 1799 named his daus. Modlian Fink and Mary Robinson, and mentioned his 'present wife's children' (BAWB 6:221).

Baker, Meshack, m. by 21 Oct 1765, [-?-], daughter of William Hamilton (BAAD 6:149).

Baker, Morris, m. by 16 Feb 1765, Elizabeth, daughter of Francis Dorsey, whose administration account of 17 Jan 1752 names an 18 year old daughter Elizabeth (MDTP 41:35; MDAD 32:10).

Baker, Morris (or Maurice), m. by 4 Oct 1767, Christian, daughter of William Grafton (BAWB 3:56; BAAD 6:280).

Baker, Nicholas, and Martha Wood were m. on 4 Jan 1741 (Harrison, "St. George's Parish Register:" 324). On 21 March 1749 Martha was named as a sister of Joshua Wood (MWB 26:99 abst. by Gibb).

Baker, Sarah, was charged with bastardy at June 1741 Court (BACP TB&TR:56).

Baker, Sarah, was charged with bastardy at Nov 1758 Court (BAMI 1757-1759:162).

Baker, Thomas, in Aug 1729 was charged with begetting a bastard on the body of Alice Carrington (BACP HWS#6:274, 277).

Bakon, Stephen, m. by 27 Dec 1787, Barbara Weaver (BALR WG#BB:97).

Balderson, Jonathan, and Mekey (Milcah), daughter of Nicholas Baker, were m. on Thurs., 25th ult. (*Baltimore Daily Repository* 1 May 1793; BAWB 6:212).

Balderston, Ely, and Esther Brown, on 12 d. 10 m, 1797 declared their intention to marry, and their parents being present gave their consent ("Minutes of Baltimore Meeting," *QRNM:*229).

Baldwin, [-?-], m. by 1 Nov 1765, Agnes, sister of Elizabeth Sanders, spinster, of Anne Arundel Co., who also named her niece Rebecca Baldwin (BAWB 4:237).

Baldwin, Abraham, and Sarah Jenny were married by license dated 26 May 1798 (BAML). On 17 Dec 1800 Sarah was named as the widow of Nathaniel Zenney [*sic*], by whom she had had two children, Ann and John (BAAD 13:263; BAOC 4:135; BOCP Petition of Abraham Baldwin, 1800), Nathaniel Jenny and Sarah Dawson were married by license dated 27 Aug 1795 (BAML).

Bale, Anthony, d. by Feb 1731 having m. Ann, sister of Johanna Hall; Ann later m. Michael Taylor of Prince George's Co. (*q.v.*) (MCHR 5:349). He d. by 11 July 1744 having m. Ann, sister of William Plummer of Gloucester Co., Va.; she m. 2nd, Michael Taylor (BALR TB#C:576).

Bale, Thomas, m. by 20 Aug 1704, Sarah, sister of Robert Gibson (BALR HW#2: 356; deposition of Thomas Bond, made 8 July 1734 in BALC HWS#3 #48).

Ball, Amos, on 27 d. 12 m. 1777, has reportedly gone out in marriage to a woman not of our Society ("Minutes of Gunpowder Meeting," *QRNM:*71). [No other marriage reference found].

Ball, Catherine, (now Catherine Randall), on 28 d. 10 m. 1786 and 25 day, 11 m 1786, was condemned for having a child in an unmarried state and afterwards having accomplished her marriage contrary to the good idea ("Minutes of Gunpowder Meeting," *QRNM:*83). See **Catherine Randall**.

Ball, Jemima. See Jemima Grilse.

Ball, Richard, m. by 1 March 1661, Mary, widow of Thomas Humphreys (BALR RM#HS:19; *Archives of Maryland* 67:134).

Ball, William, d. by Feb 1685/6 by which time his widow Elizabeth(Treearne) had m. 2nd, William Cromwell (*q.v.*), and 3rd, George Ashman (*q.v.*).

Ball, William, and Betsy Dukehart were m. [date not given] (*Maryland Journal and Baltimore Advertiser* 29 Oct 1790). William Ball and Elizabeth Dukehart were m. 21 Oct 1790 (Marriage License Returns of Rev. Daniel Kurtz, Scharf Papers, MS 1999 at MdHS). Elizabeth Ball (formerly Dukehart) on 30 d. 10 m. 1790 and 27 d 11 m. 1790 was charged with going out in marriage ("Minutes of Gunpowder Meeting," *QRNM:*89).

Ballard, Col. Robert, of Va., and Miss Plowman of Baltimore, were m. last Thurs. (*Maryland Journal and Baltimore Advertiser* 18 July 1780; Marr. Returns of Rev. William West, Scharf Papers, MS.1999 at MdHS) She was the eldest daughter of Jonathan Plowman (BOCP: Petition of Jonathan Plowman, 1787; Box 1, Folder 46). Rebecca Arnold, in her will made 17 June 1784 named her granddaughter Rebecca Ballard and the latter's sons John Plowman Ballard and Robert Edmund Ballard (BAWB 4:316). On 31 March 1787 Rebecca was named as a devisee of William Holland of Calvert Co. (BALR WG#AA:128). Rebecca's sister Mary m. William McLaughlin (*q.v.*) whose will made Dec 1794 named Ballard's sons Robert and Henry BAWB 5:233).

Bandell, Daniel, m. by 12 April 1797, Eleanor Mack, heir of James Mack (BAAD 12:306).

Banks, John, and Mary Kelly were m. on 18 Sep 1756 (Harrison, "St. Paul's Parish Register:" 72). She was a daughter of James Kelly, husbandman (BAWB 3:397).

Banks, William, and Susanna Conway were m. on 11 Sep 1788 (Marr. Returns of Rev. William West, Scharf Papers, MS.1999 at MdHS). On 31 Dec 1795 John Conway made his will naming a William Banks and naming his granddaughter Mary Banks (BAWB 6:218).

Bankson, [-?-], m. by 29 March 1753, Ariana, daughter of Hannah Hughes (BALR TR#D: 533).

Bankson, Hannah, on 12 March 1743 was named as a 'daughter-in-law' in the will of William Hughs (*q.v.*), tavern keeper, who also named his own wife Hannah as extx. (MWB 25:478 abst. by Gibb).

Bankson, Major John, was m. last Sat eve. to Miss Mickle, daughter of John Mickle, merchant (*Maryland Journal and Baltimore Advertiser* 8 May 1797).

Bankson, Joseph, m. 16 Jan 1752, Elizabeth, widow of James Slemaker (Reamy, *St. Paul's Parish Register:* 35). In Dec 1753 Eliza was named as the widow of James Slemaker of Baltimore Co. (MPL YS#7:387, YS#6:360; MDAD 41:244; MWB 27:212). In her will, dated 30 Dec 1754, Cassandra Giles named, among others, her daughter Elizabeth, wife of Joseph Bankson (MWB 29:273, abst. in *Md. Cal. of Wills* 11:80).

Bantz, [-?-], m. Catharina Franciscus, who d. 13 Sep 1794, aged 25 or 26 years old ("First German Reformed Church Register," MS. at MdHS:32).

Barber, Mary, was charged with bastardy in March 1755 and ordered to serve her master Richard Ruff for 9 mos. from April for fees arising from her having had a bastard child (BACP BB#B:15).

Barber, Thomas, in his will made 30 Sep 1799 named his brother-in-law Moses Hand as his sole legatee (BAWB 6:228).

Barclay, [-?-], m. by 7 June 1771, Mary, daughter of Adam Hoops (BAWB 3:259).

Barclay, [-?-], m. by 28 May 1794 Eleanor, daughter of John Gill (BAWB 5:467).

Bardell, John, in July 1776 was made a ward of his mother Ann Bardell (BACP Minutes, 1772, 1775-1779).

Bardley (Bardtly), Ann, was charged with bastardy at the March 1743/4 Court (BACP Liber 1743-1745:154).

Barge, Andrew, merchant of Baltimore, and Miss Susanna Miles of Elkton, were m. [date not given] (*Baltimore Daily Repository* 9 May 1793).

Barickman, Anthony, m. by lic. on 12 June 1784, Christina Baker, at St. Peter's Catholic Church, Baltimore (*Piet*: 126).

Barker, Thomas, m. by 22 Dec 1769, Mary, sister of Edward Thorp, late of Md., dec. (BALR AL#B:419).

Barker, William, m. by 5 Sep 1698, Mary, admx. of Francis Watkins (INAC 16:209; MDTP 17:202).

Barkley, Thomas, merchant, and Miss Jane M'Cormick, both of Baltimore, were m. last Thurs. by Rev Allison (*Baltimore Telegraphe* 3 Nov 1798).

Barlar, Mary, was charged with bastardy, convicted, and fined 30 shillings on 29 Dec 1753. Edmond Flanagan (*alias* Edmond Burges or Burgess) was named as the father of the child (BACP BB#A: 31).

Barlow, James, d. by 2 Nov 1723 when his extx. Joanna had m. Charles McDaniel (*q.v.*). Barlow left a daughter named Barsheba (MDAD 5:234, 8:198, 9:98; BAAD 3:21).

Barly, Mary, was charged with bastardy at the June 1729 Court (BACP HWS#6:41).

Barnaby, Elias, and Rachel Riffitt were m. on 8 June 1788 (Harrison, "St. Paul's Parish Register:" 217). Rachel Barnaby, (formerly Riffitt) on 26 d. 4 m. 1788 was charged with marrying outside the order ("Minutes of Gunpowder Meeting," *QRNM:*85).

Barnerd, James, stated he would not pay the debts of his wife Mary, who has for sundry times misconducted herself to the dishonor of my bed, and contracting debts I am unable to pay (*Federal Gazette and Baltimore Daily Advertiser* 11 Jan 1798).

Barnes, Dorsey [of Baltimore Co.], m. by 1 March 1797, Lydia [-?-], when they conv. land which had formerly belonged to Joseph Musgrove, to Nathan Musgrove (MOLR G:450-451).

Barnes, Elijah, a Private in the Revolutionary Army, was m. to Catherine Shipley on 17 Aug 1784 in St. Paul's Parish, Baltimore (Rev. War Pension Application of Catherine Barnes, widow of Elijah Barnes: W-9717).

Barnes (Barns) Ford, and Ruth Garrett were m. on 20 Oct 1743 (Harrison, "St. George's Parish Register:" 234); in his will made 24 May 1761 Ford Barnes named his wife Ruth and his brother-in-law Amos Garrett (MWB 31:530 abst. by Gibb).

Barnes (Barns), Gregory, and Elizabeth Mitchell were m. on 30 Nov 1758; their son Ford was b. on or about 4 April 1761 ("Bible Record of Barns Family of Harford Co.," BRHA:56).

Barnes, Isabella, aged 14 in Aug 1757 chose John Patterson as her guardian (BACP Minutes, 1755-1763).

Barnes, James, m. by 18 April 1723, Ketura, daughter of Adam Shipley (BALR TR#A:242).

Barnes, James, and Bethia Loney were m. on 27 May 1726 (Harrison, "St. George's Parish Register:" 258). On 23 Dec 1742 she was named as a daughter of William Loney (BAAD 3:274). James Barnes d. by 27 March 1754, at which time his admx.

Bothia (late Adams) was m. to [-?-] Scarlett (q.v.) (MDTP 36:28).

Barnes, James, m. by 6 June 1765, Elizabeth, daughter of Benjamin Culver (BALR B#O:241, 242, 282).

Barnes, Job, and Constance West were m. on 11 Oct 1722 (Harrison, "St. George's Parish Register:" 230). On 18 Feb 1722/3 Constant was named as a daughter of Robert West, Sr. (BALR IS#G:94, BALR HWS#M:9).

Barnes, Mary, was charged with bastardy at Aug Court 1733, John Hurd was the father of the child (BACP HWS#9:71).

Barnes, Philemon, m. by 20 Nov 1756 [-?-], daughter of George Ogg (BACT TR#E:232).

Barnet (or Burnet), [-?-], m. by 4 Sep 1763 Eliza, daughter of Jacob Algire (BAWB 3:26).

Barnet, Peter, m. by 19 April 1794 Mary Owings, heir of John Owings (BAAD 11:421). They were married by license dated 4 Jan 1790 (BAML).

Barnett, Hannah, (formerly Spencer), on 27 d. 6 m. 1789, was charged with marrying outside the good order ("Minutes of Gunpowder Meeting," *QRNM:*87). [No other marriage reference found].

Barney, [-?-], m. by 16 Jan 1717 Mary, daughter of Mary Stevenson of Baltimore Co., and mother of William Barney (BALR TB#E:512).

Barney, [-?-], m. by 1778 Rebecca Shelmerdine, daughter of John and Sarah of Baltimore Co. (MCHP # 644).

Barney, [-?-], m. by 7 Oct 1798, Mary daughter of Conrad Kerlinger; she was the mother of Elizabeth, Henry, and Catherine Siford (BAWB 6:138).

Barney, Absalom, m. by 6 Dec 1752 Mary, daughter of Thomas Ford (MDAD 33:223).

Barney, Benjamin, in March 1754 was charged with begetting a bastard on the body of Mary Cross *alias* Mary Heeth (BACP BB#A:29).

Barney, Benjamin, and Delilah Bosley were m. on 23 April 1758 (Harrison, "St. John's Parish Register:" 217). On 12 April 1772, Delilah was named as a daughter of Joseph Bosley (BAWB 3:393; BAAD 9:35).

Barney, John, merchant, of Baltimore, m. [date not given] Charity Stiles, daughter of Joseph Stiles of Harford Co. (*Maryland Journal and Baltimore Advertiser* 13 Aug 1784).

Barney, Joseph Bosley, and Rebecca Pickett were m. by license dated 2 Feb 1788 (BAML). He d. by 23 May 1789 when Rebecca Barney, admx., posted bond to administer his estate (BAAB 7:198).

Barney, Marcy, on 18 Nov 1748 was named as a daughter in the will of Thomas Ford, Sr. (MWB 25:480 abst. by Gibb).

Barney, Moses, and Sarah Bond were m. on 5 April 1758 (Harrison, "St. Thomas' Parish Register;" 73). Some time before 10 Aug 1781 Sarah Barney petitioned for the release of her son William from the 'draught' as he is the only support of the petitioner and six small children; her husband and eldest son have been in service for six years; she stated that William ran the risk of contracting small pox in the Army; James Calhoun also asked for the discharge of Barney (Brown Books V, 32, 33).

Barney, William, m. by May 1738, Mary, daughter of Elizabeth Stevenson (Black Books VIII: 98, 114).

Barney, William, and Frances Holland Watts were m. 26 Jan 1743 (Harrison, "St. Paul's Parish Register:" 167; PCLR DD#4:247).

Barney, William, d. by 3 June 1750 at which time his extx. Mary was m. to Richard Rutter (*q.v.*). Mary was the mother of Absolom. Benjamin, William, and Moses Barney, and Mary Butler (BAWB 3:388).

Barney, William, in Nov 1759 was charged with begetting a bastard on the body of Elizabeth Marvell (BAMI 1757-1759:242).

Barney, William, and Rebecca Ridgely were m. on 2 May 1799 (Harrison, "St. Paul's Parish Register:" 371; *Federal Gazette and Baltimore Daily Advertiser* 4 May 1799). As William B. Barney, he m. Rebecca Ridgely, daughter of Charles Ridgely of John of Baltimore Co. (MCHP # 2669, 4435).

Barney, William B., m. 1783, Mary, sister of Samuel and Thomas Chase, and daughter of Samuel and Hannah K. Chase of Baltimore Co. (MCHP # 1219, 1458, 3547).

Barnharton, Catherine, servant of George Pickett, was charged with bastardy at Nov Court 1758 (BAMI 1757-1759:161).

Barnisger, Christian, m. by 1763 Mary, daughter of John Myer of Baltimore Co. (MCHP # 3530, 3547).

Barnes. See Barnes.

Baroux, James Michael, native of Arras, m. by lic. on 16 Nov 1793, Mary Deagle, at St. Peter's Catholic Church, Baltimore (*Piet*: 126).

Barrett, [-?-], m. by 24 Aug 1754 Susannah, sister of Stephen Onion; they had a son Zacheus Barrett whom Onion called nephew (MWB 29:190 abst. by Gibb).

Barrett (Barrot), John, m. by [c1700] Alice, extx. of Nicholas Corbin (INAC 20:47; MDTP 18B:4).

Barron, William, of this city, and Miss Sally Brownley of Harford Co., were m. last Fri. eve. by Rev. Mr. Richards (*Federal Gazette and Baltimore Daily Advertiser* 2 July 1799).

Barrot. See Barrett.

Barrow, John, d. by 11 Jan 1780, naming his wife Elizabeth and his stepson Silas Baldwin (BAWB 3:405). Elizabeth Barrow, in her will made 7 Feb 1793 named her sons Silas and William Baldwin (BAWB 5:98).

Barry, [-?-], may have m. by 26 Dec 1785 [-?-], daughter of Jonathan Hanson who named a granddaughter Mary Mullin (BAWB 4:115).

Barry, Capt. John, and Mrs. Elizabeth Diffenderfer, both of Baltimore, were m. last sat. eve. (*Maryland Journal and Baltimore Advertiser* 9 March 1790; *Maryland Gazette or Baltimore General Advertiser* 12 March 1790; BALR WG#MM: 115).

Barry, John, m. by 22 Oct 1798, Elizabeth, daughter of Samuel Messersmith (BALR WG#56:356).

Barry, Lavalin, and Jemima Stansbury were m on 14 march 1795 (Marr. Register of Rev. Lewis Richards, MS.690 at MdHS). She was Jemima Gorsuch, a representative of Kerrenhappuck Gorsuch, and a widow and admx. of James Stansbury. (BAAD 12:62, 82, 220).

Barry, Redmond, m. by lic. on 27 Dec 1790 Johanna Hannecy, at St. Peter's Catholic Church, Baltimore (*Piet*: 126).

Barry, Standish, and Nancy Thompson, daughter of John Thompson of Baltimore, were m. last Sat eve. (*Maryland Journal and Baltimore Advertiser* 14 Oct 1788; *Maryland Journal and Baltimore Advertiser* 14 Oct 1788).

Barton, Elizabeth, m. 1727, William Wright (*q.v.*), 2nd, 1741. James Greer (*q.v.*), and 3rd, Heathcote Pickett (*q.v.*).

Barton, James, and Temperance Rollo were m. on 8 Oct 1730 (Harrison, "St. John's Parish Register:" 68). On 20 Oct 1734 Temperance was named as a daughter of Archibald Rollo (MWB 21:319 abst. in *Md. Cal. of Wills* 7:126).

Barton, John, m. on 23 May 1738, Ann Hitchcock (Harrison, "St. John's Parish Register:" 104). She was a daughter of William Hitchcock (BALR TB#C:664).

Barton, John, and Dorothy Nice were married by license dated 31 May 1783 (BAML). She m. 2nd, [-?-] Fews (*q.v.*)

Barton, John, m. by 26 Oct 1798 Ann, daughter of Jesse Biddle (BALR WG#58:247).

Barton, Lewis, m. Judith [-?-], She m. 2nd, William Farfarr (q.v.) (MDTP 16:13).

Barton, Lewis, and Johanna Simmons were m. on 30 June 1757 (Harrison, "St. John's Parish Register:" 215). On 28 May 1770 she was named as an heir of George Simmons (BAAD 6:188).

Barton, Selah Dorman, m., 1st, Rebecca Biddison on 27 Dec 1730, and, 2nd, Comfort Roberts on 24 Jan 1733 (Reamy, *St. Paul's Parish Register:* 150, 151). Comfort Lynch, relict of Selah Dorman Barton, and age 64, deposed on 20 July 1780. She stated that she was m. to Selah Dorman Barton by Rev. William Hooper. She always understood that her husband was the son of Lewis Barton and his wife Sarah, who was a daughter of Selah Dorman. The said Selah Dorman had another daughter who m. Michael Gorman but there were no descendants of that marriage. The deponent stated that her husband (Selah Dorman Barton) held lands which formerly belonged to Selah Dorman, and her husband was the only child of his father, and the only descendants of Selah Dorman are the deponent's children. She stated that her husband claimed that Tobias Stansbury caused him to get in liquor at Edward Day's, and Stansbury got him to write a deed for the said land, but when her husband got sober, he would not convey the land. Greenbury Barton was her son by Selah Dorman Barton (BACT 1773-1784:400).

Barton, Seth, merchant, and Sally Maxwell were m. last Thurs. eve. (*Maryland Journal and Baltimore Advertiser* 21 Dec 1790; *Maryland Gazette or Baltimore General Advertiser* 21 Dec 1790).

Barton, Susanna, (formerly Sharp), on 28 d. 3 m. 1789 was charged with marrying outside the society ("Minutes of Gunpowder Meeting," *QRNM*:86). [No other marriage reference found].

Basey, John, son and heir of John Basey of Baltimore Co., dec., has moved to Va.; he is being sued by Abraham Larsh, son of Valentine Larsh, over a mortgage on 100 a. *Buck's Purchase* (*Md. Gaz.* 28 Oct 1790).

Baseman, John, m. by 4 April 1788 [-?-], daughter of Richard Owings (BAAD 9:188).

Basket, Richard, m. Adfire Boyd on 31 Jan 1743/4 (Peden, *A Closer Look at St. John's Parish Registers:* the name is incorrectly written as Bashet in *Md. Marr., 1634-1777*).

Bataline (Batline), Joseph, and Eve Elcon were married by license dated 8 June 1791 (BAML); on 27 Feb 1793 Bataline's wife was named as a daughter of George Elgar (Ilgers?) (BAWB 5:91).

Bateman, Henry, m. by 4 April 1792, [-?-], who received an equal share (£58.9.0) of the estate of Thomas Gittings (BAAD 11:18).

Battee, [-?-], m. by 5 April 1789, Ellen, dau, of George Stansbury (BAWB 4:358).

Battista, John, of Baltimore, stated he would not pay the debts of his wife Charlotte who has eloped from him (*Maryland Gazette or Baltimore General Advertiser* 20 June 1788).

Bauduy, Louis Alexander Amelie, native of St. Domingo, son of John Baptiste and Helene (Curon), m. by lic. on 15 April 1799, Victoire Agatha Marguerite Darnaud, native of St. Domingo, daughter of Stephen and Martha Mary Frances (Laulaigne), at St. Peter's Catholic Church, Baltimore (*Piet*: 127).

Baum, Pet., m. 23 June 1783 An. Barb. Hahn (*Saint Mary's Church, Silver Run, Carroll County* :35).

Baur, Christian, m. by 14 Feb 1790, Salome Junglin (*Reformed and Lutheran Congregations at Manchester, Baltimore County, Maryland (Now Carroll County)*: 285).

Bausman, Lorentz, and Catherine Riz were m. on 27 Oct 1789 ("First German Reformed Church, Baltimore," *MGSB:*194). Lawrence [*sic*] Bausman his will proved 27 Sep 1797 named his brother-in-law Lewis Shryer (BAWB 6:32).

Bautain, Nancy, admx., on 21 Sep 1799 posted bond to administer the estate of James Williams (BAAD 9:4).

Baxley. George, and Mary Merryman were m. on 5 Sep 1793 (Marr. Returns of Rev. John Hagerty, Scharf Papers, MS.1999 at MdHS). Mary was a daughter of Joseph Merryman (BAWB 6:159).

Baxley, John, Jr., merchant, and Polly Stevenson, both of Baltimore, were m. yesterday afternoon by Rev. Hagerty (*Baltimore Daily Repository* 17 July 1793).

Baxley, Samuel, and Catherine Sharmiller were married by license dated 1 Dec 1784 (BAML). She was a daughter of Gotlieb Sharmiller (BALR WG#FF:180).

Baxter, Edmund, m. by 8 May 1760 Susannah, widow of William King (BALR B#P: 567).

Baxter, Elizabeth, was charged with bastardy at the June 1743 Court and confessed to bastardy at Aug Court 1746 (BACP TB#D:185, TB&TR#1:125-126).

Baxter, Greenbury, of Ohio. m. by 1789 Hannah Butler, daughter of Absalom and Susannah Butler of Baltimore Co. (MCHP # 5143, 5419, 5583).

Baxter, John, in March 1743/4 was charged with, and confessed to, begetting a bastard on the body of Mary Brown (BACP 1743-1745:172).

Baxter, Nicholas, son of Nicholas Baxter, aged 18, on 14 Aug 1788 chose John Ready as his guardian. Josias Green and John Bowen were sureties (BAOC 2:79).

Baxter, Nicholas, and Sarah Perigo were m. on 2 Feb 1792 (Marr. Register of Rev. Lewis Richards, MS.690 at MdHS). On 21 Feb 1796 John Perigo named his granddaughter Ellender Baxter in his will (BAWB 5:360).

Baxter, Samuel, m. by lic. on 21 Aug 1779 Sarah Chenoweth, who d. 9 Dec 1830, aged 72; their son Greenbury was b. on 16 Nov 1780 ("Baxter Family Bible," *HMGB* 12 (3) (July 1941) 37-40).

Bay, Andrew, of Albany, New York, formerly of Baltimore Co., m. by 3 Nov 1771 Sarah [-?-], by whom they were the parents of Elihu Hall Bay (BALR AL#D:44).

Bay, Margaret, in March 1768 was guilty of bastardy (BAMI 1768-1769:12).

Bay, Thomas, m. by 14 Sep 1769 Frances, daughter of Eric Erickson (MDAD 61:384; BALR AL#D:39).

Bayley, Cassandra, (late Johns), on 5 d. 11 m. 1789 was reported to have been m. by a Baptist Preacher ("Minutes of Deer Creek Meeting," *QRNM:*147). [No other marriage reference found].

Baylis, Augustin, and Elizabeth Brown were married by license dated 4 Dec 1785 (BAML). Elizabeth Baylis, *admx. de bonis non,* on 16 April 1795 posted bond to administer that part of the estate of Martha Brown that had not been administered by Augustin Baylis (BAAB 8:732).

Baylor, William, m. by banns on 10 June 1783, Mary Wyster, at St. Peter's Catholic

Church, Baltimore (*Piet:* 127).

Bayly, Elisha T., and Jennet [-?-] were m. 1 Sep 1791 ("Bayly Family Bible," *MGSB* 40 (2) (Spring 1999).252)

Bayly, Thomas, on 23 June 1718 was named as a cousin in the will of George Westall, planter (MWB 14:713 abst. in *Md. Cal. of Wills* 4:185).

Bayne, William, m. by 8 Nov 1762, Lydia, admins. with Peter Miles of Amos Johnson (BFD 5:52).

Bays, Elinor, was charged with bastardy in 1765. Samuel Harryman was also to appear (BAMI 1765:1, 20). John Bays, who had d. by March 1765, had m. Eleanor Harryman on 12 Sep 1748 Harrison, "St. Paul's,": 161).

Baze, [-?-], m. by 29 Oct 1742, Ann, daughter of Zachariah Gray (MWB 25:330 abst. by Gibb).

Beach, Henry, on 6 Oct 1767, was summoned to appear before the vestry of St. George's Parish for unlawful cohabitation. Jane Beach was summoned as evidence; on 5 March 1770 Henry Beach was summoned to appear before the vestry of St. George's Parish for unlawful cohabitation with Elizabeth Dixon (Reamy, *St. George's Parish Register:* 110, 111).

Beal, Benjamin, of Woodberry Twp., Huntingdon Co., Pa., m. by 24 Nov 1794 Ann, widow of John Bartle [Bardell?] of Baltimore Co. (BALR WG#QQ:1).

Beal, John, m. by 9 Oct 1724 Elizabeth, sister of Andrew, Ann, and Hannah Norwood (BALR IS#G:387).

Beal, Samuel, stated he would not pay the debts of his wife Ann (*Federal Gazette and Baltimore Daily Advertiser* 31 March 1799).

Beale, John, and Keziah Wooden, in Nov 1760 were fined for begetting a bastard (BAMI 1757-1763)

Beale, Josias, m. by 31 Jan 1770 Millicent, granddaughter of Clement Hill of Prince George's Co. (BALR AL#B:67).

Beale, Peter, m. by 17 Dec 1783 Catherine, daughter of Anthony Haines (BAWB 4:521; BAAD 11:51).

Beall, Lloyd, and Betsy, daughter of Thomas Jones, were m. last Sun. in Patapsco Neck (*Maryland Journal and Baltimore Advertiser* 6 May 1785).

Beall, Sarah, was named as a sister in the will, made 4 June 1704, of Robert Gibson (MWB 3:236 abst. in Md. Cal. of Wills 3:37).

Bealy, [-?-], m. by 1 May 1765 Nelly, daughter of Edw. Flanagan (BAWB 3:28).

Beam, George, and Sarah McAllister were married by license dated 19 Jan 1782 (BAML). She was a daughter of Joseph McAllister((BAWB 3:560).

Beamer, Susanna, on 9 May 1790 was named as a granddaughter in the will of Frederick Caley (BAWB 3:421).

Bear, Michael, m. by 13 June 1769 [-?-], heir of Esther Whistler, widow of Ulrich Whistler (BAAD 7:30).

Beecher, John, m. Edith, widow of Joseph Williams; on 24 May 1693 the posted bond to administer the estate of Joseph Williams (*q.v.*) (BAAB 4:62). In her will made 23 May 1694, Edith Beecher of Patapsco River, Baltimore Co. left her son Richard Gest or Gist in charge of her brother Richard Cromwell (Her will was recorded in BALR RM#HS:550 abst. in *Md. Cal. of Wills* 4:240).

Beard, Capt. Alexander, m. last Fri. eve. at Fell's Point, Molly Bride (*Maryland Journal and Baltimore Advertiser* 27 July 1790; *Maryland Gazette or Baltimore General Advertiser* 27 July 1790; Marr. Returns of Rev. William West, Scharf Papers, MS.1999 at MdHS).

Beasman (Baysman), John, on 5 Oct 1786 was named as a son-in-law in the will of Richard Owings (BAWB 4:180).

Beasman, Thomas, m. by 9 Dec 1789 [-?-], daughter of Loveless Gorsuch, and heir of Nathan Gorsuch (BAAD 10:88, 250).

Beasman, William, m. by 21 Oct 1765 [-?-], daughter of William Hamilton (BAAD 6:149).

Beason. See Besson.

Beatty, Thomas S., Esq., of George-Town, was m. Thurs. eve. last at Epsom by the Rev. Mr. Oliver, to Miss Achsah C. Holliday, daughter of John R. Holliday, Esq. (*Federal Intelligencer and Baltimore Daily Gazette* 10 Nov 1795).

Beaudu, William, a native of Bordeaux, m. by lic. on 2 Aug 1796, Mary Ann Hubon, a native of Martinico at St. Peter's Catholic Church, Baltimore (*Piet:* 127).

Beaumee, Bon Albert Briois, m. by lic. on 22 March 1796, Sarah Lyons Fluker at St. Peter's Catholic Church, Baltimore (*Piet:* 127).

Beaumont, Joseph, d. by 20 Feb 1775, by which date his admx. Elizabeth had m. Robert Henderson (*q.v.*) (MDTP 20:227).

Beaupre, Lewis (son of Lewis Nan Rochefort, Counselor of the King, and Mary Bouchereau), m. by lic. on 14 Oct 1795, Victoire Bardan (daughter of John Baptiste and Frances Collette Lamonie) at St. Peter's Catholic Church, Baltimore (*Piet:* 127).

Beaven, John, d. by 14 Jan 1779; his widow, Elizabeth, m. by that date John Ford, who because of sundry disputes, quarrels and animosities between him and his wife Elizabeth, gave her full power to marry again, and to receive all debts due her former husband, John Beaven (BALR WG#E:90). He may be the John Beven [*sic*] who m. Elizabeth Freeman on 5 Oct 1760 (Harrison, "St. John's,": 220).

Beaven, John, m. by 3 Nov 1793 Sarah, widow of Benjamin Bennett (BALR RM#HS: 361, IR#AM: 192).

Beavens, Joseph, was given an allowance for caring for Sarah Beavens (Levy Lists for 1736, 1737, and 1739).

Beaver, John, and Sarah Hawkins were m. on 19 Sep 1749 (Harrison, "St. John's Parish Register:" 199). She was a daughter of Robert Hawkins (BAWB 2:344).

Beaver, John, died by 2 April 1791, leaving three sons: John, who obtained letters of administration on his father's estate, and Martin and Adam. He also left two daughters, Frances, and Judith, now wife of John Plumb (BOCP Petition of Martin and Adam Beaver, 1793).

Beaver, William, Jr., m. Blanch Duly [*sic*] in Oct 1740 (Harrison, "St. George's Parish Register:" 320). On 19 Aug 1741 Blanch was named as the admx. of William Duly or Dooley (i) (MDTP 31:207).

Beazley (Beemsley), Thomas, m. by 14 July 1772 Mary [-?-], who seems to have m. 2nd, James Kelly (*q.v.*), now dec.; According to depositions, Beazley had runaway and was still alive in a part of Southern Va, near Carolina (MDTP 44:481-187).

Beck, John, m. by lic. on 6 Dec 1794 Anne Miller, both natives of Germany, at St. Peter's Catholic Church, Baltimore (*Piet:* 127).

Beck, Matthew, and Ann Horner were m. on 10 Feb 1740 (Harrison, "St. John's Parish Register:" 134). She was the widow and admx. of Nicholas Horner (*q.v.*) (MDAD 18:403, 21:158; BAAD 4:112) She m. 3rd, on 14 July 1748 Henry Waters (q.v.) (Harrison, "St. John's Parish Register:" 197).

Becker (Beker), Johann Georg, m. by 2 May 1790 Juliana Cuntzin ("Reformed and Lutheran Congregations at Manchester, Baltimore (now Carroll) Co.,"*MGSB* 35:285).

Beckley, James, and Ann Campbell were married by license dated 11 Nov 1797 (BAML). On 14 Aug 1800 Ann was named as a legatee of James Campbell (BAAD 13:317).

Beckley, Matthias, m. by 15 April 1795 Juliana Gittinger, a representtaive of John Gittinger (BAAD 12:4).

Beddoes, Sarah, was charged with unlawful cohabitation with Godfrey Vine by the Vestry of St. George's Parish in Nov 1735. They appeared before the Vestry in July 1737 but could not prove their marriage, but then in Oct 1737 a certificate was produced showing they had been married by Rev. James Cox, minister of St. Paul's Parish, Queen Anne's Co. on 14 Feb 1733 (Reamy, *St. George's Parish Register:* 103, 104). John Beddoe had m. Sarah Litten on 3 Dec 1724 (Reamy, *St. George's Parish Register:* 26). Godfrey and Sarah Vine were the parents of (Reamy, *St. George's Parish Register:* 49, 60): Godfrey, b. 5 July 1733; Sarah, b. 6 Sep 1736; and John, b. 7 March 1738).

Bedigo[?], [-?-], m. by 14 Oct 1769 Alice, daughter of John Edwards (MWB 38:33, abst. in *Md. Cal. of Wills* 14:140).

Beecher, John, m. by 21 Feb 1693 Edith, widow of Christopher Gist, and of Joseph Williams (BALR RM#HS:417; MDTP 15C:88, 135).

Beedle, Edward, d. by 30 Dec 1696, leaving two daus.: Martha, extx. of George Goldsmith, and wife of John Hall, and Mary, widow of George Utie (BALR IS#IK:241, 245; BACP G#1:201).

Beeman, James, and Miss Amelia Johnston, both of Fell's Point, were m. last eve, by Rev. Bend (*Maryland Journal and Baltimore Advertiser* 18 Aug 1795).

Beeson (Besson), Nicholas, m. by 12 Dec 1722 Diana, admins. of Matthew Hall or Hale (*q.v.*) (BAAD 1:73).

Begnall, Michael, m. by lic. on 21 June 1798 Anne Cromwell at St. Peter's Catholic Church, Baltimore (*Piet:* 127).

Behn, John H., of Lubeck, was m. last eve. by Rev. Mr. Allison, to Miss Violet Bryden, daughter of James Bryden of this city (*Federal Gazette and Baltimore Daily Advertiser* 19 Sep 1798).

Beker, See Becker.

Belcher, John, m. Mary Perkins, widow, in Feb 1706 (Harrison, "St. George's Parish Register:" 201). In 1708 Mary was named as the admx. of Richard Perkins (MDTP 21:27; INAC 28:260). Perkins had m. Mary, admx. of Thomas Gash (MDTP 19C:219).

Bell, [-?-], m. by 29 July 1782, Rebecca, daughter of Edward Wann (Wonn) (BAWB 5:73).

Bell, [-?-], m. by 31 Dec 1784, Ketura, daughter of John Price, Sr. (BAWB 4:422).

Bell, Edward, and Nancy Kennedy, both of Fell's Point, were m. last eve. by Rev. Richards (*Baltimore American* 5 Aug 1799).

Bell, Henry, and Priscilla Parks were married by license dated 1 Nov 1783 (BAML). She was a daughter of John Parks (BAWB 4:314).

Bell, Jacob, and Elizabeth Rowles were m. on 18 Feb 1727 in St Paul's Parish (Reamy, *St. Paul's,* p 29); she m. 2nd, [-?-] Graham.

Bell, John, m. by 29 July 1746 Susannah, daughter of John Tye, who named his grandsons John, Francis, and Arthur Bell (MWB 22:143 abst. in *Md. Cal. of Wills* 7:67, BALR TB#E:119).

Bell, John, who served in the Maryland Regiment under Capt. Ghiselin, was m. to Catherine Doyle on 6 Jan 1773 by Parson Chase in St. Paul's Parish. The births of their children were recorded in a prayer book by Richard Bell. The children were: Susanna, b. 23 July 1774; Richard, b. 8 Nov 1776; John, b. 10 Jan 1779; Isaiah, b. 27 Sep 1782, Jehu, b. 2 Nov 1784, Jesse, b. 11 Aug 1787, Clarissa, b. 13 Nov 1789, Cecilius, b. 2 March 1792, Edward, b. 14 April 1795, Mary, b. 27 Oct 1797, Harriet, b. 5 June 1779, Sidney, b. 14 June 1802 (Rev. War Pension Application of Catherine Bell, widow of John Bell: W-9437).

Bell, Samuel, of Baltimore, and Miss Elizabeth M'Gee of Philadelphia, were m. last Tues. eve., by Rev. Dr. Rogers (*The Philadelphia Gazette and Universal Daily Advertiser* 3 Nov 1796).

Bell, William, was charged with fornication and bastardy, and was fined, in 1762 (BAMI 1755-1763).

Belleville, Capt. Lewis, m. on 7 Feb 1800, Mary Ann Faure at St. Peter's Catholic Church, Baltimore (*Piet*: 127).

Belloc, Francis, planter of Hispaniola, m. last Sun. eve. Polly Barney of Baltimore (*Maryland Journal and Baltimore Advertiser* 20 Oct 1789).

Belt, Benoni, son of Sarah Belt, was charged with bastardy and fined at the Nov 1758 Court (BAMI 1755-1763: 162).

Belt, Joseph, on 22 day 2 mo. 1794 was condemned for being married by a hireling minister ("Minutes of Gunpowder Meeting," *QRNM*:95). Joseph Belt and Ellin Randall were m. by lic. dated 30 Sep 1793 (BAML).

Belt, Leonard, m. by 23 Feb 1798 Hannah, daughter of Mary Parish (BALR WG#55:199).

Belt, Lucy, daughter of John and Milcah, on 22 day, 4 mo., 1772, was charged with having sworn a child to a man and have got one unmarried ("Minutes of Gunpowder Meeting," *QRNM*:62).

Belt, Mary, on 29 day. 6 mo. 1793 was charged with outgoing in marriage ("Minutes of Gunpowder Meeting," *QRNM*:94). **See James Peddicoat.**

Belt, Rachel. See Samuel Hooker.

Belt, Rebecca, now Tipton, on 30 day, 5 mo. 1778 was reported to have gone out in marriage to a person not of our Society. On 25 day 7 mo. 1778 was condemned for having her marriage solemnized by a priest ("Minutes of Gunpowder Meeting," *QRNM:*72). See Aquila Tipton.

Belt, Sarah, was charged with bastardy at the June 1738 Court (BACP HWS#6:16, 38), She was the mother of Benoni Belt (see above).

Belt, Sarah, was charged with bastardy at the Nov 1758 Court and fined (BAMI 1757-1759:162).

Belton, William, and Frances Smith were m. on 11 Sep 1790 (Marr. Returns of Rev. William West, Scharf Papers, MS. 1999 at MdHS) On 14 June 1792 Margaret was named as a daughter of Francis Smith, skinner, glover, and breeches maker of Baltimore Town (BAWB 4:383; BAAD 11:81).

Bembridge, Christopher, in Nov 1695 was charged with begetting a bastard on the body of Elizabeth Stimson (BACP G#1:503). He d. by 13 Dec 1701, having m. Jone (Joan) admx. of John Bay or Boy; she m. by that date Daniel Cranley (or Crawley) (*q.v.*).

BenAli, Susanna, admx., on 17 Dec 1800 posted bond to administer the estate of Jacob M. Tobbes (BAAB 9:44).

Bencil, Balser, m. by 26 Oct 1778 Sophia, admx. of Jacob Creeder of Baltimore Co., dec. (BALR WG#C:31). Balcer Bencil and Sophia Krider were married by license dated 28 Feb 1778 (BAML).

Bener, Henry, m. by banns on 1 Dec 1793 Elizabeth Heimlin, at St. Peter's Catholic Church, Baltimore (*Piet:* 127).

Benjar, Robert, on 6 March 1676 was named as a son-in-law in the will of Margaret Therrell (Thurrrold) of Back River, Baltimore Co. (MWB 5:347, abst. in *Md. Cal. of Wills* 1:201; MDTP 10:36). Margaret was the widow of Richard Thurrol.

Bengar (Benjar), Robert, m. by 29 Feb 1677, Katherine, relict and admx. of John Chadwell (Shadwell) (INAC 4:631, 632, 7A:9; BAAD 2:41; MDTP 9:335).

Benger, Robert, of Cecil Co., m. by May 1688 [-?-], the relict of Nicholas Shaw (MDTP 14:72).

Benger, Robert, d. by 31 March 1744, having m. Deborah, mother of Jane Johnson (who m. Daniel Scott (*q.v.*), and of Elizabeth Shaw (BALR TB#C:471).

Benillant, Stephen, native of Cap Francois, St. Domingo, son of Peter and Ann (Lecroix), m. by lic. on 27 Feb 1796, Clare Theresa Pissard, native of Marseille, France, widow of [-?-] Argentel, and daughter of Raimond and Catherine (Chailan), at St. Peter's Catholic Church, Baltimore (*Piet:* 127).

Benned, [-?-], m. by April 1799 [-?-], sister of Michael Fisher; they had a daughter Esther (BAWB 6:182).

Bennett, [-?-], d. by 29 Jan 1756 having m. Elinor, widow of John Durbin (*q.v.*) and of Alexander Hill (*q.v.*), and mother of John Hill (BALR BB#1:521).

Bennett, [-?-], m. by 9 Jan 1781 Catherine, daughter of Jacob Young, Sr. (BAWB 3:429).

Bennett, George, m. by 7 Dec 1798, Mary [-?-], to whom John Hart, in his will, made 7 Dec 1798 left a tract *Christworth,* and whom he named extx. (BAWB 6:236). Mary Bennett, extx. on 27 Nov 1799 posted bond to administer the estate of John Hart (BAAB 9:17).

Bennett, James, merchant, and Miss M. Wright, both of this town, were m. at Norfolk [date not given] (*Maryland Journal and Baltimore Advertiser* 25 July 1795).

Bennett, Nancy, on 22 Aug 1794 was named as one of the children in the nuncupative will of Christopher Curtz (BAWB 5:163).

Bennett, Patrick, a relation of Felix Coskery, m. by 22 Dec 1782, Mary [-?-], who was named in Coskery's will (BAWB 3:531).

Benson, Benjamin, m. by 20 May 1799 Hannah, daughter of Abraham Scott (BAWB 7:176).

Benson, James, son of Benjamin and Hannah, and Elizabeth, daughter of Mordecai and Rachel Price of Gunpowder Forest were m. on 30 day, 4 mo. 1794 (Bliss Forbush, "Records of Gunpowder Meeting," at MdHS; BAWB 5:379).

Benson, Richard, and Miss Catherine Smith, both of Baltimore, were m. last Thus. eve. by Rev. Bonsal (*Baltimore Daily Repository* 17 Oct 1793).

Benson, William, of Prince George's Co., m. by 15 March 1736, Elizabeth, mother of Zachariah Wade (BALR IS#IK:427).

Bentalou, Paul, m. by 22 April 1796 Catherine, daughter of Jacob Keeports (BALR WG#VV:418).

Bentheim, Paul, m. by banns on 2 Aug 1793 Mary Steiger at St. Peter's Catholic Church, Baltimore (*Piet:* 127).

Bentley, John, d. by 26 April 1765 by which time his widow and admx. Tamar had m. John Carter (*q.v.*) (BAAD 6:271, 7:248).

Bentley, Michael, and Eleanor Caton, both natives of Ireland, were m. by lic. 9 Oct 1796, at St. Peter's Catholic Church, Baltimore (*Piet*: 127).

Bentley, Stephen, m. by Nov 1693 Ann, relict of Philip [Piffions or Pitstow], formerly the wife of William Pearl (BACP F#1:300, 307). Stephen Bentley, of Baltimore Co., aged about c57. deposed on 19 Jan 1714/5 regarding the bounds of William Pearle's land; he had lived in these parts for 21 years and had lived on *Upper Spring Neck* and that he had m. William Pearle's mother (MCHR CL:108). He had m. by Nov 1693, Ann, relict of Philip [Piffions?], formerly the wife of William Pearl (BACP F#L:300, 307). She m. 4th [-?-] Fenton (**See Amy Fenton**).

Bergebeil, Jacob, m. by 27 Dec 1786 Catharina Dillin ("Reformed and Lutheran Congregations at Manchester, Baltimore County, Maryland (Now Carroll County:" 282).

Bergman, Joseph, m. by banns on 28 Nov 1786 Catherine Steiger at St. Peter's Catholic Church, Baltimore (*Piet*: 127).

Berman, Matthew, m. by lic. on 25 Nov 1783 Ann Duliar at St. Peter's Catholic Church, Baltimore (*Piet*: 127).

Bernard, Charles, m. on 4 Dec 1784 Mary White at St. Peter's Catholic Church, Baltimore (*Piet*: 127). She m. 2nd, [-?-] Heinisler (*q.v.*).

Bernett, Jacob, m. by lic. 1 Dec 1793 Mary Thompson at St. Peter's Catholic Church, Baltimore (*Piet*: 127).

Berridge, William, of Baltimore, stated he would not pay the debts of his wife Anne (*Maryland Journal and Baltimore Advertiser* 27 May 1788). William Berridge and Ann Adams were married by license dated 12 June 1784 (BAML).

Berry, George, and Mary Cox were m. on 6 Feb 1714 (Harrison, "St. John's Parish Register:" 4). On 24 May 1714 they posted bond to administer the estate of Joseph Cox (BAAB 1:280; see also (MDTP 22:365).

Berry, Hannah, in 1761 was convicted of bastardy (BAMI 1755-1763).

Berry, John, m. by banns on 25 July 1791 Mary Spence at St. Peter's Catholic Church, Baltimore (*Piet*: 127).

Bertholin, Joseph, m. by lic. on 11 June 1791 Eve Elcon at St. Peter's Catholic Church, Baltimore (*Piet*: 127).

Bertrand, John Peter, b. at St. Germain de Montivillers, Diocese of Rouen, son of Peter Lewis and Mary Martha (Pougal), m. by lic. 17 Feb 1795, Victoire Sophie Vatmel [nee Valand], b. at Havre de Grace, France, daughter of Lewis and Angelica (Godefray), at St. Peter's Catholic Church, Baltimore (*Piet*: 127; BAML).

Besson (Beason), Nicholas, and Diana Hale were m. on 3 Sep 1722 (Harrison, "St. Margaret's Parish Register," Anne Arundel Co., at MdHS: 102). On 12 Dec 1722 Diana was named as the admx. of William Hutchings (*q.v.*) and of Matthew Hale (*q.v.*) or Hall (MDAD 5:83; BALR RM#HS:73).

Bestland, Ann, on 26 Feb 1756 was named as a sister in the will of Hubbard Brewer (MWB 30:56 abst. by Gibb).

Betts, Solomon, and Araminta Alexander were m. by lic. dated 24 Nov 1796 [last Thurs. by Rev. Bend] (BAML; BALR WG#57:52; *Maryland Journal and Baltimore Advertiser* 26 Nov 1796).

Bevan, Jesse, m. by 24 May 1775 Martha, admx. of Esrom Hendrickson (*q.v.*) (MINV 121:354, 359).

Bevan (Bevans), John, m. by 3 Nov 1682 Sarah, daughter of Benjamin Bennett (BALR IR#AM:92, RM#HS:361).

Bevan, Mr. Richard, was m. last eve. by Rev. Mr. Richards, to Mrs. Ann Guffey, both of this town (*Federal Intelligencer and Baltimore Daily Gazette* 30 Dec 1795).

Bevans, [-?-], m. by 2 March 1747, Rachel, daughter of William Denton who also named his granddaughter Rachel Bevans; **N.B.:** John Bevan, Jr., witnessed the will (MWB 25:206 abst. by Gibb).

Bevans (Bevins), James, and Mary Rusk were married by license dated 10 Jan 1793 (BAML). On 24 July 1793 Mary Rusk was the admx. of Thomas Rusk (BAAD 11:294, 449).

Beven, John, and Elizabeth Freeman were m. on 5 Oct 1760 (Harrison, "St. John's Parish Register:" 220). She m. 2nd John Ford (*q.v.*).

Biays, James, was m. Thurs., 11th inst., at Fells Point, to Sally Jackson (*Maryland Journal and Baltimore Advertiser* 18 June 1784). Sarah was a daughter of Abraham Jackson of Fell's Point (BAWB 4:275).

Biays, James, and Miss Trimble, both of Fell's Point, were m. last Thurs. (*Federal Gazette and Baltimore Advertiser* 14 May 1795).

Biays, Joseph, m. by 17 Feb 1800 Elizabeth who was one of the heirs-at-law of Cornelius Clopper; Nicholas Clopper, John Clopper, and Edward N. Clopper were the other heirs at law (BALR WG#61:380).

Bidot, John Peter, m. by lic. 26 March 1788, Peggy Tonerey at St. Peter's Catholic Church, Baltimore (*Piet:* 127).

Bier, Philip, Jr., of Baltimore, and Miss Polly Miller, daughter of Major Miller of Frederick Town, were m. last sun. eve. by Rev. Schneider (*Baltimore Telegraphe* 16 Nov 1798).

Bigger, Gilbert, and Sarah Rice were m. on 7 May 1791 ("Register of the First Presbyterian Church, Baltimore, " MS. at MdHS). Sarah Bigger, (formerly Rice).has gone out in marriage with a man not in membership ("Minutes of Gunpowder Meeting," *QRNM:* 91). Gllbert Bigger and Sally Rice were m. last Sat, eve. by Rev. Dr. Allison (*Maryland Gazette or Baltimore General Advertiser* 10 May 1791).

Bignall, Joseph, and Eleanor Smith were m. 19 Feb 1780 (Marr. Lic. Return of Rev. William West). In May 1791 Bignall stated he would not pay the debts of his wife Eleanor, who has eloped (*Maryland Gazette or Baltimore General Advertiser* 10 May 1791).

Bignell (Bignell), Rebecca, was charged with bastardy at the June 1731 Court and confessed at the March 1731/2 Court (BACP HWS#7:156, 236). She m. Robert Hambleton on 15 Nov 1733 (Harrison, "St. George's Parish Register:" 234).

Billingsley (Billingslea), [-?-], m. by 37 March 1766 Asenath, daughter of Samuel Howell (MWB 35:219 abst. in *Md. Cal. of Wills* 13:165).

Billingsley, James, m. Elizabeth Matthews on 14 Sep 1797 ("Day Bible," *The* Notebook 15 (2) (June 1883) 9; *MBR* 2:24-27).

Billingsley, Walter, m. Sarah Love on 27 Aug 1742 (Harrison, "St. George's Parish Register:" 325). She was widow of Robert Love and mother of John, Ruth and Tamar Love (BALR TB#C; 5, 6, 7).

Billmaker, William, and Lydia James were married by license dated 21 March 1792 (BAML). In 1792 Lydia. wife of William Bell Mickes [*sic*], was named as one of the representatives of Hannah James (BOCP Petition of Henry Newman, 1792).

Billmeyer, Michael, m. by 11 May 1787 Mary, sister of John Shryer (BAAD 9:48).

Bilson, John, and Ann [-?-] were m. by 1 Jan 1780 when their son William was b. ("Pearce Family Bible," *HABFR* 3:74; "William Bilson Bible," MBR 2:10-11).

Bingan, Peter, m. by 5 Sep 1749 Elizabeth, widow of William Little (PCLR EI#8:618).

Bingdon, John, m. by 23 Dec 1742 [-?-], daughter of William Bond, Sr., of Baltimore Co. (MDAD 19:266).

Birchfield. See Burchfield.

Bird, John, m. by Nov 1680 Eliza, extx. of Henry Lewis (*q.v.*) (*ARMD* 69:270, 366; INAC 7B:8).

Bird, John, m. by Nov 1694, [-?-], widow of James Armstrong (*q.v.*) (BACP D:212).

Birely, Conrad, m. by 16 May 1795 Mary, daughter of Philip Deale (BAWB 4:83; BAAD 12:9).

Birmingham, Christopher, stated he would not pay the debts of his wife Sarah (*Maryland Journal and Baltimore Advertiser* 1 Nov 1793).

Birmingham, James, m. by 28 Dec 1787, Rebecca, who received an equal share of the estate of Robert McClung (BAAD 10:168).

Birmingham, John, widower, m. by lic. 7 Aug 1799 Ruth Wilson, widow at St. Peter's Catholic Church, Baltimore (*Piet*: 127).

Bisco, [-?-], d. by 2 May 1732, having m. Ann, daughter of Thomas Jackson of St. Mary's Co., by whom he had a son James Bisco; she m. 2nd, Owen Smithson (*q.v.*) (BALR IS#L:256).

Bishe, Joseph, d. by 1789 leaving a widow and admx. Nancy Bishe, who has since m. Stephen Mallett (*q.v.*) (BOCP Petition of Peter Deshong Peter [P---?], 1792).

Bishop, Jesse, m. by 15 May 1770 Frances, admins. of James Hambleton (MDTP 43L534).

Bishop, Richard, mariner, m. by lic. on 19 Oct 1796, Elizabeth Young of Fell's Point, at St. Peter's Catholic Church, Baltimore (*Piet*: 127). Capt. Richard Bishop was m. last eve. to Miss Elizabeth Young, both of Fell's Point (*Federal Gazette and Baltimore Daily Advertiser* 10 Oct 1796; see also BALR WG#56:351).

Bishop, Robert, m. Elizabeth Day on 22 Sep 1742 (Harrison, "St. John's Parish Register:" 124). She was the widow and extx. of Nicholas Day (*q.v.*).

Bishop, Thomas, m. by 23 Aug 1751, Margaret, execs. of Hugh Morgan of Baltimore Co. (MDAD 30:224),

Bisset, Major David, and Mrs. Ann Adkinson [*sic*] were m. on 30 Jan 1755 (Harrison, "St. George's Parish Register:" 350). She was the relict of John Atkinson (*q.v.*) (BALR BB#I:411).

Bitchie, Peter, of Baltimore Co., stated that his wife Resian had eloped from his bed and board and was staying with John Ribble (*Maryland Journal and Baltimore Advertiser* 13 March 1781).

Bizouard, Joseph Yves, m. by lic. on 25 Aug 1794, Reine Paterson at St. Peter's Catholic Church, Baltimore (*Piet*: 127).

Black, James, and Miss Mary Carroll, both of this town, were m. last Sat. eve. by Rev. Mr. Bend (*Maryland Journal and Baltimore Advertiser* 10 June 1795).

Blair, John, mariner, m. by lic. on 25 Sep 1796, Catherine Cronan, both natives of Ireland at St. Peter's Catholic Church, Baltimore (*Piet*: 127).

Blair, William, m. by 3 June 1765, Mary, daughter of Alexander Hanna, weaver, who named Mary's children Elizabeth. and William Blair (BAWB 3:22; BAAD 7:178).

Blizard, John, of Baltimore Co., stated he would not pay the debts of his wife Chloe, who has eloped from his bed and board without just cause (*Federal Intelligencer and Baltimore Daily Gazette* 22 Jan 1795).

Blood, Richard, m. by 1756 Mary, widow of Richard Marshall; Mary m. 2nd. Joseph Foresight (*q.v.*) (Deposition of William Marshall, *alias* Johnson (*ARMD* 31:174-179).

Blossom, Peter, m. by lic. 30 Jan 1791, Mary Magdalen Leblanc at St. Peter's Catholic Church, Baltimore (*Piet*: 127).

Boardman, [-?-], m. by 20 March 1773 Catherine, daughter of Robert Stephenson, farmer, (BAWB 3:258).

Boaz, Peter, of York Co., Pa., m. by 25 Aug 1773 Eliz., daughter of Margaret Dentler of York Co., Pa., but now resident in Baltimore Town (BAWB 3:241).

Boblitz, Peter, m. by 14 Dec 1785 [-?-], heir of John Markee (BAAD 8:173).

Body (Boddy), Peter, and Mary Allender were m. on 25 Aug 1757 (Harrison, "St. John's Parish Register:" 216). Peter Body died by 21 Oct 1761, when Tho. Jones, admin, posted a bond for £100. Arch. Buchanan was the surety. (BAAB 1:209)

Body (Boddy), Stephen, and Elizabeth [-?-] were m. on 10 Feb 1728 (Harrison, "St. Paul's Parish Register:" 147). She was the widow of Lewis Owings (*q.v.*) and m. 3rd, Luke Trotten (*q.v.*). On 29 Oct 1765 Eliz. Trotten named her grandsons Stephen and Joshua Boddy (BAWB 3:44).

Body, Stephen, orphan of Peter and Mary, in Nov 1775 was over 14 when he chose Dixon Stansbury as his guardian (BACP Minutes, 1772, 1775-1781, 160).

Bogwell, Thomas, and Margaret Brian of Fell's Point were m. last eve. by Rev, Bonsall (*Baltimore Daily Repository* 9 May 1793).

Boislandry, Robert Charles LeGrand, native of Orleans, widower, son of Damien LeGrand and Margaret (Tassin), was m. by lic. on 17 Sep 1796 to Louise Frances Buscaille, native of Port du Paix, daughter of James Lewis and Mary Catherine (LeGaigneur) at St. Peter's Catholic Church, Baltimore (*Piet*: 127).

Boles, Jacob, m, by 1 Aug 1749 [-?-], widow of James Scarfe of Baltimore Co. (MDAD 27:1).

Bolton, [-?-], of Anne Arundel Co., m. by 10 Feb 1684/5, Elizabeth, widow of Richard Bennett (BALR RM#HS:110).

Bolton (Boulton), Charles Mathias, m. Ann Higginson on 4 July 1729 (Harrison, "St. John's Pariah Register:" 137; Harrison, "St. George's Parish Register:" 308). She was the admx. of John Higginson (MDTP 31:44; BAAD 4:26).

Bolton, John, m. by Nov 1685, Dorothy Crandon (BACP D:358).

Bolton. See also Boulton.

Bonaday, James, and Frances Carback, in May 1758 were reported by Thos. Merrideth as living together in a scandalous manner; they were cited to appear before the next vestry (Harrison, "St. John's and St. George's Parish Vestry Proceedings:" 139).

Bond, [-?-], m. by 25 Aug 1785 Mary, daughter of John Hughes (BAWB 4:526).

Bond, [-?-], m. by 22 Aug 1792 Rachel, daughter of Thomas Cole (BAWB 5:53).

Bond, Amelia. See Amelia Moore.

Bond, Barnett, then residing in London, according to the deposition of his widow Alice, now Grimes, aged 55, who deposed on 4 April 1771 that in 1736 she was married by a Rev. Foster to Barnett Bond then residing in London. By Barnet Bond she had issue: William, Barnet, Mary, and Thomas Bond. Her sons William and Barnett died in their infancy before 1743, and as of 1 Jan 1765 Thomas Bond is her only son living. Her husband Barnet Bond was a mariner and master of a vessel, *Coomes* that he sailed from London to Md. After the death of his father, William Bond, which happened about 3 years after her [the deponent's] marriage Barnet continued to sail from London to this province until the year 1745, when he died in VA. After

Barnet's death the deponent married William Grimes (*q.v.*) who is also dead (BAEJ: "Thomas Bond: Harritt's Fancy, Laurence, Buck Range, and Addition").

Bond, Barnet, and Sarah Harryman were married by license dated 27 Dec 1785 (Marr. Returns of Rev. William West, Scharf Papers, MS.1999 at MdHS). On 29 Feb 1788 Barnet Bond's wife was named as the widow and admx. of Josias Harryman (BAAD 9:163).

Bond, Benjamin, m. Clemency Taylor 28 May 1737 (Harrison, "St. John's Parish Register:" 92). She was a sister of Martin Taylor, dec., and daughter of Martin Taylor (in admin. account of Robert Robertson of Baltimore Co.) (MDAD 18:12; BAAD 4:53). On 17 Dec 1748 Clemency was named as a daughter of Sarah Robertson (MWB 25:543 abst. by Gibb). Robert Robertson had m. Sarah Taylor on 9 Nov 1721 (Harrison, "St. John's Parish Register:" 19). (BAAD 4:53).

Bond, Benjamin, m. by 1 Dec 1749 daughter of Henry Butler of Baltimore Co. (MDAD 27:252).

Bond, Benjamin, m. by 9 Dec 1789 [-?-], daughter of Loveless Gorsuch (BAAD 10:88).

Bond, Buckler, m. by 3 Nov 1779 Mary, daughter of Tobias Stansbury and sister of Tobias Stansbury (BALR WG#E:16). N.B.: Buckler Bond and Charity Bond were m. on 17 April 1770 (Harrison, "St. John's Parish Register:" 260).

Bond, Charles, d. by 1784; his children, Elizabeth, Edward, and Barzilla [Bazil], had been made wards of James Campbell, but on 22 Feb 1787 he had resigned and Josias Grover was appointed guardian (BAOC 2:15). Bond's widow Sarah m. 2nd, by 1785 Nicholas Miller (*q.v.*) (BPET: Charles Bond, petition, 1785, Box 1, Folder 17; BAAD 9:197).

Bond, Christopher, and Sarah Pindell were married on 13 Dec 1787 (BAML). On 11 Oct 1790 Sarah received share of £32.6.9 from the estate of John Pindell (BAAD 10:286, 281, 12:231).

Bond, Daniel, and Patience Bosley were m. on 1 Nov 1759 (Harrison, "St. John's Parish Register:" 219). She was a daughter of James Bosley (BAAD 6:131; MDAD 48:74).

Bond, Edward, and Catherine Pindell were m. on 5 Feb 1778 (Marr. Returns of Rev. Thomas Chase, Scharf Papers, MS.1999 at MdHS) On 11 Oct 1790 Catherine received share of £32.6.9 from the estate of John Pindell (BAAD 10:286, 281). On 4 Feb 1797, Catharine rec'd an equal share of the estate of Eleanor Pindell (BAAD 12:231).

Bond, Henry, and Elizabeth Gorsuch were m. on 5 March 1778 (Marr. Returns of Rev. Thomas Chase, Scharf Papers, MS.1999 at MdHS) m. by 9 Dec 1789, [-?-], daughter of Loveless Gorsuch (BAAD 10:88).

Bond, Jacob, and Frances Partridge were m. on 28 Dec 1747 (Harrison, "St. Paul's Parish Register:" 161). She was a daughter of Buckler and Jane Partridge, sister of William Partridge, of Baltimore Co. (BAWB 2:335; MDAD 46:57, 53:167; BAAD 6:166, 7:177).

Bond, James, m Sarah [-?-], were m. by 11 Nov 1774 when their son William Leech Bond was b. ("Family Bible of James Bond." *Gen. of Penna. Families from the Pennsylvania Genealogical Magazine,* Baltimore: Genealogical Publishing Co., 3:581-582).

Bond, James, m. Martha Wilmer on 8 Dec 1782 ("Family Bible of James Bond." *Gen. of Penna. Families from the Pennsylvania Genealogical Magazine,* Baltimore: Genealogical Publishing Co., 3:581-582).

Bond, James, merchant, and Juliana M'Hard, both of Baltimore, were m. Thurs. eve. (*Baltimore American* 15 July 1799).

Bond, John, m. by Aug 1711, Mary, extx. of Samuel Standiford (MDTP 22:42). Mary m. 3rd by 8 June 1722, John Wesley (INAC 32C:42; MDAD 4:210).

Bond, John, and Isabella Robinson were m. on 21 Feb 1733 (Harrison, "St. John's Parish Register:" 82). Isabella m. 2nd, by 20 July 1740 George Presbury (*q.v.*).

Bond, John, son of Thomas, and Alizanna Webster, daughter of John, were m. 26 d., 1 m. (March) 1734 ("Records of Nottingham Meeting," at MdHS).

Bond, John, on 16 July 1773 entered an ante-nuptial contract with Elizabeth Hunt, mother of Samuel and Thomas Hunt (BALR AL#G: 505).

Bond, John, son of Joshua, dec., of Fairfax Co., Va., warned his guardians, John and Ann Dodd (*q.v.*), not to pay Nicodemus Bond any money arising by virtue of a valuation of lands (*Maryland Gazette or Baltimore General Advertiser* 20 July 1787).

Bond, John, revoked a power of attorney he had given to William Moore, who had m. Bond's daughter; Bond also mentioned money due him from the estate of Barney Riley, dec., and he mentioned the estate of Col. John Hall, administered by Benedict E. Hall on behalf of Bond's mother (*Maryland Journal and Baltimore Advertiser* 23 sep 1788).

Bond, John, m. by 15 Feb 1792 [-?-], heir of Richard Bond (BAAD 10:544).

Bond, John, m. by 13 June 1795 Rachel Cole, daughter of Thomas Cole (BAWB 5:53; BAAD 12:18).

Bond, Joshua, m. by 6 Sep 1758 Ann, daughter of Buckler and Jane Partridge, sister of William Partridge (BAWB 2:335 ; MDAD 46:57, 53:167; BAAD 7:177).

Bond, Joshua, m. by 5 Aug 1767 Ann, sister of Moses Groom and daughter of Moses Groom, Sr. (BALR B#Q:158).

Bond, Joshua, married Anne [-?-], who married 2nd, John Dodd on 7 June 1782 (Marr. Returns of Rev. William West, Scharf Papers, MS.1999 at MdHS). They were guardians of John Bond of Joshua (see above).

Bond, Luke, and Frances Webster were m. on 18 July 1762 (Harrison, "St. John's Parish Register:" 223; "Family Bible of James Bond," *Gen. of Penna. Families from the Pennsylvania Genealogical Magazine,* Baltimore: Genealogical Publishing Co., 3:581-582).

Bond, Nicodemus, and Rachel Stevenson were m. on 1 Jan 1765 (Harrison, "St. Thomas Parish Register:" 73) She was a daughter of Richard King Stevenson (BAWB 3:337). In Aug 1787 Nicodemus bond refuted the charges made by John Bond of Joshua, and mentioned his own son Richard (*Maryland Gazette or Baltimore General Advertiser* 3 Aug 1787).

Bond, Peter, m. by 18 June 1678 Alice, widow of 1st, [-?-] Gill, by whom she had a son Steven, and 2nd, William Drury, who left a daughter Christian Drury (*ARMD* 67:407; MWB 3:109, abst. in *Md. Cal. of Wills* 1:175). She married 4th, Philip Washington.

Bond, Peter, d. c.1718 having m. Eleanor, daughter of Richard Gwynn (*BCF:* 47). She m. 2nd, Hill Savage (*q.v.*).

Bond, Peter, m. by 8 March 1730/1, Hester, daughter of Isaac Butterworth (MWB 19:627; MDAD 10:691). Hester, widow and admx. of Peter Bond, m. 2nd, Caleb Hughes (*q.v.*) (BAAD 3:66).

Bond, Peter, and Susanna Butler were m. on 1 Aug 1735 (Harrison, "St. Paul's Parish Register:" 153). She was a daughter of Henry Butler of Baltimore Co. (MDAD 27:252). Susanna m. 2nd, John Pitts (*q.v.*).

Bond, Peter, son of Peter, dec., in June 1756 chose John Dorsey as his guardian (BAMI 1755-1763).

Bond, Samuel, of Peter, m. Charity Clark on 9 Feb 1766 (Harrison, "St. Thomas' Parish Register:" 73). She received an equal share of the estate of Clare Clarke (BAAD 11:116).

Bond, Susan, in April 1796 was made guardian of William, Tobias, Alesy, Joshua, and Mary Bond (BAOC 3:187).

Bond, Thomas, Jr., and Elizabeth Scott were m. on 13 April 1725 (Harrison, "St. John's Parish Register:" 36). On 13 March 1744 Elizabeth was named as a daughter of Daniel Scott (MWB 24:81 abst. by Gibb).

Bond, Thomas, on 28 d. 12 m. 1763 had a complaint made against him of a young woman laying bastard child to his charge ("Minutes of Gunpowder Meeting," *QRNM*: 42).

Bond, Thomas, "the 3rd," and Catherine Fell were m. on 3 Feb 1765 (Harrison, "St. John's Parish Register:" 227). She was a daughter of William Fell, dec. (Gen. Court Western Shore Land Records TBH#1:166). Thomas Bond and Catherine [-?-], were m. by 6 July 1779 when their daughter Catherine was b. ("Allen-Raymond Family Bible," *HABFR* 2:3). On 9 Dec 1773 Thomas Bond gave property to his sister[-in-law] Jenet Few, wife of Isaac Few (*q.v.*), and to her children (BACT 1773-1784:85).

Bond, Thomas, son of John, and Rebecca Stansbury were m. on 19 Dec 1771 (Harrison, "St. John's Parish Register:"263). On 3 Nov 1779 Rebecca was named as a daughter of Tobias Stansbury and sister of Tobias Stansbury (BALR WG#E:16). On 26 d., 2 m. 1772, was charged with going out in marriage, contrary to the order ("Minutes of Gunpowder Meeting," *QRNM:*62).

Bond, Thomas, and Sarah Jordan were m. on 24 July 1783 (Marr. Returns of Rev. William West, Scharf Papers, MS.1999 at MdHS). Sarah married, 2nd, James Gregory (*q.v.*).

Bond, William, m. by 8 March 1710 Mary, heiress of Thomas, Daniel, and William Westbury (BALR TR#A:63).

Bond, William, in Aug 1711 was charged with begetting a bastard on the body of Mulatto Bess (BACP IS#B:247).

Bond, William, m. Elizabeth [-?-] on 17 March 1730 ("The Family Bible of James Bond," *Gen. of Penna. Families from the Pennsylvania Genealogical Magazine,* Baltimore: Genealogical Publishing Co., 3:581-582).

Bond, William, m. by 25 March 1742, Elizabeth, daughter of Luke Stansbury who named a grandson Luke Bond (MWB 22:464 abst. in *Md. Cal. of Wills* 8:169; MDAD 20:35). On 16 April 1759 William Bond was named as the father of Luke, Tobias, and Cassandra Bond, and of Priscilla Worthington, a granddaughter of Jane Stansbury (MWB 30:684 abst. by Gibb).

Bond, William, of William, at March 1761 Court was appointed guardian to his own children (BAMI 1755-1763).

Bond, William, and Sarah Wrongs were m. on 16 Nov 1771 (Harrison, "St. John's Parish Register:" 263). On 26 d. 2 m. 1772 William Bond, son of John, was charged with going out in marriage, contrary to the order ("Minutes of Gunpowder Meeting," *QRNM:*62).

Bond, William, d. by 13 March 1778 at which time his admx. Susanna m. 2nd, Isaac Hammond (*q.v.*).

Bond, William, of Samuel, on 26 d. 3 m. 1796, was reported to have married contrary to the good order ("Minutes of Gunpowder Meeting," *QRNM:*98). [No other marriage reference found].

Bondfield. See Bonfield.

Bone, Elizabeth, in June 1760 confessed to bearing a bastard mulatto child named Lucy who was one year old on 15 July 1760. In Nov 1760 Eliza was sold to William Coe, and her child was sold (BAMI 1755-1763).

Bone, Thomas, m. by 3 July 1751, Sarah, sister of John Cockey, Jr., (MDAD 30:112).

Bonfield (Bondfield), John, m. by 10 April 1771 Elizabeth, daughter of John Ensor (BAWB 3:257).

Bonfield, John, and Cassandra Stansbury were m. on 23 Dec 1783 (Marr. Returns of Rev. William West, Scharf Papers, MS 1999 at MdHS). On 30 May 1797 Cassandra was named as a daughter of Richardson Stansbury (BAWB 5:305; BAAD 12:412).

Bonham, Samuel, of Hanover Co., N.C., m. by 31 Oct 1767 Tomlinson, granddaughter and sole heiress of Edward Carter, late of Baltimore Co., dec. (BALR B#Q;290).

Bonnaday, Alice, servant of John Roberts, was discharged from service in Aug [1711?]); in June 1712 she was indicted for bastardy, naming John Hall as the father of her child; her son John Bonnaday was 2 years old in June 1709 and was bound out to serve John Roberts until age 21 (BACP IS#A:184, 314, IS#B:40).

Bonnaday (Bonaday), John, and Frances Carback were charged with living together in a scandalous manner by Thomas Meredith who informed the vestry of St. John's Parish on 2 May 1758 (Harrison, "St. John's Vestry Proceedings:" 140).

Bonner, Hugh, m. by lic. on 12 Aug 1796, Mary Silk at St. Peter's Catholic Church, Baltimore (*Piet:* 127).

Bonner, William, conveyed property to his bro. Barnaby Bonner on 26 Sep 1769 (BACT (BACT B#G:296).

Bonsall (Bonsell), Jesse, and Mary Stapleton were m. on 2 June 1795 (Register of First Presbyterian Church, Baltimore. MS at MdHS). Mary Bonsall (formerly Stapleton), on 24 d. 4 m. 1796 was charged with having her marriage accomplished contrary to the good order ("Minutes of Baltimore Meeting," *QRNM:*226).

Bonsall, Robert, merchant, was m. last eve. by Rev. Mr. McClaskey, to Miss Hatty Fonerden, both of Baltimore (*Baltimore Daily Intelligencer* 14 Feb 1794).

Boon. See Boone.

Boone, Eleanor, on 7 May 1782 were named as a niece in the will of Richard Croxall (BAWB 4:36).

Boone, John, m. by 5 June 1707 Jane, widow of 1st, William Choice (*q.v.*), and 2nd, John Durham (*q.v.*), and only daughter and heir of Francis Trippols [Trippas] (BALR RM#HS:553, IR#AM:60).

Boone (Boon), John Cockey Robert Burly, and Elizabeth Hale were married by license dated 16 June 1791 (Marr. Returns of Rev. John Hagerty, Scharf Papers, MS.1999 at MdHS). In Nov 1792 John Cockey Robert Burly 'Boon' stated he would not pay the debts of his wife Elizabeth (*Maryland Journal and Baltimore Advertiser* 6 Nov 1792).

Boone (Boon), John Cockey Robert Burley, m. by 29 April 1796, Elizabeth, daughter of Richard Demmitt (BALR WG#VV:310).

Boone, Thomas, m. by 28 May 1748, Sarah, daughter of Capt. John Cockey of Baltimore Co., and sister of John Cockey, Jr. and of Peter Cockey (MDAD 24:317, 30:112, 41:457).

Boos, Henrich, m. by Sep 1787, Dorothea Baumgärtnerin ("First Record Book for the Reformed and Lutheran and Congregations at Manchester, Baltimore (Now Carroll Co.," *MGSB* 35:283).

Boothby, Edward, m. by 7 Sep 1686, Elizabeth, widow of Col. Nathaniel Utie (*q.v.*) of Baltimore Co. and of Henry Johnson (*q.v.*) (INAC 12:143, 145, 19½B:67, 28:143; BAAD 2:118). Elizabeth was a sister of George Goldsmith and the mother of Frances who m. 1st, Bechley, and 2nd, Dr. Josias Middlemore (*q.v.*) (BALR BB#1:426).

Boram, Aaron, son of John and Ann, both dec., on 24 d. 4 m. 1794, announced his intention to marry Elizabeth Johns, daughter of Nathan and Elizabeth ("Minutes of Deer Creek Meeting," *QRNM:*154).

Border, John, m. by 25 April 1789, Margaret, daughter of Rudolph Hook (BAAD 9:325).

Borderie, Bernard, merchant of Bordeaux, m. by lic. on 4 Jan 1794, Elizabeth Bulger of Montgomery Co., Md., at St. Peter's Catholic Church, Baltimore (*Piet:* 127). Bernard Borderie advertised he would not pay the debts of his wife Betsy (*Baltimore Daily Intelligencer* 8 July 1794).

Bordley, Beale, m. by 22 Sep 1759, Margaret Chew (AALR BB#2:292).

Bordley, Maj. John, of Kent Co. was m. last eve. by Rev. Mr. Bend to Miss Catharine Starck, daughter of Mr. John Starck of this city (*Federal Gazette and Baltimore Daily Advertiser* 3 Aug 1798).

Bordley, Martha, servant of Robert West, Jr., in June 1732 was tried for bastardy (BACP HWS#7:298).

Bordley, William C., Esq., of Chesterfield, Queen Anne's Co., was m. last eve. by the Rev. Mr. Ireland to Miss Margaret Keener (*Federal Gazette and Baltimore Daily Advertiser* 11 July 1798). On 18 Feb 1800 Margaret was named as a legatee of Melchor Keener (BAAD 13:194).

Boreing. See Boring.

Boren, Reuben, m. by 10 Aug 1768, Anna Tronin ("First Record Book for the Reformed and Lutheran and Congregations at Manchester, Baltimore (Now Carroll) Co.," MGSB 35:272).

Borie, Joseph, native of Point Petre, Island of Guadeloupe, m. by lic. on 30 Aug 1794, Margaret Lockerman at St. Peter's Catholic Church, Baltimore (*Piet:* 127).

Boring, |-?-|, m. by 24 June 1798 Rebecca, daughter of Jacob Cox (BAWB 6:121).

Boring, Absolom, m. by 2 June 1790 Sarah, admx. of James Chilcote (BAAD 10:150).

Boring, Ezekiel, in 1761 was fined for bastardy (BAMI 1755-1763).

Boring, James, m. by 4 March 1719 Jane, daughter and coheir of Daniel Welsh (BALR TR#DS:196). See John Boring below.

Boring, James, and Rebecca Gain, widow, were m. on 5 Aug 1734 Harrison, "St. Paul's Parish Register:" 152). Rebecca was named as the widow of William Gain (*q.v.*). She m. 3rd, John Frazier (*q.v.*) (*BCF:* 36).

Boring, James, and Martha Wheeler were m. on 25 Dec 1736 (Harrison, "St. Paul's Parish Register:" 155). She was a daughter of William Wheeler (BAAD 4:35).

Boring, James, m. by 19 March 1774, Sarah, widow of Luke Tipton (*q.v.*), and mother of Thomas Tipton (BALR AL#K:167).

Boring, John, mariner, m. by 22 Sep 1679 Margaret, relict and admx. of Roger Sidwell (INAC 6:423).

Boring, John, m. by 15 Sep 1711 Mary, daughter of John Kemp of Baltimore Co. (MWB 4:239; BALR TR#A:171).

Boring, John, m. by 4 March 1719 Jane, daughter and coheir of Daniel Welsh, late of Baltimore Co., dec. (BALR TR#DS:196). See James Boring above.

Boring (Boreing), John, aged about 50, deposed on 7 July 1732 naming his father-in-law John Ferry who had been living when Boring was 11 years old (BALC HWS#3 #36).

Boring, John, m. by 17 Oct 1774 Avarilla, daughter of Charles Robinson (BALR AL#L: 208).

Boring, Joshua, m. by 21 Sep 1787 Ann, daughter of Thomas Lane (BAAD 9:107).

Boring, Mary, was charged with bastardy at Nov 1740 Court (BACP HWS#TR:351).

Boring, Reuben, m. by 4 June 1770, [-?-], daughter of Abraham Vaughn (BAAD 6:217).

Boring, Thomas, and Mary Haile were m. on 21 Jan 1730 (Harrison, "St. Paul's Parish Register:" 156). Thomas d. by 5 Oct 1775; Mary left land to her eldest son James Boring (BALR AL#N:384).

Born, Adam, m. by 13 Sep 1767, Apollonia Penzin ("First Record Book for the Reformed and Lutheran and Congregations at Manchester, Baltimore (Now Carroll) Co.," *MGSB* 35: 271). **See George Born below.**

Born, George, m. by 18 June 1765 Appolonia Penzin ("First Record Book for the Reformed and Lutheran and Congregations at Manchester, Baltimore (Now Carroll) County, *MGSB* 35: 270). **See Adam Born above.**

Born, George, m. by 5 March 1760, Catharina Jungin ("First Record Book for the Reformed and Lutheran and Congregations at Manchester, Baltimore (Now Carroll) Co.," *MGSB* 35: 265).

Born, Joh., m. by 27 Oct 1763, Maria Elisabeta Hochshiltin ("First Record Book for the Reformed and Lutheran and Congregations at Manchester, Baltimore (Now Carroll) Co.," *MGSB* 35: 268).

Borth, Henry, of Baltimore, stated he would not pay the debts of his wife Elizabeth (*Maryland Journal and Baltimore Advertiser* 4 Jan 1785).

Bose, Jacob, d. by 1800, leaving a daughter Catherine Bose, and other children, who are all wards of George Decker (BOCP Petition of George Decker, 1800).

Bosley, [-?-], m. by 9 April 1751 Elizabeth, daughter of William Demmitt (MWB 28:209).

Bosley, [-?-], m. by 16 Dec 1788 Rachel daughter of John Gorsuch (BAWB 5:371).

Bosley, [-?-], m. by 2 April 1781 Elizabeth, daughter of Joseph Norris (BAWB 4:31).

Bosley, [-?-], m. by 2 April 1781 Willimine, daughter of Joseph Norris (BAWB 4:31).

Bosley, [-?-], m. by 6 Dec 1782 Rachel, daughter of John Wilmot (BAWB 3:550).

Bosley, [-?-], m. by 22 Aug 1792 Ann, daughter of Thomas Cole (BAWB 5:53).

Bosley, Charles, m. by 3 Aug 1736, Elizabeth, daughter of William Cox, and sister of Jacob Cox (BALR HWS#M:418; MWB 31:750 abst. by Gibb).

Bosley, Daniel, orphan son of Joseph, in April 1793 chose Edward Owings as his guardian (BAOC 3:46).

Bosley, Elijah, m. by 5 March 1795 [-?-], legatee of Ruth Ingram (BAAD 11:523).

Bosley, James, m. by 23 Feb 1787 Ann, daughter of Samuel Gott (BAWB 4:225; BAAD 9:205).

Bosley, John, d. by 15 April 1775 having m. Hannah, widow of William Tipton (*q.v.*); Hannah's will of that date named her sons Samuel and Mordecai Tipton, and her daughter Sarah, now wife of Christopher Cole (BAWB 3:325).

Bosley, John, and Nancy Cole were married by license dated 9 Sep 1782 (BAML). She was a daughter of Thomas Cole (BAWB 5:53; BAAD 11:352, 12:18).

Bosley, John, and Susannah Price were m. by lic. dated 27 July 1785 (BAML). Susanna Bosley, formerly Price, on 29 d. 10 m. 1785 was charged with being married contrary to the good order ("Minutes of Gunpowder Meeting," *QRNM*:81).

Bosley, Joseph, m. by 7 Feb 1745 Mary, dau. of Joshua Hall; they were the parents of a son Joshua Bosley (BALR BB#I: 510).

Bosley, Joseph, died by 12 Aug 1777 leaving a widow Elizabeth, since m. to Amos Ogden, and a daughter Belinda Bosley; on 14 Feb 1788 Charles Gorsuch pet. the court that he be made guardian of Belinda (BOCP Petition re Joseph Bosley, 1788, Box 2, Folder 53).

Bosley, Joshua, and Ann Gott were m. on 4 Nov 1779 (Harrison, "St. James Parish Register," Anne Arundel Co., MS. at MdHS: 415). On 6 Sep 1793 Ann was named as a daughter of Rachel Gott (BAWB 6:2).

Bosley, Mary, was charged with bastardy at the Nov 1720 Court (BACP IS#C:405).

Bosley, Thomas, and Mary Richards were m. 13 Dec 1770 (Harrison, "St. John's Parish Register:" 261). In April 1776 Bosley stated that his wife Mary had left him (*Dunlap's Maryland Gazette* 16 April 1776).

Bosley (Boozley, Bossley), William, on the last Sat. in Feb 1736 with Mary Brown was summoned before the Vestry of St. George's Parish and promised to refrain from all unlawful practices. On 6 June 1737 William Bossley and Mary Brown were ordered returned to the Court for not separating and refraining from each other's company (Reamy, *St. George's Parish Register:* 103, 104).

Bosley, William, died by 1795 leaving a leasehold property "for one life," that has never been sold. In 1795 Vincent Trapnall petitioned the court that the property be sold and dividend made among the heirs. The petition was also signed by Elizabeth Chenoweth, Charles Wells, James Headington, and Arthur Chenoweth, Jr. (BOCP Petition of Vincent Trapnall, 1795).

Bosman, Edward, m. by 29 July 1785, Mary, admx. of John Shields (BAAD 8:196).

Bossell, William, on 30 May 1797 was named as a grandson in the will of Richardson Stansbury (BAWB 5:505).

Bossey, Jane, was charged with bastardy at the June 1734 Court (BACP HWS#9:253).

Boston, Samuel, on 4 May in the 43rd year of Cecilius [Lord Baltimore] posted bond to admin. the estate of his wife Mary, formerly Mary Goldsmith, relict and admx. of Capt. George Goldsmith (BAAB 1:62; MDTP 4B:21). In his will dated 6 Jan 1676 Boston named George Goldsmith his son-in-law and Mary Goldsmith his daughter-in-law (MWB 5:175 abst. in *Md. Cal. of Wills* 1:186).

Botner, Capt. John, and Elizabeth Sherwood were m. last Thurs. at Fell's Point (*Baltimore Telegraphe* 9 April 1796).

Boswell, William, on 2 May 1798 received a share of £77.15.3 from the estate of Richardson Stansbury, who named his grandson William 'Bossell' in his will dated 30 Jan 1797 (BAAD 12:412; BAWB 5:505).

Bosworth, John, m. by 3 Dec 1745 Mary, daughter of William Robinson (BALR TB#D: 428).

Boucher, Susanna, servant of Thomas Sellman, was charged with bastardy at the March 1759 Court, for having a mulatto bastard child named Richard Boucher (BAMI 1757-1759:187).

Boudrau, Charles, m. by lic. on 9 Sep 1787 Mary Yau at St. Peter's Catholic Church, Baltimore (*Piet*: 128).

Bouis, John, was m. Thurs. eve. by Rev. Mr. Kurtz, to Martha Mitchell, both of this city (*Federal Gazette and Baltimore Daily Advertiser* 6 Dec 1800).

Bourdillon, Rev. Benedict, of Baltimore Co., m. by 14 June 1751 Janettee Jansen (MDAD 30:105). Rev. Benedict Bordillon, Rector of St. Paul's Parish in Balto., was dec.; James Richard advertised a sale of property at the house of Mrs. Jane Bourdillon (*Md. Gaz.* 4 Feb 1746). His eldest son Andrew Theodore Bourdillon, second son William Benedict Bourdillon, and widow Jane Bourdillon had empowered Daniel and Walter Dulany to sell the property of the dec. (Annapolis *Maryland Gazette* 12 April 1764).

Bourgeois, Antony Chapeau, native of Conne Province, m. by lic. on 4 April 1794, Anna Savon Parce, native of St. Heule, Diocese of Lisberon, France, at St. Peter's Catholic Church, Baltimore (*Piet*: 128).

Bourne, Sylvanus, was m. last eve. to Miss Rebecca Haslett (*Federal Gazette and Baltimore Daily Advertiser* 18 Oct 1797).

Bowen, Benjamin, m. by 19 April 1703 [-?-], widow of Nathaniel Ruxton (MDTP 19A:166).

Bowen, Benjamin, and Mary Carr were m. 4 d. 8 m. 1744 (Records of Gunpowder Monthly Meeting, at MdHS). Benjamin d. leaving a will made 9 Jan 1770, having m. Mary, daughter and devisee of Thomas Carr, dec., and leaving two sons Benjamin and Joshua Bowen (BALR AL#G:208).

Bowen, Benjamin, and Elizabeth Merryman were married by license dated 12 April 1792 (BAML). Elizabeth was a daughter of Joseph Merryman (BAWB 6:159).

Bowen, Benjamin, m. by 6 Feb 1797 Mary, daughter of Edward Talbott (BAWB 6:20; BAAD 13:5).

Bowen, Elizabeth, servant of Thomas Allender, was charged with bastardy at the Nov 1756 Court and found guilty of having born a mulatto child named Sarah, Sarah was sold to Thomas Allender to the age of 21 ; Elizabeth Bowen was charged with bastardy at the Nov 1757 Court; she had borne Nathan Bone [*sic*] who was fathered by a black man; in June 1760 she confessed to having borne a mulatto bastard named Lucy Bone (BACP BB#C:322; BAMI 1757-1759:74, 100; BAMI 1755-1763).

Bowen, Elizabeth. See Galloway, Elizabeth.

Bowen, Jacob, of Calvert Co., m, by 15 July 1760 Mary Parran Abbott, natural daughter of John Parran of Calvert Co. (BALR B#O:597).

Bowen, John, and Milcah Claxton (Clarkson) were m. on 7 Oct 1699 (Harrison, "St. James Parish Register," Anne Arundel Co., MS. at MdHS: 297). On 10 May 1706 Milcah was named as a daughter of Robert Clarkson of Anne Arundel Co. (BALR RM#HS:549).

Bowen, John, m. by 22 Jan 1742, Rosanna, widow of Jonas Robertson (*q.v.*) (BALR TB#C: 96). She was the mother of Rosanna and Rebecca Robertson, and widow of Jonas Robertson (BALR TB#C:72, 96). She m. 3rd, John Ogle (*q.v.*).

Bowen, John B. and Sarah Marshall, both of Baltimore, were m. last eve. (*Baltimore American* 8 July 1799).

Bowen, Jonas, of Baltimore Co., m. by 26 March 1699, Martha, mother of Lawrence Wolden (MWB 6:228 abst. in *Md. Cal. of Wills* 2:171).

Bowen (Bowin), Jonas, m. by 6 Oct 1702, Anne, admx. of William Story (INAC 23:96),

Bowen, Josias, Sr., of Patapsco Neck, aged 62, and Sarah Stansbury, aged 33, daughter of Tobias Stansbury of the same place, were m. Sat., 24h inst. (*Baltimore Daily Repository* 27 Dec 1791). They had entered into a marriage contract and agreed on a marriage settlement on 22 Dec 1791 (BALR WG#HH:78). She was a daughter of Tobias Stansbury (BAWB 6:173).

Bowen, Nathan, m. by6 Feb 1760 Mary, daughter of Sabrett and Mary Sollers (MWB 30:860 abst. by Gibb).; BAWB 3:242).

Bowen, Peter, of Baltimore City, on 14 July 1800, set free his wife Dinah and two children, Ephraim and Julia, who had been conveyed to him by a bill of sale given by Dennis Sollers of Frederick Co. (BACT WG#7).

Bowen, Sabret, and Elizabeth Humphrey were m. by lic. dated 4 Jan 1792 (BAML). Elizabeth Bowen, formerly Humphrey, on 26 d. 2 m. 1792 reportedly had her marriage accomplished by a hireling minister ("Minutes of Gunpowder Meeting," *QRNM*:92).

Bowen, Solomon, and Temperance Ensor were m. on 28 Nov 1751 (Harrison, "St. Thomas Parish Register:" 71). She was a daughter of John Ensor (BAWB 3:257).

Bowen, Solomon, and Jemima Merryman were m. on 20 June 1786 (Marr. Returns of Rev. William Gill, Scharf Papers, MS.1999 at MdHS). Jemima was a daughter of Joseph Merryman (BAWB 6:159).

Bowen, Tabitha, was charged with bastardy at the June 1750 Court (BACP TR#5:2; TR#6:25-26).

Bower, Barnard, on 1 Sep 1763 was appointed attorney by his father James Bower (BACP BB#F:204).

Bowles, Richard, of Baltimore Co., dec., by May 1795 when William Shaw (*q.v.*) advertised he had m. the only surviving child of the dec., and had the sole right to administer the estate (*Maryland Journal and Baltimore Advertiser* 8 May 1795).

Bowley, [-?-], m. by 9 Oct 1759 Elizabeth, daughter of Darby Lux, who also named a grandson Daniel Bowley in his will (MWB 27:403 abst. by Gibb). On 5 May 1773 Elizabeth was named as a daughter of Ann Lux of Baltimore Town, and sister of William Lux (BAWB 3:357, 4:43).

Bowman, Waltara, on 25 Feb 1786 was named as cousin, residuary legatee, and extx. of Christian Deans (BAWB 4:176). On 18 Oct 1786 Waltara Bowman, extx., posted bond to administer Dean's estate (BAAB 6:363).

Box, Nicholas, m. by banns 14 Oct 1787 Mary Oxford at St. Peter's Catholic Church, Baltimore (*Piet*: 128). Nicholas Boxx, of Fell's Point, stated he would not pay the debts of his wife Mary (*Maryland Journal and Baltimore Advertiser* 9 Aug 1791).

Boyce, Ann Rebecca, in April 1795 was made a ward of Eleanor Boyce (BAOC 3:152).

Boyce, John, Esq., of Harford Co., was m. on Thurs., 19th inst., by Rev. Wilmer, Miss Rogers, daughter of Benjamin Rogers of Baltimore Co. (*Maryland Journal and Baltimore Advertiser* 24 Jan 1786).

Boyce, Roger, in his will made 16 Sep 1766 named his wife's brother John Addison Smith (MWB 38:694, abst. in *Md. Cal. of Wills* 14:223).

Boyce, Roger, aged 15, son of Roger, in March 1775 chose Alexander Cowan as his guardian; Cowan was also appointed guardian of John and Ann Boyce, children of the aforesaid Roger (BAMI 1772, 1775-1781: 113).

Boyd, [-?-], m. by 14 June 1674 [-?-], widow of [-?-] Norwood (INAC 1:48).

Boyd, [-?-], m. by 1 Oct 1759 [-?-], daughter of John Cooper who named his grandsons Cooper Boyd and John Boyd (MWB 30:752 abst. by Gibb).

Boyd, [-?-], d. by 9 July 1752, having m. Elinor Carroll, daughter of Charles Carroll, Esq., dec.; they were the parents of Benjamin Boyd of Prince George's Co. (BALR TR#D:339).

Boyd, **Abraham,** of Montgomery Co. stated in Aug 1783 that he would not pay the debts of his wife Sarah (*Maryland Gazette or Baltimore General Advertiser* 1 Aug 1783). On 8 June 1785 Boyd conveyed [property] Daniel Dady for the maintenance of the said Sarah (BACT 1785-1788, MS 2865, MdHS: 84).

Boyd, **John,** and Anna Little were m. on 8 May 1777 (First Presbyterian Church of Baltimore, MS. at MdHS: 5). Boyd, of Baltimore Co., practitioner of physic, m. by 26 June 1777, Ann, widow of John Little, inn holder (BALR WG#A: 252). In his will dated 19 Jan 1790, Boyd named his wife's sister Mary Drury, his own sisters Mary Stewart (and her son William Stewart), Jane Culberson, and Elizabeth Smith (BAWB 4:404).

Boyd, **John,** d. by 1783 having m. Mary, daughter of John Wooden. She m. 2nd, Daniel Shead (*q.v.*) BAWB 4:426; BAAD 10:541).

Boyd, **Robert,** m. by 6 Dec 1742, Ruth Bayes, legatee of Christopher Shaw of Baltimore Co., dec. (BALR TB#C:223).

Boyer, **David,** and Mrs. Ann Kinkaid, of Baltimore, were m. last eve. by Rev. the Rev. Mr. Hargrove (*Baltimore American* 9 Dec 1800).

Boyer, **John,** and Agnes Boyes were married by license dated 26 Aug 1785 (BAML). Agnes Boyer, on 12 Nov 1785 was conveyed land by her mother, Margaret Hall IBALR WG#X:546).

Boyer, **John,** on 11 April 1799 was a legatee of Robert Mack (BAAD 13:28).

Boyle, **James,** d. in Sep 1783 leaving a widow Mary, who on 13 June 1787 pet. the court that her husband d. leaving a will and naming Richard Ridgely and James Toole, execs. At the time her husband d., Mary was *enciente,* and has since given birth to son James. She was appointed guardian on 18 Aug 1785 (BOCP Petition of James Boyle, 1787, Box 2, Folder 5).

Boyle, **William,** m. by banns on 23 Dec 1787 Mary Burk at St. Peter's Catholic Church, Baltimore (*Piet*: 128).

Boyle, **William,** and Mary Evans were married on 9 Dev 1792 (Register of First Presbyterian Church, MS. at MdHS, p 3). In Dec 1793 Boyle stated he would not pay the debts of his wife Mary Ann, who had eloped (*Baltimore Daily Intelligencer* 27 Dec 1793), W. Boyle

Boyreau, **John Joseph,** m. by lic. on 11 June 1792 Mary Marzial at St. Peter's Catholic Church, Baltimore (*Piet*: 128).

Brabie (Brabo), **Nicholas,** of the District of Southwark, in the County of Philadelphia, ship caulker, m. by 8 Sep 1783, Elizabeth, widow of James Bonfield, carpenter, of Baltimore Town (BACT 1773-1784:432).

Bracke, **Ferdinand,** was m. 2nd inst. by Rev. Dr. Allison to Miss Hannah Cornwall, both of this city (*Federal Gazette and Baltimore Daily Advertiser* 8 April 1799).

Brackett, **Mary,** orphan daughter of John Brackett, in Aug 1792 chose Christian Baum as her guardian (BAOC 3:7).

Brackman, **Anthony,** m. by lic. on 8 Sep 1793 Ann Hendericks at St. Peter's Catholic Church, Baltimore (*Piet*: 128).

Bradbury, **Stephen,** native of Mass., m. by lic. on 6 Oct 1798, Margaret Colgan at St. Peter's Catholic Church, Baltimore (*Piet*: 128).

Bradford, Elizabeth, had three illegitimate children, born in Susquehanna Lower Hundred: Barbara, b. 1 Dec 1753 or 1758; Mary, b. 15 Nov 1757, and William Daphier Bradford, b. 13 Dec 1759. Thomas Brown paid a criminal fine in Nov 1760 (BAMI 1755-1763, pp. 20, 21).

Bradford, George, and Margaret Talbot were m. by lic. dated 20 April 1785 (HAML). Margaret Bradford (formerly Talbot), on 5 d. 11 m. 1789 produced a paper condemning her outgoing in marriage ("Minutes of Deer Creek Meeting," *QRNM:*147).

Bradford, William, and Catherine Osborne made a prenuptial agreement on 4 May 1751 (BACT TR#E:37). She was a daughter of Henry Rhodes, and when Bradford d. by 2 May 1761, she was noted as being the mother of Benjamin Osborne (BALR B#I:107).

Bradford, William, and Sarah McComas were m. on 16 Feb 1764 (Harrison, "St. John's Parish Register:" 226). She was a daughter of Daniel McComas (MWB 33:341; BAWB 3:20; BAAD 7:192).

Bradhurst, Capt. Benjamin, m. Sun., 14th inst., Miss Delilah Young (*Maryland Gazette or Baltimore General Advertiser* 23 March 1790).

Bradley, Hannah, was charged with bastardy at the Nov 1757 Court and fined for having borne a bastard child named William Bradley (BACP TB&TR#1:163; BAMI 1755-1763).

Bradley, John, and Elizabeth Jones were m. on 15 Dec 1746 (Harrison, "St. Paul's Parish Register:" 160). In Nov1751 Bradley, living in the Forks of Gunpowder, on 20 Nov 1751, stated he would not be responsible for debts of wife Elizabeth, who had eloped (BACT TR#E:51).

Bradley, Robert, and Ruth Howard were m. by Rev. Allison by license dated 17 April 1787 (BAML). Ruth was a daughter of Charles Howard, whose will dated 2 Feb 1799 named a grandson Robert Bradley (BAWB 6:161).

Brady, James, m. by 25 Aug 1785 Elizabeth, daughter of John Hughes and heir of Benjamin Hughes (BAWB 4:526; BAAD 12:293).

Brady, John, m. by lic. on 25 Aug 1793 Mary McFee at St. Peter's Catholic Church, Baltimore (*Piet:* 128).

Bragg, Hannah, was charged with bastardy at the March 1739/40 Court (BACP HWS&TR:140, 236).

Bragg, Sarah, was charged with bastardy at the March 1723/4 Court and named Reuben Hassal or Hassell as the father of her child at the June 1724 Court BACP IS&TW#1:201, 330).

Bramwell, George, and Susanna Fortt were m. on 7 March 1750 (Harrison, "St. Thomas Parish Register :" 71). She was the relict and extx. of Samuel Fort, collar-maker of Baltimore Co., dec. (BALR TR#C:532). In his will dated 29 March 1769 and proved 24 Sep 1770 Bramwell named his wife Susanna, his children Henry and Mary, sons-in-law [*i.e.*step-sons] Richard and Samuel Fortt, daughter-in-law Ruth Ford. Son Henry was to administer the estate. John Pitts, John Murray, Sophia Bond, and Thomas Towson, Jr., witnessed the will (MWB 38:70, abst. in *Md. Cal. of Wills* 14:145).

Branch, John, and Rebecca Strawble were married by license dated 29 Feb 1788 (BAML). By 5 June 1789 Rebecca was named as the widow of Zachariah Strouble; the said John Branch hath since abandoned her (BALR WG#DD:643).

Brand, Samuel, d. by 29 April 1693 having m. Mary, widow of John Hammond (*q.v.*); she later m by that date 3ʳᵈ, Edward Reeves (*q.v.*), and 4ᵗʰ Richard Askew (*q.v.*) (MDTP 14:124, 15A:8, 26, 27; BALR IR#AM:68; BACP F#1:128, G#1:84).

Brandt, Abraham, made a will on 12 Jan 1766, naming his wife Sharlett, widow of [-?-] Walt; he also named Barbery Weaver and the children he had by her: Catherine Brandt, Modelianor Brandt; and Elizabeth Brandt (BAWB 2:287).

Brangwell, Peter, m. by 30 April [1683?] Elizabeth Kemb (BACP D:94).

Brannon, Patrick, m. by 10 May 1767, [-?-], daughter of Jacob Hanson (BAAD 6:234). As Patrick Brenna, his wife was named as a daughter of Sarah Tayman of Baltimore Co. (MDAD 31:118).

Brannon, Patrick, and Elizabeth Johnston [*sic*] were m. on 11 Aug 1769 (Harrison, "St. John's Parish Register:" 259). Patrick Brannon and Elizabeth Johnson, on 23 Feb 1768 were accused by Elizabeth's sister Martha Johnson, of unlawful cohabitation (Reamy, *St. George's Parish Register:* 110).

Brannock, Patrick, d. by 1796, leaving as his nearest relation in this country Patrick Ragan, who petitioned that letters of admin. be granted to him (BOCP Petition of Patrick Ragan, 1796).

Branson, William, and Peggy Smith, daughter of Peter Smith, were m. on Sun. eve. (*Maryland Journal and Baltimore Advertiser* 4 Jan 1791),

Brashears, Nathan, m. by 10 Nov 1767 Esther, admx. of William Sappington (*q.v.*) (MDTP 42:260).

Brashear(s) (Brashiers), Thomas, and Sarah Constance were m. on 13 Oct 1726 (Harrison, "St. George's Parish Register:" 262). In 1726 William Grafton conveyed 100 a. of *Grafton's Gift* to his friend John Constant and wife Susanna for life; then to their daughter Susanna; then to John Constant, Jr.; Grafton also conv. 50 a. to John and Susanna's daughter Sarah, wife of Thomas Brashiers (BALR IS#H:381).

Brashier, Jane, was aged 6 in Nov 1710 when she was bound to serve Sarah Day (BCCP IS#A:181).

Brashier (Brasher, Brazier), Jane, was charged with bastardy and she was fined on 5 March 1744/5; she was charged again at the Nov 1746 Court (BACP 1743-1745:154, 480, TB&TR#1:20).

Brashier, Thomas, son of William and Elizabeth, dec., aged about 11 next 1 Sept. in June 1712 was bound to John Webster to age 25 (BACP IS#A: 315).

Brason, Babier?, m. by 16 Feb 1799 Mary Drebert, who received her full share of the estate of Adam Forney (BAAD 12:541). She was the widow of Christian Drepert (*q.v.*).

Brawn. See Brown.

Breard, Michael, an officer in the French Navy, and Miss Sophia Delor, daughter of Mr. Delor, late Commissary of the French marine, were m. by lic. on 17 Dec 1792, Mon. eve. by the Rt. Rev. Bishop Carroll (*Baltimore Daily Repository* 20 Dec 1792; at St. Peter's Catholic Church, Baltimore (*Piet:* 128).

Breidenbaugh, John, m. by lic. on 4 Nov 1798, Anne Moran at St. Peter's Catholic Church, Baltimore (*Piet:* 128).

Bremont, John, native of Rau in Bearn, son of Bernard and Martha (Dauhorat), m. by lic. on 19 Nov 1793, Frances Elizabeth Delesfauris, daughter of John Martin and Radegonde (Richer) at St. Peter's Catholic Church, Baltimore (*Piet:* 128).

Brenszen, Jacob, m. by 30 Jan 1799, [-?-] Forney (First German Reformed Church, Register, MS at MdHS: 24).

Brereton, Thomas, original and ancient broker, was m. Mon. 26th ult., to Sally, daughter of Thomas Marshall of Northampton Co., Va.(*Maryland Journal and Baltimore Advertiser* 6 March 1781).

Brerewood, Thomas, Jr., m. by 31 Aug 1731 Charlotte, granddaughter of Lady Margaret Baltimore (BALR IS#L:222). In his will made 8 Aug 1746 he named his daughter Charlotte, and a grandson William Brerewood (MWB 25:4 abst. by Gibb).

Bressforth, Jonathan, of Sheffield, m. by 16 Aug 1774, Ann daughter of Jonathan White, clerk of Charles Co. (BALR AL#L:454).

Brett, Martha, was charged with bastardy and fined at the Nov 1757 Court (BAMI 1757-1759:74).

Brevitt, John, of Wolverhampton, Staffordshire, and Elizabeth Skatt were m. before 28 June 1717 when their daughter Sarah was born ("Brevitt Bible," deposited at the MdHS; *The Notebook* (9) (4) (Dec 1993) 38).

Brevitt, John, and Mary Swope were married by license dated 4 May 1784 (BAML). On 3 Nov 1787 Brevitt's wife was named as one who received a legacy from the estate of John Wilkes (BAAD 9:115). John Wilkes in his will, made 25 Feb 1774, left Mary, 3rd daughter of Benedict Swope £10 (BAWB 3:290).

Brevitt, Joseph, son of John and Sarah (Skatt), was b. 30 March 1729 and m. 2nd, Ann Wilkes of Autherly near Wolverhampton, ("of the blood of John Wilkes the English patriot), were m. some time before 29 Nov 1760 when their son John was born ("Brevitt Bible," deposited at the MdHS; *The Notebook* (9) (4) (Dec 1993): 38).

Brevitt, Dr. Joseph, son of Joseph, m. Cassandra Woodland on 29 Nov 1798 ("Joseph Brevitt Bible Record," in *MBR* 1:44-45). Dr. Brevitt of this city was m. at Abingdon on Thurs. eve. last by Rev. Dr. Allen, to Miss Cassandra Webster Woodland of Harford Co. (*Federal Gazette and Baltimore Daily Advertiser* 1 Dec 1798).

Brian (Briant), James, m. 4 July 1754 Mary Raven (Peden, *A Closer Look at St. John's Parish Registers, 1701-1801*). She was a daughter of Luke Raven who named a granddaughter Sarah in his will (BAWB 2:349).

Brian (Bryan), Mary, was charged with bastardy at the March 1720/1 Court (BACP IS#C:435).

Briant, Hannah, on 14 March 1738 was named as a daughter in the will of John Simkins (MWB 22:39 abst. in *Md. Cal. of Wills* 8:20).

Brice, James, and Mary Johnson had been m. on 6 Jan 1742 (Harrison, "St. George's Parish Register:" 327). Mary m. 2nd, Thomas Renshaw (*q.v.*). Mary was a daughter of Thomas Johnson, Sr., of Deer Creek (BAWB 3:63).

Brice, John, Jr., of Annapolis, was m. 19th inst. at Lilac Hill, Calvert Co., by Rev. Mr. Scott, to Miss Sarah Lane, late of this town (*Baltimore Daily Intelligencer* 28 April 1794).

Bricker, Anthony, m. by 26 March 1799 Margaretta, daughter of Helfrich Gramer of Mannheim Twp., York Co., Pa. (BALR WG#58:47).

Brien (Bryan), Luke, and Eleanor Harryman were m. on 6 Jan 1780 (Marr. Returns of Rev. William West, Scharf Papers, MS. 1999 at MdHS); on 29 Nov 1794 Eleanor was named as a daughter of George Harryman (BAWB 5:236; BOCP Petition of George Harryman, 1799).

Brierly, Robert, in his will, made 4 Sep 1764 named his aunt Ann Dawtha [*sic*] *(BAWB* 2:330).

Briggs, James, was m. last eve. by Rev. Dr. Allison, to Miss Temperance Ensor (*Federal Gazette and Baltimore Daily Advertiser* 6 Dec 1797).

Brinton, Joseph, son of Moses and Eliner of Lancaster Co., Pa., on 5 d. 9 m. 1784, announced his intention to marry Susanna Rigbie, daughter of James and Elizabeth, the latter dec.; his parents and her father gave their consent ("Minutes of Deer Creek Meeting," *QRNM*:142).

Britain (Britton), [-?-], m. by 1799, Mary, widow of Matthew Miller (BOCP Petition of Mary Britton, 1799).

Britain (Britton), Abraham, m. by 24 July 1770, Hannah, admx. of William Tolley Towson (MINV 104:358).

Britain (Britton), Nicholas, m. by 17 Oct 1774, Alethia, relict of Thomas Finley (*q.v.*) by whom she had a son Thomas Finley, Jr. (MDAD 47:155; BALR AL#L:199).

Britain (Brittain, Button), Richard, and Temperance Talbott were married by license dated 25 March 1782 (BAML). On 13 March 1799 Temperance was named as a daughter of Edward Talbott (BAAD 13:5; BAWB 6:20).

Brittain. See Britain.

Britton, See Britain.

Broad, John, m. by Nov 1692, Barbara, relict of Dennis Garrett (BACP F#1:276).

Broad, John, m. by 13 Oct 1739, Jemima, granddaughter of Joseph Peake (BALR HWS#1-A:336).

Broad, Thomas, m. by 23 Sep 1723 Anna, daughter of Matthew Hawkins, who named his daus. Mary, Dinah, Ann and Elizabeth in his will dated 14 April 1705 and proved 24 April 1705 (BALR IS#G:208; MWB 3:446).

Broadhurst, [-?-], m. by 6 Dec 1723, Katherine, widow of Reiner Skaats of Schenectady, Albany, N. Y., and mother of Gideon Skaats (BALR IS#G:286).

Brock, Elizabeth, servant to Lance Todd, was charged with bastardy at the Aug 1722 Court and named fellow servant as the father of her child; Elizabeth Brock, servant to Charles Rockhold, was charged with bastardy at the March 1724/5 Court. Her son William Brock, aged 16 in April 1737, was bound out to John Wooley in Aug 1737 (BACP IS&TW#1:306, IS&TW#4:98, (BACP HWS#1A;98).

Brock, Rachel, on 22 March 1760 was named as a granddaughter in the will of Mary Bowen (MWB 31:748 abst. by Gibb).

Brock, Thomas, and Mary Perrigo were m. on 15 Feb 1787 (Marr. Register of Rev. Lewis Richards, MS.690 at MdHS). On 12 April 1791 Mary received an equal share of the estate of Nathan Perigo (BAAD 10:329).

Brogden, Ann, was charged with having borne two children out of wedlock at the Nov 1722 Court and named John Mahan as the father; she was charged again at the March 1733/4 Court and allowed 50 lbs. of tobacco a month for her support as she was too lame to support herself. She was charged again at the June 1740 Court and presented at the Aug 1740 Court (BACP IS&TW#2: 21, HWS#9:183, 256, 263, HWS#TR:226, 330).

Broker (Brocar), Penellipia, servant to John Campbell, was charged with bastardy at the Nov 1746 Court and on 3 March 17467 was ordered to be whipped (BACP TB&TR#1:320, 398).

Brokes. See Brooks.

Brooke, Basil, of Montgomery Co., and Miss Maria Patrick of Baltimore, were m. last Fri. at Joshua Hervey's (*Federal Gazette and Baltimore Advertiser* 27 Nov 1797; (Marr. Register of Rev. Lewis Richards, MS.690 at MdHS).

Brooks, Ann, was charged with bastardy in 1750, and at the 5 June 1750 Court Charles Croxall was named as the father of her child (BACP TR#5:28).

Brooks, Humphrey, m. by 23 Aug 1773 Mary, daughter of James McAllister (BALR AL#1: 54, WG#Y: 255).

Brooks, Isaac, and Sarah Haywood, on 14 d. 11 m. 1799 declared their intention to marry ("Minutes of Baltimore Meeting," *QRNM:* 234).

Brooks, Joseph, on 24 March 1733/4 was named as a son of Ann Woodall in the will of Ralph Woodall (MWB 21:97 abst. in *Md. Cal. of Wills* 7:86).

Brooks, Joseph, and Priscilla Gardner were married by license dated 28 Aug 1786 (BAML). John Gardner, in his will dated 22 Jan 1798 named his son-in-law Joseph Brooks (BAWB 6:162).

Brooks, William, and Mary Magdalene Bracket were married by license dated 20 Jan 1781 (BAML). **N.B.:** On 27 July 1784 Mary Magdalene Brooks was named as a daughter of Rowland Smith, stone mason (BAWB 4:7). On 4 Oct 1788, Mary Magdalene was named as the widow of Capt. John Brackett (BAAD 9:241).

Brooks, William, m. by lic. on 24 Jan 1792, Elizabeth Jennings at St. Peter's Catholic Church, Baltimore (*Piet:* 238).

Brothers, Austin, m. by 17 Oct 1792, Sarah, who received an equal share of the estate of Joseph Bardell (BAAD 11:145).

Brown, [-?-], m. by 24 Jan 1732/3, Mary, daughter of Timothy Keen (MWB 20:730 abst. in *Md. Cal. of Wills* 7:29).

Brown, [-?-], of Prince George's Co., m. by 20 March 1734, Verlinda, daughter of Robert Doyne of Charles Co. (BALR HWS#M:42, TB#E:340).

Brown, [-?-]. m. by 19 Sep 1785, Sarah, daughter of Peter Gosnell (BAWB 4:228).

Brown, Absolom, and Sarah Shepherd were m. on 19 Jan 1728/9 (Harrison, "St. George's Parish Register:" 246). On 13 Jan 1731/2 Sarah was named as a daughter of Rowland Shepherd (Shephard) MWB 20:347 abst. in *Md. Cal. of Wills* 6:215).

Brown, Absolom, and Margaret Hanson were m. on 5 Dec 1752 (Harrison, "St. George's Parish Register:" 354). She was a daughter of Jacob Hanson (BAAD 6:234).

Brown, Alexander, cabinet-maker of this town, was m. last Thurs. by Dr. Allison, to Miss Ann Jones of Baltimore Co. (*Federal Intelligencer and Baltimore Daily Gazette* 25 March 1795).

Brown, Benjamin, on 27 d. 7 m. 1774 was reported to have taken the Oath [?] and had a child laid to his charge by a young woman ("Minutes of Gunpowder Monthly Meeting," *QRNM:*65).

Brown, Cornelius, m. by 12 Jan 1787 Elizabeth, daughter of Conrad Smith BAAD 8:347).

Brown, David, and Elizabeth Matthews, on 27 d. 1 m. 1776 declared their intention to marry ("Minutes of Gunpowder Monthly Meeting," *QRNM:*66).

Brown, David, and Jemima Elder were m. on 7 Nov 1791 (Marr. Register of Rev. Lewis Richards, MS.690 at MdHS). On 16 Feb 1796 Jemima was named as a daughter of John Elder (BAAD 12:101).

Brown, Dixon, and Sarah Kingsbury were m. on 7 Aug 1777 (Liesenring, "Maryland Marriages," at MdHS: 68). She was a sister of John Kingsbury, and had a son John Kingsbury Brown, who Kingsbury called nephew, and a daughter Ann, called niece (BAWB 4:414).

Brown, Edward, and Sarah Richards were m. on 15 March 1785 (Marr. Returns of Rev. William West, Scharf Papers, MS. 1999 at MdHS). Brown stated that on or about 15 March 1785 he married Sarah Richards, daughter of Richard Richards (MCHP 724).

Brown, Frederick, and Sarah Wilson were m. by lic. dated 18 Feb 1788 (BAML). Sarah Wilson, daughter of Joseph, on 28 d, 2 m. 1788 was reported to have been m. to a man not of our society with the assistance of a Methodist Preacher ("Minutes of Deer Creek Meeting," *QRNM:*145).

Brown, Gabriel, and Mary Keen were m. on 10 Feb 1730 (Harrison, "St. George's Parish Register:" 256). She was a daughter of Timothy Keen (MWB 20:730).

Brown, George, m. by 6 July 1727 Mary, daughter of Edward Stevenson, whose widow had m. Henry Sater (MDTP 28:44, 271).

Brown, George, d. by 13 June 1764, having m. Mary, sister of Robert Dutton (BAWB 3:129).

Brown, George Frederick, d. by 2 Aug 1762 when Mary Brown, admx., signed in German when she posted bond to administer his estate. Both the widow and the son Jacob Frederick Brown swore they did not know what had become of the deceased's will (BAAB 1:202).

Brown, Grace. See John Smart,

Brown, Henry, and Achsah Sollers were m. on 25 March 1783 (Marr. Returns of Rev, William West, Scharf Papers, MS. 1999 at MdHS). On 25 April 1796 Achsah was named as a daughter of Francis Sollers (BAWB 6:87).

Brown, Hephzibah. See Perine, Maulden.

Brown, Jacob, m. by 8 Sep 1775 Catherine, daughter of Edward Stocksdale (MCHP-478; BAAD 8:324).

Brown, Jacob Frederick, m. by 15 Nov 1790 Catharine Barbara, sister of Christian Scott and of Mary Alder (BAWB 5:35). On 7 Feb 1791 Barbara, wife of Jacob Brown, received an equal share of the estate of John Wright (BAAD 10:286).

Brown, James, and Eliza Morgan were m. on 16 Jan 1758 (Harrison, "St. George's Parish Register:" 363). She m. 2nd, Josiah Lyon (*q.v.*).

Brown, James, son of Abel died leaving a will dated 26 April 1782 and proved 29 May 1782. He named Hugh Finley and Elizabeth Twist as execs., and acknowledged Elizabeth, William, Mary, Charlotte. Ann, and Rebecca Brown as children of Elizabeth Twist, which he hereby acknowledged as his; he also named his brothers Abel, John, Jacob, Elias and Moses (BAWB 3:484; BAOC 2:50).

Brown, James, and Elizabeth Stansbury were married on 19 Dec 1782 (Marr. Returns of Rev. William West, Scharf Papers, MS.1999 at MdHS). On 18 Aug 1798 Elizabeth Brown received an equal share of £20.8.10 from the estate of Isaac Stansbury (BAAD 12:471). Elizabeth Stansbury, in her will made 26 Aug 1799 named a granddaughter Elizabeth Brown (BAWB 6:229).

Brown, James, m. by lic. on 14 April 1793, Hannah Jaffris at St. Peter's Catholic Church, Baltimore (*Piet:* 128).

Brown, James, and Catherine Dukehart on 14 d. 3 m. 1799 declared their intention to marry ("Minutes of Baltimore Meeting," *QRNM:*233).

Brown, Jesse, and Dorothy Matthews on 26 d. 3 m. 1791 declared their intention to marry ("Minutes of Gunpowder Meeting," *QRNM:*90).

Brown, John, and Elizabeth Sickelmore were m. on 18 Nov 1705 (Harrison, "St. George's Parish Register:" 206). He was a son of Thomas and Margaret ([-?-]) Brown, and Margaret m. 2nd, Anthony Drew. On 15 Jan 1721 John Brown was named as the father of Margaret Drew's grandsons Thomas Brown, Augustine, and Gabriel (Gambrall) Brown (MWB 17:217 abst. in *Md. Cal. of Wills* 5:102).

Brown, John, Jr., of Anne Arundel Co., m. by 21 Feb 1718, Milcah, daughter and sole heir of Robert Clarkson, dec. (BALR TR#DS: 67).

Brown, Dr. John, in June 1733 was charged with begetting a bastard on the body of Denny Downs (or Downes) (BACP HWS#9:2).

Brown, John, m. by 15 May 1769 Margaret, widow and extx. of Uriah Davis (BAWB 3:97; MDAD 60:301). John Browne, on 28 d. 3 m. 1770, was charged with being married by a priest ("Minutes of Gunpowder Monthly Meeting," *QRNM:*59).

Brown, John, stay maker, stated he would not pay the debts of his wife Catherine Brown, *alias* Hurly (*Maryland Journal and Baltimore Advertiser* 2 Nov 1779).

Brown, John, and Jane Lynch were married by license dated 16 June 1781 (BAML). On 8 Nov 1796 Robuck Lynch named his daughter Jane Brown (BAWB 5:504).

Brown, John, wheelwright of West Nottingham Twp., Chester Co., Pa., m. by 14 d. 6 m. 1794, Mary, sister of Stephen McDade of Monongahela Co., Pickett Settlement, Va., and of John McDade, late of Fell's Point, dec., who left a widow Matilda (BACT 1791-1794, MS 2865.1 at MdHS*:* 357).

Brown, John, m. by 14 Oct 1797, Rebecca, coheir of John Naylor, Sr., of Baltimore Co. (BALR WG#53:474; BAAD 12:526).

Brown, John, was m. last eve. by Right Rev. Bishop Carroll, to Miss Mary Rosenstiel both of this city (*Federal Gazette and Baltimore Daily Advertiser* 26 Nov 1798). They were m. by lic. on 25 Nov 1798 at St. Peter's Catholic Church, Baltimore (*Piet:* 128).

Brown, John, and Mary Read were m. on 29 July 1799 (Richards' Marr. Register). Mary Brown, formerly Read, on 12 d. 12 m. 1799 had a complaint made that she married contrary to the rules of our discipline ("Minutes of Baltimore Meeting," *QRNM:*236).

Brown, John, m. by 22 Nov 1800, Catherine Boblitz, legatee of Charles Boblitz (BAAD 13:342).

Brow, John Dixon, in Feb 1796 was made a ward of Dixon Brown (BAOC 3:180).

Brown, Joshua, m. by 14 Jan 1722 Margaret, sister of William Chew of Baltimore Co. (BAAD 1:109).

Brown, Joshua, son of Joshua and Hannah, both dec., on 25 d. 12 m. 1800 announced his intention to marry Sarah Ely, relict of Hugh Ely ("Minutes of Deer Creek Meeting," *QRNM:*162).

Brown, Josias, and Jehosheba Kirk were m. on 16 Aug 1790 (Register of First Presbyterian Church, Baltimore, MS at MdHS*:* 2). By 13 Aug 1798 Jehosheba was named as a devisee of George Wells, Sr. (BALR WG#57:285). In his will, made 24 Oct 1783 George Wells left personalty to his daughter Jehosheba Kirk(BAWB 3:578). Jehosheba was a widow of Nathaniel Kirk (*q.v.*).

Brown, Margaret, was charged with bastardy at the June 1730 Court (BACP HWS#6:415).

Brown, Maria, *alias* **Sylvester,** orphan, aged 8, in Feb 1795 was bound to Laurence Bausman to learn housework (BAOC 3:138).

Brown, Mary. See John Baxter; see also William Bosley.

Brown, Mary, on 13 Sep 1743 was named as a daughter in the will of Thomas Biddison (MWB 23:289 abst. in *Md. Cal. of Wills* 8:237).

Brown, Mary, on 23 d. 2 m. 1782, hath gone out in marriage ("Minutes of Gunpowder Meeting," *QRNM:*75, 76). **See John Davis.**

Brown, Moses, m. by lic. on 30 April 1797 Mary Snowden at St. Peter's Catholic Church, Baltimore (*Piet:* 128).

Brown, Nicholas, d. by 10 Sep 1687 having m. by 11 Oct 1680 Ann, admx. of Dennis Inglish (MDTP 12A:162; INAC 9:427).

Brown, Peregrine, on 27 Jan 1745 was named as a son in the will of Rachel Paca (MWB 24:440 abst. by Gibb).

Brown, Perry, James Brown, and Samuel Brown were named as grandsons in the will of Mary Buchannan, widow of Archibald Buchannan (MWB 30:698 abst. in *Md. Cal. of Wills* 7:23).

Brown, Richard, joyner, and Catherine Small on 5 Feb 1771 were summoned by the vestry for unlawful cohabitation (Reamy, *St. George's Parish Register:* 111).

Brown, Richard, of Anne Arundel Co., and Miss Honor Price, daughter of Absolom Price of Baltimore Co., were m. last Thurs. (*Baltimore Daily Repository* 2 March 1793).

Brown, Samuel, of this city, was m. Tues. eve. by Rev. Mr. Pasket, to Polly Wheeler, of Harford Co. (*Federal Gazette and Baltimore Daily Advertiser* 13 Nov 1800).

Brown, Solomon, m. by 1 March 1771, Huldah, daughter of Ralph and Huldah Smith (BAWB 3:193, 248).

Brown, Thomas, and Susanna Higginson were m. on 19 June 1739 (Harrison, "St. George's Parish Register:" 308). She m. 2nd, Daniel Robinson (*q.v.*), and 3rd, Garrett Garrettson (*q.v.*).

Brown, Thomas, woodcutter, in Feb 1747, promised to turn away Mary Gordon immediately (Reamy, *St. George's Parish Register:* 106).

Brown, Thomas, and Miss Rebecca Bay, both of Gunpowder Falls, Baltimore Co., were m. Mon. eve. last (*Federal Intelligencer and Baltimore Daily Gazette* 26 June 1795).

Brown, Thomas, and Miss Rebecca Martin, both of Baltimore Co., were m. last Thurs. eve. (*Baltimore Telegraphe* 21 Sep 1795).

Brown, Thomas, m. by lic. on 4 May 1797, Mary Colgan at St. Peter's Catholic Church, Baltimore (*Piet:* 128).

Brown, William, and Elizabeth Lacy on 25 d. 1 m. 1775 declared their intention to marry ("Minutes of Gunpowder Monthly Meeting,"*QRNM:*65).

Brown, William, in his will made 4 Oct 1794 named his wife Martha, children William and Mary Brown, and Hannah Hewitt and Hannah's daughter Sarah Chandler (BAWB 5:206).

Brown, William, of Baltimore and Miss Nancy Loughridge, daughter of Mr. Abraham Loughridge, were m. Thurs. eve., at Carlisle by Rev. Dr. Davidson (*Carlisle Weekly Gazette* 18 Jan 1797).

Brucebanks, Abraham, in June 1744 was charged with begetting a bastard on the body of Martha Thomas BACP 1743-1745:243).

Brucebanks (Brusebanks, Brushbanks). Ann; see Luke Griffin.

Bruchs, Wilhelm, m. by 1 Dec 1781, Maria Magdalena, daughter of Ruland and Anna Maria Schmit, who as grandparents were sponsors of Ruland Bruchs, b. 1 Dec 1781 ("First German Reformed Church Register," MS. at MdHS: 6).

Bruff, William, m. by 11 March 1796 Catherine, widow of Nicholas Jones (BALR WG#UU:559; BAAD 13:10).

Bruhns, A. H., stated he would not pay the debts of his wife Maria Eliza Saloman Bruhns who had behaved so disagreeably that it was impossible to live with her (*Federal Gazette and Baltimore Daily Advertiser* 4 Nov 1800).

Bruner, Peter, m. by 18 Nov 1783 Sophia Sittlemeyer, granddaughter of Mary [-?-] who was the widow of Sebastian Sittlemeyer (BALR WG#T:8-9).

Bryant, [-?-], m. by 1 Sep 1760 Mary, daughter of Luke Raven (MWB 31:123).

Bryson, James, m. by 15 Feb 1791 [-?-], who received an equal share of the estate of Richard Bond (BAAD 10:544).

Bryson, John, and Catherine Green were married by license dated 25 March 1786 (BAML). Bryson, of Baltimore, stated he would not pay the debts of his wife Catherine (*Maryland Journal and Baltimore Advertiser* 11 Aug 1786). Catherine Bryson refuted the charges made by her husband (*Maryland Journal and Baltimore Advertiser* 22 Aug 1786).

Bryson, Nathan G., merchant, and Mrs. Susanna Perkins, both of Baltimore, were m. 20th inst. by Rev. Dr. Allison (*Baltimore American* 25 Oct 1799).

Buchanan, Andrew, and Susannah Lawson were m. on 20 July 1761 Harrison, "St. Paul's Parish Register :" 168). They were the parents of Eleanor Buchanan, who on 5 Sep 1760 \was named as a granddaughter in the will of Alexander Lawson (BAWB 2:337; see also Annapolis *Maryland Gazette* 24 July 1760).

Buchanan (Buchaman, Burhaman), Archibald, m. by 30 Sep 1706 Mary, admx. of Thomas Prebbell (Preble) (*q.v.*) (INAC 25:416).

Buchanan, Archibald, Jr., and Anne Roberts were m. 28 April 1729 (Harrison, "St. George's Parish Register:" 250). She was a daughter of John Roberts (*q.v.*) (MDAD 11:101, BAAD 3:99; MDAD 11:101).

Buchanan, Dr. George, of Baltimore, m. last Thurs. eve. in Philadelphia, Letitia McKean, second daughter of the Hon. Thomas McKean, Chief Justice of Penna. (*Maryland Journal and Baltimore Advertiser* 16 June 1789).

Buchanan, James, merchant, m. last Mon. eve., Susannah Young of Philadelphia (*Maryland Journal and Baltimore Advertiser* 30 Nov 1787). She was b. 20 April 1767 in Philadelphia, daughter of John and Mary Ann (Bedford) Young ("The John and Mary Ann (Bedford) Young Bible Records," *Gen. of Penna. Families,* 3:433- ff..)

Buchanan, James A., merchant, and Elizabeth Calhoun, daughter of James Calhoun, were m. last Tues. eve. by Rev. Dr. Allison (*Maryland Journal and Baltimore Advertiser* 4 Jan 1793).

Buchanan, Lloyd, and Miss Rachel Lawson were married a few days ago in Baltimore Town (Annapolis *Maryland Gazette* 14 July 1757).

Buchanan, William, m. by 3 Dec 1778 Peggy Hill (BALR WG#C:423).

Buchanan, William, Esq., and Hepzibah Perine were m. on 10 Nov 1799 (Marr. Register of Rev. Lewis Richards, MS.690 at MdHS). William Buchanan of Baltimore Co., was m. last eve. to Miss H. Prian of this city (*Federal Gazette and Baltimore Daily Advertiser* 11 Nov 1799). The couple had executed a marriage settlement on 4 Nov 1799 (BALR WG#59:102). On 22 March 1800 Hepzibah was named as the admx. of Malden Perine (*q.v.*) (BAAD 13:221).

Buchman, George, m. by lic. on 28 March 1796 Barbara Fisher at St. Peter's Catholic Church, Baltimore (*Piet*: 128).

Bucholtz, George, m. by lic. on 14 Oct 1798 Elizabeth Butcher at St. Peter's Catholic Church, Baltimore (*Piet*: 128).

Buck, [-?-], m. by 15 April 1761 Susanna, daughter of Benjamin Meed (Meade, Meads) of Baltimore Co. (BAWB 2:177; MWB 31:1084).

Buck, [-?-], m. by 4 Sep 1783 Eliz., daughter of Patrick Hannon of Fell's Point (BAWB 4:28).

Buck, Benjamin, b. 10 Oct 1741 (1744?), d. 24 Dec 1807 in his 64th year, and Dorcas
Sutton, b. 4 Sep 1747, d. 7 April 1824, in her 77th year were m. on 10 Feb 1763
(Harrison, "St. John's Parish Register:" 224; "Buck Bibles," *The Notebook* 11 (3)
(June 1995) 22). On 27 Feb 1764 she was named as the only child of Christopher
Sutton, whose estate was administered by Buck (MDAD 50:309).

Buck, Christopher, m. by 12 Dec 1795 Keziah Gorsuch, a rep. of Kerenhappuck
Gorsuch (BAAD 12:82). They were married by license dated 9 Oct 1790 (BAML).

Buck (Burk), Edward, m. by 21 Feb 1711 [-?-], admx. of John Anderson (MDTP 22:85;
INAC 33A:69). In April 1715 she was called the admx. of John Anderton [*sic*]
(MDTP 22:448).

Buck, John, and Susanna Ingram were m. on 11 Feb 1742 (Harrison, "St. John's Parish
Register:" 143. John Buck d. 26 Sep 1793 in his 77th year, and Susanna d. 15 Oct
1793 in her 75th year. Their son Benjamin was b. 10 Oct 1744 ("Buck Bibles," *The
Notebook* 11 (3) (June 1995) 22).

Buck, John, of Bideford, Co. Devon, m. [date not given], Judith, daughter of William
Pawley; John and Judith had a son George (BALR B#K:202).

Buck, John, of B, b. 25 Sep 1768, son of Benjamin and Dorcas, m. 1st, on 19 Nov 1790,
Catherine [-?-], b. 2 March 1766, d. 7 Aug 1799, aged 33 years and 6 mos. ("Buck
Bibles," *The Notebook* 11 (3) (June 1995) 22; MGRC 31:178.).

Buck, John, d. by 13 Aug 1793 having begotten a bastard child on the body of Mary
Mattox (BAAD 11:302).

Buck, John, age 17 years, 9 mos., in Feb 1793 was bound to Peter Mackenheimer
(BOCP 3:30). He may be the John Buck who, in Feb 1793, chose Joel Green as his
guardian (BCOP 3:32).

Buck, John, Jr., of Fell's Point, and Sophia Winks of Baltimore Co. were m. 25 Aug
(*Baltimore American* 30 Aug 1799).

Buck, Joshua, b. 5 April 1756, and Sarah Crook, b. 20 Aug 1758, were m. on 11 June
1778 ("Buck Bibles," *The Notebook* 11 (3) (June 1995) 22; MGRC1:11).

Buck, William, orphan of James Buck, in Feb 1793 chose Thomas Hood as his guardian
(BOCP 3:30). As William Buck, aged 15, in Feb 1793 he was bound to Thomas
Hood (BOCP 3:31).

Bucker[?], Capt. Joseph, aged 54, and Mrs. Anderson of Fell's Point, were m. last
Thurs. eve. by Rev. Richards (*Baltimore Telegraphe* 30 July 1795).

Buckingham (Buckinham), [-?-], m. by 2 April 1726 Mary, daughter of William Slade
(MWB 20:263 abst. in *Md. Cal. of Wills* 6:202).

Buckingham, [-?-], m. by 3 Feb 1759 Avarilla, daughter of William Gosnell (BAWB
2:143).

Buckingham, Thomas, d. by 7 Nov 1750 by which time his admx. Mary had m. William
Hall (*q.v.*).

Buckingham, Thomas, and Rachel Gardner, daughter of John Gardner, were married by
license dated 21 Sep 1785 (BAML; BAWB 6:162).

Buckingham, Thomas, and Miss Mary Stouphell [Stophel], both of Baltimore, were m.
last eve. by Rev. Bend (*Baltimore Daily Repository* 4 May 1793; Harrison, "St.
Paul's Parish Register:" 266). On 28 d. 6 m. 1793 Thomas Buckingham was
reported to have accomplished his marriage to a woman not of our society with the
assistance of a hireling ("Minutes of Baltimore Meeting," *QRNM:* 221).

Buckingham, Thomas, and Mary [-?-], were m. by 16 Oct 1798 when their son Isaac
was b. ("Buckingham Bible Records," *NGSQ* 22 (2) (June 1934) 45).

Buckingham, William, m. by 1 May 1765 [-?-], daughter of Edw. Flanagan, who named grandson Charles Buckingham of William (BAWB 3:28).

Buckler, John, d. intestate by 1800. The wife of Nathaniel Andrews (*q.v.*) was entitled to a distributive share of his estate. William and Thomas Buckler obtained letters of admin. on the estate (BPET: Petition of Nathaniel Andrews 1800).

Buckler, William, merchant of Baltimore, and Nancy Hepburn, daughter of the late Thomas Hepburn, were m. 9th inst., at Port Royal, Va. (*Maryland Journal and Baltimore Advertiser* 23 Nov 1792).

Buckley, James, and Mary Leary, both natives of Ireland, were m. by lic. on 1 July 1800 at St. Peter's Catholic Church, Baltimore (*Piet*: 128).

Buckley, Lawrence, on 25 d. 8 m. 1792 was disowned for marrying with the assistance of a hireling minister ("Minutes of Gunpowder Meeting," *QRNM:*92). Lawrence Buckley and Catherine Conne [sic] were married by license dated 24 May 1792 (BAML).

Bucknall, Thomas, m. by 19 Feb 1675, Mary, relict of Edward Wheelock (*q.v.*) of Anne Arundel Co. (MDTP 7:304).

Buckner, William, and Mrs. Patience Colegate were m. 20 Sep 1724 (Harrison, "St. Paul's Parish Register:" 147). She was a daughter of Col. Richard Colegate (BAAD 1:322; PCLR PL#8:146).

Budd, Elizabeth; see Christopher Choate.

Budd, Elizabeth, and Amos Loney, execs., on 12 June 1787 posted bond to administer the estate of Dr. George Loney (BAAB 7:120).

Budd, Samuel, and Milcah Young were m. on 27 Sep 1747 by Rev. James Sterling of the lower Parish in Kent Co. (Harrison, "St. George's Parish Register: " 94). On 11 June 1760 Milcah was named as a daughter and heir of Joseph Young of Kent Co. Md. (BALR B#H:367; PCLR (PCLR DD#3:608).

Buess, Peter, m. by 14 Aug 1773, Elizabeth, daughter of John Tenley, formerly of York Co., Pa., now of Baltimore Town (BAWB 3:243).

Bughen, Engel, m. by banns on 8 Oct 1793 Mary Magdalen Hislin at St. Peter's Catholic Church, Baltimore (*Piet*: 128).

Buker, Henry, m. by 5 July 1763 Ann, daughter of Ulrick Eckler (MDAD 49:274; BAAD 6: 52).

Bull, Constantine, in March 1768 had two daughters, Mary and Catherine, who chose Robert Adair their guardian. In Nov 1768 they chose Constantine Bull as their guardian (BAMI 1768-1769).

Bull, Eleanor, before marriage Amos, on 25 d., 5 m. 1774, was reportedly married by a priest ("Minutes of Gunpowder Monthly Meeting," *QRNM:*64). [No other marriage reference found].

Bull, Isaac, and Hannah Robertson were m. on 23 Jan 1749 (Harrison, "St. John's Parish Register:" 200). On 21 June 1770 Hannah was named as a daughter of Richard Robinson [*sic*} (BAWB 3:169).

Bull, Jacob, and 'Ranrice' Bussey were m. on 17 Oct 1752 (Harrison, "St. John's Parish Register:" 206). As Rannis or Wrennes Bussey, she was named as a daughter of Edward Bussey (BAWB 4:245; BAAD 9:217).

Bull, John, and Hannah Ruff were m. on 20 Feb 1739 (Harrison, "St. John's Parish Register:" 143). On 27 July 1747 Hannah was named as a daughter of Sarah Ruff (read by Gibb as Rulf) (MWB 25:203 abst. by Gibb).

Bull, Thomas, on ?? d. 9 m. 1783 was charged with having m. outside by a hireling minister ("Minutes of Gunpowder Meeting," *QRNM*:78). [No other marriage reference found].

Bull, William, m. by 2 Sep 1774 Martha Davis, who was aged 57, when she dep. on 2 Sep 1774 that she had come into this country from England in 1738, and went to live at Thomas Brerewood's house on *My Lady's Manor*, where she lived until 1743. She stated that a lease had been given to her husband, William Bull, for the lifetimes of her husband William Bull, her daughter Martha, and one other .... . She mentioned Abraham Bull (BAEJ: Brerewood, Thomas: *My Lady's Manor*).

Bumberger, William, m. by 8 Jan 1789 Christina, daughter of John Delcher (BAWB 4: 327).

Bunbury, M. Simmons, m. by lic. on 24 Sep 1795 Ann Bride at St. Peter's Catholic Church, Baltimore (*Piet*: 128).

Bungey, [-?-], m. by 10 April 1771 Ruth, daughter of John Ensor (BAWB 3:257). Bungey d. by 25 June 1787, leaving minor child Ruth Bungey who was one of the heirs of Joseph Ensor; Nathan Griffith, guardian, filed an account (BAGA 1:33).

Bunker, Job, and Mary Anderson were m. on 29 July 1795 (Marr. Register of Rev. Lewis Richards, MS.690 at MdHS). Capt. [Joseph?] Bunker, aged 54, and Mrs. Anderson, aged 74, were m. last Thurs. eve. by Rev. Richards (*Baltimore Telegraphe* 30 July 1795).

Bunker, Capt. Moses, was m. Tues. eve. by Rev. Dr. Allison to Mrs. Margaret Franciscus, both of this city (*Federal Gazette and Baltimore Daily Advertiser* 10 May 1798).

Bunn, [-?-], m. by 31 Aug 1760 Elizabeth, daughter of John Dunn (BAWB 3:130).

Bunting, William, m. by April 1784 Billy Drew, daughter of William Andrews (BAOC 1:111).

Burchfield, Adam, and Ann Nelson were m. on 2 Oct 1753 (Harrison, "St. George's Parish Register:" 377). On 9 Feb 1754 she was named as a daughter of John Nelson (BACT TR#E:175).

Burchfield, Elias, in Aug 1718 was charged with begetting a bastard on the body of Mary Longman (BACP IS#C:23).

Burchfield (Birchfield), Thomas, and Joanna Cantwell were m. on 4 Aug 1721 (Harrison, "St. George's Parish Register:" 229). She was the extx. of Edward Cantwell (*q.v.*) of Baltimore Co. (BAAD 1:258; MDAD 4:213).

Burden, Eleanor, was charged with bastardy at the March 1708/9 Court (BACP IS#B:22).

Burdet, Benjamin, in Nov 1739 was charged with begetting a bastard on the body of Mary Walker (BACP HWS&TR: 72, 159).

Burford, James, m. by 13 June 1767, Sarah, daughter of Robert Morgan, dec. (BALR B#P: 615).

Burgess, Ann, on 28 d. 5 m. 1785 was condemned for outgoing in marriage ("Minutes of Gunpowder Meeting," *QRNM:*80). **See Edward Bussey.**

Burgess, Hugh, and Alice Moore were m. on 1 Feb 1764 (Gunpowder Monthly Meeting, at MdSA: 251). Hugh d. by 2 Aug 1772 when his widow Alice, (daughter of Mary Moore, widow of William Moore), m. 2nd, Samuel Butler (*q.v.*) (Harrison, "St. Paul's Parish Register:" 170; BAWB 3:496). In Oct 1775 Hugh's daughters, Mary, aged 11, and Ann, aged 9, were made wards of John Cornthwait (BAMI 1772, 1775-1781: 135).

Burgess, John, son of Joseph and Deborah, on 27 d. 8 m. 1795 announced his intention to marry Drusilla Morgan, daughter of John, dec., and his wife Ann ("Minutes of Deer Creek Meeting," *QRNM:*156).

Burgess, Mary, in her nuncupative will made 29 March 1794 named her sister Alice Forwood (BAWB 5:156).

Burgess, Mary. See Mary Jones.

Burgess, Ura. See Ura Butler.

Burgis, Samuel, stated he would not pay the debts of his wife Mary, who has eloped from his bed and may be in Alexandria or Charleston, S. C. (*Federal Gazette and Baltimore Daily Advertiser* 20 June 1798).

Burk, Edward. See Edward Buck.

Burk, Greenbury, and Rhoda Davis, both of Fell's Point, were m. last eve, by Rev. Bend (*Maryland Journal and Baltimore Advertiser* 18 Aug 1796).

Burk (Burke), James, m. by 11 May 1741 Ann, extx. of Christopher Randall of Baltimore Co. (MDAD 18:164; BALR HWS#1-A:30; BALR TB#A:30; MDTP 31:166). Christopher Randall m. c1719, Anne, daughter of William and Sydney (Wynne) Chew (*BCF:*528).

Burk, (Burke), John, stated he would not pay the debts of his wife Elizabeth, who had eloped from his bed and board (*Maryland Journal and Baltimore Advertiser* 26 April 1775).

Burk, John, m. by lic. 17 Nov 1784 Mary Roach at St. Peter's Catholic Church, Baltimore (*Piet:* 128).

Burk (Burke), Margaret, petitioned the Orphan's Court, that a number of "children of us being in great distress," an unworthy woman pretended compassion, and on this pretense the petitioner gave up her sister Cealia to her in Aug. Orphans Court. But how deplorable it must be to see my sister brought up by a Miss Hendricks. Let my sister be discharged from her and be bound to some decent person. NOTE: A Mrs. Grundervil [?] on Fells Point will take her. (BOCP: Petition of Margaret Burke, n.d.).

Burk (Burke), Richard, m. Ann Ryland on 16 Dec 1776 ("Richard Burke Bible Record," *MBR* 2:11).

Burk (Burke), Richard, m. by lic. on 27 April 1800, Catherine Gleeson, widow; both natives of Ireland, at St. Peter's Catholic Church, Baltimore (*Piet:* 128).

Burk, Sarah, was charged with bastardy and confessed at the March 1745/6 Court, and was ordered to be whipped (BACP 1745-1746:808-809).

Burk (Burke), Thomas, in June 1733 was charged with begetting a bastard on the body of Sarah Owings (BACP HWS#9:136).

Burk, Thomas, and Sarah Sicklemore were m. 14 April 1737 (Harrison, "St. John's Parish Register:" 84). She was a daughter of Sutton Sicklemore, planter (BAWB 3:21).

Burk, W., and Mary Lemmon were m. on 8 Nov 1764 (Harrison, "St. John's Parish Register:" 227). On 30 May 1786 Mary was named as a daughter of Alexis Lemmon, Sr. (BAWB 4:151)

Burke. See Burk.

Burneston, Isaac, merchant, and Ann Rutter of Baltimore, were m. last Tues. eve. (*Maryland Journal and Baltimore Advertiser* 20 Jan 1792).

Burnham, John, d. 19 Oct 1799, m. Rebecca Davis on 4 May 1784 by Rev. Davis ("The Burnham Bible," *The Notebook* 10 (1) (March 1994) 7).

Burns, [-?-], m. by 28 Nov 1794 Catherine, daughter of George Fisher (BAWB 6:6).

Burns, Adam, and Catherine Fisher were m. by 28 Nov 1794 when she was named as a daughter in the will of George Fisher (BAWB 6:6; BAAD 12:489).

Burns, George, of Baltimore Co. stated he would not pay the debts of his wife Catherine, who had eloped (*Md. Gaz.* 7 Sep 1769).

Burns, James, m. by lic. 28 July 1793 Jane Cummins, at St. Peter's Catholic Church, Baltimore (*Piet:* 128). Margaret Cummins, in her will, made 6 Dec 1799 named a grandson John Burns (BAWB 6:238).

Burns, Judith, was charged with bastardy in 1775 and was fined (BAMI 1772, 1775-1781:208).

Burns, Margaret, was charged with bastardy in 1775, and was fined (BAMI 1772, 1775-1781:208).

Burns, Simon, d. by 1790, leaving a relict and admx. Hannah Burns (BOCP: Petition of Hannah Burns, 1790).

Burns, Simon, m. by lic. on 15 July 1794 Mary Knowlan, both natives of Ireland at St. Peter's Catholic Church, Baltimore (*Piet:* 128).

Burnet. See Barnet.

Burnett, Ann, admx., on 8 Nov 1800 posted bond to administer the estate of James Fortescue (BAAB 9:21). She was a sister of Jane Fortescue (*q.v.*).

Burney, John, of Fell's Point, stated he would not pay the debts of his wife Mary (*Maryland Journal and Baltimore Advertiser* 16 Nov 1795).

Burney, William, m. by 4 Nov 1719, Martha, relict and extx. of William Howard (BALR TR#DS:60).

Burnham, John, m. 4 May 1784 in Baltimore Town by Rev. William West, Rebecca Davis ("Burnham Bible Record," *The Notebook* 10 (1) (March 1994) 7-8).

Burroughs, Richard, m. by 26 Feb 1719/20 Elizabeth, extx. of John Brown (*q.v.*) of Baltimore Co. (MDTP 24:110; MINV 3:241; MWB 17:217 abst. in *Md. Cal. of Wills* 5:102; BACP IS#IA:93).

Burroughs (Burrows), Thomas, and Jane Morehead were married by license dated 15 Dec 1785 (BAML). Jane was the admx. of Michael Morehead (BAAD 10:498).

Burrow, Mary, was charged with bastardy at the Nov 1723 Court (BACP IS&TW#3:75).

Burson, Catherine. See Joseph Griffith.

Burteloine, Joseph, m. by 1 April 1796 Eve Ilgar, daughter of George Ilgar (BAAD 12:131).

Burton, John, m. by 5 Dec 1744, Ann, daughter of William Hitchcock (BALR TB#C:664).

Bush, Isaac, m. by 19 Dec 1760 Elizabeth, daughter of Andrew Thompson (BAWB 2:308, 329; MDAD 47:22).

Bussey, [-?-], of Baltimore Co., m. by July 1759 Mary, widow of George Williams (*q.v.*) of Cecil Co. (MDTP 37:276).

Bussey, Edward, merchant of Harford Co., was m. last Sun. eve. to Anne Burgess of Baltimore (*Maryland Gazette or Baltimore General Advertiser* 14 Jan 1785). On 28 d. 5 m. 1785 Ann Burgess had been condemned for outgoing in marriage ("Minutes of Gunpowder Meeting," *QRNM:* 80).

Bussey, Jesse, m. by 3 July 1759 Mary, daughter of Abraham Jarrett (MDTP 37:276; MDAD 43:153).

Bussey, Richard, in 1744 was charged with begetting a bastard on the body of Elinor Watts (BACP 1743-1745:488).

Bussey, Thomas D., of Baltimore, and Mrs. Peggy Bennett of Anne Arundel Co., were m. last eve. (*Federal Gazette and Baltimore Advertiser* 5 Feb 1796).

Bussey, Thomas D., m. by 1 Oct 1799, Margaret Ashbaw (BALR WG#60:288).

Butcher, [-?-], m. by 1 March 1797 Charlotte, daughter of James Osborn (BAWB 6:97).

Butcher, Bartholomew, m. by lic. on 21 Sep 1795, Elizabeth Plume at St. Peter's Catholic Church, Baltimore (*Piet*: 128).

Butler, [-?-], m. by 13 Feb 1779 Mary, daughter of Mary Rutter (formerly Barney) (BAWB 3:388).

Butler, Absolom, admin. de bonis non, on 13 Feb 1783 posted bond to administer that part of the estate of John Wells which had not been administered by Avarilla Wells (BAAB 6:110).

Butler, Anthony, free Negro, m. on 16 April 1797 Ruth Middleton, free Mulatto, at St. Peter's Catholic Church, Baltimore (*Piet*: 128).

Butler, Charles, m. by 11 July 1758 Elizabeth, mother of Peter Cockey (MDAD 41:457). **See Charles Baker, above.**

Butler, Charles F., of Fell's Point, stated he would not pay the debts of his wife Elizabeth (*Maryland Journal and Baltimore Advertiser* 1 Oct 1794).

Butler, Elizabeth, in Aug 1795 was made guardian of John and Mary Butler (BAOC 3:155).

Butler, James, m. by 2 April 1773 Mary, admx. of James Beck (MDTP 45:47).

Butler, John, in 1746 was charged with begetting a bastard on the body of Mary Foursides (BACP TB&TR#1:246-247).

Butler, John, m. by banns on 6 Nov 1791 Margaret Coleman at St. Peter's Catholic Church, Baltimore (*Piet*: 128).

Butler, John Holpin, m. by lic. on 17 April 1792 Margaret Evans at St. Peter's Catholic Church, Baltimore (*Piet*: 128).

Butler, Joseph, m. by 1756 [-?-], daughter of Richard and Mary [-?-] Marshall; Mary m. 2nd. Joseph Foresight (Deposition of William Marshall, *alias* Johnson, in *ARMD* 31:174-179).

Butler, Joseph, and Sarah Lane were married by license dated 29 July 1783 (BAML). On 11 June 1793 she was named as a daughter of Dutton Lane (BAAD 11:281).

Butler, Joseph, m. by 1 Dec 1791 [-?-], widow of Moses Berbione (BAAD 10:480).

Butler, Mary, was charged with bastardy at the Aug 1735 Court (BACP HWS#9:305).

Butler, Nicholas, m. by 15 Feb 1791 [-?-], who received an equal share of the estate of Richard Bond (BAAD 10:544).

Butler, Samuel, and Alice, widow of Hugh Burgess (*q.v.*), were m. on 2 Aug 1772 (Harrison, "St. Paul's Parish Register:" 170; BAMI 1772, 1775-1781:135). Butler d. by 18 Dec 1782 having m. Alice, daughter of Mary Moore, widow of William (BAWB 3:496).

Butler, Ura, before marriage Burgess, on 25 d. 11 m. 1772 was charged with marrying outside the society ("Minutes of Gunpowder Monthly Meeting," *QRNM*:63). [No other marriage reference found].

Butler, Walter, m. by lic. on 4 Feb 1786 Elizabeth Finn at St. Peter's Catholic Church, Baltimore (*Piet*: 128).

Butteram, John, m. by 8 March 1710 Elizabeth, heiress of Thomas, Daniel, and William Westbury (BALR TR#A:63).

Butters (Button), John, m. by 20 April 1772 Sarah, daughter of Mary Beck, widow of Samuel Beck (MINV 110:219; BAAB 1:143; BAAD 6:278); on 6 May 1773 Sarah Butters, admx. of Mary Beck, as guardian of Henrietta Beck, infant daughter of

Samuel Beck, was paid Henrietta's share of Samuel Beck's estate (MDAD 69: 173).

Butterworth, Isaac, in his will dated 17 May 1728, named his bro.-in-law Robert Clark and his nephews Michael and Thomas Webster (MWB 19:627 abst. in *Md. Cal. of Wills* 6:100).

Butterworth, Isaac, and Jane Wheeler were m. on 18 Dec 1728 (Harrison, "St. George's Parish Register:" 340). On 16 Sep 1741 Jane was named as a daughter of Benjamin Wheeler (MWB 22:436 abst. in *Md. Cal. of Wills* 8:160; BALR TB#A:21). Jane m. 2nd, Lawrence Clark by 17 March 1748 when she administered Butterworth's estate; Isaac Butterworth left five children (BAAD 4:202).

Button, Joseph. See John Butters, above.

Button. See Brittain.

Büxler, Christian, m. by 6 Feb 1785, Barbara Krumreinen ("First Record Book for the Reformed and Lutheran and Congregations at Manchester, Baltimore (Now Carroll) Co.," *MGSB* 35:281).

Byall, William, and Elizabeth Stafford were m. on 8 Aug 1782 by Rev. William West ("Byall of Baltimore County," in MGRC 35:24, (Marr. Returns of Rev. William West, Scharf Papers, MS.1999 at MdHS).

Byas, James, m. Thurs., 10th inst., at Fell's Point, Sally Jackson (*Maryland Journal and Baltimore Advertiser* 18 June 1784).

Byerly, Conrad, m. by 6 Nov 1792 Mary Deale, legatee of Philip Deale (BAAD 11: 154).

Byfoot, William, m. by 5 March 1744, Sarah, daughter of John Hall (BALR TB#D:51).

Byrne, Mr. B. C., of the Federal Circus, and Mrs. Hamilton of Baltimore were m. Sat. by Richards (*Baltimore Intelligencer* 9 April 1798).

Byrne, Columbus John, native of Ireland, and Margaret Hankey, native of Maryland, were m. on 16 Jan 1800 at St. Peter's Catholic Church, Baltimore (*Piet*: 128).

Byrne, William, m. by lic. 3 May 1800 Catherine Carey at St. Peter's Catholic Church, Baltimore (*Piet*: 128).

Byrnes, Mary, (formerly Erwin), on 26 d. 5 m. 1787, was found guilty of unchastity and having her marriage accomplished from amongst Friends ("Minutes of Gunpowder Meeting," *QRNM:* 84). [No other marriage reference found].

Byrns, Maurice, d. intestate on 11 Sep 1794, leaving an only brother Daniel Byrns, who on 9 Dec 1794 petitioned that letters of admin. should have been granted to him and not to William Anderson (BOCP: Petition of Daniel Byrns, 1794).

"C"

Cabera, John, m. by lic. on 9 Nov 1794 Jane Mitchell (at St. Peter's Catholic Church, Baltimore (*Piet*: 128). BAML gives the groom's name as Caberra.

Cable, Jacob, stated he would not pay the debts of his wife Elizabeth, who, on Saturday evening eloped from his bed and board without the slightest cause (*Federal Gazette and Baltimore Daily Advertiser* 26 June 1797).

Cadle, Ann, and James Dorney (*q.v.*) were charged with unlawful cohabitation by the vestry of St. John's Parish on 20 April 1746 (Harrison," St. John's and St. George's Vestry Proceedings:" 24-88).

Cafferty, [-?-], m. by 12 April 1791 Catherine Clyne, admx. of David Clyne (BAAD 10:326, 327).

Cage, Martha, was charged with bastardy at the March 1693/4 Court, and named William Wilkinson as the father (BACP G#1:175-176).

Cage (Cagge), Robert, m. by 24 Oct 1687 [-?-], widow of Mark Child (*q.v.*) (MDTP 14:11). By 1696, Martha, the admx. of Robert Cage had m. 3rd, David Thurston (*q.v.*).

Caggill, John, m. by 13 Oct 1739 Mary, granddaughter of Joseph Peake (BALR HWS#1-A:336).

Cahill, George, m. by lic. 8 Dec 1793 Eleanor Murphy, both natives of Ireland at St. Peter's Catholic Church, Baltimore (*Piet*: 128).

Cain, James, on 31 March 1746, with Ann Spicer was summoned to appear before the vestry of St. George's Parish. No reason was given. James Cain and Ann Spicer were m. on 15 April 1746 (Reamy. *St. George's Parish Register:* 73, 105).

Cain, John, m. Catherine Gibson on 4 June 1769 (Harrison, "St. John's Parish Register:" 258). Catherine was the widow and admx. of Thomas Gibson (*q.v.*) (BAAD 6:230; MINV 101:232).

Cain, Maria, aged 8, daughter of Sarah Cain, in Aug 1772 was bound to James Coxe (BAMI 1772: 22).

Caither, John. See John Gaither.

Caldron, Francis, and Mary Celeston were married by license dated 14 Nov 1780 (BAML). Caldron stated he would not pay the debts of his wife Mary, who has eloped from his bed and board (*Federal Intelligencer and Baltimore Daily Gazette* 20 Jan 1795). Francis Caldron, commonly called Carter, for many years has drunk strong liquors that have brought him to an enraged insanity that has caused him to abuse his wife and children. His wife Mary Caldron or Carter asks no one to purchase anything from her husband, and asks the magistrates of Baltimore Co. not to sign any acknowledgement or contract or deed made by her husband unless she is present (*Baltimore Daily Intelligencer* 28 June 1794).

Caldwell, George, m. by 20 July 1799 Ann, sister of Sarah Hickley whose will of that date names her sister Ann Caldwell and the children she had by George Caldwell: Edmond, Eustace, Benjamin, and Emilia Caldwell (BAWB 6:216).

Caldwell, John, and Miss Caldwell, daughter of Samuel Caldwell, Esq., of Philadelphia, were m. Thurs., 16th inst. (*Maryland Gazette or Baltimore General Advertiser* 24 Oct 1788).

Caldwell (Calwell), John, cabinet-maker. and Mary Purle, both of Baltimore, were m. last eve. by Dr. Allison (*Baltimore Telegraphe* 12 Feb 1796).

Caley, Frederick, in his will made 9 May 1780, named his wife Margaret extx., and left Margaret Counselman (*q.v.*) property after his wife's death; he left George Counselman only one shilling (BAWB 3:421). Margaret Council [*sic*] [Counselman?] m. by 30 July 1796 John Denton (*q.v.*).

Calhoun, James, and Ann Gist were m. on 18 Nov 1766 (Harrison, "St. Thomas' Parish Register:" 73). On 21 Feb 1782 John Gist of Baltimore Town made a will naming his nephew William Calhoun, and his brother-in-law James Calhoun (BAWB 3:466).

Calhoun, William, merchant, late of Baltimore, and Lydia Cattle were m. 22nd ult, in Charleston (*Maryland Journal and Baltimore Advertiser* 4 Jan 1793).

Calman, Joseph, native of Treves, merchant of Cap Francois, m. by lic. June 1794 Mary Martha Ranoulleau, native of San Domingo, dau. of John Baptist Charles and Ann Margaret Patterson at St. Peter's Catholic Church, Baltimore (*Piet*: 128). BAML gives the bride's name as Renuleau.

Caltrider, [-?-], m. by 19 April 1794, Catherine, daughter of Phinsense Kepper (BAWB 5:332).

Calvert, Bethyah, in her undated will, proved 6 June 1733, named her sister Sarah Drew, and her late husband William Lenox (MWB 20:697 abst. in *Md. Cal. of Wills* 7:22).

Calvert, John, *de jure* 8th Lord Baltimore, b. 1742, d. 1790, m. 1st, in 1765, Sarah Bailey, daughter of George Bailey; she lived only a few years, and he m. 2nd, in 1772, Helen Bailey, daughter of John and Helen (Newsome) Bailey (John Bailey Calvert Nicklin, "The Calvert Family, Part II, The Untitled Line," *Maryland Genealogies* (Baltimore: Genealogical Publishing Co., 1980), 1:148).

Cameron, Esther, and Joseph Smith were charged with unlawful cohabitation by the vestry on 20 April 1747 (Harrison,"St. John's and St. George's Vestry Proceedings," MS at MdHS: 82).

Cameron, John, and Margaret Macckelltons were m. on 12 Dec 1716 (Harrison, "St. John's Parish Register:" 9). Margaret Macintosh, on 19 April 1717, posted bond to administer the estate of Daniel Macikntosh (BAAB 2:117). On 4 Dec 1717 Margaret Mackeltoes [*sic*] posted bond to administer the estate of Daniel Mackeltoes, her former husband (BAAB 2:120; MDAD 3:25; MDTP 24:165).

Campbell, Archibald, merchant, and Betsy Hindman were m. Thurs. last, 1 June (*Maryland Gazette or Baltimore General Advertiser* 6 June 1786; BAML).

Campbell, James, in March 17445/6 was charged with begetting a bastard on the body of Catherine Carroll (BACP TB&TR#1:5, Liber 1745-1746, 157).

Campbell, James, and Frances Moody were m. 6 Jan 1790 at First Presbyterian Church (First Presbyterian Church, Baltimore, MS. at MdHS: 4). Campbell stated he would not pay the debts of his wife Frances (*Maryland Gazette or Baltimore General Advertiser* 30 Nov 1790).

Campbell, John, and Miss Marian Maxwell were m. last eve., 20 May (*Maryland Journal and Baltimore Advertiser* 20 May1788; BAML).

Campbell, Phillis, was charged with bastardy at Nov Court 1728. in June 1731 her brother John Roberts (*alias* John Campbell) petitioned the court to let him take her two children, Aquila and Benjamin Campbell (BACP HWS#6:65, HWS#7:157).

Campbell, Robert, m. by lic. 18 Sep 1793, Catharine Rarity (or Ranty) at St. Peter's Catholic Church, Baltimore (*Piet*: 128; BAML).

Campble, John, about 1712 was the father-in-law of John Roberts Campble in the latter's deposition made on 29 Aug 1732,when at age 41, he deposed mentioning his father-in-law John Campble who had been living 20 years earlier (BALC HWS#3 #33).

Candron, John, m. by 20 Feb 1770, Ann [-?-], formerly wife of [-?-] [-?-] who owned Brown's Lot (BALR AL#B: 203). The deed does not mention the name of the 'former owner,' but *Brown's Lot* was formerly owned by Roland Vine.

Cannaday, Margaret, servant of Robert Green, was charged with bastardy at June 1719 Court and named John Quare as the father of her child. She was ordered to serve her master an additional 21 months (BACP IS#C: 131, 198).

Cannon, [-?-], m. by 15 Dec 1721, Barbara, daughter of John Fitzredmond (BINV 4:206; MINV 7:236).

Cannon [?], [-?-]. m. by 6 March 1784 Susanna, daughter of Abraham Andrews (BAWB 4:11).

Cannon (Canon), Robert, m. Sophia Johnson on 8 July 1725 (Harrison, "St. George's, Parish Register:" 260). She was a daughter of Daniel Johnson of Baltimore Co. (MDAD 15:203; BAAD 4:224).

Cannon (Canon), Simon, on 23 Oct 1700 was named as a son-in-law in the will of Christopher Durbin (MWB 12, part 2:236 abst. in *Md. Cal. of Wills* 3:160). On 1 April 1718 he was named as a son-in-law of John Downs; Elizabeth Cannon was named as a daughter-in-law (MWB 14:599 abst. in *Md. Cal. of Wills* 4:161).

Cannon, Thomas, d. by 18 July 1682 having m. Henrietta, widow of William Robinson (*q.v.*), and Edward Swanson (*q.v.*); she m. 4th, Edward Reeves (*q.v.*) (INAC 7C:183, 8:275; MDTP 12B:43-44, 125; BACP D:187).

Cannon, William, m. Frances Johnson on 28 Dec 1721 (Harrison, "St. George's Parish Register:" 260). She was a daughter of Daniel Johnson of Baltimore Co. (MDAD 15:203).

Cantegril, Lewis, son of John and Jane Lole, m. by banns on 4 Feb 1794 Mary Prun, daughter of John Baptist and Mary Magdalen Berquier at St. Peter's Catholic Church, Baltimore (*Piet*: 129).

Cantwell, Edward, and Joan Chattum were m. on 5 Dec 1699 (Harrison, "St. George's Parish Register:" 189). She m. 2nd, Thomas Burchfield (*q.v.*).

Cantwell, Mary, was fined 30 shillings for bastardy on 3 March 1746/7 (BACP TB&TR#1:402-403).

Cantwell, Ruth, and Samuel Sutton were charged with unlawful cohabitation on 18 July 1757 (Reamy, *St. George's Parish Register:* 108).

Cantwell, Sarah, was charged with bastardy, confessed and was fined on 4 Nov 1746 (BACP TB&TR#1:247).

Cantwell, Thomas, and Sally Smith were married by license dated 27 Aug 1795 (BAML). James Smith, in his will made 13 Dec 1800 named his daughter Sarah Cantwell, and her children Catherine Goff Cantwell and James Smith Cantwell (BAWB 6:339).

Caples, [-?-], m, by Jan 1767 [-?-], daughter of William Cole, by whom he had a daughter Alse (BALR B#N:459; BAWB 3:144).

Carback, [-?-], m. by 19 Aug 1769, Ruth, daughter of Richard Jones (BAWB 3:161); on 25 June 1770 she m. 2nd, Abraham Green (*q.v.*) (Harrison, "St. John's Parish Register:" 260).

Carback, Avarilla, was charged with bastardy at Aug Court 1765; Thomas Egleston or Eagleston was summoned to appear (BAMI 1765:18).

Carback, John Martin, and Frances Mahone were m. on 14 July 1734 (Harrison, "St. Paul's Parish Register:" 134). On 5 March 1741 Frances was named as a daughter of John Mahone (MWB 22:533 abst. in *Md. Cal. of Wills* 8:193; MDAD 22:207).

Carback, John Valentine, m. Mary Harryman on 19 Dec 1736 (Harrison "St. Paul's Parish Register:" 156). She was a daughter of John Harryman of Baltimore Co. (MDAD 28:53, 30:78, 79).

Carback, William, son of Henry and Mary, b. 17 Aug 1763, and Jane Wright, b. 12 April 1770, were married by license dated 15 Nov 1785 (BAML). In 1785, Jane Wright (now Jane Carback), was identified as an orphan girl aged 15, who chose William Carback as her guardian (BAOC 1:235; BAGA 1:2; "Carback Bible," MGRC 1:16).

Card, Joseph, of St. Catherine Court near the Tower of London, m. by 16 Jan 1770, Martha, daughter of Elizabeth Clark (BALR AL#B:416).

Carey, Dennis, m. by lic. 10 Sep 1794, Margaret Dillon at St. Peter's Catholic Church, Baltimore (*Piet*: 129).

Carey, Francis, and wife Eleanor, in 1765 were presented for [breach of?] peace (BAMI 1765:15)

Carey, James, merchant, and Patty Ellicott, daughter of John Ellicott of Baltimore Co., were m. last Wed. (*Maryland Gazette or Baltimore General Advertiser* 12 Sep 1786).

Carey, Joshua, merchant, of Baltimore, m. lately in Bucks Co., Penna., Polly Gibbs (*Maryland Journal and Baltimore Advertiser* 5 Nov 1782).

Carl, [-?-], m. by 27 Aug 1793, Mary, formerly Marvell, admx. of Francis Marvell (BAAD 11:313).

Carlisle, [-?-], m. by 19 Feb 1722 Eleanor, extx. of John Rawlings (*q.v.*).

Carlisle, David, m. by 12 March 1767, Mary, daughter of Peter Carroll, Sr. (*q.v.*) (BACT B#G:114).

Carlisle (Carlile), Elizabeth, confessed to bastardy and was fined 30 shillings in June 1750. Robert Carlile was her security (BACP TR#5:24).

Carlisle, Rev. Hugh, d. by 16 Nov 1752 at which time his admx., Mary, had m. 2nd, John Loney (q.v.) (MDTP 33-2:26).

Carlisle, Dr. John, of the Island of Jamaica, and Betsy, eldest daughter of the late Capt. Richard Lane of Baltimore, dec., were m. last eve. (*Maryland Journal and Baltimore Advertiser* 19 Feb 1790; BAML).

Carlisle, Peter, m. by 27 Oct 1771, Anne, heir of Rachel Wilmot (BAAD 7:114).

Carnan, [-?-], d. by 1 April 1772, having m. Achsah, daughter of Charles Ridgely; she m. 2nd, [-?-] Chamier (BAWB 3:201).

Carnan, [-?-], m. by 4 April 1783, Catherine, daughter of George Risteau (BAWB 5:42).

Carnan, Charles Ridgely, son of John and Achsah, b. 6 Dec 1762, and Priscilla Dorsey, daughter of Caleb and Priscilla, b. 12 July 1762, were m. ob 17 Oct 1782 "Gough-Carroll Bible Records." *MG* 2:23)

Carnan, Christopher, and Elizabeth North were m. on 13 June 1751 (Harrison, "St. Paul's Parish Register:" 165). She was the eldest daughter of Capt. Robert North (Annapolis *Maryland Gazette* 19 June 1751). She m. 2nd, Samuel Johnston (*q.v.*).

Carnan, Daniel, m. by banns on 1 Nov1786 Mary Freeman at St. Peter's Catholic Church, Baltimore (*Piet*: 129).

Carnan, John, and Acshah [-?-] were m. before 16 Jan 1755 when their daughter Prudence was b. ("Gough-Carroll Bible Records." *MG* 2:23).

Carnighan, James, was m. last Thurs. eve. by Rev. Mr. Richards, to Miss Kitty Miller, both of Baltimore (*Federal Gazette and Baltimore Daily Advertiser* 28 Oct 1797).

Carnole, Charles, m. by 17 May 1794, Ruth Stansbury Culliston, who had a legacy from Samuel Stansbury (BAAD 11:427). Charles Carnowles [*sic*] and Ruth Stansbury were married by license dated 24 Aug 1784 (BAML).

Carpenter, Mary, was charged with bastardy at the March 1742/3 Court (BACP TB#D:121).

Carr, [-?-], m. by 17 Oct 1784 Sarah, daughter of Johanna Miller, widow (BAWB 4:66).

Carr, Ann. See Ann Randall.

Carr, Aquila, on 29 d. 7 m. 1786, was charged with marrying contrary to the good order ("Minutes of Gunpowder Meeting," *QRNM:*82). Aquila Carr and Susannah Bond were m. by lic. dated 3 Sep 1796 (BAML).

Carr, Elizabeth, was disowned by the Gunpowder Meeting of Friends on 29 d. 7 m. 1768 for accompanying her brother to his marriage contrary to the good order of Friends and for having a bastard child to her and Friends dishonor (*QRNM:*58).

Carr, John, m. by 30 March 1744, Elizabeth, or Lewsey, daughter of John Clark, son of Matthew Clark and son-in-law of Elizabeth his wife, sister of James Ford (BALR TB#C:565).

Carr, Peter, of Albemarle Co., Va., m. by 31 Jan 1798, Esther Stevenson (BALR WG#55:9).

Carr, Phebe, (formerly Dyer), on 26 d. 4 m. 1788 was charged with marrying outside the order ("Minutes of Gunpowder Meeting," *QRNM:*85). [No other marriage reference found].

Carr, Rachel. See Parish, Rachel.

Carr, William, m. by 23 May 1688, Mary, relict of John Diamont (*q.v.*) (MDTP 14:72).

Carr, William, son of William, was b. 15 June 1763; in Nov 1772, with the consent of his mother, he was bound to John Forward to age 21, to learn the miller's business (BAMI 1772, 1775-1781, p.33).

Carr, William, and Sarah Harbert on 24 d. 7 m. 1792 declared their intention to marry ("Minutes of Gunpowder Meeting," *QRNM:*91).

Carre, Joseph Mary, son of Peter and Louisa Haudbois of St. Malo, m. by lic. 27 Oct 1793, Magdalen Deschamps, dau of Lewis and Mary Tibodeau at St. Peter's Catholic Church, Baltimore (*Piet*: 129).

Carrere, John, m. by lic. 18 Feb 1793 Mary Walsh at St. Peter's Catholic Church, Baltimore (*Piet*: 129).

Carrick, [-?-], m. by 20 Sep 1768, Sarah, daughter of Renaldo Monk of Baltimore Co. who named a grandson George Carrick in his will (BAWB 3:123).

Carrick, Daniel, m. by lic. 1 Oct 1796, Bridget Faherty, both natives of Ireland at St. Peter's Catholic Church, Baltimore (*Piet*: 129). BAML gives the bride's name as Farly.

Carriere, John, merchant, and Mary Walsh, daughter of Robert Walsh, all of Baltimore, were m. last eve. by Bishop Carroll (*Baltimore Daily Repository* 1March 1793).

Carrington, Alice, was charged with bastardy at Aug Court, 1729 and named Thomas Baker as the father of the child. Her daughter Joanna Carrington was b. 2 Sep 1731, and William Beesly or Boosley was named as the father. At the same time her daughter, Mary Carrington, was bound out to serve James Balch until she was 16. She was charged again at November Court, 1733, and her son James Hogg *alias* James Carrington was bound out to serve James Lee (BACP HWS#6:274, 277, HWS#9:139; Reamy. *St. George's:* 39).

Carrington, John, in Nov 1710, was charged with begetting a bastard on the body of Ann Mackarny (BACP IS#B:187).

Carroll, Catherine, confessed to bastardy and was fined on 4 June 1746 (BACP TB&TR#1:10-11).

Carroll, Charles, Jr., a son of the Hon. Charles Carroll of Carrollton, and Harriet, daughter of Benjamin Chew of Philadelphia, were m. Thurs. eve. (*Federal Gazette and Baltimore Daily Advertiser* 21 July 1800).

Carroll, Daniel, was charged with bastardy and indicted at June Court, 1744 (BACP Liber 1743-1745: 228).

Carroll, Daniel, who lived with Henry Dillon, on 9 May 1771 was named as a nephew and exec. in the latter's will (BAWB 3:198).

Carroll, Col. Daniel, of Mount Dillon, was m. a few days since, to Miss Nancy M'Cubbin, daughter of the late Zachariah M'Cubbin, Esq., of Baltimore County (*Federal Gazette and Baltimore Daily Advertiser* 28 Jan 1799). They were m. in Montgomery Co. (Harrison, "Prince George's Parish Register," Montgomery Co., MS at MdHS).

Carroll, Edward, and Mary Sullivan were m. by banns on 2 Aug 1789 at St. Peter's Catholic Church, Baltimore (*Piet*: 129).

Carroll, Elizabeth, in 1772 was fined for bastardy (BAMI 1772, 1775-1781: 84).

Carroll, Henry Hill, and Sarah Rogers were m. by license on 10 Nov 1789 at St. Peter's Catholic Church, Baltimore (*Piet*: 129).

Carroll, James, and Sophia, daughter of Harry Dorsey Gough of Baltimore Co., were m. Thurs. eve. 10th inst. at Perry Hall (*Maryland Journal and Baltimore Advertiser* 25 Dec 1787).

Carroll, Martin, and Mary Ann [-?-] were married by license dated 15 May 1784 (BAML). In Dec 1787 Carroll stated that his wife Marianna has eloped (*Maryland Journal and Baltimore Advertiser* 25 Dec 1787).

Carroll, Michael, and Nancy Drake, natives of Ireland, were m. by license dated 26 Aug 1795 at St. Peter's Catholic Church, Baltimore (*Piet*: 129).

Carroll, Peter, and Anne Hitchcock were m. 8 June 1739 (Harrison, "St. John's Parish Register:" 110). On 25 Sep 1739 Ann was named as the extx. of William Hitchcock (*q.v.*) (MDTP 31:44; see also MINV 24:161; BALR TB#C, 671; MDAD 17:298).

Carroll, Peter, on 2 Oct 1766, entered into a prenuptial contract with Elizabeth Kitely, widow, who conveyed all her property to William Kitely 'in trust' (BALR B#P:259). Peter Carroll and Eliza Kitely were married on 2 Oct 1766 in St. John's and St. George's Parish (Harrison "St. John's Parish Register:" 110). Peter Carroll advertised he would not pay the debts of his wife Elizabeth, who has eloped (Annapolis *Maryland Gazette* 23 April 1767).

Carroll, Peter, on 12 March 1767, made a deed of gift to his daughter Mary, wife of David Carlisle (*q.v.*), and to his son James Carroll (BACT B#G:114, 117).

Carroll, Thomas, and Rose Craven were m. by lic. dated 10 Aug 1787 at St. Peter's Catholic Church, Baltimore (*Piet*: 129).

Carroll, Thomas, and Sarah King were m. by lic. dated 14 Dec 1797 at St. Peter's Catholic Church, Baltimore (*Piet*: 129).

Carslake, Thomas, of Caroline Co., Md., m. by 8 Aug 1796, Margaret, daughter of Elizabeth Lease by Valentine [Lease?] [**N.B.** The deed is signed by Thomas Cradock [*sic*] and Margaret Carslake] (BALR WG#WW:551).

Carroll, William, and Margaret [-?-], were m. by 21 Jan 1792 when their son Aquilla was b. ("Aquilla Carroll Family Records," *MBR* 2:16-17).

Carson, Andrew, merchant of Baltimore, was m. last Thurs. eve. to Jane Rowland, second daughter of the late William Rowland, Esq., of Cecil Co. (*Maryland Gazette or Baltimore General Advertiser* 18 Aug 1789).

Carson, Nathaniel, and Eleanor Cresman (or Creaman) were m. by lic. dated 5 March 1791 at St. Peter's Catholic Church, Baltimore (*Piet*: 129; BAML).

Carson, William, of Baltimore Co., aged c24, m. by 20 Sep 1744, Elizabeth, aged c16, sister of Andrew Johnson, aged c8 (BALR TB#C:601).

Carter, [-?-], m. by 13 March 1764, Margaret, extx. of Benjamin Mann, whose will, dated 26 May 1761 named his wife Margaret as extx. (MDTP 40:158; BAWB 2:152).

Carter, John, m. Elizabeth [-?-]; he d. by 11 Aug 1732 and his widow Elizabeth m. 2nd, Thomas Green (*q.v.*).

Carter, John, m. by 26 April 1765, Tamar, widow and admx. of John Bentley (*q.v.*) (BAAD 6:271, 7:248; MDAD 68:163).

Carter, John, on 27 d. 5 m. 1790, was charged with having m. to a woman not of our society with the assistance of a man formerly a Methodist Preacher ("Minutes of Deer Creek Meeting," *QRNM:*148). He may be the John Carter who m. Ann Thomas on 4 March 1790 ("First Evangelical Church, Frederick, Md.;" MS. at MdHS:1117).

Carter, John, on 26 d. 8 m. 1798 announced his intention to marry Rebeccah Harlan ("Minutes of Deer Creek Meeting," *QRNM:*159).

Carter, Richard, m. by 14 Feb 1769 Rebeckah, daughter of Joseph Bankson. On 28 April 1738 Rebecca was named as a daughter of Joseph Bankson (MDAD 18:132). Hannah 'Bankston' m. William Hughes (*q.v.*) on 11 Dec 1735 (Harrison "St. Paul's Parish Register:" 154). She named her daughter Rebecca, wife of Richard Carter in her will made 14 Feb 1770 (MWB 38:110, abst. in *Md. Cal. of Wills* 14:150).

Cartwright, Abraham, and Mary Hart were married by license dated 20 Jan 1783 (BAML). In Dec 1796 Cartwright stated he would not pay the debts of his wife Mary, who had frequently absented herself in an unbecoming manner from his family, and wantonly made unlawfully [*sic*] destruction of his property (*Federal Gazette and Baltimore Daily Advertiser* 12 Dec 1796).

Carty (Cartee), Timothy, servant of George Presbury, in Nov 1737 was charged with begetting a bastard on the body of Ann Bellows (BACP HWS#1A:129, 189).

Carville, John, m. by 10 July 1701 Mary, daughter of James Phillips of Baltimore Co., and his wife Susanna, who later m. [-?-] Arnold (*q.v.*). Mary was a sister of Anthony Phillips of Baltimore Co. John was the father of Avarilla Carville, to whom, on 12 July 1701 her grandmother, Susannah Arnold, conv. a Negro boy named Ledgen (INAC 20:229; BALR HW#2:57; MWB 6:81 abst. in *Md. Cal. of Wills* 2:157, 12:304).

Casey, John, in Nov 1723, was charged with begetting a bastard on the body of Sarah Evans (BACP IS&TW#3:109).

Casey, Robert, and Elizabeth Davies (Davis) were m. by lic. dated 30 March 1796 at St. Peter's Catholic Church, Baltimore by Bishop Carroll (*Piet:* 129; *Baltimore Telegraphe* 1 April 1796).

Cassat, Peter, was m. last Thurs. eve. by Rev. John Ireland, to Miss Susanna Stansbury, all of this city (*Federal Gazette and Baltimore Daily Advertiser* 6 Jan 1798; BAML).

Cassidy, [-?-], m. by Sep 1786 Jane, widow of Robert Wood of Baltimore Co.; Jane advertised that she intended to petition the Assembly (*Maryland Journal and Baltimore Advertiser* 12 Sep 1786).

Cassidy, Patrick, and Hannah Read (Reed) were m. on 9 July 1778 (Marr. Returns of Rev. Thomas Chase, Scharf Papers, MS.1999 at MdHS). On 6 June 1791, Hannah was named as a daughter of John Daniel Reed (BAWB 5:4).

Caswell, Richard, on 11 Jan 1731 was named as a nephew in the will of William Smith (MWB 20:345 abst. in *MCW* 6:214).

Caswell, Capt. Thomas, and Mrs. Jane Leary (or Lowry), both of Fell's Point, were m. last Sat. night by Rev, Mr. Bend (*Federal Intelligencer and Baltimore Daily Gazette* 21 April 1795; BAML).

Cates, Jane (formerly Nailor), on 31 d. 5 m. 1777, hath gone out in marriage to a man not of our Society ("Minutes of Gunpowder Meeting," *QRNM:*70). [No other marriage reference found]. On 9 May 1796 Jane Catts [*sic*] was named as a daughter of John Naylor (BAWB 5:451).

Caton?, James, and Clare [-?-], both belonging to Mr. Richard Caton were m. 17 Nov 1799 at St. Peter's Catholic Church, Baltimore (*Piet:* 129).

Caton, Mark, and Ann Cherry, both natives of Ireland, were m. by lic. 28 Dec 1799 at St. Peter's Catholic Church, Baltimore (*Piet:* 129).

Caton, Richard, of Baltimore, and Polly, daughter of the Hon. Charles Carroll of Carrollton, were m. Sun. eve. last at Annapolis ((*Maryland Journal and Baltimore Advertiser* 30 Nov 1787).

Catto, George, of Cecil Co., m. by 30 May 1761 Araminta, widow of Col. Joseph Young (BALR B#1:283).

Catts. See Cates.

Causton, Esther, servant of Samuel Owings, Jr., was charged with bastardy at the March 1763 Court; she confessed to having a bastard child named William Causton who had been 1 year old on the previous November. William was sold to Samuel Owings for 20 shillings (BAMI 755-1763).

Cavenagh (Cavannah), Patrick, m. by 8 Dec 1752, Mary, acting extx, of John Renshaw (*q.v.*) (BAAD 5:259, 288; MDAD 33:309; MDTP 33-2:58).

Cavaroc, Francis, son of John and Catherine Magne, native of Tiezac, diocese of Auverne, of Cap. Francois, St. Domingo, m. by lic. dated 11 Nov 1793, Mary Sears, daughter of James and Ann of Annapolis at St. Peter's Catholic Church, Baltimore (*Piet:* 129; BAML).

Cayol, Antony, native of Marseilles, m. by license dated 7 Oct 1799, Modeste Tardieu, native of St. Domingo at St. Peter's Catholic Church, Baltimore (*Piet:* 129).

Cebron, Olivier, of the Parish of Debouches, Diocese of Nante, m. by lic. 5 May 1794, Mary Joanna Foushne Trouve, from Piffivers, Diocese of Orleans; both were lately from San Domingo at St. Peter's Catholic Church, Baltimore (*Piet:* 129).

Chabert, Anthony, in his undated will probated 26 Nov 1793, stated he was a native of Toulon, Provence, France, but lately of Jacquirie in the Parish of St. Peter de Terriers Rouge on the Island of St. Domingo, and that he had m. Rene Charlotte DeMontdieu, widow of the late M. Pillot, by whom she had two children (BAWB 5:133).

Chadbourn (Chandbourne), William, m. by 15 Nov 1673, [-?-], relict of Richard Foxon (MDTP 6:28; INAC 1:147). William Chadbourne of Cecil Co. had immigrated in 1669 and was Deputy Surveyor of Baltimore and Cecil Counties (MPL 15:308, 18:336).

Chaeld, Samuel, stated his wife Elizabeth had deserted him (*Dunlap's Maryland Gazette* 26 May 1778 supplement).

Chainey, [-?-], of Washington Co., Pa., m. by 1 Nov 1800, Elizabeth, daughter and-heir at law of John Lane and her bros. John Boreing Lane and William Lane (BALR WG#64:333).

Chalke (Choake), George, on 24 d. 4 m. 1771, was reported to have gone out in marriage with a woman of another society ("Minutes of Gunpowder Monthly Meeting," *QRNM:* 61). George Chalke and Eliz. Hughes were m. on 9 April 1771 (Harrison, "St. John's," p. 262).

Chalmers, John, Jr., m. Mary Ashbury Gilder on 2 July 1797 ("Emanuel Kent Bible," *MBR* 1:139; BAML). John Chalmers, 'the Younger,' m. by 13 July 1798, Mary Ashberry Alkin, only daughter and heir at law of Ellen Burneston (BALR WG#55:430). Mary Gilder Chalmers was the widow of 1st, [-?-] Alkin (q.v.), and 2nd Reuben Gilder (q.v.).

Chamberlain, Charles, m. Mary Guthrow (Gutrow) by lic. dated 21 June 1798, at St. Peter's Catholic Church, Baltimore (*Piet:* 129; BAML).

Chamberlain, John, m. Margaret Gittings on 31 Oct 1737 (Harrison, "St. John's Parish Register:" 120). She was a daughter of Thomas Gittings (BALR TR#C:489; BAWB 2:259).

Cambers, Arthur, of Reisterstown, was presented by his wife with triplets—one son and two daughters—who were baptized on Sunday by Rev. Dr. Allison (*Maryland Journal and Baltimore Advertiser* 31 May 1791).

Chambers, James, m. by 1 June 1764, Mary, daughter of John Tipton (BALR B3O;247, AL#N:513).

Chambers, Sarah, was charged with bastardy at the June 1734 Court (BACP HWS#9:253).

Chambers, William, m. by 18 July 1783, Mary, lately the wife of William Rowles (BALR WG#O:188).

Chambers, William, and Miss Mary McLaughlin, both of Baltimore, were m. last eve. by Rev. Bonsall (*Baltimore Daily Repository* 19 April 1793; BAML).

Chamier, Daniel, and Achsah Carnan were m. on 25 Feb 1768 (Register of First Presbyterian Church, Baltimore, at MdHS: 3). Achsah, widow of [-?-] Carnan (*q.v.*), was a daughter of Charles Ridgely (BAWB 3:201).

Chamillon, Joseph, m. Ann Meade on 6 Dec 1784, at St. Peter's Catholic Church, Baltimore (*Piet:* 129; BAML gives the bride's name as Ann Smith).

Chamness, Anthony, m. Sarah Cole on 24 Nov 1735 (Harrison "St. Paul's Parish Register:" 154). She was a daughter and heir at law of Joseph Cole who was brother of John Cole, who was the father of testator William Cole (BAWB 3:144).

Chamney, Mary, was charged with bastardy at the March 1733/4 Court and named George Egerton as the father of her child (BACP HWS#9:1283, 199). Either she or another Mary Chamney m. George Buswell on 30 Aug 1752 (Harrison, "St. John's Parish Register:" 206).

Chamney. See also Chancey.

Champion, Isaac, in June 1731 was charged with begetting a bastard on the body of Mary Fitzpatrick (BACP HWS#7:156, 168).

Chance, [-?-], m. by 20 Nov 1793 Martha, daughter of Samuel Watkins who also named a granddaughter Elizabeth Chance (BAWB 5:336).

Chancey (Chaney, Chamney), George, m. Mrs. Sarah Smith on 22 June 1706 (Harrison "St. George's Parish Register:" 201). She was the admx. of Benjamin Smith (*q.v.*), sawyer, who was admin. of William Hollis (MDTP 19C:233; INAC 28:25). Sarah was a daughter of William Hollis (*Maryland Rent Rolls,* 23).

Chancey, George, on 24 Nov 1742 was named as son in the will of Sarah Hanson who also named George's children Sarah and George (MWB 23:21 abst. in *Md. Cal. of*

Wills 8:196).

Chancey, George, m. by 8 July 1768, Mary, sister of George Little (BACT B#G:210).

Chandbourne. See Chadbourn.

Chaney, [-?-], m. by 10 Nov 1794 Elizabeth, sister of William Lane (BAWB 5:208).

Chaney, Benjamin Burgess, m. by 25 Jan 1756 Margaret Shipley, daughter of Adam Shipley of Anne Arundel Co. (BALR BB#I:565).

Chaney. See also Chancey and Cheney.

Changeur, Leon, son of Peter and Mary Samson of Bordeaux, France, m. by lic. 30 June 1795, Josephine DeGripier Monroe Motalibor, daughter of Germain deGripiere Monroe, Order of St. Louis, Lt.-Col. Inf., formerly Commandant of the King, St. Domingo at Jeremie, Port au Paix, and Elizabeth De Bey, at St. Peter's Catholic Church, Baltimore (*Piet*: 129). Leon Changeur, aged 23, born in Bordeaux, son of Peter Changeur, merchant of Bordeaux and brother of John Changeur, on 24 June 1795 executed marriage articles with Jane Josephine Moncrave Montalebor, the under age daughter of Mr. Germaine Gripiere Moncrave Montalebor, formerly Knight of [the Order] of St. Louis, and Mrs. Elizabeth Rey; Jane Josephine was born in the northern part of St, Domingo (BALR WG#SS:9).

Channell, Edward, exec, on 29 Dec 1797 posted bond to administer the estate of Elizabeth King, whose will dated 6 Dec 1797 appointed William H. Woods guardian of her only child, Elizabeth (BAAB 8:19; BAWB 6:68).

Chapman, [-?-], m. by 16 June 1761 Sophia, sister of William Wooden, and daughter of John Wooden (MWB 31:357 abst. by Abst. by Gibb; MWB 37:82 abst. in *Md. Cal. of Wills* 14:77).

Chapman, John, in March 1743/4, was charged with begetting a bastard on the body of Martha Bastock or Bostock (BACP 1743-1745, 171).

Chapman, John, and Mary Hall were m. on 17 July 1746 Harrison, "St. Paul's Parish Register:" 159). She was the widow of 1st, Thomas Gwynn (q.v.), and 2nd, William Hall (*q.v.*).

Chapman, William, on 24 d. 4 m. 1794 was charged with marrying a woman not of our society with the assistance of a hireling teacher ("Minutes of Deer Creek Meeting," *QRNM:*154). [No other marriage reference found].

Chappel, Samuel, and Sarah Tice were m. on 5 Aug 1792 (Marr. Register of Rev. Lewis Richards, MS.690 at MdHS). On 7 Aug 1797 Chappell's wife was named as Mary, mother of John Tise, aged 15 (BIND 1:225).

Chareele, Peter, free Negro, St. Domingo, and Rachel [-?-], a free mulatto of Martinico, were m. 10 Feb 1795, at St. Peter's Catholic Church, Baltimore (*Piet*: 129).

Charles, Richard, was m. last eve. by Rev. Mr. Lyle, to Elizabeth Benson, both of this city (*Federal Gazette and Baltimore Daily Advertiser* 22 April 1799).

Charnox (Charnock), Anthony, m. Hannah Hollingsworth on 14 May 1717 (Lucy H. Harrison, "St. Anne's Parish Register," Anne Arundel Co., at MdHS: 400). Hannah was a daughter of George Hollingsworth of Baltimore Co.; Anthony and Hannah's daughter Margaret m. Charles Phelps (PCLR EI#8:339).

Chase, [-?-], m. by 9 March 1789 Sarah, daughter of George Haile (BAWB 4:538).

Chase, Jeremiah, son of Richard Chase, in Aug 1765 chose Richard Moale as his guardian (BAMI 1765).

Chase, Nathaniel, slave of Samuel Chase, and Ann Leduc, were m. 2 Dec 1794, at St. Peter's Catholic Church, Baltimore (*Piet*: 129).

Chase, Capt. Thorndike, was married [date not given] to Miss Polly Jacobs of Fells Point (*Maryland Journal and Baltimore Advertiser* 18 Feb 1785).

Chase, Rev. Thomas, and Ann Birch, daughter of Thomas Birch, chirurgeon and man midwife in the Town of Warwick, Co. of Warwick, England, wre m. on 19 July 1763 (Harrison, "St. Paul's Parish Register:" 167). On 13 Sep 1770, Ann, wife of Thomas Chase was named as a niece of [Deborah?] the wife of Joseph Smith, ironmaster (MINV 104:140).

Chatman, Mary, was charged with bastardy at the March 1768 Court. The case was struck off the docket (BACP BB:12).

Cheney, [-?-], m. by 9 Sep 1759 Margaret, daughter of Patrick Montgomery (MWB 30:756 abst. by Gibb).

Cheney, Benjamin Burgess, m. by 10 July 1753, Ann, widow of Richard Acton (MDTP 33-2:140).

Chenith. See Chenoweth.

Chenoweth (Chenith), [-?-], m. by 9 March 1789, Frances, daughter of George Haile (BAWB 4:538).

Chenoweth (Chinworth), Arthur, and Sofira [Sophia], daughter of Samuel Hooker, were m. by 11 Aug 1767 (MWB 39:93, abst. in *Md. Cal. of Wills* 15:19).

Chenoweth, Arthur, m. by 10 April 1769 Ann, daughter of William Beasman (BAWB 3:112; BAAD 10:136).

Chenoweth, Arthur, and Cassandra Bosley were m. by lic. dated 24 March 1784 (BAML). She was an heir of William Bosley (BPET: Petition of Vincent Trapnall, 1795; BAAD 10:116).

Chenoweth (Chinworth), John, Sr., and Jane Wood were m. on 16 Dec 1736 Harrison, "St. Paul's Parish Register:" 156). On 29 Oct 1737 Jane was named as the admx. of William Wood, Sr. (MDTP 30:360).

Chenoweth, John, m. by 16 April 1795 Hannah Cromwell, a representative of William Cromwell (BAAD 12:7).

Chenoweth, Richard, m. by 26 Dec 1785 [-?-], daughter of Jonathan Hanson who named his granddaughter Sarah Chenoweth, daughter of Richard, in his will (BAWB 4:115).

Chenoweth, Samuel, and Elizabeth Cromwell were married by license dated 8 Oct 1785 (BAML). Elizabeth was the extx. of Stephen Cromwell (BAAD 9:70, 12:8, 133).

Chenoweth, Samuel, m. by 16 April 1795, Patience Cromwell, a representative of William Cromwell (BAAD 12:7).

Chenoweth (Chinwoth), Thomas, Jr., m. Rachel Moore on 14 Sep 1766 (Harrison, "St. John's Parish Register:" 229). She was a niece of Nicholas Ruxton Gay (BALR B#P:359; BAWB 3:151). On 26 Aug 1771 Thomas and Rachel were conveyed property by their cousin Rachel Thorpe (*q.v.*).

Chenowith (Chinnuth), William, and Elizabeth 'Ritcherson' were married by license dated 8 April 1789 (BAML). Elizabeth received a share of the estate of James Richardson (BAAD 10:536).

Cheshire, Ann, was charged with bastardy at the Nov 1772 Court (BAMI 1772, 1775-1781: 84).

Cheshire, Elizabeth, was charged with bastardy at the June 1734 Court (BACP HWS#9:265). She married John Sherelock on 30 Nov 1737 (Harrison, "St. John's Parish Register:" 104).

Chester, Elizabeth, in 1763 was convicted of bastardy (BAMI 1755-1763).

Chester, Samuel, m. Mary Coursy on 18 Nov 1776 (Harrison "St. Paul's Parish Register:" 669). She was a daughter of James Scorce [*sic*] and sister of William Scorce [*sic*] (BAWB 3:430).

Cheston, Daniel, m. by 13 Oct 1798, Mary Farrell, admx. of George Farrell (BAAD 12:502).

Chew, [-?-], m. by 27 Oct 1746 Mary, daughter of Martha Paca (MWB 24:496 abst. by Gibb).

Chew, Benjamin, son of Benjamin, and Cassandra Johns, daughter of Richard and Ann, were m. on 1 May 1750 ("Records of Nottingham Meeting," MS. at MdHS; MWB 30:367 abst. by Gibb).

Chew, Elizabeth, orphan of Joseph, in March 1761 chose Ephraim Gover as her guardian (BAMI 1755-1763).

Chew, Joseph, was charged with bastardy at the March 1744/5 Court; the mother of the child was not named (BACP Liber 1743-1745: 496).

Chew, Joseph, in his will, made 15 d., 1 m. 1753 he named his wife Sarah extx. (MWB 28:453). Sarah was m. to William Yates (*q.v.*) by 20 April 1754 (MDTP 26:32).

Chew, Phineas, m. by 26 Nov 1770, Cassandra, extx. of John Wallace (*q.v.*) (MINV 105:75).

Chilcoat (Chilcoate), [-?-], m. by 22 May 1771, Eliza, daughter of George Ensor (BAWB 3:195).

Chilcoat, Robert, and Joyce Webb were married by license dated 5 April 1781 (BAML). On 18 June 1781 Chilcoat's wife was named as Jane, lately called Jane Webb (BALR WG#K: 437).

Chilcoate, William, m. by 16 May 1795 Uleana, daughter of Philip Deale (BAWB 4:83; BAAD 11:154, 12:9).

Child, Mark, d. by 1687 when his admx. had m. 2nd, Robert Cage (*q.v.*). She m. 3rd, by 1696 David Thurston (*q.v.*).

Chilson, David, m. by 15 May 1766, Mary, daughter of John York (BALR B#G:92).

Chinworth. See Chenoweth.

Choake. See Chalk.

Choat, Edward, on 16 June 1725 warned all persons he stated he would not pay the debts of his wife Constant, who had left him (BALR IS#H:133).

Choate, Augustine, in March 1738/9 was charged with begetting a bastard on the body of Sarah Savage (BACP HWS#1A:351).

Choate, Christopher, in Aug 1711 was charged with begetting a bastard on the body of Elizabeth Budd (BACP IS#B:43).

Choate, Edward, Jr., m. by 6 Nov 1752 Elizabeth, daughter of Samuel Underwood (BALR TR#D:451; IS#L:145, 161).

Choate, Richard, and Jane Lowe were married by license dated 4 Aug 1783 (BAML). On 11 Aug 1790, she was named a representative of John Lowe (BAAD 10: 185).

Choice, William, m. Jane, daughter of Francis Trippas; he died leaving a will dated 28 Oct 1680 and proved 1 March 1681, leaving land and the rest of his estate to his wife Jane (MWB 2:177 abst. in *Md. Cal. of Wills* 1:104). Jane m. 2nd, John Durham (*q.v.*), and 3rd John Boone (*q.v.*).

Chrisman (Chriessman), [-?-], m. by 7 June 1794 Christian, daughter of Jacob Shaffer (BAWB 6:249).

Christie, Charles, and Cordelia Stokes were m. on 21 or 22 July 1754 (Harrison, "St. John's Parish Register:" 210; (Harrison, "St. George's Parish Register:" 351). She m. 2nd, Dr. Alexander Stenhouse (*q.v.*).

Christie, Gabriel, aged 16 this Nov 13, in Nov 1772 was bound to James Christie to learn the mercantile business (BAMI 1772, 1775-1781: 35).

Cimble, Samuel, m. by 21 Dec 1772 Sarah, daughter of Samuel McCarty (BAWB 3:271).

Clagett, [-?-], m. by 26 Nov 1714 Deborah, daughter of the Hon. John Dorsey of Baltimore Co. (MWB 14:26).

Clagett, Nicholas, and Rebecca Young, daughter of John and Rebecca, were m. on 11 Feb 1768; she m. 2nd, Edward Day (*q.v.*), and 3rd, John Weston (*q.v.*) ("Original Records of the Young Family of Baltimore County," HMGB 16:15-17, 16:24-27).

Clalk, [-?-], m. by 29 May 1742, Mary, daughter of Rebecca Potee (BAWB 2:80).

Clark, [-?-], m. by 4 Sep 1760, Eliz., daughter of William Jenkins (BAWB 2:258).

Clark, [-?-], m. by 22 March 1774, Isabel, sister of Isaac Hall, bricklayer (BAWB 3:336).

Clark, Aquila, m. Hannah Bull on 8 April 1760 (Harrison "St. Paul's Parish Register:" 219). On 23 March 1761 she was named as a daughter of Hannah Bull (MDAD 46:285, 47:26).

Clark, Daniel, m. by 7 June 1771 Jane, daughter of Adam Hoops (BAWB 3:259).

Clark, David, m. Salley Lewes on 23 Nov 1767 (Harrison, "St. John's Parish Register:" 231). On 20 Feb 1773 she was named as an heir of Joseph Lewis (BAAD 6:312; MDAD 68:107).

Clark, Edward, and Jemima Addison were m. by lic. 8 April 1790, at St. Peter's Catholic Church, Baltimore (*Piet*: 129; BAML).

Clark, Hannah, aged 2, orphan of John Clark, in 1772 was made a ward of Greenbury Dorsey (BAMI 1772, 1775-1781, p.13).

Clark, James, in Nov 1755 was charged with begetting a bastard on the body of Martha West (BACP BB#B:399).

Clark, James, m. by 28 Feb 1789 [-?-], who received an equal share of the estate of Gilbert Israel (BAAD 10:239).

Clark, John, son of Matthew Clark, m. by 30 March 1744, Elizabeth, sister of James Ford (BALR TB#C:565).

Clark, John, and Hannah [-?-] were m. by 10 June 1755 when their daughter Sarah was b. ("Aquila Standiford Bible," *MBR* 2:140-141).

Clark, John, and Sophia Lester were m. on 4 April 1769 (Harrison, "St. George's Parish Register:" 386). Sophia m. 2nd, Greenbury Dorsey (*q.v.*).

Clark, John, blacksmith of Baltimore Town, and Ann Mackilvene were m. last Thurs. night (*Maryland Gazette or Baltimore General Advertiser* 11 Dec 1787). They were m. in Baltimore Co. BAML).

Clark, John, m. by 27 Sep 1796 Eleanor, a representative [daughter?] of John Anderson (BAAD 12:191).

Clark, Lawrence, m. by 15 Jan 1750 Jane, extx. of Isaac Butterworth (*q.v.*) of Baltimore Co. (MDAD 29:158; MDTP 35:88).

Clark, Mary, alias Mary Poleson, confessed to bastardy at the March 1750/1 Court and was fined (BACP TB&TR#6:282).

Clark, Patrick, and Sarah Mitchell were m. by lic. dated 12 Jan 1792 at St. Peter's Catholic Church, Baltimore (*Piet*: 129).

Clark, Prudence, admx., on 6 June 1765 posted bond to administer the estate of Amos Fogg (*q.v.*) (BAAB 3:95). In his will dated 7 Aug 1762 Fogg named his daughter-in-law Prudence Clark and her children Samuel and Rebecca Clark (MWB 31:710; abst. in *Md. Cal. of Wills* 12:144).

Clark, Robert, m. Elizabeth Smithson on 5 Dec 1729 (Harrison "St. George's Parish Register:" 272). She was a daughter of Thomas Smithson of Baltimore Co. (MWB 20:568 abst. in *Md. Cal. of Wills* 6:253).

Clark, Robert, m. by 4 Sep 1760, Elizabeth, daughter of William Jenkins (MWB 31:316; BAAD 6:24; MDAD 49:399; BAWB 2:358).

Clark, Samuel, m. by 27 Dec 1773, Sophia, daughter of George Harryman, Sr.; they had sons William Clark, Samuel, and George Clark (BAWB 3:285).

Clark, Sarah, was charged with bastardy at the June 1709 Court and named Robert Clark as the father of her child (BACP IS#B:43).

Clark, William, d. by 13 Feb 1787, leaving minor child William; Samuel Clark, guardian, filed an account (BAGA 1:17).

Clarke, [-?-], m. by 11 Nov 1766 Margaret, daughter of John Chocke (BAAD 7:192).

Clarke, [-?-], m. by 11 Nov 1766 Sarah, daughter of John Chocke (BAAD 7:192).

Clarke, Francis, widower, Fifer to the Company of Artificers, garrisoned at Whetstone Point, at the Fort near Baltimore, and Mary Hagerty, were m. by banns on 15 March 1795 at St. Peter's Catholic Church, Baltimore (*Piet*: 129).

Clarke, James H., and Miss Hannah Hammond, both of Fell's Point, were m. Thurs. eve. by Rev. Riggen (*Baltimore American* 17 Aug 1799).

Clarke, Matthew, m. by 30 March 1744, (poss. as his second wife), Elizabeth, sister of James Ford (BALR TB#C:565).

Clarke, William, m. by 13 March 1792, Elizabeth, daughter of Jarvis Biddison (BAAD 11: 13). William Clarke on 20 May 1789 was named as a nephew in the will of Daniel Biddison (BAWB 4:262).

Class, John, announced his wife Elizabeth had eloped (*Maryland Journal and Baltimore Advertiser* 12 Aug 1785).

Clay, Elizabeth, was charged with bastardy in March 1743/4 and she confessed in June (BACP 1743-1745, pp. 154, 236).

Claypoole, Septimus, one of the proprietors of the *American Daily Advertiser,* was m. on the eve. of the 8th ins., to Miss Elizabeth Polk at the seat of Col. Nathaniel Ramsay, Carpenter's Point, Cecil Co. (*Federal Gazette and Baltimore Daily Advertiser* 12 June 1797).

Clayton, Joseph, and Priscilla [-?-] were m. by 1 March 1778 when their son Joseph as b. ("Clayton-Archer Family Bible," MBR 1:55; *HABFR* 2:38).

Clayton, Joseph, b. 1 March 1778, son of Joseph and Priscilla, and Sarah Wills, b. 26 June 1782, daughter of John and Susannah, were m. on 18 Aug 1796 ("Clayton-Archer Family Bible," *HABFR* 2:38; BAML).

Clemens. See Clements.

Clements, [-?-], m. by 29 Nov 1769 Mary, daughter of Thomas Wheeler (BAWB 3:171).

Clements, Josias, of Baltimore, and Sarah McSherry of Littlestown were m. last Thurs. (*Baltimore Telegraphe* 31 March 1796).

Clements (Clemens, Clemons), William, m. by 31 Jan 1748 Ann, extx. of Leonard Wheeler (*q.v.*) of Baltimore Co. (MINV 37:309; MDAD 30:222; MDTP 32:228).

Clemons. See Clements

Cleverly, Thomas, stated his wife Mary had eloped from him (*Maryland Journal and Baltimore Advertiser* 13 April 1784).

Cliborn, Mary, was charged with bastardy at the June 1732 Court (BACP HWS#7:289).

Cline, David, and Catherine Shakes, both of Fell's Point, were m. last eve. by Rev. Bend (*Baltimore American* 29 July 1799).

Cloherty, Patrick, native of Ireland, widower, was m. by lic. dated 22 April 1800, to Catherine Taylor, daughter of Philip and Catherine Taylor, at St. Peter's Catholic Church, Baltimore (*Piet:* 129).

Clougherty, Patrick, and Honor Faherty, both natives of Ireland, were m. by lic. dated 12 Nov 1795 at St. Peter's Catholic Church, Baltimore (*Piet:* 130).

Clopper, [-?-], m. by 2 June 1790 [-?-], daughter of Emanuel Stansbury, who named his granddaughter Leah Clopper (BAWB 4:513).

Close, Garrett, in March 1710/11 was charged with begetting a bastard on the body of Susanna Simpson (BACP IS#B:205, 210).

Cloyd, [-?-], m. by 19 Jan 1790, Ann, sister of Dr. Alexander Boyd (BAWB 4:404).

Clyon, David, d. leaving his daughter Catherine, now Catherine McCassidy (*q.v.*) as admx. (BOCP Petition of Catherine 'McCassady,' late Catherine Clyon, 1791)

Coale, Isaac, son of William and Sarah, the latter dec., on 3 d. 8 m. 1786, announced his intention to marry Rachel Cox, daughter of William and Mary, the former dec. ("Minutes of Deer Creek Meeting," *QRNM:*143).

Coale, Philip, son of William, on 5 d. 9 m. 1765 was lately m. by a priest to a woman not of our society ("Minutes of Deer Creek Meeting," *QRNM:*131). [No other marriage reference found].

Coale, Philip, and Elizabeth Cockey were married by license dated 1 Jan 1783 (BAML). On 6 Aug 1784 Elizabeth was named as a daughter of Thomas Cockey (BAWB 4:63).

Coale, Samuel, son of Skipwith Coale, dec., and wife Margaret, on 5 d. 9 m. 1776 announced his intention to marry Lydia Pusey, daughter of Joshua and Mary Pusey, of New Garden Meeting, dec. ("Minutes of Deer Creek Meeting," *QRNM:*137).

Coale, Samuel, son of Philip and Ann, both dec., on 27 d. 11 m. 1794 announced his intention to marry Alasanna Wilson, daughter of Thomas and Ann, the latter dec. ("Minutes of Deer Creek Meeting," *QRNM:*154-155).

Coale, Skipwith, on 1 April 1738 received chattel from William Holland, because Coale was about to marry Holland's daughter Margaret (BALR HWS#IA:63).

Coale, Skipwith, on 23 d. 3 m. 1797 was found guilty of marrying a woman not of our society by the assistance of a hireling teacher ("Minutes of Deer Creek Meeting," *QRNM:*157). Skipwith Coale m. Elizabeth Gilbert on 22 Jan 1797 (Rev. John Allen's Marr. Register). She was the widow of Michael Gilbert (*q.v.*).

Coale, Thomas, on 19 Jan 1739 was named as a brother-in-law in the will of Aquila Massey (MWB 22:145 abst. in *Md. Cal. of Wills* 8:67). Aquila Massey, son of Jonathan, and Sarah Coale, daughter of William, were m. on 7 Jan 1724/5 ("Records of West River Monthly Meeting," *QRSM:29*). Thomas Coale, in his will, made 5 April 1745, named his nephews Aquila Massey and Jonathan Massey (MWB 24:85 abst. by Gibb).

Coale, William, son of Skipwith, on 29 d. 3 m. 1769 stated he intended to marry Elizabeth Rigbie, daughter of James ("Minutes of Deer Creek Meeting," *QRNM:*133).

Coatney. See Courtney.

Coats, James, and Rachel Jackson were m. on 9 March 1793 (Marr. Register of Rev. Lewis Richards, MS.690 at MdHS). Rachel Coates, (formerly Jackson), on 30 d. 8 m. 1793, had a complaint made against her for having her marriage accomplished by the assistance of a hireling ("Minutes of Baltimore Meeting," *QRNM:*222).

Coatsworth, Caleb, Doctor of Physic, London, m. by 30 June 1705, Susannah, sister of Roger Newman, dec. (MDTP 19B:56).

Cobb, James, and Rebecca Emson were m. on 30 Oct 1709 (Harrison, "St. George's Parish Register:" 208). She was the widow John Daniell (or Darnall), James 'Empson' (*q.v.*), (INAC 32A:23; BAAD 2:147). She m. 4th, John Hawkins (*q.v.*), and 5th Gregory Farmer (*q.v.*).

Cochran, Thomas, son of Thomas, dec., in March 1745/6 was bound to George Jones, joiner to age 21; in Aug 1746 was kept by Catherine Jones (BACP for 1743-1745/6: 801; TB&TR#1:118).

Cockey, [-?-], m, by 2 April 1726 Elizabeth, daughter of William Slade (MWB 20:263 abst. in *Md. Cal. of Wills* 6:202).

Cockey, [-?-], m. by 6 Dec 1774, Susannah, daughter of Thomas Boone (BAWB 3:307).

Cockey, [-?-], m. by 17 Feb 1777 Charcilla Cockey, daughter of Penelope Deye (BAWB 3:562).

Cockey, Charles, son of Thomas and Prudence (Hill [Gill]) Cockey, was married to Urath Cockey, his cousin, daughter of Col. Edward and Eleanor Pindell Cockey, 4 Nov 1786 ("Cockey Bible," *MGSB* 26 (2) (Spring 1985)186).

Cockey, Col. Edward, and Eleanor Pindell were m. on 19 June 1753 (Harrison, "St. Thomas' Parish Register:" 71). Their daughter Urath m. Charles Cockey ("Thomas B. Cockey Bible," *MGSB* 2 26 (2) (Spring 1985) 186).

Cockey, Hannah, in July 1775 was made guardian of Ruth and William Cockey (BAMI 1772, 1775-1781: 132).

Cockey, John, m. by 14 Sep 1768 Chloe daughter of Joseph and Comfort Cromwell, widow (BAWB 3:101, 4:241). In his will Joseph Cromwell also named a granddaughter Rebecca, eldest daughter of Chloe (MWB 37:42, abst. in *Md. Cal. of Wills* 14:110).

Cockey, Joshua, of Baltimore Co., m. by 20 June 1716, Sarah, daughter of John Ray of Anne Arundel Co., dec. (AALR IB#2:283). She was a widow of Thomas Hanson (*q.v.*), and m. 3rd, by July 1725, Benjamin Tayman (*q.v.*) (BALR TR#DS:95; MDTP 17:197).

Cockey, Thomas, m. by 27 Aug 1746, Catherine, daughter of John Risteau (BALR TB#E: 276).

Cockey, Thomas, m. Prudence Gill on 15 May 1753 (Harrison "St. Thomas' Parish Register:" 71). On 12 May 1753 Cockey executed a pre-nuptial contract with Prudence Gill (BACT TR#E:93). Thomas Cockey stated his wife Prudence has eloped (*Maryland Journal and Baltimore Advertiser* 16 Oct 1776).

Cockey, Thomas Deye, and Betsy, daughter of John Cockey, Esq., were m. yesterday eve. in Baltimore Co. (*Maryland Journal and Baltimore Advertiser* 11 Jan 1788).

Cockey, Thomas Deye, m. by 18 Aug 1795, Ann, heir at law of Darby Lux (BALR WG#TT:477). Thomas Cockey Deye and Mrs. Ann Risteau were married last Tues. at the house of Darby Lux by Rev. Mr. Richards (*Baltimore Evening Post* 28 March 1793; BAML).

Cockey, William, in his will made 14 Sep 1756, named his mother Elizabeth Baker (wife of Charles Baker (*q.v.*). Cockey m. Constant [-?-], and d. by 15 Jan 1758 on which date Constant had m. 2nd, William Randall (*q.v.*) (Harrison, "St. Thomas' Parish Register:" 71).

Cockey, William, and Hannah Owings, b. 17 April 1743, daughter of Samuel and Urath, were m. 30 June 1771 by Rev. William Edmndson ("Records from an Old [Owings] Bible." *MG* 2:273).

Cockin, John, and wife Ann in Nov 1750 were allowed 1000 lbs. tob. for their maintenance (BACP TR#6:20).

Coe, William, m. by 2 Nov 1764, Susannah, daughter of Susannah Herod or Harrod (BAWB 3:13; MDAD 67:208).

Coe. See also Goe.

Coffee, John, and Miss Elizabeth Jamima Woodward were m. last eve. by Rev. Hagerty (*Baltimore Telegraphe* 18 May 1798; BAML). Joseph Perigo (*q.v.*), in his will made 12 Aug 1800 named his half-sister Sarah Parks, and her daughter Elizabeth Jemima Coffee (BAWB 6:319).

Cogen, Dennis, native of Ireland, and Mary Stewart, widow of Robert Stewart, born near Annapolis, were m. by banns on 5 July 1795, at St. Peter's Catholic Church, Baltimore (*Piet*: 130).

Coggins, [-?-], m. by Jan 1794 Margaret, daughter of John Sheppard who named his grandchildren John and Elizabeth Coggins (BAWB 6:281).

Coghlan, William, of Washington, D. C., and Catharine Kirk, were m. by lic. 10 Nov 1794, at St. Peter's Catholic Church, Baltimore (*Piet*: 130).

Cohen, Dr., and Mrs. Margaret Quisic, both of Baltimore, were m. last eve. (*Baltimore Telegraphe* 10 Aug 1797).

Cole, [-?-], m. by 28 June 1781 Sarah, daughter of Richard Hooker (BAWB 3:428).

Cole, [-?-], m. by 1 Feb 1788, Sarah, who received an equal share of the estate of John Stinchcomb (BAAD 10:319).

Cole, Angelica, on 28 Dec 1738 was named as a daughter-in-law in the will of Alexander Grant (*q.v.*) (MWB 22:26 abst. in *Md. Cal. of Wills* 8:13).

Cole, Christopher, m. by 30 July 1776 Sarah, daughter of Hannah ([-?-]) Tipton Bosley and sister of Samuel and Mordecai Tipton (BAWB 3:325; BACT 4:186).

Cole, Ezekiel, m. by 5 March 1783 Sarah, daughter of Thomas Rowland (BAWB 3:540).

Cole, James, and Sophia [-?-] were m. by 27 Nov 1783 when their son Thomas was b. ("John Hanson Bible," *MBR* 2:55).

Cole, John, m. by 23 Sep 1723 Dinah, daughter of Matthew Hawkins, who named his own daus. Mary, Dinah, Ann and Elizabeth Hawkins in his will dated 14 April 1705 and proved 24 April 1705 (BALR IS#G:208; MWB 3:446).

Cole, John, and Margaret Cunningham were m. on 27 Dec 1782 (Marr. Returns of Rev. William West, Scharf Papers, MS. 1999 at MdHS). On 9 Jan 1786 Margaret was named as a daughter of Michael Cunningham who also named a granddaughter Ann Cole (BAWB 4:125).

Cole, John, and Miss Mary McDonough, daughter of John McDonough, both of Baltimore, were m. last eve. by Rev. Dr. Allison (*Maryland Journal and Baltimore Advertiser* 7 Feb 1797).

Cole, Mordecai, m. by 21 Jan 1763 Elizabeth, daughter of Richard Bond (BAWB 2:360); on 27 July 1767 Mordecai Cole received a share of Richard Bond's estate (MDAD 57:193).

Cole, Richard Miller, and Sabina Haile were m. on 15 May 1735 (Harrison, "St. Paul's Parish Register:" 153). Cole d. by 27 Oct 1770, when his wife Sabina, daughter of Nicholas Hale, m. 2nd, by that date, Philip Deaver (*q.v.*) (BALR AL#C:105).

Cole, Skipwith, and Elizabeth Gilbert were m. on 22 Jan 1797 (Marr. Register of Rev. John Allen for St. George's Parish, Ms. at MdSA). She was the widow of Michael Gilbert (*q.v.*).

Cole, Stephen, and Rachel Gorsuch were married by license dated 3 Nov 1792 (BAML). On 8 Dec 1792 Rachel was named as a daughter of Charles and Eleanor Gorsuch; Eleanor was named as a daughter of John Bond (BAWB 5:75; BAAD 11:530).

Cole, Thomas, Jr., m. Sarah Price on 23 d. 4 m. 1747 (Records of Gunpowder Meeting, at MdSA). Sarah was a daughter of Mordecai Price and an heir of Elizabeth Price of Baltimore Co. (BALR B#H:764; BAAD 6:146).

Cole, Thomas, of West River, Anne Arundel Co., was m. last eve. at Mr. John Battery's, Patapsco Neck, to Elizabeth Dorsey of Baltimore Co. (*Federal Gazette and Baltimore Daily Advertiser* 29 Dec 1798).

Cole, Thomas, and Elizabeth Welsh, were m. Fri. eve. by Rev. Richards (*Baltimore American* 21 April 1800).

Cole, Thomas B., merchant, was m. Wed. eve. by Rev. Mr. Ireland, to Elizabeth Smith, daughter of William Smith, Esq. of this city (*Federal Gazette and Baltimore Daily Advertiser* 15 Nov 1799). Thomas B. Cole and Elizabeth Smith were m. on13 Nov 1799 (Harrison "St. Paul's Parish Register:" 380). On 21 June 1800 Elizabeth was named as an heir of Abraham Smith (BAAD 13:282).

Cole, William, m. by 4 Oct 1688, Ann, relict of David Adams of Baltimore Co. (MDTP 14:99).

Cole, William, m. by 15 June 1764, Ruth, daughter of John Cross who also named a grandson Abraham Cross of William (BAWB 2:179).

Cole (Coale), William, m. by 8 June 1790, Sarah, heir of William Harvey and legatee of Priscilla Harvey (BAAD 10:158, 386).

Cole, William, and Miss Rachel Waters, both of Baltimore Co., were m. last Thurs. eve. by Rev. Richards (*Weekly Museum* 12 Feb 1797 in *MGSB* 20 (3) (Summer 1979).

Colegate, [-?-], m. by 17 Feb 1777, Cassandra, daughter of Penelope Deye (BAWB 3:562).

Colegate, [-?-], m. by 1 March 1780 Elizabeth, daughter of Walter Moore of Gunpowder Forest, Baltimore Co., farmer (BAWB 3:450). By 8 June 1792 Elizabeth had m. 2nd, Charles Prosser (*q.v.*) (BAAD 11:61).

Colegate, [-?-], m by 25 July 1780 Honour, daughter of Edw. Tully who named his grandsons Richard and John Colegate (BAWB 3:464).

Colegate, Benjamin, m. by 15 Sep 1741 Charity, daughter of Benjamin Wheeler (BALR HWS#1-A:557; MWB 22:436 abst. in *Md. Cal. of Wills* 8:160).

Colegate, Elizabeth. See Charles Prosser.

Colegate, John, of Baltimore Co., stated he would not pay the debts of his wife Elizabeth, who had eloped (Annapolis *Maryland Gazette* 7 Sep 1769).

Colegate, Rebecca. See Murray, Rebecca.

Colegate, Richard, m. by 5 Aug 1701 Rebecca, daughter of Eleanor Herbert (BALR RM#HS:569). Rebecca m. 2nd, James Powell (*q.v.*).

Colegate, Thomas, m. Elizabeth Clarke on 3 April 1770 (Harrison, "St. John's Parish Register:" 260). She was a daughter of Robert Clarke (BALR AL#B: 609).

Coleman, [-?-], m. by 25 Aug 1740 Frances, daughter of Francis Brown, shipwright, of Back River, Baltimore Co., formerly of Va. (MWB 22:399 abst. in *Md. Cal. of Wills* 8:148).

Coleman, Duncan, m. by 16 April 1731 Sarah, admx. of Thomas Towson of Baltimore Co. (BAAD, 3:85; MDAD 11:9). On 7 Nov 1734, Coleman warned all persons he stated he would not pay the debts of his wife Sarah (BALR HWS#M:135).

Coleman, R'd (Richard?), m. Mary Hatten on 22 Aug 1765 (Harrison, "St. John's Parish Register:" 228).

Coleman, William, and Ann Labesius were m. on 31 July 1784 (First Presbyterian Church Register, mss. at MdHS: 3). She was the mother of Ann Lebesius who was a granddaughter of Ann Hammond who had died testate (BAOC Petition of John Hammond, 1800; BALR WG#V:497). John Labesius and Nancy Hammond were married by license dated 12 Sep 1778 (BAML).

Coleson, Elizabeth, was charged with bastardy at the March 1731/2 Court (BACP HS#7:224).

Colespeegle, Elizabeth, was charged with bastardy at the June 1728 Court (BACP HWS#6:31).

Colleton, Mary Ann, in 1763 was fined for fornication and bastardy (BAMI 1755-1763).

Collett, Abraham, and Hannah Curtis were married by license dated 15 Dec 1781 (BAML). 'Ann,' admx.of Abraham Collett, m. by 13 Aug 1796 Isaac Marshall (*q.v.*).

Collett, John, of Baltimore Co., d. by 1693/4, leaving an admx. Elizabeth who was also widow of Miles Gibson (*q.v.*), and formerly widow of Henry Hazlewood (*q.v.*) (INAC 12:150). She was also the widow of Richard Edmonds (*q.v.*).

Colley, [-?-], m. by 21 June 1755 Mary, daughter of John Hill, whose will of the above date names Mary's son Hugh Colley (BAWB 3:92).

Collier, James, m. by 28 March 1674, [-?-], widow of Edward Ayres (q.v.) of Bush River, Baltimore Co., who d. leaving a widow, now dec., and a daughter Elizabeth Ayres (MDTP 6:178).

Collier, John, d. by 10 March 1673 having m. Ann, widow of James Stringer (*q.v.*) of Anne Arundel Co.; she then m. by 10 March 1673 William York (*q.v.*). Collier and Ann had issue John, Philip, William, Sarah, Eliza, and Jane Collier (MDTP 6:148).

Collier, John, m. by March 1684/5 Sarah, sister of Abraham Holman and widow of George Hooper (*q.v.*) (INAC 10:168, 169; MDTP 14:101; BALR HW#2:38; BACP D:252). She later m. John Hall (*q.v.*). John and Sarah Collier were called brother and sister in the undated will (proved 1 June 1686) of Abraham Holman of BA Co. (MWB 4:219). On 23 July 1686 Sarah Collier, admx. posted bond to administer the estate of Abraham Holman (BAAB 3:215).

Collings, [-?-], m. by 1 Sep 1731, [-?-], daughter of Samuel Ward (*q.v.*), by whom he had Simeon, Samuel, and Amey Collings (MWB 20:356, abst. in *Md. Cal. of Wills* 6:217).

Collins, Francis, on 10 April 1729 was named as a son-in-law in the will of Mathew Molton (MWB 18:398 abst. in *Md. Cal. of Wills* 5:199).

Collins, George, and Sarah Bailey were m. on 26 Dec 1790 (Harrison, "St. James Parish Register: 3). On 3 Sep 1795 Sarah was named as a daughter of Thomas Bailey (BAWB 5:316).

Collins, George, widower, and Sarah Joyce, widow, were m. by lic. dated 30 Nov1799, at St. Peter's Catholic Church, Baltimore (*Piet*: 130).

Collins, James, in Aug 1716 was charged with begetting a bastard on the body of Susanna Simpson (BACP IS#1A: 56).

Collins, John, and Mary Carney were m. by lic. on 27 Jan 1785 at St. Peter's Catholic Church, Baltimore (*Piet*: 130).

Collins, Robert, on 11 April 1737 was summoned by the vestry of St. George's Parish and promised to turn Anna Sylbey away and to have no society with her whatsoever. On 6 June 1737 Collins and Sylbey were ordered returned to the Court for not separating and refraining from each other's company (Reamy, *St. George's Parish Register*:104).

Collins, Sarah [or Silence], was charged with bastardy and fined 30 shillings at the Nov 1756 Court) (BACP BB#C: 312).

Collins, Timothy, Sergeant in the Rev. Army, d. 24 Dec 1834, was m. to Elizabeth McFee on 21 April 1777 by Rev. Mr. Chase, Pastor of the Lutheran Church [*sic*] in Baltimore [N.B.: The dates given by Elizabeth Collins differ from the dates given by her son Charles Collins, who stated that his mother Elizabeth died 30 Nov 1837]; Timothy and Elizabeth had seven surviving children: Sarah, Nancy, James, Isaac, Charles, Hannah, and Elizabeth (Rev. War Pension Application of Elizabeth Collins: W-3186). Timothy Collins and Elizabeth McFee were married by license dated 21 April 1778 (BAML).

Collison, William, m. Susanna Adams on 3 Dec 1714 (Harrison, "St. John's Parish Register:" 4). She was the admx. of William Addams (MDTP 22:481).

Colp, [-?-], m. by 5 June 1789 Elizabeth, daughter of Michael Steitz (BAWB 4:364).

Coltrider, Devolt, m. by 23 Nov 1796 Catherine Kepper, daughter of Vincent Kepper (BAAD 12:219).

Colvin, Philip, and Miss Rosetta Desrameaux were m. by Right Rev. Bishop Carroll [date not given] (*Maryland Journal and Baltimore Advertiser* 4 Jan 1793). They were m. at St. Peter's Catholic Church, Baltimore (*Piet*: 130).

Combest, Keturah, was charged with bastardy at the June 1716 Court (BACP IS#C:64). Keturah, daughter of John Combest was b. at Swan Creek on 10 Oct 1695 9Reamy. *St. George's Parish Register:* 1). She may be the 'Anna Lurey' Combest whose son John was born 4 June 1715 (Reamy, *St. George's Parish Register*: 18).

Combest, Martha, was charged with bastardy at the March 1718/9 Court but refused to name the father of her son Jacob, b. 10 Nov 1718 (BACP IS#C:64). Martha Combest, daughter of John, was b. at the head of Coletts Creek on 9 Sep 1700. Her son Jacob Combest was born 10 Nov 1718 (Reamy. *St. George's Parish Register:* 7, 21).

Combest, Martha, in 1763 was convicted of bastardy (BAMI 1755-1763).

Combest, Thomas, on 11 April 1737 appeared before the Vestry of St. George's Parish and produced a certificate of his marriage with Elizabeth Thornbury, on 20 Nov 1735, the rites having been performed by Elisha Gatchell, Justice of the Peace in Pennsylvania (Reamy, *St. George's Parish Register*: 104).

Combly, James, m. by 10 Jan 1793, Jane Partridge, who received an equal share of the estate of D. B. Partridge (BAAD 11:179).

Combo, Elizabeth, servant of William Hammond, was charged with bastardy at the March 1739/40 Court and was presented at the June 1740 Court (BACP HWS#TR:140, 239-240).

Comins, John, and Christine Grogen were m. by banns on 30 Jan 1785 at St. Peter's Catholic Church, Baltimore (*Piet*: 130).

Conckin, John, on 9 Dec 1701 was conv. 50 a. of land by his father-in-law Abraham Taylor (BALR HW#2:114).

Comley, Jacob, on 27 d., 12 m., 1769, was disowned for marrying contrary to the approved rule for Friends ("Minutes of Gunpowder Monthly Meeting," *QRNM:*59). [No other marriage reference found].

Comley, John, on 27 d. 1 m. 1776 was charged with marrying a young woman of a different persuasion ("Minutes of Gunpowder Monthly Meeting," *QRNM:*66). [No other marriage reference found].

Comley. Mary. See Nicholas Merryman.

Comley, Rachel. See Hooker, Rachel.

Conaway, Charles, m. by 13 June 1787 [-?-], daughter of Solomon Stocksdale (BAAD 9:58).

Condon, Richard, and Arey Franklin were married by license dated 6 Jan 1787 (FRML). On 15 Aug 1798 'Aerey" was named as a representative of Thomas Franklin (BAAD 12:467; BALR WG#64:431).

Condron, John, m. by 20 Feb 1770 Anne, widow of [-?-] Brown (BALR AL#B:202).

Cone, Margaret, in April 1796 was made guardian of Elizabeth, Mary, and Daniel Cone; she was a daughter of Henry Cone who d. by April 1796 (BAOC 3:188).

Coney, [-?-], m. by 14 Nov 1770 Mary, daughter of John Hatton (BAWB 3:159).

Conn (Con), Hugh, m. by 1718, [-?-], Elizabeth, extx. of Thomas Todd (MDTP 23:194, 28:2-ff.).

Conn, Hugh, m. 2nd, Sabilla [-?-]. On 26 July 1718 Hugh Conn and Sibia [*sic*] Durrant signed the inventory of Anthony Durrant of Baltimore Co. as next of kin (MINV 1:492).

Connaway, [-?-], m. by 5 Sep 1779 Ruth, sister of John Owings (BAWB 3:384).

Connell, John, his wife Mary were the parents of Eliza, who, on 20 June 1761, was named in the will of William Nicholson (BAWB 2:346). Mary m. 1st, John Forty (*q.v.*) 2nd, John Connell, 3rd, William Nicholson (*q.v.*), and 4th, Elisha Hall (*q.v.*).

Connelly, Robert, and Mary Preston were m. by banns 10 July 1789 at St. Peter's Catholic Church, Baltimore (*Piet*: 130).

Conner, Arthur, and Mary Loney were m. by lic. on 12 Dec 1785 at St. Peter's Catholic Church, Baltimore (*Piet*: 130).

Conner, Margaret, servant of Luke Trotten, was charged with bastardy at the March 1740/1 Court and again at the Nov 1742 Court (BACP TB&TR:20, TB#D:59).

Connolly (Conley), Margaret, confessed to bastardy at the June 1737 Court and named Nicholas Hutchins as the father of the child; however Thomas Hands was presented for begetting a bastard on the body of Margaret Conley (BACP HWS#1A:57, 62).

Conny, Elizabeth, was charged with bastardy at the March 1746/7 Court (BACP TB&TR#1:378).

Conrod, Henry, d. by 2 Feb 1787, having m. Elizabeth [-?-], who m. 2nd, George Solomon (*q.v.*). Conrad left a minor son John, a ward of Englehardt Yeiser (BAGA 1:16; BOCP Petition re: Henry Conrod, 1787, Box 2, Folder 17)

Conrod (Conrad), Henry, son of Henry Conrad, dec., on 14 Oct 1795 was made a ward of Engelhard Yeiser (BAOC 1:228, 299-300).

Constable, Thomas, d. by 10 Feb 1756 by which time his admx. Frances had m. Thomas Pert (q.v.) (MDTP 36:267).

Constable, Thomas, m. by 6 Oct 1770 Mary Magdalen, daughter of George Frederick Brown and sister of Jacob Frederick Brown (BALR AL#B:507; BAWB 5:35). In

1792 Francis, Thomas, and Jacob Constable were legatees of Jacob Brown and Thomas Constable was appointed their guardian (BAOC 2:251).

Constantine (Constanty), Patrick, m. Ann Bond, daughter of Richard Bond, on 29 Sep 1760 (Harrison "St. Thomas' Parish Register:" 72; BAWB 2:360).

Conveatherum, Mary, servant of Thomas Sligh was charged with bastardy at the Aug 1739 Court (BACP HWS#TR:1).

Conway, America [*sic*], Esq., and Miss Polly Sadler, both of Baltimore Co., were m. recently by Rev. Richards (*Maryland Journal and Baltimore Advertiser* 4 Jan 1793; BAML).

Conway, James, was married last Sat, evening by Dr. Patrick Allison to Miss Elizabeth Atkinson, both of this town (*Baltimore Evening Post* 27 Nov 1792; the BAML gives the bride's name as Amelia Elizabeth Atkinson).

Conway, William, and Hannah Stewart were married by license dated 11 April 1795 (BAML). Hannah Conway was named as a daughter of John Stewart; she and her husband had a son, Joel, aged about 3 in 1799 (BAOC Petition of Thomas Morgan, 1799).

Conyngham, David Mayfield, m. by 17 Sep 1793 Mary, cousin of William West (BAWB 5:309).

Conyngham, Capt. John, and Peggy Mathers, daughter of Capt. Joseph Mathers of Fell's Point, were m. last Tues. eve. (*Maryland Gazette or Baltimore General Advertiser* 6 Feb 1787).

Conyngham, Capt. Robert, and Betsy Adams were married by license dated 23 May 1783 (BAML; *Maryland Journal and Baltimore Advertiser* 30 May 1783).

Cooch, William, of Newcastle Co., and Peggy, only daughter of Zebulon Hollingsworth, Sr., were m. 24th ult. (*Maryland Journal and Baltimore Advertiser* 8 Dec 1789).

Cook, [-?-], m. by 17 Jan 1785 Rachel, daughter of John Parrish, who was 'aged and infirm' (BAWB 4:87).

Cook, [-?-], m. by 28 Feb 1799 Ann, daughter of Robert Neilson (BAWB 6:167).

Cook, Elizabeth, was charged with bastardy at the March 1744/5 Court and was fined (BACP Liber 1743-1745, pp. 480-481).

Cook, Jeremiah, m. by 25 Sep 1739, Elizabeth, extx. of Philip Sindall (*q.v.*) (MDTP 31:44; MDAD 17:300).

Cook (Cooke), John, m. Sarah West on 30 Dec 1726 (Harrison, "St. George's Parish Register:" 243). She was a daughter of Robert West (BALR IS#H:395).

Cook, John, m. Mary Price on 29 Jan 1748 (Harrison "St. Paul's Parish Register:" 162). She was a daughter of John Price (BAWB 3:496).

Cook, William, aged 46, deposed on 20 Jan 1730/1, naming his father-in-law Samuel Seeley (BALC HWS#3 #26).

Cook, William, m. by 12 May 1792 [-?-], who received a share of the estate of Edward Hewitt (BAAD 11:49).

Cooke, Richard, son of William Cooke, and Miss Elizabeth Van Wyck, daughter of William Van Wyck of Baltimore, were m. Mon. eve. by Rev. Ireland (*Baltimore Telegraphe* 26 Nov 1800).

Cooke, Thomas, m. by 6 Sep 1786, [-?-], heir of John Parrish (BAAD 8:307).

Coop, Richard, m. Hannah Stansbury on 6 Dec 1747 (Harrison, "St. John's Parish Register:" 242). She was the admx. of Solomon Stansbury (*q.v.*) (MINV 37:220).

Cooper, [-?-], m. by 29 Nov 1769 Hannah, daughter of Thomas Wheeler (BAWB 3:171).

Cooper, [-?-], m. by 28 May 1794 Eleanor, daughter of John Gill (BAWB 5:467).

Cooper, John, left England about 20 years earlier, and now was urged to contact his daughter Mary, living in Baltimore (*Maryland Journal and Baltimore Advertiser* 9 Jan 1775).

Cooper, John, of Baltimore stated he would not pay the debts of his wife Ann who had behaved herself in such a manner that he could no longer live with her' her conduct had been occasioned by his 'malicious neighbors." The next door neighbor to the westward was her principal tutor (*Maryland Journal and Baltimore Advertiser* 27 June 1786).

Cooper, John, and Agnes Davidson were married by license dated 18 May 1784 (BAML). On 3 May 1787 Agnes was named as a daughter of Andrew Davidson (BAWB 4:239; BALR WG#OO:517).

Cooper, John, and Apelonia Shaffer were married by license dated 16 March 1791 (BAML). On 16 March 1791 she was named as the extx. of Christian Shaver or Schaefer (*q.v.*) (BAAD 10:485, 11:347). On 24 Sep 1793, Apolonia, extx., posted bond to administer the estate of John Adam Shaver, whose will made 20 Aug 1793 named his mother Apolonia Cooper as his extx. (BAWB 5:124; BAAB 7:466).

Cooper, Margaret, servant of Luke Trotten, in March 1740/1 was tried for bastardy (BACP TB&TR:20).

Cooper, Nicholas, and Sarah [-?-] were m. by 31 Aug 1789 when their daughter Hannah was b. ("Lukens-Cooper Family Bible," *HABFR* 2:38).

Cooper, Nicholas, son of Nicholas and Sarah, on 22 d. 9 m. 1791 announced his intention to marry Sarah Balderson, daughter of Isaiah and Martha Balderson who were present ("Minutes of Deer Creek Meeting," *QRNM:* 150).

Cooper (Copper), Stephen, m. by 13 June 1767 Susannah, daughter of Robert Morgan (BALR B#P: 615).

Copas. See Copus.

Cope, Eleanor, confessed to bastardy at the Aug 1746 Court and was ordered to be whipped. John Wilmot admitted he was the father of her child. Her daughter Elizabeth, b. 29 May 1744 was bound to serve Samuel Owings until she reached the age of 16 (BACP TB&TR#1:116, 23, 241, 248).

Cope, Jasper, Baltimore merchant, and Rebecca Shoemaker, daughter of Joseph Shoemaker of Baltimore were m. at the Friends Meeting House for the Northern District of Philadelphia on 14th inst. (*Federal Gazette and Baltimore Daily Advertiser* 23 Oct 1800).

Copeland, [-?-], m. by17 Sep 1756 Mary, daughter of George Little (MWB 3:321).

Coppersmith, Peter, m. by 9 April 1800 Elizabeth, daughter of Basil Hickman (BAAD 13:233).

Copperstone, George, of North Hundred, Baltimore Co. stated he would not pay the debts of his wife Jane (*Maryland Journal and Baltimore Advertiser* 15 Sep 1778).

Copus (Copas), John, m. by Nov 1685, Ann, widow of Matthew Wood (BACP D:356).

Copus, John, m. by 30 March 1699, Sarah, widow of Edward Teale (*q.v.*), and mother of Ales Teale (BALR TR#RA:538). Sarah m. 3rd, Patrick Murphy (*q.v.*) (BALR TR#RA:38; MDTP 19A:119; INAC 23:90).

Corbeley, Nicholas, and Hannah Kneass were m. by lic. dated 20 Nov 1790 (BAML).

Corbett?, William, m. by 26 Jan 1796 Catherine, daughter of Cornelius Leary (BALR WG#UU:275).

Corbin, [-?-], m. by 21 April 1718 Jane, daughter of William Wilkinson (MWB 14:503 abst. in *Md. Cal. of Wills* 4:162; BALR AL#A:356).

Corbin, John, m. by 29 Nov 1794 Rachel, daughter of George Harryman (BAWB 5:236; BAOC Petition of George Harryman, 1799).

Corbin, Nicholas, eldest son of Edward Corbin, on 21 June 1717 was named as grandson in the will of John Barrett of Baltimore Co. (MWB 14:544 abst. in *Md. Cal. of Wills* 4:246).

Corbin, William, and Catherine Leary were m. by license 14 July 1792, at St. Peter's Catholic Church, Baltimore (*Piet:* 130; BAML gives the bride's name as Catharine Maryann Leary).

Corbley, Nicholas, of Baltimore, and Hannah Kneass of Philadelphia were m. last Sat, eve. (*Maryland Journal and Baltimore Advertiser* 23 Nov 1790; BAML).

Cord, Abraham, on 25 Feb 1734, with Elizabeth Hargas was summoned by the Vestry of St. George's Parish, for unlawful cohabitation. On the last Sat. in Feb 1736 Abraham Cord appeared before the Vestry of St. George's Parish and promised never to have any society with Elizabeth Hargas, nor to admit her to his home or on any premises he may erect (Reamy. *St. George's Parish Register:*103). On the last Saturday in July 1737 Cord and Hargas were returned to the Court. On 2 May 1738 Patrick Kilmurry and his wife were summoned to inform the Grand Jury of what they knew to be unlawfully enacted between Cord and Hargas. On 26 June 1740 Cord and Hargas were again summoned to appear before the vestry the first Tuesday in May. On 3 Nov 1746 he was discharged for putting her away.

Cord, Abraham, and Mary Pritchard were m. 19 Feb 1733 in St. George's Parish (Reamy, *St. George's Parish Register:* 270). On 10 Aug 1734 Cord warned all persons that his wife Mary had absented herself from him, and he stated he would not pay her debts (BALR HWS#M:97). [Mary joined Abraham Cord in a deed dated 15 March 1735. Mary was a sister of Joseph Pritchard, dec. (BALR HWS#M:401, IS#IK:358).

Cord, Hannah, had a son Isaiah b. 12 Oct 1736 (Harrison, "St. George's Parish Register:" 94); Hannah m. Abraham Taylor (*q.v.*), and 2nd, Edward Munday (*q.v.*).

Cordery, Philip, stated his wife Sarah had eloped from him (*Maryland Journal and Baltimore Advertiser* 5 Jan 1779).

Corkin, Grace, (formerly Mason) on 26 d. 8 m. 1790, was condemned for going out in marriage ("Minutes of Gunpowder Meeting," *QRNM:*89). [No other marriage reference found].

Corne, John, m, by Aug 1714, Elizabeth, extx. of John Mortimer (BACP IS#IB:566).

Cornelius, John, and his wife Sarah on 17 Feb 1717 posted bond to administer the estate of Stephen White, carpenter (BAAB 4:50; MDAD 2:140; 3:507; BAAD 1:279).

Cornthwait, John, son of Thomas and Elizabeth, of Bucks Co., Penna., and Mary Matthews, daughter of Oliver and Hannah, were m. on 17 d., 4 m., 1771 ("Records of Gunpowder Meeting," MS. at MdSA; BAWB 3:446). John d. by 26 Jan 1787, leaving minor children John and Robert. Oliver Matthews, guardian, filed a guardian account (BAGA 1:14, 15).

Cornwell, Ann, was named as a daughter-in-law of Richard Gwinn in his will dated 19 Sep 1692; he left her *Gwin's Farm* (MWB 6:48 abst. in *Md. Cal. of Wills* 2:65). By about 1707 the land was held by Henry Waters (*MRR:*103).

Cosden, Alphonso, m. some time after 10 June 1685, Anne, daughter of Christopher Beanes, who was granted 1000 a. *Christopher's Camp* on that date (BALR IS#H:101).

Coskery, Arthur, d. by 14 Feb 1787 leaving minor children James, Martha, Elizabeth, and John; Francis Coskery, guardian, filed an account (BAGA 1:21, 23) On 18 April 1792 his widow Ann (nee Creaton) was entitled to a share of the estate of Robuck Lynch (BAAD 11:40).

Coskery, Francis, in his will, made 24 Feb 1797, named his niece Martha O'Brien, and named Charles O'Brien (*q.v.*) his executor (BAWB 6:230).

Coskery, John, hatter of Baltimore, and Jacoba Clementina Spalding, daughter of Henry Spalding, hatter, were m. last Mon. (*Maryland Journal and Baltimore Advertiser* 24 Feb 1792).

Costley, Alice, was charged with bastardy at the June 1733 Court (BACP HWS#9:2).

Costley, James, d. by June 1765, leaving two orphans, James, aged 16, and John, aged 13, who were bound to Richard Hill to age 21; Hill agreed to teach them to write, read, and cast accounts, and at the expiration of their time he would give them each a suit of jersey or broadcloth, two white shirts, a pair of shoes, stockings, a castor hat, and one neck cloth (BAMI 1765).

Costley, Mary, was charged with bastardy at the March 1737/8 Court and was presented at the June 1738 Court (BACP (BACP HWS#1A:169, 221).

Costley, Oliver, was charged with bastardy at the June 1733 Court (BACP HWS#9:2).

Costos, Mary, servant of William Lewis, was convicted by a jury of Negro bastardy at the June 1743 Court. Her Mulatto daughter Estre, aged about one year old in March 1743/4, was sold to William Lewis and was to serve him to age 31; Mary was to serve the county for seven years after her present servitude. She was charged with bastardy again at the Nov 1743 Court and presented at the March 1743/4 Court (BACP TB#D:185, Liber 1743-1745:71, 88-89, 155, 163).

Cotrall (Cottrall), John, and Ann Wood were m. in 1752 (Harrison, "St. John's Parish Register:" 241). In his will made 26 Nov 1766, John Cottrell named his wife Sarah, daughter-in-law Martha Wood, his son-in-law Luke Raven, his brother Thomas Cottrell and a cousin John Cottrell (BAWB 3:38). Cotrall's estate was administered on 16 April 1768, and a payment was made to the unnamed wife of John Hendrickson for her share of the estate of William Wood (MDAD 59:300).

Couch, Charles, of Baltimore, announced that he and his wife Ann had parted by mutual consent (*Maryland Journal and Baltimore Advertiser* 7 July 1786).

Coughlin, Richard, stated he would not pay the debts of his wife Mary (*Maryland Journal and Baltimore Advertiser* 21 Oct 1777).

Coulling, James, m. by 26 July 1780 Elizabeth Sims, widow of Christopher Sims (BALR WG#D:619, WG#M:316).

Coulon, John Baptist, and Mary Mangee were m. 12 Dec 1784 at St. Peter's Catholic Church, Baltimore (*Piet*: 130).

Coulson, Joseph Stump, orphan of Thomas Coulson, in Feb 1795 was made a ward of John Stump (BAOC 3:132).

Coulson, Thomas, d. by Feb 1795, leaving orphans George, Eliza, and Martha, who were made wards of their mother Martha Coulson (BAOC 3:132).

Coulter, Alexander, and Betty McCaskey, daughter of Mr. Alexander McCaskey, were m. last eve. at Fell's Point (*Maryland Journal and Baltimore Advertiser* 30 March 1792; Register of First Presbyterian Church, Baltimore, MS. at MdHS:4).

Coulter, John, Esq., and Polly M'Caskey were m. at Fell's Point last Sun. eve. (*Maryland Journal and Baltimore Advertiser* 5 Feb 1788; Register of First Presbyterian Church, Baltimore, MS. at MdHS:4; BAML).

Courney. See Courtney.

Course, John, of Kent Co., Md., on 1 d. 10 m. 1770, stated he intended to marry Cassandra Rigbie, daughter of James Rigbie who was present and gave his consent ("Minutes of Deer Creek Meeting," *QRNM*:134).

Coursey, William, m. by 27 Aug 1777, Hannah, sister of Edward Hanson (BAWB 4:107). Coursey d. by 24 Feb 1785, and Hannah m. 2nd, by that date, Samuel Wilson (*q.v.*) (BALR WG#Y:468). When Edward Hanson's estate was divided, Hannah's son John Amon 'Scorce' [*sic*] was named (BACT 1785-1788, MS 2865 at MdHS: 75).

Courtenay, Henry, and Miss Isabella Purviance were m. last eve. by Rev. Allison (*Baltimore Telegraphe* 11 Jan 1799).

Courtenay, Hercules, m. Mary Drury by license dated 16 Oct 1790 (BAML). On 13 Oct 1792. Mary Drury was named as a sister of Ann [-?-], wife of Dr. John Boyd (BAWB 4:404; BAAD 11:143).

Courtenay, John, m. Frances Greenfield on 16 Aug 1739 (Harrison "St. George's Parish Register:" 305). On 30 May 1763 they were named as heirs of William Greenfield BAWB 3:4).

Courtenay. See also Courtney.

Courtney, Hercules, on 18 June 1774 was named as a brother-in-law in the will of John Little (BAWB 3:298).

Courtney, Jonas, and Comfort Cole were m. 15 Jan 1738 (Harrison, "St. George's Parish Register:" 304). On 21 Jan 1744 their son Thomas was b. ("John Hanson Bible," *MBR* 2:55).

Courtney, Robert, and Hannah Cook were m. on 2 Oct 1740 (Harrison, "St. George's Parish Register: 315). On 6 May 1741 Hannah was named as the extx. of William Cook (MDTP 31:166).

Courtney (Courtenay), Robert, m. Betsy, daughter of Richard Burland (*Maryland Journal and Baltimore Advertiser* 5 Oct 1790; BAML). She was one of the heirs at law of Richard Burland, dec. (BALR WG#57:643).

Courtney, Thomas, m. Sarah Hanson on 22 Aug 1765 ("Hanson Bible Record," *MGSB* 3 (3) (July 1962) 26-29).

Courtney. See also Courtenay.

Covenhaven. See Covenhover.

Covenhoven, George, of Baltimore Co., stated he would not pay the debts contracted by his wife Elizabeth, who has eloped from his bed and board without any just cause or provocation (*Federal Gazette and Baltimore Daily Advertiser* 16 July 1796).

Covenhoven, Jesse, m. by 16 Aug 1787 Elizabeth, daughter of Isaac Tyson (BAAD 9:91).

Covenhover (Covenhaven), William, and Eleanor Pindell were married by license dated 29 Aug 1785 (BAML). By 11 Oct 1790, Eleanor was named as having received share of £32.6.9 from the estate of John Pindell; she was also named as an heir of Eleanor Pindell (BAAD 10:286, 281, 12:231).

Coventry, Jacob, and Hannah Finney on 5 Feb 1771 were summoned by the vestry for unlawful cohabitation (Reamy, *St. George's Parish Register:* 111).

Cowan (Cowen), Alexander, m. Elinora Boyce on 2 May 1771 (Harrison, "St. John's Parish Register:" 262). She was a daughter of Rebecca Boyce, who called Cowan son-in-law and who named grandchildren Rebecca Cowan and Roger Boyce Cowan (BAWB 3:306).

Cowan, James, and Catherine Strider were m. by lic. 30 April 1799 at St. Peter's Catholic Church, Baltimore (*Piet*: 130; BALR WG#58:263).

Cowan, Sarah, was charged with bastardy at the June 1739 Court (BACP HWS&TR;85).

Cowan, Thomas, from Derry in Ireland, a non-Catholic, and Margaret Venny, widow, both residents of Fell's Point, were m. by lic. 14 July 1796, at St. Peter's Catholic Church, Baltimore (*Piet*: 130).

Cowdray, James, m. Ann Green in Sep 1723 (Harrison, "St. John's Parish Register:" 30). In Jan 1737 she m. Thomas Dawney (Harrison "St. John's Parish Register:" 30, 92). In Aug 1719 Jane Boone, widow, had conveyed to her granddaughters Catherine, Anne, and Martha Green, daughters of Matthew Green 150 a. *Joyce Trippas*, and in 1729 Ann Cowdrey conveyed *Choice Trippas, Green's Range,* and *Levy's Tribe* to Thomas Coale (BALR IS#K:193). Ann m. 2nd, Thomas Dawney (*q.v.*).

Cowley, Thomas, of Anne Arundel Co., m. by 10 June 1772 Ann, sister of William and John Barrett (BALR AL#E:111).

Cox, [-?-], d. by 1737 when his orphan Prudence was cared for by John Carpenter (Levy List for 1737).

Cox, [-?-], m. by 11 April 1787 Ruth, daughter of Joseph Bosley (BAAD 9:35).

Cox, [-?-], d. by 2 Feb 1790, having m. Mary, whose will made on that date named her brother Mark Alexander (BAWB 4:407).

Cox, Abraham, and Cassanna [Cassandra?] Tipton were married by license dated 30 Sep 1779 (BAML). She was a daughter of Samuel Tipton whose will of 30 Oct 1799 named his granddaughters Elizabeth and Sarah Cox (BAWB 7:334).

Cox, Dinah. See William Price Young.

Cox, Edward, m. by 7 June 1723 Jane, daughter of John Broad (BALR IS#G:194).

Cox, Elizabeth, was charged with bastardy at the March 1746/7 Court (BACP TB&TR#1:379).

Cox, Hannah, was charged with bastardy at the June 1731 Court and named Zachariah Gray as the father She was charged with bastardy at the June 1739 Court, the Nov 1742 Court, and the March 1746/7 Court (BACP (BACP HWS#7:156, HWS#9: 135, HWS#TR:10, 401, TB#D:59, and TB&TR#1:378).

Cox, Isaac, Jr., on 24 d. 10 m. 1793 was charged with marrying a woman not of our society with the assistance of a Baptist Preacher ("Minutes of Deer Creek Meeting," *QRNM:*153). [No other marriage reference found].

Cox, Isaac, sea captain, and Mary Blossom, widow, were m. by lic. 12 Jan 1799 at St. Peter's Catholic Church, Baltimore (*Piet*: 130).

Cox, Israel, and Elizabeth Hopkins were married by license dated 9 Nov 1785 (BAML). On 19 Feb 1788, she was named as a daughter of Richard Hopkins (BAAD 9:161).

Cox, Jacob, m. Elizabeth Merryman on 25 Sep 1722 (Harrison "St. Paul's Parish Register:" 147). She was a daughter of Charles Merryman, whose will named a grandson Merryman Cox (MWB 18:431 abst. in *Md. Cal. of Wills* 5:208). Elizabeth Merryman Cox m. 2nd, [-?-] Smith; her will dated 22 June 1770 named a son Merryman Cox (BAWB 3:175).

Cox, James, son of Thomas and Rebecca, b. 22 Feb 1738/9, killed at the Battle of Germantown, 4 Oct 1777, while a Major of the Third Baltimore Battalion, and Mary White, widow, nee Alexander, daughter of Moses and Mary (Wallace), b. 1738, d. 20 Feb 1790, were m. 15 Aug 1765 Harrison, "St. Paul's Parish Register:"

168; "Cox Bible Record," *MGSB* 32 (1) Winter 1991: 61, 62).

Cox, James, son of James and Mary (Alexander), b. 27 June 1770, was m. last eve. by Rev, Mr. Bend, to Miss Catharine Fulford (*Federal Gazette and Baltimore Daily Advertiser* 9 Dec 1796; BAML; "Cox Bible Record," *MGSB* 32 (1) Winter 1991: 61, 62).

Cox, Jane. See Edmund Quinlan.

Cox, Mark Alexander, son of James and Mary (Alexander), b. 25 May 1766, d. 20 Oct 1798, m. Maria Gresham on 10 April 1788 ("Cox Bible Record," *MGSB* 32 (1) Winter 1991: 61, 62).

Cox, Mary, in 1737 had a child who was being nursed [cared for] for six weeks by James Boreing (Levy List for 1737),

Cox, Mary, died leaving a will dated 2 Feb 1790 and proved 23 Feb 1790, naming her children Mark Alexander, James, Mary, and Rebecca (dec.) Cox, and her brother Mark Alexander, as well as a niece Mary Dysart (BAWB 4:407). Mary was the widow of James Cox who died leaving a will dated 13 Feb 1777 and proved 10 De 1777 (BAWB 3:338).

Cox, Matthew, and Priscilla Gott were m. by 25 Nov 1789 in Baltimore ("Marr. Returns of Ezekiel Cooper, Scharf Papers, MS 1005 at MdSA;" in *MGSB* 32 (1) (Winter 1991): 6).

Cox, Merriman, stated he would not pay the debts of his wife Eleanor (*Maryland Journal and Baltimore Advertiser* 34 April 1780).

Cox, Providence, in 1762 was fined for begetting a bastard (BAMI 1775-1763),

Cox, Samuel, and Elizabeth Hopkins were m. on 10 Nov 1785 (First Presbyterian Church Parish Register, Baltimore. Transcription, 1906, at MdHS). Elizabeth Cox, formerly Hopkins, on 25 d. 2 m. 1786 was charged with being m. to a member by a priest ("Minutes of Gunpowder Meeting," *QRNM*:81).

Cox, Sarah, was charged with bastardy at the June 1719 Court (BACP IS#C:198).

Cox, Winifred, in 1765 was fined for bastardy (BAMI 1755-1763).

Cox, Zebediah, m. by 4 June 1770 [-?-], daughter of Abraham Vaughn (BAAD 6:217).

Coxill, Henry J. of Baltimore stated he would not pay the debts of his wife Mary who had left his bed and board (*Maryland Journal and Baltimore Advertiser* 1 Oct 1794).

Coxsill, Mary (*alias* Mary Hagan), was charged with bastardy at the March 1709/10 Court (BACP IS#B94).

Crabtree, Elizabeth, in 1761 was fined for bastardy (BAMI 1755-1763).

Craddock. See Cradock.

Cradock, [-?-], m. by March 1796, Ann, sister of Hannah Worthington, who in her will of that date named her sister Ann Cradock (and her children Mary, Catherine, Elizabeth, and Ann Cradock) (BAWB 5:447).

Cradock (Craddock), Rev. Thomas, m. Catherine, daughter of John and Katherine Risteau on 31 March 1746 (Harrison "St. Thomas' Parish Register:" 70; BALR TB#E:276; BAWB 2:148).

Crage, [-?-], m. by 12 March 1773 Agnes, daughter of Solomon Wheeler (BAWB 4:204).

Craig, [-?-], m. by 10 April 1793, Acheson, heir of Joseph Hayes (BAAD 11:247).

Craig (Craggs, Craggie), John, and Mary Burgess were married 27 July 1775. They had a daughter Mary Craggie. Mary Burgess Craig m. 2nd, James Fishwick (*q.v.*) (Notes from "The Craggs-Burgess- Stansbury-McElhiney Prayer Book," *MGSB* 25 (1)

(Winter 1994), 58-59).

Craine, Anne, was charged with bastardy at the June 1730 Court and presented at the Aug 1730 Court (BACP HWS#6:415, HWS#7:8).

Cramer, Edward, and Mary Britt, natives of Ireland, were m. by lic. 31 Aug 1794 at St. Peter's Catholic Church, Baltimore (*Piet*: 130).

Cranford, Ann, was charged with bastardy in 1775 (BAMI 1775-1781:26).

Cranforth, Samuel, cordwainer, and Miss Parker, both of Baltimore, were m. last eve. by Rev. Bend (*Baltimore Daily Intelligencer* 6 March 1794).

Crashow. See Croshow.

Crass, Benjamin, m. by 23 Feb 1763, Maria Preissin ("First Record Book for the Reformed and Lutheran Congregations at Manchester, Baltimore (now Carroll) Co.," *MGSB* 35:267).

Crass, Joseph, m. by 23 Feb 1763, Anna Maria Leidigin ("First Record Book for the Reformed and Lutheran Congregations at Manchester, Baltimore (now Carroll) Co.," *MGSB* 35:267).

Crawford, [-?-], d. by 20 Feb 1789 leaving a widow Agnes (who had a son Eaton Crawford, and who m. 2nd, [-?-] Westernhouse (*q.v.*) (BAWB 4:341).

Crawford, Frances, (late Johns), on 5 d. 11 m. 1789 was reported to have been m. by a Baptist Preacher ("Minutes of Deer Creek Meeting," *QRNM:*147). On 23 d. 10 m. 1794, she produced a paper condemning herself for marrying outside the society by the assistance of a hireling teacher ("Minutes of Deer Creek Meeting," *QRNM:* 154). [No other marriage reference found].

Crawley (Cranley, Crowley), Daniel, m. by 13 Dec 1701 Jone, extx. of Christopher Brumbridge (Bembridge) (*q.v.*), and admx. of John Boy or Bay (INAC 21:173, 252; MDTP 19A:51, 58).

Crayton (Cretin), John, m. by 14 Aug 1754, Martha, daughter of Patrick Lynch (BACT TR#E:144; BFD 5:403). On 16 April 1792 his four children were named as heirs in Patrick Lynch's administration account: Patrick, James and John Creaton [*sic*], and Sarah Hunter (BAAD 1111:37).

Creighton (Cretin), Ann, was charged with bastardy at the Nov 1759 Court and named John Cretin as the father (BAMI 1757-1759:241).

Creighton, Capt. William, and Minny Weary, both of Fell's Point, were m. last eve. by Rev. Bend (*Baltimore Telegraphe* 22 Aug 1800).

Cresap (Crisup), Thomas, m. Hannah Johnson on 30 April 1727 (Harrison "St. George's Parish Register:" 247). She was a daughter of Daniel Johnson of Baltimore Co. (MDAD 15:203; BALR HWS#1-A, 291).

Cretin. See Creighton.

Crisall, Peter, and Margaret Richards, were m. by lic. on 6 Oct 1790 at St. Peter's Catholic Church, Baltimore (*Piet*: 130).

Crisup. See Cresap.

Crocker, Thomas, in his will made on 10 Dec 1792 named Mary Inloes, wife of David Inloes, Charles Caples Cole, Cassandra Cole, and Elizabeth Cole as the children of his deceased wife Delilah Crocker (BAWB 5:65). Crocker's children, Sarah, Actious, and John Crocker, in May 1796 were made wards of Charles C. Coale (BAOC 3:192).

Crockett, Benjamin, merchant, was m. to Miss Jenny Donnellan, both of Baltimore (*Maryland Journal and Baltimore Advertiser* 11 March 1785). They were m. in Baltimore Co. (BAML). Jane Crockett administered the estate of Benjamin

Crockett on 1 May 1793, 8 April 1794, and 15 April 1795. In the third account she stated she was guardian to Mary, Ann, and Benjamin Crockett (BAAD 11:267, 399, 538). In April 1795 Mary Ann and Benjamin (or Mary, Ann, and Benjamin were made wards of Jane Crockett (BOCP 3:151).

Crockett, Gilbert, and Mary Chew were m. in 1727 (Records of Nottingham Monthly Meeting, MS. at MdHS). She m. 2nd, James Harrison (*q.v.*).

Crockett, John, merchant of Baltimore, and Miss Graves, daughter of Col. Richard Graves of Kent Co., were m. [date not given] (*Maryland Journal and Baltimore Advertiser* 28 Nov 1786).

Crohan, Lawrence, of Baltimore Co. stated that his wife Nancy had eloped (*Maryland Journal and Baltimore Advertiser* 18 Feb1783).

Crohan, Matthew, and Jane Armstrong were m. by license dated 12 April 1783 (BAML). In July 1783 Crohan stated he would not pay the debts of his wife Jane (*Maryland Journal and Baltimore Advertiser* 15 July 1783).

Cromby. See Abercrombie.

Crommey, [-?-], m. by 14 Nov 1770, Ann, daughter of John Hatton (BAWB 3:159).

Cromwell, [-?-], m. by 4 d. 3 m. 1733, [Elle?], daughter of Sarah Giles, and sister of John and Jacob Giles (BALR HWS#M:9).

Cromwell, [-?-], m. by 11 June 1759 Ruth, daughter of Rachel Wilmot who named her grandchildren Ruth and William Cromwell in her will (BAWB 2:348; BAAD 7:114).

Cromwell, [-?-], m. by 2 June 1784 Chloe, daughter of William Kelly (BAWB 5:425).

Cromwell, [-?-], m. by 3 May 1790 Elizabeth, daughter of John Wooden, Sr. (BAWB 4:426).

Cromwell, Alexander, and Sarah Dorsey were m. on 17 April 1733 (Garrison, "St. Margaret's Parish Register," Anne Arundel Co., at MdHS: 109). On 8 March 1742 Sarah Dorsey was named as one of the residuary legatees of John Hammond (MDTP 31:359; MDAD 19:421).

Cromwell, Dinah, aged 14 or more, daughter of Wm., in Nov 1759 chose Richard Wilmot as her guardian (BAMI 1755-1763).

Cromwell, Elizabeth, widow, in her will made 15 Dec 1792 named her daughter Elizabeth Ashman and her grandsons Edward and Richard Cockey (BAWB 6:244).

Cromwell, John, on 3 March 1745 was named as a nephew in the will of John Rattenbury (MWB 24:446 abst. by Gibb).

Cromwell, John, m. by Nov 1757, Eleanor, daughter of Thomas and Eleanor (Dorsey) Todd. Eleanor Dorsey Todd m. 1st, William Lynch (*q.v.*) (BALR B#G:91, 93, 95; BAWB 2:266).

Cromwell, John, m. by 23 July 1760 Elizabeth, daughter of Elinor Lynch (MWB 31:26 abst. by Gibb; BAAD 6:197; MDAD 49:169).

Cromwell, John, and Urath Owings were m. on 6 Dec 1787 (Harrison, "St. Thomas' Parish Register:" 75); on 26 Nov 1792 Cromwell's wife was named as a daughter of Urath Owings, widow, who also named a granddaughter Urath Cromwell (BAWB 5:70).

Cromwell, Joseph, of Joseph and Comfort, b. 2 Sep 1741 in Baltimore Co., m. 3 March 1768, by Rev. Thomas Cradock, Ann Orrick, daughter of Nicholas and Hannah, b. 16 Dec 1750 ("Wesley Stevenson Bible Recorrd," *The Notebook* 21 (3) (Fall 2005) 12-15).

Cromwell, Nathaniel, Jr., and Miss Susannah Walker, daughter of Charles Walker, of Baltimore Co. were m. last Tues. by Rev. Butler (*Baltimore Telegraphe* 19 Jan 1799).

Cromwell, Richard, of Baltimore Co. m. 26 Oct 1697 Ann Besson, b. 26 Dec 1670, daughter of Thomas and Margaret (Saughier) Besson ("Philip Jones Bible," *MdHM* 14:76-79; and *MBR* 7:101).

Cromwell, Stephen, his wife Elizabeth and their daughter Ruth were named in the will made 6 Sep 1788 of Ruth Howard (BAWB 5:442).

Cromwell (Crumwell), Thomas, m. by 2 March 1707, Jemima, relict and extx. of James Murray (INAC 28:46).

Cromwell, Thomas, in Aug 1724 was charged with begetting a bastard on the body of Elizabeth Peacock (BACP IS&TW#1:438).

Cromwell, Thomas, later of Huntingdon Co., Pa., and Ann Waters were m. on 25 May 1784 (Marr. Returns of Rev. Thomas Chase, Scharf Papers, MS. 1999 at MdHS). On 16 Jan 1796 Ann was named as a daughter of Jacob Walters of Anne Arundel Co., Pa. (BALR WG#UU:210; BAML gives the bride's name as Waters).

Cromwell, William, d. by Feb 1685/6, by which date his wife Elizabeth (Trehearne), widow of William Ball (*q.v.*), had m. George Ashman (*q.v.*).

Cromwell, William, m. by 18 Feb 1748, Constant, daughter of John Willmott (MWB 25:531 abst. by Gibb). About six years prior to 8 May 1759 Charity was named as a daughter of Constant Ashman (MDTP 37:251). On 4 Nov 1752, Constant received a portion of the estate of John Willmott of Baltimore Co. (MDAD 33:157).

Cromwell, William, m. Eliz. Risteau on 10 June 1768 (Harrison, "St. John's Parish Register:" 232). She may be the Elizabeth Cromwell mentioned on 14 May [1796?] as Elizabeth Raven, and a sister of George Risteau of Baltimore Co. (BALR WG#VV:424).

Cromwell, William, m. by 8 Dec 1774, Elizabeth, daughter of William Raven (BALR AL#M:88). Elizabeth Cromwell on 3 Oct 1791 was named as a daughter in the will of Sarah Raven (BAWB 5:296).

Cromwell, Woolgist (Weelgist), and Venetia Dorsey were m. on 10 Feb 1740 (Harrison, "St. Margaret's Parish Register," Anne Arundel Co., at MdHS: 109). On 3 March 1743 Venetia was named as a legatee of John Hammond (MDTP 31:450; MDAD 19:421).

Croney, Jeremiah, m. Mary Coleman on 23 Dec 1766 (Harrison, "St. John's Parish Register:" 230). Mary was the admx. of Richard Coleman *(q.v.)* (BAAD 7:76, 304).

Crook, James, and Rachel Bailey were m. on 13 Jan 1784 (Marr. Returns of Rev. William West, Scharf Papers, MS.1999 at MdHS); on 23 Sep 1795 Rachel was named as a daughter of Thomas Bailey (BAWB 5:316).

Crook (Crooks), John, and Rachel Owings were married by license dated 16 Oct 1781 (BAML). On 19 April 1794 she was named as an heir of John Owings (BAAD 11:421).

Crook, Joseph, m. Priscilla Galloway on 24 April 1757 (Harrison, "St. John's Parish Register:" 215). She was the admx. of Salathiel Galloway (*q.v.*) (MINV 63:629; BAAD 6:1).

Crosby, John, aged 14 on next 12 Nov, son of Richard and Elizabeth Crosby of Baltimore Co., apprenticed himself to William McNutt of Baltimore Co., to learn the business of farming; on 21 July 1769 (BACT (BACT B#G:300).

Crosby (Crosley), Robert servant to Samuel Stansbury, in June 1757 was charged with begetting a bastard on the body of Elizabeth Sedgehill (BAMI 1755-1763:37).

Croshaw, William (Crashow), m. by 19 Sep 1682, Elizabeth, relict and admx. of Thomas Russell (*q.v.*); Elizabeth had m. 1st, William Hollis (*q.v.*), and 4th, by Aug 1685, William Harris (*q.v.*) (MDTP 12B:196; INAC 7C:330; BACP D:385).

Crosillant, Joachim, native of Bordeaux, and Charlotte Round were m. by lic. on 4 Sep 1794 at St. Peter's Catholic Church, Baltimore (*Piet*: 130).

Crosley. See Crosby.

Cross, [-?-], m. by 21 May 1782, Rebecca, daughter of Michael Gladman who in his will stated he was 'far advanced in years' (BAWB 4:381).

Cross, [-?-], m. by 14 April 1783, Tabitha, daughter of Samuel Stansbury (BAWB 3:539; BAAD 8:342).

Cross, Henry, m. by 6 Aug 1747, Mary, widow of John Royston (BALR TB#E:497).

Cross, Jane, before marriage Dunkin, on 24 d. 7 m. 1771, was charged with having gone out in marriage with a man of another society ("Minutes of Gunpowder Monthly Meeting," *QRNM:*61). [No other marriage reference found].

Cross, John, m. by 12 Aug 1725, Dianah (or Dinah), admx. of John Wheeler of Baltimore Co. (MINV 11:590; MDAD 11:494; MDTP 29:180).

Cross, John, son of Joseph of York Co., was b. 10 Dec 1733, m. by Nov 1760, when he and Edith sold 50 a. *John's Adventure* to Michael Deeds (BALR B#H:433); on 14 Oct 1781 Edith was named as a daughter of William and Margaret (Sing) Wiley, sister of Richard Wiley and of Ann who m. Thomas Hunt (BALR WG#G:496).

Cross, Joseph, m. by June 1727 Sarah, daughter of Henry Matthews (through her, Cross owned *Hughes' Chance,* laid out for Joseph Hughes (BALR HWS#3:15, HWS#M:90).

Cross, Joseph, m. Elizabeth Merryman on 13 Sep 1730 (Harrison "St. Paul's," p. 149). She was a daughter of Charles Merryman of Baltimore Co. (MDAD 17:187).

Cross, Mary (*alias* Mary Heeth), confessed to bastardy at the March 1756 Court and named Benjamin Barney as the father (BACP BB#A:29).

Cross, Robert, was m. Tues. last by Rev. Mr. Ellis, to Miss Catherine Hildebrand, daughter of Jacob Hildebrand, both of this town (*Federal Intelligencer and Baltimore Daily Gazette* 5 March 1795; BAML).

Cross, Thomas, m. by June 1727, Sarah, heir of Joseph Hughes (BALC HWS#3:15). She was named as a daughter of Henry Matthews (BALR IS#L:77, HWS#M:67, 90).

Crouch, James, m. Hannah Starkey on 22 Sep 1757 (Harrison, "St. John's Parish Register:" 216). She was the widow of Joshua Starkey (BALR B#G: 497). Joshua Starkey had m. Hannah Meads on 29 Sep 1743 (Harrison, "St. John's Parish Register:" 126). Hannah Crouch was a daughter of Benjamin Meed of Baltimore Co. (MWB 31:1084; BAWB 2:177).

Crouch, Joseph, m. Mary Lynch on 3 Jan 1719 (Harrison "St. Paul's Parish Register:" 147). Mary was formerly the wife of Robuck Lynch (BALR IS#L:114). Crouch was aged about 48, when he deposed on 25 Feb 1739, mentioning his wife, formerly the wife of Robuck Lynch (BALC HWS&BB#4: #79). Mary was the mother of William Lynch (BALR IS#G:36).

Crow, James, and Rachel Tevis were m. on 11 June 1789 (Marr. Register of Rev. Lewis Richards, MS. 690 at MdHS); Robert Tevis, Sr., in his will made 25 Oct 1796 named his daughter Rachel Crow (BAWB 5:475).

Crowley. See Crawley.

Croxall, Charles, m. Rebecca Moale on 23 July 1746 (Harrison "St. Paul's Parish Register:" 159). She was a sister of Richard Moale (BALR AL#G:300; BAWB 4:133).

Croxall, Capt. Charles, and Polly Morris were m. in Baltimore Town (*Maryland Journal and Baltimore Advertiser* 31 July1781; BAML).

Croxall, James, merchant of Baltimore, and Nelly, daughter of James Gittings, Esq., of Baltimore Co., were m. last Tues. eve. (*Maryland Gazette or Baltimore General Advertiser* 14 March 1788; BAML).

Croxall, John, of Baltimore Co., and Isabella Hanna of Baltimore were m, last Sat. eve. (*Baltimore Daily Repository* 30 Nov 1791; BAML).

Croxall, Richard, and Eleanor Buchanan were m. on 12 Dec 1748 (Harrison, "St. Paul's Parish Register:" 162). On 4 Feb 1749/50, she was named as a daughter of Dr. George Buchanan (MWB 27:280 abst. by Gibb). On 7 May 1782 Eleanor was named as a sister of Andrew and Archibald Buchanan in Richard Croxall's will (BAWB 4:36).

Cruikshank, Joseph, printer, and Rachel Saunders, daughter of Joseph Saunders, late of Baltimore, were m. at the Friends Meeting House in Pine St. (*Maryland Journal and Baltimore Advertiser* 16 Jan 1797).

Crumwell. See Cromwell.

Cruse, Christopher, and Miss Margaret Bricker, both of Baltimore, were m. last Sun. eve. by Rev. Otterbein (*Baltimore Telegraphe* 30 July 1799).

Cruse, Jacob, and Mary Hoffman were married by license dated 10 Dec 1789 (BAML). In 1799 George and Mary Hoffman were execs. of Jacob Cruse (BAOC 4:58).

Crute, Robert, and Rachel Barns were m. on 18 Aug 1751 (Harrison, "St. George's Parish Register:" 382). Rachel m. 2nd, William Stevenson (*q.v.*) by 29 Aug 1764 when she administered Crute's estate (MDAD 51:235).

Culberson, [-?-], m. by 19 Jan 1790, Jane, sister of Dr. Alexander Boyd (BAWB 4:404).

Cullen, John, native of Ireland, and Judith Fenix, native of Germany, were m. by lic. 22 Aug 1796, at St. Peter's Catholic Church, Baltimore (*Piet*: 130).

Cullen (Culling), Thomas, in his will dated 4 Oct 1731 named the children of his sister Sarah: Sarah Gwin, Avis Jinkins, Thomas Jinkins, William Jinkins (MWB 20:354 abst. in *Md. Cal. of Wills* 6:216).

Cullins, Thomas, m. by 18 Sep 1796, Ann, who received an equal share of the estate of John Cummins (BAAD 12:190).

Cullison, [-?-], m. by Jan 1794, Teresia, daughter of John Sheppard (BAWB 6:281).

Cummings, [-?-], m. by 7 June 1771, Margaret, sister of Adam Hoops; they had a son Robert Cummings (BAWB 3:259).

Cummings, Thomas, grocer, of Baltimore, and Miss Polly Maxfield of Kent Co. were m. last Sun. (*Baltimore American* 11 July 1800).

Cummins, Anthony, m. by 6 Sep 1773, Mary, admx. of Benjamin Harris (MDTP 45:160). In Dec 1779 Cummins stated he would not pay the debts of his wife Mary (*Maryland Journal and Baltimore Advertiser* 28 Dec 1779).

Cummins Anthony, m. by 14 June 1785, Mary, admx. of Benjamin Morris (BAAD 8:204).

Cunnard, Edward, and Judith Hurst, with consent of her mother, on 27 d. 5 m. 1772, declared their intention to marry ("Minutes of Gunpowder Monthly Meeting," *QRNM:*63).

Cunningham, [-?-], m. by 25 Dec 1765 Mary, sister of John Tredway and daughter of Thomas Tredway (BAWB 3:64).

Cunningham, William, and Margaret Brierly were m. on [29 Dec?] 1761 (Harrison, "St. John's Parish Register:" 223). She was a daughter of Robert Brierly (MWB 41:415; abst. in *Md. Cal. of Wills* 16:414).).

Curran, James, and Mary Ann Roddy were m. by lic. 6 Feb 1800, at St. Peter's Catholic Church, Baltimore (*Piet*: 130).

Curson [poss. Curzon], Richard, Jr., and Elizabeth Moale were m. on 13 March 1794 (Harrison, "St. Paul's Parish Register:" 285). She was a daughter of John Moale (BAWB 6:114).

Curtain, Thomas, of Fell's Point, and Miss Jane Grave were m. Fri. by Rev. Richards (*Baltimore Weekly Mercury* 26 Feb 1797).

Curtis, [-?-], m. by Jan 1794 Ann, daughter of John Sheppard (BAWB 6:281).

Curtis, Benjamin, m. by 28 July 1744, Abarilla, admx. of Nicholas Gostwick (*q.v.*) (MDAD 20:419). She was widow of Nicholas Gostwick and mother of Joseph Gostwick (BALR TB#E:665).

Curtis, Benjamin, and Deborah Perrigo were m. on 1 July 1790 (Marr. Register of Rev. Lewis Richards, MS.690 at MdHS). On 21 Feb 1796 John Perigo named his daughter Deborah Curtis (BAWB 5:360).

Curtis, Daniel, m. by 18 April 1788, [-?-], daughter of Thomas Anderson (BAAD 9:196).

Curtis, Capt. Jacob, of Conn., and Elizabeth Deagan, were m. on Thurs. eve. by Dr Allison (*Baltimore American* 15 Feb 1800).

Curtis, John, m. by 22 Dec 1769, Elizabeth, a relative of Edward Thorp, late of Md., dec. (BALR AL#B:419).

Curtis, Joseph, and Mary Walker were married by license dated 17 Oct 1784 (BAML). Mary was a daughter of Joseph Walker of Middle River Upper Hundred (BAWB 6:263).

Curtis, Mary, was charged with bastardy at the Aug 1710 Court (BACP IS#B:164).

Curtis, William, and Mary Turine were m. by lic. 9 Feb 1794, at St. Peter's Catholic Church, Baltimore (*Piet*: 130).

Curtz, Jacob, of York-Town, Pa., m. last Thurs. eve. Sukey, daughter of John Schultz of Baltimore (*Maryland Gazette or Baltimore General Advertiser* 18 Nov 1788).

Cutchin, Robert, m. by 17 March 1701, Dorothy, admx. of Moses Groome (INAC 21:246; MDTP 19C:243).

Cutchin, Thomas, m. Jane Hicks on 28 Oct 1713 (Harrison "St. Paul's Parish Register:" 3; BACP IS#IB:633). She was the widow of William Hicks, and mother of Henry and Elizabeth Hicks (BALR IS#G:312).

Cutchin, Thomas, aged about 51, deposed on 1 Oct 1728, mentioning his brother-in-law Samuel Sicklemore (BALC HWS#3 #11).

"D"

Daily, James, and Catherine Kelfohl, natives of Ireland, were m. by banns 22 June 1794 at St. Peter's Catholic Church, Baltimore (*Piet:* 130).

Dakings, Joseph, and Eliza Munnings, daughter of Shadrach Munnings, Esq., of Harmony Hall, Baltimore Co., were m. last Tues. by Rev. Mr. Oliver (*Federal*

Intelligencer and Baltimore Daily Gazette 18 July 1795; BAML gives the bride's name as Mannings).

Dale, Dr. John, and Mary, daughter of Richard Colegate, Jr., were m. on 21 April 1767 (Harrison, "St. John's Parish Register:" 98). On 28 July 1767 Mary was named as a daughter of Bridget Colegate (BACT B#G:148).

Daliquet, John Baptist, native of Diocese of Auch, lately of St. Domingo, and Elizabeth McSherry, widow of Patrick McSherry, and daughter of Charles and Belinda Clements, were m. by lic. on 22 Sep 1795 at St. Peter's Catholic Church, Baltimore (*Piet:* 130). (BAML gives his name as Deliquit).

Dall, James, merchant, m. last eve., Charlotte Lane, daughter of the late Capt. Richard Lane, dec., of Baltimore (*Maryland Journal and Baltimore Advertiser* 22 Jan 1790; *Maryland Gazette or Baltimore General Advertiser* 26 Jan 1790; BAML).

Dall, James, merchant, of Baltimore, and Miss Sarah Brooke Holliday, daughter of John Robert Holliday of this county, were m. Thurs. eve. last by Rev. Mr. Coleman (*Federal Intelligencer and Baltimore Daily Gazette* 24 Nov 1794; BALR WG#UU: 445; BAML).

Dallahide (Dallahyde), [-?-], m. by 2 March 1747 Jane, daughter of William Denton (MWB 25:206 abst. by Gibb).

Dallahide, (Dellehead), Francis, m. by 13 Nov 1700 Sarah, extx. of Thomas Heath (INAC 20:68).

Dallahide (Dollahide), Francis, m. by 4 July1723 Mary, admx. of John Bradshaw of Baltimore Co. (MDTP 16:164). On 10 Dec 1740 Mary was named as the mother of John Bradshaw of Prince George's Co. (BALR HWS#1-A:470).

Dallahide (Dallihyde), Thomas, m. 23 Aug 1751 [-?-], who received a portion of the estate of William Denton of Baltimore Co. (MDAD 30:225),

Dallahyde. See Dallahide.

Dallam, John, and Mary Wilson were m. by lic. dated 13 May 1781 (HAML). Mary Dallam (late Wilson), on 3 d. 8 m. 1780, was condemned for outgoing in marriage. on 22 d. 11 m. 1792 Mary Dallam produced a paper condemning her marriage several years ago contrary to the good order ("Minutes of Deer Creek Meeting," *QRNM:*140, 151).

Dallam, Josias, aged under 14, son of William Dallam, was in court in Nov 1759 (BAMI 1755-1763).

Dallam, Josias W., Esq., of Harford Co., was m. last eve. by Rev. Mr. Mansfield, to Miss Henrietta Jones, daughter of the Hon. Thomas Jones of Baltimore Co. (*Federal Gazette and Baltimore Daily Advertiser* 16 Jan 1800).

Dallam, Richard, d. April 1714, m. Elizabeth, daughter of William Martin; she m. 2nd, William Smith (q.v.) (*BCF:*156), and 3rd, John Paca (*q.v.*).

Dallam, William, on 11 Jan 1731 was named as a son-in-law in the will of William Smith (MWB 20:345 abst. in *MCW* 6:214).

Dallam, Major William, and Ann Matthews were m. on 23 July 1754 (Harrison, "St. George's Parish Register:" 350). On 13 May 1759 Ann was named as a sister of James Matthews, and daughter of Roger Matthews (BAWB 2:254).

Dallam, Winston Smith, son of Richard and Frances Dallam, on 31 d. 10 m. 1771 announced he intended to marry Margaret Gover, daughter of Ephraim and Elizabeth Gover ("Minutes of Deer Creek Meeting," *QRNM:*135).

Dallas, Walter, m. by 24 Oct 1732, Chloe, daughter of James Crook(e) of Baltimore Co. (BAAD 3:115; MDAD 11:504).

Dalton, George, native of Newburyport, Mass., and Catherine Venny, native of Ireland, were m. by lic. 22 Jan 1798, at St. Peter's Catholic Church, Baltimore (*Piet:* 130). (BAML gives the bride's name as Vinny). Catherine m. 2nd, Daniel McMeal (*q.v.*).

Danfossy, Baltazar Maurice, native Marseilles, lately a planter of St. Domingo, and Catherine Eugenie Moreno, native of Cap Francois, were m. by lic. 7 Dec 1797 at St. Peter's Catholic Church, Baltimore (*Piet:* 130; BAML, which gives the groom's name as Danfary).

Daniels, Capt. Anthony, and Miss Anna Maria Menskie were m. 17th inst. at Baltimore by Rev. Dr. Allison (*Apollo, or the Chestertown Spy* 26 March 1793).

Danmour, Chevalier, Consul of His Most Christian Majesty for the Middle District of the United States, and Julia de Rocour, a young lady lately arrived from the West Indies, were married (*Maryland Journal and Baltimore Advertiser* 17 Dec 1782).

Dannenberg, Frederick William, and Dorothea Koenig were m. by lic. on 16 April 1795, at St. Peter's Catholic Church, Baltimore (*Piet:* 130). She was a daughter of August Koenig (BAWB 6:336).

Danney, James, in 1762 was fined for bastardy (BAMI 1755-1763).

Darby, John, and Alice Gay were m. on 3 Dec 1733 (Harrison, "St. Paul's Parish Register:" 151). On 12 April 1770 their children Alice, James, and John, of S. C., were named as nephews and niece in the will of Nicholas Ruxton Gay (BAWB 3:151).

Darby, John B. was m. last Sun. eve. 19 Jan, by Rev, Mr. Hargrove to Miss Harriott Milbourne of the New Theatre (*Federal Gazette and Baltimore Daily Advertiser* 22 Jan 1798 [1799?]; Register of New Jerusalem, Swedenborgian Church, MS. at MdHS: 4). William Hawkins, guardian of Darby, who was the son of Daniel Darby, petitioned the court for permission to sell some shares of stock (BOCP Petition of William Hawkins, 1800)

Darby, Mary, was charged with bastardy; she confessed and was fined 30 shillings at the Nov 1745 Court; she was charged with bastardy again at the Nov 1746 Court (BACP 1743-1745, TB&TR#1:220).

Dare, [-?-], m. by 27 July 1784, Katharine, daughter of Rowland Smith, stonemason of Baltimore Town (BAWB 4:7).

Dare, [-?-], m. by 9 May 1798 Priscilla, daughter of Henry Wilson (BAWB 6:234).

Dare, Elizabeth, on 30 d. 4 m. 1785 apologized for marrying a man not of this society, by a priest ("Minutes of Gunpowder Meeting," *QRNM:*80). [No other marriage reference found].

Dare, Gideon, m. by 9 May 1798 Elizabeth, daughter of Henry Wilson, whose will of that date named their children Sarah, Rachel, and Elizabeth (BAWB 6:234).

Dashiell, Capt. Henry, and Miss Mary Leeke, daughter of Nicholas Leeke of Fell's Point, were m. last Thurs. by Rev. Ireland (*Federal Gazette and Baltimore Advertiser* 26 Jan 1799).

Dassest[?], [-?-], m. by 18 Jan 1771 Annemary, eldest daughter of Philip Heir (MWB 38:481, abst. in *Md. Cal. of Wills* 14:197).

Daucer, Peter Francois, in his will made 12 Sep 1800 named his wife Selena Gunn (BAWB 6:343).

Daucy[?], [-?-], m. by 8 April 1800, Eleanor, daughter of Barbara Wood (BAWB 6:262).

Daughaday, [-?-], m. by 29 Aug 1786, Rachel, daughter of Sarah Hamilton, widow (BAWB 4:304).

Daughaday, John, blacksmith, and Sarah Taylor, were convicted of bastardy in Nov 1757 (BAMI 1755-1763).

Daughaday, John, m. by 27 Dec 1788, Rachel, formerly the wife of George Sater (*q.v.*) (BALR WG#CC:351).

Daughaday, Katherine, on 19 April 1788 was named as the mother of Joseph, Abraham, Thomas, John, and Richard Daughaday, in the will of Joseph Taylor, who named her sons as cousins (nephews?) (BAWB 4:346).

Daughaday, Thomas, and **John Daughaday,** were legatees of Joseph Taylor, and in Feb 1794 they chose Richard Taylor as their guardian (BAOC 3:88).

Daugherty, |-?-|, m. by 18 Dec 1781 Elizabeth, daughter of John Stansbury (BAWB 4:102).

Daugherty, Neal, and Mary Green. both natives of Ireland, were m. by lic. on 23 Sep 1794, at St. Peter's Catholic Church, Baltimore (*Piet:* 130).

Daugherty, William, Jr., in 1762 was fined for bastardy (BAMI 1755-1763).

Davenport, Jonathan, and Margaret Dukehart on [day not given] 1 m. 1790 declared their intention to marry ("Minutes of Gunpowder Meeting," *QRNM:*88). Capt. Jonathan Davenport of Kent Co., m. at Friends' Meeting House, Peggy Duchart [Dukehart?] of Baltimore (*Maryland Journal and Baltimore Advertiser* 5 March 1790). She was a legatee of Valerius Dukehart (BAAD 10:182).

Davenport, David, and Lydia [-?-] were m. before 13 June 1790 when their son Lewis was born ("Bible Records of the Davenport Family," MSA SC 236 1-59).

Davey. See Davoy.

David, Elizabeth, was charged with bastardy at Aug Court 1725 (BACP IS&TW#4:312).

Davidson, Andrew, and Ann Stokes were m. 18 July 1779 at the First Presbyterian Church, Baltimore ("Register of the First Presbyterian Church, Baltimore," MS. at MdHS:4). In Feb 1781 Davidson, of Baltimore Town, advertised that his wife Ann had eloped (*Md. Gaz.* 6 Feb 1781). Anne Davidson of Baltimore Town advertised that she intended to petition the General Assembly for a divorce from her husband Andrew Davidson, who for some time past had left her, married another wife and otherwise treated her ill (*Maryland Journal and Baltimore Advertiser* 13 July 1784).

Davidson, Andrew, and Miszey Donnal were married by license dated 21 Jan 1793. Andrew d. by 1787 leaving a widow Meshah, who bound her son William McCay to James Osborn (BAOC 2:39).

Davidson, James, m. by 7 Feb 1791, Christiana, who received an equal share of the estate of John Wright (BAAD 10:286).

Davidson, Job, m. Elizabeth, daughter of Nicholas Miller, by license dated 17 May 1778 (BAML; BAWB 3:459).

Davidson, John, and Eleanor Strachan were m. on 14 Sep 1769 (Harrison, "All Hallow's Parish Register," Anne Arundel Co., MS. MdHS: 148). On 8 June 1774 Elinor was named as a daughter of William and Mary Strachan (BALR AL#L:58).

Davidson, John, m. by 1794, Margaret, daughter of Christiann Scott (*q.v.*) who was a sister of John Wright (BOCP Petition of Andrew Scott, 1794).

Davidson, William, stated he would not pay the debts of his wife Delia (*Maryland Journal and Baltimore Advertiser* 7 June 1785).

Davies, Vaughan, of New York, New York, m. by 2 Dec 1723, Catherine, only daughter and heir of Gideon Skaats, dec. (BALR IS#G:283, IS#H:272; MDAD 6:94).

Davis, [-?-], m. by 16 Aug 1779 Margaret, daughter of Edward Stocksdale who named his grandson Aaron Davis (BAWB 3:376).

Davis, [-?-], m. by 20 Oct 1782 Ann, daughter of Abraham Eaglestone (BAWB 3:494). She m. 2nd, Henry Fitch (*q.v.*).

Davis, [-?-], m. by 24 Oct 1784, Ann, sister of Nathaniel Clary (BAWB 3:577).

Davis, [-?-], m. by 11 Feb 1785 Alce, daughter of John Harriman (BAWB 4:16).

Davis, [-?-], m. by 23 Sep 1791 Sarah, daughter of George James (BAWB 5:15).

Davis, [-?-],m. by 24 June 1798 Elizabeth, daughter of Jacob Cox (BAWB 6:121).

Davis, Abednego, son of Uriah, aged 11, in Aug 1768 was bound to Abraham Ensor to age of 21, and was to be taught trade of a blacksmith (BAMI 1768-1769).

Davis, Amos, m. by 5 June 1794 Teresa, sister of Otho Holland Williams (BAWB 5:180).

Davis, Amos, was m. last Sun. eve. by Rev. Mr. Richards, to Miss Mary Carson both of this city (*Federal Gazette and Baltimore Daily Advertiser* 25 Oct 1797).

Davis, Elizabeth, was charged with bastardy at the March 1724/5 Court (BACP IS&TW#4:127). Benjamin Davis, son of Elizabeth Davis, was b. 20 Jan 1724/5 (Reamy. *St. George's Parish Register:* 28).

Davis, Elizabeth, daughter of John and Mary Davis [who m. 2nd, Thomas McDaniel (*q.v.*)], in Nov 1775 was bound to William Pullen to learn the trade of seamstress (BAMI 1772, 1775-1781: 141).

Davis, Francis, and Catherine Fitzgerald were m. by banns on 13 May 1787 at St. Peter's Catholic Church, Baltimore (*Piet:* 130).

Davis, Gaither, and Miss Elizabeth Birmingham were m. Thurs. eve. by Rev. Mr. Kurtz (*Federal Gazette and Baltimore Advertiser* 8 Dec 1800).

Davis, Capt. Henry Ferguson, native of Boston, Mass., and Elizabeth Britt, were m. by lic. on 22 Jan 1795 at St. Peter's Catholic Church, Baltimore (*Piet:* 130; *Maryland Journal and Baltimore Advertiser* 24 Jan 1795).

Davis, Ignatius, m. by 26 May 1760, [-?-], who received an equal portion of the estate of James Low (MDAD 44:322).

Davis, John, d. by Nov 1775, leaving a widow who m. 2nd, Thomas McDaniel (*q.v.*) and a daughter Elizabeth who was bound to William Pullen to learn the trade of seamstress (BAMI 1772, 1775-1781:141).

Davis, John, and Mary Brown were m. on 20 Jan 1782 (Marr. Returns of Rev. William West; Scharf Papers, MS. 1999, at MdHS). Mary was named as a sister in the will of James Brown (BAWB 5:314).

Davis, John, a native of Liverpool, Eng., and Mary Burdan were m. by lic. on 18 June 1795 at St. Peter's Catholic Church, Baltimore (*Piet:* 130; BAML which gives the bride's name as Bordan).

Davis, John, and Rosanna McGinnis were m. by lic. on 19 May 1799 at St. Peter's Catholic Church, Baltimore (*Piet:* 130).

Davis, Joseph, on 26 d. 2 m. 1785 was charged with marriage by the assistance of a priest ("Minutes of Gunpowder Meeting," *QRNM*:79). [No other definite marriage reference found].

Davis, Mary, was charged with bastardy in March 1768. Jonathan Griffith was summoned to court (BAMI 1768-1769:6).

Davis, Robert, m. by 14 May 1792, [-?-], who received an equal share of the estate of Clare Clarke (BAAD11:116).

Davis, Dr. Samuel, of Shippensburg, and Miss Mary Neil, daughter of Mr. William Neil, late of Baltimore, were m. at Shippensburgh on Tues., 19th ult., by Rev. Mr. Cooper (*The Carlisle Gazette and the Western Repository of Knowledge* 6 Nov 1793).

Davis, Samuel, and Deborah Renshaw were married by license dated 8 Oct 1795 (BAML). In 1797 Deborah was the admx. of Hosea Renshaw (*q.v.*) (BAAD 12:296; BAOC 3:224; BOCP Petition of Samuel Davis, 1797). Robinson Jones Renshaw, in April 1798, chose Samuel Davis as his guardian (BAOC 4:11).

Davis, Samuel, carpenter, and Miss Mary Baker, both of Baltimore, were m. last eve. by Rev. Mr. Morrell (*Baltimore Telegraphe* 3 Oct 1799).

Davis, Sarah, of Pencader Hundred, New Castle Co., Delaware, in her will made 4 June 1795 named her granddaus. Sarah and Mary Perry (BAWB 5:362).

Davis, Sarah, on 27 d. 7 m. 1797, produced a paper condemning her misconduct in marrying a man outside the society ("Minutes of Deer Creek Meeting," *QRNM:*158). [No other marriage reference found].

Davis, Uriah, in Aug 1740 was charged with begetting a bastard on the body of Mary Watkins (BACP HWS#TR:305).

Davis, William, m. by 19 April 1770, Elizabeth [-?-], sister of Sarah Bond (MWB 37:580, abst. in *Md. Cal. of Wills* 14:124; BAWB 3:140).

Davis, William, on 24 d. 9 m. 1785, was charged that soon after his wife died he was married with the assistance of a priest to a woman whose former husband may have still been living ("Minutes of Gunpowder Meeting," *QRNM:*80). [No other marriage reference found].

Davis, Zachariah, orphan of Ann Davis, aged 12 on 6 Feb 1772, in Aug of that year was bound to William Tinker, butcher (BAMI 1772, 1775-1781: 20).

Davoy, Michael, and Ann Knowlen (Knowland) were m. by lic. on 25 Feb 1786, at St. Peter's Catholic Church, Baltimore (*Piet:* 130; BAML).

Davy, Mary, was charged with bastardy at the June 1755 Court. Thomas Hughes was summoned to court (BAMI 1765: 17).

Dawes. Mareb. See Israel Hendrick Johnson.

Dawkins, Miles, m. by 10 May 1694, Elizabeth, widow of [-?-] Goldsmith and heir of John Collett of Baltimore Co. (INAC 12:149). **See Symon Dawkins below.**

Dawkins, James, on 17 Aug 1763 conv. property to his grandson James Sollers (BALR BB#F:194).

Dawkins, Symon, m. by 1692 Elizabeth, sister of Mathew Goldsmith of Baltimore Co. (MWB 1:548, INAC 12:149). **See Miles Dawkins above**

Dawkins, William, of Calvert Co., m. by 19 Nov 1724, Ann, daughter and devisee of Richard Smith of Calvert Co., dec. (BALR IS#H:22).

Dawney, [-?-], m. by 1 Feb 1760, Mary, daughter of Blackledge Woodland of Kent Co.. now of Baltimore Co. (BAWB 3:250; MWB 39:328, abst. in *Md. Cal. of Wills* 15:65).

Dawney, John, and Lydia Swift were m. in March 1716 (Harrison, "St. John's Parish Register:" 14). On 6 July 1723 Lydia was named as a daughter of Mark Swift (BALR IS#G:205, 295).

Dawney, Thomas, m. Ann Cowdray in Sep 1737 (Harrison, "St. John's Parish Register: 39). She was the widow of James Cowdray (*q.v.*).

Dawson, [-?-], m. by 20 March 1734, Mary, daughter of Robert Doyne of Charles Co. (BALR HWS#M:42).

Dawson, Elizabeth, in 1772 was fined for bastardy; she had borne two children (BAMI 1772, 1775-1781:84).

Dawson, Martha, was charged with bastardy and having borne two children and fined at Nov Court 1772 (BAMI 1772, 1775-1781:86).

Dawson, William, was m. last Thurs. eve. by Rev. Mr. Richards, to Miss Anne Robertson (*Federal Intelligencer and Baltimore Daily Gazette* 21 March 1795).

Day, [-?-], m. by 18 Dec 1755 [-?-], daughter of Thomas Bond who named his granddaughter Ann Day in his will (MWB 30:24 abst. by Gibb).

Day, Andrew, and Bridget Collins were m. by lic. on 8 Feb 1796, at St. Peter's Catholic Church, Baltimore (*Piet:* 130).

Day, Edward, and Abarilla Taylor were m. on 22 May 1722 (Harrison, "St. John's Parish Register:" 19). He d. 24 Jan 1746, and Avarilla Day m. 2nd, Patrick Lynch (*q.v.*) ("Day Bible Record," *The Notebook,* 15 (2) (June 1999) 7-9).

Day, Edward, and Ann Fell who were married 8 Feb 1749 in St. John's Parish, Baltimore Co. (Harrison, "St. John's Parish Register:" 200). In July 1757 Day stated he would not pay the debts of his wife Anne, who had eloped from him and run him into debt (*Annapolis Maryland Gazette* 7 July 1757). She was supposed to have gone to Philadelphia (*Pa Gaz.* 30 June 1757). She had eloped again, and this time taken four children (three daughters and one son), and other property. Edward would not honor any contract made by her (*Annapolis Maryland Gazette* 20 Aug 1767; *Pa. Gaz.* 11 Dec 1760).

Day, Edward, and Rebecca Clagett were m. on 19 Sep 1771 (Harrison, "St. John's Parish Register:" 263). Rebecca m. 2nd, John Weston (*q.v.*). ("Original Records of the Young Famiy of Baltimore County," *HMGB* 16:15-17, 16:24-17).

Day, Emmory, was charged with bastardy at Nov Court 1757 and named Richard Moale as the father of her child (BAMI 1757-1759: 75).

Day, John, son of Edward, b. 25 April 1723, m. 1st, on 20 July 1742, Phillis Zana Maxwell ("Day Bible Record," *The Notebook,* 15 (2) (June 1999) 7-9; Harrison, "St. John's Parish Register:" 127). She was a daughter and coheir of James Maxwell of Baltimore Co., dec. (BALR TR#D:562). She was a granddaughter of James Maxwell (BALR BB#1:6).

Day, John, son of Edward, b. 15 April 1723, m. 2nd, on 30 Dec 1764, Sarah York [*sic*], daughter of Nicholas Horner ("Day Bible Record," *The Notebook,* 15 (2) (June 1999) 7-9; Harrison, "St. John's Parish Register:" 227, 264). Sarah was the widow of John York (BACT B#G: 92).

Day, John, m. by 28 Aug 1765, Mary, admx. of John Yarby (or Yerby) (MINV 87:254; BAAD 6:95).

Day, John, son of John Day of Edward, b. 8 or 14 Oct 1755, m. in St. John's Parish on 30 Nov 1775 Mary Gouldsmith Presbury, b. 1 July 1758, daughter of G. Gouldsmith and Elizabeth ([-?-]) Presbury ("Day Bible Record," *The Notebook,* 15 (2) (June 1999) 7-9; "John Day Bible," *MBR* 2:24-27; Harrison, "St. John's Parish Register:" 264).

Day, John, of Baltimore Co., and Agnes, daughter of the late William Young, merchant of Baltimore, were m. last Thurs. morn. in Anne Arundel Co. (*Baltimore Daily Repository* 12 March 1795).

Day, Nicholas, and Elizabeth Cox were m. on 14 July 1709 (Harrison, "St. John's Parish Register:" 42). She was the daughter and heir of Christopher Cox (BALR TB#E:63;

MDAD 21:167). Nicholas d. by 22 May 1746, and his widow Elizabeth, by whom
he had a son John Day, m. 2nd, Robert Bishop (*q.v.*) (BALR TB#E:63).

Day, Samuel, m. by 25 Feb 1752, Sarah, daughter of William Talbott (MWB 28:348
abst. by Gibb).

Deagan, George, m. by 22 April 1797 Frances, daughter of Henry Brothers, whose will
named his grandson Henry Deagan (BAWB 5:519; BAAD 12:496).

Deagan, Patrick, merchant of Baltimore, and Miss Polly McComas of Harford Co. were
m. last eve. (*Federal Gazette and Baltimore Advertiser* 25 Oct 1799).

Deagen, Peter, stated he would not pay the debts of his wife Salome as she had left his
bed and board without any just cause (*Federal Gazette and Baltimore Daily
Advertiser* 31 Jan 1799).

Deagle, Simon, and Elizabeth Boudville were m. by lic. on 9 July 1785 at St. Peter's
Catholic Church, Baltimore (*Piet:* 131; BAML gives his name as Lamn Deagle and
her name as Elizabeth Budiel).

Deal, Christian, m. by 28 July 1764 Elizabeth, daughter of Anna Mary Ash who named
her grandchildren Christian and Peter Deal (BAWB 3:41).

Deale, Christian, d. by 9 Jan 1787, leaving a minor child Christian Deal: Erasmus Uhler
was appointed guardian; account mentioned legacy left to the orphan by Mary Ash
(BAGA 1:2).

Deal, Christian, m. by 5 June 1789, Hannah, daughter of Michael Steltz (BAWB 4:364).
Christian Deale, Mary Steltz, and Philip Highjoe, execs., administered the estate of
Michael Steltz on 11 Oct 1790 (BAAD 10:209).

Deal, Eleanor, on 15 Oct 1748 was named as a daughter in the will of John Bowen
(MWB 25:455 abst. by Gibb).

Deal, Josias, of Prince George's Co., m. by Jan 1770, Millicent, granddaughter of
Clement Hill of Prince George's Co. who left Millicent the tract *Well's Camp*
(BALR AL#B:67).

Deale (Deal), Christian, m. by 28 July 1764 Elizabeth, daughter of Anna Mary Ash
(BAWB 3:41). Elizabeth m. 2nd, Joseph Miller (*q.v.*)

Deale, Jacob, and Susanna Dougherty, of Baltimore Co., were m. by lic. on 15 Nov
1798, at St. Peter's Catholic Church, Baltimore (*Piet:* 131).

Dean, [-?-], m. by 25 Oct 1762, Martha, daughter of Thomas West (BAWB 3:87).

Dean, [-?-], m. by 25 Oct 1762, Susanna, daughter of Thomas West (BAWB 3:87).

Dean, Alex., m. by 24 June 1783, Ann, daughter of Elizabeth Payne of Baltimore Town
(BAWB 3:525).

Dean, Ezekah, and Rebecca Lowndes were married by license dated 12 March 1778
(BAML). On 27 Aug 1793, Rebecca formerly Lowndes was named as the admx. of
James Lowndes of Baltimore Co. (BAAD 11:312).

Dean (Deane), Hannah, petitioned the Justices of Baltimore Co. that some years ago her
son John Deane had been apprenticed to Isaiah Jackson, in 1784, to learn the trade
of joiner and house carpenter. She believed Jackson had not treated her son right,
and wanted her son put to some other person of the same trade (BOCP Petition of
Hannah Deane, n.d.).

Dean, Hannah, widow, in her will made 10 Aug 1800 named her grandson John
Ottenburg (BAWB 6:325).

Deason, Sarah, was charged with bastardy and confessed in Aug 1746, naming Solomon
Armstrong as the father of the child (BACP TB&TR#1:132).

Deaver, [-?-], m. by 30 d., 7 m., 1751 Sarah, daughter of John Webster (MWB 29:374 abst. by Gibb).; see also (BALR B#H:297, B#P: 190). Antil and Sarah were the parents of John Deaver, Quaker, aged c35, who deposed on 30 Oct 1766 about a gift his grandfather made to his mother Sarah (BAEJ OS: Ruff, Richard, vs. Isaac Webster).

Deaver, [-?-], m. by 24 Nov 1788, Mary, daughter of Bothia Scarlett (*q.v.*).

Deaver, Daniel, on 23 July 1747 was named as a brother in the will of John Carilsle who also named Richard Deaver, son of Daniel, as a cousin (MWB 25:113, abst. by Gibb).

Deaver, John, and Perina Greenfield were m. on 21 Oct 1742 (Harrison, "St. George's Parish Register:" 325). On 14 May 1764 Perina was named as a daughter of William Greenfield (BAAD 6:99; BAWB 3:4).

Deaver, John, and Ann Bond were m. on 11 May 1756 (Harrison, "St. George's Parish Register:" 352). On 4 March 1760 Ann was named as a daughter of Peter Bond and granddaughter of Thomas Bond (BALR B#H:275).

Deaver, John, and Rebecca Talbot, widow, recorded their marriage articles on 6 Nov 1776 (BALR AL#O:298). Rebecca was the widow of Edmund Talbot (*q.v.*) and the mother of Benjamin Robinson Talbot (BALR WG#D:57).

Deaver, John, m. 11 March 1777 Susannah Talbott, who d. 9 Sep 1787 ("Deaver Bible Record," in Rev. War Pension Application, in *NGSQ* 23:52). He was a Lieut. In the 3rd Md. Regt., m. 1st, on 11 March 1777, Susannah Talbot, sister of Benjamin Robinson Talbott; she d. 9 Sep 1787. He m. 2nd, on 4 Aug 1789, Honora Wroth, who d. 14 Oct 1793; and 3rd, by license on `1 Jan 1797, Sarah Hunt, who d. 23 Oct 1851; they were the parents of Margaret Hopkins Holtzman, wife of George Holtzman of Baltimore, who was 49 years old when she deposed on 26 March 1852. John and Susanna were the parents of: John Talbott Deaver, b. 9 Sep 1787; John and Honora were the parents of: Ann b. 12 Jan 1792; John and Sarah were the parents of: Emanuel Hunt Deaver, b. 24 Jan? 1798, Job Hunt Deaver, b, 9 Jan 1801, d. 18 Aug 1801, John Hunt Deaver, b. 9 April 1804, d. 20 Aug 1804, Miriam Hunt Deaver, b. 22 Aug 1805, d. 4 Nov 1805, Miriam Deaver, b. 23 Oct, .d 24 Oct 1806 (Rev. War Pension Application of John Deaver: R-2822). (BAWB 4:309).

Deaver, John, m. by 21 Oct 1785, [-?-] who received a portion of the estate of Francis Moore (under the will of Francis Moore of Cardiff, Co. of Dublin [*sic*]) (BAAD 8:170).

Deaver, John, and Honner Wroth were m. by Rev. Hagerty on 3 Aug 1799 (Marr. Returns of Rev. John Hagerty, Scharf Papers, MS. 1999 at MdHS). They were m. on 4 Aug 1789 ("Deaver Bible Record," Rev. War Pension Appl., in *NGSQ* 23:52).

Deaver, John, m. 12 Jan 1797, Sarah Hunt ("Deaver Family Record,"*NGSQ* 23:52).

Deaver, Mary, was charged with bastardy in March Court 1730/1 (BACP IS& TW#4: 96).

Deaver, Misael, on 31 d. 12 m. 1780 was reported to have married from amongst us. On 24 d. 2 m. 1781 he admitted he had been married by a priest ("Minutes of Gunpowder Meeting," *QRNM:*74). [No other marriage reference found].

Deaver, Philip, planter, m. by 27 Oct 1770, Sabina, widow of Richard Miller Cole (*q.v.*) (by whom she had a son Richard Cole). She was a daughter of Nicholas Hale of Baltimore Co. (BALR AL#C:105, AL#L:341).

Deaver, Richard, and Sarah Pritchard were m. on 1 March 1732 (Harrison, "St. George's," p. 263). On 14 June 1735 Sarah was named as a daughter of Obadiah Prichard of Baltimore Co. (MDAD 13:178).

Deaver, Stephen, m. by 12 April 1794 [-?-], daughter of William Wheeler, who named his grandson John Deaver (BAWB 5:242).

Deaver, Thomas, and Deborah Hartley were m. on 9 June 1730 (Harrison, "St. George's Parish Register:" 282). Deborah m. 2nd, by 27 July 1747 Alexander McComas (*q.v.*) (BAAD 4:174).

Deaver, William, m. by 18 Oct 1741, Blanch, widow of William Duly or Dooley (*q.v.*) of Baltimore Co. (MDAD 18:400).

Debeaulieu, Jacque Simon Poulet, born at Magny [*sic*] Lepard, Diocese of Paris, and Catherine Mary Elizabeth Hay, born at Angouleme, France, were m. by banns on 27 Nov 1794 at St. Peter's Catholic Church, Baltimore (*Piet:* 131).

Debroim, Charles, of Va., m. by 11 Sep 1733, Christian, sister of William Buckner, dec., and of Thomas, Philip, Ann, Elizabeth, and Mary Buckner, and a widow Patience who m. 2nd, George Elliott (MDTP 29:309-310).

Debruler, Benjamin, and Semele Jackson were m. on 25 Feb 1756 (Harrison, "St. John's Parish Register:" 213). On 7 Feb 1772 Semelia was named as a daughter of Jacob Jackson (BALR AL#D:492).

Debruler, John, of St. John's Parish, Baltimore Co., m. by 15 March 1728 Mary, daughter of Thomas Greenfield, late of St. George's Parish, dec. (BALR IS#J:266).

Debruler, John, in 1772 was given an allowance for supporting Francis and Anthony Debruler, his sons (Baltimore Co. Levy List, 1772).

Debruler, William, and Diana Greenfield were m. on 23 March 1743 (Harrison, "St. John's Parish Register:" 46, 137). On 14 May 1764 she was named as a daughter of William Greenfield (MDAD 51:112; BAAD 6:99); on 1 June 1773 William Debruler's children James, Micajah, Ufan, and William Debruler were paid their share of their grandfather William Greenfield's estate (MDAD 68:85).

Decker, Frederick, in his will made 10 April 1800, named his daughters Mary Fletcher and Mary Magdalene Cassel (BAWB 7:328).

Decourse, Anna, in 1762 was fined for bastardy (BAMI 1755-1763).

Dee, Sarah, was charged with bastardy at March Court 1722/3 (BACP IS&TW#3:224).

Deems, George, and Miss Ruth Cowen, both of this county, were m. last Sun. (*Baltimore Evening Post* 29 March 1793).

Deladabat, Auguste Philipe Lasson, native of Bordeaux, and Therese St. Avoye, widow of Charles Vallerot, were m. 19 May 1794, at St. Peter's Catholic Church, Baltimore (*Piet:* 131). Auguste P. S. De Labadat and Jeanne S. L. A. Vallerot were married by license dated 19 May 1794 (BAML).

Delaporte, Francis Frederic, and Elizabeth Herbert Cooper were m. 3 May 1787, at St. Peter's Catholic Church, Baltimore (*Piet:* 131).

deLappe, Abraham, d. by 7 March 1716 by which time his widow Julian had m. James Isham (*q.v.*).

De la Serre, M., an officer at St. Onge, belonging to the French Amy, lately under the command of Gen. Count Rochambeau in America, was m. Thurs., 22nd inst. in Baltimore, to Nancy Dulany, only daughter of Daniel Dulany, Esq. (*Maryland Gazette or Baltimore General Advertiser* 30 April 1784; BAML, which gives his name as Barbier Delasera).

Delat, Augustine, and Frances Ross were m. by lic. on 12 Feb 1786, at St. Peter's Catholic Church, Baltimore (*Piet:* 131).

Delauney, James Anthony, son of the late John and Magdalen Gonisseame, and Theresa Charlotte Mary Henrietta Labourdais, were m. by lic. 30 Nov 1796 at St. Peter's Catholic Church, Baltimore (*Piet:* 131). Jacques A Delaunay and Therese C. M. H. Lebourdais were married by license dated 25 Nov 1796 (BAML).

DeLisle, Dr. F. G., was m. last Sat. eve. by Rev. Mr. Bean, to Miss Elizabeth Warren De la Roche, both of this city (*Federal Gazette and Baltimore Daily Advertiser* 8 May 1797).

DeLisle, John, and Mary Blieze were m. by lic. 18 Nov 1785 at St. Peter's Catholic Church, Baltimore (*Piet:* 131.

Dellehead. See Dallahide.

Delozier, Daniel, of Baltimore, and Miss Higginbotham [poss. a relative] of Rev. Ralph Higginbotham, Rector of St. Anne's Parish, Annapolis, were m. there last Thurs. eve. (*Maryland Journal and Baltimore Advertiser* 8 Nov 1791).

Delphy, [-?-], m. by 13 Nov 1800, Aperillah, daughter of John Buckingham (BAWB 6:327).

Delphy, John, and Ann Buckingham were married by license dated 25 Feb 1791 (BAML). Anne may have m. 2nd, [-?-] Abbitt (or Abbott) as on 13 Nov 1800 Ann Abbitt was named as a daughter in the will of John Buckingham (BAWB 6:327).

Delphy (Delphia), Richard, and Hannah Buckingham were married by license dated 31 March 1790 (BAML; Marr. Returns of Rev. Daniel Kurtz, Scharf Papers, MS.1999 at MdHS). On 13 Nov 1800 Hannah was named as a daughter of John Buckingham (BAWB 6:327).

De Marbois, Francois Barbe, Consul General of France, and Elizabeth Moore, daughter of the President of Pennsylvania, were m. last Thurs. in Philadelphia (*Maryland Gazette or Baltimore General Advertiser* 25 June 1784).

Demasters, Anthony, m. by Nov 1692, Rebecca, widow of Randolph Death (BACP F#1:325).

Demett, James, m. by 12 April 1797, Rachel, legatee of William Sinclair (BAAD 12:287).

Demmitt, Elisha, and Miss Delilah Jessop of Gunpowder Forest were m. yesterday afternoon by the Rev. Mr. Hargrove (*Federal Gazette and Baltimore Advertiser* 12 Dec 1798).

Demmitt, Lettis, in 1762 was fined for bastardy (BAMI 1755-1763).

Demmitt, Richard, and Rebecca Merryman were m. on 9 Dec 1783 (Marr. Returns of Rev. William West, Scharf Papers, MS.1999 at MdHS). Rebecca was a daughter of Joseph Merryman (BAWB 6:159).

Demmitt. Thomas, and Sophia Stansbury were m. on 26 Dec 1734 (Harrison, "St. Paul's Parish Register:" 153). Thomas and Sophia were the parents of (Reamy, *St. Paul's Parish Register:* 15): Presbury, twin, b. 15 April 1744; Stansbury, twin, b. 15 April 1744).

Deondidier, Anthony, m. by 2 Oct 1693, Martha, sister of Eliza Horton of London (MWB 2:289). Maryha m. 2nd, Thomas Richardson (*q.v.*).

Demonti, Joseph, born near Strasbourg in Alsace, and Mary Adelaide Contant, native of Rouen in Normandy, were m, by lic. 7 Nov 1798, at St. Peter's Catholic Church, Baltimore (*Piet:* 131).

Demoss, John, b. 17 Sep 1756, m. 25 Jan [poss. 1787, but definitely by Dec 1788] Lucy Chapel, b. 24 Sep 1765 ("John DeMoss Bible," *MBR* 7:43). [Marriage date was not found in BAML, HAML or this author's MM2].

Dempsey, Patrick, of Anne Arundel Co. and Elizabeth McDermot of Montgomery Co. were m. by lic. 24 Jan 1796 at St. Peter's Catholic Church, Baltimore (*Piet:* 131).

Dempsey, Thomas, and Eleanor Hoy were m. by lic. 11 July 1799 at St. Peter's Catholic Church, Baltimore (*Piet:* 131).

Denbow, [-?-], m. by 29 Dec 1739, Mary, daughter of John Norrington, Sr. (BALR HWS#1A: 323).

Denny, James, in 1762 was fined for bastardy (BAMI 1755-1763).

Denny, Neal, and Rebecca Anderson were m. by lic. 24 Nov 1796, at St. Peter's Catholic Church, Baltimore (*Piet:* 131).

Denton, [-?-], m. by 17 Jan 1752 Elizabeth, daughter of Walter James of Baltimore Co. (MDAD 32:9. 33:14).

Denton, [-?-], m. b 27 Oct 1780 Sarah, daughter of John Jones (BALR WG#F:50).

Denton, Edward, and Mary Games were m. 20 Oct 1778 (Marr, Lic. Returns of Rev. Francis Lauder: Scharf Papers, MSS 1999 at MdHS). In Dec 1778 Denton advertised that his wife Mary had eloped from him (*Maryland Journal and Baltimore Advertiser* 15 Dec 1778).

Denton, James, m. by 9 March 1677, Rebecca, widow of Thomas O'Daniel (BACP D:164; MDTP 9A:512; INAC 5:25).

Denton, James, was charged with bastardy at March Court 1733/4 (BACP HWS#9: 188).

Denton, James, m. by 29 Sep 1766, Sarah, niece of Nicholas Ruxton Gay, who conv. her part of *Gay's Inspection* (BALR B#P:342).

Denton, James, and Temperance Green were married by license dated 17 April 1795 (BAML). On 22 Aug 1795 Temperance was named as a daughter of Moses Green (BAAD 12:39).

Denton, John, and Margaret May were m. on 18 May 1784 Harrison, "St. Paul's Parish Register:" 189). She was the widow of Benjamin May *(q.v.)*, and on 30 July 1796 was named as Margaret Councilman, legatee of Frederick Caley (BAAD 12:175).

Denyard, Henry, on 1 June 1714 conv. to his son John a red cow, and he conv. a brown cow to Charles Pines. His wife Tabitha was to have all the rest of his 'goods and substance' (BALR TR#A:319). **N.B.:** He may be the Henry 'Dunard' who had, on 20 Aug 1713, bound himself to serve John Long for five years (BALR TR#A:306).

Depo, [-?-], m. by 14 Jan 1781 Ann, sister of William McCormick of Miles Hill, Harford Co., late of Co. Down, Kingdom of Ireland (BAWB 3:483).

Dermot, Charles, m. by 1 May 1694, [-?-] the widow Guilder, mentioned in the administration account of James Phillips (INAC 12:135).

Derumple, John, of Calvert Co., m. by 20 July 1738 Eleanor, daughter of William Harris of Calvert Co., widow of [-?-] Ellt *(q.v.)* and mother of Benjamin Ellt (BALR HWS#1A: 123, TR#D: 1).

Desaprade, John Francis Cabannes, Knight of the Order of St. Louis, Col. Commandant of Artillery, and Adjutant General of the southern part of St. Domingo, and Anne Joseph St. Martin Dufoureq, daughter of Simon Joseph St. Martin and Mary Ann Smith of St. Domingo, were m. by lic. 22 Oct 1798, at St. Peter's Catholic Church, Baltimore (*Piet:* 131).

Desbordes, Antony, son of John Mary Landreieve and Mary Gilles Chanssegros DeLery, native of Paris, and Mary Clare LeGardeur Tilly, daughter of Stephen Simon Legardeur and Mary Rose Agnes Lomenie deMarme, were m. by lic. on 17 Dec 1795, at St. Peter's Catholic Church, Baltimore (*Piet:* 131).

Deshields, Capt. Joseph, of this city, was m. at Alexandria on the 30th ult., by Rev, James Griffin, pastor of the R. C. Church, to Miss Mary Martin, of the latter place (*Federal Gazette and Baltimore Daily Advertiser* 14 Dec 1798).

DeSeze, John Baptist Alexis Mary, son of Alexis, Attorney General of the Council, Cap Francois, St. Domingo, and Catherine Rose Lacaze, and Mary Fortunee Louise Buron, daughter of Julian and Mary Dasmieres of Ville Franche, were m. by lic. 16 Nov 1793, at St. Peter's Catholic Church, Baltimore (*Piet:* 131; BAML, which gives his name as Desize and her name as Baron).

Despaux, Joseph, and Frances Demanche were m. by lic. 10 Sep 1793, at St. Peter's Catholic Church, Baltimore (*Piet:* 131). Joseph Despo and Frances Demarick were married by license dated 6 Sep 1793 (BAML).

Deterly, John L., d. by March 1798, leaving Peter Deterly as admin.; Peter Deterly petitioned the court that he be allowed to sell the property of the deceased in order that an equal distribution among the children of the dec. be made. The petition was signed by Peter, Elizabeth, John, Michael, Jacob Elizabeth, Catharine, Christina and Magdalena Deterly [**N.B.:** the men signed; the women made their mark] (BOCP: Petition of Peter Deterly, 1798).

Deterly, Peter, of Baltimore, cabinetmaker, and Elizabeth Reese were married by license dated 12 Sep1796 (BAML). On 8 May 1798 Elizabeth was named as a daughter of Frederick Reese of Baltimore Co., dec. (BALR WG#54:424; BAAD 12:433)

Devalcourt, Alexander, native of Paris, and Margaret Goto were m. by lic. 18 July 1794, at St. Peter's Catholic Church, Baltimore (*Piet:* 131; BAML, which gives her name as Gold).

Deveghe (Devaga, Devagh), John, m. by 7 Nov 1694, Elizabeth, daughter of Edward Ayres, and relict and admx. of William Deyson (also Deason or Dyson) (BALR RM#HS:439, IS#L:351; MDTP 16:170; BACP G#1:103).

Device, John Darch Lovel, and Margaret Summers, were m. by lic. 9 Nov 1797 at St. Peter's Catholic Church, Baltimore (*Piet:* 131; BAML, which gives his name as John Darch Live Device [*sic*]).

Devine, Charles, and Sarah [-?-] were m. by 20 Feb 1781 when their son Charles was b. ("John Hanson Bible," *MBR* 2:55).

Devorn, William, on 25 Feb 1739/40 was named as a son in the will of John Clary (MWB 22:213 abst. in *Md. Cal. of Wills* 8:93).

Dew, [-?-], m by 4 Dec 1792, Ann, daughter of Conduce Gatch (BAWB 6:47).

Dew (Due), Robert, and Esther Raven were m. on 3 Oct 1754 (Harrison, "St. John's Parish Register:" 211). On 10 May 1775 Esther was named as a sister of Luke Raven (BAAD 6:325).

Dew, Robert, Jr., and Elizabeth Stansbury were married on 23 July 1796 (Marr. Register of Rev. Lewis Richards, MS.690 at MdHS). On 13 May 1798 Elizabeth was named as a daughter of Joseph Stansbury BAWB 6:150; BAAD 13:284).

Dew, Thomas, d. by 2 June 1760 by which time his admx. Eliza had m. John Murray (*q.v.*); Dew left five children (BAAD 4:307; MDTP 37:282). Thomas Dew (probably son of Thomas), in Aug 1760 chose John Murray, collier, as his guardian (BAMI 1755-1763: 27).

Dewit, Ann. See Ann Jewit.

Dewit, Thomas, m. by 25 Jan 1791 [-?-], daughter of William Adams, who named a grandson Thomas Dewit in his will (BAWB 5:292). Catherine Adams, in her will dated 19 Aug 1795 named her granddaughter Catherine Dewit, daughter of Thomas Dewit (BAWB 5:299). Thomas and Elizabeth Dewitt were the parents of Catherine, b. 3 Jan and bapt. 24 April 1793 (Reamy, *St. Paul's Parish Register:* 70).

Diamont, John, d. by 23 May 1688 when his relict Mary had m. 2nd, William Carr (*q.v.*) (MDTP 14:72).

Dickenson, David, on 25 d. 4 m. 1795 was reported as having been married by a hireling priest to a woman not of our society ("Minutes of Gunpowder Meeting," *QRNM:*96). A David Dickinson and Eleanor Hickey were m. by lic. dated 25 March 1794 (BAML).

Dickey, John, m. by 29 June 1790, Anne, daughter of John Thompson of Muckamore, Co. Antrim, Ireland, and sister of Hugh Thompson of Baltimore (BAWB 5:63).

Dickinson, Sarah. See Samuel Wright.

Dicks, Peter, of Chester Co., Penna., in his will made 31 Oct 1875 named his brother-in-law William Swasser co-executor with his own son Abraham Dicks (MWB 38:386, abst. in *Md. Cal. of Wills* 14:184).

Dicks, Richard, son of Edmund and Catherine Dicks of Co. Norfolk, Eng., came to America in 1760 and settled at the Head of Elk in Cecil Co.; he m. Catherine Dean (BACT 1791-1794, MS 2865/1 at MdHS: 103). Catherine was a daughter of Elicksander Dean (BAWB 3:455).

Dickson, Drusilla, on 2 Nov 1766 was named as a cousin in the will of James Shepard (BAWB 3:76)

Dietz, Michel, m. by 17 March 1760 Maria Eva Staehlin ("First Record Book for the Reformed and Lutheran and Congregations at Manchester, Baltimore (Now Carroll) Co." *MGSB* 35:265).

Diffenderfer, Michael, b. 29 July 1744, d. 9 April 1800, and Dorothy [-?-], b. 20 Sep 1756 d. 4 Dec 1829, were m. on 22 Aug 1773 ("Diffenderfer Family Record," *HMGB* 14 (3) 40-41).

Diffenderfer, Peter, and Cathrina Mayer were m. on 21 Dec 1786 ("Register of First German Reformed Church, Baltimore," MS. at MdHS: 188). On 3 Nov 1787 Catherine was named as a daughter of Frederick Meyers (BAAD 9:116; BAOC 2:54).

Dillon, Henry, in his will, made 9 May 1771 named his nephew Daniel Carroll (MWB 38:384, abst. in *Md. Cal. of Wills* 14:184).

Dilly, Joh., m. by 3 Dec 1768, Catharina Himpin (First Record Book for the Reformed and Lutheran and Congregations at Manchester, Baltimore (Now Carroll) Co." *MGSB* 35:272).

Dilly, Johannes, m. by 8 May 1764, Anna Maria Heerin ("First Record Book for the Reformed and Lutheran and Congregations at Manchester, Baltimore (Now Carroll) Co." *MGSB* 35:268).

Dilworth, William, on 29 d. 5 m. 1784 had his marriage performed contrary to Friends, and it will be looked into ("Minutes of Gunpowder Meeting," *QRNM:*79). [No other marriage reference found].

Dilworth, William, and Kezia Greenfield were married by license dated 11 Sep 1788 (BAML). On 9 Feb 1791 Dilworth's wife was named as a daughter of James Greenfield (BAAD 10:290).

Dimmitt, Elisha, was m. yesterday afternoon by Rev. Mr. Hargrove, to Miss Delilah Jessop of Gunpowder Forest (*Federal Gazette and Baltimore Daily Advertiser* 12 Dec 1798).

Dimmitt (Diamint), John, d. by May 1688 when his widow Mary had m. 2nd, William Gaine (Caine) (*q.v.*) (MDTP 14:72). She m. 3rd, Thomas Stone (*q.v.*).

Dimmitt, Lettis, in 1762 paid a criminal fine for fornication and bastardy (BAMI 1755-1763).

Dimmitt, Susanna, was charged with bastardy at June Court, 1711, and again at March Court 1715 (BACP IS#B:210, 676).

Dimmitt, Viola, was charged with bastardy and fined 30 shillings in Nov 1759; she named Job Garrettson as the father (BAMI 1757-1759:242).

Dimmitt (Demmett), William, Jr., and Catherine Warden Bull were m. on 13 May 1736 (Harrison, "St. John's Parish Register:" 77). On 2 June 1742 he was conveyed property by his father-in-law Jacob Bull (BALR TB#A:151).

Disney, Thomas, aged 9 next 1 April, orphan son of William, in 1772 was bound to Thomas Bond of Barnett to age of 21 (BAMI 1772, 1775-1781: 3).

Distance, William, free Negro, and Hetty, slave of William Evans, were m. 31 May 1800, at St. Peter's Catholic Church, Baltimore (*Piet:* 131).

Ditto, Mary, was charged with bastardy and confessed at the Nov 1768 Court (BAMI 1768-1769:31).

Ditto, Peter, and Catherine Conrad were m. by lic. 18 Oct 1787 at St. Peter's Catholic Church, Baltimore (*Piet:* 131).

Diver, |-?-|, m. by 11 Oct 1799 Jane, daughter of Lawrence Oyston (BAWB 6:241).

Divers, Ann, was charged with bastardy at Nov Court 1772 (BAMI 1772, 1775-1781:84).

Divers (Dives), Christopher, and Sarah Nixon were on 24 June 1762 (Harrison, "St. John's Parish Register:" 223). On 10 June 1765 Sarah was named as the widow and admx. of Thomas Nixon (*q.v.*) of Baltimore Co. (BAAD 6:156; BACM 2:53; MDAD 52:241).

Divers (Dives), Francis, and Mary Watters were m. on 21 Nov 1753 (Harrison, "St. John's Parish Register:" 209). On 7 April 1754 Mary was named as a daughter of Godfrey Watters (MWB 29:156 abst. by Gibb).

Divers, John, and Belinda Eaglestone were m. on 8 May 1788 (Marr. Register of Rev. Lewis Richards, MS.690 at MdHS). On 10 June 1795 Divers' wife was named as an heir of Jonathan Eagleston (BAAD 11:537).

Divers, Tamson was charged with bastardy at the Nov 1768 Court; Edward Sweeting was summoned to court; all fines were paid (BAMI 1768-1769:10).

Divine, Elizabeth, admx. on 19 Nov 1794 posted bond to administer the estate of Peter Cockley (BAAB 8:672).

Dixon, Elizabeth, was charged with unlawful cohabitation with Henry Beach by the vestry of St. George's Parish on 16 March 1767 and again on 5 March 1770 (Reamy. *St. George's Parish Register:* 110, 111).

Dixon, Morris, on 5 March 1770, was summoned to appear before the vestry of St. George's Parish for unlawful cohabitation with Drewsilla Chanley (Reamy, *St. George's Parish Register:* 111).

Dixon, William, free Negro, and Elizabeth, slave of Mr. John Baptist Bernabeu. Consul of Spain for the State of Maryland, were m. 25 Feb 1796 at St. Peter's Catholic Church, Baltimore (*Piet:* 131).

Dizabeau, John, and Magdalen Holmes were m. by lic. 21 April 1798 at St. Peter's Catholic Church, Baltimore (*Piet:* 131; BAML, which gives his name as Digabeau).

Dodd, John, and Ann Bond were m. 7 June 1782 (Marr. Returns of Rev. William West, Scharf Papers, MS.1999 at MdHS). They were guardians of John Bond of Joshua (*q.v.*).

Doddridge (Dottridge), William, and Lettice Taylor were m. on 18 Sep 1717 (Harrison, "St. John's Parish Register:" 11). On 23 Dec 1717 Lettice was named as a daughter of Abraham Taylor (BALR TR#RA:435; BAAD 1:285).

Dodge, Samuel, and Ann Stansbury were married by license dated 10 Oct 1793 (BAML; BALR WG#SS:369).

Dollahide. See Dallahide.

Dolly (Dobby), Henry, and Catherine Gall (Gaul) were m. 24 April 1796 (Marr. Returns of Rev. Daniel Kurtz, Scharf Papers, MS.1999 at MdHS). In his will made 16 Nov 1797 Dolly named his wife Catherine, and her children (by a former husband), Jacob and Elizabeth Gaul, and one other step-child (BAWB 6:65). Catherine was the widow of Johan Gall (*q.v.*).

Dombrousky, Raymond, and Elizabeth Miller were m. by banns on 5 Feb 1799 at St. Peter's Catholic Church, Baltimore (*Piet:* 131).

Donahue, Henry, m. by 11 Aug 1731 Rachel, daughter of Thomas Smithson (MWB 20:568 abst. in Md. Cal. of Wills 6:253).

Donahue, Roger, m. Elizabeth Thompson on 16 Jan 1734 (Harrison, "St. George's Parish Register:" 279). She was the widow of a James Thompson (*q.v.*)

Donaldson, James, and Elizabeth Babine were m. by lic. 28 June 1791 at St. Peter's Catholic Church, Baltimore (*Piet:* 131).

Donawin, Catherine, servant of Robert Clark, was charged with bastardy at the March 1736/7 Court She was charged again at the June 1740 Court (BACP HWS#1A:36, HWS#TR:226).

Donawin (Donovan), Thomas, and Frances Hall were m. on 6 March 1731 (Harrison, "St. George's Parish Register:" 257). On 5 March 1744 Frances was named as a daughter of John Hall (BALR TB#D: 51).

Donawin. See also Donovan.

Donnally, John, m. by 18 Sep 1768 Catherine, daughter of Cornelius Lynch (BAWB 3:99). She m. 2nd, John McCann (McCain) (*q.v.*).

Donnel, John, merchant late from the East Indies, married Sarah, daughter of Thomas Elliott of Fell's Point (*Maryland Journal and Baltimore Advertiser* 18 Oct 1785).

Donnell, John, merchant, of this city, was m. at Northampton, in Va., on Mon., 15th inst., to Miss Anna F. Smith, daughter of Isaac Smith, Esq., of that place (*Federal Gazette and Baltimore Daily Advertiser* 25 Oct 1798).

Donoghue, Daniel, and Bridget Kelnan were m. by banns on 5 Sep 1790 at St. Peter's Catholic Church, Baltimore (*Piet:* 131).

Donovan, Thomas, exec., on 5 Nov 1790 posted bond to administer the estate of Johanna Clossey, whose will made 12 Oct 1790 named Thomas Donovan, her kinsman, as exec. (BAWB 4:499; BAAB 7:255).

Donovan, Valentine, on 10 April 1787 was named as nephew in the will of John Spicer BAWB 4:287).

Donovan. See also Donawin.

Dooley (Dooly), Elizabeth, confessed to bastardy at the June 1750 Court and was fined on 7 Aug 1750 (BACP TR#5:177).

Dooley, William, and Blanche Jones were m. on 15 or 21 Oct 1725 (Harrison, "St. George's Parish Register:" 237, 259). She m. 2nd, William Beaver, Jr. (*q.v.*).

Dooley. See also Duly.

Dooly. See Dooley.

Dopp, Henry, native of Germany, and Rachel Martin were m. by lic. on 16 April 1796 at St. Peter's Catholic Church, Baltimore (*Piet:* 131).

Dorman, Robert, m. by 7 Feb 1676/7 Elisabeth, extx. of James Cogill (or Covill) of Baltimore Co. (MDTP 8A:412-413). Robert was the father of Selah Dorman (*q.v.*) Elizabeth m. 3rd, Daniel Swindell.

Dorman, Selah, son of Robert Dorman, m, 1st, by 16 May 1692, Judith, admx. of Andrew Peterson (MDTP 16:173). On that day Judith Dorman, admx., posted bond to administer the estate of Andrew Peterson (BAAB 2:430). Dorman m. 2nd, by 20 July 1695, Jane, heir of Roger Sidwell (BALR RM#HS:503, TR#RA:325). On 1 Aug 1702 Elizabeth Swindell conveyed to her granddaughter Sarah Dorman one-half of her estate (BALR HW#2:151).

Dorney, James, m. on 14 May 1749 Anne Cadle (Harrison, "St. John's Parish Register:" 198, 243). In April 1747 James Dorney and Ann Cadle had been summoned by the Vestry of St. John's Parish for unlawful cohabitation. In June 1747 Dorney and Cadle appeared and were admonished with certification (Harrison, "St. John's Vestry Proceedings:" 82, 84).

Dorney, John, and Jane Blaney, born in Harford Co., were m. by lic. 25 Sep 1796 at St. Peter's Catholic Church, Baltimore (*Piet:* 131; BAML, which gives his name as John Dawney).

Dorney, William, son of John and Martha of Harford Co., and Elizabeth Green, were m. by lic. 11 Sep 1796, at St. Peter's Catholic Church, Baltimore (*Piet:* 132; BAML, which gives his name as William Dawney).

Dorrumple, John, of Calvert Co., m. by 20 July 1736 Elinor, daughter of William Harris, formerly of Calvert Co., dec. (BALR HWS#1A:123). **See John Derumple above.**

Dorsey, [-?-], m. by 30 May 1747, Sarah, extx. of Thomas Dulany, who left a minor son Dennis (MDTP 32:94).

Dorsey, [-?-], m. by 21 Nov 1761 [-?-], daughter of Morris Baker; they were the parents of: Francis Dorsey (BAWB 2:153).

Dorsey, [-?-], m. by 8 Feb 1762 Sophia, daughter of John Owings (BAWB 3:9).

Dorsey, [-?-], m. by 21 Jan 1797 Mary, daughter of Zachariah Maccubbin and a stepdaughter of Ann, second wife of Zachariah Maccubbin (*q.v.*) (BAWB 6:107).

Dorsey, [-?-], m. by 13 Jan 1785 Rebecca, daughter of Capt. Richard Lane (BAWB 4:69).

Dorsey, Aquila, in Nov 1757 was fined for begetting a bastard on the body of Ann Gardner (BAMI 1757-1759:74).

Dorsey, Bazil, m. by 31 Aug 1751 Hannah, daughter of John Crockett and sister of John Crockett, Jr. (BALR TR#D:180).

Dorsey, Bazil John, and Polly Hanes were m. on 5 Sep 1786 (First German Church, Baltimore, MS. at MdHS). Polly was a daughter of Catherine Haines (BAWB 6:346).

Dorsey, Caleb, m. Elizabeth Worthington on 25 Feb 1772 ("Dorsey Bible Record,"
MGSB 5:65-66). [This marriage actually took place in Anne Arundel Co.].

Dorsey, Charles, m. by 25 Nov 1777, Ann, admins. of Owen Elder (*q.v.*) (BAAD 7:352).

Dorsey, Edward, of Baltimore Co. m. by 23 May 1675, Sarah, daughter of Nicholas
Wyatt of Anne Arundel Co. (MDTP 8A:81).

Dorsey, Col. Edward, d. by 15 Feb 1706 by which time his widow and extx. Margaret
had m. 2nd, John Israel (*q.v.*).

Dorsey, Edward, and Deborah Maccubbin were married by license dated 8 June
1781(BAML). Deborah was a daughter of Zachariah Maccubbin and a stepdaughter
of Ann, second wife of Zachariah Maccubbin (*q.v.*) (BAWB 6:107).

Dorsey, Edward, m. by 17 Jan 1784, Betsy, daughter of Thomas Cresap of Washington
Co. (BAWB 4:398).

Dorsey, Edward, of Elk Ridge, m. last Sat., Betsy, the eldest daughter of Col. John
Dorsey of Baltimore (*Maryland Gazette or Baltimore General Advertiser* 28 March
1786).

Dorsey, Elias, and Susannah Snowden were married on 8 June 1779 (Register of First
Presbyterian Church, Baltimore. MS. at MdHS: 4). On 20 Feb 1783 Susanna was
named as a daughter of John Baptist Snowden (BALR WG#Q:225).

Dorsey, Ely (Elie), and Mary Crockett were m. on 24 Jan 1744 (Harrison, "St. John's
Parish Register:" 192). In Oct 1747 he was named as a brother-in-law of John
Crockett (MWB 25:161 abst. by Gibb). On 8 Oct 1748 Mary was named as a
daughter of John Crockett and sister of John Crockett, Jr. (BALR TR#C:104).

Dorsey, Frances, was charged with bastardy at the Aug 1721 Court (BACP IS#C:270).

Dorsey, Greenbury, son of Col. John and Comfort Dorsey, m. by 1 May 1727, Mary,
daughter of John Belt (BALR IS#H:236, 441).

Dorsey, Greenbury, m. by 17 July 1743 Sarah Fell, widow and extx. of William Fell
(*q.v.*) (BALR TR#D:368; MDAD 28:59, 28:154, 33:159). On 28 Dec 1755 Sarah
was named as a daughter of Thomas Bond (MWB 30:24 abst. by Gibb).

Dorsey, Greenbury, m. by Jan 1773 Sophia, daughter of John Clark (*q.v.*) (MDTP
45:15-16).

Dorsey, Henry (Harry) Woodward, m. Polly, daughter of Zachariah Maccubbin of
Baltimore Co. [date not given] (*Maryland Journal and Baltimore Advertiser* 28 Feb
1786). She was a legatee of Zachariah Maccubbin (BAAD 11:535).

Dorsey, John, of Cecil Co., carpenter, and Sylvia Heathcote were m. on 2 Aug 1724
(Harrison, "St. Stephen's (North Elk) Parish Parish Register:" MS. at MdHS: 330).
On 11 Dec 1727she was identified as Sarah [*sic*], relict and legatee of John
Heathcote (BALR IS#I:82).

Dorsey, John, m. by 9 Dec 1733, Comfort, legatee and extx. of John Hammond of Cecil
Co., and mother of Vincent, John Hammond, Sarah, and Venetia Dorsey (MWB
22:78, abst. in *Md. Cal. of Wills* 8:37; BAAD 3:326).

Dorsey, John, of Michael, m. 2 Dec 1792 in Baltimore Co., Jemima Gist, b. 4 May
1766, daughter of Joseph Gist ("Gist Family Record," *HMGB* 15:35-37). She was a
daughter of Joseph Gist; they were m. Sun., 2nd inst. by Rev. Richards (*Maryland
Journal and Baltimore Advertiser* 14 Dec 1792).

Dorsey, John E., and Mrs. Margaret Hudson, both of this city, were m. last Sat. eve. by
Rev. Mr. Bend (*Federal Gazette and Baltimore Daily Advertiser* 16 Dec 1799).

Dorsey, John Hammond, and Frances Watkins were m. on 16 Feb 1743 (Harrison, "St.
John's Parish Register:" 42). On 10 March 1752 Frances was named as a sister of

Mary Tolley (MDTP 25:172). Frances Hammond Dorsey [*sic*] on 20 Oct 1744 was named as a sister in the will of Mary Tolley, widow of James Tolley; John Hammond Dorsey was named as a brother-in-law (MWB 23:657 abst. by Gibb).

Dorsey, John Hammond, and Ann Maxwell were m. on 20 Jan 1772 (Harrison, "St. John's Parish Register:" 264). She was a daughter of James Maxwell (MWB 41:414; abst. in *Md. Cal. of Wills* 16:205).

Dorsey, Johnsa, and Sarah Hammond were m. on 9 March 1788 ("First German Reformed Church, Frederick," MS at MdHS: 1122). Beal Hammond in his will made 7 May 1797 named his sister Sarah Dorsey and her children Nimrod, Henrietta and Corrilla Dorsey (BAWB 6: 67).

Dorsey, Joshua, and Flora Fitzsimmons were m. on 3 Nov 1734 (Harrison, "St. Paul's Parish Register:" 152). On 11 Oct 1745 Flora was named as a daughter of Nicholas Fitzsimons (MWB 23:501 abst. in *Md. Cal. of Wills* 8:267).

Dorsey, Nicholas, and Sarah Griffith, daughter of Orlando Griffith, were m. c1740 ("The Nicholas Dorsey Bible," *The Notebook* 10 (3) (Sep 1994): 30; *MBR* 3:67-69.).

Dorsey, Orlando G., d. 19 Oct 1816, aged 58, m. by 8 Nov 1784 (when their first child was born), Mary Gaither, d. 1 Nov 1846, sister of Beale Gaither ("The Nicholas Dorsey Bible," *The Notebook* 10 (3) (Sep 1994): 29; *MBR* 3:67-69.).

Dorsey, Owen, of this city, was m. last Sun. at the farm of Mrs. Dorsey, to Miss Henrietta Dorsey of Anne Arundel Co. (*Federal Gazette and Baltimore Daily Advertiser* 17 Oct 1797).

Dorsey, Richard, of Anne Arundel Co., m. by 31 Dec 1736, Elizabeth, widow of William Nicholson, Jr. (BALR IS#IK:372).

Dorsey, Ruth, orphan dau. of Ellas Dorsey, in Oct 1793 was made a ward of Johnsa [Johnsee?] Dorsey (AOC 3:168).

Dorsey, Vincent, and Sarah Day were m. on 26 Oct 1742 (Harrison, "St. John's Parish Register:" : 124, 149). On 8 Jan 1746 Sarah was identified as a daughter of Edward Day (MWB 25:4, abst. by Gibb).

Dousiris (or Dossius), George, in his will made 25 Sep 1797 named his grand children John and Eliza Rick (BAWB 6:37).

Dottridge. See Doddridge.

Douat, Peter, of the Parish of Margot, County of Medoc, Diocese of Bordeaux, and Mary Frances of St. John Baptist du Trou, Cap Francois, Negro, were m. 10 Jan 1794 at St. Peter's Catholic Church, Baltimore (*Piet:* 132).

Douglas (Douglass), Mary, admx. on 17 March 1779 posted bond to administer the estate of Mary Richards (BAAB 4:353).

Douglas, William, m. by 7 July 1720, Mary, daughter of John Scutt (*q.v.*) and devisee of Henry Knowles (BALR TR#A, 370; TR#DS, 338; PCLR PL#8:340). On 8 June 1716 Mary was named as a daughter of Catherine Knowles (MWB 14:230 abst. in *Md. Cal. of Wills* 4:71).

Dougherty, [-?-], m. by 3 Dec 1796, Elizabeth, representative of James Stansbury (BAAD 12:220).

Dow, Robert, m. by 28 July 1755, [-?-], legatee of Joseph Ward (MDAD 38:51).

Dowell, Edward, in his will made 30 Oct 1690 named his son-in-law Oliver Harriod and his daughter-in-law Unity Harriod (Will was recorded in BALR RM#HS:332, abst. in *Md. Cal. of Wills* 4:238).

Dowell, Philip, and Mary Tydings were m. on 11 June 1702 (Harrison, "St. James Parish Register," Anne Arundel Co., MS at MdHS: 318). On 5 April 1717 Mary was named as a daughter of Richard Tydings (BALR TR#A:436, TB#E:522).

Dowell, Thomas, age 8 on 12 Jan 1772, son of Lewis Dowell, in Nov 1772 was bound to Nathaniel Martin to age 21 (BAMI 1772, 1775-1781: 41).

Dowig (Dowing), George, m. by 9 May 1783, Catherine, widow and relict of Nicholas Hasselbach (BALR WG#N:294). In Aug 1784 the Dowigs sued Richard Rogers 'in chancery.' (*Maryland Journal and Baltimore Advertiser* 15 Aug 1794; BAAD 10:289).

Dowing. See Dowig.

Downes. See Downs.

Downey, Daniel Wilson, and Ann Byron, widow, were m. by banns on 25 May 1794 at St. Peter's Catholic Church, Baltimore (*Piet:* 132).

Downs (Downes), Denny, was charged with bastardy and confessed at the June 1733 Court (BACP HWS#9:2, 15).

Downs (Downes), John, m. by 20 March 1698, Margaret [-?-]; on that day William Coventry named Downes as his brother and left the care of his son to Downs MWB 6:218 abst. in *Md. Cal. of Wills* 2:169).

Downs (Downes), John, m. by 16 June 1711, Mary, extx. of Christopher Durbin (*q.v.*) (BAAD 1:360; INAC 33A:212; BACP IS#B:308). Thomas and Christopher Durbin on 1 April 1718 were named as sons-in-law in the will of John Downs (MWB 14:599 abst. in *Md. Cal. of Wills* 4:161). Mary was also the mother of Simon Cannon (*q.v.*) and Elizabeth Cannon.

Dowse, Edward, d. by Dec 1691; his extx. m. 2nd, Thomas James (*q.v.*) (BACP F#I:111).

Doyle, Jacob, and Miss Catherine Dutro, both of this city, were m. last Thurs. eve. by Rev. D. Kurtz (*Federal Gazette and Baltimore Daily Advertiser* 22 June 1799).

Doyle, Nicholas, and Ann McDaniel, both of Baltimore Co., were m. by lic. 5 June 1794 at St. Peter's Catholic Church, Baltimore (*Piet:* 132).

Doyle, Sarah, in her will made 4 March 1796 named her daughters Margaret wife of Ephraim Murray (*q.v.*) and Elizabeth wife of Peter Armegost (*q.v.*); she mentioned her father's estate in Bucks Co., Pa, (BAWB 5:369).

Drabough, Valentine, orphan son of Michael, in Dec 1794 chose John Drabough as his guardian (BAOC 3:123).

Drebert (Dreppard), Andrew, and Katherine Ilgar were married by license dated 27 Dec 1788 (BAML). On 1 April 1796, 'Catherine' was named as a daughter of George Ilgar (BAAD 12:131).

Drebert (Drepbert), Christian, and Mary Forney were married by license dated 16 June 1792 (BAML). She was a daughter of the late Adam Forney, were m. last Sun. eve. by Rev. Kurtz (*Maryland Journal and Baltimore Advertiser* 19 June 1792; see also BAAD 11:454). On 6 Feb 1799 Mary received her full share of the estate of Adam Forney (BAAD 12:541). She m. 2nd, Babier Brason (*q.v.*).

Drehorn, John, of Baltimore stated he would not pay the debts of his wife Catherine (*Baltimore Daily Repository* 23 June 1792).

Dreiry[?], Mary, on 18 June 1774 was named as a sister-in-law in the will of John Little (BAWB 3:298).

Drew, Anthony, m. by 7 Sep 1686, Mary Ann, daughter of George Utie and niece of Col. Nathaniel Utie (INAC 12:147; MDTP 14:48).

Drew, Anthony, and Margaret Brown were m. 17 May 1709 (Harrison, "St. George's Parish Register:" 208). She was the widow of Thomas Brown and the mother of John Brown (*q.v.*). On 9 April 1711, Margaret and John Browne, were named as execs. of Thomas Browne, and in Feb 1719, as next of kin of John Brown (MDTP 21:337; MINV 3:241).

Drew, George, and Johanna Phillips were m. on [date not given] (Harrison, "St. George's Parish Register:" 287). In 1720 Jane [*sic*] was named as a daughter of Col. James Philips, of Baltimore Co..; she m. 2nd, Jacob Giles (*q.v.*) (Prov. Court Judg. 29:126-128).

Drew, George, and Hannah Lusby were m. on 26 July 1722 (Harrison, "St. George's Parish Register:" 246). In his will, proved 8 March 1764 Joseph Lusby named his nephew Anthony Drew (BAWB 2:172).

Drew, Henry, on 2 Nov 1766 was named as a cousin in the will of James Shepard (BAWB 3:76).

Drinan, Thomas, and Mary Pemston were m. by lic. 6 Jan 1793 at St. Peter's Catholic Church, Baltimore (*Piet:* 132). (BAML gives her name as Pinson).

Droboch, Valentine, aged 14 or 16, in June 1793 chose Engl'd Yeiser as his guardian (BAOC 3:54).

Drumbo, Conrad, and Caterena Neff were married by license dated 6 April 1779 (BAML). In his will, made 4 Nov 1795 Henry Neff, aged about 75 years named his daughter Molly [*sic*] Drumbo (BAWB 5:388),

Drunkord, [-?-], m. by 8 Jan 1704/5, Mary, daughter of Thomas Greenfield (MWB 3:470, abst. in *Md. Cal. of Wills* 3:53).

Drury, Rachel was charged with bastardy, confessed, and was fined at the March 1745/6 Court (BACP 1745-1746: 186).

Dryden, Mylby, and Polly Patrick, both of Baltimore, were m. Tues. eve. by Rev. Mr. Morsell (*Baltimore Telegraphe* 12 Feb 1800).

Drysdale, Robert, in his will made 3 May 1704 named his sons-in-law John Fisher and Thomas Jackson (*q.v.*) who he named his executors and to whom he left his entire estate (MWB 3:241 abst. in *Md. Cal. of Wills* 3:38).

Ducatel, Edme, m. by 8 Sep 1798, [-?-], who received payment from the estate of Frederick Estienne (BAAD 12:484).

Ducatel, Edmond, son of Edmond and Aime Magdalen Lessene, and Ann Pineau Brucourt, daughter of John and Frances Bossen Pineau, were m. by lic. on 28 May 1785, at St. Peter's Catholic Church, Baltimore (*Piet:* 132).

Duchee, Swanson, shipwright, m. by 8 Sep 1767, Ann, widow of James Ventris (BALR B#Q: 308).

Duchemin, Mr. Francois, an eminent merchant of Port-au-Prince, and Miss Margaret Mangfee of Baltimore were m. yesterday by Rev. Mr. Sewall (*Baltimore Evening Post* 11 Jan 1793). The bride's name is given as Mongeau, at St. Peter's Catholic Church, Baltimore (*Piet:* 132).

Dudney, Mary, living at the house of Owen Bright, had a child born in May 1703 (Reamy, *St. George's Parish Register:* 13).

Due. See Dew.

Duesbury, James, stated he would not pay the debts of his wife Elizabeth (*Maryland Journal and Baltimore Advertiser* 10 June 1783).

Duff, John, and Sarah Green were m. by lic. 11 Sep 1791 at St. Peter's Catholic Church, Baltimore (*Piet:* 132).

Duffy, Henry, and Mary Rourke, natives of Ireland, were m. by lic. 3 Aug 1800, at St. Peter's Catholic Church, Baltimore (*Piet:* 132).

Duffy, Owen, and Mary Williams were m. by lic. on 29 March 1788 at St. Peter's Catholic Church, Baltimore (*Piet:* 132).

Dufy, Michael Robert, late of Jerome, Island of San Domingo, in his will made 23 Feb 1796 named his natural children Arson Francis, Arson Albert, Mary Magdelain Grielle, and Joseph, the child of Rosetta, a slave (BAWB 5:361).

Duly. See also Dooley.

Dugan, Arthur, of Fell's Point, stated he would not pay the debts of his wife Mary (*Maryland Journal and Baltimore Advertiser* 22 Dec 1778).

Dugan, Cumberland, merchant, m. last Tues. eve. Peggy, eldest daughter of James Kelso of Baltimore (*Maryland Gazette or Baltimore General Advertiser* 7 Nov 1786).

Dugan, James, and Ann Gutry were m. by lic. 22 Aug 1789 at St. Peter's Catholic Church, Baltimore (*Piet:* 132).

Dugan, Patrick, merchant of this city, and Miss Polly McComas of Harford Co. were m. last eve. (*Federal Gazette and Baltimore Daily Advertiser* 15 Oct 1799).

Dukehart, Elizabeth. See William Ball.

Dukehart, John, and Parthenia Balderston on 10 d. 11 m. 1796 declared their intention to marry ("Minutes of Baltimore Meeting," *QRNM:*227). John Dukehart was m. yesterday at Friends Meeting, to Parthenia Balderston, both of this town (*Federal Gazette and Baltimore Daily Advertiser* 16 Dec 1796).

Dukehart, Margaret, on 23 d. 1 m. 1771 was condemned for going out in marriage ("Minutes of Gunpowder Monthly Meeting," *QRNM:*60). **See Jonathan Davenport.**

Dukes, Charles, m. by 17 May 1770, Violetta, daughter of Jonas Bowen (BALR AL#B:188).

Dukes, Christopher, aged 21, and Mrs. Jane Dukes, aged 76, both of Back River Neck, were m. last eve. by Rev. Richards (*Baltimore Weekly Museum* 26 March 1797).

Dulany, |-?-| (Dulaney), m. by 15 April 1761 Ann, daughter of Benjamin Meed of Baltimore Co. (MWB 31:1084; BAWB 2:177).

Dulany, Thomas, d. by 4 dec 1741 leaving a widow and admx. (or extx.) Sarah, and children, William, Elizabeth, and Thomas (BAAD 4:84, 161).

Dulohany, John, and Catherine Franklin were m. by lic. 30 April 1792 at St. Peter's Catholic Church, Baltimore (*Piet:* 132; BAML, which gives his name as John Dulshary).

Dumeste, M., a French gentleman, m. Miss Keeports of this town (*Maryland Journal and Baltimore Advertiser* 2 July 1782). (BAML gives his name as John Durmeste).

Dunbar, |-?-|, m. by 19 Dec 1736 Mary, sister of Charles Daniel (MWB 21:765 abst. in *Md. Cal. of Wills* :212).

Duncan, Ann, now 4 years old, orphan of William Duncan, in Nov 1775 was bound to Henry Zigler (BAMI 1782-1786: 153).

Duncan (Dunkin), John, m. by 26 March 1694, Ann, daughter of John Mould (BALR RM#HS:422).

Duncan (Dunkin), John, on 22 d., 1 m. 1772, was charged with being married by a priest ("Minutes of Gunpowder Meeting," *QRNM:*62). [No other marriage reference found].

Duncan, William, and Martha Talbot were married by license dated 4 Sep 1790 (BAML). On 20 April 1792 Martha was named as the widow and extx. of Benjamin Robinson Talbott (*q.v.*) (BAWB 4:309; BAAD 10:99, 11:25).

Duncan. William, and Brigid Rice were m. by lic. 2 Jan 1794 at St. Peter's Catholic Church, Baltimore (*Piet:* 132).

Dungan, Mary, late Lukins, on 28 d. 3 m. 1793 had testimony produced against her for her marriage outside the society by a hireling preacher ("Minutes of Deer Creek Meeting," *QRNM:* 152). [No other marriage reference found].

Dunham, James, m. by 16 July 1707, Margaret, extx. of William Galloway (*q.v.*) (MDTP 19C:243). Margaret was a daughter of Hendrick and Christian Enloes and sister of Abraham Enloes who d. 1709 (*BCF:* 238).

Dunkin. See also Duncan.

Dunkin. Jane. See Jane Cross.

Dunmead, John, m. by 22 April 1796, Elizabeth, daughter of Jacob Keeports (BALR WG#VV:418).

Dunsmore, Robert, petitioned the court that in 1790 he had been bound by the court to Aaron Levering to learn the trade of a merchant, but he had been kept cleaning knives and candlesticks, and washing dishes (BOCP Petition of Robert Dunsmore, 1792).

Dunn, [-?-], d. by 11 Nov 1793 when his widow Catherine m. John Gregory (*q.v.*) (Marr. Returns of Rev. William West, Scharf Papers, MS.1999 at MdHS). In her will made 1798, Caty Gregory named her children Arthur, Samuel, Hannah, and Ann Dunn, and her son Henry Gregory (BAWB 6:155).

Dunn, Daniel, and Elizabeth Park were m. by lic. 21 Oct 1798 at St. Peter's Catholic Church, Baltimore (*Piet:* 132).

Dunn, Edward, and Mary O'Hagan, natives of Ireland, were m. 14 June 1794, at St. Peter's Catholic Church, Baltimore (*Piet:* 132).

Dunn, James, m. Sally Hodges (*Maryland Journal and Baltimore Advertiser* 31 Dec 1782). (They were m. in Baltimore Co.).

Dunn, James, m. by 21 Oct 1785 [-?-], who received a portion of the estate of Francis Moore (BAAD 8:170).

Dunn, John, and Eleanor Fitzgerald, were m. by banns on 26 July 1790 at St. Peter's Catholic Church, Baltimore (*Piet:* 132).

Dunn, Michael, and Mary McGuire were m. by lic. 9 July 1788 at St. Peter's Catholic Church, Baltimore (*Piet:* 132).

Dunn, Robert, and Sarah Wakeman or Pritchard on 9 May 1762 (Harrison, "St. George's Parish Register:" 367). On that day Sarah Wakeman or Pritchard was named as an heir of Edward Wakeman (BAWB 3:130; BAAD 6:283); on 8 April 1773, Sarah and James More (*q.v.*) administered Dunn's estate (MDAD 69:175).

Dunnavan, Pierce, and Nellie Harris, were m. by lic. 20 June 1790, at St. Peter's Catholic Church, Baltimore (*Piet:* 132).

Dunphy, Richard, and Mary Smith, were m. by lic. 8 Dec 1799, at St. Peter's Catholic Church, Baltimore (*Piet:* 132).

Dunsell, Mary, servant of Christopher Duke, was charged with bastardy at the March 1733/4 Court and was presented in Aug 1734 (BACP HWS#9:188, 308).

Dunwoody, Robert, and Eleanor Kidd were m. on 20 Sep 1784 (Marriage Returns of Rev. William West, Scharf Papers, MS. 1999 at MdHS). On 6 Aug 1785 Ellen was named as the extx. of Henry Kidd (*q.v.*) (BAAD 8:226). Robert Dunwoody, of

Baltimore, stated he would not pay the debts of his wife Eleanor (*Maryland Gazette or Baltimore General Advertiser* 21 Jan 1791).

Dunwoody, Robert, and Ann McCann were married by license dated 27 Feb 1796 (BAML). In 1796 Ann was named as the admx. of John McKenna or McCann) (*q.v.*) (BOCP Petition of Adam McLane and Elijah Egon, 1796). On 12 Feb 1800 Dunwoody was named as the guardian of John McKenna (BAAD 13:16),

Dupois, Christopher, native of Havre de Grace, France, and Mary Brier, were m. by banns on 19 Jan 1796 at St. Peter's Catholic Church, Baltimore (*Piet:* 132).

Duramier, Amable Ambrose Herbert, son of John Peter Nicholas Herbert Demontign of the King's Bodyguards, and Marie Adelaid LeJaulne, native of the Parish of Lieura in Normandy, and Marie Charlotte Justine Tardieu, daughter of John Baptist Joseph, Parish of St. Louis of Teremy, St. Domingo, and Mary Ann Magdalen O-Coin, were m. by lic. 10 Nov 1800, at St. Peter's Catholic Church, Baltimore (*Piet:* 132).

Durant, Sabrina, admx. of Anthony Durant, was charged with bastardy was charged with bastardy at the Nov 1733 Court, and presented at June 1734, Aug 1734, and Nov 1734 Courts. She was charged with bastardy again at the Nov 1742 Court (BACP HWS#9:13, 153, 309, 400; TB#D:59).

Durbin, [-?-], m. by April 1784 Mary, daughter of William Andrews (BAOC 1:111).

Durbin, Christopher, d. c1709, having m. Mary, widow of [-?-] Cannon and mother of Simon Cannon (*q.v.*) and Elizabeth Cannon; she m. 3rd, John Downs (q.v.),

Durbin, Elizabeth, was charged with bastardy at the March 1733/4 Court and presented at the June 1734 Court (BACP HWS#9:264).

Durbin, John, and 'Abarillah' Scott were m. on 20 Aug 1715 (Harrison, "St. John's Parish Register:" 7). On 9 July 1725, Avarilla was named as the daughter of Daniel Scott (BAAD 3:18; MDAD 6:406).

Durbin, John, and Elinor Odan were m. on 13 Dec 1743. She m. 2nd, Alexander Hill (*q.v.*) on 10 May 1744 (Harrison, "St. John's Parish Register:" 25, 190), and 3rd, [-?-] Bennett (*q.v.*).

Durbin, John, was the father of two sons, William, aged 12 last 1 Feb, and Samuel, aged 10 last 1 Feb, who in Aug 1759 were bound to Samuel Webb (BAMI 1755-1763).

Durbin, Mary, and **Thomas Durbin,** were named as two children of Christopher Shaw in the latter's administration account of 1742 (BAAD 3:279).

Durbin, Samuel, and Ann 'Logden'[*sic*] were m. on 4 July 1723 (Harrison, "St. Paul's Parish Register:" 146). On 19 Sep 1726 Ann was named as a daughter of William Logsdon (BALR IS#H:338).

Durham, Hugh, servant of Lance Todd, in Aug 1722 and in June 1725 was charged with begetting a bastard on the body of Elizabeth Brock, a fellow servant (BACP IS&TW#1:306, IS&TW#4:224).

Durham, Jacob, m. by 29 Oct 1764, Sarah, daughter of Andrew Thompson (BFD 4:79). [But see Joshua Thompson below].

Durham, James, m. by 6 June 1693/4, Elizabeth, daughter of John Lee (BALR RM#HS: 350).

Durham, James, m. by 16 Feb 1686 [-?-], daughter of Thomas Staley, whose will date 16 Feb 1696 named Durham as a son-in-law and Durham's eldest daughter Mary, and his son James Durham (MWB 11:25 *abst. in Md. Cal. of Wills* 2:208).

Durham, James, m. by 2 Oct 1707, Margaret, extx. of William Galloway (INAC 27:107).

Durham, John, m. by Nov 1683, Jane, admx. of William Choice (*q.v.*) (BACP D:13, 14). She m. 3rd, John Boone (*q.v.*)

Durham, John, was the brother of Elizabeth Durham who m. by 2 June 1736 John Stand (Dep. of Jane Boon in BALR HWS#M:361).

Durham, Joshua, and Sarah Thompson were m. on 10 Jan 1754 (Harrison, "St. John's Parish Register:" 209). On 19 Dec 1760 Sarah was named as a daughter of Andrew Thompson (BAWB 2:329; BAAD 4:347). [But see Jacob Thompson above].

Durham, Samuel, and Eleanor Smithson were m. on 15 Jan 1723 (Harrison, "St. John's Parish Register:" 21).On 11 Aug 1731 Eleanor was named as a daughter of Thomas Smithson (MWB 20:568 abst. in *Md. Cal. of Wills* 6:253).

Durick, Mary, was charged with bastardy at the June 1739 Court (BACP HWS#TR: 401).

Durin, Mary, was charged with bastardy at the Aug 1740 Court (BACP HWS#TR:302).

Durney, James, and Ann Mineahan were m. by banns on 22 Jan 1792 at St. Peter's Catholic Church, Baltimore (*Piet:* 132).

Dutton, Isaac, and Elizabeth [-?-] were m. some time before 17 Feb 1797 when their son David was born ("Family Bible owned by Mrs. Howard Boone," BRHA: 146).

Dutton, John, son of Robert and Susanna, b. 23 Dec 1761, and Elizabeth Hughston, b. 15 d. 3 m. 1773, were m. on 16 Feb 1790 ("John Dutton Bible," in *MBR* 7:46). John Dutton on 24 d. 7 m. 1790 [was reported as having] had his marriage accomplished by a hireling ("Minutes of Gunpowder Meeting," *QRNM*:88). [

Dutton, Robert, son of Robert of Cecil Co., and Susanna Howard, daughter of Lemuel Howard were m. 24 Feb 1755 ("Records of Gunpowder Meeting," ms at MdHS: 236; the year as given as 1757 in Harrison, "St. John's Parish Register:" 177). Robert and Susann were the parents of: Robert, b. 24 Dec 1759 ("John Dutton Bible," *MBR* 7:46).

Dutton, Robert, on 13 June 1764 was named in the will of Mary Brown as her brother (MWB 37:122, abst. in *Md. Cal. of Wills* 14:81).

Dutton, Robert, on 25 d. 6 m. 1779 was charged with having an 'unlawful child' ("Minutes of Gunpowder Meeting," QRNM:73).

Dwyer, William, widower, and Elizabeth Casey, widow, were m. by lic. on 20 Feb 1798 at St. Peter's Catholic Church, Baltimore (*Piet:* 132).

Dwyer, William, widower, and Eleanor Kelly, widow, were m. by lic. on 29 Dec 1800 at St. Peter's Catholic Church, Baltimore (*Piet:* 132).

Dyer, [-?-], m. by 31 Dec 1769, Ann, daughter of Benjamin Wheeler (BAWB 3:174).

Dyer, Elizabeth. See Elizabeth Polton.

Dyer, Hester. See Gilbert Henderson.

Dyer, Phebe. See Phebe Carr.

"E"

Eager, John, m. Jemima, daughter of James Murray (*BCF:* 463); Eager d. by d. by 29 May 1723 when Jemima had m. 2nd, Philip Jones (*q.v.*) (Harrison, "St. Paul's,": 146).

Eager, Thomas, d. by 17 Feb 1709, when his widow Mary m. 2nd, Samuel Merryman (*q.v.*) (MDTP 21:208). On 19 Nov 1709 Mary was named as a daughter of Humphrey Boone and sister of Robert Boone of Baltimore Co. (MWB 12-2:205; I

Eagleston, [Henry?], d. by 4 Dec 1772, having m. Salathiel, daughter of Jarvis Biddison, by whom he was the father of Mary and Charity; his widow m. 2nd, Robert Abercrombie (*q.v.*) (BAWB 3:272).

Eagleston, John, m. by 29 March 1768, [-?-], heir of Tobias Stansbury (BAAD 7:321).

Eaglestone, Abraham, was charged with bastardy at Aug Court 1768 (BAMI 1768-1769:26).

Eaglestone, Benjamin, and Sarah Dallas were m. on 18 Aug 1764 (Harrison, "St. John's Parish Register:" 225); she m. 2nd, Nathaniel Martin (*q.v.*) (MCHP #2464).

Eaglestone, Benjamin, d. by Oct 1792 and James Osborn was appointed guardian of his orphans sons Benjamin and Walter; in Feb 1794 both sons chose James Sloane as their guardian (BAOC 3:12, 18, 82).

Eaglestone, Charity, daughter of Henry, in Nov 1775 was bound to Mary Biddison (BAMI 1772, 1775-1781: 152).

Eaglestone, John, m. by 12 April 1791 [-?-], who received one-third of the estate of Henry Oats (BAAD 10:330).

Eaglestone, Jonathan, m. by 29 March 1769 Helen, who was paid a share of her father's estate (poss. Tobias Stansbury's) (MDAD 59:221).

Eaglestone, Mary, daughter of Henry, in Nov 1775 was bound to Daniel Biddison (BAMI 1772, 1775-1781: 152)

Eanner[?], James, on 15 March 1798 was named in the administration account of Susannah Mason and received an equal share of £38.17.0½ (BAAD 13:9).

Earle, Elizabeth, servant to Aquila Massey, of Baltimore Co., who was charged with bastardy in Aug 1739 Court (BACP HWS#TR:13). She is probably Elizabeth Earl, the felon, who was transp. from London to Md. on the *Patapsco Merchant* in April 1733 (*KPMV:*57). Elizabeth Earl and Peter Golden or Golding, both of St. John's Parish, were m. 10 Oct 1742, after the banns had been published three times. They were the parents of: John, b. 27 Oct 1744, Stephen, b. 10 Aug 1746, and Elizabeth, b. 18 Aug 1749 (Harrison, "St. John's Parish Register:" 144, 157, 238, 260).

Earnest, Caleb, m. by 17 Sep 1789 Ann, granddaughter of Mayberry Helm (BAWB 4:487).

Earp, John, m. by 29 Sep 1737 Mary, daughter and coheir of William Budd of Baltimore Co. (PCLR PL#8:558).

Easterling, John, of Calvert Co. m. by 7 July 1711 Henrietta, daughter of John Broom who took up *Brooms Bloom* in Baltimore Co. (PCLR TP#4:69).

Ebbecke, John Frederick, widower, and Catherine Fry, widow, were m. by lic. 29 Dec 1800, at St. Peter's Catholic Church, Baltimore (Piet: 132).

Ebbert, John, m. in 1778, Catherine, widow of [Philip?] Hiteshew (*q.v.*), and formerly the wife of Thomas Russell (*q.v.*) (BAOC Petitions: Sam Messersmith and John Ebbert; no date). John Ebbert and Catherine 'Hitejus' were m. by lic. dated 30 March 1778 (BAML).

Ebert, George, and Margaret Jackson were m. by lic. on 3 Sep 1779 (BAML). In Sep 1782 Ebert stated that his wife Margaret had eloped (*Maryland Journal and Baltimore Advertiser* 17 Sep 1782).

Ebden, William, d. by March 1691/2, and his wife Jane m. 2nd, Michael Judd (*q.v.*). At the March 1691/2 Court a William Ebden [Jr.?] was reported as being the 'natural son' of Jane Judd (BACP F#1:165).

Eckland, Ulrich, d. by Oct 1792; his orphan children, John, Samuel, and Ulean, were made wards of Henry Sobough (BAOC 3:12).

Eckles, Mr. Andrew, of Baltimore, and Miss Eliza Nagle of Philadelphia were m. there on 31st ult. by Rev. Dr. Smith (*Federal Gazette and Baltimore Daily Advertiser* 8 Feb 1799).

Edes, William, Boston merchant, and Catherine Pennell of Fell's Point were m. on Thurs. by Rev. Richards (*Baltimore American* 22 June 1799).

Edmiston, [-?-], m. by 18 Sep 1770 Maria Graham, daughter of William and Jane Woodward of Baltimore Town; Jane Woodward named a granddaughter Jane Edmiston in her will (BAWB 3:282, 303).

Edmonds, Richard, m. by 16 Oct 1682 Elizabeth, relict and extx, of Henry Haslewood (*q.v.*) (MDTP 12B:273). On 1 May 1699 Elizabeth Gibson conv. chattel goods to her son Thomas Edmonds. Note that Elizabeth Gibson was by now the widow of Miles Gibson (*q.v.*) (BALR TR#RA: 347; INAC 12:149, 150, 151). She m. John Collett (*q.v.*).

Edward, [-?-], d. by 11 June 1773, leaving a son Philip Edward and a widow Hannah who m. 2nd. George Salmon (BALR AL#G: 42, 329).

Edwards, [-?-], m. by 21 April 1774, Catherine, daughter of George Adam Beard (BAWB 3:294).

Edwards, [-?-], m. by 12 Oct 1790, Mary, sister of Johannah Clossey (BAWB 4:499).

Edwards, James, and Ruth Stansbury were m. on 9 March 1775 (Harrison, "St. Paul's Parish Register:" 171). On 18 Aug 1798 James Edwards received an equal share of £20.8.10 from the estate of Isaac Stansbury (BAAD 12:471).

Edwards, John, and Mary Merryman were m. on 23 Jan 1727 (Harrison, "St. Paul's Parish Register:" 148). On 13 Jan 1746 Mary was named as a daughter of John Merryman, Sr. (MWB 26:102 abst. by Gibb).

Edwards, John, and Dinah Greenfield were married by license dated 15 Jan 1791 (BAML). On 9 Feb 1791 she was named as a daughter of James Greenfield (BAAD 10:290).

Edwards, Paul, m. by 20 May 1793, Mary, admx. of Joseph Sindorff (BALR WG#MM: 1). (Records of St. Peter's Catholic Church, Baltimore, state her name was Sindolph, and that they were m. by lic. 18 Sep 1792 (*Piet:* 132).

Edwards, Paul, and Sarah Travolet were m. by lic. on 10 Sep 1785 (BAML). In Feb 1796 Edwards stated he would not pay the debts of his wife Sarah (*Maryland Journal and Baltimore Advertiser* 10 Feb 1786).

Edwards, Philip, printer and proprietor of the *Baltimore Evening Post*, and Miss Ann Rawlings of Baltimore, were m. last eve. by Rev. Dr. Bend (*Baltimore Daily Repository* 29 March 1793).

Edwards, Robert, mariner, in Aug 1714 was charged with begetting a bastard on the body of Sarah Doe (BACP IS#C:3-4).

Edwards, Thomas, was m. last Thurs. eve. by Rev. Dr. Allison, to Miss Ann Gordon, both of this city (*Federal Gazette and Baltimore Daily Advertiser* 15 Sep 1798; BAML, which gives her name as Gordan).

Egerton, George, in March 1733/4 was charged with begetting a bastard on the body of Mary Chamney (BACP HWS#9:183, 199).

Eichelberger, Frederick, m. by 11 Oct 1773 Eve, daughter of George Moyers (Myers) (BAAD 6:258; MDAD 68:153).

Eiselen, Capt. Conrad, of this town was m. in Philadelphia by Rev. Bishop White, to Miss Maria Hubley [or Hobley] (*Federal Intelligencer and Baltimore Daily Gazette* 19 Nov 1795).

Eiselen, Friderich, m. by 27 March [1796?], [-?-] Kohl (Register of First German Reformed Church, Baltimore, MS. at MdHS: 20). Frederick Eislin and Sarah Cole were married by license dated 1 March 1795 (BAML).

Eiser, Richard, m. by 9 Oct 1786, [-?-], daughter of Joseph Shaule (BAAD 8:321).

Elder, Charles, and Ruth Howard were m. on 14 Feb 1769 (Harrison, "St. Thomas Parish Register:" 74). On 26 Jan 1778 Ruth was named as a daughter of Cornelius Howard (BALR WG#A:490; BAAD 9:49). Ruth Howard, in her will made 6 Sep 1788 named her daughter Violetta, wife of Joseph West (BAWB 5:442).

Elder, Owen, and Nancy Dorsey were m. on 10 April 1766 (Harrison, "St. Thomas' Parish Register:" 74). She m. 2nd, by 25 Nov 1777 Charles Dorsey (*q.v.*).

Elder, Owen, orphan son of John, in June 1794 chose John Elder as his guardian BAOC 3:99).

Elder, Robert, m. by 21 July 1775 Mary, daughter of James Taylor (MWB 41:408; abst. in *Md. Cal. of Wills* 16:204).

Elledge, Thomas, now of Bedford Co., Va., m. by 9 Oct 1764, Elizabeth, daughter and coheir of John Thornbury, dec. (BALR B#O:97).

Elless, [-?-], m. by 26 March 1770, Rachel, daughter of John Norris (BAWB 2:328).

Ellett, [-?-], m. by 24 Dec 1761, Rebecca, a residuary legatee of John Norris (BFD 3:119).

Ellicott, John, on 31 d. 12 m. 1780 was charged with having been married by a priest ("Minutes of Gunpowder Meeting," *QRNM:*74). [No other marriage reference found].

Elliott, Ann, in July 1736 was charged by the vestry of St. George's Parish with unlawful cohabitation with George Elliott. On 2 Aug 1742 Sarah, wife of John Elliott, charged her husband with unlawful cohabitation with Ann, wife of George Elliott (Harrison, "Abstracts of St. John's Parish Vestry Proceedings:" 14, 64-65).

Elliot, George, and Patience Buckner were m. 12 Jan 1732 Harrison, "St. Paul's Parish Register:" 151). He was in Va. on 11 Sep 1733 when Patience was named as the widow of William Buckner (*q.v.*), who left siblings Thomas, Philip, Ann, Elizabeth, and Mary Buckner, and Christian wife of Charles Debroim, all of Va. (MDTP 29:309).

Elliott, George: in July 1737 he and wife Anne were summoned for unlawful cohabitation (Harrison, "St. John's and St. George's Parish Vestry Proceedings").

Elliott, George, and Theresa Anderson were m. on 20 June 1769 (Harrison, "St. John's Parish Register:" 258). On 18 April 1788 Elliott's wife was named as a daughter of Thomas Anderson (BAAD 9:196).

Elliott, John, in July 1737 with wife Sarah was summoned for unlawful cohabitation. In Aug 1743 Sarah Elliott complained that her husband John unlawfully cohabited with Ann Elliott wife of George Elliott (Harrison, "St. John's and St. George's Parish Vestry Proceedings:" 65).

Elliott, Philip Lock, and Sarah Wright were m. on 24 Dec 1752 (Harrison, "St. John's Parish Register:" 206). On 10 July 1753 Sarah was named as the admx. of William Wright (*q.v.*) (MDTP 33-2:142; MDAD 35:40; BAAD 5:226).

Elliott, Thomas, and Ann Robinson were m. on 14 April 1748 (Harrison, "St. John's Parish Register:" 196). On 11 March 1772 Ann was named as a sister of Charles Robinson, and daughter of Richard Robinson (BAWB 3:169, 233).

Ellis, [-?-], m. by 26 March 1760 Rachel, daughter of John Norris (BAWB 2:328).

Ellis, Jane, in Jan 1748 was transported from London to Kent Co., MD on the *St. George,* James Dobbins, Capt. The ship was registered in Kent Co., MD, Records in March 1748 (*KPMV:*114). A servant of Samuel Owings of Baltimore Co., in Aug 1755 she was sentenced to serve an extra nine months for runaway time and for charges to the doctor for curing her French distemper (BAMI 1755-1763). She had a daughter (Harrison, "St. Thomas' Parish Register:" 19): Sarah, b. 14 Nov 1750.

Ellis, Peter, m. by 5 Aug 1679, [-?-], admx. of William Palmer (*q.v.*) (MDTP 11:154; INAC 6:462).

Ellis, William, son of Benjamin and Ann, dec., on 30 d. 12 m. 1784, announced his intention to marry Mary Cox, daughter of William and Mary, the former dec. ("Minutes of Deer Creek Meeting," *QRNM:*143).

Ellt, [-?-], d. by 20 July 1739, having m. Elinor, daughter of William Harris, and leaving a son Benjamin Ellt; Elinor m. 2nd, John Derumple (*q.v.*) of Calvert Co. (BALR HWS#IA:123).

Elmes, William, native of N. J., and Anne Frances Bourdon, born at Port au Prince, daughter of Peter, President of the Supreme Council of Port au Prince, St. Domingo, and Ann LeMaitre, were m. by lic. 12 May 1795, at St. Peter's Catholic Church, Baltimore (*Piet:* 132).

Ely, Hannah, was charged with bastardy at March 1768 Court and Isaac Robinson was summoned; she was again presented for bastardy in 1775 (BAMI 1758-1769:9. 1772, 1775-1781:204).

Ely, Joseph, and Ann (late Jones) his wife on 2 d. 7 m. 1789 were reported as having been m. by a Baptist Preacher ("Minutes of Deer Creek Meeting," *QRNM:* 146). [No other marriage reference found].

Ely, Thomas, son of Thomas, on 2 d. 11 m. 1775 announced his intention to marry Hannah Warner, daughter of Croasdale Warner ("Minutes of Deer Creek Meeting," *QRNM:*136). Thomas Ely and Hannah Warner were m. 24 d. 1 m. 1776 ("Deer Creek Meeting," *QRNM:* 34).

Ely, William, son of Thomas and Sarah, dec., on 27 d. 4 m. 1794, announced his intention to marry Martha Preston, daughter of Henry and Rachel Preston, both dec. ("Minutes of Deer Creek Meeting," *QRNM:* 154).

Emerson (Emmerson), John, and Ann Elizabeth Partridge Colegate were m. on 20 Jan 1791 (Marr. Register of Rev. Lewis Richards, MS.690 at MdHS). On 9 Dec 1794 Elizabeth Partridge was named as a daughter in the will of Thomas Colegate (BAWB 5:249).

Emerson (Emmerson), John, d. by 9 Dec 1795. Hugh McCurdy, admin., petitioned the court that the deceased left an estate valued at 898.13.7 current money, and the estate belonged to the widow and one child in England. The petitioner wanted permission to sell the estate so he could transmit the money to the widow and child (BOCP Petition of Hugh McCurdy, 1795).

Emerson, Mary, of London, in March 1730 was transported on the *Patapsco Merchant* and registered in Annapolis in Sep 1730 (KPMV: 44). In June 1734 as servant to John Price she was tried for bastardy. Her son Henry was b. by June 1732 (BACP (BACP HWS#7:297, HWS#9:264).

Emmart, Philip, and Sarah Brown were m. on 8 April 1797 (Marr. Returns of Rev. Joseph Bend, Scharf Papers, MS.1999 at MdHS; *MBR* 3:74-75).

Emmice, Philip, m. by 19 March 1764, Elizabeth, extx. of Martin Trush (also given as Thrash and Thrush) (MDAD 51:109; MINV 80:41; BAMI 1765:51; MDTP 40:266).

Emmiott (Emmitt), Samuel, m. by 4 Sep 1760, Mary, daughter of William Jenkins (MWB 31:316; BAWB 2:358).

Emmitt, Abraham, and Mary [-?-] were m. by 1 Nov 1769 when their daughter Mary was b. ("Bible Records of the Ridgely Family of Maryland." *MG* 2:300).

Emory, Robert, m. by 14 March 1722 or 1726, Ann, widow of William Hawkins (BAAD 1:146).

Empey, Johanna, widow, on 9 Feb 1746 conveyed all her goods, chattels and debts to her friend John Shaw if he would agree to maintain Johanna for her life, and to give Johanna's granddaughter Elizabeth 'Swampson' {Sampson] at age 16 livestock (BALR TB#E: 577).

Emson, James, m. by 9 July 1686, Rebecca, relict and admx. of John Daniell [or Darnall] of Calvert Co. (INAC 9:27). Rebecca m. 3rd James Cobb (*q.v.*), 4th, John Hawkins (*q.v.*), and 5th Gregory Farmer (*q.v.*).

England, George, of Gunpowder Meeting, and Catherine Hooker, on 14 d. 11 m. 1799 declared their intention to marry. On 12 d. 12 m. 1799 George England produced a certificate with the consent of his surviving parents for his marriage to Catherine Hooker ("Minutes of Baltimore Meeting," *QRNM:*234, 236).

England, Joseph, m. by 22 Jan 1721 Margaret, daughter of John Cottrell (MWB 20:49 abst. in *Md. Cal. of Wills* 6:162).

England, Joseph, m. by 22 Nov 1794, Betsy Holland, legatee of John Ensor (BALR WG#VV: 59).

Enloes, Abraham, in June 1759 was charged with begetting a bastard on the body of Rashia Morgan (BACP HWS#7:211).

Enloes, Anthony, d. by 14 Jan 1752 at which time his extx. Elizabeth was m. to William Grover (*q.v.*).

Enloes, Henry, and Mary Elliott were m. on 26 May 1763 (Harrison, "St. John's Parish Register:" 225; Peden, *A Closer Look:* 31; On 14 Jan 1785 Mary was named as a daughter of James Elliott (BAWB 4:173).

Enloes (Enlows), John, and Sarah Leggett: in Feb 1725 the vestry heard evidence against their unlawful cohabitation (Harrison, "St. John's Vestry Proceedings:" 2).

Ennalls, Andrew Skinner, of Baltimore Town, m. by 15 March 1771, Leah Hicks (DOLR 24 Old:387).

Ensey, Richard, b. 11 Sep 1757, m. Grace Jacobs, b. 20 Nov 1760, by Nov 1783 when their son William was b. ("Lot Ensey Bible Record," *MBR* 2:35-37).

Ensor, [-?-], m. by 21 Jan 1763, Jemima, daughter of Richard Bond (BAWB 2:360).

Ensor, Abraham, and Mary Merryman were m. on 30 Jan 1750 Harrison, "St. Paul's Parish Register:" 164). On 4 Feb 1774 Mary was named as a daughter of John Merryman, farmer, by whom Abraham had had children Ann and William Ensor (BAWB 3:352). In 1792 Mary received a share of the estate of John Merryman BAAD 11:1).

Ensor, Augustine Harman, orphan son of Joseph Ensor, dec., in March 1776 chose Stephen Hyland as his guardian (BAMI 1772, 1775-1781: 223).

Ensor, George, and Elizabeth Reeves were m. on 24 Dec 1739 (Harrison, "St. John's Parish Register:" 113). On 26 Sep 1760 Elizabeth was named as a daughter of William Reaves, planter (BAWB 2:174).

Ensor, George, m. by 15 Feb 1791, [-?-], who received an equal share of the estate of Richard Bond (BAAD 10:544).

Ensor, John and wife Jane, on 1 Aug 1691 posted bond to administer the estate of John Maynard (BAAB 2:133).

Ensor, John, m. by March 1709, Elizabeth, admx. of Abraham Enloes (BACP IS#B: 133).

Ensor, John, Jr., and Eleanor Todd were m. on 6 March 1753 (Harrison, "St. Paul's Parish Register:" 167). On 28 Nov 1757 Eleanor was named as a daughter of

Thomas and Eleanor (Dorsey) Todd; Eleanor Dorsey Todd m. 2nd, [-?-] Lynch (BALR B#G: 91, 93, 95; BAAD 6:197).

Ensor, John, m. by 16 Dec 1791, [-?-], heir of Thomas Gorsuch (BAAD 10:503).

Ensor, John, m. by 25 Jan 1794, Darcus, heir of Charles Gorsuch (BAAD 11:368).

Ensor, Jonathan Plowman, a natural orphan of Jonathan Plowman, aged 17 in Aug 1779 was bound to James Hawkins to learn to be a tailor (BAOC 1:37).

Ensor, Joseph, merchant of Baltimore Town, and Miss Mary Bouchelle, daughter of Peter Bouchelle, were m. on 7 April 1757 ("Joseph Ensor Bible." MGRC 33:26; Annapolis *Maryland Gazette* 14 April 1757).

Ensor, Orpha, was charged with bastardy at Nov Court, 1758 (BACP HWS#7:162). Orpha Edenfield, daughter of John Ensor m. William Markland on 19 Nov 1770 (Harrison, "St. Paul's Parish Register:" 169).

Ensor, William, m. by 24 d. 11 m. 1788, Eleanor, sister of Benjamin Powell (BAWB 4:321).

Ensor, William, and Nancy Herrington, all of Baltimore, were m. last eve. by Rev. Richards (*Baltimore Telegraphe* 3 March 1800).

Epaugh, Henry, m. by 7 Oct 1798 Elizabeth, daughter of Conrad Kerlinger (BAWB 6:138; BAAD 13:163).

Epley, Jacob, m. by 26 March 1799, Anna Mary, daughter of Helfrich Gramer of Mannheim Twp., York Co., Pa. (BALR WG#58:47).

Erikson, Eric, m. by 8 April 1730 Mary, widow and extx. of Robert Smith, from whom Mary had inherited *Levy's Tribe* and all of Smith's estate (MWB 17:55 abst. in *Md. Cal. of Wills* 5:74; BALR IS#K:210).

Erickson, Erick, and Elizabeth Baker were m. on 27 July 1745 (Harrison, "St. John's Parish Register:" 193). She m. 2nd, by 1753 Nicholas Power (*q.v.*) (MDTP 33-2:89). Frances Ann Erickson, in March 1759 was named as a niece of Charles Baker when Nicholas Power petitioned to be her guardian (BAMI 1755-1763).

Ernutt, Samuel, m. by 1 Sep 1763 [-?-], daughter of William Jenkins (MDAD 49:399).

Errell, Ann, in Nov 1719 was ordered to serve Thomas Taylor extra time for trouble she caused in having a baseborn child (BACP IS#C: 246, 249). In March 1719/20 she named William Ingle as the father (BACP IS#C: 284).

Errl [sic], [-?-], m. by 1 June 1781, Ann, sister of Mary Braddock, late of Linnen Hall St., Parish of St. Michan, Dublin, Ireland, now of Baltimore; Ann Errl, one of the execs., posted an administration bond on 12 June 1781; they had two daus., Eliz. and Mary Errl (BAWB 3:426; BAAB 5:20).

Erwin, James, and Miss Sally Cunningham, both of Baltimore, were m. last Tues. by Rev. Allison (*Baltimore Telegraphe* 7 Feb 1799).

Erwin, James, m. by 11 April 1799 Mary, widow of Matthew Seigers (BAAD 13:28).

Erwin, Mary. See Byrnes, Mary.

Escaville, James, and Mary Hargrove were m. by lic. on 7 Sep 1799 at St. Peter's Catholic Church, Baltimore (*Piet:* 132). She was named as Polly Hargrove, eldest. daughter of Rev. Mr. Hargrove, and Bishop Carroll performed the ceremony (*Federal Gazette and Baltimore Daily Advertiser* 9 Sep 1799).

Esser, [-?-], m. by 28 April 1792 Fanny, daughter of Christopher Hartman (BAWB 6:158).

Etting, Citizen Reuben, of Baltimore, and Miss Fanny Gratz of Philadelphia, were m. last Wed. (*Maryland Journal and Baltimore Advertiser* 19 Sep 1794).

Etting, Shinah, on 14 Feb 1800 was named as a legatee of Isaac Solomon. Solomon Etting was also named in the account (BAAD 13:198).

Etting, Solomon, merchant of Baltimore, and Rachel, daughter of Bernhard Gratz, merchant of Philadelphia, were m. in Philadelphia, last Wed., 26th ult. (*Baltimore Daily Repository* 2 Nov 1791, *Maryland Journal and Baltimore Advertiser* 1 Nov 1791; *Maryland Gazette or Baltimore General Advertiser* 4 Nov 1791).

Evans, [-?-], m. by 7 June 1771 Ann, sister of Adam Hoops (BAWB 3:259).

Evans, Amos, son of Griffith, on 25 d. 8 m. 1796 announced his intention to marry Rachel Tomkins, daughter of Benjamin and Mary ("Minutes of Deer Creek Meeting," *QRNM:*156).

Evans, Daniel, orphan son of Timothy, aged 9 on 15 Sep 1772, in Nov 1772 was bound to Charles Brooks to age 21 (BAMI 1772, 1775-1781: 31)

Evans, Daniel, and Miss Mary Dew, both of Baltimore Co., were m. last eve. by Rev. Bonsall (*Baltimore Evening Post* 5 April 1793). The bride's name is given as Due (*Baltimore Daily Repository* 5 April 1793).

Evans, David, b. 22 Aug 1762, son of John, and Elizabeth Barnes, b. 14 Nov 1768, were married by license dated 23 Feb 1792 (FRML). Their daughter Rachel was b. 15 Dec 1793 (Evans Family Record).

Evans, David, petitioned the court in 1792 that on 14 Feb 1782, when he was 11, he had been bound to Job Davidson to learn the trade of a cooper. His term expired in February but Davidson would not give him his freedom dues (BOCP Petition of David Evans, 1792).

Evans, Edward, d. before 17 Sep 1741, and was named in 1742 by Bray Platt Taylor as his father-in-law MDTP 31:303, 324).

Evans, Edward, and Rachel Johnson (*q.v.*) were m. on 3 Dec 1724 (Harrison, "St. George's Parish Register:" 236). On 2 June 1725 they administered the estate of John Hastings (*q.v.*), who in his will dated 24 Feb 1723 left his entire estate to Rachel Johnson (q.v.) (BAWB 3:254; BAAD 3:34; see also BAAD 3:45; BINV 4:215; MDAD 6:415). On 23 Oct 1736 Edward Evans' wife was named as a daughter of Daniel Johnson of Baltimore Co. (MDAD 15:203; BAAD 3:224).

Evans, Elizabeth (*alias* **Elizabeth Parsons**), was charged with bastardy at March Court 1733/4, and was indicted at Aug Court 1734 (BACP HWS#9:188, 308).

Evans, Griffith, of this town, was married last evening by Rev. John Hagerty to Miss Mary Burgess, daughter of Thomas Burgess late of this town, dec. (*Baltimore Evening Post* 27 Nov 1792).

Evans, Job, of Baltimore Co., m. by 16 May 1700, Sarah, late wife of John Perry of Annapolis, dec. (AALR WT#1:55).

Evans, John, son of John Evans, Sr., was b. 31 July 1768 and married Sarah Baxter Barnes on 25 Dec 1795 (Evans Family Record).

Evans, John, of Long Green, Baltimore Co., stated his wife Catherine had refused to behave herself as an obedient wife (*Maryland Journal and Baltimore Advertiser* 26 May 1778).

Evans, John, and Margaret Burke were m. by lic. 11 April 1790 at St. Peter's Catholic Church, Baltimore (Piet:132).

Evans, Joseph, merchant, and Eliza Davey of Baltimore, were m. last eve. (*Maryland Gazette or Baltimore General Advertiser* 4 Dec 1789).

Evans, Margaret, servant of William Hutchins of Baltimore Co., was tried for bastardy in Nov 1724 (BACP 1743-1745: 391).

Evans, Mary, admx., on 13 June 1765 posted bond to administer the estate of John Yerby (BAAB 4:3).

Evans, Molly, daughter of Timothy, aged 12 on 12 Sep 1772, in Nov 1772 was bound to Charles Brooks (BAMI 1772, 1775-1781: 31)

Evans, Sarah, was charged with bastardy at Nov Court 1723 and named John Casey as the father of her child (BACP IS&TW#3:109).

Evans, William, and Mary Driskill were m. on 25 July 1777 (Leisenring: 68). On 11 Dec 1794 Mary Ann was named as the sole rep. of Darby Driskell (BAAD 11:488).

Evans, William, m. by 3 June 1795, Mary Fowler, who was a daughter of Elizabeth Smith [*sic*], who d. leaving a will dated 22 June 1776 (BALR WG#RR:457).

Everard, William, merchant of Baltimore, was m. last Sat. eve. by Rev. Mr. Richards, to Eliza Ann Mills, daughter of John Mills, Esq., of the state of New York (*Federal Gazette and Baltimore Daily Advertiser* 3 June 1800).

Everest, Thomas, of the Cliffs, Calvert Co., m. by 12 May 1681 Hannah, daughter of Richard Ball (BALR RM#HS:74, IR#AM:135).

Everet, Capt. John, of Yauchel, Ireland, and Mrs. Eleanor Taylor of Baltimore were m. yesterday by Rev. Kurtz (*Baltimore Daily Repository* 9 March 1792).

Everett, Elizabeth, was charged with bastardy, confessed, and fined at Aug Court 1746; she was charged with having a bastard child "lately born of her body" at the Nov 1750 Court (BACP TB&TR#1:127-128, TR#6:25).

Everett, John, and Rebecca Poteet were m. on 31 Oct 1728 (Harrison, "St. John's Parish Register:" 67). On 9 March 1732 Rebecca was named as a sister of John Poteet, and John and Rebecca Everett had had a daughter Mary Everett (BALR IS#L:337)

Everett, Mary, was charged with bastardy at March Court 1756 (BAMI 1755-1763:2).

Everit, Samuel, and Hannah White were m. on 9 Dec 1755 (Harrison, "St. John's Parish Register:" 212). In Jan 1756, Hannah was named as the admx. of Stephen White (*q.v.*) (MDAD 39:31).

Everson, Capt. Nicholas, and Mrs. Catherine Carlbon (Carlson?), all of Baltimore, were m. yesterday eve. by Rev. Mr. Kurtz (*Baltimore Telegraphe* 13 Jan 1800; *Baltimore American* 13 Jan 1800).

Ewings, John, was m. by 29 Jan 1708 to Elizabeth, sister of Moses Groome (BALR RM#HS:633).

Ezard, Sarah, confessed to bastardy at March Court 1750, and was fined 30 shillings on 5 June 1750 (BACP TR#5:19-20).

"F"

Fabel, Claresa, on 10 Nov 1786 was named as a granddaughter in the will of Jemima Craghead (BAWB 4:250).

Faber, Christopher, of Chambersburg, Pa., d. by 8 Dec 1800, having m. Margaret, daughter of Jacob Keeports of Baltimore Town (BALR WG#65:456).

Fabre, Lewis Augustin, (son of Peter Augustin and Teresa Charlotte Testar, born at Paris), and Henrietta Terrier (daughter of Louis and Charlotte Pecoul, widow of John Hermitte), were m. by lic. 21 Feb 1795 at St. Peter's Catholic Church, Baltimore (*Piet:* 133; BAML, which gives her name as Ferrier).

Faget, John, and Catherine Elie, widow Bourges, were m. 29 May 1800 at St. Peter's Catholic Church, Baltimore (*Piet:* 133).

Faherty, Patrick, and Maria Whelan, widow of Edward the late Faherty [*sic*], natives of Ireland, now residing in Anne Arundel Co., were m. by lic. 4 Oct 1798 at St. Peter's Catholic Church, Baltimore (*Piet:* 133).

Fahnestock, Derick, m. Sarah Deardorf on 27 Feb 1777 ("Lot Ensey Bible," *MBR* 2:35-37).

Fairbanks, William, and Miss Amelia Beckley, both of Fell's Point, were m. last eve. by Rev. Bend (*Baltimore American* 2 Dec 1799).

Falkner, Samuel, and Mrs. Mary Brown, both of Baltimore, were m. last eve. by Rev. Bend (*Baltimore Telegraphe* 7 Oct 1799).

Fall (Faal), Neal, m. by 1742 Susannah, daughter of Stephen Body (MWB 23:19 abst. in *Md. Cal. of Wills* 8:196),

Falls, Dr. Moore, was m. last Sat. at Chatsworth, the seat of George Lux, Esq., to Miss Abby Biddle, daughter of the Hon. Edward Biddle, late of Penna., dec. (*Maryland Journal and Baltimore Advertiser* 16 Dec 1785).

Falls, Dr. Moore, and Mrs. Rebecca Wilson, both of Baltimore, were m. last Sat. by Dr. Allison (*Maryland Journal and Baltimore Advertiser* 26 Sep 1796). She was the widow of Stephen Wilson (*q.v.*) and the daughter of Robert Neilson (BAWB 6:165).

Farfarr, William, and wife Jane [*sic*], relict of Lewis Barton (*q.v.*), posted bond to admin, the estate of Barton on 4 March in the 4th year [c1689] of Their Majesty's Reign (BAAB 1:42; MDTP 16:173).

Farfarr (Forfare), William, m. by 11 Aug 1713 Elinor, admx. of John Harriman (INAC 34:29).

Faris, George, of York Co., Pa., m. by12 May 1777, Elizabeth, heir of John Mercer who d. testate (BALR WG#A:126).

Farlaw, Catherine, wife of Robert, for herself and children, petitioned for immediate relief (Baltimore Co. Levy List, 1772).

Farlow, Thomas, and Elizabeth Little were m. on 8 Feb 1734 (Harrison, "St. George's Parish Register:" 282). On 24 Dec 1735 she was named as the widow and extx. of James Little (*q.v.*) (MINV 21:281; MDAD 16:354; MDTP 30:346; BAAD 4:5).

Farmer, Gregory, and Rachel Emson were m. on 14 June 1723 (Harrison, "St. George's Parish Register:" 231). On 15 March 1737 Rachel was identified as the widow of 1st, John Daniell (or Darnall), of Calvert Co., 2nd, James Empson (*q.v.*), 3rd, James Cobb, and 4th John Hawkins (*q.v.*) (BALR IS#IK:371).

Farquhar, James, and Sarah Moore were married by license dated 23 March 1784 (Fred. Co. Marr. Lic.). On 8 June 1792 Sarah was named as a daughter of Ann Moore, who was the extx. of Walter Moore (BAAD 11:61).

Farr, |-?-|, m. by 9 Aug 1768 Elisabeth, daughter of James Dickson (BAWB 3:118).

Farrell, Timothy, and Catherine Blake, natives of Ireland, were m. by lic. on 10 Oct 1793, at St. Peter's Catholic Church, Baltimore (*Piet:* 133).

Faubel, Peter, m. by 24 June 1765 Margaretha Metzin ("First Record Book for the Reformed and Lutheran and Congregations at Manchester, Baltimore (Now Carroll) Co.," *MGSB* 35:270).

Fauble, George, m, by 22 Aug 1795, Mary Leichte, representative of Jacob Leichte (BAAD 12:39).

Fauble, Mr. Jacob, was m. last Sun. to Miss Margaret Hoefligh (*Federal Gazette and Baltimore Daily Advertiser* 24 May 1796).

Faupel, Melchor, m. by 25 March 1778, Sabina, prob. Meyerin, as Margaretha Meyerin, widow, grandmother, was the sponsor ("First Record Book for the Reformed and Lutheran and Congregations at Manchester, Baltimore (Now Carroll) Co.," *MGSB* 35:277).

Faur, Antoine, and Janett Ann Brotherson were m. by lic. 19 May 1787 at St. Peter's Catholic Church, Baltimore (*Piet:* 133).

Favier, John, and Mary Thompson were m. by lic. 15 Dec 1796 at St. Peter's Catholic Church, Baltimore (*Piet:* 133).

Fearson, Capt. Jesse, and Hannah Wells were married by license dated 28 May 1791 (BAML). He and Mrs. Wells, relict of George Wells, were m. Sun. eve. at Fell's

Point (*Maryland Gazette or Baltimore General Advertiser* 31 May 1791; BAAD 10:531; BALR WG#SS:193).

Feather, Henry, in 1765 was fined for bastardy (BAMI 1765).

Feather, Philip, m. by 26 Nov 1786, Anna Maria Dillien ("First Record Book for the Reformed and Lutheran and Congregations at Manchester, Baltimore (Now Carroll) Co.," *MGSB* 35:282).

Feder, Adam, m. by 8 July 1788, Anna Magdalena Heerin ("First Record Book for the Reformed and Lutheran and Congregations at Manchester, Baltimore (Now Carroll) Co.,"*MGSB* 35:283).

Feder, Philip, m. by 27 Oct 1784, Anna Maria Dillin ("First Record Book for the Reformed and Lutheran and Congregations at Manchester, Baltimore (Now Carroll) Co.,"*MGSB* 35:281).

Feitz (Feetz), Ulrich, of Baltimore Co., Md., m. by 7 Feb 1775, Eva Elizabeth, daughter of Christian Roop of York Co., Pa. (YOLR F:165).

Feik, Henry, and Elizabeth Tietzen were m. by lic. 26 Dec 1796, at St. Peter's Catholic Church, Baltimore (*Piet:* 133).

Felkes, Edward, on 19 Feb 1701/2 made a prenuptial agreement with Ann, relict and extx. of Stephen Johnson and kinswoman of Moses Groome (BALR IR#PP: 171, HW#2:119; INAC 3:366; BAAD 2:27).

Fell, Edward, and Ann Bond were m. on 3 Nov 1758 (Harrison, "St. John's Parish Register:" 218). She m. 2nd, James Giles (*q.v.*).

Fell, Margaret, in 1762 was fined for bastardy (BAMI 1755-1763).

Fell, Stephen, and Ann Edwards were married by license dated 21 Feb 1780 (HAML). In his will, made 27 Feb 1790, Stephen Fell named his daughters-in-law Elizabeth and Ann Edwards (BAWB 4:482).

Fell, William, and Sarah Bond were m. on 8 Jan 1732 Harrison, "St. Paul's Parish Register:" 151). On 18 Dec 1755 she was named as a daughter of Thomas Bond who named his grandchildren Edward Fell, Jennet Fell, and Catherine Fell in his will (MWB 30:24 abst. by Gibb). Sarah was m. by 17 Dec 1743 to Greenbury Dorsey (q.v.)

Fell, William, in his will, made 24 Sep 1786 named his mother Ann Giles, her husband James Giles (*q.v.*), and their children: Jacob Washington, Joanna, and Susannah Giles (BAWB 4:175). In 1789 Thomas Bond warned any tenants of the late Fell not to pay any rents to Edward Fell Day (*Maryland Journal and Baltimore Advertiser* 15 Sep 1789).

Felt, Jacob, m. by 21 Dec 1797, [-?-] Renecker (Conrad and Eva Renecker were sponsors) (First German Reformed Church, Register, Baltimore, MS. at MdHS:22).

Fenby (Furby), John, and Margaret Turner were married by license dated 16 May 1793 (BAML). On 21 Dec 1793, Margaret was named as the admx. of Isaac Turner (BAAD 11:359).

Fendall, James, of Bright Helmstone, Sussex, Eng., m. on 16 Dec 1686 Elizabeth. daughter of Richard and Loveday Brocklesby of Cork (BALR TR#DS:101).

Fendall, James, of Baltimore Co., stated he would not pay the debts of his wife Anne, as he was afraid she would run him into debt (Annapolis *Maryland Gazette* 27 March 1751).

Fengeas, Lewis (son of Matthew and Magdalen Prat, native of Arles, France), and Mary Jane Theresa Pelletier (daughter of Peter and Mary Theresa Charbonnet Dumas, and widow of John Baptist Victor DeBerthe DeRoujere of San Domingo), were married by banns on 30 Sep 1794 at St. Peter's Catholic Church, Baltimore (*Piet:* 133).

Fennell, Ann, on 13 Nov 1794 was named as a niece of Thomas Knightsmth Shaw (BAWB 5:213).

Fennell, John, and Sarah Miller were m. by lic. 3 Feb 1799 at St. Peter's Catholic Church, Baltimore (*Piet:* 133).

Fenton, Amy, on 16 June 1718, posted bond to administer the estate of her third husband, Stephen Bentley (*q.v.*), and widow of Philip [Piffions?] (*q.v.*) and of William Pearle (*q.v.*) (BAAB 1:68; BACP F#1:300,307).

Fenwick, [-?-], m. by 21 Aug 1761, Jane, who received a distributive share from the estate of Thomas Courtney Jenkins (BFD 3:94).

Ferrell, James, in Nov 1757 was convicted of bastardy (BAMI 1755-1763).

Ferrell, William, orphan son of Mary Leakins, had been bound by the court to Charles Carlisle to learn the trade of painter and glazier. On 18 Sep 1787 Mary Leakins petitioned the court that Carlisle had sent her son away with the play actors, and she wanted to the court to order Carlisle to restore her son to her (BOCP Petition of William Ferrell, 1787, Box 2, Folder 14).

Ferri, Janarius, native of Naples, Italy, and Catherine Trueman, native of Ireland, were m. by lic. 1 Dec 1800 at St. Peter's Catholic Church, Baltimore (*Piet:* 133).

Ferron, John, and Elizabeth Delanco, free mulattoes from St. Domingo, were m. by lic. 24 Feb 1800 at St. Peter's Catholic Church, Baltimore (*Piet:* 133).

Ferry, John, living about 1697 was named as the father-in-law of John Boring (who was aged 11 in 1687) in Boring's deposition made 7 July 1732 (BALC HWS#3 #36). In his will, made 1 March 1688/89, Ferry named his sons-in-law, John, James, and Thomas Boring, and daughter-in-law Mary Boring (MWB 6:227 abst. in *Md. Cal. of Wills* 2:171).

Few, Isaac, of New Castle Co., Del., and Jennet Fell were m. on 15 Aug 1754 (Harrison, "St. John's Parish Register:" 211). On 28 June 1760 Jennet was named as a dau, of William Fell, and sister of Edward Fell (BALR B#H: 277; BAWB 3:29). On 9 Dec 1773 Thomas Bond of Thomas (*q.v.*) gave property to his sister Jenet Few, wife of Isaac Few (*q.v.*), and to her children (BACT 1773-1784:85).

Few, William, m. by 2 July 1750 Mary, daughter of Benjamin Wheeler of Baltimore Co. (BALR TR#C:546).

Fewis, [-?-], m. by 9 March 1791 Dorothy, formerly Dorothy Nice, extx. of David Nice (BAAD 10:309).

Fews, [-?-], m. by 18 June 1791, Dorothy (Nice), widow of John Barton (*q.v.*) (BAAD 10:400).

Ficke, Herman, of this city, was m. last eve. by Right Rev. Bishop Carroll to Miss Nancy Cain of Harford Co. (*Federal Gazette and Baltimore Daily Advertiser* 4 Dec 1799). He was a native of Germany; they were m. by lic. 3 Dec 1799 at St. Peter's Catholic Church, Baltimore (*Piet:* 133).

Field, Sarah, in 1761 was fined for fornication and bastardy (BAMI 1755-1763).

Fife, James, stated he would not pay the debts of his wife Mary who had eloped (*Baltimore Daily Intelligencer* 29 Aug 1794). Mary Fife stated that she had never eloped from her husband's bed and board until of late when he entertained Whortleberry Bell and Rachel Brett, both women of ill fame (*Maryland Journal and Baltimore Advertiser* 5 Sep 1794).

Fifer, George, and Magdalen Connet were m. by banns on 24 June 1800 at St. Peter's Catholic Church, Baltimore (*Piet:* 133).

Fink, [-?-], m. by 21 Sep 1799 Modlian (Madalena), daughter of Matthias Baker (BAWB 6:221).

Finley (Finly), Capt. James, was m. last eve. by Rev. Mr. Curtis, to Catherine Gantz, both of this city (*Federal Gazette and Baltimore Daily Advertiser* 20 Sep 1798).

Finley, Lydia, servant to John Miller, was charged with bastardy at the Nov 1724 Court (BACP IS&TW#4:32).

Finley, Thomas, and Althea Kidd were m. on 22 July 1747 Harrison, "St. Paul's Parish Register:" 160). They had a son Thomas Finley, Jr. and Althea m. 2nd, by 17 Oct 1774, Nicholas Britton (Britain) (*q.v.*) (MDAD 47:155; BALR AL#L:199). In June 1762 Thomas Finley's orphans, Agnes, Thomas, and William Finley, were made wards of Nicholas 'Brittan' (BAMI, 1755-1763).

Finney, Hannah, was charged with unlawful cohabitation with Jacob Coventry on 5 Feb 1771by the vestry of St. George's Parish (Reamy, *St. George's Parish Register*: 111).

Finsham, [-?-], m. by 5 Nov 1738, Elizabeth, mother of Phoebe Ingerom [Ingram?] and Robert and Elizabeth Whitehead (MWB 22:28 abst. in *Md. Cal. of Wills* 8:14). Pheobe was the widow of William Ingram (*q.v.*).

Firby, Margaret, admx., on 1 Nov 1800 posted bond to administer the estate of John Eagen (BAAB 9:91).

Fischer. See under Fisher.

Fisha (Pristo), Joseph, m. by 2 May 1785 Ann, administrator of John Granger (*q.v.*) (BAAB 6:266).

Fisher, Anna Maria, servant, in Nov 1756 was fined for bastardy (BAMI 1755-1763). She may be the Hannah Mariah Fisher, servant of John Griffin, who in Nov 1759 was ordered to serve extra time to repay her master for his trouble when she had a bastard (BACP BB#C:313).

Fisher (Fischer), Daniel, m. by 17 March 1760 Elizabeta Kertin ("First Record Book for the Reformed and Lutheran and Congregations at Manchester, Baltimore (Now Carroll) Co.," *MGSB* 35:265).

Fisher (Fischer), George, m. by 15 March 1760, Anna Maria Lahrin ("First Record Book for the Reformed and Lutheran and Congregations at Manchester, Baltimore (Now Carroll) Co." *MGSB* 35:265).

Fisher, Hannah, on 28 d. 3 m. 1794 was charged with bastardy being in an unmarried state ("Minutes of Baltimore Meeting," *QRNM:*222-223).

Fisher, James, and Ann Wells were m. by lic. 31 May 1787 at St. Peter's Catholic Church, Baltimore (*Piet:* 133).

Fisher, James, and Sarah Stewart were m. on 19 Jan 1800 (Marr. Register of Rev. Lewis Richards, MS.690 at MdHS). On 6 Aug 1800 Sarah was named as a representative of John Stewart (BAAD 13:307). On 11 d. 12 m. 1800 James Stewart had a complaint made that Fisher had his marriage accomplished contrary to the good order of Friends ("Minutes of Baltimore Meeting," *QRNM:*239).

Fisher (Fischer), Johannes, m. by 24 June 1760, Anna Catharina Staelzin ("First Record Book for the Reformed and Lutheran and Congregations at Manchester, Baltimore (Now Carroll) Co.," *MGSB* 35:265).

Fisher, Michael, in his will made 18 April 1799 named his sister's sons Jacob Houchs and Michael Houchs, to brother's daus.: Annamary Stover, Magdaline Smooth (or

Smeeth); to sister's daughter Esther Benned, his wife Cleary and her sister's daughter Clara Smeath (BAWB 6:182).

Fisher, Ruth. See Thomas Gilbert.

Fisher, Thomas, and Amelia Whiteacre, widow of Peter Whiteacre (*q.v.*), were m. on 18 Feb 1761 (Harrison, "St. George's Parish Register:" 369; MDTP 39:33).

Fisher, Thomas, and Miss Elizabeth Yates, both of this city were m. last eve, by Rev. Mr. Ireland (*Federal Gazette and Baltimore Daily Advertiser* 15 Nov 1799).

Fisher, William, in 1761 was fined for fornication and bastardy (BAMI 1755-1763).

Fisher, William, Jr., of Anne Arundel Co., m. by 29 Aug 1768 Patience, widow of George Cole, son of Richard Miller Cole (BALR AL#A: 19).

Fishwick (Fitchwick), James, and Mary Craig were married on 11 Dec 1787 (Harrison, "St. Paul's Parish Register:" 216). On 13 Nov 1795, Mary was named as the widow of [-?-] Craggie, by whom she had a daughter Mary Craggie (BAWB 6:306; Notes from "The Craggs-Burgess-Stansbury-McElhiney Prayer Book," in *MGSB* 25 (1) (Winter 1994), 58-59). **See John Craig.**

Fitch, Ai [*sic*] and Ann Mercer were m. on 27 May 1800 (Marr. Returns of Rev. Daniel Kurtz, Scharf Papers, MS. 1999 at MdHS). On 6 Dec 1800 Nancy Mercer was named as the admx. of Benjamin Mercer (*q.v.*) (BAAD 13:342).

Fitch, Henry, and Ruth Bailey were m. 28 Feb 1758 (Harrison, "St. John's Parish Register:" 217). On 13 March 1771 Ruth was named as a daughter of Thomas Bailey (BAWB 3:182). She m. 2nd, Joseph Hill (*q.v.*) by 7 April 1774 (BAAD 7:300).

Fitch, Henry, and Ann Eaglestone were married by license dated 30 Jan 1784 (BAML). On 12 April 1785 Ann was named as a daughter of Abraham Eaglestone, and [prob.] widow of [-?-] Davis (*q.v.*) (BAAD 8:164; BAWB 3:494).

Fite, Andrew, of Baltimore Co., dec., had been conveyed part of *Gist's Range* by Henry Fite, now also dec.; Abigail Fite, widow and admx., gave notice that the property now belonged to his children, Mary Ann, John, Elizabeth, and Andrew, all minors (*Maryland Journal and Baltimore Advertiser* 26 March 1792).

Fite, Jacob, of Baltimore, and Nancy Reinecker of Penna. were m. yesterday morning (*Maryland Journal and Baltimore Advertiser* 11 March 1793).

Fitzgerald, Garrett, and Miss Myers, both natives of Ireland, were married last eve. by the Rev. Mr. Beeston (*Baltimore Daily Intelligencer* 6 March 1794; see also *Piet:* 133; BAML, which gives her name as Margaret Myers).

Fitzgerald, James, d. by 4 July 1786 having m. Jane, daughter of Jane MacGee (*q.v.*); Jane Fitzgerald m. on the above date William Jacob (*q.v.*) (BAAD 9:231; BAWB 5:491).

Fitzgerald, John, in his will dated 13 July 1788, proved 5 June 1791, stated he had m. Anna Mariah Margarita Boucherie, only daughter of John Boucherie, Esq., who owned 1000 a. at the Three Rivers in Canada, called *Bouchier's Platt;* she d. shortly, leaving an only son by me, John Fitzgerald; will gives history of legal battles over the land (BAWB 4:547).

Fitzgerald, Richard, and Catherine Butler were m. by banns on 27 Sep 1784 at St. Peter's Catholic Church, Baltimore (*Piet:* 133)..

Fitzgerald, Richard, native of Ireland, and Ann Cooper, native of Va., were m. by lic. 12 Oct 1796, at St. Peter's Catholic Church, Baltimore (*Piet:* 133).

Fitzgerald, Richard, and Margaret Curry of Baltimore Co. were m. by lic. 22 Oct 1798 at St. Peter's Catholic Church, Baltimore (*Piet:* 133; BAML, which gives her name as Corrie).

Fitzpatrick, John, and Mary Marheim were m. by banns on 20 Aug 1786 at St. Peter's Catholic Church, Baltimore (*Piet:* 133).

Fitzpatrick, Mary, was charged with bastardy at Nov Court 1757 (BACP TB#D:8, 44).

Fitzpatrick (Fitchpatrick), William, was bound by the court to a certain Joseph Beaston, who mistreated his apprentice, according to a petition filed 12 Feb 1788 by Nathan Fitzpatrick, uncle of the said William (BOCP Petition of William Fitchpatrick, 1788, Box 2, Folder 56). On 14 Aug 1788, William, age 9 last May, was discharged from Joseph Beaston and bound to Nathan Fitzpatrick, shoemaker (BOCP 2:80).

Fitzredmond, John, d. by 16 Dec 1721, leaving Barbara Fitzredmond as his admx.; his inventory mentions a son Alexander Britson, and a daughter Barbara Cannon (MINV 7:236).

Fitzsimmons, Nicholas, m., 1st, by 3 April 1693 Martha, relict and admx. (or extx.) of Joseph Heathcote (*q.v.*); Martha posted bond to administer Heathcote's estate (BAAB 208; INAC 13A:195, 196). She was a daughter and extx. of Thomas Morgan of Baltimore Co. (MWB 7:392; MDTP 17:69). By March 1717 Fitzsimmons had m. 2nd, Elizabeth [-?-] (BACP IS#IA:235).

Flahavan, Richard, was m. by lic. 27 Dec 1799 to Catherine Baldwin, widow, both natives of Ireland, at St. Peter's Catholic Church, Baltimore (*Piet:* 133).

Flaherty, Patrick, was m. by lic. 8 Sep 1794 to Catherine Conner, natives of Ireland, at St. Peter's Catholic Church, Baltimore (*Piet:* 133).

Flanagan, Edmond (*alias* **Edmond Burges** or **Burgess),** in Dec 1753 was charged with begetting a bastard on the body of Mary Barlar (BACP BB#A:31).

Flannegan (Flaningan), Charles, m. by 14 Aug 1754 Ann, daughter of Patrick Lynch (BACT TR#E: 143; BAWB 3:52). On 16 April 1792 Ann Flannigan received a share of Patrick Lynch's estate for the use of Edward and Ann Flannigan (BAAD 11:40).

Flannegan, Edward, aged over 14, orphan son of Charles, in March 1772 chose William Cockey as his guardian (BAMI 1772, 1775-1781: 9)

Flax, Michael, and Margaret Brannar were m. 11 June 1780 (Marriage License Returns of Rev. William West, filed 19 Nov 1780; Scharf Papers). In March 1794 Flax and his wife Margaret advertised that they were legally separated (*Baltimore Daily Intelligencer* 6 March 1794; *Baltimore Daily Intelligencer* 6 March 1794).

Fleetwood, Benjamin, m. by 8 July 1772 Hannah, daughter of Reuben and Sarah Perkins (BALR AL#E: 320).

Fleming, George, in 1781 petitioned Gov. Thomas Sim Lee that he had been left possession of a house by his uncle Simon Vashon jointly with Mary Coghlan, who by her 'reputed ill behavior,' caused Fleming to strike her ("Petition of George Fleming," Maryland State Papers: Red Books XXBI, 113, portfolio).

Fletcher, William, and Melcha Botts were m. by lic. 20 Feb 1800 at St. Peter's Catholic Church, Baltimore (*Piet:* 133).

Fleury, Sebastian, and Magdalen Sapen were m. by lic. 3 June 1786 at St. Peter's Catholic Church, Baltimore (*Piet:* 133).

Flin, Frederic, and Mary Wright were m. by banns 14 May 1784 at St. Peter's Catholic Church, Baltimore (*Piet:* 133).

Flinn, James, m. by 10 June 1795, [-?-], widow of Lot Owings (BAAD 12:14).

Flint, Ann, was charged with bastardy and indicted at the Aug 1744 Court (BACP 1743-1744: 293).

Floyd, Ana, daughter of Rachel Floyd [see below], on 28 d. 9 m. 1776 has gone out in marriage to a man not of our society ("Minutes of Gunpowder Meeting," *QRNM:* 68). [No other marriage reference found].

Floyd, Caleb, and Mary Lee were m. on 31 May 1793 (Marr. Register of Rev. Lewis Richards, MS.690 at MdHS). On 28 d. 6 m. 1793 Caleb Floyd was reported to have accomplished his marriage to a woman not of our society with the assistance of a hireling ("Minutes of Baltimore Meeting," *QRNM:* 221). [No other marriage reference found.]

Floyd, Charles, and Elizabeth Dunn, natives of Ireland, were m. by lic. 5 Oct 1794 at St. Peter's Catholic Church, Baltimore (*Piet:* 133).

Floyd, James, stated he would not pay the debts of his wife Eleanor, who had eloped from him (*Maryland Journal and Baltimore Advertiser* 25 May 1790).

Floyd, Joseph, and Nancy Wheeler were married by license dated 21 Nov 1787 (BAML). On 6 March 1788 Ann received her thirds of the estate of Solomon Wheeler (BAAD 9:171).

Floyd, Joseph, and Catherine Logue were m. by lic. 9 Dec 1794 at St. Peter's Catholic Church, Baltimore (*Piet:* 133).

Floyd, Rachel, mother of Ana [see above] on 28 d. 9 m. 1776 has gone out in marriage to a man not of our society ("Minutes of Gunpowder Meeting," *QRNM:* 68).

Floyd, Thomas, m. Zipporah Hilyard; she m. 2nd, Alexander Baker (*q.v.*), and 3rd Henry Maynard (*q.v.*) (BALR HWS#1-A:137, BB#1:570; John F. Dorman, "The Maynard Family of Frederick County, Maryland, *NGSQ* 48:177-ff.).

Floyd, Thomas, and Rachel Daughaday were m. on 23 d., 4 m. 1755 ("Records of Gunpowder Meeting," MS. at MdHS: 49). John Floyd and Joseph Floyd, on 19 April 1788 were named as cousins in the will of Joseph Taylor who had also named some Daughadays as cousins in his will (BAWB 4:346). Rachel's brothers John and Thomas Daughaday were among the witnesses ("Records of Gunpowder Meeting," MS. at MdHS: 49).

Flud, William, aged 12 last Jan, son of Michael, in June 1758 was bound to Zachariah Maccubbin (BAMI 1755-1763).

Flynn, John, and Margaret Riley, natives of Co. Cork, Ireland, were m. by lic. 2 March 1794 at St. Peter's Catholic Church, Baltimore (*Piet:* 133).

Fogerty, Edward, widower, and Judith Mehin, widow, both natives of Ireland, were m. by lic. 30 Oct 1797 at St. Peter's Catholic Church, Baltimore (*Piet:* 133; BAML, which gives her name as Judy Mekin).

Fogg, Amos, and Eleanor Young were m. on 15 July1742 (Harrison, "St. Mary Ann's (North Elk) Parish," Cecil Co., MS. at MdHS: 290). In his will made 7 Aug 1762, Fogg named his wife Eleanor extx., and left her one-third of his estate; the other two-thirds he left to his daughter-in-law Prudence Clarke and her two children Samuel and Rebecca Clarke (BAWB 2:136). His inventory dated 10 May 1763 was signed by William Young and Prudence Clark as next of kin (MINV 80:312, 315).

Foldweilder, Francis, and Magdalen Wintzeiler were married by banns 6 Feb 1785, at St. Peter's Catholic Church, Baltimore (*Piet:* 133). He d. by Jan 1800 and Magdalen m. 2nd, Joseph Baker (*q.v.*).

Foley, Joseph, and Mary Burnet were m. 3 Aug 1795 (Harrison, "St. Paul's Parish Register:" 307). In Sep 1795 Foley stated he would not pay the debts of his wife Mary as she had eloped from his bed and board (*Maryland Journal and Baltimore Advertiser* 26 Sep 1795).

Folger, Capt. Frederick, who d. 5 Aug 1797, and Isabella Emmitt, who d. 7 Sep 1794, were m. on 7 March 1782 by Rev. Dr. P. Allison ("Bible Records of the Ridgely Family of Maryland." *MG* 2:301; *Maryland Journal and Baltimore Advertiser* 12 March 1782).

Foose, John, and Augustina Riddle were married by license dated 14 June 1796 at St. Peter's Catholic Church, Baltimore (*Piet:* 134).

Foose, William, and Martha Merrit of Baltimore Co. were married by license dated 4 Nov 1798 at St. Peter's Catholic Church, Baltimore (*Piet:* 134).

Forbes, James, orphan of James Forbes, in July 1796 chose Elizabeth Forbes as his guardian (BAOC 3:198).

Ford, |-?-|, m. by 17 Feb 1777 Charlotte Cockey, daughter of Penelope Deye (BAWB 3:562). Ford d. by 1787 when letters of admin. were granted to Charlotte Ford (Unpub. notes by Robert T. Nave who graciously made them available to the compiler; see also Barnes, *Baltimore Co. Families:* 223).

Ford (Foard), [-?-], m. by 13 Feb 1779 Ruth, daughter of Mary Rutter (formerly Barney) (BAWB 3:388).

Ford, |-?-|, m. by March 1781, Esther, daughter of William Jessop, collier (BAWB 3:438).

Ford, |-?-|, m. by 22 Aug 1792 Sarah, daughter of Thomas Cole who named his grand-children Eleanor, John, Mary, and Joshua Ford in his will (BAWB 5:53).

Ford, |-?-|, m. by 17 June 1796 Margaret, legatee of William Sinclair; she was the mother of two children: Charles Randall and Joseph McClung (BAAD 12:161).

Ford, Abraham, m. by 17 Feb 1736, Mary, sister of Joseph Pritchard (BALR IS#IK: 358).

Ford, Abraham, m. by 22 Nov 1794 Martha Grimes one of the reps. of James Grimes (BAAD 11:478).

Ford, Benjamin, m. by 13 Nov 1775 Rachel, daughter of John Tipton (BALR AL#N:513).

Ford, Edmund, and Catherine Bond were m. on 7 Sep 1784 ("Hance Nelson Bible," *MBR* 5:128; "Register of First German Reformed Church, Baltimore," MS. at MdHS; BAML). Catherine was the daughter and heir of William Bond of Thomas (BAAD 8:257).

Ford, John, and Elizabeth Bevens were m. 27 Oct 1778 (Marr. Returns of Rev. Thomas Chase, Scharf Papers, MS. 1999 at MdHS). On 14 Jan 1779, John Ford stated that he and his wife Elizabeth, formerly the wife of John Beaven (*q.v.*), because of sundry disputes, quarrels and animosities between John and Elizabeth, he was granting Elizabeth leave to marry again and receive all debts due John Beaven (BALR WG#E:90). **See John Beven.**

Ford, Joseph, son of William and Rosanna, on 20 d. 2 m. 1794 announced his intention to marry Frances Coale, daughter of Philip and Ann, dec. ("Minutes of Deer Creek Meeting," *QRNM:* 154).

Ford, Joshua, and Sarah Cole were married by license dated 10 June 1786 ("Register of First German Church, Baltimore," MS at MdHS: 186). On 27 Aug 1792 Sarah was named as a daughter of Thomas Cole (BAWB 5:53; BAAD 11:352). Eleanor, John,

Mary, and Joshua Ford, in June 1793 were legatees of Thomas Cole, dec., and Joshua Ford was appointed their guardian (BAOC 3:50).

Ford, Lloyd, m. by May 1768 Mary, daughter of Alexander Grant (BALR AL#A:594; BALR WG#A:362).

Ford, Margaret, in Dec 1795 was made ward of Thomas Batney (BAOC 3:173).

Ford, Mark, on 26 Aug 1738, with Thomas Phelps, was summoned to the vestry of St. George's Parish to declare that they both had been married to her who is now called Rose Phelps. She was first married to [-?-] Swift, and she eloped from him and Phelps declared he married the said Rose on 18 May 1710. (Harrison, "St. John's and St. George's Parish Register Vestry Proceedings," MS. at the MdHS).

Ford, Mordecai (written as Mordelia), m. by 9 Nov 1752, Ruth, legatee of William Barney and daughter of William and Mary Barney (MDAD 31:161, 33:161).

Ford, Mordecai, m. by 13 June 1792 Margaret, admx. of Thomas Riston (BAAD 11:71).

Ford, Mordecai, in Dec 1795 chose Christian Singery as his guardian (BAOC 3:173).

Ford, Raymond, and Peggy Poddewang were married by license dated 28 May 1784, at St. Peter's Catholic Church, Baltimore (*Piet:* 134; BAML, which gives his name as Romman Ford).

Ford, Sarah, was charged with bastardy at the Aug 1746 Court (BACP TB&TR#1:116).

Ford, Thomas, was presented [indicted] for fornication at the Nov 1772 Court (BAMI 1772: 87).

Ford, Thomas Cockey Deye, and Achsah Cockey were m. on 20 Dec 1781 (Marr. Returns of Rev. William West, Scharf Papers, MS.1999 at MdHS). On 6 Aug 1784 Achsah was named as a daughter of Thomas Cockey (BAWB 4:63).

Ford, William, m. by 12 Nov 1751, [-?-], admx. of Isaac Wright (MDTP 35:123). On 10 July 1753, [-?-]; they were ordered to take out letters of administration on the estate of Isaac Wright (MDTP 33-2:131).

Ford, William, and Jane Holmes, natives of Ireland, were married by license dated 11 Aug 1798, at St. Peter's Catholic Church, Baltimore (*Piet:* 134).

Foreman, Elizabeth, on 22 Sep 1798 received £19.6.3½ from the estate of George Fisher (BAAD 12:489).

Foreman, Robert, son of John and Elizabeth, and Mary Naylor, daughter of John and Jane, were m. on 18 d. 3 m. 1766 (Card Index to Nottingham Meeting, at MdHS; Records of Gunpowder Meeting at MdHS: 254). On 9 May 1796 Mary was named as a daughter of John Naylor, Sr., of Baltimore Co. (BAWB 5:451; BALR WG#53:474; BAAD 12:526).

Foreman, Valentine, b. 5 Sep 1774, and Rebecca Lucas, b. 27 Aug 1777, were m. on 14 Oct 1798. Their son Thomas was b. on 9 Nov 1799 ("Valentine Foreman Bible," in *MBR* 7:63; Reamy, *St. Paul's Parish Register:* 122).

Foresight, Joseph, and Mary Marshall were m. on 19 Aug 1731 (Harrison, "St. George's Parish Register:" 259). She was the widow of Richard Marshall who d. by 1730; Mary was the mother of William Marshall, and three daus. (*ARMD* 31:174-179). She m. 3rd, Richard Blood (*q.v.*).

Forman, Charles, of Baltimore, was m. last Sat. eve. at Philadelphia, by Rev. Dr. Smith, to Miss Sarah Wolf of the latter city (*Federal Gazette and Baltimore Daily Advertiser* 26 June 1799).

Forman, William, of Chestertown, Kent Co., m. last Sat. eve., Jane, daughter of the late William Spear (*Maryland Journal and Baltimore Advertiser* 23 Nov 1790; BAML).

Forrester, George, m. Cassandra Gardiner on 8 April 1789 ("Records of First German Church:" 189, *MGSB* 16 (2) (May 1975) 65-ff.). She m. 2nd, Benjamin Ricketts (*q.v.*).

Forsidal, Elias, was charged at March Court 1724/5 with fathering an illegitimate child (BACP IS&TW#4:127).

Forster, Patience, was charged with bastardy at the March 1730/1 Court (BACP HS#7:96, 105). Her son John Forster was born 22 Jan 1720/1 (Reamy, *St. Paul's Parish Register*: 20).

Forsyth, Jacob, was m. last Thurs. eve. by Rev. Parrott, to Miss Sally Cooper, both of this city (*Federal Gazette and Baltimore Daily Advertiser* 25 Nov 1797).

Fortescue, Jane, d. by 1800 leaving a sister Ann Barnet or Burnet, and a brother Henry Manley (BOCP: Petition of Ann Burnet, Baltimore Co., 1800).

Fortney, Jacob, m. by 22 April 1797 Catherine, daughter of Henry Brothers (BAWB 5:519; BAAD 12:496).

Forty, John, d. by 10 March 1754 by which time his admx. Mary had m. Elisha Hall (*q.v.*); After Forty's death Mary m. 2nd, John Connell (*q.v.*), 3rd. William Nicholson (*q.v.*), and 4th Elisha Hall (*q.v.*) (MINV 87:342; BAAD 7:181).

Forwood, Jacob, son of Samuel, m. by 5 d. 7 m. 1781 Mary Warner, daughter of Benjamin, who was reported to have gone out in marriage to a man not of our society ("Minutes of Deer Creek Meeting," *QRNM:* 141). [No other marriage reference found].

Forwood, John, b. 1 April 1762 near Wilmington, Delaware, d. 22 May 1835, m. on 8 March 1785, Hannah Forwood, his cousin, b. 6 Oct 1767, d. 4 May 1829 ("John Forwood Bible." *MBR* 1:82-85).

Forwood, Samuel, and Mary Murray were m. by lic. dated 28 Oct 1794 (HAML). Mary Forwood (late Murray), on 26 d. 2 m. 1795 was reported to have gone out in marriage to a man not of our society ("Minutes of Deer Creek Meeting," *QRNM:* 155).

Forwood, William, of Newcastle Co., Pa. [*sic*], m. by 20 Oct 1770 Sarah, daughter of Robert Clark (BALR AL#B:540).

Fosbender, Peter, and Hedwig Myer were married by banns 6 Aug 1798 at St. Peter's Catholic Church, Baltimore (*Piet:* 134).

Fosbinder, Peter, widower, and Elizabeth Butcher, were married by license dated 30 Dec 1800, at St. Peter's Catholic Church, Baltimore (*Piet:* 134).

Fossey, John, and Elizabeth Mitchell were married by license dated 24 Jan 1798 at St. Peter's Catholic Church, Baltimore (*Piet:* 134; BAML). Both of Fell's Point, they were m. last evening by the Rev. Mr. Passmore (*Federal Gazette and Baltimore Advertiser* 25 Jan 1798).

Foster, [-?-], m. by 17 Jan 1784 Sarah, daughter of Thomas Cresap of Washington Co. (BAWB 4:398).

Foster, Capt. James, was m. last Wed. eve. by the Rev. Mr. Ireland, to Miss Rebecca [Shehanasey?], both of this city (*Federal Gazette and Baltimore Daily Advertiser* 23 Sep 1799).

Foster, Capt. Joseph, and Sally, eldest daughter of Capt. Elijah Tull, were m. [in Baltimore Co.] (*Maryland Journal and Baltimore Advertiser* 31 Dec 1782).

Foster, William, and Sarah Walker were married by license dated 2 April 1782 (BAML). In Oct 1788 Foster, of Baltimore, stated he would not pay the debts of his wife Sarah (*Maryland Gazette or Baltimore General Advertiser* 28 Oct 1788).

Fottrell, Edward, and Achsah Woodward were m. on 10 May 1739 in Anne Arundel Co. (Leisenring, "List of Marriages," MS. at MdHS: 246). On 22 July 1741 Achsah was named as the admx. of Amos Woodward (q.v.) (BAAD 5: 86).

Fountain, Mary, was charged with bastardy at the March 1723/4 Court and presented at the June 1724 Court (BACP IS&TW#3:201, 332).

Fouracres, Laurence, m. by 10 March 1730 Rachel, daughter of William Hill of Cecil Co., and granddaughter of Samuel Hill (BALR IS#L:211).

Foulks, John, aged 11, orphan of John Foulks, in Nov 1772 was bound to Samuel Caldwell, blacksmith (BAMI 1772: 30).

Fountain, Collier, of Somerset Co., died leaving a will dated 3 Aug 1781 and proved 18 Aug 1781, naming his brother John Masson Fountain, and his nephews Nicholas and William Tull, children of his sister Barbara Tull (BAWB 3:420). Bridget Tull, admx. with will annexed, posted bond to administer his estate on 7 July 1784 (BAAB 6:166).

Foursides, Mary, was charged with bastardy and confessed at the Nov 1746 Court (BACP TB&TR#1:246).

Fowler, [-?-], m. by 29 Nov 1782, Thamar, sister of George Harryman, and daughter of George Harryman, Sr. (BALR WG#M:10).

Fowler, Benjamin, merchant of Pittsburgh, and Miss Mary Hughes of Baltimore were m. Thurs. eve. by Rev. Richards (*Maryland Journal and Baltimore Advertiser* 26 March 1796).

Fowler, George, and Eleanor Hammond were married by license dated 16 April 1791 (BAML). On 13 June 1792 Eleanor was named as the admx. of Thos. Hammond (BAAD 11:70). Thomas Hammond and Eleanor Hopham were m. on 17 April 1783 (Marr. Returns of Rev. William West, Scharf Papers, MS 1999 at MdHS).

Fowler, Michael, in 1763 was convicted of bastardy (BAMI 1755-1763).

Fowler, Richard, and Mary Fitch were m. on 31 Dec 1754 (Harrison, "St. John's Parish Register:" 211). On 9 April 1787 Mary was named as a daughter of William Fitch, who described himself as 'being very ancient' (BAWB 4:284; BAAD 9:287).

Fowler, Walter, of Queen St., Fell's Point, stated he would not pay the debts of his wife Margaret, who had eloped from him on 22nd inst. (*Maryland Journal and Baltimore Advertiser* 24 Aug 1787).

Fownes, John, merchant of London, was m. last week at Philadelphia, by Rev. Bishop Butler, to Mrs. Sarah Thomas of Fell's Point (*Federal Gazette and Baltimore Daily Advertiser* 7 Jan 1799).

Foy, [-?-], m. by 5 Oct 1733 Rebecca, daughter of Peter and Rebecca Puttee (Potee) (MWB 22:160 abst. in *Md. Cal. of Wills* 8:75; 30:445 abst. by Gibb).

Foy, Eleanor, in Aug 1792 was appointed guardian of Catherine, Elizabeth, Peter, and two other children [names illegible] of Michael Foy BAOC 2:232).

Foy, Miles, had an ante-nuptial contract with Frances Grant, widow of Hugh Grant (q.v.) of Baltimore Co., dec.; they were m. by 18 May 1730 (BALR IS#J:317; IS#K:306). Frances was aged 60 when she deposed on 22 Sep 1736, that she was the widow and extx. of Daniel Johnson (q.v.) (BALC HWS#3 #56; MDAD 15:203; BAAD 3:224).

Foy, Michael, and Elizabeth Asple [*sic*] were married by license on 8 March 1787 at St. Peter's Catholic Church, Baltimore (*Piet:* 134).

Fraher, Edmond, and Kitty Dillon, natives of Ireland, were married by license on 1 July 1800 at St. Peter's Catholic Church, Baltimore (*Piet:* 134).

Frails, Joseph, on 15 March 1798 was named as the administrator of Susannah Mason and received an equal share of £38.17.0½ of the estate (BAAD 13:9).

Francis, William, and Sarah Bosman were married by license dated 31 Dec 1784 (BAML). On 12 Oct 1797 Sarah was named as a daughter of Edward Bosman (BAWB 6:16).

Franciscus, George, m. by 31 Oct 1791 [-?-], daughter of John Schleich, whose will of that date named his grandson John Franciscus of George (BAWB 7:118).

Frankenberger, Henry, m. by 26 April 1794 Sarah, legatee of Edward Punteny, dec. (BALR WG#OO:461).

Franklin, Charles, and Catherine Counselman were m. on 26 April 1792 (Marr. Returns of Rev. John Hagerty, Scharf Papers, MS.1999 at MdHS). On 6 July 1794 Catherine was named as a daughter of George Counselman (BAWB 5:197).

Franklin, James, on 18 Feb 1748 was named as a grandson of John Willmott (MWB 25:531 abst. by Gibb).

Franklin, James, d. intestate before 18 Feb 1795, when Sarah Smith, *admx. de bonis non* of Ruth Ingram, and surviving admx. of Franklin, petitioned the court, stating that when Franklin had died, William Gibson and others searched for a will. They found a pocket book containing some accounts of a legacy left by Ruth Ingram to her brother Benjamin Franklin. Gibson gave the papers to Henry Hill Carroll. Smith petitions that Carroll turn the pocket book and/or accounts over to her (BOCP Petition of Sarah Smith, 1795).

Franklin (Frankland), Thomas, and Ruth Willmot were m. 26 Oct 1729 (Harrison, "St. Paul's Parish Register:" 149). Thomas Franklin m. 2nd, by 8 May 1744 Ruth, admx. of Peasley Ingram (*q.v.*) (MDTP 31:476; *BCF:* 228; MINV 26:1;MDAD 20:217, 32:320). On 11 June 1759 Rachel Wilmot named a grandson James Franklin in her will (BAWB 2:348).

Franklin, Thomas, and Margaret Counselman were m. on 1 June 1786 (Marr. Returns of Rev. William West, Scharf Papers, MS.1999 at MdHS); on 6 July 1794 Margaret was named as a daughter of George Counselman (BAWB 5:197).

Fraser, Eleanor, late of the Island of New Providence in the Bahamas, in her will made 23 May 1795 named her natural son Alexander McKenzie, by John McKenzie of New Providence, the child she is now 'aciene' [*enciente*] with, and her three half sisters, Patty, Mary, and Catherine Towson, daughters. of Susanna Towson now living in Baltimore (BAWB 5:353).

Fraser, John, d. by 6 Jan 1717, having m. Mary, widow of Dennis Duskins (BALR TR#RA:523).

Frasher, [-?-], m. [-?-], daughter of Elizabeth Price, by whom he was the father of Alexander, Mary, Sarah, and John Frasher (BACT TR#E:206).

Frashier. See Frazier.

Fraisizor. See Frazier.

Frasor, John, m. by 16 June 1761 Eleanor, sister of William Wooden (MWB 31:357 abst. by Gibb). Frasor d. by 29 Aug 1760 when John Wooden named his daughter Eleanor, widow of John Frazor, in his will (MWB 37:82 abst. in *Md. Cal. of Wills* 14:77)

Frazer, Alexander, brother of John Frazer, d. by 23 Sep 1779 leaving a widow Susannah who was described in John Frazer's will as having m. 2nd, [-?-] Towson (BAWB 3:552).

Frazer, Alexander, aged over 14, orphan of Hugh Frazer, on 20 Sep 1787 chose Philip
Rogers as his guardian (BAOC 2:40).

Frazier, George, m. by 21 Oct 1775, Mary, daughter of Jonathan Hughes (BALR AL#F:
329-337).

Frazier, Hugh, m. Ruth [-?-], who m. 2nd, Stephen Moore (*q.v.*), and 3rd, Clement
Skerrett (*q.v.*) (BAWB 3:448; BAOC 2:40. 43).

Frashier, James (or John), m. by 25 Sep 1739, Rebecca, admx. of James Boreing (q.v.)
(MDTP 31:44). John Frazier, aged c50, deposed on 29 Aug 1763 that he had m. the
widow of James Boring (BALR B#N:134). On 14 Aug 1775, Job Garrison named
Frazier as his uncle (BALR WG#V:206; MDAD 18:401, 19:505; MINV 24:160;
BAAD 3:256, 4:122).

Frazier (Fraisizor), John, m. by 20 Jan 1775 Urath, daughter of Elizabeth Boring
(BAWB 4:108).

Frazier, Joshua, formerly a resident of Annapolis, in his will made 17 Feb 1791 named
his sister Elizabeth Tootell and niece Mary Middleton (BAWB 6:171).

Frazier, William, Lieutenant in the Revolutionary War in the 5th Maryland Regiment,
died on 25 Sep 1807; married on 11 Feb 1779 Henrietta Maria Johnson, who was
born 16 Aug 1760 (Rev. War Pension Application of Henrietta Johnson: W3797).

Free Negro Chance, d. by 8 March 1797 when George Stansbury posted bond to
administer his estate (BAAB 8:73). On 25 June 1798 Tausan Couple, one of his
heirs and legal representatives, petitioned the court on the above date that he had
applied to George Stansbury, administrator of the dec., for his share of the estate,
but without effect. He asked the court to compel George Stansbury to close the
administration; Stansbury replied that he did not know if Couple was legally
entitled to a share of the estate, but if Couple could prove his right, Stansbury
would be glad to pay him his share (BOCP Tausan Couple, *vs.* George Stansbury,
1798).

Freeborne, Thomas, m. by Jan 1703/4 Priscilla (nee Thomas), widow of Richard
Kilburne (*q.v.*) (AAJU G:278, 284; MDAD 3:338). Priscilla m. 3rd, Samuel Howell
(q.v.). On 13 May 1720, Priscilla was named as a sister of David Thomas of
Baltimore Co. (MWB 16:36 abst. in *Md. Cal. of Wills* 5:6).

Freeburger, Jacob, and Mary Parks were m. on 23 Feb 1799 (Marr. Register of Rev.
Lewis Richards, MS.690 at MdHS). She was a daughter of Sarah Parks who was
named as a half-sister in the will of Joseph Perigo made 12 Aug 1800 (BAWB
6:319).

Freeland, James, m. by 14 Nov 1786, a sister of John Kingsbury, and had a son John
Kingsbury Freeland, who Kingsbury called nephew (BAWB 4:414).

Freeland, Mary, was charged with bastardy at the Nov 1708 Court; William Talbot
posted bond and assumed responsibility for raising the child (BACP IS#B:17).

Freeman, [-?-], m. by 28 Nov 1794 Elizabeth, daughter of George Fisher (BAWB 6:6).

Freeman, James, son of Richard Freeman of Calvert Co., on 17 April 1703 was
conveyed 50 a. in Calvert Co. by his grandmother Mary Clarke, widow, of
Baltimore Co. (BALR HW#2:237).

Freeman, Maria, servant to Andrew Lendrum, at the March 1761 Court was tried for
having a mulatto child, named Stephen Price Freeman (BAMI 1755-1763).

French, Benjamin, and Mary 'Abbey Crombie.' [*sic*] were m. by lic. on 3 Nov 1784
(BAML). On 11 Aug 1790 Benjamin French was paid an equal share of the estate
of Robert Abercrombie (BAAD 10:184).

French, James, and Arianna Bankson were m. sometime after 1752. On 16 April 1738 Ariana Bankson was named as one of the children of Joseph Bankson (MDAD 16:132). Hannah 'Bankston' m. William Hughes on 11 Dec 1735 (Harrison, "St. Paul's,": 154). On 14 Feb 1770 Areanna was named as a daughter of Hannah Hughes, widow of Baltimore Town (MWB 38:110; BAWB 3:158).

Frengert, Nicholas, m. by 22 June 1776 Mary Elizabeth, dau, of Theobald Schneider of Mannheim Twp., York Co., Pa. (BAWB 4:18).

Friday, John, and Elizabeth Boughan were married by banns on 4 Jan 1791 at St. Peter's Catholic Church, Baltimore (*Piet:* 134).

Friend, James, m. by March 1683/4 Jane, relict of Ambrose Gillett (BACP D:141).

Fringer, Michael, m. by 6 Nov 1792 Peggy Deale, legatee of Philip Deale (BAAD 11:154, 12:9).

Frisbie. See Frisby.

Frisby (Frisbie), [-?-], m. by 13 Nov 1754 [-?-], sister of George Wells, and had a son Peregrine (BALR BB#1: 349).

Frisby, Thomas, m. by 24 March 1703 Frances, daughter of Col. George Wells (MDTP 19A:165).

Frisby, Thomas Peregrine, son of Peregrine Frisby, in Nov 1760 chose Greenbury Dorsey as his guardian (BAMI 1755-1763: 40).

Frisby, William, m. by 12 June 1719 [-?-], daughter of George Wells (BAAD 1:54; MDAD 2:451).

Frissel, [-?-], m. by 5 Aug 1717 Sarah, daughter of Ambrose Nelson (MWB 19:704 abst. in *Md. Cal. of Wills* 6:112).

Frizle. See Frizzell.

Frizell, John, of Baltimore Co., m. by 24 June 1745 Elizabeth, daughter of John Gale of Baltimore Co. (AALR RB#2:133).

Frizzell, James, m. by May 1696 Elizabeth, extx. of William York (*q.v.*) (MDTP 16:171).

Frizzell (Frizle), James, m. by Nov 1692, Mary [*sic*], mother of William York and extx. of William York, and extx. of Jacob Looton (BACP G#1:490; MDTP 16:171; BACP F#1:316).

Frizzle, Hannah, on 8 April 1800 posted a bond as guardian of John, Nimrod, Honor and Elizabeth Ann Frizzle, orphans of John Frizzle, Sr. Stephen Gill and Benjamin Bond were sureties (Baltimore Co. Guardian Bonds WB#2).

Frogg, [-?-], m. by 19 March 1780 Catherine, daughter of Yocum Youn (BAWB 3:433).

Frost, Joseph, and Mary Baker were m. on 2 Oct 1761 (Harrison, "St. John's Parish Register:" 22. She m. 2nd, by 7 Oct 1793 Joseph Hilton (*q.v.*).

Fugate, Edward, and Elizabeth Bacon were m. on 12 Jan 1758 (Harrison, "St. John's Parish Register:" 216). On 28 Feb 1772 Elizabeth was named as a daughter of Martin Bacon (BAWB 4:106).

Fugate (Fucatt), Peter, m. by 4 July 1694, Frances, daughter of John Mould (BALR RM#HS:419).

Fulford, John, stated he would not pay the debts of his wife Mary, who had eloped from his bed and board (*Maryland Journal and Baltimore Advertiser* 16 Sep 1785).

Fuller, Henry, and Elizabeth Cox were m. on 27 Aug 1738 (Harrison, "St. John's Parish Register:" 98). On 28 May 1742 she was named as the widow of Joseph Cox of Baltimore Co. (MDAD 18:283).

Fullhart, Jacob, and Elizabeth Jacobs were married by banns 8 Nov 1789 at St. Peter's Catholic Church, Baltimore (*Piet:* 134).

Fulton, John, and Hannah Norris were m. on 4 Aug 1754 (Harrison, "St. John's Parish Register:" 211). On 5 Dec 1761 Hannah was named as a daughter of Edward Norris (BAWB 3:3).

Fulton, William, and Mrs. Mary Davidson, consort of the late Andrew Davidson of Baltimore, were m. 6th inst. (*Baltimore American* 14 Nov 1800).

Fuss (?), John, m. by 26 Oct 1798 Augustiana, daughter of Jesse Biddle (BALR WG#58: 247). John Forse and Augustine Biddle were married by license dated 10 June 1796 (BAML).

Fusselbaugh, John, and Barbara Zigler, both of Baltimore, were m. last eve. by Rev. Kurtz (*Baltimore Telegraphe* 23 June 1800).

"G"

Gabriel, Margaret, was charged with bastardy at the Nov 1738 Court and stated that the father of her child was dead (BACP HWS#1A:320).

Gadd, Thomas, and Christiana Ditto were m. on 22 Jan 1732 (Harrison, "St. John's Parish Register:" 69). On 25 March 1743 Christiana was named as the mother of Abraham Ditto (BALR TB#C:195).

Gadd, William, for support of his children was on the levy list (Balto. Co. Levy List, 1772).

Gaddis, Paul, on 5 March 1770, was summoned to appear before the vestry of St. George's Parish for unlawful cohabitation with Margaret McCoobs [later called McCall, widow] (Reamy, *St. George's Parish Register:* 111).

Gafford, Joseph, and Mary York, of Baltimore Co., were m. by lic. 13 April 1800 at St. Peter's Catholic Church, Baltimore (*Piet:* 134).

Gaine (or Caine), William, of Baltimore Co. married by May 1688 Mary, relict of John Diamint or Dimmitt (MDTP 14:72). She m. 3rd, Thomas Stone (*q.v.*).

Gaine, William, m. on 1 Aug 1727 Rebecca Harkins [Hawkins] Harrison, "St. Paul's Parish Register:" 150). She m. 2nd, James Boring (q.v.), and 3rd, John Frazier (*q.v.*).

Gaine (Gain), William, was charged with bastardy at the Aug 1750 Court (BACP TR#5:151).

Gaither (Caither), John, and Jane Buck were m. on 21 Aug 1701 (Harrison, "All Hallow's Parish Register, Anne Arundel Co.," MS. At MdHS: 57, 247). Jane was a daughter of [-?-] and Katherine Buck; Katherine m. 2nd, Theophilus Kitten. On 27 July1713 Jane 'Caither' received her portion from the estate of Theophilus Kitten (INAC 34:211).

Galbraith, John, of Baltimore Town, m. by 21 Jan 1785 Eliz., daughter of James Beaty; John had a son Thomas, a minor, believed to be in the Kingdom of Ireland (BAWB 4:46).

Galbraith, William, of Baltimore Town, in his will made 24 July 1780 named his wife as Hester Ross and stated she was the mother of William Noble Galbraith and Thomas Galbraith (BAWB 4:102).

Galbraith, William Noble, of Baltimore, and Miss Mary Range of Penna. were m. a few days ago (*Baltimore Daily Intelligencer* 1 Nov 1793).

Gale, John, and Elizabeth Ashman were m. on 25 June 1713 (Harrison, "All Hallow's Parish Register," Anne Arundel Co., at MdHS: 267). On 14 Dec 1714 Elizabeth was named as a sister of William and Joshua Cromwell, and John Ashman of Baltimore Co. (MWB 13:732 abst. in *Md. Cal. of Wills* 4:18).

Gall, Johan, and Catherine Schaffer were m. in 1788 ("Register of Zion Lutheran Church," MS. at MdHS: 388). Catherine m. 2nd, Henry Dolly, whose will made 16 Nov 1797 named his wife Catherine, and her children (by a former husband), Jacob and Elizabeth Gaul, and one other step-child (BAWB 6:65).

Gallagar, Charles, of Baltimore, stated that he would not pay the debts of his wife (*Maryland Journal and Baltimore Advertiser* 20 May 1788).

Gallagher, John, and Phoebe Baxley were married by banns 24 May 1795 at St. Peter's Catholic Church, Baltimore (*Piet:* 134).

Gallahampton, Elizabeth, was charged with bastardy and confessed on 6 March 1745/6; she was ordered to be whipped. Samuel Jarvis, the father of her child, confessed and was fined 30 shillings. As servant to Mary Keen she was charged with bastardy again and confessed on 5 Aug 1746 and again she was ordered to be whipped (BACP 1745-1746:814, TB&TR#1:133).

Gallaher, Mary, in 1775 was fined for bastardy (BAMI 1772, 1775-1781:204).

Gallahone, Catherine, mulatto, confessed at the June 1750 Court to having a child lately born of her body. She was sentenced to be sold for seven years after her present servitude; her child Margaret Gallahone was sold to Parker Hall for 31 years (BACP TR#5:11).

Gallaspie, Robert, and Eliz. Maxwell were m. on 6 Nov 1753 (Harrison, "St. John's Parish Register:" 209). On 18 July 1756, Elizabeth was named as a daughter of David Maxwell (MWB 30:116 abst. by Gibb).

Gallet, John Baptist, and Mary Celestin were married by banns 9 May 1784 at St. Peter's Catholic Church, Baltimore (*Piet:* 134).

Gallion, Keziah, was charged with bastardy at the Nov 1759 court (BAMI 1757-1759: 237).

Gallion, Samuel, m. by 3 July 1773 Eliz., daughter of John Garrettson; they had a daughter Sarah Gallion (BAWB 3:279).

Galloway, Anne, was charged with bastardy in March 1723/4 and at June 1724 Court named Patrick Lynch as the father (BACP IS&TW#3:201,330).

Galloway, Elizabeth, (formerly Bowen), hath so far erred as to consummate her marriage contrary to the rules of our discipline: 25 d. 6 m. 1776 ("Minutes of Gunpowder Meeting," *QRNM:* 67). [No other marriage reference found].

Galloway, James, son of Moses, m. by 1 June 1782 Mary, daughter of William Andrew (BALR WG#H:445).

Galloway, James, age 11, son of James Galloway, dec., on 11 Dec 1787 was made a ward of John Adamson (BOCP 2:46). He is probably the same James Galloway, orphan son of James, who chose Moses Galloway as his guardian in Nov 1794 (BOCP 3:121).

Galloway, John, and Wealthy Mildues were m. on 24 Oct 1780 (Marr. Returns of Rev. William West, Scharf Papers, MS 1999 at MdHS). She was a daughter of Aquila and Elizabeth Mildews (BAAD 9:19; BAWB 7:379).

Galloway, Joseph, of Anne Arundel Co., and Susanna Paca were m. on 18 Oct 1722 (Harrison, "St. John's Parish Register:" 19). Susannah was named as a sister of John Paca (BALR IS#IK:269).

Galloway, Moses, and Mary Nicholson were m. on 6 April 1750 (Harrison, "St. John's Parish Register:" 201). On 4 Jan 1756 Mary was named as a niece of Elizabeth Hines, widow of Thomas Hines (MWB 30:28 abst. by Gibb).

Galloway, Moses, and Pamela Owings were married by license dated 6 March 1782 (BAML). On 13 Feb 1788, Pamela was named as the admx. of John Owings, who had no children, but left eleven brothers and sisters (BAAD 9:153).

Galloway, Salathiel, and Priscilla James were m. on 28 Sep 1753 (Harrison, "St. John's Parish Register:" 208). She m. 2nd, Joseph Crooks (*q.v.*).

Galloway, Salathiel, and Mary Galloway were m. on 9 Nov 1797 (Marr. Register of Rev. Lewis Richards, MS.690 at MdHS). In 1798 Mary was named as a daughter of James Galloway (BPET: Salathiel and Mary Galloway vs. Walter and Mary Presbury, 1798).

Galloway, William, d. by 14 July 1705 having m. Margaret, daughter of Hendrick and Christian Enloes and sister of Abraham Enloes who d. 1709 (*BCF*:238). She m. 2nd, James Durham (*q.v.*).

Galloway, William, d. by Oct 1793 when his orphan children, Elijah, Sarah, Jemima, Elisha and Elihu Galloway, were made wards of Mary Galloway (BOCP 3:63).

Galloway, William, and Ann Waller (nee Taylor) were married by license dated 6 June 1792 (BAML). He and Mrs. Ann Waller, widow of the late John Waller (*q.v.*), were m. in Baltimore Co. [date not given] (*Maryland Journal and Baltimore Advertiser* 15 June 1792).

Gambrall, Sarah, on 2 July 1730 was named as a kinwoman in the will of Jane (Jean) Vandever (MWB 20:56 abst. in Md. Cal. of Wills 6:163).

Gambrill, [-?-], m. by 26 Jan 1762 Honor, daughter of Tobias Stansbury 'the Elder' (BAWB 2:167; BAAD 7:321).

Gambrill, Augustine, and Maria Baldwin were married by license dated 20 July 1795 (AAML). She was Maria Graham Woodward who married Henry Baldwin by license dated 25 Jan 1790 (AAML). William Garret Woodward, in his will made 22 July 1799 named his son-in-law Augustine Gambrill and grandchildren Eliza Baldwin, William Baldwin, George Garrett Gambrill, Mary Gambrill, Stevens Gambrill, William Woodward Warfield and Juliet Warfield (BAWB 6:208).

Ganby. See Gunby.

Ganteaume, James, native of France, and Elizabeth Casey, native of Ireland, were m. by lic. 10 Nov 1797 at St. Peter's Catholic Church, Baltimore (*Piet:* 134; BAML, which gives her name as Elizabeth Carey).

Gantz, Adam, m. by 19 March 1794 Mary Lindenberger (BAAD 11:389).

Garber, Mary, wife of John V. Garber, claimed her husband was already married to another woman at the time of their marriage (*Maryland Journal and Baltimore Advertiser* 6 July 1779).

Gardiner, Robert, orphan son of Sarah, now wife of John McDonald, had been bound some years ago to Robert Sands, carpenter, who has misbehaved, abused, and stinted the said orphan boy (BOCP Petition of Robert Gardiner, 1788, Box 2, Folder 34).

Gardner, Ann, was charged with bastardy at the Nov 1757 Court, and named Aquila Dorsey as the father of the child (BAMI 1757-1759:74).

Gardner, James, merchant of Augusta, Ga., and Sarah Hill Hodgkin, second daughter of Thomas Brooke Hodgkin of Baltimore Co., were lately m. at George Town, Ga. (*Maryland Journal and Baltimore Advertiser* 20 Dec 1793; BAWB 7:415).

Gardner, John, m. by 1759 Katherine, daughter of William and Sarah Hamilton of Baltimore Co. (MWB 30:737 abst. by Gibb; BAAD 6:149, 7:287; BAWB 2:315, 4:304).

Gardner, Capt. Obadiah, and Miss Deborah Gottier (or Gautier) were m. last Fri. eve. at Fell's Point, by Rev. Dr. Allison (*Maryland Gazette or Baltimore General Advertiser* 7 June 1791; *Maryland Journal and Baltimore Advertiser* 7 June 1791). Obed Gardiner and Deborah Gottier were married by license dated 3 June 1791 (BAML).

Gardner, Sarah, was charged with bastardy at the Nov 1758 Court (BAMI 1757-1759:162).

Gardner, Susanna, confessed to bastardy and was ordered on 4 June 1746 was sentenced to receive 10 lashes on the bare back. John Hannesea admitted he was the father of the child (BACP TB&TR#1:9, 10).

Garland, John, and Mary Ann Lyston were m. by lic. 11 Nov 1790 at St. Peter's Catholic Church, Baltimore (*Piet:* 134).

Garland, William, d. by 12 Aug 1751 when his estate was administered by Henry Garland; he left four children: James, aged 20; Susannah, 13; Francis, 10; and Catherine, 2½ (BAAD 4:276).

Garlick, Thomas, of Barnsley, Co. York, m. by 27 Nov 1771 Edith, sister of Anthony Rhodes (BALR AL#E:204).

Garnons, William, orphan, petitioned the court that he had been bound as an apprentice to Samuel Brown, carver. He complained of his treatment and added that his mother and aunt had never been paid (BOCP Petition of William Garnons, 1791).

Garnous, William, and Jane Tune were m. 19 Feb 1794 in St. Paul's Parish (Harrison, "St. Paul's Parish Register:" 281). William Garnons [*sic*] of Fell's Point, stated that he would not pay the debts of his wife Jane (*Fells Point Telegraphe* 17 April 1795).

Garrett, [-?-], m. by 15 Feb 1774 Mary, daughter of Morris (Maurice) Baker (MWB 39:716, abst. in *Md. Cal. of Wills* 15:145).

Garrett, Amos, m. by 9 Aug 1791 [-?-], who received an equal share of the estate of John Ayres (BAAD 10:418).

Garrett, Bennett, d. by 1 Nov 1744 by which time his widow Martha had m. 2nd, by 23 Dec 1742 [-?-] Todd, and 3rd, by 1 Nov 1744 George Garrettson (*q.v.*) (*BCF:*517).

Garrett, Bennett, m. by 2 April 1736, Avarilla, daughter of John Walston; on 10 Sep 1741 she was referred to as admx. of William Loney (*q.v.*) (BAAD 3:274; 4:97; BALR, HWS#M, 424; MDAD 18:395; MDTP 31:202).

Garrett, Dennis, m. by 1 March 1691/2, Barbara Stone, who was conveyed property by Thomas Stone (BALR RM#HS, 341).

Garrett, Henry, son of Richard Garrett, lately deceased, on 22 June 1710 was given a cow and a calf called 'Strawberry' by Lawrence Draper (BALR 22 June 1710).

Garrett, Henry, and Mary Butterworth were m. on 19 Dec 1728 (Harrison, "St. George's Parish Register:" 247, 340). On 8 March 1730/1 Mary was named as a daughter of Isaac Butterworth of Baltimore Co. (MWB 19:627; MDAD 10:691; BALR TB#D:300).

Garrett, James, m. by 11 Aug 1675 Johanna, daughter of George and Mary Peake of Baltimore Co. (INAC 1:409).

Garrett, John, and Margaret Baker were m. on 22 Nov 1759 (Harrison, "St. John's Parish Register:" 219). She was a daughter of Morris (Maurice) Baker (MWB 39:716, abst. in *Md. Cal. of Wills* 15:145).

Garrettson, Garrett, m. on 5 Dec 1702 Elizabeth Freeborn ("Garrettson Bible Record," (1845), MGRC 1979: 1; Harrison, "St. George's Parish Register:" 198). She was a sister of Richard Freeborn (BALR RM#HS:661).

Garrettson, Garrett, and Mrs. Susannah Robinson, widow of Capt. Daniel Robinson (q.v.), were m. on 12 March 1760 (Harrison, "St. George's Parish Register:" 381); Susannah had m. 1st, Thomas Brown (*q.v.*).

Garrettson, George, and Mrs. Martha Todd were m. in 1 Nov 1744 (Harrison, "St. George's Parish Register:" 341). Martha was a daughter of James Presbury (*q.v.*) and his wife Martha Presbury, and had m. 1st, Bennett Garrett and, 2nd, [-?-] Todd (BAAD 3:274; *BCF:*517). On 16 July 1755 Martha, a daughter of George Garrettson, d. by Nov 1759. George's widow Martha was made guardian of his children: George, Garrett, Mary Goldsmith, Goldsmith, and Frances. His daughter Freenotha Garrettson, chose her mother as her guardian (BAMI 1755-1763; MWB 24:542 abst. by Gibb).

Garrettson, James, and Catherine Nelson were m. on 24 April 1746 (Harrison, "St. George's Parish Register:" 342). On 19 Jan 1754 she was named as a daughter of John Nelson (BACT TR#E:175-176).

Garrettson, (Garrison), Job, in Nov 1759, was charged with begetting a bastard on the body of Viola Dimmit; in Nov 1760 he was charged with begetting a bastard on the body of Annastatia Oram (BAMI 1755-1763, 1757-1759:242),

Garrettson, John, and Sarah Merryarter [Mariarte?] were m. on 21 April 1742 (Harrison, "St. George's Parish Register:" 324; "Garrettson Bible Record (1845)," n MGRC 1979: 1). Sarah was a widow of Edward Merriarter *(q.v.)*. On 24 Nov 1742 Sarah was named as a daughter of Sarah Hanson, and granddaughter of Sarah Tayman, formerly Sarah Cockey who later m. [-?-] Tayman (MWB 23:21 abst. in *Md. Cal. of Wills* 8:196; BALR TB#D:311).

Garrettson, John, in Nov 1750 was charged with begetting a bastard on the body of Elizabeth Orum (BAMI 1757-1759: 242).

Garrison, Job, aged c30, deposed on 14 Aug 1775 mentioning his uncle John Frazier (BALR WG#V:206).

Garrison, Job, m. by 1787, Mary Arrison Cox of Baltimore Co. (MCHP#2177).

Garrison, Paul, and Elizabeth 'Frazer' were m. on 8 May 1735 (Harrison, "St. Paul's Parish Register:" 155). They were the parents of Job Garrison (*q.v.*).

Garrison. See also Garrettson.

Garts, Peter, son of Charles Garts, merchant of Baltimore, m. 25th ult. at Fredericksburg, Va., Peggy, dau of Robert Lilly, merchant of the latter place (*Maryland Gazette or Baltimore General Advertiser* 5 Dec 1788). Margaret Garts died in Fredericksburg, Va., wife of Peter Garts, late of Baltimore (*Maryland Journal and Baltimore Advertiser* 10 Nov 1789).

Garvise (Gerviss), Ann, was charged with bastardy at the June 1732 Court and again at the Nov 1734 Court (BACP HWS#7:288, HWS#9:350).

Gash (Gush?), Michael, m. by 3 Dec 1755 Elizabeth, admx. of Garvais Gilbert (*q.v.*) (MINV 60:335; MDAD 40:138).

Gash, Nicholas, in his will dated 19 Sep 1769 referred to his 'old woman' Hannah Shaw, and named her children Thomas and Ann Shaw (BAWB 3:103). Thomas Shaw Gash, admin., on 8 Sep 1781 posted bond to administer the estate of Hannah Gash (BAAB 5:113),.

Gash, Rachel. See Floyd, Rachel, mother of Ana.

Gash, Thomas, d. by Feb 1706 leaving a widow Mary who m. 2nd, Richard Perkins (q.v.) and 3rd, on Feb 1706, John Belcher (*q.v.*).

Gash, Thomas, d. by Feb 1796, leaving two orphans who chose John Buck or Busk as their guardian. The children were Basil and Rachel (BOCP 3:187).

Gash, William, son of Conrad, was 8 years old on 13 Dec 1755; in March 1756 he was bound to John Hammond Dorsey to age 21 (BAMI 1755-1763).

Gassaway, Nicholas, m. some time after 2 July 1773, as her second husband, Mary Day, widow of Levin Matthews (*q.v.*) ("Day Bible Record, *The Notebook* 15 (2) (June 1999) 7-9).

Gassaway, Nicholas, of Anne Arundel Co., and Pamelia Berry, daughter of Richard Berry of Montgomery Co., were m. Thurs., 28th ult., by the Rev. Mr. Reed (*Baltimore Daily Intelligencer* 4 Dec 1793).

Gatch, Philip, was born 2 March 1751 and married Elizabeth Smith on 14 Feb 1778; she was born 29 Dec 1752 ("Gatch Family Record," *MGSB* 44 (4) (Fall 2003) 497.

Gaul, [-?-], m. by 7 April 1784, Appolonia, daughter and extx. of Henry Brince (BAWB 4:271; BAAB 5:14). Apelonia Gaul, extx., on 7 April 1784 posted bond to administer the estate of Henry Brince (BAAB 5:15). In his will, made 24 Feb 1784 Henry Brice named his only child, a daughter Abelonia, and a grandchild Abelonia Kilbork (BAWB 4:27).

Gauline, John Baptist (son of John Baptist Roch, weigher of the Town of Marseilles, and Ann Armand, native of Marseilles, lately planter of Grande Riviere, St. Domingo) and Marie Pauline Justine Betzie Lender (daughter of the late Dominic and D. Soumillard, lately from Petite Rivierede l'Artbonite, St. Domingo), were m. by lic. 22 Nov 1796 at St. Peter's Catholic Church, Baltimore (*Piet:* 134). John Baptiste Gaulisa and Pauline Justine Leuder were married by license dated 19 Nov 1796 (BAML).

Gavan, Matthew, and Ann Fitzgerald, natives of Ireland, were m. by lic. 4 Oct 1795 at St. Peter's Catholic Church, Baltimore (*Piet:* 134). (BAML gives his name as Matthew Gavin).

Gay, John, m. by 3 Sep 1701 Frances, heir of Nathaniel Ruxton (BALR HW#2:90). She m. 2nd, James Moore (*q.v.*).

Gay, John, in March 1723/4 was charged with begetting a bastard on the body of Sarah West (BACP IS&TW#3:213).

Gay, Nicholas Ruxton, and Ann Lux were m. on 21 Sep 1751 (Harrison, "St. Paul's Parish Register:" 165). On 5 May 1773 Ann was named as a sister of William Lux (BAWB 3:357).

Gayer, Percy Fredrick, b. 29 Sep 1764 Ann Elizabeth [-?-], some time before 6 July 1786 when their daughter Ann Elizabeth was born ("Baxter Family Bible," *HMGB* 12 (3) (July 1941) 37-40).

Gaynor, Hugh, and Eleanor Burk were married by banns 17 Aug 1788 at St. Peter's Catholic Church, Baltimore (*Piet:* 134).

Geanty? John Baptist, and Elizabeth [-?-], free French Negro woman, of St. Domingo, were m. 20 Jan 1798 at St. Peter's Catholic Church, Baltimore (*Piet:* 134).

Gear, James, m. by 27 April 1742, Eliza, extx. of William Wright (q.v.) (MDTP 31:278).

Gears, Daniel, m. by 5 Aug 1723, Elizabeth, daughter of Daniel Benson of Anne Arundel Co. (BALR IS#G:172).

Geary, James, m. by 11 Aug 1790, [-?-], representative of John Lowe (BAAD 10:185).

Geddes, James, of Baltimore, stated that he would not pay the debts of his wife Margaret who was cohabiting with a certain James Cunningham as his wife (*Maryland Journal and Baltimore Advertiser* 25 Jan 1793). James Geddes [*sic*] and Margaret

Flax were m. on 19 Oct 1786 (Marriage License Returns of Rev. William West, filed 16 Nov 1786: Scharf Papers). **N,B,:** The *Maryland Journal* of 18 Jan 1793 gives the husband's name as William Geddes, and the 'other man' as John Cunningham.

Geer, Abigail, in Aug 1733 petitioned the court that she had been bound out by her mother Catherine Geer to serve Mary Tolly to age 21. She was now aged 22 and wanted her freedom. At the sane time she was charged with having had four bastard children (BACP HWS#9:68, 76).

Geere, Katherine, was charged with bastardy at the Aug 1728 Court (BACP HWS#6:32).

Geese, Capt. Peter, was m. yesterday eve. by Rev. Dr. Allison, to Mrs. Susanna Deiter, both of Fell's Point (*Federal Intelligencer and Baltimore Daily Gazette* 5 June 1795).

Geoghegan, Ambrose, m. by 13 July 1722 Katherine, extx. of Pierce Welch (BAAD 2:369; MINV 8:208; MDTP 27:85; MINV 8:208).

George, Joshua, and Betsy, fourth daughter of the Rev. Mr. Thompson, were m. this day at Cecil "Cecil – 21 Dec 1786" (*Maryland Journal and Baltimore Advertiser* 26 Dec 1786).

Gerard, Peter, and Magdalen Mamillon were m. by lic. 20 April 1783 at St. Peter's Catholic Church, Baltimore (*Piet:* 134).

Gerber, Charles, and Catherine Smelser were m. by lic. 13 March 1786 at St. Peter's Catholic Church, Baltimore (*Piet:* 134).

Gerlach, John, and Mary Keilholtz were m. by lic. 7 April 1796 at St. Peter's Catholic Church, Baltimore (*Piet:* 134).

Gerock, Samuel, merchant, and Sarah Wallace were m. last Tues. eve. by Rev. Dr. Cutting. "Newbern, N. C, 27 Dec" (*Maryland Journal and Baltimore Advertiser* 1 Feb 1788).

Gerviss. See Garvise.

Gethier, Georg, m. by 27 Nov 1790, Anna Maria Leineweberin ("First Record Book for the Reformed and Lutheran and Congregations at Manchester, Baltimore (Now Carroll) Co.," *MGSB* 35:285).

Getyear, Peter, by 19 April 1794 [-?-], daughter of Phinsense Kepper, who named his grandchildren Mary, John, Jacob, Elizabeth, Magdelan and Eva Getyear (BAWB 5:332). Peter Getyear d. by Oct 1796 leaving the following children who were made wards of Peter Getyear: John, Jacob, Elizabeth, Mary, Eve, and Matlain (BOCP 3:200).

Ghequier, Charles, late of the city of Hamburg but now a citizen of Baltimore, and Henrietta Haley of Cecil Co. were m. last Sun. eve. (*Maryland Journal and Baltimore Advertiser* 8 Feb 1785; BAML).

Giant, John, on 13 Nov 1750 was summoned to appear before the vestry of St. George's Parish for unlawful cohabitation with [-?-] [-?-]. "He was not found by the church warden" (Reamy, *St. George's Parish Register:* 106).

Gibson, Ann, servant of Thomas Hatchman, was charged with bastardy at the June 1734 Court (BACP HWS#9:253, 267).

Gibson, Elizabeth, admx., on 29 Aug 1698 posted bond to administer the estate of Lewis Jarman (BAAB 3:372).

Gibson, Francis, in his will dated 30 May 1761 named his daughter Frances O'Donnell (BAWB 3:37).

Gibson, Col. George, d. by 17 Sep 1793, having m. Ann, sister of William West (BAWB 5:309).

Gibson, Margaret, was charged with bastardy at the Aug 1715 Court and named James Richardson as the father of her child (BACP IS#B:626).

Gibson, Miles, on 19 May 1676 was conveyed land by Thomas Thurston in consideration of a marriage between Gibson and Ann, daughter of Thomas Thurston (BALR G#J:330).

Gibson, Miles, m. by 30 May1677 [-?-], daughter of Thomas Todd (MDTP 9A:164).

Gibson, Miles, d. by 1693/4 having m. Elizabeth, widow of John Collett (*q.v.*), Henry Hazlewood (*q.v.*), John Collett (*q.v.*). and of Richard Edmonds (*q.v.*) (INAC 12:149, 150, 151).

Gibson, Robert, m. Mrs. Mary Goldsmith on 15 Dec 1702 (Harrison, "St. George's Parish Register:" 197). She later m. George Wells (*q.v.*) and by 1718 William Marshall (*q.v.*).

Gibson, Thomas, and Katherine [*sic*] Demorce were m. on 22 Dec 1761 (Harrison, "St. John's Parish Register:" 222). By 4 June 1769 she had m. John Cain (q.v.).

Gilbert, [-?-], m. by March 1721 or 1723 Rebecca, mother of Sarah Howe (BACP IS#TW#I: 16).

Gilbert, Charles, and Elizabeth Hawkins were m. on 27 Sep 1744 (Harrison, "St. George's Parish Register:" 338). On 10 May 1761 Elizabeth was named as a daughter of Robert Hawkins (BAWB 2:344).

Gilbert, Jarvis, and Elizabeth Preston were m. 10 June 1735 (Harrison, ("St. George's Parish Register:" 283). On 3 Aug 1769 Elizabeth was named as a daughter of James Preston (BFD 5:101). Jarvis Gilbert d. by March 1758 leaving these orphans: Margaret, Jarvis, Sarah, Preston, Hannah, Elizabeth, Michael, Samuel and Ann (BAMI 1755-1763). His admx. Elizabeth m. by Feb 1756 Michael Gash (*q.v.*) (MDTP 36:267).

Gilbert, John, m. by 30 d., 7 m., 1751 [-?-], daughter of John Webster, who also named a granddaughter Martha Gilbert (MWB 29:374 abst. by Gibb). **N.B.:** A Samuel Gilbert and Martha Webster were m. on 26 April 1733 (Harrison, "St. George's Parish Register:" 262).

Gilbert, Michael, and Mary Taylor were m. on 23 Nov 1738 (Harrison, "St. George's Parish Register:" 303). On 15 Dec 1739 Mary was named as a daughter of Martin Taylor, Sr., and heir of Martin Taylor, Jr. (BALR HWS#1-A:324). She was a sister of Martin Taylor, dec., and daughter of Martin Taylor (in admin. account of Robert Robertson of Baltimore Co.) (MDAD 18:12).

Gilbert, Michael, m. 28 Nov 1782 Elizabeth Presbury; she m. 2nd, on 22 Jan 1797, Skipwith Cole (*q.v.*) (Rev. War. Pens. App. of Michael Gilbert, Cont, Line, W-3947).

Gilbert, Thomas, and Ruth Fisher were m. 29 Oct 1790 (Marriage License Returns of Rev. Daniel Kurtz, Scharf Papers, MS 1999 at MdHS). Ruth Gilbert, formerly Fisher, on 29 d. 1 m. 1791, was charged with going out in marriage ("Minutes of Gunpowder Meeting," *QRNM:*90).

Gilbraith, John, and Hannah Clarke were m. by lic. 19 July 1800, at St. Peter's Catholic Church, Baltimore (*Piet:* 134).

Gilcrash. See Gilcrest.

Gilcresh. See Gilcrest.

Gilcrest, (Gilcresh), Robert, d. by 24 Dec 1770, m. by 30 Nov 1753 Helena, admx. of Capt. George Uriell (*q.v.*), and sister of John Welsh (MDTP 33-2:204). Gilcrest (Gilcresh) d. by Aug 1769 when Helen Gilcresh and James Gilcresh, the heir at law advertised the sale of 900 a. *Upper Marlborough* in Baltimore Co. (Annapolis *Maryland Gazette* 31 Aug 1769; BAWB 3:220).

Gilder, Ellen Kent, in Aug 1795 was made a ward of Mary Gilder (BAOC 3:164).

Gilder, Reuben, and Mary Ashberry Alkin, widow of [-?-] Alkin (*q.v.*) were married on 5 Oct 1790 ("Emanuel Kent Bible," *MBR* 1:139; *Maryland Journal and Baltimore Advertiser* 8 Oct 1790; BAML). Mary Gilder m. 3rd, John Chalmers, Jr. (*q.v.*).

Giles, [-?-], m. by 4 March 1733, Sarah, daughter of Sarah Webster (BALR HWS#M:9).

Giles, [-?-], m. by 11 Nov 1767 Martha, sister of John Hall, Jr.; she was a daughter of John Hall (BAWB 3:158; MWB 39:712; abst. in *Md. Cal. of Wills* 15:144).

Giles, Jacob, m. by 19 July 1739 Johannah, daughter of Col. James Phillips (in admin. account of Johannah Hall) (MDAD 17:181; BALR HWS#1-A:310). She was the widow of George Drew (*q.v.*).

Giles, James, and Ann Fell were m. on 12 April 1770 (Harrison, "St. George's Parish Register:" 395). She was the mother of William Fell (*q.v.*). James Giles, son of Jacob, by 5 d. 7 m. 1770 had removed to Philadelphia as an apprentice, returned to Maryland and reportedly been married by a priest ("Minutes of Deer Creek Meeting," *QRNM*:134). Ann was the relict of Edward Fell (*q.v.*) (BALR AL#C:156; MDTP 45:17-18).

Giles, John, and Sarah Welsh were m. on 1 Oct 1695 (Harrison, "St. James Parish Register," Anne Arundel Co., at MdHS: 291). On 17 March 1708 Sarah was named as a daughter of John Welch (BALR TR#A:5).

Giles, John, and Sarah Butterworth were m. on 16 Oct 1734 (Harrison, "St. George's Parish Register:" 277; Harrison, "St. Paul's Parish Register:" 152). A Quaker, he m. 2nd, by 5 June 1752, Hannah, extx. of Daniel Scott (*q.v.*) (MINV 49:31; MDTP 33-2:15). In Sep 1752 John Giles was summoned by the vestry for marrying Hannah Scott, sister to his late wife and was admonished to put her000000000 away, but he refused to do it. The clerk was ordered to make presentment to the grand jury (St. John's and St. George's Parish Register Vestry Proceedings; MS. at the MdHS).

Giles, John, m. by 22 Jan 1775 Hannah, extx. of Daniel Scott (MDAD 40:290).

Giles, Rebecca, in 1765 was tried for bastardy (BAMI 1765:1).

Giles, Thomas, warned any persons against harboring his wife Elizabeth (Annapolis *Maryland Gazette* 22 Feb 1776).

Gill, [-?-], m. by 5 April 1794 Elizabeth Gore, admx. of Jacob Gore (*q.v.*) (BAAD 11:395).

Gill, John, Jr., and Sarah Gorsuch were m. on 20 July 1758 (Harrison, "St. John's Parish Register:" 217); on 16 Dec 1788 Sarah was named as a daughter of John Gorsuch (BAWB 5:371).

Gill, Leah, formerly Price, on 24 d. 1 mo. 1770 was charged with going out in marriage contrary to rules ("Minutes of Gunpowder Monthly Meeting," *QRNM:*59). [No other marriage reference found].

Gill, Nicholas, and Elizabeth Gill were m. 13 May 1794 (Harrison, "St. Paul's Parish Register:" 287). In Oct 1795 Gill announced he would not pay the debts of his wife Elizabeth, who had left him (*Federal Intelligencer and Baltimore Daily Gazette* 17 Oct 1795).

Gill, Nicholas, announced that his brother Stephen Gill of John, had not paid a debt and that Nicholas, as bondsman 'has had to make good' the notice mentioned another brother Edward Gill (*Baltimore Daily Intelligencer* 1 Sep 1794).

Gill, Stephen, Jr., in his will dated 23 Sep 1717 named Peter Bond as his uncle (MWB 14:432 abst. in *Md. Cal. of Wills* 4:121).

Gill, Stephen, m. by 1 Dec 1749 [-?-], daughter of Capt. Henry Butler of Baltimore Co. (MDAD 27:252; BAAD 5:74).

Gill, Stephen, m. by Dec 1772 Cassandra, daughter of Dennis Garrett Cole, who also named a grandson Stephen Gill (BAWB 3:252; MWB 39:337, abst. in *Md. Cal. of Wills* 15:68).

Gill, William, and Ruth Cromwell were m. on 27 Nov 1760 (Harrison, "St. Thomas Parish Register:" 72). On 9 April 1762 Ruth was named as a daughter of William Cromwell, late of Anne Arundel Co., dec. (PCLR DD#2:70). William Gill stated his wife Ruth had deserted him (*Maryland Gazette or Baltimore General Advertiser* 22 Aug 1783).

Gillellen. See Gillyen.

Gillibourn, Thomas, m. by March 1691/2 Mary, relict and admx. of Timothy Pinder (BACP F#1:164).

Gilliland, George, stated he would not pay the debts of his wife Elizabeth (*Maryland Journal and Baltimore Advertiser* 22 March 1785).

Gillingham, John, of the Forks of the Gunpowder, stated he would not pay the debts of his wife Sarah (*Maryland Journal and Baltimore Advertiser* 29 Aug 1786).

Gillis, William, m. by 16 April 1795 Ruth Cromwell, a representative of William Cromwell (BAAD 12:7).

Gillyen (Gillellen), Peter, near Taneytown, stated that he would not pay the debts of his wife Margaret, as she might run him into debt (*Maryland Journal and Baltimore Advertiser* 23 Dec 1785, 19 May 1786).

Gilmor, William, merchant of this city, was m. Tues. last in Northampton Co., Va., to Mrs. Mary Ann Drysdale (*Federal Gazette and Baltimore Daily Advertiser* 22 Dec 1799).

Gilmore, Ann, was charged with bastardy and fined at the Nov 1759 Court (BAMI 1757-1759:240).

Gilmore, John, and Jane Smith were m. by lic. on 11 Jan 1796 (BAML), In June 1796 Gilmore stated he would not pay the debts contracted by his wife Jane (*Federal Gazette and Baltimore Daily Advertiser* 4 June 1796).

Ginge, [-?-], m. by 1 March 1797 Mary, daughter of James Osborn (BAWB 6:97).

Gippsen, Robert, m. by 15 Jan 1763, Maria Elznegret, nee Debisin ("First Record Book for the Reformed and Lutheran Congregations at Manchester, Baltimore (Now Carroll) Co." MGSB 35: 267).

Girand, Alexander, and Mary Ryan were m. by lic. 29 Oct 1797 at St. Peter's Catholic Church, Baltimore (*Piet:* 134; BAML gives their names as Alexander Geraud and Mary Byan [*sic*]).

Gist, [-?-], m. by 3 July 1738 Sarah, daughter of Joshua Howard (MWB 21:208 abst. in *Md. Cal. of Wills* 7:256).

Gist, [-?-], m. by 8 Dec 1792 Ruth, daughter of John Bond (BAWB 5:75).

Gist, Cornelius Howard, of Baltimore Town, m. last Thurs. eve. Miss Clarinda Rei-necker of McAllister's Town (*Baltimore Daily Repository* 14 July 1792).

Gist, David, and Rebecca Hammond were m. on 5 June 1785 ("Mordecai Gist Bible Record," WWBR:90; BAML). David Gist stated he would not pay the debts contracted by his wife Rebecca Gist (*Federal Intelligencer and Baltimore Daily Gazette* 11 April 1795). Rezin Hammond, in his will made 26 Sep 1794, named his sister Rebecca Gist and her son Rezin Hammond Gist who was not yet 21 (BAWB 5:432).

Gist, James, b. 20 Feb 1776, m. on 24 Nov 1799 Rachel Hammond ("Gist Family Record," *HMGB*15 (3) 35-37).

Gist, John Elder, b. 3 Jan 1761, m. 13 Nov 1783 Frances Trippe (Harrison, "St. Paul's Parish Register:" 191; "Gist Family Record," *HMGB* 15:35).

Gist, Joseph, b. 30 Sep 1738, m. 30 Aug 1759, Elizabeth Elder, b 21 March 1742 ("Gist Family Record," *HMGB* 15 (3) 35-37; Harrison, "St. Thomas Parish Register:" 73).

Gist, Joshua, and Sarah Harvey were m. on 22 Nov 1772 ("Mordecai Gist Bible Record," WWBR: 90).

Gist, Mordecai, m. by 8 Dec 1769, Cecil, sister of Christopher Carnan (Cannon) (BAWB 3:141).

Gist, Col. Mordecai, and Polly Sterrett, both of this town, were m. last Fri. eve. (*Dunlap's Maryland Gazette* 27 Jan 1778; BAML). James Sterrett, of Baltimore Town, in his will made 14 Nov 1792 named his grandson Independent Gist, son of the late Gen. Mordecai Gist and his daughter Mary (BAWB 5:435)

Gist, Mordecai, in June 1795 was made a ward of Joshua Gist (BAOC 3:158).

Gist, Nathaniel, m. by 3 July 1738 Mary, daughter of Joshua Howard (MWB 21:208 abst. in *Md. Cal. of Wills* 7:256; BAAD 4:40).

Gist, Richard, on 4 Aug 1724 warned all persons not to have any dealings with his wife Zipporah (BALR IS#G:361). Richard Gist married Zipporah Murray on 7 d., 10 m. Dec. 1704 (West River Monthly Meeting, in *QRSM:* 19). She was a sister of Josephus Murray (BALR TR#A:140).

Gist, Thomas, b. 13 July 1712, d. 24 May 1787, aged 74 y. 9 m. 11 d.; m. 27 July 1735 Susannah, b. 11 Aug 1715, d. 22 Oct 1800, aged 85 y. 10 m. and 11 d., daughter of Capt. John Cockey, sister of John and Peter Cockey (Harrison, "St. Thomas' Parish Register:" 70; "Mordecai Gist Bible Record," WWBR:90; MDAD 24:317, 30:112, 41:157, 457; MWB 24:473 abst. by Gibb).

Gist, Col. Thomas, and Penelope Deye Cockey, daughter of Joshua Cockey, dec., were m. last Thurs. in Baltimore Co. (*Maryland Journal and Baltimore Advertiser* 15 May 1792).

Gist, Thomas, and Ruth Kelly were married by license dated 29 July 1785 (BAML). On 8 Dec 1792 Ruth was named as a daughter of John Bond (BAWB 5:75; BAAD 11:438, 530).

Gist, William, and Violetta Howard were m. 22 Oct 1737 (Harrison, "St. Thomas Parish Register:" 70). On 3 July 1738 Violetta was named as a daughter of Joshua Howard (MWB 21:208 abst. in Md. Cal. of Wills 7:256; BAAD 4:40).

Gist, William, b. 6 June 1772, m. 28 Feb 1797, Margaret Tennill ("Gist Family Reord," *HMGB* 15:35).

Gittinger, Henrich, m. by 14 Nov 1786 Elizabeth Uhlerin or Ullerin ("First Record Book for the Reformed and Lutheran Congregations at Manchester, Baltimore (Now Carroll) Co.," 282, 284).

Gittinger, Jacob, m. by 10 April 1788, Elisabetha Frischin ("First Record Book for the Reformed and Lutheran Congregations at Manchester, Baltimore (Now Carroll Co.," 283).

Gittings, Archibald, son of James Gittings, Esq., and Miss Elizabeth Bosley, daughter of Elijah Bosley, all of Baltimore Co., were m. (*Baltimore Telegraphe* 14 March 1799).

Gittings, James, and Mary Gorsuch were married by license dated 5 Oct 1779 (BAML). On 16 Dec 1788 John Gorsuch named his daughter Mary Gittings (BAWB 5:371).

Gittings, James, Jr., and Harriett Sterett, second daughter of the late John Sterett, Esq., were m. last Tues. by Rev. Dr. Allison (*Baltimore Evening Post* 25 April 1793).

Gittings, Richard, merchant, m. last eve. Polly, eldest daughter of the late John Sterrett, Esq. (*Maryland Journal and Baltimore Advertiser* 21 Nov 1788). Polly Sterett was a legatee of Mary Ridgely (BAAD 11:42).

Gittings, Thomas, m. by 12 April 1747 Mary, widow of James Lynch (*q.v.*); James and Mary had a daughter Margaret Lynch (BALR TB#E:340).

Glading, Rebecca, was charged with bastardy at the Nov 1756 Court and fined 30 shillings; she named James Allen as the father of her child. Jacob Glading was her security (BACP BB#C:311).

Gladman, Thomas, and Eleanor Weer were married by license dated 28 April 1792 (BAML). She was a daughter of William Weer (BAWB 7:312).

Glanvill, Stephen, m. 31 May 1798, Sarah Stevenson (Marr. Register of Rev. Lewis Richards, MS.690 at MdHS; "Wesley Stevenson Bible Record," in *The Notebook* 21 (3) (Fall 2005) 12-15).

Glathary, John M., stone cutter, aged 85 years, and Miss Margaret Hook, aged 25 years, were m. last Thurs. eve. (*Maryland Journal and Baltimore Advertiser* 28 Nov 1795).

Glavany, Francis Remy, and Elizabeth Dechamp were m. by lic. 8 May 1791 at St. Peter's Catholic Church, Baltimore (*Piet:* 134; BAML, which gives his name as Francis Henry Glarany).

Gleeson, Morris, and Mary McDaniel were married by banns on 22 May 1788 at St. Peter's Catholic Church, Baltimore (*Piet:* 134).

Gleeson, Roger, and Catherine Bryan, widow, natives of Ireland, were married by license dated 18 June 1797 at St. Peter's Catholic Church, Baltimore (*Piet:* 134).

Glesson[?], Thomas, in 1763 was convicted of bastardy (BAMI 1755-1763).

Glenn, Robert, and Isabel [-?-], were m. by 11 Dec 1759 when their son William was b. ("James S. Quinlan Bible," *MBR* 2:44-46).

Glenn, William, b. 11 Dec 1759, son of Robert and Isabel, and Rebecca [-?-], were m. by 6 June 178-(?) when their daughter Isabel was b. ("James S. Quinlan Bible," *MBR* 2:44-46).

Glottus, Joseph, and Catherine Honour, were married by license dated 31 Aug 1800 at St. Peter's Catholic Church, Baltimore (*Piet:* 134).

Goddard, William, printer of Baltimore, was m. on last Thurs. at Cranston, by the Rev. Mr. Oliver, to Miss Abigail Angell, daughter of the late Brigadier-General Angell. "Providence, 27 May" (Frederick. *Bartgis' Maryland Gazette* 28 June 1786).

Godsgrace, William, and **Rebecca Godsgrace** on 17 Nov 1772 were named as nephew and niece in the will of William Young (MWB 39:97, abst. in *Md. Cal. of Wills* 19:20).

Goe, William, and Cassandra Jones were married by license dated 5 Oct 1790 (BAML), On 10 Dec 1790 Cassandra was named as a daughter of Richard Jones of Richard (BAWB 4:523).

Going, Elizabeth, was charged with bastardy at the June 1730 Court. Elizabeth Going, *alias* Black, was charged with bastardy again at the June 1731 Court (BACP HWS#6:415, HWS#7:165).

Golden, John, at the August 1761 Court was bound to Col. William Young for the remainder of the time he was bound to serve Roger Boyce in March 1759. Aged 17 the previous 1 Nov, he had been formerly bound to John Hall of Cranberry, Roger Boyce, and Col. William Young, in Nov 1763 he was bound to Thomas Lucas to age 21 to learn trade of carpenter (BAMI 1755-1763).

Goldsmith, [-?-], m. [c1696/7] Martha, daughter and admx. of Edward Beadle (INAC 15:182).

Golliher, Mary, was charged with bastardy in 1775 and fined (BAMI 1772, 1775-1781:204. Mary Golliger [*sic*] and Nathaniel Mucimen were married by license dated 16 Oct 1778 (BAML).

Gonet, Marcellin (son of Sebastian and Magdalen Gravier, native of Dauphine), and Louise Catherine Pallon (daughter of James and Rose Generes, natives of St. Domingo), were married by license dated 2 Jan 1799 at St. Peter's Catholic Church, Baltimore (*Piet:* 134).

Good, Adam, m. by 1796, Barbara, daughter of Abraham Fishburn (BAWB 5:410).

Gooding, Samuel, was charged with bastardy at the Nov 1756 Court (BAMI 1755-1763; BACP BB#C: 311).

Goodlin, John, m. by 7 Aug 1789 Ann, widow of James Ryan (BAAD 10:27).

Goodwin (Godwin), Benjamin, and Hannah Urquhart were m. on 6 Feb 1742 (Harrison, "St. George's Parish Register:" 331). On 27 Nov 1746 Hannah was named as a sister of James Aughard [*sic*] (MWB 25:332 abst. by Gibb).

Goodwin (Goodwine), George, and Anne Rutter were m. on 29 March 1730 (Harrison, "St. Paul's Parish Register:" 149). On by 26 Sep 1744, she was named as a daughter of Thomas Rutter who named his granddaughters Susannah and Ann Goodwin (MWB 24:547 abst. by Gibb).

Goodwin, James, and Lilly Vincent were married by license on 15 July 1798 at St. Peter's Catholic Church, Baltimore (*Piet:* 134).

Goodwin, Lyde, d. by 1 April 1772 having m. Pleasance, daughter of Charles Ridgely (BAWB 3:201).

Goodwin, Dr. Lyde, and Miss Levy, eldest daughter of Benjamin Levy of Baltimore, merchant, were m. last Thurs. eve. (*Maryland Journal and Baltimore Advertiser* 23 March 1779).

Goodwin, William, m. by 28 June 1787 [-?-], daughter of John Ridgely who named Goodwin a son-in-law and who also named a grandson William Goodwin (BAAD 9:75; BAWB 3:187).

Gordon, [-?-], of McAllister's Town, Pa., m. by 18 Sep 1779 Catherine daughter of Michael Devinbaugh of Baltimore Town (BALR WG#D:377).

Gordon, Francis, stated he would not pay the debts of his wife Nancy, who had eloped from him (*Maryland Journal and Baltimore Advertiser* 17 April [1794?]).

Gordon, John, and Sophia Myers were m. on 18 Feb 1795 (Marr. Returns of Rev. Daniel Kurtz, Scharf Papers, MS.1999 at MdHS). On 6 May 1800 John and Sophia agreed to separate (BACT WG#7:139).

Gordon, or Godwin, Philip, was charged with bastardy at the March 1765 Court (BAMI 1765: 10).

Gordon, William, cabinet maker, and Mrs. Thomasin White, relict of Col. John White, late of Ga., were m. last Wed. eve. (*Maryland Gazette or Baltimore General Advertiser* 7 May 1784; *Maryland Journal and Baltimore Advertiser* 7 May 1784). She was a legatee of Dr. Thomas Andrews (*q.v.*) (BAAD 8:142).

Gore, Cybil, in 1772 was fined for bastardy (BAMI 1772, 1775-1781:87).

Gore, Jacob, died leaving a will dated 1 Sep 1790 and proved 15 Dec 1790 naming three natural sons: Christian Gore Wason, Andrew Gore Wason, and Jacob Gore Tee (BAWB 4:505). Elizabeth Gore administered his estate on 25 Nov 1792 (BAAD 11:156). She m. 2nd [-?-] Gill (*q.v.*).

Gore, Richard, and Lettice Montgomery were m. by lic. on 20 Oct 1790 at St. Peter's Catholic Church, Baltimore (*Piet:* 134).

Gore, Richard, and Ally Landilland were m. by lic. on 8 Nov 1794 at St. Peter's Catholic Church, Baltimore (*Piet:* 134; BAML, which gives her name as Allay Sandiland).

Gormack, Michael, m. by 23 May 1696 Judith Dorman, admx. of Andrew Peterson (*q.v.*) (MDTP 16:170).

Gorman, [-?-], m. by 1 April 1705 Mary, daughter of William Galloway of Baltimore Co. (MWB 3:469 abst. in *Md. Cal. of Wills* 3:53).

Gorman, [-?-], m. by 23 Feb 1704/5 Judith, daughter of Elizabeth Swindell (or Snowdell) of Baltimore Co. (MWB 3:436 abst. *in Md. Cal. of Wills* 3:46).

Gorman, Abraham, and Elizabeth, admx. of Samuel Neil (q.v.), were m. by 15 Feb 1776 (MINV 123:345; MDTP 47:14). Gorman stated he would not pay the debts of his wife Elizabeth (*Maryland Journal and Baltimore Advertiser* 7 Oct 1783).

Gorman, Daniel P., and Alice O'Donald were m. by lic. 25 Oct 1800 at St. Peter's Catholic Church, Baltimore (*Piet:* 134).

Gorman, Sarah, was charged with bastardy at the March 1729/30 Court (BACP HWS#6:362).

Gormley, Cornelius, and Mary O'Brien were m. by lic. on 18 Sep 1796 at St. Peter's Catholic Church, Baltimore (*Piet:* 134).

Gorsuch, [-?-], m. by 27 Aug 1777 Elizabeth, sister of Edward Hanson and daughter of Jonathan Hanson (BAWB 4:107, 115).

Gorsuch, [-?-], m. by 8 Dec 1792 Mary, daughter of John Bond (BAWB 5:75, BAAD 11:530).

Gorsuch, Benjamin, m. by 8 Feb 1762, [-?-], sister of John and Elizabeth Woodward, who conveyed property to their nephew Nathan Gorsuch, youngest son of Benjamin Gorsuch (BAKR B#I: 491).

Gorsuch, Charles, m. by 8 Dec 1679 Sarah, sole heir of Thomas Cole (BALR IR#PP: 46, IR#AM:185).

Gorsuch, Charles, m. by 19 Jan 1732 Sarah, granddaughter of Barbara Broad (MWB 20:733 abst. in *Md. Cal. of Wills* 7:29).

Gorsuch, Charles, and Eleanor Bond were m. on 1 Sep 1763 (Harrison, "St. Thomas Parish Register:" 73). Charles d. by Aug 1794, leaving these orphans, who chose Charles Gorsuch as their guardian: Ann, Elizabeth, Achsah, Charles, and Belinda (BOCP 3:106).

Gorsuch, Charles, m. by 14 July 1772 Sarah, only sister of Elisha Hall (MDTP 44:487-488).

Gorsuch, Charles, and Dealley [Delia?] Dimmett were married by license dated 22 Oct 1784 (BAML). On 17 June 1796 she was named in the administration account of William Sinclair (BAAD 12:162).

Gorsuch, Charles, m. by 8 June 1790 Margaret, heir of William Harvey and legatee of Priscilla Harvey (BAAD 10:158, 386).

Gorsuch, David, and Rebecca Gorsuch were married by license dated 30 Oct 1786 (BAML). On 8 Dec 1792 Rebecca Gorsuch was named as a daughter of Charles and Eleanor Gorsuch; Eleanor was named as a daughter of John Bond (BAWB 5:75; BAAD 11:530).

Gorsuch, John, m. by 4 Feb 1774 Elizabeth, daughter of John Merryman, farmer (BAWB 3:352; BAAD 11:1).

Gorsuch, John, Jr., m. by 23 Oct 1776 Belinda, daughter of Elizabeth Bosley (BACT 1773-1784:216). On 26 April 1784 Belinda was named as a daughter of Elizabeth Bosley, widow of Charles (BAWB 4:62).

Gorsuch, John, and Mary McClung were married by license dated 3 Oct 1791 (BAML). On 16 Feb 1792, she received an equal share of the estate of Robert McClung (BAAD 10:547).

Gorsuch, Capt. Joshua, was m. last eve. by Rev. Mr. Bend, to Miss Ann Smith, both of this town (*Federal Intelligencer and Baltimore Daily Gazette* 26 June 1795). Joshua Gorsuch and Ann Smith were married by license dated 24 June 1795 (BAML). On 24 June 1800 Ann was named as a legatee of Thomas Smith (BAAD 13:277).

Gorsuch, Nicholas, d. by Dec 1797 having m. Mary, widow of Andrew Granchet, and leaving Robert Gorsuch as his admin. (Pet. of Robert Gorsuch, 1797). On 10 March 1798 when Robert Gorsuch, admin., and guardian of Gerrard and Sarah Gorsuch, infant children of the dec., pet. the court for permission to sell some furniture in order to pay the debts of the deceased (Pet. of Robert Gorsuch, 1798).

Gorsuch, Norman, and Kitty Gorsuch were married by license dated 8 Nov 1790 (BAML). On Dec 1792 Ketura Gorsuch was named as a daughter of Charles and Eleanor Gorsuch; Eleanor was named as a daughter of John Bond (BAWB 5:75; BAAD 11:530).

Gorsuch, Thomas, and Rachel McClung were married by license dated 15 Dec 1787 (BAML). On 28 Dec 1787 Rachel received an equal share of the estate of Robert McClung (BAAD 10:168).

Gorsuch, Thomas, m. by 9 Dec 1789 [-?-], daughter of Loveless Gorsuch (BAAD 10:88).

Gorsuch, William, d. by 25 Jan 1794 when his estate was administered by William Gorsuch, exec. Shares of £15.0.0 each were paid to Ruth Gorsuch wife of Charles Peregoy (m. by BAML dated 15 June 1795), Sarah Gorsuch wife of Abraham Hicks (m. by BAML dated 12 March 1781), and Darcus Gorsuch wife of John Ensor (m. 2 July 1772 at St. John's Parish (Harrison, "St. John's Parish Register:" 264]). The accountant retained a balance of £516.15.3 (BAAD 11:368).

Gostick (Gosick), Thomas, and Elizabeth Lauder were m. on 15 April 1800 (Marr. Register of Rev. Lewis Richards, MS.690 at MdHS; *Baltimore American* 21 April 1800).

Gosnell, Avarilla, was charged with bastardy at the June 1739 Court and presented at the March 1739/40 Court (BACP HWS#TR:158, 401).

Gosnell, Peter, Jr., m. by 31 March 1759 Dinah, daughter of Dutton Lane, Sr. (BALR B#G:401, B#I:298).

Gostwick, [-?-], m. by 30 March 1695 Mary, daughter of Nicholas Corbin of Baltimore Co. (MWB 7:297 abst. in *Md. Cal. of Wills* 2:126).

Gostwick (Goswick), Elizabeth, confessed to bastardy and was fined 30 shillings at the Nov 1754 Court; she named Samuel Sindall as the father of her child (BACP BB#A:450).

Gostwick, Nicholas, and Abarilla Yanstone were m. on in Dec 1720 (Harrison "St. Paul's Parish Register:" 147). She m. 2nd, Benjamin Curtis (*q.v.*) (BAAD 3:360).

Gostwick, Thomas, and Elizabeth Yanstone were m. in Sep 1717 (Harrison, "St. Paul's Parish Register:" 147). John Sergeant (Serjant), in his will, made 19 Jan 1748, named his sons-in-law John Yosten and Aquila Goswick and his daughter-in-law Ann Yosten Goswick (MWB 25:544 abst. by Gibb)

Gott, [-?-], d. by 13 March 1717 having m. Eliza, daughter of Anthony Holland; she m. by the date given Thomas Woodfield of Anne Arundel Co. (BALR TR#A:544).

Gott, [-?-], m. by 10 July 1773 Rachel, sister of Samuel Norwood, who also named a niece Rachel Gott (BAWB 3:263; MWB 29:402, abst. in *Md. Cal. of Wills* 15:81).

Gott, [-?-], m. by 7 Aug 1773 [-?-], daughter of Richard King Stevenson who named Sarah and Rachel Gott his granddaughters (BAWB 3:337)

Gott, Anthony, m. by 13 Feb 1788 [-?-], sister of Moses Galloway (BAAD 9:153, 219).

Gott, Richard, and Ruth Bond were m. on 30 April 1758 (Harrison, "St. Thomas' Parish Register:" 72). On 31 Jan 1763 Ruth was named as a daughter of Richard Bond (BAWB 2:360).

Goudain, Laurence (eldest son of William and Mary Dupre Mon Troux, born at Cap Francois), and Mary Magdalen Desobry (daughter of Hilary Joseph and Elizabeth Martin), were m. by lic. on 11 Dec 1799 at St. Peter's Catholic Church, Baltimore (*Piet:* 135).

Gough, Harry Dorsey, b. 28 Jan 1745, son of Thomas and Sophia Gough, married on 2 May 1771 Prudence Carnan, b. 16 Jan 1755, daughter of John and Acshah Carnan ("Harry Dorsey Gough Carroll Bible Record," *MBR* 5:51, *MBR* 7:69, *MHM* 25:302-304).

Gough, William, d. by 17 Feb 1793 having m. Frances Phillips, daughter of Elizabeth Fitch, widow of William Fitch. Frances Phillips Gough extx., on 10 Dec 1793 posted bond to administer the estate of Elizabeth Fitch (BAAB 8:531). Elizabeth Fitch, widow of William Fitch, in her will, dated 17 Feb 1793 names a daughter Frances Phillips Gough, widow of William Gough (BAWB 5:108). Frances Phillips Gough m. 2nd, Joseph Stansbury (*q.v.*) on 1 May 1794 Harrison, "St. Paul's Parish Register:" 287). She m. 3rd, Augustine Porter (*q.v.*).

Gould, Oliver, d. leaving a will by which he divided his property among his five children, Margaret, Paul, Samuel, Elizabeth, Joseph, and Samuel [*sic*]; he appointed Cyprian Wells and Oliver White his execs. (BOCP Petition of the execs. of Oliver Gould, 1789).

Gould, Capt. Peter, and Polly White, daughter of Capt. Joseph White were m. last eve. (*Maryland Journal and Baltimore Advertiser* 16 Dec 1791). They were m. at St. Peter's Catholic Church, Baltimore (*Piet:* 135).

Goulding, John, and Martha Gould were m. by lic. on 23 Oct 1788 at St. Peter's Catholic Church, Baltimore (*Piet:* 135).

Goulding, Patrick and Anabella Young, widow, were m. by lic. on 7 June 1794 at St. Peter's Catholic Church, Baltimore (*Piet:* 135). (BAML gives her name as Arabella Young). William Young had m. Annabella Loney by license dated 16 Jan 1784 (HAML).

Gouverner (Gouvernet), Charles, was m. last eve. by Rev. Bishop Carroll to Miss Margaretta Wells, both of this city (*Federal Gazette and Baltimore Daily Advertiser* 29 Nov 1799). He was born in the Parish of Tervey Franche Compte; they were m. at St. Peter's Catholic Church, Baltimore (*Piet:* 135).

Govane, Mary, on 12 Feb 1789 was named as niece and extx. of the will of Mary Woodward who also named Mary Govane's daughter Mary Govane, Jr. (BAWB 4:352)

Govane, William, m. by 10 Aug 1741 Ann, admx. of Capt. Thomas Homewood (*q.v.*) of Baltimore Co. (MDAD 18:284). In his will dated 8 Oct 1764 William Govane named his wife Ann and his children James (son of Mary Salisbury, but known as James Govane), and Mary (daughter of Mary Salisbury, but known as Mary Govane), and his granddaughter Jane Salisbury, daughter of Mary Salisbury; he also named a brother Lawrence Hammond (MWB 36:375 abst. in *Md. Cal. of Wills* 14:68).

Gover, |-?-|, m. by 3 Nov 1758, Elizabeth, daughter of Thomas Gittings (BAWB 2:259).

Gover, Jarret, of Harford Co., and Sally Giles of Baltimore Co. were m. last Tues. eve. by Rev. Bend (*Baltimore Evening Post* 5 April 1793; BAML, which gives his name as Gerrard Gover).

Gover, Philip, and Mary Hopkins on 30 d. 6 m. 1761 declared their intention to marry ("Minutes of Deer Creek Meeting," *QRNM:* 128).

Gover, Samuel, and Hannah Webster, daughter of Isaac [*sic*] Webster, were m. on 11 Nov 1742 ("Abstracts of Records of Nottingham Meeting," MS. at MdHS). On 27 April 1744 Hannah was named as a daughter of Jacob [*sic*] Webster (MWB 23:401 abst. in *Md. Cal. of Wills* 8:253).

Gover (Grover?), Samuel, son of Samuel, in March 1760 chose Isaac Webster, John Lee Webster, and James Webster as his guardians (BAMI 1755-1763).

Gover, Samuel, son of Philip and Mary, dec., on 22 d. 9 m. 1791, announced his intention to marry Ann Hopkins, daughter of Joseph and Elizabeth, who were present, but as they [the couple] are in some degree between first and second cousins the friends at the preparative meeting advised against it and the matter will be looked into further ("Minutes of Deer Creek Meeting," *QRNM:* 150).

Gover, William, m. by 24 April 1762, Eleanor, sister of Anthony Enloe (MDTP 35:219).

Goverman, Anthony, merchant, and Miss Henrietta Delius, both of this city, were m. last eve. by Rev. Mr. Kurtz (*Federal Gazette and Baltimore Daily Advertiser* 2 Nov 1798).

Grace, Philip, d. by 11 Jan 1787, leaving a minor child Philip Grace; Thomas Constable was appointed guardian (BAGA 1:5).

Grache, Bartholomew, native of Genoa, and Mary Ann Richards were m. by lic. on 24 April 1800 at St. Peter's Catholic Church, Baltimore (*Piet:* 135).

Graham, |-?-|, m. Elizabeth Rowles, widow of Jacob Bell (*q.v.*).

Graham Daniel, in his will made 3 Nov 1769 referred to a marriage contract made between him and his lawful wife, Elizabeth Graham on 28 Oct 1769 and witnessed by Willoughby Warren and Capt. James Curry (MWB 38:337, abst. in *Md. Cal. of Wills* 14:179).

Graham, John, and Delia [-?-] were m. by 4 July 1777 when their daughter Cassander was b. ("Frederick Ellender Bible," *MBR* 1:77-78).

Graham, John, of Calvert Co. and Miss Johnson, daughter of the Hon. Thomas Johnson, were m. at Frederick Co. (*Maryland Journal and Baltimore Advertiser* 29 Jan 1788).

Granger, John, d. by 2 May 1785 when Joseph Pisha (Peshaw) (*q.v.*) and wife Ann posted bond to administer his estate (BAAB 6:266).

Granger, Joseph, and Barbara Weaver were m. on 4 Nov 1787 (Marr. Register of Rev. Lewis Richards, MS.690 at MdHS). In 1793, Barbara was named as the mother of John Weaver (BOCP Petition of Barbara Granger, 1793). Barbara was probably the widow of George Weaver (*q.v.*).

Granget, John, d. intestate in the spring of 1785 leaving a widow named Ann, a son, and daughter, Margaret Labat, the petitioner who said that the widow Ann m. Joseph [Pisha?], and took out letters of administration; Margaret claims that the admx. has not completed her trust or made any distribution (BOCP Petition of John Granget, 1787, Box 2, Folder 29).

Grangett (Grenshed), Andrew, m. by 19 Sep 1780 Mary Eve, dau. of William Lalvely (BAWB 4:263).

Grant, Alexander and Elizabeth Cole were m. on 16 Feb 1730 (Harrison "St. Paul's Parish Register:" 150). Grant named Angelica Cole as a daughter-in-law in his will (MWB 22:26 abst. in *Md. Cal. of Wills* 8:13).

Grant, Daniel, Jr., merchant, and Isabella Neilson, daughter of Robert Neilson, both of Baltimore, were m. last eve. by Rev. Dr. Allison (*Maryland Journal and Baltimore Advertiser* 8 Aug 1794).

Grant, Hugh, m. by Aug 1728 Frances, widow of Daniel Johnson (*q.v.*) d. by 18 May 1730 when his widow Frances had an ante-nuptial contract with Miles Foy (*q.v.*) (*BCF:* 274).

Grant, John, and Jane Cunningham were m. by lic. on 8 Nov 1800 at St. Peter's Catholic Church, Baltimore (*Piet:* 135).

Grant, William, and Catherine Holland were m. on 18 Nov 1790 (Harrison, "St. James Parish Register:" 3); on 29 July 1793 Catherine was named as a daughter of John Holland, Sr. (BAWB 5:118).

Grapevine, Frederick, and Elizabeth Mathews were m. on 29 April 1787 (Marr. Register of Rev. Lewis Richards, MS.690 at MdHS). Edward Faer, in his will made 8 Dec 1799 named his daughter Elizabeth Grapevine [*sic*] and his daughter Nancy Matthews [*sic*], and named Frederick Grapevine as exec. (BAWB 7:352).

Grasmuck, Casper, d. by 2 Feb 1787, leaving minor child John; Englehardt Yeiser the guardian filed an account (BAGA 1:16).

Gray, Barbara, was charged with bastardy at the June 1746 Court (BACP TB&TR#1:2).

Gray, Catherine, was charged with bastardy at the June 1746 Court (BACP TB&TR#1: 116).

Gray, Elizabeth, in 1762 was convicted of bastardy (BAMI 1755-1763). She was charged with bastardy and fined at the March 1765 Court; Nathan Perigo was summoned to court; she was charged again at the March 1768 Court and Edward Sweeting was summoned; she confessed and was fined at June 1768 Court (BAMI 1765:9; BACP BB: 10).

Gray, James, m. in 1791, Cath. Lewel ("Records of Zion Lutheran Church." MS at MdHS). He stated that he would not pay the debts of his wife Catherine (*Maryland Journal and Baltimore Advertiser* 13 Dec 1791).

Gray, John, and Mary Dwier, natives of Ireland, were m. by lic. on 6 Nov 1796 at St. Peter's Catholic Church, Baltimore (*Piet:* 135).

Gray, Capt. John, of Georgetown, and Miss Araminta Forman of Baltimore were m. last eve.. in the latter place (*Baltimore Telegraphe* 16 Dec 1799).

Gray, Lynch, and Sarah Rutter were married by license dated 2 July 1783 (BAML). On 24 Feb 1798, she was named as the widow of Joseph Rutter (BAAD 12:389).

Gray, Lynch, and Hannah Denton were married by license dated 23 Dec 1796 (BAML). On 20 May 1799 Hannah was named as a rep. of John Denton (BAAD 13:61).

Gray, Mathias, on 5 March 1741 was named as a grandson in the will of John Mahone (MWB 22:533 abst. in *Md. Cal. of Wills* 8:193).

Gray, Samuel, and Miss Nancy Rice, both of Baltimore, were m. last Sat. eve. (*Maryland Gazette or Baltimore General Advertiser* 25 Sep 1787).

Gray, Zachariah, m. by 15 Jan 1729 Rebecca, daughter of Jonas and Ann Bowen of Baltimore Co. (MWB 19:580 abst. in *Md. Cal. of Wills* 6:92; MDAD 10:174; BALR HWS#M:464)

Gray, Zachariah, in March 1733/4 was charged with begetting a bastard on the body of Hannah Cox (BACP HWS#9:135).

Gray, Zachariah, and Mary Lynch were m. on 22 Dec 1748 (Harrison, "St. Paul's Parish Register:" 172). On 15 Nov 1770 Mary was named as a daughter of Patrick Lynch (BAAD 6:197). Zachariah and Mary were the parents of the following heirs of Patrick Lynch, named on 11 April 1792: Rebecca, Thomas (dec.), Joshua, Lynch, and James Gray (BAAD 11:37).

Gray, Zachariah, d. by Nov 1759, leaving two orphans, John and William, who chose Edward Stevenson as their guardian. In March 1755 William had been bound to Edmund Talbott to age 21 (BAMI 1755-1763).

Gray, Zachariah, of Patapsco Neck, and [-?-] [-?-], were m. by 12 Aug 1763 when their daughter Sarah was b. ("John Dutton Bible," *MBR* 7:46-50).

Greece, Ruth, in 1763 was convicted of bastardy (BAMI 1755-1763).

Green, [-?-], m. by 5 March 1700, Elizabeth, daughter of Anthony Demondidier, dec. (BALR HW#2:51).

Green, [-?-], m. by 4 March 1745/6 Susannah, daughter of Nicholas Haile (BALR TB#E:10).

Green, [-?-], m. by 10 Jan 1758, Alenor, sister of George Brown who named Alenor's children, Mary, Sarah, Susena [Susanna?], Daniel, and Eleanor Green in his will (BAWB 2:173).

Green, [-?-], m. by 13 March 1771 Mary, daughter of Thomas Bailey (BAWB 3:182).

Green, [-?-], m. by 29 Nov 1769 Sarah, daughter of Thomas Wheeler (BAWB 3:171).

Green, [-?-], m. by 8 April 1772 Ruth, daughter of William and Dinah Towson (BAWB 3:222, 532).

Green, Abraham, and Elizabeth Baxter were m. on 28 Jan 1749/50 (Harrison, "St. Paul's Parish Register:" 163). In March 1750 Abraham and Elizabeth Green were named as executors of Benjamin Bowen of Baltimore Co. (MDAD 29:217). On 26 Aug 1760 Elizabeth was named as a daughter of Edmund Baxter; Abraham and Elizabeth were the parents of Greenbury and Rachel Green (BAWB 3:297).

Green, Abraham, and Ruth Carback were m. on 25 June 1770 (Harrison, "St. John's Parish Register:" 260). On 12 April 1773 she was named as a legatee of Richard Jones (MDAD 69:194).

Green, Ann, was convicted of bastardy on 2 Feb 1754 and refused to name the father (BACP BB#A:30).

Green, Benjamin, m. by 15 March 1755 Elizabeth, daughter of David Thomas (BACT TR#E:165). She was the sister of David Thomas; Benjamin and Elizabeth were the parents of Leonard Green and David Green who was living 11 July 1768 (MINV 35:322; BALR B#Q:551; BAWB 3:109).

Green, Bennett, and Anne Jones were m. by lic. on 11 Nov 1798 at St. Peter's Catholic Church, Baltimore (*Piet:* 135).

Green, Clement, son of Benjamin and Elizabeth of Harford Co., and Rebecca Todd were m. by lic. on 8 May 1800 at St. Peter's Catholic Church, Baltimore (*Piet:* 135).

Green, Edward, his wife Mary and their son Bennett and their daughter Sarah wife of Aubrey Jones (*q.v.*), on 24 Aug 1797 were named in the will of Hannah Green, widow (BAWB 6:79).

Green, Elizabeth, servant of James Standiford, was charged with bastardy at the June 1744 Court and was fined (BACP 1743-1745:496-497).

Green, Elizabeth, servant of Rev. Thomas Chase, was charged with bastardy in Nov 1772 and was ordered to serve her master an extra year for the time of her fine, fees, and expenses of 'her lying in' when she gave birth to a son Daniel Green (BAMI 1772, 1775-1781:27, 87)

Green, Ezekiel, and Darcus Denton were married on 24 Jan 1795 (Marr. Register of Rev. Lewis Richards, MS.690 at MdHS). On 30 May 1796 she was named as a daughter of John Denton (BAWB 5:385; BAAD 13:61).

Green, George, m. by 27 July 1772 Ruth, daughter of William and Dinah Towson (BAWB 3:222, 532).

Green, Henry, m. by 31 March 1748 Elizabeth, acting extx. of David Thomas (*q.v.*) (MDTP 32:158).

Green, Henry, m. on 21 June 1788 Elizabeth Boreing. They had issue: a son Michael, and one other child who d. before Elizabeth (Rev. War Pension Application of Elizabeth Green: W25657). (They were m. in Baltimore Co.).

Green, Isaac, m. by 23 March 1771, Elizabeth, daughter of Sarah Stevens, widow (BACT B#G:358).

Green, James, and Elizabeth Addison, Negro slaves of Richard Caton, were m. 8 May 1796, at St. Peter's Catholic Church, Baltimore (*Piet:* 135).

Green, Joel, and Elizabeth, daughter of James Buck, were m. last Tues. in Baltimore Co. (*Maryland Journal and Baltimore Advertiser* 30 March 1792). She was a daughter of James Buck who was an heir of John Buck (BAAD 11:492).

Green, John, and Cloe Jones in Nov 1743 were summoned for unlawful cohabitation ("St. John's and St. George's Parish Register Vestry Proceedings," MS. at MdHS).

Green, John, on 15 Oct 1748 was named as a grandson in the will of John Bowen (MWB 25:455 abst. by Gibb).

Green, Jonas, m. by 24 June 1747 Mary, sister of Martha Bowen (BAAD 4:183). Mary Green, admx. of Jonas Bowen, posted bond to administer his estate on 27 June 1762 (BAAB 1:150).

Green, Joseph, and Mary Bowen were m. on 24 or 25 Feb 1744/5 (Harrison, "St. John's Parish Register:" 192, 240). On 27 Oct 1760 Mary was named as the admx. of

Joseph Bowen (MDTP 38:16). In 1747 Mary was named as a sister of Samuel Browne [or Browen] of Baltimore Co. (MDAD 23:345).

Green, Joseph, and Catherine Stansbury were m. on 26 March 1789 (Marr. Register of Rev. Lewis Richards, MS.690 at MdHS). On 5 May 1789 Catharine was named as a daughter of George Stansbury (BAWB 4:358).

Green, Josias, and Mary Monk published their marriage articles on 23 Nov 1796 (BALR WG#XX:655).

Green, Matthew, m. by 1 Aug 1719 Mary, daughter of Jane Boon. Matthew and Mary had three daus.: Catherine, Anne, and Martha, all named in a deed (BALR TR#DS:42).

Green, Ruth, in 1772 was fined for bastardy (BAMI 1772, 1775-1781:86).

Green, Samuel, m. by license dated 23 July 1796 Hannah, coheir of John Naylor, Sr., of Baltimore Co. (BAML, BALR WG#53:474). Green, Hannah, formerly Naylor, on 9 d, 3 m. 1797, was charged with marrying contrary to the good order ("Minutes of Baltimore Meeting," *QRNM*:228).

Green, Shadrach, b. 16 July 1747, and Rachel [-?-], b. 18 Sep 1758, were m. before 3 Jan 1777 when their daughter Elizabeth was born ("Shadrack Green Bible," in *MBR* 7:74).

Green, Susanna, was charged with bastardy and confessed at the Nov 1750 Court; her daughter Phyllis Baxter [*sic*] was born 23 March 1750 (BACP TR#6:34).

Green, Thomas, and Elizabeth Carter were m. on 11 Aug 1732 (Harrison, "St. Paul's Parish Register:" 150). On 23 April 1732 Elizabeth was named as an extx. of John Carter (*q.v.*) of Baltimore Co. (MINV 16:593; MDAD 12:4, 15:50; MDTP 29:277).

Green, Thomas, native of Charles Co., and Ann Harryman, native of Anne Arundel Co., were m. by lic. on 29 Aug 1795 at St. Peter's Catholic Church, Baltimore (*Piet:* 135).

Green, Vincent, and Elizabeth Eaglestone were m. on 15 Sep 1777 (Liesenring, "Maryland Marriages, 1777-1804," MdHS: 69). On 20 Oct 1782 Elizabeth was named as a daughter of Abraham Eaglestone (BAWB 3:494). She m. 2nd, by license dated George Rees (*q.v.*) (BAML)

Greene, Abraham, and Elizabeth Cole were married by license dated 25 Feb 1787 (BAML). On 10 Feb 1790 she was named as an heir of Salathiel Cole (BAAD 10:101).

Greene, Henry, printer of this city, was m. yesterday evening in Anne Arundel Co. to Ann Walker, daughter of Capt, James Walker of that county (*Federal Gazette and Baltimore Daily Advertiser* 6 Sep 1799).

Greenfield, [-?-], m. by 13 Feb 1761 [-?-], daughter of [Walter?] Smith, 13 Feb 1761 (BALR B#I:1).

Greenfield, [-?-], m. by 1 Feb 1768 Sophia, daughter of Samuel Smith, planter (BAWB 3:100).

Greenfield, Jacob, b. 13 Dec 1762, son of Micajah and Martha, and Elizabeth Everist were m. on 29 Sep 1791 ("Bible owned by Mrs. Clyde E. Greene," BRHA: 40; Micajah Greenfield BR, in *MBR* 1:97-98; Harrison, "St. George's Parish Register:" 396).

Greenfield, Micajah, d. 25 Dec 1772, (aged 39 as of 17 July 1772) and Martha, d. 10 April 1768 in her 27th year, and daughter of Jacob Hanson, were m. by 13 Dec 1762 when their son Jacob was born ("Micajah Greenfield Bible," *MBR* 1:97-98; BACT B#G:17; BAWB 3:16).

Greenfield, Micajah, in his will dated 11 Dec 1772 named his wife Mary and his father-in-law James Osborn (BAWB 3:255).

Greenfield, Thomas, in his will made 8 Jan 1704/5 directed that his daughter Jane was to live with her aunt Mary Pickens (MWB 3:470 abst. in *Md. Cal. of Wills* 3:54).

Greeniff, John, m. by 4 Nov 1703 Ruth, admx. of Edward Dorsey (INAC 24:178).

Greening, Samuel, m. Ann Twine on 1 March 1714 (Harrison, "St. John's Parish Register:" 5). Ann Twine was the admx. of Richard Twine on 18 Jan 1710/11 (BAAB 4:217).

Greenleafe, [-?-], m. by 5 d., 10 m. 1780 Catherine, sister of Richard Wister (BAWB 4:433).

Greenwell, Cuthbert, in Nov 1757 was fined for begetting a bastard on the body of Martha Childs (BAMI 1755-1763).

Greenwood, Thomas, and Sophia Peddicord were married by license dated 3 Sep 1782 (BAML). On 14 Nov 1786 Sophia was named as a daughter of William 'Peddicoart' (BAAD 8:336; BAAD 10:281).

Greer, [-?-], m. by 26 March 1760 Ann, daughter of John Norris (BAWB 2:328; BFD 3:119).

Greer, [-?-], m. by 9 April 1787 Ann, daughter of William Fitch, who described himself as 'being very ancient' (BAWB 4:284).

Greer, James, m. Anne, daughter of Arthur Taylor; he d. by after 6 June 1687, and Ann m. 2nd, Laurence Richardson (*q.v.*), who d. by 13 June 1705, and Anne m. 3rd, by 9 Oct 1710, Oliver Harriott (*q.v.*) (*BCF:*538; BAAD 2: 2, 134; BAAB 2:556; INAC 32A:24, 32C:135).

Greer, James, and Elizabeth Wright were m. on 28 May 1741 (Harrison, "St. John's Parish Register:" 199). She was the widow of William Wright (*q.v.*), and m. 3rd, Heathcote Pickett (*q.v.*). James Greer and Elizabeth, extx. of William Wright, administered Wright's estate (BAAD 3:267).

Greer, John, m. by 4 March 1714 Sarah [-?-] when they conveyed to Walter Bosley 75 a., part of *Arthur's Choice*; Ann Harriott the mother of John or Sarah, gave her consent; deed does not clearly state which of the two is the child of Ann (BALR TR#A:333).

Greer, John, and Cloe Jones, in Nov 1743 were summoned to answer charges of unlawful cohabitation ("St. John's and St. George's Parish Register Vestry Proceedings," MS. at MdHS: 66).

Greer, John, aged about 58, deposed on 8 Aug 1747 naming his uncle [-?-] Smithers and his father-in-law Lawrence Richardson (BALC HWS&BB#4: #109).

Greer, Moses, and Mary Bailey (Bayley) were m. in Jan 1737 (Harrison, "St. John's," p. 208); on 31 Aug 1772 Mary Greer was paid her portion of the estate of Thomas Bailey (MDAD 67:229).

Greer (Greear), William Wood, in March 1768 was named as a "natural son" in the will of William Wood (MWB 37:353 abst. in *Md. Cal. of Wills* 14:102).

Grees, Johann Phillip, m. by 15 March 1763 Anna Ettkinz ("First Record Book for the Reformed and Lutheran Congregations at Manchester, Baltimore (Now Carroll) Co.," *MGSB* 35:267).

Gregory, David. See Elizabeth Williams.

Gregory, James, and Jane Wigley were m. on 20 Nov 1790 (Marr. Register of Rev. Lewis Richards, MS.690 at MdHS). On 22 Aug 1795 Jane was named as a daughter of Edward Wigley who named a grandson Christopher Gregory in his will (BAWB 5:328).

Gregory, James, and Sarah Bond were m. on 7 May 1796 (Marr. Register of Rev. Lewis Richards, MS.690 at MdHS). On 14 Aug 1800 Sarah was named as the admx. of Thomas Bond (*q.v.*) (BAAD 13:316).

Gregory, John, and Mary Parlet were m. on 27 July 1746 (Harrison, "St. Paul's Parish Register:" 159). Gregory d. by 14 March 1761 by which time his admx. was m. to Nathaniel Hill (*q.v.*) (MDTP 38:80).

Gregory, John, and Catherine Dunn were m. on 11 Nov 1783 (Marr. Returns of Rev. William West, Scharf Papers, MS.1999 at MdHS). John Gregory, of Back River Upper Hundred, Baltimore Co., stated that he would not pay the debts of his wife Catherine, who had refused to move from Fell's Point and live with him (*Maryland Journal and Baltimore Advertiser* 18 Feb 1785). Caty Gregory, in her will made named 1798 named her children Arthur, Samuel, Hannah, and Ann Dunn, and her son Henry Gregory (BAWB 6:155).

Gregory, Peter, free Negro from St. Domingo, and Marie Louisa Crenze[?], slave of Mrs. Allaire Crenze, were m. 22 Nov 1795 at St. Peter's Catholic Church, Baltimore (*Piet:* 135).

Gregory, Simon, in his will dated 21 d. 7 m. 1736 named his mother Rebecca Powell, and his father-in-law Thomas Bab of Newcastle Co. MWB 21:695 abst. in *Md. Cal. of Wills* 7:196).

Gregory, William, and Ann Tanner were m. by lic. on 19 March 1796 at St. Peter's Catholic Church, Baltimore (*Piet:* 135).

Grehan, James, and Elizabeth Hunt were married by banns on 16 Oct 1788, at St. Peter's Catholic Church, Baltimore (*Piet:* 135).

Grenshed. See Grangett.

Grey, Elizabeth, in 1762 was convicted of bastardy. She was fined for bastardy again in 1765 (BAMI 1755-1763, 1765). In March 1768 she was again found guilty of bastardy (BAMI 1768-1769:10).

Grier. See Greer.

Griffee (Griffith), Richard, m. by 16 Aug 1779 Rachel, daughter of Edward Stocksdale (BAWB 3:376; BACT 1773-1784:303; BAAD 8:324).

Griffin, [-?-], m. by 22 May 1771 Rachel, daughter of George Ensor (BAWB 3:195).

Griffin, Abraham, and Mary Miller were m. by lic. on 11 Aug 1793 at St. Peter's Catholic Church, Baltimore (*Piet:* 135). In 1799, Mary was named as a daughter of Matthew Miller (BOCP Petition of Mary Britton, 1799).

Griffin, Charles, b. 1751, enlisted in the Maryland Flying Camp from Baltimore Co., d. 1 Sep 1843, m. Rebecca Kelly on 31 July 1781in Baltimore Co. (Rev. War Pension Application of Rebecca Griffin: W4445; BAML).

Griffin, John, and Mary Carback were m. on 27 March 1792 (Marr. Register of Rev. Lewis Richards, MS.690 at MdHS). On 11 Sep 1793 Margaret [*sic*] was named as the mother of Henry Carback (BACT 1791-1794, MS 2865/1 at MdHS: 248).

Griffin, Luke, in Nov 1756 was charged with begetting a bastard on the body of Ann Brucebanks (BAMI 1755-1763).

Griffin, Thomas, Sr., d. 12 April 1789, and Esther [-?-], d. 16 Jan 1804 in her 75th year, were m. by 17 Dec 1748 when their daughter Nancy was b. ("Thomas Griffin Bible," on *MBR* 7:76; Harrison, "St. Paul's Parish Register:" 80).

Griffin, Thomas, Jr., b. 17 Jan 1754, son of Thomas and Esther, and Margaret Shryak, born 27 June 1769 were m. on 28 Nov 1786 ("Thomas Griffin Bible," on *MBR* 7:76).

Griffin, William, and Jane Chambers were m. by license dated 16 May 1795 (BAML). William Griffin of Fell's Point, stated he would not pay the debts contracted by his wife Jane, who has eloped from his bed and board without any just provocation (*Federal Intelligencer and Baltimore Daily Gazette* 24 Sep 1795).

Griffith, [-?-], m. by 1 March 1780 Mary, daughter of Walter and Ann Moore of Gunpowder Forest, Baltimore Co., farmer (BAWB 3:450; BAAD 11:61).

Griffith, Abraham, on 25 d. 10 m. 1788 requested a certificate to marry Rachel Taylor, a member of Fairfax Monthly Meeting in Va. ("Minutes of Gunpowder Meeting," *QRNM:*86).

Griffith, Ann, on 26 d. 6 m. 1790 reportedly gone out in marriage ("Minutes of Gunpowder Meeting," *QRNM:*88). [No other marriage reference found].

Griffith, Elizabeth, in the 8 m. 1780 was charged with being married by a priest ("Minutes of Gunpowder Meeting," *QRNM:*73). [No other marriage reference found].

Griffith, George, and Diana Lane were married by license dated 23 Dec 1783 (BAML). On 11 June 1793 she was named as a daughter of Dutton Lane (BAAD 11:281).

Griffith, Henry, m. by 14 Jan 1780 Sarah, widow of Samuel Norwood of Baltimore Co., dec. (BALR WG#D:611).

Griffith, Isaac, on 24 d. 11 m. 1773 was reported to have married outside the order ("Minutes of Gunpowder Monthly Meeting," *QRNM:*64). [No other marriage reference found].

Griffith, John, m. by 1793 Eleanor, daughter of John Ensor (MCHP # 2029).

Griffith, John, and Sarah Jeffries were married by license dated 4 Oct 1798 (BAML). On May 1800 Sarah was named as the admx. of John 'Jeffers' (BAAD 13:251).

Griffith, Joseph, and Catherine (before marriage Burson) on 29 d. 7 m. 1786 were condemned for marrying outside the outside the good order ("Minutes of Gunpowder Meeting," *QRNM:*82). [No other marriage reference found].

Griffith, Kerrenhappuck, in 1772 was fined for bastardy (BAMI 1772, 1775-1781:84).

Griffith, Luke, and Mrs. Blanch Hall, widow of Parker Hall were m. on 13 Jan 1757 (Harrison, "St. George's Parish Register:" 378; MDAD 46:387). On 9 June 1761 Luke and Blanch Griffith administered the estate of Parker Hall (BAAD 4:354).

Griffith, Nathan, m. by 1793, Elizabeth, daughter of John Ensor (MCHP# 2029).

Griffith, Osborn, and Cassandra Haile were m. on 12 Aug 1790 (Marr. Register of Rev. Lewis Richards, MS.690 at MdHS). Sarah Haile, widow of Neale Haile, in her will made 10 Sep 1796 named her grandson John Griffith (BAWB 5:404).

Griffith, Samuel, m. by 21 April 1741 Mary, sister of Luke Raven (BALR HWS#1-A:490).

Griffith, Samuel, and Freenatah Garrettson were m. on 15 March 1764 (Harrison, "St. George's Parish Register:" 380). She was a daughter of Martha Garrettson (MWB 36:170 abst. in *Md. Cal. of Wills* 14:17; see also BAWB 3:62).

Griffith, Sarah, dec., left a will in which she left part of her estate for the support of Elizabeth Griffith, wife of the petitioner, and for the support, maintenance, and education of Rachel, John, Eleanor, Elizabeth, and Nathan, sons and daughters of the petitioner and his wife Elizabeth (BOCP Petition of Nathan Griffith, 1791).

Griffith, William, and Ann Frazier, daughter of the late Mr. James Frazier of this town were m. last eve. by Rev. Richards (*Baltimore Daily Repository* 30 Aug 1793).

Griffiths, Jonathan Camp, merchant of New York, was m. at Philadelphia on Thurs. eve. last by Rev. Dr. Green, to Miss Mary Harvey Ellicott, daughter of Andrew Ellicott, Esq., geographer to the United States (*Federal Gazette and Baltimore Daily Advertiser* 16 April 1800).

Grilse?, Jemima, before marriage Ball, on 25 d., 5 m. 1774 was reportedly married by a priest ("Minutes of Gunpowder Monthly Meeting," *QRNM:*64). [No other marriage reference found].

Grimes, [-?-], m. by 24 Oct 1784 Sarah, sister of Nathaniel Clary (BAWB 3:577).

Grimes, [-?-], m. by 22 Sep 1789 Sarah, daughter of Edward Oursler (BAWB 5:244).

Grimes, Honor, was charged with bastardy at the Nov 1721 Court (BACP IS#C:631).

Grimes. Nicholas, m. by 3 Oct 1780 Mary, daughter of William Parlett (BAWB 3:411; BAAD 10:256).

Grimes, William, m. by 20 April 1749 Alice, widow of Barnett Bond (*q.v.*) (AWAP:187-188; BAEJ: "Thomas Bond: *Harritt's Fancy, Laurence, Buck Range, and Addition;*" BALR AL#B:652).

Groc, John Anthony, and Catherine Mary Lemonnier, widow of Charles Chantrier of San Dominque, were m. by lic. on 28 Dec 1794 at St. Peter's Catholic Church, Baltimore (*Piet:* 135).

Gronau, Christian, printer, and Miss Peggy Commer, both of Baltimore, were m. last eve. by Rev. Trottenier (*Baltimore Telegraphe* 18 Nov 1799).

Groom, Moses, m. by 9 May 1701 Elizabeth, admx. of William Ebden (MDTP 18B:74).

Groome, Moses, had a kinswoman Ann, former wife of Stephen Johnson, who m. by 11 Feb 1704, Edward Felkes (BALR IR#PP:171, HW#2:119; BAAD 2:27; INAC 28: 23).

Groome, Moses, was named as a brother-in-law of the will of John Ewings of Baltimore Co. on 12 April 1709 (MWB 12, part 2: 143 abst. in *Md. Cal. of Wills* 3:145).

Grose, Johannes, m. by 29 Jan 1787, Rosina Hauertin ("First Record Book for the Reformed and Lutheran Congregations at Manchester, Baltimore (Now Carroll) Co.," *MGSB* 35: 282).

Grosjean, J. J., merchant, m. Polly Trickle, [date not given] (*Maryland Journal and Baltimore Advertiser* 29 Oct 1790).

Gross, Henry, and Elizabeth Isaacks were m. by lic. on 26 Sep 1794 (BAML). Henry Grass [*sic*], living near Robert Gilmore's Gunpowder Mills, Baltimore Co., stated he would not pay the debts of his wife Elizabeth, who had eloped from his bed and board on Monday night (*Federal Gazette and Baltimore Daily Advertiser* 4 April 1796).

Gross, Lieut. James, of the U. S. Frigate *Constellation* and Miss Ann Job, daughter of Mr. Morris Job of Fell's Point were m. last eve. by Rev. Allison (*Baltimore Telegraphe* 29 Jan 1798).

Gross, Lewis, and Catherine Wise of Frederick Co. were m. by lic. on 17 Dec 1795 at St. Peter's Catholic Church, Baltimore (*Piet:* 135).

Grouse (Crouse), [-?-], m. by 28 April 1792 Catherine, daughter of Christopher Hartman (BAWB 6:158).

Grover, Ann, confessed to bastardy on 7 March 1754, but refused to name the father; she was fined £3 (BACP BB#A:449)..

Grover, George, m. by 1 May 1724 Jane Russell, who had an inheritance in Va. (BALR IS#G:312).

Grover, William, and Eliz. Enloes were m. on 14 Jan 1752 (Harrison, "St. John's Parish Register:" 204). On 16 Nov 1752 Elizabeth was named as the extx. of Anthony Enloes (*q.v.*) (MDTP 33-2:25; MDAD 32:154, 33:176).

Grover. See also Gover.

Groverman, Anthony, merchant, and Miss Henrietta Delius, both of Baltimore, were m. last eve. by Rev. Kurtz (*Federal Gazette and Baltimore Daily Advertiser* 2 Sep 1798).

Groves, Capt. John, and Miss Ann Carroll, both of Fell's Point, were m. last eve. by Rev. Mr. Bend (*Baltimore Intelligencer* 20 April 1798).

Groves, William, m. by 12 Dec 1720 Dorothy [-?-], who on that day, with the consent of her husband, wrote her will, leaving part of *Harrison, Neglect* to her uncle John Rallings or Rawlings (BALR TR#DS:290: MWB 17:211 abst. in *Md. Cal. of Wills* 5:101).

Grundy, Robert, m. by [date not given], Mary (or Marg.), extx. of John Pemberton (BAAD 1:288).

Gudgeon (or Cutchin), Robert, m. by 3 Sep 1703 [-?-], admx. of Moses Groome (INAC 23:165).

Guest, John, Jr., merchant of this city, was m. last Thurs. eve. To Miss Rebecca Hall of Harford Co. (*Baltimore Evening Post* 26 Nov 1792).

Guffy, Elizabeth, orphan, in Oct 1795 was made a ward of Ann Guffy (BAOC 3:171).

Guichard (Guishard), Mark, m. by 15 Feb 1744/5 Diana, extx. of Roger Crudgington (MDTP 31:621).

Guishard, Mark, and Sarah Hendon, in Aug 176, were summoned to appear before the vestry for [some words seem to have been omitted] in an irregular manner ("St. John's and St. George's Parish Register Vestry Proceedings," MS. at the MdHS: 162).

Guishard, Mark, and Catherine McCabe were married by license dated 22 Feb 1796 (BAML). In July 1798 Catherine was named as a legatee of Phebe Hutchinson (BAAD 12:460).

Guiton (Guyton), Henry, and Sarah Holt were m. on 17 April 1738 (Harrison, "St. John's Parish Register:" 217). On 30 Oct 1765 Sarah was named as a daughter of John Holt, who also had a daughter Ann Holt (BALR B#P:64).

Gullison, Esther, widow of Thomas Gullison, dec., petitioned the Orphans Court. She stated her husband d. 23 Dec last, leaving personal property, including crops and livestock worth about 150 pounds currency. She has been greatly afflicted with some illness including hysteric fits. She was so ill when her husband died that she felt she could not administer his estate. She sent to John Merryman, Esq., who lived hear her, and asked him to take over her affairs. Now she is afraid Merryman will take the property which is rightfully hers. (BOCP Petition of Esther Gullison, n.d.).

Gunby (Ganby), Stephen, and Ann Stansbury were married on 5 May 1796 (Marr. Register of Rev. Lewis Richards, MS.690 at MdHS). On 13 May 1798 Nancy, wife of Stephen Gunby, was named as a daughter of Joseph Stansbury (BAWB 6:150; BAAD 13:284).

Guney, Mary, confessed to bastardy at the Nov 1754 Court but did not name the father (BACP BB#A:451).

Gunnell, George, Gent., m. by 24 May 1679 Jane, admx. of Thomas Overton (*q.v.*), immediately after his death; they were m. by 28 July 1679 (INAC 6:225; MDTP 11:77).

Gurtner, Jacob, m. by 15 Oct 1766 Anna Catharina Ottin ("First Record Book for the Reformed and Lutheran Congregations at Manchester, Baltimore (Now Carroll Co.," *MGSB* 35:270).

Gush. See Gash.

Guthrie (Guthrow, Guttry), Joshua, and Susanna Keener were married on 7 Dec 1783 (Marr. Return of William West, Scharf Papers, MS. 1999 at MdHS). On 6 March 1798 Susanna was named as a daughter of Melchoir Keener; they had a daughter Charlotte (BAWB 6:129; BAOC 4:101). Mrs. Susannah Guttry [*sic*], wife of Joshua Guttry, and youngest daughter of Melchoir Keener died last Thurs.; she was buried in the German Calvinist Graveyard (*Maryland Journal and Baltimore Advertiser* 27 Jan 1789).

Guthrow, John, widower, and Rebecca Joiner, widow, were m. by lic. on 20 May 1797 at St. Peter's Catholic Church, Baltimore (*Piet:* 135). (BAML gives his name as John Gutlerow).

Guttero, Ann, received an allowance in 1772 for the support of an infant child supposed to be that of John McNabb, who had absconded (Levy List for 1772).

Güttinger, Johannes, m. by 5 May 1764 Catharina Maulin ("First Record Book for the Reformed and Lutheran Congregations at Manchester, Baltimore (Now Carroll) Co.," MGSB 35:268).

Guy, William, of Charles Co., m. by 13 Oct 1752 Elizabeth, daughter of John Gibson, son of Thomas, who was a son of Thomas Gibson (BALR TR#D:516).

Guyton, Aaron, b. 27 Oct 1761 in Baltimore Co., Md., m. 6 Oct 1789 in York Dist., S.C., Margaret McCurdy, b. Dec 1773 (Guyton Bible Record, in Rev. War Pension Appl. W21237, in *NGSQ* 21:48.).

Guyton, John Holt, and Sarah Watkins were m. on 30 Oct 1787 (Harrison, "St. James Parish Register:" 1). On 20 Nov 1793 Sarah was named as a daughter of Samuel Watkins who also named a granddaughter Frances Guyton (BAWB 5:336).

Guyton. See also Guiton.

Gwin, William, and Sarah Ginkins (or Jinkins) were m. on 28 June 1721 (Harrison, "St. George's Parish Register:" 265). She was a niece of Thomas Cullen (*q.v.*).

Gwinn, Edward, m. Acshah Dorsey on 11 Dec 1789 ("Dorsey Bible Record," *Genealogy* 3 (10) (Oct 1913): 98; BAML). Achsah was b. 5 Aug 1766, daughter of Caleb and Rebecca Dorsey ("Old Dorsey Bible." contributed by Ida M. Shirk, accessed at www.biblerecords.com).

Gwinn, Hannah, was charged with bastardy at the March 1746/7 Court (BACP TB&TR#1:378).

Gwinn, John, a Sergeant in the Maryland Line, d. about 18 Sep 1800 m. on 20 Sep 1785, at First Presbyterian Church, Baltimore, by Rev, Patrick Allison, Julia Steel, and had daus. Susanna and Catherine Gwinn (Rev. War Pension Application of Julia 'Gwynn': W3802/BLWT1494-100).

Gwynn (Gwinn), Thomas, d. by 7 Feb 1726 at which time his widow Mary m. William Hall (*q.v.*).

"H"

Hagar, [-?-], m. by 30 Sep 1757 Mary Ann, who received a distributive share from the estate of Thomas Courtney Jenkins (MWB 30:368, abst. in *Md. Cal. of Wills* 11:179).

Hagare, Catherine, Rebecca, Louisa, Frances, and **Mary,** in May 1796, were made wards of William McMechen (BOCP 3:192).

Hager, John, and Susanna Gill were married by license dated 2 April 1789 (BAML). On 15 Oct 1789 Susanna was named as a daughter of Stephen Gill (BAAD 10:65).

Hagerman, Samuel, m. by 17 Feb 1798, Rebecca Wooden (BALR WG#58:482). (BAML gives his name as Samuel Hageman).

Hagerty, William, and Jenney Barrett, widow of [-?-] Nicholson, natives of Ireland, were m. by lic. on 23 April 1795 at St. Peter's Catholic Church, Baltimore (*Piet:* 135).

Hahn, Michel, m. by 4 March (1761?) Catharina Zensin ("First Record Book for the Reformed and Lutheran Congregations at Manchester, Baltimore (Now Carroll) Co.," *MGSB* 35:266).

Haile, [-?-], m. by 19 Jan 1732 Frances, daughter of Barbara Broad (MWB 20:733 abst. in *Md. Cal. of Wills* 7:29).

Haile, Neal, m. by 17 Oct 1774 Sarah, daughter of Charles Robinson (BALR AL#L:208).

Haile, Samuel, orphan of Ann Haile, aged 14 next 2 Nov, in Aug 1768 was bound to James Wood to age 21 to learn trade of blacksmith (BAMI 1768-1769).

Haile, Stephen, aged 14 next 2 Nov [prob. the son of Ann Haile], in Aug 1768 was bound to James Wood (BAMI 1768-1769).

Haile. See also Hale.

Hailey, Peter, and Margaret Leary were m. by lic. on 28 Nov 1790 at St. Peter's Catholic Church, Baltimore (*Piet:* 135).

Haines, Catherine, in her will made 13 Nov 1800 named her granddaughter Eleanor Gunnet, her sons-in-law Alexander Walters and Basil John Dorsey (*q.v.*) (BAWB 6:346).

Haines (Hains), Daniel, son of Joseph and Elizabeth Hains of West Nottingham Meeting, Chester Co., Pa., and Mary Price, daughter of Mordecai, were m. on 25 d. 3 m. 1762 (Gunpowder Meeting, Records at MdSA: 248). On 15 Oct 1765 she was named as an heir of Elizabeth Price of Baltimore Co. (BAAD 6:146).

Haines, Daniel, and Ann Sollers were m. on 26 Jan 1782 (Marr. Returns of Rev. William West, Scharf Papers, MS.1999 at MdHS). Ann was a daughter of Francis Sollers, who in his will made 23 April 1796 named his grandsons Francis and William Haines (BAWB 6:87).

Haines (variously written as Haims,Homes, Homs, and Kime), George, in 1798, was guardian to Christian, Catherine, Elizabeth, George, William, John, and Jacob Homes, his infant children. It was ordered that Abraham Sitler pay the share of the estate of Barney (Bernad or Barnhart) Miller, dec., due to the said children in the right of their mother, Rosina Homes, dec., the sister of said Barney Miller (BAOC 4:21; BAAD 13:47; MCHP # 3442).

Haines (Hains), Nathan, son of Joseph, of West Nottingham, Chester Co., Pa., and Sophia Price, daughter of Mordecai, were m. on 23 d. 10 m. 1755 (West River Monthly Meeting, pub. in *MGSB,* serially beginning vol. 14, no. 2). On 15 Oct 1765 she was named as an heir of Elizabeth Price of Baltimore Co. (BAAD 6:146).

Hair, Jemima. See Thomas Sullivan.

Hakes. See Hacks.

Hale, Capt. [-?-], was m. last Thurs. eve., 11th inst., by Rev. Mr. Wilmer, to Susan Hall, daughter of Aquila Hall, Esq., at his seat at Long Green, Baltimore Co. (*Federal Gazette and Baltimore Daily Advertiser* 15 Sep 1800).

Hale, Amon, was a private under Capt. Stephenson; he was b. 16 June 1759 and d. 4 Dec 1843; m. Mary [-?-], d. 19 Jan 1849, on 30 Sep 1785; The Family Bible gives the dates of birth of Amon and his children: Elizabeth, b. 1 Sep 1786; Uratha, b. 11 Sep 1788; Jesse, b. 16 Oct 1791; Micajah N., b. 20 March 1793; Robert G., b. 11 Nov 1795; Mary, b. 14 Dec 1797; Joshua, b. 10 Feb 1800; Prisse, b. 8 Aug 1802; Amon C., b. 11 March 1705; Ruth, b. 11 Nov 1787 (Rev. War Pension Application of Mary Hale W227).

Hale, George, Jr., m. by 31 May 1777, Ann, daughter of Alexander Grant of Baltimore Co., dec. (BALR WG#A:362).

Hale, George, brickmaker, m. by 23 Feb 1784, Jane, mother of Eliz. Everington and Jonathan Anderson (BAWB 3:587).

Hale, Matthew, d. by 3 Sep 1722 when his admx. Diana had m. Nicholas Besson (*q.v.*) (MDAD 5:83; BALR RM#HS:73).

Hale, Matthew, m. by 17 Oct 1774 Rebecca, daughter of Charles Robinson (BALR AL#L: 208).

Hale. See also Haile.

Haley, William, aged 12 next 11 June, orphan of Edward, in March 1760 was bound to Thomas Matthews to learn the art of husbandry (BAMI 1755-1763: 10).

Hall, [-?-], d, by 29 June 1745, having m. [-?-], coheir of William Cockey of Anne Arundel Co. (BALR TB#D:250).

Hall, [-?-], m. by 24 June 1772 Ann, daughter of James Mayes of Baltimore Co. (BALR AL#E:127).

Hall, [-?-], m. by 6 May 1791 Priscilla Woodfield, sister of Thomas Woodfield and niece of Nathaniel Phipps (BAWB 5:21).

Hall, [-?-], m. by 8 Dec 1792 Sarah, daughter of John Bond (BAWB 5:75).

Hall, Ann, of Somerset Co., in her will made 20 June 1799 named her daughter Elizabeth Maddox and grandson Levin Hall Brittingham (BAWB 6:196).

Hall, Aquila, and Johanna Kemp, widow of [-?-] Kemp (*q.v.*), were m. on 17 Dec 1720 (Harrison, "St. George's Parish Register:" 230). In 1720 Johanna was named as the widow of Col. James Phillips of Baltimore Co. (PCJU 29:125-128; MDAD 8:297, 10:274). On 27 July 1731 Johanna was named as guardian and mother to John Kemp and Richard Kemp (MDTP 29:108).

Hall, Aquila, and Sophia White were m. on 14 Feb 1750 (Harrison, "St. George's Parish Register:" 50). Mrs. Sophia Hall, relict of the late Aquila Hall, Esq., of Harford Co., and sister of the Rev. Dr. White of Philadelphia, d. early this morning [7 Jan 1785] (*Maryland Journal and Baltimore Advertiser* 11 Jan 1785).

Hall, Aquila, m. by 26 July 1781 Ann, daughter of Walter Tolley who also named grandchildren Walter Tolley Hall and Martha Susanna Hall (BAWB 3:507).

Hall, Avarilla, on 7 April 1747 posted bond to administer the estate of Thomas Maccroy (BAAB 2:179).

Hall, Benjamin, stated he would not pay the debts of his wife Lucretia, who had behaved in an improper manner (*Federal Gazette and Baltimore Daily Advertiser* 29 Dec 1798).

Hall, Daniel, d. about 22 months ago, leaving his widow, Rebecca (the petitioner), and a child about 11 days old, and a debt owed by Robert Long. She asks that she be paid her thirds of the money due, and also a third for the maintenance of the child (BOCP Petition of Rebecca Hall, 1790).

Hall, Edward, and Sarah Phillips were m. 2 Sep 1756 (Harrison, "St. George's Parish Register:" 364). Sarah m. 2nd, Daniel Magee (*q.v.*), and on 14 Jan 1764 they posted bond to administer Hall's estate (BAAB 3:316).

Hall, Edward, and Nancy Shaw, both of Fell's Point, were m. last eve. by Rev. Riggen (*Baltimore American* 26 Aug 1799).

Hall, Elijah, ship-carpenter, and his heirs have inherited about 200 a. of land in Anne Arundel Co., on the Patapsco River, now in the possession of Captain Thomas Mortimer of Baltimore Town, who claims the land [under the will?] of Charles Hall, but whereof only one-half of the land was willed to him. Elijah and Charles Hall are cousins and served their apprenticeship to ship carpenters on Fells Point. The land was willed to them by their grandfather Nathan Pumphrey; Elijah Hall served his time about 20 years ago with a Mr. Wells, ship carpenter, from whence he went about 18 years ago to Chincoteague to repair a vessel burnt down by the British. He is or was a married man and had children. This notice was placed by Elijah's friend James Bonadye (*Federal Intelligencer and Baltimore Daily Gazette* 23 Oct 1795).

Hall, Elisha, and Mary Nicholson were m. on 13 May 1762 Harrison, "St. Paul's Parish Register:" 167). Mary was the widow of 1st, John Forty (*q.v.*), 2nd, John Connell (*q.v.*), and 3rd, William Nicholson (*q.v.*) (MDTP 41:220, 42:29; MWB 31:363; BAAD 6:118, 7:191; MINV 80:401, 402; MINV 87:342; BAAD 7:181; BAAB 3:103).

Hall, George, and Elizabeth Robinson were married by license dated 9 May 1788 (BAML). On 1 May 1789 Elizabeth was named as the widow and admx. of George Robinson (BAAD 9:327; BALR WG#TT: 554).

Hall, James White, of Harford Co., and Mrs. Stokes of Havre de Grace were m. Thurs., 20th inst. (*Maryland Journal and Baltimore Advertiser* 28 Oct 1785).

Hall, John, and wife Sarah, on 7 June 1687 posted bond to administer the estate of John Collier (*q.v.*) (BAAB 1:312). On 9 Aug 1688 Sarah was named as the extx. of Abraham Holman (INAC 10:169). In his undated will, proved 1 June 1686, Abraham Holman named his sister Sarah Collier, brother John Collier, Isabella Hopper [Hooper], Elizabeth Taylor and Daniel Wine. Edward Alley, William York and William Taylor witnessed the will (MWB 4:219, abst. in *Md. Cal. of Wills,* 2:6). Sarah was the admx. of John Collier, George Hooper (*q.v.*), and Abraham Holman (INAC 10:168, 169; MDTP 14:101). She was the mother of Isabella Hooper and Ann Collier (BALR HW#2:38).

Hall, John, and Martha Gouldsmith were m. on 18 July 1693 (Harrison, "St. George's Parish Register:" 178). By 1695 Martha was named as the daughter and admx. of Edward Beadle, and extx. of George Goldsmith (INAC 10:454, 15:182). On 10 July 1697, John and Martha posted bond to administer the estate of Mary Utie (BAAB 4:194).

Hall, John, in June 1712 was charged with begetting a bastard on the body of Alice Bonnaday (BACP IS#B:40).

Hall, John, in his will dated 24 Jan 1717/8 named his mother Jane Novell and his uncle John Rawlins (MWB 14:605 abst. in *Md. Cal. of Wills* 4:162).

Hall, John, Jr., and Mrs. Hannah Johns were m. on 26 Nov 1734 (Harrison, "St. George's Parish Register:" 286). On 27 Oct 1735 Hannah was named as the extx. of Abraham Johns (*q.v.*) of Baltimore Co. She was also the widow of Asael Maxwell (*q.v.*) (MDAD 14:1, BAAD 2:214, 3:214, 4:75; BALR HWS#M:110, TR#C:188, 329).

Hall, John, and Susanna Marshall were m. on 2 June 1742 (Harrison, "St. George's Parish Register:" 326). On 23 Dec 1746 Hall was named as a son-in-law of Mary Marshall (MWB 25:555 abst. by Gibb).

Hall, John, and 'Mrs.' Barthiah Stansbury were m. on 9 Aug 1743 (Harrison, "St. George's Parish Register:" 341). On 16 April 1759 he was named as a son-in-law of Jane Stansbury, and the father of Sophia, Martha, Elizabeth, John Biddle, and Josias Hall (MWB 30:684 abst. by Gibb).

Hall, John, m. by 15 June 1792 Jane, admx. of John Joy (*q.v.*) (BAAD 11:88).

Hall, John, and Susanna Lynch were m. by lic. on 17 Nov 1795 at St. Peter's Catholic Church, Baltimore (*Piet:* 135).

Hall, John, mariner, and Juliana Townsend, widow, were m. by lic. on 7 Feb 1798 at St. Peter's Catholic Church, Baltimore (*Piet:* 135).

Hall, Joshua, m. by 6 Jan 1738 Dinah, daughter of John Spicer (MWB 22:144, abst. in *Md. Cal. of Wills* 8:68). On 9 Nov 1742 Dinah was named as the mother of Mary Spicer (BALR TB#C:63).

Hall, Joshua, m. by 8 Dec 1792, Sarah, daughter of John Bond (BAWB 5:75; BAAD 11:530).

Hall, Col. Josias Carvil, of Harford Co., and Miss Smith, eldest daughter of William Smith, Esq., of this town, were m. [date not given] (*Maryland Journal and Baltimore Advertiser* 21 March 1780).

Hall, Parker, m. Blanch Carvill, daughter of John and Mary (Phillips) Carvill (*BCF:*293); he d. by 9 June 1761, leaving three children all of age, when his estate was administered by Luke and Blanch Griffith (*q.v.*) (BAAD 4:35)

Hall, Philip, and Sarah Frazier were m. on 2 June 1772 (Harrison, "St. Paul's Parish Register:" 177). On 14 Jan 1779, Sarah was named as a daughter of John Frazier (*q.v.*) and on 23 Sep 1779 as a sister of John Frazier, late of the Island of New Providence, merchant (BAWB 3:552; BALR WG#D:11).

Hall, William, and Mary Gwynn were m. on 7 Feb 1726 (Harrison, "St. Margaret's Parish Register," Anne Arundel Co.: 104). On 7 Nov 1750 Mary was named as the widow of Thomas Gwinn (*q.v.*); she m. 3rd, John Chapman (*q.v.*) (BAAD 3:92, 5:127; MDAD 8:248, 9:291; BAAD 3:92).

Hall, William, and Mary Merryman were m. on 17 Dec 1734 (Harrison, "St. Paul's Parish Register:" 152). On 3 Aug 1739 she was named as a daughter of Charles Merryman of Baltimore Co. (MDAD 17:187).

Hall, William, m. by 7 Nov 1750 Mary, admx. of Thomas Buckingham (*q.v.*) of Baltimore Co. (MDAD 29:5).

Hall, William, and Sarah Steed were m. by lic. dated 6 Aug 1783 (BAML). Hall stated he would not pay the debts of his wife Sarah (*Maryland Journal and Baltimore Advertiser* 29 June 1784).

Halton, Thomas, of Baltimore, stated he would not pay the debts of his wife Mary (*Maryland Journal and Baltimore Advertiser* 25 Dec 1793).

Hamby, Elizabeth, was charged with bastardy at March Court 1741/2, again in March Court 1742/3, and presented in June 1743 (BACP TB&TR:294, TB#D:121, 196).

Hamilton, [-?-], m. by 8 Jan 1771 Elizabeth, sister of Alexander Cummings (BAWB 3:294).

Hamilton, [-?-], m. by 20 Sep 1795 Rachel, daughter of Nicholas Baker (BAWB 6:212).

Hamilton, Ann, was charged with bastardy at the Nov 1758 Court and named Joseph Morgan as the father of her child (BAMI 1757-1759:164).

Hamilton, James, and Elizabeth McCracken were married by license dated 13 Oct 1779 (BAML). In June 1785 Hamilton stated he would not pay the debts of his wife Elizabeth (*Maryland Gazette or Baltimore General Advertiser* 16 June 1785).

Hamilton, James, and Cassandra Bond were married by license dated 27 June 1788 (BAML). On 15 Oct 1788 Cassandra was named as a daughter of Elizabeth Bond (BAWB 4:200; BAAD 9:245).

Hamilton, Capt. John A., and Peggy, daughter of Peter Shepherd, Esq., of this town, were m. [date not given] (*Maryland Journal and Baltimore Advertiser* 14 Aug 1782). (BAML gives his name as John Agnu [Agnew?] Hamilton).

Hamilton, Levi, of Charles Co., and Abigail Barru were m. by lic. on 27 Dec 1797 at St. Peter's Catholic Church, Baltimore (*Piet:* 135).

Hamilton, Robert, merchant of Alexandria, and Miss Esther Gray, late of Baltimore, were m. Thurs. last (*Dunlap's American Daily Advertiser* 29 Sep 1794).

Hamilton, Samuel, and Elizabeth Baker were married by license dated 4 Jan 1786 (BAML). She was a daughter of Nicholas Baker (BAWB 6:212).

Hamilton, William, m. by 25 May 1754 Kerrenhapuck, daughter of George Bayly (Bailey) (MWB 29:179 abst. by Abst. by Gibb; *BCF:297*). On 4 June 1768 she was named as a sister of Jabez Bailey (BAWB 3:107).

Hamilton, William, pilot, and Mrs. Maria Sullivan, both of Fell's Point, were m. on Sun. by Rev. Bend (*Baltimore American* 28 May 1799).

Hamin, [-?-], m. by 1 Feb 1797 Ann daughter of John McGregory (BAWB 5:527).

Hamlin, Peter, and Mary Koaler were m. by lic. on 23 Feb 1800 at St. Peter's Catholic Church, Baltimore (*Piet:* 135).

Hammond, Abraham George, of Baltimore Co., m. by 19 Feb 1794 Mary, widow of William Andrew (*q.v.*), dec., and mother of Elizabeth Durbin William Andrew, an infant under the age of 21 (BALR WG#NN:286; BAAD 10:41).

Hammond, Benjamin, and Margaret Talbot were m. on 6 April 1735 (Harrison, "St. Paul's Parish Register:" 153). On 18 March 1736 Margaret was named as a daughter of William Talbot (BALR IS#IK:377). On 12 Nov 1761 Margaret was named as a daughter of Catherine Risteau (BAWB 2:148).

Hammond, Isaac, and Susanna Bond were married by license dated 13 March 1778 (BAML). On 8 April 1786 Susanna was named as the admx. of William Bond of Thomas (BAAD 8:257).

Hammond, John, d. by 19 Dec 1688 by which time his widow Mary had m. 2nd, Samuel Brand (*q.v.*), 3rd Richard Askew (*q.v.*), and 4th, Edward Reeves (*q.v.*).

Hammond, John, merchant, and Mrs. McConnell, were m. in this town [date not given] (*Maryland Journal and Baltimore Advertiser* 28 Nov 1783; BAML, which gives her name as Elizabeth McConnell).

Hammond, John, m. by 1 March 1793 [-?-], daughter of Catherine Barnet of Baltimore, widow, who named her grandson John Barnet Hammond in her will of that date BAWB 5:147). John Hammond, admin. with will annexed, on 4 March 1795 posted bond to administer the estate of Catherine Barnet (BAAB 8:704).

Hammond, John, Esq., was m. yesterday at Canton, the seat of Col. O'Donnell, to Miss Elizabeth Anderson (*Federal Intelligencer and Baltimore Daily Gazette* 6 March 1795).

Hammond, John, and Frances Clifford were married by banns on 7 Nov 1790 at St. Peter's Catholic Church, Baltimore (*Piet:* 135).

Hammond, John, and **Ann Hammond** d. by 28 Nov 1798 leaving Vachel Hammond and John Hammond as administrators. Joshua Dorsey and Johnza Dorsey pet. the court that the above administrators have not paid the petitioners their share of the estate due them in right of their wives, Sarah and Henrietta (BOCP Petition of Joshua and Johnza Dorsey, 1798).

Hammond, John Barnett, son of John Hammond and legatee of Catherine Barnett, in Feb 1794 was made a ward of John Hammond (BAOC 3:79).

Hammond, Lawrence, and Avarilla Simpkins were m. on 21 June 1734 (Harrison, "St. Paul's Parish Register:" 152). On 14 March 1738 Avarilla was named as a daughter of John Simkins (MWB 22:39 abst. in *Md. Cal. of Wills* 8:20; BALR TB#C:169).

Hammond, Nathan, orphan son of Rezin Hammond, in Feb 1793 chose Rebecca Hammond as his guardian (BAOC 3:27).

Hammond, Rezin, and Rebecca Hawkins were m. on 2 Sep 1760 (Harrison, "St. Margaret's Parish Register," Anne Arundel Co., MS. at MdHS: 112). Rezin Hammond of Baltimore Co., d. by June 1783 when Rebecca Hammond, admx., advertised she would settle the estate (*Maryland Journal and Baltimore Advertiser* 6 June 1783). Rebecca advertised she intended to petition the General Assembly to make valid a bargain for the sale of land sold by John and Martha Hammond to her late husband, Rezin Hammond. No deed had been given, but Martha was dead, and the right of conveyance was in her son, a minor (Annapolis *Maryland Gazette* 26 Aug 1784).

Hammond, Thomas, of Baltimore Co., Gent., m. by 21 Feb 1693 Rebecca, widow of Thomas Lightfoot or Lytfoot (*q.v.*), and daughter of John Larkin (BALR RM#HS:417; INAC 13B:23, 24; MWB 5:186).

Hammond, Thomas, on 8 Dec 1723 gave notice his wife Mary had absented herself from her habitation without his consent and 'has about ruined [him] by running [him] into debt" (BALR IS#G:207). On 29 March 1723 [prob. 1723/4] he stated that 'she was to go away and leave me; anyone may entertain or employ her, but he won't pay her board' (BALR IS#G:235).

Hammond, Thomas, son of Benjamin, died leaving a will dated 30 Oct 1784 and proved 17 Jan 1786, naming his natural son, John Hammond Gore, son of Isabella or Suva Gore; he also named Philip Hammond Brothers, son of his brother Mordecai Hammond by Mary Brothers (BAWB 4:40).

Hammond, William, and Eliza Raven were m. on 26 Aug 1735 (Harrison, "St. Paul's Parish Register:" 154). On 7 Sep 1735 Elizabeth was named as the widow of Luke Raven (*q.v.*) (MDTP 30:81).

Hammond, William, and Sarah Sheredine were m. on 9 March 1739 (Harrison, "St. Paul's Parish Register:" 156). On 5 Oct 1746 Sarah was named as a daughter of Thomas Sheredine (BALR TB#E: 185).

Hammond, William, in his will, made 30 Oct 1785 named his natural son John Hammond Gore he had by Isabella or [-?-] Gore, and he named Philip Hammond Brothers, son of his brother Mordecai Hammond by Mary Brothers (BAWB 4:40).

Hanaway, Ruth. See Ruth Hayhurst.

Hanbo, Jeremiah, m. by Oct 1704 Mary, admx. of John Clarke (MDTP 20:89). **See Jer. Hacks, above.**

Hancock, William, printer, and Ann Gavin, both of Baltimore, were m. last eve. by Rev. Ustick (*Baltimore Telegraphe* 7 Aug 1797).

Hancock. See also Harecock.

Hand (Stand), John, m. by 14 Feb. 1732 Rosanna, daughter of Jacob Grove (BAAD 3: 108).

Handlen, Patrick, and Jane James were m. by lic. on 7 July 1798 at St. Peter's Catholic Church, Baltimore (*Piet:* 135).

Handsall, Ann, was named as an heir in the will of Charles Murphy, a Sergeant of the First Maryland Regiment, made 10 Jan 1784 (BAWB 4:25). On 28 April 1784 Ann Hands [*sic*], extx., posted bond to administer Murphy's estate (BAAB 6:191).

Hands, Ephraim, m. by 5 Oct 1793 Sarah, daughter of Job Garrettson (BALR WG#MM: 218; BAML).

Hands, Thomas, in June 1737 was charged with begetting a bastard on the body of Margaret Conley (BACP HWS#1-A:62).

Hanes, [-?-], m. by 3 Dec 1792, Sibbol [?; prob. Sybil], daughter of Michael Gore (BAWB 5:96).

Haney, William, private in the Maryland Artillery in the War of the Revolution; m. Susanna Hay on 10 Oct 1788, by Rev. Daniel Kurtz, Pastor of the German Lutheran Church (Rev. War Pension Application of Susanna Hancy: W9049).

Hanly, Jeremiah, on 25 March 1724 stated that his wife had absented herself, and he would not pay her debts (BALR IS#G:242).

Hanly, Michael, and Mary Hanly were married by banns on 21 July 1792 at St. Peter's Catholic Church, Baltimore (*Piet:* 135).

Hanna, Andrew, printer, and Ann Mara were m. by lic. on 21 June 1798 at St. Peter's Catholic Church, Baltimore (*Piet:* 135; BAML, which gives her name as Ann Mayra).

Hanna, Grizelda, will petition the General Assembly for an Act allowing her to divorce her husband (*Maryland Gazette or Baltimore General Advertiser* 9 Sep 1788).

Hannah, Mary, (formerly Tucker) on 28 d.5 m. 1785 was condemned for outgoing in marriage ("Minutes of Gunpowder Meeting," *QRNM:*80). [No other marriage reference found].

Hannan, James, and Elizabeth Thomas were m. by lic. on 17 Jan 1796 at St. Peter's Catholic Church, Baltimore (*Piet:* 135).

Hannan, John, and Margaret Towers were m. by lic. on 4 Jan 1795 at St. Peter's Catholic Church, Baltimore (*Piet:* 135).

Hannan, Michael, and Janet Williams, widow, were m. by lic. on 4 April 1799 at St. Peter's Catholic Church, Baltimore (*Piet:* 135).

Hannesea, John, convict, in June 1746 was fined for begetting a bastard on the body of Susanna Gardiner (BACP TB&TR#1:9, 10).

Hansman, William, d. by 19 Sep 1761 leaving a widow and admx. (Maria) Sophia who m. 2nd, John Stover (*q.v.*) and three children (BAAD 4:339).

Hanson, [-?-], m. by 13 May 1759 Amelia, sister of James Matthews (MWB 30:825 abst. by Gibb).

Hanson, Benjamin, in Aug 1717 was charged with begetting a bastard on the body of Mary Winn (BACP IS#1A:124).

Hanson, Benjamin, in March 1743/4 was charged with begetting a bastard on the body of Katherine Ogg (BACP 1743-1745:172).

Hanson, Benjamin, m. by 25 Dec 1765 [-?-], sister of John Tredway and daughter of Thomas Tredway (BAWB 3:64).

Hanson, Hollis, and Avarilla Hollingsworth were m. on 30 Dec 1777 (Harrison, "St. George's Parish Register:" 201). On 20 Oct 1778 their son John as born ("John Hanson Bible," *MBR* 2:56).

Hanson, Jacob, was named as a son in the will of Sarah Tayman, made 14 Feb 1739, Sarah also named her daughter-in-law Sarah Hanson, and grandchildren John, Sybil, Benjamin, Hollis, Avarilla, Thomas and Jacob Hanson (MWB 24:322 abst. by Gibb).

Hanson, Jacob, and Margaret Hughes were m. on 23 Jan 1738 (Harrison, "St. George's Parish Register:" 309). On 13 Jan 1743 Margaret was named as a daughter of Samuel and Jane Hughes (who was the mother of Francis Watkins) (BAWB 3:27, 185; BALR TB#C:380). **See Samuel Hughes, below.**

Hanson, John, m. on 4 Aug 1743, Somelia Garrettson ("Hanson Bible Record," *MGSB* 3 (3) 26-29; Harrison, "St. George's Parish Register:" 332).

Hanson, John, m.[Mariah? Heriah?] Hollinsworth on 2 Dec 1762 ("Hanson Bible Record," *MGSB* 3 (3) 26-29).

Hanson, John, and Susannah Lancaster were the parents of: Somelia Lancaster, b. 7 April 1786 ("John Hanson Bible," *MBR* 2:55).

Hanson, Jonathan, son of Timothy and Barbara of Philadelphia Co. and Mary Price, daughter of Mordecai and Mary were m. on 29 d. 5 m. 1718 (Minutes of West River Meeting, in *QRSM:* 25; BAAD 2:303). Mary m. 2nd, Dr. George Walker (*q.v.*) on 14 Nov 1728 Harrison, "St. Paul's Parish Register:" 149).

Hanson, Jonathan, was charged with bastardy in Nov 1758 (BAMI 1757-1759:162).

Hanson, Mary, was named as a granddaughter of Dr. George Walker in his will dated 5 April 1743 (MWB 23:198 abst. in *Md. Cal. of Wills* 8:224).

Hanson (Handson), Thomas, of Baltimore Co., m. by 4 July 1696 Sarah, daughter of John Ray of Anne Arundel Co. (INAC 13B:105; MWB 14:6 abst. in *Md. Cal. of Wills* 4:22). She m. 2nd, Joshua Cockey (q.v.), and 3rd, Benjamin Tayman (*q.v.*).

Hanson, Thomas, m, by 6 Jan 1738 Sarah, daughter of John Spicer (MWB 22:144 abst. in *Md. Cal. of Wills* 8:67).

Harden, Elizabeth, was charged with bastardy at the June 1739 Court (BACP HWS#TR: 401).

Harden, Sarah, described one time as a servant to George Rigdon, Sr., and another time as a convict, was charged with bastardy in March Court 1738/9, Nov 1739, Nov 1745 (she confessed and was ordered to be whipped 10 times), and again In June 1750 (and was fined on 7 Aug 1750 (BACP HWS#1A:351, HWS#TR:86, Liber 1743-1745: 747, TB&TR:6, TR#5:175).

Harden, John Barton, and Ann Hughes were m. by lic. on 25 Feb 1794 at St. Peter's Catholic Church, Baltimore (*Piet:* 135).

Harden, [Severell?], and Elizabeth Price, on 11 Nov 1766 were summoned to appear before the vestry of St. George's Parish for unlawful cohabitation (Reamy. *St. George's Parish Register:* 110).

Hardesty (Hargisty), Joshua, and Kezia Taylor were m. on 6 Oct 1746 (Harrison, "St. John's Parish Register:" 196, 240). Kezia was the extx of John Taylor (*q.v.*) (MDTP 32:133; BAAD 4:176; MDAD 24:221, 26:2, 29:135, 28:49; BALR TR#C:250).

Hardesty, Lemuel, convict, in May 1755 was fined for begetting a bastard on the body of Sarah Thorn (BACP BB#B:22, 403-404).

Harding, Elias, and Cassandra Ford were married by license dated 9 Jan 1786 (FRML). On 11 Dec 1790 Cassandra was named as a legatee of John Ford (BAAD 10:240).

Harding, Matthew, and Mary Davis were m. by lic. on 1 Feb 1791 at St. Peter's Catholic Church, Baltimore (*Piet:* 135).

Hare (Harry), Edward, m. by 14 June 1713 Lidia, admx. of Zachariah Brown (INAC 34:9).

Hare, Jacob, m. by 13 Dec 1791 [-?-], who received an equal share of the estate of Christian Shaver (BAAD 10:486).

Hare, Michael, m. by 14 Oct 1796, Catherine Ansell, admx. of Valerius Ansell (BAAD 12:204).

Harecock, (Hancock?), John, in Aug 1724 was charged with begetting a bastard on the body of Ann Martin (BACP IS&TW#3:449).

Hargues, Elizabeth, was summoned by the vestry of St. George's Parish on 25 Feb 1754 for unlawful cohabitation with Abraham Cord. Neither appeared, but in Feb 1736 Cord did appear and promised never to have any society with Elizabeth Hargues nor to admit her to his home or on any premises belonging to him, nor to frequent her company elsewhere (Reamy. *St. George's Parish Register:* 105, 106).

Harks. See also Hacks and Hakes.

Harley. See Hartley.

Harman, John, m. by 4 March 1795 Sarah, widow of Jacob Anders of Baltimore Co (BALR WG#QQ:520).

Harman, William, and Sarah Powell were m. on 24 June 1744 (Harrison, "St. John's Parish Register:" 190). Harman, of Baltimore Co., aged c36, on 1 Sep 1744 leased land for the lifetimes of himself, his wife Sarah, aged c30, and her son Edward Powell, aged c3 (BALR TB#C:587). Sarah was the widow of James Powell (*q.v.*) and daughter of Richard Hewett.

Harmer, Godfrey had m. by 20 June 1662 Mary, daughter of Oliver and of Johanna Spry of Talbot Co., who named her daughter Mary Harmer and grandchildren, Sarah, Eliza, and Mary Harmer (BALR RM#HS:4; MWB 2:349; MDTP 7:51-52, 54). Mary m. 2nd, Dr. John Stansby (q.v.) and 3rd, Richard Adams (q.v.).

Harner, John, m. by 22 April 1797 Christina, daughter of Henry Brothers (BAWB 5:519; BAAD 13:42).

Harney, Joshua, merchant, and Miss Eliza Patrick, both of Baltimore, were m. Fri., 21st inst. by Rev. Willis (*Baltimore Weekly Museum* 30 April 1797). Cf. to Joshua Harvey below.

Harp, Elizabeth, was charged with bastardy at the Nov 1723 Court (BACP IS&TW#3:75).

Harriman. See Harryman.

Harrington, Cornelius, m. by 22 Nov 1708 Rebecca, admx. of Evan Miles (MDTP 21:72; MDTP 21:281).

Harriott (Harwood), Oliver, m. by 1 April 1708 Anne, widow of James Greer (*q.v.*), and admx. of Laurence Richardson (*q.v.*) (MDTP 21:6; INAC 32A: 24; BAAD 2:2).

Harriott (Harrot), William, in 1763 was fined for fornication and bastardy, and convicted of bastardy (BAMI 1755-1763).

Harris, [-?-], d. by 25 June 1754 having m. Mary Ann, mother of William Johnson (BALR B#N:267). He m. by Dec 1755 Mary Ann, widow of Philip Johnston (BALR WG#G:206).

Harris, Ann, living at the house of Timothy Keen, was charged with bastardy at the March 1724/5 Court (BACP IS&TW#4:127).

Harris, David, and Miss Crockett, both of this own, were m. [date not given] (*Maryland Journal and Baltimore Advertiser* 19 Sep 1780).

Harris, David, merchant, m. last Wed. eve. Mrs. Frances Moale, relict of Richard Moale of Baltimore (*Maryland Gazette or Baltimore General Advertiser* 29 Jan 1788).

Harris, George, and Susanna Rogers declared their intention to marry ("Minutes of Gunpowder Meeting," *QRNM*:87).

Harris, James, m. by 2 Nov 1718 Bathsheba, daughter of James Barlow (BAAD 2:311).

Harris, Katherine, servant of Ludwick Enloes, was charged with bastardy at the Dec 1691 Court, having borne three baseborn children to Dennis Bryant (BACP F#1:131).

Harris, Lloyd, and Eleanor Rogers, widow of Nicholas Rogers (*q.v.*), were m. on 4 July 1721 (Harrison, "St. Paul's Parish Register:" 148). They were m. on 4 July 1721 by Rev. William Tibbs, Rector of St. Paul's; their son, James Lloyd Harris, was born 17 July 1724, being delivered by Mary Ann Harris (Depositions of Rachel Wilmot, age c47, Mrs. Elizabeth Carter, aged c40, and Mary Ann Harris, age c50, recorded in BALR IS#L:92). Elinor was the widow and extx. of Nicholas Rogers (*q.v.*) and the step-daughter and extx. of Jabez Peirpoint (MDTP 27:49; MDAD 6:218; BAAD 3:1, 9).

Harris, Matthew, m. by 11 Oct 1745 Elizabeth, sister of Thomas Francis Roberts (BALR TB#D:374).

Harris, Nathan, m. by 15 Oct 1765 [-?-], daughter of Elizabeth Price (MDAD 53:224).

Harris, Samuel, on 27 d. 3 m., 1771, produced a certificate from West River Monthly Meeting, and his father's consent to his marrying Rachel Wilson ("Minutes of Gunpowder Monthly Meeting," *QRNM:*61). They were married at Gunpowder Meeting on 2 d. 4 m. 1771 (Gunpowder Monthly Meeting: microfilm of original records at MdHS:256).

Harris, Samuel, son of Samuel and Margaret, on 5 d. 2 m. 1785 announced his intention to marry Cassandra Gover, daughter of Ephraim and Elizabeth, the former dec. ("Minutes of Deer Creek Meeting," *QRNM:*143).

Harris, Sarah, was charged with bastardy at the Aug 1723 Court and charged again at the Aug 1725 Court, naming John Swynyard as the father of her child (BACP IS&TW#3:436, IS&TW#4:306).

Harris, Susanna, was charged with bastardy and fined at the Aug 1710 Court; Thomas Cromwell said he would pay the fine if she did not (BACP IS#B:164).

Harris, Thomas, m. by 12 July 1726 Anne, admx., of Michael Gormuccon (MDTP 27:31).

Harris, Thomas, m. by 2 Nov 1728 Bathsheba, daughter of James Barlow, Sr., of Baltimore Co. (MDAD 9:98; MWB 17:53).

Harris, Thomas, and Mary Jones appeared in May 1736 and were admonished for unlawfully cohabiting ("St. John's and St. George's Parish Register Vestry Proceedings, " MS. at the MdHS).

Harris, William, and wife Elizabeth on 5 Aug 1684 posted bond to administer the estate of William Croshaw (*q.v.*) (BAAB 1:314). On 8 April 1684, Elizabeth was named as the relict and admx. of Thomas Russell (*q.v.*), and widow of William Croshaw, she had m. 1st, William Hollis (MDTP 13: 110; INAC 7C:330, 8:214; BACP D:240, 385).

Harris, William, m. by 18 Oct 1722 Judith, extx of George Hope (*q.v.*) (BAAD 3:81).

Harris, William, d. by 15 Feb 1782 when his widow Catherine renounced right to administer his estate, and Conrad Hush posted bond to administer Harris' estate (BAAB 5:143).

Harris, William, and Mary Constable, daughter of Thomas Constable, of Baltimore, were m. last Thurs. eve. by Rev. Hagerty (*Edward's Baltimore Daily Advertiser* 15 Nov 1793).

Harrison, [-?-], m. Mary, daughter of Edward Dowse or Douce; she m. 1nd, by 1696 Thomas James (*q.v.*), and 3rd, by Sep 1707 John Hillen (*q.v.*).

Harrison, Daniel, and Miss Nelly Bunker, both of Fell's Point, were m. last eve. (*Federal Intelligencer and Baltimore Daily Gazette* 1 Jan 1795). Rachel Bunker, on behalf of her daughter Eleanor, informed the public that the rumor of the marriage was false (*Federal Intelligencer and Baltimore Daily Gazette* 3 Jan 1795).

Harrison, Daniel, was m. last Thurs. by Rev. Mr. Bend to Miss Illingworth, both of Fell's Point (*Federal Gazette and Baltimore Daily Advertiser* 5 March 1796).

Harrison, Hall Caile, was m. last eve. by Rev. Mr. Ireland, to Miss Eliza Galt, both of this city (*Federal Gazette and Baltimore Daily Advertiser* 18 March 1800).

Harrison, James, m. by 28 Dec 1744 Mary, admx. of Gilbert Crockett (*q.v.*) of Baltimore Co. (MDAD 21:44; BAAD 3:346, which gives his name as John Harrison).

Harrison, Jno., m. by 17 March 1719 Margaret, widow of Daniel Mackintosh (BAAD 1:49).

Harrison, John, and Elizabeth Row were married by banns on 10 Nov 1799 at St. Peter's Catholic Church, Baltimore (*Piet:* 136).

Harrison, Thomas, and Eliza Inloes were m. on 18 March 1783 (Marr. Returns of Rev. William West, Scharf Papers, MS.1999 at MdHS). On 18 Nov 1790 Abraham Inloes called Harrison son-in-law (BAWB 4:510).

Harry, Edward, m. by April 1715 Lydia, admx. of Zachariah Brown (MDTP 22:448).

Harryman (Haynman), Charles, and Elizabeth Raven were m. on 6 Feb 1752 (Harrison, "St. John's Parish Register:" 204). On 28 July 1755 she was named as a legatee of Joseph Ward and on 12 July 1774 as an heir of Isaac Raven (MDAD 38:51; BAAD 7:228).

Harryman, George, and Sarah Raven were m. on 17 Oct 1749 (Harrison, "St. John's Parish Register:" 199). On 5 Sep 1760 Sarah was named as a daughter of Luke Raven who also named a granddaughter Rachel Harryman (MWB 31:162 abst. by Gibb).

Harryman, George, and Ann Wilkinson were m. on 30 March 1725 Harrison, "St. Paul's Parish Register:" 148). On 20 May 1769 Ann was named as a daughter of William Wilkinson of Baltimore Co. (BALR AL#A:356).

Harryman, George, and Rachel Bond were married by license dated 8 Feb 1788 (BAML). On 8 Dec 1792 Rachel was named as a daughter of John Bond (BAWB 5:75; BAAD 11:438, 530).

Harryman, John, and Mary Eaglestone were married by license dated 2 Feb 1785 (BAML). On 15 April 1788 she was named as a daughter of Thomas Eaglestone and a legatee of Abraham Eaglestone (BAAD 9:191).

Harryman, Prudence, was charged with bastardy at the March 1736/7 Court, and named Joseph Ward as the father of her child; she confessed to having another child at the Nov 1739 Court (BACP HWS#1A:90, HWS&TR38). Her daughter Elizabeth was born on 2 Nov 1736 (Reamy, *St. Paul's Parish Register:* 12).

Harryman (Harriman), Rebecca, in 1765 was fined for bastardy (BAMI 1765).

Harryman, Robert, and Elizabeth Simkins were m. on 24 Jan 1733 (Harrison, "St. Paul's Parish Register:" 151). On 14 March 1738 Elizabeth was named as a daughter of John Simkins (MWB 22:39 abst. in *Md. Cal. of Wills* 8:20).

Harryman, Samuel, on 26 Dec 1721 was named as a son-in-law in the will of William Farfer (Farfar) (MWB 17:233 abst. in *Md. Cal. of Wills* 5:105).

Harryman, Samuel, m. by 8 Nov 1742 [-?-], daughter of Elizabeth, widow of Edward Evans (MDTP 31:321).

Harryman, Thomas, m. by 12 Aug 1727, Elizabeth, execs. of John Norton (*q.v.*), whose son, John Norton, recommended the widow as extx. (MDTP 28:73; BAAD 2:281). Thomas and Elizabeth Harryman, execs., on 15 July 1727 posted bond to administer the estate of John Norton (*q.v.*) (BAAB 2:341).

Harryman. See also Haynman.

Hart, [-?-], m. by 4 May 1703 Sarah, dau, of John Scutt of Baltimore Co. (MWB 11:339, abst. in *Md. Cal. of Wills* 3:14). After Hart's death Sarah Scutt Hart m. 2nd, by April 1735, [-?-] Owings (*q.v.*) (*ARMD* 39:308).

Hart, [-?-], m. by 12 March 1773 Sarah Ann, daughter of Solomon Wheeler (BAWB 4:204).

Hart, John, b. 6 March 1720 in Reichinberg, Bohemia, Germany [*sic*], m. 5 Oct 1744 'near Baltimore,' Catherine Greathouse, b. 17 May 1726 in Allegany Co., Md. [*sic*] ("Slemaker," *MGSB* 19 (3) (Summer 1978) 145-146).

Hart, John, stated he would not pay the debts of his wife Sarah who had left his bed and board and gone off with another person (*Federal Gazette and Baltimore Daily Advertiser* 19 April 1797).

Hart, Stephen, d. by 18 Feb 1696 when his widow Katherine had m. John Scutt (*q.v.*) (MDTP 16:214; INAC 14:142; MWB 11:339, abst. in *Md. Cal. of Wills* 3:14). On 26 Feb 1704/5 Katherine Scutt, admx., posted bond to administer the estate of Stephen Hart (*q.v.*) (BAAB 3:122). Katherine m. by 8 June 1716 Richard Owings (MWB 14:230, later m. Henry Knowles (q.v.) (MWB 13:705 abst. in *Md. Cal. of Wills* 4:14).

Harte, Samuel, of Anne Arundel Co., and Catherine Gardner were m. on 16 Aug 1742 (Harrison, "St. Margaret's Parish Register," Anne Arundel Co.: 109). On 26 Aug 1749 Catherine was named as a sister of Elizabeth Gardner and daughter of John Gardner (BALR TR#C:296).

Hartich Jacob, m. Maria Clara Wyants who d. 27 Sep 1791, aged 37 years and some months ("First German Reformed Church," MS. at MdHS: 31).

Hartley (Harley), Thomas, m. by c1756 Urath, daughter of Adam Shipley of Anne Arundel Co., who conv. them 101 a., part of *Adam's Garden* (BALR BB#I:559).

Hartley, Thomas, m. by 21 Feb 1772 [-?-], daughter of Barnet Holtzinger (BAWB 3:214; MINV 111:146).

Hartman, [-?-], m. by 13 Sep 1793 Mary Estridge, daughter of Joseph Rawlins (BAWB 5:151).

Hartman, Paul, merchant of this city, was m. last eve. by Rev. Richards to Mrs. Margaret Pryor, of Annapolis (*Federal Gazette and Baltimore Daily Advertiser* 6 March 1800).

Hartnell, James, and Ann Carty were m. by lic. on 8 Nov 1788 at St. Peter's Catholic Church, Baltimore (*Piet:* 136).

Hartway, Vitus, of Baltimore Town, d. by 28 June 1785 having m. Ann Elizabeth, sister of Charles Barnitz, and aunt of Jacob Barnitz of York Town, Pa. (BAWB 4:191).

Harvey, Joshua, merchant, was m. last eve. by Rev. Mr. Willis, to Miss Eliza Patrick, both of this city (*Federal Gazette and Baltimore Daily Advertiser* 22 April 1797). Cf. to Joshua Harney above.

Harwood, Margaret, servant of John Swynyard, was charged with bastardy at the Aug 1729 Court and again at the Aug 1733 Court (BACP HWS#6:276, HWS#9:71).

Harwood, Thomas, and Margaret Strachan were m. on 16 Jan 1772 (Harrison, "All Hallow's Parish Register," Anne Arundel Co., at MdHS: 153). On 8 June 1774 Margaret was named as a daughter of William and Mary Strachan (BALR AL#L:58).

Harwood, William, in 1762 as fined for bastardy (BAMI 1755-1763).

Hatzhog, George, and Dorothy Teinsnor were m. by lic. on 1 April 1797 at St. Peter's Catholic Church, Baltimore (*Piet:* 136). (BAML gives his name as George Hartong and her name as Dorothy Zeinsor).

Hashan, Josiah, and Lucy David were m. by lic. on 26 May 1791 at St. Peter's Catholic Church, Baltimore (*Piet:* 136; BAML, which gives his name as Jessey Hasen).

Hashman, Henry, of Baltimore Town, painter, and Sally Gloyd, daughter of Col. Daniel Gloyd of Bladensburg, were m. Sun., 7th inst. (*Maryland Journal and Baltimore Advertiser* 19 April 1793).

Haskins, Govert, merchant of this city, was m. 25th ult. to Leah Eccleston of Talbot Co. (*Federal Gazette and Baltimore Daily Advertiser* 7 Oct 1800).

Haslet, Mr. Alexander, and Mrs. Elizabeth High, both of Baltimore, were m. last eve. by Rev. Allison (*Federal Gazette and Baltimore Daily Advertiser* 16 Feb 1798).

Haslewood, Henry, d. by 12 Feb 1680 having m. Elizabeth, relict and extx. of John Collett (*q.v.*) (MDTP 12A:220, 221; INAC 7A: 361). She was also the widow of Miles Gibson (q.v.) and of Richard Edmonds (*q.v.*).

Hassal (Hassell), Reuben, in March 1723, was charged with begetting a bastard on the body of Sarah Bragg (BACP IS&TW#1:201, 330).

Hasselbach, Johannes, m. by 27 Sep 1799 [-?-] Collodin ("First German Reformed Church," MS. at MdHS: 24).

Hastings, [-?-], m. by 16 Feb 1680 Mary, relict and admx. of Thomas Biworth (MDTP 12A:223).

Hastings, John, d. by 2 June 1725 when Edward Evans (*q.v.*) and his wife Rachel administered his estate (BAAD 3:45). Hastings in his will dated 24 Feb 1723 left his entire estate to Rachel Johnson (q.v.) (BAWB 3:254; BAAD 3:34; see also BAAD 3:45; BINV 4:215; MDAD 6:415).

Hastings, Michael, m. by 30 Nov 1688 [-?-], relict of Francis Potee (Petite) (MDTP 14: 121).

Hatch, John, m. by 11 July 1709 Sarah, admx. of Edward Jones (MDTP 21:148; BAAD 1:158; INAC 31:321).

Hatch, John, m. by 9 Oct 1710 [-?-], admx. of Edward Stout (MDTP 21:281).

Hattier, Zenny (son of Edme and Francisca Pleon, native of Burgundy, France), and Magdalen Perdonne (daughter of Usard and Magdalena Boillon, native of Rochelle, France), were m. by lic. on 31 Oct 1794, at St. Peter's Catholic Church, Baltimore (*Piet:* 136). Henry Hattier and Magdalen Perenne were married by license dated 31 Oct 1794 (BAML).

Hatton (Hatten), Chainey, and 'Kez.' Bailey were m. on 31 Dec 1761 (Harrison, "St. John's Parish Register:" 223). On 13 March 1771 Kesiah was named as a daughter of Thomas Bailey (BAWB 3:182; MDAD 67:229).

Hatton (Hatten), John, and Unity Welcher were m. on 16 Nov 1765 (Harrison, "St. John's Parish Register:" 228). Unity Hatton's will dated 21 April 1774 named her daughter Unity Wilshire, her son Benjamin Wilshire, her daughter Nancy League, and her daughter Sarah Hatton (BAWB 3:296).

Hatton, John, m. by 5 Oct 1798 Ann, daughter of John Holland (BALR WG#56:270).

Hatton, Thomas, and Catherine Bailey were m. on 29 Jan 1767 (Harrison, "St. John's Parish Register:" 230). On 13 March 1771 Catherine was named as a daughter of Thomas Bailey (BAWB 3:182).

Hatton, Thomas, and Mary Ward were married by license dated 30 Aug 1784 (BAML).In Oct 1786 Hatton stated he would not pay the debts of his wife Mary (*Maryland Journal and Baltimore Advertiser* 17 Oct 1786). On 12 June 1792 Mary was named as admx. of Edward Ward (BAAD 11:66).

Hawkins, [-?-], m. by 21 March 1749 Mary, sister of Joshua Wood (MWB 26:99 abst. by Gibb).

Hawkins, Catherine, in 1762 paid a criminal fine for fornication and bastardy; she was fined in 1763 (BAMI 1755-1763).

Hawkins, Jane, was charged with bastardy at the Aug 1715 Court (BACN IS#B:624).

Hawkins, John, Jr., and Rebecca Emerson were m. on 23 Dec 1718 (Harrison, "St. George's Parish Register:" 222). She was the widow of John Daniell (or Darnall) or Calvert Co., and James Emson (*q.v.*) and James Cobb (*q.v.*) John Hawkins died leaving a will dated 19 Nov 1732 and proved 8 Aug 1733, naming among others, his wife Rebecca and his son-in-law James Cobb, not yet 21 (MWB 20:750 abst. in *Md. Cal. of Wills* 7:33). On 22 July 1737 Rebecca filed an account of his estate, citing an inventory of £8.6.0, and mentioning the estate one Cobb (MDAD 15:353). She m. 5th, Gregory Farmer (*q.v.*).

Hawkins, John, and Mary Simkins were m. on 12 June 1733 (Harrison, "St. Paul's Parish Register:" 133). On 14 March 1738 Mary was named as a daughter of John Simkins who also named a granddaughter Priscilla Hawkins (MWB 22:39 abst. in *Md. Cal. of Wills* 8:20).

Hawkins, Joseph, m. by 9 Dec 1789 Jane, daughter of Loveless Gorsuch, and heir of Nathan Gorsuch (BAAD 10:88, 250).

Hawkins, Martha, in 1765 was presented for bastardy (BAMI 1765:14).

Hawkins, Matthew, m. by 11 Oct 1745 Elizabeth, sister of Thomas Francis Roberts (BALR TB#D:374).

Hawkins, Nathan, aged upwards of 40, deposed on 7 May 1764 that when he was a small boy he had been shown a boundary by his father-in-law James Boring (BALR B#N:139).

Hawkins, Robert, and Ann Preble were m. on 15 Nov 1701 (Harrison, "St. George's Parish Register:" 217). On 17 Jan 1732 Anne was named as a daughter of Mary

Buchannan, widow of Archibald Buchanan (*q.v.*); Mary Buchannan also named a granddaughter Elizabeth Hawkins (MWB 30:698 abst. in *Md. Cal. of Wills* 7:23).

Hawkins, Robert, and Martha Davice [*sic*] were m. on 23 April 1764 (Harrison, "St. John's Parish Register:" 226). On 20 Nov 1769 Martha was named as a sister of Henry Davis (BAWB 3:149).

Hawkins, Sarah, and Eliza Hawkins, both not yet 16 years of age, on 6 March 1676 were named as daughters in the will of Margaret Therrell (Thurrold) of Back River, Baltimore Co. (MWB 5:347, abst. in *Md. Cal. of Wills* 1:201). Margaret was the widow of Richard Thurrol.

Hawkins, Thomas, and Elizabeth Giles on 25 d. 12 m., 1703/4 and again on 24 d. 1 m., 1703/4 declared their intention to marry ("Register of Cliffs Monthly Meeting," in *QRSM:* 70). On 1 April 1708 they were named as accountants of Jacob Giles (MDTP 21:5). Jacob Giles and Elizabeth Arnold declared their intention to marry on 5 d. 10 m. 1701 and again on 2 d. 11 m. 1701 ("Register of Cliffs MM," in *QRSM:* 69). On 13 May 1707 Elizabeth was named as the admx. of Jacob Giles, whose brother John Giles had lately gone to Eng. (MDTP 19C:186).

Hawkins, Thomas, and Mary Jones, on first Tues. in May 1756 were summoned to appear before the vestry of St. George's Parish for unlawful cohabitation. They were admonished by the vestry to quit their vicious course and were discharged (Reamy, *St. George's Parish Register:* 107).

Hawkins, William, m, by 18 Oct 1722, Judith, extx. of George Hope (*q.v.*) (BAAD 3:81).

Hawkins, William, exec., on 19 Nov 1796 posted bond to administer the estate of Phebe Hutchinson (BAAB 8:950; see also BAWB 5:429).

Hawley, Truman, of Kent co., m. by 29 June 1798 Ann, widow of William Ridgely, and daughter of Samuel Worthington (BALR WG#55:251; BAML).

Hay, John, and Martha Andrews were m. on 2 Sep 1777 ("Register of First German Reformed Church, Baltimore," MS. at MdHS: 69). In April 1784 Martha was named as a daughter of William Andrews (BAOC 1:111).

Hay, John, b. 18 Feb 1764 in Penna., son of Adam Hay, and Barbara Mayer, b. 18 May 1769, daughter of George Mayer, were m. in 1791; their son Samuel was b. 1 Sep 1794 ("Hay Family of Baltimore Bible Record," *MDG* 9 (4) (Oct 1968) 79).

Hayes, Edmond, m. by Nov 1710, Mary Mencham, who, when a minor, had been bound to Nathaniel Ruxton on 6 June 1699 (BACP IS#B:187).

Hayes, Jesse, m. by 7 Sep 1789 Mary, daughter of Robert McAllister (BAAD 10:52).

Hayes, John, m. by 6 Jan 1699 Abigail, widow of Thomas Scudamore (or Skidmore) (*q.v.*), and daughter of John Dixon; by Scudamore, Abigail was the mother of Penelope who m. James Todd (*q.v.*) (BALR TR#RA:418; Hodges cites PCLR EI#10:745).

Hayes, John, in his will dated 9 Jan 1726/7 named his son John Stansbury, and his daughter Elizabeth Lenox (MWB 19:70 abst. in *Md. Cal. of Wills* 6:11).

Hayes (Hays), John, and Grace Crabtree were m. on 31 Oct 1727 (Harrison, "St. George's Parish Register:" 203). She was named as a daughter of William Crabtree (BALR IS#K:20). **See John Hays below.**

Hayes, John, native of Ireland, and Mary Lankston, native of Canada, were m. by lic. on 20 July 1796 at St. Peter's Catholic Church, Baltimore (*Piet:* 136). (BAML gives her name as Mary Langston).

Hayes, Mary, admx., on 9 June 1717 posted bond to administer the estate of Philip Johnson. John Hayes was one of the sureties (BAAB 3:367).

Hayes, Walter C., and Maria Barbara Wonder were m. by lic. on 20 Nov 1800 at St. Peter's Catholic Church, Baltimore (*Piet:* 136).

Hayes, Dr. William, of the Point, and Miss Polly Stocket were m. [date not given] (*Maryland Gazette or Baltimore General Advertiser* 11 Oct 1791).

Hayes, William, and Mrs. Anne Goulding, all of Baltimore, were m. last eve. by Rev. Hargrove (*Federal Gazette and Baltimore Daily Advertiser* 15 Jan 1800).

Hayes. See also Hays.

Hayhurst, David, on 26 d. 5 m. 1787 was charged with marrying contrary to the good order ("Minutes of Gunpowder Meeting," *QRNM:*84). [No other marriage reference found].

Hayhurst, James, son of James and Ann of Gunpowder Meeting, on 31 d. 8 m. 1780 announced his intention to marry Mary Warner, daughter of Benjamin and Sarah Warner of Deer Creek Meeting ("Minutes of Deer Creek Meeting," *QRNM:*140).

Hayhurst, Ruth, (now Hanaway) on 23 d. 2 m. 1782, was reported to hath gone out in marriage ("Minutes of Gunpowder Meeting," *QRNM:*75-76). [No other marriage reference found].

Hayhurst, Sarah, now Newborough, on 29 d. 12 m. 1781was reported as having gone out in marriage ("Minutes of Gunpowder Meeting," *QRNM:*75). [No other marriage reference found].

Hayly, Thomas, and Catherine Nawlan were married by banns on 21 Sep 1786 at St. Peter's Catholic Church, Baltimore (*Piet:* 136).

Haynman, Charles, m, by 28 July 1755 [-?-], legatee of Joseph Ward (MDAD 38:51).

Hays, John, and Mary Crabtree were m. on 31 Oct 1727 (Harrison, "St. George's Parish Register:" 253). She was a daughter of William Crabtree of Baltimore Co. (BALR IS#K:20). **See John Hayes above.**

Hays, Joseph, d. by April 1793; his children John and Ellit chose Sarah Hays as their guardian; his children William and Samuel were under 14, and were made wards of Sarah Hays (BAOC 3:42).

Hays, Thomas, and Mary Norrington were m. on11 Aug 1735 (Harrison, "St. John's Parish Register:" 149). On 29 Dec 1739 she was named as a daughter of John Norrington, Sr. (BALR HWS#1A: 323).

Hays. See also Hayes.

Hayward, Joseph, and Rebecca Scott, daughter of Joseph and Hannah, were m. on 9 d. 6 m. 1757 ("Records of Gunpowder Meeting," at MdSA). On 13 d. 11 m. 1766 she was named as a daughter of Jacob [*sic*] Scott (BAWB 3:77).

Hayward, William, b. 29 March 1707, and Mary Chaney, b. 28 July 1708, were m. by 26 May 1733, when their son Joseph was b. ("Hayward Family," *HMGB* 2 (4) (Oct 1931) 28).

Hayward, William, son of Joseph Hayward, dec., and wife Rebecca, on 25 d. 3 m. 1790 announced his intention to marry Mary Husband, daughter of Joseph (dec.) and wife Mary ("Minutes of Deer Creek Meeting," *QRNM:*148).

Hayward, William, and Keziah Coates on 30 d. 4 m. 1791 declared their intention to marry ("Minutes of Gunpowder Meeting," *QRNM:*90).

Head, Bigger, of Calvert Co., m. by 22 Jan 1735 Martha, daughter of Edward Butler of Calvert Co., dec. (BALR TB#E:1).

Headington, [-?-], may have m. by 30 May 1786 Eleanor, daughter of Alexis Lemmon, Sr., who named Eleanor's two children Laban and Ruth (BAWB 4:151).

Headington, Abel, m. by 29 Nov 1794 Mary, daughter of George Harryman (BAWB 5:236; BAAD 12:183; BOCP Petition of George Harryman, 1799).

Headington, William, m. by 22 March 1790 [-?-], daughter of William Bosley (BAAD 10:116).

Headington. See also Heddinton.

Heally, Dennis, and Mary Holland were married by banns on 3 Nov 1793 at St. Peter's Catholic Church, Baltimore (*Piet:* 136).

Heard, John, comedian, and Mrs. Margaret Shields, were m. last Sat. eve. (*Maryland Journal and Baltimore Advertiser* 10 Dec 1782). John Herd and Mary [sic] Shields were married by license dated 6 Dec 1782 (BAML). Mrs. Margaret Heard, consort of John Heard of Baltimore, d. last Wed., in her 20th year (*Maryland Journal and Baltimore Advertiser* 12 Oct 1784).

Hearn, Anthony, native of Ireland, and Sarah Jenkins were m. by lic. on 18 Nov 1794 at St. Peter's Catholic Church, Baltimore (*Piet:* 136). She was a daughter of Michael Jenkins (BAWB 6:253).

Heath, James, of Cecil Co., and Susanna, daughter of John Hall of Swan Town, [prob. Baltimore Co.], were married 25 Oct 1759 (Annapolis *Md. Gaz.* 1 Nov 1759; BAWB 3:89).

Heath, James, in his will, made 23 Nov 1766 named his uncle Daniel Dulany's son Benjamin and his uncle Walter Dulany's son Daniel (BAWB 3:32).

Heath, John, in May 1795 was made a ward of Samuel Heath (BAOC 3:154).

Heathcote, Joseph, m. Martha, a daughter and extx. of Thomas Morgan of Baltimore Co. (MWB 7:392; MDTP 17:69). She m. 2nd, Nicholas Fitzsimmons (q.v.).

Hebert, John Baptist, of the Parish of Iberville, Mississippi, in his will, made 15 July 1785 named his uncle Joseph Marie Boudiot, and his uncle Peter Hebert or Hubert; he mentioned his estate in the Parish of Hiberville (BAWB 4:95).

Heddinton, Hannah, formerly Moore, on 28 d. 9 m. 1793 was condemned for being married by a hireling minister ("Minutes of Gunpowder Meeting," *QRNM*: 94). [No other marriage reference found].

Heddinton. See also Headington.

Hedge, Henry, and m. Mary Parker, were m. when the banns were pub. on Whitsunday, 1700 (Harrison, "St. George's Parish Register:" 191). She m. 2nd, John Smith (*q.v.*).

Hedge, Thomas, Clerk of Baltimore Co., was m. by Lt.-Col. Thomas Richardson some time before 30 Sep 1696 to [-?-] [-?-], when Richardson was charged by the Council of Maryland for marrying Hedge who is alleged to have had a wife living in England; the case was referred to the Attorney General, but Hedge died by July 1698, and no other action was taken (*ARMD* 20:507, 508).

Heer, Christoph, m, by 12 March 1787 Elisabetha Kehlbachin ("First Record Book for the Reformed and Lutheran Congregations at Manchester, Baltimore (Now Carroll) Co." *MGSB* 35:283).

Heide, George, merchant, and Rachel Griffith, daughter of Mr. Nathan Griffith, both of Baltimore, were m. last Wed. eve. (*Baltimore Daily Repository* 4 May 1792).

Heighe, Samuel, and wife Sarah, execs. on 15 March 1724 posted bond to administer the estate of John Israel (*q.v.*) (BAAB 3:373; MDAD 7:364, 10:299; BALR IS#J:29).

Heighoe, Philip, d. by 25 Jan 1787 leaving minor child Philip; Samuel Messersmith, guardian, filed an account (BAGA 1:9).

Heimel, Jacob, and Catherine Fisher were m. by lic. on 21 May 1798 at St. Peter's Catholic Church, Baltimore (*Piet:* 136). (BAML gives his name as Jacob Hamlin).

Heinike, Dr. F., and Miss Schroeder both of this town were m. last Fri. (*Federal Intelligencer and Baltimore Daily Gazette* 24 Nov 1794).

Heinisler, [-?-], m. by 11 Oct 1791 Mary, extx, of Charles Bernard (*q.v.*) (BAAD 9:269, 10:447).

Hellen, [-?-], m. by 10 Dec 1770 Susanna, sister of David and Thomas Aisquith (BAAD 6:187; BFD 6:33).

Hellen (Hellem[?]), David, m. by 3 June 1795 Lois[?] Upperco, daughter of Jacob Upperco (BAAD 12:12).

Helm, Maybery, m. by 8 May 1739 Ann, daughter of Edward Parish of Anne Arundel Co., dec. (MDTP 31:21). Helm d. by 8 March 1776, having m. by 28 July 1747, Ann, widow of William Pontenay (Puntany), and mother of Edward and William Puntany and grandmother of Edward and Ann Puntany, children of her son William (PCLR EI#8:333; BAWB 3:324). The will of Ann Helms, dated 8 March 1776 also named her daughter Mary Marlanell, wife of John Marlanell (*q.v.*) (MWB 41:23; abst. in Md. Cal. of Wills 16:141).

Helm, Mayberry, stated his claim to *Parrish's Fear,* which Edward Parrish devised to his daughter Ann Parrish, who was mother of the said Mayberry Helm, and who had deeded 113 a. of the land to Edward Puntenay for the latter's lifetime. After Puntany's death the land was to descend to Helm (*Maryland Gazette or Baltimore General Advertiser* 11 Jan 1791).

Helms, John, in 1762 was convicted of bastardy (BAMI 1755-1763).

Helms (Helm), Leonard, and Mary Horsman were m. by lic. dated 17 June 1791 (BAML). Mary Helms, (formerly Houstman), on 27 d. 8 m. 1791, was reported to have gone out in marriage ("Minutes of Gunpowder Meeting," *QRNM:*91). In his will dated 13 Nov 1792 Helm mentioned John Horseman as his wife's brother (BAWB 5:139).

Hemstead, Nicholas, m. by 2 Sep 1679 Elizabeth [-?-], grandmother of Enoch Spinks (BALR HW#2:159).

Henderson, Gilbert, m. on 8 Oct 1782 Esther (Hester) Dyer (Marr. Ret. of Rev. William West, Scharf Papers, MS.1999 at MdHS). Hester Henderson, (formerly Dyer), on 25 d. 1 m. 1783 was reported as having been m. by a priest to one not of our Society ("Minutes of Gunpowder Meeting," *QRNM:*70).

Henderson, Robert, and Elizabeth, admx. of Joseph Beaumont (*q.v.*), were m. by 20 Feb 1775 (MDTP 46:22).

Hendon, [-?-], m. by 3 Dec 1745 Hannah, daughter of William Robinson (BALR TB#D: 428).

Hendon, James, and Hannah Norris were m. on 7 Feb 1754 (Harrison, "St. John's Parish Register:" 209). Hannah, was named as a daughter of Benjamin and Sarah Norris, wife of Benjamin Norris, and as a sister of Joseph Norris (MWB 38:591, abst. in *Md. Cal. of Wills* 14:211; MWB 40:576; abst. in *Md. Cal. of Wills* 16:105; BAWB 3:229).

Hendon, Joseph, and Mary Crudgents were m. on 31 July 1753 (Harrison, "St. John's Parish Register:" 208). In his will made 31 Jan 1760 Hendon named his wife Mary his extx (MWB 30:836). Mary m. 2nd, by 2 May 1761 William Lynch (*q.v.*) (BAAD 4:346; MDTP 38: 101).

Hendon, Josias, father of William Hendon, in Aug 1726 was named as son-in-law in a deed from James and Elizabeth Isham (BALR IS#H:261)

Hendon, Sarah, in 1761 was convicted of bastardy (BAMI 1755-1763).

Hendrickson, Esram, d. by 24 May 1775 when his admx. Martha was m. to Jesse Bevan (*q.v.*) (MINV 121:354, 359).

Hendrickson, John, and Ruth Sing were m. on 16 Oct 1748 (Harrison, "St. John's Parish Register:" 197). On 3 March 1749 they petitioned the Prerogative Court to be granted letters of administration on the estate of Joseph Thomas (*q.v.*) (MDTP 33-1:87).

Hendrickson, John, m. by 16 April 1768 [-?-], daughter of William Wood, when she was paid her share of her father's estate, in the administration account of John Cotrall (*q.v.*) (MDAD 59:300)' he d. by 8 Jan 1786, leaving minor child; John; William Wood was appointed guardian (BAGA 1:1, 37). On 11 Jan 1787 his minor daughter Eleanor was made a ward of John Waller (BAGA 1:5).

Hendrickson, Joseph, merchant, was m. last eve. to Miss Susannah Cochran, both of this town (*Federal Gazette and Baltimore Daily Advertiser* 16 Dec 1796).

Hendrix, Absolom, stated he would not pay the debts of his wife Eleanor who had eloped from his bed and board (*Maryland Journal and Baltimore Advertiser* 2 Jan 1795).

Hendrix, Isaac, of York Co., Pa., m. by 19 Dec 1769 Jean, widow of Thomas Shea (BALR AL#A:610).

Henlen, Peter, and Sarah Collins, on 16 March 1767 were summoned to appear before the vestry of St. George's Parish for unlawful cohabitation. They appeared on 20 April 1767 and were discharged with the proviso they would never cohabit together anymore (Reamy, *St. George's Parish Register:* p. 110.).

Henninger, Jacob, of Baltimore, gave notice his wife Catherine had eloped (*Maryland Journal and Baltimore Advertiser* 11 July 1783).

Hennion, Joseph, and Margaret Hione were m. on 29 April 1787 at St. Peter's Catholic Church, Baltimore (*Piet:* 136).

Henrichs, Johann, m. by 10 Nov 1759, Catharina Ketzin ("First Record Book for the Reformed and Lutheran Congregations at Manchester, Baltimore (Now Carroll) Co." *MGSB* 35:266).

Henry, [-?-], m. by 9 Aug 1768, Margaret, daughter of James Dickson (Dixon) (BAWB 3:118).

Henry, [-?-], m. by 3 Sep 1781 Sophia, sister of Gotlip Shearmiller, butcher (BAWB 3:427).

Henry, Aaron, and Minty Butler, both Negroes, were married by banns on 23 Dec 1800 at St. Peter's Catholic Church, Baltimore (*Piet:* 136).

Henry, David, on 12 Sep 1769 was named as a cousin in the will of Joseph Smith, ironmaster (BAWB 3:168).

Henry, John, and Mary Copeland were m. on 10 Feb 1757 (Harrison, "St. John's Parish Register:" 214). Mary Henry d. by 21 Nov 1773, leaving a will naming sons George and John Copeland (BAWB 3:239).

Henry, John, on 24 Nov 1763 was named as a brother-in-law of Guy Little (MWB 32:98 abst. in *Md. Cal. of Wills* 13:16).

Henry, Thomas, and Monica Carter, both Negroes, were m. by banns on 24 Nov 1800 at St. Peter's Catholic Church, Baltimore (*Piet:* 136).

Henry, William, and Nancy Dugan, natives of Ireland, were m. by lic. on 21 Jan 1796, at St. Peter's Catholic Church, Baltimore (*Piet:* 136).

Hepburn, [-?-], m. by 2 Jan 1793 Elizabeth, daughter of William Fox of Princess Anne Co., Va. (BACT 1791-1794, MS 2865.1 at MdHS: 144).

Hepple, Lawrence, m. by 28 July 1764 Mary, daughter of Anna Mary Ash (BAWB 3:41).

Herbert, William, m. by 9 May 1796 Ann, daughter of John Naylor (BAWB 5:451).

Herman, Philip, and Elizabeth Hook were m. by lic. on 20 Oct 1788 at St. Peter's Catholic Church, Baltimore (*Piet:* 136).

Hern, Eleanor, in 1772 was fined for bastardy (BAMI 1772, 1775-1781:86).

Herner [Haines?]. John, and wife Christian, on 22 Sep 1798 received part of the estate of Henry Brother (BAAD 12:496, 13:42).

Herring, Robert, and Susan Lively were m. yesterday eve. by Rev. Mr. Kurtz (*Baltimore Daily Intelligencer* 5 Sep 1794).

Herringstraw[?], Peter, an orphan, was maintained by William Hughes (Levy List for 1739, Black Books III, 8),.

Herrington, Cornelius, m. by 25 April 1701 Rachel, daughter of Thomas Jones (BALR HW#2:105).

Herrington, Laban, in 1762 was convicted of bastardy (BAMI 1755-1763).

Herrington, Sarah, was charged with bastardy at the June 1734 Court and was presented at the Nov 1734 Court, naming Thomas Little as the father of the child (BACP HWS#9:253, 365, TB#D:186). Sarah's known children were Hannah Herrington, b. 17 Oct 1735, and Sarah Herrington, b. 15 April 1739 (Reamy. *St. George's Parish Register:* 48, 64).

Herrinshaw, Ruth, was charged with bastardy at the Nov 1733 Court and presented in March 1733/4. She may have been the mother of Peter 'Herringstrew,' an orphan, for whom William Hughes was paid £2 by the county for maintaining (BACP HWS#9:124, 198; Baltimore Co. Levy List for 1739).

Hersey (Hershey), Isaac, of New Castle Co., Pa. m. by 28 Aug 1765 Henrietta Holland, legatee of Frances Middlemore (BALR B#O:418).

Hershey. See Hersey.

Herstons, Charles, merchant, Poplar Springs, was m. last eve. by Rev. Mr. Richards to Miss Delilah Sprigg, daughter of Capt. Sprigg (*Federal Gazette and Baltimore Daily Advertiser* 6 Nov 1797).

Herther, Nathan, and Catherine Diffendolph were m. by lic. on 5 Sep 1792 at St. Peter's Catholic Church, Baltimore (*Piet:* 136).

Hertzog, Michael, and Margaret Butcher were married by banns on 27 April 1795 at St. Peter's Catholic Church, Baltimore (*Piet:* 136). Michael Hertzog stated he would not pay the debts contracted by his wife Margaret (*Federal Intelligencer and Baltimore Daily Gazette* 14 Nov 1795).

Hesson. See Hisson.

Hettinger, Michael, m. by 8 Feb 1794 Barbara, widow of David Muma (BALR WG#OO:42).

Heugh, Samuel, and wife Mary, administered the estate of John Israel (*q.v.*) on 18 April 1726 (BAAD 3:40).

Heuisler, Maximilian, and Mary Bernard were m. by lic. on 31 Aug 1792 at St. Peter's Catholic Church, Baltimore (*Piet:* 136). (BAML gives his name as Maximilian Heuiler).

Hewes, James, and Eleanor Green were m. by lic. on 19 Jan 1789 at St. Peter's Catholic Church, Baltimore (*Piet:* 136).

Hewet (Hewett, Huett), Richard, and Elizabeth Fraser were m. on 28 July 1722 (Harrison, "St. Ann's Parish Register," Anne Arundel Co., at MdHS: 419). In his will dated 3 Nov 1729 Hewett named his son-in-law John Frazer and his daughter-in-law Elizabeth Frazer (MWB 19:904 abst. in *Md. Cal. of Wills* 6:149). Elizabeth m. 3rd, Benjamin Price (*q.v.*). Charles Ridgely, exec., admin. Hewet's estate on 17 Feb 1737 and listed the widow Elizabeth, now wife of [-?-] Price, and also Eleanor, daughter of James Powell [who had m. Hewet's daughter Eleanor] (BAAD 3:250). Elizabeth Fraser Hewet m. 2nd, Charles Ridgely (*q.v.*).

Hewett, [-?-], m. by Nov 1721, Mary, daughter of Thomas Williamson (BACP IS#C:626).

Hewie, Caleb, and Miss Sarah Wilkinson, both of Baltimore, were m. yesterday evening by Rev. Mr. Lynch (*Baltimore Daily Intelligencer* 16 May 1794).

Hewit, Caleb, and Polly Moreton, both of Baltimore, were m. on Sat. (*Baltimore American* 27 Aug 1799).

Hewitt, Hannah, in 1765 was fined for bastardy (BAMI 1765).

Hewlett, John Jacob, aged 10 on 7 July 1772, son of William Hewlett, in Nov 1772 was bound to Benjamin Arnold, weaver (BAMI 1772, 1775-1781: 29)

Hewling, Jonas, dec., m. by 12 July 1726 Ann, mother of Patrick Lynch (BALR HWS#M:147).\

Heyden, James, and Miss Elizabeth Nussear, daughter of Jacob Nussear, Jr., both of this city, was m. last eve. by Rev. Bishop Carroll (*Federal Gazette and Baltimore Daily Advertiser* 21 Dec 1798). They were m. at St. Peter's Catholic Church, Baltimore (*Piet:* 136; BAML gives their names as James Hayden and Elizabeth Nussen).

Heyser, Jacob, of Baltimore, and Miss Kitty Otto of this county, were m. last Tues. by Rev. Rahauser (Elizabeth Town *Washington Spy* 17 Jan 1794).

Hick, Jonas, m. by 28 July 1764 Susanna, daughter of Anna Mary Ash who named her grandchildren Peter and Esther Hick (BAWB 3:41).

Hickley, [-?-], d. by 20 July 1799 leaving a widow Sarah whose will of that date named 'the surviving children of her late husband:' Mary Ann. Robert, and Thomas James Hickley, and her own sister Ann, wife of George Caldwell (*q.v.*) (BAWB 6:216).

Hickman, [-?-], m. by 18 May 1789 Elizabeth, sister of Abram Mumma, farmer (BAWB 4:367); on 20 Aug 1788 Elizabeth was named as a daughter of David Mumma (BAWB 5:17).

Hickman, Lawrence, d. by Dec 1797 when his orphans Anna, John, Jacob, and Joseph were made wards of David Hickman (BAOC 3:239).

Hickman, Susanna, was charged with bastardy at the Aug 1709 Court (BACP IS#B:50).

Hicks, [-?-], m. by Jan 1794 Ann, daughter of John Sheppard (BAWB 6:281).

Hicks, Abraham, and Sarah Gorsuch were married by license dated 12 March 1781 (BAML). On 25 Jan 1794 Sarah was named as an heir of Charles Gorsuch (BAAD 11:368).

Hicks, George, cordwainer, and Miss Sally Matthews, all of Baltimore, were m. last eve, by Rev. Dunkin (*Baltimore Telegraphe* 21 Oct 1799).

Hicks, James, d. by 25 April 1732 having m. Margaret, mother of William Standifer (MDTP 29:175).

Hicks, Mary, in 1762 paid a criminal fine for fornication and bastardy (BAMI 1755-1763).

Hicks, Nehemiah, and Phillisanna Hitchcock were m. on 12 June 1725 (Harrison, "St. John's Parish Register:" 72). On 6 March 1727 Philizana was named as a daughter of William Hitchcock (BALR IS#I:57, IS#L:410; MWB 22:27 abst. in *Md. Cal. of Wills* 8:145).

Hicks, Nehemiah, m by 17 Oct 1774 Elizabeth, daughter of Charles Robinson (BALR AL#L:298).

Hicks, Tamor, warned all persons from having any dealing with her children (*Federal Intelligencer and Baltimore Daily Gazette* 10 Oct 1795).

Hide, Ann, was named as a granddaughter in the undated will, proved 27 July 1691, of Joseph Simmons (MWB 7:133 abst. in *Md. Cal. of Wills* 2:98).

Higenbotham, Ralph, Jr., and Miss Isabella Presbury, niece of George G. Presbury, were m. last Thurs. by Rev. John Allen (*Federal Gazette and Baltimore Daily Advertiser* 2 March 1799).

Higgenbotham, Arthur, and Eleanor Willson were m. by lic. on 13 Aug 1792 at St. Peter's Catholic Church, Baltimore (*Piet:* 136; BAML, which gives his name as Arthur Higginbottom).

Higginbottom, [-?-], m. by 6 Oct 1753, Mary, dau. of John Serjeant, dec. (BACT TR#E: 178).

Higinbothom, Thomas, and Susanna Blundell, both of Baltimore, were m. last eve. by Rev. Bend (*Baltimore Telegraphe* 22 Jan 1800).

High, Sebastian, and Catherine White were m. by lic. on 4 Aug 1796 at St. Peter's Catholic Church, Baltimore (*Piet:* 136).

Highjoe, Philip, m. by 5 June 1789, Mary, daughter of Michael Steitz (BAWB 4:364).

Hildebrand, Jacob, m. by 1 March 1788 Maria Stoffelin ("First Record Book for the Reformed and Lutheran Congregations at Manchester, Baltimore (Now Carroll) Co." *MGSB* 35:283).

Hildebrandt, Jacob, m. by 25 May 1791 [-?-], heir of Henry Hennestophel (BAAD 10:375). As Jacob Hiltebrent [*sic*] he m. by 18 Jan 1793, Ann Mary, daughter of Henry Henninstofel who d. intestate (BALR WG#LL: 44).

Hill, Alexander, and Elioner Durbin were m. on 10 May 1744 (Harrison, "St. John's Parish Register:" 190). On 30 July 1745 Eleanor was named as the widow of John Durbin (*q.v.*) (MDTP 31:594). Alexander d. by 29 Jan 1756, leaving his widow Eleanor and a son John Hill, formerly of Baltimore Co., but now of Fawn Twp., York Co., Pa.; Eleanor m. 3rd, [-?-] Bennett (*q.v.*), who was also dec. by 29 Jan 1756 (BALR BB#I:521).

Hill, Caroline, servant of Owen Allen, in Nov 1772 was ordered to serve her master one year and six mos. for expenses for her bastardy; she was later fined (BAMI 1772, 1775-1781:42, 84).

Hill, Eleanor, was charged with bastardy at the March 1739/40 Court and presented at the June 1740 Court and again at the Aug 1740 Court (BACP HWS#TR:140, 247, 299).

Hill, George, d. by 16 March 1799 when his estate was administered by George Sears. Mary Pierce, mother and heir at law of the deceased was paid £201.15.3 (BAAD 13:7).

Hill, James, on 13 d. 2 m. 1800, had a complaint that he had his marriage accomplished by a hireling teacher ("Minutes of Baltimore Meeting," *QRNM:*236). [No other marriage reference found].

Hill, John, m. by 6 Sep 1766, Sarah, sister of Thomas Radish or Reddich, mariner, late of London, but now of Baltimore Co. (BAWB 3:36).

Hill, Joseph, m. by 31 Aug 1772 [-?-], who was paid her portion of the estate of Thomas Bailey (MDAD 67:229).

Hill, Joseph, m. by 7 April 1774 Ruth, widow and admx. of Henry Fitch (*q.v.*) (BAAD 7:275, 300).

Hill, Milcah, mulatto servant of Capt. Walter Tolley, in Aug 1762 admitted she was mother of a baseborn child by a Negro. The child was named Priscilla and was sold to Capt. Walter Tolley until she reached the age 31 (BAMI 1755-1763).

Hill, Nathaniel, m. by 26 Oct 1760 Mary, admx. of John Gregory (*q.v.*) (MINV 70:176; BAAD 4:360; BAMI 1765: 50; MDTP 38:80). John Gregory had m. Mary Parlat on 27 July 1746 (Harrison, "St. Paul's Parish Register:" 159).

Hill, Richard, and Ann Willis, both of Baltimore, were m. last eve. by Rev. Bend (*Baltimore Telegraphe* 27 June 1800).

Hill, Sarah, in March 1768 was found guilty of bastardy (BAMI 1768-1769:12).

Hill, William, d. by 25 Sep 1787 by which time his extx. Mary had m. Benjamin Lego (*q.v.*) (BAAD 2:169; INAC 27:211).

Hill, William, and Martha Green were m. in Sep 1724 (Harrison, "St. John's Parish Register:" 29). On 8 Ma0rch 1732 Martha was named as a daughter and coheir of Matthew Green, and granddaughter of Jane Boone (BALR IS#L:326).

Hillen, [-?-], m. by 29 Nov 1769 Martha, daughter of Thomas Wheeler (BAWB 3:171).

Hillen (Hilton), John, m. by 25 Sep 1707 Mary, admx. of Thomas James (INAC 27:210; BACP IS#B:18).She was a daughter of Edward Dowsc. In his will dated 19 March 1726 Hillen named his wife Mary. his brother-in-law Thomas Hines, and his three sons-in-law Walter, William, and Watkins James (MWB 19:179 abst. in *Md. Cal. of Wills* 6:27). She m. 1st, [-?-] Harrison (*q.v.*), and 2nd, Thomas James (*q.v.*).

Hillen, John, and Catherine Rusk were m. by lic. on 23 Nov 1784 at St. Peter's Catholic Church, Baltimore (*Piet:* 1360.

Hillen, Solomon, and Elizabeth Raven were m. on 7 Oct 1729 (Harrison, "St. Paul's Parish Register:" 149). On 21 April 1741 Elizabeth was named as a sister of Luke Raven (BALR HWS#1-A:490). Hillen d. by 21 Dec 1738 when his admx. had m. 2nd, Thomas Wheeler (*q.v.*).

Hillen, Thomas, of Baltimore Co., and Robinie Kennedy McHaffie, of Frederick Co., were married by lic. on 14 Dec 1794 at St. Peter's Catholic Church, Baltimore (*Piet:* 136; BAML, which gives his name as Thomas Hilton).

Hilliard, Mary, servant of John Townsen, was charged with bastardy at the March 1729/30 Court (BACP HWS#7:96).

Hilliard, Sarah, was charged with bastardy at the June 1733 Court (BACP HWS#9:15).

Hilman, John, m, by 23 Aug 1794 [-?-], who received an equal share of the estate of Jacob Sindall (BAAD 11:464).

Hilton, Joseph, m. by 7 Oct 1793 Mary Frost, admx. of Joseph Frost (*q.v.*) (BAAD 11:328).

Hilton, Mary, was charged with bastardy at the March 1719/20 Court (BACP IS#C:245).

Hilton, William, m. by 4 Aug 1787 [-?-], daughter of James Greenfield (BAAD 9:102).

Hilton. See also Hillen above.

Hiner, Nicholas, stated his wife Mary had been unruly while he was in the army, and he would not pay her debts (*Maryland Journal and Baltimore Advertiser* 9 March 1784). Nicholas Hiner (Hyner) advertised again that he would not pay the debts of his wife Mary, who had left his bed and board in 1783 and lived with Patrick Kelly until 1788 when Kelly died (*Maryland Gazette or Baltimore General Advertiser* 6 June 1788).

Hines, Elizabeth, widow of Thomas Hines, in her will made 4 Jan 1756 named her cousins James and Nathan Nicholson (MWB 30:28, abst. by Gibb).

Hines (Hynes), Francis, m. by 3 Oct 1739 Frances, daughter and heir of John Roberts, who also left daus. Ann and Lucina Roberts (BALR HWS#IA:285).

Hines, Thomas, d. by Aug 1757 when his orphan son, Thomas Horner [?], aged 9 last 1 June, in Aug 1757 was bound to Thomas Potts (BAMI 1755-1763).

Hinslow, Thomas, m. by 17 Sep 1793 Dorothy, sister of William West (BAWB 5:309).

Hinton, John, orphan boy, aged 14 next 6 March, in Sep 1795 was bound to Richard Pearce, merchant (BAOC 3:166).

Hinton, Samuel, m. Elizabeth [-?-], widow of 1st, Richard Sampson (*q.v.*), and 2nd, James Bagford (*q.v.*); she m. 4th Thomas Stone (*q.v.*) (MWB 14:43, abst. in *Md. Cal. of Wills* 4:29; BACP IS#C:4; BALR IS#H:328, 385; HWS#M:163; MWB 21:768, abst. in *Md. Cal. of Wills* 7:212).

Hipple, Lawrence, m. by 28 July 1764 Mary, daughter of Anna Mary Ash (BAWB 3:41).

Hiser, Joseph, of Baltimore, stated he would not pay the debts of his wife Sarah (*Maryland Gazette or Baltimore General Advertiser* 16 Jan 1787).

Hisey. See Hissey.

Hissey (Hisey), [-?-], m. by 19 April 1781 Rebekah, daughter of John Price (BAWB 3:486).

Hissey, Elizabeth, confessed to bastardy at the Nov 1754 Court and again at the Nov 1758 Court (BACP BB#A:451-452; BAMI 1757-1759: 162).

Hissey, Henry, m. by 19 April 1781, Rebekah, daughter of John Price (BAWB 3:486). She m. 2nd, by Oct 1783 Nicholas Smith (*q.v.*).

Hisson (or Hesson), Cornelius, and Elizabeth Weaver were m. by license dated 22 Oct 1793 (BAML). On 23 May 1797 Elizabeth was named as a daughter of Daniel Weaver (BAWB 5:512).

Hitchcock, Asael, and Sarah Norris were m. on 8 Oct 1741 or 1742 (Harrison, "St. John's Parish Register:" 130, 133). On 26 March 1760 Sarah was named as a daughter of John Norris (BAWB 2:328; BFD 3:119).

Hitchcock, George, m. by 29 July 1713 Mary, admx. of Teage Tracey (*q.v.*) (INAC 35B:29).

Hitchcock, Jemima, on 10 Nov 1786 was named as a granddaughter in the will of Jemima Craghead (BAWB 4:250).

Hitchcock, Joanna, on 6 March 1766 was named as a stepdaughter of John Rigdon (BAWB 3:55).

Hitchcock, William, and Anne Jones were m. on 7 Sep 1716 (Harrison, "St. John's Parish Register:" 9). Anne m. 2nd, Peter Carroll (q.v.),

Hitchcock, William, m. by 14 Feb 1792 [-?-], who received a share of the estate of James Richardson (BAAD 10:536).

Hiteshue, Philip, d. by 1774 leaving a widow Catherine who m. 2nd, Thomas Russell (*q.v.*), and 3rd, John Ebbert (q.v.).

Hobbs, John, on 3 March 1725, stated he stated he would not pay the debts of his wife Susanna who separated from her husband 4 or 5 years earlier, and had followed a lewd course of life (BALR IS#H:225).

Hochs, [-?-], m. by April 1799 [-?-] sister of Michael Fisher; they had a son Jacob (BAWB 6:182).

Hock, Frederic, and Mary Conrad were married by banns on 4 June 1789 at St. Peter's Catholic Church, Baltimore (*Piet:* 136).

Hocker, Nicholas, m. by 12 Oct 1755 Catherine, administrators of John Count (MDTP 36: 215). See Nicholas Hagan above.

Hodges, Joseph, m. by 11 June 1794 Elizabeth, heir of Joshua Shields (BALR WG#OO: 155). Joseph Hodg and Elizabeth Phields [*sic*] were married by license dated 7 Jan 1784 (BAML).

Hodnet, John, and Mary Teston were married by banns on 20 Nov 1797 at St. Peter's Catholic Church, Baltimore (*Piet:* 136).

Hoff, Peter, gave notice that his wife Susanna had eloped from him (*Maryland Journal and Baltimore Advertiser* 10 Dec 1782).

Hoffman (Hoofman), Adam, and Elizabeth Lane were married by license dated 18 Jan 1786 (BAML). On 11 June 1793 she was named as a daughter of Dutton Lane (BAAD 11:281).

Hoffman, Casper, living at Patapsco Ferry, gave notice that his wife Mary had eloped (*Md. Gaz.* 31 May 1759).

Hoffman, George, merchant of this city, was m. Tues. eve. last at Chestertown to Miss Margaret Eliza Tilghman, daughter of Richard Tilghman, 4th, Esq., of that place (*Federal Gazette and Baltimore Daily Advertiser* 26 April 1799).

Hoffman, Peter, Jr., was m. last Thurs. eve. by Rev. Mr. Coleman, to Miss Deborah Owings, daughter of Samuel Owings, Esq., of Baltimore Co. (*Federal Gazette and Baltimore Daily Advertiser* 18 May 1799).

Hogan, Michael, and Mary Herring were m. on 3 June 1791 at St. Peter's Catholic Church, Baltimore (*Piet:* 136).

Högel, Johannes, m, by 8 May 1760 Margareta Ickesin ("First Record Book for the Reformed and Lutheran Congregations at Manchester, Baltimore (Now Carroll) Co." *MGSB* 35:265).

Hogg, Mary, was charged with bastardy at the June 1710 Court. She named Daniel Kelly as the father (BACP IS#B:135).

Hogg, Mary, was charged with bastardy at the March 1730/1 Court and was presented at the June 1731 Court (BACP (BACP HWS#7:96, 167).

Hogg, Sarah, in 1763 was fined for fornication and bastardy (BAMI 1755-1763).

Hoize, Frederick, in Nov 1768 was charged with begetting a bastard on the body of Mary Coffy (BAMI 1768-1769:18).

Holbrook, [-?-], m. by 22 Aug 1795 Keziah, daughter of Edward Wigley, Sr. (BAWB 5:328).

Holeson, Mary, in 1768 was presented for bastardy (BAMI 1768-1769:12).

Holiday, Henry, a Negro belonging to Mr. Henry Dorsey, and Milly Ireland, a mulatto belonging to Col. Rogers, were m. 21 Jan 1796, at St. Peter's Catholic Church, Baltimore (*Piet:* 136).

Holland, [-?-], m. by 14 Jan 1781 Jane, sister of William McCormick of Miles Hill, Harford Co., late of Co. Down, Kingdom of Ireland (BAWB 3:483).

Holland, Francis, m. by 28 Feb 1716 Susannah, daughter of George Utie (BALR TR#A: 437).

Holland, Francis, who d. 12 Aug 1795, aged about 50, and Hannah Matthews were m. on 18 Nov 1770 ("Francis Holland Family Record," *HABFR* 3:63).

Holland, Francis, and Sybil West were married by license dated 18 May 1797 BAML). On 7 Feb 1799 Sybil was named as a daughter of John Holland [?; probably a clerks error for John West] (BALR WG#56:270).

Holland, John, and Elizabeth Sicklemore were m. on 23 Dec 1755 (Harrison, "St. John's Parish Register:" 213). On 9 July 1762 Elizabeth was named as a daughter of Sutton Sicklemore, planter (BAWB 3:21). On 8 June 1756 Holland stated that he would not pay the debts of his wife [-?-], who had run him into debt (BACT TR#E:204a). In Oct 18792 he stated [again] that he would not pay the debts of his wife Elizabeth (*Maryland Journal and Baltimore Advertiser* 9 Oct 1792). N.B.: The will of John Holland, dated 29 July 1793 and proved 30 Aug 1793 named children Samuel (to have *Bond's Forest*), Ann and George (to have *Bond's Security*), Sarah McCubbin, Mary Hunt, Catherine Grant, and wife Elizabeth [all other children and wife to have one shilling and no more] (BAWB 5:118).

Holland, John, was one of the heirs of Joseph Ensor; Nathan Griffith, guardian, filed an account on 25 June 1787 (BAGA 1:33).

Holland, John Thomas, orphan of Thomas Holland, aged 11 on 2 Jan 1772, in 1773 was bound to James Edwards to age 21. Edwards was to teach him soap making and tallow chandlery (BAMI 1772, 1775-1781: 61).

Holland, Otho, m. by c1684 Mehitable, daughter of John Larkin; she m. 2nd, c1703, John Pierpoint (BALR RM#HS:62; MCHR PC:668; AALR IB#2:545-546).

Holland, Otho, and Mary Howard, widow, were m. on 9 Dec 1718 (Harrison, "St. Ann's Parish Register," Anne Arundel Co., MS. at MdHS: 406). On 3 Aug 1719 Mary was named as the late wife of Charles Howard of Anne Arundel Co. (BALR TR#DS:157). Charles Howard had m. Mary Selby on 1 Aug 1715 (Harrison, "St. Ann's Parish Register," Anne Arundel Co., MS. at MdHS: 392).

Hollandsworth, Barbara, admx., on 5 Nov (1744?) posted bond to administer the estate of Philip Phillips (BAAB 2:507).

Hollandsworth, John, in June 1721 was charged with begetting a bastard on the body of Eliza Lester (BACP IS#C:498, 507).

Holler, Francis, d. by 18 June 1787 leaving minor child Francis Holler; Conrad Choke, guardian, filed an account (BAGA 1:31).

Holliday, James, and Sarah Molton had been m. on 30 Oct 1721 (Harrison, "St. George's Parish Register:" 229). On 10 April 1725 she was named as a daughter of Matthew Molton of Baltimore Co., who named a grandson Robert Holyday [*sic*] (MWB 18: 398).Sarah m., 2nd, by 1726 Abraham Lake (Leak) (q.v.).

Holliday, John Robert, m. by 6 April 1775 Eleanor Addison Smith, only daughter and heir at law of Walter Smith of Calvert Co. (BALR AL#M:319).

Holliday, Robert, and Mary Cantwell, on 3 Nov 1746 were summoned to appear before the vestry of St. George's Parish ("St. John's and St. George's Parish Register Vestry Proceedings," MS. at MdHS).

Hollingsworth, Jesse, Esq., was m. last Thurs. eve. to Mrs. Rachel Parkin (or Perkins), widow of the late Mr. Perkins if Baltimore on 30 Sep 1790 (*Maryland Journal and Baltimore Advertiser* 5 Oct 1790; *Maryland Gazette or Baltimore General Advertiser* 5 Oct 1790; (Harrison, "St. James Parish Register:" 3). Jesse Hollingsworth and Rachel Lyde Parkin were married by license dated 30 Sep 1790 (BAML). Richard Parkin had died by 16 Jan 1787, leaving a minor child Thomas Parkin; Rachel Lyde Parkin was appointed guardian (BAGA 1:8).

Hollingsworth, Samuel, merchant of Baltimore, and Miss Adams were m. at Christiana (*Maryland Journal and Baltimore Advertiser* 21 May 1782).

Hollingsworth, Zebulon, m. last eve. Betsy, daughter of Edward Ireland , merchant (*Mary-land Journal and Baltimore Advertiser* 23 April 1790).

Hollins, John, merchant, m. last Sat. in Baltimore, Jenny Smith, daughter of the Hon. John Smith (*Maryland Gazette or Baltimore General Advertiser* 6 Jan 1786). In his will, made 19 Aug 1791 John Smith named a grandchildren John Smith, William, and Mary Hollins (BAWB 5:164).

Hollis, Amos, and Martha Everett, widow and extx. of John Everett were m. on 10 June 1761 (Harrison, "St. George's Parish Register:" 369; BAAD 7:11; MDTP 43:213).

Hollis, William, d. by c1680. His widow Elizabeth m. 2nd, Thomas Russell (q.v.), 3rd, William Croshaw (*q.v.*), and 4th, William Harris (*q.v.*).

Hollis, William, m, by 11 June 1694 Mary, daughter of Abraham and Sarah Clark (BALR RM#HS:401).

Holly, Anne, widow, on 12 Sep 1704 conv. property to her kinswoman Anne Richardson (BALR HW#2:364).

Hollyday, Margaret, in Feb 1760 was convicted of bastardy; the child's name was Isaac; in March 1760 Margaret named Daniel Hare as the father (BAMI 1755-1763).

Holman, Abraham, d. by 22 Nov 1666 by which time his relict Isabel had m. 2nd, Edward Ayres (q.v.). He left an orphan son Abraham mentioned when Ayers posted bond on 20 Nov 1666 to administer the estate of Holman (BAAB 3:216).

Holman, Abraham, in his undated will filed on 1 June 1686 named his sister Sarah Collier and his brother John Collier (MWB 4:210 abst. in *Md. Cal. of Wills* 2:6).

Holmes, Anthony, and Margaret Reeves, widow of George Reeves (*q.v.*), were m. by lic. on 7 July 1795 at St. Peter's Catholic Church, Baltimore (*Piet:* 136).

Holmes, Delia, in 1768 was presented for bastardy (BAMI 1768-1769:2).

Holmes, Gabriel, and Mary Bacon were married by license dated 2 Feb 1793 (BAML). On 18 May 1793 Mary was named as a daughter of John Bacon (BAAD 11:272).

Holmes, James, and Magdalen Babin were married by banns on 12 Oct 1790 at St. Peter's Catholic Church, Baltimore (*Piet:* 136).

Holmes, John, and Margaret Germaine were m. by lic. on 7 Aug 1792 at St. Peter's Catholic Church, Baltimore (*Piet:* 136; BAML, which gives her name as Margaret German).

Holmes, John, merchant of Baltimore, m. last Wed. at Harrisburg, Pa., Miss Juliana Thompson, daughter of the late Gen. Thompson (*Carlisle Weekly Gazette* 17 Dec 1794).

Holmes, Joyce, on 24 Aug 1754 was named as a niece in the will of Stephen Onion (MWB 29:190 abst. by Gibb).

Holmes, Mary, servant to James Presbury, was charged with bastardy at the Nov 1743 Court, and was fined 30 shillings; she was charged again at the June 1750 Court (BACP Liber 1743-1745: 72, 170-171, and TR#5:2).

Holstader, Nicholas, m. by 5 July 1763 Magdalena, daughter of Ulrick Eckler (MDAD 49:274; BAAD 6:52).

Homan, Michael, m. by 14 Dec 1785 [-?-], heir of John Markee (BAAD 8:173).

Homewood, Capt. Thomas, and Ann Hammond, daughter of Charles, were m. on 16 Dec 1731 (Harrison, "St, Margaret's Parish," Anne Arundel Co., MS. at MdHS: 105). Ann m. 2nd, William Govane (*q.v.*).

Honore, Anthony, merchant, m. Thurs., 31st ult., Mrs. Maria Meighan (*Maryland Journal and Baltimore Advertiser* 8 June 1787).

Hood, Elizabeth, a poor orphan was maintained by Francis Freeman for the past year (Levy List for 1739, Black Books, III 8).

Hood, James, who d. 1819 in Anne Arundel Co., Md., and Kitty Franklin, who d. 28 Jan 1847 were m. 22 July 1784 (Marr. Returns of Rev. William West, Scharf Papers, MS.1999 at MdHS; "James Hood Bible," in *MBR* 7:85). Hood entered the service of the United States as a corporal on 5th March 1777 (Hood Bible Record in Rev. War Pension Appl. W-3816, in *NGSQ* 20:120-121).

Hood, James, and Sally, daughter of Thomas Hobbs, Esq., were m. last Thurs. at Elk Ridge by Rev. Mr. Chalmers (*Federal Intelligencer and Baltimore Daily Gazette* 2 Jan 1795; BAML).

Hoofman. See Hoffman.

Hook, Jacob, m. 23 Nov 1784 Elizabeth Campbell ("Hook Bible," *MGSB* 20 (4) (Fall 1979) 344).

Hook, Jacob, m. by 13 June 1787 [-?-], daughter of Solomon Stocksdale (BAAD 9:58).

Hook, Joseph, and Sophia Jones were m. on 8 Oct 1780 (Marr. Returns of Rev. William West, Scharf Papers, MS.1999, at MdHS). As exec., Joseph Hook, on 27 Sep 1787 posted bond to administer the estate of Hester (Esther) Jones who in her will made 3 May 1787 named her daughter Sophia, wife of Joseph Hook (BAWB 4:91, 254; BAAB 7:128; BAAD 10:68).

Hook, Joseph, and Sarah Johnson were married by banns on 25 Jan 1791 at St. Peter's Catholic Church, Baltimore (*Piet:* 136).

Hook (Hooke), Matthias. m. by 18 April 1793 Catherine, heir of Henry Hennestophel (BAAD 11:267; (BALR WG#LL:44).

Hooke, Andrew, and his wife Margaret, of Baltimore, have consented to live apart (*Maryland Gazette or Baltimore General Advertiser* 20 Feb 1784).

Hooke, John, and Sophia Honko were m. by lic. on 20 April 1795 at St. Peter's Catholic Church, Baltimore (*Piet:* 136; BAML, which gives her name as Horke).

Hooker [-?-], m. by 16 Aug 1779 Hannah, daughter of Edward Stocksdale (BAWB 3:376).

Hooker, Benjamin, m. by 24 d. 11 m. 1788 Deborah, sister of Benjamin Powell (BAWB 4:321).

Hooker, Rachel, formerly Comley, daughter of James and Mary Comley on 23 d,, 8 m., 1769, was charged with being married outside the Society by a priest ("Minutes of Gunpowder Monthly Meeting," *QRNM:*59). [No other marriage reference found].

Hooker, Richard, m. by 20 Feb 1746/7 Martha, eldest daughter of William Barney (MWB 25:57, abst. by Abst. by Gibb; MDAD 25:57, 31:161, 33:161).

Hooker, Samuel, and Rachel Belt were m. by license dated 15 Dec 1784 by Rev. West (BAML). Rachel Hooker, formerly Belt, on 29 d. 10 m. 1785, was charged with being married by a hireling priest to a man not in unity with us. On 26 d. 11 m. 1785 John Belt, son of Richard, was charged with accompanying his sister to her marriage ("Minutes of Gunpowder Meeting," *QRNM:*81).

Hooper, [-?-], d. by 1 April 1693 when his widow Sarah, mother of Isabella Hooper, m. John Hall (BALR HW#2:38).

Hooper, [-?-], m. by 24 Dec 1786, Eleanor, mother of Alexius Thompson (BOCP 1:287). Eleanor Thompson, petitioned the court on 12 Dec 1786 that some time ago she had a child named [Alexius] Thompson by a man named Hugh Green, who in his last will and testament devised a sum of money to her son. James McCannon refused to pay the interest (BPET; Green, Hugh, 1786; Box 1, Folder 33).

Hooper, George, m. Sarah, sister of Abraham Holman, and d. by March 1684/5 by which time his widow Sarah m. 2nd, John Collier (*q.v.*). She m. 3rd, John Hall (*q.v.*)

Hooper, James, and Rachael Gorsuch were married by license dated 4 Nov 1783 (BAML). On 16 Dec 1791 she was named as an heir of Thomas Gorsuch (BAAD 10:503).

Hooper, Rev. Joseph, Rector of St. Paul's Parish, in his will dated 8 July 1729 named his will dated 8 July 1729 named his mother Sarah Shorter (MWB 22:100, abst. in *Md. Cal. of Wills* 8:48).

Hooper, Sarah, and **Nicholas Hooper.** were named as grandchildren of Aberilla Merryman, widow, in her will made 13 Nov 1784 (BAWB 4:60).

Hoops, Jesse, son of David and Esther, on 28 d. 8 m. 1794 announced his intention to marry Sarah Wilson, daughter of John and Alisanna ("Minutes of Deer Creek Meeting," QRNM:154).

Hope, George, and Dorcas Turner were m. on 21 Dec 1703 (Harrison, "All Hallow's Parish Register," Anne Arundel Co., MS. at MdHS: 64).

Hope, George, and Judith Clarke were m. on 27 May 1706 (Harrison, "All Hallow's Parish Register," Anne Arundel Co., MS. at MdHS: 72). Hope d. by 10 June 1722 by which time Judith, his extx., had m. 2nd, William Hawkins (*q.v.*) or Harris (*q.v.*) or Hutchings (*q.v.*) (BAAD 3: 81; 4:142; MDTP 26:12).

Hope, James, and Anne [-?-], were m. by 29 Sep 1744 when their son Richard was born ("Hope Bible," *HABFR* 1:8).

Hope, Richard, son of James and Anne, was b. 29 Sep 1744, and Jenny [-?-], were m. on 16 June 1761 ("Hope Bible," *HABFR* 1:8).

Hopham, William, and Jane, on 8 May 1722 posted bond to administer the estate of George Newport (BAAB 2:336; BINV 5:27).

Hopkins, [-?-], m. by 23 July 1707 Eliza, daughter of John Debruler (MWB 13:84).

Hopkins, [-?-], m. by 10 May 1793 Sarah, sister of William Evans BAWB 5:112).

Hopkins, Catherine, on 30 d. 9 m. 1786 was charged with leaving her husband in an unreconciled manner without previously advising with her friends and removing a considerable distance from amongst the society without a certificate of removal ("Minutes of Gunpowder Meeting," *QRNM:*83).

Hopkins, Charles, and Ann Jenkins were m. on 23 July 1793 (Harrison, "St. James Parish Register:" 5). She was a daughter of Michael Jenkins (BAWB 6:253).

Hopkins, Major David, m. last Sat. eve. Polly, daughter of Edward Dorsey (*Maryland Journal and Baltimore Advertiser* 14 Dec 1790). (They were m. in Baltimore Co.).

Hopkins, Elizabeth. See Samuel Cox.

Hopkins, Ephraim Gover, on 26 d. 2 m. 1795, was reported to have consummated a marriage to a woman not of our society ("Minutes of Deer Creek Meeting," *QRNM:*155). [No other marriage reference found].

Hopkins, Gerard, son of Samuel, on 30 d. 11 m. 1776 was charged with fornication and being married by a priest ("Minutes of Gunpowder Meeting," *QRNM:*68). [No other marriage reference found].

Hopkins, Gerrard, son of William and Rachel, on 5 d. 5 m. 1774 announced he intended to marry Sarah Wallis, daughter of Samuel Wallis, dec., and his wife Grace ("Minutes of Deer Creek Meeting," *QRNM:*136).

Hopkins, John, son of Samuel, late of Patapsco Meeting and his wife Sarah, on 29 d. 9 m. 1768 announced his intention to marry Sarah Chew, daughter of Joseph Chew late of Deer Creek Monthly Meeting and his wife Sarah ("Minutes of Deer Creek Meeting," *QRNM:*133).

Hopkins, John, denied he was married to Sarah Evans, widow, who had lived with him off and on for 13 or 14 years, as a female friend, during which time she had stolen from him, tried to poison him...[other details of her actions are given] (*Maryland Journal and Baltimore Advertiser* 3 May 1785).

Hopkins, John, on 26 d. 7 m. 1798, was charged with having gone out in marriage to a woman not of our society with the assistance of a hireling teacher ("Minutes of Deer Creek Meeting," *QRNM:*159). John Hopkins and Eleanor Morgan were m. on 19 April 1798 (Harrison, "St. James Parish Register:" 8).

Hopkins, John Wallis, and Susannah Dallam were m. by lic. 9 Oct 1800 (HAML). Susannah Hopkins, (late Dallam), on 25 d. 12 m. 1800 was reported to have consummated her marriage with the assistance of a Baptist Preacher ("Minutes of Deer Creek Meeting," *QRNM:*162).

Hopkins, Johns, on 6 d. 4 m. 1775, requested a certificate to West River Monthly Meeting to marry a young woman of that meeting ("Minutes of Gunpowder Monthly Meeting," *QRNM:*65).

Hopkins, Johns, on 8 d. 6 m. 1797 was charged with marrying contrary to the good order of friends, and was disowned on 13 d. 7 m. 1797 ("Minutes of Baltimore Meeting," *QRNM:*229). [No other marriage reference found].

Hopkins, Joseph, son of Joseph and Ann Hopkins, on 5 d. 1 m. 1769 announced he intended to marry Elizabeth Gover, daughter of Ephraim and Elizabeth ("Minutes of Deer Creek Meeting," *QRNM:*133).

Hopkins, Joseph, son of Samuel, on 29 d. 7 m. 1780 was charged with marrying a woman not of our Society ("Minutes of Gunpowder Meeting," *QRNM:*73). Joseph Hopkins and Rebecca Bret were m on 20 Jan 1780 (Marr. Returns of Rev. William West, MS 1999 at MdHS).

Hopkins, Joseph, on 27 d. 6 m. 1799 was reported to have gone out in marriage to a woman not of our society ("Minutes of Deer Creek Meeting," *QRNM:*160). Joseph Hopkins and Sarah Morgan were m. on 18 April 1799 (Harrison, "St. James Parish Register:" 6).

Hopkins, Levin Hill, son of William and Rachel, on 2 d. 3 m. 1780 announced his intention to marry Frances Wallis, daughter of Samuel Wallis, dec., and his wife Grace ("Minutes of Deer Creek Meeting," *QRNM:*139).

Hopkins, Margaret, was charged with bastardy having had a bastard child in the care of Elizabeth Jones in Aug 1724 (BACP IS&TW#3:437).

Hopkins, Margaret. See Margaret Hunt.

Hopkins, Margaret. See Margaret Sanderson.

Hopkins, Mary, formerly Wilson, on 24 d. 1 m., 1770 was charged with marrying outside the Society ("Minutes of Gunpowder Monthly Meeting," *QRNM:*59). [No other marriage reference found].

Hopkins, Mary. See Mary Worthington.

Hopkins, Philip, on 6 d. 4 m. 1775 was charged with marrying a woman outside the Society ("Minutes of Gunpowder Monthly Meeting," *QRNM:*65) . Philip Hopkins m. Catherine Evans on 13 March 1775 ("Register of the First Presbyterian Church in Baltimore," MS at MdHS: 7).

Hopkins, Philip, on 28 d. 6 m. 1798 was charged with having gone out in marriage to a woman not of our society with the assistance of a Baptist Preacher ("Minutes of Deer Creek Meeting," *QRNM:*159). [No other marriage reference found].

Hopkins, Samuel, and Sarah Giles were m. on 2 d. 7 m 1740 ("Records Gunpowder Meeting," *QRNM;*26). On 30 d., 12th mo., 1754 Sarah was named as a daughter of Cassandra Giles who named Gerard Hopkins as a grandson in her will (MWB 29:373 abst. by Gibb) Samuel Hopkins d. by 8 Sep 1768 when Sarah was named as a daughter and devisee of John Giles (BALR B#Q:633, AL#M:564).

Hopkins, Samuel, son of Philip, dec., and wife Elizabeth, on 4 d. 5 m. 1769 announced he intended to marry Mary Gover, daughter of Ephraim and Elizabeth ("Minutes of Deer Creek Meeting," *QRNM:*133).

Hopkins, Samuel, son of William, dec. and Rachel, on 28 d. 10 m. 1790 announced his intention to marry Sarah Husband, daughter of Joseph, dec. and his wife Mary ("Minutes of Deer Creek Meeting," *QRNM:*148-9).

Hopkins, Samuel, son of Joseph, dec., and Elizabeth, on 29 d. 3 m. 1798 announced his intention to marry Rachel Worthington, daughter of John and Priscilla ("Minutes of Deer Creek Meeting," *QRNM:*158).

Hopkins, Sarah, daughter of John, on 26 d. 2 m. 1792 reportedly had her marriage accomplished by a hireling minister ("Minutes of Gunpowder Meeting," *QRNM:* 92). Sally Hopkins and Joseph Hopkins were m. by lic. dated 29 Nov 1791 (BAML).

Hopkins, William, of Baltimore Co., Gent., m. by 11 Nov 1741 Rachel, widow and extx. of Charles Daniel of Baltimore Co., dec. (AALR RB#1:112; MDTP 31:312; MDAD 19:181; BAAD 3:196).

Hoppe, Ferdinand Frederick, b. 2 Feb 1769, and Catherine Snouffer, daughter of John Snouffer, b. 13 Nov 1752 and Christian [-?-], b. 1756, were m. in 1799. Catherine m. 2nd, [-?-] Werble ("John Henry Hoppe Bible," *MBR* 3:122-124.

Horgan, Jeremiah, stated he would not pay the debts of his wife Elizabeth, who had eloped (*Maryland Journal and Baltimore Advertiser* 2 April 1795).

Horn, Thomas, m. by 8 Nov 1743 [-?-], daughter of Abigail Barton; they had a daughter Alce Horn (BALR TB#C:363).

Horne, John S., was m. last eve. by Rev. Mr. Ireland, to Mary Ridgley, all of this city (*Federal Gazette and Baltimore Daily Advertiser* 4 May 1799).

Horne, William, m. by 5 Nov 1684 Mary, heir of Thomas O'Daniel (BALR RM#HS: 101).

Horner, Nicholas, d. by 13 Nov 1741 when his widow and admx. Ann had m. Matthew Beck (q.v.) (BAAD 4:112); she m. 3rd, Henry Waters (*q.v.*).

Horner, Thomas, and Grace Anderson were m. on 27 Oct 1741 (Harrison, "St. George's Parish Register:" 320); in his will dated 16 June 1756 Horner named his daughter-in-law Sarah Anderson and named her brother Daniel Anderson as one of his execs. (MWB 30:150 abst. by Gibb).

Horsman, Mary. See Leonard Helm.

Horton, Ann, was charged with bastardy at the Aug 1717 Court (BACP IS#1A:152).

Horton, Margaret, was named as a granddaughter of William Smith in his will dated 21 Nov 1739 (MWB 23:120 abst. in *Md. Cal. of Wills* 8:212).

Horton, William, son of John and Priscilla, formerly bound to Samuel Webb, in Nov 1757 was then bound to Webb (BAMI 1755-1763).

Horze, Frederick, in June 1768 was found guilty of bastardy (BAMI 1768-1769: 18).

Hossefratz, George, and Dolly Gross were married by banns on 1 Feb 1790, at St. Peter's Catholic Church, Baltimore (*Piet:* 136).

Hotchkiss, Capt. Solomon, was m. last Mon. eve. by Rev. Mr. Hagerty to Miss Alisannah Hall, both of Fells Point (*Baltimore Daily Intelligencer* 23 Jan 1794).

Houchin (or Houchings), William, m. by 18 Dec 1722 Judith, execs. of George Hope of Baltimore Co. (MDAD 5:127, 413; BALR IS#H:89). **See Hawkins, above.**

Hough, John, merchant of this city, was m. last Thurs. eve. to Miss Rebecca Thompson of Philadelphia (*Federal Gazette and Baltimore Daily Advertiser* 27 Nov 1797).

Hough, Robert, and Frances Martin, on 11 d. 1 m. 1798 declared their intention to marry ("Minutes of Baltimore Meeting," *QRNM:*230).

Houlton, John, and Miss Sally Burns, were m. last Tues. eve. in Baltimore, by Rev. Mr. Kurtz (*Baltimore Daily Repository* 26 June 1793; *Maryland Journal and Baltimore Advertiser* 28 June 1793).

Housamer, [-?-], m. by 27 Sep 1756 [-?-], daughter of Frances Foy of Baltimore Co., and had a daughter Sarah of Frederick Co. (PCLR BT#1:26).

Houstman, Mary. See Leonard Helm.

Houton, Edward, aged 7 next 1 Dec 1757, orphan of Edward, in Nov 1758 was bound to (name not given) (BAMI 1755-1763).

Hover, Ignatius, and Rebecca Mentz were m. by lic. on 11 April 1797 at St. Peter's Catholic Church, Baltimore (*Piet:* 136; BAML, which gives his name as Sebastian Hover).

How, William, and Mary Lester were m. on 11 June 1761 (Harrison, "St. George's Parish Register:" 378). On 12 Sep 1763 she was named as a daughter of Alice Lester, the widow of George Lester (BAAD 6:59; MDAD 49:579; BACT B#G:452).

Howacres, Mary, was charged with bastardy at the Nov 1742 Court (BACP TB#D:59).

Howard, [-?-], m. by 16 Oct 1704, Hannah, daughter of Edward Dorsey of Baltimore Co. (MWB 3:725 abst. in *Md. Cal. of Wills* 3:68).

Howard, [-?-], m. by 26 April 1778 Sarah, daughter of John Hurd (BAWB 3:360).

Howard, Edmund, and Ruth Teale were m. on 27 Feb 1728 Harrison, "St. Paul's Parish Register:" 155). He d. by 12 Nov 1754 by which time his extx. had m. William Lewis (q.v.) (MDTP 36:96).

Howard, Edward, and Sidith [-?-], slave of James Cretin, of Harford Co., were m. on 26 Dec 1794, at St. Peter's Catholic Church, Baltimore (*Piet:* 136).

Howard, Gideon, m. by 23 Oct 1723 Hannah, admx. of William Orrick of Baltimore Co. (BAAD 1:116; MDAD 5:229; MDTP 26:206).

Howard, Hannah, was charged with bastardy at the Aug 1742 Court, and again in 1744 (BACP TB#D:1, 74, and Liber 1743-1745: 293).

Howard, James, m. by March 1683/4 Jane, relict of Ambrose Gillett (BACP D:141).

Howard, James Govane, merchant, was m. last Thurs. eve. by Rev. Mr. Liell, to Miss Mary Woodward Govane, both of this city (*Federal Gazette and Baltimore Daily Advertiser* 27 Oct 1798; BAML, which gives her name as Mary Govan). On 18 Jan 1800 Mary Woodward Govane was named as a legatee of Mary Woodward (BAAD 13:179).

Howard, John, m. by Aug 1759 Dorcas Sater (BALR B#G:530).

Howard, John, and Elizabeth Gassaway were m. on 17 Sep 1732 (Harrison, "All Hallow's Parish, Anne Arundel Co.," MS> at MdHS: 114). On 12 May 1764 Elizabeth was named as a legatee of Thomas Gassaway, who was a brother of Jane Saunders, widow of James Saunders, son of Robert Saunders (BALR B#N:99).

Howard, John Beale, m. by 7 Feb 1799 Margaret, daughter of John Holland (BALR WG#56:270).

Howard, John Beale, Jr., m. Margaret West on 28 Sep 1796 ("Reverend William West Bible," *MBR* 5:208).

Howard, Col. John Eager, of Baltimore, m. at Philadelphia, Miss Chew, daughter of the Hon. Benjamin Chew, Esq. (*Maryland Journal and Baltimore Advertiser* 12 June 1787).

Howard, Joshua, m. by 9 April 1793, Rebecca, daughter of Samuel Owings (BAAD 11:239).

Howard, Lemuel, and Mrs. Ann Ward were m. on 11 Jan 1730 (Harrison, "St. John's Parish Register:" 91). On 8 June 1733 Ann was named as the extx. of Edward Ward of Baltimore Co. (BAAD 1:246; MDAD 12:2; BALR TB#C:668; MDTP 29:277).

Howard, Lemuel, of Baltimore Co., m. by 2 Aug 1749 Katherine, daughter and devisee of John Greenisse [Greeneff], son and heir of James Greenisse [Greeneff] late of Baltimore Co.; Lemuel and Katherine were the parents of John Greenisse [Greeneff] Howard (AALR RB#3:161).

Howard, Lemuel, and Martha Scott were m. on 7 Dec 1760 (Harrison, "St. John's Parish Register:" 220). On 11 Aug 1762 she was named as a daughter of Aquila Scott (MDAD 48:178).

Howard, Mary, in 1762 was convicted of bastardy (BAMI 1755-1763).

Howard, Mary, on 7 May 1782 was named as a niece in the will of Richard Croxall (BAWB 4:36).

Howard, Sarah. See James McComas.

Howard, Thomas, and Catherine Johnson were m. on 4 July 1723 (Harrison, "St. Paul's Parish Register:" 146). On 8 Oct 1723 Katherine was named as the extx. of Anthony Johnson of Baltimore Co., and mother of William Johnson, who was left *Phantasco* by the last will and testament of Edward Boarman, dated 10 Jan 1702 (MDTP 26:202; MDAD 5:385; BALR IS#G:273).

Howard, William, and Mary Rooke were m. by lic. on 18 Feb 1799 at St. Peter's Catholic Church, Baltimore (*Piet:* 137).

Howell, John, of Elk Ridge gave notice that his wife Nancy had eloped from him (*Maryland Journal and Baltimore Advertiser* 13 March 1781).

Howell, Samuel, and Priscilla Freeborne were m. on 8 Dec 1720 (Harrison, "St. George's Parish Register:" 279). Priscilla was the widow of 1st, Richard Kilburne (*q.v.*), and 2nd Thomas Freeborne. On 22 Aug 1723 Priscilla, wife of Samuel Howell, filed the acct. of Richard Kilbourne as extx. (AAJU G:278, 284; MDAD 3:338). Priscilla was the sister of David Thomas of Baltimore Co. (MWB 16:76).

Howell, Samuel, on 10 Sep 1746 entered into a [prenuptial?] agreement with Sarah Durbin; he conveyed to her the following tracts: *Garrison's Neglect, Howell's Contrivance, Johnson's Bed, Johnson's Rest, Joshua Wood's Mistake,* and *Lofton's Neglect.* He also gave her a child's portion of his estate, for her and any heirs she might have by him; if she died without heirs by him, the above tracts would be divided among his male heirs; she relinquished her dower right to 1/3 of his estate (BALR TB#E:177). They were m. on 11 Sep 1747 (Harrison, "St. George's Parish Register:" 70). Sarah, m., 2nd, by 18 May 1768 William Urquhart (Virchworth) (*q.v.*) (MINV 96:155; BAAD 7:65; BAMI 4:19).

Howlett, John, m. by 2 Jan 1768 Mary, widow of [-?-] Langdon (*q.v.*), and daughter of Mary Ann Harris; the couple had a daughter Mary Howlett (BAWB 3:126; BFD

5:394). Mary Howlet d. by 22 Dec 1794 leaving Joseph Langdon as administrator. Patrick Lynch signed a receipt for 41.0.1 as his part of his mother-in-law's estate. John Howlet signed a receipt for 161.4.11 as his share of his mother's estate (BOCP Petition of Joseph Langdon, 1794).

Hubbard, John, m. by 13 Nov 1681 Margaret, relict and admx. of John Leekins (INAC 7B:157).

Hubbert, Joseph, in his will made 9 Jan 1800 named his mother Kezia Wright and a Catherine Hodson (who may have been a sister) (BAWB 6:425).

Hucken, Nicholas, and Catherine Hucken on 4 Oct 1755 posted bond to administer the estate of John Counts or Kountz (BAAB 1:396).

Hudson, James, stated he would not pay the debts of his wife Mary, who had eloped from his bed and board (*Maryland Journal and Baltimore Advertiser* 5 June 1785).

Hudson, James, and Joanna Macnamara were m. by lic. on 8 Sep 1796 at St. Peter's Catholic Church, Baltimore (*Piet:* 137).

Hudson, John, and Fanny Brown were married by license dated 21 Sep 1786 (BAML). John Hudson denied he had two wives, let alone three. His only wife was Fanny, daughter of John and Sarah Nutbrown [Brown?] (*Maryland Journal and Baltimore Advertiser* 23 June and 30 June 1789).

Hudson, Jonathan, of Baltimore, dec., left an infant heir, Jonathan Hudson; Margaret Hudson is trustee (*Md. Gaz.* 25 Sep 1794).

Hudson, Joshua, m. by 29 Sep 1766 Hannah, niece of Nicholas Ruxton Gay who on that day conveyed to his niece Hannah wife of Joshua Hudson 150 acres part *Gay's Inspection* (BALR B#P:343).

Hudson, Robert, of Anne Arundel Co., m. by 3 May 1794 Priscilla, granddaughter Of John Simkins who left her part of *Mount Organ* (BALR WG#OO:8).

Hugg, Jacob, and Elizabeth Lancaster, daughter of Sinclare Lancaster were m. by 4 Nov 1780 when their son Jacob was born ("Lambdin-Fox-Hugg Bible," *MBR* 1:146-149).

Huggins, James, m. by 5 Aug 1723 Jane, daughter of Daniel Benson of Anne Arundel Co. (BALR IS#G:172).

Hughes, [-?-], m. by 18 Dec 1755 [-?-]. daughter of Thomas Bond who named his granddaughter Sarah Hughes in his will (MWB 30:24 abst. by Gibb).

Hughes, [-?-], m. by 5 May 1773 Rebecca, sister of William Lux (BAWB 3:357).

Hughes, [-?-], m. by 5 Sep 1777 Rosana [*sic*], daughter of Francis Hays (BAWB 3:356).

Hughes, [-?-], m. by 15 Feb 1785, Margaret, daughter of William Slade, who also named a granddaughter Cassander Hughes in his will ((BAWB 4:48).

Hughes (Hughs), Caleb, m. by 17 Sep 1740 Hester, widow and admx. of Peter Bond (*q.v.*) of Baltimore Co. (MDAD 18:106; BAAD 4:61; MDTP 31:49).

Hughes, Christopher, merchant, and Peggy Sanderson, both of this town, were m. [date not given] (*Maryland Journal and Baltimore Advertiser* 26 Jan 1779). Christopher Hughes and Peggy [-?-] were m. on 20 Jan 1779 Harrison, "St. Paul's," p. 213). His wife Margaret was later identified as the daughter of Margaret Sanderson (BAWB 4:71).

Hughes (Hughs), David, Quaker, m. by 4 Dec 1729 Mary, 'not a Quaker,' relict and extx. of 1st, Thomas Jackson (*q.v.*), and 2nd, John Roberts (*q.v.*) of Baltimore Co. (MINV 15:356, MDAD 11:101, 12:128, 139, 13:301). She was the mother of Lucina Roberts (BALR HWS#1A:131).

Hughes, Elizabeth, orphan of Jonathan Hughes, in Nov 1757 was made a ward of William Presbury (BAMI 1755-1763).

Hughes, Francis, and Mary Mildews were married on 1 Jan 1782 (Marr. Returns of Rev. William West, Scharf Papers, MS.1999 at MdHS). On 28 Feb 1787 she was named as a daughter of Aquila Mildews (BAAD 9:19). She was a daughter of Elizabeth Mildews, whose will made 16 Feb 1794 Named her daughter Mrs. Mary 'Hews' and her son-in-law Frank 'Hews' (BAWB 7:379).

Hughes, Hugh, and Ann Bond were married on 6 Nov 1794 (Marr. Returns of Rev. Daniel Kurtz, Scharf Papers, MS.1999 at MdHS). On 14 Aug 1800 Ann was named as a daughter of Thomas Bond (BAAD 13:316).

Hughes, John, and Elizabeth Norris were m. on 11 Sep 1740 (Harrison, "St. George's Parish Register:" 313). On 10 Dec 1747 and again on 4 April 1770 Elizabeth was named as a daughter of Benjamin Norris and a sister on Joseph Norris (BALR TB#E: 637; MWB 38:591; MWB 40:576; abst. in *Md. Cal. of Wills* 16:105).

Hughes, John, son of John Paul Hughes, b. 21 Aug 1772, d. 26 March 1853, aged 82, and Charlotte Mitchell, b. 15 Aug 1772, daughter of William and Clemency Mitchell, were m. on 27 Dec 1796 ("Bible Record of John Hughes," *MBR* 1:122-124).

Hughes, John, native of Va., now at the Garrison at Fort McHenry, and Elizabeth Labou were m. by lic. on 7 March 1799 at St. Peter's Catholic Church, Baltimore (*Piet:* 137).

Hughes, Jonathan, and Jane Shepherd were m. on 10 Dec 1728 (Harrison, "St. George's Parish Register:" 249). Jane was a widow of Rowland Shephard (*q.v.*). On 20 July 1740 Jane was named as a sister of Martin Taylor, dec., and daughter of Martin Taylor (in admin. account of Robert Robertson of Baltimore Co.) (MDAD 18:12; BALR HWS#1-A:164).

Hughes, Joseph, on 11 d. 12 m. 1800 had a complaint made that he had his marriage accomplished contrary to the good order of Friends ("Minutes of Baltimore Meeting," *QRNM:*239). [No other marriage reference found].

Hughes, Mary, was charged with bastardy at the March 1746/7 Court (BACP TB&TR#1:478).

Hughes, Sam, and Hannah Litten, in April 1747 were summoned by the vestry to answer charges of unlawful cohabitation with each other. In June 1747 Sam Hughes was admonished with certification. In Sep 1757, Sam Hughes' wife, Jane, reported him to the vestry for unlawful cohabitation with Hanneretta Jones; the said Hughes and Jones were ordered to appear before the next vestry, and Mrs. Blond[?], Dan Treadway and wife were summoned to appear as evidences ("St. John's and St. George's Parish Register Vestry Proceedings," MS. at MdHS).

Hughes, Samuel, and Jane Scott, widow of Francis Watkins, were m. on 4 Nov 1714 (Harrison, "St. George's Parish Register:" 215). On 9 July 1725 Jane was named as a daughter of Daniel Scott of Baltimore Co. (MDAD 6:406).

Hughes (Hughs), Solomon, and Sophia Wright were m. on 7 June 1772 (Harrison, "St. John's Parish Register:" 264). She was the widow of Nathaniel Wright (*q.v.*), and a daughter of Abraham Rutledge (MWB 39:336, abst. *in Md. Cal. of Wills* 15:67; MINV 112:385).

Hughes (Hughs), William, m. Hannah 'Bankston' on 11 Dec 1735 (Harrison, "St. Paul's Parish Register:" 154). On 26 April 1738, Hannah was named as the widow and admx. of Joseph Bankson (*q.v.*) who left children Joseph, Rebecca, Ariana, and

Susanna (BAAD 4:15; MDAD 16:132). On 14 Feb 1770, Rebecca, wife of Richard Carter (*q.v.*), was named as a daughter of Hannah Hughes, widow of Baltimore Town (BAWB 3:158). Ariana Bankson m. James French (*q.v.*).

Hughes (Hughs), Capt. William, m. a few days ago, Betsy M'Kirdy, daughter of Capt. John M'Kirdy of Baltimore (*Maryland Journal and Baltimore Advertiser* 27 Nov 1789; BAML).

Hughes, Young Samuel, and Ann Cullison, both of the county, were m. by lic. on 15 Nov 1793 at St. Peter's Catholic Church, Baltimore (*Piet:* 137).

Hughs. See Hughes.

Hughston, John, of Gunpowder Neck, and Hannah Waltham were m. on 10 Dec 1771 (Harrison, "St. John's Parish Register:" 263). Their daughter Elizabeth was b. 15 March 1773 ("John Dutton Bible," *MBR* 7:46-50).

Humphrey, Elizabeth. See Sabret Bowen.

Humphrey (Humphries, Humphris), Richard, m. by 12 July 1715 Elizabeth, admx. of Henry Jones who left a widow and three children (BAAD 1:336; INAC 36C:48; BACP IS#C:342).

Humphreys, Frances, servant to William Hamilton, confessed to bastardy at the Nov 1743 Court, and in March 1743/5 was ordered to receive 15 Lashes. She was found guilty of mulatto bastardy by verdict of a jury on 5 March 1744/5. On the same day, Abigail, daughter of Frances Umphrey [*sic*] was sold to William Hamilton (BACP Liber 1743-1745: 71, 168, 471, 481-482).

Humphries, See Humphrey.

Humphris. See Humphrey.

Hunn, Francis, and Margaret James were m. on 7 July 1754 (Harrison, "St. John's Parish Register:" 210). On 24 Oct 1754 Margaret was named as the widow of Nicholas James (BALR BB#I: 333).

Hunn, Francis, d. by 24 Oct 1775 by which date his admx. Mary had m. [-?-] Pocock (*q.v.*) (MDTP 46:363).

Hunt, [-?-], m. by 17 Dec 1764 Elizabeth, mother of Walter Smith of Calvert Co. (BALR B#O:175).

Hunt, [-?-], m. by 24 July 1773 Elizabeth, daughter of Henry Chew; on this date Elizabeth conv. prop. to her son Job Hunt (BACT 1773-1784:65).

Hunt, [-?-], m. by 29 July 1793 Mary, daughter of John Holland, Sr. (BAWB 5:118).

Hunt, Elizabeth, admx., on 4 April 1797 posted bond to administer the estate of John Hendrickson (BAAB 8:367).

Hunt, Margaret, before marriage Hopkins, on 28 d. 3 m. 1771 was reported to have gone out in marriage ("Minutes of Gunpowder Monthly Meeting," *QRNM:*61). [No other marriage reference found].

Hunt, Margaret, on 27 d. 6 m. 1778 was charged with outgoing in marriage ("Minutes of Gunpowder Meeting," *QRNM:*72). [No other marriage reference found].

Hunt, Phineas, and Susanna Gott were married by license dated 8 June 1793 (BAML). On 6 Sep 1793 she was named as a daughter of Rachel Gott (BAWB 6:2). On 5 Oct 1798 she was named as a daughter of Samuel Gott (BALR WG#56:136).

Hunt, Sarah, in 1765 was fined for bastardy (BAMI 1765).

Hunt, Thomas, m. by 14 Oct 1781 Ann, daughter of William and Margaret (Sing) Wiley, sister of Richard Wiley and of Edith who m. John Cross (BALR WG#G:496).

Hunt, William, and Elizabeth Wright were m. on 1 July 1787 (Marr. Register of Rev. Lewis Richards, MS.690 at MdHS). On 16 April 1788 Elizabeth was named as the admx. of William Wright (BAAD 9:196).

Hunter, Peter, and Esther Scott were married by license dated 30 Nov 1792 (BAML). She was a daughter of Abraham Scott whose will made 20 May 1799 named a grandson Curtis Grub Hunter (BAWB 7:176).

Hunter, Peter, of Baltimore Co. stated he would petition the Assembly for an act to recover a deed for part of *Taylor's Discovery* on Winter's Run, conveyed by Richard Wiley to William Hunter, father of Peter (*Maryland Gazette or Baltimore General Advertiser* 26 Oct 1797).

Hunter, William, m. by 20 April 1722 Mary, execs. of John Webster of Baltimore Co. (BAAD 1:66; MDAD 4:146, 5:250).

Hurd, John, in Aug 1733 was charged with begetting a bastard on the body of Mary Barnes (BACP HWS#9:71).

Hurd, John, and Ruth Norwood were m. on 18 June 1739 (Harrison, "St. Thomas Parish Register:" 70). On 10 July 1773 Ruth was named as a sister of Samuel Norwood (BAWB 3:263).

Hurford, Joseph, son of John and Hannah of New Garden Meeting, Pa., on 1 d. 9 m. 1763 announced his intention to marry Naomi Greenland, daughter of Flower Greenland, dec. ("Minutes of Deer Creek Meeting," *QRNM:* 130).

Hurst, Abraham, son of John, in an undated deed was given a two year old heifer by Henry Knowles (BALR TR#A:65, 70).

Husband, Joseph, on 3 d. 3 m. 1762 requested a certificate to New Garden Meeting to marry Mary Pusey, daughter of Joshua and Mary Pusey, dec. ("Minutes of Deer Creek Meeting," *QRNM:* 129).

Husband, Joseph, on 13 d. 11 m. 1800 requested a certificate to Deer Creek Meting to marry Sarah Brown, a member thereof ("Minutes of Baltimore Meeting," *QRNM:* 238). Joseph Husband, son of Joseph, dec., and wife Mary, on 27 d. 11 m. 1800 announced his intention to marry Sarah Brown, daughter of Freeborn and Mary Brown ("Minutes of Deer Creek Meeting," *QRNM:* 162).

Husbands, Joshua, son of Joseph, dec., and Mary, on 24 d. 1 m. 1793 announced his intention to marry Margaret Jewit, daughter of Thomas and Ann Jewit ("Minutes of Deer Creek Meeting," *QRNM:* 152).

Hush, Jacob, m. by 24 Oct 1782 Margaret, admx. of Hugh Watts of Baltimore Co. (BALR WG#M:148).

Hush (Husk), John, and Catherine Councilman were married by license dated 29 May 1784 (BAML). On 5 June 1799 Catherine was named as a daughter of George Councilman (BAWB 6:218).

Huson, Mary, servant to Stephen Gill, was charged with bastardy at the Nov 1722 Court (BACP IS&TW#2:22).

Hussey, George, on 24 d. 2 m. 1781 was charged with committing fornication with Rachel Hayward and since having been married to her by a priest ("Minutes of Gunpowder Meeting," *QRNM:* 74). They were m. on 24 Jan 1781 (Harrison, "St. Paul's," p. 180).

Hussey, George, on 13 d. 2 m. 1800 had a complaint brought by Baltimore Preparative Meeting that he had his marriage accomplished by a hireling teacher to a woman who may have a former husband still living, and Hussey is publicly charged with having had by her two children in his late wife's time; he neither denied nor took pains to clear himself of ("Minutes of Baltimore Meeting," *QRNM:*236). [No other marriage reference found].

Hussey, Miriam, on 28 d. 3 m. 1794 was charged with bastardy being in an unmarried state ("Minutes of Baltimore Meeting," *QRNM:*222-223).

Hutchings, Thomas, d. by Nov 1760 leaving orphans Moses, Thomas, James, Kesiah, Ann, and Sarah Hutchings (BAMI 1755-1763: 35).

Hutchings, William, d. by 3 Sep 1722 when his admx. Diana had m. Matthew Hale (*q.v.*), and then Nicholas Besson (*q.v.*) (MDAD 5:83; BALR RM#HS:73).

Hutchings, William, m. by 10 June 1722 Judith, extx. of George Hope (*q.v.*) (BAAD 4:142; MDTP 26:12).

Hutchings, William, m. by 13 July 1772 Grace, admx. of Nathaniel Adams (MDTP 45:139-140).

Hutchins, [-?-], m. by 11 March 1772, Elizabeth, sister of Charles Robinson (BAWB 3: 233).

Hutchins, Elizabeth, was charged with bastardy at the June 1733 Court (BACP HWS#9:15).

Hutchins, John, in Nov 1768 was found guilty of bastardy (BAMI 1768-1769:26).

Hutchins, Nicholas, in June 1734 was charged with begetting a bastard on the body of Elizabeth Cheshire (BACP HWS#9:253, 309).

Hutchins, Nicholas, in June 1737 was charged with begetting a bastard on the body of Sarah Hands (or Owens); at the same time Margaret Connolly also named Hutchins as father of her child (BACP HWS&TR:57).

Hutchins, Thomas, m. by March 1709 Susanna, extx. of Thomas Richardson (BACP IS#B:120).

Hutchins, Thomas, m. by 8 April 1794 Jemima, heir of Jacob Johnson (BAAD 11:397).

Hutchinson, Joseph, m. by 28 July 1781, Kezia, daughter of Nicholas Riffett, of Middle River Upper Hundred, yeoman (BAWB 3:440).

Hutchinson, Robert, and Phebe McCabe were married by license dated 14 Aug 1779 (BAML). On 13 Oct 1786 Phebe was named as the admx. of John McCabe (BAAD 8:326, 9:212). Phebe Hutchinson of Baltimore Town, widow, in her will made 12 Nov 1796 named her children Thomas McCabe, Mary Thompson, Catherine Shaw, and John McCabe (BAWB 5:429).

Hutchison, William, of Prince George's Co., m. by 6 July 1722 Sarah, daughter of Robert Doyne of Charles Co. (BALR IS#G:88, TB#E:340).

Hyatt, William, of this city, was m. last Thurs. eve. at Chestertown, by Rev. Dr. Shields, to Rebecca Miller, daughter of the late Richard Miller, Esq., of Kent Co. (*Federal Gazette and Baltimore Daily Advertiser* 22 Nov 1800).

Hydie, George, m. by 26 Sep 1793 Rachel, daughter of Nathan and Elizabeth (Ensor) Griffith (MCHP#2029). (BAML gives his name as George Heide).

Hyland, John, son of Col. Stephen Hyland of Cecil Co., and Miss Ann Johnson, daughter of Thomas Johnson, were m. last eve. by Rev. Bend (*Federal Gazette and Baltimore Daily Advertiser* 1 Nov 1799).

Hyner. See Hiner.

Hynes. See Hines.

Hynson, Charles, m. by 13 May 1759 Anita, sister of James Matthews (MWB 30:825 abst. by Gibb).

Iams. See Ijams.

Ibach, Heinrich, m. by 15 March 1785 Elisabeth Kerlingerin ("First Record Book for the Reformed and Lutheran Congregations at Manchester, Baltimore (Now Carroll) Co." *MGSB* 35:281, 283). **N.B.:** See Henry Epaugh above.

Ibach, Henrich, m. by 15 Sep 1788 Elisabetha Gerling ("First Record Book for the Reformed and Lutheran Congregations at Manchester, Baltimore (Now Carroll) Co." *MGSB* 35:283).

Ibach, Jacob, m. by 15 Feb 1761 Anna Catherine Gussin (or Giessin) ("First Record Book for the Reformed and Lutheran Congregations at Manchester, Baltimore (Now Carroll) Co." *MGSB* 35:265).

Ibach. See also Epaugh.

Igo, William, m. by 5 Jan 1793 Elizabeth Marsh, who received an equal share of the estate of John Marsh (BAAD 11:172).

Ijams, John, m. by 15 June 1763 [-?-], widow and admx. of Nicholas Watkins (BAAD 6:49).

Ijams (Iams), William, m. by 3 June 1750 Margaret, surviving admx. of John Williams (*q.v.*) (MDAD 38:47; MDTP 36:188).

Imbleton, Edward, and Ann Bryan were m. on 28 June 1790 (Marriage License Returns of Rev. William West, filed 21 Nov 1790: Scharf Papers, MS 1999 at MdHS). In May 1792 Imbleton stated he would not pay the debts of Ann Brian, *alias* Ann Imbleton (*Baltimore Daily Repository* 8 May 1792).

Ingle, John, in 1772 was given an allowance for his support (Levy List for 1772).He was the father of at least two sons: William, aged 14 last 5 May, and John, aged 12 last 12 Nov, both of whom, in Aug 1772 were bound to John Murray, collier (BAMI 1772, 1775-1781: 17).

Ingle, William, in Nov 1719 was charged with begetting a bastard on the body of Ann Erroll (BACP IS#C: 246). At March Court, 1724, he bound out his sons John Arrindale, aged 6, and Samuel Ingle, aged 1 to serve William Wright until they reached the age of 21 (BACP IS&TW#1:128).

Ingle, William, on 13 Oct 1746 conv. land to his son William Carback *alias* William Ingle, said deed to take effect after the death of the grantor's wife Catherine (BALR TB#E:221).

Ingram, Peasley, and Ruth Hammond, daughter of Major Charles Hammond were m. on 25 June 1730 (Harrison, "St. Ann's Parish Register," Anne Arundel Co., at MdHS: 432). Ingram d. by 22 May 1744 by which time his admx. Ruth had m. Thomas Franklin (*q.v.*) (BAAD 5:10). Peasley and Ruth were probably the parents of Ruth Ingram who d. leaving a will dated 17 June 1782, proved 14 Sep 1782. She named her bros.-in-law Thomas and Benjamin Franklin; the three children of her sister-in-law Sarah Smith and James Smith; sister Sarah; Hannah Wilmott, daughter of John and Aberilla; James Franklin, exec., was to have *Ingram's Rich Neck* in Back River Neck. Thomas Love, John Wilmott, and Thomas Franklin (BAWB 3:445). In 1795 Ruth Ingram was named as a sister of Benjamin Franklin (Petition of Sarah Smith, BOCP Petitions, 1795).

Ingram, William, and Phoebe Whitehead were m. on 6 Nov 1731 (Harrison, "St. John's Parish Register:" 73). On 5 Nov 1738 Phoebe was named as a daughter in the will of Elizabeth Finsham (*q.v.*) and Robert and Elizabeth Whitehead (MWB 22:28 abst. in *Md. Cal. of Wills* 8:14).

Inloes, David, and Mary Cole were m. c1791 (Marr. Returns of Rev. John Turner, Scharf Papers, MS.1999 at MdHS). On 10 Dec 1792 Mary Inloes was named as a daughter of Delilhah Crocker, dec., wife of Thomas Crocker, and as a sister of Charles Caple Cole, Cassandra Cole, and Elizabeth Cole (BAWB 5:65).

Inloes, Henry, m. by 11 June 1791, [-?-], heir of John Hood (BAAD 10:381).

Ireland, Rev. John, and Miss Nancy Waters were m. lately in Harford Co. (*Maryland Journal and Baltimore Advertiser* 2 Oct 1787).

Ireland, Nathaniel, in Nov 1757 was convicted of bastardy (BAMI 1755-1763).

Ireland, Sarah, in March 1768 was guilty of bastardy (BAMI 1768-1769:4).

Ireland, William, m. by 3 Feb 1736/7 Mary, daughter of William Hickman (MWB 21:746 abst. in *Md. Cal. of Wills* 6:206).

Isaacs, Capt. Isaac, was m. last eve. by Rev. Mr. Bend, to Henrietta Mulakin, both of this city (*Federal Gazette and Baltimore Daily Advertiser* 8 Oct 1798).

Isham, James, m. by 7 March 1716 Julian, widow of Abraham de Lappe (BALR HW#2:291, TR#A:455).

Isham (Isum), James and Elizabeth Robinson were m. [date not given] (Harrison, "St. John's Parish Register:" 11). On 8 Nov 1722 Elizabeth was named as an admx. of William Robinson (*q.v.*) (BALR IS#H:172; MDAD 5:47; MDTP 26:81).

Isham. James, innholder, on 30 May 1738 was about to marry Mary, widow of Thomas Warren, and Isham conv. all his land and movables to his son James Isham of Philadelphia, blacksmith, at the elder Isham's decease (BALR HWS#1-A:74). They were m. on 1 June 1738 (Harrison, "St. John's Parish Register:" 91). Mary 'Issom' in a codicil dated 4 Jan 1742 was named as the mother of Thomas Jones (MWB 23:22 abst. in *Md. Cal. of Wills* 8:196).

Isoard (Tsoard), Joseph, (son of Mark and Rosalia de Fourgerer; native of Argon), and Frances Deschamps (daughter of Lewis and Mary Tibodeau) were m. by lic. on 27 Oct 1793 at St. Peter's Catholic Church, Baltimore (*Piet:* 144; BAML).

Israel, [-?-], m. by 5 June 1794 Priscilla, sister of Otho Holland Williams who named Priscilla's son Joseph (BAWB 5:180).

Israel, John, m. by 15 Feb 1706 Margaret, widow and extx. of Col. Edward Dorsey (INAC 26;147).

Israel, John, d. by 18 April 1726 when Samuel Heighe (*q.v.*) or Heugh (*q.v.*) and wife Mary, execs., administered his estate (BAAD 3:40).

Israello, Jacob, son of Angel Israello, b. 14 Feb 1746, aged 13 last 14 Feb, in Aug 1760 was bound to Jacob Myers to learn the trade of saddler (BAMI 1755-1763: 27).

Isum. See Isham.

Ives, Elizabeth, was charged with bastardy at Aug Court, 1721 (BACP IS#C:570).

"J"

Jackman, Robert, in 1762 paid a criminal fine for fornication and bastardy (BAMI 1755-1763).

Jacks, Thomas, m. by 15 Aug 1726 Elizabeth, widow of John Powell; Thomas and Elizabeth were the parents of Richard and Barbara Jacks; John and Elizabeth Powell were the parents of John and Joseph Powell (BALR IS#H: 276).

Jackson, [-?-], m. by 21 March 1771 Molly, sister of Theophilus Kitten of Anne Arundel Co. (BAWB 4:111).

Jackson, Abraham, d. by Oct 1792 leaving two daughters, Frances and Rosanna, who were made wards of William Jackson (BAOC 3:12).

Jackson, Eleanor, admx., on 23 Aug 1785 posted bond to administer the estate of Peter Blyden (BAAB 5:39).

Jackson, Elizabeth, orphan of Isaac Jackson, in March 1759 chose George Presbury as her guardian (BAMI 1755-1763).

Jackson, Henry, m. by 24 Jan 1704 Mary, sister of William Kimball of Baltimore Co. (MWB 3:432 abst. in *Md. Cal. of Wills* 3:45).

Jackson, Henry, and Clare Anderson were married by banns on 8 July 1791 at St. Peter's Catholic Church, Baltimore (*Piet:* 137).

Jackson, Isaac, and Mary Hollingsworth were m. on 17 July 1733 (Harrison, "St. John's Parish Register:" 69; BALR IS#L:36, TR#D:271).

Jackson, Isaiah, on 13 d. 10 m. 1796 was charged with accomplishing his marriage contrary to the good order ("Minutes of Baltimore Meeting," *QRNM:*227). Isaiah Jackson and Catherine Davis were married by license dated 28 Jan 1796 (BAML).

Jackson, Israel, aged 9 last 15 March, son of Phoebe Jackson, in Aug 1756 was bound to James Yoe to age 21 (BAMI 1755-1763).

Jackson, Jacob, m. on 4 Oct 1731 Frances Dallahide (Harrison, "St. John's Parish Register:" 39). In April 1744 Jacob Jackson and his present wife, who was niece to his deceased wife, were summoned by the Vestry to show cause why they should not be prosecuted for marrying contrary to the Table of Marriages. The couple appeared before the Vestry in May 1744, and had no legal defense to take, and it appeared that they had married contrary to the Table of Marriages. They were to be reported to the next county court ("St. John's and St. George's Parish Register Vestry Proceedings," MS at MdHS).

Jackson, Jemima, confessed to bastardy at June 1750 Court; she confessed to bastardy again at November Court 1754 (BACP TR#5:176-177, BB#A:450-451).

Jackson, Jemima, in 1762 paid a criminal fine for fornication and bastardy (BAMI 1755-1763).

Jackson, Jo., on 30 Oct 1750, with Ann Cole, was summoned to appear before the vestry. He appeared before the vestry on 7 May 1751 for illicit cohabitation with Ann, but stated he was married but could not produce the certificate he was given next vestry day to produce the certificate. On 20 Dec 1752 they both were summoned to appear before the vestry again. In Feb 1753 they were ordered returned to the court for unlawful cohabitation ("St. John's and St. George's Parish Register Vestry Proceedings," MS. at MdHS).

Jackson, John, m. by 5 Aug 1773, Hannah, admx. of Garrett Cruzon (MINV 121:1; BAAD 7:226).

Jackson, Joseph, on 5 May 1752 was summoned to appear before the vestry of St. George's Parish for unlawful cohabitation with Ann Coal (Reamy, S*t. George's Parish Register:* 106).

Jackson, Mary, was charged with bastardy at the Aug 1742 Court. She confessed to bastardy on 6 March 1745/6 (BACP TB#D: 8, Liber 1745-1746, pp. 800, 818). Mary Jackson's son William was born 2 June 1742. She and John Norviband were summoned to appear before the vestry on 31 March 1746 (Reamy, *St. George's Parish Register:* 67, 105).

"J"

Jackson, Robert, of Bush River m. Isabella Hooper of Cranbury Hall, after their banns were pub. on 30 July 1699 and on the first and second Sundays in Aug 1699, on 24 Aug 1699 (Reamy, *St. George's Parish Register:* 5). Benjamin Lego, aged 76, deposed on 15 Sep 1750 that he was a neighbor of Robert Jackson and Isabella his wife and they had two sons and that he had one son already called Abraham and the oldest twin was named Isaac and the younger Jacob; some time later Lego was at the house of Jonathan Massey who m. the sister of Isabella the wife of Jackson, and Massey's wife said that Robert Jackson could both read and write (BACT TR#E:7-8). William Hill, aged 48, deposed on 15 Sep 1750 that he was a neighbor to Robert Jackson, and that Robert had two sons and the older one was named Isaac; that Jonathan Massey was guardian to the said children. Hill's deposition was witnessed by Mary Jackson, widow of Isaac and Jamima Jackson widow of Jacob Jackson (BACT TR#E:8-9). John Dawney, aged 67, deposed on 15 Sep 1750 that he frequently heard the neighbors talk about the birth of Robert Jackson's twin children, Isaac and Jacob, and that Isaac was the first born (BACT TR#E:9).

Jackson, Simon, m. by 23 May 1688 Elizabeth Chadwill, eldest daughter of John Chadwill (MDTP 14:72). She m. 2nd, on 14 July 1688 Thomas Morris (*q.v.*)

Jackson, Thomas, called "son of Robert Drisdale" [*sic*], who in his will made 3 May 1704 named his sons-in-law John Fisher and Thomas Jackson as executors (MWB 3:241 abst. in *Md. Cal. of Wills* 3:38).

Jackson, Thomas, and Mary Kimball were m. on 25 July 1703 (Harrison, "St. George's Parish Register:" 199); she m. 2nd, by 24 Jan 1705 John Roberts (*q.v.*) on 11 April 1705 (Harrison, "St. George's Parish Register:" 204), and 3rd, by 13 June 1731 David Hughes (*q.v.*).

Jackson, Thomas, in March 1719/20, was named as the father of Elizabeth Jenkins' child (BACP IS#C:279, 366).

Jackson, Thomas, and Patience Harryman were m. on 14 July 1757 (Harrison, "St. John's Parish Register:" 215). Jackson d. by 27 Dec 1773, leaving Thomas and George Jackson, named as grandsons in the will of George Harryman, Sr. (BAWB 2:285).

Jackson, Capt. Thomas, of Baltimore, and Miss Elizabeth Reilly of Philadelphia were m. last eve. by Rev. Bend (*Baltimore Telegraphe* 9 Sep 1797).

Jacob, [-?-], m. by 1 Nov 1772 Catherine, daughter of Michael Mull (BAWB 3:270).

Jacob, Robert, b. 7 Dec 1766, d. Wed., 29 June 1818, and Elizabeth Hack, b. 5 Dec 1758, were m. by 31 Oct 1789 when their daughter Margaret was b. ("Robert Jacob Bible," *MBR* 7:92).

Jacob, William, 5th son of Zachariah Jacob of Anne Arundel Co., married on 19 July 1772 Mary, daughter of Renaldo Monk. Late of London, by his wife Rachel, widow of Edward Riston of *Ranger's Forest*, Baltimore Co. (Harrison, "St. Paul's Parish Register:" 176). In Oct 1773 Jacob stated he would not pay the debts of his Mary, who had departed his bed and board (*Maryland Journal and Baltimore Advertiser* 30 Oct 1773).

Jacob, William, and Jane Fitzgerald were married on 4 July 1786 (Marr. Returns of Rev. William West, Scharf Papers, MS.1999 at MdHS). On 14 Aug 1789 Jane was named as the admx. of James Fitzgerald (BAAD 9:231). On 29 Sep 1792 Jane

MacGee (*q.v.*), widow of Patrick MacGee, made her will naming her daughter Jane Jacob, wife of William Jacob (BAWB 5:491).

Jacobs, John, m. by 12 Oct 1790 [-?-], heir of George Ogg (BAAD 10:209). Helen Ogg, in her will made 2 April 1798 named her daughter Rachel Jacobs (BAWB 6:89).

Jacobs, Moses, stated he would not pay the debts of his wife Easter Jacobs as she had left his house on last Sat., and said she would not return (*Federal Gazette and Baltimore Daily Advertiser* 22 April 1800).

Jacquett, J. P., and Mrs. Rebecca Stran, both of Fell's Point, were m. last eve. by Rev. Ireland (*Baltimore Telegraphe* 19 Oct 1798).

Jalland, John, and Ruth Jane Bungy were m. on 19 Jan 1786 (Marr. Returns of Rev. William West, Scharf Papers, MS.1999 at MdHS). In his will made 26 Aug 1800 Jalland named his wife Ruth Jane and his brother-in-law John Holland (BAWB 6:296).

James, Capt. [-?-], was m. last eve. by Rev. Mr. Bruce to Miss Sarah Legard, both of this city (*Federal Gazette and Baltimore Daily Advertiser* 14 May 1800).

James, Amos, and Mary Lee on 28 d. 5 m. 1791 declared their intention to marry ("Minutes of Gunpowder Meeting," *QRNM*:90).

James, Charles, of Baltimore Co., Gent., m. by March 1670 Elizabeth, daughter and sole heir of Leonard Strong of Anne Arundel Co., merchant (MPL 14:40; *ARMD* 51:142; MDTP 5:32).

James, Edward, a black man, stated he would not pay the debts of his wife Elizabeth (*Federal Gazette and Baltimore Daily Advertiser* 20 Jan 1800).

James, George, and Mary Lemmon were married by license dated 21 Jan 1794. Mary was a daughter of Jacob Lemmon (BAWB 6:59; BAML).

James, Hannah, d. intestate leaving Henry Newman to administer her estate. He petitioned the court to sell some of her property, and has signatures from the following reps. of the dec.: Henry Newman as guardian of William James; Sally Newman; Lydia Micks and William Bell Mickes (BOCP Petition of Henry Newman, 1792).

James, Henry, (*alias*** Henry Quine),** in Nov 1741 was charged with begetting a bastard on the body of Kedemoth Merryman (BACP TB#TR:56, 183).

James, John, on 5 March 1741 was named as a grandson in the will of John Mahone (MWB 22:533 abst. in *Md. Cal. of Wills* 8:193).

James, John, m. by 2 Aug 1786 Mary, daughter of Edward Bussey (BAWB 4:245).

James, John, of the Fork of Gunpowder, stated he would not pay the debts of his wife Mary (*Maryland Journal and Baltimore Advertiser* 31 Oct 1786).

James, John, and Letitia Delworth were m. by 25 Nov 1789 in Baltimore (Marr. Returns of Ezekiel Cooper, Scharf Papers, MS. 1999 at MdSA, *MGSB* 32 (1) (Winter 1991) 6).

James, John, was m. last Sat. eve. by Rev. Mr. Bend, to Miss Maria Johns, both of this town (*Federal Intelligencer and Baltimore Daily Gazette* 12 May 1795).

James, John, and Jane Taylor, both of Baltimore were m. 2nd inst. by Rev Mr. Richards (*Federal Gazette and Baltimore Daily Advertiser* 10 June 1799).

James, Mary, in 1762 paid a criminal fine for fornication and bastardy (BAMI 1755-1763).

James, Michael, in Nov 1721 was charged with begetting a bastard on the body of Elizabeth Joy (BACP IS#C:619).

James, Michael, and Constant Shepherd were m. on 20 Aug 1736 (Harrison, "St. John's Parish Register:" 73).As the admx. of Michael James, Constant m. 2nd, Henry Stone (q.v.).

James, Thomas, m. by 20 Feb 1682, Sarah, relict and admx. of Gyles Stevens (*q.v.*) (INAC 8: 3). By 26 June 1696 he was living in Concord, Chester Co., Pa. (BALR RM#HS:524, 529, 530).

James (Jones), Thomas, m. by 1696 Mary Harrison, daughter and extx. of Edward Dowse (*q.v.*) (BALR RM#HS: 524; BACP F#1:111). She had m. 1st, [-?-] Harrison, and she m. 3rd, John Hillen (*q.v.*).

James, Thomas, m. by 11 Nov 1766 [-?-], daughter of John Charke (Chocke) (BAAD 55:277).

James, William, m. by 1 June 1750 Margaret, surviving admx. of John Williams (*q.v.*) (MDAD 35:36). His name is given as Jams [*sic*] (MINV 43:1).

James, William, on 31 d. 12 m. 1780 was charged with having been m. by a priest to a woman not of our Society ("Minutes of Gunpowder Meeting," *QRNM:* 74). William James and Rachel Bull were m. by lic. dated 15 Aug 1780 (HAML).

James, William, orphan son of Hannah James, in June 1794 was made a ward of Sarah Newman (BAOC 3:97).

Jameson, John, m. by 9 May 1753 Isabella Lombard, guardian of Elizabeth and Letitia, daughters of Henry Wetherel (MDAD 34:88).

Jameson, Martha, servant of John Watkins, was charged with bastardy at Nov 1739 Court (BACP HWS#TR:87).

Jamison, Capt. Adam, of Baltimore, was m. on Sun. eve., to Polly Johnson, daughter of Thomas Johnson of Baltimore Co. (*Maryland Gazette or Baltimore General Advertiser* 12 Sep 1786).

Jamison, John, and Ann Jackson were m. on 17 April 1794 (Richards' Marr. Register), Ann Jamison, (formerly Jackson), on 13 d. 11 m. 1794 had a complaint made against her for having her marriage accomplished contrary to the good order ("Minutes of Baltimore Meeting," *QRNM:*223).

Jamison, Mary, on 15 Aug 1798 was named as on of the representatives of Thomas Johnson in his administration account (BAAD 12:468).

Janney, Sarah, (late Wilson), on 26 d. 1 m. 1799 was found guilty of outgoing in marriage by assistance of a Baptist Teacher ("Minutes of Deer Creek Meeting," *QRNM:*161). [No other marriage reference found].

Jaquet, Dr. Jesse, of Fells Point, d. by 20 June 1798 when Patrick Bennett and Nicholas Slubey petitioned the Orphans Court that his property should be preserved for the doctor's orphan children; the subscribers were sureties for admin. by John Paul Jaquet, brother of the dec., who they discovered had a propensity for Gaming for money. They asked to be released as sureties (BOCP Petition of Patrick Bennett and Nicholas Slubey, 1798).

Jarman, John, d. by June 1794 leaving orphans: John, William, Mary, and Cassandra, who were made wards of Mary Jarman (BAOC 3:97).

Jarman, Martha, was charged with bastardy at the June 1724 Court (BACP IS&TW#3: 309).

Jarman,Thomas, and Mary Rawley were m. on 29 April 1733 (Harrison, "St. John's Parish Register:" 208). She m. 2nd, Francis Roach (*q.v.*).

Jarman, Thomas, m. by 25 April 1789 Mary, daughter of Joshua Barton (BAAD 9:326).

Jarrett, Abraham, d. by 3 July 1759 by which time his admx. Eleanor had m. Michael McGuire (*q.v.*) (MDTP 32:273).

Jarrold, [-?-], m. by 14 Feb 1769, Catherine, daughter of William Payne of Baltimore Co., who also named a granddaughter Elizabeth Jarrold (BAWB 3:61; MWB 37:418, abst. in *Md. Cal. of Wills* 14:109).

Jarrold, Mary, in 1765, petitioned for her son's freedom from Conrode Conrode (BAMI 1765: 44).

Jarrold. See also Jarratts.

Jarvis [-?-], m. by 22 Sep 1789 Elizabeth, daughter of Edward Oursler (BAWB 5:244).

Jarvis (Jarves), John, and Sarah Wright were m. on 2 July 1761 (Harrison, "St. John's Parish Register:" 222). On 11 July 1763 Sarah was named as a daughter of Jacob Wright (BAWB 3:170).

Jarvis, Philip, and Mary Conaway were m. on 9 July 1733 (Harrison, "St. Margaret's Parish," Anne Arundel Co., at MdHS: 103). Jarvis d. by 8 May 1744, by which time his admx, Mary, had m. 2nd, John Robinson (*q.v.*) (MDTP 31:476).

Jarvis, Samuel, confessed to bastardy at March 1745/6 Court and was fined on 5 Aug 1746 (BACP TB&TR:134).

Jarvis, Sarah in 1765 was presented for bastardy (BAMI 1765:2).

Jay, Hannah, formerly Wilson, on 5 d. 10 m. 1762 was charged with marrying outside the society ("Minutes of Deer Creek Meeting," *QRNM:*129). [No other marriage reference found].

Jay, Joseph, on 13 d. 10 m. 1796 was charged with accomplishing his marriage contrary to the good order ("Minutes of Baltimore Meeting," *QRNM:*227). Joseph Jay and Anne Williams were m. on 19 June 1796 (Harrison, "St. Paul's Parish Register:" 323). On 9 Aug 1797 Ann was named as the admx. of John Williams (BAAD 12:328).

Jay, Thomas, son of Stephen, on 26 d. 1 m. 1797 announced his intention to marry Sarah Wilson, daughter of Thomas and Ann, both dec. ("Minutes of Deer Creek Meeting," *QRNM:*157).

Jeff, William, and Elizabeth Aishleys [*sic;* Ashley?] were m. 29 May 1701; their daughter Margaret was b. 6 Jan 1701/2 (Harrison, "St. George's Parish Register:" 192, 193). Elizabeth m. 2nd, John Olwell (*q.v.*).

Jeff, William, and Ruth Marthews (Matthews?) were m. on 12 Aug 1697 (Harrison, "St. George's Parish Register:" 178). William Jeff, living at the head of Swan Creek was bapt. the last day of June 1700 (Harrison, "St. George's Parish Register:" 192).

Jeffers, George, mariner, and Miss Catherine Robinson were m. last eve. at Fell's Point by Rev. Dr. Allison (*Maryland Journal and Baltimore Advertiser* 29 Jan 1796).

Jeffries (Jeffery), William, and Mary Puntany were married by license dated 7 Dec 1790 (BAML; BALR WG#OO:228).

Jeger, [-?-], m. by 14 July 1780 Mary, daughter of William Millward of Christansteed, St. Croix, West Indies, merchant, now keeping store in Baltimore (BAWB 3:407).

Jenkins, [-?-], m. by 29 Nov 1769 Charity, daughter of Thomas Wheeler (BAWB 3:171).

Jenkins, Elizabeth, was charged with bastardy at March 1719/20 Court and named Thomas Jackson as the father (BACP IS#C:279, 366).

Jenkins, Elizabeth, was convicted for bastardy in 1761 (BAMI 1755-1763).

Jenkins, Francis, m. by 22 June 1770 Cassandra, daughter of William Grafton (BAAD 6:280; MDAD 68:160; BACT B#G:323).

Jenkins, Elizabeth, was charged with bastardy at March 1719/20 Court and named Thomas Jackson as the father (BACP IS#C:279, 366).

Jenkins, Elizabeth, was convicted for bastardy in 1761 (BAMI 1755-1763).

Jenkins, Francis, m. by 22 June 1770 Cassandra, daughter of William Grafton (BAAD 6:280; MDAD 68:160; BACT B#G:323).

Jenkins, Ignatius, d. by Dec 1797 leaving orphans, Francis, Jesse, Eleanor, Teresa, Oswald, Henry, and Samuel, who chose Ignatius Walter Jenkins as their guardian (BAOC 3:239).

Jenkins, William, and Mary Clarke were m. on 25 March 1758 (Harrison, "St. George's Parish Register:" 363). She m. 2nd, John Peacock (*q.v.*).

Jenkins, William, and Ann Hillen were m. by lic. on 21 April 1793 at St. Peter's Catholic Church, Baltimore (*Piet:* 137).

Jennings (Jinnings), [-?-], m. by 19 Dec 1761 Aley, daughter of Thomas Litten (MINV 76:363).

Jennings, Henry, was fined on 6 Nov 1744 for begetting a bastard on the body of [-?-] BACP 1743-1745: 390).

Jennings, Samuel Kennedy, b. 6 June 1771, son of Jacob and Mary (Kennedy) Jennings, and Mary Cox, d. 23 Jan 1771, daughter of John and Mary (Ferguson) Cox, were m. on 18 Jan 1793 ("Jennings Bible, *"HMGB* 2 (2) (April 1931) 9-10).

Jennings, William, and Hannah Rutledge were m. on 20 Aug 1770 (Harrison, "St. John's Parish Register:" 260). She was a daughter of Abraham Rutledge (MWB 39:336, abst. *in Md. Cal. of Wills* 15:67).

Jenny, Capt. Joseph, and Mary Conway, daughter of Robert, were m. by lic. on 6 March 1800 at St. Peter's Catholic Church, Baltimore (*Piet:* 137).

Jessop, Charles, and Mary Gorsuch were married by license dated 12 April 1786 (BAML). On 10 Aug 1791 Mary was named as a daughter of David Gorsuch, and a representative of Kerrenhapuck Gorsuch (BAAD 10:423, 12:82).

Jessop, Nicholas, and Miss Lydia Bosley, both of Baltimore Co., were m. last eve. by Rev. Richards (*Baltimore Telegraphe* 17 Jan 1799).

Jewell, Alice. See Joseph McClaskey.

Jewit (Dewit), Ann, on 3 d. 6 m. 1773 was to be visited about outgoing in marriage; her mother Margaret Webster and her sister Margaret Talbott were also to be visited on that account ("Minutes of Deer Creek Meeting," *QRNM:*135). On 31 d, 5 m. 1787 Ann Jewet (formerly Webster) produced a paper condemning her outgoing in marriage ("Minutes of Deer Creek Meeting," *QRNM:*144). [No other marriage reference found].

Jinnings. See Jennings.

Johns, [-?-], m. by 19 June 1745 Ann, daughter of Cassandra Cole who also named a granddaughter Cassandra Johns (MWB 24:444 abst. by Gibb).

Johns, [-?-], m. by 12 July 1774, Drusilla, heir of Isaac Raven (BAAD 7:228).

Johns, Abraham, chyrurgeon, m. by 10 Oct 1732 Hannah, daughter of Roger Mathews and sister of John Mathews (MWB 20:358 abst. in *Md. Cal. of Wills* 6:217). Hannah was the widow of 1st, Asael Maxwell (*q.v.*); she m. 3rd, on 26 Nov 1734 John Hall (*q.v.*) (BALR HWS#M:110, TR#C:188, 239; BAAD 4:75).

Johns, Ann, daughter of Richard Johns, dec., on 27 d. 4 m. 1762 was reported to have been lately m. by a priest and her sister Mary Johns was in attendance ("Minutes of Deer Creek Meeting," *QRNM:*129). [No other marriage reference found].

Johns, Nathan, on 2 d. 11 m. 1762 condemned his actions for outgoing in marriage ("Minutes of Deer Creek Meeting," *QRNM:* 129). [No other marriage reference found].

Johns, Philip, on 5 d. 6 m. 1764 was charged with outgoing in marriage ("Minutes of Deer Creek Meeting," *QRNM:* 130). [No other marriage reference found].

Johns, Richard, of the Cliffs, Calvert Co., m. by 10 June 1685 Elizabeth, sister of Paul Kinsey (BALR RM#HS: 154, 253).

Johns, Capt. Richard, was m. Thurs. eve., 9th inst., to Polly Luce (*Maryland Journal and Baltimore Advertiser* 17 April 1789). (They were m. in Baltimore Co.: BAML)

Johns, Richard, son of Nathan and Elizabeth, on 28 d. 8 m. 1794, announced his intention to marry Elizabeth Wilson, daughter of Benjamin and Elizabeth ("Minutes of Deer Creek Meeting," QRNM:154).

Johns, Skipwith, assisted by his brother Henry (who had joined the Methodists), some time before 5 d. 3 m. 1778, stole away the daughter of Nathan Rigbie and married her ("Minutes of Deer Creek Meeting," *QRNM:* 138). [No other marriage reference found].

Johnson, |-?-|, m. by 5 Aug 1717 Sarah, daughter of Ambrose Nelson: by her had two children, Ambrose and Ruth, named as grandchildren in the will of Ambrose Nelson (MWB 19:704).

Johnson, [-?-], of Kent Co., d. by 9 April 1750 having m. Beatrice, daughter of Col. St. Leger Codd of Cecil Co. (BALR TR#C:405).

Johnson, [-?-], m. by 22 Dec 1755 Hester, daughter of Robert Clark of Baltimore Co. (MWB 30:221 abst. by Gibb).

Johnson, |-?-|, m. by 30 May 1770 Cassandra, daughter of William Peddicoart (BAWB 3:320).

Johnson, |-?-|, m by 21 Aug 1797 Ann, daughter of John Almony (BAWB 6:19).

Johnson, Abraham, and Ann Butler, free Negroes, were m. 2 June 1797 at St. Peter's Catholic Church, Baltimore (*Piet:* 137).

Johnson, Absolom, and Ruth Wooden were m. on 24 Jan 1782 (Marriage Register of Rev. Lewis Richards, MS.690 at MdHS); on 3 May 1790 Ruth was named as a daughter of John Wooden, Sr. (BAWB 4:426).

Johnson, Ann. See Ana Floyd, daughter of Rachel.

Johnson, Ann. See Ann Stuart.

Johnson, Anthony, m. on 3 March 1699 Catherine Smith (*Harris and McHenry* 281, "Johnson and Johnson's Lessee vs. Howard" (which cites a now missing Register of marriages, births, and burials, of St, Paul's Parish, Baltimore Co.), *NGSQ* 53:201-202).

Johnson, Archibald, may have m. by 22 March 1766 [-?-], daughter of Adam Burchfield, who called Johnson his son-in-law (BAWB 3:42).

Johnson, Benjamin, was named as a son in the undated will (proved 5 Aug 1700) of Deborah Benger (MWB 6:374 abst. in *Md. Cal. of Wills* 2:197).

Johnson, Rev. Caleb, of Harford Co. and Mrs. Jane Shields of Baltimore were m. last Thurs. eve. by Rev. Dr. Allison (*Maryland Journal and Baltimore Advertiser* 11 Nov 1793).

Johnson, Charity, was charged with bastardy at Nov 1720 Court (BACP HWS#7:61).

Johnson, Daniel, d. by 14 Sep 1715 leaving a widow Frances who m. 2nd, Hugh Grant (*q.v.*), and 3rd, Miles Foy (*q.v.*) (*BCF:*367)..

Johnson, David, son of Thomas and Elizabeth, and Sarah Standiford, daughter of William and Elizabeth, b. 19 Oct 1756, were m. on 19 Nov 1773 ("Bible Record of David Johnson Family," in MGRC 35:70).

Johnson, Edward, Jr., and Miss Ann Plowman, both of Baltimore, were m, last eve. by Rev. John Robinson (*Maryland Journal and Baltimore Advertiser* 1 April 1791; BAML).

Johnson, Edward, of Baltimore, and Miss Mackubin, daughter of William Mackubin, were m. last eve. by Rev. Ireland (*Baltimore Telegraphe* 1 June 1798).

Johnson, Elizabeth, was charged with unlawful cohabitation with Patrick Brannon by the vestry of St. George's Parish on 23 Feb 1768. The complaint was brought by her sister Martha (Reamy, *St,. George's Parish Register:* 110).

Johnson, Henry, m. by 1 Dec 1680, Elizabeth, relict and extx. of Nathaniel Utye (Utie) (*q.v.*); she m. by 11 June 1694, Edward Boothby (*q.v.*) (MDTP 12A:196; INAC 12:143).

Johnson, Israel Hendrick, and Merab Dawes were m. by lic. dated 29 Dec 1784 (BAML). Merab Johnson, (formerly Dawes), on 28 d.5 m. 1785 was condemned for outgoing in marriage ("Minutes of Gunpowder Meeting," *QRNM:*80).

Johnson James, and Miss Ann Hall, both of Baltimore, were m. yesterday by Rev. Reid (*Baltimore Telegraphe* 26 March 1798).

Johnson, James, and Mary Ann Elizabeth [-?-], both Negroes, were m. 24 Oct 1799, at St. Peter's Catholic Church, Baltimore (*Piet:* 137).

Johnson, James, and Hannah Michael were m. by 17 Aug 1790 when their daughter Hannah was b. ("Johnson-Johnston Bible," *MBR* 1:134).

Johnson, James Isham, in April 1795 was made a ward of Jacob Johnson (BAOC 3:150).

Johnson, Jeremiah, b. 1 Jan 1725, m. by 4 March 1758 Cassandra Peddicord, b. 14 March 1735 (John Johnson, Sr., Bible, in *MBR* 7:95-96). She was a daughter of William Peddicoart (BAWB 3:320).

Johnson, Jeremiah, m. by 13 Feb 1788 Eleanor, daughter and admx. of Heighe Sollers (BAAD 9:151).

Johnson, John, m. by 18 June 1774 Hannah, admx. of Garrett Cruzon (MDTP 45:342).

Johnson, John, m. Susan West on 29 Oct 1786 ("Jeremiah and Thomas Johnson Bible Record," *MGSB* 47 (1) (Winter 2006) 6-12; "John Johnson, Sr., Bible," *MBR* 7:94).

Johnson, John, orphan of Thomas, in April 1793 chose Rinaldo Johnson as his guardian (BAOC 3:43).

Johnson, John, m. by 28 May 1800, Ann, daughter of John Almony (BAAD 13:257).

Johnson, Joseph, in Aug 1723 was charged with begetting a bastard on the body of Elizabeth Smithers (BACP IS#TW#3:422).

Johnson, Joseph, and Julia Lacely, native of Ireland, were m. by lic. on 4 Oct 1794, at St. Peter's Catholic Church, Baltimore (*Piet:* 137).

Johnson, Joseph, in his will dated 15 March 1730 named Josias Middlemore as his brother-in-law (MWB 20:215 abst. in *Md. Cal. of Wills* 6:192).

Johnson, Mark, of Anne Arundel Co., m. by 29 March 1745, Elizabeth, coheir of William Cockey of Anne Arundel Co. (BALR TB#D:250).

Johnson, Oneal, of Anne Arundel Co., m. by 29 June 1745 Mary, coheir of William Cockey of Anne Arundel Co., dec. (BALR TB#D:250).

Johnson, Peter, and Fanny Owings, both mulattoes, were m. 21 Sep 1791, at St. Peter's Catholic Church, Baltimore (*Piet:* 137) Peter Johnson stated he would not pay the debts of his wife Fanny who had eloped (*Baltimore Daily Intelligencer* 9 Jan 1794).

Johnson, Rachel, admx., on 5 June 1724 posted bond to administer the estate of John Hastings, who in his will dated 24 Feb 1723 left his entire estate to Rachel Johnson (BAWB 3:254).

Johnson, Robert, m. by 10 Nov 1767 Ann, admx. of John Golder (MDTP 42:260, 43:102 indicates the estate may be in Anne Arundel Co.).

Johnson, Samuel, m. by June 1742 Mary, widow of Garvis Gilbert (BACP TB#TR: 442).

Johnson, Stephen, m. by 19 Feb 1701/2 Ann, kinswoman of Moses Groome (BALR IR#PP: 171, HW#2:119; BAAD 2:27).

Johnson, Thomas, and Alis Bond were m. on 17 Oct 1724 (Harrison, "St. George's Parish Register:" 252). On 3 Nov 1730 Alice was named as a daughter of William Bond (BALR IS#L:56; TB#C:662; MDAD 19:266). On 19 April 1770 Alice Johnson was named as a step-daughter in the will of Sarah Bond (MWB 37:580, abst. in *Md. Cal. of Wills* 14:124).

Johnson, Thomas, Jr., and Mary Clark were m. 29 Nov 1748 (Harrison, "St. George's Parish Register:" 346). She was a legatee of Robert Clark (MWB 30:221 abst. by Gibb; BFD 2:77).

Johnson, Thomas, and Elizabeth [-?-], were m. before [date not given] when their son was b. ("Bible Record of David Johnson Family," MGRC 35:70).

Johnson, Thomas, of Baltimore Co., m. by 19 May 1770, Wealthy daughter of Mordecai Hall of Anne Arundel Co. (AALR IB#2:97).

Johnson, Thomas, m. by 6 Sep 1773 Sarah, admx. of William Kirkman (MDTP 45:160).

Johnson, Thomas, and Patience, daughter of George Harryman were m. by 27 Dec 1773 (MWB 39:727; abst. in *Md. Cal. of Wills* 15:147).

Johnson, Dr. Thomas, and Miss Ann Giles, both of Baltimore, were last Thurs. eve. by Rev. John Coleman (*Baltimore Daily Intelligencer* 24 May 1794).

Johnson, Thomas, m. by 12 April 1797 Elizabeth, legatee of William Sinclair (BAAD 12:287).

Johnson, William, m. by 5 Aug 1735 [-?-], daughter of Thomas Harris; they were the parents of a son named William (BALR HWS#M: 281).

Johnson, William, in 1761 was fined for fornication and bastardy (BAMI 1755-1763).

Johnson, William, and Sarah Brock were m. on 22 Jan 1787 (Marr. Register of Rev. Lewis Richards, MS.690 at MdHS). On 4 Jan 1790, Sarah who received an equal share of the estates of Daniel Brock and of Thomas Brock (BAAD 10:311).

Johnson, William, m. by 13 June 1792 Rachel Royston (or Riston), who received an equal share of £51.5.6¾ from the estate of Thomas Royston (or Riston) (BAAD 11:71).

Johnson, William, sailmaker, was m. last eve. by the Rev. John Ireland, to Mrs. Eleanor Aiskey (Ashley) (*Federal Gazette and Baltimore Daily Advertiser* 24 Aug 1797).

Johnston (Johnson?), George, of Baltimore, and Miss Burnham, daughter of the late Robert Burnham of New York, were m. last eve. by Rev. Ireland (*Baltimore Telegraphe* 23 July 1800).

Johnston, John W., m. by 12 April 1797 Ann, widow of John Kay (BAAD 12:289).

Johnston, Samuel, and Elizabeth Carnan, widow of Christopher Carnan (*q.v.*), entered into a marriage settlement on 7 Sep 1773 (BALR AL#I:271; BALR WG#RR:1).

Jolly, John, d. by 10 Dec 1770 having m. Janet, daughter of Thomas Kelly (BAWB 3:249).

Jones, [-?-], d. by 31 Aug 1738 by which time his widow Mary, mother of Jonathan, Lewis, and Thomas Jones, had m. 2nd, [-?-] Thomas Warren (q.v.), and 3rd, James Isham (*q.v.*) (BALR IS#IK:533, HWS#1-A:69, 70, 71).

Jones, [-?-], m. by 19 Dec 1761 Hannah, daughter of Thomas Litten (MINV 76:363).

Jones, [-?-], m. by 22 Jan 1781 Rachel, daughter of John Hendrickson (BAWB 3:442).

Jones, [-?-], m. by 1799 Sarah, daughter of George Harryman (BOCP Petition of George Harryman, 1799).

Jones, Aaron, a baseborn child who had formerly been bound to Aaron Fox, at the June 1732 Court was assigned to serve Thomas Broad; at the March 1733/4 Court he was ordered to be kept by Elizabeth Goodwin (BACP HWS#7:294, HWS#9:189).

Jones, Abraham, m. by 4 April 1792 [-?-], who received an equal share of the estate of Thomas Gittings (BAAD 11:18).

Jones, Amos, d. 12 Sep 1827, aged 57, m. by license dated 26 Aug 1783 Ann Jones, d. 2 June 1850, aged 95 years (BAML; Joseph Carroll Hopkins, 'Private Graveyard of the Amos Jones Family of Harford County," *MGSB* 20 (1) (Winter 1979) 89-92).

Jones, Ann, servant to William Petticoat, confessed to bastardy at the Aug 1743 Court, and was ordered to be whipped with 15 lashes (BACP 1743-1745:14).

Jones, Aquila, and Elizabeth Dillon on 25 d. 12 m. 1790 declared their intention to marry ("Minutes of Gunpowder Meeting," *QRNM*:89).

Jones, Antony, on 26 d. 6 m. 1800 was found guilty of marrying a woman not in membership with us, with the assistance of a Baptist Teacher ("Minutes of Deer Creek Meeting," *QRNM:*162). [No other marriage reference found].

Jones, Aubrey, m. by 24 Aug 1797 Sarah, daughter of Edward (*q.v.*) and Mary Green; with their daughter Mary Jones, were named in the will of Hannah Green, widow (BAWB 6:79).

Jones, Benjamin, m. by 2 April 1728 Elizabeth, sister of Heathcote Pickett and daughter of William Pickett (BALR, IS#I:64).

Jones, Benjamin, and Honor Kelly were m. on 23 March 1761 Harrison, "St. Thomas Parish Register:" 72). Honor was named as a daughter of James Kelly, husbandman (BAWB 3:397). On 8 Feb 1791 Honour Kelly received an equal share of the estate of James Kelly (BAAD 10:288).

Jones, Cadwallader, and Mary Ellis were m. on 23 April 1702 (Harrison, "St. George's Parish Register:" 196. Mary was named as a daughter of Peter Ellis and sister of John Ellis; Jones and his wife were the parents of Charles Jones (BALR TB#E:157).

Jones, Caleb, aged 14 next 10 April, orphan of John and Esther, in Oct 1792 chose Joseph Tomblinson as his guardian and was bound to him to learn the trade of sadler (BAOC 3:14, 15). In Feb 1795 Caleb Jones of John chose John Jones as his guardian (BAOC 3:140).

Jones, Charity, was charged with bastardy at the Aug 1728 Court and was presented that Nov (BACP HWS#6:22, 74).

Jones, Charles, d. by 2 June 1701, leaving a widow Bridget and sons Thomas and Theophilus (MWB 11:83, abst. in *Md. Cal. of Wills* 2:218). Bridget m 2nd, Edward Smith (*q.v.*).

Jones, Charles, and Frances Cobb were m. on 26 Dec 1727 (Harrison, "St. George's Parish Register:" 257). On 1 Oct 1731 Frances was named as a daughter of James

Cobb of Baltimore Co. whose widow Rebecca had m. 2nd, John Hawkins (BAAD 3:155; MDAD 12:476).

Jones, Charles, was given an allowance for his support and his wife's (Levy List of 1772).

Jones, Chloe, on 1 Nov 1743 was charged by the Vestry of St. John's Parish with John Greer; and was charged with bastardy at the Aug 1745 Court, and confessed (Harrison, "St. John's Vestry Proceedings:" 75; BACP Liber1743-1745:631-632).

Jones, Daniel, carpenter, and Miss Catherine Messersmith, both of Baltimore, were m. last Sat, evening by Rev. Mr. Kurtz (*Maryland Journal and Baltimore Advertiser* 1 Sep 1794).

Jones, David, m. by 16 Jan 1678 Anne, relict of Capt. Thomas Todd (q.v.) (INAC 7A:279). Anne m. 3rd, John Oldton (*q.v.*).

Jones, Elizabeth, was charged with bastardy at the March 1733/4 Court (BACP HWS#9:188).

Jones, Elizabeth. See James Wheeler.

Jones, Enoch, as of 13 Oct 1792 was a ward of Joseph Hook (BAAD 11:138); in April 1794 chose Thomas Bodley as his guardian (BAOC 3:88).

Jones, Esther, d. by 10 April 1792, leaving Caleb and Joshua Jones; John Walton was their guardian (BAAD 121:20).

Jones, Ezekiel, on 29 d. 1 m. 1795 was charged with marrying a woman not in membership and by a Baptist Teacher ("Minutes of Deer Creek Meeting," *QRNM:* 155). [No other marriage reference found].

Jones, Henry, m. by 26 Feb 1726 Mary, widow of Philip Pitstow (*q.v.*) (BAAD 3:59).

Jones, Henry, convict, in March 1750/1 was charged with begetting a bastard on the body of Patience Powell (BACP TR#6:289-290).

Jones, Henry, of the Parish of St. Mary Woolchurch Haw, London, m. by 31 Dec 1761 Susanna [Heyling?], widow of James Dobbins (BALR B#L:12).

Jones, Isaac, on 24 d. 4 m. 1793 was charged with having some time ago taken a woman to keep his house and that he had made a proposal of marriage to her soon after the death of his wife; that he had 'flighted' [flouted?] the advise of his friends and had m. her with the assistance of a Baptist Preacher ("Minutes of Deer Creek Meeting," *QRNM:* 152). Isaac Jones and Mary Hearn were m. by lic. dated 2 April 1793 (BAML).

Jones, Jacob, and Elizabeth 'Perrigoe' were married by license dated 7 June 1786 (BAML). On 12 Oct 1786 Elizabeth was named as a daughter of Joseph Peregoy (BACT 1785-1788, MS 2865 at MdHS: 206).

Jones, Jacob, d. by 22 Nov 1787 leaving a minor child Jacob. John Jones, guardian, filed an account (BAGA 1:37).

Jones, John, m. by 17 March 1701 Elizabeth, mother of Wolfron and John Hunt. John and Elizabeth had a son Jonas (PCLR TL#2:759).

Jones, John, admin., on 3 Aug 1714 posted bond to administer the estate of John Watts; John Watts of Anne Arundel Co. renounced his right to administer (BAAB 4:52).

Jones, John, m. by 25 July 1724 Margaret, daughter and sole heir of John Chadwell (or Shadwell), Jr., of Baltimore Co., dec., who was a son of John Chadwell, Jr. (BALR IS#G:352, IS#K:157).

Jones, John, on 9 Nov 1724, advised all persons not to trust or give credit to his wife Johanna who had eloped from him and cohabited with another man (BALR IS#H:111).

213

Jones, John, and Hannah Wooley were m. in Dec 1732 (Harrison, "St. John's Parish Register:" 82). Hannah was a daughter of John Wooley (*q.v.*) who d. by Aug 1747 (BAAB 4:117; BALR IS#L:405).

Jones, John, m. by 27 Aug 1757 Mary, niece of Nicholas Ruxton Gay (BALR B#G:36).

Jones, John, m. by 13 Jan 1762 Sarah, formerly wife of Robert Hawkins, Sr. They conveyed to Robert Hawkins one-third part of the lands which Robert, Sr., left to his wife for her life (BALR B#I:443).

Jones, John, aged 11 next March, son of Emanuel, in Nov 1768 was bound to Thomas Davis and his wife Rachel (BAMI 1768-1769).

Jones, John, denied the charges made by Henry Rutter, who was the brother of Jones' wife (*Maryland Journal and Baltimore Advertiser* 30 Dec 1777).

Jones, John, some time before he d. made a codicil to his will leaving money for the support, maintenance, and education of his three sons Joshua, Caleb, and Enoch. John Walton was admin. (BOCP Petition of John Walton, 1791).

Jones, John, m. by 29 Nov 1794 Sarah, daughter of George Harryman (BAWB 5:236; BAAD 12:183).

Jones, John, and Eleanor Taylor were m. on 28 May 1799 (Harrison, "St. Paul's Parish Register:" 371). On 5 Feb 1800 Eleanor was named as the admx. of John Taylor (*q.v.*). (BAAD 13:187).

Jones, Joseph, on 28 d. 7 m. 1791 was reported to have separated from his wife Phoebe ("Minutes of Deer Creek Meeting," *QRNM:* 149). [No other marriage reference found].

Jones, Joshua, m. by 8 June 1790 Mary, heir of William Harvey and legatee of Priscilla Harvey (BAAD 10:158, 386).

Jones, Joshua, orphan of John and Esther, in Aug 1792 chose Nicholas N. Harvey as his guardian (BAOC 1792-1798: 7).

Jones, Capt. Levin, and Miss Mary Jackson, daughter of the late Mr. Abraham Jackson, were m. last Tues. eve. at Fell's Point, by Rev. Dr. Allison (*Maryland Journal and Baltimore Advertiser* 27 May 1791; BAAD 11:322).

Jones, Mary, was charged with mulatto bastardy at the March 1723/4 Court; her child was ordered at the Aug 1724 Court to be raised by Thomas Hughes (BACP IS&TW#3:201, 438). She may be the same Mary Jones who was charged with bastardy at the Nov 1734 Court (BACP HWS#9:350).

Jones, Mary, was charged with bastardy at the Nov 1758 Court (BAMI 1757-1759:164). Aquila Jones, son of Mary, was b. 12 March 1758 (Reamy. *St. George's Parish Register:* 78).

Jones, Philip, and Jemima Eager, widow, were m. on 29 May 1723 (Harrison, "St. Paul's Parish Register:" 146). In Sep 1724, Jemima was named as the extx. of John Eager (*q.v.*) (MDTP 27:87).

Jones, Philip, m. on 2 Oct 1727 Ann Rattenbury, daughter of Dr. John and Margaret (Reamy, *St. Paul's Parish Register:* 30; Philip Jones Bible, *MdHM* 24:76-79; *MBR* 7:102). Rattenbury Jones and Nicholas Jones, on 3 March 1745 were named as nephews in the will of John Rattenbury (MWB 24:446 abst. by Gibb).

Jones, Rachel, was charged with bastardy at the March 1750/1 Court (BACP HWS#6:270).

Jones, Richard, of Baltimore, stated he would not pay the debts of his wife Eleanor (*Maryland Gazette or Baltimore General Advertiser* 13 July 1790).

Jones, Robinson, and Mary Burgess were m. 3 Aug 1780 (Marr. Returns of Rev. William West; Scharf Papers, MS 1999, at MdHS). Mary Jones, formerly Burgess, on 27 d. 1 m. 1781 was charged with marrying a man not in membership and having been m. by a priest ("Minutes of Gunpowder Meeting," *QRNM:*74). Robinson Jones m. by 6 Aug 1781, Mary, daughter of Hugh Burgess and his wife Alice, who is now Alice Butler (BALR WG#G:212).

Jones, Salsbury, and Eleanor Loney were m. by lic. on 28 April 1789 at St. Peter's Catholic Church, Baltimore (*Piet:* 137).

Jones, Samuel G., on 10 d. 10 m. 1799 was reported as having his marriage accomplished by a hireling preacher to a woman not of our society He was disowned on 10 d. 4 m. 1800 ("Minutes of Baltimore Meeting," *QRNM:*234, 237). [No other marriage reference found].

Jones, Sarah, was charged with bastardy at the March 1729/30 Court (BACP HWS#6:362).

Jones, Solomon, m. by 14 Sep 1752 Elizabeth, daughter of Thomas Keytin (BALR TR#D:502).

Jones, Solomon, matross in the Maryland Line, d. 30 Nov 1830; m. Eliza [-?-] on 10 May 1792 in Baltimore City; Solomon and Eliza were the parents of Solomon, b, 1793, and Amanda (Rev. War Pension Application of Eliza Jones: W-9080).

Jones, Thomas, m. by 7 April 1675 [-?-], relict of Walter Marcanalle (Mackenell); the relict died immediately after Walter (MDTP 8A:23).

Jones, Thomas, d. by 12 May 1740 when his extx. Mary was m. to Isaac Litton (*q.v.*) (BAAD 4.132).

Jones, Thomas, m. by 11 Nov 1766 [-?-], daughter of John Chocke (BAAD 7:192).

Jones, Thomas, blacksmith, living at the corner of Light Lane and Bank St., stated he would not pay the debts of his wife Mary (*Maryland Journal and Baltimore Advertiser* 1 April 1785).

Jones, Thomas, m. by 11 June 1794 Rebecca, heir of Joshua Shields (BALR WG#OO: 155).

Jones, William, and Eleanor Green, 'both of the (Baltimore?) county,' were m. by lic. on 10 Nov 1793 at St. Peter's Catholic Church, Baltimore (*Piet:* 137).

Jones, Wm., merchant, was m. last Sun. by Rev. Dr. Allison, to Elizabeth Leary of this city (*Federal Gazette and Baltimore Daily Advertiser* 12 Feb 1800).

Jones, Winifred, servant to Thomas Sheredine in Annapolis was charged with mulatto bastardy at the Aug 1725 Court, the June 1728 Court, and the Nov 1733 Court; at the last session her son James Jones was bound out to serve her master (BACP IS&TW#3:3132, HWS#6:16, and HWS#9:142-143).

Jordan, James, and Honor Callahan were m. by lic. on 24 Nov 1791 at St. Peter's Catholic Church, Baltimore (*Piet:* 137).

Jorse, Jack, and Frances Wagerman, were married by banns on 22 May 1792 at St. Peter's Catholic Church, Baltimore (*Piet:* 137).

Josel, John, m. by 5 Feb 1798 Mary, daughter of Simon Laudecker (BAWB 6:78).

Joy, Elizabeth, servant to William Holland, was charged with bastardy at the Nov 1721 Court and named Michael James as the father (BACP IS#C:619).

Joy, John, d. by 15 June 1792 when his admx. Jane had m. John Hall (q.v.) (BAAD 11:88).

Joyce, [-?-], d. by 24 Jan 1787 leaving a minor child Elijah Joyce; Joseph Joyce, the guardian, filed an account (BAGA 1:9).

Joyce, Comfort, in 1765 was presented for bastardy (BAMI 1765:17). In 1768 she was again presented for bastardy (BAMI 1768-1769:10).

Joyce, Richard, and Fanny Shaw were m. in May 1759 (Harrison, "St. Margaret's Parish Register," Anne Arundel Co., ms. at MdHS, p. 112). On 13 Nov 1794 Thomas Knightsmth Shaw named his nephew Thomas Joyce and his son Thomas Knightsmith Shaw Joyce, and a nephew Basil Joyce (BAWB 5:213).

Jroine?, James, and Mary Steiger were m. by lic. on 18 Feb 1799 at St. Peter's Catholic Church, Baltimore (*Piet:* 137).

Judd, Michael, m. by 2 March 1691/2 Jane, widow of William Ebden (*q.v.*) and mother of William Ebden (BACP F#1:165: BALR RM#HS:348).

Judge, Mary, daughter of Judy Judge, in March 1755 was bound to Edmund Talbot until she should come of age (BAMI 1755-1763).

"K"

Kahn, Daniel, in his will made 24 Feb 1794 named his wife Rachel Jordan (BAWB 5:158).

Kambey, Elizabeth, in 1761 was convicted of bastardy (BAMI 1755-1763).

Kean, [-?-], m. by 13 Dec 1800, Elizabeth, daughter of August Konig (BAWB 6:336).

Kearns, Charles, and Hannah Long were m. by lic. on 17 Sep 1791 at St. Peter's Catholic Church, Baltimore (*Piet:* 37).

Keating, Matthew, and Elizabeth Barlow were m. by lic. on 14 April 1798 at St. Peter's Catholic Church, Baltimore (*Piet:* 137; BAML, which gives his name as Matthew Caton).

Keaton, William, sailmaker, and Betsy Constable, both of Baltimore, were m. last eve. by Rev. John Hagerty (*Baltimore Daily Intelligencer* 1 Aug 1794).

Kebble, [-?-], child of Joseph Kebble, dec., on 15 Feb 1788 chose John Graves as guardian (BOCP 2:52).

Keen, John, of Baltimore Co., m. by 19 June 1750 Elizabeth, daughter of John Young, late of St. Mary's Co., dec. (BALR TR#C: 469, TR#D: 42).

Keen, Pollard, of Baltimore Co., m. by 19 June 1750 Mary, daughter of Dr. John Young, late of St. Mary's Co., dec. (BALR TR#C: 475, TR#D: 42).

Keene, William, m. by 15 March 1770 Sarah, widow of Thomas Gassaway (BALR AL#B: 223).

Keener, John, merchant, and Miss Shepherd, daughter of Peter Shepherd, were m. (*Maryland Journal and Baltimore Advertiser* 1 Feb 1780).

Keeports, Jacob, of Baltimore Town d. intestate on or about 8 March 1792 leaving a daughter Margaret who m. Christopher Faber of Chambersburg, Pa., who d. some time before 8 Dec 1800 (BALR WG#65:456).

Keepot (Keephost), Michael, and Ann Sutton were m. by lic. dated 29 July 1779 (BAML).Michael Keepot of Baltimore, stated that he would not pay the debts of his wife Ann (*Maryland Journal and Baltimore Advertiser* 13 Aug 1782).

Keilholtz, William, d. by Feb 1794 leaving children, Margaret, Philip, and Henry, who were made wards of Jacob Nurser (BAOC 3:79).

Keinan, Laurence, and Polly Hales were m. by lic. on 31 Oct 1799 at St. Peter's Catholic Church, Baltimore (*Piet:* 137).

Keith, Alexander, m. by 26 Feb 1708/9 Christiana, daughter of William Farfarr, whose wife was Joanna (BALR RM#HS: 636). On 16 Dec 1721 Christianne was named as a daughter of William Farfer (Farfar) who also named his grandsons Alex., and John Keeth in his will of that date (MWB 17:233 abst. in *Md. Cal. of Wills* 5:105).

Keith, David, aged 15 next 1 Jan, orphan of Florence Keith, in Aug 1757 was bound to Thomas Reeves, house carpenter (BAMI 1755-1763).

Kelinger, Georg, m. by 28 April 1790 Susanna Meyern ("First Record Book for the Reformed and Lutheran Congregations at Manchester, Baltimore (now Carroll) Co.," *MGSB* 35:285).

Kell, Jupiter, stated that he would not pay the debts of his wife Ruth (*Maryland Gazette or Baltimore General Advertiser* 23 Sep 1788).

Kelley, Thomas, m. by 17 June 1796 a daughter of Margaret Ford, a legatee of William Sinclair (BAAD 12:162).

Kelley, William, an Ensign in the Soldier's Delight Battalion of the Baltimore Co. Militia; he was later made a Captain in that Battalion, and died on 22 Feb 1818; m. on 1 Jan 1778, Martha Loveall, and they were the parents of: Sarah, b. 26 Oct 1778, d. 12 April 1791; John, b. 17 May 1781; Mary, b. 30 July 1784; Nicholas, b. 10 July 1783 d. 20 Nov 178-?: Urith, b. ...1789, d. 19 Feb 1793; Nichols, b. 11 Dec 1793; Sarah, b....; and Joshua, b. ...1799; Rachel, b. 19 April 1803; Elizabeth, b. 22 March 1807 (Rev. War Pension Application of Martha Kelley: R5831; "Kelley Bible," *NGSQ* 20:95).

Kelly, [-?-], m. by 3 Sep 1774 Elizabeth, daughter of Thomas Gorsuch (BAWB 3:315).

Kelly, [-?-], d. by 25 Aug 1778 having m. Rachel Simkins, granddaughter of John Simkins of Baltimore Co., dec. (BALR WG#B:454).

Kelly,[-?-], m. by 2 Dec 1795 Mary, daughter of Thomas Boring (BAWB 5:341).

Kelly, Daniel, in June 1710 was charged with begetting a bastard on the body of Mary Hogg (BACP IS#B:135).

Kelly (Kelley), James, d. by 14 July 1772, having m. Mary [-?-], who had formerly been m. to Thomas Beazley (*q.v.*) (or Beemsley), who according to depositions had run away and was still living in Southern Va. near Carolina (MDTP 44:481-487).

Kelly, John, orphan of James Kelly in Aug 1772 was bound to David Brown, potter (BAMI 1772, 1775-1781: 21).

Kelly, John, and Sarah Draynan were m. by lic. on 22 Feb 1794 at St. Peter's Catholic Church, Baltimore (*Piet:* 137).

Kelly, John, m. by 10 Feb 1798 Elizabeth, daughter of Wm. Clover (BAAD 12:394). John Kellen [*sic*] and Elizabeth Clower were married by license dated 21 Sep 1797 (BAML).

Kelly, Margaret, was charged with bastardy at the Nov 1772 Court and fined (BAMI 1772, 1775-1781:87).

Kelly, Mary, was charged with bastardy at the June Court, 1751 (BACP HWS#7:156).

Kelly, Patrick, and Jane Young were m. by lic. on 10 Feb 1799 at St. Peter's Catholic Church, Baltimore (*Piet:* 137).

Kelly, Ruth, was convicted of bastardy in Nov. 1757 (BAMI 1757-1759).

Kelly, Stephen, son of Thomas, age 8 last 20 April, in November 1775 was bound to John Stevenson of Edward (BAMI 1772, 1775-1781: 146).

Kelly, Thomas, son of John, age 11, last 23 June, in Nov 1775 was bound to Daniel Reese, blacksmith (BAMI 1772, 1775-1781: 146).

Kelly, Thomas, and Charity Gorsuch were married by license dated 20 Jan 1781 (BAML). On 9 Dec 1789 Kelly's [unnamed] wife was named as a daughter of Loveless Gorsuch, and heir of Nathan Gorsuch (BAAD 10:88, 250).

Kelly, Thomas, m. by 13 June 1792 Cassandra Royston (or Riston), who received an equal share of £51.5.6¾ from the estate of Thomas Royston (or Riston) (BAAD 11:71).

Kelly, Thomas, m. by 12 April 1797 Cassea, legatee of William Sinclair (BAAD 12:287).

Kelshamer, Francis, and John Kelshamer, in 1792 were legatees of Jacob Brown and Francis Kelshamer was appointed their guardian (BAOC 2:251).

Kelsheimer, Francis, m. by 7 Feb 1791 Margaret, who received an equal share of the estate of John Wright (BAAD 10:286).

Kelso, James, and Miss Elizabeth Standiford, both of Baltimore Co., were m. last Thurs. by Rev. Kurtz (*Maryland Journal and Baltimore Advertiser* 2 Aug 1793).

Kelso, Thomas, enlisted in the Army in March 1780; was m. to Penelope Rutledge (who d. 24 May 1850) in Baltimore by a Baptist minister named Davis and died 29 Jan

1847. A Family Record in Thomas Kelso's own handwriting shows that he was born 7 March 1764, Penelope Kelso was born 5 Dec 1765, and that Thomas and Penelope had issue: Jane, b. 25 Feb 1790; Elijah, b. 18 Nov 1791; Ann, b. 14 June 1793; Abraham, b. 31 May 1797; Penelope, b, 4 March 1799; Ruth B., b. 17 Jan 1802, (m. [-?-] Hitselberger, and in 1851 was living in Shelby Co., Ky.); Thomas, b. 18 March 1806; Russell [or Bussell], b. 8 April 1806; Elizabeth, b. ...Sep 1807 (Rev. War Pension Application of Thomas Kelso: W 9099). Thomas Kelso and Penelope Rutledge were married by license dated 22 April 1789 (BAML).

Kembal, Rowland, and Mary Jackson were m. on 15 May 17-(?) ((Harrison, "St. George's Parish Register:" 222). On 12 Nov 1719 Samuel Jackson made his will naming his 'son and daughter' Rowland and Mary Kimble (MWB 16:11 abst. in *Md. Cal. of Wills* 5:2).

Kemble, William, m. by 27 March 1716, Mary daughter of Humphrey Jones, who on that date conveyed 100 a. *Jones' Addition* to William and Mary's children William and Mary Kemble (BALR TR#A:389).

Kemerly (Kemmerly), Jacob, stated he would not pay the debts of his wife Catherine. [The notice was in rhyme] (*Maryland Journal and Baltimore Advertiser* 14 Feb 1785).

Kemp, [-?-], m. Johanna [-?-], whom. 2nd, James Phillips (*q.v.*), and 3rd, on 17 Dec 1720 Aquila Hall (q.v.); Johanna was the mother of John and Richard Kemp (BALR TR#DS: 287).

Kemp, Joh., m. by 10 April 1760 Anna Maria Ettchen ("First Record Book for the Reformed and Lutheran Congregations at Manchester, Baltimore (now Carroll) Co.," *MGSB* 35:265).

Kemp, John, in his will, made 1 Dec 1686 named his wife Sarah, nee Wichell (MWB 4:239 abst. in *Md. Cal. of Wills*). Sarah m. 2nd, Edward Norris (*q.v.*), 3rd. John Thomas (*q.v.*) and 4th, Thomas Matthews (*q.v.*).

Kemp, John, m. by 13 Oct 1749 Mary, granddaughter of Joseph Peake (BALR HWS#1-A:336).

Kemp, Shadrack, and **John Kemp,** in April 1794 were representatives of Priscilla Harvey, and they chose John Kemp as their guardian (BAOC 3:88).

Kemp, Shadrach, b. 4 Jan 1778, son of John, and Henrietta [-?-] were m. on 10 Dec 1799 ("Shadrach Kemp Bible," *MBR* 3:127-129).

Kenane, Maurice, saddler, late of Tipperary, Ireland, and Mary Greenfield, of Baltimore Co., were m. 12th inst. (*Baltimore Daily Repository* 24 Jan 1792).

Kenbey, Elizabeth, in 1761 was fined for fornication and bastardy (BAMI 1755-1763).

Kenely, Timothy, and Bridget Mullan, natives of Ireland, were m. by lic. on 7 April 1799 at St. Peter's Catholic Church, Baltimore (*Piet:* 137).

Kennard, Matthew, b. 22 April 1769, d. 24 July 1846, aged 77 y. 3 m. 2 d., and Mary Hawthorne, b. 12 March 1773, d. 28 Nov 1849, were m. on 24 July 794 ":Kennard Bible Records, Harford Co., Maryland" *HMGB* 3 (3) (July 1932) 17).

Kennedy, [-?-], m. by 29 April 1771 Hannah, daughter of William Jones of Upper Deer Creek Hundred (BAWB 3:253).

Kennedy, [-?-], m. by 31 Dec 1785 Margaret, daughter of Sarah Callister, and sister of Elizabeth Peale, who was the widow of G. Peale; they had a son Henry Callister Kennedy (BAWB 4:150).

Kennedy, Patrick, practitioner of physic, and Areanna French entered into marriage articles on 6 June 1772 and again on 7 Sep 1772 when they were already married (BALR AL#E:8, 386). Patrick Kennedy and Hannah [*sic*] French, widow, were m. 6 June 1772 (Harrison, "St. Paul's Parish Register:" 169) On 13 Jan 1773 Ariana was named as the extx. of Hannah Hughes, and widow of James French (MINV 110:352; BALR AL#G:71). Hannah [*sic*] Kennedy advertised that she intended to petition the General Assembly for a ratification of the marriage contract made between herself and her husband Patrick Kennedy (*Maryland Journal and Baltimore Advertiser* 10 April 1781). On 8 Dec 1796 John Lynch of Baltimore, in his will made 8 Dec 1796 named Areanna, wife of Patrick Kennedy as his 'aunt by marriage' (BAWB 5:480).

Kent, Emanuel, m. Ellen Burneston on 19 June 1788 ("Emanuel Kent Bible," *MBR* 1:139; BALR WG#II:550; BAML)

Kent, Robert, merchant, was m. last Sat. eve. by Rev. Mr. Kurtz to Miss Margaret Myers, both of this city (*Federal Gazette and Baltimore Daily Advertiser* 9 Jan 1798).

Kenter, C. F., merchant, and Miss Eliza Griffith, both of this city were m. last eve. by Rev. Mr. Richards (*Federal Gazette and Baltimore Daily Advertiser* 30 Oct 1799).

Kentler, Baltus, of Baltimore, advertised that his wife Elizabeth had eloped from his bed and board (*Baltimore Daily Repository* 2 May 1792).

Keon, [-?-], of N. C., m. by 6 June 1711 Hannah, formerly the wife of Lodowick Williams (BALR TR#DS:135).

Keon, Hannah, stated on 6 June 1711 that Edward Williams here present was the heir of Lodowick Williams, and was lawfully begotten of her body (BALR TR#A:135).

Kepler, Mr. John Tilghman, merchant, was m. Sat. eve. by Rev. John Hagerty, to Miss Mary Culverwell, daughter of Richard Culverwell, both of this town (*Federal Intelligencer and Baltimore Daily Gazette* 19 May 1795).

Kerevan, Kate, servant to John Roberts, was charged with bastardy in Aug 1719, and was ordered to be examined by Dorothy Cutchin (BACP IS#C:208).

Kerlinger, Georg, m. by 28 April 1790 Susanna Meyerin ("First Record Book for the Reformed and Lutheran and Congregations at Manchester, Baltimore (Now Carroll) Co.," *MGSB* 35:285).

Kernan, Jane, extx., on 2 March 1789 posted bond to administer the estate of Zacheus Richason (Richardson), whose will made 7 July 1788 named Jane Kernan as extx., who was to have his estate for life or widowhood (BAWB 4:343; BAAB 7:223).

Kerns, Joseph, and Anna Darrell were m. by lic. on 9 Aug 1792 at St. Peter's Catholic Church, Baltimore (*Piet:* 137).

Kerr, Thomas, m. by 21 Oct 1785, [-?-], who received a portion of the estate of Francis Moore (BAAD 8:170).

Ketcham. James, in March 1717/8 was charged with begetting a bastard on the body of Jane Lett (BACP HS#IA:237-238).

Key, James E., was m. last Thurs. by Rev. Mr. Bend, to Miss Eliza W. Smith of Baltimore (*Baltimore Daily Intelligencer* 28 April 1794; BAML)

Key, Job, m. by 5 Jan 1771 Rebecca, daughter of Benjamin Colegate (BALR AL#B:607).

Key, Hon. Philip, was m. last Thurs. eve. at Col. Ramsay's, by the Rev. Mr. Bend, to Miss Sophia Hall of this town (*Federal Gazette and Baltimore Daily Advertiser* 11 June 1796).

Keyes, Stephen, m. by 24 Dec 1789 Elizabeth, heir of William Watson, whose will, made 7 May 1784, named a daughter Elizabeth (BAWB 3:558; BAAD 10:94).

Keys, John, and Elizabeth Darrell were m. by lic. on 26 April 1792 at St. Peter's Catholic Church, Baltimore (*Piet:* 137).

Keys, Richard, gave notice that his wife Anne had eloped from his bed and board (*Baltimore Daily Intelligencer* 13 Jan 1794).

Kidd, [-?-], m. by 19 Aug 1795 Mary, daughter of John Royston (BAWB 6:104).

Kidd, Henry, and Eleanor Berry were m. on 19 Oct 1780 (Marr. Returns of Rev. William West, Scharf Papers, MS.1999 at MdHS). She m. 2nd, Robert Dunwoody (*q.v.*).

Kidd, John, and Sarah Royston were married by license dated 15 March 1780 (HAML). Sarah was named as a daughter of John Royston in his will made 19 Aug 1795 (BAWB 6:104).

Kidd, Joshua, m. by 3 April 1799 Margaret, representative of Henry Cove (BAAD 13:36).

Kiernan, [-?-], m. by 24 Dec 1799 Ketty Muller ("Register of First German Reformed Church," MS. at MdHS:25).

Kilberk, Abalon[?], on 24 Feb 1784 was named as a grandson in the will of Henry Brince (BAWB 4:27).

Kilbren (Kibren), Catherine, confessed to bastardy in Nov 1755 and named Michael Sharpner, servant to Edward Punteny, as the father of her child (BACP BB#B:401).

Kilburne, Richard, d. by Jan 1703/4, leaving a son William Kilburne, and a widow Priscilla (nee Thomas) who m. 2nd Thomas Freeborne (*q.v.*), and 3rd, Samuel Howell (*q.v.*) (AAJU G:278, 284; MDAD 3:338).

Killlen, John, and 'Polly' Tripolet, eldest dau of the widow 'Triplet,' were m. on 21 Dec 1783 (Marr. Returns of Rev. William West, Scharf Papers, MS.1999 at MdHS; *Maryland Gazette or Baltimore General Advertiser* 26 Dec 1783). In May 1791 Mary was named as a daughter of Mary Magdalen Tripolet (BAWB 5:24).

Killeon, Jacob, and Mary Newman, of Frederick Co., were m. by lic. on 28 Sep 1795 at St. Peter's Catholic Church, Baltimore (*Piet:* 137).

Killi, Simon, m. by 28 Jan 1765 Anna Maria Bohrin ("First Record Book for the Reformed and Lutheran Congregations at Manchester, Baltimore (now Carroll) Co.," *MGSB* 35:270).

Kilpatrick, James, and Barbara Thatcher on 5 Feb 1771 were summoned by the vestry for unlawful cohabitation (Reamy, *St. George's Parish Register:"* 111).

Kilty, William, m. Elizabeth Middleton in Aug 1790 ("Emanuel Kent Bible," *MBR* 1:139).

Kimball. See Kimble.

Kimble, [-?-], m. by 12 Nov 1719 Hannah, daughter of Samuel Jackson (MWB 16:11).

Kimble (Kimball), Samuel, and Jemima Barnes were m. on 19 Feb 1747 (Harrison, "St. George's Parish Register:" 352). On 16 May 1754 she was paid her filial portion of the estate of John Barnes (*q.v.*), which was administered by Bethia Scarlett, admx. (MDAD 36:257).

Kimble, Sarah, was charged with bastardy at March Court 1739/40, again at March Court 1743/4 (she confessed and was fined), and again at March Court 1745/6 (BACP HWS#TR:163, and Liber 1743-1745). Sarah Kimball [*sic*] was the mother of Sabra, b. 9 Aug 1745 (Reamy, *St. George's Parish Register:* 80).

Kimble (Kimball), William, and Sarah Hanson were m. on 1 Jan 1754 (Harrison, "St. George's Parish Register:" 354). On 10 May 1767, she was named as a daughter of Jacob Hanson (BAAD 6:234). She m. 2nd, William Pike (*q.v.*).

Kimmebright, [-?-], m. by 23 Jan 1797, Mary daughter of Elizabeth Peters (BAWB 5:478).

Kimpson, [-?-], m. by 17 Dec 1756 Susannah, daughter of William Keeper (MWB 30:246 abst. by Gibb).

King, Ann, was charged with bastardy at June Court, 1724 (BACP HWS#9:253).

King, Eleanor, was charged with bastardy three times after1739 [exact times not given] She bound out her twin children James Hill and Sarah Hill as apprentices at March Court 1744/5. She is probably identical with the Elinor Hill who was charged with bastardy at March Court 1739/40, June and Aug Courts 1740, and again at June 1743 Court, where she confessed (BACP HWS#TR: 140, 247, 299, Liber 1743-1745:471). Eleanor's twin children James Hill and Sarah Hill were b. 1 May 1743 (Harrison, "St. John's," p. 133).

King, Henry, m. by May 1698 Tabitha, daughter of Jane Long (MDTP 17:125). Another source says her name was Galvilla (BAAD 2:216).

King, Thomas, of Baltimore Co., m. between 1669 and 1673 Joane Strand, who had immigrated from Va. (MPL 17:443).

King, William, stated he would not pay the debts of his wife Elizabeth (*Maryland Journal and Baltimore Advertiser* 19 Sep 1780).

King, William, merchant of Baltimore, and Betsy, daughter of John Hammond, barrister -at-law, were m. [date not given] (*Maryland Gazette or Baltimore General Advertiser* 13 Aug 1784). William A. King and Elizabeth King advertised they intended to petition the General Assembly to vest the real estate devised by John Hammond, Esq., to the subscriber and her heirs in fee simple (Annapolis *Maryland Gazette* 17 Feb 1785). William King and Elizabeth Ann Hammond were married by license dated 4 Aug 1784 (BAML). In Aug 1791 Elizabeth was named as the mother of William Hammond (BPET: Petition of Elizabeth King, 1794).

Kinsey, Isaac, son of Joseph and Hannah, m. on 7 d. 2 m. 1789, Rachel Matthews, dau, of Thomas and Rachel (Bliss Forbush, "Abstracts of Records of Gunpowder Meeting," MS. at MdHS). On 7 May 1800 Rachel was named as an heir of Thomas Matthews (BAAD 13:252).

Kinsley, Elizabeth, and Benjamin Ricketts were charged with unlawful cohabitation by the vestry of St. John's Parish on 1 April 1771 (St. John's and St. George's Parish Register Vestry Proceedings. Typed copy of the original at the MdHS).

Kintz, Barney, and Elizabeth Shilling were m. by lic. on 12 Jan 1800 at St. Peter's Catholic Church, Baltimore (*Piet:* 137).

Kipp, John, was m. last eve. by Rev. Mr. Kurtz, to Mrs. Mary Wolslager, both of this city (*Federal Gazette and Baltimore Daily Advertiser* 16 June 1800).

Kipple, Humphrey, m. by 15 Aug 1797 Sally, daughter of James Marshall, whose will named his grandchildren James Marshall Kipple and Hannah Kipple (BAWB 6:33).

Kinsey, Jno., m. by 8 Nov 1723 Ellinor, daughter of Henry Donahue (BAAD 1:129).

Kirk, Nathaniel, m. by 24 Oct 1783 Jehoshaba, daughter of George Wells, who also named a grandson George Wells Kirk (BAWB 3:578). Jehosheba m. 2nd, Josiah Brown (*q.v.*)

Kirk, Samson, on 22 d. 8 m. 1773 appeared with a certificate from Nottingham Meeting, but was not received because he had since been married by a priest ("Minutes of Gunpowder Monthly Meeting," *QRNM:*64). [No other marriage reference found].

Kirwan, John, merchant of Baltimore, m. Polly Sewell of St. Mary's Co. [date not given] (*Maryland Journal and Baltimore Advertiser* 28 Feb 1786; BAML).

Kitchen (or Hitchen), Elizabeth, was charged with bastardy at June 1719 Court and named Stephen Yoakley as the father. She confessed and was fined at March Court 1719/20 (BACP IS#C:198,437).

Kitteman, George, of Liberty Town, will not pay the debts of his wife Charlotte, who has eloped (*Maryland Journal and Baltimore Advertiser* 23 June 1789).

Kitten, John, of Baltimore, denied he had ever been married, and he refuted the charge that he had been a deserter (from his regiment) in Baltimore (*Maryland Journal and Baltimore Advertiser* 5 July 1791).

Kline, John Henry, d. by 11 June 1789 when his relict and extx. Catherine was m. to John Stohler (*q.v.*) (BOCP: Petition of John Stoler *et uxor,* 1789).

Knight, [-?-], m. by 4 Oct 1769 Martha, daughter of John Edwards (BAWB 3:148).

Knight, [-?-], m. by 19 April 1781, Elizabeth, daughter of John Price (BAWB 3:486).

Knight, [-?-], m. by 21 d. 5 m. 1784, Sarah, daughter of Isaac Tyson (BAWB 3:567).

Knight, Benjamin, and Jane Merriman were m. on 6 Aug 1723 (Harrison, "St. Paul's Parish Register:" 146). On 9 Sep (1724?) Jane was named as the extx. of Charles Merryman (*q.v.*) of Baltimore Co. (MDAD 6:92. 9:433, 11:494, 17:187). She had m. 1st, Joseph Peake (*q.v.*).

Knight, Benjamin, convict, in March 1750/1 was charged with begetting a bastard on the body of Elizabeth Robertson (BACP TR#6:290-291).

Knight, Benjamin, and Margaret Hook were married by license dated 12 May 1784 (BAML). She was a daughter of Anthony Hook (BAWB 6:409).

Knight, John, was charged with bastardy at March Court, 1765. Sarah Jarvis was summoned. The case was struck off because the defendant had died (BAMI 1765:2).

Knight, Sarah, in her will made 4 Aug 1748 named her children Joseph, James, Thomas, Morgan and Sarah Morray, and her granddaughter Elizabeth, daughter of Thomas Morray (MWB 25:486 abst. by Gibb).

Knowles, [-?-], m. by 13 Aug 1714 Katherine, widow and next of kin of Matthias Gray (INAC 36A:92).

Knowles, [-?-], m. by 15 Dec 1743 Mary, aged 21, poss. daughter of James Fugate, who also had a daughter Ann Fugate, aged 8 years old, named in a lease for three lifetimes (BALR TB#D:440).

Knowles, Henry, m. Katherine, widow of Stephen Hart (q.v.) and John Scutt (q.v.). In his will, made 4 Jan 1713 Knowles named his daughter-in-law Mary Scutt (MWB 13:705 abst. in *Md. Cal. of Wills* 4:14).

Knox, [-?-], m. by 6 Dec 1790 Ruth Biddison, admx. of Jarvis Biddison (BAAD 10:231).

Knox, Alexander, and Elizabeth Easton were m. on 8 May 1799 ("Register of First Presbyterian Church, Baltimore," MS. at MdHS: 9). She m. 2nd, by Aug 1800 [-?-] Mouler (BAAB 9:51).

Knox, Reynolds, and Grace Coats were m. 5 Sep 1799 (Harrison, "St. Paul's Parish Register:" 377). Grace Knox, formerly Coats, on 12 d. 12 m. 1799 had a complaint made that she married contrary to the rules of our discipline ("Minutes of Baltimore Meeting," *QRNM:*236).

Knox, William, m. by 27 Feb 1782, Elizabeth, daughter of William and Elizabeth Payne and sister of Richard Payne (BAWB 4:257; BAAD 9:253, 255).

Koller, Anthony, and Maria Fifer were m. by lic. on 2 Aug 1794 at St. Peter's Catholic Church, Baltimore (*Piet:* 137).

Konecke, Nicholas, merchant, and Mrs. Catherine Thomas were m. last eve. (*Maryland Gazette or Baltimore General Advertiser* 29 April 1791; *The Pennsylvania Mercury, and Universal Advertiser* 7 May 1791).

Koneese, John, m. by 8 Dec 1787 [-?-], daughter of Michael Burns (BAAD 9:127).

Krattinger, Joh. Henrich, m. by 6 Sep 1765, Maria Margareta Utzin ("First Record Book for the Reformed and Lutheran Congregations at Manchester, Baltimore (Now Carroll) Co.," *MGSB* 35:269).

Krauss, John, and Catherine Hartman were married by banns on 23 Oct 1791, at St. Peter's Catholic Church, Baltimore (*Piet:* 137),

Kreas, Phillip, m. by 9 Nov. (year not given), Anna Ettckins ("First Record Book for the Reformed and Lutheran Congregations at Manchester, Baltimore (now Carroll) Co.," *MGSB* 35:266).

Krems, Joseph, and Christiana, daughter of John Schultz of this town were m. last eve. by Rev. Daniel Kurtz (*Baltimore Daily Intelligencer* 21 July 1794).

Kurtz, Rev. Mr. Daniel, m. last Sun. eve., Polly, daughter of Samuel Messersmith of this town (*Maryland Gazette or Baltimore General Advertiser* 10 Sep 1790).

Kyler, Daniel, m. by 11 May 1789 Nancy, widow of Josephus Murray of Frederick Co. (BALR WG#DD:14).

"L"

Labatt, John Baptist, and Margaret Granger were m. by lic. on 22 Nov 1784 at St. Peter's Catholic Church, Baltimore (*Piet:* 137). In 1787 Margaret was named as a daughter of John Granget (Granger) (BOCP Petition of John Granget, 1787, Box 2, Folder 29; BAAD 9:112).

Labesius, John, and Nancy Hammond were married by license dated 12 Sep 1778 (BAML). On 29 May 1783 Ann was named as a daughter of Ann Hammond, widow of John Hammond, who also named a granddaughter Ann' Labecious' (BAWB 4:14).

Labob (Laboob, Laboth?), Michael, Mary, Elizabeth, and Christiana, were named as the step-children of Joseph Lawrence whose will, made 20 Oct 1795, also named his wife Dorothy (BAWB 5:483). In June 1794 Christiana, Elizabeth, Mary, and Michael Labob, ages not given, were made wards of Joseph Lawrence (Baltimore Co. 3:97).

Laborde, Bernard, and Modeste Landry were m. by lic. on 16 May 1784 at St. Peter's Catholic Church, Baltimore (*Piet:* 137).

Labold, Charles, d. by Oct 1783, having m. Anna Rachina Rahm, extx. of Jacob Rahm (BAOC 1:217, 287; BOCP Petition of Peter Keener, 1795). **See Jacob Raham.**

Laboth. See Labob.

Labou, Michael, and Catherine Keffer were m. by lic. on 13 May 1800 at St. Peter's Catholic Church, Baltimore (*Piet:* 137).

Lacey, Thomas, Jr., on 30 d. 12 m. 1786, was charged with marrying contrary to the good order ("Minutes of Gunpowder Meeting," *QRNM:*83). [No other marriage reference found].

Lacy, Amos, on 29 d. 12 m. 1781was reported as having gone out in marriage ("Minutes of Gunpowder Meeting," *QRNM:*75). [No other marriage reference found].

Lacy, Thomas, and Elizabeth Hayhurst, on 25 d., 10 m. 1777 declared their intention to marry ("Minutes of Gunpowder Meeting," *QRNM:*71).

Lafee, Lewis, m. by 14 Jan 1744 Sarah, extx. of William Lowe (*q.v.*) of Baltimore Co. (MINV 30:282; MDAD 21:259). She had m. 1st, George Graves.

Lafon, Bernard, native of Bayonne, France, and Susanna Morin, widow of Mr. Balfo of San Domingo, were m. by lic. on 29 Jan 1794 at St. Peter's Catholic Church, Baltimore (*Piet:* 137). Bernard Lafen and Susannah Morine were married by license dated 29 Jan 1794 (BAML).

LaForest, Thomas, and Hannah Simmons were married by banns on 1 May 1785 at St. Peter's Catholic Church, Baltimore (*Piet:* 137).

Lagarda, John, of Baltimore, stated he would not pay the debts of his wife Mary, who had eloped from his bed and board (*Baltimore Daily Repository* 16 March 1792).

Lake, [-?-], m. by 10 April 1725 Sarah, daughter of Mathew Molton (MWB 18:398 abst. in *Md. Cal. of Wills* 5:199).

Lake, Abraham. See Abraham Leak.

Lalor, James, and Ann O'Neale, natives of Ireland, were m. by lic. on 25 Dec 1798 at St. Peter's Catholic Church, Baltimore (*Piet:* 137).

Lamar (Lemar), Capt. William, and Peggy Worthington were m. in Baltimore Co. by license dated 15 Nov 1784(*Maryland Journal and Baltimore Advertiser* 3 Dec 1784; BAML). On 2 April 1792 Margaret was named as a daughter of John Worthington (BALR WG#HH:463). Margaret or Peggy, was a sister of Hannah Worthington, whose will of that date named her sister Margaret Lamar and her children, Mary, Lueset and Sarah Lamar and appointed William Lynch and Robert North Carnan as execs (BAWB 5:447). William Lemar, admin. with will annexed, on 18 May 1797 posted bond to administer Hannah Worthingon's estate (BAAB 8:331).

Laming, Benjamin, and Nelly Ridgely were m. last Tues., 13 Jan, at Fell's Point (*Maryland Gazette or Baltimore General Advertiser* 16 Jan 1784; Marr. Returns of Rev. William West, Scharf Papers, MS.1999 at MdHS); on 19 Feb 1786 Eleanor was named as a daughter of Mary Ridgely, widow of John Ridgely (BAWB 4:189).

Lammot, [-?-], m. by 7 Oct 1798 [-?-], daughter of Conrad Kerlinger (BAWB 6:138).

Lammot, David, m. by 3 Feb 1783 Elizabeth, daughter of Philip Forney of York Co., Pa., who owned land in Baltimore Co. (BALR WG#DD:492).

Lammot, John, of Baltimore Town, m. by 3 Feb 1783 Hannah, daughter of Philip Forney of York Co., Pa., who owned land in Baltimore Co. (BALR WG#DD:492).

Lancaster, Jesse, on 31 d., 8 m, 1776, reportedly hath gone out in marriage to a woman not in membership with Friends ("Minutes of Gunpowder Meeting," *QRNM;*68). [No other marriage reference found].

Landerking, John, and Nell Bowser were m. by lic. on 30 Oct 1792 at St. Peter's Catholic Church, Baltimore (*Piet:* 137; BAML, which gives their names as John Landerkin and Nell Bouser).

Landers, William, and Elizabeth Taylor were m. by lic. on 21 April 1796 at St. Peter's Catholic Church, Baltimore (*Piet:* 137).

Landford, Michael, and Martha Lucy, widow, natives of Ireland, were m. by lic. on 20 Dec 1798 at St. Peter's Catholic Church, Baltimore (*Piet:* 137),

Landy (Landyes), John, and wife Catherine posted bond on 30 March 1706 to administer the estate of Edward Boreman (BAAB 1:170; MDTP 21:31).

Lane, [-?-], m. by 28 June 1781 Margaret, daughter of Richard Hooker (BAWB 3:428).

Lane, Dutton, m. by 5 Feb 1683 Pretiosa, daughter of Richard Tydings of Anne Arundel Co. (BALR TB#E:522, IS#G:68).

Lane, Dutton, m. by 15 Oct 1751 [-?-], daughter of John Boreing (MDAD 31:119).

Lane, Joseph, on 29 Sep 1739 was named as a bro-in-law in the will of Samuel Maccubbin (MWB 22:142 abst. in *Md. Cal. of Wills* 8:67). Lane, had m. by 8 May 1750, Rachel, daughter of Samuel Maccubbin, on which date their son Samuel Lane deposed on 8 May 1750 (MDTP 33-1:126-133).

Lane, Richard, m. by 1799 Providence, daughter of Flora Dorsey who was a daughter of Nicholas Fitzsimmons (MCHP#1799).

Lane, Samuel, of Calvert Co., and Mrs. Providence Lane of Baltimore were m. (*Maryland Journal and Baltimore Advertiser* 9 Aug 1791). (They were m. by license in Baltimore Co.)

Lang, Daniel, m, by 18 Aug 1765 Anna Schmdtin ("First Record Book for the Reformed and Lutheran Congregations at Manchester, Baltimore (now Carroll) Co.," *MGSB* 35:270).

Langdon, [-?-], m. by 2 Jan 1768 [-?-], daughter of Mary Ann Harris, and had a son Joseph Langdon. Langdon's widow m. 2nd, John Howlett (*q.v.*) (BAWB 3:126). The estate distribution of Mary Anne Harris mentioned a grandson Joseph Langdon (BFD 5:394).

Langley, Edward, rope-maker, and Sarah Cromwell, both of Baltimore, were m. Tues. eve. by Rev. John Hagerty (*Maryland Journal and Baltimore Advertiser* 15 Aug 1794). (BAML gives his name as Edmund Longley).

Langley, Mary, was charged with bastardy at March Court 1746/7 (BACP TB&TR#1: 378).

Langley, William, d. by 14 Sep 1752, having m. by 23 Oct 1725 Elinor, daughter of Solomon and Elizabeth Jones of St. Mary's Co. (said William and Elinor were the parents of John Langley), and Elizabeth Jones was the daughter of Thomas Keytin (BALR IS#H:183, TR#D:502).

Langley, William, d. by 9 Nov 1789 by which time his widow Mary, mother of Mary Langley, had m. 2nd, Robert Leakins (*q.v.*) (BALR WG#DD: 650).

Lanham, Josias, m. by 24 Feb 1720 Susannah, daughter of Anthony Drew of Baltimore Co. (BAAD 1: 151; MDAD 3:281½).

Lannay, Louis Isaac, m. by 13 March 1795 Henrietta Viedar de Saint Armand (BALR WG#RR:17).

Lansbourg, Frederick, stated he would not pay the debts of his wife Rosanna (*Maryland Journal and Baltimore Advertiser* 1 June 1783).

Lansdall, Joseph, of Baltimore, gave notice his wife Rachel had behaved in a very unbecoming manner (*Dunlap's Maryland Gazette* 21 July 1778).

Largeau, George James, m. 10 July 1783 Rachel Adams, b. c1766, d. March 1789, aged 23 (*Maryland Journal and Baltimore Advertiser* 15 July 1783, 27 March 1789; Harrison, "St. Paul's Parish Register:" 188).

Lashley, Elizabeth, was charged with bastardy at Nov 1758 Court. Her daughter was named Jemima Lashley (BAML 1757-1759:163).

Latique, [-?-], m. by 12 June 1797 Ann, widow of Jacques Brun (BAAD 12:265).

Latour, Capt. John, was m. yesterday eve. by Rev. Bend to Miss Grace Smith, both of this town (*Federal Intelligencer and Baltimore Daily Gazette* 24 Oct 1795). On 17 Feb 1798 she was named as a daughter of John Smith (BAAD 12:389).

Latourandaie, Joseph, and Mary Frances Ducasse, from St. Domingo, were m. by lic. on 23 Oct 1798 at St. Peter's Catholic Church, Baltimore (*Piet:* 138). (BAML gives his name as Joseph A. L. Dais).

Latreyte, John, and Marie Deshelds were m. by lic. on 21 July 1794 at St. Peter's Catholic Church, Baltimore (*Piet:* 138).

Laudeman, Margaret, in her will made 12 Nov 1800 named her daughters Catherine Davis, Elizabeth Fields, and Mary Sapp (BAWB 6:411).

Laurence, Wendel, and Ann Steele were m. by lic. on 28 Feb 1797 at St. Peter's Catholic Church, Baltimore (*Piet:* 138).

Laurens, Augustus, of Baltimore, advertised that his wife Mary had eloped (*Maryland Gazette or Baltimore General Advertiser* 1 Aug 1783).

Laurer, Gottfried, m. by 23 Sep 1760 [or 1761], Maria Elisabeta Welltin ("First Record Book for the Reformed and Lutheran Congregations at Manchester, Baltimore (now Carroll) Co.," *MGSB* 35:266).

Laushbaugh, Frederick, d. intestate leaving John Bridenbach as admin., and also leaving a widow and two children, who now reside in the state of Penna. (Petition of John Bridenbach, 1791, BPET).

Lavell, Michael, and Mary Bourke were m. by lic. on 25 Oct 1798 at St. Peter's Catholic Church, Baltimore (*Piet:* 138). Michael Lavele and Mary Bulk were married by license dated 25 Oct 1798 (BAML).

Lavely (Lovely), George, m. by 13 June 1769 m. Catherine, daughter of Ulrich and Esther Whistler, and widow and admx. of John Rohrer (Rohra) (*q.v.*) (BAAD 7:30; BAWB 3:72; MDTP 43:212).

Law, James, merchant and Miss Davies, both of this city were m. last Thurs. eve. by Rev. Mr. Bend (*Federal Intelligencer and Baltimore Daily Gazette* 11 July 1795).

Lawler, David, widower, and Ruth Clifton were m. by banns on 18 Oct 1795 at St. Peter's Catholic Church, Baltimore (*Piet:* 138).

Lawrassey. Mary, was charged with bastardy at March Court 1729/30, and was presented at Aug Court 1739 (BACP HWS#6:362, HWS#7:7). Sarah Lawrassey was born on 13 Aug 1728 (Reamy, *St. George's Parish Register:* 33). Mary Larrissee m. William Sympson on 12 Nov 1739 (Reamy, *St. George's Parish Register:* 59).

Lawrence, [-?-], m. by 16 Nov 1772 Urath, daughter of Samuel Owings, Sr., Gent. (BAWB 3:299).

Lawrence (Laurence), Benjamin, son of Benj. and Eliza, and Rachel 'Marriartee' were m. on 6 d.11 m. 1701/2 ("West River Monthly Meeting," MS. at MdHS). On 14 March 1720/1 Rachel was named as a sister of Daniel Mariarte at whose house Laurence died (MDTP 24:316). Rachel m. 2nd, John Norwood (*q.v.*).

Lawrence, Benjamin, m. by 9 April 1793 [-?-], dau. of Samuel Owings (BAAD 11:239).

Lawrence, Benjamin, m. by 26 Nov 1792 Urath, daughter of Urath Owings, widow, who also named a granddaughter Elizabeth Lawrence (BAWB 5:70).

Lawrence, John, formerly of Great Britain, in his will made 20 Sep 1797 named his wife Esther and daughter Sophia, his wife's only lawful heir, and his daughter Susannah, now wife of James Mills (*q.v.*) (BAWB 6:126).

Lawrence, Leaven, and Sarah Dorsey were married on 19 Aug 1786. Sarah was born 31 Oct 1763, daughter of Caleb and Rebecca Dorsey ("Old Dorsey Bible." contributed by Ida M. Shirk, accessed at <www.biblerecords.com>; BAML).

Lawrence, Vernel, and Margaret Robinson were married by banns on 23 Nov 1788 at St. Peter's Catholic Church, Baltimore (*Piet:* 138),

Lawson, Alexander, a young gentleman of Baltimore, was married a few days ago to Miss Elizabeth Brown, only daughter of Charles Brown of Queen Anne's Co. (Annapolis *Maryland Gazette* 20 Jan 1763).

Lawson, Alexander, eldest son of James Lawson of Banff, Scotland, m. 13 Nov 1785 Dorothy Smith, daughter of Walter ("Alexander Lawson Bible Recrod," FCA at MdHS).

Lawson, Moses, and Mary Taylor were m. 26 Jan 1763 in the Lutheran Church at York Co. (Lawson Records at the York Co., Pa., Historical Society). Mary Lawson was named as a cousin in the will of Joseph Taylor, made 19 April 1788 (BAWB 4:346).

Lawson, Richard, and Mrs. Diana Parkinson, both of Baltimore, were m. last Sat, eve. (*Maryland Gazette or Baltimore General Advertiser* 1 Nov 1791; *Maryland Journal and Baltimore Advertiser* 1 Nov 1791; BAML)

Lawson, Robert, and Elizabeth McAllister, natives of Ireland, were m. by lic. on 12 Feb 1798 at St. Peter's Catholic Church, Baltimore (*Piet:* 138). They were m. last evening by the Rev. Bishop Carroll (*Federal Gazette and Baltimore Advertiser* 13 Feb 1789).

Lawyer, John Casper, m. by 28 Nov 1794 Ann, daughter of George Fisher (BAWB 6:6; BAAD 12:489).

Lawyer, Philip, m. by 28 Nov 1794 Clare, daughter of George Fisher (BAWB 6:6; BAAD 12:489).

Laxec, Lewis. See Lewis Lafee.

Lay, Henry, and Mary Deal were m. by lic. on 27 July 1799 at St. Peter's Catholic Church, Baltimore (*Piet:* 138).

Laypold. See Labold.

Leach, Philip, and Sarah Nearn were m. 1 June 1756 (Harrison, "St. John's Parish Register:" 213). On 18 Aug 1756 Leach stated that his wife Sarah had eloped from him and he would not pay her debts (BACT TR#E:214).

Leach, Richard Henry, of Savanna, Ga. attorney-at-law, and Mrs. Johanna Loeffler (nee Marsello) of Amsterdam, were m. in Baltimore on Thurs., 2nd inst., by Rev. Dr. Ireland (*Federal Gazette and Baltimore Daily Advertiser* 3 Jan 1800).

League, [-?-], m. by 21 April 1774 Nancy, daughter of Unity [-?-] Wilshire Hatton (BAWB 3:296).

League, James, and Elinor Enloes were m. on 2 May 1759 (Harrison, "St. John's Parish Register:" 218). On 11 Jan 1771 Elinor was named as a daughter of Anthony Enloes (BALR AL#C:121).

Leak (Lake), Abraham, m. by 31 March 1726 Sarah, admx. of James Hollyday (*q.v.*) of Baltimore Co. (BAAD 3:31; MDAD 6:297). Sarah Leak was charged with bastardy at June Court, 1731. Her children were Mary Leak, b. 31 Jan 1721 (may be the Mary Leak who m. Peter Hendlen on 6 Aug 1758), and Grace Leak, b. April 1731 (BACP HWS#7: 156; Reamy, *St. George's Parish Register:* 43, 44, 80). Sarah Leak and Immanuel Jones were the parents of: Cordelia, b. 7 Nov 1728, Anne, b. 30 Jan 1734, and Immanuel, b. 13 March 1737 (Reamy, *St. George's Parish Register:* 45, 45).

Leakins, [-?-], m. by 18 Sep 1787 Mary, widow of [-?-] Ferrell and mother of William Ferrell (*q.v.*) (BPET: Ferrell, William; Box 2, folder 14).

Leakins, John, on 6 March 1676 was named as a son-in-law in the will of Margaret Therrell (Thurrold) of Back River, Baltimore Co., and was the father of John Leakins, Jr., whom Margaret Therrell called grandson (MWB 5:347, abst. in Md. Cal. of Wills 1:201). Margaret was the widow of Richard Thurrol.

Leakins, John, m. by 18 Sep 1703 Elizabeth, admx. of John Enlow (INAC 24:135; BAAD 2:230).

Leakins, John, merchant, and Betsy Irwin, both of this town, were m. (*Maryland Journal and Baltimore Advertiser* 8 Oct 1784). (BAML gives her name as Elizabeth H. Irwin).

Leakins, Robert, m. by 9 Nov 1789 Mary, relict of William Langley (*q.v.*), and mother of Mary Langley (BALR WG#DD: 650).

Leary, Andrew, and Mary Dempsey of Anne Arundel Co. were m. by lic. on 28 Aug 1796 at St. Peter's Catholic Church, Baltimore (*Piet:* 138; BAML).

Leary, Daniel, and Mary McBride were m. by lic. on 9 Dec 1790 at St. Peter's Catholic Church, Baltimore (*Piet:* 138).

Lease, Leonard, m. by 3 Feb 1783 Louise, daughter of Philip Forney of York Co., Pa., who owned land in Baltimore Co. (BALR WG#DD:492).

Leaso, Matthew, and Mary Joice were m. by lic. on 7 Oct 1787 at St. Peter's Catholic Church, Baltimore (*Piet:* 138).

LeClaire, Lewis Sebastian, (surgeon, son of Peter and Mary Falher, native of Cannes in Brittany), and Jane Julia Rollin Demonbos (daughter of Charles Augustus Rollin and Elizabeth de Toyan) were m. by lic. on 6 Feb 1798 at St. Peter's Catholic Church, Baltimore (*Piet:* 138). (BAML gives her name as Jeaune J. R. De Narbes).

Lee, |-?-|, m. by 31 d. 1 m. 1763 Eliz., daughter of Eliz. Gover (BAWB 2:186).

Lee, |-?-|, m. by 4 June 1763 Mary, sister of Edward Hall (BAWB 2:365).

Lee, |-?-|, m. by 17 Oct 1784 Elizabeth, daughter of Johanna Miller, widow (BAWB 4:66).

Lee, |-?-|, m. by 11 May 1787 Mary, daughter of Zachariah Strouble (BAWB 4:272).

Lee, Ann, servant of Richard Jones was charged with bastardy in Aug Court, 1745 (BACP 1743-1745:629).

Lee, Cassandra. See Cassandra Morgan.

Lee, Charles, and Martha Wilson were m. by lic. dated 16 Jan 1792 (HAML). Martha Wilson, Jr., on 29 d. 3 m. 1792 has reported to have let out her affections to a man not of our society and accomplished her marriage contrary to the good order ("Minutes of Deer Creek Meeting," *QRNM:* 150).

Lee, Corbin, and Mrs. Eleanor Thornton were m. on 31 Jan 1754 (Harrison, "St. John's Parish Register:" 210). In his will made 24 July 1769 William Thornton named his cousin Eleanor Lee, wife of Corbin Lee (MWB 37:80 abst. in *Md. Cal. of Wills* 14:77). Eleanor m. 2nd John Skinner (*q.v.*).

Lee, Elizabeth, servant of Robert West, was charged with bastardy in March 1731/2 Court and again at March Court, 1736/7 (BACP HWS#1A: 1, 56; HWS#7: p. 225). Elizabeth was the mother of: Mary, b. 8 Nov 1732, and Margaret, b. 27 May 1736 (Harrison, "St. George's Parish Register:" 73, 96).

Lee, George, and Mary [-?-], were m. by 6 Oct 1794 when their son Benedict was b. ("Benedict Lee Bible," *MBR* 1:149-150).

Lee, Isaac, son of James, on 5 d. 4 m. 1766 was lately m. by a priest to a woman not of our society ("Minutes of Deer Creek Meeting," *QRNM:* 131). [No other marriage reference found].

Lee, James, and Nancy Riley, both of Baltimore, were m. a few days ago (*Maryland Journal and Baltimore Advertiser* 3 April 1792). They were m. in Baltimore Co. by a license dated 28 March 1792.

Lee, John, and Alice Norris were m. on 4 April 1733 (Harrison, "St. George's Parish Register:" 266). He d. by 29 Aug 1741 when Alice Lester, wife of George Lester (q.v.) administered Lee's estate (BAAD 4:118).

Lee, John, m. by 11 May 1787 Mary, daughter of Zachariah Strouble (BAWB 4:272; BAAD 9:182).

Lee, John, son of Samuel, and Sebella Lee on 25 d. 8 m. 1790 declared their intention to marry ("Minutes of Gunpowder Meeting," *QRNM:* 89).

Lee, Mary, servant of Constance Cockey, was charged with bastardy at Nov 1750 Court and again at Nov 1756 Court. One record states she swore the father was John Pribble, Jr., servant to Mr. Owings; another that William Payne was the father; they were all fined 30 shillings at Nov 1750 Court (BAMI 1755-1763; BACP BB#C:312, TR#6: 1, 4). Mary Lee was the mother of; Sarah, b. 4 Dec 1750; John, b. 25 Oct 1756, and Seaborn, b 31 Oct 1759 (Reamy, *St. George's Parish Register:* 90).

Lee, Mary, was convicted of bastardy in 1761 (BAMI 1755-1763).

Lee, Mary. See Mary Wilson.

Lee, Rachel. See John Spicer.

Lee, Samuel, m. by 13 Sep 1763 Mary, sister of Edward Hall who died without issue (MDTP 39:435).

Lee, Susannah, was charged with bastardy at June Court, 1750 (BACP TR#5:2).

Lee, Thomas, Jr., eldest son of Thomas Sim Lee, Esq., and Eleanor Cromwell were m. by lic. in Oct 1796 at St. Peter's Catholic Church, Baltimore (*Piet:* 138).

Lee, William, on 30 d. 5 m., 1789 was charged with marrying outside the good order ("Minutes of Gunpowder Meeting," *QRNM:*87). William Lee and Margaret Day of Harford Co. were m. 4 Jan 1789 (Reamy, *St. James Parish Register:* 1).

LeFort, Louis Francois Isidore, was m. last eve. by Rev. Mr. Ireland to Mrs. Frances Deschamps, both of this city (*Federal Gazette and Baltimore Daily Advertiser* 13 July 1799).

Legatt (Legett), Bridget, was charged with bastardy at March 1736/7 Court (BACP HWS#1A: 1, 56).

Legatt, Sutton, and Hannah Green were m. on 7 April 1763 (Harrison, "St. John's Parish Register:" 224). She was a daughter of Isaac Green (BAWB 6:277).

Legett, Sarah, was cited for unlawful cohabitation with John Enlows by the vestry of St. John's Parish in April 1736 ((Harrison, "St. John's, Vestry Proceedings" pp. 2-3).

Lego (Leigo), Benjamin, m. by 25 Sep 1707 Mary, extx. of William Hill (*q.v.*) (BAAD 2:169; INAC 27:211).

Lego, Cordelia, in 1763 was convicted of bastardy (BAMI 1755-1763).

Lego Mary, was charged with bastardy at March 1733/4 Court. Benjamin Lego, her father, agreed to be responsible for her illegitimate child (BACP HWS#9:197).

Lego, Ruth, daughter of Benjamin Lego, was charged with bastardy at Nov 1733 Court (BACP HWS#1A:399).

Lego, Spencer, and **Benjamin Lego,** orphans of Benjamin ego, in Aug 1759 chose Robert Adair as their guardian (BAMI 1755-1763).

LeGuen, Jacob, and Margaret Woodhouse were m. by lic. on 13 May 1799 at St. Peter's Catholic Church, Baltimore (*Piet:* 138).

Leigo. See Lego.

Lemar. See Lamar.

Lemmon, Alexis, and Rachel Jones were married by license dated 9 Dec 1777 (BAML). In 1786 Rachel was named as formerly Jones, extx. of Jacob Jones who left a son Jacob Jones, now a ward of John Jones (BAOC 1:259: BAAD 9:239). Jacob Jones had m. Rachel Cottrell on 10 Feb 1742 (Harrison, "St. John's Parish Register:" 125).

Lemmon, Johanna, was charged with bastardy at the March 1733/4 Court and named Thomas Whitehead as the father of her child (BACP HWS#9:198). Her daughter Floria Lemmon was born 15 May 1733 (Reamy, *St. Thomas' Parish Register*: 8).

Lemmon, Capt. John, and Mrs. Esther Lawrence, both of Fell's Point, were m. Sun by Rev. Richards (*Baltimore Telegraphe* 12 Nov 1799).

Lemmon, Joshua, merchant, and Sally Priestman, both of this town, were m. (*Maryland Journal and Baltimore Advertiser* 24 Dec 1782; BAML).

Lemmon, Thomas, and Comfort Foster were married by license dated 15 Oct 1793 (BAML). On 29 Dec 1796 Comfort was named as a daughter of John Foster (BALR WG#YY:309).

LeMoine, Peter, native of France, and Elizabeth Monge were m. by lic. on 20 Feb 1798 at St. Peter's Catholic Church, Baltimore (*Piet:* 138).

Lendrum, Rev. Andrew, and Jane Burney were m. on 18 Oct 1749 at Newcastle on Delaware by the Rev, George Ross (Harrison, "St. George's Parish Register:" 366). On 13 sep 1`757 Jane (Jean) was named as a daughter in the will of Robert Berney [*sic*], formerly of Newcastle upon Delaware, but now of Baltimore Co., who also named a grandson Robert Birney Lendrum (MWB 30"369 abst. by Gibb).

Lenehan, Timothy, and Mary Ryan were m. by lic. on 13 June 1798 at St. Peter's Catholic Church, Baltimore (*Piet:* 138). (BAML gives his name as Timothy Lanahan).

L'Engle, John, native of Fort Dauphin, St. Domingo, and Suzanna Guilman, native of Cap Francois, St. Domingo, Parish of Our Lady, were m. by lic. on 2 Dec 1793 at St. Peter's Catholic Church, Baltimore (*Piet:* 137).

Lenox, [-?-], m. by 9 Jan 1726/7 Elizabeth, who was called daughter Elizabeth Lenox in the will of John Hayes (MWB 19:70 abst. in *Md. Cal. of Wills* 6:11).

Lenox, James, and Honour Lenox, administrators, on 12 May 1728 posted bond to administer the estate of Jacob Peacock (*q.v.*) (BAAB 2:456; MDTP 28:213).

Lenox, James, m. by 22 Jan 1735 Mary, daughter of Robuck Lynch (BALR HWS#M:371).

Lenox (Lennox), Richard, m. by 6 March 1706 Mary, sister of James Richardson and daughter of Col. Thomas Richardson, dec. (BALR IR#AM:40, TR#DS:212).

Lenox, Richard, m. by 27 Jan 1724 Tamar (Thamar), widow and extx. of William Wilkinson of Baltimore Co. and admx. of Frances Keys (BAAD 1:94, BAAD 2:335; MDAD 6:296; 7:103; MDTP 27:1258)..

Lenox, William, m. by 24 Feb 1720 Bethiah, daughter of Anthony Drew of Baltimore Co. (MDAD 3:281 1/2).

Leopold, Charles, of Baltimore, advertised his wife's repeated elopements (*Maryland Journal and Baltimore Advertiser* 30 Jan 1787).

Leppard, William, stated he would not pay the debts contracted by his wife Charlotte, who had eloped from his bed and board (*Federal Gazette and Baltimore Daily Advertiser* 16 Aug 1796).

Lerew, James, and Miss Elizabeth Kantz, both of Baltimore, were m. last Tues. by Rev. Bend (*Baltimore Telegraphe* 17 Oct 1799).

Lester, Eliza, was charged with bastardy at the June 1721 Court; at first she named John Hollandsworth as the father, then recanted and named an Indian named Sackelah as the father (BACP IS#C:498, 507).

Lester, George, and Alice Lee were m. on 8 Dec 1737 (Harrison, "St. George's Parish Register:" 129). On 4 Feb 1737 [1737/8?], Alice was called sister-in-law in the will of Henry Millain, whose estate she administered (MWB 21:840 abst. in *Md. Cal. of Wills* 7:235; MDTP 30:389, 397). In Aug 1741 Alice was the widow and admx. of

John Lea or Lee (*q.v.*) (BAAD 4:1218); she also claimed the balance of Henry Millain's estate as residuary legatee (MDAD 18:390, 391). Henry Millen had m. Mary Norris on 5 July 1720 (Harrison, "St. George's Parish Register:" 225).

Lester, Peter, and Anne [-?-] were m. 8 May 1713 (Harrison, "St. George's Parish Register:" 214). Peter Lester d. by 2 June 1735 leaving his admx. Ann and two children George and Mary (BAAD 3:196). Ann Lester, in her will made 25 May 1749 named her son Henry Hail and grandson Thomas Hail, her daughter Mary Sinclair, son-in-law James Sinclair, and grandchildren, Ann and Lester Sinclair (MWB 27:84 abst. by Gibb).

Lester, William, cabinet maker, and Miss Elizabeth Johnson, both of Fell's Point, were m. last Tues. eve, by Rev. Bend (*Baltimore Telegraphe* 12 Aug 1797).

Let, John, native of Cueta in Provence, and Mary Brongier, widow Nonnier, born at Hieres in Provence, France, were m. by lic. on 25 Aug 1799 at St. Peter's Catholic Church, Baltimore (*Piet:* 138).

Lett, Eleanor, mulatto, aged 4 years, daughter of Elizabeth Lett, in 1772 was bound to Mary Barkever (BAMI 1772, 1775-1781: 21).

Lett, Jane, was charged with bastardy at March 1717/8 Court and named James Ketcham as the father (BACP IS#1A:237-238).

Lett, Mary, was charged with bastardy at the Aug 1728 Court, and again Nov 1728. Her children, Sarah Lett and Zachariah Lett were bound out to serve William Rogers at the March 1730/1 Court (BACP HWS#6: 22, 74; HWS#7: 97). Zachariah and Margret Lett were the parents of (Reamy, *St. Paul's Parish Register*: 16): Luzana, b. 27 April 1741; Vashti (daughter), b. 1 Jan 1743, and Daniel, b. 29 Oct 1745.

Lett, Sabra, was charged with bastardy at the June 1732 Court and again at the March 1736/7 Court (BACP (BACP HWS#7:289, HWS#1A:19).

Lettick, Peter, d. by 16 May 1763 when his estate was distributed by the admx. Elizabeth wife of John Seigler (*q.v.*) (BFD 4:7).

Lively, George, m. by 13 June 1769 Catherine, extx. of John Rohra (*q.v.*) (BAAD 7:33). Catherine was *admin. de bonis non* of Esther, widow of Ulrich Whistler (BAAD 7:30).

Levering, Aaron, d. by 1795 when Hannah and Nathan Levering, his administrators, petitioned the court to sell one-half of a lot of ground (Pet. of Hannah Levering and Nathan Levering, 1795, BPET).

Levering, E.?, on 23 April 1800 was named as an heir of John Brown (BAAD 13:244).

Leverington, Enoch, and Miss Hannah Brown were m. last eve. by Rev. Dr. Allison (*Baltimore Telegraphe* 29 Jan 1800).

Levingston. See Livingston.

Levy, Isaac, of New York d. prior to 1796, leaving a will by which he appointed Sampson, Moses, and Asher Levy his execs. Moses Levy renounced the executorship, and Sampson Levy was dead. Asher Levy was dead, and by his will appointed Matthias Williamson and wife Henrietta as execs. They complained that Benjamin Levy of Baltimore Town obtained false letters of admin. Benjamin Levy filed a reply that he did not know if Williamson and his wife were execs. of Asher Levy or not, but he (Benj. Levy) did obtain letters of admin., and he did admin. the estate of Asher Levy. Benjamin Levy swore "on the five books of Moses," that his testimony was true. He enclosed a copy of his final admin. account dated 9 April 1795. It mentioned sums received from Dr. Leonard Hollyday and son, money due from a late Capt. Robert Etherington, and money due from Nathan Levy and David

Franks. (BOCP Petition of Matthias Williamson and wife Henrietta, Pet., BA, 1796).

Lewin, Mary, was charged with bastardy at the Aug 1736 (or 1738) Court (BACP HWS#1A:19).

Lewis, Benjamin, m. by 16 Feb 1796 Helen, daughter of John Elder (BAAD 12:101).

Lewis, Catherine, was charged with bastardy at the June 1723 Court (BACP IS&TW#2: 331).

Lewis, Charles, of Conn., was m. last Thurs. eve. to Miss Margaret Barron (Barnes?) of this city (*Federal Gazette and Baltimore Daily Advertiser* 20 Nov 1797; BAML).

Lewis, Henry, d. by Nov 1680 when his extx, Eliza, had m. 2nd, John Bird (*q.v.*) (*ARMD* 69:270, 366; INAC 7B:8).

Lewis, Henry, of Baltimore Co., m. by 13 Dec 1700 Sarah, daughter and heir of William Jones who d. leaving a will dated 22 March 1684 (AALR WT#1:105, WT#2:527).

Lewis, Henry, m. by 21 Nov 1730 Caturah, daughter of Robert Parker (BALR IS#L:50).

Lewis, John, and Mary Young were married by license dated 16 Feb 1789 (BAML). On 28 Nov 1799 Mary was named as the admx. of John Young (BAAD 10:81). A John Young and Mary Kelly had been married by license dated 19 June 1778 (BAML).

Lewis, Mary, was charged with bastardy at the March 1746/7 Court (BACP TB&TR#1: 378).

Lewis, Philip, and Sally Barton, both of Baltimore, were m. on Mon. by Rev. Hagerty (*Baltimore American* 30 April 1800).

Lewis, Richard, son of Richard and Elizabeth, late of England, and Betty Giles, son of John and Sarah, were m. on 15 d. 3 m. 1723 (Records of West River Monthly Meeting, QRSM; MWB 18:429 abst. in *Md. Cal. of Wills* 5:208).

Lewis, Richard, m. by 22 Dec 1778 Catherine, widow and admx. of William Harris of Baltimore Co., dec. (BALR WG#C:236; BAAD 8:83).

Lewis, Thomas, m. by 21 July 1781 Elizabeth, daughter of John Moore (BALR WG#G:194).

Lewis, William, m. by 12 Nov 1754 Ruth, extx. of Edmund Howard (*q.v.*) (MDTP 36:96; on 5 Nov 1755 his name was given as Edmond Harris: MDTP 36:235; MDAD 38:251).

Lewis, William, aged 6, on 14 Oct. 1785 was bound to Martin Lowdenslager, weaver (BAOC WB#1, 227).

Lewis, William Young, merchant, and Miss Stewart, daughter of Dr. William Stewart, lately from Europe, were m. in Baltimore (*General Magazine and Impartial Review,* June 1798, in *MGSB* 20 (3) (Summer 1979).

Lewthwaite, See Luther, below.

Leypold, Samuel F., and Miss Breidenbaugh, both of Baltimore, were m. last eve. by Rev. Mr. Kurtz (*Baltimore Telegraphe* 19 Oct 1798).

Lick, Peter, and Rosanna Willis were married by banns on 1 Nov 1790 at St. Peter's Catholic Church, Baltimore (*Piet:* 138).

Liddle, John, and Catherine Foy of Fell's Point were m. by lic. on 26 May 1796 at St. Peter's Catholic Church, Baltimore (*Piet:* 138).

Liggat, Samuel, merchant of Baltimore, and Jenny Parks, daughter of John Parks, merchant, were m. a few days ago at Frederick (*Maryland Journal and Baltimore Advertiser* 25 Dec 1787). A merchant of Baltimore, Liggat died last Tues., 29th ult. at Frederick Town, in his 25th year, leaving a young wife (*Maryland Journal and*

Baltimore Advertiser 27 Oct 1789). Jane Liggatt, admx., advertised she would settle the estate (*Maryland Journal and Baltimore Advertiser* 27 Oct 1799).

Lightner, George, was guardian of Margaret Marvell, and was fined by the court for not settling her guardian account (BOCP Pet. of George Lightner, 1793).

Lile, Jacob, m. by 10 Aug 1798 Barbara Smith, legatee of Leonard Smith (BAAD 12:465).

Lilley, Samuel, m. by 20 Feb 1799 Belinda, admx of Elijah Walker (*q.v.*) (BAAD 12:547).

Lillington, John, m. by 23 May 1689, Elizabeth, widow of John Taylor (MDTP 14:148).

Limes, Barnet, and Margaret Turin were m. by lic. on 30 April 1785 at St. Peter's Catholic Church, Baltimore (*Piet:* 138). (BAML gives her name as Margaret Turvine).

Linch. See Lynch.

Linden, Robert, m. by 5 Aug 1767 Rebecca, sister of Moses Groom and daughter of Moses Groom, Sr. (BALR B#Q:158).

Lindenberger, George, m. by 7 Feb 1791 Susanna, who received an equal share of the estate of John Wright (BAAD 10:286).

Lindenberger, Capt. George, and Miss Ann Stevenson, eldest daughter of Dr. Henry Stevenson, were m. last eve. by Rev. Bend (*Maryland Journal and Baltimore Advertiser* 9 Jan 1795; BAML).

Lindsey, Champoneyss, d. by 27 July 1775 by which time his admx. Susan had m. Elijah Minor (*q.v.*) (MDTP 46:236).

Lindsey (Linsey), John, m. by 21 April 1798 Elizabeth, extx. of Elizabeth Barrows (BAAD 12:412).

Liner, Peter, and Barbara Whitemasters were married by banns on 8 Jan 1786 at St. Peter's Catholic Church, Baltimore (*Piet:* 138).

Lintall (Lontall), [-?-], m. by 31 Jan 1720 Mary, daughter of Thomas Williamson (BAAD 3:278).

Lippi, Conrad, m. by 13 Feb 176, Maria Elisabeta Weinsbergerin ("First Record Book for the Reformed and Lutheran Congregations at Manchester, Baltimore (now Carroll) Co." *MGSB* 35:269).

Liston, James, m. by 11 May 1790 Sarah, legatee of Henry Pearson (BALR WG#FF: 96).

Litten, [-?-], m. by 19 Nov 1732 Ann, daughter of John Hawkins (MWB 20:750).

Littig. Jost, d. by Feb 1794 when Philip Littig, his heir at law advertised a sale of real estate in Fell's Point (*Baltimore Daily Intelligencer* 5 Feb 1794).

Littig (Lydig). Philip, m. by 27 May 1769 Elizabeth, eldest daughter of George Frederick and Mary Brown of Baltimore Co. (BALR AL#A:233).

Littig, Philip, d. by 9 June 1784 leaving a widow Elizabeth Margaret and sons Philip and George; on that day his widow leased land (BALR WG#LL:59).

Little, [-?-], m. by 10 May 1761 Elizabeth, daughter of Michael Webster, Quaker (BAWB 2:176).

Little, [-?-], m. by 6 Dec 1781, Rachel, daughter of John Colegate, farmer (BAWB 3:470).

Little (Litle), Guy, and Eliza Ruff were m. on 25 March 1751 (Harrison, "St. John's Parish Register:" 271). On 7 Dec 1752 she was named as the admx. of Daniel Ratt (prob. Ruff) (*q.v.*) (MDTP 32-3:32; MDAD 30:158, 33:429).

Little, Henry, m. by 1 Aug 1761 Mary Sims, daughter of William and Mary Sims (who named Henry Little as her son-in-law in her will (MWB 31:441 abst. by Gibb); Mary Little came into court on 16 Oct 1763 and claimed that she m. Henry Little in St. Paul's Parish when she was only 12 years old and she renounced her marriage (BACT B#G, 1763-1773).

Little, James, d. by 24 Dec 1735 when his widow Elizabeth had m. Thomas Farlow (*q.v.*) (MINV 21:281; MDAD 16:354; MDTP 30:346).

Little, Jane, was charged with bastardy at the March 1738/9 and March 1739/40 Courts (BACP HWS#1A:351, HWS#TR:157).

Little, Peter, was m. last eve. by Rev. Mr. Richards, to Miss Arabella Hughes, both of this city (*Federal Gazette and Baltimore Daily Advertiser* 25 Aug 1797; BAML, which gives her name as Anna Bella Hughes).

Little, Thomas, and Mary Shepard were m. on 27 June 1731 (Harrison, "St. George's Parish Register:" 257). On 13 Jan 1731/2 Mary was named as a daughter of Rowland Shepherd of Baltimore Co. (MWB 20:347 abst. in *Md. Cal. of Wills* 6:215).

Little, Thomas, in Nov 1734, was charged with begetting a bastard on the body of Sarah Herrington (BACP HWS#9:350).

Little, Thomas, and Avarilla Osborn were m. on 28 Feb 1737 (Harrison, "St. George's Parish Register:" 295). On 15 Jan 1750 Avarilla was named as a daughter of William Osborn/Osburn of Baltimore Co. (MDAD 29:136).

Little, Thomas and Sarah Hughes on 26 June 1746 were ordered to appear before the vestry of St. George's Parish the first Tuesday in September. On 3 Nov 1746 he was discharged for putting her away ("St. John's and St. George's Parish Register Vestry Proceedings," MS. at MdHS). **N.B.:** Thomas Little m. by 14 April 1762, Sarah, daughter of Samuel and Jane Hughes (who was the mother of Francis Watkins), and had a son Thomas Little (BAWB 3:27, 185). In his will, made 23 March 1764, Thomas Little stated that he had a daughter born to Sarah Hughes before he was married to her, and he wanted her to be called by his name, and leaves the child to his daughter Mary (MWB 32:294 abst. in *Md. Cal. of Wills* 13:31). Samuel Hughes, in his will, made 15 Jan 1771 named his daughter Sarah and her heirs by Thomas Little (MWB 38:193, abst. in *Md. Cal. of Wills* 14:161).

Little, Thomas, m. by [date not given] Mary, daughter of James and Margaret Calder, dec. (MCHP # 5328).

Littlejohn, Dr. Miles, and Miss Sally Payne, were m. last Wed. eve. (*Maryland Journal and Baltimore Advertiser* 9 Jan 1795; BAML, which gives her name as Sarah Paine).

Littlejohn, Thomas, and Sarah McCarty were married by license dated 28 March 1796 (BAML). On 24 June 1797 Sarah was named as the widow of William McCarty (BAAD 12:316).

Litton (Litten), [-?-], m. by 19 Nov 1732 Ann, daughter of John Hawkins (MWB 20:760 abst. in *Md. Cal. of Wills* 7:33).

Litton, Ann, was indicted for bastardy at the Aug 1765 Court (BAMI 1765:17).

Litton, Hannah, daughter of Thomas Litton was charged with bastardy at the Aug 1742 Court and a bill was presented against her at the March 1743/4 Court; she was indicted again at the Nov 1746 Court (BACP TB#D:8, Liber 1743-1745:154, and TB&TR#1:220).

Litton, Isaac, m. by 17 March 1745 Mary, extx. of Thomas Jones (*q.v.*) (MDTP 31:630; see also MDAD 22:336). On 11 Jan 1750/1 Isaac Litton stated he would not be responsible for his wife Mary Litton (BACT TR#E:21).

Litton, Thomas, Jr., m. by 31 July 1742 Margaret, accountants of the estate of Seaborn Tucker (*q.v.*) of Baltimore Co. (MDTP 31:295; MDAD 19:193).

Litzenger, Henry, and Darcus Warner were m. by lic. on 12 Feb 1786 at St. Peter's Catholic Church, Baltimore (*Piet:* 138).

Lizenger, William, and Elizabeth Shreagley were m. by lic. on 31 Jan 1788 at St. Peter's Catholic Church, Baltimore (*Piet:* 138; BAML, which gives his name as William Litzinger).

Livers, Arnold, born in Frederick Co., and Polly Stansbury were m. by lic. on 23 Sep 1798 at St. Peter's Catholic Church, Baltimore (*Piet:* 138).

Livingston, John, of Livingston Twp., Columbia Co., N. Y., m. by 29 April 1799 Mary, widow of Matthew Ridley (BALR WG#59:208).

Livingston, Mr. Paul Bartholomew Hymen, merchant of Baltimore, was m. Sun. eve. To Miss Letitia Smith of Fells Point (*Federal Intelligencer and Baltimore Daily Gazette* 21 April 1795). The bride's name is given as Lehlia Smith at St. Peter's Catholic Church, Baltimore (*Piet:* 138).

Lloyd, [-?-], d. by 6 Feb 1744 having m. Elizabeth, widow of William Holland (PCLR EI#8:34).

Lloyd John, and wife Elizabeth, extx., on 29 Sep 1737 posted bond to administer the estate of Theophilus Jones (BAWB 3:377; MDTP 30:354).

Lloyd (Loyde), Robert, and Kitty Shaw were m. by lic. on 12 June 1791 at St. Peter's Catholic Church, Baltimore (*Piet:* 138).

Lloyd, Sarah, servant of Samuel Cooper was charged with bastardy at the March 1736/7 Court and presented at the June 1737 Court (BACP (BACP HWS#1A:1, 56).

Lloyd (Loyd), Rev. Thomas, of Denbigh Co., Eng., m. by 25 May 1721 Mary, only daughter of Rev. Evan Evans of St. George's Parish Baltimore Co. (MWB 17:207 abst. in *Md. Cal. of Wills* 5:101).

Lloyd, Thomas, and Nancy Price were married by license dated 13 Nov 1793 (BAML). On 12 May 1798 Ann was named as a daughter of Absolom and Martha Price (BALR WG#54:435).

Lloyd (Loyde), William, and Mary Walsh were married by banns on 1 Nov 1790 at St. Peter's Catholic Church, Baltimore (*Piet:* 138).

Lloyd, William, widower, and Elizabeth Walter, widow, were m. by lic. on 14 March 1799 at St. Peter's Catholic Church, Baltimore (*Piet:* 138).

Lock, Sarah, was charged with bastardy at the June 1765 Court and John Parks was summoned (BAMI 1765:14).

Lock, Thomas, and Miss Sarah Duncan, were m. last eve. by Rev. Hagerty (*Baltimore Daily Intelligencer* 13 Dec 1793). (They were m. by BAML in Baltimore Co.)

Lorkitt, John, m. by 19 Sep 1692 [-?-], daughter of Richard Green [Gwinn?] of Baltimore Co. (MWB 6:48 abst. in *Md. Cal. of Wills* 2:65).

Loe. See Lowe.

Loftin, Elizabeth, was charged with bastardy at the March 1731/2 Court (BACP HWS#7:225).

Logan, [-?-], m. by 5 Sep 1760 [-?-], sister of Alexander Lawson (BAWB 2:337).

Logan, Neil, and Mary White, natives of Ireland, were m. by lic. on 15 Oct 1796 at St. Peter's Catholic Church, Baltimore (*Piet:* 138).

Logsdon, Job, and Patience Helms were m. by lic. on 21 Sep 1790 at St. Peter's Catholic Church, Baltimore (*Piet:* 138; BAML, which gives his name as Jeb Logsdon).

Logsdon, John, and Margaret Wooley were m. on 9 Oct 1735 (Harrison, "St. Paul's Parish Register:" 154). Margaret was a daughter of John Wooley (*q.v.*) who d. by Aug 1747 (BAAB 4:117).

Logsdon, William, m. by 17 May 1758 Ann, daughter of Henry Davis (BALR B#G:237).

Loney, Amos, and Mary Donellan were m. 28 Nov 1782; their son John was b. 7 July 1792 (Marr. Returns of Rev. William West, Scharf Papers, MS.1999 at MdHS; "Amos Loney Bible," *MBR* 7:113).

Loney, John, m. by 16 Nov 1752 Mary, admx. of Rev. Hugh Carlisle (*q.v.*) (MDTP 33-2:26; MDAD 32:211, 40:445 where her name is given as Allery).

Loney, William, m. by 22 April 1700 Jane sole heir of [Thomas] Overton (BALR HW#2:54, 61).

Loney, William, m. by 27 April 1706 Arabella, daughter of John Walston (Harrison, "St. George's Parish Register:" 201, gives his name as William Love). She m. 2nd, Bennett Garrett (*q.v.*).

Long, [-?-], m. by 1 May 1723 Jane, formerly Tealle, acct. of John Tealle of Baltimore Co. (MINV 8:207).

Long, [-?-], m. by 18 Dec 1781 Ann, daughter of John Stansbury (BAWB 4:102).

Long, Abraham, on 22 Aug 1794 was named as one of the children in the nuncupative will of Christopher Curtz (BAWB 5:163).

Long, James, on 10 June 1778 bought land in Baltimore Town from James Moore and his wife Cassandra of Kent Co. Cassandra was sister and heir at law of Robert Adair of Baltimore Co. (BALR WG#B:294).

Long, James, m. by 7 Jan 1794, Patience, widow of Roger Horace Pratt of Baltimore Co. (BALR WG#NN:594).

Long, John, m. by 20 April 1780 Eleanor, formerly Eleanor Moore (BALR WG#E:264).

Long, John, m. by 18 Nov 1783 Elizabeth Sittlemeyer, granddaughter of Mary [-?-] who was the widow of Sebastian Sittlemeyer (BALR WG#T:8-9).

Long, John, and Elizabeth Partridge were married by license dated 9 Nov 1791 (BAML). On 6 March 1793 Elizabeth was named as the admx. of Danbury B. Partridge (*q.v.*) (BAAD 11: 225).

Long, John, m. by 16 Feb 1793 Ann Stansbury, who was mentioned in the administration acct. of John Stansbury (BAAD 11:206).

Long, John, and his daughter Jane were named in the 1798 will of Thomas Hamm of Back River Neck (BAWB 6:247).

Long, Kennedy, merchant of Baltimore, was m. last eve. by Rev. Dr. Green, to Miss Eliza Kennedy, daughter of Mr. Andrew Kennedy of this city (*Federal Gazette and Baltimore Daily Advertiser* 20 Nov 1797).

Long, Robert, b. 31 July 1733, m. 28 Jan 1768, Elizabeth Edwards ("Nicholas Dorsey Bible," *The Notebook* 10 (3) (Sep 1994); *MBR* 3:67-69).

Long, Robert, was charged with bastardy at the March 1768 Court (BAMI 1768-1769:9). Robert Long, in his will, made 13 Jan 1779 named his natural son Robert Carey Long, and his bros. Andrew and James Long, and a sister Jane Parkhill (BAWB 3:389).

Long, Robert, by 4 Sep 1782 had a marriage contract with Mary [-?-], who named her children John and Mary Norwood in her will (BAWB 3:526).

Long, Robert Carey, and Miss Sarah Carnigher, both of Baltimore, were m. on Thurs. by Rev. Richards (*Baltimore Telegraphe* 11 Oct 1797).

Long, Samuel and Mary Cummins were married by license dated (BAML). Margaret Cummins, in her will made 6 Dec 1799 named her granddaughter Jane Long (BAWB 6:238).

Long, Sewell, m. by 31 Aug 1747 Margaret, daughter of Richard Acton MDTP 32:116, 132).

Long, Thomas, d. by 14 April 1747 having m. Jane, widow of John Dixon (Prov. Court Judgments EI#10#1:743-746).

Long, Thomas, son of John, was named as a nephew on 6 April 1787, in the will of Richard Stansbury (BAWB 4:233).

Long, Thomas, and Elizabeth Johnston were m. by lic. on 18 Oct 1792 at St. Peter's Catholic Church, Baltimore (*Piet:* 138; BAML, which gives her name as Elizabeth Inkston).

Longsworth, Sarah, in 1762 was convicted of bastardy (BAMI 1755-1763).

Lontall. See Lintall.

Lorentz, Ferdinand, a solder in the Maryland Line, served nearly three years in the German Regiment and died about 1805. He m. Elizabeth [-?-] at the R. C. Church in Baltimore in 1780 or 1781.An Extract of the Baptismal Record of the Cathedral in Baltimore shows the births and baptisms of the children of Ferdinand and Elizabeth: Wendel, b. 2 Nov, bapt. 13 Nov 1783; Elizabeth, b. 4 Jan, bapt. 23 Jan 1786; and Ann, b. 28 Feb, bapt. 4 March 1792 (Rev. War Pension Application of Elizabeth Lorentz: W9140).

Lorentz, Wendel, enlisted in the German Regiment on 12 July 1776 and served until 1779 and died 15 March 1833. He m. Ann Steele in Baltimore Co. on 28 Feb 1797. In 1820 Wendell Lawrence stated his wife was sickly, and he had four daughters: Rachel, aged 19; Elizabeth, aged 14; Ann, aged 7; and Mary, aged 4; and two sons: George Washington, aged 10, and Jacob, aged 2 (Rev. War Pension Application of Ann Lorentz: W9113/BLWT8517-160-55).

Lorman, William, merchant, and Miss Mary Fulford, both of Baltimore, were m. last eve. by Rev. Dr. Bend (*Baltimore Daily Intelligencer* 4 April 1794).

Lotten (Loton), Jacob, d. by 16 April 169, leaving a widow Elizabeth and three children (*BCF:*411). Elizabeth m. 2nd, William York (*q.v.*), and 3rd, James Frizzle (*q.v.*).

Lotzinger, Hannah, orphan daughter of Christian Lotzinger, in Dec 1794 was made a ward of Frederick Decker (BAOC 3:122).

Loubies (Lubies), Philip, and Mary Helm or Mary Adams were married by license dated 25 April 1785 (BAML gives both names for the wife). On 25 Sep 1795 Mary was named as a granddaughter of Mayberry Helm (BALR WG#TT: 15).

Louchly, Selina, was charged with bastardy at the Nov 1758 Court; her daughter was named Elizabeth Louchly (BAMI 1757-1759:162).

Louderman, Frederick, in June 1795 was made a ward of John Louderman (BAOC 3:158).

Louderman, John Christian, b. 1761 in Reisterstown, Md., and Mrs. Ann King (possibly the Anne Barnes who was b. 4 Feb 1765 in Frederick Town, Md.) were m. on 18 Jan 1791; their daughter Margaret was b. 14 Nov 1791; Ann Barnes Louderman d. 5 Jan 1832 ("John Louderman Bible," *MBR* 7:116; BAML).

Love, [-?-], m. by 4 Oct 1771 Margaret, daughter of Daniel Preston (BAWB 3:211).

Love, John, in his will dated 2 March 1708 named his wife Alice and her son John Brassha (MWB 12. Part 2:44 abst. in *Md. Cal. of Wills* 3:131).

Love, John, in Nov 1756 was fined for begetting a bastard on the body of Clara Billingslea (BAMI 1755-1763).

Love, Miles, stated he would not pay the debts of his wife Rachel (*Maryland Journal and Baltimore Advertiser* 13 March 1775).

Love, Robert, m. by June 1693 Jane, daughter of Thomas Thurston (BACP F#1:415, 489).

Love, Robert, and Sarah Bond were m. on 9 June 1729 (Harrison, "St. John's Parish Register:" 63). As Robert's widow and the mother of John, Ruth, and Tamar Love, she m. 2nd, on 27 Aug 1742 Walter Billingsley *(q.v.)* (Harrison, "St. George's Parish Register:" 325; BALR TB#C; 5, 6, 7). On 9 June 1729 Sarah was named as a daughter of William Bond (BALR IS#L:58; see also MDAD 19:266).

Love, Thomas, m. by 1701 [-?-], admins. of John Skellds (MDTP 19A:79).

Love, William, and Ann, daughter of Abraham Delap were m. by 22 July 1707 (INAC 27:28). William Love died leaving a will dated 23 Feb 1708 and proved 2 March 1708/9. He named his wife Ann and a daughter Juliana (MWB 12:317 abst. in *Md. Cal. of Wills* 3:117). Ann m. 2nd, John McComas *(q.v.)*.

Loveall, [-?-], m. by 25 Oct 1762 Mary, daughter of Thomas West (BAWB 3:87).

Lovedon, Thomas, in his will made 28 Nov 1798 named his wife Mary and his step-son John Wilson (BAWB 6:149).

Lovely. See Lavely.

Low, John, m, by 12 Sep 1715 [-?-], daughter of Daniel Robinson (MWB 14:212 abst. in *Md. Cal. of Wills* 4:65).

Lowden, Wealthy, was charged with bastardy at the March 1768 Court (BAMI 1768-1769:11).

Lowe, [-?-], m. by 26 March 1760 Mary, daughter of John Norris (BAWB 2:328; BFD 3:119).

Lowe, Ann, in 1763 was convicted of bastardy (BAMI 1755-1763).

Lowe, John, and Hannah Hewit were married by license dated 18 Aug 1778 (BAML). On 12 May 1792 she was named as having received a share of the estate of Edward Hewitt (BAAD 11:49).

Lowe (Loe), Thomas, m. by 24 April 1702 Elizabeth, admx. of John Shields (INAC 21:372).

Lowe, Thomas, and Thamar Love were m. in 1728/9 (Harrison, "St. John's Parish Register:" 63). On 14 Oct 1726 Tamar was named as a daughter of John Love (BALR TB#C:522; BAAD 2:318; MDTP 28:403).

Lowe, Thomas, was charged with bastardy at the June 1734 Court (BACP HWS#9:253).

Lowe (Low), Thomas, and Sarah Mainer were m. in 1753 or in Jan 1754 (Harrison, "St. John's," pp. 209, 242). On 9 Dec 1769 Sarah was named as a sister of John Mainer (BAWB 3:164).

Lowe, William, m. by 22 July 1707 Anne, daughter of Abraham Delap of Baltimore Co. (INAC 27:28).

Lowe, William, m. on or by 28 Feb 1736 Sarah, admx. of George Graves (*BCF:* 413). She m. 3rd, Lewis Lafee *(q.v.)*.

Lowe, William, m. by 7 June 1744 Temperance, daughter of William Pickett (BALR TB#C: 522).

Lowe (Low), William, and Ann 'Davice' were m. on 30 Jan 1746 (Harrison, "St. John's Parish Register:" 121). On 20 Nov 1769 Ann was named as a sister of Henry Davis (BAWB 3:149).

Lowry, Samuel, d. by 25 June 1773 having m. by 4 March 1772 Margaret, admx. of Hugh McKinnie (BAAB 2:306; MDAD 68:171; MDTP 45:55).

Lowry, Capt. Samuel, was m. last eve. by Rev. Hargrove, to Mrs. Agnes Cooper of Fell's Point (*Federal Gazette and Baltimore Daily Advertiser* 13 Sep 1798; BALR WG#59:243).

Loyd. See Lloyd.

Loyde. See Lloyd.

Lubies. See Loubies.

Lucas, Thomas, and Mary Chamberlain were m. on 2 March 1762 (Harrison, "St. John's Parish Register:" 223). On 12 Oct 1774 Mary was named as a daughter of John Chamberlain (BAWB 3:314).

Lucy, Esther, was presented for mulatto bastardy at the June 1765 Court and again Aug 1765 Court (BAMI 1765:16).

Ludig, Philip, m. by 6 Oct 1770 Elizabeth, daughter of George Frederick Brown (BALR AL#B:507).

Lukens. See Lukins.

Lukins (Lukens), Moses, son of Benjamin and Alice, who were present, on 25 d. 3 m. 1790 announced his intention to marry Sarah Tompkins, daughter of Benjamin and Sarah ("Minutes of Deer Creek Meeting," *QRNM:* 148).

Lukins, Charles, son of Benjamin and Alice, on 21 d. 2 m. 1793 announced his intention to marry Sarah Coale, daughter of Philip, dec., and his wife Ann ("Minutes of Deer Creek Meeting," *QRNM:* 152).

Lusby, Robert, m. by 20 Sep 1700 [-?-], daughter of Stephen Johnson of Baltimore Co. (MWB 11:150 abst. in *Md. Cal. of Wills* 2:228).

Lusby, Robert, m. by 8 April 1718 Mary, daughter of Lawrence Draper of Baltimore Co., who also named a granddaughter Hannah Lusby (MWB 13:559 abst. in *Md. Cal. of Wills* 3:247).

Lusby, Robert, and Eliz. Hughes were m. on 30 May 1765 (Harrison, "St. John's Parish Register:" 228). On 9 Jan 1769 Elizabeth was named as a daughter of Jonathan Hughes (BALR AL#A: 146, AL#F:329-337).

Luther (Lewthwaite?), Capt. Christopher, and Mrs. Agnes Carlisle, both of Baltimore, were m. last Sun. by Rev, Allison (*Baltimore Telegraphe* 12 July 1797; *Federal Gazette and Baltimore Daily Advertiser* 10 July 1797). 'Christian' Lewthwaite and Agnes Carlisle were married by license dated 7 July 1797 (BAML).

Luttig, John C., merchant, and Miss Sally Prett, both of Baltimore, were m. last evening by the Rev. Mr. Bend (*Federal Gazette and Baltimore Advertiser* 22 Jan 1798). (BAML gives her name as Sally Pratt).

Lutton, King, of Baltimore, and Providence Baker of *The Forest* were m. yesterday se'ennight (*Maryland Gazette or Baltimore General Advertiser* 17 Aug 1784).

Lutz, Andreas, and Susanna Mumma were m. on 25 Nov 1784 ("First German Reformed Church, Baltimore," MS. at MdHS: 184); on 20 Aug 1788 Susannah was named as a daughter of David Mumma (BAWB 5:17); 18 May 1789 Susan was named as a sister of Abram Mumma, farmer (BAWB 4:367). She m. 2nd, Adam Riley (*q.v.*).

Lutz, Valentine, and Appolonia Heiperin were married by banns on 29 Oct 1786 at St. Peter's Catholic Church, Baltimore (*Piet:* 138).

Lux, [-?-], m. by 1 Nov 1765, Ann, sister of Elizabeth Sanders who also named a niece Ann Lux in her will IBAWB 4:237).

Lux, Darby, m. by 1 April 1772 Rachel, daughter of Charles Ridgely (BAWB 3:201; BALR WG#LL:252; PCLR DD#4:233).

Lux, Darby, and Miss Mary Nicholson were m. last Wed. eve. by Rev. Richards (*Baltimore Telegraphe* 23 Feb 1798).

Lux, George, of Baltimore, and Miss Biddle, daughter of the Hon. Edward Biddle, were m. at Philadelphia (*Maryland Journal and Baltimore Advertiser* 29 June 1779).

Lux, William, and Agnes Walker were m. on 16 July 1752 (Harrison, "St. Paul's Parish Register:" 165). On 9 May 1754 Agnes was named as a daughter of Dr. George Walker (PCLR EI#9B:466; BALR AL#A:9).

Lux, Capt. William, on 12 April 1770 was named as a brother-in-law in the will of Nicholas Ruxton Gay (BAWB 3:151).

Lyal, John, on 10 Nov 1751, conveyed livestock and furniture to his son Edmond Cook (BACT TR#3:5).

Lydig. See Littig.

Lyle, Robert, merchant, was m. to Miss Martha Hewitt of Bladensburg (*Maryland Journal and Baltimore Advertiser* 29 Nov 1785).

Lyles, Elizabeth, was charged with bastardy at the Aug 1728 Court (BACP HWS#6:22).

Lynch (Linch), [-?-], m. by 5 May 1789 Ruth, a daughter of George Stansbury (BAWB 4:358).

Lynch, [-?-], m. by Jan 1794 Mary, daughter of John Sheppard of *My Lady's Manor* (BAWB 6:28).

Lynch, Cornelius, and Cassandra Johns, [both?] of Baltimore Co., were m. by lic. on 12 May1800 at St. Peter's Catholic Church, Baltimore (*Piet:* 138).

Lynch, Hugh, m. by 18 Dec 1780 [-?-], heir of John Owings (BAAD 8:67).

Lynch (Linch), James, m. by 29 Jan 1732 Mary, daughter of James Lee who named a granddaughter Mary Linch (MWB 20:567 abst. in *Md. Cal. of Wills* 6: 253).Mary m. 2nd, James Gittings (*q.v.*).

Lynch, James, m. by 12 April 1747 Margaret, daughter of Mary Gittings (BALR TB#E: 340).

Lynch, James, and Comfort Barton were m. on 18 Nov 1762 (Harrison, "St. John's Parish Register:" 224). Comfort Lynch, relict of Selah Dorman Barton, and aged 64, deposed on 20 July 1780 concerning her marriage to Selah Dorman Barton by Rev. William Hooper (BACT 1773-1784:400).

Lynch, James, and Bridget Hurley, natives of Ireland, were m. by lic. on 12 Sep 1795 at St. Peter's Catholic Church, Baltimore (*Piet:* 138; BAML, which gives her name as Bridget Garvey).

Lynch, John, m. by 16 Oct 1769 Mary, extx. of John Webster (BFD 5:224).

Lynch, John, of Baltimore Town, in his will made 8 Dec 1796 named Arance Kennedy, wife of Patrick Kennedy, 'his aunt by marriage' (BAWB 5:480).

Lynch, Joshua, and Henrietta Maria Stansbury were married by license dated 1 May 1798 (BAML). On 27 Nov 1799 Henrietta was named as the widow of Daniel Stansbury in the administration account of Thomas Stansbury (BAAD 13:161).

Lynch, Mary, servant of Nathan Bowen was charged with bastardy at the Nov 1756 Court; she was fined. Either she or another Mary Lynch, now servant of Robert

Freight, was charged with bastardy at the Nov 1757 Court (BAMI 1757-1759:75; BAMI 1755-1763; BACP BB#C:313).

Lynch, Patrick, in March 1723/4 was charged with begetting a bastard on the body of Ann Galloway (BACP IS&TW#3:201, 330).

Lynch (Linch), Patrick, and Martha Bowen were m. in 1722 (Harrison, "St. Paul's Parish Register:" 122). On 15 Jan 1729 Martha was named as a daughter of Jonas and Ann Bowen of Baltimore Co. (MWB 19:580; MDAD 10:174; BALR HWS#M:464). Patrick and Martha were the parents of a daughter Martha Lynch (MWB 19:580 abst. in Md. Cal. of Wills 6:92).

Lynch, Patrick, m. by 7 Dec 1744 Sarah, widow of Benjamin Bowen (MDAD 21:41).

Lynch, Patrick, and Avarilla Day were m. on 20 April 1747 (Harrison, "St. John's Parish Register:" 196). On 12 June 1748 Avarilla was named as the widow of Edward Day (*q.v.*) and mother of Edward Day (BAAD 4:190; BALR B#K:486). On 9 March 1753 Avarilla was named as the daughter and heir at law of John Taylor (BALR TR#D:522).

Lynch, Patrick, and Elizabeth Howlet were m. on 7 Dec 1786 (Marr. Register of Rev. Lewis Richards, MS.690 at MdHS). On 22 Dec 1794 Lynch signed a receipt for his share of the estate of his mother-in-law Mary Howlet (BOCP Petition of Joseph Langdon, 1794).

Lynch, Patrick, and Elizabeth Walsh were married by banns on 24 Dec 1797 at St. Peter's Catholic Church, Baltimore (*Piet:* 139).

Lynch, Robuck, and Jemima Stansbury were m. on 16 Aug 1747 Harrison, "St. Paul's Parish Register:" 160). On 21 Feb 1748 Jemima was named as a daughter of Thomas Stansbury BAWB 3:46; BFD 5:231; BALR WG#GG:59).

Lynch (Linch), William, and Elinor Todd were m. on 6 Sep 1740 (Harrison, "St. Paul's Parish Register:" 164). On 4 Aug 1741 Elinor was named as the extx. of Thomas Todd *(q.v.).* Eleanor Dorsey Todd, daughter of Caleb and Eleanor (Warfield) Dorsey) m. 3rd, John Cromwell (*q.v.*) (BALR B#G: 91, 93, 95; BAWB 2:266).

Lynch, William, m. by 8 Jan 1761 Mary, extx. of Joseph Hendon (*q.v.*) (BFD 3:69; BAAD 4:346; MDAD 46:348; MDTP 38:101).

Lynn, Josias, m. by 1764 Elizabeth, admx. of James Brown (BFD 4:78).

Lyon, [-?-], m. by 6 June 1775 Elizabeth, daughter of Edward Morgan (MWB 40:401, abst. in *Md. Cal. of Wills* 16:68).

Lyon, Josias (Josiah), and Elizabeth Brown were m. on 16 Oct 1763 (Harrison, "St. George's Parish Register:" 380). On 12 May 1764 Elizabeth was named as the admx. of James Brown (*q.v.*) (MDTP 40:257: see also MDAD 51:342; BAMI 1765:53).

Lyon, Robert, and Eliz. Warren, in April 1763 were summoned by the vestry for unlawful cohabitation ("St. John's and St. George's Parish Register Vestry Proceedings, " MS. at the MdHS).

Lyon, Samuel, and Hanna Thomas were m. by 25 Nov 1789 in Baltimore (Marr. Returns of Ezekiel Cooper, MdSA S1005/19999-002-312, pub. in *MGSB* 32 (1) (Winter 1991) 6).

Lyon, Samuel, merchant of Baltimore, was m. at Wilmington on 3rd, inst. by Rev. Dr. Read, to Hetty W. Broom, daughter of Jacob Broom of that borough (*Federal Gazette and Baltimore Daily Advertiser* 14 March 1800).

Lyon, William, was married last evening by Rev, Mr. Allison to Miss Rachel M'Coy, both of this town (*Federal Intelligencer and Baltimore Daily Gazette* 11 March 1795).

Lyons, John, and Joanna Ragan, natives of Ireland, were m. by lic. on 24 Jan 1797 at St. Peter's Catholic Church, Baltimore (*Piet:* 139). (BAML gives her name as Johanna Ragoin).

Lytfoot, Thomas, m. by 29 April 1685 Rebecca, daughter of John Larkin; she m. 2nd, Thomas Hammond (*q.v.*) (BALR RM#HS:417; INAC 13B:23, 24; MWB 5:186). In his will dated 23 March 1686/7 Lytfoot named his wife Rebecca and his sister-in-law Eliza Larkin (MWB 4:272 abst. in *Md. Cal. of Wills* 2:19).

Lytle, Thomas, was charged with bastardy, confessed, and was fined 30 shillings (BACP Court Proceedings, 1745-1756, pp. 811-812).

"M"

M'... names are filed as Mc...
Mac'... names are filed as Mc...

Mack, James, m. by 7 June 1788 Margaret, extx. of James Hammond, shipwright (BAAD 9:210).

Mackadoe, J., and Miss Nancy Spencer of Fell's Point were m. last Tues. eve. (*Maryland Journal and Baltimore Advertiser* 4 Sep 1795; BAML).

Mackarny, Ann, was charged with bastardy at the Nov 1710 Court, and named John Carrington as the father of her child (BACP IS#B: 187).

Mackelfresh, [-?-], m. by 19 Feb 1764 Sarah, daughter of Thomas Bennett (BAWB 2:170).

Mackelfresh, John, and Margaret Madeira were married by license dated 17 Dec 1790 (BAML). On 17 May 1792 Margaret who received an equal share of the estate of Jacob 'Medairy' (BAAD 11:52).

Mackenheimer, John, m. by 14 Dec 1790, Susanna, daughter of William Clause (BAAD 10:243).

Mackenheimer, Peter, and Catherine Lindenberger (BAML). On 18 July 1795 Catherine was named as a daughter of George Lindenberger (BAWB 5:393).

Mackey, Hugh, and Sarah Henry were m. by lic. on 19 Nov 1795 at St. Peter's Catholic Church, Baltimore (*Piet:* 139).

Mackey, William, of Berkeley Co., Va., m. by 5 Nov 1799 Ruth, daughter of Stephen and Elizabeth Cromwell of Baltimore Co., Md. (BALR WG#60:398).

Mackie, John, and Elizabeth Hollingsworth were m. by lic. on 10 July 1787 at St. Peter's Catholic Church, Baltimore (*Piet:* 139).

Mackin, James, mariner, and Margaret Kellagrew, native of Ireland, were m. by lic. on 21 July 1800 at St. Peter's Catholic Church, Baltimore (*Piet:* 139).

Maclone, James, aged 23, in his will dated 28 March 1724 named his father-in-law Matthew Organ (MWB 18:395 abst. in *Md. Cal. of Wills* 5:198).

Madden, [-?-], m. by 24 Oct 1784 Mary, sister of Nathaniel Clary (BAWB 3:577).

Madden, John, and Elizabeth Host were married by banns on 28 Nov 1790 at St. Peter's Catholic Church, Baltimore (*Piet:* 139).

Maddy, John, of Baltimore Co., m. by Feb 1711 Ann, extx. of Robert Gardiner of Baltimore Co. (MDTP 22:81, 82; INAC 33A:231; BAAD 1:12, 364; BACP IS#C: 342).

Maeller, Adophus, merchant, and Miss Eliza McGlathery of Baltimore were m. at New Bremen on 5th inst. (*Baltimore Telegraphe* 14 April 1798)

Magamus [?], Henry, m. by 9 April 1800 Susanna, daughter of Basil Hickman (BAAD 13:233).

Magee (McGee. McGhee), Daniel, m. by 14 Jan 1764 Sarah, extx. of Edward Hall (*q.v.*) (BAWB 2:365; BAAD 3:316; MINV 83:229; BALR AL#A: 696; MDTP 30:153, 45:15-16).

Magers. See Majors.

Mahan, Edward, m. by 1 July 1718 Ann, the admx of Samuel Greening (Grinning, Gunning) of Baltimore Co. (MDAD 1:23). Edward Massey [*sic*] m. by March 1718, Ann, admx. of Samuel Greening (BACP IS#IA: 253).

Mahany (Mahiney), Timothy, was charged with bastardy and fined in 1775 (BAMI 1772, 1775-1781: 208).

Mahann. See Mahone.

Mahone (Mahanne), John, in Nov 1722 was charged with begetting a bastard on the body of Ann Brogden (Brogdon). On 5 March 1741/2 John Brogden (Brogdon) was named in the will of John Mahone (BACP IS&TW#2:21; MWB 22:533).

Maidwell, [-?-], m. by June 1784 [-?-], heir of the estate of Peter Bond (BAOC 1:210).

Maidwell, James, m. by 21 Dec 1781 Temperance, daughter of William Carter, Sr. (BAWB 3:467).

Majers. See Majors.

Majors (Magers, Majers), Elias, and Diana Bosley were m. on 8 Sep 1763 (Harrison, "St. John's Parish Register:" 225). On 12 April 1772 Diana was named as a daughter of Joseph Bosley (BAWB 3:292; BAAD 9:35).

Majors (Mayjors), John, and Rebecca Pollard on 26 May 1756 (Harrison, "St. John's Parish Register:" 213). On 21 March 1763 Rebecca was named as a daughter of John Pollard (BALR B#L: 103).

Majors, John, and Rachel Backster were married by banns on 8 Feb 1799 at St. Peter's Catholic Church, Baltimore (*Piet:* 139).

Mallet, Thomas, and Nancy Pluschan were m. by lic. on 28 Dec 1790 at St. Peter's Catholic Church, Baltimore (*Piet:* 139).

Mallett, Stephen, m. by 1789 Nancy, widow and admx. of Joseph Bishe (*q.v.*) (BPET: Petitions of Peter Deshong and Peter P---, 1792).

Mallonee, Dennis, m. by 15 Feb 1792 [-?-], who received an equal share of the estate of Richard Bond (BAAD 10:544).

Mallonee (Malance, Mallane, Mallence), Emanuel and Margaret Reeves were m. on 11 or 13 Feb 1749/50 (Harrison, "St. John's Parish Register:" 244, 250). On 26 Sep 1760 Margaret was named as a daughter of William Reaves; Emanuel and Margaret were the parents of a daughter Elizabeth 'Malance' (BAWB 2:174).

Mallonee (Mallanee), John, and Edith Cole were m. on 6 or 8 Nov 1743 (Harrison, "St. John's Parish Register:" 198, 243). In Dec 1772 Edith was named as a daughter of Dennis Garrett Cole (BAWB 3:252).

Malloney, John, m. by 23 Sep 1773 [-?-], daughter of Mary Brown (BALR AL#I: 246).

Malone, [-?-], and Lucy Belt were m. on 28 June 1788 (Marr. Returns of Rev. John Turner, Scharf Papers, MS.1999 at MdHS). On 24 Sep 1788 Lucy was named as a daughter of John Belt (BAWB 4:350).

Malony, James, and Avarilla League were m. by lic. on 19 May 1793 at St. Peter's Catholic Church, Baltimore (*Piet:* 139).

Malony, James, widower, and Catherine Veal, widow, were m. by lic. on 9 Dec 1798 at St. Peter's Catholic Church, Baltimore (*Piet:* 139).

Manchote, John, native of Bordeaux, and Mary Viney were m. by lic. on 16 Aug 1794 at St. Peter's Catholic Church, Baltimore (*Piet:* 139).

Mangroll (Mungrill), Mary, was charged with bastardy at June Court 1740, and again in 1744 (BACP TB&TR: 226, Liber 1743-1745: 227).

Mann, Frederick, was m. last eve. by Rev. Mr. Kurtz, to Miss Campbell, both of the city (*Federal Gazette and Baltimore Daily Advertiser* 24 June 1797).

Mann, Zachariah, of Baltimore, stated he would not pay the debts of his wife Mary Ann (*Maryland Journal and Baltimore Advertiser* (*Maryland Journal and Baltimore Advertiser* 20 Sep 1791).

Manning (Mannan), Dorothy, servant of Philip Jones, was charged with bastardy in 1744. She was fined and her master was her security (BACP 1743-1745:228, 306-307).

Manns, Charles, of Baltimore Co., m. by 6 Sep 1768 Elizabeth, daughter of Joseph Meade of Anne Arundel Co. (PCLR DD#4:463).

Manwaring, Jacob, late of London, in his will proved 8 Aug 1797 named his wife Mary, late Mary Whitchurch, and his two sons by Eleanor Hill, Jacob and George Henry Manwaring, and his son by his wife named William Whitchurch (BAWB 6:13).

Manyfold, Eleanor, on 31 d. 12 m. 1772 produced a paper condemning her misconduct for outgoing in marriage ("Minutes of Deer Creek Meeting," *QRNM*: 135). [No other marriage reference found].

March, Andrew, and Rebecca Stock, both of (Anne Arundel Co.?), were m. by lic. on 23 Nov 1795 at St. Peter's Catholic Church, Baltimore (*Piet:* 139).

March (Marsh?), John, on 12 July 1738 was mentioned in the admin. account of James Maxwell as having a bond for a legacy left him as the only living child of Juliana Dehaws (BAAD 4:18).

March. see also Marsh.

Marchant, Peter Stephen (son of Thomas and Mary Ann Chaille, planter from St. Domingo), and Mary Magdalen Martha Mallet (daughter of Francis and Mary Jane Yronet; widow of [-?-] Hug [*sic*]), were m. by lic. on 20 Oct 1798 at St. Peter's Catholic Church, Baltimore (*Piet:* 139).

Marean, Jonas, was m. last Sun. eve. by Rev. Mr. Kurtz, to Miss Maria Gartuen of this county (*Federal Intelligencer and Baltimore Daily Gazette* 29 Dec 1795).

Margolle, John Baptist. and Mary Ann Ocain were m. by lic. on 18 Nov 1789 at St. Peter's Catholic Church, Baltimore (*Piet:* 139).

Mariarte, Rachel, on 24 Nov 1742 was named as a granddaughter in the will of Sarah Hanson (MWB 23:21 abst. in *Md. Cal. of Wills* 8:196).

Mariarte, Sarah, on 14 Feb 1739 was named as a granddaughter in the will of Sarah Tayman (MWB 24:322 abst. by Gibb).

Markell, John, and Sarah Bender were married by license dated 26 March 1778 (BAML). Markell stated he would not pay the debts of his wife Sarah as she had been "led by the persuasions of her father and other people who [he thought] might mind their own business and look at home" (*Maryland Journal and Baltimore Advertiser* 23 May 1786).

Markin, Samuel, gave notice his wife Elizabeth had absconded from his bed and board (*Dunlap's Maryland Gazette* 14 April 1778).

Markland, William, and Orpha Edenfield, dau. of John Ensor, were m. on 19 Nov 1770 (Harrison, "St. Paul's Parish Register:" 169). On 10 April 1771 John Ensor named his grandchildren John, Jonathan and Nathan Markland in his will (BAWB 3:257).

Marlanell, John, m by 8 March 1776 Mary, daughter of Ann, widow of Marbry Helms (*q.v.*); Ann's will also named a grandson William Marlanell MWB 41:23; abst. in *Md. Cal. of Wills* 16:141).

Marr, William, private in the Maryland Line, was about 65 years old when he applied for a pension stating he had enlisted in the Capt. Nathaniel Ramsey's Regiment in April 1776. In June 1838 Airey Marr, aged 74, made a deposition stating she had m. William Marr on 14 June 1784, and that he d. on 3 July 1819 (Rev. War Pension Application of Airey Marr: W3838). William Marr and Arrey Owings were married by license dated 14 June 1784 (BAML).

Marriott, William, son of William, had been bound to Rudolph Hook, who in Nov 1775 was reported as dec. (BAMI 1772, 1775-1781: 151)

Marsh, [-?-], m. by 14 Oct 1727 Ann, daughter of Richard King (BALR IS#I: 20).

Marsh, John, and Cathe. Hewit were m. on 3 May 1784 (Marr. Returns of Rev. William West, MS. 1999 at MdHS). On 12 May 1792, Marsh's wife received a share of the estate of Edward Hewitt (BAAD 11:49).

Marsh, John, and Susannah were m. some time before 1 Oct 1792 when their daughter Matilda was b. ("Bible Records of the Davenport Family," MSA SC 236 1-59).

Marsh, Joseph, Jr., and Hannah, daughter of Adam Hubley, were m. [date not given] (*Baltimore Daily Repository* 23 Nov 1791).

Marsh, Joshua, was commissioned Captain of a militia company in Baltimore Co., and died 5 Nov 1828; he m. Temperance Harryman on 11 Dec 1785 at her father's residence. Joshua and Temperance were the parents of: Reshaw [?], William, Stephen, Rebecca, Elijah, Sarah, Grafton, Dennis, Josiah, Ellen, Joshua, [two children whose names were illegible], and Benedict (Rev. War Pension Application of Temperance Marsh: R6924). Temperance was a daughter of George Harryman (BAWB 5:236).

Marsh, Providence, was charged with bastardy at Nov Court, 1740 (BACP HWS#TR: 351).

Marsh (March), Prudence, was charged with bastardy at the Aug 1746 Court. She confessed on 3 March 1746/7 and was fined 30 shillings. She m. Edward Wann on 23 July 1747 (BACP TB&TR#1:116, 395-396; Reamy, *St. Paul's Parish Register:* 34).

Marsh, Richard, son of John, in Nov 1744, and again in Nov 1746 was charged with unlawful cohabitation with Ann Roberts (BACP Liber 1743-1745: 93; TB&TR#1: 220).

Marsh, Thomas, and Sophia Corbin were m. on 10 Feb 1745 (Harrison, "St. John's Parish Register:" 240). On 26 Sep 1798 he was named as a representative of Abraham Corbin (who had d. intestate (BAAD 12:495).

Marsh, William, on 13 d. 2 m. 1800, had a complaint that he had his marriage accomplished by a hireling teacher ("Minutes of Baltimore Meeting," *QRNM:*236). William Marsh and Ann Naylor were m. 14 Aug 1799 (Marr. Returns of Rev. Daniel Kurtz, Scharf Papers MS 1999 at MdHS).

Marsh. See also March.

Marshall, [-?-], m. by 5 Oct 1794 Mary, sister of Robert Clark Cooper (BAWB 5:312).

Marshall, [-?-], m. by 24 June 1798 Rachel, daughter of Jacob Cox (BAWB 6:121).

Marshall, Isaac, m. by 13 Aug 1796 Ann, admx. of Abraham Collett (*q.v.*) (BAAD 11:301).

Marshall, Joanna, was charged with bastardy at Nov 1719 Court and fined (BACP IS#B:186).

Marshall, Mary, extx., on 7 June 1721 posted bond to administer the estate of William Marshall (BAAB 2:137). Query if he could be the William Marshall who m. Mrs. Mary Wells on 19 June 1718 (Harrison, "*St. George's Parish Register,*" p. 221).

Marshall, Mrs. Mary, on 4 Jan 1728 was named as a daughter-in-law in the will of John Hall (MWB 21:792 abst. in *Md. Cal. of Wills* 7:220).

Marshall, Thomas, and Sarah Bull were m. on 3 ct 1740 (Harrison, "St. John's Parish Register:" 154): on 22 Nov 1756 Sarah was named as a daughter of Jacob Bull (MWB 30:223 abst. by Gibb).

Marshall, William, and Mrs. Mary Wells were m. on 19 June 1718 (Harrison, "St. George's Parish Register:" 221). In Aug 1719 Mary was named as the admx. of George Wells (*q.v.*) of Baltimore Co. (MDTP 24:32; MDAD 2:451, 3:4). Mary was a daughter of George and Martha (Beedle) Gouldsmith (*BCF:*424).

Marshall, William, b. c1725, m. by 1756 Elizabeth, daughter of William Deale (*ARMD* 31:174-179).

Marticq, John, and Mary Shammo Nery were m. by lic. on 1 Feb 1798 at St. Peter's Catholic Church, Baltimore (*Piet:* 139; BAML gives their names as John Mirceall and Mary Shammo).

Martin, Alexander, native of Va., and Mary Gibson were m. by lic. on 2 Oct 1796 at St. Peter's Catholic Church, Baltimore (*Piet:* 139).

Martin, Ann, was charged with bastardy at the Aug 1724 Court naming John Harecock or Hancock as the father of the child; she was ordered to have 15 lashes well laid on until the blood appeared; she was charged again at June 1732 Court, and again at March 1736/7 Court (BACP IS&TW#3:438, 449, IS&TW#4:32, 42, and HWS#1A:10).

Martin, Benjamin, and Deborah Dalton were married by banns on 21 Aug 1791 at St. Peter's Catholic Church, Baltimore (*Piet:* 139).

Martin, Catherine Reed, d. by 20 Aug 1800, leaving the following heirs, each of whom received a payment of $98.00: George Reese (*q.v.*), the admin.; Sarah Thompson; Abraham Eaglestone; Benjamin Eaglestone; and Walter Eaglestone (BAAD 13:323).

Martin, James, stated he would not pay the debts of his wife Elizabeth (*Maryland Journal and Baltimore Advertiser* 31 Aug 1779).

Martin, Martha, on 11 June 1773 posted bond to administer the estate of Thomas Kelley (BAAB 2:2).

Martin, Nathaniel, m. Sarah Dallas, widow of Benjamin Eaglestone (*q.v.*) (MCHP#2464).

Martin, Nathaniel, m. by 8 March 1774 Mary, admx. of Tobias Stansbury (*q.v.*) (MDTP 45:292).

Martin, Thomas, and Mary Stokes were married by license dated 8 Sep 1791 (BAML). In Feb 1797 Martin stated he would not pay the debts of Mary Stoaks who had assumed the name of his wife (*Federal Gazette and Baltimore Daily Advertiser* 22 Feb 1797).

Marvell, Elizabeth, was charged with bastardy at the Nov 1759 Court; she named William Barney as the father of her son William Marvell (BAMI 1757-1759: 242).

Mashan, Joseph, and Cristina Seighoffer, natives of Germany, were married by banns on 20 Oct 1794 at St. Peter's Catholic Church, Baltimore (*Piet:* 139).

Mason, [-?-], m. by 8 May 1775 Cornelia, admx. of William Presbury (*q.v.*) (MDAD 72:117).

Mason, Abraham, late of Philadelphia, and Miss Sally Hayes of this town were m. (*Maryland Journal and Baltimore Advertiser* 24 Sep 1782).

Mason, George, of New Garden Meeting, son of George Mason later of the same meeting, dec., and his wife Jane, on 5 d. 11 m. 1778, announced his intention to marry Susannah Hopkins, daughter of William Hopkins, of Deer Creek Meeting ("Minutes of Deer Creek Meeting," *QRNM:* 139).

Mason, Grace, on 24 d. 7 m. 1790 hath gone out in marriage ("Minutes of Gunpowder Meeting," *QRNM:* 88). **See Grace Corkin.**

Mason, James, and Rachel Scott on 29 d. 1 m. 1780 declared their intention to marry ("Minutes of Gunpowder Meeting," *QRNM:* 73). James Mason, son of George and Jane, and Rachel Scott, daughter of Abraham and Elizabeth, were m. on 2 d. 4 m. 1780. Abraham Scott's will named his daughter Rachel Mason and her two daus. Elizabeth and Rachel ("Records of Gunpowder Meeting," MS at MdHS; BAWB 7:176)

Mason, John, and Frances Allen were m. on 20 Dec 1733 (Harrison, "St. John's Parish Register:" 67). On 29 Sep 1735 Frances was named as the admx. of Nathaniel Allen (*q.v.*) of Baltimore Co. (BAAD 3:178; MDAD 14:223).

Mason, John, and Ann Howard on 31 d., 8 m., 1776 declared their intention to marry ("Minutes of Gunpowder Meeting," *QRNM:* 68).

Mason, Michael, m. by 23 Feb 1777 [-?-], daughter of William Bell (BAWB 3:436).

Massey, Anna, (now Bull), on 2 d. 11 mo. 1786, has m. a man not of our society before a Baptist Preacher ("Minutes of Deer Creek Meeting," *QRNM:* 144). [No other marriage reference found].

Massey, Aquila, son of Jonathan and Cassandra dec., on 29 d. 8 m. 1793 announced his intention to marry Anna Rigbie, daughter of James and Sarah, dec. ("Minutes of Deer Creek Meeting," *QRNM:* 153).

Massey, Aquila, d. by 5 d. 2 m. 1761, having m. Sarah Boulton, daughter of Isaac Boulton; she m., 2nd, by that date James Rigbie (*q.v.*), who received a payment for Aquila's son Isaac from the estate of Benjamin Vanhorn (MDAD 68:165).

Massey, Isaac, son of Aquila and Sarah, dec., on 1 d. 5 m. 1788 announced his intention to marry Margaret Webster, daughter of Isaac and Sarah, dec. ("Minutes of Deer Creek Meeting," *QRNM:* 145).

Massey, Jonathan, m. by 15 Sep 1750 [-?-], sister of Isabella, wife of Robert Jackson, 15 Sep 1750 (BACT TR#E:7). Jonathan 'Marcy' had m. Mrs. Ann Collier on 25 Nov 1701 (Harrison, "St. George's Parish Register:" 196). On 1 April 1693 Sarah Hall, wife of John, conveyed 100 a. *Holmwood* to her daughter Isabella Hooper; if Isabella died under age the land was to go to her sister Ann Collier, then to John Burley, son of Stephen Burley, late of Severn; Sarah was the widow of John Hall, widow and admx. of John Collier and of George Hooper (BALR HW#2: 38). Robert Jackson had m. Isabella Hooper on 24 Aug 1699 (Harrison, "*St. George's Parish Register*," p. 188). On 1 April 1693 John Hall conveyed 28 a. *Hall's Ridge,* part of a warrant for 640 a., to his daughter-in-law Isabella Hooper. If she dies without lawfully begotten heirs, land to go to her sister Ann Collier. If Ann died without legitimate heirs, land would revert to John Hall; if Hall bought 31 a.

247

Waterton's Angle, formerly belonging to John Waterton, (and gave it to Isabella) she was to give her sister Ann an equal amount of above 218 a. (BALR HW#2: 122). On 1 April 1748 Isaac Jackson conveyed 50 a. *Hall's Ridge* to Benj. Lego, Jr. (BALR TB#E: 704).

Massey, Jonathan, son of Aquila, on 5 d. 5 m. 1763 intends to marry Cassandra Webster, daughter of Isaac ("Minutes of Deer Creek Meeting," *QRNM:*130); he d. by 3 d. 9 m. 1772 when Cassandra Massey was reported as having gone out in marriage to a man not of our society ("Minutes of Deer Creek Meeting," *QRNM:*135); on 9 June 1773 Jonathan and Cassandra Woodland administered Massey's estate (MDAD 68:187).

Massey, Jonathan Collier, in March 1755 chose Aquila Massey as his guardian (BAMI 1755-1763: 3).

Masterman, William, of New Brook St., London, banker, m. by 8 d., 9 m., 1786 Lydia, daughter of Daniel Mildred (BAWB 4:331).

Mathers, William, and Miss Ann Farris, both of Baltimore, were m. last Thurs. eve. by Rev. Richards (*Federal Gazette and Baltimore Daily Advertiser* 7 June 1799).

Mathews. See Matthews.

Mattax, Lucretia, was charged with bastardy at the March 1768 court (BACP BB:6).

Matthaeus, Joseph, m. by 2 April 1763, Gertraut Eberhardtin ("First Record Book for the Reformed and Lutheran Congregations at Manchester, Baltimore (now Carroll) Co.," *MGSB* 35:267).

Matthes, [-?-], m. by 1 March 1796 Ann, daughter of Mordecai Price of Gunpowder Forest (BAWB 5:379).

Matthews, [-?-], m. by 19 Sep 1769 Catherine, daughter of Nicholas Gash 'otherwise the daughter of Hannah Shaw;' Thomas and his wife were the parents of Thomas, Rachel Catherine, Ann and Rebecca (BAWB 3:103).

Matthews, Daniel, and Martha Davis declared their intention to marry on 24 d., 2 m., 1776 ("Minutes of Gunpowder Meeting," *QRNM:*67).

Matthews, Daniel, on 22 d. 2 m. 1783 was reported to have had an unlawful child lid to his charge by an unmarried woman and had left these parts ("Minutes of Gunpowder Meeting," *QRNM*: 77).

Matthews, Daniel, son of Thomas, on 29 d. 12 m. 1787 requested a certificate to Marry Susanna Bartlett of Third Haven Monthly Meeting ("Minutes of Gunpowder Meeting," *QRNM:*84).

Matthews, Francis, and Mary Carr on 27 d. 9 m. 1777 declared their intention to marry ("Minutes of Gunpowder Meeting," *QRNM:*70).

Matthews, George, and Sarah Nailor, on 25 d., 10 m. 1777 declared their intention to marry ("Minutes of Gunpowder Meeting," *QRNM*: 71). On 9 May 1796 Sarah was named as a daughter of John Naylor, Sr., of Baltimore Co. (BAWB 5:451).BALR WG#53:474).

Matthews, Jesse, and Milkah Belt on 28 d. 12 m. 1793 declared their intention to marry ("Minutes of Gunpowder Meeting," *QRNM*: 94).

Matthews, John, and Ann Maxwell were m. on 18 April 1737 (Harrison, "St. George's Parish Register:" 295). On 12 July 1738 Ann was named as a daughter of Col. James Maxwell (MDAD 16:187; BAAD 4:75; MDTP 30:360).

Matthews (Mathews), Capt. John, and Milcah Lusby were m. on 23 Feb 1748 (Harrison, "St. George's Parish Register:" 350). Milcah was named as a sister of

John Lusby; John and Milcah were the parents of Aquila, John, Milcah, and Bennett Matthews (BAWB 2:172; BFD 4:127).

Matthews, John, and Leah Price on 30 d. 10 m. 1790 declared their intention to marry ("Minutes of Gunpowder Meeting," *QRNM:* 89).

Matthews, Levin, m. 29 Nov 1764, as her first husband, Mary Day, b. 5 Feb 1744, daughter of John and Phillis Zana; Mary m. 2nd, Nicholas Gassaway (*q.v.*) ("Day Bible, in *The Notebook* 15 (2) (June 1999) 7-9; "John Day Bible," *MBR* 2: 24-27; Harrison, "St. George's Parish Register:" 366).

Matthews, Mordecai, on 25 d. 10 m. 1788 requested a certificate to marry Ruth Hussey, a member of Warrington MM in Pa. ("Minutes of Gunpowder Meeting," *QRNM:*86).

Matthews, Patrick, and Elizabeth Matthews were m. on 5 July 1790 at St. Peter's Catholic Church, Baltimore (*Piet:* 139).

Matthews, Samuel, son of George and Dorothy, and Ann Price, daughter of Mordecai and Rachel, were m. 1 d 12 m. 1779 (Bliss Forbush, "Records of Gunpowder Meeting," MS. at MdHS; BAWB 5:379).

Matthews, Thomas, m. by Nov 1718, Sarah (nee Wichell), widow of 1st, John Kemp (*q.v.*), 2nd, Edward Norris (*q.v.*), and 3rd, widow and extx. of John Thomas (*q.v.*) (BACP IS#IA:55; MDTP 27:259).

Matthews, Thomas, and Rachel Price were m. on 26 d. 11 m. 1751 ("Records of Gunpowder Meeting," MS. at MdSA). On 15 Oct 1765 Matthews' wife was named as an heir of Elizabeth Price of Baltimore Co. (BAAD 6:146).

Matthews, Thomas, d. by July 1775; his sons Mordecai, Daniel, and John, chose their mother Rachel Matthews as their guardian; she was also made guardian of Jesse, Rachel, Ely, Elizabeth, Thomas, and William, orphans of Thomas (BAMI 1775-1781: 130)

Matthews, Thomas, and Ann Humphries on 27 d. 9 m. 1775 declared their intention to marry ("Minutes of Gunpowder Monthly Meeting," *QRNM:*66).

Matthews, Thomas, on 25 d. 4 m. 1795 was reported to have been married by a hireling priest to a woman not of our society ("Minutes of Gunpowder Meeting," *QRNM:*96). Thomas Matthews and Ann Gill were m. by lic. dated 2 Feb 1795 (BAML).

Matthews, William, and Elizabeth Hanway on 26 d. 10 m. 1793 declared their intention to marry ("Minutes of Gunpowder Meeting," *QRNM:*94).

Matthews, William, on 3 d. 8 m. 1774 m. Ann, widow of Aquila Price ("Records of Gunpowder Monthly Meeting." MS. at MdHS; BAOC Petition of William Matthews 1794). On 1 March 1796 Ann was named as a daughter of Mordecai Price of Gunpowder Forest (BAWB 5:379).

Matthey, Frederick, gave notice his wife Mary had eloped from him on Tues., 10th inst. (*Dunlap's Maryland Gazette* 15 Dec 1778).

Mattocks, |-?-|, m. by 11 Feb 1785 Sarah, daughter of John Harriman (BAWB 4:16).

Mattox, John, in his will, made 5 Sep 1774 named his wife Mary, but mentions sons or children by his former wife (MWB 40176; abst. in *Md. Cal. of Wills* 16:36).

Mattox, Lucretia, in 1768 was presented for bastardy (BAMI 1768-1769:6).

Mattson, Matthias, blacksmith, of Pa., in 1706 was declared to be the brother of Matthias Devoss, late of Baltimore Co., and had been so regarded for 40 years; signed by Abell Pearce, Andrew Willson, and John Nambe. In a separate document

Christopher Mounts and Calbert Cox made oath that Matthias Devoss, so commonly called, is the brother of Andrew Mattson (BALR IS#G:58).

Maud, Daniel, of the City of London, and Magdalen Stevens were m. on 17 Aug 1710 ("Records of Third Haven Meeting, Society of Friends," MdSA: 447). On 14 June 1762, Daniel and His wife, daughter of William Stevens of Talbot Co., and were the parents of a son Daniel who was living in Baltimore Co. on the above date (DOLR 18 Old:176).

Maulsby, Elinor, on 25 d. 8 m. 1792 was condemned for marrying outside the good order to a man not in membership and having a child born too soon after marriage ("Minutes of Gunpowder Meeting," *QRNM*:92). Elinor Maulsby and Maurice Maulsby were m. by lic. dated 22 March 1792 (HAML).

Maulsby, William, on 30 d. 7 m. 1796 has married contrary to the good order ("Minutes of Gunpowder Meeting," *QRNM:*98). [No other marriage reference found].

Maxfield, Rev. John, m. last Thurs. Miss Rachel Roder [Rober?], both of Baltimore Co. (*Federal Intelligencer and Baltimore Daily Gazette* 6 Dec 1794).

Maxwell, [-?-], m. by 9 Sep 1759 Rebecca, daughter of Patrick Montgomery (MWB 30:756 abst. by Gibb).

Maxwell, Asael, one of the sons of Col. James Maxwell, d. leaving a widow Hannah (nee Matthews); she m. 2nd, prior to 9 Aug 1734 Abraham Johns (*q.v.*); she m. 3rd, on 26 Nov 1734 John Hall, Jr. (*q.v.*) (Harrison, "St. George's Parish Register:" 286; MDTP 30:360).

Maxwell, Col. James, was named as a brother-in-aw of the will of John Ewings of Baltimore Co. on 12 April 1709 (MWB 12, part 2: 143 abst. in *Md. Cal. of Wills* 3:145).

Maxwell, James, m. by 9 April 1711, [-?-], with Moses Groome, were named as execs. of John Ewings (MDTP 21:336).

Maxwell, James, on 30 Sep 1712 conveyed 50 a. to his son-in-law Spry Godfrey Gundry (BALR TR#A:207).

Maxwell, James, m. by 1 Jan 1719 Ann, kinswoman of Ann Felkes, widow; James and Ann had issue: Asael (a son), Elizabeth, James, Ann, and Robert (MWB 16:249 abst. in *Md. Cal. of Wills* 5:32).

Maxwell, James, m. by 23 Oct 1723 Mary, daughter of John March (Marsh) of Kent Co., chirurgeon, when their daughter Phillis Zana was born ("Day Bible," *The* Notebook 15 (2) (June 1993) 9; KELR JS#16:317). Mary m. 2nd, by Nov 1733 William Savory (*q.v.*)

Maxwell, James, in April 1747, with Johannah Rigbie was summoned for unlawful cohabitation. In June 1747 Maxwell appeared and was admonished with certification. In July 1749 Maxwell and Susannah Rigbie were summoned for unlawful cohabitation. In Aug 1749 Maxwell appeared and stated that Rigbie was his housekeeper. The vestry gave him until 1 Nov next to put her away and provide himself with someone else to keep his house (St. John's and *St. George's Parish Register* Parish Register Vestry Proceedings. Typed copy of the original at the MdHS).

Maxwell, James, merchant, and Nancy, daughter of Daniel Grant of this town, were m. [date not given] (*Maryland Journal and Baltimore Advertiser* 17 Dec 1782). They were married by license dated 12 Dec 1682 (BAML).

Maxwell, Samuel, m. by 29 Sep 1720 Mary, daughter and admx. of Henry and Tabitha (Long) King (MDAD 3:356; BAAD 2:13).

May, Benjamin, and Margaret Counselman, legatee of Frederick Caley, were m. on 31 Dec 1781(Marr. Returns of Rev. William West, Scharf Papers, MS. 1999 at MdHS: 5). She m. 2nd John Denton (q.v.).

May, Elizabeth, in April 1795 was made guardian of Benjamin, Abraham, Diveyce [?], and Juliana May (BAOC 3:151).

Maydwell, John, m. by 21 Dec 1781 Temperance, daughter of William Carter, Sr. (BAWB 3:467).

Mayel, Joseph Anthony, and Margaret Dashield were m. by lic. on 1 Nov 1798 at St. Peter's Catholic Church, Baltimore (*Piet:* 139). (BAML gives his name as Joseph Anthony).

Mayer, Johannes, m. by 8 May 1785 Anna Maria Willin ("First Record Book for the Reformed and Lutheran Congregations at Manchester, Baltimore (now Carroll) Co.," *MGSB* 35:281).

Mayes, [-?-], m. by 6 Dec 1770 Mary, daughter of Antill Deaver (BAWB 3:177).

Mayjors. See Majors.

Mays, James, m. by 7 June 1771 Isabel, daughter of Adam Hoops (BAWB 3:259).

Maynard, Henry, of Anne Arundel Co., m. by 27 Feb 1707 Sarah, widow and extx. of Robert Hopkins (INAC 28:41).

Maynard, Henry, m. by 11 June 1756, Zepporah Hillyard, widow of 1st, Thomas Floyd (*q.v.*), and 2nd, by 1750, Alexander Baker (*q.v.*) (BALR HWS#1-A:137, BB#1:570; John F. Dorman, "The Maynard Family of Frederick County, Maryland," *NGSQ* 48:177 ff.).

McAllister, Charles, and Elizabeth Trainer, natives of Ireland, were m. by lic. on 21 Jan 1796 at St. Peter's Catholic Church, Baltimore (*Piet:* 139).

McAllister, John, d. by 13 June 1787 when his sons John and Lloyd, both under 14, were made wards of Jacob and Mary Davis; on 4 Aug 1787, Thomas Rutter and Andrew Barnett testified that both bys had been willed a tract called *Darbyshire* (BAOC 2:21, 32-33).

McBride, [-?-], m. by 31 Aug 1760 [-?-], daughter of John Dunn, who named his grandsons John and David McBride in his will (MWB 31:176 abst. by Gibb).

McCabe, John, d. by 14 Aug 1779 when his widow Phebe and Robert Hutchinson were m. by lic. (BAML). Phebe Hutchinson of Baltimore Town, widow, in her will made 12 Nov 1796 named her children Thomas McCabe, Mary Thompson, Catherine Shaw, and John McCabe (BAWB 5:429; BAAD 13:201).

McCabe, Thomas, orphan, son of John McCabe, in Aug 1792 chose Phebe Hutchinson as is guardian (BAOC 3:2).

McCallum, [-?-], m. by 10 April 1773 Mary, daughter of Huldah Smith (who was a widow of Ralph Smith (BAWB 3:248).

McCan (McKenna), John, and Ann Johnson were m. on 4 Jan 1790 (Marr. Returns of Rev. William West, Scharf Papers, MS 1999 at MdHS).

McCan, John, and Ann Egan were remarried [*sic*] on 29 March 1791 at St. Peter's Catholic Church, Baltimore (*Piet:* 139).

McCandless, George, m. by 15 Sep 1770 Sarah (daughter of James Patterson), by whom he had a son Robert McCandless (BACT B#G:350).

McCann, Daniel, d. by Nov 1757 when his widow Ann McCann was made guardian of his orphans Patrick and Ann (BAMI 1755-1763).

McCann (McCain), John, m. by 9 Aug 1786 Catherine, admx. of John Donnolly *(q.v.)* (BAAD 8:296, 11:326).

McCannon, Catherine, in 1772 was fined for bastardy (BAMI 1772, 1775-1781: 84).

McCarter, Margaret, orphan daughter of William, in Sep 1795 was made a ward of William Singleton (BAOC 3:167).

McCarter, William, and [-?-], daughter of Robert Slater of Baltimore some time before 4 Nov 1780; they had two children; McCarter and his wife moved to New York from Philadelphia and left the two children in Baltimore ("Petition of Robert Slater," Red Books XXVIII, 82).

McCartey, John, m. by 16 March 1795 Rebecca, daughter of John Jordon (BAWB 5:282).

McCarthy, George, and Mary Cooper were m. by lic. on 30 Nov 1797 at St. Peter's Catholic Church, Baltimore (*Piet:* 139).

McCarty, Michael, and Helen O'Brien were m. by lic. on 10 April 1796 at St. Peter's Catholic Church, Baltimore (*Piet:* 139).

McCassady [-?-], m. by 1791, Catherine, daughter of David Clyon (BPET: Petition of Catherine McCassady, late Catherine Clyon, 1791).

McCausland (M'Causland), Marcus, merchant, and Polly Priestman were m. in Baltimore Town (*Maryland Journal and Baltimore Advertiser* 3 Dec, 7 Dec 1784). (BAML gives her name as Polly Presstman).

McCay, [-?-], d. by 21 Jan 1793, leaving son William and a widow Mesha or Miszey who by that time was the widow of Andrew Davidson (*q.v.*).

McClain, John, on 15 Aug 1769 stated he would not pay the debts of his wife Sarah (BACT B#G:298).

McClain, Roger, and Eleanor Connely were m. by lic. on 25 Nov 1795 at St. Peter's Catholic Church, Baltimore (*Piet:* 139).

McClain (or Macclain), William, d. by 17 Oct 1754 when his extx. had m. 2nd [-?-] Williams (*q.v.*) (MDTP 36:56).

McClaskey, Joseph, and Alice Jewell were m. by lic. dated 11 Sep 1788 (BAML). Alice McClaskey, (formerly Jewell), on 27 d. 12 m. 1788 was found guilty in going out in marriage ("Minutes of Gunpowder Meeting," *QRNM:* 86).

McClellan, John, and Mary [-?-] were m. by 6 Aug 1762 when their son William was b. ("John McClellan Bible," *MBR* 7:119). On 3 Nov 1770, Mary was named as a daughter of Mayberry and Ann Helms, and sister of Leonard Helms (BALR AL#B: 732; BAWB 3:324, 4:487, 5:139).

McClennan. See McClellan.

McClure, David, m. by 19 March 1770 heir of Alexander Hannah (BAAD 7:178).

McClure (M'Clure), John C., and Miss Mary Ann Thornburgh, both of this city, were m. last eve. by Rev. Dr. Allison (*Federal Gazette and Baltimore Daily Advertiser* 7 Dec 1798; BAML, which gives their names as John McSure and Mary Ann Thornbury).

McComas, Alexander, and Hannah Whitaker were m. on 23 Aug 1728 (Harrison, "St. John's Parish Register:" 38). She m. 2nd, Thomas Miles (*q.v.*).

McComas, Alexander, m. by 8 June 1747 Deborah, admx. of Thomas Deaver (*q.v.*) (MDTP 32:96; MDAD 24:70; BAAD 4:174).

McComas, Ann, widow of John, on 10 Dec 741 conveyed personalty to her children William, Alexander, Daniel and Mary, and William and Alexander were to take care of Daniel and Mary until they were 16 (BALR TB#A:57).

McComas (Maccomas), Aquila, and Sarah Preston were m. on 2 Jan 1752 (Harrison, "St. John's Parish Register:" 204). On 17 Sep 1766 Sarah was named as a daughter of James Preston (BAWB 3:48; BFD 5:101).

McComas (Maccomas), Daniel, and Martha Scott were m. on 26 Dec 1734 (Harrison, "St. John's Parish Register:" 119). On 13 March 1744 Martha was named as a daughter of Daniel Scott (MWB 24:81 abst. by Gibb). On 2 May 1758 Martha was named as a daughter of Elizabeth Scott (MWB 30:493).

McComas, Daniel, son of Alexander McComas, Sr., and Hannah Taylor were m. on 15 March 1753 (Harrison, "St. John's Parish Register:" 207). On 8 April 1771 Hannah was named as a sister of Thomas Taylor (BALR AL#C: 250).

McComas, Daniel, and Ann Miles were m. on 10 Oct 1758 (Harrison, "St. John's Parish Register:" 217). His extx. (admx.?) Ann, m. John Poteet (*q.v.*) on 20 April 1762 (Harrison, "St. John's Parish Register:" 223; MDTP 39:208).

McComas, James, and Sarah Howard were m. 29 March 1794 (Harrison, "St. James Parish Register:"). Sarah McComas, formerly Howard, on 29 d. 9 m. 1794 was condemned for being m. by a hireling teacher to a man not of our society ("Minutes of Gunpowder Meeting," *QRNM:*95).

McComas, John, m. by June 1713 Ann, extx. of John Edwards (BACP IS#B:383).

McComas, John, m. by March 1719/20 Ann, mother of Julian Love [and widow of William Love (*q.v.*)] (BACP IS#C:280).

McComas, Moses, m. by 31 Oct 1766 [-?-], daughter of Daniel McComas (BAAD 7:192).

McComas, Sarah, on 25 d. 4 m. 1795 was reported as having been married by a hireling priest to a man not of our society ("Minutes of Gunpowder Meeting," *QRNM:*96). [No other marriage reference found].

McComas, William, and Hannah Deaver were m. on 27 July 1742 (Harrison, "St. George's Parish Register:" 342). On 6 Dec 1770 Hannah was named as a daughter of Antill Deaver (BAWB 3:177).

McComas, William, of Harford Co., m. by 3 Aug 1785 Hannah, widow of Zacheus Onion (*q.v.*), dec. (BALR WG#Y:152).

McComas, William. See William Maccubbin.

McComsey, Robert, and Catherine Warner were married by license dated 18 April 1785 (FRML). In Aug 1786 he stated that he would not pay the debts of his wife Catherine (*Maryland Journal and Baltimore Advertiser* 4 Aug 1786).

McConnell, Charles, merchant, and Betsy Barnet, both of Baltimore, were m. last Thurs. (*Maryland Gazette or Baltimore General Advertiser* 21 Nov 1775).

McConnell, John, orphan of Charles McConnell, in Feb 1795 chose John Hammond as his guardian (BAOC 3:139).

McConnell, John, and Miss Sarah Leret, both of Baltimore, were m. last eve. by Rev. Mr. Ireland (*Federal Gazette and Baltimore Daily Advertiser* 17 June 1799).

McConniken, John, and Eleanor Long were m. on 20 Sep 1762 Harrison, "St. Paul's Parish Register:" 168). On 29 Oct 1765 Elinor was named as a daughter of Eliz. Trotten (BAWB 3:44). Eleanor Owings m. 1st, John Long (*q.v.*) on 8 March 1735 Harrison, "St. Paul's," p. 155). Eleanor's mother had m. 1st, Lewis Owings, 2nd, Stephen Body, and 3rd, Luke Trotten (*BCF:*410).

McCool (McCoob, McCall), Margaret, on 5 March 1770 was charged with unlawful cohabitation with Paul Gaddis by the vestry of St. George's Parish; on 4 June 1770 the Vestry decided that they should be presented to the Grand Jury for unlawful cohabitation (Reamy, *St. George's Parish Register*: 111).

McCormick (M'Cormick), James, Jr., and Rachel Ridgely Lux were m. 12 April 1798 by the Rev. Andrew Thos. McCormick ("James McCormick Family Bible," *HABFR* 2:37; *Federal Gazette and Baltimore Daily Advertiser* 16 April 1798; BAML).

McCoy, William, and Rachel Joice were m. on 30 May 1793 (Marr. Returns of Rev. John Hagerty, Scharf Papers, MS.1999 at MdHS). On 13 Nov 1794 Rachel was named as a niece of Thomas Knightsmth Shaw (BAWB 5:213).

McCoy (M'Coy), John, and Sarah Wade were married by license dated 21 July 1790 (BAML) In April 1795 McCoy stated he would not pay the debts of his wife Sarah (*Federal Gazette and Baltimore Daily Advertiser* 4 April 1795).

McCoy, Robert, and Cassander [*sic*] Cole were m. by lic. dated 9 Jan 1797 (HAML). Cassandra Coale on 23 d. 3 m. 1797 was found guilty of marrying a man not in membership by the assistance of a Methodist teacher ("Minutes of Deer Creek Meeting," *QRNM:*157). On 23 d. 11 m. 1797 Cassandra McCoy produced a paper condemning herself for having gone out in marriage to a man not of our society with the assistance of a Methodist Preacher ("Minutes of Deer Creek Meeting," *QRNM:*158).

McCreary (MacCreery), Thomas, and Susanna Nelson were m. on 21 April 1792 Harrison, "St. Paul's," p. 256). Susanna was a daughter of Benjamin and Margaret Nelson; Margaret m. 2nd, Thomas Winning (*q.v.*).

McCreary (M'Creary), William, merchant, was m. to Miss Letitia Nelson, daughter of Robert Nelson, of Fell's Point, merchant (*Maryland Journal and Baltimore Advertiser* 23 Sep 1785). However, Robert Neilson, in his will, made 28 Feb 1799 named a Thomas McCreary [*sic*] as a son-in-law (BAWB 6:167).

McCubbin, James, son of Nicholas and Mary (Clare), b. Dec 1761 or 1762, and Sophia Gough, daughter of Harry D. and Prudence, b. 2 Aug 1772, were m. in Dec 1787 "Gough-Carroll Bible Records." *MG* 2:23).

McCubbin (MacCubbin, McKubbin), James, and Lydia Collins were m. by lic. on 5 Feb 1795 at St. Peter's Catholic Church, Baltimore (*Piet:* 140).

McCubbin (MacCubbin), John, and Sarah Holland were m. on 29 Jan 1761 (Harrison, "St. John's Parish Register:" 221); on 29 July 1793 Sarah was named as a daughter of John Holland, Sr. (BAWB 5:118).

McCubbin (Maccubbin), Samuel, m. by 2 Feb 1731/2 Mary, daughter of Edward Parish, and sister of William Parish, dec. (BALR IS#L:187).

McCubbin (MacCubbin), William, son of William McComas [*sic*], in 1755 chose Anthony Rhodes as his guardian (BAMI 1755-1763).

McCubbin (MacCubbin), Zachariah, and Ann Ottay were m. on 22 Jan 1778 (Marr. Returns of Rev. Thomas Chase, Scharf Papers, MS.1999 at MdHS), In her will made 21 Jan 1797 Ann MacCubbin named Zachariah MacCubbin, son of her late husband Zachariah, her late brother William Ottay and his wife Ann Ottay of Great Britain; her step-daus. Sarah Maccubbin, Deborah Dorsey and Mary Dorsey (BAWB 6:107).

McCubbin (MacCubbin), Zachariah, and Sarah Norwood were m. on 7 Nov 1745 Harrison, "St. Paul's Parish Register:" 158).

McCulla (M'Culla), John, and Miss Margaret Logan, late from Ireland, now all of Baltimore, were m. Thurs. by Rev. Richards (*Baltimore Telegraphe* 4 March 1800).

McCullogh, David, on 19 July 1775 was named as a son-in-law in the will of Robert Russell (MWB 40:399; abst. in *Md. Cal. of Wills* 16:68).

McCurdy, Hugh, merchant of Baltimore, was m. yesterday eve. at Fayetteville, the seat of James M'Henry, Esq., to Miss Allison, daughter of the late I. [or J.] Allison, Esq., of Philadelphia (*Baltimore Daily Intelligencer* 18 June 1794; BAML).

McDaniel, [-?-], m. by 3 March 1776 Mary, daughter of David Thomas (MWB 41:37; abst. in *Md. Cal. of Wills* 16:144).

McDaniel, Charles, m. by 2 Nov 1723 Johannah, extx. of James Barlow, Sr. (*q.v.*), of BA Co. (MDAD 5:234, 8:198, 9:98).

McDaniel (MacDaniel), Hugh, of Prince George's Co., m. by 13 March 1737 Elizabeth, relict of John Yates (BALR HWS#1-A:59).

McDaniel, Thomas, m. by Nov 1775 Mary, widow of John Davis, whose daughter Elizabeth in Nov 1775 was bound to William Pullen to learn the trade of seamstress (BAMI 1772, 1775-1781: 141).

McDermott, Grace, on 21 d. 2 m. 1794 was charged with bastardy as her husband was not present ("Minutes of Baltimore Meeting," *QRNM:*222).

McDermott, Henry, was m. last Tues. [5 Dec.] by the Rev. Bishop Carroll, to Miss Esmy Jordan, both of this city (*Federal Gazette and Baltimore Daily Advertiser* 7 Dec 1797). They were natives of Ireland at St. Peter's Catholic Church, Baltimore (*Piet:* 139).

McDermott, John, and Catherine Joyce, natives of Ireland, were m. by lic. on 18 Sep 1797 at St. Peter's Catholic Church, Baltimore (*Piet:* 139).

McDermott, Capt. Thomas, and Jane Cunningham were m. Sun. by Rev. Ellison [Allison] (*Baltimore American* 28 May 1799).

McDonald, John, m. by 1788, Sarah, mother of Robert Gardiner (BOCP Petition of Robert Gardiner, 1788, Box 2, Folder 34).

McDonald, John, native of Harford Co., Md., and Frances English, native of New Jersey, widow, were married by banns on 26 Feb 1795 at St. Peter's Catholic Church, Baltimore (*Piet:* 139).

McDonogh, John, and Bridget Connelly were m. by lic. on 26 Dec 1799 at St. Peter's Catholic Church, Baltimore (*Piet:* 139).

McDoon, Joseph, and Rosanna Hughes, widow, natives of Ireland were m. by lic. on 5 Oct 1796 at St. Peter's Catholic Church, Baltimore (*Piet:* 139).

McDowall (M'Dowal), Thomas, and Mrs. Catherine Chisroe, both of Fell's Point, were m. last eve by the Rev. Mr. Kurtz (*Federal Gazette and Baltimore Advertiser* 27 Feb 1798). (BAML gives their names as Thomas McDowell and Catherine Chesu; Marr. Returns of Rev. Daniel Kurtz, MS. 1999 ay MdHS, give her name as Cath. Chesroe).

McDowell (M'Dowell), George, of Baltimore, and Susanna Hanse of Philadelphia were m. there last Tues. eve. by Rev. Smith (*Baltimore Daily Intelligencer* 20 Oct 1794)

McElderry, Thomas, merchant of Baltimore, m. last Sat eve. Betsy, daughter of John Parks, merchant (*Maryland Gazette or Baltimore General Advertiser* 19 June 1787).

McEvoy (M'Evoy), James, and Mary Anne Hickley, both of Baltimore, were m. last Thurs. (*Federal Gazette and Baltimore Daily Advertiser* 5 July 1800). She was *admin. de bonis non* of James Hickley (BAAD 13:338). James Hickey [*sic*] had m. Mary Ann Linch on 14 Sep 1789 (Frederick Co. Marr. Lic.).

McFadden, [-?-], m. by 1 March 1771, Hannah, daughter of Ralph Smith and Huldah ([-?-]) Smith (BAWB 3:193, 248).

McFadon, Alexander, d. by 1785. Richardson Stuart and James Armstrong were execs.; they petitioned that Robert D--- and James McFadon have wrongfully obtained sundry goods and chattels of the dec. (BOCP Petition of Alexander McFaden, 1781, 1785, Box 1, Folder 2).

McFadon (M'Fadon), Capt. James, and Rebecca (Becky) Sligh were m. a few days since, 25 May 1783 in this town (*Maryland Journal and Baltimore Advertiser* 30 May 1783; Marr. Returns of Rev. William West, MS. 1999 at MdHS).

McFadon (M'Fadon), John, and Miss Priscilla Wilson, both of Baltimore, were m. last eve. by Rev. Allison (*Federal Gazette and Baltimore Daily Advertiser* 21 Dec 1798).

McFadon, William, on 16 April 1789 was made a ward of John McFadon (BAOC 2:113).

McFadon (M'Fadon), William, and Miss Nancy Ellick were m. last Sat. eve. (*Baltimore Daily Repository* 7 Aug 1792).

McFarlin (M'Farlin), Edward, and Nancy Tull were m. last eve. (*Maryland Gazette or Baltimore General Advertiser* 19 Dec 1783; BAML, which gives his name as Edward McFarlen).

McFarlin, Edward, and Ann Tull were m. by lic. on 18 Dec 1783 at St. Peter's Catholic Church, Baltimore (*Piet:* 139).

McFarlin, Michael, and Peggy Brand were m. by lic. on 27 Dec 1787 at St. Peter's Catholic Church, Baltimore (*Piet:* 139).

McGarrett (M'Garrett), Thomas, and Elizabeth Gray, both of Baltimore, were m. last eve. by the Rev. Dr. Allison (*Federal Gazette and Baltimore Advertiser* 28 Feb 1798).

McGarretty (M'Garretty), Thomas, and Miss Elizabeth Gray, both of Baltimore, were m. last eve. by Rev. Allison (*Federal Gazette and Baltimore Daily Advertiser* 28 Feb 1798).

McGaw, Sarah, of *My Lady's Manor,* in her will made 3 March 1797, named her sister Mary Madden and her children James and Mary Madden, her nephew Alexander Young, son of her brother Robert Young, her brother-in-law John Giving, and Robert McGaw, son of John and Sarah (BAWB 7:236).

McGee (MacGee), Jane, late of York Co., Pa., in her will made 29 Sep 1792 named her late husband of Patrick MacGee of Chanceford Twp., York Co., her daughter Jane Jacob, wife of William Jacob (*q.v.*), and daughter Elizabeth Macknulty (BAWB 5:491)

McGee. See also Magee.

McGill, Charles, and Margaret Lazaur were m. by lic. on 24 June 1786 at St. Peter's Catholic Church, Baltimore (*Piet:* 139; BAML, which gives her name as Margaret Lasseuir).

McGill, Richard, and Peggy Elsin were m. by banns on 29 June 1789 at St. Peter's Catholic Church, Baltimore (*Piet:* 139).

McGovern, Emanuel, and Elizabeth Chattel were m. by lic. on 6 March 1789 at St. Peter's Catholic Church, Baltimore (*Piet:* 139).

McGrath, James, and Catherine Commin, natives of Ireland, were m. by lic. on 17 Jan 1798 at St. Peter's Catholic Church, Baltimore (*Piet:* 140).

McGrath. Michael, and Margaret Carroll were m. by lic. on 21 Feb 1792 at St. Peter's Catholic Church, Baltimore (*Piet:* 140).

McGregory, John, in his will made 1 Feb 1797 named his daus. Ann Hamin and Susannah Ricketts (BAWB 5:527).

McGrill, Patrick, m. by 18 April 1792 Ann, widow of Arthur Coskery (BAAD 11:40).

McGuire (Macguire, McQuie), Michael, m. by 3 July 1759, Eleanor, the admx. of Abraham Jarrett (MDTP 37:273; BAAD 4:254MDAD 43:153; MINV 68:221).

McGuire, Hugh, and Nancy McMechen were m. by lic. on 8 Jan 1792 at St. Peter's Catholic Church, Baltimore (*Piet:* 140).

McGuire, Roger, and Eleanor Casey were m. by lic. on 22 Oct 1795 at St. Peter's Catholic Church, Baltimore (*Piet:* 140).

McGuire. See also Maguire.

McHenry, Dennis, native of Ireland, and Mary Young were m. by lic. on 7 Oct 1794 at St. Peter's Catholic Church, Baltimore (*Piet:* 140).

McHerge, John, m. by 24 Feb 1764 Mary, daughter of Andrew McGill, farmer (BAWB 2:181).

McIlvaine (Miclevane), David, convict, in Feb 1754 was fined for begetting a bastard on the body of Mary Murphy (BACP BB#A:438, 463).

McInney (McImsey), Joseph, m. by 20 Feb 1773 Elizabeth, heir of Joseph Lewis (BAAD 6:312; MDAD 68:107).

McKean, John, m. by 15 Sep 1796 Ann Helms (BALR WG#YY:86).

McKenna, John, d. by 14 Oct 1795 when Ann Mckenna was made admx., and Adam McLane and Elijah Egon were sureties. Ann has since married to Robert Dunwoody who McLane and Egon fear had wasted McKenna's estate. The petitioners wanted Dunwoody to give counter security (BOCP Petition of Adam McLane and Elijah Egon, 1796).

McKenney (McKiny), Jane, servant of James Moore, was charged with bastardy at the Aug 1736 Court and again at the Aug 1737 Court (BACP HWS#1A:97). Her daughter Martha McKenney was b. 25 Aug 1738 and prob. d. on 30 Sep 1741 (Reamy, *St. George's Parish Register:* 50, 65). Aaron Porter and Jane McKenny were m. on 19 Aug [year not given, but prob. 1740 or 1741] (Reamy, *St. George's Parish Register:* 63). Aaron and Jane were the parents of Thomas Porter, b. 9 Jan 1742 (Reamy, *St. George's Parish Register* p. 68).

McKennsey. See McKenzie.

McKenzie (M'Kenzie), Benjamin, stated he would not pay the debts of his wife Susanna Butler M'Kenzie (*Baltimore Daily Intelligencer* 4 April 1794). In Dec 1796 he stated again that his wife Susanna Butler [*sic*] had eloped from his bed and board without any lawful cause and he stated [again] he would not pay any debts of her contracting (*Federal Gazette and Baltimore Daily Advertiser* 12 Dec 1796). Susanna M'Kenzie (McKennsey), admx., on 18 July 1798 posted bond to administer the estate of Benjamin McKennsey, but she signed the bond as Susanna Trimble (BAAB 8:337).

McKenzie (MacKenzie), Dr. Colin, of Baltimore, and Miss Sally Pinkerton of Chester Co., Pa., were m. last Thurs. eve. by Rev. Allison (*Federal Gazette and Baltimore Daily Advertiser* 25 May 1799).

McKenzie, John, and Elizabeth Warner were m. by lic. on 4 Aug 1795 at St. Peter's Catholic Church, Baltimore (*Piet:* 140).

McKenzie, John, m. by 19 March 1794 Anne, daughter of Zachariah Strauble (BALR WG#NN:356).

McKenzie, Roger, and Ann Martin were m. by lic. on 22 July 1793 at St. Peter's Catholic Church, Baltimore (*Piet:* 140).

McKewen, Owen, and Elizabeth Crisman were m. by lic. on 19 July 1796 at St. Peter's Catholic Church, Baltimore (*Piet:* 140).

McKey, [-?-], m. by 26 d., 9 m. 1770, Margaret Dunkin who was reportedly m. by a priest ("Minutes of Gunpowder Monthly Meeting," *QRNM:*60). [No other marriage reference found].

McKiernan, Michael, and Mary Bowman were married by banns on 26 Jan 1793 at St. Peter's Catholic Church, Baltimore (*Piet:* 140).

McKim, Alexander, served as a private in the Baltimore Independent Cadets; he d. in Baltimore on 18 April 1832; he m, Catherine Sarah Davey on 20 July 1783; Rev. William West was the minister; They were the parents of Catherine M. Singleton and Elizabeth Dubois (Rev. War Pension Application of Sarah McKim: R6758). She was a daughter of Elizabeth Davey (BAAD 9:70).

McKim (M'Kim), John, Jr., of Baltimore, merchant, and Miss Margaret Telfair, daughter of Mrs. Elizabeth Telfair of Philadelphia, were m. Thurs. eve., 11th inst, by Rev. Dr. Ashbel Green (*The Federal Gazette, and Philadelphia Evening Post* 12 July 1793).

McKim, John, and Mary Love on 13 d. 8 m. 1795 declared their intention to marry ("Minutes of Baltimore Meeting," *QRNM:* 225). John McKim, merchant, was m. yesterday at the Friends Meeting, to Mary Love, both of this town (*Federal Intelligencer and Baltimore Daily Gazette* 25 Sep 1795).

McKinley, Neale, and Margaret King were m. by lic. on 2 Dec 1794 at St. Peter's Catholic Church, Baltimore (*Piet:* 140).

McKinney, Christian, was charged with bastardy at the Nov 1759 Court (BAMI 1757-1759:241-242).

McKinnon, Daniel, is separated from his wife Ruth because she brought into the family an adulterous child, begotten about the beginning of June 1758 (while Daniel was in Britain), and was born 2 March 1759; Daniel stated he would not pay the debts of his wife (Annapolis *Md. Gaz.* 29 March 1759).

McKinsey, Jno., m. by 8 Nov 1723 Eleanor, daughter of Henry Donahue (BAAD 1:129, 176).

McKubbin. See McCubbin.

McLane, Alexander, m. by 8 Aug 1786, Kezia, widow of Samuel Haslet who left five children: James age 13, Mary, 12, Ann, 8, Joseph, 6, and Samuel, 4 (BPET: Petition re Samuel Haslet, 1786; BAAD 8:289).

McLane (M'Lane), [Hector?], m. by 9 June 1697 Sarah, daughter of Thomas Morgan of Baltimore Co. (MWB 7:392).

McLane, Hector, m. as his second wife Amy Norman, daughter of George and Johanna ([-?-]) Norman (*BCF:* 440). Amy m. 2nd, by Nov 1724 John Townsend (*q.v.*).

McLaughlin (M'Laughlin), William, was m. by Rev. William West, to Mary (Polly), daughter of the late Jonathan Plowman (*Maryland Gazette or Baltimore General Advertiser* 23 Jan 1787; (Marr. Returns of Rev. William West, Scharf Papers, MS.1999 at MdHS). Mary's sister, Rebecca Plowman, m. Robert Ballard (*q.v.*) on 13 July 1780 (Marr. Returns of Rev. William West, Scharf Papers, MS.1999 at MdHS). In his will made in Dec 1794 McLaughlin named his wife's nephews

Robert and Henry Ballard (BAWB 5:233). Mary McLaughlin, in her will made 26 March 1798 named John, Henry, William, and Edward Ballard her sister's children; also John Plowman, son of her brother Jonathan Plowman (BAWB 6:169).

McLaughlin, William, exec., on 12 Feb 1794 posted bond to administer the estate of Catherine Barnet (BAAB 8:564).

McLening, John, m. by 14 June 1763 Mary, daughter of Maybury and Ann Helm (BALR (BALR B#M:114).

McLochlin, Hugh, was charged with bastardy at the Nov 1758 Court (BAMI 1757-1759:162).

McMab, Jane, aged 8 last 28 March, daughter of Thomas, in June 1758 was bound to Thomas Brierly (BAMI 1755-1763).

McMahan, Esther, was charged with bastardy at the March 1768 Court (BACP BB:1).

McMahon, Patrick, and Nancy Brown were m. by lic. on 12 Sep 1792 at St. Peter's Catholic Church, Baltimore (*Piet:* 140).

McMeal, Daniel, and Catherine Dalton, widow, were m. by lic. on 27 Nov 1800 at St. Peter's Catholic Church, Baltimore (*Piet:* 140). She was a widow of George Dalton (*q.v.*).

McMechen (M'Mechen), William, Esq., was m. last eve. by Rev. Mr. Ireland to Eleanor B. Armstead, all of this city (*Federal Gazette and Baltimore Daily Advertiser* 21 Feb 1800).

McMullen, Alexander, and Hannah Stringhar were m. on 1 June 1776 Harrison, "St. Paul's Parish Register:" 172), Alexander and Hannah McMullen, administrators, on 16 April 1787 posted bond to administer the estate of William Reed (BAAB 7:93).

McMullen, Patrick, and Jane McDonough were m. by lic. on 16 May 1785 at St. Peter's Catholic Church, Baltimore (*Piet:* 140).

McMullen, Peter, and Catherine O'Hara were married by banns on 4 Aug 1785 at St. Peter's Catholic Church, Baltimore (*Piet:* 140).

McMullen, Thomas, m. by 25 Nov 1761 Margaret, sister of John Maxwell (BAWB 2:139).

McNamara, John, and Judith Clarke, [both?] of Baltimore Co., were m. by lic. on 29 March 1796 at St. Peter's Catholic Church, Baltimore (*Piet:* 140).

McNamara, Matthew, and Ann Glassby were m. by lic. on 15 June 1793 at St. Peter's Catholic Church, Baltimore (*Piet:* 140).

McQuie. See McGuire.

McQuinn, William, m. by 1 Aug 1788 Jane Hendricks (F. Edward Wright, "Pardons by the Governor," *MGSB* 32 (3) (Summer 1991) 351).

McQuinn, William, widower, and Elizabeth Rasford, widow, were m. by lic. on 27 Feb 1797 at St. Peter's Catholic Church, Baltimore (*Piet:* 140).

McSherry, Patrick, of York Co., Penna., m. last Sun. eve. Betsy Clements of Baltimore (*Maryland Journal and Baltimore Advertiser* 13 April 1790). She was a daughter of Charles and Belinda Clements; they were m. by lic. on 11 April 1790 at St. Peter's Catholic Church, Baltimore (*Piet:* 130, 140). Elizabeth m. 2nd, John Baptist Daliquet (*q.v.*).

McSherry, Richard, late of Baltimore, merchant, now of Berkeley Co., Va., and Anastatia Lilly, daughter of Richard Lilly of Frederick Co., were m. [date not given] (*Maryland Journal and Baltimore Advertiser* 5 Aug 1791).

McSwaine, Catherine, in March 1760 was the illegitimate daughter of Mary McSwaine; Barnett Boner was the surety for the fees (BAMI 1755-1763: 14).

McSwaine, Dennis, m. by 10 Aug 1772 Mary, admx. of John Skipton (MINV 109:275; BAAD 7:135; MDAD 67:221).

Mead, Ann, was charged with bastardy at the March 1736/7 Court (BACP (BACP HWS#1A:1).

Mead, Edward, and 'Darcass' Evins were m. on 13 Oct 1713 (Harrison, "St. James Parish Register" Anne Arundel Co., MS. at MdHS: 3). On 6 Nov 1746 Darkas [Dorcas] was named as a daughter of John Ewing and his wife Elizabeth; Elizabeth was a daughter of Moses Groome; Darkas d. by the above date, leaving a son James Mead (BALR TB#E:188, TR#D:406).

Mead, Ed. (or Meed), in July 1737 with Catherine Baker were summoned for unlawful cohabitation, for more than seven years (St. John's and *St. George's Parish Register* Parish Register Vestry Proceedings. Typed copy of the original at the MdHS).

Mead, Joseph, in his will dated 17 Sep 1737 named Benjamin Cadle as his brother (MWB 21:828 abst. in abst. in *Md. Cal. of Wills* 7:231).

Meadohan, Benjamin, on 21 Feb 1738 was named as a father-in-law in the will of John Ingram (MWB 22:160 abst. in *Md. Cal. of Wills* 8:75).

Meads, [-?-], m. by 3 Sep 1767 Susan [Eufan?], daughter of Mary Shepherd (BACT B#G:149; BALR B#Q:6).

Meads, Jeffery, stated he would not pay the debts of his wife Lucy, who about four years ago, without any just cause, had absconded from his bed and board and had cohabited with other persons (*Federal Gazette and Baltimore Daily Advertiser* 12 June 1797).

Meaks (Micks), William Bell, and Lydia James were m. on 21 March 1792 (Harrison, "St. Paul's Parish Register:" 255). On 21 Oct 1793 Lydia was named as a daughter of Hannah James of Baltimore Co., dec. (BALR WG#MM:315).

Medcalfe (Metcalfe), John, and Mary Norris were m. on 6 Aug 1725 ((Harrison, "St. James Parish Register," Anne Arundel Co., MS. at MdHS: 377). On 10 June 1740 Medcalf's wife was named as a daughter of John Norris, and Medcalfe had died leaving a daughter Mary Medcalfe (BALR HWS#1A:397).

Meeling, John Godfrey, stated he would not pay the debts of his wife Cassandra as she had eloped from his bed and board (*Maryland Gazette or Baltimore General Advertiser* 25 July 1783). Cassandra Meeling advertised that no one should take notice of her husband's publication as he "[was] well-known by many people to be crackbrained" (*Maryland Gazette or Baltimore General Advertiser* 25 July 1783).

Melancy, John, and Catherine Towel were married by banns on 14 Sep 1786 at St. Peter's Catholic Church, Baltimore (*Piet:* 140).

Melton, Sarah, was charged with bastardy in 1720 having had a baseborn daughter, Leana Melton, who was born 10 April 1720 and 'left with John Harper' (Harrison, "St. John's Parish Parish Register:" 56).

Meneur, William, and Polly Fry, both of Baltimore, were m. Fri. by Rev. Richards (*Baltimore American* 21 April 1800).

Mentz, Joseph, on 16 Feb 1794 was named as a son-in-law in the will of Elizabeth Mildews (BAWB 7:379).

Mera, Frederic, and Mary Sneider were married by banns on 20 May 1793 at St. Peter's Catholic Church, Baltimore (*Piet:* 140).

Mercer, Benjamin James, and Anna Strophel (Stophel) were married by license dated 17 May 1790; they were actually m. on 18 May 1790 (BAML; Marr. Returns of Rev. William West, Scharf Papers, MS. 1999 at MdHS).

Mercer, John, and Miss Elizabeth Pearpoint, both of this county, were m. last eve. by Rev. Bend (*Baltimore Evening Post* 12 June 1799).

Mercer, Richard, m. by 12 May 1757 [-?-], legatee of Edward Richards (MDAD 41:20).

Mercier. See Mercer.

Meredith, [-?-], m. by 30 Oct 1799 Sarah, daughter of Samuel Tipton (BAWB 7:7:334).

Meredith, Samuel, and Jemima Taylor were m. 2 Feb 1748 Harrison, "St. Paul's Parish Register:" 162). Joseph Taylor named Jemima Meredith as a cousin in his will dated 19 April 1788 (BAWB 4:436).

Merriarter, Edward, and Sarah Hanson were m. on 17 Feb 1736 (Harrison, "St. George's Parish Register:" 293). Sarah m. 2nd, John Garrettson (*q.v.*). On 24 Nov 1742 Sarah was named as a daughter of Sarah Hanson, and granddaughter of Sarah Tayman, formerly Sarah Cockey who later m. [-?-] Tayman (MWB 23:21 abst. in *Md. Cal. of Wills* 8:196; BALR TB#D:311).

Merrick, Patrick, stated he would not pay the debts of his wife Ann as she had behaved in an unbecoming manner (*Baltimore Daily Intelligencer* 15 April 1794). Merrick and Ann Hamilton were m. by lic. on 20 Oct 1790 at St. Peter's Catholic Church, Baltimore (*Piet:* 140).

Merrick, William, and Catherine Deasmond were m. by lic. on 4 Sep 1790 at St. Peter's Catholic Church, Baltimore (*Piet:* 140; BAML, which gives her name as Catherine Dearmona).

Merriken, Hugh, and Ann Westall were m. in Nov 1719 (Harrison, "St. Margaret's Parish Register," Anne Arundel Co.: 100). On 23 Dec 1719 Anne was named as the extx. of George Westall (*q.v.*) of Baltimore Co. (MDAD 2:372; MDAD 3:18; MDTP 24:97).

Merriken, Joshua, boatwright, and Dinah Day were m. on 24 June 1718 (Harrison, "St. John's Parish Register:" 11). On 4 Nov 1720 Dinah was named as a daughter of Nicholas Day (BALR TR#DS:251).

Merryman, Caleb, and Mary Merryman were m. in 1786 ("Records of Zion Lutheran Church," MS. at MdHS: 387). On 13 April 1792 Mary was named as an heir of Nicholas Merryman (BAAD 11:33).

Merryman (Merriman), Charles, m. by 28 Feb 170, Jane, widow and extx. of Joseph Peake (*q.v.*), and extx. of Jane Long (INAC 21:185; BAAD 2:34, 216). Jane m. 3rd, Benjamin Knight (*q.v.*).

Merryman, Elijah, m. by 7 Feb 1775 Frances, daughter of John Ensor (BALR AL#M: 74).

Merryman, John, m. by 12 April 1702, Martha, daughter of Martha Bowen, widow of Baltimore Co. (MWB 3:2 abst. in *Md. Cal. of Wills* 3:30).

Merryman, John, and Sarah Smith, widow of Capt. John Addison Smith were m. on 9 Dec 1777; John Addison Smith and Sarah, daughter of William Rogers had been m. on 17 Oct 1765 (Harrison, "St. Paul's Parish Register:" 184).

Merryman, Joseph, convict, in July 1755, was fined for begetting a bastard on the body of Rachel Carter, convict (BACP BB#B:400-401).

Merryman, Kedemoth, was charged with bastardy at the June 1741 Court. Henry Quine, alias Henry James, admitted he was the father of the child (BACP TB&TR:56, 183).

Merryman, Keturah, was charged with bastardy at the March 1740/1 Court (BACP TB&TR:211).

Merryman, Luke, a private in the Maryland Line, d. 23 Nov 1813; he was m. to Elizabeth Gorsuch in Baltimore Co. on 27 Jan 1794, by Rev. Bend; they had a son Caleb Merryman, age 52 in 1849, and two other children born prior to him, the first in 1795 (Rev. War Pension Application of Elizabeth Merryman: W2648).

Merryman, Micajah, m. by 1793 Mary, daughter of John Ensor (MCHP# 2029).

Merryman, Micajah, advertised that he intended to petition the Assembly for an act enabling him to lease land in Baltimore Town that belongs to his children: Sarah, Moses, Eleanor, Mary, and Micajah, all under the age of 21 (*Maryland Journal and Baltimore Advertiser* 17 Sep 1793). He advertised he would sell the land that descended to his children from their mother Mary Merryman, dec. (*Maryland Journal and Baltimore Advertiser* 17 Oct 1794).

Merryman, Nicholas, and Avarilla Raven were m. 1 May 1755 (Harrison, "St. John's Parish Register:" 212). On 5 Sep 1760 Avarilla was named as a daughter of Luke Raven (BAWB 2: 349).

Merryman, Nicholas, and Mary Comley were m. on 21 Feb 1792 (Marriage Register of Rev. Lewis Richards, Pastor of First Baptist Church, Baltimore, 1784-1818. MS 690 at MdHS). Mary Merryman, formerly Comley, on 31 d. 3 m. 1792, reportedly on 26 d. 2 m. 1792 reportedly had her marriage accomplished by a hireling minister ("Minutes of Gunpowder Meeting," *QRNM*:92). On 11 Oct 1796 Mary Comly was named as an heir of Keziah Hooker BAAD 12:196).

Merryman, Nicholas, and Deborah Ensor were married by license dated 5 Feb 1778 (BAML). In 1793 Deborah was named as a daughter of John Ensor (MCHP# 2029).

Merryman, Samuel, m. by 17 Feb 1709 Mary, widow of Thomas Eager (*q.v.*) (MDTP 21:208). On 19 Nov 1709 Mary was named as a daughter of Humphrey Boone and sister of Robert Boone of Baltimore Co. (MWB 12-2:205; INAC 32B:249).

Merryman, William, merchant, and Miss Ann Presbury, daughter of George G. Presbury, all of this city, were m. Thurs. eve, by Rev. Mr. Ireland (*Federal Gazette and Baltimore Daily Advertiser* 8 Feb. 1800).

Mery, Frederic and Eva Rosenbyke, widow, were married by banns on 27 July 1794 at St. Peter's Catholic Church, Baltimore (*Piet:* 140).

Messersmith, William, merchant, and Miss Frances Cromwell of Baltimore Co., were m. last Thurs. eve. by Rev Mr. Kurtz (*Baltimore Daily Intelligencer* 14 Jan 1794).

Messonier, Henry, and Betsy, dau, of Dr, Wiesenthal of Baltimore, were m. [date not given] (*Maryland Journal and Baltimore Advertiser* 17 Aug 1781). Henry Messonier and Elizabeth Wiesenthal were married by license dated 1 Aug 1782 (BAML). Elizabeth Messonier, consort of Henry Messonier and dau, of Dr. Charles F. Wiesenthal, d. last Tues. eve. (*Maryland Gazette or Baltimore General Advertiser* 2 Nov 1787).

Metcalfe. See Medcalfe.

Meyers (Myers), Charles, and Elizabeth Garrols were m. on 30 Dec 1786 (Register of First Presbyterian Church, Baltimore at MdHS, 10). On 28 Oct 1788 Elizabeth Jarrold [*sic*] was named as a legatee of Richard Payne and of William Payne (BAAD 9:253, 255). In his will dated 14 Feb 1769 and proved 17 Dec 1769 William Payne of Baltimore Town named his wife Elizabeth, sons Robert and

Richard, daughter Elizabeth, daughter Catherine Jarrold, and granddaughter Elizabeth Jarrold (BAWB 3:61).

Meyers. See also Myers.

Michael, [-?-], m. by 21 d. 5 m. 1784 Tacey, daughter of Isaac Tyson (BAWB 3:567).

Mickle, Robert, was m. last eve. by Rev. Dr. Allison, to Miss Eliza Etting, both of this town (*Federal Intelligencer and Baltimore Daily Gazette* 25 Dec 1795).

Middlemore, Josiah, and Mrs. Frances Beechley [*sic*] were m. on 9 Oct 1720 (Harrison, "St. John's Parish Register:" 33). On 12 Jan 1724/5 Frances was named as the only daughter and heir of Edward Boothby of Baltimore Co., dec. (MDTP 27:119).

Middleton, Elizabeth, was charged with bastardy at the Nov 1772 Court and fined £1.10.0 (BAMI 1772, 1775-1781:86).

Miers, Ann, was charged with mulatto bastardy and confessed at the Aug 1755 Court; her daughter Martha Miers was sold to John Gorsuch and ordered to serve him to age 31 (BAMI 1755-1763).

Miers, James, of Kent Co., Md., m. by 18 July 1795 Rebecca Briscoe (BALR WG#SS: 335).

Mifflin, Daniel, of Accomack Co., Va., on 8 d. 10 m. 1789 announced his intention to marry Mary Husband, relict of Joseph Husband, dec. ("Minutes of Deer Creek Meeting," *QRNM:*147).

Miles, [-?-], m. by 5 Oct 1733 Catherine, daughter of Peter Puttee (Potee) (MWB 22:160 abst. in *Md. Cal. of Wills* 8:75). Catherine was also the daughter of Rebecca Potee (MWB 30:445 abst. by Gibb).

Miles, [-?-], m. by 7 Jan 1733/4 Mary, mother of John Miles Youngblood (BALR HWS#M:16).

Miles, [-?-], m. by 21 Sep 1747 Eleanor, dau. of William McComas (MWB 25:488 abst. by Gibb). On 24 March 1749, Elinor was described as aged 25, daughter of William McComas of Baltimore Co. (MDAD 27:336; BAAD 5:75).

Miles, Charles, m. by 20 April 1709 Mary, daughter of William Pecket of Baltimore Co. (MWB 13:132 abst. in *Md. Cal. of Wills* 3:180; MDAD 8:60).

Miles, Evan, and Elizabeth Davis were m. on 24 July 1726 (Harrison, "St. George's Parish Register:" p. 244). Elizabeth m. 2nd, on 18 Sep 1739, Robert Price (*q.v.*).

Miles, Jacob, and Hannah McComas were m. on 10 Nov 1748 (Harrison, "St. John's Parish Register:" 198, 243). On 18 Oct 1760 Hannah was named as a daughter of Alexander McComas (MWB 31:179, abst. by Gibb).

Miles, John, and Miss Mary Dewees, both of Baltimore, were m. Thurs. eve. by Rev. Richards (*Baltimore Telegraphe* 28 Dec 1799).

Miles, Thomas, in Nov 1718 was charged with begetting a bastard on the body of Sarah Litton (BACP IS#C:31). Sarah's daughter, Martha Litton, was b. 27 April 1718. Martha 'Litten' m. George Cole on 2 March 1732 (Reamy. *St. George's Parish Register*: 19, 26).

Miles, Thomas, as son and devisee of John Miles, dec., on 7 Aug 1733 conv. to Mary Miles, widow of John Miles and to John Miles Youngblood the tract *Miles*, which John Miles had given to Mary Miles for her life and then to John Miles Youngblood. Thomas Miles' wife Catherine consented (BALR IS#L:419).

Miles, Thomas, in Aug 1744 was fined for begetting a bastard on the body of Ann Robertson (BACP 1743-1745: 228, 312).

Miles, Thomas, and Margaret Taylor were m. on 11 Oct 1744 (Harrison, "St. John's Parish Register:" 191). On 5 May 1761 Margaret was named as the mother of Elizabeth Taylor, and daughter of Ulick Burk (BAWB 2:117).

Miles, Thomas, Quaker, m. by 18 Oct 1760 Hannah (not a Quaker), daughter and extx. of Alexander McComas (*q.v.*) (BAWB 2:352; BAAD 4:365 MDTP 38:252; MDAD 47:447).

Miles, Thomas, and Hannah Thompson were m. in Dec 1771 (Harrison, "St. John's Parish Register:" 263). Hannah Miles, before marriage Thomson, on 25 d. 12 m. 1771, was charged with marrying outside the Society ("Minutes of Gunpowder Meeting," *QRNM:*61).

Miles, Zachary, and Rebecca Bell were married by license dated 18 June 1793 (BAML). On 26 Dec 1796 Rebecca was named as a daughter of William Preston; Miles was guardian of the grandchildren (BAWB 5:465; BAAD 13:11). William Preston, in his will dated 26 Dec 1796 and proved 31 Dec 1796 named his wife Ann and his step-daughter Rebecca, wife of Zachary Miles (BAWB 5:465).

Miller, [-?-], m. by 22 Sep 1789 Mary, daughter of Edward Oursler (BAWB 5:244).

Miller, [-?-], m. by 14 May 1799 Catherine, daughter of Jacob Spindler (BAWB 6:294).

Miller, Adolphus, and Miss Eliza M'Glathery of Baltimore were m. 5th inst. at New Bremen (*Federal Gazette and Baltimore Daily Advertiser* 13 April 1798. **See Maeller, Adolphus, above.**

Miller, Catherine, formerly Catherine Mackenheimer, extx., on 11 April 1792 posted bond to administer the estate of Gabriel Mackenheimer, whose will, made 9 Sep 1773 and was proved on 10 April 1792, named his wife Catherine as extx. (BAWB 5:39; BAAB 7:368).

Miller, George, m. by 17 Jan 1784 Jane, dau. of Robert Cresap and niece of Thomas Cresap (BAWB 4:398).

Miller, George, and Sarah Oyston were m. on 28 Sep 1786 (Marr. Returns of Rev. William West, Scharf Papers, MS.1999 at MdHS). Sarah was a daughter of Lawrence Oyston (BAWB 6:241).

Miller, George, and Margaret Frazier were m. by lic. on 12 Oct 1794 at St. Peter's Catholic Church, Baltimore (*Piet:* 140).

Miller, Gottlieb, m. by 10 March 1787, Anna Juliana Märtzin ("First Record Book for the Reformed and Lutheran Congregations at Manchester, Baltimore (now Carroll) Co.," *MGSB* 35:282).

Miller, Henry, and Ann Fields, both of the county, were m. by lic. on 8 June 1794 at St. Peter's Catholic Church, Baltimore (*Piet:* 140).

Miller, Jacob, and Margaret Dentlinger were married by license dated 8 Oct 1778 (Frederick Co. Marr, Lic.). In 1792 Margaret was named as a daughter of Catherine Dentlinger whose estate was admin. by Anthony Clyne; Jacob and Margaret complained about the admin. (BOCP Petition of Jacob Miller and wife Margaret, 1792).

Miller, Jacob, in June 1795 was made guardian of Henry, Peter, Michael, and Catherine Miller (BAOC 3:156).

Miller, John, and Elizabeth Rebecca Webster were m. Tues., 18th June by Rev. Walter McPherson. By this marriage the oldest of twelve brothers ands sisters was married by the youngest, both widowers, and by this event, the said Miller became son to his son William Cox, who by his last marriage became son, nephew, and brother to his wife's oldest sister (*Maryland Gazette or Baltimore General Advertiser* 30 Aug 1791).

Miller, John, and Sarah McCloud were m. by lic. on 1 Aug 1791 at St. Peter's Catholic Church, Baltimore (*Piet:* 140).

Miller, Jon., and Hannah Hendon, in May 1758 were reported by Thos. Meredith as living together in a scandalous manner; they were cited to appear before the next vestry ("St. John's and St. George's Parish Vestry Proceedings," MS. at MdHS).

Miller, Joseph, m. by 26 Nov 1770 Elizabeth, extx. of Christian Dale (Deale) (*q.v.*) (MINV 105:86, 114:82). On 28 July 1764 Mary Ann Ash made a will naming her daughter Elizabeth wife of Christian Deale, and her grandchildren Christian and Peter [sic] Deale (BAWB 3:41).

Miller, Joseph, and Frances Wilson were m. by lic. dated 16 Sep 1775 (HAML). Frances Miller, late Wilson, on 3 d. 11 m. 1785 was reported as having m. a man not of our society, by a Baptist Preacher ("Minutes of Deer Creek Meeting," *QRNM:* 143).

Miller, Joshua, son of William Miller, in Oct 1792 was made ward of Nathaniel Marsh (BAOC 3:12).

Miller, Matthias, and Barbara Warner were m. by lic. dated 12 Jan 1784 (BAML). On [date not given] Barbara was named as the admx. of George Warner (BAAD 10:70).

Miller, Michael, m. by 15 Jan 1733 Elizabeth, daughter of Mary Tolley (MWB 21:34 abst. in *Md. Cal. of Wills* 7:74). On 17 Jan 1733 Elizabeth was named as a sister of Thomas Tolley (MWB 21:193 abst. in *Md. Cal. of Wills* 7:104). On 20 Oct 1744 Elizabeth Miller was named as the sister of her dead husband in the will of Mary Tolley, widow of James Tolley (MWB 23:657 abst. by Gibb). On 10 March 1752 Elizabeth was named as a sister of James Tolley (MDTP 35:172).

Miller, Michael, (son of Donald and Catherine), and Elizabeth Harken (daughter of Jacob and Adelaide), were m. by lic. on 4 June 1795 at St. Peter's Catholic Church, Baltimore (*Piet:* 140).

Miller, Nicholas, living in Pa., m. by 1785 Sarah, widow of Charles Bond (*q.v.*) (BPET: Charles Bond, petition, 1785, Box 1, Folder 17; BAAD 9:197).

Miller, Rudick, and Margaret Miller, execs., on 9 Aug 1785, posted bond to administer the estate of Rudy Brubach (BAAB 5:41). In his will, made 29 Aug 1795 Rudy Brubeck named his daughter Margaret Miller and named Rudick and Margaret Miller as execs. (BAWB 4:401).

Miller, Samuel, and Mary Burk were m. by lic. on 2 Aug 1783 at St. Peter's Catholic Church, Baltimore (*Piet:* 140).

Miller, Susanna, was charged with bastardy at the March 1768 Court (BAMI 1768-1769:7).

Miller, Thomas, of French Lane near Charles St., Baltimore, stated he would not pay the debts of his wife Ann, who by the "bad advice and tales of scandalous persons had separated herself from her husband (*Maryland Journal and Baltimore Advertiser* 18 May 1792).

Miller, Warrick, son of Robert and Ruth, of Chester Co., Pa., m. on 29 d. 4 m. 1762, Elizabeth, daughter of Mordecai and Elizabeth Price (Records of Gunpowder Meeting at MdSA). On 5 Oct 1765, Miller's wife was named as an heir of Elizabeth Price of Baltimore Co. (BAAD 6:146).

Miller, William, of Carlisle, Pa., m. by 17 Sep 1793, Mary, niece of William West (BAWB 5:309).

Milleret, Cosmo, of the Parish of Margot, Co. of Medoc, Diocese of Bordeaux, but from Cap Francois, and Mary Ann Granger of St. John Baptist du Trou, Cap Francois, were m. by lic. on 20 April 1783 at St. Peter's Catholic Church, Baltimore (*Piet:* 140).

Millhuse, Bartholomew, m. Bridget [-?-], who m. 2nd, John Parks (*q.v.*) on 29 Oct 1743 (Harrison, "St. John's Parish Register:" 189).

Millhues, Greenbury, m. by 21 Jan 1777 Mary, daughter of Nathan Sinklair (BAWB 3:465).

Mills, James, and Susannah Lawrence were m. on 14 Feb 1796 (Marr. Register of Rev. Lewis Richards, MS.690 at MdHS). She was a daughter of John Lawrence (*q.v.*) (BAWB 6:126).

Mills, Peter, m. by 4 Jan 1756 Anne, sister of Elizabeth Hines, widow of Thomas Hines (MWB 30:28 abst. by Gibb).

Mills, Thomas, m. by Nov 1761 Susanna, extx, of Alexander McComas (MINV 77:188).

Milner, Ann, was charged with bastardy at the Nov 1711 Court, and again in March 1719/20; she admitted she had born an illegitimate child in Cecil Co. in Aug 1720 (BACP IS#B:266, 314, IS#C:279, 365).

Miniere, John James Joseph, and Jane Mary Anne Mathias, natives of Cap Francois, St. Domingo, were m. by lic. on 26 Sep 1796 at St. Peter's Catholic Church, Baltimore (*Piet:* 140; BAML).

Minor, Elijah, and Susan, admx. of Champoneyss Lindsey (*q.v.*), were m. ny 27 July 1775 (MDTP 236).

Minor, John, m. by 5 June 1794, sister of Otho Holland Williams, who named Minor his brother-in-law (BAWB 5:180).

Mitchell, [-?-], m. by 2 Sep 1748 Hannah, daughter of Ford Barnes (MWB 26:119 abst. by Gibb).

Mitchell, [-?-], m. by 4 Feb 1748/9 Prudence, daughter of John Harryman (MWB 25:540 abst. by Gibb). On 5 April 1750 Prudence, aged 35, was named as a daughter of John Harryman of Baltimore Co. (MDAD 28:53).

Mitchell, Alexander, merchant, and Miss Eliza Torrence, daughter of Charles Torrence, both of Baltimore, were m. last eve. by Rev. Allison (*Baltimore Telegraphe* 20 Dec 1799).

Mitchell, Elizabeth, was charged with bastardy at the Nov 1759 Court (BAMI 1755-1763:240).

Mitchell, (Capt.) John, of Va., and Mary Daffin were m. by license dated 14 May 1782 (*Maryland Journal and Baltimore Advertiser* 21 May 1782; BAML).

Mitchell, John, Jr., m. by 14 Nov 1786 a sister of John Kingsbury, and had a son John, whom Kingsbury called nephew (BAWB 4:414).

Mitchell, John J., m. by 8 March 1783 Mary, daughter of Joseph Bankson (BALR WG#L: 469).

Mitchell, Peter, stated he would not pay the debts of his wife Barbara, who had left him (*Baltimore Daily Repository* 16 May 1792).

Mitchell, Thomas, and Ann [-?-] were m. by 8 Feb 1719 when their son Thomas was born ("Thomas Mitchell Bible," *MBR* 3:126-127).

Mitchell, Thomas, and Hannah Osborn were m. on 24 Dec 1742 (Harrison, "St. George's Parish Register:" 329). Hannah, wife of Thomas, was b. 14 Oct 1721; Their son Kent Mitchell was b. 8 May 1742; their daughter Mary was b. 8 April 1752 ("Thomas Mitchell Bible," *MBR* 3:126-127).

Mitchell, William, and Clemency [-?-], were m. some time before 25 March 1772 when their daughter Charlotte, who m. John Hughes, was b. ("Bible Record of John Hughes," BRHA:46).

Mitchell, William, and Eliza Calver were m. on 24 May 1787 (Marr. Returns of Rev. William West, Scharf Papers, MS. 1999 at MdHS). On 15 Nov 1791 Elizabeth was named as the admx. of William Calver (Colver), who left a son Henry Colver (BAAD 10:477; BAOC 2:215, 220).

Mitzler, Nicholas, and Jacobena Frolich were married by license dated 9 Sep 1785 (BAML). On 17 June 1786 Jacobena was named as the extx. of Christian Frolich (BAAD 8:276).

Moale, Mr. John, and Miss Helen North were married 25 May 1758 at Baltimore Town (Annapolis *Maryland Gazette* 1 June 1758). She was a sister and co-heir of Thomas North, late of Baltimore Co., dec. (BALR B#P: 108).

Moale, Richard, in Nov 1757 was fined for begetting a bastard on the body of Emmory Day, servant to William Lux (BAMI 1757-1759:75).

Moale, Richard H., was m. last eve. by Rev. Mr. Ireland, to Miss [Judith Carter] Armistead, both of this city (*Federal Gazette and Baltimore Daily Advertiser* 17 April 1797 (BAML).

Moale, S., was m. last eve. to Miss Ann Howard, daughter of S. H. Howard of Annapolis (*Federal Gazette and Baltimore Daily Advertiser* 23 Sep 1796).

Moale, Thomas, of Baltimore Town, and Nelly Owings, daughter of Samuel Owings of Baltimore Co., were m. Thursday, 21st March by Rev. Bend (Chestertown *Apollo* 26 March 1793).

Mobley, Mordecai, and Elizabeth Brown were m. on 23 April 1789 (Marr. Register of Rev. Lewis Richards, MS.690 at MdHS). She was a daughter of John Brown (BAWB 6:377).

Mockbie, John, of Baltimore Co., and Nancy Howard, daughter of the late John Howard of Anne Arundel Co., were m. 20th inst. (*Maryland Journal and Baltimore Advertiser* 28 Jan 1791; BAML).

Mohlar, Peter, in his will made 10 Sep 1773 named his brother-in-law Peter Schels of York, Penna., as co-exec. (BAWB 3:272, abst. by Jean K. Brandau in *MGSB* 28 (2) (Spring 1987) 222-223).

Mohler, Jacob, b. 5 April 1745, son of Lewis and Ann (Huntzinger) Mohler, married on 4 April 1768, Elizabeth Tschudy, b. 17 March 1743, daughter of Winbert and Elizabeth (Rover) Tschudy (Tschudy Family Record; "First German Reformed Church,: MS. at MdHS: 4).

Mohr, Christoph, m. by 14 Dec 1765 Margareta Schreinein ("First Record Book for the Reformed and Lutheran Congregations at Manchester, Baltimore (now Carroll) Co.," *MGSB* 35:269).

Mohr, Henrich, m. by 11 Dec 1786 Elizabeth Kruterin ("First Record Book for the Reformed and Lutheran Congregations at Manchester, Baltimore (now Carroll) Co.," *MGSB* 35:282).

Mollholland. See Mulholland.

Molone, [-?-], m. by 30 Nov 1747 Sarah, daughter of John Wooley of Baltimore Co. (MDAD 24:187).

Monk, Renaldo, m. by 12 Nov 1754 Rachel, extx. of Edward Riston or Reaston (*q.v.*) (MDTP 36:96; MINV 60:325; MDAD 38:34).

Monk, Richard, and Agnes Taylor were m. on 26 June 1756 (Harrison, "St. George's Parish Register:" 355). She was a daughter of James Taylor (MWB 41:408; abst. in *Md. Cal. of Wills* 16:204).

Montgomery, [-?-], m. by 13 Sep 1783 [-?-], daughter of Samuel Smith who named his grandchildren Robert, William, Samuel, John, James, Boyd, Sidney, Polly, and Peggy Buchanan (BAWB 3:568)

Montgomery, Robert, m. by 27 June 1726 Alice, extx. of Thomas Smith (*q.v.*) (BAAD 3:55; MDAD 7:463; MDTP 27:326).

Montgomery, William, d. by March 1775 when his widow Elizabeth was chosen guardian of his daughter Elizabeth, and of Martha Montgomery (BAMI 1772, 1775-1781: 115)

Montouroy, Lewis Jacynthe, and Mary Clare Rabar DeBeaumale were m. by lic. on 7 Oct 1794 at St. Peter's Catholic Church, Baltimore (*Piet:* 140; (BAML, which gives their names as Louis Montonroy and Marie Claire de Rabar de Bomale).

Moody, Robert, and Lucretia Butler, both of Fell's Point, were m. last eve. by Rev. Bend (*Baltimore American* 7 June 1799).

Mooney, William, and Miss Polly Slaymaker, both of this city, were m. last eve. by the Rev. Mr. Beeston (*Federal Gazette and Baltimore Daily Advertiser* 29 June 1798). They were m. by lic. on 28 June 1798 at St. Peter's Catholic Church, Baltimore (*Piet:* 140).

Moorcock, [-?-], m. by 25 May 1732 Susanna, mother of Thomas and Richard Demmitt (BALR IS#L:264, 266, HWS#M:85).

Moore, [-?-], m. by 27 Oct 1771 Ruth, heir of Rachel Wilmot (BAAD 7:114).

Moore, Alice. See Abigail Stevenson.

Moore, Amelia (formerly Bond), on 28 d. 12 m. 1776 has reportedly gone out in marriage to a man not of our Society ("Minutes of Gunpowder Meeting," *QRNM:* 69). [No other marriage reference found].

Moore, David, son of William, on 29 d. 6 m. 1776 has reportedly gone out in marriage to a woman of our society. On 31 d., 8 m., 1776 he was reportedly married by a priest to a woman of our society ("Minutes of Gunpowder Meeting," *QRNM:*67, 68). [No other marriage reference found].

Moore, Eleanor, on 18 July 1767 was named daughter of James Moore, who was a half-brother of Nicholas Ruxton Gay; James Moore was also the father of Ruxton Moore, James Francis Moore, and John Gay Moore (BALR B#P:681, 683, 685, 688).

Moore, George, of Alexandria, Va., m. last Sun. eve., Lydia, daughter of William Winchester of Baltimore (*Maryland Journal and Baltimore Advertiser* 28 Dec 1790).

Moore, Hannah, late of Dublin Ireland, in her will made 13 June 1785, named her bros. and sisters in Ireland: James, Humphrey, and Jane Templeton and Alice Templeton *alias* Lemeriks (BAWB 4:104).

Moore, Hannah, on 30 d. 3 m. 1792 was condemned for being married by a hireling ("Minutes of Gunpowder Meeting," *QRNM:*93). **See Hannah Heddington.**

Moore, Henry, m. by 31 March 1756 Agnes, mother of James Taylor (and widow of Lawrence Taylor (q.v.) (BACT TR#E:193).

Moore, James, m. by 20 April 1722 Frances, admx. of Jno. Gay of Baltimore Co. (MDAD 4:147).

Moore, James, Jr., and Hannah Willmott were m. on 28 Aug 1744 (Harrison, "St. John's Parish Register:" 133). On 18 Feb 1748 Hannah was named as a daughter of John Willmott (MWB 25:531 abst. by Gibb). On 4 April 1750 Hannah was named as a daughter of John and Rachel Wilmot of Baltimore Co. (MDAD 28:1; BAWB 2:348).

Moore, James, m. by 8 April 1773 Sarah, widow of Robert Dunn (*q.v.*) and the heir of Edward Wakeman (BAAD 6:283). Robert Dunn had m. Sarah Wakeman or Pritchard on 9 May 1762 (Harrison, "St. George's Parish Register:" 367).

Moore, James Francis, and Ann Standiford were m. on 18 Feb 1773 (Harrison, "St. John's Parish Register:" 265). On 30 Oct 1775 Ann was named as a daughter of William Standiford (BAWB 3:330).

Moore, John, of Kent Co., m. by 8 March 1768 Cassandra, daughter of Cassandra Adair who was also the mother of Robert Adair of Baltimore Co. (MDTP 42:351). Moore's wife Cassandra was the sister and heir at law of Robert Adair, dec. (BALR AL#C:620, WG#B:294, WG#C:387).

Moore, John, m. by 27 d. 10 m. 1773 Phebe, daughter of Josiah Dyer (Minutes of Gunpowder Monthly Meeting: *QRNM:*64).

Moore, John, son of Walter, on 27 d. 9 m. 1772, was charged with abandoning his wife and children and may have taken with him a young woman in a scandalous manner ("Minutes of Gunpowder Monthly Meeting," *QRNM:*63).

Moore, John, stated he would petition the Assembly to confirm a deed from Aquila Carr to Walter Moore, dec., father of the said John Moore (*Maryland Journal and Baltimore Advertiser* 5 April 1785).

Moore, John, m. by Sep 1788 [-?-], dau. of John Bond, who on the above date revoked the power of atty. he gave Moore (*Maryland Journal and Baltimore Advertiser* 23 Sep 1788).

Moore, Nicholas Ruxton, Lieutenant and then Captain of Cavalry in the Revolutionary War; d. 11 Oct 1816. He was m. on 25 Dec 1793 by Patrick Allison to Sarah Kelso, who d. Nov 1839, aged 72 (Revolutionary War Pension Application of Sarah Moore: W 26275).

Moore, Philip, Esq., of this city, was m. Tues. eve. last by Rev. Mr. Coleman, to Miss Delia Hall, second daughter of Aquila Hall, Esq., of Harford Co. (*Federal Gazette and Baltimore Daily Advertiser* 2 May 1799).

Moore, Stephen, on 27 d. 9 m. 1775 was charged with having been m. by a priest ("Minutes of Gunpowder Monthly Meeting," *QRNM:*66). [No other marriage reference found].

Moore, Stephen, died leaving a will dated 13 March 1782 and proved 8 May 1782, naming his wife Ruth, his son William, and his stepson Alexander Frazier (BAWB 3:448). Ruth [the widow of Hugh Frazier (q.v.)], m. 3rd, Clement Skerrett (q.v.) by 2 Nov 1787 when she and her husband were ordered to pay Philip Rogers, guardian of William Moore and Alexander Frazier their share of their deceased father's estates (BAOC 2:43).

Moore, Thomas, on 31 d. 8 m. 1793 had a child laid to his charge in an unmarried state ("Minutes of Gunpowder Meeting," *QRNM:*94).

Moore, William, gave notice that anyone indebted to him or to William Moore, Sr., of Baltimore, should pay at once (*Maryland Journal and Baltimore Advertiser* 23-30 Oct 1773).

Moore, William, was m. last eve. to Miss Catherine Leypold, daughter of John Leypold, Esq. of Baltimore (*Baltimore Daily Intelligencer* 7 March 1794).

Morancy, Joseph, and Ann Sparrow were married by banns on 12 Jan 1785 at St. Peter's Catholic Church, Baltimore (*Piet:* 140).

More, Mrs. [-?-], m. by 11 Oct 1799, [-?-], who was one of three legatees of James Fortune to receive a payment of $1111.11 (BAAD 13:139). The legatee was Mrs. More, sister of the testator, living in Co. Wexford, Ireland (BAWB 6:53).

More, Francis, m. by 30 Oct 1775 Ann, daughter of William Standiford MWB 41:24; abst. in *Md. Cal. of Wills* 16:141).

More, Patrick, and Ann Murray were married by banns on 24 Jan 1790 at St. Peter's Catholic Church, Baltimore (*Piet:* 140).

Moreland (Morland), Alexander, of Baltimore Co., stated he would not pay the debts of his wife Jane, who had eloped from him, and now had returned to him, but only to do him greater damage (*Md. Gaz.* 30 Sep 1762).

Morgan (Morgain), [-?-], m. by 22 Sep 1755 Anne, daughter of Edward Richards (MWB 30:26 abst. by Abst. by Gibb).; BFD 2:57).

Morgan, [-?-], m. by 12 Aug 1788 Violetta, daughter of Sophia Robinson, widow (BAWB 4:402).

Morgan, Cassandra, late Lee, on 31 d. 1 m. 1771 was reported as married to man not of our society ("Minutes of Deer Creek Meeting," *QRNM:* 134). [No other marriage reference found]. **N.B.:** a Cassandra Lee Morgan m. Zaccheus Onion Bond on 19 Jan 1797 (Harrison, "St. James' Parish Register:" 7).

Morgan, Edward, m. by 31 May 1742 Sarah, daughter of Abraham Simmons (MWB 27:405; BALR TB#A:173, 175).

Morgan, Henry, and Sarah Pike were m. 14 May 1744 (Harrison, "St John's Parish Register:" 190). Cecill Bryan, aged 72, deposed on 22 June 1773 that she had delivered all the children born to Capt. Henry and Sarah Morgan; they were: Henry, who d. in his minority without leaving any survivors; James, now living at Fell's Point, a ship-builder; Philip; and William, who also d. in his minority without leaving any survivors (BACT 1773-1784:33). William Barney, aged 54, deposed on 22 June 1773 that in 1744, 1745, and 1746 he had transacted business with Henry Morgan and that Henry and his wife went abroad to be married. Barney also mentioned John Hammond Dorsey and Henry and Sarah's son James (BACT 1773-1784:33).

Morgan, James, mariner, in his will made 11 May 1798 named Esther and Thomas Sanderson, children of Esther (BAWB 7:35).

Morgan, Jesse, on 12 d. 5 m. 1796 was charged with marrying outside the good order ("Minutes of Baltimore Meeting," *QRNM:* 226). Jesse Morgan and Sarah Scott were married by license dated 19 Aug 1795 (BAML).

Morgan, John, m. by 9 Dec 1745 Flora, widow of Joseph Peregoy (*q.v.*) of Baltimore Co. (MDAD 22:51; BAAD 5:37).

Morgan, John, Jr., and Ann Matthews, daughter of William, on 9 d. 8 m. 1798 declared their intention to marry. Their marriage was reported on 13 d. 9 m. 1798 as having been accomplished ("Minutes of Baltimore Meeting," *QRNM:* 231).

Morgan, Joseph, in Nov 1758, was charged with begetting a bastard on the body of Ann Hamilton (BAMI 1757-1759:164).

Morgan, Rashia, was charged with bastardy at the June 1759 Court and named Abraham Enloes as the father of her child (BACP HWS#7:211).

Morgan, Sarah, daughter of Lydia Morgan, on 5 d. 6 m. 1784 was reported for having accomplished her marriage by a Baptist Preacher to a man not of our society ("Minutes of Deer Creek Meeting," *QRNM:*142). [No other marriage reference found].

Morgan, Thomas, on 13 d. 8 m. 1795 requested a certificate in order to marry Sarah Amoss, daughter of William Amoss, Jr., of Gunpowder Meeting ("Minutes of Baltimore Meeting," *QRNM:*225). They declared their intention to marry on 29 d. 8 m. 1795 ("Minutes of Gunpowder Meeting," *QRNM:*97).

Morgan, William, and Sarah Price on 26 d. 2 m. 1791 declared their intention to marry ("Minutes of Gunpowder Meeting," *QRNM:*90). William Morgan, son of Benjamin and Jane, m. on 30 d. 3 m 1791, Sarah Price, daughter of Mordecai and Rachel Bliss Forbush, "Records of Gunpowder Meeting," MS. at MdHS; BAWB 5:379).

Morgan, William, and Hannah Matthews were married by license dated 10 Dec 1796 (BAML). Hannah Matthews (now Morgan), on 14 d. 9 m. 1797, was charged with marrying contrary to the good order ("Minutes of Baltimore Meeting," *QRNM:*229). William Morgan, merchant of Fell's Point, was m. last Sun. eve. by Rev. Mr. Bonsall to Miss Hannah Matthews of this town (*Federal Gazette and Baltimore Daily Advertiser* 15 Dec 1796).

Morgan, William, m. by 19 Aug 1797 Katy, admx. of John Baker (BAAD 12:331).

Morkaboy, [-?-], m. by 11 March 1778 Eleanor, the sister of William Wells who also named her two sons William and George (BAWB 3:361).

Morres, Mark. See Mark Morris.

Morris, Benjamin, m. by 6 June 1798, Elizabeth, a representative of Daniel Weaver (BAAD 12:438).

Morris, Eleanor, was named in Dec 1781 as the grandmother of John Merryman; in Feb 1782 she was named as the mother of Miss Catherine Rogers, who was aged 60 (BALR WG#H:438, 440).

Morris, James, son of Edward, in March 1757 was bound to Henry Ruff (BAMI 1755-1763).

Morris, John, and Sarah Deaver were m. on 17 May 1748 (Harrison, "St. John's Parish Register:" 197). Sarah was a daughter of Antill and Sarah Deaver, and named a granddaughter Margaret Morris (BAWB 3:177: MWB 34:179, abst. in *Md. Cal. of Wills* 13:118). John and Sarah were the parents of: Sarah Morris, who, as of 5 Jan 1774, was unmarried when she was conveyed property, including a lot in Fells Point by her uncle John Deaver (BALR AL#H:448).

Morris, John A., printer, m. last Mon. eve. Ann Field, both of this city (*Federal Gazette and Baltimore Daily Advertiser* 15 April 1797).

Morris, Mark, m. by 21 April 1780 Joanna, widow of Yocum Yown (BALR WG#G: 31).

Morris, Mark, m. by 10 Feb 1792 Catherine, widow of Cornelius Leary (BAAD 10:525). They were married by license dated 11 Feb 1786 (BAML).

Morris, Mary, was charged with bastardy at the March 1723/4 Court, at the March 1730/1 Court, and again at the June 1732 Court (BACP IS&TW#3:201, 331, (BACP HWS#7:96, 156, 288).

Morris, Thomas, and Elizabeth Jackson were m. on 14 July 1698 (Harrison, "St. George's Parish Register:" 178). In June 1711 Elizabeth was named as the widow of Simeon Jackson (*q.v.*) (BACP IS#B:210).

Morris, William, and Rebecca Rock were m. on 10 Sep 1800 (Marr. Register of Rev. Lewis Richards, MS.690 at MdHS). In his will, made 29 Sep 1800 William Morris of Old Town named his wife Rebecca Morris otherwise Rebecca Rock, and her uncle William Day (BAWB 6:300).

Morrison, Alice, was charged with bastardy at the March 1741 Court (BACP TB&TR:294).

Morrison, Patrick, and Priscilla Constable, widow, were m. by lic. on 12 July 1796 at St. Peter's Catholic Church, Baltimore (*Piet:* 140).

Mortimer, Edward, m. by 7 Aug 1741 Eleanor, mother of Easter Bray (BALR HWS#1A:536).

Morton, Jacob, m. by 23 Nov 1796 Mary, daughter of Vincent Tepper (BAAD 12:219).

Morton, John Andrew, was married last Mon. eve. by Rev. Richards, to Miss Mary Grangett, both of this town (*Federal Intelligencer and Baltimore Daily Gazette* 28 Jan 1795). In June 1797 Mary was named as a daughter of Andrew Granget (BAOC Petition of John Moreton, 1797).

Morton (Moreton), Nathaniel, of Baltimore, and Miss Sally Copeland of Harford Co. were m. 1ˢᵗ inst. by Rev. Mr. Allen (*Federal Gazette and Baltimore Advertiser* 3 March 1798).

Morton, William, formerly of York Co., Va., but now of Baltimore Co., in his will, made 2 April 1750 stated his children William and Elizabeth were to be sent to their grandfather Jacob Harrington until they 'were fit to go to trades' (MWB 28:30 abst. by Gibb).

Morving, Jane, was charged with bastardy at the March 1683/4 Court (BACP D:131).

Moss, John Frederick, and Nancy Wheeler were married by license dated 27 July 1784 (BAML). On 24 May 1790 Frederick Moss' wife was named as an heir of Samuel Wheeler (BAAD 10:149).

Mossman, Archibald, d. by May 1775 leaving two daughters, Margaret and Mary, who were made wards of John McClellan (BAMI 1772, 1775-1781: 120)

Motherby, Charles, m. by 27 April 1742, Priscilla, extx. of John Simkins (MDTP 31:278).

Motherby, Charles, and Ann Strange were ordered to appear at the vestry held the first Tues. in Sep 1749, to give their reasons for unlawful cohabitation. William Ambrose and Susanna Hague were also summoned to give evidence. On 3 Oct 1749, Motherby was ordered by the vestry to put the said Ann Strange away and not to cohabit with her or frequent her company. On 6 Feb 1749/50, Motherby was still persisting in his obstinacy. In July 1750, Motherby and Strange were still unlawfully cohabiting (Reamy. *St. Thomas'*: *pp.* 113, 114, 116, 118, 123). On 25 Feb 1755 he stated that his wife Ann had eloped (BACT TR#E: 185).

Mouler, Elizabeth, admx., on 2 Aug 1800 posted bond to administer the estate of Alexander Knox (*q.v.*) (BAAB 9:51).

Mounseuer, Elizabeth, servant of Charles Ridgely, was charged with bastardy at the March 1738/9 Court (BACP (BACP HWS#1A:351, HWS#TR:11).

Mountfield, John, m. by 15 June 1698 Ann, widow of Thomas Morris (BALR IS#IK: 251).

Moutray, Ann, was charged with bastardy at the Nov 1717 Court (BACP IS#1A:204).

Mulatto Bess, servant to the Widow Day, was charged with bastardy at the Aug 1711 Court and named William Bond as the father (BACP IS#B:2470.

Muilatto Nann, servant to Thomas Sheredine, confessed to bastardy and on 3 March 1746/7 was ordered to serve for the county for seven years after her present servitude. Her child, Mulatto Rachel, was sold to Thomas Sheredine until she was 31. (BACP TB%TR#1:396).

Mulatto Posen, was charged with bastardy at the June 1718 Court and her three children, born out of wedlock, Mulattos Ann, Rebecca, and Joseph, were ordered bound to serve Rebecca Day (BACP (BACP HWS#1A;226).

Mulatto Ruth, servant to John Hawkins of Robert, confessed to bastardy on 3 March 1746/7; she confessed to bastardy again the June 1750 Court (BACP TR#6:28, TB&TR#1:416-417).

Mulhern, Bernard, and Susanna Randall were m. by lic. on 30 July 1797 at St. Peter's Catholic Church, Baltimore (*Piet:* 140).

Mullan, Henry, and Susan O'Brien, natives of Co. Tyrone, were m. by lic. on 28 Dec 1799 at St. Peter's Catholic Church, Baltimore (*Piet.* 140).

Mulholland (Molholland), Charles, in Aug 1744 was charged with begetting a bastard on the body of Elizabeth Claron (BACP 1743-1745:320).

Mullen (or Muller), Samuel, merchant, and Rachel Botner, daughter of Elias Botner of Baltimore, were m. last eve. by Rev. Bend (*Baltimore Telegraphe* 7 March 1800; the *Baltimore American* of 7 March 1800 gives his name as Muller).

Mullin, [-?-], may have m. by 26 Dec 1785 [-?-], daughter of Jonathan Hanson who named a granddaughter Mary Mullin in his will (BAWB 4:115)

Mullins, Mary, widow of William Mullins, m. by 1791 Jonas Osborne (*q.v.*) (BOCP: Petition of Mary Mullins, 1791).

Multshire (Multshair), Sarah, servant to William Murphy, confessed to bastardy at the March 1743/4 Court (BACP 1743-1745:71,168).

Mumma, Barbara, will petition the Assembly for a law to prevent her husband, David Mumma, from conveying his property away from his wife and children (*Maryland Journal and Baltimore Advertiser* 20 Oct 1789). David Mumma and Barbara Hickman were married by license dated 8 July 1783 (BAML).

Mummery, Thomas, of Hager's Town, and Kitty Fishburn of Baltimore were m. last eve. by Rev. Kurtz (*Baltimore Telegraphe* 14 July 1797).

Mummy, Benjamin, of Baltimore, stated he would not pay the debts of his wife Barbara (*Maryland Journal and Baltimore Advertiser* 10 Nov 1786).

Mummy, Christopher, m. by 4 Aug 1783 Rebecca, sister of Elizabeth and Marcella Owings (BAWB 3:523).

Mummy, Samuel, blacksmith, m. by 11 Nov 1782 [-?-], sister of Ephraim Owings; they were the parents of Thomas, Joshua, Jesse, and Elizabeth Mummy (BAWB 3:567).

Münche, Georg Phillip, m. by 27 March 1767 Elisabeta Schneiderin ("First Record Book for the Reformed and Lutheran Congregations at Manchester, Baltimore (now Carroll) Co." *MGSB* 35:270, 271 where his name is given as Mönche).

Munday, Edward, d. by 9 Aug 1757 having m. Hannah [-?-], who in her will of that date named her former husband, and her children Francis and Thomas Taylor, and a son Isaac [Isaiah] Cord (MWB 30:371 abst. by Gibb).

Munnikhuysen, John, of Baltimore, merchant and Miss Mary Howard, daughter of Thomas Gassaway Howard, Esq., of Baltimore Co., were m. Thurs. eve. last at the dwelling house of Mr. Thomas Sadler, by Rev. John Ireland (*Federal Gazette and Baltimore Daily Advertiser* 4 March 1799).

Munroe, Margaret, was charged with bastardy at the Nov 1750 Court and confessed at the March 1750/1 Court (BACP TR#6:1, 283-284).

Munsch, Joh. Adam, m. by 9 Dec 1766 Anna Margaret Stamlerin ("First Record Book for the Reformed and Lutheran Congregations at Manchester, Baltimore (now Carroll) Co.," *MGSB* 35:270).

Munson, Joel M., and Ann Swan, widow of Matthew Swan (*q.v.*), entered into marriage articles on 12 Aug 1797 (BALR WG#51:570). Joel M. Munson, was m. last Sun. eve. by Rev. Mr. Richards, to Mrs. Ann Swan of this city (*Federal Gazette and Baltimore Daily Advertiser* 16 Aug 1797).

Murphey, [-?-], m. by 20 Feb 1754 Mary, mother of James Godfrey (BACT TR#E:123),

Murphey, Catherine, servant to Col. Nathan Rigbie, confessed to bastardy in 1746 (BACP TB&TR#1:393-394).

Murphey, William, on 5 June 1749 was called son-in-law in the will of Francis Dorsey (MWB 27:132 abst. by Gibb).

Murphy, [-?-], m. by 11 Oct 1799 Mary, who was one of three legatees of James Fortune to receive a payment of $1111.11 (BAAD 13:139). She was Mary Murphy, sister of the testator, living in Co. Wexford, Ireland (BAWB 6:53).

Murphy, Daniel, and Charlotte Weaver were m. 20 Feb 1798 (Richards' Marr. register at MdHS). On 6 June 1798 Charlotte was named as a representative of Daniel Weaver (BAAD 12:438).

Murphy, Dorcas, was charged with bastardy at the March 1739/40 Court (BACP HWS#TR#150).

Murphy, Edward, of Cecil Co., m. by 2 Oct 1715 Jane, daughter of Thomas Greenfield (BALR TR#A:376).

Murphy, James, m. by 18 March 1768 Hannah, daughter of William Cole of Nottingham, whose will was written and recorded in Baltimore Co., Md. ("Chester County Wills."*MGSB* 35 (4) (Fall 1994) 577).

Murphy, James, m. by 25 Dec 1779 Eleanor, daughter of James Kelly, husbandman (BAWB 3:397; BAAD 10:288).

Murphy, John, and Miss Ann Warmingham, both of Baltimore, were m. last eve. by Rev. Dr. McCloskey (*Baltimore Daily Intelligencer* 8 Nov 1793).

Murphy, John, and Mary Healy, natives of Ireland, were m. by lic. on 6 June 1799 at St. Peter's Catholic Church, Baltimore (*Piet:* 140).

Murphy, Mary, was charged with bastardy at the March 1754 Court, and confessed to having a child out of wedlock with David Musselman (BACP BB#A:27). She may be the Mary Murphy, spinner who, on 20 Feb 1754 bound her son James Godfrey, aged 2 years, 5 months, to William Ray and his wife Martha, until the boy was 21 (BACT TR#E:123).

Murphy, Patrick, m. by 1702 Sarah, widow of Edward Teale, and admx. of John Copas (MDTP 19A:119; INAC 23:90; BALR TR#RA:38).

Murphy, Patrick, and Susanna Kearns were m. by lic. on 20 June 1790 at St. Peter's Catholic Church, Baltimore (*Piet:* 141).

Murphy, William, m. by 10 Sep 1774 Mary, admx. of Moses Campbell (BAAD 7:224).

Murra, John. See John Murray.

Murray, [-?-], m. by 19 April 1732 Mary, daughter of William Wheeler (MWB 21:894 abst. in *Md. Cal. of Wills* 7:252).

Murray, [-?-], Mary, daughter of Dutton Lane by 27 June 1759 (BACT B#G:484).

Murray, [-?-], m. by 2 Sep 1761 Margaret, dau, of Philip Jones who named his granddaughter Elizabeth, daughter of Margaret (BAWB 2:121; MWB 31:568 abst. by Gibb).

Murray, Archibald, on 26 d. 2 m. 1795 was reported as having accomplished his marriage contrary to the good order ("Minutes of Deer Creek Meeting," *QRNM:*155). [No other marriage reference found].

Murray, Edward, and Mary Morton were married by license dated 3 Sep 1779 (BAML). In his will made 24 Oct 1794 Murray named his step-daus. Adeline Geist and Margaret and Mary Morton (BAWB 5:202). Mrs. Mary Murray, wife of Edward Murray, merchant, d. last Wed. morning in Baltimore, and was buried in St. Paul's Churchyard (*Maryland Journal and Baltimore Advertiser* 13 April 1790).

Murray, Ephraim, of Washington Co., Tenn., and Margaret Doyle were m. by license dated 18 March 1788 (BAML); on 22 Dec 1789 Margaret was named as a daughter of Richard Doyle of Pipe Creek and in 1796 as a daughter of Sarah Doyle (BAWB 5:3, 369), On 30 July 1796 Margaret was named as a daughter of Richard and Sarah Doyle, and sister of Mary Doyle, all of Baltimore Co., dec. (BALR WG#XX:444).

Murray, Francis, and Jane Hutton were m. by lic. on 16 Oct 1795 at St. Peter's Catholic Church, Baltimore (*Piet:* 141).

Murray, Frederick, m. by 9 April 1793, Elizabeth, daughter of Anthony Haines (BAAD 11:240, 12:277).

Murray, John, m. by 2 June 1760 Elizabeth, admx. of Thomas Dew (*q.v.*), and mother of William Dew and Elizabeth Dew, a minor orphan (MDAD 44:319; MDTP 37:282; BAAD 4:307; BALR B#K:126; BACM 1).

Murray, John, m. by 22 Sep 1761 [-?-], daughter of John Long (BAAD 4:342; MDAD 47:19).

Murray, John, m. by 29 Oct 1765 Ruth, daughter of Elizabeth Trotten (BAWB 3:44; MDAD 59:285).

Murray (Murra), John, on 28 d. 2 m. 1782 was charged with several offenses including having gone out in marriage to a young woman not of our society and having been m. by a Baptist Preacher ("Minutes of Deer Creek Meeting," *QRNM:*141). [No other marriage reference found].

Murray, John, b. 29 Jan 1751, d. 9 Feb 1833, and Diana Cox, b. 15 July 1750, were m. by 8 March 1769 when their daughter Elizabeth was born ("Murray Bible."*The Notebook* 9 (4) (Dec 1993) 40). Diana was a daughter of Jacob Cox (BAWB 6:121).

Murray, Josephus, m. by 17 Dec 1725 Sarah, daughter of Joseph Hawkins (MWB 18:433 abst. in *Md. Cal. of Wills* 5:209). On 12 Feb 1732 she was named as egatee of Joseph Hawkins of BACo (MDAD 11:633).

Murray, Josephus, Jr., m. by 20 Aug 1747 Margaret, widow of John Rattenbury (*q.v.*) (BAAD 4:168; BALR TR#C:91).

Murray, Melchizedek, son of James and Jemima, dec., and Sophia Giles, daughter of John and Sarah, were m. on 13 d. 9 m. 1723 (Records of West River Monthly Meeting, *QRSM:*26; MWB 18:429 abst. in *Md. Cal. of Wills* 5:208).

Murray, Rebecca, before marriage Colegate, on 22 d., 1 m. 1772, was charged with being married by a priest ("Minutes of Gunpowder Meeting," *QRNM:*62). She was a daughter of John Colegate, farmer (BAWB 3:470). [No other marriage reference found].

Murray, Zachariah, was charged with bastardy at the March 1768 Court (BAMI 1768-1769:6).

Murray (Murrey), Zachariah, and Margaret Simmons were m. on 27 May 1767 (Harrison, "St. John's Parish Register:" 219). On 28 May 1770 Margaret was named as an heir of George Simmonds (BAAD 6:188).

Musselman, David, in March 1754 was charged with begetting a bastard on the body of Mary Murphy (BACP BB#A:27).

Mutchner, [-?-], m. by 14 Dec 1791 Alice, admx. of David Johnson (BAAD 10:490).

Myerly, [-?-], m. by 7 June 1794 Magdalen, daughter of Jacob Shaffer (BAWB 6:249).

Myers (Miers), [-?-], m. by 21 July 1775 Henrietta, daughter of James Taylor whose will named grandchildren James and Laama Miers (MWB 41:408; abst. in *Md. Cal. of Wills* 16:204).

Myers, [-?-], m. by 11 May 1787 Sarah (Sary), daughter of Zachariah Strouble (BAWB 4:272).

Myers, Charles, merchant of Baltimore, m. Betsy, only of the late Capt. Thomas Jarold (*Maryland Journal and Baltimore Advertiser* 2 Jan 1787).

Myers, Daniel, m. by 6 Nov 1792, m. by 6 Nov 1792 Elizabeth, legatee of Philip Deale (BAAD 11:154).

Myers (Myre), Jacob, m. by 13 June 1769 [-?-], daughter of Ulrick and Esther Whistler (BAAD 7:30; MDAD 61:165).

Myers, Jacob, Esq., was m. 1st inst. by the Rev. Dr. Hopkins, to Miss Eliza Ross, daughter of David Ross, Esq., of Cumberland Co., Va. (*Federal Gazette and Baltimore Daily Advertiser* 11 May 1797).

Myers, Jacob, was m. last eve. by Rev. Mr. Morrell, to Sarah Warren, both of this city (*Federal Gazette and Baltimore Daily Advertiser* 6 Dec 1800).

Myers, John, was given an allowance for keeping an orphan child named Elizabeth Taylor (Levy List for 1772).

Myers, Joseph, tailor, was m. last Sun. eve. by Rev. Mr. Otterbein to Miss Catherine Small (*Federal Gazette and Baltimore Daily Advertiser* 19July 1796).

Myers, Marazin, on 16 May 1795 received an equal share of estate of Philip Deale (BAAD 12:9).

Myers, Peter Nelson, and Elizabeth Lapstein were m. by lic. on 11 Dec 1798 at St. Peter's Catholic Church, Baltimore (*Piet:* 141).

Myers, Philip, native of Germany, and Hannah Henly were m. by lic. on 5 Nov 1798 at St. Peter's Catholic Church, Baltimore (*Piet:* 141).

Myers, See also Meyers.

Myles, Zachary, merchant of this city, was m. last eve. at his own house by Rev. Mr. Morrell, to Miss Jane M'Machan of Harford Co. (*Federal Gazette and Baltimore Daily Advertiser* 12 Sep 1799).

Myrick, [-?-], m. by 1 April 1797 Lilley, admx. of George Reese (BAAD 12:249).

"N"

Nabb, Elisha, and Mary [-?-] were m. by 29 Aug 1785 when their daughter Rebecca was b. ("John Day Bible," *MBR* 2:24-27).

Nace, [-?-], m. by 26 Dec 1798 Catherine, daughter of Peter Fowble (BAWB 6:210).

Nace, Major William, was m. last eve. by Rev. Mr. Butler, to Miss Elizabeth Mury [prob. Murray], both of Baltimore Co. (*Federal Gazette and Baltimore Daily Advertiser* 14 July 1797).

Nailor, Jane. See Jane Cates.

Nailor, Samuel, on 31 d. 7 m. 1795 was reported as having been married by a hireling priest to a woman not of our society ("Minutes of Gunpowder Meeting," *QRNM:*96). Samuel Naylor [*sic*] and Rebecca Perrigoe were m. by lic. dated 14 Jan 1795 (BAML).

Nappert, Samuel, m. by 10 Aug 1791, Elizabeth Bell who received an equal share of the estate of William Bell (BAAD 10:427).

Nash, [-?-], m. by 3 May 1787 Eliz., daughter of Andrew Davidson of Baltimore Town (BAWB 4:239).

Nash, Elizabeth, was charged with bastardy at Aug Court, 1742 (BACP TB#D:1, 9).

Naylor, James, of Gunpowder Meeting and Margaret Marsh on 12 d. 12 m. 1799 announced their intention to marry ("Minutes of Baltimore Meeting," *QRNM:*236).

Neal, Abner, and Miss Barbara Reed, both of this city, were m. last Thurs. by Rev. Mr. Reed (*Federal Gazette and Baltimore Daily Advertiser* 3 July 1799).

Neale, Edward, and Elizabeth Martin were m. by lic. on 26 Jan 1796 at St. Peter's Catholic Church, Baltimore (*Piet:* 141).

Neale, Eleanor, was charged with bastardy having born a child at the house of Samuel Dorsey in 1720; she was charged again at the Aug 1723 Court (BACP IS#C:436, IS&TW#2:437).

Nearn. See Nern.

Neary, Peter, and Polly Shamms (Shammond) were m. on 1 Aug 1784 (Marr. Returns of Rev. William West, Scharf Papers, MS.1999 at MdHS). Mary Nary [*sic*], admx. with will annexed, on 31 Jan 1798, posted bond to administer the estate of Mary Rose Shammond (BAAB 8:383; see also BAWB 6:77).

Neece, [-?-], m. by 4 Nov 1795 Elizabeth, daughter of Henry Neff (BAWB 5:388).

Neess, Johannes, m. by 23 April 1790 Catherina Faubelin ("First Record Book for the Reformed and Lutheran Congregations at Manchester, Baltimore (now Carroll) Co.," *MGSB* 35:285).

Negro Alexius, Bishop Carroll's servant, m. 30 Nov 1799 Free Negro Henrietta, Mulatto woman at St. Peter's Catholic Church, Baltimore (*Piet:* 126).

Negro George, was charged with bastardy in 1711 and was named as the father of Mary Rye's child (BACP IS#B:245).

Negro Hector, m. 28 Dec 1799 Negro Marie Louise at St. Peter's Catholic Church, Baltimore (*Piet:* 126).

Negro Jean Jacques, m. 26 April 1800 Negro Mary Agnes at St. Peter's Catholic Church, Baltimore (*Piet:* 126) .

Negro Mingo, was charged with bastardy in 1714 and was named as the father of Mary Wenham's children (BACP IS#B: 505, 537).

Neighbours, Henry, and Ann Knott of Baltimore Co. were m. by lic. on 24 Dec 1794 at St. Peter's Catholic Church, Baltimore (*Piet:* 141).

Neil, Samuel, d. by 22 Feb 1776 by which time his widow [-?-], had m. Abraham Gorman (*q.v.*) (MDTP 47:14).

Neill, Michael, and Eleanor McCarthy, natives of Ireland, were m. by lic. on 12 June 1799 at St. Peter's Catholic Church, Baltimore (*Piet:* 141).

Nelson, Benjamin, d. by 5 Feb 1782 leaving an admx. Margaret, wife of John Winning (*q.v.*) whose will dated 15 Jan 1787 named a 'daughter-in-law' Susanna Nelson (BAAB 2:375; BAWB 4:369).

Nelson, Benjamin, student at law, in his will made 10 Sep 1783 named Dr. Ephraim Howard of Elk Ridge his uncle (BAWB 3:590).

Nelson, John, and Frances Rhodes were m. 12 Jan 1718 (Harrison, "St. John's Parish Register:" 9). On 7 Nov 1734 Frances was named as a sister of Henry Rhodes (BALR HWS#M: 131).

Nelson, John, in 1763 was fined for fornication and bastardy (BAMI 1755-1763).

Nern (Nearn), Elizabeth, was charged with bastardy, confessed, and was fined at the March 1745/6 Court (BACP Liber 1743-1745, pp. 806-806). Priscilla Nearn, daughter of Elizabeth Nearn, was b. 12 Sep 1745 (Harrison, "St. John's Parish Register:" 147).

Nevis, Hezekiah, and Ann Clark were married by license dated 4 Dec 1790 (BAML). Ann was named as a daughter of Samuel Clark on 28 Sep 1795 (BAWB 6:90). Sophia Clark in her will made 2 June 1798 named her daughter Ann Nevis, and named her grandchildren William and Sophia Nevis (BAWB 6:127).

Newborough, Sarah. See Sarah Hayhurst.

Newell, Mary, was charged with bastardy at Nov Court 1740 (BACP HWS#TR:350).

Newgate, Jonathan, in 1721 was charged with begetting a bastard on the body of Mary Long (BACP IS&TW#1:9).

Newman, Ann, servant of James Poteete, was charged with bastardy at the Aug 1744 Court. She was ordered to be whipped with 15 lashes (BACP 1743-1745:283, 389).

Newman, Catherine, was charged with bastardy at the Nov 1719 Court (BACP IS#C:245).

Newman (Nunin), Dennis, m. by 19 Sep 1709 Katherine, widow and extx, of Thomas Knightsmith (BAAD 1:348, 2:104; INAC 30:18, 33A:79; BAWB 1:140: MDTP 21:143).

Newman, Henry, and Sarah James were married on or about 23 Aug 1791 (Marr. Returns of Rev. William West, Scharf Papers, MS.1999 at MdHS). On 22 Jan 1794 Sarah Newman, admx. posted bond to administer the estate of Hannah James (BAAB 8:561; BOCP Petition of Henry Newman, 1792)

Newman, Thomas, b. 16 May 1744, in Nov 1757 was bound to Abraham Jarrett (BAMI 1755-1763).

Newsome, John, and Ann Stinchcomb were m. on 16 Feb 1715 (Harrison, "St. George's Parish Register:" 220). She m. 2nd, William Smith (*q.v.*).

Newton, Ann, aged 8 last 5 Nov, daughter of Ann Newton, in Nov 1763 was bound to William Aisquith to age 16 (BAMI 1755-1763).

Newton, Mary, in 1761 was fined for fornication and bastardy (BAMI 1755-1763).

Newton, Capt. William, and Mrs. Rachel Lawrence were m. [date not given] (*Maryland Journal and Baltimore Advertiser* 31 Dec 1782). William Newton and Rachel Lawrence were m. on 24 Dec 1782 ("Register of First Presbyterian Church, Baltimore," MS. at MdHS: 11).

Nice, Cornelius, and Elizabeth Webster were m. by lic. dated 26 March 1785 (BAML). In July Nice gave notice that his wife Elizabeth had deserted him (*Maryland Gazette or Baltimore General Advertiser* 8 July 1785).

Nicholas, [-?-], m. by 21 Jan 1772 Mary, daughter of Charles Ridgely (BALR AL#D:475).

Nicholas, Col. George, of Va., and Polly, daughter of John Smith of Baltimore, were m. [date not given] (*Maryland Journal and Baltimore Advertiser* 5 Jan 1779). In his will made 23 Aug 1791 John Smith named his daughter Margaret [*sic*] Nicholas and his grandsons Smith Nicholas and Carey Nicholas (BAWB 5:164).

Nicholas, Philip N., Esq., of Va., was m. last eve. by Rev. Dr. Allison, to Miss Mary Spear of this city (*Federal Gazette and Baltimore Daily Advertiser* 19 Feb 1799).

Nicholls (Nicholson), John, d. by Nov 1693 when his extx. Mary had m. 2nd, John Warfoote (*q.v.*).

Nichols, Henry, and Miss R. Smith, both of Baltimore, were m. on last Thurs. eve. (*Baltimore Daily Intelligencer* 7 Dec 1793).

Nicholson, Benjamin, m. Mary, daughter of John Ridgely (BAWB 3:187). On 19 Feb 1786 Polly was named as a daughter of Mary Ridgely who was the widow of John Ridgely (BAWB 4:189).

Nicholson, James, in 1763 was convicted of bastardy (BAMI 1755-1763).

Nicholson, John, of Baltimore, merchant, was m. Sun., 26th ult., to Susanna Peachey, daughter of Col. William Peachey of Milden Hall, Richmond Co., Va. (*Maryland Journal and Baltimore Advertiser* 8 May 1789).

Nicholson, Dr. John, and Matilda Smith, both of Baltimore Co., were m. last eve. at Blenheim Hall by Rev. Mr. Coleman (*Baltimore Daily Intelligencer* 26 March 1794). On 1 Aug 1798 Matilda Heath Smith was named in the in administration account of Sarah Smith, *adm. de b. n.* of James Smith (BAAD 12:463). In 1795 he was named as a son-in-law of Sarah Smith, surviving admx. of Benjamin Franklin (Answer of George Fitzhugh, BOCP Petitions, 1795).

Nicholson, John, m. by 5 March 1795 [-?-], legatee of Ruth Ingram (BAAD 11:523).

Nicholson, Nathan, and Ruth Bond were m. on 16 March 1749 (Harrison, "St. John's Parish Register:" 201). By 30 Oct 1765 Ruth was named as a daughter of William Bond and sister of Cassandra Bond (BAWB 5:12; see also BALR TR#D:386).

Nicholson, Nathan, m. by 26 Jan 1765 Ruth Stansbury (BACT B#G:42).

Nicholson, Nicholas, m. by 10 June 1772 Mary, sister of William and John Barrett (BALR AL#E:111).

Nicholson, William, and Mary, widow of John Connell (*q.v.*), were m. on 24 April 1750 Harrison, "St. Paul's Parish Register:" 164). She m. 1st, John Forty (*q.v.*), 2nd, John Connell (*q.v.*), and, 4th, by 11 Jan 1763 Elisha Hall (*q.v.*. (MWB 31:363; BAAD 6:118, 7:191; MINV 80:401, 402).

Nicklin, Philip, and Juliana, daughter of Benjamin Chew, Esq., were m. last Tues. eve. in Philadelphia by Rev. Dr. White (*Baltimore Evening Post* 4 April 1793).

Nicodemus, John Louis, and, Ann Maria Neff were married by license dated 24 Dec 1784; she was a daughter of Henry Neff (FRML; "Nicodemus Bible Record," *MGSB* 39 (1) 73; BAWB 5:388).

Nicolle, John Baptist, native of the Island of Guadeloupe, and Mary Glace, native of Angouleme, France, were m. by lic. on 12 Aug 1799 at St. Peter's Catholic Church, Baltimore (*Piet:* 141).

Nicolls, James, and Charlotte Graham, daughter of Charles Graham Esq., were m. a few days ago at Lower Marlborough in Calvert Co. (*Maryland Journal and Baltimore Advertiser* 5 July 1791).

Nicols (Nicholls), Henry, Esq., m. Thursday eve. last Miss R. Smith of this town (*Baltimore Daily Intelligencer* 7 Dec 1793). Henry Nicols and Rebecca Smith were

m. on 5 Dec 1793 (Harrison, "St. Paul's Parish Register:" 279). On 21 Dec 1795 [1796?] Richard Smith named Rebecca Nicols as his sister (BAWB 6:13).

Niger, Michael, and Sarah Morgan were m. on 18 Jan 1793 (Harrison, "St. James' Parish Register:" 5). Sarah Niger, formerly Morgan, on 21 d. 2 m. 1793 was found guilty of marrying a man not of our society with the assistance of a hireling preacher ("Minutes of Deer Creek Meeting," *QRNM:* 152).

Ninde, James, and Miss Catherine Blyth, both of Fell's Point, were m. last eve. by Rev. Richards (*Federal Gazette and Baltimore Daily Advertiser* 27 Feb 1797).

Niser, Abraham, in Feb 1796 was made a ward of Michael Grauer (BAOC 3:181).

Nixon, [-?-], m. by 7 Nov 1766 Permelia, daughter of Christopher Divers (BAWB 3:33).

Nixon, (Nixson) Thomas, and Sarah Thompson were m. on 23 July 1747 (Harrison, "St. John's Parish Register:" 161).On 24 June 1762 she m. Christopher Divers (*q.v.*).

Noble, Anthony, merchant of Baltimore, d. by 1785 having m. Hettey, sister of Jno. McAlister (BPET; Noble, Anthony, 1785, Box 1, Folder 18).

Noel, Louis Philippe, m. by 3 May 1798 Marie Flore Eugenie Estienne, legatee of Frederick Estienne (BAAD 12:428).

Noland, Thomas, m. by 23 Sep 1723 Mary, daughter of Matthew Hawkins who named his daughters Mary, Dinah, Ann and Elizabeth in his will dated 14 April 1705 and proved 24 April 1705 (BALR IS#G:208; MWB 3:446).

Noll, Anton, m. by 24 Sep 1764[?] Maria Magdalena Prenlin ("First Record Book for the Reformed and Lutheran Congregations at Manchester, Baltimore (now Carroll) Co.," *MGSB* 35:268).

Noll, Anton, m. by 24 Feb 1768 Maria Magdalena Brünnle ("First Record Book for the Reformed and Lutheran Congregations at Manchester, Baltimore (now Carroll) Co.," *MGSB* 35:271).

Noll, Franss., m. by 15 Aug 1784 Elisabeth Reinhardtin ("First Record Book for the Reformed and Lutheran Congregations at Manchester, Baltimore (now Carroll) Co.," *MGSB* 35:281).

Noonan, Edward, and Mary Fitzpatrick, natives of Ireland, were m. by lic. on 11 May 1797 at St. Peter's Catholic Church, Baltimore (*Piet:* 141).

Norbury, George, and Mary Burgess were married by license dated 22 Sep 1798 (BAML). Mary Norbury, formerly Burgess, on 10 d. 1 m. 1799 reportedly had her marriage accomplished contrary to the good order ("Minutes of Baltimore Meeting," *QRNM:*232).

Norquay, Magnus, and Jane Trotman were m. on 17 July 1795 ("Register of First Presbyterian Church, Baltimore," MS. at MdHS: 11). Jane was named as the widow of George Trotman (BAOC Petitions: Norquay, Magnus, 1795).

Norrington, Francis, and Mary Everett were m. on 19 Feb 1749/50 (Harrison, "St. John's Parish Register:" 200, 244); on 10 March 1758 Mary was named as a daughter in the will of John Everett (MWB 30:482 abst. by Gibb).

Norrington, Mary, was indicted for bastardy in March 1733/4 and tried in June (BACP IS&TW#4:121). Mary Norrington m. Thomas Hayes on 11 Aug 1735 (Harrison, "St. John's Parish Register:" 99, 149). Thomas and Mary were the parents of: James, b. 21 Oct 1728; Edmund, b. 21 or 22 Nov 1739; Elizabeth, b. 12 Feb 1745; and Mary, b. 15 July 1747 (Harrison, "St. John's Parish Register:" 149, 153).

Norris, [-?-], may have m. by 1 May 1763 Elizabeth, daughter of William Kitely (BAWB 2:367; BFD 4:96).

Norris, [-?-], m. by 2 Sep 1793 Elizabeth of Bourbon Co., Ky., daughter of Thomas
Cole, dec., of Baltimore Co. (BACT 1791-1794, MS 2865.1 at MdHS: 263; BAAD
12:18).

Norris, **Abraham,** and Rebecca Cross were married by license dated 22 Jan 1783
(BAML). On 15 Feb 1792 Rebecca was named as the admx. of Henry Cross
(BAAD 10:542).

Norris, **Edward,** m. 2nd, c1689, Sarah Wichell, widow of John Kemp (*BCF:*471). Sarah
m. 3rd, John Thomas (*q.v.*), and 4th, Thomas Matthews (*q.v.*).

Norris, **Edward,** m. by 13 March 1744 Hannah, daughter of Daniel Scott (MWB 24:81
abst. by Gibb). On 2 May 1759 Hannah was named as a named as a daughter in the
will of Elizabeth Scott (MWB 30:493).

Norris, **Edward,** and Elizabeth Amos were m. 21 Nov 1771 (Harrison, "St. John's Parish
Register:" 263). Elizabeth Norris, before marriage Amos, on 25 d. 12 m. 1771, was
charged with marrying outside the Society ("Minutes of Gunpowder Meeting,"
*QRNM:*62).

Norris, **Elizabeth,** on 25 d. 7 m. 1795 was reported as having as having been married by
a hireling priest ("Minutes of Gunpowder Meeting," *QRNM:*97). [No other
marriage reference found].

Norris, **James,** and Elizabeth Davis were m. on 1 Jan 1744 (Harrison, "St. John's Parish
Register:" 191). On 20 Nov 1769 Elizabeth was named as a sister of Henry Davis
(BAWB 3:149).

Norris, **James,** son of Edward, and Philizanna Barton were m. on 2 Aug 1750 (Harrison,
"St. John's Parish Register:" 201). On 3 Dec 1756 Phyllis was named as a daughter
of James Barton who d. intestate, and who was a son of Thomas Barton (BALR
BB#I:620).

Norris, **James,** son of Edward, m. by 4 April 1770 Sarah, granddaughter of Benjamin
Norris (MWB 38:591).

Norris, **Lloyd,** merchant of this city, was m. last eve. by Rev. Mr. Ireland, to Miss Jane
Peterkin of Fell's Point (*Federal Gazette and Baltimore Daily Advertiser* 8 Nov
1799).

Norris, **Sarah,** was charged with bastardy, confessed, and fined, on 4 Nov 1746 (BACP
TB&TR#1:245-246).

Norris, **Sarah,** aged over 16, daughter of Thomas Norris, dec., in Nov 1772 chose Joseph
Norris her guardian (BAMI 1772, 1775-1781: 62)

Norris, **Thomas,** and Elizabeth McComas were m. on 20 Dec 1736 (Harrison, "St. John's
Parish Register:" 76). On 8 Oct 1760 Elizabeth was named as a daughter of
Alexander McComas of Baltimore Co. (MWB 31:179). On 26 April 1762,
Elizabeth Norris was paid a sum by Thomas and Hannah Miles [Hannah was the
widow of Alexander McComas] (BAAD 4:365).

Norris, **Thomas,** and Avarilla Scott were m. on 10 Oct 1738 (Harrison, "St. John's Parish
Register:" 120). On 6 April 1744 Avarilla was named as a daughter of Nathaniel
and Avarilla (Raven) Scott (BALR TB#C:471).

Norris, **Thomas,** in Nov 1756 was charged with begetting a bastard on the body of
Rebecca Potee (BACP BB#C:311). They were m. at St. John's Parish on 11 Sep
1757 (Harrison, "St. John's Parish Register:" 216).

Norris, **Thomas,** son of John and Sarah, b. 5 d. 6 m. 1769, m. 22 d., 11 m., 1792, Ann
Cowman, b. 24 d. 7 m. 1771 ("William Thomas Watson Bible," *MBR* 2:169-171).

Norris, William, of Va., and Miss Sally Schaeffer, daughter of Baltzer Schaeffer, of this city, were m. last eve. by Rev, Dr. Allison (*Federal Gazette and Baltimore Daily Advertiser* 27 Dec 1799; *Baltimore Telegraphe* 6 Feb 1799).

Norton, Dennis, and Margaret Murphy were m. by lic. on 12 March 1797 at St. Peter's Catholic Church, Baltimore (*Piet:* 141).

Norton, John, in his will proved 3 April 1727 named his wife Elizabeth as extx. (MWB 19:97 abst. in *Md. Cal. of Wills* 6:15). Thomas and Elizabeth Harryman (*q.v.*), execs., on 15 July 1727 posted bond to administer the estate of John Norton (BAAB 2:341).

Norton, Stephen, on 29 d. 2 m. 1776 announced his intention to marry Sophia Jay, daughter of Thomas Jay, dec. ("Minutes of Deer Creek Meeting," *QRNM:* 137).

Norton, William, and Elizabeth Clark were m. on 1 Feb 1722 (Harrison, "St. George's Parish Register:" 269). On 23 Oct 1735 Elizabeth was named as the mother of Ford Barnes (BALR HWS#M: 323). Elizabeth Clark was the widow of Matthias Clark and of Job Barnes, and the daughter of James Ford (*BCF:*27).

Norton, William, and Sarah West were m. by lic. on 20 April 1784 at St. Peter's Catholic Church, Baltimore (*Piet:* 141).

Norvill, James, and Mary Jackson, on 31 March 1746 were summoned to appear before the vestry of St. George's Parish. No reason was given. On 3 Nov 1746 Norvill and Jackson were returned to Jos. George at the Nov Court ("St. John's and St. George's Parish Register Vestry Proceedings," MS. at the MdHS).

Norvill, William, and Sarah Cantwell, on 3 Nov 1746 were summoned to appear before the vestry of St. George's Parish. In July 1748 they were summoned again to appear before the vestry of St. John's Parish ("St. John's and St. George's Parish Register Vestry Proceedings," MS. at the MdHS).

Norwood, [-?-], d. by 3 Nov 1729 leaving a widow Ruth, sister of Richard Owings (BALR IS#K:113).

Norwood, Edward, m. by 16 Nov 1763 Mary, sister and residuary legatee of Samuel Gaither, late of Annapolis (PCLR DD#3:195).

Norwood, Edward, d. by July 1775 leaving children John and Mary who were made wards of Robert Long (BAMI 1772, 1775-1781: 127)

Norwood, Elijah, and Rachel Price were m. on 6 Oct 1787 (Marr. Register of Rev. Lewis Richards, MS.690 at MdHS). On 12 May 1798 Rachel was named as a daughter of Absolom and Martha Price (BALR WG#54:435, WG#56L178).

Norwood, John, m. by Nov 1724, Rachel, admx. of Benjamin Lawrence (MDTP 27:110; BAAD 3:113).

Norwood, Philip, in Nov 1754 was charged with begetting a bastard on the body of Mary Odle (BACP BB#A: 448-449).

Norwood, Samuel, m. by 14 Feb 1769 Susannah, daughter of Joseph Bankson. Susannah Bankson was named as a daughter of Joseph Bankson on 26 April 1738 (MDAD 16:132). Hannah 'Bankston' m. William Hughes on 11 Dec 1735 (Harrison, "St. Paul's Parish Register:" 154). Susanna, wife of Samuel Norwood was named as a daughter in the will of Hannah Hughes, widow of Baltimore Town (BAWB 3:158).

Nower, Andrew, m. by 27 March 1790, [-?-], legatee of John Fowle (BAAD 10:117).

Nowilman, Tamasin, on 9 Feb 1696 was named as a granddaughter in the will of Richard Adams of Baltimore Co. (MWB 7:255 abst. in *Md. Cal. of Wills* 2:118).

Nunin. See Newman.

Nussear, Jacob, Sr., and Catherine Kapler were m. by lic. on 26 March 1799 at St. Peter's Catholic Church, Baltimore (*Piet:* 141).

"O"

Oakerson, Joanna on 4 Oct 1743 was named as a niece of Anne Bond (MWB 23:564 abst. in *Md. Cal. of Wills* 8:276); as Joanna Hitchcock she was named as a stepdaughter in the will of John Rigdon (*q.v.*) who had m. Elizabeth 'Oachison' in 1740 (MWB 34:439).

Oaks, Edward, of Boston, New England, m. by 12 May1794 Elizabeth, daughter of Andrew Davidson of Baltimore Co. (BALR WG#OO: 517).

Oats, Peter, m. by 8 Dec 1787 [-?-], daughter of Michael Burns (BAAD 9:127).

O'Brian, Joseph D., widower, and Mary Flattery were m. by lic. on 15 May 1796 at St. Peter's Catholic Church, Baltimore (*Piet:* 141).

O'Brian, Patrick, and Benea Johnson were m. by lic. on 15 Aug 1793 at St. Peter's Catholic Church, Baltimore (*Piet:* 141).

O'Brien, Charles, merchant, and Miss Polly Coskery were m. last Sun. eve. at Fell's Point (*Maryland Journal and Baltimore Advertiser* 7 Feb 1792). They were m. 5 Feb 1792 at St. Peter's Catholic Church, Baltimore (*Piet:* 141). Charles O'Brian, exec., on 25 Nov 1799 posted bond to administer the estate of Francis Coskery (*q.v.*), who named his niece Martha O'Brien and his nephew Charles O'Brien in his will (BAWB 6:230; BAAB 7:15).

O'Brien, John, and Hannah Walsh were married by banns on 23 Sep 1792 at St. Peter's Catholic Church, Baltimore (*Piet:* 141).

O'Brien, Michael, and Margaret Hook were m. by lic. on 1 Dec 1791 at St. Peter's Catholic Church, Baltimore (*Piet:* 141).

O'Bryan, Ann, was charged with bastardy at the March 1765 Court, confessed, and was fined (BAMI 1765: 9).

O'Bryan, Mary, was charged with bastardy at the June 1757 Court (BAMI 1757-1759:35).

O'Connor, Michael, and Catherine Walsh, widow, [both?] of Fell's Point, were m. by lic. on 18 Feb 1798 at St. Peter's Catholic Church, Baltimore (*Piet:* 141; BAML, which gives her name as Catherine Welsh).

Odenbaugh, Jonas, d. by 11 Jan 1787 when his minor son Charles Odenbuagh was made a ward of Henry Wilson (BAGA 1:4).

Odle, Elizabeth, was indicted for bastardy in 1775 for having borne three children out of wedlock (BAMI 1772, 1775-1781:204).

Odle, Mary, confessed to bastardy in Nov Court 1754, She was fined 30 shillings as was Philip Norwood, the father of her child. Mary's mother, Elizabeth was her security (BACP BB#A:448-449).

Odle, William, and Miss Rachel Waters, both of Baltimore, were m. last eve. by Rev. Richards (*Federal Gazette and Baltimore Daily Advertiser* 10 Feb 1797).

O'Donnell, [-?-], m. by 30 May 1766 Frances, daughter of Francis Gibson (MWB 35:37 abst. in *Md. Cal. of Wills* 13:1420).

O'Donnell, John, Esq., an eminent merchant, late from the East Indies, was m. to Miss Sally Elliott, daughter of Thomas Elliott, Esq., of Fell's Point (*Maryland Journal and Baltimore Advertiser* 18 Oct 1785). Capt. John O'Donnell, of the ship *Pallas,* lately arrived from the East Indies (*Maryland Gazette or Baltimore General Advertiser* 18 Oct 1785).

Offert, Charles, and Rose Richards were m. on 12 Dec 1784 at St. Peter's Catholic Church, Baltimore (*Piet:* 141).

Ogden, Amos, m. by 14 Feb 1788 Elizabeth, widow of Joseph Bosley (BPET: Petition re Joseph Bosley, 1788, Box 2, folder 53).

Ogg, Francis, m. by 3 March 1710 Katherine, relict and admx. of Henry Rhodes (*q.v.*) (INAC 32B:48; BAAD 1:161).

Ogg, Francis, and Mary Ogg on 5 June 1723 posted bond to admin. the estate of William Beard (or Beardy) (BAAB 1:78; MDTP 26:176; MDAD 7:462).

Ogg, George, m. by 15 Oct 1759 Helen, daughter of William and Sarah Hamilton (BAWB 2:315, 4:304). Hellen Ogg in her will made 2 April 1798 named her grandchildren George and Hellen Sater, children of Charles, and her daughter Rachel Jacobs (BAWB 6:92).

Ogg, Katherine, was charged with bastardy and confessed at the March 1743/4 Court, and was fined 30 shillings (BACP 1743-1745:172).

Ogg, William, m. by 10 April 1769 Sarah, daughter of William Beasman (BAWB 3:112; BAAD 9:121).

Ogier, John, of Baltimore, silversmith, and Catherine Reese were m. on 4 Jan 1797 (Harrison, "St. Paul's Parish Register:" 354). On 8 May 1798 Catherine was named as a daughter of Frederick Reese of Baltimore Co., dec. (BALR WG#54:424).

Ogilvie (Ogleby) [*sic*], Francis, and Charlotte McCoy were m. on 5 Feb 1794 (Marr. Lic. Return of Rev. Francis Allison: Scharf Papers, MS. 1999 at MdHS). In Dec 1795 Ogilvie advertised that his wife Charlotte had eloped from his bed and board (*Maryland Journal and Baltimore Advertiser* 24 Dec 1795). Charlotte Mecoy [*sic*] stated that Charlotte Ogilvie had been driven to leave Francis by ill usage (*Maryland Journal and Baltimore Advertiser* 30 Dec 1795).

Ogle, John, m. by 24 June 1743 Rosannah, admx. of Jonas Robinson (*q.v.*) of Baltimore Co.. and of John Bowen (*q.v.*) (BAAD 3:259; MDAD 19:413; MDTP 31:385).

Okely,Thomas, in April 1741 with Prewdence (Penhoue?), was summoned to appear before the vestry on the first Tuesday in May 1741 ("St. John's and St. George's Parish Register Vestry Proceedings, " MS. at the MdHS).

Oldham, Edward, and Mary Ensor, daughter of Joseph and Mary, were m. on 21 Nov 1784 at Nicholas Merryman's ("Joseph Ensor Bible." MGRC 33:26).

Oldham, Mr. John, and Miss Nancy Albright were m. last Sun. eve. by Mr. Daniel Kurtz (*Federal Intelligencer and Baltimore Daily Gazette* 14 April 1795).

Oldham, William, and Ruth Talbott were m. on 1 April 1754 (Harrison, "St. John's Parish Register:" 209). On 17 April 1773 Ruth was named as a sister of Thomas Talbott who named Edward Oldham as his sister's son (BAWB 3:267).

Oldton, John, m. by Sep 1693 Ann, widow of Thomas Todd (*q.v.*) and then extx. of David Jones (q.v.) (BACP G#1:126).

Oless (Oleff), Robert, of Gunpowder Hundred, cooper, m. by 4 June 1695 Margaret, widow of William Westbury (*q.v.*), mother of Em Westbury, and daughter of Thomas O'Daniel (BALR RM#HS:466; BACP G#1:215).

Oliff, Mary, was charged with bastardy and found guilty at the March 1709/10 Court, and William Talbott paid her fine (BACP IS#B:94).

Oliver, John, and Rachel Machanin were m. by lic. on 26 April 1792 at St. Peter's Catholic Church, Baltimore (*Piet:* 141; BAML, which gives her name as Rachel Mathman).

Oliver, John, d. by 1793 leaving two orphans, John, and Mary, both under the age of 14, who in April 1793 were made wards of Richard Thralls (BOCP 3:39).

Ollive, John Baptist, native of St. Aignan, Brittany, and Louise Thiron, widow of Geanty, native of Port de Paix, St. Domingo, were married by license dated 12 Oct 1795 at St. Peter's Catholic Church, Baltimore (*Piet:* 141). John B. Ollives and Louise Epiron were married by license dated 12 Oct 1795 (BAML).

Olwell (Olivell) , John, of Anne Arundel Co., m. by 10 April 1710 Elizabeth, widow of William Jeff (or Geff) (*q.v.*) of Baltimore Co. (BALR TR#A:162).

O'Mely (or O'Malley), Briant, m. by 14 March 1667/8 Ann, widow of Abraham Morgan (BALR IR#PP: 70; *BCF:* 480).

O'Neal, Henry, and Sarah Hennyse, on 6 May 1746 were summoned to appear before the next vestry of St. George's Parish. On 5 Aug 1746 Henry O'Neal was discharged by the vestry for putting Sarah Hannessey away ("St. John's and St. George's Parish Register Vestry Proceedings," MS. at the MdHS).

O'Neale, Felix, and Rose Morgan were m. by lic. on 9 Oct 1798 at St. Peter's Catholic Church, Baltimore (*Piet:* 141).

O'Neill (O'Neale), Bernard and Margaret O'Brian, of Fell's Point, were m. by lic. on 21 March 1796 at St. Peter's Catholic Church, Baltimore (*Piet:* 141; *Maryland Journal and Baltimore Advertiser* 24 March 1796).

Onion, John Barret, and Juliet Pendegrass were m. on 21 March 1784 ("Edward M. Onion Bible," *MBR* 5:131).

Onion, Stephen, d. by 16 May 1757 at which time his extx. Deborah m. 2nd, Joseph Smith (*q.v.*).

Onion, Stephen, and Kitty Cross were m. [date not given] (*Maryland Journal and Baltimore Advertiser* 1 July 1783). Stephen Onion and Kitty Crone [*sic*] were m. 26 June 1783 (Marr. Returns of Rev. Patrick Allison, MS. 1699 at MdHS).

Onion, Thomas Bond, m. by 7 March 1788 Elizabeth, daughter of Achsah Chamier (BALR WG#BB:352).

Onion, Zacheus, and Hannah Bond were m. on 2 Dec 1757 (Harrison, "St. John's Parish Register:" 175). Hannah m. 2nd, William McComas (*q.v.*).

Onion, Zacheus Barrett, in Dec 1757 was judged to be over 14. He chose Thomas, William, Joshua, and Jacob Bond as guardians (BAMI 1755-1763).

Onions, Thomas, and Miss M'Call of this town were m. [date not given] (*Maryland Journal and Baltimore Advertiser* 21 Oct 1781). Thomas Onion and Elizabeth McCall were married by license dated 6 Aug 1781 (BAML).

Oram, Anastatia, and Job Garrettson appeared in court on conviction of bastardy in Nov 1760. She swore that Job was the father of her child, and he was fined £5.7.6 (BAMI 1755-1763).

Oram, Arnold, and Elizabeth League were m. on 2 April 1795 (Marr. Register of Rev. Lewis Richards, MS.690 at MdHS). On 3 Sep 1800 Elizabeth was named as a representative of Josias League (BAAD 13:329).

Oram (Orum), Elizabeth, was charged with bastardy at the Nov1759 Court, and named John Garrettson as the father of her child (BAMI 1757-1759:242).

Oram, Henry, m. by 4 Jan 1763 Ann Statia, extx. of Dearing Haws (BAWB 3:78; MDTP 42:151; BAAB 3:292).

Oram, Henry, and Sarah Diver were m. on 7 Nov 1765 (Harrison, "St. John's Parish Register:" 228). On 7 Nov 1766 Oram was named as a son-in-law in the will of Christopher Divers (BAWB 3:33).

Orban, Henry, and Catherine Hock were m. by lic. on 24 April 1786 at St. Peter's Catholic Church, Baltimore (*Piet:* 141). She was a daughter of Anthony Hook (BAWB 6:409).

Orchard, William, m. by March 1666/7 Susanna [-?-]; he d. by 12 June 1668, and Susanna m. 2nd, James Phillips (*q.v.*), and 3rd, Benjamin Arnold (*q.v.*) (*BCF:*482).

Organ, Catherine, was charged with bastardy at the June 1729 Court, and again at the June 1733 Court; at the latter she denied the charges (BACP HWS#6:146, HWS#9:14).

Organ, Matthew, m. by 27 April 1705 Katherine, extx. of John Carrington, and admx. of Turlow Michael Owen (INAC 25:48, 68; MDTP 19B:37, 88; BAAD 2:166, 227; MCHR 4:304).

Organ, Matthew, in a deed dated 1 Feb 1724 referred to *Furlough's Chance* which had been willed to him by his son-in-law Capt. James Maclone, dec. (BALR IS#H:4).

Orr, James, and Angeline Malsby on 28 d. 2 m. 1789 declared their intention to marry ("Minutes of Gunpowder Meeting," *QRNM:*86).

Orrick, John, and Susannah Hammond were m. on 15 Dec 1719 (Harrison, "St. Margaret's Parish Register," Anne Arundel Co., MS. at MdHS: 166). On 20 Dec 1724 Susannah was named as a daughter of Thomas Hammond (MWB 18:350; abst. in *Md. Cal. of Wills* 5:186).

Orrick, Nicholas, son of Jno. and Susanna, b. 1 May 1725, d. 1 Feb 1781, m. 1st, 1 May 1749, by Rev, Thomas Chase, Hannah Cromwell, b. April 1729, d. 2 Dec 1762 He m. 2nd, on 16 March 1769, Mary Bell (Wesley Stevenson BR in *The Notebook* 21 (3) (Fall 2005) 12-15).

Orsbourne. See Osborne.

Ort, Conrad, and Elizabeth Pillier were married by banns on 10 April 1787 at St. Peter's Catholic Church, Baltimore (*Piet:* 141).

Osborn, [-?-], m. by 7 March 1691 Rebecca, daughter of John Hill of Baltimore Co. (MWB 7:127 abst. in *Md. Cal. of Wills* 2:97).

Osborn, [-?-], m. by 14 April 1762 Jane, daughter of Samuel and Jane Hughes who was the mother of Francis Watkins (BAWB 3:27, 185).

Osborn, John, m. by 20 May 1779 Ruth, daughter of John Frazier, farmer, who named their son John as his grandson (BAWB 4:85).

Osborn, John, Jr., and Mary Armigost were m. on 19 May 1785 (Marr. Returns of Rev. William West, Scharf Papers, MS. 1699 at MdHS). On 13 April 1791 she was named as a daughter of Christ[ophe]r Armigost (BAAD 10:355).

Osborn, Jonas, m. by 1791 Mary, widow and extx. of James Mullins (BPET: Petition of Mary Mullins, 1791; BAAD 11:110).

Osborn (Osbourne), William, and Avarilla [-?-] were m. on 24 Jan 1710 (Harrison, "St. George's Parish Register:" 248). Osborn died by 5 Nov 1724 on which day Avarilla was named as a sister of William Hollis, and leaving a son William (BALR IS#H:28).

Osborne (Orsborne), Elisha, m. by 14 March 1783 [-?-]. widow of Joseph Ward and mother of Mary Ann Ward (BAWB 3:547).

Osborne, William, m. by 1693/4 Margaret, widow of John Wallston (*q.v.*) (JAC 12:139; MDTP 16:98). She m. 3rd, William Wise (*q.v.*)

Osborne, William, and 'Cathurinah' Rhodes were m. on 1 March 1727/8 (Harrison, "St. George's Parish Register:" 245). On 7 Nov 1734 Catherine was named as a daughter of Henry and Catherine Rhodes and sister of Henry, Frances and Ann Rhodes (BALR HWS#M:131).

Osborne, William, and Mary [-?-] were m. some time before 4 May 1768 when their daughter Cordelia was b. ("Micajah Greenfield Bible," *MBR* 1:97-98).

Osbourne, William, m. by 31 Oct 1693 Margaret, extx. of John Walston (MDTP 15C:5).

Ottenbaugh, Elizabeth, aged 12 last 1 March, daughter of Jonas[?] and Catherine, in Nov 1775 was bound to Frederick Heller (BAMI 1772, 1775-1778: 154).

Ottey, William, in his will, made 31 Dec 1772 named his wife Ann, his sister Ann, and his cousins Jane Henderson and Ann Hudson (MWB 39:100, abst. in *Md. Cal. of Wills* 15:20).

Oulton, Ann, aged 6½, orphan of Edward Oulton, in Nov 1756 was bound to William Barney to age 16 (BAMI 1755-1763).

Oursler, Edward, and Ruth Owings, daughter of Richard and Sarah (Knowles) Owings were m. on 21 Nov 1734 (Oursler BR, *in NGSQ* 5:53-64).

Oursler, William, and Mary Parker were m. on [18?] Jan 1778 (Marr. Returns of Rev. William West, Scharf Papers, MS. 1699 at MdHS). On 16 June 1792 she received an equal share of the estate of Alexander Parker (BAAD 11:93).

Overton, John, and Mary Weaver were m. by lic. on 23 July 1793 at St. Peter's Catholic Church, Baltimore *(Piet:* 141).

Overton, Thomas, m. by 5 June 1676 Jane, who joined him in sale of part Beaver Neck, formerly sold by John Mascord and his wife Jane (BALR TR#RA.127, 235). Jane m. 2nd, George Gunnell (*q.v.*).

Overy, John, m. by 8 April 1772 Catherine [-?-], who, on 8 April 1772, was named in the will of William Towson as the mother of Isaac Towson Overy and William Towson Allen; William Towson did not want John Overy to be supported from Towson's estate (BAWB 3:222).

Overy, William, and Miss Elizabeth Sheppard were m. last Thurs. by Rev. Hargrove (*Federal Gazette and Baltimore Daily Advertiser* 26 Dec 1800).

Owens, William, and Miss Mary Enright, both of this city were m. Sat. eve. by Rev. Mr. Richards (*Federal Gazette and Baltimore Daily Advertiser* 14 Oct 1799).

Owing, [-?-], m. by 14 March 1742 Sarah, daughter of Richard Gott (BAWB 3:417).

Owings, [-?-], m. by April 1735 Mary, widow of [-?-] Hart (*q.v.*), and daughter of John Scutt of Baltimore Co. (*ARMD* 39:308).

Owings, [-?-], m. by 12 Sep 1778 Elizabeth, daughter of David How (BAWB 3:378).

Owings, [-?-], m. by 2 June 1784 Elizabeth, daughter of William Kelly (BAWB 5:425).

Owings, [-?-], m. by 26 Aug 1794 Ruth, sister of Elias Dorsey who named Ruth's son Peregrine Owings (BAWB 5:193).

Owings, Caleb, m. Susannah Walters on 20 Nov 1768 ("Owings Bible Record." *NGSQ* 5 (4) (Jan 1917) 63).

Owings, John, m. by 11 July 1758, Mary, sister of Peter Cockey of Baltimore Co. (MDAD 41:457).

Owings (Owen), John, and Pamela Cheyne were m. on 12 Nov 1761 (Harrison, "St. John's Parish Register:" 222). She m. 2nd, by 6 March 1782 Moses Galloway (*q.v.*) (BAML). On 13 Feb 1788, Pamela Galloway was named as the admx. of John Owings, who had no children, but left eleven brothers and sisters (BAAD 9:153).

Owings, John Cockey, m. by 27 March 1772 Colegate Deye, daughter of Thomas Colegate, sister of Charlotte Deye Colegate, and niece of Honour Colegate (BALR AL#D:640).

Owings, Joshua, and Mary Cockey were m. on 9 March 1735 (Harrison, "St. Paul's Parish Register:" 155). On 22 May 1740 Mary was named as a daughter of John Cockey (MWB 24:473 abst. by Abst. by Gibb); MDAD 27:152, 30:112).

Owings, Lewis, m. Elizabeth Gurney[*sic*]; she m. 2nd, Stephen Body (*q.v.*), and 3rd, Luke Trotten (*q.v.*). **N.B.:** Lewis Owens and Eliza Quiney [*sic*] were m. on 19 June 1720 (Harrison, "St. Anne's Parish Register," Anne Arundel Co., MS. at MdHS:412).

Owings, Nicholas, merchant of this town, m. Fanny Risteau of Baltimore Co. (*Maryland Journal and Baltimore Advertiser* 24 Feb 1786). Frances Owings, wife of Nicholas Owings, d. in Baltimore Co. (*Maryland Journal and Baltimore Advertiser* 29 April 1788).

Owings, Nicholas, and Sophia Dorsey were m. 20 July 1794 ("Dorsey Bible," pub. in *Genealogy* 3 (10) (Oct 1913): 98).

Owings, Samuel, son of Richard, b. 1 April 1702, and Urath Randall, daughter of Thomas Randall and wife, were m. 1 Jan 1729 ("Urath Randall Owings Bible." *MG* 2:270).

Owings, Samuel, and Ruth Cockey were m. 22 March 1791 ("Records from an Old [Owings] Bible." *MG* 2:272). She was a daughter of the late William Cockey (*Maryland Journal and Baltimore Advertiser* 25 March 1791).

Owings, Samuel, and Miss Mary Govane both of Baltimore, were m. last Sat. eve. (*Federal Gazette and Baltimore Daily Advertiser* 10 April 1797). She was the niece and extx. of Mary Woodward (BAWB 4:352; BAAD 13:179).

Owings, Sarah, was charged with bastardy at the Aug 1733 Court and named Thomas Burke as the father of her child; she was charged again at the March 1736/7 court and presented at the Aug 1737 Court (BACP HWS#9:76, HWS#1A:1, 101).

Owings, Sarah, on 4 Jan 1713 was named as a daughter-in-law of Henry Knowles who also named his wife Catherine (MWB 13:705 abst. in *Md. Cal. of Wills* 4:14). On 8 June 1716 she was named as a daughter in the will of Catherine Knowles who also named Sarah's children, Richard, Ruth and Steven as her grandchildren (MWB 14:230 abst. in *Md. Cal. of Wills* 4:71).

Owings (Owen), Stephen, and Lucy Jones were married by license dated 13 June 1781 (BAML). On 10 Dec 1790 Lucey [*sic*] was named as a daughter of Richard Jones of Richard (BAWB 4:523).

Owings, Thomas, b. 28 Oct 1740, son of Samuel and Urath, and Ruth Lawrence, b. 23 Dec 1745, were m. on 27 Nov 1760 ("Owings Bible Record," *HMGB* 3 (3) (July 1932) 18).

Owings, Thomas, m. by 7 May 1800, Sarah, heir of Thomas Matthews (BAAD 13:252).

Owings, Zachariah, aged 16 next 1 March, son of Samuel Owings, dec., in Nov 1758 was bound to Eleanor Frazier (BAMI 1755-1763).

Oxley, Margaret, was charged with bastardy at the June 1737 Court (BACP HWS#1A:54).

Oyston, Lawrence, m. by 16 April 1788 Rebecca, admx. of Nathan Perigo (*q.v.*) (BAAD 9:318).

"P"

Paca, [-?-], m. by 5 Oct 1746 Elizabeth, daughter of Thomas Sheredine (BALR TB#E: 185).

Paca, Aquila, and Martha Phillips were m. on 11 Sep 1699 (Harrison, "St. George's Parish Register:" 199). On 10 July 1701 Martha was named as a daughter of James Phillips (INAC 20:229). On 22 Sep 1706, Martha was named as a daughter of Susanna Arnold of Spesutia Hundred, who named her granddaughter Mary Paca (MWB 12:301 abst. in *Md. Cal. of Wills* 3:115).

Paca, Aquila, m. by 4 Nov 1725 Frances, daughter of John Stokes (BALR IS#H:200). John Paca on 25 Aug 1745 was named as a grandson in the will of Susannah Stokes (MWB 24:441 abst. by Gibb).

Paca, Aquila, of Baltimore Co., Gent., m. by 23 June 1732 Rachel, widow of John Brown, and mother of Peregrine Brown; she was a dau, of William Blay (KELR JS#16:237; *ARMD* 37:382).

Paca, John, and Elizabeth Smith were m. on 2 Nov 1732 (Harrison, "St. John's Parish Register:" 148). On 20 Oct 1736 Eliza was named as the extx. of William Smith (BAAD 3:216). She had m. 1st, Richard Dallam (*q.v.*).

Paca, Rachel, admx., on 3 Nov 1744 posted bond to administer the estate of Stephen Wilkinson (BAAB 4:118).

Paca, Rachel, in her will made 27 Jan 1745 named her six cousins: John Tilden, Catherine Tilden, William Blay Tilden, William Weatherhead, Samuel Weatherhead, and John Weatherhead (MWB 24:440 abst. by Gibb).

Paca. See also Peece.

Pacquinet, Michael, of Bath Co., N. C., m. by 27 Dec 1726, Mary, daughter of Richard Tydings, dec., and "loving cousin" of John Belt (BALR IS#J:36, 61).

Pagez, John, (son of Martin and Mary Duhalde, living in France, a native of Jean de Lux, France), and Mary Button (daughter of Oliver, dec., and Mary Celestine), were m. by lic. on 12 June 1795 at St. Peter's Catholic Church, Baltimore (*Piet:* 141).

Pain, Martha, on 3 d. 2 m. 1761, denied granting permission for her son, John Pain to marry outside the society ("Minutes of Deer Creek Meeting," *QRNM:* 128). [No other marriage reference found].

Painter, [-?-], m. by 12 April 1799 Betsy, daughter of John Hoos or Hoss (BAWB 6:180).

Palmer, Abraham, shipwright of Baltimore, d. by 5 Feb 1762 when his 'wife or reputed widow' Sarah, and Sarah's daughter Rebecca, wife of John Stewart, were named in the will of Thomas Clindinning (MWB 31:570 abst. by Gibb).

Palmer, William, d. by 5 Aug 1679 by which date his admx. had m. Peter Ellis (*q.v.*) (MDTP 11:154; INAC 6:462).

> **Pannell, Edward,** m. by 14 Dec 1787 Sarah, who received a legacy from the estate of Margaret McCulloch (BAAD 9:131). Sarah was a sister of James McCulloch (BAWB 6:72).

> **Pannell, John,** m. by 30 Dec 1790 Elizabeth, heir of Benjamin Nelson (BAAD 10:230).

Pannell, Capt. John, and Margaret, daughter of Conrad Smull, both of Baltimore, were m. Tues. eve. by Rev. Trulconter (*Maryland Journal and Baltimore Advertiser* 24 Dec 1795).

Pappin, [-?-], m. by 12 May 1757 Sarah, legatee of Edward Richards (BFD 2:57).

Paris, Elizabeth, was charged with bastardy in Aug 1740 (BACP HWS&TR:291). Her son Joshua Paris was b. 16 May 1740 (Reamy, *St. George's Parish Register:* 72).

Paris, Sarah, (late Thomas), on 22 d. 9 m. 1796 was reported as having gone out in marriage with the assistance of a hireling minister ("Minutes of Deer Creek Meeting," *QRNM:*157). [No other marriage reference found].

Parish. See Parrish.

Parker, [-?-], m. by 11 April 1795 Elizabeth, daughter of Hellen Bailey (BAWB 6:405).

Parker, Aletha Smith, stated that some years ago, in 1779, she had executed a deed of conveyance, to her grandchildren Gabriel Parker and Walter Smith Parker, the only children of her dec. son Walter Smith Parker. The deed was recorded in PG Cl., and mentioned Elizabeth Parker, widow of her son Walter Smith Parker. Included with the petition was a copy of the deed (BOCP Petition of Althea Parker, 1791).

Parker, Elizabeth, servant of Robert Clarke, was charged with bastardy at the June 1724 Court. She named David Pearce, also a servant to Robert Clarke, as the father of her child. Her son James Parker, aged 17, was bound out to serve Robert Clark to the age of 21 (BACP IS&TW#3:333, IS&TW#4:305).

Parker, John, of Calvert Co., d. by 12 March 1724 having m. some time after 10 June 1685 and by 3 Nov 1701, Mary, daughter of Christopher Beanes, who was granted 1000 a. *Christopher's Camp* on that date (BALR IS#H:101).

Parker, John, m. by 3 Nov 1701 Isabel, admx. of Thomas Smith (INAC 28:150, 152).

Parker, Robert, merchant, and Miss Margaret Millward of this city, were m. last eve. by Rev. Mr. Reed (*Federal Gazette and Baltimore Daily Advertiser* 24 Aug 1798; The *Baltimore Telegraphe* 24 Aug 1798 gives the bride's name as Millford and the Minster's name as Hagerty).

Parkhill, [-?-], m. by 13 Jan 1779 Jane, sister of Robert Long (BAWB 3:389).

Parkin, Richard, of Baltimore Co., d. by May 1775 when Rachel Lyde Parkin and Richard William Parkin, administrators, advertised they would settle estate (*Maryland Journal and Baltimore Advertiser* 3 May 1775). On 21 Dec 1776 Rachel Lyde was named as a daughter of Pleasance Goodwin (BAWB 3:354). On 16 Jan 1787 Parkin's minor child Thomas Parkin was made a ward of Rachel Lyde Parkin (BAGA 1:8). Rachel Lyde Parkin m. 2nd, Jesse Hollingsworth (*q.v.*). Thomas Parkin, in his will made, 29 June 1797 named his mother Rachel Hollingsworth (BAWB 6:8).

Parkinson, Edward, and Dinah James were m. on 17 July 1785 (Marr. Returns of Rev. William West, Scharf Papers, MS.1999 at MdHS). On 23 Sep 1791 Dinah was named as a daughter of George James (BAWB 5:15).

Parks, [-?-], m. by 10 May 1775 Millicent, sister of Luke Raven and heir of Isaac Raven (BAAD 6:325, 7:228).

Parks, Benjamin, and Eleanor Jones were m. on 2 Oct 1783 (Marr. Ret. of Rev. William West, Scharf Papers, MS. 1999 at MdHS). On 3 May 1787 Eleanor was named as a daughter of John and Esther (Hester) Jones (BAWB 4:91, 254; BAAD 10:68, 11:138).

Parks, Edmund (Edward?), and Elizabeth Sinkler (Sinklair) were m. on 9 July 1764 (Harrison, "St. John's Parish Register:" 226). On 21 Jan 1777 Elizabeth was named as a daughter of Nathan Sinklair (BAWB 3:465).

Parks, Elisha, and Rachel Brannon were m. on 17 March 1785 (Marr. Ret. of Rev. William West, Scharf Papers, MS. 1699 at MdHS). Parks d. by 16 June 1788, having m. [-?-], widow of (James ?) Brannon, and having been the guardian of William, Cassandra, Elizabeth, Thomas, Avarilla, and James Brannon (BAAD 9:293).

Parks, Frederick, and Rachel Parks were married by license dated 1 Dec 1787 (BAML). On 14 Feb 1789 Rachel was named as the extx. of Elisha Parks and admx. of James Brannon (BAAD 9:293, 11:81). Elisha Parks and Rachel Brannon were married by license dated 2 March 1785 (BAML).

Parks, John, and Bridget Millhughs (Milhews) were m. on 29 Oct 1743 (Harrison, "St. John's Parish Register:" 189). On 21 June 1744 Bridget was named as the extx. of Bartholomew Millhuse (*q.v.*) (MDTP 31:502; MINV 29:406; MDAD 20:418).

Parks, John, and Kezia Rutledge were m. on 3 Nov 1761 (Harrison, "St. John's Parish Register:" 222). On 25 Aug 1774 the unnamed wife of John Parks was listed as a legatee of John Rutledge (MDAD 70:414).

Parks, John, and Mary Stewart were m. on 1 May 1796 Harrison, "St. Paul's Parish Register:" 323). She was a daughter of Charles Stewart (BAWB 6:482).

Parks, Peter, and Priscilla Jones were m. on 13 Oct 1790; their son Joshua was b. 29 Aug 1791 ("Peter Parks Bible," *MBR* 1:189-196; BAML).

Parks, Philip, m. by 12 April 1791 Elizabeth, admx. of Peter Slegle (BAAD 10:333).

Parks, Philip, m. by 18 Jan 1793 Elizabeth, daughter of Henry Henninstofel, who d. intestate (BALR WG#LL:44).

Parlett, [-?-], m. by 3 Feb 1734 Mary, daughter of Henry Fitch, who was the grandfather of William Parlett (BALR HWS#M:166).

Parlett, William, m. by 14 Oct 1751, Sarah, representative of Charles Gorsuch of Baltimore Co. (MDAD 31:109). On 17 Feb 1753 he acknowledged receipt from Sarah Gorsuch, admx. of Charles Gorsuch, of his wife's full balance of her fortune (BACT TR#E:95).

Parr, Elizabeth, and Anthony Durant were charged by the vestry of St. George's Parish with unlawful cohabitation (Reamy, *St. George's Parish Register:* 111).

Parran, John, of Calvert Co. had two natural daughters: Esther Parran Abbott and Mary Parran Abbott, who m. by 15 July 1760 Jacob Bowen of Calvert Co. (BALR B#O:597).

Parrish, [-?-], m. by 16 Jan 1754 Citurah [Keturah], daughter of Samuel Merryman (MWB 29:876 abst. by Gibb).

Parrish, Edward, and Elizabeth Gill were m. on 3 May 1735 (Harrison, "St. Paul's Parish Register:" 153). On 13 Oct 1736 Elizabeth was named as a daughter of Stephen Gill of Baltimore Co. (MDAD 15:136).

Parrish (Parish), Edward , m. by 5 April 1750 [-?-], due a portion of the estate of John Harryman of Baltimore Co. (MDAD 28:53).

Parrish, (Parish) Edward, m. by 28 Feb 1789 [-?-], who received an equal share of the estate of Gilbert Israel (BAAD 10:239).

Parrish, John, son of William, m. 6 d. 1 m. 1744 Mary Price, daughter of John ("Records of Gunpowder Meeting," *QRNM:*27; BAWB 4:422).

Parrish, Mordecai, and Rachel Malloney on 27 d. 9 m. 1775 declared their intention to marry (Minutes of Gunpowder Monthly Meeting: *QRNM:*66).

Parrish, Nicholas, on 25 d. 5 m. 1793 was charged with going out in marriage with a woman not of our society ("Minutes of Gunpowder Meeting," *QRNM:*94). Nicholas Parrish and Elizabeth Johnson were m. by lic. dated 8 Dec 1792 (BAML).

Parrish (Parish), Rachel, formerly Carr, on 24 d. 2 m. 1768, was reported to Gunpowder Meeting had been married unto her cousin by a priest ("Minutes of Gunpowder Meeting," *QRNM:*58). [No other marriage reference found].

Parrish (Parish), Richard. m. by 28 Feb 1789, [-?-], who received an equal share of the estate of Gilbert Israel (BAAD 10:239).

Parsons, Abner, and Rachel Dyer, on 27 d. 3 m. 1790 declared their intention to marry ("Minutes of Gunpowder Meeting," *QRNM:*88).

Parsons, Ann, was charged with bastardy in the June 1738 Court (BACP HWS#1A: 221).

Parsons, Gainor, (late Lukins) on 26 d. 4 m. 1798 was reported to have accomplished her marriage with the assistance of a Baptist Preacher ("Minutes of Deer Creek Meeting," *QRNM:*159). [No other marriage reference found].

Parsons, Mary, was charged with bastardy at the Aug 1738 Court (BACP HWS#1A: 274).

Partrick, George, some three years before 1795 deserted his wife Elizabeth, leaving her with five children to support; the two eldest were William and John Partrick (BAOC Petition of Elizabeth Partrick, 1795).

Partridge (Patrudge), [-?-], m. by 6 Feb 1760 Ann, daughter of Sabrett Sollers (MWB 30:860 abst. by Gibb).

Partridge, [-?-], m. by 14 March 1776, Lettisha, daughter of John Smith (BAWB 3:347).

Partridge, [-?-], m. by 14 Oct 1794 Catherine, daughter of Tobias Stansbury who named his grandsons Dob [*sic*] and William Partridge (BAWB 6:173).

Partridge, Buckler, m. by 4 June 1747 Jane, the widow and admx. of Joseph Penhallow of Baltimore Co. (MDAD 23:253, 259).

Partridge, Daubney B., and Elizabeth Porter had been m. on 4 March 1785 (Marr. Register of Rev. Lewis Richards, MS.690 at MdHS). She m. 2nd, John Long (*q.v.*).

Partridge, Francis, late of Baltimore, merchant, m. 19th ult. at Elkton, Hannah, daughter of the Hon. Joseph Gilpin (*Maryland Journal and Baltimore Advertiser* 8 Dec 1789).

Partridge, Job, son of Daubney B. Partridge, dec., in May 1796 was made a ward of William Partridge (BAOC 3:193).

Partridge, William, in his will made 20 Sep 1777 named William Partridge Smith, son of Rebecca Smith, widow (BAWB 5:351).

Partridge, William, and Ann Wells were m. on 8 Jan 1795 (Marr. Register of Rev. Lewis Richards, MS.690 at MdHS). Ann Partridge (formerly Wells), on 14 d. 1 m. 1796, was reported to have had her marriage accomplished by the assistance of a hireling ("Minutes of Baltimore Meeting," *QRNM:*225-226).

Ann, daughter of John Wells, was under the age of 21, but was named as a daughter in Wells' will on 19 Aug 1796 (MCHP 44; BAWB 5:419).

Partridge, William Brown, bricklayer, was m. last eve. by Rev. Mr. Richards, to Miss Nancy Wells, daughter of John Wells, Esq. (*Federal Intelligencer and Baltimore Daily Gazette* 9 Jan 1795).

Pascal, Paul Francis Victor, native of La Rochelle France, and Margaret Morel, widow St. Bris, native of Cap Francois, St. Domingo, were m. by lic. on 6 May 1796 at St. Peter's Catholic Church, Baltimore (*Piet:* 141). (BAML gives her name as Mme. Marg't. Adelaide Morel).

Pascault, L., of Baltimore, was in Cap Francois on 9 April 1790 and was paid a legacy by Dominique Arcambeau, exec. of Joseph Pascault, who was uncle of the said l. Pascault (*Baltimore Daily Repository* 4 May 1793).

Pascault, Lewis Felix, and Mary Ann Magdalen Sly were m. (or remarried) on 22 Dec 1789 in the presence of Charles Ghequiene [prob. Ghequiere] and Richard Ratien at St. Peter's Catholic Church, Baltimore (*Piet:* 141).

Pasquinet, Michael, of Bath Co., N. C., m. by 12 Feb 1727, Charity, daughter and devisee of Richard Tydings, Sr. (BALR IS#1:61).

Passmore, Rebecca, was charged with bastardy at the Nov 1738 Court (BACP HWS#1A:307). She m. Thomas Wodgworth in Jan 1741 (Harrison, "St. John's Parish Register:" 141).

Patridge. See Partridge.

Patten, George, d. on or about 19 Feb 1778 having m. [-?-], the mother of the wife of Nathaniel Smith. George Patten made his Last Will and Testament, making bequests to Thomas Patten, Moses Patten, Mrs. Agnew, David Stewart, Nathaniel Smith, and to a Mrs. Butts. Evidently Thomas Patten had accused them of acting hastily in applying for letters of administration of George Patten's estate. Stewart and Smith, in their response filed 23 May 1780, stated that George Patten departed this life on or about 19 Feb 1778 at which time the libellant, Thomas Patten, was out of state. Stewart and Smith waited until May 1778, and no one applying for letters of administration, they did so. (BOCP: Petition of George Patten, 1778; Box 1, folder 1).

Patterson, [-?-], m. by17 Sep 1756 Jean, daughter of George Little (MWB 30:321 abst. by Gibb).

Patterson, William, and Marey [*sic*] Smith were m. 17 Aug 1773 ("Patterson Family Bible [1]," *HABFR* 1:10).

Patterson, William, merchant, and Miss Spear, daughter of William Spear, Esq., of this town, were m. [date not given] (*Maryland Journal and Baltimore Advertiser* 25 May 1779). William Patterson and Dorcas Spear were married by license dated 15 May 1779 (BAML).

Patton (Hatton?), Zachariah, m. by 18 June 1800 Alie, admx. of John Burtles (BAAD 13:286).

Paublitz, Charles, m. by 13 June 1792 [-?-], who received an equal share of the estate of John Markee (BAAD 11:80).

Paul, Peter, of Fell's Point, stated he would not pay the debts of his wife Elizabeth (*Baltimore Daily Intelligencer* 21 Oct 1794).

Pauling, Sarah, was charged with bastardy at the March 1730/1 Court (BACP IS&TW#4:243).

Paulson, Andrew, m. 27 Nov 1758 [-?-], daughter of John Evans (MDAD 44:227).

Paum, |-?-|, m. by 11 April 1799 Catherine, daughter of Charles Boblitz (BAWB 6:225).

Pawmer, Thomas, on 5 Jan 1741 was summoned by the vestry of St. George's Parish to show cause why he unlawfully cohabited with [name not given] (Reamy, *St. George's Parish Register:* 104).

Pawson, William, of Prince George's Co., m. by 15 March 1736 Elizabeth, mother of Zachariah Wade (BALR IS#IK:427).

Payne, William, servant of S. Owings, in Nov 1756 was fined for begetting a bastard on the body of Mary Young (BACP BB#C:312).

Peacock, Elizabeth, was charged with bastardy at the Nov 1723 Court, and was summoned to answer the charge in March Court 1723/4 (BACP IS&TW#3:212).

Peacock, Jacob, and Honor Arden, widow, were m. on 26 Oct 1720 Harrison, "St. Paul's Parish Register:" 147). James and Honour Lenox (*q.v.*), administrators, on 12 May 1728 posted bond to administer Jacob Peacock's estate (BAAB 2:456).

Peacock, Jacob, and Mary Gardner were m. on 27 June 1793 Harrison, "St. Paul's Parish Register:" 269). She was a daughter of John Gardner (BAWB 6:162).

Peacock, John, m. by 2 Oct 1769 Mary, admx. of William Jenkins (*q.v.*) (BAAD 7:43; MDTP 43:332).

Peacock, Luke, and Constant Sickelmore were m. on 26 July 1753 (Harrison, "St. John's Parish Register:" 208). On 9 July 1762 Constant Love was named as a daughter of Sutton Sickelmore (BAWB 3:21). Sutton Sickelmore Peacock on 9 July 1762 was named as a grandson of Sutton Sickelmore (BAAD 5:304).

Peake, Joseph, m. by 23 Aug 1697 Jane, extx. of her mother Jane Long (MDTP 17:33). Jane m. 2nd, Charles Merryman (q.v.), and 3rd, Benjamin Knight (q.v.).

Peale, Charles W., Esq., of Baltimore, and Elizabeth DePeyster, daughter of William DePeyster, merchant of New York, were m. in New York [date not given] (*Maryland Journal and Baltimore Advertiser* 10 June 1791).

Peale, Mr. Raphaelle, and Miss M. M'Glathery, both of Baltimore, were m. on Thurs. eve. by Rev. J. B. Smith (*Federal Gazette and Baltimore Daily Advertiser* 31 May 1797).

Pearce, |-?-|, m. by Dec 1772 Rachel, daughter of Dennis Garrett Cole (BAWB 3:252, 4:204).

Pearce, |-?-|, m. by 12 March 1773 Rachel, daughter of Solomon Wheeler (BAWB 4:204).

Pearce, Charles, and Drusilla Stansbury were m. 3 Sep 1793 (Marr. Register of Rev. Lewis Richards, MS.690 at MdHS). On 30 May 1797 Drusilla was named as a daughter of Richardson Stansbury (BAWB 5:505).

Pearce, David, in June 1724 was charged with begetting a bastard on the body of Elizabeth Parker (BACP IS&TW#3:333).

Pearce, Elizabeth, was charged with bastardy at the March 1710/11Court (BACP IS#B:205).

Pearce (Piers), Thomas, and Elizabeth Cummins were m. on 20 April 1795 (Harrison, "St. Paul's Parish Register:" 301). On 29 Aug 1795 Elizabeth was named as the admx. of Alexander Cummins (BAAD 12:42, 97).

Pearle, William, d. by Nov 1693; his widow Ann, m. 2nd, Philip Pissions [Pitstow] (*q.v.*), 3rd, Stephen Bentley (*q.v.*) (BACP F#1:300, 307), and 4th, [-?-] Fenton (*q.v.*).

Pearson, Mary, admx., on 15 April 1797 posted bond to administer the estates of John Reason, and of Thomas Pearson (BAAB 8:76, 77).

Pearson, Simon, and Sarah Shaw (Schaw) were m. on 25 July 1715 (Harrison, "St. John's Parish Register:" 7). Pearson and his wife Sarah, administrators, on 15 Nov 1715 posted bond to administer the estate of Thomas Shaw (q.v.) who had m. Sarah, daughter of Thomas Thurston (*BCF:*572; BAWB 3:422). On 27 May 1723 Pearson gave public notice that his wife Sarah had absented herself from his person (BALR IS#G:142).

Pearson, Simon, aged about 71, deposed on 2 April 1731 mentioning his mother-in-law Margaret Anlis [Owless or Oless] (BALC HWS#3 #29).

Pease, Capt. Dennis, and Mrs. Margaret Edwards, both of this town, were m. Sat, eve. last by Rev. Kurtz (*Federal Intelligencer and Baltimore Daily Gazette* 18 Aug 1795).

Peck, John, and Eleanor Piper were m. by lic. on 3 March 1791 at St. Peter's Catholic Church, Baltimore (*Piet:* 141).

Peck, John, stated he would not pay the debts of his wife Anne Catherine, who last Friday had eloped from his bed and board without any just cause and went off in company with five men, who took with them a large quantity of his property (*Federal Intelligencer and Baltimore Daily Gazette* 29 Jan 1795).

Peddicoat, James, and Mary Belt were m. 28 April 1793 (Marriage Register of Rev. Lewis Richards, MS. 690 at MdHS). Mary Peddicoat, formerly Belt, on 28 d. 9 m. 1793 was condemned for marrying by a hireling minister to a man not of our society ("Minutes of Gunpowder Meeting," *QRNM:*94).

Peddicord, Alisere was the mother of an illegitimate child, born in Soldier's Delight Hundred (BAMI 1755-1763).

Peddicord, William, d. by15 Feb 1787 leaving minor child Benedict; Thomas Greenwood was the guardian and filed an account (BAGA 1:24).

Peduzi, Peter, native of Austrian Lombardy in Italy, and Sally Shaw were m. by lic. on 5 Sep 1797 at St. Peter's Catholic Church, Baltimore (*Piet:* 141; BAML, which gives his name as Peter Paduze).

Peece (or Price), [-?-]. m. by 4 Sep 1763 Hannah, daughter of John Algire (BAWB 3:26).

Peerpont. See Pierpoint.

Peirpoint. See Pierpoint.

Pempillion, Thomas, and Mary Love were m. by lic. on 19 Feb 1788 at St. Peter's Catholic Church, Baltimore (*Piet:* 141).

Pencil, Baltzer, m. by 31 March 1780 Sophia, orphan and coheir of William Hensman (BALR WG#E:207). Elizabeth Peters of Baltimore Town, in her will made 23 Jan 1797 named her brother-in-law 'Balzner' Pencil (BAWB 5:478).

Pendegrass, Patrick, m. by 18 Sep 1796 Margaret, who received an equal share of the estate of John Cummins (BAAD 12:190). They were m. on 25 Sep 1787 (Marr. Returns of Rev. William West, Scharf Papers, MS. 1999 at MdHS). Margaret Cummins, in her will made 6 Dec 1799 named her granddaus. Mary and Margaret Pendergrass (BAWB 6:238).

Pendigrass (Pindergist), Luke, and Rachel Simmons were m. on 26 Jan 1768 (Harrison, "St. John's Parish Register:" 231); on 28 May 1770 his wife was named as an heir of George Simmonds (BAAD 6:188; MDAD 64:1).

Pennel, John, and Elizabeth Nelson were married by license dated 24 Jan 1781(BAML). On 4 Nov 1793 Elizabeth was named as a daughter of Margaret Winning [formerly Nelson] who also named a grandson Benjamin Pennel (BAWB 5:144).

Pennnell, Sarah, on 23 March 1784 was named as an aunt in the will of Margaret McCulloch (BAWB 4:26).

Pennetho, Joseph, and Mary Landry were m. by lic. on 2 Aug 1783 at St. Peter's Catholic Church, Baltimore (*Piet:* 141).

Pennington, Amos, on 29 d. 1 m. 1791 was charged with going out in marriage ("Minutes of Gunpowder Meeting," *QRNM:*90). [No other marriage reference found].

Pennington, Josias, and Jemima Hanson were m. on 24 Feb 1771 (Harrison, "St. Paul's Parish Register:" 170). On 27 Aug 1777 Jemima was named as a sister of Edward Hanson and daughter of Jonathan Hanson who called Pennington a son-in-law (BAWB 4:107; BALR WG#EE:238). Jemima Pennington's five children were mentioned in a division of the estate of Edward Hanson (BACT 1785-1788, MD 2865 at MdHS: 75).

Pennington, William, m. by 10 Aug 1791 Rosanna Bell, who received an equal share of the estate of William Bell (BAAD 10:427).

Penry, Margaret, admx., in Oct 1671 posted bond to administer the estate of Francis Wright (BAAB 4:71).

Pepper, Francis, of Baltimore, and Mrs. Susan Conklin of Philadelphia, were m. Thurs. eve., 15th ult., by Rev. Mr. Collin (*The Philadelphia Minerva* 1 Oct 1796).

Percy, [-?-], m. by 10 Dec 1770 Mary, sister of David Aisquith (BAAD 6:187).

Perdue, Prudence, was charged with bastardy at the June 1740 Court and presented at the Aug 1740 Court (BACP HWS#TR:226, 304).

Perdue, Sarah, was charged with bastardy at the June 1750 Court and fined at the Aug 1750 Court (BACP IS#C:15, IS#TW#3:96).

Perdue (Purdue), Walter, in Nov 1742, with Sarah Armager, was to be summoned for unlawful cohabitation ("St. John's and St. George's Parish Register Vestry Proceedings," MS. at the MdHS).

Peregoy, [-?-], m. by 2 June 1764 Eliz., daughter of William Wheeler (BAWB 3:75).

Peregoy (Perigo, Perrrigoe), Andrew, Jr., and Alice Edwards were m. on 17 April 1750 (Harrison, "St. John's Parish Register:" 201). On 14 Oct 1769 Alice was named as a daughter of John Edwards (BAWB 3:148).

Peregoy, Charles, son of Joseph, b. 18 Dec 1764, m. by May 1786 Ruth [-?-], b. 6 May 1766 ("John Read Bible" *MBR* 1:201-202; BAML gives date of license as 15 June 1785).

Peregoy (Perrigoe), Edward, d. by 29 May 1750 at which time his widow Avarilla had m. Samuel Sollers (*q.v.*).

Peregoy (Perigo), James, m. by 7 Dec 1789 Jemima, daughter of Solomon Wheeler (BAAD 10:85).

Peregoy (Perigo), John, in his will made 21 Feb 1796 named his daughter Deborah Curtis, and his granddaughter Ellender Baxter, and his brother William Sollers (BAWB 5:360).

Peregoy, Joseph, and Flora Ryder were m. on 17 Feb 1735 (Harrison, "St. Paul's Parish Register:" 155). She m. 2nd, John Morgan (*q.v.*)

Peregoy (Perrigo), Joseph, and Jemima Woodward were married by license dated 9 May 1783 (BAML). On 23 June 1786 Jemima was named as the extx. of John Woodward (BAAD 8:280, 11:186). In his will made 12 Aug 1800 Perigo named his half-sister Sarah Parks, and her daughter Elizabeth Jemima Coffee (*q.v.*) and a niece Sarah Jenkins (BAWB 6:319).

Peregoy (Perigo), Joseph, and Mary Gorsuch were married by license dated 27 April 1785 (BAML). On 8 Dec 1792 Mary Gorsuch was named as a daughter of Charles and Eleanor Gorsuch; Eleanor was named as a daughter of John Bond (BAWB 5:75; BAAD 11:530).

Peregoy, Joseph, exec., on 3 March 1798 posted bond to administer the estate of Hugh Burgoyne (BAAB 8:345). Peregoy was named as the residuary legatee in Burgoyne's will made 6 July 1797 (BAWB 6:80).

Peregoy (Perigo), Nathan, and Rebecca Evans were m. on 7 Dec 1757 (Harrison, "St. Paul's Parish Register:" 167).

Perian[?], [-?-], m. by 6 Sep 1793 Sarah, daughter of Rachel Gott (BAWB 6:2).

Perigo, Perrigo. See Peregoy.

Perine, Hannah (now Stewart), on 30 d. 11 m. 1776, reportedly hath gone out in marriage with a man of our society ("Minutes of Gunpowder Meeting," *QRNM:* 68). [No other marriage reference found].

Perine, Maulden, and Hephzibah Brown were m. on 22 Oct 1793 (Marr. Register of Rev. Lewis Richards, MS.690 at MdHS). On 24 d. 1 m. 1794 he was charged with accomplishing his marriage by the assistance of a hireling ("Minutes of Baltimore Meeting," *QRNM:*222). On 11 d. 12 m 1794 a complaint was made against Hephzibah Perine, formerly Brown, for having her marriage accomplished contrary to the good order ("Minutes of Baltimore Meeting," *QRNM:*224). Hepzibah m. 2nd, William Buchanan (*q.v.*).

Perine, Peter, on 14 d. 6 m. 1798 was charged with having his marriage accomplished contrary to the good order ("Minutes of Baltimore Meeting," *QRNM:*231). Peter Perine and Mary Howard were married by license dated 17 Nov 1797 (BAML).

Perine, Peter, and Margaret Perine were m. on 2 Dec 1798 (Marr. Register of Rev. Lewis Richards, MS.690 at MdHS). On 12 June 1800 Margaret was named as the admx. of Simon Perine (BAAD 3:275).

Perine, William, m. by 23 Feb 1787 Sarah, daughter of Samuel Gott (BAWB 4:225; BAAD 9:205).

Perine, William, m. by 18 Jan 1788 [-?-], widow of Samuel Lewiston (BAAD 9:146).

Perkins, Reuben, and wife Sarah, on 10 Dec 1771 conveyed land to his son-in-law Richard Seward or Sword (BALR AL#D:657, AL#E:397).

Perkins, Richard, d. by Feb 1706 having m. Mary, admx. of Thomas Gash (*q.v.*) (MDTP 19C:219). She m. 3rd, John Belcher (*q.v.*) (Harrison, "St. George's Parish Register:" 201).

Perkins, William, m. by 22 Jan 1721 Elizabeth, daughter of John Cottrell who also named his granddaughter Mary Perkins MWB 20:49 abst. in *Md. Cal. of Wills* 6:162).

Perkins, William, was indicted for fornication at the Nov 1772 Court and fined; he was charged again in 1774 by the Vestry of St. George's Parish on suspicion of illegal cohabitation with Sarah Durbin; they agreed to separate and remove all cause for further suspicion (BAMI 1772-1781: 84; Reamy, *St. George's Parish Register:* 112).

Perpont. See Pierpoint,

Perrigo. See Peregoy.

Perrigoe. See Peregoy.

Perry, John, stated he would not pay the debts of his wife [unnamed] (*Maryland Journal and Baltimore Advertiser* 16 Sep 1785).

Perry, Mary, was charged with bastardy at the March 1743/4 Court (BACP 1743-1745: 154).

Pert, Thomas, m. by 10 Feb 1756, Frances, admx. of Thomas Constable (*q.v.*) (MDTP 36:267; MDAD 39:29).

Perting, Peter, and Mary Field were m. by lic. on 28 Feb 1797 at St. Peter's Catholic Church, Baltimore (*Piet:* 141).

Peryne. See Perine.

Peshaw, Joseph, and Ann Grainger were married by license dated 12 Oct 1784 (BAML). On 2 May 1785 as administrators, they posted bond to administer the estate of John Granger (*q.v.*) (BAAB 6:266). In 1787 Ann was named as the widow of John Granget (Granger) (BOCP Petition of John Granget, 1787, Box 2, Folder 29).

Peter, David, and Miss Johns were m. 17th inst. (*Federal Gazette and Baltimore Daily Advertiser* 20 Sep 1799).

Peters, Daniel, of Baltimore Town, and Elizabeth Shriver were married by license dated 16 May 1781 (BAML), On 28 July 1790 Elizabeth was named as the widow of Michael Schriber (Shriver) (*q.v.*) (BALR WG#FF:292; BAAD 11:52).

Peters, George, and Polly Trimble were married by license dated 25 March 1796 (BAML). Mary Peters, formerly Trimble, on 8 d. 12 m. 1796 was charged with marrying contrary to the good order ("Minutes of Baltimore Meeting," *QRNM*:227).

Peters, John, m. by Oct 1701 Hester, mother of John Fuller (BALR HW#2:93).

Peters (Peter), Thomas, of Philadelphia, and Rebecca Johnson of Baltimore Co., were m. on 30 Oct 1783 (Marr. Returns of Rev. William West, Scharf Papers, MS.1699 at MdHS; *Maryland Gazette or Baltimore General Advertiser* 31 Oct 1783). She was a daughter of Dr, Edward Johnson and of Ann Johnson (BAWB 6:57, 7:218).

Peterson, Andrew, d. by 16 May 1692 when Judith Dorman, admx., posted bond to administer his estate (BAAB 2:430). She m. 2nd by 1696 Michael Gormack (*q.v.*).

Peterson, John, and Margaret Holmes were m. by lic. on 15 April 1800 at St. Peter's Catholic Church, Baltimore (*Piet:* 141).

Petticoate, [-?-], m. by 8 Feb 1762 Hannah, daughter of John Owings (BAWB 3:9).

Petticoate, [-?-], m. by 26 Oct 1704 Sarah, daughter of Edward Dorsey MWB 3:725 abst. in *Md. Cal. of Wills* 3:68).

Petty, Ann, servant of John Fuller, was charged with bastardy at the June 1743 Court, and sentenced at the Aug 1743 Court to be given 15 lashes on the bare back (BACP TB#D:185, Liber 1743-1745, pp. 13-14).

Petty, Constant, on 25 Aug 1746 was named as the extx. of William Mattingley (MDTP 31:676). Constant Pilley [*sic*], extx. of William Mattingly, on 26 Aug 1746 posted bond to administer his estate (BAAB 2:184).

Petty, John, age 13, orphan of Francis Petty, in Nov 1762 was bound to Tobias Stansbury, Jr., to age 21 to learn the trade of weaver (BAMI 1755-1763).

Peverell, Daniel, d. by 2 May 16792 leaving a widow Hannah and a daughter Sarah (BALR RM#HS#1:350, abst. in *Md. Cal. of Wills* 4:239). Hannah m. 2nd, George Smith (*q.v.*), and 3rd David Thomas (q.v.).

Phelps, Avinton, and Rachel Muckledory were m. on 23 April 1730 (Harrison, "St. George's Parish Register:" 251). On 5 Aug 1741 they sold 50 a. *Rachel's Delight* which had been surveyed in 1725 for John Muckeldory (BALR HWS#M:4, HWS#1-A:519). In April 1762 Edward Morgan, exec. of Thomas Phelps, advertised he was holding money for Avington Phelps, supposed to be living in Carolina (Annapolis *Maryland Gazette* 8 April 1762).

Phelps, Charles, m. by 12 Aug 1747 Margaret, daughter of Anthony Charnox and his wife Hannah, daughter of George Hollingsworth (PCLR EI#8:339).

Phelps, Capt. John Parker, was m. last Thurs. eve. to Hannah Jacobs, daughter of William Jacobs of Fell's Point (*Maryland Gazette or Baltimore General Advertiser* 5 Jan 1790).

Phelps, Thomas, on 26 Aug 1738,with Mark Ford, was summoned to the vestry of St. George's Parish to declare that they both had been married to her who is now called Rose Phelps. She was first married to [-?-] Swift, and she eloped from him and Phelps declared he married the said Rose on 18 May 1710 (Reamy, *St. George's Parish Register:* 104).

Phillips, Elizabeth, was charged with bastardy at the March 1746/7 court BACP TB&TR#1:378).

Phillips, Henry, m. by 22 July 1786 Mary mother of Stephen Jacob Poolly (BAWB 4:155).

Phillips, James, m. Susanna, widow of William Orchard and d. by 1696 at which time his widow Susanna, mother of Anthony and James Phillips and Mary Carville had m. Dr. Benjamin Arnold (*q.v.*). (*BCF:*503).

Phillips, James, m. by 8 June 1701 Bethia, who was named daughter-in-law in the will of Mark Richardson, who also named his wife Susanna (MWB 12:6, abst. in *Md. Cal. of Wills* 3:73). In his will dated 121 Sep 1674 George Utie named his wife Susanna and his children, George, Mary Ann, and Bethia (MWB (MWB 9:60 abst. in *Md. Cal. of Wills* 1:206). Mark Richardson m. by June 1683. Susanna, extx. of Johanna Goldsmith and widow and extx. of George Utye (BACP D:45; MDTP 13:479; INAC 10:170). On 4 Oct 1684 Susanna, wife of Mark Richardson, was named as a daughter in the will of Johanna Goldsmith (MWB 6:26 abst. in *Md. Cal. of Wills* 2:35).

Phillips, James, on 12 Aug 1717 was named as a brother-in-law of Richard Cromwell (MWB 14:396 abst. in *Md. Cal. of Wills* 4:112).

Phillips, Col. James, d. by 12 Dec 1720 having m. Johanna, mother of John and Richard Kemp (BALR TR#DS:287). Johanna m. 3rd, Aquila Hall (*q.v.*)

Phillips, James, m. by 24 Nov 1788 Bothia, daughter of Bothia Scarlett (*q.v.*), whose will also named James Phillips, Jr., and Sarah Phillips of Boston, children of James and Bothia (BAWB 4:508).

Phillips, Samuel, and Rosanna Harris were m. on 27 July 1793 (Marr. Returns of Rev. John Hagerty, Scharf Papers, MS. 1999 at MdHS). On 3 May 1794 Rosanna was named as an heir of William Harris (BAAD 11:424).

Phillips, William, in his will, proved 23 Feb 1788 William Phillips named James Phillips and Patience Phillips as his execs. on 26 March 1788 Patience Phillips renounced the will and claimed her thirds (BAWB 4:291).. Patience m. 2nd, on 2 April 1789 Luke Wages (*q.v.*).

Philpot, Bryan, ensign in Capt. Smith's Co., and in Smallwood's Regiment; m. Elizabeth Johnson on 16 Nov 1796 in Baltimore Co.; he d. on or about 11 April 1811; Bryan and Elizabeth were the parents of Mary Ann, wife of John Frazier, living 11 Jan 1849 in her 52nd year; John Philpot, b. Oct 1801; Elizabeth, widow of J. Gowan Blanchard; Clarissa, wife of Nicholas R. Merryman; Edward Philpot, and one other child (Rev. War Pension Application of Elizabeth Philpot: W5543).

Philpott, Thomas, was m. last eve. by Rev. Mr. Hagerty, to Maria Jacob, both of this city (*Federal Gazette and Baltimore Daily Advertiser* 25 May 1799).

Phippen, [-?-], m. by 22 Sep 1755 Sarah, daughter of Edward Richards (MWB 30:26 abst. by Gibb).

Piat, John Baptist, and Peggy Chameau were m. by lic. on 20 Sep1790 at St. Peter's Catholic Church, Baltimore (*Piet:* 141).

Picke, William, m. by 3 May 1765 [-?-], extx. of William Kimble, whose will dated 3 Jan 1761 appoints his unnamed wife as extx., and whose admin. bond was posted by Sarah Kimble, extx., with will attached (MDTP 41:94; BAWB 2:334; BAAB 2:11).

Pickersgill, John, and Miss Polly Young, were m. last Fri. [date not given] (*Maryland Journal and Baltimore Advertiser* 9 Oct 1795). They were m. on 2 Oct 1793 (Harrison, "St. Paul's Parish Register:" 311).

Picket, George, d. by 17 Aug 1717 having m. [Mary?], daughter of Sarah Spinks [who was a widow Stansbury] and sister of Luke Stansbury (INAC 39C:73).

Pickett, George, and Barbara Gorsuch were m. on 16 Feb 1751 (Harrison, "St. John's Parish Register:" 203). On 14 Oct 1751 Barbara was named as a representative of Charles Gorsuch of Baltimore Co. (MDAD 31:109). On 17 Feb 1753 George Pickett acknowledged receipt from Sarah Gorsuch, admx. of Charles Gorsuch, of his wife's full balance of her fortune (BACT TR#E:95). On 11 May 1760 Barbara, sister of David Gorsuch was so named in the will of Launcelott Wattson (BAWB 2:141). Barbara m. 2nd, John Wilkerson (*q.v.*) (MDTP 43:256).

Pickett, George, m. a few days ago at Richmond, Va., Mrs. Margaret Flint, late of Baltimore (*Maryland Journal and Baltimore Advertiser* 3 Nov 1789).

Pickett, Heathcote, and Elizabeth Wright were m. on 26 Jan 1742 (Harrison, "St. John's Parish Register:" 125). On 27 July 1743 Elizabeth was named as the admx. of William Wright (*q.v.*) and of James Greer (*q.v.*) (MINV 28:141; MDAD 20:411, 22:18; BAAD 3:267, 312).

Pickett, Lucretia, in 1762 and again in 1763 was convicted of bastardy (BAMI 1755-1763).

Pickett, William, m. some time after 1700 [-?-], heiress of Joseph Heathcote (*MRR* 41).

Pickett, William, m. by 9 Sep 1724 [-?-], widow of Gideon Skaats of Baltimore Co. (MDAD 6:94).

Pickett, William, and Jemima Deaver were m. by license dated 13 Dec 1777 (BAML). On 23 Nov 1784 Jemimah was named as a daughter of Philip Deaver (BAWB 4:6).

Pierce, [-?-], m. by 17 Dec 1756 Mary, daughter of William Keeper (MWB 30:246 abst. by Gibb).

Pierce, [-?-], m. by 16 March 1799 Mary, mother and heir at law of Benjamin Hill (*q.v.*) (BAAD 13:7).

Pierce, Humphrey, merchant, married Nancy Williamson, both of Baltimore [date not given] (*Maryland Journal and Baltimore Advertiser* 7 Aug 1789). They were m. on 6 Aug 1791 (Register of First Presbyterian Church, Baltimore," MS. at MdHS: 11).

Pierce, Levi, of Boston, was m. last eve. by Rev. Dr. Allison to Miss Mary Elizabeth Williamson of this city (*Federal Gazette and Baltimore Daily Advertiser* 13 Sep 1798).

Piercy, [-?-], m. by 10 Dec 1770 Mary, sister of Thomas Aisquith (BFD 6:33).

Pierpoint, [-?-], m. by 27 March 1792 Jemima, heir and representative of John Penn of Baltimore Co. (BACT 1791-1794, MS 2865.1 at MdHS: 46).

Pierpoint, Abraham, in 1760 was charged with having a child laid to him ("Minutes of Gunpowder Meeting," *QRNM:*40).

Pierpoint, Ann, on 27 d. 6 m. was 'guilty of having a child before marriage' ("Minutes of Gunpowder Meeting," *QRNM:*61).

Pierpoint (Peirpoint, Perpont) , Charles, m. by 24 Nov 1720 Sidney, sister, next of kin, and admx. of William Chew of Baltimore Co. (BAAB 1:294; MDTP 24:284; MDAD 6:225; MINV 5:87).

Pierpoint (Peirpoint), Jabez, died leaving a will dated 1 Oct 1730 and proved 24 April 1721. He named Elinor Rogers, daughter of his wife, as extx. He also named his five sisters, Sidney, Eliza Dea, Mary Davis, Sarah Warfield, and Eliza. He named his grand-daughters-in-law Elinor Rogers and Sarah Rogers (MWB 16:388 abst. in *Md. Cal. of Wills* 5:48).

Pierpoint (Peerpont), Thomas, and Miss Margaret Wells, both of this town were m. last Sun. eve. by Rev. Kurtz (*Baltimore Daily Intelligencer* 30 Sep 1794). She was under age of 21, daughter of John Wells (MCHP 44). On 13 d, 11 m. 1794 a complaint was made against him and his wife Margaret for having their marriage accomplished against contrary to the good order ("Minutes of Baltimore Meeting," *QRNM:* 223). Margaret was named as a daughter in the will of John Wells, made 19 Aug 1796 (BAWB 5:419).

Piers. See Pearce.

Pike, William, m. by 27 March 1740 Ann, widow of Abraham Whitaker (*q.v.*) (MINV 25:231; MDAD 18:394; BAAD 4:120; MDTP 31:198). On 29 May 1742 Ann was named as a daughter of Rebecca Puttee (MWB 30:445 abst. by Gibb).

Pike, William, m. by 9 April 1765 Sarah, extx. of William Kimble (*q.v.*) (BAAD 6:186).

Pilkington, Thomas, and Mary Workman, were m. on 31 March 1785 (Marr. Returns of Rev. William West, Scharf Papers, MS. 1999 at MdHS). On 31

Jan 1786 Mary was named as a sister of Hugh Workman (BAWB 4:129; BPET: Hugh Workman, 1787, Box 1, folder 48)

Piller, Phillip, m. by (date not given), Elisabeta Ettckins ("First Record Book for the Reformed and Lutheran Congregations at Manchester, Baltimore (now Carroll) Co.," *MGSB* 35:266).

Pimple, [-?-], m. by 3 Sep 1775 Delilah, daughter of James Richardson (BAWB 3:317).

Pindall, John, may have m. by 27 July 1767 [-?-], daughter of Richard Bond since two sons of John Pindall received a share of Richard Bond's estate (MDAD 57:193).

Pindall, Joshua, in April 1796 was made a ward of Richard Bond, Jr. (BAOC 3:187).

Pindall, Margaret, in Feb 1796 was made guardian of Elizabeth and Thomas Pindall (BAOC 3:181).

Pindell, John, and Eleanor Gill who were m. 6 Nov 1757 (Harrison, "St. Thomas' Parish Register:" 71). Pindell stated his wife Eleanor had eloped (*Maryland Gazette or Baltimore General Advertiser* 20 Jan 1786; BACT 1785-1788, MS 2865, MdHS: 112). On 28 May 1794 Eleanor Pindell was named as a daughter of John Gill (BAWB 5:467).

Pines, Tabitha, in June 1768 was fined for (BAMI 1768-1769:20).

Pinkton [?], Isaac, in Nov 1756 was bound to Thomas Talbot for 4 years (BAMI 1768-1769).

Pinkton, Margaret, was charged with bastardy at the March 1737/8 Court (BACP (BACP HWS#1A:168).

Pinkston, William, and Martha Nelson were m. on 4 March 1716/7 (Harrison, "St. Ann's Parish Register," Anne Arundel Co. MS. at MdHS: 398). On 15 Aug 1717 Martha was named as a daughter of Ambrose Nelson of Baltimore Co. (MWB 19:704, abst. in *Md. Cal. of Wills* 6:112).

Piper, John, and Susanna Coney were m. by lic. on 30 Nov 1789 at St. Peter's Catholic Church, Baltimore (*Piet:* 142).

Piper, William, made his will on 7 Jan 1785 naming wife Elizabeth and brother-in-law Valentine Hiss (BAWB 4:56).

Pisha, Joseph, m. by 11 Oct 1787 Ann, daughter and admx. of John Granger (BAAD 9:112).

Pissions, See Pitstow.

Pitchey, Abraham, m. by 27 Jan 1785 Barbara, daughter of Jacob Liechte, farmer, whose will stipulated that Pitchey was to have no part of his [daughter's?] until they had begotten children (BAWB 4:296).

Pitstow (Pissions), Philip (or William), m. by Nov 1693, Ann, relict of William Pearle (*q.v.*); she m. 3ʳᵈ Stephen Bentley (*q.v.*) (BACP F#1:307). She m. 4ᵗʰ, [-?-] Fenton (*q.v.*).

Pitstow, Philip, d. by 26 Feb 1726 when Henry Jones and wife Mary admin. his estate (BAAD 3:59); his widow Mary m. 2ⁿᵈ, Henry Jones (*q.v.*).

Pitstow, Philip Love, exec., on 11 Aug 1794 posted bond to administer the estate of Robert Love Pitstow (BAAB 8:607). Philip Love Pitstow was named as a son in the will of Robert Love Pitstow (BAWB 5:175).

Pitts, John, and Susanna Bond were m. on 6 Feb 1766 (Harrison, "St. Thomas' Parish Register:" 73). On 1 Sep 1766 Susanna was named as the extx. of

Peter Bond (BAAD 7:200; N.B.: BAAD 55:210 gives her name as Eve). In his will, made 29 July 1785 John Pits named his step-children Susanna and Sophia Bond (BAWB 4:80). Susanna was probably the widow of Peter Bond (*q.v.*).

Pitts, Rebecka, before marriage Price, on 23 d. 12 m. 1772 was charged with having married a man of another society ("Minutes of Gunpowder Monthly Meeting," *QRNM*:63). [No other marriage reference found].

Placide, Paul, native of Marseilles, France, and Louisa Devenois, native of Nismes, France, were m. by lic. on 19 Sep 1797 at St. Peter's Catholic Church, Baltimore (*Piet:* 142). (BAML gives her name as Louise Duvernous).

Plaisted, Mary, challenged the allegations of her husband Mordecai that she had run him into debt (*Maryland Journal and Baltimore Advertiser* 19 March 1790).

Plant, Elizabeth, living at the house of John Giles, was charged with bastardy at the Nov 1724 Court (BACP IS&TW#4:32).

Plater, George, m, by 13 May 1760, Elizabeth, widow of John Carpenter (BALR B#H:115).

Platt, Dorothy, was charged with bastardy at the June 1768 Court (BAMI 1768-1769:21).

Pleasants, Robert, son of Thomas and Mary, and Mary Webster, daughter of Isaac and Margaret, were m. on 14 April 1748 ("Abstracts of Nottingham Meeting," MS. at MdHS; MWB 30:754 abst. by Abst. by Gibb; BAAD 7:4).

Plowman, John, and Sarah Chambers were m. on 3 May 1736 Harrison, "St. Paul's Parish Register:" 155). John was a brother of the half-blood of Richard Stevenson Vickory (*q.v.*) (BAAB 4:195). On 11 Nov 1736 Sarah Chambers received a payment from the estate of Richard Stevenson Vickory (MDAD 15:235). Richard King Stevenson had inherited *Jack's Double Purchase,* or *Selset,* which descended to him by the death of Richard Stevenson Vickory, and on 3 Aug 1740 he conveyed 50 a. of *Jack's Double Purchase* to his cousins John and Jonathan Plowman (BALR HWS#1-A:438).

Plowman, Jonathan, and wife Ann on 13 Feb 1714 conveyed a cow to their son Richard Vickory (BALR TR#A:359).

Plowman, Jonathan, merchant, of Baltimore, was married last Thurs. to Miss Rebecca Arnold, eldest daughter of Mr. David Arnold (Annapolis *Maryland Gazette* 14 Oct 1762). She was a sister of David Arnold of Calvert Co. who named his nephew Jonathan Plowman and nieces Rebecca, Mary, and Ann Plowman in his will (BAWB 3:318). Rebecca Arnold, in her will made 17 June 1784, named her grandchildren Ann, Mary Ann, Jonathan, and Rebecca, children of the late Jonathan Plowman (BAWB 4:316).

Plowman, Jonathan, died owning a dwelling house and a lot on the east side of Jones Falls, and other assorted tracts of land. He left a son and heir, Jonathan Plowman, and Edward Johnson and William McLaughlin, trustees, advertised a sale of property (*Maryland Journal and Baltimore Advertiser* 26 Oct 1787).

Plowman, Jonathan, m. by 11 Nov 1797 Martha, heir of Benjamin Hughes (BAAD 12:293).

Plowman, Mary, was charged with bastardy at the June 1729 Court and the child was bound to Lloyd Harris (BACP HWS#6:142).

Plowright, Ann, was presented at the Aug 1756 Court for having borne three baseborn mulatto children: George, aged 8; Nero, aged 6; and Roger, aged 4; her children were sold to William Rogers for 20 shillings each and ordered to serve him until they arrived at the age of 31 (BACP BB#C:233, BAMI 1755-1763).

Plumb, John, m. by 2 April 1791 Judith, daughter of John Beaver (BOCP: Petition of Martin and Adam Beaver, 1793).

Plummer, Ann, (late Wallice) on 28 d. 8 m. 1800 was reported to have gone out in marriage to a man not of our society with the assistance of a hireling teacher ("Minutes of Deer Creek Meeting," *QRNM*:162). [No other marriage reference found].

Plummer, Thomas, of Prince George's Co., m. by 26 Aug 1703 Elizabeth, daughter of George Yate of Anne Arundel Co. (BALR HW#2: 309).

Plunkett, John, son of Mary Plunkett who was the daughter of William Plunkett formerly of Baltimore Co., was named in the will of Adam Magaw (BAWB 3:490).

Plushart, Ann, widow of Joseph Plushart, refuted the charge made by a madman, John Miller *alias* Peter Mallet or Stephen Maller that she had forsaken his company, because he already had a wife and two children in Normandy, and had turned her and her orphan children out of his house (*Maryland Journal and Baltimore Advertiser* 22 May 1792).

Poak, [-?-], m. by 12 Sep 1769 Mary, a sister of Joseph Smith, ironmaster, who also named a nephew Joseph Poak in his will (BAWB 3:165; MWB 37:469, abst. in *Md. Cal. of Wills* 14:114).

Poang [?], Charles, of Belfast, m. by 11 April 1776 Elizabeth, sister of Thomas Ewing (BAWB 4:402).

Pocock, [-?-], m. by 24 Oct 1775 Mary, admx. of Francis Hunn (*q.v.*) (MDTP 36:363).

Pocock, James, and Rebecca Biddison were married by license dated 7 Jan 1783 (BAML). She was a daughter of Thomas Biddison (BAWB 6:401).

Pocock, Joshua, administrator with will annexed on 24 Sep 1796 posted bond to administer the estate of Elizabeth Beattle (Beedle) (BAAB 8:917). Elizabeth Beedle, spinster, in her undated will, proved 24 Sep 1796, left to Joshua Pocock the estate left to her by an uncle; the rest of her estate was to be divided equally between John and Jemima Pocock, children of Joshua Pocock (BAWB 5:405).

Poe, David, was Assistant Deputy Quarter Master General of the United States during the Revolutionary War; m. Elizabeth [-?-], who died by 8 May 1837; David and Elizabeth were the parents of: (1) Eliza, m. Henry Herring, and had: Elizabeth Rebecca Herring, Louis David Herring, Henry Herring, Jr., Emily Virginia Herring; and George Augustus Herring; (2) David Poe, Jr., dec., who was the father of Edgar Allan Poe, and Rosalie Poe, and (3) Maria wife of [-?-] Clemm (Rev. War Pension Application of Elizabeth Poe: R8293).

Poirier, Peter, died leaving a will dated 1 March 1796 and proved 9 April 1796. He named his wife Margaret Belliste and her children, and named his wife Margaret as extx. Samuel Mangee De Velcourt, Peter Gold and J. B, Binoit witnessed the will (BAWB 5:374). A native of Nova Scotia, aged 66 years and 10 mo., he died 19 March 1796 and was buried 20 March 1796 at St.

Peter's Catholic Church, Baltimore (*Piet:* 196). Margaret Belleste, extx., on 9 April 1796 posted bond to administer the estate of Peter Poirier (Povier) (BAAB 8:856). Margaret Poirvier [*sic*], widow, native of Nova Scotia, died 5 Feb 1799 and was buried 6 March 1799 at St. Peter's Catholic Church, Baltimore (*Piet:* 193).

Poloke, John, m by 17 Jan 1732 Sarah, daughter of Mary Buchannan, widow of Archibald Buchannan; Mary Buchannan also named a grandson Joseph Poloke (MWB 20:698 abst. in *Md. Cal. of Wills* 7:23).

Polson, Hannah, was charged with bastardy at the June 1743 Court; as a servant to Edward Day, she was charged again and confessed at the Nov 1745 Court when she was ordered to serve the county for seven years after her servitude; her child, Nan Polson, was sold to Edward Day until she was 31; as a servant to Avarilla Day she confessed in March 1746/7, and was ordered to serve another seven years for seven years after her present servitude; her negro child Rachel Polson was sold to Avarilla Day until she was 31; Hannah also had a bastard child named Joseph Polson (BACP TB#D:203, Liber 1745-1746, pp. 734-748-749; and TB&TR#1:417).

Polson, Mary, was charged with bastardy at the March 1765 Court (BAMI 1765:11).

Polson, Rebecca, was charged with bastardy at the Aug 1742 Court and again at the March 1750/1 Court (BACP TB#D:1, 73, TR#6: 270).

Polton, Elizabeth, before marriage Dyer, on 28 d. 3 m. 1771 was reported to have gone out in marriage ("Minutes of Gunpowder Meeting," *QRNM:* 61).

Polton, Thomas Ridgely, and Sarah Bryan were m. by lic. on 3 July 1799 at St. Peter's Catholic Church, Baltimore (*Piet:* 142).

Pompey, William, d. by 14 Nov 1786 having m. a sister of John Kingsbury, and having a son John, who Kingsbury called nephew, and a daughter Ann Brashears, called niece (BAWB 4:414).

Ponsiby, Thomas, and Ann Phillips were m. by lic. on 20 Sep 1795 at St. Peter's Catholic Church, Baltimore (*Piet:* 142).

Ponteny. See Puntany.

Pontenay. see Puntany.

Pontler, Anthony, (son of Robert Andrew and Mary Teresa Pascal, a native of L'Alais in Languedoc), and Mary Catherine Duplan, widow Lassiteau, daughter of Francis and Charlotte DuRoche, native of Grand Riviere, St. Domingo), were m. by lic. on 19 Feb 1795 at St. Peter's Catholic Church, Baltimore (*Piet:* 142).

Pool, Joseph, comb maker in Baltimore advertised for the return of his runaway son Joseph, aged 13 (*Baltimore Telegraphe* 28 July 1795).

Poole, Henry, m. by 22 Sep 1775 Elizabeth daughter of Luke Mercer (Mercier) (BAWB 3:305).

Pope. Morris, and wife Catherine, formerly Catherine Loucresy, posted bond to administer the estate of Patrick Loucresy (BAAB 7:71).

Port, Daniel, and Isabella Barclay were m. in Baltimore Co. by 23 Nov 1789 (Marr, Returns of Ezekiel Cooper, Scharf Papers, MS 1999 at MdHS).

Porter, [-?-], m. by 21 Feb 1777 [-?-], sister of John Mercer, by who he had a son John Mercer Porter (BAWB 3:349).

Porter, [-?-], m. by 17 Jan 1785 Mary, daughter of John Parrish, who was 'aged and infirm' (BAWB 4:87).

Porter, [-?-], m. by 19 April 1794 Mary Ann, daughter of Phinsense Kepper (BAWB 5:332).

Porter, Augustine, and Frances Stansbury were m. on 16 Jan 1800 (Marr. Register of Rev. Lewis Richards, MS.690 at MdHS). On 25 June 1800 Frances was named as the extx. of Joseph Stansbury BAAD 13:284). Frances Phillips had m. 1ˢᵗ, William Gough (*q.v.*).

Porter, James, in his will made 24 Dec 1798 named his sister Rebecca, wife of Levy Cammell (Cathell or Camell) of Worcester Co. (BAWB 6:154).

Porter, Louis, orphan of Louis Porter, in June 1794 chose Catherine Porter as his guardian (BAOC 3:100).

Porter, Richard, m. by 6 Sep 1786 [-?-], heir of John Parrish (BAAD 8:307).

Potee, Lewis, Jr., and Catherine Green were m. on 12 June 1722 ((Harrison, "St. John's Parish Register:" 19). On 2 Nov 1726 Katherine [*sic*] was named as a daughter and coheir of Matthew Green, and granddaughter and grantee of Jane Boon (BALR IS#H:298).

Poteet, John, and Ann McComas were m. on 20 April 1762 (Harrison, "St. John's Parish Register:" 223). On 21 Jan 1763 Ann was named as the extx. of Daniel McComas (*q.v.*) (MDTP 39:208; see also BAAD 6:70; MDAD 49:173; BFD 4:10).

Poteet, John, m. by 1 Oct 1772 Hannah, widow of Charles Simmons, and daughter of Edward Smith (BALR AL#F: 138).

Poteet, Susanna, daughter of Francis, some time prior to 1692 was the ward of Benjamin Stanley; in Nov. 1692 Anthony Johnson petitioned to be her guardian; she died in mysterious circumstances, and in March 1692/3 Johnson's wife was tried for her murder; later Anthony Johnson was also tried (BACP F#1: 304, 347, 411).

Poteet, Thomas, and Elizabeth Taylor were m. on 24 Dec 1761 (Harrison, "St. John's Parish Register:" 223). On 8 April 1771 Elizabeth was named as a sister of Thomas Taylor (BALR AL#C:250).

Poteet, William, and Jane [*sic*] Stewart were m. on 12 June 1733 (Harrison, "St. George's Parish Register:" 268). Poteet d. by 1 Dec 1744 by which time Jane, now called Johanna had m. John Ramsey, Jr. (*q.v.*)

Pothain, Peter Francis, lately from St. Domingo, and Sarah Jervis of Baltimore Co. were m. by lic. on 19 March 1800 at St. Peter's Catholic Church, Baltimore (*Piet:* 142).

Pott, John, m, by 1 Sep 1766, [-?-], extx. of Peter Bond (BFD 5:8).

Potter, John, and Miss Kitty Snyder, both of Baltimore, were m. last eve. by Rev. Reed (*Maryland Journal and Baltimore Advertiser* 4 Dec 1795).

Potter, Dr. Nathaniel, of this city, and Miss Kitty Goldsborough, were m. in Talbot at Belleair, the seat of Mrs. Catherine Goldsborough, on Sun. eve. June 5, by Rev. Mr. Bowie (*Federal Gazette and Baltimore Daily Advertiser* 22 June 1798).

Pouder, Jacob, m. by 16 May 1795 Christian, daughter of Philip Deale (BAWB 4:83; BAAD 11:154, 12:9).

Poulson (Poleson), Cornelius, of Frederick Co. and Ann Emson were m. on 23 Dec 1720 (Harrison, "St. George's Parish Register:" 226). On 16 July 1757 Ann was named as a daughter and co-heiress of James Empson (BALR B#G:22).

Powell, [-?-], m. by 21 d. 7 m. 1736 Rebecca, mother of Simon Gregory (MWB 21:695).

Powell, [-?-], of Chester Co., Pa., m. by 16 Sep 1794 Rachel, sister of John Griffith (BAWB 5:188)

Powell, [-?-], m. by 16 March 1795 Martha, daughter of John Jordon (BAWB 5:282).

Powell, James, m. by 21 Jan 1724 Rebecca, extx. of Richard Colegate (*q.v.*) of Baltimore Co., dec. (BALR IS#H:9; MDAD 8:107; MDTP 27:77).

Powell, James, m. by 17 Oct 1737 Eleanor, daughter of Richard Hewitt (BAAD 3:250). Eleanor m. 2nd, William Harman (*q.v.*). James Powell's daughter Eleanor was paid from the estate of Richard Hewitt (BAAD 3:250).

Powell, John, m. by 29 Oct 1725 Phillis Temple, who was named in the will of Edward Weildy or Wilde (BALR IS#H:196-200, IS#L:110).

Powell, John, m. by 15 May 1734 Elizabeth, relict and widow of John Poteet, Sr., dec. (BALR HWS#M: 55).

Power, James, of Cecil Co., m. by 24 March 1746 Sarah, daughter of George Linegar of Kent Co. (BALR TB#E:537).

Power, Nicholas, m. by 11 April 1753 Elizabeth, extx. of Errick Errrickson (*q.v.*) (MDTP 33-2:89, 36:234; MDAD 33:427, 38:249).

Power, Patrick, and Margaret Gowen, were married by banns on 13 Sep 1788 at St. Peter's Catholic Church, Baltimore (*Piet:* 142).

Powers, John, of Philadelphia, and Miss Elizabeth A. Sloan of Baltimore were m. on Sat, by Rev. Bend (*Baltimore American* 27 Jan 1799).

Powley, Daniel, and Jane Logue were m. by lic. on 15 May 1800 at St. Peter's Catholic Church, Baltimore (*Piet:* 142).

Pratt, Frederick, merchant of Baltimore, and Fanny McCarty of Richmond Co., Va., were m. last eve. (*Maryland Journal and Baltimore Advertiser* 14 June 1791).

Pratten, Carolina Frederica, widow of Thomas Pratten and daughter of Dr. Charles Frederick Wiesenthal, petitioned the court that she was never summoned to be present at the appraisement of her father's personal property and when the appraisement was presented to her to sign, she absolutely refused to sign, as she had been told, and she knew from her own knowledge that some of the items had been omitted. Andrew Wiesenthal (her brother) applied several times for her to sign, but she refused. Andrew Wiesenthal promised her several times that the omitted items should be added. Andrew Wiesenthal promised "upon the Toe of a Brother and his Honour that every justice should be done. She finally signed the inventory, but the omitted items were never added to the inventory. The petitioner wanted the admx. to admit in court that some of the items have been signed (BOCP Petition of Mrs. Pratten, 1791).

Prebble, (Phibble?), John, m. by 1730 Ann, daughter of John Gallion (MWB 20:263).

Preble, Thomas, d. by Sep 1706; his widow Mary m. 2nd, Archibald Buchanan (*q.v.*).

Preiss, Johann, m. by 22 June 1762, Sophia Maerimann ("First Record Book for the Reformed and Lutheran Congregations at Manchester, Baltimore (now Carroll) Co.," *MGSB* 35:267).

Presbury, George, m. by 23 May 1736 Mary, admx. of John Nicholson (MDAD 16:137).

Presbury, George, m. by 20 July 1740 Isabella, admx. of John Bond (*q.v.*) (MDTP 31:109; MDAD 18:78, 19:492; MINV 25:42). On 5 March 1745 she was named as Isabella, daughter of William Robinson (BALR TB#E:34).

Presbury, George Goldsmith, and Elizabeth Ferguson were married by license dated 27 July 1786 (HAML; BALR WG#Z:680).

Presbury, Goldsmith, and Elizabeth Tolley were m. on 10 June 1756 (Harrison, "St. George's Parish Register:" 207). On 26 July 1781 Presbury's wife was named as a daughter of Walter Tolley who also named a grandson Walter Goldsmith Presbury (BAWB 3:507).

Presbury, James, and Martha Goldsmith were m. on 26 Feb 1708 (Harrison, "St. George's Parish Register:" 207). On 8 Feb 1709/10 Martha was named as a daughter of George Goldsmith who was the brother of Elizabeth Boothby (*q.v.*) who was the mother of Frances who m. Dr. Josias Middlemore (BALR TR#A:206; BB#I:426).

Presbury, Joseph, and Eleanor Carlisle were m. on 11 July 1723 (Harrison, "St. John's Parish Register:" On 10 April 1724 Elinor was named as the extx. of Joseph Rawlings (MDTP 27:24).

Presbury, Joseph, on 23 March 1737/8 was named as son-in-law in the will of Henry Weatherall (MWB 21:877 abst. in *Md. Cal. of Wills* 7:246). Henry Wetherall and Mrs. Ellen Presbury were m. on 20 Dec 1724 (Harrison, "St. John's Parish Register:" 25).

Presbury, Joseph, and Sarah Pycraft were m. on 11 Jan 1749 (Harrison, "St. John's Parish Register:" 200). In May 1766 Sarah was named as a daughter of Thomas Pycroft; Joseph and Sarah were the parents of Thomas Pycroft Prebsury and James Presbury (BAWB 3:5).

Presbury, Walter, son of George G. Presbury, Esq., was m. last eve. by Rev. John Ireland, to Mrs. Mary Galloway, both of Middle River Neck, Baltimore Co. (*Federal Gazette and Baltimore Daily Advertiser* 1 Sep 1797). On 18 July 1798 Mary Galloway was named as the admx. of James Galloway (BAAD 12:454). James Galloway had m. Mary Chine on 5 Sep 1790 (Harrison, "St. James' Parish Register:" 2).

Presbury, William, and Clemency Hughes were m. on 16 Jan 1757 (Harrison, "St. John's Parish Register:" 214), On 9 Jan 1769 Clemency was named as a daughter of Jonathan Hughes (BALR AL#A:146).

Presbury, William, and Cordelia Debruler were m. on 3 Sep 1771 (Harrison, "St. John's Parish Register:" 262). On 16 Feb 1772 Cordelia was named as a daughter of Wm. Debruler, Sr. (BAWB 3:324). 'Cornelia' Presbury m. [-?-] Mason (*q.v.*) by 8 May 1775.

Preshaw, John, and Ann Granger were m. by lic. dated 12 Oct 1784 (BAML). On 2 May 1785 they administered the estate of John Granger (BAAD 6:66). On 1 Feb 1794 her son Matthew was bound to George Rea, cooper, for seven years (BIND 1:7).

Press, Henry, son of Henry and Sophia, on 18 Feb 1792 chose Jacob Deiler [Deter?] as his guardian (BAOC 2:234). In Dec 1793 he chose Sophia Press as his guardian. At the same time he was bound to William Weatherly, cooper (BAOC 3:72, 74).

Presstman, George, and Frances Stokes, widow, entered into a marriage contract on 25 July 1777 (BALR WG#A:217).

Presstman, Thomas, m. by 15 Jan 1800 Phebe Kelly, extx. of Andrew Kelly (BAAD 13:178). Thomas Presstman and Phebe Kelly were m. on 9 March 1797 (Richards' Marr. Register; *Federal Gazette and Baltimore Daily Advertiser* 11 March 1797).

Preston, [-?-], m. some time after 10 Aug 1669 [-?-], heiress of Joseph Hughes (*Md. Rent Rolls,* 62).

Preston, Bernard (Barnett), and Sarah Ruff were m. on 28 Dec 1749 (Harrison, "St. George's Parish Register:" 366; Harrison, "St. John's Parish Register:" 200). Sarah was a daughter of Richard Ruff (MDTP 33-1:82). On 13 April 1752 Sarah was named as a sister of Richard Ruff and the daughter of Richard Ruff (BALR TR#D:344).

Preston, Daniel, and Ann Grafton were m. on 5 Jan 1737 (Harrison, "St. John's Parish Register:" 264); on 6 May 1773 she was admx. of William Grafton's estate (MDAD 68:160). Ann Preston, admx., on 27 June 1772 posted bond to administer the estate of William Grafton (BAAB 3:189). William Grafton had died leaving a will dated 4 Oct 1767 and proved 26 Oct 1767 in which he named his daughter Ann and her husband Daniel Preston (MWB 36:175 abst. in *Md. Cal. of Wills* 14:18).

Preston, James, m. by 9 July 1725 Sarah, daughter of Daniel Scott (BAAD 3:18).

Preston, James, and Sarah Putteet were m. on 15 May 1733 (Harrison, "St. George's Parish Register:" 268). On 5 Oct 1733 Sarah was named as a daughter of Peter Puttee (MWB 22:160 abst. in *Md. Cal. of Wills* 8:75). She was also named in the 1742 will of Rebecca Puttee (MWB 30:445).

Preston, James, and Clemency Bond were m. on 30 March 1749 (Harrison, "St. John's Parish Register:" 198). Preston's administration account of 23 Aug 1768 shows a payment to his unnamed wife for her portion of the estate of her father Benjamin Bond and of the estate of her brother John Bond (MDAD 58:219).

Preston, James, Jr., and Ann Lusby were m. on 13 May 1762 (Harrison, "St. John's Parish Register:" 223). Ann was a sister of John Lusby whose will made 25 March 1775 named his sister's son, James Lusby (MWB 40:577; abst. in *Md. Cal. of Wills* 16:105).

Preston, Luke, son of Thomas Preston, dec., on 25 Jan 1752 apprenticed himself to Sam'l McCarty to the age of 21 (BAMI 1755-1763).

Preston, Thomas, and Elizabeth Deaver were m. on 9 Dec 1721 (Harrison, "St. John's Parish Register:" 20). On 3 Jan 1731/2 Elizabeth was named as a daughter of John Deaver (MWB 20:350 abst. in *Md. Cal. of Wills* 6:215).

Preston, Thomas, formerly held land on Winter's Run, Broad Neck, Gunpowder Neck, and several parts of Harford Co. The heirs of his children, Thomas Preston and Mary Skates, are urged to contact the printer (*Maryland Journal and Baltimore Advertiser* 2 Dec 1791).

Preston, Thomas, and Margaret Connolly were married by banns on 7 Sep 1794 at St. Peter's Catholic Church, Baltimore (*Piet:* 142). Thomas Preston, about five feet, six inches high, has left his lawful wife and gone off with another woman, taking $20.00 out of the house of Anthony Connelly, near George Beem's Tavern on the Turnpike Road. Margaret Preston warns all persons she stated he would not pay the debts of Thomas Preston (*Federal Gazette and Baltimore Daily Advertiser* 5 Sep 1796).

Preston, William, m. [-?-], mother of Rebecca Bell who m. Zachary Miles (*q.v.*). Preston, in his will made 26 Dec 1796. named his wife Ann and his stepdaughter Rebecca, wife of Zachary Miles (BAWB 5:465).

Pribble, James, m. by 12 Jun 1758 [-?-], a daughter of James Laws (MDAD 41:446; BAAD 6:2½).

Pribble (Philbble), John, m, by 1730 Ann, daughter of John Gallion (MWB 20:263 abst. in *Md. Cal. of Wills* 6:201).

Pribble, John, on 17 Jan 1732 was named as a son, and Sarah and Thomas Pribble were named as grandchildren in the will of Mary Buchannan, widow of Archibald Buchannan (MWB 30:698 abst. in *Md. Cal. of Wills* 7:23).

Pribble, John, Jr., in Nov 1756 was charged with begetting a bastard on the body of Mary Lee (BACP BB#C:312, TR#6:1, 41).

Pribble, John, m. by 23 Aug 1769 [-?-], daughter of James Preston (BAAD 7:314).

Price, [-?-], m. by 5 Sep 1763 Patty, daughter of Richard Demmett (MWB 34:215 abst. in *Md. Cal. of Wills* 13:122).

Price, [-?-], m. by 12 Sep 1778 Ann, daughter of David How (BAWB 3:378).

Price, [-?-], m. by 1 March 1780 Ann, daughter of Walter Moore of Gunpowder Forest, Baltimore Co., farmer (BAWB 3:450; BAAD 11:61).

Price, [-?-], m. by 1 Oct 1781 Susanna, daughter of Richard Chenoweth, blacksmith (BAWB 3:434).

Price, [-?-], m. by 12 Oct 1786, Helena, daughter of Joseph Peregoy (BACT 1785-1788, MS 2865 at MdHS: 206).

Price, [-?-], m. by 27 Aug 1792 Sophia, daughter of Thomas Cole (BAWB 5:53).

Price, Aquila, d. by March 1773 leaving a widow Ann, and a daughter Leah. In 1794 William Matthews petitioned the court stating that Aquila, d. in 1773, leaving a widow and one child, an heiress. His brother Mordecai Price prevailed on the widow to let him administer the estate, and to be guardian of the child. The widow chose her third part of the land, on which there was no dwelling house. William Matthews petitioned the court in 1794 stating he m. the widow and built a house on the land. Mordecai Price told him that Matthews had no right to build on the land or commit waste [*i.e.,* cut down trees]. Now Mordecai Price's ward has chosen Matthews as her guardian (BOCP Petition of William Matthews, 1794).

Price, Benjamin, and Elizabeth Hewett were m. on 22 June 1730 (Harrison, "St. Paul's Parish Register:" 150). On 17 Oct 1737 Elizabeth was named as the widow of Richard Hewitt (BAAD 3:250).

Price, Benjamin, m. by 7 June 1762 [-?-], daughter of James Bosley (MDAD 48:74; BAAD 6:131).

Price, Israel, and Hannah Brown, on 13 d 4 m. 1797 declared their intention to marry ("Minutes of Baltimore Meeting," *QRNM:*228).

Price, John, Jr., son of John, and Urith Cole were m. 26 d. 1 m. 1753 ("Abstracts of Gunpowder Meeting," MS. at MdHS). In Dec 1772 Urith was named as a daughter of Dennis Garrett Cole (BAWB 3:252).

Price, John, m. by 20 April 1798 Sarah Sanderson (BALR WG#56:180).

Price, Joshua, on 29 d. 5 m. 1784 was disowned for having been m. by a hireling priest ("Minutes of Gunpowder Meeting," *QRNM:* 79). Joshua Price and Martha Lemmon were m. by lic. dated 20 Jan 1784 (BAML).

Price, Leah. See Gill, Leah.

Price, Mordecai, son of Mordecai and Elizabeth, and Rachel Moore, daughter of Walter and Ann, were m. on 27 d. 12 m. 1759 ("Records of Gunpowder Monthly Meeting," *QRNM:*47; BAWB 3:450).

Price, Mordecai, son of John and Rebecca, and Angelina Tipton, daughter of William and Angeline were m. on 1 d. 1 m. 1772 ("Records of Gunpowder Meeting," MS. at MdHS: 258). William Tipton, in his will made 17 Aug 1796 named his son-in-law Mordecai Price (BAWB 5:509).

Price, Mordecai, of Mordecai, and Charity Comly on 25 d. 7 m. 1795 were reported as having as having been married by a hireling priest ("Minutes of Gunpowder Meeting," *QRNM:*97). [No other marriage reference found].

Price, Nathan, and Ruth Thomas were m. on 17 Feb 1785 (Marr. Returns of Rev. William West, Scharf Papers, MS.1999 at MdHS). She was a daughter of John Thomas (BAWB 7:185).

Price, Nathaniel, m. by 22 Feb 1791 Elizabeth, widow of James Harryman (who left a son David Harryman (BALR WG#FF:504).

Price, Nathaniel, of Middletown Township, Bucks Co., son of Nathaniel Price, m. 13th day of 12th month, 1792, Mary Spicer, daughter of James and Rachel Spicer, of Maryland ("Minutes of Middleton Meeting, Bucks Co., Pa.," *MGSB* 34 (3) (Spring 1993) 201).

Price, Peter, stated he would not pay the debts of his wife Mary Maria (*Maryland Journal and Baltimore Advertiser* 17 March 1783).

Price. Rebecka. See Rebecka Pitts.

Price, Robert, and Elizabeth Miles were m. 18 Sep 1739 (Harrison, "St. John's Parish Register:" 127). On 5 April 1740 Elizabeth was named as the admx. of Evan Miles (q.v.) (MDTP 31:88).

Price, Susanna. See John Bosley.

Price, Thomas, and Keturah Merryman were m. on 1 July 1732 Harrison, "St. Paul's Parish Register:" 151). On 16 Jan 1754 Rebecca was named as a daughter of Samuel Merryman (MWB 29:876 abst. by Gibb).

Price, William, m. by 13 June 1795 Sophia Cole, representative of Thomas Cole (BAAD 12:18).

Price, Zachariah, and Sarah Richardson were married by license dated 22 Oct 1783 (BAML). On 14 Feb 1792 she received a share of the estate of James Richardson (BAAD 10:536).

Prichard. See Pritchard.

Priery, Mary, on 13 June 1774 was named as a sister-in-law of John Little of Baltimore Town (MWB 40:108; abst. in *Md. Cal. of Wills* 16:23).

Prigg, William, and Martha Morgan were m. on 21 or 22 Nov 1749 (Harrison, "St. George's Parish Register:" 364; (Harrison, "St. John's Parish Register:" 199). She was a daughter of Edward Morgan (MWB 40:401, abst. in *Md. Cal. of Wills* 16:69).

Prill, Frederick, m. by 15 Oct 1791 Elizabeth, daughter of Conrad Smith of Baltimore Co. (BALR WG#GG:569).

Prince, Thomas, son of John and Alice, now aged 9, in Nov 1775 was bound to Daniel Stansbury, shoemaker (BAMI 1772, 1775-1781: 152).

Prindell, John, m. by 1767, Eleanor, legatee of Richard Bond (BFD 5:74).

Pringle, Capt. James, of the *Pallas,* East Indiaman, was m. to Miss Sally Forsythe of Fell's Point, a daughter of Robert Forsythe (*Maryland Journal and Baltimore Advertiser* 18 Nov 1785; BAAD 9:168).

Pringle, Mark, merchant, was m. last eve. By the Rev. Mr. Ireland at Willow Brook, the seat of Mr. Thorowgood Smith, to Miss Lucy Stith, both of this city (*Federal Gazette and Baltimore Daily Advertiser* 7 July 1797).

Prior, Thomas, of Baltimore Co., m. by 7 Aug 1671 Margaret, daughter and sole heir of Rowland Reynolds of Anne Arundel Co. (AALR IH#1:302).

Pristo. See Fisha.

Pritchard, Elizabeth, was charged with bastardy at the March 1742/3 Court and again the Aug 1745 Court; she was the mother of Elizabeth, b. 28 Jan 1743/4, and Sarah, b. 17 March 1744/5 (BACP TB#D: 121, 135, 185; Reamy, *St. George's Parish Register:* 7).

Pritchard (Prichard), Herbert, m. by 23 Jan 172-, Mary, daughter of John Arden, who left 'sons and daus.' (BALR IS#G:81).

Pritchard, James, on 22 Sep 1743 was named as a son-in-law of John Durbin, Sr. (MWB 23:286 abst. in *Md. Cal. of Wills* 8:236). James Pritchard and Elizabeth Durbin were m. on 1 May 1735 (Harrison, "St. George's," p. 283).

Pritchard, Obadiah, and Elizabeth Litten were m. on 7 Feb 1733 (Harrison, "St. George's Parish Register:" 269). On 29 Jan 1756 Elizabeth was named as a daughter in the will of Thomas Litten who named his grandchildren Samuel and Ann Pritchard (MWB 31:419 abst. by Gibb).

Pritchard, Samuel, and Isabella Cotrall were m. on 13 July 1735 (Harrison, "St. George's Parish Register:" 283). On 23 March 1765 Isabella was named as a daughter of John Cotterall (BALR B#O).

Pritchard, Stephen James, on 9 Dec 1753 was named as a son-in-law in the will of Edward Wakeman, chirurgeon (MWB 29:26 abst. by Gibb).

Pritchert, Margaret, on 22 d. 8 m., 1770 was condemned for outgoing in marriage ("Minutes of Gunpowder Meeting," QRNM: 60). [No other marriage reference found].

Probert, James, and Mrs. Mary Veale, both of Baltimore, were m. last eve. by Rev. Bend (*Baltimore American* 14 June 1799).

Proctor, Izak, on 12 d. 9 m. 1799 requested a certificate in order to marry Rebecca Farquhar, a member of Falls Monthly Meeting in Bucks Co., Pa. ("Minutes of Baltimore Meeting," *QRNM:*234). Izak Proctor of Baltimore, Md., son of Stephen Proctor, dec., and his wife Rebecca, both late of York, Eng., m. 13th day, 11 mo., 1799, Rebecca Farquhar, daughter of Adam and Elizabeth Farquhar of Falls Twp., Bucks Co., Pa. ("Records of Falls Monthly Meeting, Bucks Co., Pa.," *MGSB* 35 (1) (Winter 1994) 55).

Proctor, Margaret, servant of Edmund Talbott, was charged with bastardy at the June 1740 Court and presented at the Aug 1740 Court (BACP TB#TR: 266, 303).

Prosser (Proser), Charles, and Elizabeth Colegate were m. by lic. dated 26 Oct 1782 (BAML). Elizabeth Proser [*sic*], formerly Colegate, on 30 d. 11 m. 1782 was reported as having gone out in marriage to a man not of our membership("Minutes of Gunpowder Meeting," *QRNM:*76). She was the widow of [-?-] Colegate (*q.v.*) and daughter of Walter Moore of Gunpowder Forest, Baltimore Co., farmer (BAWB 3:450; BAAD 11:61).

Prouin, Andrew, and Mary Ann Fournachon were m. by lic. on 7 Aug 1792 at St. Peter's Catholic Church, Baltimore (*Piet:* 142).

Prout, William, merchant of Baltimore, and Sarah Slater, daughter of Jonathan Slater, were m. last Tues. eve. at *Bradford's Rest,* Montgomery Co. (*Baltimore Evening Post* 10 May 1793).

Prudhomme, John Baptist, and Mary Glodine Babineau were m. by lic. on 14 Aug 1793 at St. Peter's Catholic Church, Baltimore (*Piet:* 142; BAML, which gives their names as John Baptiste Prudheimme and Mary Gledine).

Pryon, Peter, and Mrs. Margaret Cole, both of Fell's Point, were m. last Sat. (*Maryland Journal and Baltimore Advertiser* 24 March 1796).

Publitz, Peter, m. by 13 June 1792 [-?-], who received an equal share of the estate of John Markee (BAAD 11:80).

Publitz, Stophel, m. by 13 Dec 1791 [-?-], who received an equal share of the estate of Christian Shaver (BAAD 10:486).

Pue, Dr. Arthur, was m. at Auburn last eve, by Rev. Mr. Lyell, to Rebecca Ridgely Buchanan (*Federal Gazette and Baltimore Daily Advertiser* 13 Nov 1800).

Puelly, [-?-], m. by 12 Aug 1788 Mary, admx. of Daniel Ross (*q.v.*) (BAAD 9:288).

Puggsley, [-?-], of Baltimore Co., m. by 1792, Isabella Ackworth (MCHP 551).

Pugh, Jacob, on 14 d. 2 m. 1799 reportedly had his marriage accomplished contrary to the good order ("Minutes of Baltimore Meeting," *QRNM:*232). Jacob Pugh and Elizabeth Morgan were married by license dated 15 Sep 1798 (BAML).

Pumphrey, Mary, lately called Mary Cockey, on 16 May 1720 posted bond to administer the estate of William Cockey (BAAB 1:303; MDTP 24:175; BALR IS#H:32).

Pumphrey, Joseph, m. by 19 Dec 1741 Ann, daughter of William Cockey of Anne Arundel Co. (PCLR EI#3:279; TB#D:250).

Pumphrey, Nathan, m. by 14 Aug 1722 Mary, admx. of William Cockey (MDTP 26:20; MDAD 4:183, 6:13).

Pumphrey, Sylvanus, in March 1718/9, was charged with begetting a bastard on the body of Sarah Cockey (BACP IS#C:62).

Puntany, [-?-], d. by 8 March 1776; m. Ann [-?-], who m. 2nd, Marbry (Maybury) Helms, and whose will made 8 March 1776, named her son Edward Puntany and her grandchildren Edward and Ann Puntany (MWB 41:23; abst. in *Md. Cal. of Wills* 16:141).

Puntany, William, d. by 8 Jan 1730 having m. Ann, daughter of Edward Parrish (BALR IS#L: 90).

Puntany (Pontaney), William, and Sarah Wooden were m. on 29 Sep 1745 Harrison, "St. Paul's Parish Register:" 157). She was a daughter of John Wooden, whose will dated 29 Aug 1760 named his grandson Edward Puntany, son of his daughter Sarah (MWB 37:82 abst. in *Md. Cal. of Wills* 14:77).

Puntany (Ponteny), William, of Baltimore Town, advertised that his wife Susanna had eloped from his bed and board (Annapolis *Maryland Gazette* 20 Oct 1763).

Purdue. See Perdue.

Purveal, Gideon, on 2 d. 2 m. 1775 announced that he intended to marry Mary Harris, daughter of Samuel and Margaret Harris ("Minutes of Deer Creek Meeting," *QRNM:* 136).

Purviance, James, and Miss Eliza Young, both of Baltimore, were m. last eve. by Rev. Allison (*Baltimore Telegraphe* 24 Nov 1797).

Purviance, John, Esq. was m. last eve. by Rev. Dr. Allison, to Miss A. Dugan, daughter of Cumberland Dugan, Esq. (*Federal Gazette and Baltimore Daily Advertiser* 4 Jan 1799).

Purviance, Matthew, and Juliet Caton were m. on 8 Jan 1799 at St. Peter's Catholic Church, Baltimore (*Piet:* 142).

Pusey, George, late of New Garden MM, son of John, dec. and Catherine, on 3 d. 8 m. 1769 intends to marry Sarah Cox, daughter of William and Mary ("Minutes of Deer Creek Meeting," *QRNM:* 133).

Puttee. See Potee.

"Q"

Quare, John, in June 1719 was charged with begetting a bastard on the body of Margaret Cannaday (BACP IS#C:198).

Quay, Thomas, had been bound to William Davidson, house carpenter; on 14 March 1787 Quay's mother Eleanor Summers petitioned the court that her son would be of age on 1 July 1788, and he had not been taught the trade as he was supposed to (BOCP Petition of Thomas Quay, 1787, Box 2, Folder 1).

Queen, Edward, a free Negro, and Slave Ann of Charles Wells were m. on 12 Nov 1797 at St. Peter's Catholic Church, Baltimore (*Piet:* 142)

Quick, Elizabeth, servant of Lance Todd, was charged with bastardy at the March 1724/5 Court (BACP IS&TW#4:127).

Quine, Henry. See Henry James.

Quine, William, on 21 Feb 1738 was named as a brother-in-law in the will of John Ingram (MWB 22:160 abst. in *Md. Cal. of Wills* 8:75).

Quinlan, Edmond, and Jane Cox were married by banns on 30 Jan 1790 at St. Peter's Catholic Church, Baltimore (*Piet:* 142). Jane Quinlan, (formerly Cox), on 27 d. 3 m. 1790 was condemned for being married by a hireling ("Minutes of Gunpowder Meeting," *QRNM:* 88).

Quinlin, Philip, convict, in Nov 1754 was charged with begetting a bastard on the body of Elizabeth Port (BACP BB#A:20-21).

Quinlin, Philip, m. by Aug 1758 Charity, daughter of Isaac Butterworth (BALR B#H:221).

Quirk, Peter, and Margaret Chaney were m. by lic. on 10 July 1792 at St. Peter's Catholic Church, Baltimore (*Piet:* 142).

"R"

Rabba, Simon, had warned the public not to trust his wife Sally, who replied that she has never asked anyone to credit her on her husband's account, and he has treated her in a most contemptuous manner and left her and the children destitute of all assistance for four months (*Federal Gazette and Baltimore Daily Advertiser* 1 Nov 1800).

Raddad, Matthew, in his will made 14 Sep1797 named Catherine Adams (not yet 16), 'daughter of my mother' by Alexander Adams of Baltimore, and George and Elizabeth Adams, brother and sister of Catherine. His uncles Lawrence and John Bousman were named execs. (BAWB 6:27).

Ragan, Michael, and Mary Fitzpatrick, natives of Ireland, were married by banns on 4 Feb 1799 at St. Peter's Catholic Church, Baltimore (*Piet:* 142).

Raham, Jacob, m. by 8 Dec 1787 [-?-], daughter of Charles Leybold (BAWB 4:292). **See Charles Labold.**

Ralph, Isaac, m. by 4 Aug 1752 Keziah, admx. of Moses Rutter (*q.v.*) (MINV 50:35).

Ramo, Jean, free Mulatto, and Magdalaine, Mulatto, were m. on 27 May 1800 at St. Peter's Catholic Church, Baltimore (*Piet:* 142).

Ramsay, Col. Dennis, merchant, was m. to Miss Jenny Taylor, daughter of Capt. Jesse Taylor (*Maryland Journal and Baltimore Advertiser* 29 Nov 1785).

Ramsay, William, d. by 25 May 1772 when Sarah Ramsay, admx., signed she would posted bond to administer Ramsay's estate, but in the 'Condition" of the bond her name is given as Sarah Thompson. James Thompson and Sam Thompson were sureties (BAAB 5:223).

Ramsey, [-?-], m. by 31 Aug 1772 Sarah, daughter of Samuel Durham (MWB 39:16, abst. in *Md. Cal. of Wills* 15:3).

Ramsey, [-?-], m. by 8 April 1800, Mary, daughter of Barbara Wood (BAWB 6:262).

Ramsey, Charles, m. by 1 March 1691 Elizabeth, relict of John Walley (*q.v.*) and daughter of Thomas Thurston (BALR RM#HS:340; INAC 13A:317).

Ramsey, John, Jr., m. by 1 Dec 1744 Johanna, admx. of William Poteet (*q.v.*) of Baltimore Co. (MDAD 21:39; BAAD 5:4). (MDAD 21:39; BAAD 5:4).

Randall, [-?-], m. by 14 March 1706 Hannah, sister of Thomas Bale (MWB 12:220 abst. in *Md. Cal. of Wills* 3:102).

Randall, [-?-], m. by 24 Sep 1788 Sarah, daughter of John Belt (BAWB 4:350).

Randall, [-?-], m. by 20 Sep 1795 Rebecca, daughter of Nicholas Baker (BAWB 6L212).

Randall, Ann, formerly Carr, on 25 d. 10 m. 1788, was charged with going out in marriage ("Minutes of Gunpowder Meeting," *QRNM:*86). [No other marriage reference found].

Randall, Catherine, formerly Ball, on 25 d. 11 m. 1786 was condemned for outgoing in marriage ("Minutes of Gunpowder Meeting," *QRNM:*83). [No other marriage reference found].

Randall, Charles, m. by 13 June 1792 Dinah Royston (or Riston), who received an equal share of £51.5.6¾ from the estate of Thomas Royston (or Riston) (BAAD 11:71).

Randall, Chas., m. by 12 April 1797 Dinah Ford, legatee of William Sinclair (BAAD 12:287).

Randall, Christopher, m. by 14 Jan 1722 Ann, sister of William Chew of BA Co. (BAAD 1:109). Ann m. 2nd, James Burk (Burke) (*q.v.*).

Randall, Israel, was m. Sat. eve. by Rev. Mr. Bend, to Miss Delilah Lee, both of this town (*Federal Gazette and Baltimore Daily Advertiser* 27 June 1796).

Randall, Thomas Beal, Esq., was m. last Thurs. eve. by Rev. Mr. Lisle, to Martha Thomas, both of this city (*Federal Gazette and Baltimore Daily Advertiser* 31 Dec 1800).

Randall, William, and Constant Cockey were m. on 15 Jan 1758 (Harrison, "St. Thomas Parish Register:" 71). On 27 July 1761 Constant was named as the widow and admx. of William Cockey (*q.v.*) (MDTP 38:152; MWB 30:151; BAAD 6:209).

Randall, William, aged under 14, son of Richard Randall, on 16 June 1787 was made a ward of Richard Randall (BAOC 2:73).

Rankin, Elizabeth, on 23 March 1784 was named as grandmother in the will of Margaret McCulloch (BAWB 4:26).

Rapinot, Michael, born at Fougeres, Parish of St. Leonard, Prov. of Brittany, Diocese of Rennes, and Mary Rose Pellerin, born Isle of Grenada, Parish of Our Lady of the Assumption, District of Marquis, were m. by lic. on 27 Dec 1786 at St. Peter's Catholic Church, Baltimore (*Piet:* 142).

Rardin, William, and Rachel Miller were m. by lic. on 6 Oct 1792 at St. Peter's Catholic Church, Baltimore (*Piet:* 142).

Raredon, John, and Honor Raredon [*sic*] were married by banns on 10 Aug 1788 at St. Peter's Catholic Church, Baltimore (*Piet:* 142).

Rattenbury, John, m. 30 Dec 1701 Margaret Besson, b. 31 Jan 1673/4, daughter of Thomas and Margaret (Saughier) Besson ("Philip Jones Bible," *MdHM* 14:76-79, *MBR* 7:101).

Rattenbury, John, in Nov 1712 was charged with begetting a bastard on the body of Margaret Durham (BACP IS#B:335).

Rattebury, John, and Margaret Jones were m. on 3 Nov 1745 Harrison, "St. Paul's Parish Register:" 15). Rattenbury d. testate leaving his wife Margaret and her father, Capt. Philip Jones, joint execs., but Margaret declined to serve, and 4 June 1746 Jones posted bond to administer Rattenbury's estate (BAAB 5:173). Margaret m. 2nd, Josephus Murray (*q.v.*).

Raven, Esther, on 7 Dec 1708 was named as a daughter in the will of Thomas Preston (MWB 13:155 abst. in *Md. Cal. of Wills* 3:185).

Raven, Isaac, m. by 7 Feb 1748/9 Letitia, daughter of Joseph Ward of Back River; they were the parents of Luke, Elizabeth, Letitia, Hester, Kezia, Abarilla, and Drusilla Raven (MWB 29:70 abst. by Gibb).

Raven, Luke, 'a member of the Church of England,' on 13 March 1724/5 stated he had been married for some years to Elizabeth, daughter of Thomas and Mary Hughes; she has absented herself from me and the care of her family since 9 Dec 1724; he excludes her from her thirds, and will no longer pay her debts. John Stokes, Clerk of the Court, wrote that the above was countermanded and entered by mistake (BALR IS#H:30). Raven repeated this posting on 15 Nov 1725 (BALR IS#H:207). Eliza Raven m. 2nd, William Hammond (*q.v.*).

Raven, Luke, Jr., m. by 21 April 1728 Sarah, daughter of Thomas (?) Major (BAAD 2:309; MDAD 9:327, in admin. account of James Crook; AALR RD#2:86).

Raven, Luke, m. by 17 April 1796 Eleanor Harryman, legatee of George Harryman (BAAD 12:183).

Rawlings, Dorothy (or Dority), was charged with bastardy in March 1743 and was fined on 5 June 1734 (BACP Liber 1743-1745: 154, 237).

Rawlings, John, and Eleanor Ridgely were m. on 13 Jan 1712 (Harrison, "All Hallows Parish Register," MS. at MdHS: 272). He d. by 19 Feb 1722 when Eleanor Carlisle (*q.v.*), extx., posted bond to administer his estate (BAAB 4:347).

Rawlings, William, m. by 22 Aug 1795 Temperance, daughter of Edward Wigley (BAWB 5:328).

Rawlings. See also Rollins.

Ray, William, m. by 31 Aug 1760 Martha, daughter of John Dunn (BAWB 3:130; MDAD 60:295).

Ray, William, of Alexandria, Va., m. by 14 July 1794 Ann Puntenay of Baltimore Co. (WG#OO:463).

Raymond, Dr. Frederick, was married in Baltimore by Rev. Mr. Bend, to Miss Rachel Cannon of this town (*Baltimore Evening Post* 28 Nov 1792).

Rea, William, and Mary Gardiner were m. by lic. on 5 Nov 1792 at St. Peter's Catholic Church, Baltimore (*Piet:* 142).

Read, John, m. Catherine [-?-] by 30 April 1773 when their daughter Sarah was b. ("John Read Bible," *MBR* 1:201-202).

Read (Reed), John, and Martha Rolam [*sic*] were married by license dated 18 Nov 1779 (BAML). On 5 March 1783 Martha was named as a daughter of Thomas Rowland (BAWB 3:540).

Read, John, and Eliza Jackson were m. on 12 April 1757 (Harrison, "St. George's Parish Register:" 355). John Read of *My Lady's Manor* gave notice his wife Elizabeth had left him (*Maryland Journal and Baltimore Advertiser* 1 Oct 1784). John Reed [*sic*], of *My Lady's Manor* again gave notice that his wife Elizabeth had eloped from him (*Maryland Journal and Baltimore Advertiser* 11 March 1785).

Read (Reed), Joseph, and Agnes Miller were m. 28 March 1774 (Marr. Register of Rev. Lewis Richards, MS.690 at MdHS). On 6 Dec 1785 Agnes was named as a daughter of Hugh Miller, yeoman (BAWB 4:391).

Read, Larkin, and Edith Perigo were m. 5 May 1796 (Marr. Register of Rev. Lewis Richards, MS.690 at MdHS). On 13 d. 10 m. 1796 Larkin Read was charged with accomplishing his marriage contrary to the good order; he was disowned on 12 d. 10 m. 1797 ("Minutes of Baltimore Meeting," *QRNM:*227, 229).

Read (Reed), Matthew, and Elizabeth Lucas were m. by lic. dated 20 May 1793 (BAML). Matthew, a Protestant, and Elizabeth Lucas were m. at St. Peter's Catholic Church, Baltimore (*Piet:* 142). In Sep 1794 Matthew Read stated he would not pay the debts of his wife Elizabeth, who has eloped from his bed and board without any reason (*Baltimore Daily Intelligencer* 11 Sep 1794).

Read. See also Reed.

Ready, John, m. by 21 March 1778 Rachel, admx. of Benjamin Baxter (BAAD 8:7, 11:230).

Reaston, Edward, d. by 12 Nov 1754 by which time his extx. Rachel had m. 2nd, Renaldo Monk (*q.v.*) (MDTP 36:96).

Reaves, See Reeves.

Rebald, Nicholas, m. by 13 Dec 1791 [-?-], who received an equal share of the estate of Christian Shaver (BAAD 10:486).

Red, Jacob, and Ann Pierpoint, on 23 d. 8 m. 1773, declared their intention to marry (Minutes of Gunpowder Monthly Meeting: *QRNM:*64).

Redman, Mary Ann, was charged with bastardy at March Court 1765. Joseph Norris, constable, was summoned (BAMI 1765: 11).

Redstone, Mary, warned all persons she would not pay the debts of her husband Samuel Redstone and she disowned him as her husband (*Baltimore Daily Intelligencer* 22 March 1794).

Reed, George, and Dinah Lane were m. on 7 Nov 1790 (Marr. Returns of Rev. John Hagerty, Scharf Papers, MS. 1999 at MdHS). On 23 July 1782 [*sic*] Dinah was named as a daughter of John Lane who d. owning *Williams' Forest,* and *Addition to William* (BALR WG#64:472).

Reed, Capt. James, and Nelly Taylor of Baltimore were m. Tues. eve., 13th inst. (*Maryland Journal and Baltimore Advertiser* 23 April 1790).

Reed, Nelson, and Nancy Steyer were m. on 8 June 1790 (Marriage Returns of Henry Wills, Scharf Papers, MS. 1999 at MdHS). On 11 March 1799 Nancy was named as the widow of George Steyer (BALR WG#57:662).

Reed, Robert, of Philadelphia, and Miss Catherine Connor of Baltimore, were m. by Rev. William Marshall [date not given] (*The Philadelphia Minerva* 24 Sep 1796).

Reed. See also Read.

Rees, David, on 30 d. 8 m. 1788 was charged with having a child in an unmarried state ("Minutes of Gunpowder Meeting," *QRNM:*86).

Rees, David, of Baltimore, merchant, and Mrs. Mary Rothery were m. last Thurs. by Rev. Emerson at Portsmouth (*Maryland Journal and Baltimore Advertiser* 25 Nov 1788).

Rees, John, and wife Ann on 27 d. 1 m. 1787 apologized for marrying contrary to the order of Friends ("Minutes of Gunpowder Meeting," *QRNM:*84). See below.

Rees, John Evan, and Ann Lacey, a member of Little Falls Preparative Meeting were m. by a priest ("Minutes of Gunpowder Meeting," *QRNM:*80). See above.

Rees, Joseph, and Mary Rea on 25 d. 2 m. 1786 were disowned for being m. by a hireling minister ("Minutes of Gunpowder Meeting," *QRNM:*81). [No other marriage reference found].

Rees. See Also Reese.

Reese, [-?-], m. by 7 June 1794 Dorothy, daughter of Jacob Shaffer (BAWB 6:249).

Reese, [-?-], m. by 2 May 1798 Drusilla, legatee of Richardson Stansbury BAAD 12:412).

Reese, Daniel, on 30 d. 4 m. 1796 was reported as having married contrary to the good order, and joined the Methodist Society ("Minutes of Gunpowder Meeting," *QRNM:*98). [No other marriage reference found].

Reese, Daniel, and Elizabeth Bond were married by license dated 28 July 1790 (BAML). On 14 Aug 1800 Elizabeth was named as an heir of Thomas Bond (BAAD 13:316).

Reese, George, and Ann Reese were married by license dated 7 March 1778 (BAML). On 2 Sep 1779 Ann was named as the admx. of Henry Reese of Baltimore Co. (BALR WG#D:232).

Reese, George, and Elizabeth Eaglestone were married by license dated 20 Feb 1784 (BAML). On 12 April 1785 Elizabeth was named as a legatee of Abraham Eaglestone [She was probably a widow of Vincent Green (*q.v.*)] (BAWB 3:494; BAAD 8:164).

Reese, George, admin., on 20 Nov 1799 posted bond to administer the estate of Catherine Reed Martin (BAAB 9:15).

Reese, Henry, was allowed a sum for the support of Bridget Thompson's child named Thomas from 19 Feb to 1 April (Baltimore Co. 1772 Levy List).

Reese, Henry, and Mary Burtell [*sic*] were married by license dated 19 May 1791 (BAML). On 18 June 1800 Mary Burtles received one-third of the estate of John Burtles (BAAD 13:286).

Reese, John, was m. last eve. by Rev. Mr. Bend, to Miss Elizabeth Rush (Rusk?), all of this place (*Federal Gazette and Baltimore Daily Advertiser* 4 Feb 1799).

Reese, John, of Baltimore, was m. last Thurs. eve. by Rev. Mr. Hinch, to Miss Polly Zacharia, near Westminster, Frederick Co. (*Federal Gazette and Baltimore Daily Advertiser* 30 Nov 1799).

Reese, Margaret, (late Morgan), on 27 d. 3 m. 1794 was found guilty of marrying a man not in membership with us, with the assistance of a Baptist teacher ("Minutes of Deer Creek Meeting," *QRNM:* 154). [No other marriage reference found].

Reese, Mary, daughter of Christian Reese, dec., in May 1976 chose John Reese as her guardian (BAOC 3:194).

Reese, Solomon, and his wife were allowed a sum for their support (Baltimore Co. Levy List 1772).

Reese, William, and Ann O'Herd were m. on 10 July 1746 (Harrison, "St. George's Parish Register:" 353). William Reese (Reice) on 27 Nov 1742 was named as a brother-in-law of John Aughard (MWB 25:332 abst. by Gibb).

Reese. See also Rees.

Reeves, [-?-], d. by 25 Dec 1779 having m. Prudence, daughter of James Kelly, husbandman (BAWB 3:397; BAAD 10:288).

Reeves, Anthony, and Elizabeth McKenzie were m. on 2 May 1793 Harrison, "St. Paul's Parish Register:" 266). As administrator, on 22 Dec 1798 he posted bond to administer that part of the estate of Benjamin McKinsey which had not been administered by Susanna McKinsey, dec. (BAAB 8:446).

Reeves, Edward, m. by 18 July 1682 Henrietta, widow and admx. of Thomas Cannon (*q.v.*), and of William Robinson (*q.v.*) and Edward Swanson (*q.v.*) (INAC 7C:183; BACP D:187; BALR RM#HS:58).

Reeves, Edward, d. by 19 Dec 1688, leaving a widow Mary who had m. 1st, John Hammond (*q.v.*), 2nd, Samuel Brand (*q.v.*), and 4th, Richard Askew (*q.v.*) (MDTP 14:124, 15A:8, 26, 27; BALR IR#AM:68; BACP F#1:128, G#1:84).

Reeves, George, and Margaret Miller were married by banns on 18 Sep 1792 at St. Peter's Catholic Church, Baltimore (*Piet:* 142). Margaret m. 2nd, Anthony Holmes (*q.v.*).

Reeves, Josias, and Letitia Raven were m. on 11 Jan 1756 (Harrison, "St. John's Parish Register:" 213). On 12 July 1774 Letitia was named as an heir of Isaac Raven and sister of Luke Raven (BAAD 6:3257:228).

Reeves, Richard, and Margaret Orc were married by license dated 9 Feb 1791 (BAML). In Aug 1795 Reeves stated he would not pay the debts of his wife Margaret (*Federal Intelligencer and Baltimore Daily Gazette* 10 Aug 1795).

Reeves (Reaves), William, on 12 Dec 1728 was named as a son in the will of Jonas Bowen (MWB 19:580 abst. in *Md. Cal. of Wills* 6:92).

Reeves, William, and his marriage to Mary Gott was stopped for bigamy c1745 ("St. John's and St. George's Parish Register Vestry Proceedings," MS. at the MdHS).

Reeves, Capt. William, of this place, was m. last eve. to Miss Abigail Grate of York Co., Penna. (*Federal Intelligencer and Baltimore Daily Gazette* 24 April 1795). They were m. by lic. on 23 April 1795 at St. Peter's Catholic Church, Baltimore (*Piet:* 142).

Regain, Michael, and Catherine O'Donnel were married by banns on 17 July 1791 at St. Peter's Catholic Church, Baltimore (*Piet:* 142).

Reger, [-?-], m. by 2 Dec 1771 Mary, daughter of Susanna Rantz, late of Va., now of Baltimore; they had children John and Susanna Reger (BAWB 3:263).

Reid (Reed), Robert, and Catherine Conner were m. on 12 Sep 1796 (Marriage Register of Rev. Lewis Richards, MS. 690 at MdHS). In June 1797 Reid stated he would not pay the debts of his wife Catherine by reason of her conduct (*Federal Gazette and Baltimore Daily Advertiser* 14 June 1797),

Reigart, John, of Penna., was m. yesterday by the Rev. Mr. [Altonier?] to Miss Ann Mary Keener, daughter of Christian Keener of Baltimore Co. (*Federal Gazette and Baltimore Daily Advertiser* 12 April 1799).

Reilly, John, and Mary Landragan, natives of Ireland, were m. by lic. on 25 Sep 1797 at St. Peter's Catholic Church, Baltimore (*Piet:* 142; BAML, which gives her name as Mary Lundragan).

Reily, William, in 1775 was a Sergeant in Baltimore Co. Militia; later was a Captain in the Maryland Line during the Revolutionary War; he d. 8 July 1824; m. Barbara Hodgkin on 28 Sep 1791 at Bloomsbury, near Baltimore, the seat of her father Thomas Brooke Hodgkin; their first child, Clajon Reily, was b. in Augusta, Ga., on 10 Aug 1792; their second child, William Reily, was b. at the same place on 16 Sep 1794, d. 27 July 1795; their third child was John Reily, b. 23 March 1797 at Philadelphia; 'our Creole daughter' was b. 12 June 1794; a son Th. B. Reily applied for a pension on behalf of his mother (Rev. War Pension Application of Barbara Reily: W26377; Harrison, "St. Paul's," p. 254; BAWB 7:415).

Reinecker, Conrad, and Eve Fite were married by license dated 7 Jan 1790 (BAML). On 12 June 1792 Eve received a share of the estate of Henry Fite (BAAD 11:69, 532).

Reinecker, George, m. by 6 June 1792 Elizabeth, daughter of Henry Fite; he was guardian of Mary, Ann, John, Elizabeth, and Andrew Fite, orphans of Andrew Fite (BAAD 11:69).

Reister, Philip, m. Eve [-?-] on 21 March 1773 ("Owings Family Bible," *HMGB* 3 (3) (July 1932) 18-20).

Renaud, John, of Petersburg, Va., and Ariana Finegan, widow, were m. by lic. on 27 Aug 1796 at St. Peter's Catholic Church, Baltimore (*Piet:* 142). She may be the Ariana Finegan who was m. to Samuel Peniston by BAML dated 18 Aug 1798).

Renaudet, Peter Abraham, (son of Peter and Mary Merlat, Parish of Arce in Saint-Onge), and Ann Guttrow (daughter of Joseph and Ann Tibodeau), were m. by lic. on 17 Nov 1793 at St. Peter's Catholic Church, Baltimore (*Piet:* 142).

Rener, Sebastian, and Juliana Witherhoolt were m. by lic. on 15 Dec 1796 at St. Peter's Catholic Church, Baltimore (*Piet:* 142).

Renker, Henry, and Christiana Nieslem were m. by lic. on 4 April 1799 at St. Peter's Catholic Church, Baltimore (*Piet:* 142).

Renshaw, [-?-], m. by 30 May 1774 Mary, daughter of Alice Johnson (MWB 40:321; abst. in *Md. Cal. of Wills* 16:58).

Renshaw, Abraham, and Ann Hawkins were m. on 15 June 1738 (Harrison, "St. George's Parish Register:" 290). On 10 May 1761 Ann was named as a daughter of Robert Hawkins (BAWB 2:344).

Renshaw, Cassandra, was charged with bastardy at June Court 1765. Thomas Hughes was summoned (BAMI 1765, p.16).

Renshaw, Hosea, stated he would not pay the debts of his wife Deborah who has eloped from his bed and board without just cause. He warns all persons who harbor her do so at their peril (*Federal Intelligencer and Baltimore Daily Gazette* 21 Feb 1795). He d. by 8 Oct 1795, leaving a son Robinson Jones Renshaw and a widow Deborah who m. 2nd, Samuel Davis (*q.v.*) by a license dated 8 Oct 1795 (*q.v.*) (BAML).

Renshaw, James, and Nelly Coale, both of Baltimore, were m. last Sun. eve. by Rev. Richards (*Baltimore Telegraphe* 26 Jan 1796).

Renshaw, James, exec., on 18 March 1797 posted bond to administer the estate of Jeremiah Pickett (BAAB 8:109). In his will made 24 Dec 1794 Jeremiah Pickett of Knox Co., Tenn., named Renshaw exec. and sole legatee (BAWB 5:494)

Renshaw, John, and Mary Litten were m. on 27 March 1735 (Harrison, "St. George's Parish Register:" 281). He d. by 10 Feb 1753 when his extx. Mary had m. 2nd, Patrick Cavannah (*q.v.*) (MDTP 333-2:58; BAAD 4:319).

Renshaw, Philip, and Ruth 'German' were m. on 12 March 1784 Harrison, "St. Paul's Parish Register:" 187); on 20 Feb 1790 Ruth was named as a daughter of John Jarman (BAWB 5:49).

Renshaw, Robert, and Mary Anderson were married by license dated 12 Feb 1782 (HAML). On 27 Sep 1796 Mary received an equal share of the estate of John Anderson (BAAD 12:191).

Renshaw, Thomas, and Frances Clark were m. on 29 Jan 1739 (Harrison, "St. George's Parish Register:" 275). On 22 Dec 1755 Frances was named as a daughter of Robert Clark of Baltimore Co. (MWB 30:221 abst. by Gibb; BFD 2:77).

Renshaw, Thomas, m. by 17 Nov 1771 Mary, widow of James Brice (*q.v.*) (BACT B#G:359).

Repold, George, m. by 12 July 1800, Martha, a representative of Bernhard Stanhoof (BAAD 13: 297).

Reston, James, m. by 9 July 1725, Sarah, daughter of Daniel Scott of Baltimore Co. (MDAD 6:406).

Retaker, Adam, of Baltimore Co., stated he would not pay the debts of his wife Mary (*Maryland Journal and Baltimore Advertiser* 26 Sep 1788).

Rey, Charles, native of Montpelier in Languidoc, and Elizabeth Beaupre, late from Jeremie, St. Domingo, were m. by lic. on 26 March 1796 at St. Peter's Catholic Church, Baltimore (*Piet:* 142).

Reynaud, Francis Regis Benedict, and Mary Dubourg, widow Carrie, natives of France, were m. by lic. on 12 April 1798 at St. Peter's Catholic Church, Baltimore (*Piet:* 142).

Reynolds, John, m. by 11 March 1684/5 Providence, relict and extx. of Robert Davidge of Anne Arundel Co. (BALR RM#HS:127).

Reynolds, Thomas, servant to Luke Trotten, in Nov 1757 was fined for begetting a bastard on the body of Ann Young (BAMI 1757-1759: 75).

Rhea, Benjamin, on 25 d. 2 m. 1786 was charged with marrying contrary to rules ("Minutes of Gunpowder Meeting," *QRNM*:81-82).

Rhea, Joseph, and Elizabeth Conn were m. by lic. dated 13 Jan 1783 (BAML). On 26 d. 7 m. 1783 Rhea was reported for marrying outside the society ("Minutes of Gunpowder Meeting," *QRNM:*78).

Rheem (Riehm), Jacob, exec., on 8 Oct 1796 posted bond to administer the estate of John Martin Baker (BAAB 8:928). John Martin Baker, formerly of Dorset [Dorchester Co.?], in his will made 1 July1777 named his nephews Philip, Jacob, ad William Rheem, sons of Christopher Rheem, and named his brother-in-law Christopher Rheem as exec. (BAWB 5:406).

Rhoads, William, m. by 2 Nov 1726 [-?-], daughter of Henry Matthews (MINV 11:675; BALR IS#L:185).

Rhodes, [-?-], m. by Nov 1756 Ann, mother of Thomas Robuck, who was bound to Aquila McComas (BAMI 1757-1759).

Rhodes (Rodes), Henry, and Katherine Stockett were m. 15 Jan 1697/8 (Harrison, "All Hallow's Parish Register, "Anne Arundel Co., MS.at MdHS: 39). Henry Rhodes d. by 10 Sep 1712 when James Carroll conveyed 200 a. *Binn* to Frances, Ann, and Catherine Rhodes, daus. of Henry, stating that Henry Rhodes in his life time had paid £20 for the land, but no deed had been made, and now the mother of the girls, their cousin Thomas Stockett, and other relatives alleged that it was the said Henry's intent that the said children should have the 200 a. (BALR TR#A:203).

Rhodes, Richard, and Sarah Whitaker were m. 9 Feb 1740 (Harrison, "St. John's Parish Register:" 111). However, on 18 Oct 1760 Sarah was named as a daughter of Alexander McComas (BAWB 2:352; MDAD 47:447). On 26 April 1762, Richard Rhodes was paid for his wife by Thomas and Hannah Miles [Hannah was the widow of Alexander McComas] (BAAD 4:365).

Rhody, Henry, was m. last eve, by Rev. Mr. Kurtz, to Maria Falsgraff, both of this city (*Federal Gazette and Baltimore Daily Advertiser* 8 Oct 1800).

Rhote [Rhole?], Caspar, m. by 24 April 1792 [-?-], widow of Matthias Miller (BAAD 11:92).

Rice, James, and Elizabeth Davenport were married by license dated 26 Oct 1794 (BAML). Elizabeth Rice, (formerly Davenport), on 9 d. 4 m. 1795, had a complaint made against her for having her marriage accomplished contrary to the good order to a man not of our society ("Minutes of Baltimore Meeting," *QRNM:*224).

Rice, Joseph, m. last Sat. Nancy, eldest daughter of John Gray of Baltimore (*Maryland Journal and Baltimore Advertiser* 19 Feb 1788; Annapolis *Maryland Gazette* 19 Feb 1788).

Rice, Sarah. See Gilbert Bigger.

Rice, Ulrick, m. by 31 May 1776 Mary Ann, widow of John Rudy Calman *alias* Coleman (BALR AL#O:13).

Richard, John, late of Jeremie [Jeromie?] in the Island of Santo Domingo, in his will made 31 Dec 1795 named his wife Marie Joanna Chapoteau and mentioned 'alL his children' (BAWB 5:345). John Richard, a native of La Rochelle, France, d. 5 Jan and was bur. 6 Jan 1796,, aged 48 years at St. Peter's Catholic Church, Baltimore (*Piet:* 194).

Richards, [-?-], m. by 24 Oct 1784 Catherine, sister of Nathaniel Clary (BAWB 3:577).

Richards, Mr. A., Baltimore merchant, and Polly Barry were m. on 9 Sep by Rev. Richards (*Baltimore American* 12 Sep 1800).

Richards, Benjamin, m. Ann [-?-] by 24 June 1731 when their son Edward was b. ("Edward Richards Bible," *MBR* 3:160-161). On 3 Aug 1739 Richards' wife was named as a daughter of Charles Merryman of Baltimore Co. (MDAD 17:187).

Richards, Edmond, m. by 18 Jan 1731 Susannah, relict of Francis Crossing of Exon, Eng., and mother of Thomas Crossing who patented land in Md., and of John Crossing, tailor of Exon, Eng., who was the next heir of her son Thomas Crossing (BALR IS#L:275).

Richards, George, of Crigglestone in the parish of Sandal Magna, Yorkshire, Eng.., m. by 27 Nov 1771 Martha, sister of Anthony Rhodes (BALR AL#E:204).

Richards, John, and Ann Mills were m. by lic. on 28 May 1799 at St. Peter's Catholic Church, Baltimore (*Piet:* 143).

Richards, Joseph, and Margaret Berbine were m. by lic. on 3 June 1797 at St. Peter's Catholic Church, Baltimore (*Piet:* 143).

Richards, Richard, m. on 14 July 1754 Sarah Hooker ("Edward Richards Bible," *MBR* 3:160-161; Harrison, "St. John's Parish Register:" 211). She was a daughter of Samuel Hooker (MWB 39:93, abst. in *Md. Cal. of Wills* 15:19).

Richards (Rickards), William, on 3 Oct 1738 was summoned and appeared before the vestry of St. George's Parish. Not having his certificate of marriage he consented to be married again ("St. John's and St. George's Parish Register Vestry Proceedings," MS. at the MdHS).

Richardson, [-?-], m. by 21 April 1752 Unity, daughter of John Legatt, Sr. (MWB 30:81 abst. by Gibb).

Richardson, [-?-], m. by 22 July 1775, Tabitha, sister of Jeremiah Sheredine (MWB 40:403; abst. in *Md. Cal. of Wills* 16:69).

Richardson, Aubrey, m. by 14 Jan 1779 Mary, daughter of John Frazer (BALR WG#D:11).

Richardson, Benjamin, of Harford Co., and Betsy Howard, daughter of John B. Howard of Baltimore, were m. last Sun. eve. by Rev. Mr. Campbell (*Baltimore Telegraphe* 18 June 1795).

Richardson, Daniel, son of William and Elizabeth, and Elizabeth Welsh, daughter of John and Mary, were m. 4 d. 12 m. 1691 ("Records of West River Monthly Meeting," *QRSM:* 15; BALR TR#A:5, 33).

Richardson, Elizabeth, was charged with bastardy at the June 1711Court (BACP IS#B: 210).

Richardson, Fielder, son of Richard and Mary, and Miriam Griffith, daughter of Abraham and Mary, were m. 31 d. 10 m. 1798 (Bliss Forbush, "Minutes of Gunpowder Meeting," MS. at MdHS; BAWB 6:268).

Richardson, James, in Aug 1715, was charged with begetting a bastard on the body of Margaret Gibson (BACP IS#B: 626).

Richardson, James, a tailor, and Mary Ruff, widow of Richard Ruff, (*q.v.*) were m. on 31 May 1759 (Harrison, "St. George's Parish Register:" 367; MDTP 38:17).

Richardson, Laurence, m. Ann, widow of James Greer (*q.v.*); Richardson d. by 13 June 1705, and Anne m. 3rd Oliver Harriott (BAAD 2: 2, 134; BAAB 2:556; INAC 32A:24, 32C:135).

Richardson, Margaret Hill, daughter of Nathan Richardson, dec., and his wife Hannah, had let out her affections to a man not of our society and was married to him by a priest. The next meeting showed her name as Margaret Hill Bradford ("Minutes of Deer Creek Meeting," *QRNM:* 138). Margaret Richardson and William Bradford were m. by lic. dated 1778 (HAML).

Richardson, Mark, had m. by June 1683 Susanna, extx. of Johanna Goldsmith and widow and extx. of George Utye (Utie) (*q.v.*) (BACP D:45; MDTP 13:479; INAC 10:170; MWB 6:26 abst. in *Md. Cal. of Wills* 2:35). She m. 3rd, Thomas Wainwright (*q.v.*).

Richardson, Nathan, son of William and Margaret, m. on 30 d. 8 m. 1735, Elizabeth Crockett, daughter of John and Mary ("Records of West River Meeting," *QRSM:*31). In Oct 1747 Richardson was named as a brother-in-law in the will of John Crockett who also named Nathan's son Nathan (MWB 25:161 abst. by Gibb).

Richardson, Nathan, and Hannah Webster Gover, widow of Samuel Gover, and daughter of Isaac Webster were m. 20 April 1749 ("Records of Nottingham Meeting," MS. at MdHS; BAAD 7:4).In his will dated 7 Jan 1756 Nathan Richardson named his mother-in-law Margaret Webster (MWB 30:118 abst. by

Gibb). Hannah was named as a daughter in the will of Isaac Webster made 29 d. 3
m. 1755 (MWB 30:754 abst. by Gibb).

Richardson, Robert R., merchant, and Eliza Ridgely, all of Baltimore, were m. last Sun.
eve. by Rev. Bend (*Baltimore Telegraphe* 29 March 1796).

Richardson, Samuel, was named as brother-in-law in the will of Thomas Coale, made 5
April 1745 (MWB 24:85 abst. by Gibb).

Richardson, Samuel, and Sarah Davis were m. on 30 Dec 1755 (Harrison, "St. George's
Parish Register:" 375; but Harrison, in "St. John's Parish Register:" 214 gives the
date as 30 Dec 1756). On 20 Nov 1769 Sarah was named as a sister of Henry Davis
(BAWB 3:149).

Richardson, Thomas, m. by 9 May 1685 Rachel, admx. of John Tower (BALR
RM#HS:216).

Richardson, Col. Thomas, m. by 25 Oct 1697 Martha, extx. of Anthony Demondidier
(*q.v.*) (MDTP 17:54).

Richardson, Thomas, and Sarah Standifor were m. on 20 May 1720 (Harrison, "St.
John's Parish Register:" 19). On 12 Nov 1728 Sarah was named as a daughter of
Samuel Standiver [*sic*] (MDTP 28:277).

Richardson, William, and Mary Davis were m. on 27 March 1759 (Harrison, "St. John's
Parish Register:" 218). On 20 Nov 1769 Mary was named as a sister of Henry
Davis (BAWB 3:149).

Richen (Kichen), Sarah, servant of Priscilla Simkins, was charged with bastardy at Nov
Court, 1738, and again at Aug Court, 1729 (BACP HWS#1A;307, HWS#TR:12).

Richmond, |-?-|, |-?-|, m. by 19 Aug 1796 Eleanor, sister of John Wells (BAWB 5:419).

Ricketts, |-?-|, m. by 1 Feb 1797 Susannah, daughter of John McGregory (BAWB
5:527).

Ricketts, Benjamin, and Elinor Maxwell were m. on 18 Oct 1746 (Harrison, "St. John's
Parish Register:" 151). On 7 June 1753 Eleanor was named as a daughter and
coheir of James Maxwell of Baltimore Co., dec. (BALR TR#D:562). She was a
granddaughter of James Maxwell (BALR BB#1:6). Elizabeth Ricketts and Hannah
Meritor Ricketts, daughters of Benjamin Ricketts, on 3 March 1759 were conveyed
part of *Day's Privilege* by their uncle John Day of Edward (BALR BB#1:647).
John Day of Edward had m. Philizanna Maxwell on 20 July 1742 (Harrison, "St.
John's Parish Register:" 127).

Ricketts, Benjamin, m. by 6 Aug 1753 Elizabeth, extx. of Hugh McDoggle [*sic*]
(MDAD 34:243).

Ricketts, Benjamin, and Ely Kinsley in April 1771 were summoned to appear before the
vestry in May 1761 for unlawful cohabitation ("St. John's and St. George's Parish
Register Vestry Proceedings," MS. at the MdHS).

Ricketts, Benjamin, m. Cassandra Forrester in St. Paul's Parish on 29 Sep 1791
(Harrison, "St. Paul's Parish Register:" 64). She was the admx. of George Forrester
(*q.v.*) of Anne Arundel Co., dec. (*Maryland Journal and Baltimore Advertiser* 2
March 1792).

Ricketts, Samuel, and Hannah Mead were m. 24 Dec 1753 (Harrison, "St. John's Parish
Register:" 209). On 5 April 1760 Hannah was named as a daughter of Edward
Meads (BAWB 2:264). Ricketts, as *admin. de bonis non.* filed an account of
Edward Mead's estate on 18 April 1767 (MDAD 56:307).

Riddell, Robert, of Baltimore, was m. on Sun. eve. by Rev. Dr. West, to Miss Mary
Hawksworth (*Maryland Gazette or Baltimore General Advertiser* 14 March 1786).

Riddle, Maria, confessed to bastardy at the Nov 1754 Court, but refused to name the father (BACP BB#A:452).

Ridge, Jonathan, of Baltimore, and his wife Eleanor have parted by mutual consent (*Maryland Journal and Baltimore Advertiser* 18 Sep 1787).

Ridgely, Charles, m. by 17 Feb 1737/8, Elizabeth, execs. of Richard Hewett (*q.v.*) (MDTP 30:386).

Ridgely, Col. Charles, m. by 24 June 1755 Lydia Stringer, extx. of Dr. Samuel Stringer of Anne Arundel Co. or Baltimore Co. (MINV 59:12; MDAD 38:52).

Ridgely, Charles, son of William, m. by 10 July 1773 Ruth, daughter of Samuel Norwood (BAWB 3:263; BALR WG#59:360).

Ridgely, Charles, not yet 14, in April 1793 was made a ward of Richard Gittings (BAOC 3:42).

Ridgely, Henry, m. in Baltimore Miss Matilda Chase, daughter of the Hon. Samuel Chase (*Maryland Journal and Baltimore Advertiser* 12 June 1787; *Maryland Gazette or Baltimore General Advertiser* 12 June 1787).

Ridgely, John, and Mary [-?-] were m. by 24 Nov 1764 when their son John was born ("Bible Records of the Ridgely Family of Maryland." *MG* 2:300).

Ridgely, John, b. 24 Nov 1764, son of John and Mary, and Mary Emmitt, b. 1 Nov 1769, were m. on 15 Jan 1791 ("Bible Records of the Ridgely Family of Maryland." *MG* 2:300; BAML).

Ridgely, John, d. by March 1775, leaving a son William who chose Charles Ridgely of John as his guardian; Charles Ridgely of John was also made guardian of John Ridgely's children Eleanor and John (BAMI 1772, 1775-1781: 119).

Ridgely, John, d. by 19 Feb 1786 when his widow Mary made her will, mentioning the will of her brother Edward Dorsey, and naming her grandchildren, Polly, Harriet, and Andrew Sterrett (BAWB 4:189).

Ridgely, Mordecai, of Anne Arundel Co. was m. last eve. by Rev. Mr. Hagerty to Mary Wellmore of this city (*Federal Gazette and Baltimore Daily Advertiser* 14 Dec 1798).

Ridgely, William, son of John, in his will made 3 Jan 1797 named his brother-in-law John Tolley Worthington (BAWB 5:511)

Ridley, Essex Sherborne, orphan of Matthew Ridley, in Feb 1793 chose Catherine Ridley as his guardian (BAOC 3:31).

Ridley, Matthew, merchant of Baltimore, m. a few days ago at the seat of His Excellency Governor Livingston, near Elizabeth-Town, N.J., Catherine Livingston, daughter of the Governor (*Maryland Journal and Baltimore Advertiser* 1 May 1787). Catherine was a sister of Susan Livingston of Baltimore Co., and mother of Susanna Ann Ridley and Matilda Frances Ridley (BACT 1791-1794, MS 2865.1 at MdHS: 395). Matthew Ridley d. leaving the following heirs, all infants in the State of New York: Essex Shetburne, Susanna, Ann Ridley, and Matilda Frances Ridley (*Maryland Journal and Baltimore Advertiser* 27 July 1795).

Riely. See Riley.

Rien, Mary, confessed to bastardy at the Nov 1754 Court; she was fined but refused to name the father (BACP BB#A: 451).

Riess, Adam, m. by 15 April 1766 [-?-], daughter of Jost and Sara Runckel ("Reformed Congregation of Saint Benjamin's Known as Kreider's Church at Pipe Creek, Maryland [Westminster]," *MGSB* 35:437).

Riffitt, Rachel. See Elias Barbaby.

Rigbie, Cassandra, daughter of Nathan and Sarah, on 4 d. 6 m. 1767 was reported to have gone out in marriage ("Minutes of Deer Creek Meeting," *QRNM:*132). [No other marriage reference found].

Rigbie, Hannah, on 1 d. 6 m. 1775 was stated to have gone out in marriage by a priest to man not of our society ("Minutes of Deer Creek Meeting," *QRNM:*136). [No other marriage reference found].

Rigbie, James, on 16 Feb 1743 posted bond to administer the estate of Samuel Cooper during the minority of Lydia Cooper (BAAB 1:358).

Rigbie, James, son of Nathan, dec., on 30 d. 12 m. 1760, announced his intention to marry Sarah Massey, widow of Aquila Massey (*q.v.*), dec., and daughter of Isaac Bolton of Bucks Co., Pa. ("Minutes of Deer Creek Meeting," *QRNM:*127); they were m. on 5 d., 2 m., 1761 ("Records of Deer Creek Meeting," MS. at MdHS: 2). On 6 May 1773 James Rigbie was paid from the estate of Benjamin VanHorn for Isaac Massey, infant of Aquila, and son-in-law to Rigbie (MDAD 68:165).

Rigbie, Johanna, was charged with bastardy at the June 1742 Court, and confessed in Aug 1744, and confessed again in Aug 1746 (BACP 1743-1745:228, 306, TB&TR#1:126-127, and TB#D:195).

Rigbie, Nathan, m. by 26 July 1734 Cassandra, daughter of Philip Coale of Baltimore Co. (BAAD 3:172; MDAD 12:393). On 19 June 1745 Cassandra was named as a daughter of Cassandra Cole, who also named a granddaughter Susannah Rigbie (MWB 24:444 abst. by Gibb).

Rigbie, Col. Nathan, of Baltimore Co., m. by 16 Feb 1749 Sabina, widow and extx. of William Rumsey of Cecil Co. (CELR 7:160). Sabrinah was a daughter of Benjamin and Margaret Blaidenburgh (Harrison, "St. Stephen's Parish Register," Cecil Co., MS. at MdHS).

Rigbie, Sarah, on 8 May 1775 was named as a sister in the will of Nathaniel Giles (MWB 40:319; abst. in *Md. Cal. of Wills* 16:58).

Rigdon, [-?-], m. by 29 July 1757 Ann, eldest daughter of Margaret Leasie (MWB 30:401 abst. by Gibb).

Rigdon, Benjamin, and Elizabeth [-?-], were m. by 29 Jan 1799 when their son Thomas Baker Rigdon was b. ("John Forwood Bible," *MBR* 1:82-85).

Rigdon, John, m. by 23 Aug 1742 [-?-], daughter of William Bond (BAAD 3:271). On 3 Oct 1743 Elizabeth Rigdon was named as a sister of Anne Bond (MWB 28:564 abst. in *Md. Cal. of Wills* 8:276).

Rigdon, John, and Elizabeth Oachison (Oakerson, Okinson) were m. on 11 March 1740 (Harrison, "St. George's Parish Register:" 319). In her will made 1743 Ann Bond named a sister Elizabeth Rigdon and a niece Joanna Oachison (MWB 23:564); in his will made 26 March 1766 Rigdon named his wife Elizabeth and a step-daughter Johanna Hitchcock (MWB 34:439 abst. in *Md. Cal. of Wills* 13:134).

Right. See Wright.

Riley, Adam, m. by 16 Aug 1792 Susanna, admx. of Andrew Lutz (*q.v.*) (BAAD 11:114).

Riley, James, and Ann Lee, both of Baltimore, were m. last eve. by Rev. Hagerty (*Maryland Journal and Baltimore Advertiser* 30 March 1792).

Riley, Stephen, who served under Capt. Graybill in the Revolutionary War, d. 2 March 1840, having m. Mary Hook on 2 Jan 1783 by Rev. Mr. West (Rev. War Pension Application of Mary Hook, W9255).

Riley (Riely), William, and Sarah Dukehart were m. on 7 Oct 1784 (Marr. Returns of Rev. John Hagerty, Scharf Papers, MS.1999 at MdHS). On 10 Aug 1790 Sarah was named as a legatee of Valerius Dukehart (BAAD 10:182).

Rily, [-?-], m. by 8 Jan 1789 Catherine, daughter of John Delcher (BAWB 4:327).

Ringgold, Thomas, and Mary Gittings were married by license dated 9 Feb 1795 (BAML). Mary 'Gettings' was named as a daughter of James 'Gettings' of Baltimore Co. (MCHP # 4234).

Rinsinger, Abraham, m. by 13 June 1769 [-?-], heir of Esther Whistler, widow of Ulrich Whistler (BAAD 7:30).

Risteau, [-?-], m. by 2 June 1773 Catherine, daughter of William and Elizabeth Cromwell (BALR AL#G: 400).

Risteau, George, and Frances Todd were m. on 7 Aug 1757 (Harrison, "St. Thomas Parish Register:" 71). In Nov 1757 Frances was named as a daughter of Thomas and Eleanor (Dorsey) Todd (BALR B#G: 91, 93, 95; BAWB 2:266; MDAD 49:169).

Risteau, George, and Ann Lux were m. on 3 April 1787 (Marr. Returns of Rev. William West, Scharf Papers, MS. 1299 at MdHS). In his will, made 27 Nov 1788, George Risteau named his daughter Rebecca Ridgely Risteau and his brother-in-law William Lux BAWB 4:356). In Feb 1795 Rebecca Ridgely Risteau was made a ward of William Lux (BAOC 3:139).

Risteau, Isaac, and Elizabeth Raven were m. on 21 Feb 1748 (Harrison, "St. John's Parish Register:" 179). On 2 June 1748 Elizabeth was named as a daughter of Abraham Raven (BALR TR#C: 182).

Risteau, John, m. by 16 Dec 1723 Catherine, widow of William Talbott (*q.v.*), and daughter of George Ogg, Sr. (BALR IS#IK: 377; BALR IS#G:232).

Risteau, Capt. John Talbot, of Baltimore Co., was m. last Tues. eve. to Miss Betsy Denny (*Maryland Journal and Baltimore Advertiser* 28 Jan 1785).

Risteau, Talbot (Talbert), and Mary Stokes were m. 20 June 1745 (Harrison, "St. John's Parish Register:" 194). On 7 Sep1750 Mary was named as the admx. of Humphrey Wells Stokes (*q.v.*) (MDTP 33-1:198).

Risteau, Talbot, m. by 3 Feb 1752 Susannah, admx. of Winston Smith of Baltimore Co. (MDAD 32:85). She had m. 1st, George Risteau (*q.v.*).

Rister, [-?-], m. by 19 March 1780 Mary, daughter of Yocum Youn (BAWB 3:433).

Riston. See also Royston.

Ritchey, Abraham, m. by 27 Jan 1785 Barbara, daughter of Jacob Liechte who stipulated that Ritchey was to have no part of his daughter's estate 'until they have begotten children' (BAWB 4:296).

Ritter, John, m. by 1783 [-?-], daughter of Andrew Shroyer of Baltimore Co., dec., and the petitioner's father had m. the relict of said Shroyer. The petitioner's father is now dead, and his widow, Kenyet Ritter, has taken letters of admin. on Andrew Shroyer's estate (BPET Petition of John Ritter 1793).

Ritter, Ludwig, m. by 28 Jan 1765 Barbara Schauerin ("First Record Book for the Reformed and Lutheran Congregations at Manchester, Baltimore (now Carroll) Co.," *MGSB* 35:269).

Roach, Francis, and Mary Jarman were m. on 17 Sep 1754 (Harrison, "St. John's Parish Register:" 211). On 7 July 1755 Mary was named as the admx. of Thomas Jarman (*q.v.*) (MINV 59:17).

Roach, James, and Ruth Jordan were m. on 24 Sep 1789 (Marr. Register of Rev. Lewis Richards, MS.690 at MdHS). On 16 March 1795 Ruth was named as a daughter of John 'Jordon' (BAWB 5:282).

Roach, Mary, servant of Luke Raven, was charged with bastardy at the March 1736/7 Court (BACP HWS#1A:39).

Robb, William, merchant, and Elizabeth Garts, daughter of Charles Garts, were m. last eve. by Rev. Dr. Allison (*Maryland Journal and Baltimore Advertiser* 15 April 1791). The groom's name was given as William Ross (*Maryland Gazette or Baltimore General Advertiser* 15 April 1791).

Roberson (Robinson), [-?-], m. by 14 May 1759 Sophia, widow of Thomas Demmitt (*q.v.*) and mother of William, Richard and Rachel Demmitt, and heir of Tobias Stansbury (BALR B#G:414; BAAD 7:321). On 26 Jan 1762 Sophia was named as a daughter of Tobias Stansbury, the Elder (BAWB 2:167). Sophia d. by 12 Aug 1788 naming her children, Violetta Morgan, and William, Ellin, Stansbury, Nancy Demmitt, Mary Cooke, and Comfort Night, a granddaughter Mary Morgan, and nephew Caleb Stansbury (BAWB 4:402).

Robeson[?], Jane, in 1763 was convicted of bastardy (BAMI 1755-1763).

Robert, Conrad, and Mar. Magdaline Frankfurtherin were m. on 2 March 1784 ("Transcript of Zion Evangelical Lutheran Church," by Pastor Frederick Weiser, MS. at MdHS: 82). On 3 Dec 1794 Magdaline was named as a daughter of Nicholas Frankforter (BAWB 5:225).

Roberts, [-?-], m. by 30 March 1695 Eliza, daughter of Nicholas Corbin (MWB 7:297 abst. in *Md. Cal. of Wills* 2:126).

Roberts, Benjamin, and Clarenda Ann McKain were m. on 4 Feb 1776 ("Roberts Bible Records," *HMGB* 12 (3) (July 1941) 35-36).

Roberts, Billingsley, and Betty Manen [Maynor?] were m. on 2 March 1748 (Harrison, "St. John's Parish Register:" 49). On 9 Dec 1769 Mary was named as a sister of John Maynor (BAWB 3:164).

Roberts, Charles, servant of Charles Bosley and Jno. Bosley, Jr., in Nov 1755 was charged with begetting a bastard on the body of Mary Wiley (BACP BB#B:400, BB#C:313).

Roberts, Conrod, m. by 11 Oct 1796 Mary, heir of Nicholas Frankforter (BAAD 12:198).

Roberts, Frances, was charged with bastardy at the Nov 1738 Court (BACP HWS#1A:307).

Roberts, James, d. by 9 Nov 1757 when Sarah Waters, admx., posted bond to administer his estate (BAAB 5:219).

Roberts, James, son of Richardson Roberts at the Nov 1761 Court was made levy free (BAMI 1755-1763).

Roberts, John, m. by 13 Feb 1705 Mary ,widow of Thomas Jackson (*q.v.*) who was a son-in-law of Robert Drysdale; inherited *Drysdale's Habitation* from Robert Drysdale (BALR IR#AM:20; INAC 25:348). Drysdale, in his will, made 3 May 1704 named his sons-in-law John Fisher and Thomas Jackson as executors (MWB 3:241 abst. in *Md. Cal. of Wills* 3:38). Roberts and his wife Mary, extx., on 12 April 1705 posted bond to administer the estate of Thomas Jackson (BAAB 3:357). Roberts d. by 19 June 1731 when his estate was administered by David Hughes (*q.v.*) and wife Mary; Roberts had a daughter Mary who m. William Talbot (*q.v.*), and a daughter who m. Archibald Buchanan (*q.v.*).

Roberts, John, and Elizabeth Baker on 28 July 1750 were summoned to appear at the next vestry meeting to make their defense for unlawful cohabitation (Reamy, *St. Thomas' Parish Register:* 123).

Roberts, John, son of Peter, dec., in Aug 1772 was bound to John Gray of Joppa to learn the trade of a carpenter (BAMI 1772, 1775-1781: 24)

Roberts, John, m. by 25 April 1789 Sarah, widow and admx. of Joshua Barton (BAAD 9:326).

Roberts, John. See Elizabeth Baker.

Roberts, Levy, and Elizabeth Flood were married by license dated 9 July 1778 (BAML). Roberts, of Baltimore, stated he would not pay the debts of his wife Elizabeth, who had behaved in a manner unbecoming the marriage state; she had deserted him....[a list of other offences is given] (*Maryland Journal and Baltimore Advertiser* 4 July 1786).

Roberts, Owen, and Miss Margaret Pawson, both of Baltimore, were m. last Sat. eve. (*Baltimore Telegraphe* 15 June 1795).

Roberts, Peter, d. by 14 June 1766 having m. Araminta, sister of Joseph Fling; they were the parents of John and Samuel Roberts, called nephews by Fling; Araminta m. 2nd, John Jacob Summers (*q.v.*) (BAWB 3:66).

Roberts, Thomas, m. by 3 Oct 1780 Sarah, daughter of William Parlet and a representative of Sarah Parlet (BAWB 3:411; BAAD 12:435). He is almost certainly the Thomas Robertson whose wife, on 17 Dec 1790, received an equal share of the estate of William Parlett (BAAD 10:256).

Roberts, William, and Cathr. McCumsy had an illegitimate son; William, b. 17 Dec 1790, bapt. 23 May 1795 ("Records of Emanuel, or Baust's Church, Carroll County, 1792-1800," *MGSB* 35:262).

Robertson (Robinson?), Daniel, and Elizabeth Webster on 29 d. 6 m. 1768 were reported to have been married by a priest ("Minutes of Deer Creek Meeting," *QRNM:* 133). Daniel Robertson and Elizabeth Webster were m. on 18 d. 8 m. 1768 ("Marriages of Cliffs Monthly Meeting," *MGSB* beginning vol. 16).

Robertson, Elizabeth, was charged with bastardy and confessed at the March 1750/1 Court (BACP TR#6:293).

Robertson, John, and Mariah Wilson were m. by license dated 16 Dec 1793 (BAML). John Robertson of Fell's Point stated he would not pay the debts of his wife Maria, who had eloped from his bed and board (*Baltimore Daily Intelligencer* 17 Jan 1794).

Robertson, Robert, and Sarah Taylor were m. on 9 Nov 1721 (Harrison, "St. John's Parish Register:" 19). On 2 July 1723 Sarah was named as the widow and admx. of Martin Taylor (MDAD 5:179; BAAD 1:110). Martin and Sarah Taylor had a son Martin Taylor. Robert Robertson bequeathed property to John Robertson living at Glasgow, Scotland. On 2 May 1711 Robert Robertson, writing from Burlington, sent a letter to his father, stating that 'by overpersuasion' Robert was to come away from his father; he had served in time in Pennsylvania (BALR TR#D 197-). Robert 'Robinson' m. by 15 May 1736, Sarah, mother of Martin and Clemence Taylor (MWB 21:655 abst. in *Md. Cal. of Wills* 7:189).

Robinett, Prissilla, formerly Worthington, daughter of Priscilla Worthington, on 29 d. 3 m. 1792 has reported to have let out her affections to a man not of our society and accomplished her marriage contrary to the good order ("Minutes of Deer Creek Meeting," *QRNM:* 150). [No other marriage reference found].

Robinson, [-?-], son of Elugy [*sic*] Robinson, in Aug 1758 was bound to Thomas Simmons on a trial basis; in March 1760 his mother petitioned the court that he be released and the court granted her petition (BAMI 1755-1763: 9).

Robinson, [-?-], m. by 5 Sep 1760 [-?-], sister of Alexander Lawson (BAWB 2:337).

Robinson, Abraham, and Sarah Simpson were m. on 18 Sep 1744 (Harrison, "St. George's Parish Register:" 337). On 15 March 1764 Sarah Robinson was named as a daughter of Elizabeth Church, widow of John Church (BAWB 2:183).

Robinson, Alexander, merchant of Baltimore, m. Thurs., 8th inst. at Walnut Grove in Frederick Co., Va., to Mrs. Priscilla Booth (*Maryland Journal and Baltimore Advertiser* 17 June 1788). Priscilla, wife of Alexander Robinson, merchant of Baltimore, d. 7th inst. at Walnut Grove, Frederick Co. (*Maryland Journal and Baltimore Advertiser* 23 July 1790).

Robinson, "Citizen" Alexander, of Baltimore, and Miss Angelica Peale, daughter of Mr. Peale of Philadelphia, were m. there on Tues., 15h inst. (*Maryland Journal and Baltimore Advertiser* 18 July 1794).

Robinson, Charles, m. by 26 July 1726 Judith, widow and admx. of William Welch (*q.v.*) (MDTP 28:310, 32:95).

Robinson, Charles, stated he was b. 1756 in Harford Co. (and his birth was recorded in a Family Bible which is now in the house where Col. William Hutchins was living); he served as a private in the Maryland Militia during the Rev. War, m. Mephytica Galloway, daughter of Aquila Galloway, on 30 June 1787 and d. 1834 (Rev. War Pension Application of Mephytica Robinson, W9267/BLWT6042-160-55).

Robinson, Capt. Daniel, and Susannah Brown were m. on 18 July 1751 (Harrison, "St. George's Parish Register:" 366, 385); she was the widow of Thomas Brown (*q.v.*), and m. 3rd, Garrett Garrettson (*q.v.*).

Robinson, Daniel. See Daniel Robertson.

Robinson, Ephraim, and Eve Dale were m. by lic. on 19 Dec 1786 at St. Peter's Catholic Church, Baltimore (*Piet:* 143).

Robinson, George, d. by 9 May 1788 at which time his widow and admx. Elizabeth had m. 2nd, George Hall (*q.v.*) (BAML).

Robinson, George, d. by 15 June 1788 by which time his widow Rosanna had m. 2nd, William Savory (*q.v.*).

Robinson, Jemima, confessed to bastardy at the Nov 1755 Court, but would not name the father of the child (BACP BB#B:399).

Robinson, John, m. by 17 April 1738 Mary Jarvis. Mary Robinson, lately Mary Jarvis, now wife of John Robinson, on 17 April 1738 posted bond to administer the estate of Philip Jarvis (*q.v.*) (BAAB 3:374; see also MDTP 30:404, 31:476; BAAD 3:380; MINV 29:6).

Robinson, John, m. by 1 Dec 1749 [-?-], daughter of Henry Butler of Baltimore Co. (MDAD 27:252; BAAD 5:74).

Robinson, John, of Chambersburg, Pa., and Mary Baker, daughter of Mathias and Mary, were m. by lic. on 30 May 1797 at St. Peter's Catholic Church, Baltimore (*Piet:* 143; BAWB 6:221; (Marr. Returns of Rev. Francis Beeston, Scharf Papers, MS.1999 at MdHS).

Robinson, Jonas, d. by 24 June 1741 by which time his admx. Rosanna m. 3rd, John Ogle (*q.v.*). She was the admx. of John Bowen (MDAD 19:413; MDTP 31:385).

Robinson, Richard, on 11 Sep 1756, recorded that he would not be responsible for the debts of his wife Mary (BACT TR#E:220).

Robinson, Richard, m. by 15 May 1731 Elizabeth, daughter of Edward Smith (BALR AL#F: 138). On 15 May 1731 he was named as son-in-law and next of kin of Edward Smith of Baltimore Co. (MINV 16:473).

Robinson, Susanna, admx., on 1 May 1701 posted bond to administer the estate of Thomas Peort (BAAB 2:418).

Robinson, Thomas, son of Elugah (Eliza?) Robinson, 1765, was ordered to be discharged from service of John Quearns; his mother was to bring her son to next court to be bound to a good master (BAMI 1772, 1775-1781: 44).

Robinson, William, in his will dated 24 April 1671 named his wife Henerica (Henrietta) (MWB 1:623 abst. in *Md. Cal. of Wills* 1:67). She m. 2nd, Edward Swanson (*q.v.*), 3rd, Thomas Cannon (*q.v.*), and 4th, Edward Reeves (*q.v.*).

Robinson, William, m. by 5 April 1711 Mary, admx. of William Macarty (MDTP 21:344)

Robinson, William, d. by 8 Nov 1722 at which time his admx. Elizabeth had m. James Isham (*q.v.*).

Robinson, William, in Aug 1728 was named by Elizabeth Robinson as the father of her child (BACP HWS#6:32).

Robinson, William, m. by 28 July 1747 Temperance, daughter of Archibald Rollo (MWB 25:114 abst. by Gibb).; BALR BB#1:631).

Robuck, Thomas, aged 7 last Aug., orphan of Ann Rhodes [*sic*] in Nov 1756 was bound to Aquila McComas (BAMI 1755-1763).

Rock, Thomas, and Rebecca Reed were m. in St. James' Parish on 29 May 1791 (Harrison, "St. James' Parish Register:" 3). Rock stated he would not pay the debts of his wife Rebecca (*Maryland Journal and Baltimore Advertiser* 2 April 1794).

Rockhold, John, m. by 5 Aug 1752 Elizabeth Elinor, daughter of Edmund Talbot (BALR TR#D:414).

Rockhold, [-?-], d. by 1787, and Edward Stansbury was appointed guardian to Lancelot Todd Rockhold and Moses Rockhold. Edward Johnson, physician, was surety (BOCP Answer of Dr. Edward Johnson, 1794).

Rockhold, Thomas, of Baltimore Co., m. by 14 Oct 1710 [-?-], daughter of Sarah Clark (AALR PK:321).

Roddy, James, m. by 13 Sep 1783 [-?-], daughter of Samuel Smith, who named his grandchildren Samuel, John, Esther, Mary and Dorcas Roddy (BAWB 3:568).

Roe, Walter, merchant of Baltimore, and Miss Donaldson of Philadelphia, were m. last Tues. at that city (*Maryland Journal and Baltimore Advertiser* 19 April 1785).

Roger, [-?-], m. by 2 Dec 1772 Mary, daughter of Susannah Rantz, late of Va., but now of Baltimore Co., who also named her grandchildren John and Susannah Roger (MWB 39:107, abst. in Md. Cal. of Wills 15:22).

Rogers, [-?-], m. by 29 July 1797 Elizabeth, mother of James Hamilton (BAAD 12:319).

Rogers, Allen, and Rebecca Evans were m. on 11 April 1792 (Register of First Presbyterian Church, Baltimore," MS. at MdHS: 5). Rogers stated he would not pay the debts of his wife Rebecca who was taking methods of disgracing and ruining him (*Federal Gazette and Baltimore Daily Advertiser* 11 July 1797).

Rogers, Grace, in 1728 had a mulatto child named Ishmael Rogers who was being cared for by Jacob Bull (BACP HWS#6:30).

Rogers, Jacob, of Bedford, Great Britain, m. by 14 Aug 1747 Mary, daughter of John Copson, *als.* Weaver (BALR TB#E:202, TR#C:453).

Rogers, James, m. by Nov 1692 Mary [-?-], who bore him a child and was then deserted by him (BACP D:F#1:320).

Rogers, James Lloyd, eldest son of Nicholas Rogers, dec., of Baltimore Co., and now a Student of Civil Law at the College of Glasgow, on 17 July 1769, appointed John Merryman, Jr., his atty. (BACT B#G:310).

Rogers, John, and Mary Barbine were m. by lic. on 3 Oct 1793 at St. Peter's Catholic Church, Baltimore (*Piet:* 143).

Rogers, Mordecai, on 26 d. 8 m. 1786 was condemned for being married by a hireling minister ("Minutes of Gunpowder Meeting," *QRNM:*82). [No other marriage reference found].

Rogers, Nicholas, m. by 1 Oct 1720 Ellinor, daughter of the wife of Jabez Pierpoint (Peirpoint),whose will of that date named Eleanor, daughter of his wife, as extx., and also named Eleanor's children William, Catherine, Ellinor, and Sarah (MWB 16:388 abst. in *Md. Cal. of Wills* 5:48). Ellinor Rogers, extx., on 24 April 1721 posted bond to administer the estate of Jabez Pierpoint (BAAB 2:441). Eleanor m. 2nd, Lloyd Harris (*q.v.*) on 4 July 1721 Harrison, "St. Paul's Parish Register:" 148).

Rogers, Nicholas, and Henrietta Jones were m. on 18 Aug 1745 (Harrison, "St. Paul's Parish Register:" 56). On 18 Feb 1763 Henrietta was named as a daughter of Philip and Anne Jones and a sister of Thomas Jones (BAWB 2:121, 163; MWB 30:503 abst. by Gibb).

Rogers, William, m. by 13 Aug 1736 [-?-], daughter of Stephen Gill (BAAD 3:220; MDAD 5:136).

Rohrer (Rohra), John, d. by 4 April 1767, naming his wife Catherine as extx. (BAWB 3:72). Catherine was a daughter of Ulrick and Esther Whistler, and m. 2nd, by 17 March 1769 George Lavely (Lovely) (*q.v.*) (BAAD 7:30; BAWB 3:72; MDTP 43:212)

Roles. See Rowles.

Rollins (Rawlings), William, m. by 22 Aug 1795 Temperance, daughter of Edward Wigley, Sr. (BAWB 5:328; BAAD 12:309).

Rollins. See also Rawlings.

Rollo, Rebecca, daughter of Archibald Rollo who d. testate by 17 Aug 1747, was charged with bastardy at the March 1736/7 Court, again at the June 1750 Court; she had a daughter Temperance, born 20 Feb 1739/40 (BACP TB#5:182; *BCF:*556).

Rool, Frederick, m. by 13 April 1796 Catherine, extx. of Henry Ansell (BAAD 12:135).

Roper, Sarah, was charged with bastardy at the Aug 1717 Court (BACP IS#1A;152).

Rosensteel, George, Jr., merchant, was m. last eve. by Rev. Mr. Beeston, to Miss Barbara White, both of this city; they were m. by lic. on 30 Nov at St. Peter's Catholic Church, Baltimore (*Federal Gazette and Baltimore Daily Advertiser* 1 Dec 1797; *Piet:* 143).

Rosensteel, John, and Margaret Myers were m. by lic. on 30 Sep 1798 at St. Peter's Catholic Church, Baltimore (*Piet:* 143).

Ross, Charles, m. by 19 Jan 1782 Eve, daughter of Conrad Smith, dec. (BALR WG#H:32).

Ross, Charles, and Polly Smith, both of this town, were m. last Thurs. eve. by Rev. Mr. Richards (*Baltimore Daily Intelligencer* 26 April 1794).

Ross, Daniel, and Mary West were m. on 29 May 1785 (Marr. Returns of Rev. William West, Scharf Papers. MS. 1999 at MdHS). Mary m. 2nd, by 12 Aug 1788 [-?-] Puelly (*q.v.*).

Ross, Richard, of Bladensburg, m. last Wed. eve. in Baltimore, Mrs. Sarah Brereton of Baltimore (*Maryland Gazette or Baltimore General Advertiser* 6 Nov 1788).

Thomas Brereton and Sarah Marshall were married by license dated 26 Feb 1781 (BAML).

Ross, **William,** merchant, and Miss Betsy Garts, daughter of Charles Garts, merchant of Baltimore, were m. last eve. (*Maryland Gazette or Baltimore General Advertiser* 15 April 1791).

Rotch, **George,** and Catherine Green were m. by lic. on 31 July 1790 at St. Peter's Catholic Church, Baltimore (*Piet:* 143).

Roth, **Jacob,** m. by 22 June 1776 Mary Martha, oldest daughter of Theobald Schneider of Mannheim Twp., York Co., Pa. (BAWB 4:18).

Rouse, **John,** m. Sarah Cochran on 9 Jan 1800; both were of Baltimore Co. ("Rouse Family Bible," *MGSB* 48 (1) (Winter 2007) 67-72).

Rowan, **John,** and Elizabeth Stokes were married by banns on 16 Feb 1794 at St. Peter's Catholic Church, Baltimore (*Piet:* 143).

Rowe (Row), **James,** and Lydda Johnson on 2 March 1740 were summoned to appear before the vestry of St. George's Parish. Capt. Cole was summoned to give evidence ("St. John's and St. George's Parish Register Vestry Proceedings," MS. at the MdHS).

Rowles, [-?-], m. by 20 Sep 1795 Sarah, daughter of Nicholas Baker (BAWB 6L212).

Rowles, **Jacob,** m. by 23 April 1750 Patience, admx. of Nathaniel Stinchcomb (*q.v.*) (MDTP 33-1:122; MDAD 28:127; BALR AL#D:257).

Rowles, **Jacob,** and Mary Scarff were m. on 28 Sep 1746 Harrison, "St. Paul's Parish Register." 159). On 13 Nov 1750 Rowles was named as the administrator of James Scarff (*q.v.*) (MDTP 34:36).

Rowles, **Mary,** was charged with bastardy at the March 1733/4 Court (BACP HWS#9: 188).

Rowles (Roles), **Ruth,** daughter of Jacob Rowles, was charged with bastardy in Nov 1757 and Jethro Lynch Wilkinson was named as father. In Nov 1760 Ruth Rowles (Roles) and George Stansbury were charged with bastardy and each was fined 30 shillings. Ruth had had a daughter Ann Rowles, born in Aug 1760. In 1762 another bastard child was born but Ruth did not name the father (BAAD 5:54; BAMI 1755-1763:42, 74; BAMI 1768-1769).

Royston, [-?-], m. by 12 April 1797 Mary, legatee of William Sinclair (BAAD 12:287).

Royston, **Abraham,** m. by 13 April 1791 Susanna, admx. of Elijah Hughes (BAAD

Royston, **John,** m. by 10 March 1697, Anne, relict and extx. of Roland Thornborough (INAC 16:25, 94).

Royston, **John,** and Ruth McClung were married by license dated 18 Dec 1784 (BAML). On 28 Dec 1787 Ruth received an equal share of the estate of Robert McClung (BAAD 10:168).

Royston, **John,** m. by 17 June 1796 one of the children of Margaret Ford, a legatee of William Sinclair (BAAD 12:162).

Royston. See also Riston.

Ruark, **Patrick,** d. by 8 March 1732 when Thomas Robinson posted bond to administer his estate, Ruark's widow Ann having renounced the right of administration (BAAB 4:332).

Rub (Rup), **Henrich,** m. by 15 June 1786 Catharina Nollin ("First Record Book for the Reformed and Lutheran Congregations at Manchester, Baltimore (now Carroll) Co.," *MGSB* 35:282, 283).

Rub, Michael, m. by 3 Jan 1788 Magdalena Tannerin (First Record Book for the Reformed and Lutheran Congregations at Manchester, Baltimore (now Carroll) Co., " *MGSB* 35:283).

Ruckle, John, merchant, and Miss Eleanor Dorsey, both of Baltimore, were m. last eve. by Rev. Mr. Reed (*Baltimore Telegraphe* 16 Nov 1798).

Ruckle, Thomas, painter, and Miss Mary Chambers were m. last eve. by Rev. Reed (*Federal Gazette and Baltimore Daily Advertiser* 28 Nov 1798).

Ruff, Daniel, and Elizabeth Webster were m. on 11 May 1740 (Harrison, "St. George's Parish Register:" 315). On 7 Dec 1752 his admx., Eliza, had m.2nd, Guy Little (*q.v.*). Daniel and Eliza were the parents of Hannah Ruff who on 10 May 1761 was named as a granddaughter of Michael Webster, Quaker (BAWB 2:176).

Ruff, Henry, and Hannah Preston were m. on 28 July 1759 (Harrison, "St. George's Parish Register:" 369). On 17 Sep 1766 Hannah was named as a daughter of James Preston (BAWB 3:48; BFD 5:101).

Ruff, Richard, m. after c1700 and before 4 Sep 1733 Sarah, daughter and heiress of Daniel Peverell (*MRR* 20; BALR IS#L:426).

Ruff, Richard, son of Richard, in March 1757 chose Jno. Paca as his guardian (BAMI 1755-1763).

Ruff, Richard, d. by 31 May 1759 on which date his widow m. James Richardson (*q.v.*) (Harrison, "St. George's Parish Register:" 367; MDTP 38:17).

Ruff, Sarah, on 13 May 1720 was named as a daughter-in-law in the will of David Thomas, who also named Daniel and John Ruff (MWB 16:36 abst. in *Md. Cal. of Wills* 5:6).

Ruisinger, Abraham, m. by 13 June 1769 [-?-], daughter of Esther Whistler (MDAD 61:165).

Rumage, Nicholas, and Priscilla Mildews were married by license dated 28 April 1785 (BAML). On 28 Feb 1787 she was named as a daughter of Aquila Mildews (BAAD 9:19).

Rumney, [-?-] [Nathaniel?], m. by 22 Nov 1755 [-?-], daughter of Joanna Croxall who named her grandchildren Elizabeth and Mary Rumney (MWB 30:53 abst. by Gibb).

Rumney, Elizabeth, and Rachel Rumney, on 7 May 1782 were named as nieces in the will of Richard Croxall (BAWB 4:36).

Rumney, Mary, on 14 Oct 1748 was named as a sister in the will of James [Carroll] Croxall (MWB 25:465 abst. by Gibb).

Rumsey, Benjamin, of Charlestown, Cecil Co., and Mary, daughter of Col. John and Hannah Hall of Cecil Co., were m. on 24 May 1768 (Harrison, "St. Mary Ann's Parish, Cecil Co.," p. 312; BALR AL#A:429).

Rumsey, John, m. by 22 June 1771 Martha, daughter of John Hall (BALR AL#C:523).

Runkel, Jacob, m. by 15 Nov 1775 Eva, daughter of Anna Barbara Buttelin, who was grandmother and sponsor of Jost Runckel, child of Jacob and Eva ("Reformed Congregation of Saint Benjamin's Known as Kreider's Church at Pipe Creek, Maryland [Westminster]," *MGSB* 35:438).

Runnells, Nicholas, m. by 10 June 1795 Rachel Renn, representative of Lot Owings (BAAD 12:14).

Rup. See Rub.

Rupper, Jacob, and Bridget Lynch were married by banns on 8 Jan 1792 at St. Peter's Catholic Church, Baltimore (*Piet:* 143).

Rush, Charles, m. by 22 Jan 1791 Magdalena, devisee of Gotliep Shearmiller (BALR WG#FF: 326).

Rusk, Robert, and Barbara Alstock of Baltimore were m. last Thurs. eve. by Rev. Kurtz (*Maryland Journal and Baltimore Advertiser* 8 Sep 1794)

Russell, [-?-], m. by 5 May 1773 Frances, sister of William Lux (BAWB 3:357).

Russell, [-?-], m. by 26 Dec 1797 Frances, daughter of Robert McCulloh who was a brother of James McCulloh (BAWB 6:72).

Russell, Francis, m. by 1 Aug 1732 Elizabeth, mother of John Ryley, whose aunt was Lucy Bailey, wife of John Bailey (BALR IS#L: 267).

Russell, Samuel, native of Boston, and Sarah German were m. by lic. on 13 Feb 1798 at St. Peter's Catholic Church, Baltimore (*Piet:* 143).

Russell, Thomas, m. by 12 Oct 1680 Elizabeth, relict of William Hollis (MDTP 12A: 164; INAC 7B:168; BAAB 4:350). She m. 3rd, William Croshaw (*q.v.*), and 4th, William Harris (*q.v.*).

Russell, Thomas, m. Catherine, widow and extx. of Philip Hiteshew in 1774. Russell ran away, and Catherine m. 3rd, John Ebbert (*q.v.*) (BOCP Petition of Sam. Messersmith and John Ebbert, [date not given]).John Ebbert and Catherine Hitshue were married by license dated 10 March 1778 (BAML).

Russell, Thomas, of Baltimore, and Miss Moale, daughter of John Moale. Esq., of Baltimore Co., were m. [date not given] (*Maryland Journal and Baltimore Advertiser* 17 Oct 1780). Thomas Russell and Rebecca Moale were m. on 12 Oct 1780 (Marr. Returns of Rev. Thomas Chase, Scharf Papers, MS.1999 at MdHS). Thomas Russell d. by Ref 1795 when his children John Moale Russell and Thomas Russell were made wards of Samuel Moale (BAOC 3:139; see also BAWB 6:114).

Russell, Capt. William, of Boston, and Catherine Dagan, daughter of George Dagan of Baltimore, were m. last Wed eve. by Rev. Dr. Allison (*Maryland Journal and Baltimore Advertiser* 19 Dec 1795).

Rust, John, and Mary Patterson were married on 9 July 1782 (Marr. Returns of Rev. William West, Scharf Papers, MS.1999 at MdHS). On 5 Jan 1793 Mary was named as the widow of John Patterson (BALR WG#KK: 157).

Rutledge, (Rutlidge), Thomas, and Mary Matthews were m. by license dated 23 Nov 1782 (BAML). Rutledge stated his wife Mary had eloped (*Maryland Journal and Baltimore Advertiser* 24 Aug 1784, 31 Aug 1784).

Rutlis, Worten, of Baltimore Co. advertised his wife Hannah had eloped from him with Peter Hines (Annapolis *Maryland Gazette* 21 Jan 1746).

Rutter, [-?-], m. by 27 Aug 1777 Mary, sister of Edward Hanson (BAWB 4:107). On 26 Dec 1785 Rutter's wife was named as a daughter of Jonathan Hanson who named his grandson Jonathan Rutter (BAWB 4:115).

Rutter, [-?-], m. by 13 Dec 1794 Catherine, daughter of Nicholas Frankforter (BAWB 5:225).

Rutter, Edward, counselor a law, and Ruth Ann Potts of Md. were m. Thurs., 28th ult. at the seat of Thomas Rutter at Pottsgrove, Penna. (*Maryland Journal and Baltimore Advertiser* 3 July 1792).

Rutter, Henry, and Christina Nice were married by license dated 22 Nov 1779 (Marr. Returns of Rev. William West, Scharf Papers, MS.1999 at MdHS). On 2 Dec 1780 Christiana was named as the widow and admx. of Christopher Nice (BALR WG#F:95).

Rutter, John, exec., on 15 Oct 1794 posted bond to administer the estate of Mary Hanson (BAAB 8:649). Mary Hanson, widow, in her will made 3 Oct 1794 named Elizabeth Hanson Rutter, wife of John, Jonathan Hanson Rutter, Thomas Bodley [?] Rutter, and Mary Hanson Rutter, daughter of John (BAWB 5:197).

Rutter, Capt. Josias, and Mary, daughter of Josias Pennington, both of Baltimore, were m. last eve. by Rev. Bend (*Baltimore Telegraphe* 25 May 1796).

Rutter, Moses, d. by 4 Aug 1752 at which time his admx. Keziah was m. to Isaac Ralph (*q.v.*).

Rutter, Richard, and Mary Barney were m, on 3 June 1750 (Harrison, "St. Paul's Parish Register:" 164). On 9 Nov 1752 Mary was named as the extx. of William Barney (*q.v.*) (MDTP 33-2:19).On 13 Aug 1754 Rutter stated that he and his wife Mary were separated; she was formerly Mary Barney, and was the mother of Absolom Barney (BALR TR#E:105, 217, 218). Rutter d. by 10 Sep 1761 when his estate was admin. by William Isgrig, exec. Rutter left four children, Esther, Henry, Thomas, and Moses (BAAD 4:347).

Rutter, Solomon, was charged with bastardy at the Nov 1756 Court (BAMI 1757-1759:161).

Rutter, Capt. Solomon, m. last Thurs. Peggy Reitenauer, daughter of Nicholas Reitenaur (*Maryland Journal and Baltimore Advertiser* 16 Dec 1788).

Rutter, Thomas, Jr., m. last Sat. eve., Polly Graybill, youngest daughter of Philip Graybill of Baltimore (*Maryland Gazette or Baltimore General Advertiser* 20 Nov 1787).

Ryan, James, enlisted as a private in Capt. Hamilton's Co., of the Fifth Maryland Regiment, m. March 1774 Eleanor Green at a church in Baltimore Co. called Mary's Chapel, but the marriage was never recorded. Ryan died a short time after his return from his Revolutionary service, and she later married another Revolutionary soldier named Joseph Harper. Thomas Johnson testified that James and Eleanor had two sons before the Rev. War. Joshua Tracey testified that one of the sons was a Joshua Ryan who had worked with Tracey. (Rev. War Pension Application of Eleanor Harper, W11205).

Ryan, James, and Mary Purcell, natives of Ireland, were m. by lic. on 14 Oct 1798 at St. Peter's Catholic Church, Baltimore (*Piet:* 143).

Ryan, John, m. by 10 Nov 1748 Ann, daughter of Edward Wilburn and sister of William Wilburn (BALR TR#C:112, BB#I:70).

Ryan, Margaret, was charged with bastardy at the March 1721/2 Court (BACP IS&TW#1:31).

Ryan, Mary, in 1762 was convicted of bastardy (BAMI 1755-1763).

Ryan, Peter, aged 13, son of John Ryan, dec., in Aug 1762, was bound to Philip Gover (BAMI 1755-1763).

Ryan (Ryon), Sarah, before marriage Spicer, on 27 d. 1 m. 1773 was charged with having gone out in marriage (Minutes of Gunpowder Monthly Meeting: *QRNM:* 63). On 27 d. 9 m. 1777 she condemned her own actions when she con-summated her marriage with one not of our Society before an hireling minister ("Minutes of Gunpowder Meeting," *QRNM:*70). [No other marriage reference found].

Rye, Mary, servant of James Phillips, was charged with mulatto bastardy at the Aug 17111 and named Negro George, a slave of the said Phillips as the father of the child (BACP IS#B:245).

Ryland, [-?-], m. by 5 May 1761, Mary, daughter of Ulick Burk, planter (BAWB 2:117).

Ryland, Arthur, m. by 5 Oct 1798 Elizabeth, daughter of Samuel Gott (BALR WG#56:136).

Ryon, Sarah. See Sarah Ryan.

"S"

Sackeld, Agnes, was charged with bastardy at the March 1716/7 Court and named Thomas Taylor as the father of her child (BACP HWS#TR:95).

Sadler, Thomas, merchant of Baltimore, and Elizabeth, daughter of Thomas G. Howard of Long Green, Baltimore Co., were m. Thurs., 6th inst., by Rev. John Coleman (*Baltimore Daily Intelligencer* 12 Nov 1793).

Sagasay, Margaret, extx., on 9 April 1795 posted bond to administer the estate of John Johanna Ludwick Vansile, whose will dated 21 March 1795 named Margaret Sagasvay [*sic*] as sole legatee and extx. (BAAB 8:722; BAWB 5:247).

Salisbury, Capt. Daniel, and Miss Polly Hall, daughter of Isaac Hall, all of Fell's Point, were m. last Wed. by Rev. Riggen (*Baltimore American* 17 Aug 1799).

Salmon, George, m. by 11 June 1773 Hannah, now dec., daughter of Philip Jones and mother of Philip Edward (BALR AL#G:42, 329).

Salvan, Joseph Lewis, native of Courbon in Provence, and Lucy Jane Deshayes, native of Port au Prince, St. Domingo, were m. by lic. on 19 Dec, 1795 at St. Peter's Catholic Church, Baltimore (*Piet:* 143).

Sampson, |-?-|, m. by 18 Aug 1783 Eliz., daughter of Daniel Collett (BAWB 3:555).

Sampson, Emanuel, m. by 13 June 1792 Cassandra, who received an equal share of the estate of Thomas Riston (BAAD 11:71).

Sampson, George, and Miss Catherine Dysart, both of Baltimore, were m. last Sat. eve. by Rev. John Hagerty (*Baltimore Daily Intelligencer* 21 July 1794).

Sampson, George, administrator with will annexed, on 21 Nov 1798 posted bond to administer the estate of William Woods, Jr. (BAAB 8:468). Woods' will, dated 4 Oct 1796 named David Stewart and Archibald Campbell of Baltimore and Thomas Irwin and Capt. Francis Blackwell as execs. (BAWB 6:143).

Sampson, Jacob, m. by 14 Nov 1786 a sister of John Kingsbury, and had a son John Sampson, who Kingsbury called nephew, and a daughter Martha, called niece (BAWB 4:414).

Sampson, Jacob, administrator, on 25 Oct 1797 posted bond to administer the estate of Mary Freeland (BAAB 8:33).

Sampson, Richard, d. by 8 March 1714; he m. Elizabeth [-?-] who m. 2nd, James Bagford (*q.v.*), 3rd, Samuel Hinton (*q.v.*), and, 4th, Thomas Stone (*q.v.*) (MWB 14:43, abst. in *Md. Cal. of Wills* 4:29; BACP IS#C:4; BALR IS#H:328, 385; HWS#M:163; MWB 21:768, abst. in *Md. Cal. of Wills* 7:212).

Sampson, Richard, m. by 21 Feb 1790 Rachel, daughter of Robert Love Pitstow BAWB 5:175).

Sampson, Richard, administrator, on 10 April 1793 posted bond to administer that part of the estate of Thomas Riston that had not been administered by Mary Riston (BAAB 7:436).

Sanders, Edward, and Christian 'Beardy' were m. on 29 Oct 1728 (Harrison, "St. George's Parish Register:" 249). On 4 Aug 1735 Christian Beard was mentioned in the administration account of Francis Ogg of Baltimore Co. (MDAD 13:303).

Sanders, James, and Ruth Andrews were m. on 11 Feb 1782 in St. Paul's Parish

(Harrison, "St. Paul's Parish Register:" 188). In Feb 1784 Sanders stated that he would not pay the debts of his wife Ruth (*Maryland Journal and Baltimore Advertiser* 24 Feb 1784).

Sanders (Saunders), Thomas, m. by 9 May 1758 Elizabeth, daughter of Antil and Sarah Deaver (BALR B#G:134; BAWB 3:177). Elizabeth was a daughter of Sarah Deaver and granddaughter of John Webster (BALR (BALR B#H:297, B#P:190).

Sanders. See also Saunders.

Sanderson, Thomas, m. by 17 April 1800 Margaret, daughter of Gerrard Hopkins (BAWB 6:260). Margaret Sanderson, (formerly Hopkins), on 30 d. 6 m. 1787, was charged with marrying contrary to the good order ("Minutes of Gunpowder Meeting," *QRNM:* 84). [No other marriage reference found].

Sandozo, John, died leaving a will dated 4 Oct 1784 and proved 14 Sep 1789, naming his mother-in-law Catherine Butler, and his nephews and nieces Ann Margaret, Elizabeth, John, and William Hauck, and Henry and Margaret Arnold (BAWB 4:376).

Sands, [-?-], m. by 29 June 1765 Frances, daughter of Francis Bright, who owned land on Kent Island; in her will of that date, Frances Sands named her son Alexander Sands and a granddaughter Martha Smith (BAWB 3:165).

Sands, Samuel, m. 1st, by 12 April 1794 Mary [-?-] ("The Sands Bible," *The Notebook* 10 (2) (June 1994): 22).

Sands, Samuel, m. 2nd, by 26 Aug 1797 Areanna [-?-], who d. 7 June 1839 in her 88th year ("The Sands Bible," *The Notebook* 10 (2) (June 1994): 22)

Sanger, Capt. Seth, of Boston, and Miss Kitty Elkins of Baltimore, were m. [date not given] (*Maryland Journal and Baltimore Advertiser* 8 Aug 1794).

Sappington (Sappenton), Roger, on 25 Nov 1774 was named as a grandson in the will of Rebecca Boyce (BAWB 3:306).

Sappington, William, d. by 10 Nov 1767 when his admx. Esther had m. Nathan Brashears (q.v.) (MDTP 42:260).

Sater, Charles, m. by 12 Oct 1790 [-?-], heir of George Ogg (BAAD 10:209). Hellen Ogg, in her will made 2 April 1798 named her grandchildren George and Hellen Sater, children of Charles, and her daughter Rachel Jacobs (BAWB 6:92).

Sater, George, m. by 15 Oct 1759 Rachel, daughter of William Hamilton (BAWB 2:315). By 27 Dec 1788 Rachel had m. 2nd, John Daughady (*q.v.*).

Sater (Satyr), Henry, m. by June 1718 Mary, extx. of Edward Stevenson (*q.v.*) (BACP IS#IA:316; BAAD 1:182; MDTP 27:66; MDAD 8:541).

Sater, Henry, d. by Dec 1792 when his sons Henry and Thomas chose Hannah Sater as their guardian; his children Joseph, Sarah, and John were made wards of Hannah Sater (BAOC 3:18).

Satyr. See Sater.

Saunders, James, convict, in March 1750/1, was fined for begetting a bastard on the body of Mary Polson (Poulson), *alias* Mary Clark (BACP TR#6:288-289).

Saunders, Robert, of Anne Arundel Co., m. by 4 June 1745 Rebecca, sister of Moses Groome and daughter of Moses Groome; Robert and Rebecca conveyed 300 a. to 'their son' Darby Lux (BALR TB#D:338). Darby Lux and Anne Sanders were m. on 16 May 1722 (Harrison, "All Hallows Parish Register," Anne Arundel Co., MS at MdHS: 90).

Saunders. See also Sanders.

Savage, Dennis, widower, and Ann Moore were m. by lic. on 12 May 1799 at St. Peter's Catholic Church, Baltimore (*Piet:* 143).

Savage, George, m. by 14 June 1798 Frances, admx. of William Cummins (BAAD 12:443).

Savage, Hill, m. by 1 March 1719 Elinor, extx. of Peter Bond (*q.v.*) (MINV 3:216; MDAD 3:205, 6:53).

Savage, Hill, the illegitimate son of Sarah Savage (see below), was b, 22 Dec 1738; he was charged with bastardy at March Court 1765 (BAMI 1765:2).

Savage, Peter, widower, and Elizabeth Kenny, widow, natives of Ireland, were m. by lic. on 17 June 1800 at St. Peter's Catholic Church, Baltimore (*Piet:* 143).

Savage. Sarah, was charged with bastardy at March Court 1738/9, and indicted at June Court in June 1739. Her son Hill Savage (see above) was b. 22 Dec 1738. Augustine Choat, (*q.v.*), was the father (BACP HWS#1A:351).

Savage, William, died leaving a will dated 17 Aug 1784 and proved 8 Feb 1785 naming his wife Margaret as extx. (BAWB 4:68). Margaret m. 2nd. John Stokes (*q.v.*); on 8 Aug 1785 John and Margaret Stokes posted bond to administer William Savage's estate (BAAB 6:250).

Savage, William, stated he would not pay the debts of his wife Frances, who had taken up with another man in his absence (*Maryland Journal and Baltimore Advertiser* 14 Oct 1785).

Savory, William, m. by 17 Nov 1733 Mary, the widow and relict of James Maxwell (*q.v.*) of Baltimore Co. (MDAD 12:130). Mary Savory d. 24 July 1753 ("Day Bible." *The Notebook* 15 (2) (June 1999) 9).

Savory, William, in March 1753 appeared before the vestry, to answer charges of unlawful cohabitation with Mary Mead. He promised she would not live at his house any longer (Harrison, "St. John's and St. George's Parish Register Vestry Proceedings," p. 117).

Savory, William, and Rosanna Robinson were m. on 25 July 1787 (Marr. Register of Rev. Lewis Richards, MS.690 at MdHS). On 15 June 1788 Rosanna was named as the admx. of George Robinson (BAAD 9:213, 11:6; BOCP: Robinson, George, 1788, Box 2, Folder 65; BAAD 11:6).

Scanlan, James, was m. last Sat. eve. by Rev. Mr. Kurtz, to Mary Pearson, both of this city (*Federal Gazette and Baltimore Daily Advertiser* 27 Nov 1797).

Scarff, James, d. by 13 Nov 1750 when Jacob Rowles (*q.v.*) (who had m. Mary Scarff) was named as the admin. of Scarff's estate (MDTP 34:36).

Scarlett, [-?-], m. by 27 March 1754, Bothia [-?-], late Bothia Adams (q.v.), admx of James Barnes (*q.v.*) (MDTP 36:28; MDAD 36:257 which gives her former husband's name as John Barnes). Bothia was the mother of Bothia, wife of James Phillips (*q.v.*), James, William, and Ford Barnes, and Rachel Stephenson (*q.v.*) and Mary Deaver (*q.v.*) (BAWB 4:508; MDTP 36:28).

Schaefer, Christian, m. by 24 Nov 1763, Mar. Appolon Haefnerin ("First Record Book for the Reformed and Lutheran Congregations at Manchester, Baltimore (now Carroll) Co.,"*MGSB* 35:268). She m. 2nd, John Cooper (*q.v.*).

Schaefer, George Michael, m. by 8 June 1786, Maria Elisabeth Bleyin ("First Record Book for the Reformed and Lutheran Congregations at Manchester, Baltimore (now Carroll) Co.," *MGSB* 35:282).

Schaefer, Jacob, m. by 8 June 1764, Anna Dillin ("First Record Book for the Reformed and Lutheran Congregations at Manchester, Baltimore (now Carroll) Co.," *MGSB* 35:268).

Schafer, Baltser, and Eleanor Larsh were married by license dated 24 Feb 1781 (BAML). On 27 Jan 1782 Eleanor was named as an heir of Valentine Larsch (BAAD 8:154).

Scheidecker, Joseph, m. by 27 Dec 1793 Eve Barbara, daughter of Conrad Smith, dec. (BALR WG#MM: 540).

Scheiecker (Sheldecker), Joseph, and Barbara Brown were m. on 29 Dec 1793 (Marr. License Returns of Rev. Daniel Kurtz; Scharf Papers, MS.1999 at MdHS).

Schildtacker, Joseph, stated he would not pay the debts of his wife Eve Barbara, who had eloped from his bed and board without any just cause (*Federal Gazette and Baltimore Daily Advertiser* 12 April 1796).

Schilling, Christian, m. by 12 May 1764, Elisabeta Morri (or Marry) ("First Record Book for the Reformed and Lutheran Congregations at Manchester, Baltimore (now Carroll) Co.," *MGSB* 35:268, 270).

Schits, Peter, of York Town, Pa., on 10 Sep 1773 was named as a brother-in-law of Jacob Mohlar of Baltimore Town (BAWB 3:272).

Schlegel, Christian, of Baltimore, m. Charlotte Wolf of Lancaster Co., Pa. on 14 Oct 1786 ("City of Lancaster Reformed Church Records," *MGSB* 34 (4) (Fall 1993) 407; "Minutes of Falls Meeting," Bucks Co., Pa.).

Schleich, John, in his will made 31 Oct 1791 named his daughter Catherine, by his wife Catherine, his daughter Sophia, his grandson John Allen, son of Solomon, and his grandson John Franciscus, son of George (BAWB 7:118).

Schlotthauer, Nicolaus, m. by 25 Oct 1766, Anna Elisabeta Nollin ("First Record Book for the Reformed and Lutheran Congregations at Manchester, Baltimore (now Carroll) Co.," *MGSB* 35:270).

Schmall, Adam, m. by 13 Feb 1760, Johanna Dorothea Zimmermanin ("First Record Book for the Reformed and Lutheran Congregations at Manchester, Baltimore (now Carroll) Co.," *MGSB* 35:265).

Schneider, Abraham, m. by 14 June 1787 Elisabetha Stoffelin ("First Record Book for the Reformed and Lutheran Congregations at Manchester, Baltimore (now Carroll) Co.," *MGSB* 35:283).

Schneider, Friedrich, m. by 3 Jan 1787 Maria Margaretha Grünnewaldin ("First Record Book for the Reformed and Lutheran Congregations at Manchester, Baltimore (now Carroll) Co.," *MGSB* 35:283).

Schneider, Michael, m. by 11 Dec 1787 Catharina Eckerin ("First Record Book for the Reformed and Lutheran Congregations at Manchester, Baltimore (now Carroll) Co.," *MGSB* 35:283).

Schriber, Michael, m. by 31 March 1780, Elizabeth, daughter of William Hensman (BALR WG#E:207).

Schroeder, Charles, letter carrier, and Miss Catherine Hauptman, from Penna., were m. last eve. by Rev. Kurtz (*Baltimore Telegraphe* 25 May 1799).

Schroeder, Henry, of Baltimore Town, was m. last Sun. at Frederick Town to Miss Polly Schley of that place (*Federal Intelligencer and Baltimore Daily Gazette* 9 April 1795).

Schroeder, Herman Henry, and Sus. Schwartz were m. on 30 Oct 1785 ("Register of First German Evang. Lutheran Church, Frederick," MS. at MdHS: 1167). On 9

Nov 1794 Susanna Schwarz [Schroeder] who was buried 9 Nov 1794, aged 28 y, 7 m. ("First German Reformed Church Register," MS. at MdHS: 33).

Schunck, John, m. by 18 May 1789 Nancy, sister of Abram Mumma, farmer (BAWB 4:367).

Schwob, [-?-] (possibly Benedict), m. by 11 Dec 1759 [-?-], daughter of Geo. Welcker and his wife who were sponsors for their grandson Johannes Schwob ("Reformed congregation of Saint Benjamin's Known as Kreider's Church at Pipe Creek, Maryland [Westminster]," *MGSB* 35:437).

Scooly, Reuben, and Esther Lacey on 24 d. 9 m.1785 declared their intention to marry ("Minutes of Gunpowder Meeting," *QRNM:*80).

Scott, [-?-], m. by 15 Nov 1790 Christian, sister of Catherine Barbara Brown, wife of Jacob Frederick Brown (BAWB 5:35). In 1794 Christiann was named as a sister of John Wright and as the mother of Margaret wife of John Davidson (*q.v.*) (BOCP Petition of Andrew Scott, 1794).

Scott, Amos, and Rachel Price were married by license dated 18 April 1789 (BAML). On 1 March 1796 Rachel was named as a daughter of Mordecai Price of Gunpowder Forest (BAWB 5:379).

Scott, Andrew, and Priscilla Colvin were m. by lic. dated 13 July 1786 (BAML).In June 1797 he stated he had removed goods from his house, and would not pay the debts of his wife Priscilla (*Maryland Journal and Baltimore Advertiser* 22 June 1787). Priscilla Scott, formerly Colvin, refuted her husband's charges (*Maryland Journal and Baltimore Advertiser* 26 June 1787).

Scott, Aquila, d. by Nov 1762 when Mordecai Amos was made guardian of Elizabeth, Aquila, James, Rebecca, and Sarah Scott (BAMI 1755-1763).

Scott, Aquila, son of Aquila, in March 1768 chose Lemuel Howard as his guardian (BAMI 1768-1769).

Scott, Daniel, Jr., m. by 5 Sep 1707 Elizabeth, admx. of Robert Love (INAC 17:110).

Scott, Daniel, d. by 4 Nov 1723 when his widow Jane renounced her right to administer his estate, so Daniel Scott posted a bond (BAAB 3:434).

Scott, Daniel, and Hannah Butterworth were m. on 27 Jan 1740 (Harrison, "St. John's Parish Register:" 147). On 15 May 1742 Hannah was named as a daughter of Isaac Butterworth (BALR TB#A:196). Scott d. by 21 Oct 1752 when his extx. Hannah was m. to John Giles (*q.v.*).

Scott, Daniel, m. by 6 April 1744, Jane Johnson, who called Elizabeth Shaw (*q.v.*) her sister; Jane and Elizabeth called Deborah Benger (*q.v.*) mother (BALR TB#C:471).

Scott, Daniel, orphan of Aquila Scott, in Nov 1760 chose Joshua Bond as his guardian (BAMI 1755-1763: 40).

Scott, Esther, on 29 d. 12 m. 1792 was condemned for going out in marriage ("Minutes of Gunpowder Meeting," *QRNM:*93). She and Peter Hunter were m. by lic. on 30 Nov 1792 (BAML).

Scott, George, of Baltimore, informed the public that he was keeping the tanyard formerly kept by his father Michael Scott (*Maryland Journal and Baltimore Advertiser* 2 Jan 1775).

Scott, James, and Ann Wheeler were m. on 18 Feb 1741 (Harrison, "St. George's Parish Register:" 322). On 16 Dec 1745 Anna was named as a daughter of Benjamin Wheeler (BALR TB#D:432).

Scott, John, m. by 16 Dec 1745 Ann [-?-], who joined him in selling 80 a. *St. Omer's,*
which Benjamin Wheeler had conv. to his daughter Ann Wheeler on 15 Sep 1741
(BALR HWS#1-A:588, TB#D:432).

Scott, John, Esq. attorney-at-law, lately m. Betsy Goodwin Dorsey of Baltimore Co.
(*Maryland Gazette or Baltimore General Advertiser* 23 May 1788).

Scott, Joseph, son of Jacob and Hannah, on 30 d. 3 m. 1762 stated he intended to marry Ann
Hayward ("Minutes of Deer Creek Meeting," *QRNM:*129).

Scott, Joseph, Jr., on 9 d. 7 m. 1795 was charged with marrying contrary to the good
order ("Minutes of Baltimore Meeting," *QRNM:*224). Joseph Scott and Hannah
Morris were married by license dated 4 March 1795 (BAML).

Scott, Nathaniel, son of Daniel and Jane (Johnson) Scott, m. by 6 April 1744 Avarilla,
daughter of Luke Raven; they had a daughter Avarilla Scott who m. Thomas Norris
(*q.v.*) (BALR TB#C:471).

Scott, Rossiter, on 28 d. 2 m. 1789 requested a certificate to Gwynned Monthly Meeting,
Pa., to marry Edith Lukens ("Minutes of Gunpowder Meeting," *QRNM:*86).

Scott, Thomas, and Elizabeth Matthews declared their intention to marry ("Minutes of
Gunpowder Meeting," *QRNM:*93). On 7 May 1800 Elizabeth was named as an heir
of Thomas Matthews (BAAD 13: 252).

Scott, William, on 29 d. 12 m. 1787 was charged with having been married by a hireling
minister ("Minutes of Gunpowder Meeting," *QRNM:*84). William Scott and Sarah
Merryman were m. 6 Dec 1787 (Marriage Register of Rev. Lewis Richards, Pastor
of First Baptist Church, Baltimore, 1784-1818. MS 690 at MdHS). She was a sister
of Samuel and Nicholas Merryman (BALR WG#HH:385; BAOC 2:185).

Scrivener, Robert, m. by 25 Aug 1769 Juliana, admx. of John Bailey (MDTP 43:335).

Scrivener, William, m. by 30 March 1744 Elizabeth, coheir of John Clark, son of
Matthew Clark who m. Elizabeth, sister of James Ford, late of Anne Arundel Co.,
dec (BALR TB#C:565).

Scrogs, Alexander, and Nancy McElroy were m. on 20 Feb 1794 ("Register of First
Presbyterian Church, Baltimore," MS. at MdHS: 13; *Baltimore Daily Intelligencer*
21 Feb 1794).

Scroggs, John, of Baltimore Co., m. by 4 May 1789 Frances, daughter of Andrew Hooke
(BALR WG#DD:91).

Scudamore (Skidmore), Thomas, d. by 1 Nov 1743, having m. [-?-], only daughter of
John Dixon of Baltimore Co.; she m. 2nd, John Hayes (*q.v.*) (PCLR EI#10:745).
Jane Long, widow of John Dixon and now wife of Thomas Long named her
granddaughter in her will dated 19 May 1696 (MWB 7:141 abst. in *Md. Cal. of
Wills* 2:100).

Scutt, John, m. by 18 Feb 1696 Katherine, relict of Stephen Hart (*q.v.*) (MDTP 16:214;
INAC 14:142). John and Katherine were the parents of: Mary, m. William Douglas
(*q.v.*). Katherine m. 3rd, Henry Knowles (*q.v.*).

Seabrook, William, came to Md., and m. 1st, by Jan. 1737/8 Jemima, daughter of Capt.
Richard Gist. Jemima d. by 1749 and William m. 2nd, Zipporah, b. 11 June 1729,
eld. daughter of Nathaniel and Mary Davis (Richard S. Wheeler, "Seabrooks of
Maryland and Pennsylvania," *MGSB* 34 (2) 140; BALR TB#A:132).

Seale, James, m. by 12 June 1753 Sarah, heir of Henry O'Neale (BACT TR#E:120).

Seamer (Symore), Elizabeth, was charged with bastardy at June 1721 Court and named
(Capt.) Richard Smithers as the father of her child. In Nov 1722 she petitioned the
court and state she was carrying a bastard child and named Smithers as the father.

She was presented for bastardy at the March 172/3 Court (BACP IS#C:50, IS&TW#3: 15, 215, 436). Elizabeth Seamer (Seamore) was the mother of Sophia Seamer, b. 26 Sep 1720, and Thomas Seamore, d. 1723 (Reamy, *St. George's Parish Register:* 21, 31).

Sedgehill, Elizabeth, servant to Samuel Stansbury, was charged with bastardy at June Court 1737 and named Robert Crosbie or Croslie, also a servant to Samuel Stansbury, as the father of the child (BAMI 1755-1763: 37).

Sedgwick, [-?-], m. by 7 Sep 1763, Dorcas, sister of James Sollers (BAWB 2:166).

Seeley, Samuel, on 20 Jan 1730/1 was named as father-in-law some 30 years prior to this date in a deposition by William Cook (BALC HWS#3 #26).

Seigler. See Sigler.

Selman. See Sellman.

Sellman, [-?-], m. by 12 Dec 1750 Charity, daughter of Richard Tydings (BALR TR#D, 107). See Michael Pasquinet, elsewhere in this work.

Sellman, Gassaway, m. by 10 March 1768 Catherine, widow and extx. of Francis Davis, Sr. (BAAD 8:59, 294).

Sellman, Johnzee, and Mrs. Sarah Rollins, both of Baltimore, were m. last eve. (*Baltimore Daily Repository* 15 Feb 1792).

Sellman, Peter, and Elizabeth Cole, free Mulattoes, were m. by lic. on 27 June 1799 at St. Peter's Catholic Church, Baltimore (*Piet:* 143).

Sellman (Selman), Thomas, m. by 25 Jan 1756 Ruth Shipley, daughter of Adam Shipley (BALR BB#I:567).

Semons, [-?-], m. by 12 May 1757 Elizabeth, legatee of Edward Richards (BFD 2:57).

Sempstress, Elizabeth, was charged with bastardy at March Court 1765. Godfrey Watters was summoned (BAMI 1765:6).

Senz. See Zentz.

Sergant, John, m. by 3 Feb 1684 Elizabeth [-?-], to whom Edward Reeves conveyed property 'for love and affection' (BALR RM#HS:109).

Sergeant, John, and Elizabeth Gostwick were m. on 4 Feb 1732 (Harrison, "St. Paul's Parish Register:" 150). On 30 Aug 1733 Elizabeth Sergeant, admx. posted bond to administer the estate of Thomas Gostwick (q.v.) (BAAB 3:135; see also BAAD 3:229; MDAD 14:402).

Sergeant, John, m. by 16 June 1766 Mary, legatee of James Dawkins (BFD 4:126).

Seton, John Curson, of Baltimore, and Miss Ann Wise of Summer Hill, near Alexandria, were m. last Sun. at Georgetown, Md., by Rev. Mr. Balch (*Federal Gazette and Baltimore Daily Advertiser* 9 Jan 1800).

Settlemine, Christopher, stated he would not pay the debts of his wife Elizabeth (*Maryland Journal and Baltimore Advertiser* 25 Nov 1783).

Sewell, Sarah, was charged with bastardy at the March 1736/7 Court (BACP HWS#1A:20).

Sewell, William, stated he would not pay the debts of his wife Mary Ann (*Maryland Journal and Baltimore Advertiser* 29 Aug 1786).

Shade. See Shead.

Shaffer, [-?-], m. by 15 Nov 1790 Elizabeth Margaret, sister of Jacob Frederick Brown (BAWB 5:35).

Shammand, Mary Rose, in her will made 26 June 1797 named her four surviving children, incl. Elisabeth Shammand Preratery[*sic*] and Margaret Prette; money due them from their father's share of his patrimony in Bordeaux, France (BAWB 6:77).

Shanly, Jeffrey D., of Long Green, Baltimore Co.,, denied the report that he had a wife in Ireland still living; she died some time ago, and Mr. Gilbert Bigger of Market St. Baltimore, and the widow Eleanor Ellerton, also of Baltimore, would attest to that (*Maryland Journal and Baltimore Advertiser* 1 Oct 1793).

Shardle, William, was m. last eve. by Rev. Mr. Kurtz, to Martha Wilson, both of this city (*Federal Gazette and Baltimore Daily Advertiser* 30 Aug 1800).

Sharp, [-?-], d. by April 1793 when his children, George, John, Hannah, and Micajah, all under 14, were made wards of Matthew Sparks (BAOC 3:42).

Sharp, John, son of Thomas and Susanna, the latter dec., on 23 d. 4 m. 1795, announced his intention to marry Elizabeth Walton, relict of William Walton ("Minutes of Deer Creek Meeting," *QRNM:*155).

Sharp, Capt. Peter, of Talbot Co., and Miss Dickinson, only daughter of Capt. Brittingham Dickinson of this town, were m. last Thurs. eve. (*Maryland Journal and Baltimore Advertiser* 1 April 1783).

Sharp, Thomas, Jr., on 26 d. 3 m. 1791, being in an unmarried state, hath a child laid to his charge. He was so reported again on 28 d. 4 m. 1792 ("Minutes of Gunpowder Meeting," *QRNM:*90, 92).

Sharp, William, on 29 d. 12 m. 1781 was reported as having gone out in marriage ("Minutes of Gunpowder Meeting," *QRNM:*75). [No other marriage reference found].

Sharper, Enoch, and Mary Beard were m. by license on 22 July 1783 (BAML).In May 1784 Sharper stated his wife Mary (formerly Mary Beard) had eloped (*Maryland Journal and Baltimore Advertiser* 18 May 1784).

Sharpless, Benjamin, son of Benjamin of Pa., on 6 d. 10 m. 1774, announced he intended to marry Sarah Rigbie, daughter of James Rigbie of Harford Co. ("Minutes of Deer Creek Meeting," *QRNM:* 136). Sharpless had d. by 28 d. 1 m. 1782 and it was announced that Samuel Wallis (*q.v.*) intended to m. Sarah Rigbie Sharpless ("Minutes of Deer Creek Meeting," *QRNM:* 141).

Sharpner, Michael, servant to Edward Puntney in May 1755 was fined for begetting a bastard on the body of Catherine Kibren, servant, to William Rogers (BACP BB#B:401, 404).

Sharrer, Conrad, m. by 28 July 1764 Catherine, daughter of Anna Mary Ash (BAWB 3:41).

Shauck, John, m. by 3 July 1790 Mary, daughter of Jacob Epaugh (BAWB 4:496; BAAD 10:401).

Shavers, Abraham, m. by Aug 1718 Mary, extx. of Henry Dukes (BACP IS#IA:19).

Shaw, [-?-], m. by 15 Feb 1749, Eleanor, widow of Thomas Joyce of Anne Arundel Co. MINV 43:68).

Shaw, Capt. [-?-], of Baltimore, was m. at Philadelphia on Friday eve. by Right Rev. Bishop White, to Miss Eliza Palmer, daughter of Thomas Palmer of this city (*Federal Gazette and Baltimore Daily Advertiser* 13 Aug 1798).

Shaw, Catherine, was charged with bastardy at the Aug 1728 Court and John Moorcock agreed at the Nov 1728 Court to be responsible for bringing up the child. She was charged again at the Aug 1733 Court at the March 1736/7 Court, and was presented at the June 1737 Court; she was charged with Negro bastardy at the March 1737/8 Court (the name of the slave was not given); the child was to be sold and bound out until the age of 31 and Catherine was sold and bound to serve for seven years. As a servant to William Grafton she was charged with bastardy at the Nov 1738 Court.

She was charged with Negro bastardy and confessed at the Aug 1745 Court, and she was ordered to serve for the use of the county for seven years after her present term of service. Her child, Temperance Shaw, was sold to William Grafton until she should arrive at the age of 31. Catherine was charged with bastardy again at the Nov 1746 Court, and again as a servant to William Grafton she was charged again and confessed to having a Mulatto child born of her body at the June 1750 Court; she was ordered to be sold again for seven years after her present servitude (BACP HWS#6:22, 74, HWS#9:69, HWS#1A: 35, 173, 321, Liber 1745-1746: 645, TB&TR#1:220, TB&TR#5:10).

Shaw, Daniel, d. by 5 May 1739. Ann Shaw delivered up her right to administer his estate to Charles Green, who on 5 May 1739 posted bond to administer Shaw's estate (BAAB 5:265).

Shaw, Hannah, was charged with bastardy at the June 1739 Court, the Aug 1739 Court, and again at the Nov 1741 Court; As a servant to William Grafton she admitted at the March 1741/2 Court to having had child by a slave; her child, now one year old was sold to William Grafton to age 32. She was charged with bastardy again at the March 1746/7 Court (BACP HWS#6:401, TB#TR:152,333, and TB&TR#1:378).

Shaw, John, of Cecil Co., m. by 1700 Elizabeth, daughter of John Johnson of Baltimore Co.; Johnson's widow m. 2nd, Robert Benger, and Elizabeth was named as daughter in the undated will of Deborah Benger (q.v.) (MWB 6:372 abst. in *Md. Cal. of Wills* 2:197).

Shaw, John, m. by 17 March 1730 Bridget, daughter of Thomas Knightsmith (MSA Baltimore Co. Rent Roll # 2, 1658-1771: 370).

Shaw, Mary, a free black woman, was charged with bastardy at the March 1710/11 Court (BACP IS#B:205, 214).

Shaw, Mary, was charged with bastardy at the June 1724 and Nov 1724 Courts. As a servant to Christopher Durbin she was again charged with bastardy at the June 1730 Court. Her son, Weymouth Shaw, was bound to serve William Wright in Nov 1736 (BACP IS#TW#3:309, IS&TW#4:42, HWS#6:41().

Shaw, Thomas, m. Sarah daughter of Thomas Thurston (*BCF:*572). On 15 Nov 1715 Simon Pearson (*q.v.*) and wife Sarah, administrators, posted bond to administer the estate of Thomas Shaw (BAAB 3:422).

Shaw, Thomas Knightsmith, aged 14 next 13 March, son of Thomas Shaw, dec., in Nov. 1757 was made ward of William Shaw (BAMI 1755-1763).

Shaw, Thomas Knightsmith, and Sarah Stansbury were m. by license dated 31 Dec 1777 (BAML). On 30 May 1797 Sarah Shaw was named as a daughter of Richardson Stansbury (BAWB 5:505; BAAD 12:412).

Shaw. Upton, son of Thomas, with the advice and consent of his father on 7 Feb 1752 bound himself to Dr. Thomas Thornton, for seven years to learn the art and mystery 'he now [Thornton] followeth' (BACT TR#E:58).

Shaw, William, and Rachel Rowles were m. 19 Oct 1784 (Marr. Returns of Rev. Thomas Chase, Scharf Papers, MS. 1999 at MdHS). William Shaw advertised he had married the only surviving child of Richard Rowles of Baltimore Co., dec., and he has the sole right to settle the estate (*Maryland Journal and Baltimore Advertiser* 8 May 1795).

Shay, James, and Mary Green, natives of Ireland, were m. by lic. on 29 June 1794 at St. Peter's Catholic Church, Baltimore (*Piet:* 143).

Shea, Daniel, and Elizabeth Lurden were m. by lic. on 22 April 1786 at St. Peter's Catholic Church, Baltimore (*Piet:* 1443).

Shead (Shade), Daniel, and Mary Boyd were m. on 30 Oct 1783 (Marr. Returns of Rev. William West, Scharf Papers, MS.1999 at MdHS); on 3 May 1790 Polly was named as a daughter of John Wooden, Sr. (BAWB 4:426). On 14 Feb 1792 Mary was named as formerly Mary Boyd, admx. of John Boyd (*q.v.*) (BAAD 10:541).

Shean, David, and Matto [Matte] Kenochen were m. by lic. on 21 Dec 1785 at St. Peter's Catholic Church, Baltimore (*Piet:* 143).

Shee, Berthes, of Philadelphia, Pa. m. by 19 April 1775 Cecilia, daughter of Thomas Parks, merchant (BALR AL#L:513).

Shegay, Jacob, m. by 13 June 1769 [Judith], heir of Esther Whistler, widow of Ulrich Whistler (BAAD 7:30).

Shehm, Mary [*sic*], m. by 18 Sep 1796 Jane (or June), who rec'd an equal share of the estate of John Cummins (BAAD 12:190).

Shenaman, [-?-], m. by 23 Dec 1785 Juliana, admx. of Jacob Foubler (BAAD 8:169).

Shephard, Rowland, and Jane Taylor were m. on 22 June 1727 (Harrison, "St. George's Parish Register:" 244). On 20 July 1740 Jane was named as a sister of Martin Taylor, dec., and daughter of Martin Taylor (in the administration account of the estate of Robert Robertson of Baltimore Co.) (MDAD 18:12; BALR HWS#1-A:164). Jane m. 2nd, Jonathan Hughes (*q.v.*)

Shepherd, Edward Fletcher, aged 10 last Christmas Day, in Aug 1772 was bound to John Clements, barber (BAMI 1772, 1775-1781: 20).

Shepherd, John, and Eleanor Melony were m. 13 Oct 1787 by Rev. Lewis Richards (Marriage Register of Rev. Lewis, Pastor of First Baptist Church, Baltimore, 1784-1818. MS 690 at MdHS). Eleanor Shepherd advertised that she was leaving her husband, John Shepherd, because he had used her in a scandalous manner (*Federal Intelligencer and Baltimore Daily Gazette* 4 July 1795).

Shepherd, John, m. by 18 April 1788 [-?-], dau. of Thomas Anderson (BAAD 9:196).

Shepherd (Sheapard), Mary, servant of William Fell or Few confessed to bastardy at the Aug 1743 Court and ordered to be whipped on the bare back. She confessed to bastardy again at the June 1746 Court and was ordered to be whipped (BACP Liber 1743-1745: 14-15, BACP TB&TR#1: 11).

Shepherd, Mary, in 1761 was convicted of bastardy (BAMI 1755-1763).

Sheppard, John, and Mary Bryan were m. on 13 May 1780 by Rev. William West (Marriage License Returns of Rev. William West filed 19 Nov 1780: Scharf Papers, MdHS). In Oct 1780 Sheppard stated that he would not pay the debts of his wife Mary (*Maryland Journal and Baltimore Advertiser* 3 Oct 1780).

Sheppard, Sarah, admx., on 20 Sep 1794 posted bond to administer the estate of Michael Finlay (BAAB 8:630).

Sheppard, Thomas, and Nancy Amos were m. by lic. dated 31 Oct 1795 (BAML). Ann Shepherd [*sic*] formerly Amoss [*sic*] on 27 d. 2 m. 1796 were reported as having as gone out in marriage with a man [not] in profession with us ("Minutes of Gunpowder Meeting," *QRNM:*97). T. Shepherd and Nancy Amos were m. yesterday eve, (*Maryland Journal and Baltimore Advertiser* 2 Nov 1795). Thomas Sheppard and Nancy Amos were m. 1 Nov 1795 (Richards' Marr. Register). On 12

d. 5 m. 1796 Thomas Sheppard was charged with marrying outside the good order ("Minutes of Baltimore Meeting," *QRNM:*226).

Sherberly, William, and Miss Margaret Ballard, both of Fell's Point, were m. Sun., 24th inst., by Rev. Toy (*Baltimore Telegraphe* 1 March 1799).

Sheredine, Thomas, m. by 21 June 1754 Ann, daughter of Capt. John Cromwell of Anne Arundel Co., dec. (BALR BB#1:248; BAWB 3:164).

Sherwood, [-?-], m. by 10 Dec 1770 Ann, sister of David and Thomas Aisquith (BAAD 6:187; BFD 6:33).

Shetz, Martin, m. by 22 June 1776 Margaret, daughter of Theobald Schneider of Manheim Twp., York Co., Pa. (BAWB 4:18).

Shields, [-?-], m. by 4 Jan 1790 Mary, who received an equal share of the estate of Daniel Brock and of Thomas Brock (BAAD 10:311).

Shields, Henry, d. by 2 Sep 1725 when his estate was administered by Humphrey Yates (*q.v.*) and his wife Lawrana (BAAD 3:37).

Shields, Solomon, d. by 19 Oct 1751 at which time his admx. Elizabeth was m. to Jacob Sindall (*q.v.*). (MDTP 35:111).

Shilling, Tobias, and Catherine Lawrence were married by banns on 26 Dec 1787 at St. Peter's Catholic Church, Baltimore (*Piet:* 143).

Shipley, [-?-], m. by 4 Aug 1783 Rachel, sister of Elizabeth and Marcella Owings (BAWB 3:523).

Shipley, Adam, on 4 May 1760 was named as a son-in-law of Margaret Whips (MWB 32:99 abst. in *Md. Cal. of Wills* 13:16).

Shipley, Adam, m. by 9 Sep 1785 Ann, daughter of Peter Gosnell (BAWB 4:228).

Shipley, Charles, and Jenny Grymes were m. on 31 Oct 1782 (Marr. Returns of Rev. William West, Scharf Papers, MS.1999 at MdHS). In July 1794 Jennet was named as a representative of James Grimes (BAAD 11:478).

Shipley, Elizabeth, on 1 Oct 1785 was named as an heir of John Knox (BAAD 8:227).

Shipley, George, m. by 20 Nov 1756 Catherine, daughter of George Ogg (BACT TR#E: 228 ff.).

Shipley, Henry, of Anne Arundel Co., brother of Adam Shipley, was m. to Ruth Howard in Aug 1782, in Baltimore, by Parson West (Rev. War Pension Application of Ruth Shipley, widow of Henry: W-6046).

Shipley, Rezin, and Eleanor Brooks were m. by lic. on 3 April 1790 at St. Peter's Catholic Church, Baltimore (*Piet:* 143).

Shipley, Mr. Richard, and Miss Elizabeth Jones, both of this town, were m. last Thurs. eve. By Rev. Mr. John Hagerty (*Federal Intelligencer and Baltimore Daily Gazette* 23 May 1795).

Shipley, Robert, of Baltimore Co., m. by 12 Oct 1710 Elizabeth, daughter of Charles Stephens (Stevens), and sister of William Stephens (Stevens) (AALR PK:296).

Shipley, Samuel, Sr., m. by 4 May 1760 [-?-], daughter of Margaret Whips (BAWB 2:187).

Shipley, Susanna, on 1 Oct 1785 was named as an heir of John Knox (BAAD 8:227).

Shipley, William, m. by 20 Nov 1756 Rebecca, daughter of George Ogg (BACT TR#E: 228-ff.).

Shirk, Peter, and Margaret Chaney were married by license dated 10 July 1792 (BAML). She m. 2nd, James Adams (*q.v.*).

Shock, Mr. Henry, was m. last eve. by Rev. Mr. Willis, to Miss Hannah Spicer, both of this city (*Federal Gazette and Baltimore Daily Advertiser* 21 April 1797).

Shoemaker, Ignatius, native of Hirsingen, Alsace, and Louise Shaffer, native of Erhelen, Germany, were m. by lic. on 15 Feb 1795 at St. Peter's Catholic Church, Baltimore (*Piet:* 143).

Shoemaker, Jacob, stated that he would not pay the debts of his wife Lucy, who had eloped from his bed and board without any just cause (*Federal Intelligencer and Baltimore Daily Gazette* 31 Oct 1795).

Shoen, Mary, servant of Edward Roberts, was charged with bastardy at the Nov 1729 Court (BACP HWS#6: 314).

Shorb, Andrew, and Juliana Golden were m. by lic. on 24 May 1798 at St. Peter's Catholic Church, Baltimore (*Piet:* 143).

Shorp, John, and Catherine Groff were married by banns on 10 Oct 1786 at St. Peter's Catholic Church, Baltimore (*Piet:* 143).

Shorter, [-?-], m. by 8 July 1739 Sarah, mother of Rev. Joseph Hooper, Rector of St. Paul's Parish, Baltimore Co., and of Sarah Hooper (MWB 22:100).

Showers, John, m. by 8 Dec 1787 [-?-], daughter of Michael Burns (BAAD 9:127).

Shrakes, Tedrick, of Baltimore stated that he would not pay the debts of his wife Margaret (*Maryland Journal and Baltimore Advertiser* 31 July 1787).

Shriber, Michael, m. by 31 March 1780 Elizabeth, orphan and coheir of William Hensman (BALR WG#E:207).

Shrim (Shum), Adam, m. by 27 March 1790 [-?-], legatee of John Fowle (BAAD 10:117).

Shriver, Ludick [Ludwick?], m. by 3 Feb 1783 Mary, daughter of Philip Forney of York Co., Pa., who owned land in Baltimore Co. (BALR WG#DD:492).

Shriver, Michael, d. by 16 May 1792 when his admx. Elizabeth had m. 2nd, Daniel Peters (*q.v.*) (BAAD 11:52).

Shroeter, Charles, letter carrier, was m. last eve. by Rev. Kurtz, to Miss Catherine Hauptmann, from Hanover, Pa. (*Federal Gazette and Baltimore Daily Advertiser* 25 May 1799).

Shroyer, George, d. some time in the year 1771 leaving a son George, the petitioner, as exec., and another son Andrew (BOCP Petition of George Shroyer, 1793).

Shultz, Andrew, and Mary Miller were married by license dated 15 Aug 1778 (BAML; BALR WG#C:322).

Shryock, Dr. Jacob, and Miss Elizabeth Dutro, both of Baltimore, were m. last Thurs. eve. by Rev. Dr. Kurtz (*Baltimore Daily Repository* 28 Sep 1793).

Shute, John, merchant, in his will, made 27 June 1763 named his half-brother Thomas Dicas (BAWB 3:1).

Sides (Sends), Aaron, exec., on 18 April 1791 posted bond to administer the estate of John Daniel Reed, whose will made 6 June 1791and proved 28 July 1791 [*sic*] named Sides as exec. (BAWB 5:4; BAAB 7:318).

Sieg, Peter, and Mary Weiss were m. by lic. on 3 Sep 1800 at St. Peter's Catholic Church, Baltimore (*Piet:* 143).

Siegfried, Charles Louis, and Charlotte Frazier were m. on 26 March 1798 (Harrison, "St. Paul's Parish Register:" 356). On 1 June 1800 Charlotte was named as a daughter of Alexander Frazier who owned *Todd's Forest* and *Deep Point* (MCHP 1544). However F. H. Siegfried [*sic*] and Miss Charlotte Frazier, of Baltimore., were m. last Mon. eve. by the Rev. Mr. Ireland (*Federal Gazette and Baltimore Advertiser* 29 March 1798).

Siegler. See Sigler.

Sier (Sue), [-?-], m. by 12 May 1757 Rachel, legatee of Edward Richards (BFD 2:57).

Sigler (Seigler, Segler), John, m. by 10 May 1763 Elizabeth, extx. of Peter Lettick (*q.v.*) (or Littig) (MDTP 39:108; MDAD 49:235; BAAD 6:43).

Simm, [-?-], m. by 11 April 1776 Margery, sister of Thomas Ewing (BAWB 4:402).

Simmonds. See Simmons.

Simmons, [-?-], d. by 18 Aug 1782 having m. Belinda, daughter of John Ford, Sr. (BAWB 3:456).

Simmons, Charles, m. by 5 June 1704 [-?-], admx. of Thomas Jones (INAC 3:413; BAAD 1:238).

Simmons, Charles, on 15 May 1731 was named as son-in-law and next of kin of Edward Smith of Baltimore Co. (MINV 16:473). Simmons d. by 1 Oct 1772, having m. Hannah, daughter of Edward Smith; Hannah m. 2nd, John Poteet (*q.v.*) (BALR AL#F:138),

Simmons, Charles, and Elizabeth Poteet were m. on 19 Oct 1742 (Harrison, "St. John's Parish Register:" 124, 144).

Simmons (Simmonds), Thomas, and Priscilla McComas were m. 6 Feb 1753 (Harrison, "St. John's Parish Register:" 207). On 18 Oct 1760 Priscilla was named as a daughter of Alexander McComas (BAWB 2:352; MDAD 47:447). On 26 April 1762, Thomas Simmons was paid for his wife's share [of Alexander McComas' estate] by Thomas and Hannah Miles [Hannah was the widow of Alexander McComas] (BAAD 4:365).

Simms, [-?-], m. by 19 July 1778 Ann, daughter of Samuel Carson Davey, merchant of Baltimore Town (BAWB 3:364).

Simonds, See Simmons.

Simons, [-?-], m. by 22 Sep 1755 Elizabeth, daughter of Edward Richards (MWB 30:26 abst. by Gibb).

Simpkin, [-?-], m. by 3 Sep 1774 Mary, daughter of Thomas Gorsuch (BAWB 3:315).

Simpson, James, merchant of Baltimore, was m. Thurs. eve., 21st inst. at Mt. Serenity, Lancaster Co., Pa. to Miss Clingan, daughter of the late James Clingan (*Maryland Journal and Baltimore Advertiser* 29 Jan 1790).

Simpson, Dr. John, and Elizabeth Durbin William Andrew were m. on 13 Feb 1794 (Marr. Register of Rev. Lewis Richards, MS.690 at MdHS). John Simpson entered into a marriage contract with Elizabeth Durbin William Andrew on 13 Feb 1794. She was a sister of Abarilla Andrew and Abraham Andrew. Abraham George Hammond had m. Mary Andrew, widow of William Andrew who had d. testate, and mother of Elizabeth Durbin William Andrew (BALR WG#NN: 286). In Feb 1794 Elizabeth Durbin William Simpson, formerly Andrew, orphan daughter of William Andrew, chose her husband Dr. John Simpson as her guardian (BAOC 3:81).

Simpson, Richard, in May 1793 Prudence Kelly brought a Bible in which his age was listed, showing he was of full age; in Oct 1793 he was discharged from Samuel Owings (BAOC 3:64).

Simpson, Sarah, was charged with bastardy at the Aug 1743 Court (BACP 1743-1745L 395). Sarah Simpson was the mother of Thomas Simpson, b. 11 June 1737 (Reamy, *St. George's Parish Register:* 55).

Simpson, Susanna, was charged with bastardy at the March 1710/11 Court and named Garret Close as the father. She was charged again at the Aug 1716 Court and named James Collins as the father (BACP IS#B: 305, 210, IS#IA:56). Susanna's daughter, Sarah Collins Simpson, was born 27 Feb 1715 (Reamy, *St. George's Parish Register:* 18).

Simpson, Thomas, Edward Pontany, Jr., son of William, John Curtis, Conrad Hush and George Fight cautioned all persons from buying Simpson's estate or any portion of his estate from Sarah Ward or any of her children or her sons-in-law. Edward Pontany, Sr., and the said Sarah Ward had cohabited together, and Pontany has since d. Sarah Ward now styles herself Sarah Pontany, but the records of St. Paul's Parish show her to be Sarah Ward (*Maryland Journal and Baltimore Advertiser* 12 Nov 1784).

Simpson, William, m. by 17 Jan 1732 Elizabeth, a daughter named in the will of Mary Buchannan, widow of Archibald Buchannan; Mary also named a granddaughter Hannah Simpson (MWB 30:698 abst. in *Md. Cal. of Wills* 7:23)

Sims, John, m. by 7 June 1771 Sarah, daughter of Adam Hoops (BAWB 3:259).

Sims, Richard, m. by 5 April 1676 [-?-], daughter of John Taylor who called Richard Sims' two children his grandchildren (MWB 5:36 abst. in *Md. Cal. of Wills* 1:170).

Sinclair (Sinkler). James, and Mary Lester were m. on 25 Dec 1742 (Harrison, St. George's Parish Register:" 332). On 15 May 1749 Mary was named as a daughter of Ann Lester, who also named her grandchildren Ann and Lester Sinclair (Sinkler) (MWB 27:84 abst. by Gibb).

Sinclair, Robert, and Kitty Pancose [*sic*] were m. 6 Sep 1795 (Marr. Register of Rev. Lewis Richards, MS.690 at MdHS). Esther Sinclair, (formerly Pancoast, on 9 d. 6 m. 1796 was charged with marrying outside the good order ("Minutes of Baltimore Meeting," *QRNM:*226). Robert Sinclair and Miss Hetty Pancoast, both of this town, were m. last Sun. eve. by Rev. Mr. Richards (*Federal Intelligencer and Baltimore Daily Gazette* 8 Sep 1795).

Sinclair, William, and Mary Norris were m. in March 1769 (Harrison, "St. John's Parish Register:" 258). On 21 April 1781 Sinclair's wife was named as a daughter of Joseph Norris, who left one child's part of his estate to William Sinclair's daughter Willimina (BAWB 4:31).

Sinclair, William, of Baltimore Town died, and his estate was being administered by Philip Gibbons who had m. Sinclair's widow Margaret (*Maryland Journal and Baltimore Advertiser* 4 June 1782, 6 Aug 1782).

Sinclair (Sinklair), William, warned all persons not to buy any Negroes from his son Moses (*Maryland Journal and Baltimore Advertiser* 12 Oct 1784).

Sindall, David, and Urith Cook were m. on 4 Dec 1791(Lewis Richards' Marriage Register, MS. 690 at MdHS). Urith m. 2nd, William Weatherby (*q.v.*)

Sindall (Lyndall, Sydall), Jacob, m. by 19 Oct 1751 Elizabeth, admx. of Solomon Shields (*q.v.*) of Baltimore Co. (MDAD 31:121, 33:234).

Sindall, Jacob, d. leaving an orphan son Joseph, now of age, who now petition the court on behalf of his mother Temperance Sindall, a lunatic, and sister of William Culleston (BOCP Petition of Joseph Sindall, 1792).

Sindall, Jane, was indicted for bastardy at the Nov 1734 Court (BACP HWS#9:350).

Sindall, Joseph, and Mary Hooke were m. by lic. on 24 Sep 1787 at St. Peter's Catholic Church, Baltimore (*Piet:* 143).

Sindall (Shindall), Philip, on 7 Nov 1713 was named as a son-in-law in the will of Jane Peacock of Baltimore Co. (MWB 13:620 abst. in *Md. Cal. of Wills* 3:257). He m. by 22 July 1721 Catherine, daughter of Jacob Peacock (BAAD 1:203, 239).

Sindall, Philip, d. by 5 Nov 1739 leaving orphans Anne[?], Samuel, and Mary, and his widow and extx. Elizabeth who had m. 2nd, Jeremiah Cook (Cooke) (*q.v.*) (BAAD 3:206).

Sindall, Samuel, in Nov 1754 was charged with begetting a bastard on the body of Elizabeth Goswick (BACP BB#A:450).

Sindall, William, m. by 3 May 1773 Rebecca, daughter of William Johnson (BAAD 6:260).

Sindorf, [-?-], d. by Aug 1793 when his children Elizabeth and Joseph were made wards of Henry Orban (BAOC 3:57).

Sing, [-?-], m. by 25 Oct 1762 Johanna, daughter of Thomas West (BAWB 3:87).

Sing, Margaret, in 1726 was named as a granddaughter in the will of Richard Taylor (MWB 19:781 abst. in *Md. Cal. of Wills* 6:131). Margaret m. William Wiley (q.v.) on 23 Dec 1734 (Harrison, "St. Paul's Parish Register:" 152).

Singleton, William, and Elizabeth Slater, daughter of William Slater of Baltimore, were m. yesterday, 20th inst. at Baltimore, by Rev. Bend (Chestertown *Apollo* 26 March 1793).

Sitler, Benjamin, orphan of Benjamin, in Dec 1793 chose Mathias Sitler as his guardian (BAOC 3:74).

Sitler, John, petitioned the court that in the year 1786 he had been bound to a certain Christopher Raborg to learn the trade of coppersmith, but he has not been kept at a trade, but forced to do chores, and his term is almost up (BAOC: Petition of John Sitler, 1789).

Sittlemyer, [-?-], m. by 15 Oct 1791 Eve Barbara, daughter of Conrad Smith of Baltimore Co. (BALR WG#GG:569).

Skats, [-?-], m. by 7 Dec 1798 Sarah, dau. of Thomas Preston who also named a granddaughter Katherine Skats (MWB 13:155 abst. in *Md. Cal. of Wills* 3:185).

Skelton, Israel, d. leaving a will in which he named his widow Mary (MWB 12:15 abst. in *Md. Cal. of Wills* 3:74). On 30 July 1682 Hannah Skelton [*sic*] *alias* Gray, on 30 July 1682 posted bond to administer the estate of John Gray. Israel Skelton was one of the sureties (BAAB 3:121).

Skerner, Conrad, m. by 28 July 1764. Catherine, daughter of Anna Mary Ash (BAWB 3:41).

Skerrett, Clement, and Ruth Moore were married by license dated 16 Feb 1784 (BAML). In 1786 Ruth was the widow of Hugh Frazier (*q.v.*) and the widow and extx. of Stephen Moore (*q.v.*), who left an orphan, William, who chose Clement Skerrett as his guardian; Alexander Frazier may have also been a child (BAOC 1:242, 2:44; BAAD 9:120).

Skillman, Robert, and Mrs. Sailors, both of Baltimore, were m. last Sun. by Rev. Allison (*Baltimore Telegraphe* 27 Dec 1797).

Skinner, John, m. by 16 June 1778 Eleanor, widow of Corbin Lee (*q.v.*) (BALR WG#B:443).

Skinner, Capt. Thomas, late of New York, m. last Tues. eve. Betsy Crockett of Baltimore (*Maryland Journal and Baltimore Advertiser* 6 Oct 1786).

Skipwith, George, m. by 10 Oct 1683 Elizabeth, daughter of Thomas Thurston (BALR RM#HS:55, 60, G#J:331).

Slade, Thomas, and Hannah Miles were m. on 29 Sep 1748 (Harrison, "St. John's Parish Register:" 197). On 14 March 1766 Hannah was named as a daughter of Thomas Miles of Orange Co, N.C. (BAWB 3:74).

Slater (Slayter), William, m. by 20 Oct 1782 Charity, daughter of Abraham Eaglestone (BAWB 3:494).

Slater, William, and Hannah James were m. on 30 May 1787 (Marr. Returns of Rev. William West, Scharf Papers, MS.1999 at MdHS); on 23 Sep 1791 Hannah was named as a dau, of George James (BAWB 5:15).

Slave Charles, of Solomon Hillen, and Slave Henny, slave to John Wallace, were m. on 9 Nov 1793 at St. Peter's Catholic Church, Baltimore (*Piet:* 136).

Slave David, slave of David Moore, and Clare Butler, a free Negro woman, were m. on 30 April 1799 at St. Peter's Catholic Church, Baltimore (*Piet:* 140).

Slave George, slave of Archibald Campbell, m. 24 Dec 1797, Free Negro Jane Reed at St. Peter's Catholic Church, Baltimore (*Piet:* 128).

Slave Ignatius, slave of Rev. Beeston, m. 26 May 1795, Slave Catherine, slave of Rev. Nagot at St. Peter's Catholic Church, Baltimore (*Piet:* 127).

Slave Isaac of Christian Keener, and Eleanor Butler, free Negro, were m. 4 June 1796 at St. Peter's Catholic Church, Baltimore (*Piet:* 136).

Slave Jack, of Col. John Eager Howard, and Lukey [-?-], were m. on 18 Dec 1798 at St. Peter's Catholic Church, Baltimore (*Piet:* 136).

Slave Lewis John, slave to Mrs. Dulomgueval, a French lady from St. Domingo, and Melany (Dulongueval?), were m. 24 June 1795 at St. Peter's Catholic Church, Baltimore (*Piet:* 132).

Slave Moses, and Slave Grace, slave(s?) of Thomas McElderry, were m. on 9 June 1798 at St. Peter's Catholic Church, Baltimore (*Piet:* 139).

Slave Peter, and Jane [Lawson?], slave of Richard Lawson, were m. 20 Nov 1799 at St. Peter's Catholic Church, Baltimore (*Piet:* 138).

Slave Samuel, of Rt. Rev. Bishop Carroll, and Free Mulatto Appolonia were m. 21 Dec 1793 at St. Peter's Catholic Church, Baltimore (*Piet:* 129).

Slayter. See Slater.

Slee, Joseph, m. Elizabeth, sister of Capt. Nathaniel Richardson, whose property *Hill's Forest,* is now confiscated (*Maryland Journal and Baltimore Advertiser* 20 Aug 1782).

Slemaker, James, b. 21 Jan 1716 in Liverpool, Eng., d. Sep1752, aged 36 years, m. on 15 Sep 1745, Elizabeth Giles, b. 22 May 1726 in Baltimore Town, m. 2nd, [-?-] Webster, d, 1787, aged 61 years (Harrison, "St. Paul's Parish Register:" 157; "Slemaker" *MGSB* 19 (3) (Summer 1978)145-146). Elizabeth m. 2nd, Michael Webster (*q.v.*).

Slemaker, James, and Clarinda Zuile were m. on 3 May 1791(Marr. Returns of Rev. Daniel Kurtz, Scharf Papers, MS. 1999 at MdHS). On 10 June 1792 Cassandra was named as the extx. of William Zuill (*q.v.*) (BAAD 11:91).

Slemaker, John, son of James and Elizabeth (Giles) Slemaker, was b. 13 July 1746 in Baltimore Town, and drowned in the Chesapeake, aged 42 years; m. on 4 June 1767, Mary Hart, daughter of John and Catherine (Greathouse) Hart, b. 29 Feb 1748, d. 13 Nov 1784, age 36 years and 8 mos. ("Slemaker." *MGSB* 19 (3) (ummer 1978) 145-146).

Slider, [-?-], m. by 6 Sep 1786 Sarah, heir of John Parrish (BAAD 8:307).

Slider, Mary, Slider was tried for bastardy three years before her marriage. Before her marriage, Mary was the mother of: Christopher Slyder, born 18 July 1727. She was indicted for bastardy in June 1730 and tried in Aug 1730. Her second child,

Esther, was born a year before her marriage (BACP HWS#6:415, HS#7:8, (Reamy, *St. Paul's Parish Register*: 10).

Sly, [-?-], m. by 8 April 1800, Sarah, daughter of Barbara Wood (BAWB 6:262).

Small, James, and Ann Cresman were m. by lic. on 29 May 1789 at St. Peter's Catholic Church, Baltimore (*Piet:* 143). Ann Small advertised she had left her husband because he had beat her and turned her out of doors, and brought her to a foul disorder, which modesty forbade her from naming (*Federal Intelligencer and Baltimore Daily Gazette* 18 June 1795). John Small denied the charges made by his wife, by whom he had had three children; she "was a prudent woman until she took up drinking." He stated his wife denied putting the notice in the paper, and she says her sister Stiger made her do it (*Federal Intelligencer and Baltimore Daily Gazette* 23 June 1795). Matthias Stiger and Mary Crissman [*sic*] were married by license dated 12 Oct 1793 (BAML).

Smallshaw, Sarah, servant of William Murphy, was charged with bastardy at the March 1744/5 Court, and ordered to be whipped (BACP 1743-1745:499).

Smallwood, Samuel, in Nov 1714 was charged with begetting a bastard on the body of Elizabeth Stevenson (BACP IS#B:192, 577).

Smart, John, in June 1710 was charged with begetting a bastard on the body of Grace Brown (BACP IS#B:136).

Smeak, John, m. by 28 Nov 1794 Molly, daughter of George Fisher (BAWB 6:6; BAAD 12:489).

Smith, [-?-], m. by 7 Aug 1773 Mary, daughter of Richard King Stevenson (BAWB 3:337).

Smith, [-?-], m. by 19 Jan 1790, Eliz., sister of Dr. Alexander Boyd (BAWB 4:404).

Smith, Andrew, carpenter of Baltimore, stated that he intended to petition the Assembly for a divorce from his wife Amelia, who had deserted him (*Maryland Journal and Baltimore Advertiser* 24 Sep 1794).

Smith, Ann, was charged with bastardy at the June 1737 Court at the Nov 1738 Court, and at the June 1743 Court (Baltimore Co. (BACP HWS#1A:62, HWS#TR:154, and TB#D:185).

Smith, Benjamin, d. by 22 June 1706, when his admx. Sarah had m. 2nd, George Chancey (q.v.). She was a daughter of William Hollis (*Maryland Rent Rolls:* 23).

Smith, Caleb, and Eliza Oyston were m. on 4 May 1784 (Marr. Returns of Rev. William West, Scharf Papers, MS.1999 at MdHS) Eliza was a daughter of Lawrence Oyston (BAWB 6:241).

Smith, Catherine, was charged with bastardy at the Nov 1737 Court and at the Aug 1742 Court (BACP (BACP HWS#1A:129, and TB#D:1, 74).

Smith, Charles, m. by 12 July 1749, Margaret, daughter of Frances Brown (BAAD 5:58).

Smith, Daniel, m. by 17 June 1766 Flora, daughter of Patrick Lynch (BAWB 3:52; BAAD 6:197; BFD 5:403). On 16 April 1792 Daniel's four children were named in the administration account of Patrick Lynch; Basil, Patrick, Prudence, and Flora (BAAD 11:37).

Smith, Edward, m. by 29 April 1703, Bridget (or Margaret), relict and extx. of Charles Jones (*q.v.*) (INAC 23:50; BAAD 1:297). On 15 Feb 1728/9 Bridget was named as the mother of Theophilus Jones (MWB 21:545 abst. in *Md. Cal. of Wills* 7:169).

Smith, Edward, and Mrs. Catherine Webster were m. in Philadelphia (*Baltimore Telegraphe* 17 May 1799).

Smith, Elizabeth, confessed to bastardy at the Nov 1750 Court, and confessed on 27 July 1754 (BACP TR#6:27, BB#1A:449).

Smith, Elizabeth, in 1763 was convicted of bastardy (BAMI 1755-1763).

Smith, Elizabeth, was charged with bastardy at the March 1765 court, and presented at the Aug 1765 Court (BAMI 1765, pp. 1, 16).

Smith, Emanuel, in his will dated 19 April 1704 named his wife Susan, son-in-law William Teague and daughters-in-law Catherine and Ann Teague (MWB 3:235 abst. in *Md. Cal. of Wills* 3:37).

Smith, Frances, was charged with bastardy at the June 1730 Court (BACP HWS#6:415).

Smith, Frances, formerly Dallam, daughter of Margaret Dallam, on 29 d. 3 m. 1792 has reported to have let out her affections to a man not of our society and accomplished her marriage contrary to the good order; the marriage was performed at her mother's house. On 24 d. 1 m. 1793 Margaret Dallam was disowned for allowing her daughter's marriage in her won house to a man not of our society ("Minutes of Deer Creek Meeting," *QRNM:* 150, 152). [No other marriage reference found].

Smith, Francis, and wife Elizabeth on 8 Sep 1690 posted bond to administer the estate of Daniel Lawrence (BAAB 2:113; MDTP 16:170).

Smith, Francis, m. by 15 Oct 1766 Elizabeth, extx. of Henry Fingan (or Finnegan) (BAAD 7:197; BAAD 55:218; MINV 89:157).

Smith, George, m. by 15 May 1694 Hannah, extx. of Daniel Peverell (MDTP 15C:65). She was the mother of Sarah Peverill (BALR RM#HS#1, MWB 3:238, abst. in *Md. Cal. of Wills* 3:37). Hannah m. 3rd, David Thomas (*q.v.*).

Smith, George, a convict, in Aug 1746 was charged with begetting a bastard on the body of Jane Wilson (BACP TB&TR#1:2, 129).

Smith, George, merchant of McAllister's Town, was m. last eve. by Rev. Mr. Kurtz. to Miss Mary Frick, daughter of Peter Frick. of Baltimore, merchant (*Baltimore Evening Post* 6 Dec 1792; *Baltimore Daily Repository* 6 Dec 1792).

Smith, Henry, and Elizabeth Stout were m. by license dated 11 Jan 1783 (BAML). In April 1794, Smith stated he would not pay the debts of his wife Elizabeth (*Maryland Journal and Baltimore Advertiser* 21 April 1794).

Smith, Isaac, aged 9 next 1 Sep. son of Joseph, in June 1759 was bound to Samuel Tate (BAMI 1755-1763).

Smith, Isaac, merchant of Baltimore, and Mary Hopkinson. daughter of the late Francis Hopkinson of Bordentown, N.J., were m. at that city on Tues.. 3rd inst. (*Baltimore Daily Intelligencer* 12 Nov 1794; [Philadelphia] *Aurora General Advertiser* 11 Nov 1794).

Smith, James, m. by 14 June 1792 [-?-], who received an equal share of the estate of Mary Hayes (BAAD 11:88).

Smith, Job, m. by 15 Oct 1791 Rebecca, dau. of Conrad Smith of Baltimore Co. (BALR WG#GG:569).

.**Smith, John,** and Mary Hedge were m. on 2 Feb 1709/10 (Harrison, "St. George's Parish Register:" 208). On 25 Oct 1711 Mary was named as the admx. of Henry Hedge (INAC 32B:270; BAAD 1:378).

Smith, John, m. by 22 Feb 1719 Dorothy, admx of Thomas Williamson (MDAD 2:449; MDTP 24:301; BACP IS#G:626).

Smith, John, and Margaret Scarff were m. on 18 Dec 1752 (Harrison, "St. John's Parish Register:" 206). She was named as an heir of Nicholas Scarf (BAAD 4:243)

Smith, John, orphan son of John Smith, in Aug 1794 chose Caleb Smith as his guardian (BAOC 3:106).

Smith, John, m. by 10 June 1795 Delilah Eaglestone, heir of Jonathan Eaglestone (BAAD 11:537).

Smith, Joseph, and Esther Cameron, in April 1747 were summoned by the vestry to answer charges of unlawful cohabitation with each other ("St. John's and St. George's Parish Register Vestry Proceedings," MS. at the MdHS).

Smith, Joseph, and Deborah Onion were m. on 16 May 1757 (Harrison, "St. John's Parish Register:" 42). On 17 Aug 1757 Deborah was identified as the extx. of Stephen Onion (*q.v.*) (MDTP 36:411; see also BAAD 6:88; MINV 83:56).

Smith, Joseph, was m. last eve. by Rev. Mr. Ireland, to Winifred McCarthy, both of this city(*Federal Gazette and Baltimore Daily Advertiser* 12 April 1799).

Smith, Lambert, merchant of this town, was married last evening by Rev. Mr. Collman [Coleman?] to Elizabeth Gittings, daughter of James Gittings, Esq. (*Baltimore Evening Post* 7 Nov 1792).

Smith, Larkin H., b. 3 Aug 1774, m. 6 July 1796, Rachel Nicholson, b. 10 Oct 1776 ("Larkin H. Smith Bible," *MBR* 7: 1760). Larkin Smith of this county, was m. a few evenings ago, in this town, by Rev. Mr. Bend, to Miss Rachel Nicholson, daughter of Thomas Nicholson, Esq., of Kent Co., Eastern Shore (*Federal Gazette and Baltimore Daily Advertiser* 12 July 1796; (Harrison, "St. Paul's Parish Register:" 327).

Smith, Mary Magdlane [*sic*], on 4 Oct 1765 posted bond to administer the estate of Mathias Colman (BAAB 1:401).

Smith, Nathaniel, and Eliz'th Webster were m. on 11 March 1752 (Harrison, "St. George's Parish Register:" 357). Nathaniel and Elizabeth Smith on [date not given] were conveyed property by Samuel Webster who called Nathaniel Smith son-in-law (BACT B#G: 235).

Smith, Nicholas, and Rebecca Hissey were m. on 28 Oct 1783 (Marr. Returns of Rev. William West, Scharf Papers, MS.1999 at MdHS). On 16 June 1791 Rebecca was named as the extx. of Henry Hissey (*q.v.*) (BAAD 10:383, 11:194).

Smith, Richard, m. by 1 May 1765, Mary, daughter of Edward Flanagan; grandson John Smith of Richard was named in Flanagan's will (BAWB 3:28).

Smith, Capt. Richard, and Miss Polly Beavans were m. last Sun. at Fell's Point (*Maryland Gazette or Baltimore General Advertiser* 27 Sep 1791).

Smith, Richard, mariner, in his will made 21 Dec (1795? or 1796?), named his half-sister Elizabeth Merryman, his half-brother Nicholas Rogers Merryman, and his sister Rebecca Nicols [See Henry Nicols] (BAWB 6:13).

Smith, Robert, m. by 6 Dec 1785 [-?-], daughter of Hugh Miller, yeoman, by whom he had: Hugh, John, Agnes, Mary, Margaret, and Elizabeth Smith (BAWB 4:391).

Smith, Robert, Esq., and Peggy, daughter of the Hon. William Smith of Baltimore, were m. by Rev. Dr. Allison last Tues. (*Maryland Journal and Baltimore Advertiser* 10 Dec 1790).

Smith, Samuel, and Elizabeth Cox were m. on 3 Sep 1727 (Harrison, "St. Paul's Parish Register:" 150). In his will made 1 Feb 1768 named his wife Elizabeth and his children, including a daughter Sophia Greenfield (BAWB 3:100). Elizabeth Smith, in her will made 22 June 1770 named her children Merryman Cox and Sophia Greenfield (BAWB 3:175).

Smith, Samuel, and Avarilla Beck were m. on 30 Aug 1738 (Harrison, "St. John's Parish Register:" 123). On 4 Nov 1749 she was named as a daughter of Matthew Beck (MDAD 27:133). On 6 Oct 1770 'Abarilla' was named as a sister of Charles Beck (BAWB 3:139).

Smith, Samuel, and Tabitha Wheeler were m. on 10 June 1783 (Marr. Returns of Rev. William West, Scharf Papers, MS. 1999 at MdHS). On 7 Dec 1789 Tabitha was named as a daughter of Solomon Wheeler (BAAD 10:85).

Smith, Col. Samuel, and Miss Peggy Spear, daughter of William Spear, Esq., of this town were m. (*Maryland Journal and Baltimore Advertiser* 5 Jan 1779).

Smith, Samuel R., was m. last eve. by Rev. Mr. Richards, to Miss Ann Sitler, both of this town (*Federal Gazette and Baltimore Daily Advertiser* 20 May 1796; Marr. Register of Rev. Lewis Richards, MS.690 at MdHS). She was a daughter of Abraham Sitler or Citler (BAWB 6:243).

Smith, Thomas, d. by 27 June 1726 when his execs. Robert (*q.v.*) and Alice Montgomery, administered his estate (BAAD 3:55).

Smith, Thomas, m. by 22 June 1770 Margaret, daughter of William Grafton (BAAD 6:280; MDAD 68:160; BACT B#G: 323).

Smith, Thomas, of Baltimore, stated that he would not pay the debts of his wife Mary (*Maryland Journal and Baltimore Advertiser* 15 Oct 1790).

Smith, Walter, in his will made 13 Aug 1770 named his mother Elizabeth Hunt, and his brothers-in-law Henry, Job, Samuel, and Phineas Hunt (BAWB 3:217).

Smith, William, m. by 3 Aug 1723 Mary, widow of John Newsom (*q.v.*) (MDTP 26:175).

Smith, William, m. by 19 May 1726 Elizabeth, widow and admx. of Richard Dallam (*q.v.*) (MDTP 27:294). She m. 3rd, John Paca (*q.v.*).

Smith, William, and 'Eilce' Smith were m. on 22 May 1729 (Harrison, "St. Paul's Parish Register:" 149). On 1 Sep 1770 Alice was named as a daughter of Thomas Smith, dec. (PCLR DD#5:42).

Smith, William, judged to be 14 years old, son of Vincent Smith, in Nov 1761 chose Susannah Risteau as his guardian (BAMI 1755-1763).

Smith, William, and Rosanna Bosman were married by license dated 28 Jan 1795 (BAML). On 12 Oct 1797 Rosanna was named as a daughter of Edward Bosman who also named Rosanna's daughter Sarah Smith (BAWB 6:16).

Smith, William R., was m. last eve. by Rev. Mr. Ireland, to Margaret Dugan, daughter of Cumberland Dugan, Esq., of this city (*Federal Gazette and Baltimore Daily Advertiser* 3 Oct 1798).

Smith, Winston, m. on 18 July 1743 Mrs. Susannah Stokes (Harrison, "St. George's Parish Register:" 337). On 17 March 1743 Susannah was named as the widow and extx. of George Stokes (*q.v.*) (MDTP 31:457). Susanna m. 3rd, Talbot Risteau (*q.v.*).

Smith, Winston, and Miss Cassandra Dallam, both of Harford Co., were m. last Thurs. by Rev. Ireland (*Federal Gazette and Baltimore Daily Advertiser* 29 Oct 1796).

Smithee, Sarah, was charged with bastardy at the Nov 1772 Court (BAMI 1772, 1775-1781: 86).

Smithers, Elizabeth, living at the house of Sarah Cockey, was charged with bastardy at the Aug 1723 Court, and named Joseph Johnson as the father (BACP IS&TW#3:422).

Smithers, Richard, and Blanche Wells were m. on 14 Feb 1700 (Harrison, St. George's Parish Register:" 196). On 12 June 1719 Blanche was named as a daughter of George Wells (MDAD 2:451). Smithers d. by 13 Feb 1726, having m. Blanch, daughter of Col. George Wells, and died leaving a son John Smithers of Kent Co. (BALR IS#H:385, BB#I:349).

Smithers, Richard, in June 1721 was charged with begetting a bastard on the body of Eliza Symore. In Nov 1722 he was charged with begetting a bastard on the body of Elizabeth Seamer (BACP IS#C:50, IS&TW#3:15).

Smithers, Richard, m. by Aug 1732 Mary, daughter of James Phillips of Baltimore Co. (*ARMD* 37:568).

Smithson, [-?-], m. by 4 Oct 1767 Mary, daughter of William Grafton (BAWB 3:56).

Smithson, Daniel, and Susannah Taylor were m. on 3 Feb 1785 (Smithson: Rumsey Records Book, MGRC 6:67).

Smithson, Nathaniel, and Mary Bull were m. on 24 or 26 Jan 1779 (Smithson: Rumsey Records Book, MGRC 6:67).

Smithson, Owen, m. by 2 May 1732 Ann, widow of [-?-] Bisco (*q.v.*) and daughter of Thomas Jackson (BALR IS#L:256).

Smithson, Thomas, m. by 9 July 1725 Ann, daughter of Daniel Scott of Baltimore Co. (MDAD 6:406).

Smithson, Thomas, and Sarah Bond were m. on 22 Jan 1767 (Harrison, "St. John's Parish Register:" 230). On 23 Aug 1769 she was named as a daughter of Benjamin Bond and sister of John Bond (BAAD 7:314).

Smythe, Samuel, merchant, and Miss Betsy Wignell, daughter of Capt. James Wignell of Baltimore, were m. at Baltimore on the 15th inst. (*The Pennsylvania Mercury, and Philadelphia Price-Current* 27 Oct 1791).

Snider, Abraham, m. by 18 Jan 1793 Mary Elizabeth, daughter of Henry Henninstofel, who d. intestate (BALR WG#LL:44).

Snider, Mathias, was m. last eve. by Rev. Dr. Kurtz, to Elizabeth Dayley both of this city (*Federal Gazette and Baltimore Daily Advertiser* 8 Oct 1800).

Snowdell (Swindell?), Elizabeth, in her will made 23 Feb 1704/5 named her daughter Judith Gorman (MWB 3:436 abst. in *Md. Cal. of Wills* 3:46).

Snowden, Richard, of Prince George's Co., son of Samuel and Elizabeth, on 30 d. 5 m. 1782 announced his intention to marry Hannah Moore Hopkins, daughter of William and Rachel, of Harford Co.; the parents of the young woman gave their consent ("Minutes of Deer Creek Meeting," QRNM:141).

Snyder (Schneider), Andrew, and Christina Trorbach [*sic*] were m. on 28 April 1794 (Marr. Returns of Rev. Daniel Kirtz, Scharf Papers, MS.1999 at MdHS). On 17 June 1797 Snyder's wife was named as an heir of Michael Drawback (BAAD 12:250).

Snyder, Valentine, and Mrs. [Eliza] Jones, both of Baltimore, were m. on Thurs. by Rev. Kurtz (*Baltimore Telegraphe* 22 Dec 1800).

Snuggrass, William, and Miss Catherine Hart, both of Baltimore, were m. last Thurs. by Rev. Allison (*Baltimore Telegraphe* 9 Dec 1797).

Sollers, [-?-], m. by 10 June 1766 [-?-], daughter of James Dawkins, whose administration account named grandchildren Ann, Mary, and Ellen Sollers (MDAD 54:53). James Sollers, in his will dated 7 Sep 1763 named his grandfather James Dawkins (MWB 32: 149 abst. in *Md. Cal. of Wills* 13:23).

Sollers, Basil, and Susanna Owings, both of Baltimore Co., were m. last Tues. by Rev. Coleman (*Baltimore Telegraphe* 31 March 1800).

Sollers, Elisha, and Miss Sarah Partridge, both of Baltimore Co., were m. last eve. by the Rev. Mr. Richards (*Federal Gazette and Baltimore Advertiser* 4 May 1798).

Sollers, Francis, m. by 12 Aug 1751 Elizabeth, sister of Jonas Bowen and daughter of Mary Bowen (BAWB 2:156, 3:413, 5:85; MWB 28:21 abst. by Gibb).

Sollers, Heighe (or Hugh), m. by 24 Oct 1750 Elizabeth, daughter of Buckler and Elizabeth Partridge, and sister of William Partridge (BAWB 2:335; BAAD 4:323, 6:6, 166, 7:177; MDAD 42:126, 46:57, 53:167).

Sollers, Joseph, on 2 Sep 1746 was summoned with Eleanor Sollers to make their defense for unlawful cohabitation; Eleanor did not appear (Reamy, *St. Thomas' Parish Register:* 101).

Sollers, Joseph, d. by Aug 1765 leaving an orphan Joseph, who chose Michael Fowle as his guardian (BAMI 1755-1763).

Sollers, Joseph, m. by 10 Jan 1793 Ann Partridge, who received an equal share of the estate of D. B. Partridge (BAAD 11:179).

Sollers, Joseph, d. by Feb 1794 leaving a son Elijah who in Feb 1794 chose William Partridge as his guardian (BOCP:3:79).

Sollers, Mary, d. by 31 March 1775 when Sabrett Sollers, admin., posted bond to administer her estate, Heighe Sollers, the original exec., having renounced the right to admin. IBAAB 5:322).

Sollers, Samuel, m. by 29 May 1750, Avarilla, widow and admx. of Edward Peregoy (*q.v.*) (Perrigoe) (MDTP 33-1:145; MDAD 28:98, 35:265).

Sollers (Sollars), Samuel, m. by 16 Sep 1758 Mary admx. of Thomas Tonge (*q.v.*) (MDTP 37:66;. **N.B.:** MDTP 37:144 gives his name as Solomon Sollars, and MDAD 42:90 gives his name as Sabrett Sollers).

Sollers, Thomas, m. by 1 April 1779 Ariana, sister of Elizabeth Howard and Eleanor Sheredine (BALR WG#C:519). In his will, made 13 April 1781, Sollers named his wife Ariana, who as extx. posted an administration bond on 15 June 1783 (BAWB 3:535; BAAB6:62). By 31 May 1781 Ariana had m. 2nd, Jacob Walters (*q.v.*). Thomas Sollers had a son Thomas, aged 19 in 1786 (BAOC 1:286). Ariana Walters, in her will made 19 March 1798 named her children Ariana, Eleanor, Helen, Thomas, and Sabrit Sollers and her daughter Sarah Trotten (BAWB 6:93).

Sollers (or Sellers), William, and Susannah Wells were married by license dated 3 Sep 1778 (BAML); on 19 Aug 1796 she was named as a sister in the will of John Wells (BAWB 5:419).

Solomon, Elkin, merchant, and Abigail Hasleton of Baltimore, were m. last eve. by Rev. Ralph (*Baltimore Daily Repository* 3 Jan 1793).

Solomon, George, m. by 30 Nov 1789 Elizabeth, daughter of John Fowle (BAAD 10:84). On 7 April 1790 Elizabeth was named as the relict of Henry Conrod (BALR WG#EE:283; BPET; Conrod, Henry, 1787; Box 2, folder 17).

Somervell, James, of Baltimore, and Mary Ralph were married (*Maryland Journal and Baltimore Advertiser* 30 Jan 1787).

Souder, Jacob, m. by 6 Nov 1792 Christian Deale, legatee of Philip Deale (BAAD 11:154).

Spain (Pain?), Constabella, was charged with bastardy at the March 1728/9 Court (BACP (BACP HWS#1A:351, HWS#TR:407).

Sparks, Matthew, and 'Providence' Sharp were married by license dated 23 March 1786 (BAML). On 10 April 1793 Prudence was named as the admx. of John Sharp (BAAD 11:243).

Spavold, Dr. James, m. by 29 July 1766 Margaret, extx. of Moses Hill (MDTP 41:364. 408; BAAD 7:281). In May 1767 Thomas Spavold of Baltimore Co., advertised that his wife Margaret had eloped (Annapolis *Maryland Gazette* 14 May 1767).

Spear, John, and Elizabeth Smith were m. on 14 Sep 1779 ("Register of First Presbyterian Church, Baltimore," MS. at MdHS: 13). In his will, made 19 Aug 1791 John Smith named his daughter Elizabeth wife of John Spear and granddaughter Mary Spear (BAWB 5:164).

Spear, Joseph, was m. last eve. by Rev. Dr. Allison, to Miss B. Spear (*Federal Gazette and Baltimore Daily Advertiser* 11 Jan 1798).

Spears, Sarah, was charged with bastardy at the March 1733/4 Court (BACP HWS#9:215).

Speck, John, m. by 2 March 1782 Catharine, extx. of Jacob Schewff [?] (BAAB 4:358).

Spellard, Matthias, and Winifred Gleeson were m. by lic. on 24 Sep 1797 at St. Peter's Catholic Church, Baltimore (*Piet:* 143).

Spellman, William, orphan of William Spellman of St. Mary's Co., in Aug 1762 was bound to Capt. Septimus Noel (BAMI 1755-1763).

Spence, Capt. Peter, of N.Y., and Miss Eliza Jervis of Baltimore were m. last eve. by Rev. Ireland (*Baltimore American* 13 Nov 1799).

Spencer, Hannah, on 28 d. 2 m. 1789 was charged with marrying outside the order ("Minutes of Gunpowder Meeting," *QRNM:*86). **See Hannah Barnett.**

Spencer, William, and Elizabeth Ward were m. on 2 July 1776 (Harrison, "St. James Parish Register," Anne Arundel Co.: 413 at MdHS). On 14 March 1783 Elizabeth was named as a daughter of Joseph Ward and a sister of Mary Ann Ward (BAWB 3:547).

Spencer, Zachariah, and 'Christian' Cobb were m. on 2 Feb 1728 (Harrison, "St. George's Parish Register:" 255). On 1 Oct 1734 'Charity' was named as a daughter of James Cobb (MDAD 12:476).

Spicer, [-?-], m. by 26 Dec 1785 [-?-], daughter of Jonathan Hanson who named his granddaughter Esther Spicer (BAWB 4:115).

Spicer, [-?-], m. by 12 Oct 1790, Rebecca, sister of Johannah Clossey (BAWB 4:499).

Spicer, Ann, was charged with bastardy in 1756, having borne two bastard children (BAMI 1755-1763).

Spicer, Elizabeth, on 22 d. 11 m. 1775 was reported to have had a baseborn child (Minutes of Gunpowder Monthly Meeting: *QRNM:*66).

Spicer, John, and Rachel Spicer (formerly Lee) on 25 d. 8 m. 1792 were disowned for marrying outside the good order ("Minutes of Gunpowder Meeting," *QRNM:*92). John Spicer and Rachel Lee were m. 22 Dec 1791 (Marr. Lic. Returns of Rev. Daniel Kurtz filed 1 Nov 1782, Scharf Papers, MS 1999 at MdHS).

Spicer, Sarah. See Sarah Ryan.

Spicer, Thomas, m. by 13 Feb 1793 [-?-], who received an equal share of the estate of Henry Hissey (BAAD 11:194).

Spindler (Spindle), John, and Sophia Royston were m. by lic. dated 7 May 791 (BAML). On 19 Aug 1795 Sophia was named as a daughter of John Royston (BAWB 6:104).

Spinks, Enoch, on 5 Aug 1702 conv. to John Taylor 100 a. that had formerly belonged to his grandparents Nicholas and Elizabeth Hemstead (BALR HW#2:159). He may have been a son of Roger and Eliza (Hemstead) Spink. He m. by 9 Oct 1710 Sarah (Raven), admx. of Tobias Starnbrough (See *BCF:* 598; MDTP 21:281).

Sprenckel, Johan Henrich, m. by 10 Dec 1791 Chreta Göttigorn ('First Record Book for the Reformed and Lutheran Congregations at Manchester, Baltimore (now Carroll) Co.," *MGSB* 35:286).

Spring, Elizabeth, aged 9, daughter of Jacob Spring, in Nov 1763 was bound to Joseph Peck (BAMI 1755-1763).

Sprusbanks. See Brucebanks.

Spurrier, [-?-], m. by 24 Oct 1784 Anastasia, sister of Nathaniel Clary (BAWB 3:577).

Spurrier, Levin, and Eleanor Clarey [*sic*] were married by license dated 7 March 1780 (Frederick Co. Marriage Licenses). On 24 Oct 1784 Eleanor was named as a sister of Nathaniel Clary (BAWB 3:577).

Squirrell, Elizabeth, in Nov 1762 was convicted of bastardy (BAMI 1755-1763).

Staab, Philip, and Catherine Kraus were married by banns on 9 May 1790 at St. Peter's Catholic Church, Baltimore (*Piet:* 143).

Stafford, [-?-], m. by 11 Oct 1799 Ann who was one of two legatees of James Fortune to receive a payment of $2666.66 (BAAD 13:139). She was Ann Stafford, sister of the testator, living in the Parish of Tantrim, Co. Wexford, Ireland (BAWB 6:53).

Staley, [-?-], m. by 25 April 1701 Mary, widow of Thomas Jones (BALR HW#2:105).

Staley, Thomas, and Robert Owlas, administrators, on 12 Jan 1694 posted bond to administer the estate of Mary Walford, relict of 1st, John Nichols, and 2nd, John Warfoot or Walford (*q.v.*) (BAAB 4:74).

Stamford, James, m. by 15 Nov 1727 Mary, mother of John Fuller (BALR IS#J:28).

Stand (or Hand), John, m. by 14 Feb 1732, Rosanna, daughter of Jacob Grove (BAAD 3: 108).

Stand, John, m. by 2 June 1736 Elizabeth Durham, sister of John Durham; John and Elizabeth were the parents of John Stand (Deposition of Jane Boon in BALR HWS#M: 361).

Standiford, Aquila, son of William and Christian, b. 15 Aug 1740, m. on 27 Dec 1764, Sarah Clark, daughter of John and Hannah, b 10 June 1744 ("Aquila Standiford Bible," *MBR* 2:140-141).

Standiford, Archibald, and Eliz. Armstrong were m. on 25 June 1754 (Harrison, "St. John's Parish Register:" 214). On 27 Nov 1754 she was named as the admx. of William Armstrong (*q.v.*) (MDTP 36:120; MINV 9:221; MDAD 37:51).

Standiford, Dela, on 19 April 1783 was named in the will of Samuel Stansbury (BAWB 3:539).

Standiford, Ephraim, d. by 2 Aug 1744 at which time his admx. m. Solomon Armstrong (*q.v.*).

Standiford, James, and Martha Watkins were m. on 6 Oct 1737 (Harrison, "St. John's Parish Register:" 102). On 27 Aug 1753 Martha was named as a sister of William Watkins (BACT TR#E:111; MWB 29:154 abst. by Gibb).

Standiford (Standford), John, m. by 24 April 1706 Margaret, daughter of Israel Skelton who named his grandson Skelton Standiford (MWB 12:15 abst. in *Md. Cal. of Wills* 3:74; BAAD 2:131).

Standiford, John, and Jemima 'Robertson' were m. on 11 Jan 1759 (Harrison, "St. John's Parish Register:" 218). On 11 March 1772 Jemima was named as a sister of Charles Robinson, and daughter of Richard Robinson (BAWB 3:169, 233).

Standiford, Samuel, d. by Aug 1711 when his widow Mary had m. 2nd, John Bond *q.v.*); she m. 3rd John Wesley (*q.v.*).

Standiford (Standefor), Samuel, and Ann Rollo were m. on 30 Nov 1732 (Harrison, "St. John's Parish Register:" 73). On 28 July 1747, Mary Ann Standiford was named as a daughter of Archibald Rollo (MWB 25:114 abst. by Gibb).

Standiford, Skelton, and Mary Richardson were m. on 5 Nov 1772 (Harrison, "St. John's Parish Register:" 265). On 3 Sep 1775 Mary was named as a daughter of James Richardson (BAWB 3:317). On 14 Feb 1792 Skelton's wife received a share of the estate of James Richardson (BAAD 10:536).

Standiford, William, and Christiana Wright were m. on 8 Dec 1740 (Harrison, "St. John's Parish Register:" 116). On 26 April 1742 Christiana was named as the admx. of Thomas Wright (*q.v.*) of Baltimore Co. (MDAD 19:40, 22:232; MINV 28:310). Christiana was a daughter of William and Hannah Clark ("Aquila Standiford Bible," *MBR* 2:140-141).

Standiford, William, and Elizabeth Carlisle were m. on 16 July 1750 (Harrison, "St. John's Parish Register:" 201). Their daughter Sarah was b. on 19 Oct 1756 and m. David Johnson (*q.v.*) ("Bible Record of David Johnson Family," in MGRC 35:70).

Standish, Mary, servant of John Norrington, was charged with bastardy at the Aug 1740 Court (BACP HWS#TR:365).

Stane, John, m. by 14 Feb 1732 Rosanna, daughter of Jacob Groce of Baltimore Co. (MDAD 11:635).

Stanesby, Dr. John, m. by Aug 1675 Mary, widow of Godfrey Harmer and daughter and sole heir of Johanna Spry; Mary was the dau. of Oliver and Johanna Spry (BALR RM#HS:10; MDTP 7:51-52; MWB 4:755; INAC 4:564). Mary m. by Dec 1691 2nd, Richard Adams (*q.v.*) (BACP F#1:146).

Stansbury, [-?-], m. by 30 May 1786 Ruth, daughter of Alexis Lemmon, Sr. (BAWB 4:151).

Stansbury, [-?-], m. by 23 Feb 1787 Rachel, daughter of Samuel Gott (BAWB 4:225).

Stansbury, Avarilla, was charged with bastardy at the Nov 1756 Court and was fined (BAMI 1755-1763; BACP BB#C:313).

Stansbury, Daniel, of Baltimore, stated he would not pay the debts of his wife Sarah, who had eloped from his bed and board (*Maryland Journal and Baltimore Advertiser* 19 Dec 1774).

Stansbury, Daniel, and Elizabeth Stansbury were m. on 1 May 1788 (Marr. Register of Rev. Lewis Richards, MS.690 at MdHS). On 26 May 1789, Elizabeth was named as the extx. of Richard Stansbury (BAAD 9:314). Elizabeth, widow of Richard Stansbury, was mentioned in the administration account of John Stansbury (BAAD 11:206). Richard Stansbury and Elizabeth Garrettson were m. on 20 Feb 1787 (Marr. Register of Rev. Lewis Richards, MS.690 at MdHS). On 30 June 1797 Elizabeth was named as a daughter of Job Garrettson (BALR WG#52:153).

Stansbury, David, d. by Feb 1796 leaving orphans, Jane, Daniel, and others, who were made wards of Henrietta Stansbury (BAOC 3:188).

Stansbury, Dixon, and Penelope Body were m. on 4 Jan 1740/1 (Harrison, "St. John's Parish Register:" 140). In 1742 Penelope was named as a daughter of Stephen Body (MWB 23:19 abst. in *Md. Cal. of Wills* 8:196; MDAD 20:171). On 29 Oct 1765 Penelope was named as a daughter of Eliz. Trotten [wife of Luke Trotten (*q.v.*)] (BAWB 3:44). On 23 August 1786 Penelope was named as a coheir of Alanson

[Hanson?] Body, and sister of Ann who m. [-?-], Watts and was the mother of John Watts (BALR WG#Z:257).

Stansbury, Dixon, m. by 2 Aug 1786 Easter, daughter of Edward Bussey (BAWB 3:494, 4:245; BAAD 9:217).

Stansbury, Edmond, d. by 27 Jan 1787 leaving minor children Mary, and Jane Stansbury; Thomas Stansbury, the guardian, filed an account (BAGA 1:10, 11).

Stansbury, Edmund, m. by 13 Feb 1799, [-?-], widow of Thomas Talbott (BAAD 12:542).

Stansbury, Elijah, and Sarah Gorsuch were m. on 27 Dec 1779 (Marr. Returns of Rev. William West, Scharf Papers, MS.1999 at MdHS). On 5 May 1784 Sarah was named as a daughter of David Gorsuch who named a grandson Charles Stansbury in his will (BAWB 4:3).

Stansbury, Elijah, and Elizabeth Gorsuch were married by license dated 15 Nov 1783 (BAML). On 12 Dec 1795, Elizabeth was named as a representative of Kerrenhapuck Gorsuch (BAAD 12:82).

Stansbury, George, in Nov 1760 was convicted of bastardy with Ruth Rowles (BAMI 1755-1763:42).

Stansbury, George, and Mary [-?-] were m. by 24 Dec 1770 when their son Darius was b. ("Bible Records – The Stansbury Family," MGRC 33:227-228).

Stansbury, George, m. by 20 Oct 1783 Mary, daughter of Abraham Eaglestone (BAWB 3:494; see also BAAD 9:191).

Stansbury, Jacob, exec., on 18 April 1798 posted bond to administer the estate of Sarah Raven (BAAB 8:342).

Stansbury, James, and Jemima Gorsuch were m on 7 Feb 1789 (Marr. Register of Rev. Lewis Richards, MS.690 at MdHS). On 10 Aug 1791 she was named as a daughter of David Gorsuch (BAAD 10:423).

Stansbury, John, and Dorcas Sater were m. by license datd 16 April 1791 (BAML). On 13 Dec 1792 Dorcas who received an equal share of the estate of Henry Sater (BAAD 11:166).

Stansbury, Joseph, son of John, m. (prob. 2nd) Frances Phillips Gough on 1 May 1794 Harrison, "St. Paul's Parish Register:" 87). Frances was the daughter of Elizabeth widow of William Fitch, and the widow of William Gough (*q.v.*). Frances m. 3rd, Augustine Porter (*q.v.*).

Stansbury, Luke, d. by 19 Aug 1786 when Catherine Stansbury and Daniel Stansbury posted bond to administer his estate; Charles Stansbury and Thomas Corcoran were sureties (BAAB 6:386).

Stansbury, Richardson, and Mary Raven were m. on 12 Feb 1747 (Harrison, "St. John's Parish Register:" 196). On 7 Feb 1748/9 Mary was named as a daughter of Isaac and Letitia Raven, and granddaughter of Joseph Ward of Back River (MWB 29:70 abst. by Gibb). On 12 July 1774 Mary was named as an heir of Isaac Raven (BAAD 7:228).

Stansbury, Samuel, in 1763 was fined for fornication and bastardy (BAMI 1755-1763). In March 1768 he was charged with begetting a bastard on the body of Mary Ann Culester [Cullison] (BACP BB:10). See Samuel Stansbury below.

Stansbury, Samuel, and Ann Culleson were m. on 24 May 1777 (Harrison, "St. Paul's Parish Register:" 173). Mary Ann Culester was charged with bastardy at the June 1765 Court, and again at the March 1768 Court (BAMI 1765: 17; BACP BB:11). Jasper Stansbury Culston (Cullison), Polly Stansbury Culston (Cullison) and Ruth Stansbury Culston (Cullison), on 19 April 1783 were named as children in the will of Samuel Stansbury (BAWB 3:539). Samuel Stansbury of Middle River Upper Hundred stated that he would not pay the debts of his wife Mary Ann (*Maryland Journal and Baltimore Advertiser* 2 May 1780).

Stansbury, Solomon, and Hannah Hix [Hicks?] were m. on 27 Oct 1743 (Harrison, "St. John's Parish Register:" 189). She m. 2nd, by 6 Dec 1747 Richard Coop (*q.v.*)

Stansbury, Thomas, m. by 1 Nov 1743 Jane, daughter of John Hayes and his wife Abigail, widow of Thomas Scudamore, and daughter of John Dixon of Baltimore Co. (PCLR EI#10, 745; Provincial Court Judgments EI#10#1:743-746).

Stansbury, Thomas, and Hannah Gorsuch were m. 2 March 1735 Harrison, "St. Paul's Parish Register:" ," p. 155). On 14 Oct 1751 Thomas's wife was named as a representative of Charles Gorsuch of Baltimore Co. (MDAD 31:109).

Stansbury, Thomas, m. by 28 May 1791 Rachel, daughter of Samuel and Rachel Gott (BAAD 9:205; BAWB 6:2).

Stansbury, Thomas, m. by 4 Oct 1792, Ruth, who received an equal share of the estate of Alexis Lemmon (BAAD 11:128).

Stansbury, Tobias, and Mary Hammond were m. on 27 April 1746 Harrison, "St. Paul's Parish Register:" 166), She was a daughter of Katherine Hammond, widow (QALR RT#C:178). She m. 2nd, by 15 March 1775 Nathaniel Martin (*q.v.*) (MDTP 46:229).

Stansbury, Tobias, and Miss Arianna Sollers, both of this county, were m. last eve. by Rev. Mr. Richards (*Federal Gazette and Baltimore Daily Advertiser* 11 Dec 1799).

Stansbury, William, and Elizabeth Ensor were m. on 14 Feb 1739/40 (Harrison, "St. Paul's Parish Register:" 164). On 10 April 1771 Elizabeth was named as a daughter of John Ensor, who also named his grandson John Ensor Stansbury (BAWB 3:257).

Stansbury, William, m. by 28 May 1791, [-?-], daughter of Samuel Gott (BAAD 9:205).

Stansby. See Stanesby.

Stanton, Sarah, was charged with bastardy at the Nov 1742 Court, and confessed to bastardy again at the Aug 1746 Court (BACP TB#D:59; TB&TR#1:116, 394-395).

Stapleton, John, aged 10 last June, son of Bartholomew and Mary, in Nov 1766 was bound to George Gardner, book keeper (BAMI 1765-1766: 229).

Starkey, John, and Elizabeth Boyle were m. on 1 Jan 1707 (Harrison, "All Hallows Parish Register," Anne Arundel Co., MS. at MdHS: 76). Starkey d. by 14 May 1733 when Elizabeth Starkey, 'being on in years,' renounced the right to administer the estate in favor of Joshua Starkey, son and heir of John; on 6 June 1733 Joshua Starkey posted bond to administer John Starkey's estate (BAAB 5:269).

Starkey, Jonathan, and Mary Simmons were m. on 23 June 1757 (Harrison, "St. John's Parish Register:" 215). On 28 May 1770 she was named as a daughter of George Simmonds (BAAD 6:188; MDAD 64:81).

Starkey, Jonathan, and Hannah Starkey, widow of Joshua Starkey, dec., were admonished for unlawful cohabitation together, and were admonished by the vestry 'not to come together no more' ("St. John's and St. George's Parish Register Vestry Proceedings," MS. at the MdHS).

Starkey, Joshua, married on 29 Sep 1743 Hannah Meads (Harrison, "St. John's Parish Register:" 126). In March 1753 Jonathan Starkey and Hannah Starkey, widow of Joshua Starkey were summoned by the Vestry of St. John's Parish for unlawful cohabitation, and were admonished to separate from each other and not to come together any more ("St. John's and St. George's Parish Register Vestry Proceedings." MS. at MdHS). Hannah Meads m. 2nd, James Crouch (*q.v.*).

Starr, Eunice, formerly Fisher on 10 d. 10 m. 1799 was reported as having married contrary to the good order ("Minutes of Baltimore Meeting," *QRNM:*234).A William Starr and an Anna Fisher were m. on 21 June 1799 (Register of Zion Lutheran Church, Baltimore at MdHS: 405).

Stauck, Jacob, m. by 1797 Catherine, sister and one of the heirs of Barnhart Miller, who also left brothers John Miller and George Miller, and another sister Rosina, also dec., who had m. George Haines (*q.v.*) (BOCP Petition of the heirs of Bernard Miller 1797; MCHP #3442).

Steare, John, and Rachel Fifer, natives of Germany were m. by lic. on 29 June 1794 at St. Peter's Catholic Church, Baltimore (*Piet:* 143).

Steele, Mary, servant of Edward Wakeman, was charged with bastardy at the Aug 1739 Court (BACP HWS#TR:1, 327).

Steffe, Harman, and Rebecca Griffith were married by license dated 12 May 1790 (BAML). On 2 Jan 1791 Rebecca was named as a daughter of John Griffith (BAWB 5:32).

Steiger, Jacob, and Catherine Tichner were married by banns on 9 Oct 1786 at St. Peter's Catholic Church, Baltimore (*Piet:* 143).

Steiger, John, and Elizabeth Stephenson were married by banns on 3 June 1783 at St. Peter's Catholic Church, Baltimore (*Piet:* 143).

Steiger, Mattias, and Mary Crissman were m. by lic. on 13 Oct 1793 at St. Peter's Catholic Church, Baltimore (*Piet:* 143).

Stein, Henry, of Frederick Co., m. by 18 Oct 1760 or 1761 Anna Catharina Matthesin ("First Record Book for the Reformed and Lutheran Congregations at Manchester, Baltimore (now Carroll) Co.," *MGSB* 35:266).

Stenhouse, Dr. Alexander, and Cordelia Christie, widow, were m. on 21 June 1761 (Harrison, "St. George's Parish Register:" 370). On 8 April 1763 Cordelia was named as the widow of Charles Christie (*q.v.*) (BALR B#M:234). On 7 Mat 1763 the wife of Dr, Alexander Stenhouse received an equal share of John Stokes' estate (MDAD 49:233).

Stephens, Abram, m. by 3 July 1790, Catoron [Catherine], daughter of Jacob Epaugh (BAWB 4:496; BAAD 10:401).

Stephens, Ann, daughter of William Stephens, dec., in April 1794 was made a ward of Jeremiah Elliott (BAOC 3:87)

Stephenson, [-?-], m. by 11 June 1786 Mary, sister of John Price of Mordecai (BAWB 4:502).

Stephenson, [-?-], m. by 24 Nov 1788 Rachel, daughter of Bothia Scarlett (*q.v.*).

Stephenson (Stevenson), William, and Rachel (Barns) Crute, widow of Robert Crute, were m. on 21 June 1762 (Harrison, "St. George's Parish Register:" 383) In 1765 Rachel was named as the admx. of Robert Crute (*q.v.*) (BAMI 1765:53).

Stephenson. See also Stevenson.

Sterling, Mary Richards, was charged with bastardy at the Nov 1738 Court (BACP HWS#1A:307).

Sterling. See also Stirling.

Sterett, Samuel, Esq., of Baltimore, and Rebecca, daughter of the late Isaac Sears of New York were m. Thurs., 20th inst at New York by the Right Rev. Bishop Provost (*Maryland Journal and Baltimore Advertiser* 1 June 1790).

Sterrett, Capt. Clement, an officer who served with [great?] reputation in the American Army, and Mrs. Ruth Moore of Baltimore, were m. (*Maryland Journal and Baltimore Advertiser* 24 Feb 1784).

Stevens, Ephraim (Ep'rm), and Temperance Green were m. on 28 Jan 1768 (Harrison, "St. John's Parish Register:" 231). She was a daughter of Isaac Green (BAWB 6:277).

Stevens, Ephraim, and Milcah Dashiell, daughter of Louther and Anna Dashiell of Wicomico Creek, were m. on 18 April 1773 (Harrison, "Coventry Parish," Somerset Co., MS. at MdHS: 167). On 9 Dec 1780 he was named as a brother-in-law of William Augustus Dashiell, a surgeon in the Continental Army, who also named Ephraim's sons Arthur and John (BAWB 3:395).

Stevens, Gyles, d. by 20 Feb 1682 by which date his relict ad admx. Sarah had m. Thomas James (*q.v.*).

Stevens, Mary, was charged with bastardy at the Nov 1733 Court (BACP HWS#9:135).

Stevens, Rezin, m. by 21 June 1782 Sarah, niece and heir of John Hood of Anne Arundel Co. (BALR WG#K:375; BAAD 10:381).

Stevenson, [-?-], m. by 10 Dec 1770 Sarah, daughter of Thomas Kelly; they had a daughter Nancy Stevenson (BAWB 3:249).

Stevenson (Stephenson), [-?-], m. by 16 Nov 1772 Rachel, daughter of Samuel Owings, Sr., Gent. (BAWB 3:299).

Stevenson, [-?-], m. by 7 Oct 1778 Mary, daughter of Mary Bowen, widow (BAWB 4:355).

Stevenson, [-?-], m. by 31 Dec 1784 Ann, daughter of John Price, Sr. (BAWB 4:422).

Stevenson, [-?-], m. by 18 Dec 1781 Jane, dau. of John Stansbury (BAWB 4:102).

Stevenson, [-?-], m. by 26 Nov 1792 Rachel, daughter of Urath Owings, widow, who also named granddaughter Urath Stevenson (BAWB 5:70).

Stevenson, Edward, d. by 1718 when his extx. Mary had m. 2nd, Henry Sater (*q.v.*).

Stevenson, Dr. George, and Hetty Smith, daughter of John Smith of this town were m. last eve. (*Maryland Gazette or Baltimore General Advertiser* 4 Feb 1791). Dr. George Stevenson, eldest son of Henry Stevenson of Baltimore, d. Mon. night in his 26th year (*Maryland Journal and Baltimore Advertiser* 25 Nov 1791).

Stevenson, George, m. 1 May 1794 Margaret Cromwell ("Wesley Stevenson Bible Record," *The Notebook* 21 (3) (Fall 2005) 12-15).

Stevenson, Dr. Henry, m. [-?-], who on 7 May 1763 received an equal share of John Stokes' estate (MDAD 49:233).

Stevenson, Henry, and Anne Caulk as of 9 Oct 1794 stated they were intending to marry (BALR WG#P:248). Dr. Henry Stevenson and Ann Caulk were married by license dated 8 Oct 1794 (BAML). On 6 Jan 1797 Ann was named as the admx. of Joseph Chalk [*sic*] (BAAD 12:273).

Stevenson, Henry, m. by 16 Feb 1793 Jane Stansbury, who was mentioned in the administration account of John Stansbury (BAAD 11:206).

Stevenson, Henry, m. by 9 April 179, Rachel, heir of Samuel Owings (BAAD 11:239; BALR WG#UU:64).

Stevenson, Dr. Henry, in Feb 1795 was made guardian of his own children Cosmo and Juliana Stevenson (BAC 3:139).

Stevenson, John, merchant, and Eleanor Hall, both of Fell's Point, were m. last eve. (*Baltimore American* 26 Sep 1799).

Stevenson, Joseph, and Urath, daughter of Henry Stevenson, Esq., were m. last Sun. eve. by Rev. Lewis Richards (*Federal Intelligencer and Baltimore Daily Gazette* 3 March 1795).

Stevenson, Joshua, and Mary Spencer, both of Baltimore, were m. last Sun. by Rev. Morrell (*Baltimore Telegraphe* 20 May 1800).

Stevenson, Josiah, was married last Sun. eve. by Rev. Lewis Richards, to Miss Urath Stevenson, daughter of Henry Stevenson, Esq. (*Federal Intelligencer and Baltimore Daily Gazette* 3 March 1795).

Stevenson, Nicholas, and Mary Moore were married by license dated 20 Dec 1782 (BAML). On 25 Sep 1797 Nicholas was described as of Sullivan Co., Tenn., and Mary was named as a daughter of John Moore of Frederick Co., dec. (BALR WG#52: 204).

Stevenson, Ralph, m. by 2 Jan 1701 Mary, daughter of Thomas Bruff (MWB 11:241 abst. in *Md. Cal. of Wills* 2:246).

Stevenson, William, and Abarilla [*sic*] Moore were m. by lic. dated 10 Oct 1788 (BAML). Abigail [*sic*] Stevenson, formerly Moore, on 27 d. 12 m. 1788 was found guilty in going out in marriage ("Minutes of Gunpowder Meeting," *QRNM:*86).

Stevenson, Capt. William, and Ann Foster, both of Baltimore were m. Thurs. (*Baltimore American* 28 Feb 1800).

Stevenson. See also Stephenson.

Steward (Stewart, Stuart), Ann, (formerly Norris or Morris) on 27 d. 5 m. 1800 was found guilty of accomplishing her marriage to a man not of our society ("Minutes of Deer Creek Meeting," *QRNM:*161). [No other marriage reference found].

Steward, Elizabeth, was charged with bastardy at the March 1743/4 Court (BACP 1743-`1745:154, 389, 800).

Stewart, [-?-], m. by 5 May 1773 Sarah, sister of William Lux (BAWB 3:357).

Stewart, [-?-], m. by 19 Jan 1790 Martha, sister of Dr. John Boyd, by whom he had a son William Stewart (BAWB 4:404).

Stewart, Capt. Alexander, m. by 12 April 1758 Sarah, sister-in-law of Nicholas Ruxton Gay (BALR B#G:201).

Stewart, Archibald, merchant, and Sally Neilson, daughter of Robert Neilson, merchant, were m. last eve. in Baltimore (*Maryland Journal and Baltimore Advertiser* 25 Nov 1791).

Stewart, Charles, and Rachel Merryman were married by license dated 17 Oct 1778 (BAML). In his will made 2 May 1798 Stewart named his wife Rachel, and his brother-in-law John Merryman (BAWB 6:482).

Stewart, Cicley, was charged with bastardy at the Aug 1720 Court and named John Wilde as the father (BACP IS#C:365).

Stewart, David C., merchant of this city, was m. last eve by Rev. Dr. Allison, to Miss Jane Purviance, daughter of Robert Purviance, Esq. (*Federal Gazette and Baltimore Daily Advertiser* 17 May 1799).

Stewart, Elizabeth, mulatto child of Elizabeth Stewart who had run away; she was bound to serve John and Ann Norris to the age of 21 (BACP IS#1A:61).

Stewart, Elizabeth, confessed to bastardy and was fined on 4 June 1746 (BACP TB&TR#1:7).

Stewart, Hannah. See Hannah Perine.

Stewart, Isabella, was charged with bastardy at the Aug 1715 Court (BACP IS#B:624).

Stewart, James, and Mary Wood were m. on 10 Feb 1741 (Harrison, "St. George's Parish Register:" 324). On 27 April 1742 Mary was named as the admx. of Joshua Wood (*q.v.*) (MDTP 31:278).

Stewart, James, and Eleanor Ewing were m. by lic. on 25 Dec 1785 at St. Peter's Catholic Church, Baltimore (*Piet:* 143).

Stewart, James, and Margaret Britt were m. by lic. on 15 Aug 1793 at St. Peter's Catholic Church, Baltimore (*Piet:* 143). She was the admx. of Robert [Brit?], late of Baltimore Co., dec. (BALR WG#RR:526; BAAD 12:210).

Stewart, John, tailor, m. by 5 Feb 1762 Rebecca, named as a daughter of Sarah Palmer, in the will of Thomas Clendenning (BAWB 2:149).

Stewart, John, and Miss Sarah Clark, both of Baltimore, were m. last Sun. (*Baltimore Telegraphe* 29 Nov 1798).

Stewart, John, merchant of this city, was m. last Tues. by Rev. Bishop White at the seat of David H. Cunningham, Esq., near Philadelphia, to Miss Helen West (*Federal Gazette and Baltimore Daily Advertiser* 10 July 1799).

Stewart, Margaret, was charged with bastardy at the Nov 1719 Court (BACP IS#C:245).

Steyer, George, in his will made 1 May 1785 named his wife Nancy, sister of Isaac and Joseph Burneston, and daughter of Ann Burneston (BAWB 4:157).

Stille, [-?-], m. by 19 Jan 1790 Mary, sister of Dr. Alexander Boyd (BAWB 4:404).

Stillinger, Jacob, and Christiana Lebough were m. by lic. on 28 Feb 1797 at St. Peter's Catholic Church, Baltimore (*Piet:* 143).

Stimson, Elizabeth, was charged with bastardy at the Nov 1695 Court and named Christopher Bembridge as the father (BACP G#1:503).

Stinchcomb, Aquila, m. by 3 Nov 1779 Catherine, daughter of Tobias Stansbury and sister of Tobias Stansbury (BALR WG#E:16).

Stinchcomb, Enoch, and Sarah Howard were married by license dated 5 March 1792 (BAML). Sarah was a daughter of Charles Howard (BAWB 6:161).

Stinchcomb. George, and Abarilla Andrew, daughter of William Andrew entered into a marriage contract on 23 June 1783 (BALR WG#R:20). In June 1783 Stinchcomb stated he would not pay a bond his wife Avarilla Andrew gave to Abraham Andrew as it was for a tract of land that Andrew had not legal right nor claim to (*Maryland Journal and Baltimore Advertiser* 18 June 1784).

Stinchcomb, John, on 5 May 1720 was named as a son-in-law of Edward Teal (MWB 16:253 abst. in *Md. Cal. of Wills* 5:33).

Stinchcomb, John, m. by 1736 Katherine, daughter of Hector McClaine of Baltimore Co. (BALR HWS#M:122, 302, HWS#1-A:122). On 25 Jan 1749/50 'Catherine' was named as a sister of William Macclan (McLean) (MWB 28:220 abst. by Gibb).

Stinchcomb, Nathaniel, and Patience Rowles [*sic*] were m. on 15 Jan 1733 (Harrison, "St. Paul's Parish Register:" 151). She m. 2nd, by 21 April 1750 Jacob Rowles (*q.v.*) (MDTP 33-1:122).

Stinchcomb, Patience, was charged with bastardy at the June 1757 Court, Nathaniel Stinchcomb agreed to be financially responsible for the child (BAMI 1757-1759:30).

Stinchcomb, Thomas, and Ruth Owings were m. on 23 April 1778 (Marr. Returns of Rev. Thomas Chase, Scharf Papers, MS.1999 at MdHS). On 5 Sep 1779 Ruth was named as a daughter of John Owings (BAWB 3:384; BAAD 8:67).

Stirling (Sterling), James, merchant, and Miss Eliza Gibson were m. at Baltimore on 19 May 1782 (Marr. Returns of Rev. William West, Scharf Papers, MS,1999 at MdHS; *Maryland Journal and Baltimore Advertiser* 21 May 1782).

Stivers, Adam, on 22 Sep 1798 received £19.6.3½ from the estate of George Fisher (BAAD 12:489).

Stobo, Capt. Jacob, and Sally Hughes were m. (*Maryland Journal and Baltimore Advertiser* 14 Oct 1783)

Stockdale, Thomas, and Mary Patrick, on 26 d. 10 m, 1776 declared their intention to marry on 28 d. 9 m. 1776. On 30 d. 11 m., 1776 Stockdale produced his mother's consent to marry ("Minutes of Gunpowder Meeting," *QRNM:*68).

Stockett, Capt. Henry, and Miss Barbara M'Kenzie were m. last eve. by Rev. Mr. Richards (*Federal Intelligencer and Baltimore Daily Gazette* 27 Dec 1794).

Stockett, Thomas, and Damaris Welch, daughter of John and Mary, were m. on 9 April 1700 (Harrison, "All Hallow's Parish Parish Register:" Anne Arundel Co.: 54; BALR TR#A: 5).

Stocksdale (Stoxsdill), [-?-], m. by 3 Feb 1759 Sarah, daughter of William Gosnell (BAWB 2:143).

Stocksdale, John, was charged with bastardy at the Aug 1728 Court (BACP HWS#6:37).

Stockton, Samuel, and Catherine [-?-] were m. by 29 March 1794 when their daughter Esther Cox was b. ("Amos Loney Bible," *MBR* 7:113-115).

Stohler (Stoler), John, m. by 11 June 1789 Catherine, relict of John Henry Kline (*q.v.*) (BPET: Petition of John Stoler, *et uxor,* 1789; BAAD 10:11).

Stokes, David, on 25 d. 12 m. 1800 was reported to have gone out in his marriage to a woman not of our society by the assistance of a Baptist Preacher ("Minutes of Deer Creek Meeting," *QRNM:*162). David Stokes and Sarah Johns were m. by lic. dated 9 May 1800 (HAML).

Stokes, George, d. by 14 Sep 1741 having m. by 19 July 1739 Susanna, daughter of James Phillips (BALR HWS#IA:42; MDAD 17:181). She m. 2nd, Winston Smith (*q.v.*). She was the mother of Cordelia and Frances Stokes (MDAD 20:82; MINV 35:327; BAAD 4:177; BACT TR#E:48-50).

Stokes, Humphrey Wells, son of John and Susanna Stokes, and Mary Knight, daughter of Steven and Sarah Knight, were m. on 31 Dec 1730 (Harrison, "St. John's Parish Register:" 78). Mary Stokes, admx. of Humphrey Wells Stokes, m. 2nd, on 20 June 1745 Talbot Risteau (*q.v.*).

Stokes, John, on 20 Jan 1716 named his nephew John Smithers of Kent Co., Gent. (KELR JS#X:75).

Stokes, John, the Elder, m. by 17 March 1718 Susanna Wells, daughter of George Wells (BALR RM#HS:632, IS#G:212, IS#L:418). James Ives left *Beaver Neck, i*n his will, dated 4 March 1703/4 and proved 13 March 1704, to Susanna Wells (MWB 3:4).

Stokes, John, in Aug 1750, was charged with begetting a bastard on the body of Elizabeth Tolson (BACP TR#5:182).

Stokes, John, and Margaret Savage were married by license dated 10 Oct 1784 (BAML). Between 17 Aug 1784 and 18 Aug 1785 Margaret was named as the widow and extx. of William Savage (*q.v.*) (BAWB 4:68; BAAB 6:250; BALR WG#Z:169).

Stokes, Joseph, and Hannah Harvey, daughter of John and Esther, b. 11 April 1746, were m. on 19 April 1770 ("John Barclay Bible," *MBR* 2:3-6).

Stokes, Robert, and Rebecca Young were m. on 15 Aug 1756 (Harrison, "St. George's Parish Register:" 351). She m. 2nd, Samuel Young (*q.v.*) on 9 April 1765 (Harrison, "St. John's," p. 227). She was a dau,. of William Young, whose will of 17 Nov 1772 named his Stokes grandchildren (MWB 39:97, abst. in *Md. Cal. of Wills* 15:20).

Stokes, Robert Young, on 15 Feb 1776 was named as a son-in-law in the will of Samuel Young who had m. his mother, Rebecca Stokes (BAWB 3:487). Robert Young Stokes and Sarah, daughter of Clement Brooke, were m. by license dated 24 May 1781 (HAML; BALR WG#K:39).

Stoler. See Stohler.

Stolter, Mary'n (Margaret?), in 1775 was fined for bastardy (BAMI 1772, 1775-1781:206).

Stonall, William, and Polly Ensor, both of Fell's Point, were m. last eve. by Rev. Bend (*Baltimore Telegraphe* 14 March 1796).

Stone, [-?-], of Charles Co., d. by 4 Feb 1739, having m. Catherine, daughter of Richard Boughton, late of Charles Co., dec. (BALR HWS#1A:341).

Stone, [-?-], m. by 26 Nov 1792 Hannah, daughter of Urath Owings, widow (BAWB 5:70).

Stone, Henry, d. by 12 July 1726 by which time his admx. Jane had m. Charles Yates (*q.v.*) (MDTP 27:310).

Stone, Henry, and Constance James were m. on 2 July 1740 (Harrison, "St. George's Parish Register:" 313). On 8 May 1744 Constant was named as the admx. of Michael James (*q.v.*) (MDTP 31:476).

Stone, Thomas, m. by 23 May 1696 Mary, extx. of William Gaine (Caine, Gayne) (*q.v.*) (MDTP 16:170). She had m. 1st, John Dimmitt (Diamint) (*q.v.*).

Stone, Thomas, m. Elizabeth [-?-], widow of 1st, Richard Sampson (q.v.), 2nd, James Bagford (q.v.), and 3rd Samuel Hinton (*q.v.*) (MWB 14:43, abst. in *Md. Cal. of Wills* 4:29; BACP IS#C:4; BALR IS#H:328, 385; HWS#M:163; MWB 21:768, abst. in *Md. Cal. of Wills* 7:212).

Stone, Thomas, and Henrietta, widow of John Jenkins, late of Baltimore Co., were m. by lic. on 29 Jan 1796 at St. Peter's Catholic Church, Baltimore (*Piet:* 143).

Stone, William, and Hannah Cockey were m. on 21 April 1778 (Marr. Returns of Thomas Chase, Scharf Papers, MS.1911 at MdHS). In 1787 Hannah, formerly Cockey, was named as the guardian of her children Ruth and William Cockey; Ruth Cockey, aged 16, chose William Stone as her guardian (BAOC 2:2, 16). On 9 April 1793 Hannah Stone was named as an heir of Samuel Owings (BAAD 11:239).

Stoney, [-?-], m. by 22 Sep 1755 Patience, daughter of Edward Richards (MWB 30:26 abst. by Gibb).

Storm, George, and Margaret 'Armagost' were married by license dated 24 July 1784 (BAML). On 13 April 1791 Peggy was named as the admx. of Christ'r Armigost (BAAD 10:355).

Story, Elizabeth, was charged with bastardy at the March 1750/1 Court (BACP TR#6:270).

Story, Capt. George, and Miss Christiana Dashiell, daughter of Capt. Benjamin Dashiell, both of Fell's Point, were m. last Tues. eve by Rev. Mr. Bend (*Federal Intelligencer and Baltimore Daily Gazette* 6 Aug 1795).

Story, Jane, was charged was charged with bastardy at the June 1744 Court and named John Watts as the father of her child; she was charged again at the March 1746/7 court (BACP 1743-1745:227, 323, TB&TR#1:378).

Story, Joshua, in 1763 was convicted of bastardy (BAMI 1755-1763).

Story, Thomas, and Patience Richards were m. on 13 Jan 1743/4 (Harrison, "All Saints Parish Register," Frederick Co., MS. at MdHS: 12). On 12 May 1757 Patience was named as a legatee of Edward Richards (MDAD 41:20; BFD 2:57). Richard Richards, administrator, on 15 Aug 1797 posted bond to administer the estate of Patience Story (BAAB 8:275).

Stouart, Tomas, was named by Elizabeth Tomsin as the father of her daughter Elizabeth Schünckly, who was b. 20 Nov 1779 and bapt. 30 Dec 1779 ("First German Reformed Church Register," MS. at MdHS:4).

Stout, John, will not pay the debts of his wife Mary (*Federal Gazette and Baltimore Daily Advertiser* 19 Oct 1799).

Stover, [-?-], m. by April 1799 [-?-], sister of Michael Fisher; they had a daughter Annamary (BAWB 6:182).

Stover, John, m. by 19 Sep 1761 Sophia, admx. of William Hansman (*q.v.*) (MDAD 47:20; BAAD 4:339).

Stoxsdill. See Stocksdale.

Strahan, Jane, extx., on 11 Feb 1795 posted bond to administer the estate of Simon Quinn (BAAB 8:692). In his will made 21 Feb 1793 and proved 11 Feb 1795 Simon Quinn left all his estate, real and personal to Jane Strahan for her lifetime, and then son Thomas Quinn. Daniel Chambers and Joseph Carnaby witnessed the will (BAWB 5:231).

Strain, Robert, admin., on 7 Aug 1799 posted bond to administer the estate of Benjamin Hood (BAAB 8:488).

Stran, Capt. John, and Rebecca Johnson, daughter of William Johnson, sailmaker, of Fell's Point, were m. last Thurs. eve. (*Maryland Gazette or Baltimore General Advertiser* 5 Oct 1790).

Strasman, [-?-], m. by 12 Oct 1785 Mary, daughter of Mathias Sittler (BAWB 4:261).

Stratton, William, native of Boston, and Mary Howard, native of Ireland, were m. by lic. on 21 Feb 1797 at St. Peter's Catholic Church, Baltimore (*Piet:* 143).

Strawbridge, Joseph, m. by 7 Sep 1696 Sarah, extx. of John Arden (*q.v.*) (INAC 14:152). In her will made 30 March 1699, Sarah, widow of Joseph Strawbridge named her daughter Mary 'Harding,' son Samuel 'Harding,' and the latter's father John 'Harding' (MWB 6:260 abst. in *Md. Cal. of Wills* 2:178).

Street, Capt. Benjamin, late of the 11th Penna. Regiment and Patty Cambridge were m. (*Maryland Journal and Baltimore Advertiser* 17 Dec 1782).

Streett (Strutt), Elizabeth, confessed to Negro bastardy at the Nov 1743 Court, her son Benjamin, aged about 9 months old, was sold to John Ensor on 1 Nov 1743, to serve him to the age of 31 (BACP 1743-1745:82).

Streney, Nicholas, and Mary Green were m. by lic. on 16 May 1788 at St. Peter's Catholic Church, Baltimore (*Piet:* 143).

Strider, [-?-], m. by 5 Feb 1798 Catherine, daughter of Simon Laudecker (BAWB 6:78).

Strider, [-?-], m. by 5 Feb 1798 Mary, daughter of Simon Laudecker (BAWB 6:78).

Stringer, James, of Anne Arundel Co. m. Ann [-?-], who m. 2nd, John Collier (*q.v.*), and 3rd, William York (*q.v.*).

Stroman (Strawman), John, and Mary Sitler were married by license dated 3 June 1778 (BAML). On 12 Oct 1785 Mary was named as a daughter of Matthias Sitler of Baltimore Town (BAWB 4:261).

Strotee, John, m. by 28 July 1765 Catherine, admx. of John Henry Cline (or John Hendrick Clyne) (MINV 86:174).

Stroub, Jacob, aged c10, son of Jacob Stroub, dec., in Aug 1765 was bound to John Fowle to age 21 (BAMI 1765).

Strouble, Zachariah, [son of Zachariah] on 11 Dec 1788 came into court and chose John Lee as his guardian (BAOC 2:91).

Stuart, Ann, late Johnson, daughter of Benjamin Johnson, on 3 d. 1 m. 1771 was reported as having married a man not of our society ("Minutes of Deer Creek Meeting," *QRNM*:134). [No other marriage reference found].

Stuart (Stewart), James, and Mary Wood were m. on 10 Feb 1741 (Harrison, "St. George's Parish Register:" 324). On 5 May 1742 Mary was named as an admx. or extx. of Joshua Wood (*q.v.*) (MINV 26:570).

Stuart (Stewart), James, and Eleanor Ewing were m. in Baltimore Co. by license dated 23 Dec 1785 (BAML). Stuart warned all persons from "crediting, employing, harboring, or dealing or holding any conversations with' his wife Eleanor, who resided in Lovely Lane (*Maryland Gazette or Baltimore General Advertiser* 8 Nov 1791).

Stuart, Mr. John, of Carlisle, bookbinder, was m. last Thurs. by Rev. Mr. Ellis, to Miss Mary Boney of Baltimore (*Federal Intelligencer and Baltimore Daily Gazette* 29 April 1795).

Stuart, William, m. by 16 Aug 1792 Ann Thompson, who received an equal share of the estate of John Thompson (BAAD 11:112).

Stump, Hannah, (late Wilson), on 25 d. 10 m. 1798 was reported to have gone out in marriage to a man not of our society ("Minutes of Deer Creek Meeting," QRNM:159). [No other marriage reference found].

Stump, John, and Cassandra Wilson were m. on 2 Oct 1779 ("Williams-Neilson Family Bible," *MBR* 1:225-226; "Register of First Presbyterian Church, Baltimore," MS. at MdHS: 13). Henry Wilson, in his will, made 9 May 1798, named his daughter Cassandra wife of John Stump and his granddaughter Priscilla Stump (BAWB 6:234).

Stupuy, Peter, (son of John Baptist and Ann Deval; widower of Catherine Chadwick of Conn.), and Catherine Duharlay (daughter of John Baptist and Barbara Perigo; widow of Bartholomew Camiran), were m. by lic. on 26 July 1798 at St. Peter's Catholic Church, Baltimore (*Piet:* 144).

Sturgess, Thomas, keeper of the Three Tun Tavern, Baltimore, will not pay the debts of his wife Mary (*Maryland Journal and Baltimore Advertiser* 25 March 1785). Thomas Sturgiss and Marian Thompson were m. by lic. dated 24 Feb 1781 (BAML).

Sturmay, Margaret, was charged with bastardy at the Nov 1758 Court; her son was named Jeremiah (BAMI 1757-1759:163). {See also Elizabeth Toff *alias* Margaret Stormie.

Sue, [-?-], m. by 22 Sep 1755 Rachel, daughter of Edward Richards (MWB 30:26 abst. by Gibb).

Sulaven. See Sullivan.

Sullivan, Daniel, m. by 13 Oct 1752 Winifred, legatee of Miles Foy and heir of Robert Brierly (BALR TR#D: 434).

Sullivan (Sulavan, Sulaven), Elizabeth, confessed to bastardy at the March 1754 Court but refused to name the father of her child. Nevertheless, on 2 March 1754 John Watson was convicted by the oath of Elizabeth Sulaven as the father (BACP BB#A:29-30).

Sullivan, I. P., and Miss Harriot Lannaway were m. Sat. eve. (*Federal Gazette and Baltimore Daily Advertiser* 14 Oct 1799).

Sullivan, Julian, was charged with bastardy at the Nov 1712 Court (BACP IS#B: 334).

Sullivan, Margaret, admx., on 24 Oct 1800 posted bond to administer the estate of James Day (BAAB 9:86).

Sullivan, Thomas, and Jemima Heir were m. by lic. dated 13 April 1791 (BAML). On 24 d. 7 m. 1791 Jemima Sullivan, formerly Hair [*sic*], was reported as having gone out in marriage with a man not in membership ("Minutes of Gunpowder Meeting," *QRNM:*91).

Sumers, John, m. by 24 June 1719 [-?-], admx. of Andrew Berry (MDTP 24:1).

Summers, Eleanor, admx., on 24 Nov 1785 posted bond to administer the estate of James Quay (BAAB 6:336). In March 1787, [-?-] Summers, mother of Thomas Quay petitioned (BOCP: Petition of Thomas Quay, 1787, Box 2, folder 1).

Summers, John Jacob, and Araminta Roberts were m. on 27 April 1766 (Harrison, "St. John's Parish Register:" 229). On 14 June 1766 Araminta was identified as the widow of Peter Roberts (*q.v.*) and sister of Joseph Fling (BAWB 3:66).

Summers, William, m. Viola [-?-]; when he d. by 7 Aug 1737 Viola enounced her right to administer and Francis Street posted an administration bond (BAAB 3:430).

Sutherland, Edward, and Eleanor Stockdell [*sic*] were m. on 10 Sep 1776 ("Register of First Presbyterian Church, Baltimore," MS. at MdHS: 12). On 9 Oct 1786 Ellen was named as a daughter of Edward Stocksdale (BAAD 8:324).

Suthod, [-?-], (Capt.), of Baltimore, was m. last Tues. eve. by Rev. Mr. Ireland, to Mrs. Speck of this city (*Federal Gazette and Baltimore Daily Advertiser* 26 June 1800).

Sutton, Thomas, d. by 4 Feb 1732 when his admx. Dorcas [-?-], had m. 2nd, Joseph Thomas (*q.v.*) (BAAD 3:142).

Swan, Frederick Andrew, m. by 2 Dec 1771 Catherine, daughter of Susanna Rantz, late of Va., now of Baltimore Co. (BAWB 3:263).

Swan, Major John, of Baltimore, and Eliza Maxwell of Myrtle Grove of Talbot Co., were m. at the latter place on 12th inst. (*Maryland Journal and Baltimore Advertiser* 17 July 1787).

Swan, Joseph, merchant, and Nancy Maxwell were m. last eve. (*Maryland Journal and Baltimore Advertiser* 8 Oct 1790).

Swan, Matthew, merchant, and Ann M'Kean, both of this town, were m. last Thurs. eve. (*Maryland Gazette or Baltimore General Advertiser* 10 Sep 1784). Matthew Swan d. by Feb 1796 when his orphans Matthew, William, and John, were made wards of Ann Swan (BAOC 3:179). Ann Swan m. 2nd, Joel Munson (*q.v.*).

Swan, Samuel, and Susanna Punteney were m. on 7 May 1778 (Marr. Ret. of Rev. Thomas Chase, Scharf Papers, MS. 1999 at MdHS). On 17 March 1795 he was identified as 'of Easton in Talbot Co.' (BALR WG#RR:134).

Swan, Thomas, of St. Mary's Co., m. by 17 Nov 1745 Elizabeth, daughter of Edward Butler of Calvert Co. (BALR TB#D:412).

Swanson (Swanstone), Edward, m. by 23 Nov 1675, Henrietta, widow of William Robinson (*q.v.*) (MDTP 5:229; INAC 1:472). Henrietta m. 3rd, Thomas Cannon (*q.v.*), and 4th, Edward Reeves (*q.v.*).

Swanstone. See Swanson.

Swazy, Edward, m. by 20 March 1788 Mary, daughter of John Fulford (BAAD 9:176).

Sweeny, [-?-], m. by 29 Sep 1789 [-?-], daughter of Daniel McComesky, whose will of that date named a grandson Daniel Sweeny (BAWB 4:427),

Sweeny, Edward, and Elizabeth Blatchford were m. by lic. on 1 Oct 1796 at St. Peter's Catholic Church, Baltimore (*Piet:* 144).

Sweeny, Hugh, and Priscilla Hook were m. by lic. on 19 July 1789 at St. Peter's Catholic Church, Baltimore (*Piet:* 144).

Sweenyard, See Swinyard.

Sweetin, [-?-]. m. by 7 Oct 1778 Ann, daughter of Mary Bowen (BAWB 4:355).

Sweeting, Edward, in 1762 paid a criminal fine for fornication and bastardy (BAMI 1755-1763).

Sweeting, Thomas, of this city, and Miss Catherine Wineman of the county, were m. last eve, by Rev. Dr. Allison (*Federal Gazette and Baltimore Daily Advertiser* 15 Nov 1799).

Sweetser, John, of Boston, Co. Suffolk, Mass., and wife Katherine, stated about 1785 that Katherine was the daughter of Benjamin Andrews of Boston. Benjamin was the son of Thomas Andrews and wife Ruth, both dec. Benjamin was the brother of Jedediah Andrews, also dec. Jedediah was the father of Ephraim Andrews, of Deer Creek, Md., physician, also dec. John Sweetser and his wife, on 20 Jan 1785, gave power of atty. to Henry Andrews to collect any property due them by the death of said Ephraim (BACT Liber 1785-1788, MS 2865 at MdHS; 508). In 1786 John Sweetser, Jr., of the Commonwealth of Massachusetts, petitioned the court that on 23 Aug 1753 he m. Catherine Andrews, cousin of the deceased, and a daughter, of Benjamin Andrews, dec., uncle of said dec. The petitioner stated that his wife was the [nearest] relation of Ephraim Andrews, and he was entitled to administer the estate (BOCP Petition of Ephraim Andrews, 1786, Box 1, Folder 30).

Sweitzer, Benjamin, m. by 20 Jan 1785 Katherine, daughter of Benjamin and Katherine Andrews of Boston, dec. Benjamin Andrews was the son of Thomas and Ruth Andrews and the brother of Jedediah Andrews who was the father of Ephraim Andrews of Deer Creek, Md., physician (BACT 1773-1784:508).

Swift, Mark, m, by 16 Feb 1696 Eliza, niece of Thomas Staley (MWB 11:25; abst. in *Md. Cal. of Wills* 2:208). Elizabeth Swift, widow and admx., posted an administration bond on 22 April 1708 (BAAB 3:448). She d. soon after that and on 13 June 1708 Abraham Taylor posted a bond to administer both their estates (BAAB 3:437).

Swinyard (Sweenyard), John, m. by 28 Oct 1712 Lucy, extx. of Francis Pottee (INAC 33B:65; BAAD 1:354).

Swinyard, John, in Aug 1725 was charged with begetting a bastard on the body of Sarah Harris. He was charged with bastardy again in June 1731 (BACP IS&TW#4:306; HWS#7:156).

Swope, Benedict, Jr., and Margaret Keener were married by license dated 13 Dec 1777 (BAML). On 6 March 1798 Margaret was named as a daughter of Melchoir Keener (BAWB 6:129).

Sybell, Lodowick, aged about 10, son of Lodowick Sybell, in June 1756 was bound to Valentine Larsh (BAMI 1755-1763).

Symes, Jane, on 19 July 1775 was named as a daughter in the will of Robert Russell (MWB 40:399; abst. in *Md. Cal. of Wills* 16:68).

Sydall. See Sindall.

Sylva, Francis, and Catharine O'Brian were m. by lic. on 30 Nov 1799 at St. Peter's Catholic Church, Baltimore (*Piet:* 144).

<h2 style="text-align:center">"T"</h2>

Taaffe, Robert, of Ardee, Co. of Lowth, Ireland, m. by 8 Sep 1766 Achsah, daughter of Edward Fottrell of Baltimore Co., dec. (PCLR DD#4:192). Robert Taafe of Violet Hill, Co. Meath, Ireland, deposed on 17 Feb 1775 that he was the father and natural guardian of Stephen Taafe, a minor under the sage of 21; he stated that in 1758 he had m. Achsah Fottrell, daughter and sole heir of Edward Fottrell of Baltimore Co., and that he and Achsah had one son, Stephen, now 14, and two daughters, all living, but Achsah had died, and Robert Taafe claimed he was entitled to his wife's estate (BALR AL#N:274).

Tagart, John, merchant of Baltimore, and Polly Williamson of Baltimore Co. were m. last Sat. (*Maryland Journal and Baltimore Advertiser* 15 Oct 1790).

Talbee (Talbie), Samuel, and Elizabeth Hitchcock were m. on 1 Dec 1736 (Harrison, "St. John's Parish Register:" 90). On 5 Dec 1744 Elizabeth was named as a daughter of William Hitchcock (BALR TB#C: 664).

Talbot, [-?-], m. by 12 Oct 1790 Temperance, sister of Johannah Clossey (BAWB 4:499).

Talbot (Talbott), [-?-], m. by 10 Dec 1790 Rachel, daughter of Richard Jones of Richard (BAWB 4:523).

Talbot (Talbott), Benjamin, m. by 21 June 1781 Sarah, sister of Capt. William Wilmot (BAWB 3:547; BAAD 9:236).

Talbot, Benjamin R., and Martha Deaver were married by license dated 9 June 1778 (BAML). On 16 Oct 1782 Martha, was named as a daughter of John Deaver, who also named a granddaughter Ann Talbot (BAWB 3:476). In his will dated 1788 Benjamin Robinson Talbott named his step-brother John Deaver and his nephew John Talbott Deaver (BAWB 4:309). Martha m. 2^(nd), William Duncan (*q.v.*).

Talbot, Edmond, m. by 9 Feb 1712 Mary, daughter of William Cook (AALR IB#2:24). Mary m. 2^(nd), by March 1732 John Taylor (*q.v.*).

Talbot, Edmund, and Rebecca Robinson on were m. on 18 June 1752 (Harrison, "St. Paul's Parish Register:" 165). They were the parents of Benjamin Robinson Talbot (BALR WG#D: 57). Rebecca may have m. 2^(nd), John Deaver (*q.v.*).

Talbot (Talbott), Edmund, in Nov 1760 was named by Hannah Waters as the father of her illegitimate daughter (BAMI 1755-1763:33).

Talbot, Edward, and Margaret Slade were m. on 7 April 1763 (Harrison, "St. John's Parish Register:" 224). On 5 Feb 1785 Edward Talbott was named as a grandson in the will of William Slade (BAWB 4:48).

Talbot (Talbott), James, m. by 10 Dec 1787 Sarah, admx. of Robert Forsyth, late of Baltimore Town (BALR WG#Z:677).

Talbot (Talbott), John, and Prudence Colegate were m. on 17 Feb 1723 (Harrison, "All Hallow's Parish Register," Anne Arundel Co., MS. at MdHS: 98). On 10 Jan 1726 Prudence was named as a daughter of Col. Richard Colegate of Baltimore Co. (MDAD 8:107; BAAD 1:322).

Talbot (Talbott), John, son of John and Mary, and Margaret Webster, daughter of Isaac and Margaret, were m. on 22 Oct 1741 (Nottingham Monthly Meeting at MdHS; BALR BB#I: 424, AL#I:4 24; BAAD 7:4).

Talbot (Talbott), John, and Hannah Bosley were m. by 14 March 1781 when their son William was b. ("Alexander and Ann Morrison Family [Bible]," MGRC 33:20-24).

Talbot (Talbut), John, and Miss Mary Slade, all of Baltimore, were m. last Thurs. by Rev. Davis (*Baltimore Telegraphe* 15 Nov 1797).

Talbot (Talbott), William, in his will dated 8 Nov 1713 named his brother-in-law George Ogg, and named his father-in-law George Ogg as one of his executors (MWB 13:642 abst. in *Md. Cal. of Wills* 4:4). On 16 Dec 1723 Catherine was named as a daughter of George Ogg; she m. 2nd, John Risteau (*q.v.*). William's daughter Margaret m. Benjamin Hammond (BALR IS#1K:377, IS#G: 56).

Talbot, William, and Mary Roberts were m. on 31 Jan 1729 (Harrison, "St. John's Parish Register:" 40). On 9 Feb 1728 [1728/9] Mary was named as the eldest daughter of John Roberts (MWB 19:585 abst. in *Md. Cal. of Wills* 6:93; MDAD 11:101).

Talbott. See Talbot.

Talbut. See Talbot.

Tamer, Benjamin, m. by 24 Dec 1789 Rachel, heir of William Watson (BAAD 10:94).

Tankard, Elizabeth, *alias* **Tyler,** admx., on 4 Sep 1786 posted bond to administer the estate of William Tankard; Littleton Tyler was a surety (BAAB 6:378).

Tanner, George, m. Hannah Scott before a magistrate some time before 26 d. 6 m. 1770 because Hannah made oath she was with child by Scott (QRNM 60, cites Abstracts of Gunpowder Monthly Meeting). [No other marriage reference found].

Tanner, Mary, servant of Richard Deaver, confessed to bastardy at March Court 1745/6, and was sentenced to be whipped with 10 lashes on 4 June 1746 (BACP Liber 1743-1745: 800, TB&TR#1:6-7).

Tarre [Torre?], Levin, of Snow Hill, was m. last Fri. eve. by Rev, Mr. Hagerty to Miss Rosetta Duplessis of this town (*Federal Intelligencer and Baltimore Daily Gazette* 5 Jan 1795). (BAML gives her name as Rosella Tuplessa).

Tarrington, [-?-], m. by 6 March 1784 Mary, daughter of Abraham Andrews (BAWB 4:11).

Tate, Andrew, m. by 9 Jan 1786, Jean, daughter of Michael Cunningham, by whom he had a daughter Ann Tate (BAWB 4:125).

Tate, David, and Elizabeth Sinclair were m. on 15 March 1768 (Harrison, "St. John's Parish Register:" 231). On 7 May 1771 Elizabeth was named as a daughter of Mary Sinclair (BAWB 3:181).

Tate, Capt. James, and Betsey Coulter were m. last Tues. eve. at Fell's Point (*Maryland Journal and Baltimore Advertiser* 2 Feb 1782).

Tate, John, of the Baltimore Barrens stated he would not pay the debts of his wife Meriam (*Maryland Journal and Baltimore Advertiser* 30 Dec 1774).

Tatlow, Joseph, of Baltimore, stated he would not pay the debts of his wife Mary (*Maryland Journal and Baltimore Advertiser* 4 Jan 1788).

Taylard, William, on 31 May 1742 was named as a son-in-law to Abraham Simmons (BALR TB#A:173, 175).

Taylor, [-?-], d. by 25 March 1747, having m. Verlinda, daughter of Robert Doyne; she m. 2nd, [-?-] Brown (BALR TB#E: 340)

Taylor, [-?-], m by 4 Dec 1792 Sarah, daughter of Conduce Gatch (BAWB 6:47).

Taylor, [-?-], m. by 20 May 1800 Ann, daughter of Abraham Griffith (BAWB 6:268).

Taylor, Abraham, and wife [Jane] on 9 June 1699 posted bond to administer the estate of John Armstrong (BAAB 1:29; INAC 20:253).

Taylor, Abraham, son and orphan of Lawrence Taylor, dec., being 16 on 22 Oct 1723, with the consent of his mother Agnes, on 5 June 1732, bound himself to William

Cook, joiner, as an apprentice to William Cook to age 21 as a joiner and carpenter (BALR IS#L:253).

Taylor, Abraham, m. Hannah Cord (*q.v.*); she m. 2nd Edward Munday (*q.v.*).

Taylor, Abraham, on 17 Nov 1774 was charged by the vestry with unlawful cohabitation with Martha Whayland (Reamy, *St. George's Parish Register:* 112).

Taylor, Aquila, and Sarah Holland were m. by 25 Nov 1789 in Baltimore (Marr. Returns of Ezekiel Cooper, MdSA S1005/19999-002-312, pub. in *MGSB* 32 (1) (Winter 1991) 6).

Taylor, Arthur, m. by 3 March 1683/4 Frances, mother of James Smithers (BALR RM#HS:68).

Taylor, Bray Platt, m. by 1742 [-?-], daughter of Edward and Eliza Evans of Baltimore Co. (MDTP 31:324; MDTP 31:303, 324).

Taylor, Charles, m. by 10 June 1762 Elizabeth, admx. of William Montgomery (MDTP 38:394; BFD 3:147; BAAD 6:136; BACM 2:51).

Taylor, Elizabeth, on 30 Jan 1764 was paid as a legatee of 'Ellick' Burk (MDAD 50:268).

Taylor, Frances, was charged with bastardy at June Court 1731 (BACP HWS#7:155).

Taylor, Francis, and Elizabeth Whitaker were m. on 6 Oct 1729 ((Harrison, "St. George's Parish Register:" 254). In May 1732 they administered the estate of Mark Whitaker (*q.v.*). About 1729 Francis Taylor had a prenuptial contract with Elizabeth Whitacre, admx. of Mark Whitecar (Whitseer) of Baltimore Co. (BALR IS#K: 109; MDTP 29:89; MDAD 11:433).

Taylor, George, and Martha Goldsmith were m. on 24 Nov 1792 (Marr. Register of Rev. Lewis Richards, MS.690 at MdHS). She was a daughter of Thomas Goldsmith (BAWB 6:279).

Taylor, Jacob, and Sarah Thompson were m. on 21 March 1779 ("The Burnham Bible." *The Notebook* 10 (1) (March 1994) 7).

Taylor, James, m. by 15 July 1739 Mary, widow of John Thomas, and mother of Moses Thomas, who will be 18 next 26 June; said Moses signed his name when he was apprenticed to William Daugherty, tailor to age 21 (BALR HWS#1A:230).

Taylor, James, m. 1st, Mary Foster, now dec., by whom he had a son James Taylor; on 4 May 1747 he entered into a prenuptial contract with Sarah Kimball, daughter of Rowland Kimble (BALR TB#E:380). James Taylor m. 2nd, Sarah Kemball on 9 May 1747 (Reamy, *St. George's Parish Register:* 80). On 31 March 1746 James Taylor and Sarah Kembal were summoned by the Vestry ("St. John's and St. George's Parish Register Vestry Proceedings," MS. at the MdHS). On 6 March 1764 Sarah was named as a daughter of Hannah Kimble, widow (BAWB 2:175).

Taylor, James, in Nov 1756 was fined for begetting a bastard on the body of Sarah Pike (BAMI 1755-1763).

Taylor, John, and his wife Elizabeth, execs., on 3 Aug 1710 posted bond to administer the estate of William Pecket (Pickett) (BAAB 2:419; BACP IS#B: 213, 216; MDTP 21:291, 22:145; INAC 36A:164; MDTP 27:232; MDAD 8:60; BAAD 1:9).

Taylor, John, was charged with incontinence with Mary Gilbert at the Aug 1725 Court (BACP IS&TW#4:306).

Taylor, John, m, by 9 March 1732 Mary, relict of Edward Talbot [*i.e.*, Edmond Talbot] (*q.v.*) (BALR IS#L: 392).

Taylor, John, m. by 20 June 1736 Kezia, daughter of Charles Simmons (MWB 21:876 abst. in *Md. Cal. of Wills* 7:246). In his will, made 19 March 1745 John Taylor named his son Charles and the latter's uncle George Simmons (MWB 24:221 abst. by Gibb). By 6 Oct 1746, his widow Kezia had m. Joshua Hardesty (*q.v.*) of Baltimore Co. (MDTP 32:133; MDAD 24:262).

Taylor, John, and Elizabeth Norris were m. on 18 Oct 1757 (Harrison, "St. John's Parish Register:" 216). On 5 Dec 1761 Elizabeth was named as a daughter of Edward Norris (BAWB 3:3).

Taylor, John, and Elinor Hooper were married on 10 Oct 1790 (Marr. Returns of Rev. William West, Scharf Papers, MS.1999 at MdHS). Eleanor m. 2nd, on 28 May 1799 John Jones (q.v.).

Taylor, Lawrence, and Agnes Montague were m. on 7 Feb 1703/4 (Harrison, "St. George's Parish Register:" 200). As the mother of James Taylor she m. 2nd, by 31 March 1756, Henry Moore (*q.v.*).

Taylor, Matthew, and Mary Smith were m. by lic. on 20 Oct 1790 at St. Peter's Catholic Church, Baltimore (*Piet:* 144).

Taylor, Michael, In Aug 1728 was charged with begetting a bastard on the body of Ann White (BACP HWS#6:38).

Taylor, Michael, on 15 June 1723 in hopes of setting a final end to all unhappy disputes and debates heretofore had by us or hereafter might be: conveyed to his wife Ann Taylor all the estate she had on 1 Feb 17--, the date of their marriage (BALR IS#G:190).

Taylor, Michael, of Prince George's Co., m. by Feb 1731, Ann, widow of Anthony Bale (*q.v.*) of Baltimore Co. (MCHR 5:340-347). He d. by 17 July 1744 leaving Ann, widow and residuary legatee of Anthony Bale; Kemp Plummer of Gloucester Co., Va., was her brother and heir-at-law (BALR TB#C:570, 576).

Taylor, Richard, and Eleanor Spicer were m. on 9 Jan 1788 (Marr. Returns of Rev. William West, Scharf Papers, MS.1999 at MdHS). On 10 April 1787 Eleanor was named as a sister of John Spicer who named Eleanor's daughter Hannah Spicer [*sic*] (BAWB 4:287).

Taylor, Robert, m. 2 Nov 1773 Mary Ridley ("Wesley Stevenson Bible," *The Notebook* 21 (3) (Fall 2005) 12-15).

Taylor, Robert, merchant, and Miss Frances Etting, both of Baltimore, were m. last Thurs. eve. (*Baltimore Daily Repository* 9 March 1793).

Taylor, Thomas, m. by 12 April 1714 Elizabeth, widow and extx. of Edward Welch (INAC 35A:130; BAAD 1:1; BACP IS#B: 513).

Taylor, Thomas, in March 1716/7, was charged with begetting a bastard on the body of Agnes Sackield (BACP HWS#TR:95).

Taylor, Thomas, d. by 22 July 1725 at which time his widow and admx. Elizabeth had m. William Anglin (*q.v.*).

Taylor, Thomas, m. by 20 Feb 1729 [-?-], daughter of Mary Price (BAAD 2:247).

Taylor, Thomas, m. by 21 Dec 1799 Hannah, sister of Nicholas Cromwell (BALR WG#60:614).

Taylor, William, of Prince George's Co., m. by 10 June 1772 Esther, sister of William and John Barrett (BALR AL#E:111).

Taylor, William, merchant, and Hannah Judah, both of this town, were m last Thurs. eve. (*Maryland Journal and Baltimore Advertiser* 14 Jan 1783).

Taylor, William, Jr., merchant of Shelburne, was m. last eve. by Rev. Dr. Davis, to Martha Richards, daughter of the Rev. Lewis Richards of this city (*Federal Gazette and Baltimore Daily Advertiser* 20 Aug 1800).

Tayman, Benjamin, m. by July 1725 Sarah (nee Ray), extx. of Joshua Cockey (*q.v.*), and widow of Thomas Hanson (*q.v.*) (MDTP 17:197). On 21 Aug 1745, Sarah, formerly Sarah Cockey, conv. land to her grandchildren John, Benjamin, and Sarah Hanson; Sarah Hanson had m. by the above date John Garrettson (BALR TR#DS:95; IS#G:182, TB#D:311).

Teal, [-?-], m. by March 1781 Elizabeth, daughter of William Jessop, collier (BAWB 3:438).

Teal, Edward, m. by 28 April 1720 Hannah, widow and admx. of Nathaniel Stinchcomb (BALR TR#DS:209: BACP IS#B:274, 297). On 8 Nov 1722 Hannah was named as a sister of Thomas Randall of Baltimore Co., and on 20 Sep 1735 as a sister of Christopher Randall (MINV 9:118, 24:257).

Teale, Edward, d. by Nov 1685, leaving a daughter Ales and a widow Sarah who m. 2nd, John Copas or Copus (*q.v.*), and 3rd, Patrick Murphy (*q.v.*) (BALR TR#RA:38; MDTP 19A:119; INAC 23:90). Ales Teale on 13 March 1699 was named as daughter-in-law of John Copus (BALR TR#RA:338).

Teale, Emanuel, and Catherine Johnson were m. on 24 Dec 1734 Harrison, "St. Paul's Parish Register:" 153). On 23 d. 8 m. 1786, Catherine was named as a sister of Thomas Johnson and of Mary Williams whose will of that date named her sister Catherine Teale and John Teale of Emanuel in her will (BAWB 4:494)

Tee(s) (Tea), John, in 1761 paid a sum to the mother of a bastard child he bought (BAMI 1755- 1763).

Tees, Mary, in 1765 petitioned on behalf of her son against Thomas Goldsmith (BAMI 1772, 1775-1781: 45).

Temple, Susanna, servant of Daniel Scott, was charged with bastardy at Aug 1724 Court. and indicted at Nov 1724 Court; she named Abraham Whitacre as the father of her child (BACP IS&B:137, IS&TW#3:438, IS&TW#4:631). Susanna, daughter of Thomas Temple, was b. 21 Aug 1699 at Rumley Creek; her son Michael Temple was born 11 July 1724 (Reamy, *St. George's Parish Register:* 5, 35).

Templeton, Margaret, in 1762 was fined for bastardy (BAMI 1755-1763).

Teves, [-?-], m. by 19 Feb 1764 Ann, daughter of Thomas Bennett (BAWB 2:170).

Tevis, Robert, and Margaret [-?-] were m. before 8 Nov 1744 when their daughter Hamutal was born (Kathleen Field, "A Record of Tevis Births," *MGSB* 35 (2) (Spring 1994) 242).

Thackham, Mary, was charged with bastardy in 1775 and fined £1.10.0 (BAMI 1772, 1775-1781).

Thacker, [-?-], m. by 17 Nov 1725 Hannah, daughter of Christopher Gardiner (MWB 18:430 abst. in *Md. Cal. of Wills* 5:208).

Thismose, [-?-], m by 4 Dec 1792 Elizabeth, daughter of Conduce Gatch (BAWB 6:47).

Thomas, [-?-], m. by 31 Dec 1769 Jane, daughter of Benjamin Wheeler (BAWB 3:174).

Thomas, [-?-], m by 19 Aug 1795 Margaret, daughter of John Royston (BAWB 6:104).

Thomas, Benjamin, his wife Elizabeth, and their son Joseph, on 24 Aug 1797 were named in the will of Hannah Green, widow (BAWB 6:79).

Thomas, David, m. by 25 July 1706 Hannah, extx. of George Smith (BAAD 1:232; INAC 25:343). In June 1714 Hannah was named as the mother of William Smith (BACP IS#B:507). Hannah had m., 1st, Daniel Peverell (*q.v.*), and 2nd, George Smith (*q.v.*) (*BCF:*586-587).

Thomas, David, m. by 1719 Ann Lister, widow of Richard Freeborne of Baltimore Co. (MDAD 3:26).

Thomas, David, and Elizabeth Wheeler were m. in Feb 1732 (Harrison, "St. George's Parish Register:" 268). On 15 Sep 1741 Eliz. was named as a daughter of Benjamin Wheeler (BALR HWS#1A: 555). On 16 Sep 1741 Elizabeth was named as a daughter of Benjamin Wheeler (MWB 22:436 abst. in *Md. Cal. of Wills* 8:160). As acting extx. she m. 2nd, by 31 March 1748 Henry Green (*q.v.*) (MDTP 32:158).

Thomas, David, d. by March 1761 when his daughter Hannah chose Ignatius Wheeler as her guardian; his dau Mary chose Benjamin Green as hers, and his son Benjamin chose his brother David Thomas as his (BAMI 1755-1763).

Thomas, Francis, m. by 11 May 1769 Mary, widow and admx. of Mathias Galman? Calman [Colman?] (BALR AL#A:276, 501). On 9 May 1783 he was resident in York Co., Pa., with his wife, Mary, widow and admx. of Mathias Galman of Baltimore Co., dec, (BALR WG#N:294).

Thomas, James Warner, m. by 13 Sep 1793 Rebecca Hutchinson, daughter of Joseph Rawlins (BAWB 5:151).

Thomas, John, m. by April 1698 [-?-], widow of Edward Norris of Baltimore Co. (MDTP 17:82). Sarah, widow of 1st, John Kemp (*q.v.*) and 2nd, Edward Norris (*q.v.*) (MDTP 17:82). She m. 4th, Thomas Matthews (q.v.).

Thomas, John, m. by July 1721 Mary, daughter of Samuel Jackson (BALR IS#G:33).

Thomas, John, and Eliz. Toolson [c1747/8] were returned to Jos. George for the Nov. court ("St. John's and St. George's Par St. John's and St. George's Parish Register Vestry Proceedings," MS.at the MdHS).

Thomas, John, m. by 14 May 1753,Sarah, only daughter and heir of Thomas Savage (BALR TR#D:548).

Thomas, John, received payment for supporting Ann Brucebanks, orphan of Francis Brucebanks for 8 mos. (Levy List for 1772).

Thomas, Joseph, and Dorcas Sutton were m. on 4 Feb 1732 Harrison, "St. Paul's Parish Register:" 150). Dorcas was the admx. of Thomas Sutton (*q.v.*) (BAAD 3:142; MDAD 12:172). In his will made 4 July 1748 Thomas named his daughter Ruth Sing, who later m. John Hendrickson (*q.v.*) (MWB 25:395). On 3 March 1749 Ruth Sing was named as the extx. of Joseph Thomas (MDTP 33-1:87, 33A:102). Ruth Sing was born 24 Aug 1729, a daughter of Mary Sing who was tried for bastardy in Nov 1729 and again in Nov 1733 (BACP HWS#6:315, HWS#9:134; Harrison, "St. Paul's Parish Register:" 133).

Thomas, Martha, was charged with bastardy at the June 1744 Court and named Abraham Brucebanks as the father of her child. She was charged again in March 1745/6, and confessed at the June 1746 Court (BACP Liber 1743-1745: 228, 243, 800, TB&TR#1:7-8). Her son John Thomas was born in 1746/7 (Harrison, "St. John's," p. 132).

Thomas, Martha, was charged with bastardy at the Nov 1772 Court (BAMI 1772, 1775-1781:85).

Thomas, Philip, and Kitty Myers were m. [date not given] (*Maryland Journal and Baltimore Advertiser* 1 July 1783). Philip Thomas and Catherine Myers were married by license dated 25 June 1783 (BAML). On 14 April 1787 she was named as a daughter of Jacob Myers (BAWB 4:268).

Thomas, Robert, and Jane Freeborn were m. on 18 Jan 1704 (Harrison, "St. Ann's Parish Register," Anne Arundel Co., MS. at MdHS: 389). On 13 June 1720 Jane was named as a sister of Richard Freeborne (BALR RM#HS: 661).

Thomas, Samuel, on 11 d. 5 m. 1797 was disowned for publicly attending plays and for having his marriage accomplished contrary to the good order ("Minutes of Baltimore Meeting," *QRNM:*228). He may be the Samuel Thomas who m. Hannah Ewalt by Kent Co. Marriage License (MM2:226).

Thomas, William, of Montgomery Co. , was m. Fri., 15th inst., by Rev. Mr. Richards, to Miss M. Patrick of this city (*Federal Gazette and Baltimore Daily Advertiser* 22 Nov 1799).

Thompson, [-?-], of Prince George's Co., d. by 18 Dec 1771 having m. Lettice, sister of Corbin Lee of Baltimore Co., and daughter of Philip Lee (DOLR 24:Old 405).

Thompson, [-?-], m. by 20 Oct 1795 Ritty [*sic*], mother of Charlotte Lindsey, who was bound to John Kerr, schoolmaster, to learn sewing, knitting, and housework (BIND 1:85).

Thompson, [-?-], m. by 22 Aug 1798 Susannah, mother of Alisana Johnson (BIND 1:391).

Thompson, Alexius, son of Eleanor Thompson now Hooper, on 24 Dec 1786 was to receive from James W. Cannon, administrator of Hugh Green, the above interest on a loan every year from 12 Oct 1784 until Alexius should arrive at age 21 (BAOC 1:287). Alexius, son of Eleanor Hooper by a former husband, now dec., was bound by the court to George Ryan without the knowledge or consent of the petitioner (BOCP Petition of Eleanor Hooper, 1790).

Thompson, Amos, and Miss Nancy Deegan, of Harford Co. were m. last Tues. by Rev. Richards (*Baltimore Telegraphe* 31 Oct 1799).

Thompson, Andrew, m. Ann Norrington who was b. 8 May 1748, d. 29 May 1807 ("The Burnham Bible." *The Notebook* 10 (1) (March 1994) 8).

Thompson, Daniel, m. by 11 Nov 1766 [-?-], daughter of John Chocke (BAAD 7:192).

Thompson, Edward, was charged with bastardy at the Nov 1759 Court and fined (BAMI 1757-1759:178).

Thompson, Edward, and Elizabeth [-?-] were m. by 18 Sep 1776 when their son Henry was b. ("Henry Thompson Bible," *MBR* 7:185-189).

Thompson, Henry, of Baltimore, and Miss Bowly, dau of Daniel Bowly, Esq., of *Furley,* were m. last eve. (*Federal Gazette and Baltimore Advertiser* 30 March 1798).

Thompson, James, and Elizabeth Gilbert were m. on 30 Oct 1727 (Harrison, "St. George's Parish Register:" 252). Elizabeth m. 2nd, Roger Donahue (q.v.). James and Elizabeth were the parents of: James Thompson, who on 25 Dec 1740 was named as a son-in-law in the will of Roger Donahue (*q.v.*) (MWB 25:490 abst. by Gibb).

Thompson, James, and Hannah Jay were m. by lic. in 1788 (HAML). Hannah Jay (now Thompson), daughter of Stephen Jay, has gone out in marriage to a man not of our society with the assistance of a priest ("Minutes of Deer Creek Meeting," *QRNM:*145).

Thompson, James, of the House of Wilmans, Thompson, and Co., was m. yesterday by Rev. Kurtz to Miss Maria Adelaide Munnings of Harmony Hall, Baltimore Co. (*Baltimore Daily Intelligencer* 21 March 1794).

Thompson, John, and Eliza Parks were m. on 14 June 1787 (Marr. Returns of Rev. William West, Scharf papers, MS. 1999 at MdHS). On 10 Oct 1787 Elizabeth was named as a daughter of John Parks (BAWB 4:314).

Thompson, Joseph, m. by 5 July 1761 Elizabeth, daughter and devisee of Anthony Enloes (BALR B#I:462).

Thompson, Mary, was given an allowance for keeping James and Mary Chapel (Levy List for 1772).

Thompson, Capt. Nathaniel, of the ship *Swift Packet,* and Elizabeth, daughter of the late Abraham Jackson of Fell's Point, were m. last Sat. eve. (*Baltimore Daily Repository* 31 July 1792; BAAD 11:322).

Thompson, Robert, m. by 21 Feb 1795 Catherine, widow of William Askew (BALR WG#QQ:436).

Thompson, Sabra, was charged with bastardy at the Aug 1746 Court, and confessed at the Nov 1746 Court; she was sentenced to be whipped on the bare back (BACP Criminal Proceedings 1757-1759:116, TB&TR#1:240-241).

Thompson, Sarah, on 12 July 1774 was named as the admx. of William Ramsey (MDTP 46:127-128).

Thompson, Tabitha, a free mulatto, confessed in Feb 1776 (or 1777) to having borne three mulatto bastard children: Jem Thompson, aged about 11; Saul Thompson, (sold in Aug 1773 to John Addison Smith); and Esther, aged about 2; Tabitha was ordered to serve her mistress Sarah Smith for another 21 years, and Jem and Esther were sold to Mrs. Smith and ordered to serve her until they reached the age of 31 (BAMI 1772, 1775-1781: 234).

Thompson, Thomas, and Elizabeth Willmott were married by license dated 28 Jan 1780 (HAML) On 6 Dec 1782 Elizabeth was named as a daughter of John Wilmot (BAWB 3:550).

Thompson, Thomas, and Elizabeth Adams were m. by lic. dated 25 Dec 1780 (BAML). In June 1781 Thompson stated that his wife Elizabeth had eloped (*Maryland Journal and Baltimore Advertiser* 4 June 1781).

Thompson, William, m. by 10 May 1770 [-?-], who was paid her portion of Charles Bond's estate (MDAD 63:174).

Thompson, William, and Miss Polly Poe, both of this town, were m. last Sat. eve. (*Maryland Journal and Baltimore Advertiser* 18 March 1791).

Thompson, William, watchmaker, was m. last eve. by Rev. Mr. Kurtz, to Miss Maria Miltenberger, both of this city (*Federal Gazette and Baltimore Daily Advertiser* 12 May 1797).

Thompson, Capt. William, was m. last eve. by Rev. Mr. Bend, to Mrs. Anderson, both of this city (*Federal Gazette and Baltimore Daily Advertiser* 11 Aug 1797).

Thompson. See also Thomson.

Thomson, George, m, by 35 July 1798 Mary, legatee of Phebe Hutchinson (BAAD 12:460).

Thomson, Hannah. See Miles, Hannah.

Thomson. See also Thompson.

Thorn, Jane, confessed to bastardy on 31 May 1755 (BACP BB#B: 402-403).

Thorn, Sarah, *alias* Ann Thorn, confessed to bastardy at the June 1755 Court, and named Lemuel Hardesty as the father; she was fined £3 current money at the Nov 1755 Court, and was charged again at the March 1755/6 Court (BACP BB#B: 22, 403).

Thornborough (Thornberry), [-?-], m. by May 1680, Sara, widow of John Woodhouse (MDTP 12A:38).

Thornborough, Ann, was charged with bastardy at the June 1742 Court and was presented at the June 1743 Court (BACP TB#TR:309, Liber 1743-1745:84).

Thornbrough (Thombrough), William, of Baltimore stated he would not pay the debts of his wife Ann, who has eloped (*Maryland Gazette or Baltimore General Advertiser* 4 March 1791).

Thornburg, William, m. by 4 Oct 1795 Nancy, sister of George (Gweem?) (BAWB 5:332).

Thornburgh, Joseph, on 11 d. 10 m. 1798 requested a certificate to Indian Spring Meeting in order to marry Cassandra Ellicott, a member thereof ("Minutes of Baltimore Meeting," *QRNM:*231). Joseph Thornburg, merchant, of this city, was m. Fri., 21st inst. at the Friends Mtg. House on Elk Ridge, to Cassandra Ellicott of Baltimore Co. (*Federal Gazette and Baltimore Daily Advertiser* 23 Nov 1798).

Thornbury, John, and Elizabeth Taylor, daughter of Joseph and Barbara (Billington) Taylor of Lancaster Co., Va., were m. by 10 Dec 1726 (George H. S, King, *Marriages of Richmond County, Virginia, 1668-1853* (1964): 209). Thornbury d. by 21 Nov 1730; his widow Elizabeth renounced the right to administer, so on that date Luke Stansbury posted bond to administer Thornbury's estate (BAAB 4:220). Elizabeth Thornbury, wife of John, d. 12 March 1731 Reamy, *St. Paul's Parish Register:* 41).

Thornbury, Robert, and Magdalen Barbin were m. by lic. on 25 May 1786 at St. Peter's Catholic Church, Baltimore (*Piet:* 144).

Thornbury, Roland, d. by March 1733/4 leaving the following orphans: Mary Ann, aged 3 last 22 March, bound to William Brown; John, also aged 3 last 22 March, bound to William Kemp and wife; Thomas, aged 9, bound to Edward Evans; and Baly, aged 13 (BALR HWS#9:245, 246))

Thornton, Ann, in March 1759 bound her two children, Elizabeth, aged 6, and John, aged 2, to Thomas Archer (BAMI 1755-1763).

Thornton, Constant, was charged with bastardy at the Nov 1757 Court (BAMI 1757-1759:74).

Thornton, Jane, was charged with bastardy at the March 1731/2 Court (BACP HWS#7:225).

Thornton, William, m. Eleanor [-?-] who m. 2nd. Corbin Lee (*q.v.*) on 31 Jan 1754.

Thornton, William, in his will dated 24 Jan 1769 left Sarah Heighe who 'formerly lived in my family,' £20 to be paid 12 mos. after Thornton's decease, and £12 a year for life, provided she give up to my exec. William the son of the said Sarah who is commonly known as William Thornton and 'in common report is my son,' and is now at board in Baltimore Town (BAWB 3:116)

Thorpe, Edward, and Catherine Cullings were m. on 6 Jan 1731 (Harrison, "St. George's Parish Register:" 259). On 6 May 1732 they posted bond to administer the estate of Thomas Cullens (*q.v.*) (BAAB 1:328; MDTP 29:193; MINV 16:585; MDAD 14:326).

Thorpe, Rachel, on 26 Aug 1771 conveyed property to her cousins Thomas Chenoweth (*q.v.*) and wife Rachel (BACT B#G:365).

Thrasher, [-?-], m. by 3 June 1756 [-?-], daughter of Elizabeth Price, who on that day conv. property to her grandchildren Mary, Sarah, and John Thrasher (BACT TR#E:206).

Thurcall, Thomas, m. by Aug 1684 Jane, daughter of Thomas O'Daniel and step-daughter of James Denton (BACP D:164; BALR RM#HS:188).

Thurston, David, m. by 23 May 1696 Martha, admx. of Robert Cage (*q.v.*) (MDTP 16:170). She had m. 1st, Mark Child (*q.v.*).

Thwaite, Mary, on 30 Sep 1672 posted bond to administer the estate of William Boulden (BAAB 1:59).

Tibbles, John, m. by 10 April 1798 Mary, devisee of Jacob Brown (BALR WG#VV:22).

Tibbett, James, m. by 11 June 1787 Sarah, admx. of Robert Forsyth (BAAD 9: 55).

Tibbett, Walter, and Delilah Green were married by license dated 2 July 1783 (BAML). She was a daughter of Isaac Green (BAWB 6:277).

Ticklin, William, a Protestant, and Eleanor Crawley were m. by lic. on 27 Nov 1795 at St. Peter's Catholic Church, Baltimore (*Piet:* 144).

Tilbury, Sarah, servant of William Petticoat, was charged with bastardy at the March 1746/7 Court, and was presented at the June 1737 Court (BACP HWS#1A:1, 55).

Tilden, John, son of Luke Tilden, was m. last Thurs. eve. by Rev. Mr. Bend to Eliza Angelica Barrier [?] (*Federal Gazette and Baltimore Daily Advertiser* 24 Nov 1800).

Tilly, Mary, was charged with bastardy at the Nov 1737 Court (BACP HWS#1A:129, 189).

Tilyard, John, of Kent Co., m. by 3 Nov 1698 Mary, daughter of George Green (BALR TR#RA:308).

Timanes, [-?-], m. by 3 Sep 1781 Dorothety [*sic*], sister of Gotlip Shearmiller, butcher (BAWB 3:427).

Tippar, Edgar, m. by March 1714/5 Elizabeth, admx. of William Pritchard (BACP IS#B:612; MDTP 22:448).

Tipton, [-?-], m. by 11 June 1786 Esther, sister of John Price of Mordecai (BAWB 4:502).

Tipton, [-?-], m. by 2 Dec 1795 Ruth, daughter of Thomas Boring (BAWB 5:341).

Tipton, Aquila, and Rebecca Belt (*q.v.*) were m. by lic. dated 6 May 1778 (BAML).

Tipton, Aquila, m. by 8 Dec 1792, Mary, daughter of John Bond (BAWB 5:75; BAAD 11:530).

Tipton, Jabez Murray, and Rebecca Lemmon were married by license dated 16 Jan 1781 (BAML). On 30 May 1786 Rebecca was named as a daughter of Alexis Lemmon, Sr. (BAWB 4:151).

Tipton, Luke, and Sarah Boston were m. on 26 Dec 1749 (Harrison, "St. Paul's Parish Register:" 163). They had at least one son, Thomas Tipton; Sarah m. 2nd, James Boring (*q.v.*) (BALR AL#K: 167). Shadrach Boston Tipton [prob. another son], aged 17 last Oct, in March 1772 was bound to Josias Pennington to learn the trade of millwright (BAMI 1772, 1775-1781: 7).

Tipton, Jonathan, administrator, on 30 Sep 1726 posted bond to administer the estate of William Tipton; on 8 June 1726, Hannah Tipton gave up the right to administer her husband's estate to her father-in-law Jonathan Tipton (BAAB 4:200).

Tipton. Rebecca. See Rebecca Belt.

Tipton, Sarah, was charged with bastardy at the Nov 1757 Court and was fined 30 shillings (BAMI 1757-1759:73).

Tipton, William, d. by 8 June 1726; he m. Hannah [-?-], who m. 2nd, John Bosley (*q.v.*); Hannah Bosley's will dated 30 July 1776 named her sons Samuel and Mordecai Tipton, and her daughter Sarah, wife of Christopher Cole (BAWB 3:325).

Todd, [-?-], m. by 23 Dec 1742, Martha, admx. of Bennett Garrett (*q.v.*) (BAAD 3:274); she m. 3rd, George Garrettson (*q.v.*).

Todd, [-?-], m. by 13 Aug 1759 Sarah, daughter of Robert Wilkinson (BAWB 2:275).

Todd, [-?-], m. by 26 Oct 1785 Elizabeth, daughter of John Stevenson (BAWB 4:147).

Todd, Benjamin, and Eleanor Ford were married by license dated 10 Dec 1781 (BAML). On 18 Aug 1782 Eleanor was named as a daughter of John Ford, Sr. (BAWB 3:456). Benjamin Todd stated that his wife Eleanor, through the persuasion of some evil persons, had eloped from his bed and board last April, and he stated he would not pay any debts of her contracting (*Federal Gazette and Baltimore Daily Advertiser* 27 June 1796).

Todd, James, m. by 6 Jan 1699 Penelope, daughter of Thomas and Abigail Scudamore; Abigail had m. 2nd, John Hayes (*q.v.*) (BALR TR#RA:418).

Todd, Lancelot, of Anne Arundel Co., m. by 5 March 1684, Sarah, daughter and heir of Thomas Phelps (BALR RM#HS:116).

Todd, Owen, son of James Todd, Esq., of Philadelphia., and Nancy Bibell (or Besett), both of Baltimore, were m. by Rev. Richards (*Baltimore Telegraphe* 22 April, 23 April 1800).

Todd, Thomas, m. prob. by 1657 Anne, daughter of Rev. John and Anne (Lovelace) Gorsuch; she m. 2nd, David Jones (*q.v.*), and 3rd, John Oldton (*q.v.*) (BALR IS#IK:57; *BDML* 2:836).

Todd, Thomas, m. by Nov 1757 Eleanor Dorsey, daughter of Caleb Dorsey (BALR (BACT B#G: 91, 93, 95; *BCF:* 644). Todd d. by 6 Sep 1740 when his widow and extx. Eleanor m. 2nd, William Linch (*q.v.*). Thomas and Eleanor had had a son William Todd (Harrison, "St. Paul's Parish Register:" 164). Eleanor was named as the extx. of Thomas Todd (MDTP 31:204; BAAD 3:375; MINV 26:98; MDAD 18:255).

Todd, Thomas, m. by 9 March 1763, [-?-], heir of Elinor Lynch (BAAD 6:197).

Todd, William, aged 10, orphan of David, in Nov 1762 was bound to James Heron, carpenter, to age 21 (BAMI 1755-1763).

Toff, Elizabeth (*alias* Margaret Stormay), was charged with bastardy and fined 30 shillings at the Nov 1757 Court (BAMI 1755-1763).

Toker, John, on 12 June 1764 was summoned to appear before the vestry of St. George's Parish for unlawful cohabitation with a Negro woman (Reamy, *St. George's Parish Register:* 109).

Tolley, Edward C., of Harford Co., and Miss Worthington of Baltimore Co. were m. Sun., 22nd ult. (*Maryland Journal and Baltimore Advertiser* 3 Sep 1784). Mrs. Elizabeth Tolley, wife of Edward Carvel Tolley, d. last Sun. at Bloomsbury, the seat of John Cradock, in her 23rd year (*Maryland Journal and Baltimore Advertiser* 25 Nov 1785). Hannah Worthington, in her will made March 1796, named her niece Elizabeth Mary Tolly (BAWB 5:447).

Tolley, Thomas, m. by 18 June 1720 Mary, sister of Richard Freeborne (BALR RM#HS:661, IS#G:115).

Tolley, Walter, and Martha Hall were m. on 22 Dec 1751 (Harrison, "St. George's Parish Register:" 349). On 30 Jan 1755 Martha was named as a daughter of Avarilla Hall, who also named a grandson Edward Carvill Tolley in her will (MWB 29:311 abst. by Gibb).

Tolson, Elizabeth, was charged with bastardy at the June 1750 Court and named John Stokes as the father of her child (BACP TR#5:23, 182).

Tomarus, Lawrence, m. by 10 March 1732 Rachel, daughter and heir of William Hill of Cecil Co., and granddaughter of Samuel Hill of Cecil Co. (BALR IS#L:211).

Tomblinson, Capt. Samuel, of Portsmouth, was m. last Sun. eve. by Rev. Mr. Bend, to Miss Hannah Fox of this town (*Federal Gazette and Baltimore Daily Advertiser* 22 March 1796).

Tombs. Charles, m. by 6 Dec 1768 Catharine, admx. of Jonas Otenpock (Odenback) (joiner) (MINV 99:169B).

Tomlinson, Joseph, and Miss Peggy Noel were m. last eve. (*Maryland Gazette or Baltimore General Advertiser* 29 April 1791).

Tomlinson, William, m. by 29 July 1797 Jennet, sister of James Hamilton (BAAD 12:319).

Tompkins, John, and Sarah Burgess on 30 d. 4 m. 1799 announced their intention to marry. Mary Tompkins gave her consent and Joseph Burgess sent a few lines giving his consent ("Minutes of Deer Creek Meeting," *QRNM:146*).

Tonge, Thomas, d. by 16 Sep 1758 by which time his admx. Mary had m. 2nd, Samuel Sollars (*q.v.*) (MDTP 27:144).

Toogood, Josias, and Mary Purnell were m. on 3 Oct 1698 (Harrison, "St. James Parish Register:" Anne Arundel Co., MS. at the MdhS: 372). Mary was the widow of Richard Purnell who d. by 14 Feb 1702, leaving his widow Mary, now the wife of Toogood (AALR WT#2:21). On 17 March 1708 Mary was named as a daughter of John Welsh (BALR TR#A:5).

Tool, Daniel, was m. last Tues. eve. to Miss Betty Smith, both of this town (*Federal Intelligencer and Baltimore Daily Gazette* 8 Jan 1795). Daniel Tool advertised that his wife Elizabeth had deserted him (*Federal Intelligencer and Baltimore Daily Gazette* 17 April 1795).

Toole, James, merchant, and Mrs. Hetty Noble were m. [date not given] (*Maryland Journal and Baltimore Advertiser* 19 Dec 1786). They were m. by lic. on 12 Dec 1786 at St. Peter's Catholic Church, Baltimore (*Piet:* 144). Mrs. Hetty Toole, wife of James Toole of Baltimore, d. yesterday in her 27th year (*Maryland Journal and Baltimore Advertiser* 8 Jan 1788).

Toole, James, merchant of Baltimore, and Mrs. Susanna Moore were m. last Sat eve. (*Maryland Journal and Baltimore Advertiser* 12 Aug 1788). On 10 June 1789 Susanna was named as the extx. of Robert Moore (BAAD 10:4).

Toon, Samuel, of Chelsea, and Miss Tennant of Canton were m. last eve. by Rev. Bend (*Baltimore Telegraphe* 25 March 1799.

Top, John, and Sarah Carty were m. on 4 Jan 1786 at St. Peter's Catholic Church, Baltimore (*Piet:* 144).

Tornquist, George, and Anna Margaretha Elkins were m. on 7 Aug 1800 (Harrison, "St. James Parish Register:" 9). On 8 Dec 1800 Margaret was named as a daughter of John and Mary (Keeports) Elkins (BALR WG#65:456).

Touchstone, Richard, and Sarah Johnson were m. on 25 Feb 1717 (Harrison, "St. George's Parish Register:" 256). On 23 Oct 1736 she was named as a daughter of Daniel Johnson of Baltimore Co. (MDAD 15:203).

Tourneroche, Francis Mary Teembard, Baron of St. Marguerite, and Adeline Morton, native of England, were m. by lic. on 17 May 1794 at St. Peter's Catholic Church, Baltimore (*Piet:* 144).

Towers, Capt. George, was m. last Thurs. eve. to Miss Mary Aiken of this town (*Federal Intelligencer and Baltimore Daily Gazette* 10 Jan 1795).

Towers, Capt. John, and Elizabeth Hannah were m. last Sat. eve. by Rev. Mr. Bend (*Baltimore Daily Repository* 21 Aug 1792).

Townsend, John, m. by 19 Nov 1724 Amy, extx. of Hector McClane (*q.v.*) of Baltimore Co. (MDAD 6:223; MDTP 29:246).

Townsend, Joseph, and Polly, daughter of George Matthews, were m. yesterday at Friends' Meeting (*Maryland Journal and Baltimore Advertiser* 1 June 1787).

Towson, [-?-], m. by 23 Sep 1779 Susannah, widow of Alexander Frazier, brother of John Frazier (*q.v.*), late of the Island of New Providence, merchant (BAWB 3:552).

Towson, [-?-], m. by 30 March 1787, Elizabeth, daughter of Charles Baker (BAWB 4:394).

Towson, Charles, son of William, in March 1775 chose Thomas Bailey as his guardian (BAMI 1772, 1775-1781: 119).

Towson, Ezekiel, m. by 3 May 14 Sep 1768 Ruth, daughter of Joseph and Comfort Cromwell, widow of Baltimore Co. (BAWB 3:101, 4:241; MWB 37:427, abst. in *Md. Cal. of Wills* 14:102).

Towson, Jacob, and Jane Boyd were m. last Sat. eve. (*Maryland Journal and Baltimore Advertiser* 2 April 1788).

Towson, Thomas, stated he would not pay the debts of his wife Elizabeth (*Maryland Journal and Baltimore Advertiser* 16 Oct 1783). Elizabeth Towson stated she has not left her husband, but he refused to support her and her two children. She denied the scandalous accusation made by him concerning her and Dr. John Cradock's Negro, and the following persons who knew her attested to her good character. /s/ Dr. John Cradock,, George Hammond, Ann Cromwell, Jeremiah Johnson, *et al* (*Maryland Journal and Baltimore Advertiser* 7 Oct 1783).

Towson, William, and Ruth Gott were m. on 24 Feb 1735 (Harrison, "St. Paul's Parish Register:" 155). On 24 March 1742 Ruth was named as a daughter of Richard Gott (MWB 28:106 abst. by Gibb).

Towson, William, was charged with bastardy and confessed at the March 1743/4 Court (BACP 1743-1745:172-173).

Towson, William, m. by 18 Feb 1748 Dinah, daughter of John Willmott (MWB 25:531 abst. by Abst. by Gibb; MDAD 28:1, 33:153). She was a sister of Rachel Therep (BAWB 2:348, 3:532). On 27 Oct 1771 Ruth was named as an heir of Rachel Wilmot (BAAD 7:114).

Towson, William, son of William and Dinah Wilmot, was b. c1743 and d. in 1767; he m. Frances [-?-] (*BCF:* 648). James Peregoy (Perrigoe), administrator, on 7 Dec 1770, posted bond to administer the estate of Francis Towson (*alias* Perrigoe) (BAAB 2:526).

Tracey, [-?-], m. by 2 Dec 1795 Milenda, daughter of Thomas Boring (BAWB 5:341).

Tracey, Basil, and Mary Cammell [*sic*] were married by license dated 4 Aug 1781 (BAML) On 27 July 1797 Mary was named as a daughter and one of the heirs at law of James Campbell (BALR WG#51:448).

Tracey, Teague, and Mary James were m. on 3 Nov 1694 (Harrison, "St. James Parish Register," Anne Arundel Co., MS. at MdHS: 298). Mary m. 2nd, George Hitchcock (*q.v.*).

Tracey, Thomas, and Susanna Hawkins were m. on 15 Jan 1701 (Harrison, "St. James Parish Register," Anne Arundel Co., MS. at MdHS: 317). On 4 May 1702 she was named as the extx. of Augustine Hawkins (MDTP 19A:79).

Tracy, Henry, b. 23 Nov 1773, and Alice Leffingwell, b 8 Aug 1775, were m. on 21 May 1795 ("Henry Tracy and Alice Tracy Bible," MGRC 33:28).

Tracy, Susannah, was charged with bastardy at the June 1731 Court (BACP HWS#7:156).

Trapnall, Hannah, was charged with bastardy at the June 1729 Court (BACP HWS#6:41).

Trapnall, Vincent, exec., on 21 Nov 1794 posted bond to administer the estate of William Lane (BAAB 8:679).

Trapnall (Trapman), William, m. by 2 Nov 1764 Elizabeth, daughter of Susannah Herod or Harrod (BAWB 3:13; MDAD 67:208).

Trapnall, William, and Honor Wheeler were m. on 14 Oct 1779 ("Register of First Presbyterian Church, Baltimore," MS. at MdHS, 14). On 29 July 1795 Hannah [Duer?] was named as a representative of William Wheeler (BAAD 12:33).

Treacle, [-?-], m. by 28 June 1781 Ruth, daughter of Richard Hooker (BAWB 3:428).

Treadway (Tredway), [-?-], m. by 21 Sep 1747 Elizabeth, daughter of William McComas (MWB 25:488 abst. by Abst. by Gibb; BAAD 5:75).

Treadway, Aaron, in Aug 1761 chose his father Thomas as his guardian (BAMI 1755-1763).

Treadway, Daniel, and Sarah Norris were m. on 2 Aug 1744 (Harrison, "St. John's Parish Register:" 191). On 5 Dec 1761 Sarah was named as a daughter of Edward Norris (BAWB 3:3).

Treadway, Richard, m. by June 1713 Jane, mother of John Smith (BACP IS#B:379).

Treadway, Thomas, m. by 24 March 1749 Elizabeth, aged 31, daughter of William McComas of Baltimore Co. (MDAD 27:336, 28:335).

Treagle, Mary, was charged with bastardy and confessed at the March 1745/6 Court; William Arnold admitted he was the father of her child (BACP 1745-1746:805-806, TB&TR#1:5).

Tredway. See Treadway.

Triel (Trierle), Mary, was charged with bastardy at the Aug 1742 Court, and as Mary Trierle was charged at the June 1747 Court (BACP TB#D:8, TB&TR:434).

Treen, Henry, stated he would not pay the debts of his wife Catherine, who had lived in a criminal state with one William Collins, plasterer (*Maryland Journal and Baltimore Advertiser* 20 Jan 1774).

Trimble, John, son of Isaac and Elizabeth, b. 17 d, 7 m., 1774, m. 15 d, 3 m. 1798 at Friends Meeting House, Elizabeth Brown, daughter of David and Elizabeth, b. 15 d, 5 m., 1778 ("John Trimble Bible," *MBR* 2:160-161).

Trimble, John, and Elizabeth Brown on 8 d. 2 m. 1798 declared their intention to marry ("Minutes of Baltimore Meeting," *QRNM*:230).

Trimble, John, of William, on 8 d. 2 m. 1798 was reported to having accomplished his marriage contrary to the good order, and on 14 d. 6 m. 1798 it was reported that previous to his outgoing in marriage he had cohabited with another woman at a tavern whilst unmarried under the pretense that she was his wife ("Minutes of Baltimore Meeting," *QRNM*:230). A John Trimble and Lydia Brick were married by license dated 5 Aug 1797 (BAML).

Trimble, John, and Julia Hugo were married by license dated 18 Oct 1798 (BAML). Julia Trimble, formerly Hugo, on 10 d. 1 m. 1799 reportedly had her marriage accomplished contrary to the good order ("Minutes of Baltimore Meeting," *QRNM*:232).

Trimble, William, and Hannah Collins were married by license dated 8 Feb 1786 (BAML). On 12 June 1787 Hannah was named as the extx. of James Collins (BAAD 10:317).

Tripolet, John, m. by 12 May 1792 [-?-], who received a share of the estate of Edward Hewitt (BAAD 11:49).

Trippas, Francis, d. by 11 Dec 1672 by which time his widow Anne had m. Thomas Armiger (q.v.). Jane Trippas (Trippers) on 4 March 1675 was called daughter-in-law by Thomas Armiger (MWB 5:52 abst. in *Md. Cal. of Wills* 1:172).

Trisler, George, merchant of this place, was m. last eve. by Rev. Kurtz, to Miss Kitty Breidenbaugh, daughter of John Breidenbaugh of this town (*Baltimore Daily Intelligencer* 28 March 1794).

Trott, Alexander, and Sarah Traverse were m. by lic. on 10 May 1788 at St. Peter's Catholic Church, Baltimore (*Piet:* 144).

Trott, Elizabeth, servant to Dr. Josias Middlemore, was charged with bastardy at the Aug 1728 Court at the March 1729/30 Court, and again at the June 1734 Court (BACP HWS#6:32, 2362, HWS#9:253, 309).

Trotten, John, and Sarah Sollers were married by license dated 5 March 1793 (BAML). Sarah was a daughter of Thomas and Ariana Sollers (*q.v.*).

Trotten, John, admin., on 16 Oct 1798 posted bond to administer that part of the estate of Christian Davis which had not been administered by Mary Davis, now dec. (BAAB 8:460).

Trotten, Luke, m. by 15 Jan 1739 Ruth, daughter and heir at law of Joseph Heathcote (MWB 28:237 abst. by Gibb).

Trotten, Luke, and Elizabeth Body were m. on 15 Jan 1744 (Harrison, "St. John's Parish Register:" 192). On 30 May 1747 Elizabeth was named as the extx. of Stephen Body of Baltimore Co. (MDTP 32:93; MDAD 32:273). Elizabeth was the widow of 1st, Lewis Owings (*q.v.*), and 2nd, Stephen Body (*q.v.*). In her will, made 29 Oct 1765, She named her daughters Eleanor McConnikin, Jenny Long and Penelope Stansbury, and grandchildren, Stephen and Joshua Body, Elizabeth and Edmund Stansbury, Ruth Murray, Penelope Watts, and Jean and John Long (MWB 34:22 abst. in *Md. Cal. of Wills* 13:101).

Trotten, Luke, and Susanna Long were m. on 10 Feb 1754 (Harrison, "St. Paul's Parish Register:" 166). On 22 Sep 1761 Susannah was named as a daughter of John Long (MDAD 47:19; BAAD 4:342).

Trotten, Susanna, widow, in her will made 20 Sep 1790 and a codicil named her grandsons Luke Trotten Lenox, Richardson Lenox, John Lenox, Luke Trotten Dorsey, John Carr and Thomas Carr, brothers of Susanna, and granddaughter Susanna Trotten Carr (BAWB 5:322).

Troup, [-?-], m. by 25 May 1787 Elizabeth, sister of Margaret Nichols, spinster (BAWB 4:258).

Truelock, John, cabinetmaker, and Miss Sidney Walker of Anne Arundel Co. were m. last eve. at Elk Ridge by Rev. Bend (*Baltimore Telegraphe* 31 Aug 1798).

Truit, Mr. George, was m. Sun. eve. last by Rev. Mr. Richards, to Mrs. Ann Rollins, both of Fell's Point (*Federal Gazette and Baltimore Daily Advertiser* 22 March 1796).

Trulock, Mr. Daniel, was m. last Thurs. by Rev. John Hagerty, to Mrs. Lydia Stevens, both of this town (*Federal Intelligencer and Baltimore Daily Gazette* 22 June 1795).

Trumbo, John, stated he would not pay the debts contracted by his wife Catherine Trumbo, and warned all persons not to harbor his wife (*Federal Intelligencer and Baltimore Daily Gazette* 28 July 1795).

Trump, John, and Miss Lydia Branson, both of Baltimore, were m. last eve. by Rev. Kurtz (*Baltimore Telegraphe* 4 Dec 1799).

Tschudi, Weinbert, son of Weinbert and Anna (Reinegrin) Tschudi, bapt. 31 Aug 1710, m. 30 April 1736, Elisabet Rorerin, b. 16 Feb 1716, daughter of Martin and Anna (Jantzin) Rorer ("First Reformed Church, Baltimore," MS. at MdHS: 2 (which contains the "Tschudy Family Record").

Tschudy, Martin, m. by 4 Feb 1783 Magdalena, daughter of George Myers (BAAD 8:111).

Tsop[?], John, of Baltimore, stated he would not pay the debts of his wife Sarah who had eloped from his bed and board (*Maryland Journal and Baltimore Advertiser* 24 June 1791).

Tsoard. See Isoard.

Tucker, David, and Mary Ward were m. on 22 March 1789 (Marriage Register of Rev. Lewis Richards, Pastor of First Baptist Church, Baltimore, 1784-1818. MS 690 at MdHS). On 30 d. 5 m. 1789 Tucker was charged with marrying outside the good order ("Minutes of Gunpowder Meeting," *QRNM:*87). On 5 April 1800 Tucker, as administrator, posted bond to administer the estates of Edward Ward and James Ward (BAAB 9:114, 115).

Tucker, Mary. See Mary Hannah.

Tucker, Seaborn, and Margaret Cobb were m. on 2 April 1730 (Harrison, "St. George's Parish Register:" 157). On 1 Oct 1734 Margaret was named as a daughter of James Cobb of Baltimore Co. (MDAD 12:476). Margaret m. 2nd, by 30 Sep 1742 Thomas Litton, Jr. (BAAD 3:294).

Tudor, Humphrey, m. by 31 March 1733 Dorcas, daughter of John Ingram (MWB 20:700 abst. in *Md. Cal. of Wills* 7:23). On 21 Feb 1738 Tudor was named as a brother-in-law in the will of John Ingram who named his sister Dorcas 'Tabor' (MWB 22:160 abst. in *Md. Cal. of Wills* 8:75). Dorcas Tudor was charged with bastardy at the March 1742/3 Court and confessed at the March 1743/4 Court (BACP TB#D: 121, 1743-1745:166). Dorcas m. 2nd, Abraham Wright on 23 May 1745 (Harrison, "St. John's Parish Register:" 193, 240).

Tudor, Thomas, and Mary Edwards were m. on 15 Feb 1758 (Harrison, "St. John's Parish Register:" 217). On 14 Oct 1769 Mary was named as a daughter of John Edwards (BAWB 3:148).

Tuke, John, of York, surveyor, m. by 8 d., 9 m., 1786 Sarah, daughter of Daniel Mildred (BAWB 4:331).

Tull, Elijah, m. by 3 Aug 1781, Barbara [or Bridget?], sister of Collier Fountain, mariner of Somerset Co., and had by her two sons: Nicholas and William Tull (BAWB 3:420). Bridget [sic] Tull, admx., on 7 July 1783 posted bond to administer the estate of Collier Fountain (BAAB 6:166). On 8 Jan 1784 she posted bond to administer the estate of Elijah Tull (BAAB 6:195).

Tullen, John, and Genevieve Melanson were m. by lic. on 16 May 1784 at St. Peter's Catholic Church, Baltimore (*Piet:* 144).

Tunis, John, and Martha Hill were m. on 21 Aug 1755 (Harrison, "St. John's Parish Register:" 212). In March 1765 Martha was named as a daughter of William Hill (BAWB 3:24).

Turbell, Sarah, was charged with bastardy at the June 1731 Court (BACP IS&TW#4:156).

Turbett, Isaac, was charged with bastardy at the Aug 1738 Court (BACP (BACP HWS#1A:267).

Turmener, William, stated he would not pay the debts of his wife Maria (*Maryland Journal and Baltimore Advertiser* 15 May 1795).

Turnbull, Robert, of Petersburg, Va., and Mrs. Sarah Buchanan were m. last Mon. at the seat of John Robert Holliday in Baltimore Co. (*Maryland Journal and Baltimore Advertiser* 19 March 1790). They had recorded their marriage articles on 13 March 1790 (BALR WG#EE: 252). On 14 Aug 1790 Sarah was named as the widow of Archibald Buchanan (BAAD 9:41, 141, 298, 10:194). Archibald Buchanan and Sarah Lee were m. on 10 March 1768 (Harrison, "St. John's Parish Register:" 231).

Turner, Ann, was charged with bastardy at the June 1741 Court and confessed at the Nov 1741 Court (BACP TB&TR:56, 173).

Turner, Francis, and Ruth Bradley were married on 11 Nov 1790 (Marr. Register of Rev. Lewis Richards, MS.690 at MdHS). On 12 July 1797 Ruth was named as the widow of Robert Bradley (*q.v.*). (BAAD 12:318). Ruth was a daughter of Charles Howard, whose will dated 2 Feb 1799 named a daughter Ruth Turner and a grandson Robert Bradley (BAWB 6:161).

Turner, Isaac, d. by Dec 1793 when his orphans, Isaac, Lydia, and Sophia were made wards of George Reese (BAOC 3:74). His admx., Margaret, m. John Fenby or Furby (*q.v.*).

Turner, James, m. Sarah, daughter of James and Margaret Calder, dec. (MCHP # 5328).

Turner, James, m. by 11 Oct 1796, Christian Frankforter who received a share of the estate of Nicholas Frankforter (BAAD 12:198).

Twine, Ann, was charged with bastardy at the June 1711 Court and again at the Nov 1712 Court (BACP IS#B:210,334).

Twist, Elizabeth, on 26 April 1782 was named as co-executor of the will of James Brown (*q.v.*) of Abel, who acknowledged that her children: Elizabeth, William, Marry, Charlotte, Ann, and Rebecca were his (BAWB 3:484). Elizabeth Twist, extx., on 5 March 1783 posted bond to administer the estate of James Brown (*q.v.*) (BAAB 5:18).

Twitt, Catherine, was charged with bastardy at the Nov 1739 Court (BACP (BACP HWS#7:49).

Tye, John, and Presiotia Hitchcock were m. on 11 Dec 1735 (Harrison, "St. Paul's Parish Register:" 154). On 12 Feb 1746 Presiotia was named as a daughter of George Hitchcock (BALR IS#IK: 356). On 23 d. 8 m. [Oct] 1747 George Hitchcock, miller, named his grandchildren, George, Elinor, Susannah (MWB 25:164 abst. by Gibb).

Tyler, Elizabeth, was charged with bastardy at the Aug 1723 Court (BACP IS&TW#3:438).

Tyson, Dorothy, now Webster, on 29 d. 3 m. 1794 was found guilty of marriage by a hireling to a man not in profession with us ("Minutes of Gunpowder Meeting," *QRNM:*95). [No other marriage reference found].

Tyson, Elisha, and Mary Amos, on 28 d. 9 m. 1776 declared their intention to marry ("Minutes of Gunpowder Meeting," *QRNM:*68).

Tyson, Henry S., native of England, and Sabina O'Connor, native of Ireland, were m. by lic. on 9 Aug 1786 at St. Peter's Catholic Church, Baltimore (*Piet:* 144).

Tyson, Isaac, on 14 d. 9 m. 1797 requested a certificate to Indian Spring Monthly Meeting in order to m. Elizabeth Thomas, a member thereof ("Minutes of Baltimore Meeting," *QRNM:*229). Isaac Tyson, merchant of this city, was m. last Wed. to Miss Eliza Thomas, daughter of Evan Thomas of Montgomery Co. (*Federal Gazette and Baltimore Daily Advertiser* 11 Nov 1797).

Tyson, Jacob, on 27 d. 1 m. 1781 was reported as having 'gone so far astray as to have a child laid to his charge, which he doth not deny ("Minutes of Gunpowder Meeting," *QRNM:*74).

Tyson, Jacob, and Ann Perine, on 29 d. 11 m. 1793 declared their intention to marry ("Minutes of Baltimore Meeting," *QRNM:*222).

Tyson, Nathan, merchant, and Sally Jackson, both of Baltimore, were m. last Thurs. eve. by Rev. Dr. Allison (*Federal Gazette and Baltimore Advertiser* 27 Jan 1798). They were married by license dated 24 Jan 1798 (BAML). Sarah Tyson, formerly Jackson, on 11 d. 10 m. 1798 had a complaint made that she married contrary to the good order ("Minutes of Baltimore Meeting," *QRNM:*231-232).

"U"

Uhler, Andrew, m. by 7 Oct 1798 Catherine, daughter of Conrad Kerlinger (BAWB 6:138; BAAD 13:163).

Uhler, Erasmus, and Polly Neace, eldest daughter of George Neace of this town, were m. (*Maryland Journal and Baltimore Advertiser* 29 July 1783). Erasmus Uhler m. on 14 July 1783, Mary Nace (Watts BR, in MGRC 3:64).

Uhler, Philip, and Miss Mary Botner, both of Baltimore, were m. last evening by Rev. Kurtz (*Baltimore Daily Repository* 21 June 1793).

Underwood, John, m. by 4 March 1695 [-?-], relict of Henry Wollin (MDTP 16:142).

Underwood, John, and Miss Elizabeth Davis, both of Baltimore, were m. last Saturday evening (*Maryland Journal and Baltimore Advertiser* 8 May 1792).

Underwood, Mary, (formerly Hicks), on 25 d. 10 m. 1793 had a complaint made against her for having her marriage accomplished by the assistance of a hireling with a member of our society ("Minutes of Baltimore Meeting," *QRNM:*222). [No other marriage reference found].

Underwood, Nehemiah, and Mary Price on 26 d. 1 m. 1788 declared their intention to marry ("Minutes of Gunpowder Meeting," *QRNM:* 85).

Uriel, Capt. George, and Elliner Welch were m. on 24 July 1734 Harrison, "St. Paul's Parish Register:" 152). Uriel d. by 30 Nov 1753 by which time his admx. Helena [*sic*] had m. 2nd, Robert Gilcresh (q.v.) (MDTP 33-2:204).

Urquhart (Virchworth), William, m. by 18 May 1768 Sarah, extx. of Samuel Howell (*q.v.*) (MINV 96:155; BAAD 7:65; BAMI 1768-1769:19).

Utie (Uty), George, m. by 12 Oct 1670 Susanna, daughter of Samuel Goldsmith (MWB 1:442, abst. in *Md. Cal. of Wills* 1:62; MDTP 5:93). She m. 2nd, Mark Richardson (*q.v.*), and 3rd, Thomas Wainwright (*q.v.*).

Utie, George, d. by [c1696/7] having m. Mary, daughter and admx. of Edward Beadle (INAC 15:182; BALR IS#IK: 241, 245; *BCF:* 35).

Utie, Nathaniel, m. Mary [-?-] who m. 2nd, Henry Johnson (*q.v.*), and 3rd, Edward Boothby (*q.v.*) (MDTP 12A:196; INAC 12:143).

Utz, Enrich Jacob, m. by 25 Feb 176, Maria Barbara Angling ("First Record Book for the Reformed and Lutheran Congregations at Manchester, Baltimore (now Carroll) County," *MGSB*: 35: 266).

Utz, Peter, m. by 1 June 1762, Elisabeth Bornin ("First Record Book for the Reformed and Lutheran Congregations at Manchester, Baltimore (now Carroll) County," *MGSB*: 35: 267).

"V"

Van Bibber, Abraham, Esq., of this town was m. yesterday eve. at the seat of Mrs. Rebecca Young, to Miss Polly Young. They are expected to arrive this eve. at their house in Hanover St. (*Federal Intelligencer and Baltimore Daily Gazette* 23 Nov 1795). They were m. by lic. on 22 Nov 1795 at St. Peter's Catholic Church, Baltimore (*Piet*: 144). Abraham Van Bibber and Mary Young recorded their marriage articles in Nov 1795 (BALR WG#TT: 447).

Van Bibber, Andrew, and Sally, daughter of Ezekiel Forman, Esq., were m. a few days ago at Chester Town, Kent Co. (*Maryland Journal and Baltimore Advertiser* 26 Feb 1790).

Van Bibber, James, merchant, and Betsey, daughter of Edward Dorsey, were married (*Maryland Journal and Baltimore Advertiser* 27 Feb 1787). Mrs. Elizabeth Van Bibber, consort of James Van Bibber of Baltimore, and daughter of Edward Dorsey, d. last Thurs., in her 24th year at the seat of her brother Edward Dorsey (*Maryland Journal and Baltimore Advertiser* 16 Feb 1790).

Van Deaver (Vandiver, Vanidear), Jacob, m. by 26 Nov 1718 Jane, widow and admx. of John Gill (BAAD 1:142; MDAD 2:369; MCHR 4:301).

Vandel, Daniel, m. by 11 April 1799, legatee of Robert Mack (BAAD 13:28).

Van Horne, Benjamin, and Martha Tunis were m. on 29 Aug 1768 (Harrison, "St. John's Parish Register:" 232). In his will, made 11 Oct 1771 Van Horne named his wife Martha, and mentioned his children 'by his first wife' (MWB 38:369, abst. in *Md. Cal. of Wills* 14:182).

Van Sickleton, Gilbert, m. by 28 Feb 1768 Mary, widow of James Shepherd who was a son of Christopher Shepherd, who was a son of Rowland Shepherd (BALR B#Q: 125).

Van Wyck, William, m. by 13 Sep 1793 Elizabeth, daughter of Joseph Rawlins (BAWB 5:151).

Vaughn, Abraham, on 30 April 1753, recorded that he would not be responsible for the debts of his wife Edith (BACT TR#E: 92).

Vaughn, Abraham, m. by 2 June 1764 [-?-], daughter of William Wheeler (BAWB 3:75).

Vaughn (Vaughan), Christopher, m. 14 May 1752 Mary Richards ("Edward Richards Bible," *MBR* 3:160-161). On 22 Sep 1755 Mary was named as a legatee of Edward Richards (MWB 30:26 abst. by Gibb; MDAD 41:20).

Vaughn (Vaughan), Gist, and Rachel Norris were m. on 2 March 1769 (Harrison, "St. John's Parish Register:" 258). On 4 April 1781 Rachel was named as a daughter of Joseph Norris (BAWB 4:31).

Vaughn, Thomas, was charged with bastardy at the Nov 1759 Court (BAMI 1757-1759:241).

Veares, Mary, was charged with bastardy at Aug Court 1717 (BACP IS#IA: 152).

Veintry, Francis, and Susanna Brand were married by banns on 6 Feb 1785 at St. Peter's Catholic Church, Baltimore (*Piet:* 144).

Veirs, Hezekiah, and Ann Clarke were m. by Oct 1791 (Marr Ret. of Rev. John Robinson, Scharf Papers, MS. 1999 at MdHS). On 28 Sep 1795Ann was named as a daughter of Samuel Clark (BAWB 6:90).

Verly, George, and Elizabeth Freeman were married by banns on 6 May 1795 at St. Peter's Catholic Church, Baltimore (*Piet:* 144).

Vickory, John, was m. to Ann [-?-] when they witnessed the will of John Harryman on 4 Feb 1710/11 (MWB 13:158 abst. in *Md. Cal. of Wills* 3:184). John Vickory died leaving a will dated 5 Nov 1711 and proved 12 Jan 1711/2. He left *Jack's Double Purchase* to his son Richard Stevenson Vickory and his heirs. His wife Ann was named extx., and was left his personal estate for life. If his son should die without issue, the land was to pass to Richard King Stevenson, son of Edward and Mary Stevenson (MWB 13:244 abst. in *Md. Cal. of Wills* 3:216).

Vickory, Richard Stevenson, d. by 2 March 1735 when George Buchanan, administrator, posted bond to administer his estate (BAAB 4:195). On 25 April 1736; his brother of the half-blood, John Plowman renounced his right of administration (MDTP 30:147).

Vickers, Amos, in his will made 22 March 1800 named his nephews William Jones Dutton and Benjamin Vickers Dutton (BAWB 6:287).

Viers, Hezekiah, m. by 28 Sep 1795 Ann, daughter of Samuel Clark (BAWB 6:90; BAAD 13:12, 13).

Villeneuve, Lewis, and Jeanne Antoinette Groc, free French Mullatoes, were m. by lic. on 24 June 1800 at St. Peter's Catholic Church, Baltimore (*Piet:* 144).

Vine, Godfrey: on 11 April 1737 George Farmer, Church Warden, was ordered by the vestry of St. George's Parish to inquire whether Godfrey Vine and Sarah Beddo cohabit together still. On 6 June 1737 Vine and Beddo were summoned to appear at the next vestry and answer their contempt. On 5 July 1737 Vine and Beddo appeared, but could not prove their marriage. The vestry was pleased to give them until the last Saturday of the month to produce a certificate. On 4 Oct 1737 Godfrey Vine and Sarah Beddo produced a certificate to show they had been married on 14 Feb 1733 by Rev. James Cox, minister of St. Paul's Parish in Queen Anne's Co. (Reamy, *St. George' Parish Registers:* 104).

Viner (Winer), Jane, was charged with bastardy at the March 1743/4 Court; she confessed on 5 June 1744 and was ordered to be whipped with 15 lashes (BACP 1743-1745, pp. 154, 237-238). Her son Henry Viner was b. 20 Feb 1743 (Reamy, *St. George's Parish Register:* 74).

Virchworth. See Urquhart.

Vizer, [-?-], m. by 9 April 1787 Sarah, daughter of William Fitch, who described himself as 'being very ancient' (BAWB 4:284).

Vogel, Mr., and Miss Mary Fowble, both of Baltimore, were married on Wednesday evening by Rev. Kurtz (*Baltimore Telegraphe* 18 Aug 1797).

Voghea, John, m. by 1 May 1694 Elizabeth, relict and admx. of William Deyson (MDTP 15C:52, 16:170). (See Devegha, John).

Volkman, Mr. P. A., merchant of this city, was m. last Thurs. at New Bremen, to Miss Sophia Amelung, daughter of J. P. Amelung, Esq. (*Federal Gazette and Baltimore Daily Advertiser* 16 Aug 1797).

Vomijim, Jeremiah, and Miss Mary Kittleman were m. on Sun. eve. by Rev. Richards (*Baltimore Telegraphe* 19 Nov 1799).

Vouchell, [-?-], m. by 3 Aug 1769, [-?-], sister of Moses Goodwin whose administration account of that date showed payments to his sister's children, Augustine. Obadiah, David, Joseph, John, and Mary Vouchell (MDAD 62:254).

"W"

Waddle, Mr. William, was m. yesterday eve. to Miss Sally Cox, both of the town (*Federal Intelligencer and Baltimore Daily Gazette* 15 Jan 1795).

Wade, John, native of Santa Cruce, widower, and Charlotte Rossiter, daughter of Thomas and Charlotte, both dec., were m. by lic. on 7 Aug 1800 at St. Peter's Catholic Church, Baltimore (*Piet:* 144).

Wagers, Francis, and Patience Logsdan [*i.e.,* Logsdon] were married by banns on 7 Sep 1791 at St. Peter's Catholic Church, Baltimore (*Piet:* 144).

Wagers, William, m. by 22 Sep 1775 Ann, daughter of Luke Mercer (Mercier) (BAWB 3:305).

Wages, Luke (Luck), and Patience Phillips were m. on 2 April 1789 (Marr, Returns of Rev. William West, Scharf Papers, MS. 1999 at MdHS). On 25 May 1789 Patience was named as the extx. of William Phillips (*q.v.*) (BAAD 9:330, 10:310).

Waggoner, Herman, m. by 12 June 1792, Mary daughter of Henry Fite (BAAD 11:69).

Waggoner, John Andrew, of Baltimore, will not pay the debts of his wife Meilche (*Maryland Gazette or Baltimore General Advertiser* 21 June 1791). Andrew Wagner and Milkey Moberry were m. by lic. dated 16 Nov 1787 (BAML)

Waggoner, Michael, m. by 17 Dec 1783 Barbara, daughter of Anthony Haines (BAWB 4:521).

Waggoner, Yost, m. by 24 Dec 1787 [Margaret? widow], who received her thirds of the estate of Andrew Welthy (q.v.) (BAAD 9:140).

Wagner, Andrew, advertises his wife Margaret has left him (*Federal Intelligencer and Baltimore Daily Gazette* 25 March 1795).

Wagner, Jacob, Esq., of the City of Philadelphia, was m. last eve. by Rev. Mr. Kurtz, to Miss Rachel Raborg, daughter of Christopher Raborg of this City (*Federal Gazette and Baltimore Daily Advertiser* 8 Aug 1798).

Wainwright, Thomas, and Susanna Richardson were m. on 21 Jan 1705/6 (Harrison, "St. George's Parish Register:" 201, 203). On 26 Aug 1706 they posted bond to administer the estate of Mark Richardson (q.v.) (BAAB 2:539; INAC 26:82; MDTP 21:186). Susanna had m. 1st, George Utie (*q.v.*).

Wakefield, Robinson, of Darlington, Bishopric of Durham (Eng,), m. by 25 April 1763 Ann, daughter of Edward Fell, formerly of Md. (PCLR DD#3:143). **See following entry.**

Wakefield, Robinson, late of Sunderland near the Sea, Co. Durham, now of Northfield, Co. Northumberland, m. by 2 Aug 1769 Ann, widow of Edward Fell (BACT B#G:254). **See previous entry.**

Wakeman, Dr. Edward, and Elizabeth Prichard, on 26 June 1746 were returned to [-?-] at the August Court ("St. John's and St. George's Parish Register Vestry Proceedings," MS. at the MdHS.).

Walcox. See Wallox.

Walker, [-?-], m. by 9 Oct 1786 Elizabeth, daughter of Joseph Shaule (BAAD 8:321).

Walker, [-?-], m. by 11 Sep 1800 Jemima, daughter of Elizabeth Miller, spinster and widow (BAWB 6:341).

Walker, Charles, b. 9 Nov 1744, m. on 1 Sep 1772 by Rev. William Edmiston, Ann Cradock, b. 23 Feb 1755 ("Walker-Cradock Bible Record," at MdHS; *MGSB* 39 (4) 530-534).

Walker, Charles, of Baltimore, and Miss Mary Woodward were m. last Thurs. eve. by Rev. John Hagerty (*Baltimore Evening Post* 3 May 1793). Charles Walker and Mary Woodard [*sic*] were m. 2 May 1793 (Marr. Returns of Rev. John Hagerty, Scharf Papers, MS.199 at MdHS). Charles Walker m. by 7 March 1800 Mary, daughter of John Woodward (BALR WG#61:275).

Walker, Elijah, and Belinda Magar were married by license dated 14 Feb 1793 (BAML). He d. by 20 Feb 1799, by which date Belinda had m. 2nd, Samuel Lilley (*q.v.*) (BAAD 12:547).

Walker, Dr. George, and Mary Hanson were m. 14 Nov 1728 Harrison, "St. Paul's Parish Register:" 149). On 28 May 1730 Mary was named as the admx. of Jonathan Hanson (q.v.) of Baltimore Co., and mother of Mary Hanson (MDAD 10:279, 11:689, 692; BALR TB#D:142).

Walker, Dr. James, b. 11 May 1705 in Peterhead, Scotland, m. 26 Aug 1731, Susanna Gardner, b. 12 March 1713 in Md., daughter of John Gardener of Anne Arundel Co. ("Reverend William West Bible," *MBR* 5:208; "Walker-Cradock Bible," *MGSB* 39 (4) 530; PCLR PL#8:89).

Walker, Jesse, and Mary Price were m. on 10 July 1787 (Marr. Register of Rev. Lewis Richards, MS.690 at MdHS). On 12 May 1798 Mary was named as a daughter of Absolom and Martha Price (BALR WG#54:435).

Walker, Maple (Mabel), servant of Maurice Baker, was charged with bastardy at Aug Court 1739 and indicted at Nov Court 1759 (BACP HWS&TR:2, 88).

Walker, Mary, was charged with bastardy at June Court, 1739, and again at Aug Court 1739; she was indicted at Nov Court 1739 (BACP HWS#1A: 54, HS&TR: 2, 87).

Walker, Philip, advertised his wife Comfort had left him (*Dunlap's Maryland Gazette* 11 Feb 1777). Again, he would not pay the debts of his wife Comfort (*Maryland Journal and Baltimore Advertiser* 6 Aug 1782).

Walker, Rachel, in 1757 had two children: George, aged 9, bound to Edward [-?-], and Jonathan, aged 6, bound to Ephraim Gover (BAMI 1755-1763).

Walker, Rebecca, in Jan 1798 was bound to Belinda Walker (BAOC 3:248).

Walker, Robert, and Sarah Murphy were m. by lic. on 11 July 1793 at St. Peter's Catholic Church, Baltimore (*Piet:* 144).

Walker, Samuel, merchant, was married this evening by the Rev. Patrick Allison, to Miss Fanny S. Smith, daughter of Nathaniel Smith (*Baltimore Evening Post* 25 Oct 1792).

Walker, William, sailmaker, and Nacky Pumphrey, both of Baltimore, were m. last eve. by Rev. John Hagerty (*Federal Intelligencer and Baltimore Daily Gazette* 4 July 1795). William Walker and Achsah Pumphrey were married by license dated 1 July 1795 (BAML).

Wall, Jacob, and Miss Hannah Jones, both of Baltimore, were m. last eve. by Rev. Mr. Lynch (*Baltimore Daily Repository* 22 March 1793).

Wallace, Cassandra, widow of John Wallace, on 31 d. 8 m. 1769 was reported as having been married by a priest ("Minutes of Deer Creek Meeting," QRNM: 134). [No other marriage reference found].

Waller, Basil, and Sarah Waller were m. on 28 June 1778 (Marr. Returns of Rev. Thomas Chase, Scharf Papers, MS. 1999 at MdHS). On 10 Oct 1787 Sarah was named as a daughter of John Parks (BAWB 4:314).

Waller, John, m. on 24 July 1779 Ann Taylor ("Watts Bible Record," MGRC 3:64). She m. 2nd, William Galloway (q.v.).

Walley (Wolley), John, m. by 1 March 1691 Elizabeth, daughter of Thomas Thurston. She m. 2nd, Charles Ramsey (q.v.) (BALR RM#HS:340; BACP F#1:152: INAC 13A:317).

Wallford. See Warfoot.

Wallis, Elizabeth, was charged with bastardy at the June 1738 Court (BACP HWS#1A: 221).

Wallis, Experience, servant to Col. Hall, was charged with bastardy at the Aug 1740 Court and presented at the Nov 1740 Court (BACP HWS#TR: 290, 361).

Wallis, John, son of Samuel, dec., on 3 d. 11 m. 1761, announced his intention to marry Cassandra Coale, daughter of Skipwith Coale, dec. ("Minutes of Deer Creek Meeting," *QRNM:* 128). John Wallace (Wallis), son of Samuel, and Cassandra Coale, daughter of Skipwith and Margaret, were m. on 3 d. 12 m. 1761 ("Records of Deer Creek Meeting," at MdSA: 6). Cassandra m. 2nd, Phineas Chew (q.v.).

Wallis, Randall, and Ann Worthington were m. by lic. dated 1 June 1795 (HAML). Ann Wallis (late Worthington) on 25 d. 6 m. 1795 was reported to have gone out in marriage to a man not of our society with the assistance of a Baptist teacher ("Minutes of Deer Creek Meeting," *QRNM:* 155-156).

Wallis, Samuel, of Kent Co., son of Samuel and Elizabeth, late of Kent Co., dec. on 28 d. 2 m. 1782, announced his intention to marry Sarah Sharpless, widow of Benjamin Sharpless (*q.v.*), and a daughter of James Rigbie ("Minutes of Deer Creek Meeting," *QRNM:* 141).

Wallox, John, and Elizabeth Jones were m. on 5 Aug 1731 (Harrison, "St. George's Parish Register:" 263). On 31 July 1742 Eliza, now dec., was named as the widow and admx. of Jacob Jones (BAAD 3:29; MDAD 19:191; MDTP 31:295, 313).

Wallston, John, d. by March 1693/4, leaving a widow Margaret who m.2nd, William Osborne (*q.v.*) (*BCF:* 483-484), and 3rd William Wise (*q.v.*).

Wallwin, John Hutchinson, m. by 13 Sep 1793 Ann, daughter of Joseph Rawlins (BAWB 5:151).

Walong, Henry, was charged with bastardy at the June 1750 Court (BACP TR#5:2).

Walsh, Edward, and Catherine Conway were m. by lic. on 9 April 1787 at St. Peter's Catholic Church, Baltimore (*Piet:* 144).

Walsh, Maurice, and Elizabeth Lee, natives of Ireland, were married by banns on 2 Aug 1795 at St. Peter's Catholic Church, Baltimore (*Piet:* 144).

Walsh, Michael, and Anna Catharina Fasbender of Baltimore Co., were m. by lic. on 27 July 1800 at St. Peter's Catholic Church, Baltimore (*Piet:* 144).

Walsh, Peter, and Sarah Cannon, widow, natives of Ireland, were married by banns on 19 June 1796 at St. Peter's Catholic Church, Baltimore (*Piet:* 144).

Walsh, Robert, of Fell's Point, and Miss Steel, were m. last eve. (*Maryland Gazette or Baltimore General Advertiser* 31 Oct 1783). Robert Walsh and Elizabeth Steel were m. by lic. on 1 Nov 1783 at St. Peter's Catholic Church, Baltimore (*Piet:* 144).

Walter, Charles, merchant, was m. last Mon. eve. by Rev. Mr. Ireland, to Mrs. Elizabeth Heidey, both of this city (*Federal Gazette and Baltimore Daily Advertiser* 2 Aug 1799).

Walter, David, m. by 7 March 1786, Anna Maria Winkin ("First Record Book for the Reformed and Lutheran Congregations at Manchester, Baltimore (now Carroll) Co.," *MGSB* 35:282).

Walter, Jacob, m. by 7 March 1765 Catherina Glasserin ("First Record Book for the Reformed and Lutheran Congregations at Manchester, Baltimore (now Carroll) Co.," *MGSB* 35:269; on p. 271 her name is given as Blasserin).

Walter, Jacob, and Sarah Peacock, daughter of Luke Peacock, dec., entered into a marriage contract in 1799 (BACT WG#7:222).

Walters, Alexander, on 11 Nov 1800 was named as a son-in-law of Catherine Haines (BAWB 6:346).

Walters, Jacob, and Ariana Sollers, widow, entered their marriage articles on 1 April 1785 (BALR WG#330). On 31 May 1787 Ariana was named as the extx. of Thomas Sollers (q.v.) (BAAD 9:52). Ariana Walters, in her will made 19 March 1798 named her children Ariana, Eleanor, Helen, Thomas, and Sabrit Sollers and her daughter Sarah Trotten (BAWB 6:93).

Waltham, Thomas, m. by 7 June 1753 Elizabeth, daughter and coheir of James Maxwell of Baltimore Co., dec. (BALR TR#D: 562). She was a grand-daughter of James Maxwell (BALR BB#1:6).

Walton, Elisha, and Elizabeth Tompkins on 5 d. 2 m. 1789 were reported to have been m. by a magistrate ("Minutes of Deer Creek Meeting," QRNM:146). [No other marriage reference found].

Walton, John, m. by 3 May 1787 Ann Jones, daughter and legatee of John and Esther (Hester) Jones (BAWB 4:91, 254; BAAD 10:68, 11:138).

Walton, John, and Barbara Hook were m. by lic. on 1 April 1793 at St. Peter's Catholic Church, Baltimore (*Piet:* 144). She was a daughter of Anthony Hook (BAWB 6:409).

Wammagham, Thomas, on 17 Nov 1774 was charged by the vestry of St. George's Parish with suspicion of illegal cohabitation with Ann Soward (or Howard). On 6 Dec 1774 he produced a certificate stating he had been married by Rev. John Davis to Ann Dulany on 27 Nov 1774 (Reamy, *St. George's Parish Register:* 112).

Wante, Charles Stephen Peter, (widower, native of Gravelines, son of Charles and Mary Ann Audibert, b. in 1756), and Mary Rose Debreuil (widow LaFitte, daughter of John Baptist and Felicity Fauche, native of Petite Anne, St. Domingo), were m. by lic. on 28 July 1796 at St. Peter's Catholic Church, Baltimore (*Piet:* 144).

Wantling, [-?-], m. by 11 Sep 1800 Margaret, daughter of Elizabeth Miller, spinster and widow (BAWB 6:341).

Warburton, Susanna, bore an illegitimate mulatto child about June 1757 and in Nov 1760 was sold into slavery for three years (BAMI 1755-1763: 33).

Ward, Catherine, was charged with bastardy at the Aug 1738 Court (BACP HWS#1A:267).

Ward, Edward, d. by 31 Jan 1788, leaving minor children Sarah, Edward, James, William, and Elizabeth. George Franciscus, guardian, filed an account (BAGA 1:38, 40). In 1786 young Edward, now 15, chose David Tucker as his guardian (BOCP Petition of Edward Ward, 1791).

Ward, Elizabeth, was charged with bastardy at the Nov 1730 Court BACP HWS#7:49).

Ward, Jane, was charged with bastardy at the March 1738/9 Court (BACP HWS#1A:351). Jane was the mother of Eleanor Ward, b. May 1738 Reamy, *St. George's Parish Register:* 61).

Ward, Joseph, in March 1738/9 was charged with begetting a bastard on the body of Prudence Harryman (BACP HWS#TR:38).

Ward, Mary, was charged with bastardy at the March 1740/1 Court and presented at the June 1741 Court. She was charged with bastardy again at the March 1745/6 Court (BACP TB#TR: 2, 78; Liber 1743-1745: 809). She was the mother of Rosanna, b. 27 Jan 1740/1 and William, b. 9 Oct 1745 (both in St. John's Parish (*BCF:* 664).

Ward, Samuel, in his will dated 1 Sep 1731 named his grandchildren: Simeon Collings, Samuel Collings, Amey Collings, and Hannah Ashbrook (MWB 20:356, abst. in *Md. Cal. of Wills* 6:217).

Ward, Sutton Sickelmore, on 9 July 1762 was named as a grandson of Sutton Sickelmore (BAAD 5:304).

Warfield, George F., merchant, and Miss Rebecca Brown of Baltimore Co., were m. yesterday by Rev. Mr. Richards (*Federal Intelligencer and Baltimore Daily Gazette* 2 Nov 1795).

Warfoot (Warfoote, Warforte, Wallford), John, m. by Nov 1693 Mary, extx. of John Nicholson (or Nicholls) (q.v.) (BACP G#1:165; INAC 14:154; MDTP 16:200; BAAD 2:33).

Warking, Harman, m. by 1792 [-?-], daughter of Henry Fite, whose estate was being administered by George Reinecker (BOCP Petition of Herman Warking, 1792).

Warner, Aaron, son of Crosdale and Mary, on 23 d. 9 m. 1790 announced his intention to marry Achsah Morgan, daughter of John Morgan, dec. and wife Mary ("Minutes of Deer Creek Meeting," *QRNM:* 148).

Warner, Asa, on 27 d. 9 m. 1798 was reported to have gone out in marriage to a woman not of our society ("Minutes of Deer Creek Meeting," *QRNM:* 159). Asa Warner and Milly Sweeny were m. by lic. dated 4 Aug 1798 (HAML).

Warner, Croasdal, Jr., on 28 d. 7 m. 1791 was reported to have gone out in marriage to a woman not of our society, and accomplished the same by a Baptist Preacher ("Minutes of Deer Creek Meeting," *QRNM:* 149). [No other marriage reference found].

Warner, Cuthbert, son of Joseph and Ruth, on 30 d. 9 m. 1773 stated he intended to marry Rachel Hill, daughter of William and Mary Hill ("Minutes of Deer Creek Meeting," *QRNM:* 135).

Warner, George, admin., on 18 March 1790 posted bond to administer the estate of Barbara W..., otherwise Barbara Role (BAAB 7:286). **N.B.:** A George Warner and Elizabeth Waggoner were married by license dated 23 May 1794 (FRML).

Warner, Martha. See Jacob Forwood.

Warner, William, and Jane Hicks were m. on 19 Sep 1793 (Marr. Register of Rev. Lewis Richards, MS.690 at MdHS). Jane Warner, (formerly Hicks), on 27 d. 12 m. 1793 had a complaint made against her for having her marriage accomplished by the assistance of a hireling to a man not of our society. His name was James ("Minutes of Baltimore Meeting," QRNM: 222).

Warrell, Henry, m. by 21 April 1769 Julietha, daughter of John and Julietha Spicer (BALR (BALR AL#A: 465).

Warren, Thomas, d. by 31 Aug 1738 having m. Mary, mother of Jonathan, Lewis, and Thomas Jones (BALR IS#IK: 533, HWS#1-A :69, 70, 71).

Warters. See Waters.

Washington, Herman, m. by 12 June 1795 [-?-], heir of Henry Fite (BAAD 12:30).

Washington, Philip, m. by 14 May 1707, Alice (formerly Alice Bond), extx. of Peter Bond (INAC 26:330; BAAD 2:82).

Waterhouse, William, and Ann Butler, on 12 d. 4 m. 1798 declared their intention to marry ("Minutes of Baltimore Meeting," QRNM:230).

Waters, [-?-], m. by 5 Oct 1778 Eleanor, daughter of Mary Bowen (BAWB 4:355).

Waters, (Warters?), [-?-], m. by 6 Dec 1781 Ann, daughter of John Colegate, farmer (BAWB 3:470).

Waters, [-?-], m. by 28 March 1798 Elizabeth, daughter of Mary Woodward and guardian of Mary, Sophia, Joseph, and James Waters (BAWB 6:98; BAAD 13:215).

Waters (Warters), Hannah, confessed to bastardy at the June 1755 Court and named Abraham Isaac Whitacre as the father (BACP BB#B:401).

Waters, Henry, and Ann Beck were m. on 14 July 1748 (Harrison, "St. John's Parish Register:" 197). On 26 Oct 1748 Ann was named as the admx. of Mat. (Matthew) Beck (q.v.) (MINV 37:213).

Waters, James, merchant of Baltimore, and Eliza Beshares of Prince George's Co., were m. (*Maryland Journal and Baltimore Advertiser* 13 Jan 1792).

Waters, Martin, and Dianna Harroman [*sic*] were married by banns on 5 March 1791 at St. Peter's Catholic Church, Baltimore (*Piet:* 144).

Waters, Philip, on 14 Oct 1786 executed a deed of gift to the children he had by his late wife Anne: James Waters and Ann Waters (BACT 1785-1788, MS 2865 at MdHS: 213).

Waters, Philip, and Nelly Hincks were m. on 9 Sep 1789 (Harrison, "St. Paul's Parish Register:" 221). Mary Hincks, in her will made 28 March 1798 named her daughter Eleanor Waters and her grandchildren Joseph, James, and Mary Sophia Waters (BAWB 6:89).

Waters, Dr. Richard, m. 2 June 1785 Margaret Smith ("Baxter Bible Record," *HMGB* 12:37).

Waterson, Robert, and Jane Faris, both of Baltimore, were m. on Thurs. by Rev. Smith (*Baltimore American* 19 July 1800; the *Baltimore Telegraphe* of 19 July 1800 gives the groom's name as William Waterson).

Watkins, [-?-], m. by 25 Feb 1723/4 Mary, daughter of William Wright (MWB 18:263 abst. in *Md. Cal. of Wills* 5:166).

Watkins, Archibald Washington, and Elizabeth Parsons, both of Fell's Point, were m. last eve. by Rev. Riggin (*Baltimore American* 28 June 1799).

Watkins, Daniel Scott, and Eliz. 'Hatten'. were m. on 29 Dec 1761 (Harrison, "St. John's Parish Register:" 223). On 14 Nov 1770 Eliza was named as a daughter of John Hatton (BAWB 3:159).

Watkins, Esau, of Chester Co., Pa., m. by 9 April 1750 Mary, heir of St. Leger Codd (BALR TR#C:405).

Watkins, Francis, m by 7 June 1681 Christiana Waites, daughter of the wife of Thomas Long (BALR IR#AM: 121; BALR IR#AM:123 gives her name as Christiana Wright).

Watkins, John, m. by 9 Nov 1742 Margaret, daughter of William Loney (BAAD 3:263).

Watkins, John, m. by 13 May 1760 Hester Carpenter, Jr., heir of Elizabeth Carpenter (the widow of John Carpenter) who m. George Plater (BALR B#H:115).

Watkins, John, and Purify Greenfield were m. on 9 Oct 1754 (Harrison, "St. George's Parish Register:" 355). On 30 May 1763 he was named as an heir of William Greenfield (BAWB 3:4). On 14 May 1764, John's wife was named as a daughter of William Greenfield (BAAD 6:99; MDAD 51:112).

Watkins, Nicholas, d. by 15 June 1763 by which time his widow and admx. had m. 2nd, John Ijams (q.v.) (BAAD 6:49).

Watkins, Rebecca, on 26 Jan 1787 was named as a daughter-in-law in the will of Elisha Parks (BAWB 4:224).

Watkins, Richard, and Elizabeth Beddo, daughter of Absolom Beddo of Montgomery Co. were m. last Thurs. (*Federal Gazette and Baltimore Daily Advertiser* 18 March 1800).

Watkins, Thomas, and Elizabeth Spurrier, daughter of William Spurrier, both of Elk Ridge, were m. last Thurs. by Rev. Bend (*Federal Gazette and Baltimore Daily Advertiser* 23 March 1799).

Watkins, Uriah, in March 1738/9 was named as the father of Mary Watkins' illegitimate child (BACP (BACP HWS#1A:3511, HWS#TR:306).

Watson, John, in March 1754 was charged with begetting a bastard on the body of Elizabeth Sulaven [Sullivan?] (BACP BB#A:30).

Watson, Mary, was charged with bastardy at the Aug 1740 Court, and Ulick Burke submitted a bill for the child's care (BACP HWS&TR: 295).

Watson, William, and Bethia Thornbury were m. on 5 May 1757 (Harrison, "St. John's Parish Register:" 215). Jean Butler, widow, for love and affection, on 2 Oct 1772 conveyed property to William Watson and wife Bethiah (BACT Liber 1773-1784, MS 2865 at MdHS: 421).

Watters, Catharine, in 1765 complained that Thomas McCool had used her child ill (BAMI 1765: 46).

Watts, [-?-], m. by 5 Oct 1778 Sarah, daughter of Mary Bowen (BAWB 4:355).

Watts, Benjamin, will not pay the debts contracted by his wife Susannah, she being guilty of many misdemeanors (*Federal Gazette and Baltimore Daily Advertiser* 28 Nov 1796). Benjamin Watts and Susanna Griffin were m. 13 July 1794 (Harrison, "St. Paul's Parish Register:" 291).

Watts, Edward, Esq., of Port Tobacco. was m. last eve. by the Rev. Mr. Ireland to Elizabeth Aisquith, daughter of Mr. William Aisquith, of this city (*Federal Gazette and Baltimore Daily Advertiser* 10 July 1797).

Watts, George, and Mary Thompson were married by banns on 22 May 1791 at St. Peter's Catholic Church, Baltimore (*Piet:* 144).

Watts, John, and Anne Body were m. on 15 April 1743 (Harrison, "St. Paul's Parish Register:" 166). On 23 Aug 1786 Ann was named as a coheir of Alanson [Hanson?] Body, and sister of Penelope wife of Dixon Stansbury. Ann Watts was the mother of John Watts (BALR WG#Z: 257). Dixon Stansbury had m. Penelope Body on 4 Jan 1740/1 (Harrison, "St. John's Parish Register:" 170). On 29 Oct 1765 Eliz. Trotten named a granddaughter Penelope Watts (BAWB 3:44).

Watts, John, in Aug 1744 was charged with begetting a bastard on the body of Jane Story (BACP 1743-1745:323).

Watts, John, d. by 8 May 1767 when Sarah Watts, admx., posted an admin. bond for £1000., with Edward Sweeting and Solomon Bowen as sureties (BAAB 4:133). By his first wife John Watts was the father of: John, b. 21 Jan 1746, Edward, b. 24 March 1749, and Penelope, b. 5 April 1751 (Reamy, *St. Paul's Parish Register:* 21). Sarah Watts filed an account on 2 Nov 1767 citing an inventory of £426.10.4, and listing payments of £28.8.8 (MDAD 57:379). She filed a second account on 21 June 1768, listing payments of £40.3.9, and mentioning nine children (MDAD 58:230). Sarah Watts, widow of John Watts, petitioned the Orphans Court, stating that she and her husband had six children: Josias, b. 23 Jan 1751, Dickinson, b. 17 March 1752, d. 4 March 1784, Beal, b. 29 Jan 1760, has been gone to sea for 6 or 7 years, Thomas, b. 28 Feb 1762, Nathaniel, b. 1 July 1764, and Benjamin, b. 23 Sep 1766.Her husband had three other children by a former wife. When her husband died, the petitioner was left with about £38 in the inventory and had six children to raise and educate, which she did. Her son Benjamin is in a good trade, and will be free 12 months and 8 days from now. She refutes the claim of her stepson John to claim his share of Beal Watts' estate. She mentioned doctors' bills and inoculation for the small pox. She asks to be acquitted from the claims of her stepson. (BOCP Petition of Sarah Watts, [date not given]).

Watts, John, son of John Watts who had d. intestate in 1767, stated that Sarah Watts, stepmother of the petitioner, admin. the estate, and in the final account there was a balance of £516.7.4. In 1780 Bale Watts, the petitioner's brother, and one of the representatives of the deceased went to sea, and has not been heard from for the past 5 years. In 1783 Dickinson Watts [another] of your petitioner's brothers, and rep. of the deceased, died intestate without having received his legal share of his father's estate. The petitioner claims to be entitled to his brothers' shares of John Watts' estate (BOCP Petition of John Watts, [date not given]).

Watts, Sarah, in March 1772 was fined for bastardy; the child died (BAMI 1772, 1775-1781: 9)

Watts, Thomas, and Lydia Bowen were married by license dated 3 Sep 1783 (BAML). On 9 Aug 1791, Thomas Watts' wife received an equal share of the estate of Nathan Bowen (BAAD 10:419).

Way, Michael, and Mary Way were married by license dated 23 July 1781 (BAML). On 30 Nov 1789 Mary was named as a daughter of John Fowle (BAAD 10:84).

Wayman, Hezekiah, and Elizabeth were m. by 9 Nov 1800 when their daughter Elizabeth was b. ("Benedict Lee Bible," *MBR* 1:149-150).

Weadge. See Wedge.

Weary, William, and Miss Ann Merritt, both of Fell's Point, were m. last eve. by Rev. Bend (*Baltimore American* 20 Sep 1799).

Weasly. See Wesley.

Weatherly (Wetherby), Daniel, and Elizabeth Gorsuch were married by license dated 7 Dec 1785 (BAML). On 10 Aug 1791 Elizabeth was named as the extx. of David Gorsuch (BAAD 10:423). On 23 June 1786, Weatherly's wife was named as a daughter of John Woodward (BAAD 8:280). Daniel Wetherby warned all persons from dealing with his wife, formerly Elizabeth Gorsuch (*Maryland Journal and Baltimore Advertiser* 22 April 1791).

Weaver, Barbara, extx of Adam Brandt, on 3 Jan 1775 posted bond to administer the estate (BAAB 1:269). She m. by 1787 Stephen Bahon or Bahn (q.v.).

Weaver, Daniel, of Baltimore, will not be responsible for the debts of his wife Eve (*Maryland Gazette or Baltimore General Advertiser* 9 July 1790).

Weaver, George, and Barbara Bearinger were married by license dated 8 Feb 1783 (FCML), Barbara m. 2nd, Joseph Granger (q.v.)

Weaver, Lewis, and Eliza Lambert were m. on 13 June 1794 (Marr. Returns of Rev. David Kurtz, Scharf Papers, MS.1999 at MdHS). Lewis Weaver and his wife

Elizabeth, on 20 Dec 1796, recorded a deed stating that they have agreed mutually to live apart (BALR WG#YY: 174). Lewis Weaver stated he would not pay the debts of his wife Elizabeth (*Federal Gazette and Baltimore Daily Advertiser* 11 Feb 1797). Lewis Weaver and Elizabeth Lombord were m. by lic. dated 13 June 1794 (BAML).

Webb, Hannah, daughter of James Webb, on 31 d., 3 m. 1774, was reported as guilty of outgoing in marriage ("Minutes of Deer Creek Meeting," *QRNM:* 136). [No other marriage reference found].

Webb, James, married Eleanor Row in 1778. The marriage was sworn to on 4 May 1784, by Catherine Holland (Harrison, "St. Paul's Parish Register:" 186). In Aug 1779 Webb stated that he would not pay the debts of his wife Ellinor because of the remarks of a certain Philip Walters Henerman (*Maryland Journal and Baltimore Advertiser* 31 Aug 1779).

Webb, Mary, daughter of James and Mary, on 31 d. 10 m. 1776 was announced to have been married by a priest to man not of our society ("Minutes of Deer Creek Meeting," *QRNM:* 137). [No other marriage reference found].

Webb. Moses, on 27 d. 11 m. 1800 was reported to have accomplished his marriage to a woman not of our society by the assistance of a Baptist Preacher ("Minutes of Deer Creek Meeting," *QRNM:* 162). [No other marriage reference found].

Webb, Richard, of Deer Creek MM, and Mary Maulsby on 31 d. 10 m. 1789 declared their intention to marry ("Minutes of Gunpowder Meeting," *QRNM:* 87). In April 1794 Richard and Mary were admins. of John Maulsby (BALR WG#OO: 6). On 31 Nov 1799 Mary Maulsby, was named as the acting admx. of John Maulsby (BAAD 13:158).

Weber, Georg, m. by 5 May 1790, Barbara Rubin ("First Record Book for the Reformed and Lutheran Congregations at Manchester, Baltimore (now Carroll) Co.," *MGSB* 35:285).

Webster, Dorothy. See Dorothy Tyson.

Webster, Isaac, Sr., m. by 19 Jan 1732 Margaret, daughter of James Lee, by whom he had a son Isaac Webster b. by 1755 (BALR BB#I: 508; MWB 20:567 abst. in *Md. Cal. of Wills* 6: 253).

Webster, Isaac, on 3 d. 1 m. 1788 stated it had been his lot to be m. by a hireling priest ("Minutes of Deer Creek Meeting," *QRNM:* 145). [No other marriage reference found].

Webster, Isaac, of Deer Creek Meeting, and Elizabeth Hopkins of Baltimore Meeting, on 14 d. 3 m. 1799 declared their intention to marry ("Minutes of Baltimore Meeting," *QRNM:* 233).

Webster, James, in his will made 12 Oct 1795 named his daughter Mary, wife of Nathan Lufborogh of Philadelphia (BAWB 7:50).

Webster, John, of Roan Oak, in June 1758 had his son John bound to Michael Webster and in Aug 1757 his son Michael, aged 13 next 15 Jan, bound to Daniel Anderson house carpenter (BAMI 1755-1763).

Webster, John Skinner, and Elizabeth Thornburgh were m. 12 June 1800 (Harrison, "St. Paul's Parish Register:" 387). Elizabeth Webster, formerly Thornburgh, on 13 d. 11 mo. 1800 had a complaint made for her marrying with the assistance of a hireling ("Minutes of Baltimore Meeting," *QRNM:* 238). John Skinner Webster, Esq., of Harford Co., was m. this forenoon by Rev. Mr. Ireland, to Elizabeth Thornburg, daughter of Joseph Thornburg, merchant, of this city (*Federal Gazette and Baltimore Daily Advertiser* 12 June 1800).

Webster, Joseph, on 28 d. 6 m. 1792 was reported to have been m. by a hireling preacher ("Minutes of Deer Creek Meeting," *QRNM:* 151). Joseph Webster and Martha Chauncey were m. by lic. dated 30 May 1792 (HAML).

Webster, Michael, m. by 3 March 1728 Elizabeth, daughter of Nathaniel Giles (BALR IS#1: 283; MWB 20:105 abst. in *Md. Cal. of Wills* 6:172).

Webster, Michael, mariner, m. by 8 Sep 1760 Elizabeth, daughter of John Giles, dec. (BALR B#Q: 633). On 29 March 1765 Elizabeth was named as the admx. of Joseph Bankson (BALR B#O: 136). Joseph Bankson and Elizabeth Slemaker, widow of James Slemaker (*q.v.*) were m. on 16 Jan 1752 (Harrison, "St. Paul's Parish Register:" 166). In her will made Aug 1786, Elizabeth Webster named her sons John Slemaker and James and Joseph Bankson, her daughter Mary Mitchell, and her grandchildren James, Charles, and Arianan [sic] Slemaker (BAWB 4:324).

Webster, Richard, m. by 10 Feb 1773 [-?-], daughter of Alice Lester (BACT B#G:452).

Webster, Samuel, on 20 d. 2 m. 1794 was found guilty of marrying a woman contrary to the good order. as Samuel, son of Isaac, he was charged with marrying with the assistance of a hireling teacher ("Minutes of Deer Creek Meeting," *QRNM:* 154). [No other marriage reference found].

Wedge, Joseph, and Mary Jubill were m. by lic. on 18 Jan 1787 at St. Peter's Catholic Church, Baltimore (*Piet:* 144). Joseph Weadge [sic], stated he would not pay the debts of his wife Mary, formerly Mary Juble. "Now, Devil, do your worst" (*Maryland Journal and Baltimore Advertiser* 13 July 1790).

Weeks, John, m. by 21 Feb 1790 Mary, daughter of Robert Love Pitstow (BAWB 5:175).

Weems, James, m. by 21 Jan 1750 Ann, admx. of Thomas Crompton (in the administration account of James Scarff (MDAD 29:137).

Wegley, [-?-], m. by 11 Jan 1787 Elizabeth, daughter of Christopher Duke (BAWB 4:290).

Weickel, Frantz, m. by 5 Sep 1765 Anna Elisabeta Dornbachin ("First Record Book for the Reformed and Lutheran Congregations at Manchester, Baltimore (now Carroll) Co.," *MGSB* 35:269).

Weir, Thomas, m. by 1 May 1790 [-?-], dau of William Beasman (BAAD 10:136).

Weiss, Adam, m. by 21 March 1760, Maria Elisabeth Grafin ("First Record Book for the Reformed and Lutheran Congregations at Manchester, Baltimore (now Carroll) Co.," *MGSB* 35:265).

Weiss, Peter, m. by 8 Feb 1788, Anna Maria Meyerin ("First Record Book for the Reformed and Lutheran Congregations at Manchester, Baltimore (now Carroll) Co.," *MGSB* 35:283).

Welch, [-?-], m. by 27 July 1784, Margaret, daughter of Rowland Smith, stone-mason (BAWB 4:7).

Welch, Ann, was charged with bastardy at the Nov 1734 Court (BACP HWS#9:350, 365).

Welch, John, and Betsy Davis were married by license dated 3 Sep 1783 (BAML). On 5 July 1788 he was identified as a 'natural son' of John Welch, the testator, and who had m. Betsy Davis of Montgomery Co., daughter of Thomas Davis, dec. (BAWB 4:165).

Welch, Thomas, b. 5 Nov 1742 son of Francis and Mary, and Mary Mitchell, b. 8 April 1752, daughter of Thomas and Hannah, were m. on 11 May 1788 ("Thomas Mitchell Bible," *MBR* 3:126-128).

Welch, William, m. Judith [-?-], and d. by 26 July 1726 at which time she had m. 2nd, Charles Robinson (q.v.) (MDTP 28:310, 32:95).

Welch, William, on 19 April 1783 was named as a grandson in the will of Samuel Stansbury (BAWB 3:539)

Welch, William, m. by 16 Dec 1791 [-?-], heir of Thomas Gorsuch (BAAD 10:503).

Wellmore, William, was m. last Thurs. eve. by Rev. Mr. Hagerty, to Miss Ann Ridgely, both of this city (*Federal Gazette and Baltimore Daily Advertiser* 23 Nov 1797).

Wells, [-?-], m. by 1763 Leah, daughter of Henry Owings (BAWB 2:185; MWB 31:1096).

Wells, Benjamin, m. by 1 Dec 1749 daughter of Henry Butler of Baltimore Co. (MDAD 27:252).

Wells, Charles, m. by 3 June 1726 Sarah, extx. of Anthony Arnold (q.v.) of Baltimore Co. (BAAD 3:62; MINV 10:105; MDAD 7:461). She was also the admx. or extx. of John Wright (q.v.) of Baltimore Co. (MINV 11:255; MDTP 27:326).

Wells, Charles, m. by 16 Feb 1765 Sarah, daughter of Francis Dorsey, whose administration account of 17 Jan 1752 names a 20 year old daughter Sarah (MDTP 41: 35; MDAD 32:10).

Wells, Charles, m. by 10 Nov 1794 Nancy, sister of William Lane (BAWB 5:208).

Wells, Cornelius, and Charlotte Craighead were m. on 13 Feb 1783 Harrison, "St. Paul's Parish Register:" 184). On 10 Nov 1786 Charlotte was named as a daughter of Jemima Craghead who also named a granddaughter Harriet Wells (BAWB 4:250). Charlotte Wells, extx., on 14 June 1787 posted bond to administer Jemima Craghead's estate (BAAB 7:107).

Wells, Cyprian, b. 5 Nov 1752 and Margaret White, b. 19 Oct 1762 were m. on 13 Sep 1778 (Marr. Returns of Rev. Thomas Chase, Scharf Papers, ms 1999 at MdHS; "Cyprian Wells Bible," *MBR* 7:200).

Wells, Capt. George, m. by 12 Oct 1670 Blanch. daughter of Samuel and Johanna Goldsmith (MWB 1:442, abst. in *Md. Cal. of Wills* 1:62; MDTP 5;93; MWB 6:26 abst. in *Md. Cal. of Wills* 2:35). On 16 Dec 1702 Blanche Wells, admx., posted bond to administer the estate of Michael Foy (BAAB 3:68).

Wells, George, Jr., m. by 6 July 1708, Mary, widow and extx. of Robert Gibson (q.v.) of Baltimore Co. (INAC 28:142; MDTP 21:29; BAAD 1:121).

Wells, George, shipwright of Fell's Point, now residing in Philadelphia, d. by 1 Nov 1783 having m. Lydia, sister of Mary Holton (BAWB 3:578).

Wells, James, m. by 6 Oct 1789 Catherine, a legatee of Richard Owings (BAAD 10:60).

Wells, John, m. by 9 April 1762 Dinah, daughter of William Cromwell, late of Anne Arundel Co., dec. (PCLR DD#2:70; MDTP 43:528; BAAD 12:7).

Wells, John, and Rachel Gassaway, on 28 d. 9 m. 1776 declared their intention to marry ("Minutes of Gunpowder Meeting," *QRNM:* 68). John Wells of Baltimore and Rachel Gazaway [*sic*] of Elk Ridge were m. last Tues. (*Dunlap's Maryland Gazette* 5 Nov 1776).

Wells, Joseph, m. by 3 March 1791 Rosanna, who received a share of the estate of Jacob Sindall, who left a widow Temperance (BAAD 10:308).

Wells, Mary, was charged with bastardy at the Aug 1728 Court (BACP HWS#6:33).

Wells, Richard, Jr., m, by 7 Aug 1754 Jane, daughter of Jane Renshaw, who, on 7 Aug 1754, for love and affection, conv. to Cassandra, Lurana, Elizabeth, and Susanna Wells, daughters of Richard Wells, Jr. and his wife Jane (who was a daughter of said Jane Renshaw) (BACT TR#E:150).

Wells, Thomas, and Elizabeth Howard were m. on 16 Sep 1736 (Harrison, "St. Paul's Parish Register:" 155). On 3 July 1738 Elizabeth was named as a daughter of Joshua Howard (MWB 21:208 abst. in *Md. Cal. of Wills* 7:256).

Wells, William, m. by 4 Sep 1760 Sarah, daughter of William Jenkins (MWB 31:316).

Wells, William, m. by 1 Sep 1763 Fenecil [Rachel?], daughter of William Jenkins (BAAD 6:24).

Welsh, [-?-], m. by 9 Jan 1781 Sarah, daughter of Jacob Young, Sr. (BAWB 3:429).

Welsh, Edward, and Prudence Walker were m. by lic. dated 3 Jan 1789 (BAML). Welsh stated he would not pay the debts of his wife Prudence, who had eloped (*Maryland Journal and Baltimore Advertiser* 15 Sep 1789). Prudence Welsh refuted the charges made by her husband Edward (*Maryland Journal and Baltimore Advertiser* 25 Sep 1789).

Welsh, Capt. John, of this county, and Elizabeth Davis of Montgomery Co. were m. 16th inst. (*Maryland Journal and Baltimore Advertiser* 26 Sep 1783).

Welsh, Marcus, of Baltimore, stated that he would not pay the debts of his wife Hannah, "who hath behaved herself in a dishonorable manner towards me, and may from her natural depravity of mind," may seek to injure me by running me further into debt (*Maryland Journal and Baltimore Advertiser* 26 May 1786).

Welsh, Rezin, m. by 22 March 1778 Ruth, daughter of Francis Davis, Sr., planter of Frederick Co. (BAWB 3:370).

Welsh, Sarah, d. by 18 June 1798; John Welsh was her administrator. The following representatives each received an equal share of 37.19.3: John Welsh, the administrator, William Phillips, Nathan Morris, Mary Welsh, and another John Welsh (BAAD 12:445).

Welthy, Andrew, in his will made 2 Nov 177, left his wife Margaret his entire estate for her life or widowhood (BAWB 3:221). She almost certainly m. 2nd, Yost Waggoner (q.v.).

Wenham, Dinah, was charged with bastardy at the June 1714 Court and named Negro Mingo, a slave of Solomon Sparrow as the father of her child. She was charged again at the Aug 1718 Court (BACP IS#B:505, 53, IS#C:4).

Wersel, Dr. Charles, and Polly Yeiser, daughter of Frederick Yeiser of Baltimore, were m. last Fri. eve. by Rev. Richards (*Baltimore Telegraphe* 17 Sep 1795).

Wesley (Weasly, Wisely), John, m. 8 June 1722 Mary, widow of 1st, Samuel Standiford (q.v.), and 2nd, John Bond (q.v.) (BAWB 1:169; BAAD 1:229, 4:210; MDTP 28:277).

West, Easter, was charged with bastardy at the March 1730/1 Court (BACP (BACP HWS#7:96).

West, George, on 29 d. 7 m. 1790 was reported to have gone out in marriage to a woman not of our society by the assistance of a magistrate ("Minutes of Deer Creek Meeting," *QRNM:* 148). [No other marriage reference found].

West, Hugh, and Sybil Harrison, daughter of Capt. William Harrison and Sarah Halley, were m. on 29 Dec 1725 ("Rev. William West Bible," *MBR* 5:208).

West, James, and Mary [-?-] were m. by 26 Feb 1783 when their daughter Mary was b. ("Henry Thompson Bible," *MBR* 7:185-189).

West, James, Esq., of Baltimore, was m. at Philadelphia last Tues. by Rt. Rev. Bishop White, to Miss Maria Blodget, daughter of Samuel Blodget of that city (*Federal Gazette and Baltimore Daily Advertiser* 10 Feb 1798).

West, Joel, and Miss Julian Francisca Rapp, both of Baltimore, were m. last eve. by Rev. Bend (*Federal Gazette and Baltimore Daily Advertiser* 20 July 1798).

West, John, m. by 13 Oct 1671 Ann widow and relict of Henry Jones and was granted administration on his estate. (MDTP 5:95-96).

West, John, of Prince George's Co., joiner, m. by 22 March 1730 Ann Dews (BALR IS#L:88).

West, Capt. John, m. by12 March 1746 Elizabeth, daughter and residuary legatee of Samuel Maccubbin, Jr. (MDTP 32:62, 33-1:126, 131; BAAD 4:208).

West, Joseph, of Baltimore Town, merchant, and Violetta Howard of Baltimore Co. were m. last Thurs. eve. (*Maryland Journal and Baltimore Advertiser* 14 Dec 1784; see also BALR WG#W: 206 and BAAD 9:49). Ruth Howard, in her will made 6 Sep 1788 named her daughter Violetta, wife of Joseph West (BAWB 5:442).

West, Martha, was charged with bastardy at the Nov 1755 Court and named James Clark as the father of her child (BACP HWS#9:398).

West, Robert, and Sarah Spinks were m. on 10 Nov 1695 (Harrison, "St. George's Parish Register:" 236). On 29 May 1758 Sarah was named as the sister and heir-at-law of Enoch Spinks, dec. (AALR BB#1:141).

West, Sarah, daughter of Robert West, was born 24 Oct 1701 (Reamy, *St. George's Parish Register:* 11). She was charged with bastardy at the June 1721 Court and stated that her father's servant was the father of her child. She was charged again at the March 1723/4 Court and named John Gay as the father of the child (BACP IS#C:49, IS&TW#3:213. She was the mother of: Moses was born 28 March 1721, and Daniel, b. 17 Dec 1734 (Reamy, *St. George's Parish Register:* 21, 23). Daniel West, *alias* Daniel Gay was made levy free at the Nov 1745 Court (BACP 1743-1745:743).

West, Stephen, of Prince George's Co., in his will dated 31 Dec 1789 named Capt. Richard Williams as the father of his (West's) wife (BAWB 4:401).

West, Stephen, of Annapolis, and Nancy Pue, daughter of Dr. Pue of Baltimore, were m. last eve. by Rev. Dr. Bend (*Baltimore Daily Intelligencer* 28 Nov 1794).

West, William, m. Susanna Walker on 28 April 1769 ("Reverend William West Bible," *MBR* 5:208).

Westall, George, and Ann Jacob were m. on 23 Oct 1711 (Harrison, "All Hallow's Parish Register," Anne Arundel Co., MS. at MdHS: 78). Ann m. 2nd, Hugh Merriken (*q.v.*).

Westbury, William, m. by 9 March 1677 Margaret, daughter and heiress of Thomas O'Daniel; he d. by 4 June 1695, and Margaret m. 2nd, Robert Olesse (q.v.) (MDTP 9A:512; BALR RM#HS:466).

Westcombe, Samuel, and Sarah Thomas were m. on 19 Jan 1732 (Harrison, "St. George's Parish Register:" 79). He is almost certainly the Samuel Winthrop (Wintrap) Westcombe who d. by Dec 1743 when Thomas Clayton, posted bond to administer the estate of Samuel Winthrop (Wintrap) Westcombe. On 17 Nov 1743 Sarah Winthrop (Wintrap) [sic] Westcombe renounced the right to administer her husband's estate (BAAB 4:142).

Westernhouse, [-?-], m. by 20 Feb 1789 Agnes, widow of [-?-] Crawford (q.v.), and sister of John Eaton (BAWB 4:341).

Westfield, Mary, aged 9, orphan of William Westfield,, on 25 Nov 1762 was bound to James Heron and wife Mary to age 16 (BAMI 1755-1763).

Weston, John, and Rebecca Day were m. on 6 Feb 1783 (Marr. Returns of Rev. William West, Scharf Papers, MS. 1999 at MdHS; "Original Records of the Young Family of Baltimore County," HMGB 16:15-17, 16:24-27). On 11 July 1789 Rebecca was named as the extx. of Edward Day (q.v.) (BAAD 10:5; **N.B.**: BAAD 8:62, 335 state that Edward Day had d. by 1780).

Wetherby. See Weatherly.

Wethereall, John, m. Sarah Day on 29 Dec 1785 ("Day Bible," The Notebook 15 (2) (June 1999) 9; MBR 2:24-27). Their marriage license was dated 8 Dec 1785 (BAML).

Wewer, George, m. by 12 Aug 1786 Barbara Ruppin ("First Record Book for the Reformed and Lutheran Congregations at Manchester, Baltimore (now Carroll) Co.," *MGSB* 35:282).

Weyand, Peter, m. by 8 Sep 1796 Anna Maria, daughter of Anna Maria Steeg, who was grandmother and sponsor of the child (First German Reformed Church at MdHS: 21).

Whaland, [-?-], m. by 10 April 1773 Elizabeth, daughter of Huldah Smith (who was a widow of Ralph Smith (BAWB 3:248).

Whaland, Thomas, of Kent Co. in his will made 25 Nov 1800 named his nephew Thomas Bishop (BAWB 7:155).

Whalen, [-?-], m. by 1 March 1771 Elizabeth, daughter of Ralph Smith (BAWB 3:193).

Wharton, Moore, and Miss Waln, eldest daughter of Mr. Waln of Baltimore were m. last eve. (*Baltimore Evening Post* 3 Oct 1792).

Whatnaby?, [-?-],m. by 21 Dec 1799 Rachel, legatee and granddaughter of Elizabeth Barrow (BAWB 5:98; BAAD 13: 168).

Whayland, Ann, was charged with bastardy at the Nov 1750 Court and Stephen White confessed to being the father (BACP TR#6:40, 60).

Whayland, Patrick, m. by 2 Nov 1726, Catherine, daughter of Henry Matthews (MINV 11:675; BALR IS#L: 208, HWS#M: 90).

Wheeler, [-?-], m. by 23 d. 11 m. 1770 Elizabeth Dutton who had reportedly gone out in marriage ("Minutes of Gunpowder Meeting," QRNM: 60). [No other marriage reference found].

Wheeler, James, and Elizabeth Jones were m. by lic. dated 20 Jan 1796 (BAML). Elizabeth Wheeler, formerly Jones, on 27 d. 2 m. 1796 was reported as having as having been married by a hireling priest to a man not of our society ("Minutes of Gunpowder Meeting," *QRNM:* 97).

Wheeler, Leonard, and Ann Bond were m. 16 Feb 1741 (Harrison, "St. George's Parish Register:" 322). In his will dated 1 Sep 1747 Wheeler named his wife Ann as one of his execs. (MWB 25:205 abst. in *Md. Cal. of Wills* 9:30).

Wheeler, Leonard, son of Leonard, in March 1762 chose Thomas Bond as his guardian (BAMI 1755-1763).

Wheeler, Solomon, m. 22 d. 11 m., 1745 Rachel Taylor (Quaker Marr. Cert. recorded in BACT TR#E:210).

Wheeler, Thomas, and Elizabeth Hillen were m. on 21 Dec 1748 Harrison, "St. Paul's Parish Register:" 162). On 20 Jan 1748 she was named as the admx. of Solomon Hillen (Hellen) (q.v.) (MDTP 33-2:18; MINV 44:318; MDAD 33:155).

Wheeler, Thomas, m. by 2 May 1758, Sarah, daughter of Elizabeth Scott (MWB 30:493). On 13 March 1744 Sarah was named as a daughter of Daniel Scott (MWB 24:81 abst. by Gibb).

Wheeler, Wayson, and Martha Hughes were married by license dated 27 April 1782 (BAML). On 25 Aug 1785 Martha was named as a daughter of John Hughes (BAWB 4:526). On 11 Nov 1797 Wayson's wife was named as an heir of Benjamin Hughes (BAAD 12:293).

Wheeler, William, Jr., m. by 9 April 1726 Constant, admx. of Stephen Price and sister of John Price, of Baltimore Co. (BALR IS#H:246; MDAD 9:437).

Wheelock, Edward, of Anne Arundel Co., d. by 27 March 1676, by which time his widow Mary, mother of Edward Wheelock, had m. 2nd, Thomas Bucknall (q.v.) (INAC 2:18; MDTP 4C:122, 8:19, 9:159; MWB 4:20).

Whelan, Bartholomew, and Bridget Flaharty, natives of Ireland, were m. by lic. on 23 Nov 1794 at St. Peter's Catholic Church, Baltimore (*Piet:* 144).

Whelan, Basil, and Catherine Riddlemoser were m. by lic. on 11 Feb 1800 at St. Peter's Catholic Church, Baltimore (*Piet:* 144; *Baltimore American* 12 Feb 1800).

Whelan, Laurance, and Elizabeth Williams were m. by lic. on 30 Nov 1787 at St. Peter's Catholic Church, Baltimore (*Piet:* 144).

Wheymer, Philip, carpenter, m. by 28 Dec 1792, Susannah, daughter of Valentine Larsh (BALR WG#KK:114). Philip Vanor [sic] and Susannah Larsh were married by license dated 31 March 1781 (BAML).

Whiffen, Joseph, and Susanna Knight were m. on 30 Oct 1791 (Harrison, "St. Paul's Parish Register:" 254). In 1794 Susanna was named as the mother of Joshua and Susanna Knight (BOCP Petition of Charles Fenton, 1794).

Whiffing, Thomas, and Elizabeth Pontany were married by license dated 31 Dec 1791 (BAML). On 6 Dec 1794 Elizabeth was named as the widow of Edward Pontenay and mother of Lydia and Sarah Pontenay (BALR WG#PP: 504).

Whips, John, m. by 20 Nov 1756 Sarah, daughter of George Ogg (BACT TR#E: 228ff.).

Whitaker (Whiteaker), [-?-], m. by 5 Oct 1733 Ann, daughter of Peter Puttee (Potee) (MWB 22:160 abst. in *Md. Cal. of Wills* 8:75).

Whitaker, [-?-], m. by 15 Feb 1774 Martha, daughter of Morris (Maurice) Baker MWB 39:716, abst. in *Md. Cal. of Wills* 15:145).

Whitaker, Abraham, in Nov 1724 was charged with begetting a bastard on the body of Susanna Temple (BACP IS&TW#4:32).

Whitaker, Abraham, and Ann Poteet were m. on 15 July 1725 (Harrison, "St. John's Parish Register:" 19). Ann Whitaker m. 2nd, by 27 March 1740, William Pike (q.v.).

Whitaker (Whitacre), Abraham Isaac, in June 1755 was charged with begetting a bastard on the body of Hannah Watters (BACP BB:B:401-402).

Whitaker, Charles, and Mary Kembal were m. on 30 Jan 1717/8 (Harrison, "St. George's Parish Register:" 221). On 5 March 1727/8 Mary was named as a daughter of William and Mary (Jones) Kemble (BALR TR#A: 389 and IS#1: 95).

Whitaker, David, exec., on 25 Oct 1797 posted bond to administer the estate of Martha Davidson (BAAB 8:46).

Whitaker, Isaac, and Ann [-?-], were m. by 6 Jan 1792 when their daughter Rachel was b. ("Aquilla Carroll Family Records," MBR 2:16-17).

Whitaker (Whitacar), John, m. by 18 Oct 1760, Mary, daughter of Alexander McComas (BAWB 2:352; MWB 31:179; MDAD 47:447). On 26 April 1762, John

Whitaker was paid for his wife by Thomas and Hannah Miles [Hannah was the widow of Alexander McComas] (BAAD 4:365).

Whitaker, Mark, and Elizabeth Emson were m. on 13 Feb 1717 (Harrison, "St. George's Parish Register:" 220). He d. by May 1732 leaving five children, and his widow Elizabeth who m. 2nd, Francis Taylor (q.v.) (BAAD 3:1170).

Whitaker (Whitacre), Peter, and Amelia Hitchcock were m. on 10 or 12 Feb 1744/5 (Harrison, "St. John's Parish Register:" 192, 240). Amelia m. 2nd, Thomas Fisher (q.v.).

White, [-?-], m. by 12 April 1774 Sarah, daughter of Benjamin Culver (MWB 39:783, abst. in *Md. Cal. of Wills* 15:159).

White, Ann, was charged with bastardy at the Aug 1728 Court and named Michael Taylor as the father of her child (BACP HWS#6:38).

White, James, and Honor King, widow of David King, natives of Ireland, were m. by lic. on 25 Dec 1799 at St. Peter's Catholic Church, Baltimore (*Piet:* 145).

White, Jane, was charged with bastardy at the March 1741/2 Court (BACP TB#TR:294).

White, Capt. Joseph, Jr., and Rosetta Landry were m. by lic. on 14 Feb 1799 at St. Peter's Catholic Church, Baltimore (*Piet:* 145; *Baltimore Telegraphe* 15 Feb 1799).

White, Mary, was charged with bastardy at the March 1718/9 Court, and seems to have borne another child by March 1721/2 (BACP IS#C: 63, IS&TW#1:33).

White, Michael, and Miss Julian Leary of Baltimore, were m. last Tues. by Rev. Bend (*Baltimore Telegraphe* 24 Feb 1798).

White, Robert, and Kezia Wooden were m. on 19 Sep 1782 (Marr. Returns of Rev. William West, Scharf Papers, MS.1999 at MdHS). On 3 May 1790 John Wooden named a grandson Robert White in his will (BAWB 4:425).

White, Capt. Samuel, and Ann Parran Hellen, daughter of David Hellen of Fell's Point, were m. [date not given] (*Maryland Journal and Baltimore Advertiser* 25 Oct 25 Oct 1785). Samuel White and Ann Parren Hellen were m. on 9 Oct 1785 (Marr. Returns of Rev. William West, Scharf Papers. MS. 1999 at MdHS).

White, Capt. Simon, and Jane Lowe, both of this town, were m. [date not given] (*Maryland Journal and Baltimore Advertiser* 1 Aug 1783). Simon White and Jane Lowe were m. on 24 July 1783 (Marr. Returns of Rev. William West, Scharf Papers. MS. 1999 at MdHS).

White, Stephen, in Nov 1750 was charged with begetting a bastard on the body of Ann Whayland (BACP TR#6:40).

White, Stephen, and Hannah Baker were m. on 1 Jan 1751 (Harrison, "St. John's Parish Register:" 202, 241).

White, Thomas, m. by 5 June 1731, Sophia, daughter of John Hall (BALR IS#L:105).

White, William, and Ann White, widow, had their banns published in June 1699 (Harrison, "St. George's Parish Register:" 187). On 20 Feb 1699 [1699/1700], Ann was named as the admx. of Samuel Baker (INAC 19½B:108).

White, William, and Mary Settlemire were m. on 17 July 1782 (Marr. Returns of Rev. William West, Scharf Papers. MS. 1999 at MdHS). On 18 Nov 1783 Mary Sittlemeyer was named as a granddaughter of Mary [-?-] who was the widow of Sebastian Sittlemeyer (BALR WG#T: 8-9).

Whitehead, Eliza (Elizabeth), was charged with bastardy at the March 1723/4 Court and presented at the June 1724 Court (BACP IS&TW#3:201, 309).

Whitehead, Elizabeth, on 5 Nov 1738 was named as a daughter in the will of Elizabeth Finsham (MWB 22:28 abst. in *Md. Cal. of Wills* 8:14). On 24 Nov 1739, Elizabeth

Whitehead, admx., posted bond to administer the estate of William Ingram (q.v.) (BAAB 3:383).

Whitehead, Frances, was charged with bastardy at the Nov 1728 Court (BACP HWS#6:65).

Whitehead, Thomas, in March 1733/4, was charged with begetting a bastard on the body of Johanna Lemmon (BACP HWS#9:199).

Whitlock, Mr., and Miss Montgomery, both of Baltimore. were m. last Sun. by Rev. Ellison (*Baltimore American* 17 April 1800).

Wholestocks , Hannah, servant to Michael Gormacon, was charged with bastardy at the Aug 1724 Court and was presented at the Nov 1724 Court at which time she was sentenced to receive 15 lashes (BACP IS&TW#4:43).

Wiath, Elizabeth, was charged with bastardy in 1722/3 (BACP IS&TW#2:231).

Widerstrand, Thomas, and Mary Charlotte Darington were m. by lic. on 1 Dec 1795 at St. Peter's Catholic Church, Baltimore (*Piet:* 145).

Wiesenthal, Dr. Andrew, of Baltimore, and Miss Sally Van Dyke of Chester were m. last Tues. at Hilltop (*Maryland Journal and Baltimore Advertiser* 7 May 1796).

Wiffen. See Whiffen.

Wiggans, Bazaleel, on 23 d. 4 m. 1795 was reported as having m. a woman not of our society with the assistance of a Baptist teacher ("Minutes of Deer Creek Meeting," *QRNM:* 155). [No other marriage reference found].

Wiggins, Joseph, and Ann Bruce on 24 d. 12 m. announced their intention to marry ("Minutes of Deer Creek Meeting," *QRNM:* 159).

Wigley, Edward, and Mary Eaglestone were married by license dated 2 Sep 18783 IBAML). On 15 April 1788 Edward's wife was named as a legatee of Abraham Eaglestone (BAAD 9:191).

Wigley (Wegley), Isaac, m. by 11 Jan 1787 Elizabeth, daughter of Christopher Duke (BAWB 4:290; BAAD 9:246).

Wild, Sarah, was charged with bastardy at the Nov 1759 Court (BAMI 1757-1759:240).

Wilde, John, in Aug 1720 was charged with begetting a bastard on the body of Cicely Stewart (BACP IS#C: 365).

Wilderson, [-?-], m. by 16 Dec 1798 Uliana [?], daughter of Joseph Baker (BAWB 6:165).

Wile, William, m. by 12 April 1797 Sarah, legatee of William Sinclair (BAAD 12:287).

Wiley, George, merchant, and Jane Smith, both of Baltimore, were m. last eve. by Rev. Bend (*Maryland Journal and Baltimore Advertiser* 27 Dec 1793).

Wiley, Henry, of Baltimore, and Mrs. Goodrich, late of Philadelphia, were m. last Sat. (*Maryland Journal and Baltimore Advertiser* 4 Jan 1791).

Wiley, Henry, m. by 1792, [-?-], sister of John Davis (BOCP: Petition of Henry Wiley, 1792).

Wiley (Wile), Walter, and Susanna Norris were m. on 29 Dec 1763 (Harrison, "St. John's Parish Register:" 226). On 21 April 1781 Walter Wiley's six children he had by Susannah Norris were mentioned in the will of Joseph Norris (BAWB 4:31).

Wiley, Walter, m. by 10 Feb 1790 Sarah Cole, admx. of Salathiel Cole (BAAD 10:101).

Wiley, William, and Margaret Sing were m. on 23 Dec 1734 (Harrison, "St. Paul's Parish Register:" 152). Margaret Wiley on 29 Oct 1745 gave consent for John Daugherty, age 15, to be indentured for six years to Samuel Collier, blacksmith, to learn the art and mystery of a blacksmith (BALR TB#D:331). In 1726 Margaret Sing was named as a granddaughter of Richard Taylor (MWB 19:781 abst. in *Md. Cal. of*

Wills 6:131). William and Margaret were the parents of: Richard, d. s. p., by 14 Oct 1781, Edith, who m. John Cross (q.v.), and Ann, who m. Thomas Hunt (q.v.) (BALR WG#G: 496).

Wilford, Eleanor, in Nov 1762 was convicted of bastardy (BAMI 1755-1763).

Wilhelm, Jacob, and Catherine Otten were m. by lic. on 22 May 1800 at St. Peter's Catholic Church, Baltimore (*Piet:* 145).

Wilk, Peter, and Catherine M'Guire, both of Baltimore, were m. last eve. by Rev. Bend (*Baltimore Telegraphe* 26 Feb 1800).

Wilkie, Thomas, of N. C., m. by 10 May 1769, Flanetta [or Frenella], daughter of Samuel Howell (BALR AL#A:226).

Wilkins, [-?-], m. by 14 June 1791 Deborah, who received an equal share of the estate of Moses McCubbin (BAAD 10:382).

Wilkins, Dr. Henry, was m. last eve. by Rt. Rev. Bishop Asbury to Miss Hetty Owings, eldest daughter of Samuel Owings of Baltimore (*Federal Gazette and Baltimore Daily Advertiser* 4 Nov 1796).

Wilkinson, Jethro Lynch, was named as the father of Ruth Rowles' child in Nov 1757 (BAMI 1755-1763; BAMI 1757-1759: 74).

Wilkinson (Wilkerson), John, m. by 10 March 1769 Barbara, admx. of George Pickett (q.v.) (BAAD 7:61; MDTP 43:256).

Wilkinson, Joshua, hatter, and Miss Ann Patrick, both of Baltimore, were m. last Sat. eve. by Rev. William Lynch (*Maryland Journal and Baltimore Advertiser* 28 Feb 1792).

Wilkinson, Phillisanna, daughter of Tamar Wilknson, was charged with bastardy at the June 1733 Court; her son was Jethro Lynch Wilkinson; she was charged again at the June 1738 Court (BACP HWS#9:14, (BACP HWS#1A:237).

Wilkinson, Sarah, was charged with bastardy at the March 1729/30 Court (BACP HWS#6:362).

Wilkinson, William, m. by 3 April 1682 Elizabeth, daughter of Abraham and Sarah Clarke (MDTP 12B:18, 211).

Wilkinson, William, in March 1693 was charged with begetting a bastard on the body of Martha Cage (BACP G#1:175-176).

Wilkinson, William, d. by 14 Sep 1725 hen his widow Tamar had m. 2nd Richard Lenox (q.v.). Tamar (Thamar) Wilkinson on 10 April 1722 posted bond to administer the estate of Francis Keys (BAAB 2:20). [No proof has been found that she was the widow of Francis Keys].

Willcox (Wilcocks), James, and Sarah Gray were m. by lic. dated 28 Oct 1789 (BAML) Willcox, of Fell's Point, stated he would not pay the debts of his wife Sarah (*Maryland Journal and Baltimore Advertiser* 12 Aug 1791).

Wilett, John, and Deborah Butler, both of Baltimore, were m. last eve. by Rev. Richards (*Baltimore Telegraphe* 16 July 1800).

Willey, Frederick, m. by 2 Oct 1791 Mary, daughter and devisee of Casper Grasmuck (BALR WG#GG:563).

Williams, [-?-], m. by 17 Oct 1754 Mary, extx. of William Macclain (q.v.) (MDTP 36:86; MDAD 36:434).

Williams, [-?-], m. by 23 d. 8 m. 1786 Mary, sister of Thomas Johnson; Mary's will of that date named her sister Catherine Teal, and John Teal, son of Emanuel Teal (q.v.) (BAWB 4:392).

Williams, [-?-], m. by 23 Jan 1799 Elizabeth, daughter of John Rozer (BAWB 6:164).

Williams, Andrew, and Elizabeth Duncan, all of this city, were m. last eve. by Rev. Dr. Allison (*Federal Gazette and Baltimore Daily Advertiser* 1 April 1799).

Williams, Benjamin, and Prudence Gorsuch were married by license dated 20 Jan 1789 (BAML). On 9 Dec 1789 she was named as a daughter of Loveless Gorsuch, and heir of Nathan Gorsuch (BAAD 10:88, 250).

Williams, Christopher, stated he would not pay the debts of his wife Nancy (*Federal Intelligencer and Baltimore Daily Gazette* 11 May 1795).

Williams, David, m. by 16 Dec 1798 Mary, daughter of Joseph Baker who also named Mary's children Thomas, Abraham, and David (BAWB 6:165).

Williams, Elizabeth, on 26 d. 12 m. 1789 was disowned for being married by a hireling ("Minutes of Gunpowder Meeting," QRNM:88). Elizabeth Williams and David Gregory were m. by lic. dated 6 June 1789 (BAML).

Williams, Ennion, and Hannah Hayward on 30 d. 4 m. 1785 declared their intention to marry ("Minutes of Gunpowder Meeting," *QRNM:* 80).

Williams, George, of Cecil Co., d. by July 1759 leaving a widow Mary who m. 2nd [-?-] Bussey (q.v.) of Baltimore Co. (MDTP 37:276).

Williams, Isaac, and Rebecca Hayward, in 9 m. 1783 declared their intention to marry ("Minutes of Gunpowder Meeting," *QRNM:* 78).

Williams, Jacob, m. by 25 Sep 1798 Mary, daughter and one of the devisees of William Clower (BALR WG#56:93). Jacob Williams and Polly Clower were married by license dated 22 June 1797 (BAML).

Williams, John, and Margaret Clark were m. on 2 Dec 1736 (Harrison, "St. George's Parish Register:" 290). Margaret, admx. of John Williams, m, 2nd, William James (q.v.). or Iams (q.v.) by 1 Aug 1755 MDTP 36:188).

Williams, John, son of John, and Betty Jones were m. on 27 Dec 1767 (Harrison, "Coventry Parish Register," Somerset Co. at MdHS: 189). On 29 March 1779 Betty was named as a sister of Benjamin Jones, mariner, of Somerset Co. (BAWB 3:423).

Williams, John, and Ann Seymer were m. on 10 June 1770 (Harrison, "St. Paul's Parish Register:" 170). John Williams of Baltimore Town stated he would not pay the debts of his wife Ann, "who (had) behaved herself so indecently that he could not live with her" (*Maryland Journal and Baltimore Advertiser* 8 Jan 1774).

Williams, John, and Ann Wells were m. on 17 March 1785 (Harrison, "St. Paul's Parish Register:" 52). On 10 Aug 1791 Ann was named as the admx. of Kingsman Wells (BAAD 10:417).

Williams, John, and Janet Malcom were m. by lic. on 13 Oct 1788 at St. Peter's Catholic Church, Baltimore (*Piet:* 145).

Williams, John, of Fell's Point, stated that he would not be responsible for the debts of his wife Hannah (*Federal Gazette and Baltimore Daily Advertiser* 7 Dec 1790; *Maryland Gazette or Baltimore General Advertiser* 11 Jan 1791).

Williams, John, and Rosanna Costen were m. on 2 June 1791 ("Williams-Neilson Family Bible," *MBR 1:225-226; HABFR* 3:82).

Williams, Joseph, m. 2nd, Edith Cromwell, widow of Richard Gist; she m. 3rd, John Beecher (q.v.) (Christopher Johnston, "The Gist Family," *MdHM* 8 (1913) 372-373).

Williams, Joseph, and Rose Blossom were married by banns on 20 Dec 1783 at St. Peter's Catholic Church, Baltimore (*Piet:* 145).

Williams, Lodowick, of Baltimore Co., m. by 10 March 1673 Mary, daughter and heir of James Stringer of Anne Arundel Co., and Stringer's wife Ann who m. 2nd, William York, and 3rd, John Collier (MDTP 6:42, 148).

Williams, Lodowick, d. by 6 June 1711; his widow Hannah, now Hannah Keon, alias Dictus Keon, was now living in N. C. (statements by William Wilkinson and John Bevans made on the date above: BALR TR#A:135). On 5 Dec 1717 Nicholas Rogers atty. For Edward Williams, of Paspotank R., Sawyers Creek, N. C., son of Lodowick Williams, late of Carolina, conv. 350 a. to Richard Colegate (BALR TR#A: 447, 448).

Williams, Mary, servant of William Connell, was charged with bastardy at the Nov 1730 Court and presented at the March 1730/1 Court (BACP (BACP HWS#7:49, 236). Martha Williams, daughter of Mary, was born 31 [sic] June 1731 (Reamy, *St. Paul's Parish Register:* 5).

Williams, Mary, servant of Nicholas Britton, was charged with bastardy at the Nov 1757 Court (BAMI 1757-1759:73).

Williams, Gen. Oho H., was m. last Tues. eve. to Miss Polly Smith, daughter of the Hon. William Smith, Esq., of Baltimore (*Maryland Journal and Baltimore Advertiser* 21 Oct 1785).

Williams, Ruth, on 29 Dec 1773 posted bond as the admx. of William Wheeler (MDTP 45:35).

Williams, Sarah, was charged with bastardy and then was discharged on 3 March 1746/7 (BACP TB&TR#1:410)

Williams, Thomas, of St. Mary's Co., m. by 15 July 1703, Elizabeth, daughter and heir at law of Mathias DeCosta of Baltimore Co., and later of St. Mary's Co. (PCLR TL#2:786).

Williams, William, m. by 17 Oct 1754 Mary, extx. of William Matthau (BAAD 4:232).

Williams, William, of Baltimore Town stated that he would not be responsible for the debts of his wife Lucy (*Maryland Journal and Baltimore Advertiser* 26 Nov 1782).

Williams, William, was m. last eve. by Rev. Mr. Roberts, to Miss Susan Ridgaway, both of this city (*Federal Gazette and Baltimore Daily Advertiser* 16 June 1800).

Williams, Capt. William N., of Baltimore, and Sally Hinson, daughter of Mary Hinson of Mount Ararat, Kent Co., were m. Thurs., 23rd inst., by Rev. Ferguson (*Baltimore American* 31 May 1799).

Williamson, David, merchant of Baltimore, and Miss Juliet Mullet, native of Flanders, were m. Tues. morn. by Bishop Carroll (*Maryland Journal and Baltimore Advertiser* 16 Dec 1795). He was a merchant and a widower and she was a native of Dixonuyde, Flanders; they were m. by lic. on 15 Dec 1795 at St. Peter's Catholic Church, Baltimore (*Piet:* 145).

Williamson, Michael, m. by 14 Dec 1787 Ann, who received a legacy from the estate of Margaret McCulloch (BAAD 9:131). On 23 March 1784 Ann Williamson had been named as an aunt in the will of Margaret McCulloch (BAWB 4:26). 26 Nov 1797 Ann's brother James McCulloch named her children Isabella and Elizabeth Williamson (BAWB 6:72).

Willing, Capt. Leonard, and Margaret Anderson, of Fell's Point, were m. by lic. on 9 Nov 1800 at St. Peter's Catholic Church, Baltimore (*Piet:* 144; *Baltimore Telegraphe* 10 Nov 1800).

Willis, George, m. by 8 June 1786 Sarah, widow of Matthew Smith (BALR WG#Z: 268).

Willis, Henry, of Philadelphia, and Nancy Hollingsworth, daughter of Jesse Hollingsworth of Baltimore, were m. last Fri. eve. by Rev. Nelson Reed (*Maryland Journal and Baltimore Advertiser* 20 March 1792).

Willis, John, and Nancy Mill, both of Fell's Point, were m. yesterday by Rev. Allison (*Baltimore Telegraphe* 13 Dec 1798).

Willis, William, m. by 3 Aug 178, Jane, daughter of Elizabeth Payne, admx. of George Payne (BALR WG#G:420).

Willits, Samuel, son of Henry and Sarah, late of Exeter Monthly Meeting in Bucks Co., Pa., intends to marry Ann Rigbie, daughter of Nathan and Cassandra, late of Deer Creek MM, dec. ("Minutes of Deer Creek Meeting," *QRNM:* 133).

Willmott. See Wilmot.

Willox, Henry, and Miss Catherine Bain, all of Baltimore, were m. last Thurs. by Rev. D. E. Reese (*Baltimore American* 20 March 1795).

Wills, John, and Susannah [-?-] were m. by 26 Sep 1782 when their daughter Sarah was b. ("Clayton-Archer Family Bible," *HABFR* 2:38).

Willson. See under Wilson.

Wilmot, John (Willmott), Jr., in Nov 1746 was fined for begetting a bastard on the body of Ellinor Cope (BACP TB&TR#1:248).

Wilmot, John, m, by 11 Nov 1772 Avarilla, daughter and devisee of Thomas Carr, dec. (BALR AL#G: 208).

Wilmot, John, and Hannah Wheeler were m. on 3 Jan 1788 (Harrison, "St. Paul's Parish Register:" 216). On 7 Dec 1789 Hannah was named as a daughter of Solomon Wheeler (BAAD 10:85).

Wilmot (Wilmott), Richard, and Mary Gittings were m. on 22 Dec 1741 (Harrison, "St. John's Parish Register:" 151, 168). On 3 Nov 1758 Mary was named as a daughter of Thomas Gittings (BAWB 2:259).

Wilmot (Willmott), Robert, m. by 9 May 1696, Jane, mother of John Cooper (MWB 7:198 abst. in *Md. Cal. of Wills* 2:110).

Wilmot (Wilmott), Robert, and Sarah Merryman were m. on 15 Dec 1748 (Harrison, "St. Paul's," p. 162). On 4 Feb 1774 Sarah was named as a daughter of John Merryman (BAWB 3:252; BAAD 11:1).

Wilshire, [-?-], m. by 15 June 1774 Unity, daughter of Unity Hatten (MWB 39:723, abst. in *Md. Cal. of Wills* 15:146).

Wilson, [-?-], m. by 31st of 1ˢᵗ mo., 1763 Cassandra, daughter of Eliza Gover (BAWB 2:186).

Wilson, [-?-], m. by the 31 d. 1 m. 1763 Priscilla, daughter of Eliza Gover (BAWB 2:186).

Wilson, [-?-], m. by 12 April 1774 Lydia, daughter of Benjamin Culver (MWB 39:783, abst. in *Md. Cal. of Wills* 15:159).

Wilson, [-?-], m. by 8 July 1783 Elizabeth, daughter of Thomas Gittings (BAWB 4:1).

Wilson, [-?-], m. by 19 May 1786 Ann, widow and extx. of John Hopkins (BAAD 8:275, 354).

Wilson, [-?-], m. by 30 June 1796 Zania, daughter of John Denton IBAWB 5:385).

Wilson, Andrew, m. by 6 June 1765 Lydia, daughter of Benjamin and Ann Culver (BALR AL#D: 78).

Wilson, Andrew, and Elizabeth Graham were m. on 16 July 1777 (Leisenring, "List of Marriages:" 68). On 4 March 1778 they posted bond to administer the estate of John Graham (BAAB 3:305).

Wilson, Ann, admx., on 22 May 1784 posted bond to administer the estate of John Potts (BAAB 6:186). On 20 May 1785 she posted bond to administer the estate of John Hopkins who in his will made 5 May 1795 left his entire estate, real and personal, to Ann Wilson, widow, whom he named his extx (BAWB 4:45; BAAB 6:325).

Wilson, Ann, daughter of John Wilson (son of Joseph), on 1 d. 2 m. 1787 was reported to have been m. by a Presbyterian minister ("Minutes of Deer Creek Meeting," *QRNM:* 144). [No other marriage reference found].

Wilson, Benjamin, of Harford Co. and Betsey, daughter of William Worthington of Baltimore Co., were m. last Thurs. (*Maryland Journal and Baltimore Advertiser* 15 Aug 1786).

Wilson, Christopher, son of John and Alisanna, on 30 d. 7 m. 1789 announced his intention to marry Margaret Coale, daughter of Skipwith and Sarah Coale ("Minutes of Deer Creek Meeting," *QRNM:* 146).

Wilson, Cordelia William, admx., on 3 May 1773 posted bond to administer the estate of John Wilson (BAAB 4:84), On 26 Jan 1774 Samuel Smith, administrator, posted bond to administer the estate of Cordelia William Wilson (BAAB 4:97).

Wilson (Willson), Capt. David, and Miss Ann Partridge, both of Baltimore, were m. last eve. by Bishop Carroll (*Baltimore Daily Intelligencer* 30 April 1794). They were m. by lic. on 29 April 1794 at St. Peter's Catholic Church, Baltimore (*Piet:* 145). He was a sea captain, and she was a daughter of Buckler Partridge, dec. (BALR WG#55:197).

Wilson, Elizabeth, servant of John Cook, was charged with bastardy at the June 1734 Court (BACP HWS#9:267).

Wilson, Elizabeth, otherwise known as Elizabeth D. Silver, d. by 30 Oct 1789 when Dr. Henry Stevenson, administrator on 30 Oct 1789 posted bond to administer her estate (BAAB 7:170).

Wilson, Elizabeth, on 25 d. 8 m. 1791 produced a paper condemning her outgoing in marriage. On 28 d. 3 m. 1791 she stated that he had let out her affections to her first cousin, a man not of our society, and she was m. by the assistance of a Baptist Preacher ("Minutes of Deer Creek Meeting," *QRNM:* 149-150). [No other marriage reference found].

Wilson, Elizabeth. See Elizabeth Adair.

Wilson, Garret, of Baltimore Town, will not pay the debts of his wife Rose (Annapolis *Maryland Gazette* 21 Aug 1760). Garret Wilson m. Rosanna Smith on 21 Jan 1745 (Harrison, "St. Paul's Parish Register:" 158).

Wilson, Hannah, on 31 d. 8 m. 1762 was reported as having m. a man not of this society ("Minutes of Deer Creek Meeting," *QRNM:* 129). **See Hannah Jay.**

Wilson, Henry, in his will made 9 May 1798 named his granddaus. Priscilla Hopkins, Priscilla Stump, daughter Priscilla Worthington wife of John (q.v.); great-granddaughters Priscilla and Elizabeth Robinett, daughter Cassandra Stump wife of John (q.v.), daughter Elizabeth Dare wife of Gideon (q.v.) and her children Sarah, Rachel and Elizabeth; daughter Priscilla Dare (q.v.); grandson Samuel Harris; grandson Henry Hopkins, son-in-law John Stump (BAWB 6:234).

Wilson, Humphrey, m. 25 Dec 1791 Cassandra Ady, b. 2 Sep 1771 ("Ady Bibles," *MGSB* 20 (3) (Summer 1979) 238).

Wilson, Isabella, in 1762 was convicted of bastardy (BAMI 1755-1763).

Wilson, James, m. by 10 Feb 1770 Elizabeth, mother of Edward Fleetwood Shepperd (BAWB 3:177).

Wilson, James, and Miss Mary Reidenhour, both of Baltimore, were m. last Sat eve by
Rev. Kurtz (*Baltimore Daily Intelligencer* 30 Sep 1794)

Wilson (Willson), James, widower, and Catherine Shilling, widow, were m. by lic. on 8
Dec 1799 at St. Peter's Catholic Church, Baltimore (*Piet:* 145).

Wilson, James, and Mrs. Mary Davis, both of Baltimore, were m. last eve. by Rev. Bend
(*Baltimore American* 27 June 1800).

Wilson, James, was m. last eve. by Rev. Mr. Richards, to Mary Shields, both of this city
(*Federal Gazette and Baltimore Daily Advertiser* 31 Dec 1800).

Wilson, Jane, was charged with bastardy at the March 1723/4 Court, again at the Aug
1730 Court, and then in June 1746. At the latter Court George Smith confessed to
being the father of her child (BACP IS&TW#3:291 232; BACP HWS#7:7, 49, and
TB&TR: 49. 128). She was the mother of Hezekiah, b. 18 Nov 1723, and Sarah, b.
12 May 1725 (Reamy, *St. George's Parish Register:* 27).

Wilson (Willson), John, and Susannah Gittings (Harrison, "St. John's Parish Register:"
193). On 3 Nov 1758 Susannah was named as a daughter of Thomas Gittings, who
named his grandson Gittings Wilson in his will (BAWB 2:259).

Wilson, John, son of our late old friend Christopher Wilson of Old England, dec., on 2 d.
10 m. 1764 intends to marry Alisanna Webb [sic; prob. Webster], daughter of Isaac
Webster, dec., and Margaret ("Minutes of Deer Creek Meeting," *QRNM:* 130).

Wilson, John, joiner, on 27 d. 3 m. 1771 requested a certificate to Nottingham Meeting
so he could marry a Friend there ("Minutes of Gunpowder Monthly Meeting,"
QRNM: 61).

Wilson (Willson), John, m. by 12 June 1784 Elizabeth, sister of William Jennings
(BAWB 4:1).

Wilson, John, m. by 20 May 1799 Zana, representative. of John Denton (BAAD 13:61).

Wilson, John W., on 27 d. 3 m. 1800 requested a certificate to Baltimore Meeting in order
for marriage with Lucretia Tyson ("Minutes of Deer Creek Meeting," *QRNM:* 161).
John W. Wilson of Harford Co. was m. this day at Friend's Meeting House, to Miss
Lucretia Tyson of this city (*Federal Gazette and Baltimore Daily Advertiser* 15
May 1800).

Wilson, John Webster, Jr., of Deer Creek Meeting, and Lucretia Tyson on 10 d. 4 m.
1800 declared their intention to marry ("Minutes of Baltimore Meeting," *QRNM:*
237).

Wilson, Martha, Jr.: See Charles Lee.

Wilson, Mary, was charged with bastardy at the June 1724 Court (BACP
IS&TW#3:127).

Wilson, Mary, late Lee, on 2 d. 11 m. 1775 was announced to have gone out in marriage
by a priest to her first cousin ("Minutes of Deer Creek Meeting," *QRNM:* 136). [No
other marriage reference found]. On 1 d. 2 m. 1776 Elizabeth Lee was questioned
about the clearness of her daughter's marriage ("Minutes of Deer Creek Meeting,"
QRNM: 137).

Wilson, Mary, (late Talbot), on 28 d. 2 m. 1782 was charged with outgoing in marriage
("Minutes of Deer Creek Meeting," *QRNM:* 141). [No other marriage reference
found].

Wilson, Mary. See Hopkins, Mary.

Wilson, Samuel, m. by 11 Aug 1731 Rebecca, daughter of Thomas Smithson (MWB
20:568 abst. in *Md. Cal. of Wills* 6:253).

Wilson, Samuel, m. by 24 Feb 1785, Hannah, widow of William Coursey (q.v.) and sister of Edward Hanson (BALR WG#Y: 468). When Edward Hanson's estate was divided, Hannah Wilson's daughter Elizabeth Wilson was named (BACT 1785-1788, MS 2865 at MdHS: 75). On 26 Dec 1785 Wilson's wife was named as a daughter of Jonathan Hanson (BAWB 4:115).

Wilson, Sarah, was named as the eldest daughter of George Brown's sister in his will (BAWB 2:173).

Wilson, Sarah. See Frederick Brown.

Wilson, Solomon, and Frances 'Judy' were married by license dated 29 Aug 1795 (BAML). On 4 June 1800 Frances was named as a legatee of John Tschudy (BAAD 13:262).

Wilson, Sophia, alias Jane Smith was charged with bastardy at the March 1754 court, and her mulatto children Elizabeth Wilson (or Smith), and Aquila Wilson (or Smith), were sold to William Rogers (BACP BB#A:15, 20, 26).

Wilson, Stephen, of Baltimore, and Miss Rebecca Neilson of Fell's Point, were m. a few days ago (*Maryland Gazette or Baltimore General Advertiser* 21 Feb 1786). She was a daughter of William Neilson, and m. 2nd, Moore Falls (*q.v.*) (BAWB 6:167).

Wilson, Stephen, d. by Jan 1798 when his orphans, Eliza, Isabella, Robert, and Armanella, were made wards of More Falls BAOC 3:246).

Wilson, Thomas, Ann Dorum were m. by lic. dated 11 Aug 1783 (BAML). Wilson stated that he would not pay the debts of his wife Ann (*Maryland Journal and Baltimore Advertiser* 29 June 1790).

Wilson, Thomas, son of Peter Wilson, dec. and his wife Ann, of Old England, announced his intention to marry Sarah Richardson, daughter of Nathan, dec., and wife Hannah ("Minutes of Deer Creek Meeting," *QRNM:* 145).

Wilson, William, on 23 d. 2 m. 1782, hath gone out in marriage ("Minutes of Gunpowder Meeting," *QRNM:* 75). [No other marriage reference found].

Wilson, William, on 27 d. 4 m. 1797 was found guilty of accomplishing his marriage with the assistance of a Baptist teacher ("Minutes of Deer Creek Meeting," *QRNM:* 157). [No other marriage reference found].

Wilson, William, was m. yesterday eve. by Rev. Mr. Bend, to Susanna Wolf, both of this city (*Federal Gazette and Baltimore Daily Advertiser* 15 Sep 1800).

Wimfet, Charles, and Ann Chaney were m. by lic. on 2 March 1794 at St. Peter's Catholic Church, Baltimore (*Piet:* 145; BAML which gives his name as Charles Wimsel).

Wimmer, John, of Berkeley Co., Va., m. by 8 April 1782 Catherine, daughter of Michael Devenbaugh of Baltimore Co. (BALR WG#H: 214).

Wimsett, James, m. by 14 March 1783 Ann, daughter of Joseph Ward and sister of Mary Ann Ward (BAWB 3:547).

Winchester, James, and Susan [-?-] were m. by 14 May 1783 when their daughter Maria Eliza was b. ("James Winchester Bible," *MBR* 7:207).

Winchester, James, executor, on 6 April 1798 posted bond to administer the estate of Mary McLaughlin (BAAB 8:412).

Winchester, William, m. 21 July 1749 Lydia Richards ("Edward Richards Bible," *MBR* 3:160-161; MDAD 41:20; BFD 2:57; MWB 30:26 abst. by Gibb).

Windley Richard, m. by 5 April 1676 [-?-], daughter of John Taylor who called Richard Windley's one child his grandchild (MWB 65:36 abst. in *Md. Cal. of Wills* 1:170).

On 22 Feb 1677 Mary was named as the sister of Arthur Taylor and aunt of John Taylor (BALR RM#HS:467).

Winespear, William, in June 1711 was named as the father of the child of Mary Mattocks (alias Mary Shorter) (BACP IS#B: 210, 251).

Winn, Christopher, and Margaret Gould were m. by lic. on 9 Sep 1787 at St. Peter's Catholic Church, Baltimore (*Piet:* 145).

Winn, Mary, was charged with bastardy at the Aug 1717 court and named Benjamin Hanson as the father of her child (BACP IS#1A: 124).

Winning, John, m. after 16 May 1775 and before 5 Feb 1782 Margaret, admx. of Benjamin Nelson (BAAB 2:375; *Maryland Journal and Baltimore Advertiser* 5 Feb 1782). In his will dated 15 Jan 1787 Winning named a 'daughter-in-law' Susannah Nelson, and then referred to her as his newly adopted daughter (BAWB 4:369). In her will dated 4 Nov 1795 Margaret Winning named her daughters Susanna McCreary and Elizabeth [formerly Nelson] Pennel, wife of John, and grandson Benjamin Pennel (BAWB 5:144).

Wise, [-?-], m. by 18 Nov 1783 Barbara [-?-] Sittlemeyer, daughter-in-law of Mary [-?-] who was the widow of Sebastian Sittlemeyer (BALR WG#T:8-9).

Wise, Felix, and Barbara Gross were m. by lic. on 26 Aug 1792 at St. Peter's Catholic Church, Baltimore (*Piet:* 145).

Wise, Michael, and Catherine Young, natives of Germany, were m. by lic. on 8 Feb 1796 at St. Peter's Catholic Church, Baltimore (*Piet:* 145).

Wise, William, planter, m. by 8 March 1705 Margaret, extx. of William Osborn (*q.v.*) (INAC 25:317). She had m. 1st, John Wallston (*q.v.*)

Wise (Wyse), William, native of Ireland, ship captain, and Rachel Morrison were m. by lic. on 29 May 1794 at St. Peter's Catholic Church, Baltimore (*Piet:* 145).

With, Elizabeth, confessed to bastardy at the June 1746 Court and was fined 30 shillings); she confessed again at the March 1750/1 Court and was fined (BACP TB&TR#1:1, 126, TB&TR#6:1, 284-285).

Withers, Michael, m. Charlotte, daughter of James and Margaret Calder, dec. of Baltimore Co. (MCHP # 5328).

Wolden, [-?-], d. by 26 March 1699 leaving a widow and Martha, mother of Lawrence Wolden; she m. 2nd, Jonas Bowen (q.v.) (MWB 6:228 abst. in *Md. Cal. of Wills* 2:171).

Woford. See Wooford.

Wolf, [-?-], m. by 8 May 1799 Elizabeth, one of the representatives of John Gittinger; Elizabeth had two daughters: Catherine and Elizabeth Wolf (BAAD 13:48).

Wolley. See Walley.

Wonn, Edward, m. by 5 Jan 1793 Rachel Marsh, who received an equal share of the estate of John Marsh (BAAD 11:172).

Wood, [-?-], m. by 23 Jan 1730/1 Eliza, daughter of Edward Wilbourne (MWB 20:154).

Wood, [-?-], m. by 22 Dec 1798 Elizabeth, sister of Caleb Hewett (BAWB 7:356).

Wood, Charles, on 7 Jan 1675 was called son-in-law in the will of John Lee of Baltimore Co. (MWB 5:100 abst. in *Md. Cal. of Wills* 1:178).

Wood, Charles, and Eleanor Eaglestone were m. on 26 Jan 1793 ((Marr. Register of Rev. Lewis Richards, MS.690 at MdHS). On 10 June 1795 Eleanor was named as an heir of Jonathan Eaglestone (BAAD 11:537).

Wood, Eady, was charged with bastardy at the March 1730/1 Court (BACP (BACP HWS#7:96).

Wood, Isaac, on 14 Jan 17--, granted to his brother Joshua Wood a release of any engagements he had under Baltimore Co. Court of Isaac's being bound apprentice to him (BALR TRD#DS: 341).

Wood, James, was charged with bastardy at the Nov 1759 Court (BAMI 1757-1759:240).

Wood, John, m. by 28 July 1683 Elizabeth, sole daughter of Edward Swanson (BALR IR#AM: 67).

Wood, John Rigbie, and Ann Shyor [sic] were m. by lic. dated 30 March 1785 (BAML). Wood had m. the widow Shrier, and had since turned his wife out of doors. She has offered herself as a housekeeper to any genteel family. She stated she had paid her husband's debts for the past seven years (*Baltimore Daily Repository* 2 June 1792).

Wood, Joshua, and Priscilla West were m. on 15April 1729 (Harrison, "St. George's Parish Register:" 249). He m. 2nd, Mary Garrett in Sep 1732 (Harrison, "St. George's, Parish Register:" 270). Mary m. 2nd, James Stewart (q.v.) on 10 Feb 1741 (Harrison, "St. George's Parish Register:" 324).

Wood, Mary, was charged with bastardy at the Aug 1719 Court; she was ordered to be whipped and to serve Lawrence Taylor an additional five months (BACP IS#C: 219).

Wood, Robert, and Jane Dunn were m. on 19 May 1783 (Reamy, *St. Paul's Parish Register:* 191). Wood d. by Sep 1786 when his widow Jane, now Jane Cassidy, stated she would petition the Assembly (*Maryland Journal and Baltimore Advertiser* 12 Sep 1786). She m. 2nd, [-?-] Cassidy (*q.v.*).

Wood, Warnal, and Thamer Smith were m. on 28 May 1754 (Harrison, "St. Paul's Parish Register:" 165). On 27 Aug 1772 Tamar Wood was given one acre of Perkins's Valley by her father William Smith (BALR AL#E:328).

Wood, William, died leaving a will dated March 1768 and proved 14 May 1769. He named his natural son William Wood Greer (BAWB 3:114).

Wood, William, and Mary Smith on 2 d. 4 m. 1781 declared their intention to marry ("Minutes of Gunpowder Meeting," *QRNM:* 74).

Wood, William H., and Anna Maria Bond were m. last Tues., 30 Jan at the residence of Thomas Bond of John (*Baltimore Telegraphe* 6 Feb 1798).

Wooden, [-?-], m. by 31 Jan 1774 Sarah, named as the eldest daughter of Dixon Brown (BAWB 3:281).

Wooden, [-?-], m. by 31 Dec 1784 Rachel, daughter of John Price (BAWB 4:422).

Wooden, Charles, m. by 10 June 1795 Nancy Owings, representative of Lot Owings (BAAD 12:14).

Wooden, John, and Rachel Hooper were married by license dated 31 June 1790 (BAML). In March 1791 John and Rachel were named as administrators of James Hooper of Baltimore Co. (*Maryland Gazette or Baltimore General Advertiser* 1 March 1791; BAAD 10:441, 11:322). James Hooper and Rachel Gorsuch were married by license dated 4 Nov 1783 (BAML).

Wooden, Mary, was charged with bastardy at the Aug 1746 Court(BACP TB&TR#1:117).

Wooden, Solomon, and Sarah Gresham were m. on 17 Aug 1726 (Harrison, "All Hallows Parish Register," MS. at MdHS: 103). On 12 April 1729 Sarah was named as a daughter of John Gresham, Jr, (KELR JS#X:345).

Woodfield, Thomas, of Anne Arundel Co., m. by 13 March 1717 Eliza, lately Eliza Gott, daughter and devisee of Anthony Holland of Anne Arundel Co. (BALR TR#A: 544).

Woodfield, Thomas, on 6 May 1791 was named as a brother of Priscilla Woodfield, now Hall, and a nephew of Nathaniel Phipps (BAWB 5:21).

Woodland, Jonathan, m. by 9 Jan 1773 Cassandra, admx. of Jonathan Massey (MINV 111:419-420; MDAD 68:167).

Woodland, Rachel, youngest daughter of Christiana Woodland, in June 1760 chose James Dawney as her guardian (BAMI 1755-1763: 17).

Woodward, Amos, and Mrs. Achsah Dorsey. daughter of Mrs. Caleb Dorsey, were m. on 3 April 1728 (Harrison, "St. Ann's Parish Register," Anne Arundel Co., MS. at MdHS: 429),. She m. 2nd, Edward Fottrell (q.v.).

Woodward, John, in his will, made 30 Oct 1780 named his wife Jemima as co-exec. with his son Thomas (BAWB 3:468). Jemima m. 2nd, Joseph Peregoy (q.v.).

Woodward, John, on 15 Aug 1798 was named as on of the representatives of Thomas Johnson in his administration account (BAAD 12:468).

Woodward, Mary, in her will made 12 Feb 1789 named her niece Mary Govane, Sr, as her extx. (BAWB 4:352).

Wooford (Woford), William, in Nov 1746 was charged with unlawful cohabitation with Abigail Draper (BACP TB&TR#1:221).

Woolsey, George, on 5 March 1772 posted a bond as administrator of Susanna Bryan alias Susanna Shink (MDTP 44:342).

Wooley, John, m. Ann [-?-], and d. by 19 Aug 1747 when John Jones (q.v.) and John Logsdon (q.v.), administrators, on 19 Aug 1747 posted bond to administer the estate of John Wooley. Ann Wooley, widow of John, renounced the right to administer in favor of her sons-in-law John Jones (q.v.) and John Logsdon (q.v.) (BAAB 4:117).

Woolf, Peter, on 12 April 1748 was summoned to appear before the vestry and was discharged by putting away his housekeeper ("St. John's and St. George's Parish Register Vestry Proceedings," MS. at MdHS.).

Woolrick, [-?-], m. by 28 Feb 1778 Sarah, daughter of Job Evans (BALR WG#B: 155).

Woolry, [-?-], m. by 7 June 1794, Catherine, daughter of Jacob Shaffer (BAWB 6:249).

Wooton, [-?-], of Exmouth, Co. Devon, Eng., m. by 30 Jan 1729, Mary, sister of Thomas Bale (BALR IS#L: 429).

Wordley, [-?-], m. by 21 Feb 1790 Ruth, daughter of Robert Love Pitstow who named his grandchildren Moses, Francis, Robert and Ann Wordley (BAWB 5:175).

Working, Herman, m. by 1792 [-?-], daughter of Henry Fite (BOCP Petition of Herman Warking, 1792).

Worrall, Samuel, d. by Aug 1755 when his son Martin, aged 13 was bound to Alex. McComas (BAMI 1755-1763).

Worrell, [-?-], m. by 6 June 1745, Mary, mother of Erick White (BALR TB#D: 112).

Worrell, Amon, d. by 1794. In 1793, with his family, he called at the house of Emanuel Cook and Isaiah Cook. At that time Worrell suffered from the complaint that was probably the cause of his death in Feb 1794. His family, consisting of three small children, is still at the house of the petitioners, who administered Worrell's estate. They now, in 1796, petitioned the court for permission to sell the personal estate (BOCP Petition of Emanuel Cook and Isaiah Cook, 1796).

Worthington, Charles, and Hammutal Hammond were m. on 12 Nov 1728 ("Charles Worthington Family Record," *MGSB* 23 (1) (Winter 1982) 73).

Worthington, Charles, and Sarah Chew were m. on 5 Oct 1732 ("Charles Worthington Family Record," *MGSB* 23 (1) Winter 1982) 73).

Worthington, John, m. by 9 March 1763 Mary, legatee of Eleanor Lynch, and daughter of Capt. Thomas Todd (BALR B#P: 208; MDAD 49:169; BAAD 6:197). Mary was named as a daughter in the will made 23 July 1760 of Eliner Lynch (MWB 31:26 abst. by Gibb).

Worthington, John, on 31 d. 8 m. 1769 requested a certificate to go to Gunpowder Monthly Meeting to marry Priscilla Wilson, daughter of Henry Wilson ("Minutes of Deer Creek Meeting," *QRNM:* 134). John Worthington, son of Charles, of Deer Creek, and Priscilla Wilson, daughter of Henry, were m. on 7 Nov 1770 (Abstracts of Records of Gunpowder Meeting at MdHS; Charles Worthington Family Record, MGSB 23 (1) (Winter 1982) 74). Henry Wilson, in his will, made 9 May 1798, named his daughter Priscilla, wife of John Worthington (BAWB 6:234).

Worthington, Mary, late Hopkins, on 1 d. 8 m. 1765 was condemned for outgoing in marriage ("Minutes of Deer Creek Meeting," *QRNM:* 131). [No other marriage reference found].

Worthington, Samuel, and Mary Tolley were m. on 17 Jan 1759 (Harrison, "St. John's Parish Register:" 218). On 26 July 1781 Mary was named as a daughter of Walter Tolley who named grandchildren Walter, Thomas Tolley, James Tolley, John and Martha Worthington (BAWB 3:507). Hannah Worthington, in her will made March 1796, named her niece Elizabeth Mary Tolly (BAWB 5:447).

Worthington, Sarah, on 5 d. 10 m. 1786 was reported as having m. a man not of our society, by a Baptist Preacher, and attended a dancing school ("Minutes of Deer Creek Meeting," *QRNM:* 143). [No other marriage reference found].

Worthington, Sarah, now Johnson, on 3 d. 2 m. 1790, was m. to a man not of our society by a Baptist Preacher ("Minutes of Deer Creek Meeting," *QRNM:* 147-8). [No other marriage reference found].

Worthington, Vachel, and Priscilla Bond were m. on 17 Nov 1757 (Harrison, "St. John's Parish Register:" 216); on 16 April 1759 Priscilla was named as a daughter of William Bond and a granddaughter of Jane Stansbury (MWB 30:684 abst. by Gibb).

Worthington, William, and Hannah Cromwell were m. on 30 June 1734 Harrison, "St. Paul's Parish Register:" 152). Their son John was b. Nov 1735 ("Jones Bible Records.: *MG* 2:109). On 1 10 June 1736 Hannah was named as the widow and extx. of Capt. John Cromwell, and mother of Margaret, John, Hannah, and Ann Cromwell (BALR IS#IK:444; BAAD 3: 318).

Worthington, William, m. by 5 May 1770 Sarah, granddaughter of Abraham Raven (BALR AL#B:171).

Worthington, William, and Elizabeth Dempsey were m. by lic. dated 2 June 1781 (BAML). Worthington stated that he would not pay the debts of his wife Elizabeth (*Maryland Journal and Baltimore Advertiser* 20 Jan 1789).

Wortland, [-?-], m. by 26 Sep 1795 Jemima, daughter of John Thomas, whose will of that date named his Jemima and her daughter Sarah Wortland (BAWB 7:185).

Wright, [-?-], m. by 21 April 1752 Sarah, daughter of John Legatt, Sr. (MWB 30:81 abst. by Gibb).

Wright, [-?-], (given as Right), m. by 9 Dec 1769 Mary, sister of John Maynard (BAWB 3:164).

Wright, [-?-], m. by 22 Jan 1781 Elizabeth, daughter of John Hendrickson (BAWB 3:442).

Wright, Blois, on 1 Nov 1722, declared that his wife Sarah has been absent from his home and family for about three years and has spread untrue stories about him; he will not pay her debts (BALR IS#G: 49).

Wright, Henry, administrator, on 18 Sep 1704 posted bond to administer the estates of William York and his wife Elizabeth (BAAB 4:16).

Wright, John, on 16 May 1685, executed an prenuptial contract with Jane Claridge, widow (BALR RM#HS: 136).

Wright, John, d. by 11 Feb 1722 when Sarah Arnold, admx., posted and administration bond (BAAB 3:60). Sarah m. 2nd, Anthony Arnold (q.v.) and 3rd, Charles Wells (q.v.).

Wright, John, in his will dated 29 Nov 1744 named his brother Cooper Oram and his cousin John Oram (MWB 23:643 abst. by Gibb).

Wright, Joseph, of Reister's Town, stated his wife Mary had absconded (*Maryland Journal and Baltimore Advertiser* 30 Nov 1779).

Wright, Nathaniel, and Sophia Rutledge were m. on 11 Aril 1769 (Harrison, "St. John's Parish Register:" 258). She was a daughter of Abraham Rutledge (MWB 39:336, abst. in *Md. Cal. of Wills* 15:67). She m. 2nd, Solomon Hughes (q.v.).

Wright, Samuel, coach and chair maker, and Polly Shriver, step-daughter of Daniel Peters of this town, were m. last sat. (*Maryland Journal and Baltimore Advertiser* 7 Jan 1791).

Wright, Samuel, and Sarah Dickinson were m. by lic. dated 15 Feb 1794 (BAML). Sarah Wright (Right), formerly Dickinson, on 29 d. 8 m. 1795 was reported as having as having been married by a hireling priest ("Minutes of Gunpowder Meeting," *QRNM:* 97).

Wright, Thomas, and Christian Enloes were m. on 5 May 1735 (Harrison, "St. John's Parish Register:" 77). By 8 Dec 1740 Christian, admx. of Wright, had m. 2nd, William Standiford (q.v.).

Wright, William, and Elizabeth Barton were m. on 7 May 1727 (Harrison, "St. John's Parish Register:" 26). She m. 2nd, by 27 April 1742, James Greer (q.v.), and 3rd, Heathcote Pickett (q.v.).

Wright, William, son of Bloyce Wright, m. Sarah Day on 28 Feb 1738 (Harrison, "St. John's Parish Register:" 136). Wright d. by 24 Dec 1752 on which date his widow Sarah m. 2nd, Philip Lock Elliott (q.v.) (MDTP 33-2:142; MDAD 35:40; BAAD 5:226).

Wright, William, son of William at the August 1761 Court was made a ward of Josias Slade (BAMI 1755-1763).

Wyle, Greenbury, m. by 16 Feb 1792 [-?-], who received an equal share of the estate of John Talbot of John (BAAD 10:544).

Wyman, Samuel, will not pay the debts of his wife Jane (*Maryland Journal and Baltimore Advertiser* 15 Aug 1783).

Wyse. See Wise.

"Y"

Yanda, John Peter, (son of Joseph, formerly an officer of the infantry in the service of the Emperor, lately from St. Domingo, resident of Limoges, and the late Catherine Arenima), and Margarate Aimee Leclerc (daughter of Francis of Plaisance and the late Marguerite Perigault, widow of Rosier Rostaing from Plaisance, St. Domingo), were m. by lic. on 2 Nov 1785 at St. Peter's Catholic Church, Baltimore (*Piet:* 145).

Yates, [-?-], m. by 6 Dec 1770, Ann, daughter of Antill Deaver (BAWB 3:177).

Yates, Charles, m. by 12 July 1726 Jane, admins. of Henry Stone (*q.v.*) (MDTP 27:310).

Yates, George, d. by 3 Nov 1726 by which time his extx. Ruth had m. Joseph Ary (*q.v.*).

Yates, George, m. by 6 May 1766, Ann, daughter of Sarah Deaver who named a granddaughter Sarah Yates (BAWB 3:47).

Yates (Yeats), Humphrey, m. by 2 Sep 1725 Lawrana, admx. of Henry Shields (*q.v.*) (BAAD 3:37).

Yates (Yeats), Joseph, m. Catherine Herrett on 15 Sep 1735 (Reamy, *St. George's Parish Register:* 47, but Harrison, "St. John's Parish Register:" 117 gives the date as 14 Sep 1736 and the bride's name as Catherine Turret). Joseph Yeats died 9 Nov 1740 or, more likely, in Oct 1748 (Harrison, "St. John's Parish Register:" 138, 157). A Joseph Yates was made exempt from the levy in Nov 1737 (BACP (BACP HWS#1A: 133). Joseph and Catherine were the parents of George Gilbert Yates, b. 21 April 1738 (Harrison, "St. John's Parish Register:" 138). Marshall Lemmon deposed on 20 Nov 1744 that he had been at school with Catherine Terrett, lately Yates, in Lincolnshire, and that her father as the younger brother of Sir John Terwhitt. Catherine's father had married against his father's wishes to a woman named Gilbert, sister of Joshua and George Gilbert of London. He stated that Catherine had married Joseph Yates in Baltimore Co., and had a son George Gilbert Yates (BACT 1773-1784:12). Ann Shea deposed on 10 Nov 1744 that she had known the Terretts in Lincolnshire (BACT 1773-1784:13). James Osborn deposed on 21 Aug 1772 that Catherine Terrett had come to Maryland over 40 years ago and had been married to Joseph Yeats for over 30 years (BACT 1773-1784:14). Elizabeth Gundry deposed on 14 Aug 1772 that she was present on or about 1738 when Catherine Yates, then living at the house of John Atkinson on Bush River Neck had been taken in labor and had had a son George Gilbert Yates, now living in Baltimore Co. (BACT 1773-1784:15). On 24 Aug 1772 George Gilbert Yates promised to pay Ishmael Morris one-half of any estate Morris might obtain for him from any (Terwhitt) property in Eng. (BACT 1773-1784:16). In a separate power of attorney executed 24 Aug 1772 Yates stated that his mother left Great Britain in 1728 on a vessel commanded by Capt. Weston. She married Joseph Yates in 1736, and Yates died shortly after the birth of the child and Catherine died intestate about 1746 (BACT 1773-1784:17).

Yates, Major Thomas, m. by 4 April 1787 Mary, daughter of Jacob Myers (BAWB 4:268).

Yates, Thomas, on 6 Feb 1799 stated he intended to marry Mary Atkinson (BALR WG#57:425). They were m. last Wed. eve. by Rev. Ireland (*Baltimore Telegraphe* 8 Feb 1799).

Yates, William, m. by 20 April 1754, Sarah, extx. of Joseph Chew (q.v.) (MDTP 26:32; MINV 62:123; MDAD 41:22).

Yates (Yeats), William, and Ann Thornbury were m. on either 5 Aug or 8 Sep 1744 (Harrison, "St. John's Parish Register:" 191, 239). Yates was in Bedford Co., Va., on 1 Aug 1764 when Ann was named as the daughter of John Thornbury, dec., who was the oldest son of Roland Thornborough of Baltimore Co., dec. (BALR B#O: 121).

Yeaman, Mr., of Alexandria, and Miss Mary Evans of Baltimore, were m. last Thurs. by Rev. Richards (*Baltimore Weekly Museum* 19 March 1797; **N.B.:** The *Federal Gazette and Baltimore Daily Advertiser* 17 March 1797 reports the groom's name as Yeatman).

Yeats. See Yates.

Yeiser, Englehart, and Catherine Keener, both of Baltimore, were married. By a recent marriage in St. Mary's Co., the lady is become sister-in-law to her own mother, and the gentleman a son-in-law to his own sister (*Maryland Journal and Baltimore Advertiser* 20 Aug 1773). On 6 March 1798 Catherine was named as a daughter of Melchoir Keener (BAWB 6:129).

Yeiser, Engelhard, Jr., and Miss Margaret Swope, daughter of Benedict Swope, Jr., were m. 3rd ult., near Danville, Ky. (*Federal Gazette and Baltimore Daily Advertiser* 2 Nov 1799). On 12 April 1800 Margaret was named as a legatee of Melchor Keener (BAAD 13:241).

Yellott, Capt. Jeremiah, and Polly Hollingsworth, eldest daughter of Jesse Holingsworth of this town, merchant, were married last Thursday evening (*Maryland Journal and Baltimore Advertiser* 27 Feb 1781; see also BALR WG#N: 31).

Yeo (Yoe), James, and Rebecca Rollo were m. on 25 May 1755 (Harrison, "St. John's Parish Register:" 212). On 14 June 1763 Rebecca was named as a devisee of Archibald Rollo (BALR B#M: 137).

Yeo, John, m. by 21 Oct 1680, Semelia, relict and admx. of Ruthen Garrettson, by whom she had a son Garrett FitzGarrett (INAC 7A:283; BALR RM#HS: 62).

Yeomans, Seth, gave notice that a certain Anne Yeomans claimed to be his wife, but he did not cohabit with her (*Dunlap's Maryland Gazette* 20 Feb 1776),

Yerby, Capt. William, of Lancaster Co., Va., and Elizabeth White, daughter of Capt. Joseph White of Baltimore, were m. by lic. on 9 Aug 1798 at St. Peter's Catholic Church, Baltimore (*Piet:* 145; *Baltimore Telegraphe* 16 Aug 1798).

Yoakley, Capt. Stephen, in Aug 1719 was charged with bastardy and named as the father of Elizabeth Kitchin (or Hitchin's) child (BACP IS#C: 131, 136, 138).

Yoakly, John, on 15 Sep 1774 was named as a stepson in the will of James Brown (MWB 40:655, abst. in *Md. Cal. of Wills* 16:14).

Yoner, Mr. Samuel, was m. last Thurs. eve. by Rev. Mr. Otterbein, to Miss Polly Stover (*Federal Gazette and Baltimore Daily Advertiser* 25 June 1796).

Yorick, George, was charged with bastardy at the March 1768 Court (BACP BB: 4).

York, [-?-], m. by 24 April 1706 Hannah, daughter of Israel Skelton (MWB 12:15 abst. in *Md. Cal. of Wills* 3:74).

York, George, and Eliner Meads were m. in Feb 1738 (Harrison, "St. John's Parish Register:" 136). On 5 March 1744, Elinor (poss. mother of Joseph and James Mead), was named as a daughter of James Hackett. On 19 June 1751 Eleanor was called one of the coheirs of Edward Selby, Sr., and Edward Selby, Jr. (BALR TB#D: 49, TR#D: 168).

York, John, and Sarah Horner were m. on 16 Oct 1752 (Harrison, "St. John's Parish Register:" 204). She m. 2nd, John Day of Edward (Edward (*q.v.*).

York, John, d. by 25 Dec 1766 leaving a daughter Mary, wife of David Chilson (*q.v.*), who on that day conv. their share of York's estate to John Day (BACT B#G: 92).

York, Mary, alias Mary Minson, was charged with bastardy at the June 1740 Court (BACP HWS#TR: 226).

York, William, m. by 10 March 1673, Ann, widow of, 1st, James Stringer of Anne Arundel Co., and 2nd, John Collier; Ann was the mother of Mary who m. Lodowick Williams (MDTP 4A: 37, 6:42, 148).

York, William, m. by June 1692, [-?-], relict of John Wood (BACP F#1:186, 187).

York, William, m. by Sep 1695, Elizabeth, extx. of Jacob Looton (BACP G#1:490; MDTP 16:171). She m. 3rd, James Frizzle (*q.v.*).

York, William, and Elizabeth Debruler were m. on 1 Jan 1733 (Harrison, "St. John's Parish Register:" 76). On 13 Jan 1734 Elizabeth was named as a daughter of George Debruler (MWB 21:397 abst. in *Md. Cal. of Wills* 7:142).

Young, Frederick, administrator of Andrew Elleckson, retained the balance of the estate as heir of the deceased (BAAD 13:308).

Young, Jacob, m. by 25 July 1780 Eleanor, daughter of Edw. Tully who named his grandchildren John Tully, Mary, Ann, Jacob, Edward, Michael, and Joseph Young (BAWB 3:464).

Young, Jacob, m. by 15 June 1787, [-?-], who received an equal share of the estate of Beale Watts, and who received a payment from the estate of Dickinson Watts (BAAD 9:62, 63).

Young, Jesse, of Fell's Point, and Miss Jane M'Donogh were m. on Sat by Rev. Dr. Allison (*Maryland Journal and Baltimore Advertiser* 1 Feb 1796).

Young, John, and Rebecca [-?-], were m. by 9 Sep 1735 when their daughter Elizabeth was b. ("Original Records of the Young Family of Baltimore County," HMGB 16:15-17, 16:24-27).

Young, John, d. by 13 Aug 1788 leaving a daughter Elizabeth who chose Mary Young as her guardian. On the same day, Ralph Young, age 4 years, 6 mos., was made a ward of Mary Young (BOCP 2:77). In Oct 1793 the orphans of John Young, Ralph and Elizabeth Young were made wards of James Allen. In Oct 1794 they were made wards of Patrick Bennett (BOCP 3:65, 114).

Young, John, and Tabitha Oyson (Oyster) were m. on 17 Sep 1795 (Marr. Register of Rev. Lewis Richards, MS. 690 at MdHS). Tabitha was a daughter of Lawrence Oyston (BAWB 6:241).

Young, John H., m. by 27 March 1788, Elizabeth, extx. of Ralph Story (BAAD 10:195; BOCP Petition of John H. Young and Elizabeth Young [c1789]).

Young, Joseph, orphan of Samuel Young, in March 1757 chose Samuel Young as his guardian (BAMI 1755-1763).

Young, Joseph, orphan of William Young, in July 1775 was made ward of John Barney (BAMI 1772, 1775-1781: 130).

Young, Joseph, and Miss Eliza Ridgely, were married last evening by Rev. Mr. Bend at "Pilgrim's Choice" (*Baltimore Daily Intelligencer* 12 Sep 1794; *Maryland Journal and Baltimore Advertiser* 12 Sep 1794).

Young, Mary, *alias* Mary Enloes, was charged with bastardy at the March 1719/20 Court and in June 1721 her husband appeared in Court (BACP IS#C: 279, 435, 524).

Young, Samuel, and Rebecca Stokes were m. on 9 April 1765 (Harrison, "St. John's Parish Register:" 227). In his will, made 15 Feb 1776 Samuel Young named his son-in-law Robert Young Stokes (BAWB 3:487). Rebecca was the widow of Robert Stokes (*q.v.*).

Young, Samuel, d. by 17 June 1784 when Rebecca Arnold in her will named him her deceased son, and named her grandsons Samuel and Henry Young (BAWB 4:316).

Young, Samuel, m. by 21 Nov 1799, Rebecca, widow and *admx. de bonis non* of Robert Clark Cooper (BAWB 5:312; BAAD 13:157).

Young, William, of Calvert Co., m. by 1 Aug 1737, Clare Tasker, who was a daughter of Nicholas Sewell (BALR IS#IK: 481, HWS#M: 50). In his will, made 7 Nov 1772 William Young named his wife Clare and his nephew William Godsgrace and niece Rebecca Godsgrace (BAWB 3:234).

Young, William, merchant of Baltimore, and Arabella Loney of Harford Co., were m. (*Maryland Journal and Baltimore Advertiser* 28 Jan 1783).

Young, William, warned all persons from harboring his runaway son Robert (*Maryland Journal and Baltimore Advertiser* 15 May 1795).

Young, William Price, and Dinah Cox were m. by lic. on 17 April 1785 (BAML). Dinah Young, (formerly Cox), on 26 d. 4 m. 1788 was charged with marrying outside the order ("Minutes of Gunpowder Meeting," *QRNM:* 85).

Youngblood, John Miles, on 17 Jan 1734 was named as a son by Mary Miles (BALR HWS#M: 16).

"Z"

Zacharie, Stephen, and Ann Waters, daughter of the late Ann Harding Waters, dec., entered into their marriage articles on 12 May 1787. Philip Waters and James Waters were also named in the document. (BALR WG#AA: 201). Zacharie, a French merchant who had lately arrived here from Holland, and Ann Waters, daughter of Philip Waters, merchant, were married last Sat. evening (*Maryland Journal and Baltimore Advertiser* 15 May 1787). They were m. by lic. on 12 May 1787 at St. Peter's Catholic Church, Baltimore (*Piet:* 145). Zacharie, executor, on 1 June 1796 posted bond to administer the estate of Elizabeth Waters (BAAB 8:876).

Zeigler (Ziegler), John, and Ann Kris [*sic*] were in Nov 1788 (Marr. Returns of Rev. Daniel Kurtz, Scharf Papers, MS. 1999 at MdHS). On 17 Oct 1791 Ann was named as having formerly been Ann Keys (BALR WG#HH:192).

Zeller, Andrew, m. by 3 July 1790, Johanna, daughter of Jacob Epaugh (BAWB 4:496).

Zenk, [-?-], m. by 4 Sep 1763, Margaret, daughter of Jacob Algire (BAWB 3:26).

Zenk, John, on 4 Sep 1763 was named as stepson in the will of John Algire, who had m. Hannah [-?-]. (BAWB 3:26),

Zentz, Christian, m. by 20 Dec 1762 Magdalena Walterin ("First Record Book for the Reformed and Lutheran Congregations at Manchester, Baltimore (now Carroll) Co.," *MGSB* 35:267).

Zentz (Senz), Joh. Peter, m, by 29 April 1765 Maria Eva Fritschin ("First Record Book for the Reformed and Lutheran Congregations at Manchester, Baltimore (now Carroll) Co.," *MGSB* 35:269).

Zep, Francis, on 28 April 1794 was named as a son-in-law in the will of Leonard Sabel of North Hundred (BAWB 5:260).

Zep, Leonhart, m. by 7 Dec 1798, [Turtete?] Stenern ("Reformed Congregation of Saint Benjamin's, Known as Kreider's, Church at Pipe Creek, Maryland [Westminster]," *MGSB* 35:440).

Zimmerman, [-?-], m. by 4 Sep 1763 Katherine, daughter of Jacob Algire (BAWB 3:26).

Zimmerman, Henry, and wife Mary, on 1 Aug 1800 agreed to separate (BACT WG#7:272).

Zobst, John, advertised that his wife Carolina had left him (*Maryland Gazette or Baltimore General Advertiser* 5 Nov 1784).

Zollickoffer, John Conrad de, merchant, and Caroline Tripolet, both of Baltimore, were married last evening (*Maryland Gazette or Baltimore General Advertiser* 23 Jan 1784; BAML). In May 1791 Caroline was named as a daughter of Mary Magdalen Tripolet (BAWB 5:24; BAAD 12:288).

Zorn, Christian, in his will made 29 Dec 1800 named his wife Eve and his brother-in-law Frederick Anspach (BAWB 6:351).

Zuill, William, and Clarinda Kingslane were married by license dated 29 April 1786 (BAML). She m. 2nd, James Slemaker (*q.v.*).

Zurbuchen, Henrich, m. by 8 Feb 1765, Anna Ecklerin ("First Record Book for the Reformed and Lutheran Congregations at Manchester, Baltimore (now Carroll) Co.," *MGSB* 35:269).

Zweiler, James, and Catharina Christina Gonderman, both of Baltimore, were m. yesterday (*Baltimore American* 11 Aug 1800).

Zwisler, James, of Baltimore, and Miss Ann Albers of Bremen, were married last evening by Rev. Mr. Kurtz (*Federal Intelligencer and Baltimore Daily Gazette* 9 April 1795).

Appendix 1: The Merry Widows of Baltimore County

This chart was compiled to help me understand the sequel of marriages for many of the women mentioned in the text, and also to assist in the proper indexing of their names. Sometime different accounts give differing order of the marriages and variations in the spelling of names. Although I did not tabulate the marriages of men or the innumerable second marriages of women, I did find that 63 women were married three times; eight were married four times and one woman had five husbands.

Married 3 Times

Ann [-?-] m. 1st, James Stringer, 2nd, William York, and 3rd, John Collier.

Ann [-?-] m. 1st. Nicholas Horner, 2nd, Matthew Beck, and 3rd, Henry Waters.

Ann Gorsuch, m. 1st, Thomas Todd, 2nd, David Jones, and 3rd, John Oldton.

Ann Taylor m. 1st, James Greer, 2nd, Laurence Richardson, and 3rd, Oliver Harriott.

Bothia (Bethia) Loney, m. 1st, James Barnes, 2nd, [-?-] Adams, and 3rd, [-?-] Scarlett.

Diana [-?-] m. 1st Matthew Hale, 2nd, William Hutchings, and 3rd Nicholas Beason (Besson).

Edith Cromwell m. 1st, Richard Gist, 2nd, Joseph Williams, and 3rd, John Beecher.

Eleanor Dorsey m. 1st Thomas Todd, 2nd, William Lynch, and 3rd John Cromwell.

Eleanor Gurney m. 1st, Lewis Owings, 2nd, Stephen Body, and 3rd, Luke Trotten.

Elinor Odan m. 1st John Durbin, 2nd Alexander Hill, and 3rd, [?] Bennett.

Elizabeth [-?-] m. 1st James Cogell, 2nd, Robert Dorman, and 3rd, Daniel Swindell.

Elizabeth [-?-] m. 1st, Jacob Loton, 2nd, by 16 April 1694, 2nd, William York, and 3rd, James Frizzle.

Elizabeth [-?-] m. 1st, [-?-] Frazier, 2nd, Richard Hewet, and 3rd Benjamin Price.

Elizabeth [-?-] m. 1st Philip Hiteshue, 2nd, Thomas Russell, and 3rd, John Ebbert.

Elizabeth Barton m. 1st, in 1727, William Wright, 2nd, 1741. James Greer, and 3rd, Heathcote Pickett.

Elizabeth Ford m. 1st, Job Barnes, 2nd, Matthias Clark, and 3rd William Norton.

Elizabeth Giles, m. 1st, James Slemaker, 2nd, Joseph Bankson, and 3rd, Michael Webster.

Elizabeth Goldsmith m. 1st, Nathaniel Utie, 2nd, Henry Johnson, and Edward Boothby.

Elizabeth Gurney m. 1st, Levi Owings, 2nd, Stephen Body, and 3rd, Luke Trotten.

Elizabeth Martin m. 1st, Richard Dallam, 2nd, William Smith, and 3rd, John Paca.

Elizabeth Trehearne m. 1st, William Ball, 2nd, William Cromwell, and 3rd, George Ashman.

Frances [-?-] m. 1st, Daniel Johnson, 2nd, Hugh Grant, and 3rd, Miles Foy.

Frances Phillips m. 1st, William Gough, 2nd, Joseph Stansbury, and 3rd, Augustine Porter.

Hannah [-?-] m. 1st, Daniel Peverell, 2nd, George Smith, and 3rd, David Thomas.

Hannah Matthews m. 1st, Asael Maxwell, 2nd, Abraham Johns, and 3rd, John Hall, Jr.

Isabel [-?-] m. 1st, Abraham Holman, 2nd, Edward Ayres, and 3rd, James Collier.

Jane [-?-] m. 1st, [-?-] Waites or Wright, 2nd, John Dixon, and 3rd, Thomas Long.

Jane Long m. 1st, Joseph Peake, 2nd, Charles Merryman, and 3rd, Benjamin Knight.

Jane Trippas m. 1st, William Choice, 2nd, John Durham, and 3rd, John Boone.

Jemima Morgan m. 1st, James Murray, 2nd, Thomas Cromwell, and 3rd, Patrick Simpson.

Joan [-?-] m. 1st, John Bay, 2nd, Christopher Bembridge, and 3rd, Daniel Crawley.

Johanna [-?-] m. 1st, James Phillips, 2nd, [-?-] Kemp, and 3rd, Aquila Hall.

Katherine [-?-] m. 1st, Stephen Hart, 2nd, John Scutt, and 3rd, Henry Knowles.

Margaret [-?-] m. 1st, John Wallston, 2nd, William Osborne, and 3rd, William Wise.
Martha [-?-] m. 1st, Mark Child, 2nd, Robert Cage, and 3rd, David Thurston.
Mary [-?-] m. 1st, John Dimmitt (Diamint), 2nd, William Gaine, and 3rd, Thomas Stone.
Mary [-?-] m. 1st, [-?-] Cannon; 2nd, Christopher Durbin; and 3rd, John Downes.
Mary [-?-] m. 1st, Thomas Gwynn, 2nd, William Hall, and 3rd, John Chapman.
Mary [-?-] m. 1st, [-?-] Jones, 2nd, Thomas Warren, and 3rd, James Isham.
Mary [-?-] m. 1st, Samuel Standiford, 2nd, John Bond, and 3rd, John Wesley.
Mary [-?-] m. 1st, Richard Marshall, 2nd, Joseph Foresight, and 3rd, Richard Blood.
Mary [-?-] m. 1st, Thomas Gash, 2nd, Richard Perkins, and 3rd, John Belcher.
Mary Ashbury m. 1st, [-?-] Alkin, 2nd, Reuben Gilder, and 3rd John Chalmers.
Mary Dowse m. 1st, [-?-] Harrison, 2nd, Thomas James, and 3rd, John Hillen.
Mary Goldsmith m. 1st, Robert Gibson, 2nd, George Wells, and 3rd, William Marshall
Mary Hill m. 1st, James Crouch, 2nd, John Rowles, and 3rd, Philip Jones.
Mary Kimball m. 1st, Thomas Jackson, 2nd, John Roberts, 3rd David Hughes.
Mary Spry m. 1st Godfrey Harmer, 2nd, Dr. John Stansby, and 3rd, Richard Adams.
Priscilla Thomas m. 1st, Richard Kilburne, 2nd, Thomas Freeborne, and 3rd, Samuel Howell.
Rebecca Harkins m. 1st, William Gain, 2nd, James Boring, and 3rd, James (or John) Frazier.
Rebecca Young m. 1st, Nicholas Clagett, 2nd, Edward Day, and 3rd, John Weston.
Rosanna [-?-] m. 1st, Jonas Robinson (Robertson?), 2nd, John Bowen, and 3rd, John Ogle.
Ruth [-?-] m. 1st, Hugh Frazier, 2nd, Stephen Moore, and 3rd Clement Skerrett.
Sarah [-?-] m. 1st, Edward Teale, 2nd, John Copus, and 3rd, Patrick Murphy.
Sarah [-?-] m. 1st, George Graves, 2nd, William Lowe, and 3rd, Lewis Lafee.
Sarah [-?-] m. 1st, John Wright, 2nd, Anthony Arnold, and 3rd, Charles Wells.
Sarah Holman m. 1st, George Hooper, 2nd, John Collier, and 3rd, John Hall.
Sarah Ray m. 1st, Thomas Hanson, 2nd, John Cockey, and 3rd, Benjamin Tayman.
Susanna [-?-] m. 1st, George Stokes, 2nd, Winston Smith, and 3rd Talbot Risteau.
Susanna [-?-] m. 1st William Orchard, 2nd, James Phillips, and 3rd, Benjamin Arnold.
Susanna Goldsmith m. 1st, George Utie, 2nd, Mark Richardson, and 3rd, Thomas Wainwright.
Susanna Higginson m. 1st, Thomas Brown, 2nd, Daniel Robinson, and 3rd, Garrett Garrettson.
Zipporah Hilyard m. 1st, Thomas Floyd, 2nd, Alexander Baker, and 3rd, Henry Maynard.

Married 4 Times
Alice [-?-] m. 1st, [-?-] Gill, 2nd, William Drury, 3rd, Peter Bond, and 4th, Philip Washington.
Ann/Amy [-?-] m. 1st, William Pearl, 2nd, Philip Pitstow (Pissons), 3rd, by Nov 1693, Stephen Bentley, and 4th, [-?-] Fenton.
Elizabeth [-?-] m. 1st, William Hollis, 2nd, Thomas Russell, 3rd, William Croshaw, and 4th, William Harris.
Elizabeth [-?-] m. 1st, John Collett, 2nd, Miles Gibson, 3rd, Richard Edmunds, and 4th, Henry Hazlewood.
Elizabeth [-?-] m. 1st, Richard Sampson, 2nd, James Bagford, 3rd, Samuel Hinton, and 4th, Thomas Stone.
Henrietta [-?-] m. 1st, William Robinson, 2nd, Edward Swanson, 3rd, Thomas Cannon, and 4th, Edward Reeves.

Mary [-?-] m. 1st, John Hammond, 2nd John Brand, 3rd, Edward Reeves, and 4th, Richard Askew.

Mary [-?-] m. 1st, John Forty, 2nd, John Connell, 3rd, William Nicholson, and 4th, Elisha Hall.

Sarah Wichell m. 1st, by 1 Dec 1686, John Kemp, 2nd, Edward Norris, 3rd. John Thomas, and 4th, Thomas Matthews.

Married 5 Times

Rebecca [-?-] m. 1st, John Daniell (or Darnall), 2nd, James Emson, 3rd, James Cobb, 4th, John Hawkins, and 5th, Gregory Farmer.

= = 0 = =

Appendix 2: Gone Out in Marriage

A number of members of the Society of Friends married "outside of meeting,' 'contrary to discipline,' or 'were married by a hireling minister.' As this chart shows, it has not always been possible to determine exactly when or where such marriages took place.

Gone out in Marriage	Men	Women
Total entries	95	109
Marr. Not Found	50	57
% Not Found	52.6%	52.2%
Marriage Found	45	52
% Found	47.3%	47.7%
No. in Balto. Co.	37	43
No. in Harford Co.	7	12
No. Elsewhere	1	

= = 0 = =

Appendix 3: Marital Discord

Marriages were not always happy, even in 'the good old days.' In the days before newspapers, some of the earliest notices of unhappy relationships were recorded in the land records, perhaps because when the husband wanted to record his intentions of not paying the debts of his wife, the land record liber was the book most likely to be open in the court house.

A: Length of marriage not known. B: Married under 1 year; C: Married under 2 years; D: Married under 5 years; E: Married under 10 years; F Married over 10 years.

Years	Total	A	B	C	D	E	F
1659-1776	38	24	2	1	3	4	4
%		63.1%	5.2%	2.6%	7.8%	10.5%	10.5
1777-1783	46	33	5	4	2	1	1
%		71.7%	10.8%	8.6%	4.3%	2.1%	2.1%
1784-1800	152	88	15	11	15	13	***9
%		57.8%	9.8%	7,2%	9.8%	8.5%	5.9%

It will be noted that as the 18th century progressed more and more couples were found to put their problems, separation, infidelity, abusive behavior, on record. As the following examples show, it was not just the 'newly weds' who had problems.

In the first time period 1659-1776, Thomas and Prudence Cockey had been married 22 years.
For the years 1777-1783, William and Ruth Gill had been married for 23 Years.
In the third time span, 1784-1800, John and Eleanor Pindell had been married for 31 years.

$$= = 0 = =$$

Barkever: Mary 231
Barkley: Jane M'Cormick 16; Thomas 16
Barkley: See also Barclay.
Barlar: Mary 16, 127
Barlo:, Barsheba 16; Bathsheba 172; Elizabeth 216; James 16, 172, 255; Joanna [-?-] 16
Barly: Mary 16
Barnaby: Elias 16, 325; Rachel Riffitt 16
Barnerd,: James 16; Mary [-?-] 16
Barnes: [-?-] Ogg 17; Ann 237; Avarilla 12; Bethia Loney 16; Bothia [-?-] Barnes 339; Catherine Shipley 16; Constance West 17; Dorsey 16; Elijah 16; Elizabeth 120; Elizabeth Culver 17; Elizabeth Mitchell 16; Ford 16, 282, 339; Gregory 16; Hannah 266; Isabella 16; James 16, 17, 339, 429; Jemima 220; Job 17, 282, 429; John 220, 339; Ketura Shipley 16; Lydia [-?-] 16; Margaret 232; Mary 17, 199; Philemon 17; Ruth Garrett 16; Sarah Baxter 120; William 339
Barnes: See also Barns.
Barnet: Catherine [-?-] 167; [-?-] 17; Ann 131; Betsy 253; Catherine 259; Eliza Algire 17; Mary Owings 17; Peter 17
Barnett: Andrew 251; Catherine [-?-] 168; Hannah 359; Hannah Spencer 17
Barney: [-?-] 17; Absalom 17, 18, 336; Benjamin 17, 18, 87; Charity Stiles 17; Delilah Bosley 17; Frances Holland Watts 17; John 17, 425; Joseph Bosley 17; Marcy Ford 17; Martha 190; Mary [-?-] 18, 129, 130, 336; Mary Chase 18; Mary Ford 17; Mary Kerlinger 17; Mary Stevenson 17; Moses 17, 18; Polly 24; Rebecca Ridgely 18; Rebecca Shelmerdine 17; Ruth 130; Sarah Bond 17; William 17, 18, 130, 190, 246, 270, 287, 336; William B. 18
Barnharton: Catherine 18
Barnisger: Christian 18; Mary Myer 18

Barnitz: Ann Elizabeth 175; Charles 175; Jacob 175
Barns: Ford 16, 266; Gregory 16; Rachel 364
Barns: See also Barnes.
Baron: See also Buron.
Baroux: James Michael 18; Mary Deagle 18
Barrett:[-?-] 18; Alice [-?-] Corbin 18; Ann 82; Esther 377; Jenney 163; John 18, 79, 82, 279, 377; Mary 279; Susannah Onion 17; William 82, 279, 377; Zacheus 18
Barrier: Eliza Angelica 383
Barron; Margaret 232; Sally Brownley 18; William 18
Barrot: See Barrett.
Barrott: See Barrett.
Barrow: Elizabeth 1; Elizabeth [-?-] 407; Elizabeth [-?-] Baldwin 18; John 18
Barrows: Elizabeth 233
Barru: Abigail 167
Barry: [-?-] 18; [-?-] Hanson 18; John 18; Elizabeth [-?-] Diffenderfer 18; Elizabeth Messersmith 18; Jemima Gorsuch Stansbury 18; Johanna Hannecy 18; John 18; Lavalin 18; Nancy Thompson 18; Polly 322; Redmon 18; Standish 18
Bartle: Ann [-?-] 21; John 21
Bartlett: Susanna 248
Barton: Abigail [-?-] 193; Ann Biddle 19; Ann Hitchcock 19; Comfort [-?-] 240; Comfort Roberts 19; Dorothy Nice 19, 124; Elizabeth 18; Greenbury 19; James 19, 281; Jane [-?-] 122; Johanna Simmons 19; John 19, 124; Joshua 206, 329; Judith [-?-] 19; Lewis 19, 122; Mary 206; Philizanna 281; Rebecca Biddison 19; Sally 232; Sally Maxwell 19; Sarah [-?-] 329; Sarah Dorman 19, 240; Seth 19; Susanna Sharp 19; Temperance Rollo 19; Thomas 281
Baseman: [-?-] Owings 19; John 19
Basey; John 19

Carty: Ann 175; Sarah 385; Timothy 62

Carvill: Blanch 166; John 166; Mary Phillips 166

Carville: Avarilla 62; John 62; Mary 299; Mary Phillips 9, 62

Casey: Eleanor 257; Elizabeth 138; Elizabeth [-?-] 113; Elizabeth Davies 62; Casey, John 62, 121; Robert 62

Cassat: Peter 62; Susanna Stansbury 62

Cassel: Mary Magdalene Decker 98

Cassidy: [-?-] 62; Hannah Read 62; Hannah Reed 62; Jane Dunn Wood 62, 419; Cassidy, Patrick 62

Caswell: Jane [-?-] Leary 63; Richard 63; Thomas 63

Cates: Jane 277; ane Nailor 63

Cathell. See Cammell.

Caton: Ann Cherry 63; Clare [-?-] 63; Eleanor 26; James, 63; Juliet 314; Mark 63; Matthew 216; Polly Carroll 63; Richard 63, 155

Cattle: Lydia 56

Catto: Araminta [-?-] Young 63; George 63

Catts: Jane Naylor 63

Catts; See also Cates.

Caulk: Anne 365

Causton: Esther 63; William 63

Cavannah: Mary Litten Renshaw 321; Patrick 321

Cavannah. See also Cavenagh.

Cavaroc: Catherine Magne 63; Francis 63; John 63; Mary Sears 63

Cavenagh: Mary [-?-] Renshaw 63; Patrick 63

Cavenagh. See also Cavannah.

Cayol: Antony 63; Modeste Tardieu 63

Cebron,: Mary Joanna Foushne Trouve 63; Olivier 63

Celestin: Mary 137

Celeston: Mary 56

Chabert,: Anthony 63; Rene Charlotte DeMontdieu Pilot 63

Chadbourne, [-?-] Foxon 63; William 63

Chadbourne. See also Chandbourne.

Chadwell: John 25, 213; Katherine [-?-] 25; Margaret 213

Chadwell. See also Chadwil; Shadwell.

Chadwick, Catherine 371

Chadwil: Elizabeth 204; John 204

Chadwil. See also Chadwell, Shadwell.

Chaeld: Elizabeth [-?-] 63; Samuel 63

Chailan: Catherine 25; Mary Ann 244

Chainey: [-?-] 63

Chalk: Ann 365; Joseph 365

Chalke: Eliz. Hughes 64; George 64

Chalmers: John 3, 64, 144, 430; Mary Burneston Ashberry Alkin Gilder 3, 64, 144, 430

Chamberlain: Charles 64; John 64, 239; Margaret Gittings 64; Mary 239; Mary Guthrow 64

Chambers: Daniel 370; James 64; Jane 159; Mary [-?-] Rowles 64; Mary McLaughlin 64; Mary Tipton 64; Sarah 64, 303; William 64

Chameau: Peggy 299

Chamier: [-?-] 59; Achsah 285; Achsah Ridgely Carnan 59, 64; Daniel 64; Elizabeth 285

Chamillon: Ann Meade 64; Joseph 64

Chamness: Anthony 64; Sarah Cole 64

Chamney: George 64; Mary 64, 115

Chamney. See also Chancey.

Champion: Isaac 64

Chance: [-?-] 64; Elizabeth 64; Martha Watkins 64

Chancey: George 64, 65, 353; Mary Little 65; Sarah 64; Sarah Hollis Smith 64, 353

Chandbourne: William 63

Chandbourne. See also Chadbourn.

Chandler: Sarah [-?-] 47

Chaney: [-?-] 65; Ann 417; Benjamin Burgess 65; Elizabeth Lane 65; George 64; Margaret 314, 347; Margaret Montgomery 66; Margaret Shipley 65; Mary 178; Susan 6

Chaney. See also Chancey, Cheney, Sheney.

Changeuir: Jane Josephine Moncrave Montalebor 65; John 65; Josephine DeGripier Monroe Motalibor 65; Leon 65; Mary Samson 65; Peter 65

Chanley: Drewsilla 103

Channell: Edward 65

Chantrier: Catherine Mary Lemonnier 160; Charles 160

Chapel: James 381; Lucy 100; Mary

Davey: Ann 349; Catherine Sarah 258;
Eliza 120; Elizabeth [-?-] 258;
Samuel Carson 349
Davey. See also Davoy.
Davice. See Davis.
David: Elizabeth 92; Lucy 175;
Thomas 213
Davidge: Providence [-?-] 321;
Robert 321
Davidson: Agnes 78; Andrew 78, 92,
136, 252, 277, 283; Ann Stokes 92;
Christiana [-?-] 92; Delia [-?-] 92;
Eleanor Strachan 92; Eliz. 277;
Elizabeth 283; Elizabeth Miller 92;
James 92; Job 92, 120; John 341;
John 92; Margaret Scott 92, 341
Martha 408; Mary [-?-] 136;
Mesha[-?-] McCay 52; Meshaw
Donnal 92; Miszey Donnal 92;
William 92
Davies; Catherine Skaats 92; Elizabeth
62; Vaughan 92
Davis: Aaron 93; Abednego 93; Alce
Harriman 93; Amos 93; Ann 236;
Ann Clary 93; Ann Davis 94; Ann
Eaglestone 93, 126; Benjamin 93;
Betsy 403; Catherine 203, 225;
Catherine [-?-] 343; Catherine
Fitzgerald 93; Christian 388; Deborah
[-?-] Renshaw 94, 320; Elizabeth 62
93, 255, 281, 391, 405; Elizabeth
[-?-] 94; Elizabeth Birmingham 93;
Elizabeth Britt 93; Elizabeth Cox 93;
Francis 93, 343, 405; Gaither 93;
Henry 177, 236, 239, 281, 324;
Henry Ferguson 93; Ignatius 93;
Jacob 251; John 46, 93, 255, 410;
Joseph 93; Margaret [-?-] 46;
Margaret Stocksdale 93; Martha 51,
248; Mary 93, 171, 324, 388;
Mary [-?-] 93, 251. 255, 342, 416;
Mary Baker 94; Mary Brown 93;
Mary Burdan 93; Mary Carson 93;
Mary Neil 94; Mary Pierpoint 301;
Nathaniel 342; Rachel [-?-] 213;
Rebecca 52, 53; Rhoda 52; Robert
93; Rosanna McGinnis 93; Ruth 405;
Samuel 94, 320; Sarah 94, 324; Sarah
James93; Teresa Williams 93;
Thomas 403; Uriah 46, 93, 94

William 94; Zachariah 94; Zipporah
342
Davoy: Ann Knowlen 94; Michael 94
Davoy. See also Davy.
Davy: Mary 94
Dawes: Merab (Mareb) 94, 210
Dawkins: Ann Smith 94; Elizabeth
[-?-] Goldsmith 94; James 94, 343,
357; Miles 94; Symon 94; William
94
Dawney: Ann Green Cowdray 82, 94;
James 420; John 94, 105, 204;
Lydia Swift 94; Mary Woodland 94;
Thomas 82, 94; William 105
Dawson: Anne Robertson 95; Elizabeth
95; Martha 95; Mary Doyne 94;
Sarah 14; William 95
Dawtha: Ann 42
Day; Abarilla Taylor 95; Agnes Young
95; Andrew 95; Ann 95; Ann Fell 95
Anna 4; Avarilla 4; Avarilla [-?-]
305; Avarilla Taylor 241; Bridget
Collins 95; Dinah 261; Edward 4, 19,
68, 95, 107, 241, 305, 324, 407, 425,
430; Edward Fell 123; Elizabeth 95;
Elizabeth [-?-] 96; Emmory 95, 267;
James 372; Jane 4; John 95, 96, 249,
324, 425; Margaret 229; Mary [-?-]
Yarby 95; Mary Gouldsmith
Presbury 95; Mary Matthews
Gassaway 141; Nicholas 95, 96, 261;
Philizanna Maxwell 324; Phillis Zana
[-?-] 249; Phillis Zana Maxwell 95;
Rebecca 273, 407; Rebecca Clagett
95; Samuel 96; Sarah 41, 107, 407,
422; Sarah Horner York 95, 425:
Sarah Talbott 96; William 272
Dayley: Elizabeth 357
Dea: Eliza Pierpoint 301
Deagan: Elizabeth 89; Frances Brothers
96; George 96; Henry 96; Patrick 96;
Polly McComas 96
Deagen: Peter 96; Salome [-?-] 96
Deagle: Elizabeth Boudville 96; Lamm
96; Mary 18; Simon 96
Deal: Christian 96; Eleanor Bowen 96;
Elizabeth 96; Hannah Steltz 96;
Josias 96; Mary 227; Millicent [-?-]
96; Peter 96
Deal. See also Deale.

101

Devag(h)a. See Deveghe.

Deval: Ann 371

Devalcourt: Alexander 101; Margaret Goto 101

Deveghe: Elizabeth Ayres Deyson 101; John 101, 393

DeVelcourt: Samuel Mangee 304

Devenbaugh: Catherine 417; Michael 417

Devenois: Louisa 303

Device: John Darch Lovel 101

Device, Margaret Summers 101; John Darch Live 101

Devinbaugh; Catherine 148; Michael 148

Devine: Charles 101; Divine, Elizabeth 103; Sarah [-?-] 101

Devorn: William 101

Devoss: Matthias 249, 250

Dew(s): Ann 406; Ann Gatch 101; Eliza [-?-] 101; Elizabeth 275; Elizabeth [-?-] 275; Elizabeth Stansbury 101; Esther Raven 101; Mary 120; Robert 101; Thomas 101, 275; William 275

Dewees: Mary 253

Dewit: [-?-] Adams 102; Ann 102; Catherine 102; Thomas 102

Dewit. See also Jewit.

Dews: Ann 406

Deye: Cassandra 73; Charcilla Cockey 71, 129; Colegate 288; Penelope 71; Penelope [-?-] 73, 129

Deyson:Elizabeth [-?-] 393; Elizabeth Ayres 101; William 101, 393

Deyson: William 101

Diamint: John 136, 369, 430; Mary [-?-] 136; Mary [-?-] Gaine Stone 369

Diamint. See also Dimmit.

Diamont: John 60, 102; Mary [-?-] 60, 102

Diamont: See also Dimmit.

Dicas: Thomas 348

Dickenson: David 102; Eleanor Hickey 102

Dickey: Ann Thompson 102; John 102

Dickinson: Brittingham 344; Sarah 102, 422

Dicks: Abraham 102; Catherine [-?-] 102; Catherine Dean 102; Edmund 102; Peter 102; Richard 102

Dickson: Drusilla 10; Elizabeth 122; James 122, 181; Margaret 181

Dickson. See also Dixon.

Dieter; Susanna [-?-] 142

Dietz: Maria Eva Staehlin 102; Michel 102

Diffenderfer: Cathrina Mayer 102; Dorothy [-?-] 102; Elizabeth [-?-] 18; Eve 3; Michael 3, 102; Peter 102

Diffendolph: Catherine 182

Digabeau. See Dizabeau.

Dillen: Anna Maria 123

Dillin: Anna 340; Anna Maria 123; Catharina 25

Dillon: Elizabeth 212; Henry 61, 102; Kitty 132; Margaret 59

Dilly: Anna Maria Heerin 102: Catharina Himpin 102; Joh. 102; Johannes 10

Dilworh; Letitia 205; Kezia Greenfield 102; William 102

Dimmitt: Catherine Warden Bull 103; Delilah Jessop 103; Elisha 103; John 103,136, 369, 430; Lettis 103; Mary [-?-] 103, 136; Mary [-?-] Gaine Stone 369; Susanna 103 Viola 103, 140; William 103

Disney: Thomas 103; William 103

Distance: Hetty [-?-] 103; William 103

Ditto: Abraham 136; Catherine Conrad 103; Christiana [-?-] 136; Mary 103; Ditto, Peter 103

Diver: Jane Oyston 103

Divers: Ann 103; Belinda Eaglestone 103; Christopher 103, 280, 286; Francis 103; John 103; Mary Watters 103; Permelia 280; Sarah [-?-] Nixon 103; Sarah Thompson Nixon 280; Tamson 103

Dives. See Divers.

Divine. See Devine.

Dixon: Abigail 177; Elizabeth 21, 103; Elizabeth [-?-] 103; Jane [-?-] 237; John 177, 237, 342, 363, 429; Morris 103; William 103

Dixon. See also Dickson.

Dizabeau: John 104; Magdalen Holmes

Fahnestock: Derick 121; Sarah Deardorf 121
Fairbanks: Amelia Beckley 121; William 121
Falher: Mary 228
Falkner: Mary [-?-] Brown 122; Samuel 122
Fall: Neal 122; Susannah Body 122
Falls: Abby Biddle 122; Moore 122, 417; Rebecca Neilson Wilson 122, 417
Falsgraff: Maria 322
Farfar(r), Elinor [-?-] Harriman 122; Jane [-?-] Barton 122; Judith [-?-] Barton 19; William 19, 122, 174, 216
Farfer. See Farfar.
Faris: Elizabeth [-?-] 122; George 122
Farlaw: Catherine [-?-] 122; Robert 122
Farlow: Elizabeth [-?-] Little 122, 234; Thomas 12, 234
Farly, Bridget 60
Farmer, Gregory 71, 118, 122, 176, 339, 431; Rachel [-?-] Daniell (Darnall) Emson Cobb Hawklns 71, 118, 122, 431
Farquhar: Adam 312; Elizabeth [-?-] 312; James 122; Rebecca 312; Sarah Moore 122
Farr: Elisabeth Dickson 122
Farrell: Catherine Blake 122; George 67; Mary [-?-] 67; Timothy122
Farris: Ann 248
Fasbender: Anna Catharine 396
Faubel: Margaretha Metzin 122; Peter 122
Faubel. See also Fauble.
Faubelin: Catherina 277
Fauble: George 122; Jacob 122; Margaret Hoefligh 122; Mary Leichte 122
Fauble. See also Faubel, Faubel.
Fauche: Felicity 397
Faupel: Melchor 122; Sabina Meyerin 122
Faur(e): Antoine 122; Janett Ann Brotherson 122; Mary Ann 24
Favier: John 122; Mary Thompson 122
Fearson: Hannah [-?-] Wells 122; Jesse 22
Feather: Anna Maria Dillien 123;

Henry 123; Philip 123
Federl Adam 12; Anna Maria Dillin 133; Philip 123
Feetz. See Feitz.
Feik: Elizabeth Tietzen 1234; Henry 123
Feitz: Eva Elizabeth Roop 123; Ulrich 123
Felkes: Ann [-?-] 250; Ann [-?-] Johnson 160; Edward 123, 160
Fell: Ann 95, 394; Ann [-?-] 144, 394; Ann [-?-] Edwards 123; Ann Bond 123; Catherine 32, 124; Edward 123, 144, 394; Jennet 123, 124; Margaret 123; Sarah Bond 123; Sarah Bond Dorsey 106; Stephen 123; William 32, 123, 124, 144, 346
Felt: [-?-] Renecker 123; Jacob 123
Fenby: John 123, 390; Margaret [-?-] 390; Margaret [-?-] Turner 123
Fendall: Anne [-?-] 123; Elizabeth Brocklesby 123; James 123
Fengeas: Lewis 123; Magdalen Pratt 123; Mary Jane Theresa Pelletier 123; Matthew 123
Fenix: Judith 88
Fennell: Ann 124; John 124; Sarah Miller 124
Fenton: Ann Amy [-?-] Pearl Pitstiow (Pissons) Bentley 25, 124, 295, 302,, 430
Fenwick: Jan [-?-] 124
Ferguson: Elizabeth 308; Mary 208
Ferrell: James 124; Mary [-?-] 227; William 124, 227
Ferri: Catherine Trueman 124; Janarius 124
Ferrier. See Terrier.
Ferron: Elizabeth Delanco 124; John 124
Ferry: John 35, 124
Few: Isaac 32, 124; Jenet [-?-] 32; Jenet Bond 124; Jennet Fell 124; Mary Wheeler 124; William 124, 346
Fewis: Dorothy [-?-] Nice 124
Fews: [-?-] 19; Fews, Dorothy Nice Barton 19, 124
Ficke: Herman 124; Nancy Cain 124
Field(s), Ann 264, 271; Elizabeth 225; Mary 298; Sarah 124

Humphries, Umphrey.
Humphries: Ann 249
Humphries. See also Humphrey.
Humphris. See Humphrey.
Hunn: Francis 198, 304; Margaret [-?-]
James 198; Mary [-?-] 198
Hunt: Ann Wiley 87, 198, 411;
Elizabeth 158; Elizabeth [-?-] 31,
213, 356; Elizabeth [-?-] Hendrickson
198; Elizabeth [-?-] Smith 198;
Elizabeth [-?-] Wright 199; Elizabeth
Chew 198; Henry 356; Job 198, 356;
John 213; Margaret 192, 198;
Margaret Hopkins 198; Mary
Holland 188, 198; Phineas 198, 356;
Samuel 31, 356; Sarah 97, 198;
Susanna 198; Thomas 31, 87, 198,
411; William 199; Wolfron 213
Hunter: Curtis Grub 199; Esther Scott
199, 341; Mary [-?-] 199; Peter 199,
341; Sarah Crayton 84; William 199
Huntziner: Ann 267
Hurd: John 17, 194, 199; Ruth
Norwood 199; Sarah 194;
Hurford: Hannah [-?-] 199; John 199;
Joseph 199
Hurley: Bridget 240
Hurst: Abraham 199; John 199; Judith
88
Husband: Joseph 178, 193, 199, 263;
Mary 178, 193; Mary [-?-] 178, 199,
263; Sarah 193
Husbands: Joshua 199; Mary [-?-] 199
Hush: Catherine Councilman 199;
Conrad 173, 350; Jacob 199; John
199; Margaret [-?-] Watts 199
Husk. See Hush.
Huson: Mary 199
Hussey: George 199; Miriam 200;
Rachel Hayward 199; Ruth 249
Hutchings: Ann 5, 200; Grace [-?-]
Adams 200: James 200; Judith Clarke
Hope 191, 200; Kesiah 200; Moses
200; Nicholas 5; Sarah 200; Thomas
200; William 26, 191, 200, 429
Hutchins: Elizabeth 200; Elizabeth
Robinson 200; Jemima [-?-] 200;
John 200; Nicholas 76, 200; Susanna
[-?-] Richardson 200; Thomas 200;

William 120, 330
Hutchinson: Joseph 200; Kezia Rifflett
200; Phebe 161, 177, 381; Phebe
[-?-] McCabe 200, 251; Rebecca 379;
Robert 200, 251; Sarah Doyne 200;
William 200
Hutton: Jane 275
Hyatt: Rebecca Miller 200; William
200
Hydie: George 200; Rachel Griffith
200
Hyland: Ann Johnson 200; John 200;
Stephen 118, 200
Hyner. See Hiner.
Hynes. See Hines.
Hynson, Anita Matthews 200; Charle
200
Iams: Margaret Clark Williams 412;
William 412
Iams. See also Ijams.
Ibach: Anna Catherine Gussin 201;
Elisabeth Kerlingerin 201; Elisabetha
Gerling 201; He(i)nrich 201; Jacob
201
Ibach. See also Epaugh.
Ickesin: Margareta 187
Igo: Elizabeth Marsh 201; William 201
Ijams: John 201, 400; Margaret [-?-]
Williams 201; William 201
Ilgar: Catherine 108; Eve 53; George
19, 53, 108; Katherine 108
Illingworth: [-?-] 173
Imbleton: Ann Bryan 201; Edward 201
Ingerom. See Ingram.
Ingle: Catherine 201; John 201; Samuel
201; William 119, 201
Inglish: Ann [-?-] 47; Dennis 47
Ingram: Dorcas 389; John 260, 389;
Peasley 133, 201; Phoebe Whitehead
125, 201; Ruth 35, 279; Ruth [-?-]
133; Ruth Franklin 133; Ruth
Hammond 201; Susanna 49; William
125, 201, 410
Inkston: Elizabeth 237
Inloes: Abraham 172; Anthony 380;
David 84, 202; Eliza 173; Elizabeth
380; Henry 202; Mary [-?-] 84; Mary
Cole 202
Inloes. See also Enloes, Enlows.

Jansen: Janette 37
Jantzin: Anna 389
Jaquet: Jesse 206; John Paul 206
Jaquet. See also Jacquett.
Jarman: Cassandra 206; John 206, 321;
  Lewis, 142: Martha 206; Mary 206,
  327; Mary Barton 206; Mary Rawley
  206; Ruth 321; Thomas 206, 327;
  William 206
Jarold: Betsy 276; Thomas 276
Jarold. See also Jarrold.
Jarratts: [-?-] 206; Elizabeth 206
Jarratts. See also Jarrold.
Jarrett: Abraham 53, 207, 257, 278;
  Marthes [Martha?] Bussey 206; Mary
  53
Jarrold: Catherine 263; Catherine
  Payne 207; Elizabeth 207, 262, 263;
  Mary 207
Jarrold. See also Jarold, Jarratts.
Jarves. See Jarvis.
Jarvis: Elizabeth Oursler 206; John
  207; Mary 330; Mary Conaway 207;
  Philip 207, 330; Samuel 137, 207;
  Sarah 207, 222; Sarah Wright 207
Jay: Anne [-?-] Williams 207;
  Hannah 380; Hannah Wilson 207;
  Joseph 207; Sophia 282; Stephen 207,
  380; Thomas 207, 282
Jeff: Elizabeth [-?-] 285; Elizabeth
  Aishleys 297; Margaret 207; Ruth
  Matthews 207; William 207,
  285
Jeffers: Catherine Robinson 207;
  George 207; John 159
Jeffery. See Jeffries.
Jeffries: John 159; Mary Puntany 207;
  Sarah [-?-] 159; William 207;
Jeger: Mary Millward 207
Jenkins: Ann 191; Ann Hillen 208;
  Cassandra 207; Charity Wheeler 207;
  Eleanor 208; Eliz. 68; Elizabeth 69,
  204, 207; Francis 207, 208; Henrietta
  [-?-] 369; Henry 208; Ignatius 208;
  Ignatius Walter 208; Jesse 208; John
  369; Mary 117; Mary Clarke 208,
  308; Michael 179, 191; Oswald 208;
  Samuel 208; Sarah 179, 297, 405;
  Teresa 208; Thomas Courtney 124,

163; William 68, 69, 117, 119, 208,
  294, 405
Jenkins. See also Jinkins.
Jennings: Aley Litten 208; Elizabeth
  44, 416; Hannah Rutledge 208;
  Henry 208; Jacob 108; Mary Cox
  208; Mary Kennedy 208; Samuel
  Kennedy 208; William 208, 416
Jenny: Joseph 208; Mary Conway 208;
  Nathaniel 14; Sarah Dawson 14
Jenny. See also Zenney.
Jervice: Hannah 4
Jervis: Eliza 359
Jessop: Charles 208; Delilah 99, 103;
  Elizabeth 378: Esther 129; Lydia
  Bosley 208; Mary Gorsuch 208;
  Nicholas 208; William 129, 378
Jewell: Alice 208, 252; Ann Webster
  208
Jewit: Ann 102; Ann [-?-] 199;
  Ann Webster 208; Margaret 199;
  Thomas 199
Jinkins: Avis 88; Sarah 162; Thomas
  88; William 88
Jinkins. See also Jenkins.
Jinnings. See Jennings.
Job: Ann 160; Morris 160
Johns: Abraham 166, 208, 250;
  Ann [-?-] 67; Ann Cole 208;
  Cassandra 20, 67, 208, 240; Drusilla
  Raven, 208; Elizabeth 34; Elizabeth
  [-?-] 34, 209; Johns, Elizabeth Kinsey
  208; Frances 84; Hannah [-?-] 166;
  Hannah Matthews Maxwell 208;
  Henry 209; Maria 205; Mary 208;
  Nathan 34, 208, 209: Philip 208;
  Polly Luce 209; Richard 67, 208,
  209; Sarah 367; Skipwith 209
Johnson: Abraham 209; Absolom 209;
  Alice [-?-] 320; Alice Bond 211; Alis
  Bond 211; Alisana 380; Ambrose
  209; Amos 13, 21; Andrew 62; Ann
  109, 200, 251, 371; Ann [-?-] 123,
  160, 210, 211, 298; Ann [-?-]
  Johnson 123; Ann Almony 209, 210;
  Ann Butler 209; Johnson,Ann Giles
  211; Ann Hall 210; Ann Plowman
  209; Anthony 195, 209; Archibald
  209; Beatrice Codd 209; Benea 283;

M'... names are often filed as Mc...
Mac'... names are often filed as Mc...
Macarty: William 331
Macckelltons: Margaret 57
Macckelltons. See also Mackeltoes,
  Mackintosh.
Macclain: William 411
Macllain: Se also Maclane, McClain(e),
  McLane, McLean.
Maccroy, Thomas 164
Maccubbin: Elizabeth 406
Maccubbin. See also Mc Cubbin.
Machanin: Rachel 285
Mack: Eleanor 15; James 15, 242;
  Margaret [-?-] Hammond 242; Robert
  39, 392
Mackadoe: J. 242; Nancy Spencer 242
Mackarny: Ann 60, 24
Mackelfresh: John 242; Margaret 242
Mackenell: Walter 215
Mackenheimer: Catherine
  Lindenberger 242; Gabriel 2645;
  John 242; Peter 49, 242; Susanna
  Alter 5; Susanna Clause 242
Mackenzie. See McKenzie,
Mackey: Hugh 242; Ruth Cromwell
  242; Sarah Henry 242; William 242
Mackie: Elizabeth Hollingsworth 242;
  John 242
Mackilvene: Ann 68
Mackin: James 242; Margaret
  Kellagrew 242
Mackintosh: Daniel 57, 173; Margaret
  [-?-] 57, 173
Mackintosh. See also Macckelltons,
  Mackeltoes.
Macknulty: Elizabeth 256
Mackubin: William 209
Mackubin. See also McCubbin.
Maclane: Hector 12; Sarah 12
Maclane. See also Macclain,
  McClain(e), McLane, McLean
Maclone: James 242, 286
Macnamara: Joanna 196
Madden: [-?-] 242; Elizabeth Host 242;
  John 242; Mary Clary 242
Maddox: Elizabeth [-?-] 164
Maddy: Ann [-?-] Gardiner 242;
  Margaret 242
Maeller: Adolphus 243, 264; Eliza
  McGlathery 243
Maerimann: Sophia 307

Maerrimann. See also Merryman.
Magamus: Henry 243; Susanna
  Hickman 243
Magar: Belinda 395
Magaw: Adam 304
Magee: Daniel 165, 243; Sarah [-?-]
  Hall 243; Sarah Phillips Hall 165
Magee. See also McGee, McGhee.
Mahan: Ann [-?-] Greening 243;
  Edward 243; John 43
Mahanne. See Mahone.
Mahany: Timothy 243
Mahiney. See Mahany.
Mahone: John 58, 154, 205, 243
Mahones: Frances 58
Maidwell: [-?-] 243; James 243;
  Temperance Carter 243
Maidwell. See also Maydwell.
Mainer: John 238; Sarah 238
Majers. See Majors.
Major(s): Diana Bosley 243; Elias 243;
  John 243; Rachel Baxter 243;
  Rebecca Pollard 243; Sarah 316;
  Thomas 316
Malance. See Malonee.
Malcom: Janet 412
Mallane. See Mallonee.
Mallanee. See Mallonee.
Mallence. See Mallone.
Maller: Setphen 304
Mallet: Francis 244; Mary Jane Yronet
  244; Nancy Pluschan 243; Peter 304;
  Thomas 243
Mallett: Nancy [-?-] Bishe 28, 243;
  Stephen 38, 243
Mallonee: Dennis 243; Edith Cole 243;
  Elizabeth 243; Emanuel 243; John
  243; Margaret Reeves 243
Malloney: john 243; Rachel 292
Malone: Eliza [-?-] 8; John 8; Lucy
  Belt 243
Malony: Avarila League 243; Catherine
  [-?-] Veal 244; James 143, 244
Malsby: Angeline 286
Malsby. See also Maulsby.
Mamillon: Magdalen 142
Manchote: John 244; Mary Viney 244
Mangee; Mary 80
Mangfee: Margaret 109
Mangroll: Mary 244
Manley: Henry 131
Mann: [-?-] Campbell 244; Benjamin

McCain. See McCann.

McCall: Elizabeth 285; Margaret [-?-] 136

McCall. See also McCool.

McCallum: Mary Smith 251

McCan: Ann Egan 251; Ann Johnson 251; John 251

McCan. See also McCann.

McCandless: George 251; Robert 251; Sarah Patterson 251

McCann: Ann 251; Ann [-?-] 112, 251; Catherine [-?-] 251; Catherine Lynch Donnally 104; Daniel 251; John 104, 112, 251; Patrick 2, 51

McCann. See also McCan.

McCannon: Catherine 252; James 191

McCarter: Margaret 252; William 252

McCartey: John 252; Rebecca Jordon 252

McCarthy: Eleanor 277; George 252; Mary Cooper 252; Winifred 155

McCarty: Fanny 307; Helen O'Brien 252; Michael 252; Sam'l 309; Samuel 68; Sarah [-?-] 234; William 234

McCaskey: Alexander 80; Betty 80; Polly 80

McCassady: Catherine Clyon 70, 252

McCassidy: Catherine Clyon 70

McCausland: Marcus 252; Polly Priestman 252

McCay: Mesha [-?-] 252; Miszey [-?-] 252; William 92, 252

McClain(e): Eleanor Connely 252; Hector 367; John 252; Katherine 367; Roger 252; Sarah [-?-] 252; William 252

McClain(e). See also Macclain, McLane, McLane, McLean

McClaske: Alice Jewell 252; Joseph 208, 252

McClellan: John 252, 272; Mary Helms 252; William 252

McClennan. See McClellan.

McCloud: Sarah 265

McClung: Joseph 129; Mary 150; Rachel 150; Robert 28, 150, 333; Ruth 333

McClure: David 252; John C. 252; Mary Ann Thornburgh 252

McComas: Alex 420; Alexander 98, 252, 253, 263, 264, 266, 281, 322,

349, 408, 409; Ann 306; Ann [-?-] 252, 253; Ann [-?-] Love 253; Ann deLap Love 238; Ann Miles 253; Aquila 253m321, 331; Daniel 6, 40, 252, 253, 306; Deborah [-?-] 252; Deborah Hartley Deaver 98; Eleanor (Elinor) 263; Elizabeth 281, 387; Hannah 6, 263, 264; Hannah [-?-] 322, 349, 409; Hannah [-?-] Onion 253; Hannah Bond 285; Hannah Deavwer 253; Hannah Taylor 253; Hannah Whitaker 252; James 195, 253; John 238, 252, 253; Martha 6; Martha Scott 253; Mary 252, 408; Moses 253; Polly 96, 110; Priscilla 349; Sarah 40, 253, 322; Sarah Howard 253; Sarah Preston 253; William 6, 252, 253, 254, 263, 285, 387

McComesky: Daniel 373; Catherine 253

McComsey: Robert 253

McComsey. See also McCumsy.

McConnell: Betsy Barnet253; Charles 253; Elizabeth 167; John 253; Sarah Leret 253

McConniken: Eleanor Owings Long 253; John 253

McConnikin: Eleanor 388

McCoob. See McCoobs, McCool.

McCoobs: Margaret 136.

McCoobs. See also McCool.

McCool: Margaret 136

McCormick; Ann 100; James 254; Jane 16, 187; Rachel Ridgely Lux 254; William 100, 187

McCoy: Cassander Cole 254; Charlotte 284; John 254; Rachel 242; Rachel Joice 154; Robert 254; Sarah Wade 254; William 254

McCracken: Elizabeth 167

McCreary: Letitia Nelson 254; Susanna Nelson 254, 418; Thomas 254; William 254

McCubbin: Ann [-?-] 195, 196; Ann Ottay 254; Lydia Collins 254; Mary Clare 254; Mary Parrish 254; Moses 411; Nancy 61; Nicholas 254; Polly 106; Rachel 224; Samuel 224, 254, 406; Sarah 254; Sarah Holland 188, 254; Sarah Norwood 254; Sophia Gough 254; William 253, 254;

Margaret Smith 279; Mary Ridgely 278; Mary Spear 279; Philip N. 279; Polly Smith 279; Smith 279
Nicholls: John 279, 398; Mary [-?-] 279
Nicholls. See also Nichols, Nicols.
Nichols: Elizabeth 388; Henry 279; John 360; Margaret 388; R. Smith 279
Nichols. See also Nicholls, Nicols.
Nicholson: Benjamin 279; Elizabeth [-?-] 107; James 186, 279; Jenney Barrett 163; John 279, 398; Mary 137, 240; Mary (Polly) Ridgely 279; Mary [-?-] Connell 279; Mary Barrett 279; Matilda Heath Smith 279; Nathan 186, 279; Nicholas 279; Rachel 355; Ruth Bond 279; Ruth Stansbury 279; Susanna Peachey 279; Thomas 355; William 76, 107, 131, 165, 279, 431
Nicholson. See also Nicholls.
Nicklin: Juliana Chew 279; Philip 279
Nicodemus: Ann Maria Neff 279; John Louis 279
Nicolle: John Baptist 279; Mary Glace 279
Nicolls: Charlotte Graham 279; James 279
Nicols: Henry 279, 355; Rebecca 355; Rebecca Smith 279, 280
Nicols; See also Nicholls.
Nieslem: Christiana 320
Niger: Michael 280; Sarah Morgan 280
Night: Comfort 328
Ninde: Catherine Blyth 280; James 280
Niser; Abraham 280
Nixon: Permelia Divers 280; Sarah [-?-] 103; Sarah Thompson 280; Thomas 103, 280
Nixson. See Nixon.
Noble: Anthony 280; Hettey McAlister 280; Hetty [-?-] 385
Noel: Louis Philippe 280; Marie Flore Eugenie Estienne 280; Peggy 385; Septimus 359
Noland: Mary Hawkins 280; Thomas 280

Noll: Anton 280; Elisabeth Reinhardtin 280; Frans. 280; Maria Magdalena Brünnle 280; Maria Magdalena Prenlin 280
Nollin: Anna Elisabeta 340; Catharina 333
Nonnier; Mary Brongier 231
Noonan; Edward 280; Mary Fitzpatrick 280
Norbury: George 280; Mary Burgess 280
Norman; Amy 258; George 258; Johanna [-?-] 258
Norquay: Jane [-?-] Trotman 280; Magnus 280
Norrington: Ann 380; Francis 280; John 100, 178, 361; Mary 100, 178, 280; Mary Everett 280
Norris: Abraham 281; Alice 228; Ann 157, 366; Ann [-?-] 366; Ann Cowman 281; Avarilla Scott 281, 342; Benjamin 180, 197, 281; Edward 136, 218, 249, 281, 377, 379, 387, 431; Elizabeth 35, 197, 377; Elizabeth Amos 281; Elizabeth Cole 281; Elizabeth Davis 281; Elizabeth Kitely 280; Elizabeth McComas 281; Hannah 136, 180; Hannah Scott 281; James 281; Jane Peterkin 281; John 116, 157, 186, 238, 260, 366; Joseph 35, 197, 281, 317, 350, 392, 410; Lloyd 281; Mary 231, 238, 260, 350; Philizanna Barton 281; Rachel 116, 392; Rebecca [-?-] 281; Rebecca Potee 281; Sally Schaeffer 282; Sarah 186, 281, 387; Sarah [-?-] 180, 281; Sarah Wichell 281; Susanna 410; Susannah 10; Thomas 281, 342; William 282; Willimene 35
North: Elizabeth 59; Helen 267; Robert 59; Thomas 267
Norton: Dennis 282; Elizabeth [-?-] 282: Elizabeth Ford Barnes Clark 282, 429; John 174, 282; Margaret Murphy 282; Sarah West 282; Stephen, 282; William 282, 429
Norviband: John 203
Norvill: James 282; William 282
Norwood: [-?-] 38; Andrew 21; Ann

Mary Howard 297; Maulden 297;
Peter 297; Sarah Gott 297; Simon
297; William 297
Perkins: Elizabeth Cottrell 298;
Hannah 127; Mary 298; Mary [-?-]
Gash 297; Reuben 127, 297; Richard
23, 141, 297, 430; Sarah [-?-] 127,
297; Susanna [-?-] 48; William 298
Perpont. See Pierpoint,
Perrigo(e): Deborah 89; F rances 386;
Mary 43; Nathan 43; Rebecca 277
Perrigo(e). See Peregoy, Perigo(e)..
Perry: John 120, 298; Mary 94, 298;
Sarah 94; Sarah [-?-] 120
Pert: Frances [-?-] 298; Frances [-?-]
Constable 76; Thomas 76, 298
Perting: Peter 298
Peryne. See Perine.
Peshaw: Ann [-?-] Grainger 298;
Joseph 298
Peshaw. See also Pisha.
Peter: [-?-] John 298; David, 298
Peter. See also Peters.
Peterkin: Jane 281
Peters: Daniel 298, 348, 422; Elizabeth
295; Elizabeth [-?-] 220, 348;
Elizabeth [-?-] Shriver 298; George
298; Hester [-?-] 298; John 298;
Mary 220; Polly Trimble 298;
Rebecca Johnson 298; Thomas 298
Peters. See also Peter.
Peterson: Andrew 105, 149, 298; John
298; Judith [-?-] 105; Margaret
Holmes 298
Petite. See Potee.
Petticoat(e), Hannah Owings 298;
Sarah Dorsey 299; William 212, 383
Petticoat(e). See also Peddicoard,
Peddicord, Petticord.
Petty: Ann 199; Constant 299; Francis
299: John 299
Petty. See also Pilly.
Peverell: Daniel 299, 334, 354, 378,
429; Hannah [-?-] 299; Sarah 299,
334, Sarah 354
Phelps: Avin(g)ton 299; Charles 65,
299; Hannah Jacobs 299; John Parker
299: Margaret Charnox 299:
Margaret Charock 65; Rachel

Muckledory 299; Rose 299; Rose
[-?-] Swift130; Sarah 384; Thomas
130, 299, 384
Phibble. See Prebble.
Phields: Elizabeth 187
Phillip: William 405
Phillips: Ann 305; Anthony 9, 62, 299;
Bethia Utie 299; Bothia [-?-] 339;
Bothia Scarlett 299; Elizabeth 299;
Henry 299; James 9, 62, 100, 109,
144, 164, 218, 286, 289, 299, 300,
336, 339, 357, 367, 429, 430;
Johanna 109; Johanna [-?-] 299;
Martha 289; Mary 62, 166, 357;
Mary [-?-] 299; Patience 394;
Patience [-?-] 299; Philip188;
Rosanna Harris 299; Samuel 299;
Sarah 165, 299; Susanna 367;
Susanna [-?-] 9, 62, 299; William
299, 394
Philpot(t), Bryan 299; Edward 299;
Elizabeth Johnson 299; John 299;
Maria Jacob 299; Thomas 299
Phippen: Sarah Richards 299
Phipps: Nathaniel 164, 420
Piat: John Baptist 299; Peggy Chameau
299
Picke: Sarah [-?-] Kimble 299; William
299
Pickens: Mary 157
Pickersgill; John 299; Polly Young 299
Picket(t): Barbara Gorsuch 299;
Elizabeth 212; Elizabeth Barton
Wright Greer 18, 157, 299, 422, 429;
George 18, 299, 411; Heathcote 18,
157, 212, 299, 422, 429; Jemima
Deaver 301; Jeremiah 321; Lucretia
299; Margaret [-?-] Flint 299; Mary
Spinks 299; Rebecca 17; Temperance
238; William 212, 238, 301
Picket(t). See also Pecket.
Pidergist. See Pendigrass.
Pierce: Humphrey 301; Levi 301; Mary
[-?-] 301; Mary [-?-] Hill 184; Mary
Elizabeth 301; Mary Keeper 301;
Nancy Williamson 301
Pierce. See also Pearce.
Piercy: Mary Aisquith 301
Pierpoint: Abraham 301; Ann 301,

Peter 339; Sarah 67, 339, 379;
Thomas 379; William 339, 367
Savory: Mary March Maxwell 250,
339; Rosanna [-?-] Robinson 330,
339; William 250, 330, 339
Scanlan: James 339; Mary Pearson 339
Scarfe: James 29
Scarff; James 333, 339, 403; Margaret
354; Mary 333, 339; Nicholas 354
Scarlett; [-?-] 339; Bethia 220; Bothia
[-?-] 364; Bothia (Bethia) Loney
Barnes Adams 17, 97, 339, 429;
Mary 97; Rachel 364
Schaefer; Anna Dillin 340; Apelonia
[-?-] 78; Christian 339; George
Michael 339; Jacob 340; Mar.
Appolon Haefnerin 339; Maria
Elisabeth Bleyin 339
Schaeffer: Baltzer 282; Christian 78;
Sally 282
Schafer; Baltser 340; Eleanor Larsh
340
Schauerin; Barbara 327
Schaw: See Shaw.
Scheidecker; Eve Barbara Smith 340;
Joseph 340
Scheiecker; Barbara Brown 340;
Joseph 340
Schels: Peter 267
Schewff: Jacob 359
Schildtacker; Eve Barbara [-?-] 340;
Joseph 340
Schilling; Christian 340; Elisabeta
Morri 340
Schits; Peter 340
Schlegel; Charlotte Wolf 340; Christian
340
Schleich: [-?-] 4; Catherine 340;
Catherine [-?-] 340; John 4, 133, 340;
Sophia 340
Schley: Polly 340
Schlotthauer: Anna Elisabeta Nollin
340; Nicolaus 340
Schmall; Adam 340; Johanna Dorothea
Zimmermanin 340
Schmidtin: Anna 225
Schmit: Anna Maria [-?-] 47; Maria
Magdalena 47; Ruland 47
Grunnewaldin 340
Schneider; Abraham 340; Catharina

Eckerin 340; Elisabetha Stoffelin
340; Friedrich 340; Margaret 347;
Maria Margaretha; Mary Elizabeth
135; Mary Martha 333; Michael 340;
Theobald 135, 333, 347
Schneider: See also Snyder.
Schneiderin: Elisabeta 273
Schreiber: See Shriver.
Schreinen: Margareta 267
Schriber; Elizabeth Hensman 340;
Michael 340
Schroeder; [-?-] 180; Catherine
Hauptman 340; Charles 340; Henry
340; Herman Henry 340; Polly
Schley 340: Sus. Schwartz 340;
Susanna Schwarz 341
Schultz: Christiana 223; John 89, 223;
Sukey 89
Schunck: John 342; Nancy Mumma
341
Schunckly: Elizabeth 370
Schwartz: Sus. 340; Susanna 341
Schwob: Benedict 341; Johannes 341
Scooly: Reuben 341
Scorce; James 67; John Amon 81;
Mary 67; William 67
Scott: Abarillah 112: Abraham 25, 199,
247; Amos 341; Andrew 92, 341;
Ann 357; Ann [-?-] 342; Ann
Wheeler 341; Aquila 195, 341;
Avarilla 112, 281, 342; Avarilla
Raven 281, 342; Betsy Goodwin
Dorsey 342; Christian 45; Christiann
[-?-] 92; Christiann Wright 341;
Daniel 25, 32, 112, 144, 197, 253,
281, 309, 321, 341, 342, 357, 378,
408; Elizabeth 6, 32, 341; Elizabeth
[-?-] 247, 253, 281, 341, 408; Esther
199, 341; George 341; Hannah 25,
375; Hannah [-?-] 144, 178, 342;
Hannah Butterworth 341; Hannah
Morris 342; Jacob 178, 342; James
341; Jane 197; Jane [-?-] 341; Jane
Johnson 25, 341, 342; John 342;
Joseph 178, 342; Margaret 92, 341;
Martha 195, 253; Mary 6; Michael
341; Nathaniel 281, 342; Priscilla
Colvin 341; Rachel 247; Rachel Price
341; Rebecca 178, 341; Rossiter 342;
Sarah 270, 309, 321, 341, 408; Sarah

Stockton: Catherine [-?-] 367;
  Esther Cox 367; Samuel 367
Stoffelin: Elisabetha 340; Maria 184
Stohler: Catherine [-?-] Kline 222, 367;
  John 222, 367
Stokes: Ann 92; Cordelia 68, 367;
  David 367; Elizabeth 333; Frances
  289, 367; Frances [-?-] 309; George
  356, 367, 430; Hannah Harvey 367;
  Humphrey Wells 327, 367; John 289,
  316, 339, 364, 365, 367, 384; Joseph
  367; Margaret [-?-] Savage 339, 367;
  Mary 327; Mary Knight 367; Rebecca
  [-?-] 426; Rebecca Young 369;
  Robert 369, 426; Robert Young 369,
  426; Sarah Brooke 369; Sarah Johns
  367; Susanna [-?-] 367; Susanna
  Phillips 367; Susanna Wells 367;
  Susannah [-?-] 289
Stoler. See Stohler.
Stolter: Margaret 369; Mary'n 369
Stonall: Polly Ensor 369; William 369
Stone: Barbara 138; Catherine
  Boughton 369; Constant Shepherd
  James 205, 309; Elizabeth [-?-]
  Sampson Bagford Hinton 12, 186,
  337, 430; Hannah [-?-] Cockey 369;
  Hannah Owings 369; Henrietta [-?-]
  Jenkins 369; Henry 205, 369, 423;
  Mary [-?-] 369; Mary [-?-] Dimmitt
  (Diamint) Gaine 130, 136, 430;
  Thomas 12, 103, 138, 186, 337, 369,
  430; William 369
Stoney: Patience Richards 369
Stophel. See Stouphell, Strophel.
Storm: George 369; Margaret [-?-]
  Armagost 369
Stormay: Margaret 384
Stormie: Margaret 371
Story: Anne [-?-] 38; Christiana
  Dashiell 369; Elizabeth 369;
  George 369; Jane 370, 400; Joshua\
  370; Patience Richards 370; Ralph
  425; Thomas 370; William 38
Stouart: Tomas 370
Stouphell: Mary 49
Stout: Edward 175; Elizabeth 354;
  John 370; Mary [-?-] 370
Stover: [-?-] Fisher 370; Annamary
  370; Annamary [-?-] 125; John 169,
  370; Maria Sophia [-?-] 169; Polly

424; Sophia [-?-] 370
Stoxsdill. See Stocksdale.
Strachan: Eleanor 92; Margarate 175;
  Mary [-?-] 92, 175; William 92, 175
Strahan: Jane 370
Strain: Robert 370
Stran: John 370; Rebecca Johnson 370;
  Rebecca Stran 205
Strand: Joane 221
Strange: Ann 272
Strasman: Mary Sittler 370
Stratton: Mary Howard 370; William
  370
Strauble: Anne 258; Zachariah 258
Strawble. See also Strouble.
Strawbridge: Joseph 8, 370: Sarah [-?-]
  370: Sarah [-?-] Arden 8
Strawman. See Stroman.
Street(t): Benjamin 370; Elizabeth 370;
  Francis 372; Patty Cambridge 370
Streney: Mary Green 370;
  Nicholas 370
Strider: Catherine 82; Catherine
  Laudecker 370; Mary Laudecker 370
Stringer: Ann [-?-] 370; James 370,
  413, 425, 429; Lydia [-?-] 325;
  Samuel 325
Stringhar: Hannah 259
Stroman: John 371; Mary Sitler 372
Strong: Elizabeth 205; Leonard 205
Strophel: Anna 261
Strotee: Catherine [-?-] 371; John 371
Stroub: Jacob 371
Strouble: Mary 228; Rebecca [-?-] 40;
  Sarah 276; Zachariah 40, 228, 276,
  371
Strouble. See also Strawble.
Strutt. See Streett.
Stuart: Ann 209; Ann Johnson 371;
  Ann Thompson 371; Eleanor Ewing
  371; James 371; John 371; Mary
  Boney 3712; Mary Wood 371;
  Richardson 256; William 371
Stuart. See also Steward, Stewart.
Stump: Cassandra Wilson 371, 415;
  Hannah Wilson 371; John 80, 371,
  415; Priscilla 371, 415
Stupuy: Ann Deval 371; Catherine
  Chadwick 371; Catherine Duharlay
  Camiran 371; John Baptist 371;
  Peter 371

Elizabeth Taylor 382; John 116, 382, 424; Magdalen Barbin 382; Mary Ann 252, 382; Robert 382; Roland 382; Thomas 382

Thornbury. See also Thornborough, Thornbbrough, Thornburg(h).

Thornton: Ann 382; Constant 382; Eleanor 228; Eleanor [-?-] 382; Elizabeth 382; Jane 382; John 382; Thomas 345; William 228, 382

Thorp: Edward 16, 89; Mary 16

Thorpe: Catherine Cullings 382; Edward 382; Rachel 66, 382

Thrash. See Trush.

Thrasher: [-?-] Price 382; John 382; Mary 382; Sarah 382

Thrush. See Trush.

Thurcall: Jane O'Daniel 382; Thomas 382

Thurol: Margaret [-?-] 25; Richard 25

Thurrol(d): Margaret [-?-] 177; Richard 177

Thurrol: Margaret [-?-] 227; Richard 227

Thurrold: Margaret 25

Thurrold. See also Therrell.

Thurston: Ann 143; David 56, 67, 382, 430; Elizabeth 351, 396; Jane 238; Martha [-?-] Child Cage 56, 67, 382, 430; Sarah 345; Thomas 143, 238, 345, 351, 396

Thwaite: Mary 383

Tibbett: Delilah Green 383; James 383; Sarah [-?-] 383; Walter 383

Tibbles: John 383; Mary [-?-] 383; Mary Alter 5

Tibodeau: Ann 320; Mary 60, 202

Tice: John 65; Mary [-?-] 65; Sarah 65

Tice. See also Tise.

Tichner: Catherine 364

Ticklin: Eleanor Crawley 383; William 383

Tietzen: Elizabeth 123

Tilbury: Sarah 383

Tilden: Catherine 289; Eliza Angelica Barrier 383; John 289, 83; Luke 383; William Blay 289

Tilghman: Margaret Eliza 187; Richard 187

Tillard: Ann 5

Tilly: Mary 383; Mary Rose Agnes

Lomenie deMarme 101; Stephen Simon Legardeur 101

Tilyard: John 383; Mary Green 383

Timanes: Dorothety Shearmiller 383

Tinker; William 94

Tipper: Edgar 383; Elizabeth [-?-] 383

Tipton: Aquila 24, 383; Cassandra 82; Esther Price 383; Hannah [-?-] 36, 383; Jabez Murray 383; John 64, 129; Jonathan 383; Luke 34, 383; Mary 64; Mary Bond 383; Mordecai 36, 71, 383; Rachel 129; Rebecca 383; Rebecca Belt 24, 383; Rebecca Lemmon 383; Ruth Boring 383; Samuel 36, 71, 82, 261, 383; Sarah 36, 261, 383; Sarah [-?-] 34; Sarah Boston 383; Shadrach Boston 383; Thomas 34, 383; William 36, 383

Tise: John 65

Tise. See also Tice.

Tobbes: Jacob M. 25

Todd: Anne Gorsuch 384; Benjamin 384; David 38; Eleanor 118; Eleanor Dorsey 85. 119, 241, 327, 384: Eleanor Ford 384; Elizabeth [-?-] 76; Elizabeth Stevenson 383; Frances 327; James 177, 384; Lance 43, 112; Lancelot 384; Martha [-?-] Garrett 383; Nancy Besett 384; Nancy Bibell 384; Owen 384; Penelope Scudamore 177, 384; Rebecca 155; Sarah Phelps 384; Sarah Wilkinson 383; Thomas 76, 85, 119, 143, 213, 241, 284, 327, 384, 421, 429; William 384

Toff: Elizabeth 371, 384

Toker: John 384

Tolley: [-?-] Worthington 384; Edward C. 384; Edward Carvel 384; Elizabeth 265; Elizabeth [-?-] 384; James 107, 265; Martha Hall 384; Mary 421; Mary [-?-] 107, 265; Mary Freeborne 384; Sophia 4; Thomas 265, 384; Walter 4, 185, 384, 421

Tolley. See also Tolly.

Tolly: Elizabeth Mary 384, 421; Mary 142

Tolly. See also Tolley.

Tolson: Elizabeth 367, 384

Tomarus: Lawrence 384; Rachel Hill 384

Tomblinson: Hannah Fox 385:

CPSIA information can be obtained at www.ICGtesting.com
Printed in the USA
BVOW03s1804060414

349814BV00009B/127/P